THE CAMBRIDGE HISTORY OF CHINA

General Editors

DENIS TWITCHETT and JOHN K. FAIRBANK

Volume 12

Republican China 1912–1949, Part 1

THE CAMBRIDGE
HISTORY OF
CHINA

Volume 12
Republican China 1912–1949, Part 1

edited by
JOHN K. FAIRBANK

CAMBRIDGE UNIVERSITY PRESS
CAMBRIDGE
NEW YORK   NEW ROCHELLE
MELBOURNE   SYDNEY

Published by the Press Syndicate of the University of Cambridge
The Pitt Building, Trumpington Street, Cambridge CB2 IRP
32 East 57th Street, New York, NY 10022, USA
10 Stamford Road, Oakleigh, Melbourne 3166, Australia

© Cambridge University Press 1983

First published 1983
Reprinted 1987

Printed in the United States of America

Library of Congress catalogue card number: 76-29852

British Library Cataloguing in Publication Data

The Cambridge history of China.
Vol. 12: Republican China 1912-1949
Pt 1
1. China - History
I. Fairbank, John K.
951 DS735
ISBN 0 521 23541 3

GENERAL EDITORS' PREFACE

As the modern world grows more interconnected, historical understanding of it becomes ever more necessary and the historian's task ever
more complex. Fact and theory affect each other even as sources pro-
liferate and knowledge increases. Merely to summarize what is known
becomes an awesome task, yet a factual basis of knowledge is increasingly
essential for historical thinking.

Since the beginning of the century, the Cambridge histories have set
a pattern in the English-reading world for multi-volume series containing
chapters written by specialists under the guidance of volume editors. *The
Cambridge Modern History*, planned by Lord Acton, appeared in sixteen
volumes between 1902 and 1912. It was followed by *The Cambridge Ancient
History*, *The Cambridge Medieval History*, *The Cambridge History of English
Literature*, and Cambridge Histories of India, of Poland, and of the British
Empire. The original *Modern History* has now been replaced by *The New
Cambridge Modern History* in twelve volumes, and *The Cambridge Economic
History of Europe* is now being completed. Other Cambridge Histories
recently undertaken include a history of Islam, of Arabic literature, of the
Bible treated as a central document of and influence on Western civiliza-
tion, and of Iran and China.

In the case of China, Western historians face a special problem. The
history of Chinese civilization is more extensive and complex than that
of any single Western nation, and only slightly less ramified than the
history of European civilization as a whole. The Chinese historical record
is immensely detailed and extensive, and Chinese historical scholarship has
been highly developed and sophisticated for many centuries. Yet until
recent decades the study of China in the West, despite the important
pioneer work of European sinologists, had hardly progressed beyond the
translation of some few classical historical texts, and the outline history
of the major dynasties and their institutions.

Recently Western scholars have drawn more fully upon the rich traditions of historical scholarship in China and also in Japan, and greatly
advanced both our detailed knowledge of past events and institutions,

and also our critical understanding of traditional historiography. In addition, the present generation of Western historians of China can also draw upon the new outlooks and techniques of modern Western historical scholarship, and upon recent developments in the social sciences, while continuing to build upon the solid foundations of rapidly progressing European, Japanese and Chinese sinological studies. Recent historical events, too, have given prominence to new problems, while throwing into question many older conceptions. Under these multiple impacts the Western revolution in Chinese studies is steadily gathering momentum.

When *The Cambridge History of China* was first planned in 1966, the aim was to provide a substantial account of the history of China as a bench mark for the Western history-reading public: an account of the current state of knowledge in six volumes. Since then the out-pouring of current research, the application of new methods, and the extension of scholarship into new fields, have further stimulated Chinese historical studies. This growth is indicated by the fact that the History has now become a planned sixteen volumes, but will still leave out such topics as the history of art and of literature, many aspects of economics and technology, and all the riches of local history.

The striking advances in our knowledge of China's past over the last decade will continue and accelerate. Western historians of this great and complex subject are justified in their efforts by the needs of their own peoples for greater and deeper understanding of China. Chinese history belongs to the world, not only as a right and necessity, but also as a subject of compelling interest.

JOHN K. FAIRBANK
DENIS TWITCHETT

March 1982

CONTENTS

MAPS

TABLES

PREFACE TO VOLUME 12

On romanization

One achievement of the revolution has been to set up an official system for transcription of Chinese sounds into alphabetic writing. This system, known as *pinyin*, one hopes may bring uniformity into a formerly chaotic situation, in which the sinologists of each foreign power had devised their own national systems of romanization – English, French, German, Russian, etc.

In the English-reading world the Wade-Giles romanization after the turn of the century gradually became accepted for scholarly work, despite its idiosyncrasies – for instance, its use of an apostrophe as an aspiration mark to distinguish, for example, T (written in Wade–Giles T') from D (Wade-Giles T), P (P') from B (P), K from G, etc. Despite this clumsy feature, Wade-Giles became by 1949 the most widely used system, enshrined in countless reference works, official documents, and the general literature of the field. For example, the four major biographical dictionaries in English of Chinese personages from 1368 to 1965 (totalling eleven volumes) all use Wade-Giles. Moreover, because of the foreign presence in China, the historical record is partly non-Chinese. It is for this reason – that Wade-Giles is still the dominant system in some of the sources and in the research tools of the period covered in this volume – that we continue to use it here. The use of the new *pinyin* system in this volume would greatly complicate the work of researchers.

Acknowledgements

The editor is most indebted to the authors for their unremitting patience and cooperation, so necessary for this sort of enterprise; to Katherine Frost Bruner for indexing and to Joan Hill for administrative and editorial assistance; to Chiang Yung-chen of the Harvard Graduate School for essential bibliographical assistance and to Winston Hsieh, the University of Missouri, and Guy Alitto, the University of Chicago, for bibliographic consultation. We are indebted for support of editorial costs to the Ford Foundation and to the National Endowment for the Humanities through the American Council of Learned Societies. A working conference of contributors was held in Cambridge, Mass. in August 1976 with the assistance of the Social Science Research Council. During the gestation period earlier versions of chapters 2, 3 and 12 were published as separate booklets. Now they are born again.

J K F

CHAPTER 1

MARITIME AND CONTINENTAL IN CHINA'S HISTORY

The 37 years from 1912 to 1949 are known as the period of the Chinese Republic in order to distinguish them from the periods of more stable central government which came before and after. These years were marked by civil war, revolution and invasion at the military-political level, and by change and growth in the economic, social, intellectual and cultural spheres. If we could neatly set forth in this first chapter the major historical issues, events and Chinese achievements in these various realms, the following chapters might be almost unnecessary. In that case, however, the cart would be in front of the horses.

Our new view of the republic must come from several angles of approach. Only one is pursued in this introductory chapter, yet it appears to serve as a central and necessary starting point.

THE PROBLEM OF FOREIGN INFLUENCE

China's modern problem of adjustment has been that of a dominant, majority civilization that rather suddenly found itself in a minority position in the world. Acceptance of outside 'modern' ways was made difficult by the massive persistence of deeply-rooted Chinese ways. The issue of outer versus inner absorbed major attention at the time and still confronts historians as a thorny problem of definition and analysis.

Anyone comparing the Chinese Republic of 1912–49 with the late Ch'ing period that preceded it or with the People's Republic that followed will be struck by the degree of foreign influence upon and even participation in Chinese life during these years. The Boxer peace settlement of 1901 had marked the end of blind resistance to foreign privilege under the unequal treaties; students flocked to Tokyo, Peking proclaimed foreign-style reforms, and both weakened the old order. After the Revolution of 1911 the outside world's influence on the early republic is almost too obvious to catalogue: the revolutionaries avoided prolonged civil war lest it invite foreign intervention; they tried in 1912 to inaugurate a constitutional, parliamentary republic based on foreign models; President

Yuan Shih-k'ai's foreign loans raised controversy; the New Culture movement after 1917 was led by scholars returned from abroad; the May Fourth movement of 1919 was triggered by power politics at Versailles; the Chinese Communist Party (CCP) was founded in 1921 under Comintern prompting; Sun Yat-sen reorganized the Kuomintang (KMT) after 1923 with Soviet help; the Nationalist Revolution 1925–27 was inspired by patriotic anti-imperialism. Truly, the early republic was moved by foreign influences that were almost as pervasive as the Japanese invasion was to become after 1931.

Yet the term 'foreign' is highly ambiguous and may trap us in needless argument. It requires careful definition. For example, among the 'foreign influences' just listed, some were events abroad, some were models seen abroad and imitated in China, some were ideas of foreign origin which animated Chinese returned from overseas, some were events in China in which foreign people or ideas played a part. The situation was not simple.

Since the 'foreign' elements in Chinese life during this period were so widespread, clarity demands that we make a series of distinctions or propositions. First of all, most readers of these pages probably still perceive China as a distinct culture, persistent in its own ways, different from 'the West'. This assumption, reinforced by common observation, stems from the holistic image of 'China' conveyed by Jesuit writers during the Enlightenment and further developed by European Sinology. It represents an acceptance in the West of an image of China as an integrated society and culture, an image that formed the central myth of the state and was sedulously propagated by its learned ruling class.[1] Still dominant in Chinese thinking at the turn of the century, this idea of 'China' as a distinct cultural entity made 'foreign' into something more than the mere political distinction that it sometimes was among Western nations.

Second, we must distinguish the actual foreign presence. There were many foreigners within the country – scores of thousands residing in the major cities, most of which were treaty ports partially foreign-run; hundreds were employed by successive Chinese governments; and several thousand missionaries were at stations in the interior. Add to these the garrisons of foreign troops and foreign naval vessels on China's inland waterways, and we can better imagine the 'semi-colonial' aspect of China under the unequal treaties that continued to give the foreigners their

---

1 On Sinology and the 'self-image of Chinese civilization', see Arthur F. Wright, 'The study of Chinese civilization', *Journal of the History of Ideas*, 21.2 (April–June 1960) 233–55. In developing this essay I have greatly benefited from comments of Marie Claire Bergère, Mark Elvin, Albert Feuerwerker, Kwang-Ching Liu, Philip A. Kuhn, Denis Twitchett and Wang Gungwu.

special status and privileges. This volume devotes a chapter simply to describing 'the foreign presence'. By any definition it had many of the features of a self-contained sub-culture transplanted and flourishing symbiotically in Chinese surroundings.

From this picture of the foreign establishment with its own way of life we can understand why the Nationalist Revolution of the 1920s erupted in anti-imperialism. The imperialist presence served as a target for a more unified revolutionary effort.

Yet this revolutionary effort itself represented other foreign influences. The revolution had always had foreign helpers. The Revolutionary Alliance led by Sun Yat-sen was organized among Chinese youths in Tokyo in 1905 under Japanese prompting. It was financed by Chinese merchant communities overseas and used the protection of the foreign administrations in Hong Kong and Shanghai. Later the emissaries of the Soviet revolution inspired both the founding of the CCP and the reorganization of the KMT. Thus, the revolution used foreigners, their aid, ideas and methods to attack the foreign establishment as its target within the country.

A third distinction or proposition, however, is that China's history had to be made by Chinese themselves, not by foreigners. Indeed, when the history of this period was recorded in Chinese, a funny thing happened – the foreigners were almost lost to sight. The inspector-general of customs, Sir Francis Aglen, might collect and even impound the Maritime Customs revenue. Sun's adviser, Michael Borodin, might draft the KMT constitution. The Soviet General Blyukher ('Galen') might work out Chiang Kai-shek's battle plans. But none of them, though in positions of considerable authority, was Chinese. All were played down if not pretty generally left out of the Chinese record. This historical facelessness of the foreigners in China not only reflected modern patriotic pride, denying outsiders a basic role in Chinese life. It also conformed with a long tradition that the Marco Polos and Ibn Batutas who turned up from Western Eurasia had no place in the Chinese record because they were outside the culture. China's society retained its integrity. It was bounded by the Chinese language and writing system. Foreign individuals figured in its history only when, like Matteo Ricci or Robert Hart, they spoke and wrote Chinese sufficiently well to be documented.

There was a colourful history of the foreigners-in-China, but it was their history, not China's. When the Anglo-American ADC (Amateur Dramatic Club) in the International Settlement governed by the Shanghai Municipal Council put on the *Pirates of Penzance* with stentorian eclat, it was an event in China, but not in Chinese history. The foreigners' experience was separate from the Chinese experience. Ibsen's *A doll's house* had influence because Hu Shih brought it within the cultural gates.

This amounts to saying that Chinese history is not one's idea of what happened in China but, rather, one's idea of what happened to the Chinese people. According to this view, the vital entities of modern times are the peoples with their national states and cultures. It is natural for most national chroniclers of events to follow the thread of their own ethnic-cultural development. Foreigners are extraneous and temporary. Witness the fact that the missionaries, the foreign employees, and the treaty-port residents all subsequently disappeared from the Chinese scene just as thoroughly as the European colonial administrations of the late nineteenth century disappeared from their colonies in the mid twentieth century.

A fourth proposition is thus in order: that foreign influences if they were to affect the Chinese people must be conveyed in the Chinese language and writing system. Here China's long experience of 'barbarian' contact had developed time-tested ways of thought and response. For example, *nei* (inside) and *wai* (outside) were very ancient Chinese categories, widely applied both geographically and figuratively. Thus *wai-kuo* (foreign states) lay outside China (Chung-kuo, the central state), but foreign rulers who kotowed could become *wai-fan* (outer feudatories).[2] In his person the Son of Heaven must be a sage within (in character) and a hero without (in action), just as the superior man must first study to cultivate himself (*hsiu-shen*) in the inner realm and then strive by his example to bring peace to the world (*p'ing t'ien-hsia*) in the outer realm. The cognate categories of *nei* and *wai* allowed Chinese thinking to respond to domestic or to foreign stimuli, all the while remaining purely Chinese.[3] A similar pair of terms proved useful in handling Westernization in the formula popularized by Chang Chih-tung; 'Chinese learning for the fundamentals (*t'i*), Western learning for practical use (*yung*).' Since *t'i* and *yung*, substance and function, were really meant to be aspects of a single entity, Chang misapplied these terms. Never mind, it helped Westernize China.

Foreign influences invading China thus had to pass through the eye of the linguistic needle. Translation of a foreign idea often verged upon its Sinification. Just as the Indo-European languages modernized to meet modern needs, so Chinese created new terms, many incorporated from

2 Lien-sheng Yang, 'Historical notes on the Chinese world order', in John King Fairbank, ed. *The Chinese world order: traditional China's foreign relations*, 21.
3 On 'the inner and outer realms' in philosophy see Benjamin Schwartz, 'Some polarities in Confucian thought', in David S. Nivison and Arthur F. Wright, eds. *Confucianism in action*, 54–8. On *nei* and *wai* separating traditional and foreign-induced matters of government, see for example Chang Shou-yung *et al.* comps. *Huang-ch'ao chang-ku hui-pien* (Collected historical records of the imperial dynasty), 3 vols.

Japanese, to carry new meanings. Yet the ancient characters, when used for a new phrase, could not shed all of their accumulated connotations.

For example, foreign faiths entering China have had remarkable difficulties over their key terms. Christian missionaries struggled long and hard to find the best term for God, who was certainly central to their enterprise. Catholics used 'Lord of Heaven' (T'ien-chu), Protestants split between 'Lord on High' (Shang-ti) and 'Deity' (Shen). Again, the sacred terms of Western liberalism, 'freedom' (*tzu-yu*) and 'individualism' (*ko-jen chu-i*), when translated, as in Japan, retained a connotation of wilful irresponsibility in the service of a doctrine of everyone for himself. Proper Confucians were appalled. The Western virtue of individualism came through as selfish licence without a sense of duty.

The idea of rights was newly developed even in the modern West, but in China it had so little background that a new term had to be invented for it. The American missionary W. A. P. Martin in translating Wheaton's *Elements of International Law* in 1864 used *ch'üan-li* and soon after it was used in Japan (*kenri*). But of course these characters already had established meanings and their combination seemed to say 'power-profit' or at least 'privilege-benefit'. This made the assertion of one's rights (*ch'üan-li*) seem like a selfish power play.[4]

Witness finally the central Marxist term 'proletariat', which originally meant the poor of ancient Rome and retains in English an urban connotation. Translated into Chinese as 'propertyless class' (*wu-ch'an chieh-chi*), the proletariat in Mao's China properly embraced the poor peasantry, no doubt a useful adaptation. We have hardly begun to study the Sinicizing role of translation as a filter of foreign influences on China.

A fifth proposition is that foreign influences operated in China primarily by affecting the conduct of Chinese individuals. Groups of persons playing new social roles were the harbingers of change, but they emerged only gradually in the late Ch'ing. To the classic quadrumvirate of scholar, farmer, artisan and merchant were now added all manner of hybrid roles. A trained officer-corps produced scholar-soldiers. Foreign universities sent back a scholar-intelligentsia, many of whom were alienated from the official establishment. Scientific training produced technicians who were scholar-artisans. Meanwhile merchants not only continued to buy official status, some officials became merchant-entrepreneurs. Revolutionists also arose as a distinct professional group, as well as journalists and modern-style politicians.[5]

---

4 Wang Gungwu, *Power, rights and duties in Chinese history*, the 40th George Ernest Morrison Lecture in Ethnology 1979 (Canberra: Australian National University, 1979), 3–4.
5 Cp. M. Bastid, *CHOC*, vol. 11, ch. 10.

In short, the specialization of modern life broke up the old social structure. Specialization discredited the Confucian ideal of an elite united by classical learning just as roughly as in the United States it had denied the Jacksonian ideal of an egalitarian education for all.[6]

All the new roles involved dealing with foreign matters or learning from abroad. Compradors and Chinese Christians (sometimes identical) emerged in the treaty ports, followed by journalists and returned students who had been abroad, all of them under foreign influence. Technology became the key to new developments whether military, industrial, administrative or educational, and nearly all of it came from the West, even when mediated through Japan. By the twentieth century, leaders of Young China like T'ang Shao-i and Wu T'ing-fang, who negotiated the revolutionary settlement in 1912, were speaking English, which they had practised respectively at Hartford, Connecticut and the Inns of Court, London.[7]

To the modern fragmentation of specialized social roles was added the diversity of foreign models and stimuli now made available by the expansion of international contact. Modernity, so various in itself, now came at China in widely different national forms. Nineteenth-century China had been subjected to the Anglo-American-French-Russian examples of patriotic naval and diplomatic officers, aggressively self-righteous missionaries, and merchants piously devoted to material profit, but all had been within the confines of one civilization from the West. Now the scene was immensely broadened: ex-samurai ideals of bushido were picked up by young patriots like Chiang Kai-shek at the Japanese officers' training academy. Populist concerns of Russian *narodniki* animated early Marxists like Li Ta-chao. Rabindranath Tagore brought his Hindu message of mystic unity, though with few takers. A Buddhist revival was promoted under the monk T'ai Hsu. A women's higher education movement fostered contact with Smith College and others of the Seven Sisters. Echoes of the New Poetry movement in the United States, the European vogue of Esperanto as a vehicle for global communication, all sorts of fashions and groundswells from abroad rippled among China's new urban intellectuals and men of affairs. The resulting flux of values and

---

6 John Higham, 'The matrix of specialization', in Alexandra Oleson and John Voss, eds. *The organization of knowledge in modern America, 1860–1920.*
7 Paul A. Cohen analyses the careers of early reformers of the 'littoral' and 'hinterland' in ch. 9 of his *Between tradition and modernity: Wang T'ao and reform in late Ch'ing China.* See also Louis T. Sigel, 'T'ang Shao-yi (1860–1938): the diplomacy of Chinese nationalism' (Harvard University, Ph.D. dissertation, 1972), 92 *et seq.*; Linda Shin, 'China in transition: the role of Wu T'ing-fang (1842–1922)' (University of California Los Angeles, Ph.D. dissertation, 1970).

morals, the blurring of self-images, made Chinese actors often ambivalent, facing two ways, and confused foreign observers accordingly.

In the midst of all of this confusion, however, we may discern a sixth proposition, that the Chinese when responding to foreign stimuli, whether in the Chinese language or by their conduct, had to fashion their modern ways out of Chinese elements, old or new, available within themselves if not actually in the local scene.

To begin with, not even the most foreignized Chinese could lose his sense of Chinese identity. Living abroad only increased it. Cultural friction generated patriotic fire. The most sincere patriot was Sun Yat-sen, who had had the least experience of Chinese tradition and the most of modern nationalism abroad.

Something more is involved here than patriotic motives, however. The mystery of human thought in general seems to be performed with a generous use of analogy, as when location in time is expressed in the terms of before and after (behind) originally used to denote location in space. On time's ladder we 'see' historical events 'preceding' and 'following' one another. Analogical and metaphorical thinking leads us to imagine the lesser known in terms of the better known – in short, to cross the cultural gap between native and foreign, we have to think mainly with whatever is already in our heads.[8] Thus, we find one Chinese patriot after another not only motivated by cultural pride but also required by his own thought processes to find in China the analogues, equivalents or Chinese counterpart of things perceived abroad.[9]

Mid-nineteenth century xenophobes took refuge in the old rationale that essentials of Western science must have been derived from ancient China. In arguing for Western scientific training some accordingly declared that Western sciences had borrowed their roots from ancient Chinese mathematics. To outflank the xenophobes, the modernizer's trick was to smuggle things Western into China as having been originally Chinese. K'ang Yu-wei perfected it when he found the modern Western ideal of Progress in the ancient Chinese theory of the three ages (see volume 11, page 288). Thus in their own minds Chinese modernizers had to confront the foreign culture with whatever equivalents they could muster from China. John Dewey's student Hu Shih, the most fearless

---

8 The psychology and thought processes of cultural contact seem extraordinarily under-studied in the case of China. For a popular discussion of metaphoric thinking, see Julian Jaynes, *The origin of consciousness in the breakdown of the bicameral mind.* Cp. p. 50: 'The concepts of science are all . . . abstract concepts generated by concrete metaphors'; p. 53: 'understanding a thing is arriving at a familiarizing metaphor for it'.

9 The Chinese search for equivalence with the West especially interested the late Joseph R. Levenson, *Confucian China and its modern fate.*

iconoclast and winnower of China's heritage, wrote his Columbia Ph.D. thesis on 'The Development of the Logical Method in Ancient China'.

Of course the early Westernization and later modernization movements soon learned to be discriminating. At first Europe and America had converged upon China as an alien society which (despite its extensive internal variety) had developed a commercial-industrial-military dynamism that seemed to be a product of its whole alien culture. The steam engine, representative government and Christianity at first glance seemed tied together, and 'Western' culture came onto the Chinese horizon looking more unified and therefore more menacing than it later turned out to be. Its menace seemed to require that China become commercial-industrial-military in self-defence.

But the very diversity of 'the West' made it clear that Westernization had to be selective; and the criterion of selection proved generally to be the compatability of Western ways with Chinese needs, so that imported things could take root and become Chinese. Foreign borrowings (*wai*) had to fit into the domestic scene (*nei*).

Indeed, one is tempted to assert that even in modern China innovation inspired from abroad still had to come as 'change within tradition'.[10] For even the most startling break with tradition still occurred within the day-to-day continuum of inherited Chinese ways and circumstances. The end of footbinding and the emancipation of women, the writing of the vernacular *pai-hua*, loyalty to nation instead of to monarch, renunciation of filial piety, all found support from within the Chinese cultural realm. The pace of change might produce vertigo, alarm and iconoclasm but it was still change in China by Chinese people immersed in Chinese speech and writing.

This suggests a final proposition, that the most natural way to meet the West on equal terms was to follow a Chinese minority tradition which had more in common with Western ways of commerce and violent competition than with Chinese ideals of bureaucracy and harmonious compromise. For example, one peculiarly menacing aspect of the 'Western Ocean' (Hsi-yang) people in the early contact at Canton was that their uncouth and greedy ways appealed to tendencies deeply latent among the Cantonese populace. The outright commercialism of the Western 'barbarians' met a quick response among the shopkeepers in Hog Lane behind the opulent ghetto of the Thirteen Factories. Once Indian opium was brought by the private merchants in the Country (local) trade from India, com-

---

10 E. A. Kracke, Jr. used this phrase (as distinct from modern Westernization) to characterize Sung urbanization and attendant changes in 'Sung society: change within tradition', *FEQ*, 14.4 (Aug. 1955) 479–88.

mercial greed fostered the growth of the opium trade on both sides. It became the great bilateral Sino-foreign joint enterprise of the nineteenth century, and it succeeded far beyond anyone's fears or foresight.

It requires only a modicum of imagination to see the Cantonese opium entrepreneur, who did his bit to usher China into modern international commerce, as the inheritor of a Chinese tradition that had much in common with the Western trading world. Some of the seemingly 'foreign influences' on the Republican Revolution may turn out at second glance to have coincided with or grown from older Chinese trends that shared certain traits with the foreigners. In what follows we can only indicate the dimensions of this historical problem.

MARITIME CHINA AS A MINOR TRADITION

Under piecemeal fragmentation by the social sciences and humanities, 'China' as a cultural entity has been dissolving into a sub-universe of great diversity. The holistic image is being supplanted by a great variety of discoveries; and research now deals with localities, cities, provinces, regions or macro-regions as useful areas for analysis.[11] Similarly the dominant agrarian-bureaucratic order of the Chinese heartland is being contrasted with peripheral and minority traditions in areas on China's frontiers.

The north-west Great Wall border zone was a peripheral area where intensive dry farming gave way to pastoralism. South-West China had been a peripheral area where irrigated rice culture gave way to the sub-tropical slash-and-burn agriculture of the hill tribes. Other such areas could be defined, for example, on the boundary of the semi-nomadic mixed economy of hunting, fishing and agriculture among the Tungusic tribes in the north-east. Of all these areas, however, the north-western steppe frontier had been the most important in history because pastoralism had produced the cavalry that could invade and rule North China. In contrast, the south-east coast had seen Chinese moving out overseas but no foreign invasions before the 1830s.

Maritime China was a peripheral region along the south-east coast. The swampy estuaries of the Yellow River north of Shantung and of the Yellow or Huai Rivers to the south inhibit coastal settlement and seafaring. North China generally lacks coastal mountains and rivers of the

11 In G. William Skinner's 'Regional urbanization in nineteenth-century China', nine macro-regions were devoted to 'sedentary agriculture' (p. 212), 'in essentially agrarian regional systems' (p. 253). Overseas trade is, thus far, peripheral to his study of urbanization. See G. William Skinner, ed. *The City in Late Imperial China.*

sort that make harbours on the Chekiang-Fukien coast. It also lacks export products such as tea, silk and ceramic ware. By the nineteenth century there was an extensive coastal trade between the Shanghai-Ningpo area and southern Manchuria. But Shantung and Liaotung did not bulk large in international trade. By this criterion the main region of our concern here stretched from the Yangtze delta to Hainan Island. It included, however, the offshore islands of the Pescadores and Taiwan, with Kyūshū, the Liu-ch'iu (Ryūkyū) islands, and Luzon as an outer fringe.[12]

In certain matters of style and tradition these peripheral or frontier regions contrasted with the dominant agrarian-bureaucratic heartland. Its distinctive and durable quality of collective cohesion needs to be recognized before we proceed with a lesser tradition. This majority order was the great achievement of early Chinese genius, more finely wrought than any other way of life in East Asia. It featured the imperial monarchy as its 'order-shaping moral centre',[13] and the Confucian three bonds (loyalty to the monarch, filial piety, wifely devotion to husbands) as its teaching of social order. The bedrock of this society was its extended family system. The oligarchic power of great clans was supplanted only in late T'ang and early Sung by the power of government to select the ruling class through the examination system.[14] Thereafter the classically-indoctrinated officials were the emperor's local agents while landowning and degree-holding gentry families were the backbone of the local elite.

Modern studies have of course broken through the Confucian crust of rule-by-virtue and normative harmony. They reveal an Old Order in which the mass of the common people were often wracked by natural calamity and local disorder – periodic starvation, banditry, inter-village feuds, chronic misery in the village, tyranny within the family, rapacious exploitation by landlords, corruption in officialdom.[15] However, this sordid picture of reality only highlights the persistence, if not success, of the classical propaganda as to how things ought to be.

Since the old China's normative ideals have contributed so heavily to the available Chinese and foreign writings on China (see, for example, volume 10, chapter 1), let us note here only their comparative efficacy in sustaining the dominant agrarian-bureaucratic tradition and its ruling class.

12 As defined by John E. Wills, Jr. in 'Maritime China from Wang Chih to Shih Lang: themes in peripheral history', 203–38 in Jonathan D. Spence and John E. Wills, Jr. eds. *From Ming to Ch'ing: conquest, region and continuity in seventeenth-century China.* See p. 206.
13 The phrase is from Hao Chang in *JAS*, 39.2 (Feb. 1980) 260.
14 David G. Johnson, *The medieval Chinese oligarchy*, 149–52. E. A. Kracke, Jr. estimated the civil service at 12,700 men in 1046. *Civil service in early Sung China 960–1067*, 55.
15 See for example the grim details in Jonathan D. Spence, *The death of woman Wang*, 39–48 et passim.

China's ruling-class supremacy had come down from the most ancient times. The roles of warrior-rulers and of recording scribes (literati) who assisted them in government appeared clearly at the dawn of Chinese society in the Shang.[16] The superior men of the upper class and the ordinary men of the common people figured in the classics of the Chou period. The universal kingship of the Son of Heaven and administration by his bureaucracy become well-established under the Han.[17] Step by step the ruling-class edifice was constructed, based on the philosophical premises of the Confucian canon, buttressed by the many practices subsumed under the examination system. The final emergence under the Ming and Ch'ing of a degree-holding gentry class, indoctrinated in loyalty to the throne and trained to sustain the socio-political order, is the best-known aspect of Chinese social history.[18] Much of the record (nearly all of which was produced from the ruling-class point of view) illustrates how comprehensively the scholar-official stratum, hardly 5 per cent of the population, dominated the military, the commercial and all the other groups in Chinese society.

This social order which every right-thinking Chinese strove to uphold included the subordination of women by men, of youth by age, of the individual by the family, of the peasant and the soldier by the scholarly degree-holder, and of the whole society by the imperial bureaucracy. This domination was all the more permanent because of its great flexibility, which allowed peasants to buy land, let almost every man compete to enter the examinations, acknowledged the indispensability of mothers and mothers-in-law, and permitted merchants to buy their way into the degree-holding class. The ruling class, in short, had learned how to perpetuate itself by absorbing the talent of Chinese society. Landlords, merchants, craftsmen and priests had little power independent of the official class, partly, of course, because landlord, merchant and official roles were normally represented among the sons of leading lineages. Familism in fact cemented the society together both at the village level and among the ruling class, and at the same time it provided channels of

---

16 By 2000 BC cities had grown up in several regions of China, especially Honan, Shantung, Kiangsu and Hupei, with 'city life, metallurgy, writing, and great art style made possible by a highly stratified society'. Kwang-chih Chang, *The archaeology of ancient China*, 217.

17 'Mental labor became the symbol of superior status. . . . Mencius characterized those who performed mental labor as "great men" or *chün-tzu* in contrast to the "small men" or *hsiao-jen*. This notion . . . had been widely accepted in Chinese society for centuries'. T'ung-tsu Ch'ü, *Han social structure*, 64.

18 For a graphic account of examinations under the Ch'ing, see Ichisada Miyazaki, trans. by Conrad Schirokauer, *China's examination hell: the civil service examinations of imperial China*; also Ping-ti Ho, *The ladder of success in imperial China: aspects of social mobility 1368–1911*.

mobility between the two.[19] The old China was not only agrarian-bureau-cratic but also familistic and rooted in the land. It contrasted with the sparseness of population and greater physical mobility of both the Inner Asian and the seafaring frontier zones.

Stereotypes like these reflect the long practice of imperial Confucianism in laying down normative principles of social order to socialize and indoctrinate the people. The diversity of Chinese life now appears to have been far greater than the chroniclers indicated. The great variety of geographic environments, local customs, architectural styles, spoken dialects, currency systems, crops, crafts, transportation and technology is only beginning to be explored. Nevertheless, China's long unity as a state derived from the ubiquitous acceptance of the agricultural peasant village, the lineage structure, the thin ruling stratum, the classical litera-ture, the official speech (*kuan-hua*), and the Confucian hierarchy of social statuses including the imperial supremacy. Clearly we confront here a triumph of teaching and administration over local particularism, or per-haps we should call it a symbiosis of universal and local, of high culture and popular cultures. In short, the great central tradition enshrined in orthodox writings and imperial utterances had learned how to live with and stay on top of minor traditions decentralized both among the villages and on the frontiers.

Let us now try to establish the identity and trace the growth of Mari-time China. It was distinguished first of all by features peculiar to the sea. Thus fish crops under the sea's surface and the highways over it were less restrictively located, less controllable in ancient times than crops and highways on the land. Meanwhile the energy cost in overcoming friction and moving vehicles was far less on water using the wind than it was on land using the footsteps of man or beast. Consequently a ship was cheaper to use and less controllable by others than a cart, pound for pound, and a small group of sailors could move goods that on land would require a considerable caravan. For trading enterprise the sea offered economic rewards superior to land trade. This principle was of course acknowledged in the great Chinese development of waterways for river and canal trans-port across the land.

At the same time, however, weather on the sea was more dangerous than by land, where the installations of highways or post routes, inns or caravanserai were far more reliable and supportive. Most of all, the land ways (and land waterways) could be controlled by large-scale govern-

---

19 See Maurice Freedman, *The study of Chinese society: essays by Maurice Freedman*, e.g. 'the richer and the stronger the lineage, the more it was likely to be differentiated into rich and poor, strong and weak', 339.

ment that positioned troops and tax collectors, while the seaways until recent times were controllable only as the configuration of sea-coasts permitted. In fine, the sea rewarded even small-scale enterprise and initiative, the continent facilitated bureaucratic government. The latter could add control of the sea to its control of the land only by developing naval power, which to be effective required a comparatively great investment in equipment and technology.

Such elementary factors, and the lack of rival naval powers nearby, led the early Chinese state to neglect the sea and leave it to the use of private bodies. The junk trade along the China coast and to South-East Asia grew up in private hands. Unlike the Inner Asian steppe where Mongol power called forth Chinese punitive expeditions, China's sea-coast seldom required such projections of state power.

On the other hand, the old assumption that prehistoric China was a land-bound society of North China, out of touch with the sea, has been spectacularly shattered by the archaeological revolution of recent decades. Excavations of Neolithic cultures that relied upon farming, used pottery, and made stone implements by grinding show their presence not only on the North China plain but also on the south-east China coast as a 'parallel regional development . . . especially in Taiwan.' Indeed, the Ta-p'en-k'eng neolithic site in Taipei county with its cord-marked pottery dated in the early third millennium BC is the type site for all the south-east coast.[20] This shows a clear Neolithic capacity for sea travel of no mean proportions. Maritime China for all practical purposes is as old as Continental China.[21]

No doubt the Canton and Yangtze deltas very early saw something like the port-to-port enterprise that Braudel characterizes as 'tramping' along the Mediterranean coasts.[22] But in the Mediterranean, as well as in the Baltic and the shallow seas of Malaya–Indonesia, rival cities and states could 'profit from their relations with each other through trading, piracy, plunder, raiding to force better conditions of trade, and colonization',[23] whereas the comparable situation best recorded in China was the inland naval relations among rival kingdoms along the lower Yangtze as in late Yuan times – hardly a genuine equivalent.[24]

20 Kwang-chih Chang, *The archaeology of ancient China*, 83; see also 85–91, 'The Ta-p'en-k'eng culture of the southeastern coast'.
21 As late as 1980 one may find ignorant references to 'that realm of Maritime China which forms a minor tradition roughly half as old as the great tradition of the continent. . .' (J.K. Fairbank in *CHOC* 11, Introduction).
22 Fernand Braudel, *The Mediterranean and the Mediterranean world in the age of Philip II*, 1.104.
23 Wills, 'Maritime China', 208.
24 Edward L. Dreyer, 'The Poyang campaign, 1363: inland naval warfare in the founding of the Ming dynasty', 202–42, in Frank A. Kierman, Jr. and John K. Fairbank, eds. *Chinese ways in warfare*.

Meanwhile, long-distance seafaring in Maritime China was at first inhibited by the distance to other centres of trade. China remained isolated, roughly 500 miles across dangerous seas from Kyūshū or Luzon, more than twice as far from Siam, and connected with Vietnam better by land than by sea. The fact that no major societies were within reach overseas during the first two millennia of Shang and Chou history, down to and even after the Ch'in unification of 221 BC and the setting up of the early Han empire, robbed seafaring of any strategic urgency. It remained a minor part of the early Chinese civilization. Armies of Han Wu-ti were mainly concerned with the Hsiung-nu in Inner Asia. Han maritime expeditions were sent to North Vietnam, to the South China coast, and to North Korea but this rudimentary naval power was still a sideshow compared with the Han expeditions sent beyond the Great Wall by land.[25]

China's early trade to South Asia grew up in Arab hands. Traders and crews arriving in China from West Asia in the seventh to ninth centuries used Persian as their lingua franca; and this was still true in Polo's day four centuries later. Sīrāf on the Persian Gulf was the main western emporium, later Hormuz. The large 'Persian ships' impressed the Chinese, who then had none comparable. The biggest came from Ceylon. They were 200 feet long and could carry 600 or 700 men.[26]

China's subsequent development in naval architecture and nautical technology confronts us with a persistent paradox (by European standards): China's achieving a capability for overseas expansion, and her failure to so expand in the early fifteenth century.[27]

Noted by many, studied by few, this paradox begins with the early superiority of Chinese nautical technology over that of medieval Europe. Chinese ships from very early on had flat bottoms, no keels, and transverse bulkheads (like the sections of a split bamboo) which easily formed watertight compartments. They also developed as early as the Han a balanced sternpost rudder such as was not seen in the West until a thousand years after its use in China. Meanwhile the compass was developed in

---

25 Michael Loewe, *Military operations in the Han period*, 3; *ibid.* 'The campaigns of Han Wu-ti', 67–122 in Kierman and Fairbank, eds. *Chinese ways in warfare*. For a collection of early Chinese textual references to sea contact with the south see Wang Gungwu, 'The Nanhai trade', *Journal of the Malayan Branch of the Royal Asiatic Society*, 31 (1958) pt 2.1–135. Professor Wang suggests the Yueh people should be identified as '"not yet Chinese" (to borrow Lattimore's phrase) from Ningpo to Hanoi before the Han. They were still mainly so along the coast until the T'ang. This is why Fukien-Kwangtung people still call themselves "T'ang-jen".' [Personal communication.]

26 Edward H. Schafer, *The golden peaches of Samarkand: a study of T'ang exotica*, 12–13. Cp. M. Elvin, *The pattern of the Chinese past*, 135–9.

27 On this major conundrum Joseph R. Levenson's paperback *European expansion and the counter-example of Asia, 1300–1600*, assembled key excerpts from a score of scholars under categories of 'technology', 'religion', 'spirit' and 'social structure'.

China and its use in navigation there was recorded at least a century earlier than in the West.[28] This early superiority to European nautical technology and naval architecture was part and parcel of a general Chinese technological superiority during the Sung. Chinese seamanship had already had a long development on the Yangtze and other inland waterways as well as on the China coast, where one had to deal with the monsoons and their punctuation by typhoons. Chinese traders in the era before Columbus faced longer voyages and rougher seas than the Europeans. The Taiwan Straits, for example, can make the Bay of Biscay seem like a mill-pond. The T'ang sea route to Japan was undoubtedly as challenging as any voyage in the Mediterranean.

China's early maritime age was the three centuries from c. 1150 to c. 1450, after the Southern Sung dynasty was forced south in 1127 from Kaifeng to Hangchow and became more dependent on sea trade. No doubt the Arab expansion under Islam in the waters of both the Mediterranean and the Indian Ocean had been a common stimulus to both European and Chinese seafaring. But the more advanced civilization of China put Chinese maritime activity at first ahead of the fragmented and impecunious efforts of the Europeans. By the time the Crusades and their attendant commerce had brought Italian seapower into the Eastern Mediterranean, the Southern Sung had developed better ships and larger fleets. They finally set up an overall naval command in 1132, although it still secured its fleet less by building than by hiring or taking over merchant vessels. The government built harbours, encouraged foreign trade and taxed it through superintendencies of merchant shipping set up in nine ports.[29]

The early efflorescence of Maritime China under the Southern Sung was incorporated after 1279 into the Mongol empire. China's naval power and her sea trade went ahead, as part of the Mongols' continued effort at global expansion. The Mongol naval attack on Japan in 1274 used a fleet of 900 ships which transported 250,000 soldiers. After the capture of 800 vessels of the Sung fleet in 1279, the Mongol expedition against Japan in 1281 sent out 4,400 ships – far more fighting men than Europe had ever seen afloat. The Mongol fleet of some 1,000 ships sent to Java in 1292 was a bigger expedition than any pre-Columbian counterpart in Europe.[30]

28 Joseph Needham, et al. Science and civilisation in China, 4 pt 3 sec. 29: 'Nautical technology', 379 ff. On the median rudder, see 650 ff. On the compass, 562 ff.
29 On the Sung and Yuan navies see the pioneer work of J. P. Lo (Lo Jung-pang), especially 'The emergence of China as a sea power during the late Sung and early Yuan periods', FEQ, 14.4 (1955) 489–504; 'Maritime commerce and its relation to the Sung navy', Journal of the Economic and Social History of the Orient, 12.1 (1969) 57–101; and 'The decline of the early Ming navy', Oriens extremus, 5.2 (Dec. 1958) 149–68.
30 Needham, Science and civilisation, 4. pt 3.477.

Mongol seapower was followed by that of the early Ming and the seven great maritime expeditions sent into and across the Indian Ocean in the years 1405–33. Chinese seafaring was then pre-eminent. The ocean-going junk of this period, for example, was typically 250 feet long by 110 feet broad and of 25 feet draught, displacing around 1,250 tons. It might have six masts up to 90 feet high and a dozen or more watertight compartments. On a long voyage it might average 4.4 knots. Such a vessel was clearly superior to the ships of pre-Columbian Europe.[31] Maritime China had come of age and at that time was potentially the world's top seapower, ahead of the Portuguese and Spanish.

European naval power over-running the globe after 1492 was thus a late Ming phenomenon chronologically, a sudden explosion powered by a dynamism of technological advance, national rivalries, religious zeal and capitalist enterprise that was not equally present in China. But European expansion was a cumulative process, slow at first, and it penetrated the Far East after Albuquerque took Malacca in 1511 only by the default of Chinese seapower. For China's maritime activity, despite its qualitative superiority to that of Europe as late as 1430, was still a minor tradition in the Chinese state and society. Once the Ming rulers had expelled the Mongol dynasts and demonstrated their early expansive capacity both by land and by sea, they found themselves saddled still with the menace of Mongol cavalry on their Inner Asian frontier. The recrudescence of this military power, which captured the emperor and besieged Peking in 1449, reconfirmed the dominant agrarian-bureaucratic nature of the Chinese realm. Near 'the Great Wall an armed society developed. The northern frontier became the fixation, the virtual obsession of many Chinese statesmen throughout the mid and late Ming.' This 'poisoned Sino-Mongol relationship' affected all the rest of China's foreign contact.[32]

Maritime China, for all its precocity, remained a subordinate and even marginal appendage of Continental China. Most indicative was the fact that shipbuilding, seafaring and foreign trade remained of marginal interest to scholars. The sea and sea-craft made no appeal to the Chinese literati. Maritime contact with Japan and South-East Asia had become of note to chroniclers only in the T'ang. Arab merchants at Canton and Zayton (Ch'üan-chou) became noteworthy only in the Sung. In this turning inwards, the seafaring-commercial life that had grown up with Maritime China was disesteemed and disregarded.

The eclipse of the government's seaward expansion by the landward

---

31 J.V.G. Mills, *Ma Huan, Ying-yai sheng-lan, The overall survey of the ocean's shores (1433)*, 303 ff.
32 Frederick W. Mote, 'The T'u-mu incident of 1449', 243–72 in Kierman and Fairbank, *Chinese ways in warfare*. See 270–2.

orientation of the Chinese empire was evidenced in many ways. The Ming naval expeditions of 1405–33 had been exceptional exploits handled by palace eunuchs like the great Cheng-ho, a Muslim who was not of the regular bureaucracy. Jealous bureaucrats all but destroyed the record of his voyages. Private Chinese sea trade continued to grow on the eastern and western junk routes to Java and Malacca, where the Portuguese after 1511 found a multitude of Chinese vessels and merchants already active. The Ming government, however, gave foreign trade no support but taxed and regulated it without any policy of encouragement. Chinese were forbidden to go out to sea to trade. Indeed the dogma arose that foreign trade was permitted only in connection with tribute missions from foreign rulers.

In the 1550s when 'Japanese pirates' (*wo-k'ou*) appeared on the China coast, most of them being in fact Chinese, the Ming dealt with them defensively like raiders from the steppe on the Great Wall frontier. Smuggling flourished, but trade was interdicted to 'starve them out' and at one time local populations were ordered to withdraw inland from the coast, resulting in considerable resettlement and economic dislocation.[33] 'To officials, the sea represented problems, not opportunities, and statecraft stopped, if not at the water's edge, certainly short of the high seas. *Pao-chia* and other registration and control techniques; forts, garrisons and coastal control squadrons; and management of government shipyards were among the foci of their interest. Chinese seafarers' solid knowledge of areas beyond the seas rarely found its way into discussions of statecraft.'[34]

To historians of the Ming, China's failure to expand like Europe after 1450 is no mystery once one takes account of the local facts, beginning with the traditional institutions and values of the dominant agrarian-bureaucratic culture. Without benefit of such a concept of culture, however, the problem remains murky indeed.[35]

33 Kwan-wai So. *Japanese piracy in Ming China during the 16th century*, ch. 3.
34 Wills, 'Maritime China', 215.
35 For example, Immanuel Wallerstein, *The modern world-system: capitalist agriculture and the origins of the European world-economy in the 16th century*, 38–47, cites 17 Western scholars, none of them primarily concerned with Ming history, as to why the Chinese failed to expand like the Portuguese and Spanish. Since he has no category of 'culture' as the overall configuration due to the interplay of economy, polity, social structure, values and other aspects of a society, Wallerstein concludes in a quandary that there was no 'significant difference between Europe and China in the fifteenth century on certain base points: population, area, state of technology (both in agriculture and in naval engineering). To the extent that there were differences it would be hard to use them to account for the magnitude of the difference of development in the coming centuries . . . the difference in value systems seems both grossly exaggerated and, to the extent it existed, once again not to account for the different consequences. . .'.

Our thumbnail sketch of Maritime China's history enters a new phase with the arrival of Europeans in East Asian waters, especially of the Dutch and British East India Companies after 1600. This coincided with Japan's brief but vigorous overseas expansion and a recrudescence of Chinese seapower on the south-east coast. During the Ming to Ch'ing transition of the seventeenth century, however, the leadership was taken not by Ming emperors or Manchu conquerors but by a succession of local Chinese pirate leaders. Their exploits bespoke the size and value of the growing international trade of East Asia that drew Batavia, Malacca, Macao, Amoy, Nagasaki, Hirado, Manila (and Acapulco) into contact. But this growth of naval-commercial power on the maritime frontier was in private hands. It climaxed in the career of Cheng Ch'eng-kung ('Koxinga'), who in 1659 invaded the Yangtze with over 1,000 vessels and unavailingly besieged Nanking before his death in 1661.

With the final establishment of Manchu rule in China, the continental anti-seafaring view was reconfirmed. All overseas trade was banned until 1684, the size of naval vessels was restricted, and as the Manchu rulers became Confucian emperors they reaffirmed the Chinese empire's agrarian-bureaucratic ideals. In foreign relations these assumed 'that the civilized order prevailing in China was one of ritual or propriety and this order must be insulated from contamination by the disorder outside.' The aim was therefore 'to prevent contact, not profit from it, to control foreigners, not cooperate with them', and this led to a Chinese style of 'unilateral decision making and bureaucratic regulation, not negotiation and commitment by treaty'.[36]

Here we see the peripheral culture of Inner Asian tribal nomadism and semi-nomadism reinforcing the anti-seafaring tradition of the Chinese heartland. It is commonly observed that the Mongol and Manchu conquests strengthened the despotism of the Chinese monarchy. By the same token the Manchus gave little or no encouragement to seafaring enterprise. The result was the continued subordination of seafaring as part and parcel of the continued domination of the coast by the continent and of the merchant by the bureaucrat. The Ch'ing remained strategically preoccupied with Inner Asia.[37]

The customary dependence of merchants on officials within China, however, did not prevent the Chinese commercial diaspora into South-East Asia, where the mandarins had no thought of following merchants across the water. China's foreign trade since the Sung had of course been

---

36 John E. Wills, Jr. *Pepper, guns and parleys: the Dutch East India Company and China 1622–1681*, 207.
37 As depicted in *CHOC* vol. 10, chs. 2, 7 and 8.

a function of the growth of domestic trade. No market overseas could rival the continental empire's home market. The early growth of trade within China from the eighth to thirteenth centuries had been on the whole successfully contained by the bureaucratic state, but thereafter domestic commerce increasingly escaped from bureaucratic controls. During the Ming special products of one region such as Fukien teas and Chekiang silks, or of one producing centre like porcelain from Ching-te-chen in Kiangsi, were distributed over the empire by long-distance trading firms. The Yangtze and the Grand Canal were only the most prominent arteries of this growing domestic trade, which made China by the eighteenth century a semi-free-trade area bigger than Europe. In short, the agrarian-bureaucratic tradition of the Chinese state now rested upon a vibrant commercial economy, which officials acknowledged in their private arrangements more fully than in their ideological pronouncements. The Ch'ing could still decry the potentialities of seafaring but tea, silk and porcelain exports, and rice and opium imports betrayed the real situation – the enormous and largely self-sufficient domestic trade of the Middle Kingdom was ready for a greater degree of international exchange, and the South China merchants who emerged in the European colonies in South-East Asia were eager to be its agents.

This expansion of Maritime China created the main channel by which Western trade and enterprise later invaded the Middle Kingdom. Study of it has hardly begun but various outlines are discernible.[38] Chinese in Siam soon became magnates in the eighteenth-century rice trade to China, extensive Chinese immigration occurred, and eventually Taksin, who largely reunited the country and reigned for 14 years after 1767, was half Chinese and proud of it. Chinese traders became prominent in all the junk trade's ports-of-call down the Malay peninsula and around to Penang. After 1819 Singapore proved a success for its founder, T. S. Raffles, when the Chinese moved in. Manila under the Spaniards lived for a time in fear of the Chinese pirate Limahong because so much of its trade was in Chinese hands. The Acapulco galleon trade made its profit from Chinese silk exports as well as Mexican silver imports to China.

During the three centuries from 1600 to 1900 when European colonialism took over South-East Asia, the Overseas Chinese were an essential part of the act. All of the colonial powers – Portugal, Spain, Holland, Great Britain and even France – during their hey-day in South-East Asia found the Chinese empire paid them no mind but Chinese merchants handled their local retail trade and often served as tax-collectors, conces-

---

38 One may still profit from the judicious survey of Sir George Sansom, *The Western world and Japan: a study in the interaction of European and Asiatic cultures*. See pt 1, 'Europe and Asia'.

sionaires and middlemen vis-à-vis the native peoples. By the nineteenth century, when Western shipping in the 'coolie' trade moved still more Chinese migrants into the area, the overseas communities of Maritime China constituted a local commercial power even though unsupervised by the Manchu government.

Thus we derive an image of the agrarian-bureaucratic empire sedulously preserving its ideological structure on the continent even while its domestic commerce through its coastal fringe was being drawn into integral relations with the developing commercial-military world of maritime trade, rivalries among nations, colonialism and technological innovation in the service of largely European capitalism.

THE TREATY-PORT MIXTURE

What perspective do these broad themes and images provide for China's modern experience? The treaty system of the century 1842–1943 can be viewed as a mediating device that cushioned the shock of cultural contact between China and the commercial West. As suggested in volume 10,[39] the system was as much Chinese as foreign in origin, only the situation grew beyond Ch'ing control. Through the legal institution of extraterritoriality the foreigners in the ports were given a privileged status comparable to that of the literati-official ruling class itself. Missionaries and Confucian scholars, for example, both had immunity from the magistrate's bastinado. Foreign gunboats could not be kept out. In this way the foreigners in China became assimilated into the new power structure in which the treaty powers exercised certain aspects of sovereignty within the synarchic (multi-governed) Chinese state.

The treaty ports, administered mainly by foreigners but peopled mainly by Chinese, were products of cultural symbiosis, junction points where Western expansion joined forces with the growth of Maritime China. This hybrid China grew up after 1842 in the new commercial cities at the nodes of China's largely water-borne commerce. Shanghai and the other treaty ports were reminiscent of Penang, Malacca, Singapore, Batavia, Manila and other European entrepôts where earlier Chinese traders had made their way successfully. The extension of Western naval-political power to the China coast formed a nurturing matrix for modern-style Chinese trade and enterprise. All of these ports were foci of an international commercial growth in which the Chinese participated more and more.[40]

39 CHOC 10.375–85, 'China's first "unequal treaty" settlement (1835)'; and ch. 5.
40 On European expansion via the trading port network, see Rhoads Murphey, *The outsiders:*

It is now recognized that Chinese capital mixed with foreign capital in this development, and that the comprador was the foreign firm's actual manager, not a mere hired hand. The treaty ports were joint Sino-foreign achievements. They represented on Chinese soil in their 'semi-colonial' way a tacit partnership of Westerners and Chinese even more active than the Sino-foreign relationships that had emerged in the European colonies in South-East Asia. As in Hong Kong, so in Shanghai, Hankow and elsewhere, Western naval power and commerce-minded administration provided a political matrix within which Chinese enterprise supplied a dynamic economic element. The Westerners in their style sought a free and open market with a published customs tariff and no licensed monopolies – keeping the Chinese bureaucrats at bay. Their compradors in Chinese style knew the local network of personal interests and relationships and, while often claiming the foreigners' privileges of free trade, could make use of necessary connections in the complex Chinese structures of bureaucracy and social hierarchy.[41]

So much was the treaty-port growth a joint Sino-foreign enterprise that foreign colonialism was stopped in its tracks. Western investment in treaty-port China remained marginal as the capitalists of London, Paris and New York found better opportunities in newer, less crowded lands like the United States and Argentina. When J. M. Forbes of Russell and Company after 1845 invested his profits from the opium trade in Middle Western railways, he was following the main chance. It was not to be found in China. Semi-colonialism in China was in large part a political phenomenon of special privilege; it was less clearly an economic phenomenon of one-sided exploitation. The full colonialism of foreign-run plantations producing for export never developed. The overall economic impact of imperialism, especially the balance between oppressive exploitation and stimulus to economic growth, remains much debated.[42]

The umbilical connection between the China treaty ports and the international trade of South-East Asia has not been adequately explored. Except for the staple trade carried by the East Indiamen between London and Canton, European and at first even American trade to the Far East

the Western experience in India and China, ch. 2. The most detailed study of the growth of the commercial credit network to 1840 is W. E. Cheong, Mandarins and merchants: Jardine Matheson & Co., a China agency of the early nineteenth century.

41 W. E. Cheong notes that by 1838 'Practices in trade and contracts well understood by then at Canton by both Westerners and Chinese, had to be fashioned anew with the merchants on the coast . . . one is struck by the close approximation of the functions of these Chinese agents and brokers on whom Jardine's . . . increasingly depended, to the latter day comprador of the treaty ports'. See his Mandarins and merchants, 138.

42 This issue is posed in Chi-ming Hou, Foreign investment and economic development in China 1840–1937. There is a large literature.

passed through the Indian Ocean and mingled with the local, Arab, Indian and Chinese commerce that had long been established in South-East Asia. Early American traders from Salem or Philadelphia might call at Penang, Bencoolen, Achin, Singapore, Batavia or Manila *en route* to and from Macao and Canton. British-Indian and Parsee opium distributors supplied South-East Asia as well as China from the East India Company production.

The nineteenth-century communities of the Overseas Chinese (*hua-ch'iao*, 'Chinese sojourners' abroad) were built up by Western as well as Chinese and local trade, including the Sino-foreign 'coolie trade' of the mid nineteenth century. As with opium imports, the export of cargoes of contract labourers required Chinese and Western private cooperation and eventually provoked joint official regulation. But such shipments were only a late increment in the seaborne commerce of the China coast.

We know something of the coast trade of Ningpo merchants to obtain soy beans from Manchuria, and of the tribute trade with the island kingdom of Liu Ch'iu (Okinawa) which masked a Chinese exchange with Japan. Chinese trade from the Fukien ports, especially Amoy, with the Nan-yang ('southern ocean', the whole area now called South-East Asia) generally overshadowed that of Canton. The import of Siamese rice at Canton, again within the bulging framework of tributary relations, had in the eighteenth century already become a staple trade as important as the tea and silk exports via Canton to London in the ships of the British East India Company.[43]

All of this bespoke a Chinese entrepreneurship in sea trade that was largely beyond bureaucratic regulation. The Ch'ing writ did not run overseas. The hazards of seafaring, the alien peoples to be dealt with abroad, the high personal risk and lack of official protection, were all rather similar to the conditions faced by Western maritime traders. However, where the Western nations developed naval power, bases and empires to protect their merchants, the Chinese could only rely upon their own community solidarity in alien ports, and often got the worst of it. They were massacred at Manila as well as elsewhere and persevered often on sufferance. But the commercial spirit was as strong in them as in the Western adventurers and entrepreneurial administrators in Asia. It has been suggested that Confucianism had bequeathed to Chinese scholars an inner tension as powerful as that which impelled the Puri-

43 In comparison with the eye-opening pioneer work of G. William Skinner, *Chinese society in Thailand: an analytical history* (1957), the 1977 publication of Sarasin Viraphol, *Tribute and profit: Sino-Siamese trade, 1652–1853*, *inter alia*, puts the study of Chinese-Thai relations on an entirely new source basis now awaiting research. See Viraphol's 'bibliographical note', 342–60.

tans.[44] Presumably there was a comparable drive among Chinese merchants in their search for success.

Either this drive for success or their speculative impulse, for which they are famous, made Chinese merchants the chief actors in the treaty-port trade. The early comprador-managers of the new Western trade came from the mixed pidgin-English milieu of Canton-Macao. But the growth of Shanghai was led by Chekiang merchant-bankers from Ningpo, the southern anchor of the coast trade to Manchuria. Very soon after China's final opening in 1860 the big firms like Jardine, Matheson and Company found it needless to staff the smaller ports with the usual young Scotsmen because their Cantonese or Ningpo compradors could handle the trade just as well alone.

The growth of treaty-port trade in China brought with it the new technology of transport and industry, a new knowledge of foreign nations, and so a growth of nationalism. The pioneer geographies of missionaries like Gutzlaff and Bridgman stimulated the production of the early geographies of Wei Yuan and Hsu Chi-yü, which in the 1840s anticipated the translation programmes of the Kiangnan Arsenal and the Society for the Diffusion of Christian and General Knowledge (SDK) in later decades. Christian reformers and journalists like Wang T'ao arose under foreign influence in Hong Kong and the treaty ports to urge the cause of Chinese nationalism. Sun Yat-sen came from near the earliest foreign port, Macao, and was educated abroad in Honolulu and Hong Kong. That most of his active life was lived outside China, although he was the chief apostle of its modern nationalism, illustrates how China's Westernizers generally were men of the coastal frontier.

The new ideas conveyed by such forerunners were neither all-foreign nor all-Chinese in origin. Wei and Hsu showed proper statecraftsmen's interest in Western technology. Wang and Sun were concerned about popular participation in government. The twentieth-century Chinese reformers' slogan 'Science and Democracy' had its nineteenth-century antecedents both in China and abroad.

China's maritime connections thus not only served as the channels of the Western invasion, they also drew a new Chinese leadership into the new port cities like Shanghai, Tientsin, Kiukiang and Hankow. As more and more students went to Japan and the West to study how to save their homeland, they were drawn away from the rural scene with which

44 In finding a Confucian ethic similar to the Protestant ethic, Thomas A. Metzger even suggests 'China's transformative vision of modernization was itself rooted in tradition' – a lively topic. See 'Review symposium' on Thomas A. Metzger's *Escape from predicament: Neo-Confucianism and China's evolving political culture*, in *JAS*, 39.2 (Feb. 1980) 235–90. See 282.

China's gentry ruling class had ordinarily retained contact. China's new modernizers generally lost their agricultural roots. In the end many were deracinated. The young revolutionaries of the Kuomintang generation from 1895 onwards were typically urban products less acquainted with the peasant villages. In their effort to save China by Westernization they mastered many aspects of Western learning and technology but often found themselves out of touch with the Chinese common people. But their demands for constitutional government, for railway building under Chinese control, for the recovery of sovereign rights impaired by the unequal treaties, all contributed to the extinction both of the Manchu dynasty and of the monarchy of the Son of Heaven. All these nationalistic demands showed foreign influence.

The first phase of the Chinese revolution in this way represented both Chinese and foreign influences conveyed largely through the medium of Maritime China. The treaty ports reinforced and gave scope to the Chinese tradition of overseas trade free of bureaucratic control abroad. This minor tradition of maritime enterprise and economic growth, most evident to foreigners originally at Singapore and Canton and also in the opium and coolie trades, contributed to the hybrid society of the treaty ports and nurtured the Westernization movement as well as the early Chinese Christian church. It fostered individualism and an interest in scientific technology at the same time that it aroused patriotism and pride of culture.

We cannot yet describe in detail the 'maritime' impact on Chinese business organization and practice. But certain broad effects are already apparent. Because the Chinese patriots who sprang from this background were seldom rooted in the villages, their new nationalism concentrated its hopes upon the Chinese state-and-culture as a whole, 'China' as against the outside nations. The mechanical devices of industry and the political institutions of constitutional democracy both seemed at first to be essential importations for the salvation of 'China'. This first generation after 1900 had little concept of or desire for basic social revolution. Sufficient unto the day was the problem of creating a unified Chinese nation-state and its necessary economic base.

For this purpose of national salvation China's central tradition of course had much to offer. The aim of nation-building could be subsumed under the ancient Legalist slogan 'enrich the state, strengthen the military' (*fu-kuo ch'iang-ping*), as had been done in Japan. Projects for this purpose appeared as new applications of the Ming and Ch'ing administrators' art of statecraft, which extolled learning 'of practical use in the administration of society' (*ching-shih chih yung*). In practice this often involved in time-honoured fashion the management and manipulation of the populace. Popular training under firm safeguards was foreseen as a necessary prerequisite for modern self-government. By some this was given the name 'tutelage'. Thus China's bureaucratic tradition seemed to offer help in the pursuit of the Western goal of popular participation.

Emerging from this background, the Revolution of 1911 shares the ambivalence of the treaty-port era as a whole. In form it is more an end than a beginning. To some degree it is the petering out of a dynasty, although to some degree it is a triumph of nationalism and other influences coming by sea to the port cities of China's littoral along the coast and up the Yangtze. Revolutionary organizing is chiefly by returned students from Japan. Financing comes from Overseas Chinese communities. Ideas like constitutionalism and the Three People's Principles of Dr Sun come from the liberal West. Yet those who attain power in the provincial assemblies of 1911 are not the revolutionaries but the new merchant gentry, while military men become governors. They all believe in the economic and military development visible in Japan and the industrializing Western nations, but violent revolution is not what they desire.

The business class that emerges is similarly ambivalent. Modern-style Chinese banks become active auxiliaries of government finance, buying bond issues at large discounts and creating a new class of financiers who hover on the borderline between simple, bureaucratic capitalism and actual industrial enterprise. For a time in the 1920s, as our chapter 12 below indicates, the ideology of liberalism is as widely embraced among Shanghai merchants as among Peking intellectuals.

From the 1890s we may discern several features of modern Chinese life associated with or coloured by the maritime tradition: first, the propriety and prestige of things foreign, including Christianity, then the spreading sense of nationalism and of the struggle for survival among nations. With this came ideas of progress and the vital role of science and technology, concepts of individualism less bound by family ties and, more vaguely, of political rights and constitutional government. Finally, underlying all of these was the independent respectability of capitalist enterprise and its need for legal safeguards.

The mere recital of such themes, which figure prominently in this volume, suggests the limitations of Maritime China vis-à-vis the problems of the great heartland. Deep within China the issue was not simply to develop and apply more broadly an urban way of life and institutions of trade that had long been nurtured in China's old society and its foreign contact. On the contrary, the issue among the peasant villages was one of continuity versus disruption, how to remake the traditional order to take account of modern technology, modern egalitarianism and political participation. This was an issue, as we now see, of social transformation and regeneration; in the end, of revolution.

But social revolution was not espoused in 1911. One reason was still the ingrained political passivity of the peasant masses and their lack of leadership. Another reason was the patriotic fear that prolonged disorder would invite foreign intervention. Revolutionaries of all camps therefore 'accepted the compromise that stopped the revolution short and brought Yuan Shih-k'ai to power. The determining factor was the foreign omnipresence.'[45]

Yet, being foreign, the foreign omnipresence remained superficial to the vast mass of agrarian China. The traditional rural society kept on its way in its own style, not yet disrupted by urban-inspired changes. The new leaders of Chinese nationalism in the 1920s were not produced directly from it nor concerned primarily with its problems. Peasant China, in short, proved to be a further bourne, beyond the purview and capacity of urban-centred and foreign-inspired revolutionaries. We leave it beyond the scope of this introductory essay.

China's social revolution was a long time coming. It could not easily find a foreign model. Insofar as China's peasant mass was uniquely large, dense and imperturbable, the ingredients of social revolution had to be mobilized mainly from within the old society. This could not be done quickly but only in proportion as the immemorial agrarian society was infiltrated by urban-maritime ideas (like that of material progress), subjected to greater commercialism, upset by new values (like women's equality) and shattered by warfare, rapine and destruction. So much had to be torn down and shown up! Yet even then the agrarian society could never be a clean slate awaiting fresh writing. The new message had to use old terms in a fresh way and create its new order out of old ingredients.

Insofar as Maritime China was a channel for change, it started something it could not finish. The rebel tradition in the old agrarian-bureaucratic China had been that of millenarian sects like the White Lotus Society in the north and of brotherhoods among places of trade like the Triad Society in the south. This rebel tradition had been secret and fanatical, too often in the negative guise of Boxerism, profoundly anti-intellectual and likely to degenerate into local feuding.[46] What happens in the twentieth century to revolutionize the major agrarian-bureaucratic tradition

45 Mary Clabaugh Wright, *China in revolution: the first phase 1900–1913*, 55.
46 For a recent close look at Boxer phenomena see Mark Elvin, 'Mandarins and millennarians: reflections on the Boxer uprising of 1899–1900', *Journal of the Anthropological Society of Oxford*, 10.3 (1979) 115–38.

of the Chinese heartland is thus another universe of discourse and research. It is even more complex and multi-faceted than China's minor maritime tradition that we have just been sketching. We are just beginning to understand its structures of folk religion, familism and local economy.

In the present volume the next two chapters, on the Chinese economy and the foreign presence, provide a framework for both volume 12 and volume 13 by covering their subjects down into the late 1940s. The following three chapters deal with President Yuan Shih-k'ai, the Peking government and the warlords – mainly North China politics – to 1928. Chapters 7, 8 and 9 then pursue developments in thought and in literature from the 1890s to 1928, while chapters 10 and 11 concern the early communist movement and the complex course of the Nationalist Revolution in the tumultuous mid 1920s. The volume concludes with the checkered career of the business class, mainly in Shanghai, into the 1930s.

Volume 13, in addition to the history of the Nationalist government, the Japanese invasion, and the rise of the CCP, will consider certain aspects of the early republic not dealt with here. These include the transformation of the local order (whatever happened to the gentry class?), the nature of the peasant movement, the growth of the modern scientific-academic community, the vicissitudes of China's foreign relations centring around the aggression of Japan, and the great Sino-Japanese and KMT-CCP conflicts between 1937 and 1949. Even this further range of subject matter may leave us hard put to trace the revolutionary processes at work in the remnants of China's ancient rural society. Perhaps we can understand how even the communist movement in China, though posited on a faith in social revolution, found the secret of success only after 1928. In the context outlined above, Mao Tse-tung's task thereafter was how to supplant or 'modernize' China's continental tradition, the agrarian-bureaucratic and local-commercial order of the heartland. In the effort he confronted the heritage of Maritime China, the industrial technology and foreign trade of port cities, though they no longer seemed a minor tradition.

Plainly, abstractions such as Maritime and Continental China have fuzzy edges – they are suggestive rhetoric rather than analytic cutting tools. Yet they cast light on a major puzzle of China's twentieth-century history – the shifting convergence-cum-conflict between the industrial and the social revolutions. No doubt two traditions – one, the scientific-technological development of material things, the other, a moral crusade to change social class structure – are interwoven in most revolutions. But the tortuous gyrations of politics in recent decades suggest that modern China lies peculiarly on a fault line between deep-laid continental and maritime traditions.

CHAPTER 2

ECONOMIC TRENDS, 1912–49

INTRODUCTION: AN OVERVIEW

To survey the history of the Chinese economy from the end of the Manchu dynasty to the establishment of the People's Republic is inevitably to tell a tale in a minor key. The years prior to 1949 saw no 'take-off' towards sustained growth of aggregate output and the possibility of increased individual welfare that might accompany it. At best, the great majority of Chinese merely sustained and reproduced themselves at the subsistence level to which, the callous might say, they had long since become accustomed. In the bitter decade of war and civil war which began in the mid 1930s, the standard of life for many fell short even of that customary level.[1]

A cautious weighing of what little is definitely known suggests that aggregate output grew only slowly during 1912–49, and that there was no increase in per capita income. Nor was there any downward trend in average income. Although a small modern industrial and transport sector, which first appeared in the late nineteenth century, continued to grow at a comparatively rapid rate, its impact was minimal before 1949. The relative factor supplies of land, labour and capital remained basically unaltered. The occupational distribution of the population was hardly changed; nor in spite of some expansion of the urban population was the urban-rural ratio significantly disturbed during these four decades. While some new products were introduced from abroad and from domestic factories, quantitatively they were a mere dribble, and they scarcely affected the quality of life. Institutions for the creation of credit remained few and feeble; the organization of a unified national market was never achieved. Foreign trade was relatively unimportant to the majority of the population. Throughout rural China a demographic

---

1 This chapter excludes any consideration of communist-controlled China which included areas inhabited by some 90 million people in 1945 and operated in part with different economic assumptions. See Peter Schran, *Guerrilla economy: the development of the Shensi-Kansu-Ninghsia border region, 1937–1945.*

pattern of high birth rates and high death rates persisted. Economic hardship, in rural China in particular, was endemic, and probably grew more critical after the outbreak of war in 1937. Yet in the absence of a profound transformation of values in a significant portion of the elite leadership of Chinese society, which led ultimately to the harnessing of this distress to political ends not directly determined by the processes of the economy itself, there is no good reason to believe that the economic system would either have collapsed catastrophically or advanced rapidly towards modern economic growth. As a system, China's economy which was 'pre-modern' even in the mid twentieth century ceased to be viable only after 1949 – and then as a consequence of explicit political choice by the victorious Communist Party and not primarily as a result of lethal economic contradictions.

While the quantitative indicators do not show large changes during the republican era, China in 1949 was nevertheless different from China in 1912. The small industrial and transport sector and, perhaps even more, the reservoir of technical skills and of experience with complex economic organizations – the hundreds of thousands of workers, technicians and managers who had themselves 'become modern' – provided a base upon which the People's Republic could and did build.

As a crude first approximation, the Chinese economy prior to 1949 may be described as consisting of a large agricultural (or rural) sector encompassing approximately 75 per cent of the population and a much smaller non-agricultural (or urban) sector with its principal base in the semi-modern treaty-port cities. Rural China grew the agricultural products which constituted 65 per cent of national output, and also made use of the handicrafts, petty trade and old-fashioned transport. To the urban sector was attached, with ties of varying strength, an agricultural hinterland. It was located mainly along rivers and railways leading to the ports, and may be differentiated from the mass of rural China by the greater degree to which it traded with the coastal and riverine cities of the urban sector.

The agricultural sector was composed mainly of 60 to 70 million family farms. Perhaps one-half were owner-operated, one-quarter were farmed by part-owners who rented varying portions of their land, and the remaining quarter was cultivated by tenant farmers. These families lived in the several hundred thousand villages that filled most of the landscape of the arable parts of China. In the course of the first half of the twentieth century the average size of these farms decreased as the growth of population exceeded the increments to arable land. Only a few areas in rural China (in the regions of dense population) lacked agglomerated settle-

MAP 2.   Provinces of China under the Republic

ments – parts of Szechwan, for example, where scattered farmsteads were the norm. The typical landscape was dotted with clusters of houses arranged along one or more streets that were surrounded by the village fields. So closely spaced were the villages in the areas of densest settlement that one was usually within sight of another. In response to local disorder in the nineteenth century many villages, first in North China and then also in the south, had erected protective walls so that the village was defined in terms of the inhabitants living within its earthen or brick ramparts. This definition proved compatible with the lineage system insofar as many village populations shared the same or a small number of different surnames. The boundaries between the fields of the residents of one village and those owned by its closest neighbours were not, however, so unambiguously distinguishable. In the course of time farm land changed hands, and it was not unusual for the mortgagee (and possible eventual owner) of property in village A to be a resident of village B, or even of village X at some distance removed from A.

This indeterminacy of village boundaries began to change only in the latter part of the nineteenth century when increased tax demands by hsien (county) governments made it essential that the villages be concerned about the precise areas in which the new levies would be collected. Even in the twentieth century, while more formal village organizations were elaborated, the rural village was usually not an effective political unit, certainly not for the purpose of organizing its human and material resources for economic development. Indeed, the frequent inability of higher levels of government before 1949 to penetrate into the basic 'natural' units of Chinese society except to collect taxes was one factor perpetuating China's traditional economy into the middle of the twentieth century.

Household and village were natural social units, not imposed by the state as the revived *pao-chia* (registration and police) system (see volume 10, page 29) was from the 1920s onwards; but the peasant's horizon was not bounded by them. The normal limits of social interaction were not the village boundaries, but rather the borders of a higher order community composed of several (a dozen or more) villages and the market town which served them. A high proportion of China's farm households produced all or much of their own food, but grains, cash crops, local agricultural specialties, as well as the products of household handicraft – perhaps 30 per cent by value of farm output – were regularly marketed. The peasant sector in fact consisted of a large number of local market areas, each one roughly defined by a radius equal to the distance which a peasant buyer or seller and his products might cover on foot in one day.

The markets were normally periodic rather than continuous, occurring every few days according to one of several scheduling systems that were characteristic of different regions in China. Skinner, who refers to these basic units as 'standard marketing areas' (SMA), has suggested that 'the rural countryside of late traditional China can be viewed as a grid of approximately 70,000 hexagonal cells, each an economic system focused on a standard market.'[2] The bulk of the trading in standard markets consisted of a horizontal exchange of goods among peasants. To some extent there was an upward flow out of the SMA of handicraft items and local agricultural specialties; the principal outflow of staples, however, consisted of tax grains to the government level of the economy. Increasingly in the late-nineteenth and twentieth centuries the SMA was the ultimate destination of new commodities either manufactured in the treaty ports or imported from abroad.

To the limited extent that rural China began to produce staples for export, including technical crops for the treaty-port factories, these tended to move in new commercial channels alternative to the traditional periodic markets. In the agricultural hinterland of the east coast treaty ports, in particular, a modern town economy developed alongside the periodic-marketing economy. But in the vast area of rural China the traditional market structure was flourishing with few signs of decay right down to 1949, a strong indication that the rural economy had not been substantially transformed. The peasant household in the mid twentieth century probably depended more on commodities not produced by itself or by its neighbours than was the case 50 years earlier. But, because there was little real improvement in transportation at the local level, the primary marketing area was not enlarged so as to bring about a radical replacement of standard markets by modern commercial channels organized around larger regional marketing complexes.

Non-agricultural, or 'urban', does not necessarily imply 'modern'. At the beginning of the nineteenth century perhaps as many as 12 million people, 3 to 4 per cent of the then 350 million Chinese, lived in cities with populations of 30,000 or more. With few exceptions, these cities were primarily administrative centres – the national capital, Peking, with nearly one million inhabitants, major provincial capitals, and the largest prefectural (*fu*) cities. Some were simultaneously important centres of inter-provincial and inter-regional commerce like Nanking, Soochow, Hankow, Canton, Foochow, Hangchow, Chungking, Chengtu and Sian. These cities were the loci of the highest officials of the empire, the major military garrisons, the wealthiest merchant groups, and the most skilled artisans. Their populations included, too, prominent non-official gentry, lesser merchants, the numerous underlings who staffed the government yamens, labourers and transport workers, as well as the little-studied literate stratum of monks, priests, jobless lower-degree holders, failed examination candidates, demobilized military officers, and the like who were part of the 'transients, migrants and outsiders'[3] so prominent in the traditional Chinese city. But the patterns of late-Ch'ing city life, political and economic, greatly resembled what they had been under the Sung dynasty, five centuries earlier.

From the mid nineteenth century onwards, as a consequence of the establishment of a foreign presence in China, the Chinese city began to add modern economic, political and cultural roles to those which continued from late-traditional times. The total number of urban residents grew slowly in the course of the nineteenth century, at a rate not much greater than total population growth; and then more rapidly between 1900 and 1938, at almost twice the average population growth rate. Cities with populations over 50,000 in 1938 included approximately 27.3 million inhabitants, 5 to 6 per cent of a total population of 500 million. These same cities had had perhaps 16.8 million inhabitants at the turn of the century, 4 to 5 per cent of a 430 million population. The difference suggests an annual growth rate for all large cities of about 1.4 per cent. China's 6 largest cities – Shanghai, Peking, Tientsin, Canton, Nanking, and Hankow – however, were growing at rates of 2 to 7 per cent per annum in the 1930s.[4]

By the start of the First World War 92 cities had been formally opened to foreign trade (see below, page 241) and while some of these 'treaty ports' were places of minor importance, a high proportion of China's largest cities were among them. (Some notable exceptions were Sian, Kaifeng, Peking, Taiyuan, Wuhsi, Shaoshing, Nanchang, Chengtu). The treaty ports were the termini of the railway lines which began to appear in the 1890s, and of the steam shipping which spread along China's coast and on the Yangtze and West Rivers. Foreign commercial firms opened branches and agencies in the larger treaty ports, and under the provisions of the Treaty of Shimonoseki of 1895, foreigners were per-

---

3 The characterization is Mark Elvin's, in Mark Elvin and G. William Skinner, eds. *The Chinese city between two worlds*, 3.

4 These are surely very rough estimates, but they are consistent with what little hard data are available. See Gilbert Rozman, *Urban networks in Ch'ing China and Tokugawa Japan*, 99–104; Dwight H. Perkins, *Agricultural development in China, 1368–1968*, app. E: Urban population statistics (1900–58), 290–6; and H. O. Kung, 'The growth of population in six large Chinese cities', *Chinese Economic Journal*, 20.3 (March 1937) 301–14.

mitted to operate manufacturing enterprises (some had done so illegally before 1896). Chinese firms specializing in foreign trade and its adjuncts made their appearance parallel to the arrival of the foreigner. While not restricted to the open ports, most of the small but growing Chinese-owned industrial sector which began to appear in the 1870s was also located in these same cities. In the shadow of the modern factories, Chinese and foreign, handicraft workshops flourished either as sub-contractors or, as in the case of cotton weaving, as major customers for the output of the new spinning mills. The processing of exports, too, still largely a handicraft operation, burgeoned in the major port cities. For a small number of urban dwellers, in addition to manufacturing and commerce a number of new occupations in the free professions, in jour-nalism and publishing, and in modern educational and cultural insti-tutions, gradually came into being.

But this modern industrial, commercial and transport sector for the most part remained confined to the treaty ports. Only to a very limited degree did it replace traditional handicrafts, existing marketing systems, or transport by human and animal backs, carts, sampans, and junks. There was almost no spill-over into the agricultural sector, for example, in the form of improved technology (new seeds, chemical fertilizer, modern water control, farm machinery) or more efficient organization (credit, stable marketing, rationalized land use).[5] The fluctuations of world markets for silver or for China's agricultural exports, experienced directly first in the treaty ports, could at times send ripples of influence into the countryside. Overall, however, the peasant sector and the treaty-port economy remained only very loosely linked until 1949.

POPULATION

Diminishing returns have probably been reached in the manipulation of available Chinese population statistics. The census-registration of 1953-4 which reported a population of 583 million for mainland China, is the nearest to an accurate count of the population of China that has ever been made. This large number is at odds with such estimates as the Kuomintang official figure of 463,493,000 for 1948; but this figure together with several dozen other official and private estimates have been based more on guesswork than was the 1953-4 census, whatever its technical short-

5 Rhoads Murphey, *The outsiders: the Western experience in India and China*, provides a major reexamination of the treaty-port experience.

comings.[6] A population of approximately 580 million in 1953 fits quite well a putative average increase of 0.8 per cent per year between 1912 and 1953, such a rate as might be expected from a demographic situation of slow but irregular growth resulting from the difference between high and fluctuating death rates and high but relatively stable birth rates. While no statistical data are available, it appears likely that population growth was sufficiently greater than this average during the Yuan Shih-k'ai presidency (1912–16), the Nanking government decade (1928–37), and the first years of the People's Republic (1950–8) to compensate for the probable negative demographic effects of the warlord period and the Second World War and civil war of 1937–49. Starting with approximately 430 million people in 1912, the population of mainland China in 1933 was some 500 million, and grew to about 580 million in 1953.

Liu and Yeh have made detailed estimates of the occupational distribution of the total population for 1933 (see table 1). Judging from more fragmentary data for individual provinces or cities for the previous two decades, this distribution was largely unchanged during the republican period.

Of a total working population in 1933 of 259.21 million, 204.91 million or 79 per cent actually engaged in farming and 54.3 million (including man-labour units apportioned from joint occupations) or 21 per cent followed non-agricultural pursuits. Of the total population 73 per cent lived in families having agriculture as their main occupation, while 27 per cent were members of non-agricultural families. Although twentieth-century China experienced some industrial growth in the treaty ports, and some development of mining and railway transport, the small numbers engaged in these occupations even in 1933 suggests that the occupational distribution of China's population as a whole had changed little from what it had been at the end of the Ch'ing dynasty. By way of contrast, in the United States only 21.4 per cent of those 10 years old and over gainfully occupied were engaged in agriculture in 1930. To find figures even remotely comparable to those of China in 1933 one would need to look at America in 1820 or 1830 when 70 per cent of the labour force worked in agriculture.

6 About 470 million seems to be a charmed number for official population estimates in the 1920s and 1930s: the Nanking government Ministry of the Interior attempted a 'census' in 1928, which produced an estimate of 474,787,386 based on 'reports' from 16 provinces and special municipalities and guesses by the ministry for 17 provinces. The same ministry published a figure of 471,245,763 in 1938 compiled from local 'reports' for 1936–7.

TABLE I

Occupational distribution, 1933

		% of
	millions	500 million
Total population	500.00	100.00
A. *Agricultural population*	365.00	73.00
1. Working population, aged 7–64	212.30	42.46
a. Agriculture only	118.78	23.76
b. Joint agriculture and subsidiary occupations	93.52	18.70
i. Agriculture	86.13	17.23
ii. Industry* = man-labour	3.61	0.72
iii. Trade units apportioned	1.66	0.33
iv. Transport to each part of	1.14	0.23
v. Other non-agricultural joint occupations		
occupations†	0.98	0.20
2. Children under 7	71.21	14.24
3. Students, aged 7 and over	5.13	1.02
4. Aged 65 and over	10.99	2.20
5. Unemployed or idle, aged 7–64‡	65.36	13.07
B. *Non-agricultural population*	135.00	27.00
1. Working population, aged 7–64§	46.91	9.38
a. Factories	1.13	0.23
b. Handicrafts	12.13	2.43
c. Mining	0.77	0.15
d. Utilities	0.04	0.01
e. Construction	1.55	0.31
f. Trade	13.22	2.64
g. Transport	10.16	2.03
h. Other non-agricultural occupations	7.91	1.58
2. Children		
a. Under 7	26.33	5.26
b. Under 12	43.86	8.77
3. Students		
a. Aged 7 and over	5.74	1.15
b. Aged 12 and over	0.60	0.12
4. Aged 65 and over	4.08	0.82
5. Unemployed or idle‡		
a. Aged 7–64	51.94	10.39
b. Aged 12–64	39.56	7.91

* Manufacturing, home industries, mining, utilities and construction
† Professional and public service, etc.
‡ Including housewives
§ Actual age of the working non-agricultural population falls mostly within the range 12–64; the age of 7 is taken as the lower limit merely for the convenience of grouping on the same basis as the agricultural working population
Source: Liu Ta-chung and Yeh Kung-chia, *The economy of the Chinese mainland: national income and economic development, 1933–1959*, 185 and 188, tables 54 and 55.

TABLE 2

Domestic product, 1933 (billion 1933 Chinese $)

Net value added in:	Liu-Yeh		Ou
1. Agriculture	18.76		12.59
2. Factories	0.64		
a. Producers' goods		0.16 ⎱	0.38
b. Consumers' goods		0.47 ⎰	
3. Handicrafts	2.04		
a. Identified portion		1.24 ⎱	1.36
b. Others		0.80 ⎰	
4. Mining	0.21		0.24
5. Utilities	0.13		0.15
6. Construction	0.34		0.22
7. Modern transport and communications	0.43 ⎱		
8. Old-fashioned transport	1.20 ⎰		0.92
9. Trade	2.71		
a. Trading stores and restaurants		1.75	2.54
b. Peddlers		0.96	
10. Government administration	0.82		0.64
11. Finance	0.21		0.20
12. Personal services	0.34		0.31
13. Residential rents	1.03		0.93
(Less: double counting of banking services)			(−0.17)
Net domestic product	28.86		20.32
Depreciation	1.02		1.45
Gross domestic product	29.88		21.77

Sources: Ou Pao-san's 1948 Harvard Ph.D. thesis, 'Capital formation and consumers' outlay in China', 204–11, summarizes the data in his *Chung-kuo kuo-min so-te, i-chiu-san-san-nien* (China's national income, 1933) and takes account of his later revisions. Liu Ta-chung and Yeh Kung-chia, *The economy of the Chinese mainland*, 66, table 8.

NATIONAL INCOME

Two major independent estimates of China's national income in the republican period have been made by Liu Ta-chung and Yeh Kung-chia, and by Ou Pao-san (Wu Pao-san) (see table 2). The aggregates differ widely – the larger estimate is about 40 per cent greater than the smaller – but the only important difference between the two is value added in agriculture. Both estimates are for 1933 only.

The probably more reliable Liu-Yeh data may be summarized as follows: agriculture of course bulked greatest in the 1933 net domestic product, contributing 65 per cent in 1933 prices. All 'industry' (factories, handicrafts, mining, utilities) contributed 10.5 per cent. Trade was third with 9.4 per cent. Other sectors ranked as follows: transport 5.6 per cent; finance, personal service and rent 5.6 per cent; government administration 2.8 per cent; and construction 1.2 per cent. Another way of stating the composition of national income in 1933 is to note that the modern non-agricultural sectors (very generously defined as factories, mining, utilities, construction, modern trade and transport, trading stores, restaurants and modern financial institutions) contributed only 12.6 per cent of the total. Agriculture, traditional non-agricultural sectors (handicrafts, old-fashioned transport, peddlers, traditional financial institutions, personal services, rent) and government administration accounted for 87.4 per cent. The structure of China's mainland economy before 1949 was also typical of a pre-industrial society when looked at from the expenditure side. By end use, 91 per cent of gross domestic expenditure in 1933 went to personal consumption. Communal services and government consumption together accounted for 4 per cent, while gross investment totalled 5 per cent.

To what degree 1933, a depression year, may be characteristic of the entire republican period is perhaps questionable, but no comparably complete national income estimates for any other year have been attempted. Perkins, however, has converted the Liu-Yeh data into 1957 prices, substituted his own somewhat lower farm output figures,[7] and added estimates for 1914-18 with results that suggest a slowly growing gross domestic product during the republican era, and one which was also changing slightly in composition (table 3).

The absolute values shown in tables 2 and 3 are not comparable because one is stated in 1933 and the other in 1957 prices. In addition, the 1914-18 figures are constructed from plausible guesses as well as true estimates. But the overwhelming predominance of the traditional sectors up to 1949, and the quantitatively small but qualitatively significant changes over four decades which these tables imply, fit very well with other information about the separate sectors of the Chinese economy under the republic presented in the remaining sections of this chapter.[8] Modern manufacturing and mining grew steadily from modest late-nineteenth century beginnings until the outbreak of war with Japan in 1937. In Manchuria this growth continued and even accelerated during the war. Modern transport, railways and steam ships, experienced a comparable expansion, not replacing traditional communications but supplementing them. A

---

7 The largest discrepancy between the Liu-Yeh and Ou estimates is in the figures for net value added by agriculture, and within agriculture for the value of crops. While Ou's figures are probably too low, Perkins has made a plausible case that those of Liu-Yeh are based on too high a grain-yield estimate for 1933. Perkins, *Agricultural development in China*, 29-32 and app. D.

8 This summary discussion follows Dwight H. Perkins, 'Growth and changing structure of China's twentieth-century economy', in Perkins, ed. *China's modern economy in historical perspective*, 116-25.

TABLE 3

Gross domestic product, 1914–18, 1933, 1952 (1957 prices)

Sector	1914–1918		1933		1952	
	Billion 1957 yuan					
Manufacturing +*	8.5		11.77		17.23	
Modern†		1.3		4.54		11.11
Agriculture	29.9		35.23		31.58	
Services	10.0		12.52		17.07	
Depreciation‡	—		2.19		—	
GDP	48.4		61.71		65.88	
	Ratio to GDP					
Manufacturing +	0.176		0.198		0.262	
Modern		0.027		0.074		0.169
Agricultural	0.618		0.592		0.459	
Services	0.207		0.210		0.259	
GDP	1.000		1.000		1.000	

* M + =industry (modern and pre-modern manufacturing, mining and utilities) + transport
† Modern=factory output, mining, utilities and modern transport
‡ Not netted out of the individual sectors except for 1933; distributed among the sectors in proportion to their net products in order to calculate the ratios in the lower half of the table.
Source: Dwight H. Perkins, 'Growth and changing structure of China's twentieth-century economy', in Perkins, ed. *China's modern economy in historical perspective*, 117, table 1.

modern financial sector, banking in particular, largely supplanted traditional banking in urban China in the course of the first half of the twentieth century. But even in 1933 Perkins estimates the contribution of the modern sectors (more narrowly defined than in my summary of the Liu-Yeh data in that he excludes modern services) as only 7 per cent of gross domestic product. This was more than twice the 3 per cent of 1914–18 but still minuscule.

The growth of total GDP between 1912 and 1949 therefore, came also from increased output by the traditional sectors, mainly agriculture and handicrafts. Agricultural production grew slowly, but with annual and regional variations due to weather and politico-military circumstances, in the first decades of the twentieth century. The largest increases occurred in newly developed areas such as Manchuria and parts of south-western China. Elsewhere the value of agricultural output was augmented by the increased production of cash crops. For reasons suggested below it is extremely unlikely that total handicraft output, as opposed to its relative share, declined between 1912 and 1949. The contrary is more plausible.

If we compare the estimates of gross domestic product in table 3 with population estimates of 430 million in 1912, 500 million in 1933, and 572 million in 1952, we find per capita GDP in each of these years was on the order of (in 1957 prices) 113, 123 and 115 *yuan* respectively. Given the possibility of potential error in all of this data, the best estimates now available do not show any pronounced upward or downward trend in per capita GDP in the decades covered by this chapter if one omits the 12 years of war and civil war which began in 1937. During this period per capita output and income in some parts of China probably fell sharply. Some notably articulate groups were adversely affected, especially teachers and government employees on fixed salaries which did not keep up with the level of inflation; but urban workers fared relatively well after the war and before the final collapse of 1948-9.

In the wake of the Japanese invasion North China saw a crippling of farm production and a breakdown of the commercial links between town and countryside. During the civil war of 1946-9 agricultural and commercial conditions were probably worse in that region, where the fighting was centred, than elsewhere in China. After 1940 crop production began to decline in unoccupied China, and averaged about 9 per cent below 1939 for the remainder of the war. The introduction of a land tax in kind and compulsory grain purchases in 1942, together with accelerated military conscription which caused severe labour shortages, appear to have reduced the real income of peasants. But industrial production in Nationalist-controlled areas in the interior, beginning from a low base, grew until 1942 or 1943. In the post-war period, the resumption of inflation in 1946 and its runaway character during 1948-9 had much more serious consequences in the coastal, urban sector than in the rural interior of South and West China where total output probably changed little although flows of food and agricultural raw materials to the cities were curtailed as the value of the currency precipitously declined.[9]

It is possible that the income of a significant part of the population was declining while average per capita GDP remained constant or rose slightly. But in the rural areas and among the majority farming population 'there is no convincing evidence that landlords were garnering an increasing share of the product during the first half of the twentieth century. The limited available data, in fact, suggest that the rate of tenancy

9 Ou Pao-san (Wu Pao-san), 'Chung-kuo kuo-min so-te, 1933, 1936, chi 1946' (China's national income, 1933, 1936, and 1946), *She-hui k'o-hsueh tsa-chih*, 9.2 (December 1947) 12-30, estimates national income in 1946 as 6% lower than 1933 (in 1933 prices). On Shanghai workers, see A. Doak Barnett, *China on the eve of communist takeover*, 78-80; on the North China rural economy during 1937-49, Ramon H. Myers, *The Chinese peasant economy: agricultural development in Hopei and Shantung, 1890-1949*, 278-87; on wartime unoccupied China and post-war inflation, Chang Kia-ngau, *The inflationary spiral: the experience of China, 1939-1950*, 59-103.

might even have declined slightly, and that in periods of political turmoil landlords often had difficulty collecting their rents.'[10]

Allegiances were certainly changed during 1937–49, but even then not primarily because the economy could not support China's population at the prevailing (and low) standard of living in the absence of severe man-made or natural disasters. The rapid recovery which by 1952 had returned output to peak pre-1949 levels was based almost entirely on the success of a new and effective government in restoring the production of existing enterprises, not on new investment. For the rest of the four decades before 1949, civil war in the 1920s and early 1930s, droughts (for example, in 1920–1 in North China), floods (for example, of the Yangtze River in 1931), and other natural disasters indeed undermined the general welfare of the Chinese people, but not necessarily their material welfare, a distinction of substantial importance. Even a slightly rising income is poor compensation for the heightened personal insecurity occasioned by political turmoil and warfare, while on the contrary a low but stable per capita income may be acceptable if offered in a context of greater personal and national security.

INDUSTRY

In describing the Chinese economy in the closing years of the Ch'ing dynasty, we noted that at least 549 Chinese-owned private and semi-official manufacturing and mining enterprises using mechanical power were inaugurated between 1895 and 1913. The total initial capitalization of these firms was Ch.$120,288,000.[11] In addition, 96 foreign-owned and 40 Sino-foreign enterprises established in the same period had an initial capitalization of Ch.$103,153,000. This was of course only a crude estimate, from a variety of contemporary official and non-official sources.

Two similar tabulations, which exclude modern mines but include arsenals and utilities, suggest an appreciable expansion of Chinese-owned modern industry during and immediately following the First World War. The first notes 698 factories with an initial capitalization of Ch.$330,824,000 and 270,717 workers in 1913, while the second, 1,759 factories with an initial capitalization of Ch.$500,620,000 and 557,622 workers in

10 Perkins, 'Growth and changing structure of China's twentieth-century economy', 124, who cites Myers, *The Chinese peasant economy*, 234–40, and Perkins, *Agricultural development in China,* ch. 5.

11 A. Feuerwerker, 'Economic trends in the late Ch'ing empire, 1870–1911', *CHOC*, vol. 11, ch. 1.

1920.[12] Concentration on war production by the European powers and the shipping shortage reduced the flow of exports to China and provided an enhanced opportunity for Chinese-owned industry to expand. While orders for equipment were placed earlier – capital goods still came mainly from abroad – the opening of most new plants had to await the end of the war and the actual arrival of the machinery ordered.

Foreign-owned and Sino-foreign enterprises also increased during the first decade of the republic, but little direct investment occurred between 1914 and 1918. The largest increments came immediately after the First World War when, for example, revisions of the Chinese tariff in 1918 and 1922, raising the import duty on the finer count yarns which Japan had been exporting to China, served as an inducement for Japan to open new textile mills in China.

Like both the Chinese- and foreign-owned factories established in the latter part of the Ch'ing dynasty, factories (and mines) opened in the second decade of the twentieth century were heavily concentrated in Shanghai and Tientsin, and in other places in Kiangsu, Liaoning, Hopei, Kwangtung, Shantung, and Hupei, that is, mainly in the coastal and Yangtze valley provinces.[13]

The first and only industrial census in republican China, for the year 1933, was made by investigators of the Institute of Economic and Statistical Research under the direction of D. K. Lieu (Liu Ta-chün). It was based on statistical information gathered directly from factory managers and, apart from its exclusion of all foreign-owned firms, as well as Manchuria, Kansu, Sinkiang, Yunnan, Kweichow, Ninghsia, Tsinghai, Tibet and Mongolia (none of these except Manchuria had any significant number of modern factories), is considered to be fairly reliable. Published in 1937 Lieu's survey recorded 2,435 Chinese-owned factories capitalized at Ch.$406,926,634 with a gross output valued at Ch.$ 1,113,974,413 and employing 493,257 workers.[14] These factories were concentrated in the coastal provinces, and especially in Shanghai which accounted for 1,186 of the plants surveyed. More than 80 per cent of Chinese-owned industry in 1933 was located in the eastern and south-eastern coastal provinces and Liaoning in Manchuria; and this proportion would be higher still if foreign-owned establishments (which were, of course, limited to the treaty ports) were included in the estimate.

12 Ch'en Chen *et al.* comps. *Chung-kuo chin-tai kung-yeh shih tzu-liao* (Source materials on the history of modern industry in China; hereafter *CKCT*), 1.55–56.
13 Nankai Institute of Economics, *Nankai weekly statistical service*, 4.33 (17 August 1931) 157–8.
14 Liu Ta-chün (D. K. Lieu), *Chung-kuo kung-yeh tiao-ch'a pao-kao* (Report on a survey of China's industry). 'Factory' was defined according to the 1929 Factory Law as an enterprise using mechanical power and employing 30 or more workers.

In his study of China's national income in 1933 Ou Pao-san supplemented Lieu's survey by adding estimates for foreign-owned factories in China proper and for factories in Manchuria and the other omitted provinces. His revised estimate reported a total of 3,841 factories (3,167 Chinese-owned and 674 foreign-owned), with a gross output valued at Ch.$2,186,159,000 (Chinese: $1,415,459,000; foreign: $770,700,000) and employing 738,029 workers.[15]

Liu Ta-chung and Yeh Kung-chia have provided a further revision of Lieu's survey in table 4, which shows the gross value of output and the number of workers in the several branches of China's modern industrial sector in 1933. Manufacturing establishments using mechanical power, regardless of the number of workers in each, in China proper and Manchuria produced a gross output valued at Ch.$2,645,400,000 in 1933 and employed a total of 1,075,800 workers. Although Liu-Yeh, in contrast to Lieu and Ou, exclude utilities from their estimate, their totals are substantially higher. This results in part from their broader definition of a factory, from better coverage of Manchuria, and from the utilization of sources other than Lieu's survey for their cotton yarn, cotton cloth, cement, pig iron and steel data.

For the remaining years before 1949 strictly comparable data are unavailable, in particular there are none on the total value of output. The Ministry of Economic Affairs of the Nationalist Government reported in 1937 that as of that year 3,935 factories (excluding mines but including utilities and arsenals) had registered with the ministry under the Factory Law. They employed 457,063 workers and had a total capitalization of Ch.$377,938,000.[16] Of the 3,935 plants, 1,235 (31 per cent) were located in Shanghai, 2,063 (52 per cent) elsewhere in the coastal provinces, and 637 (17 per cent) in the interior. Textiles and food products accounted for 55 per cent of the total capitalization of the registered factories. It is unclear to what extent the world depression affected China during the years 1933–6. The sizeable wartime damage, the fall in production, and the stagnation of new investment under Japanese occupation in such manufacturing centres as Shanghai, Tientsin and Wuhan after 1937 can be inferred from local and partial qualitative evidence. Similarly, the efforts of the Nationalist government to develop a manufacturing base,

15 Ou Pao-san (Wu Pao-san), *Chung-kuo kuo-min so-te i-chiu-san-san-nien* (China's national income, 1933), vol. 1. Tables 1–2 following p. 64; table 5, pp. 70–1; additional data in Ou, 'Chung-kuo kuo-min so-te i-chiu-san-san hsiu-cheng' (Corrections to China's national income, 1933), *She-hui k'o-hsueh tsa-chih*, 9.2 (Dec. 1947) 130–6, 144–7, which incorporated the estimates of Wang Fu-sun, 'Chan-ch'ien Chung-kuo kung-yeh sheng-ch'an-chung wai-ch'ang sheng-ch'an ti pi-chung wen-t'i' (The proportion of industrial production by foreign-owned factories in total industrial production in pre-war China), *Chung-yang yin-hang yueh-pao*, 2.3 (March 1947) 1–19.
16 *CKCT*, 4. 92.

TABLE 4

Output and employment in modern industry, 1933

| | Gross value of output (million 1933 Ch.$) | | | | Number of workers (1,000) | | | |
| | China Proper | | | | China Proper | | | |
	Chinese-owned	Foreign-owned	Manchuria	Total	Chinese-owned	Foreign-owned	Manchuria	Total
Producers' Goods								
Lumber	4.4	5.6	11.6	21.6	1.2	1.5	2.3	5.0
Machinery, including transport equipment	55.4	9.9	27.2	92.5	45.7	5.2	14.4	65.3
Ferrous metals and metal products	29.4	1.4	18.1	48.9	15.5	0.4	11.8	27.7
Small electrical appliances	1.3	0.8	—	2.1	0.7	0.3	—	1.0
Stone, clay and glass products	44.5	1.6	9.7	55.8	34.7	1.1	8.9	44.7
Chemicals and chemical products	58.5	10.0	19.1	87.6	5.6	2.4	4.2	12.2
Textile products	15.3	—	1.6	16.9	4.3	—	0.4	4.7
Leather	37.0	8.1	1.0	46.1	4.5	0.9	0.7	6.1
Paper, paper products, printing	72.0	10.7	3.4	86.1	42.0	3.6	0.8	46.4
Metal coins	41.0	—	—	41.0	0.2	—	—	0.2
Total	358.8	48.1	91.7	498.5	154.4	15.4	43.5	213.3
Consumers' Goods								
Wood products	1.2	0.5	0.9	2.6	0.5	0.2	0.8	1.5
Metal products	12.6	1.4	1.6	15.6	4.4	0.5	0.7	5.6
Small electrical appliances	11.9	7.2	0.1	19.2	5.9	2.7	*	8.6
Chinaware and pottery	1.3	0.2	0.7	2.2	1.3	—	1.9	3.2
Chemicals and chemical products	65.3	17.2	4.4	86.9	38.4	7.3	4.9	50.6
Textile products	605.4	257.8	70.6	933.8	380.1	104.7	38.8	523.6
Clothing and attire	101.1	4.6	3.4	109.1	101.7	2.0	3.5	107.2
Leather and rubber products	36.2	2.2	—	38.4	15.1	0.7	—	15.8
Food products	436.3	39.1	158.7	634.1	51.2	8.6	21.6	81.4
Tobacco products, wine, liquor	124.9	117.3	36.0	278.2	20.3	19.0	8.4	47.7
Paper products	2.9	0.5	7.9	11.3	1.8	0.2	4.7	6.7
Miscellaneous	13.5	1.3	0.7	15.5	8.1	1.8	0.7	10.6
Total	1,412.6	449.3	285.0	2,146.9	628.8	147.7	86.0	862.5
Overall	1,771.4	497.4	376.7	2,645.4	785.2	163.1	129.5	1,075.8

* Less than 100 workers

Source: Liu Ta-chung and Yeh Kung-chia, *The economy of the Chinese mainland*, 142–3 and 426–8.

largely war-related industry, in unoccupied China were widely but incompletely reported.

During 1938–40, 448 'factories' and 12,182 'technicians' moved inland to Szechwan, Hunan, Kwangsi and Shensi along with the retreating Nationalist government and armies. At the beginning of 1943 the Ministry of Economic Affairs in Chungking issued an industrial report which, although it lacks output data, gives some indication of wartime developments in unoccupied China. Of the 3,758 factories with 241,662 workers reported, 590 were in existence in 1937, and 3,168 were established during 1938–42. Their total capitalization, allowing for a ten-fold increase in the index of prices, was approximately equal to that of Shanghai's Chinese-owned industries in 1933, and the number of workers was also about the same. The majority of these factories were located in Szechwan (1,654), Hunan (501), Shensi (385) and Kwangsi (292), but others were widely dispersed throughout the Kuomintang-controlled areas. In contrast to the consumers' goods orientation of pre-war industry, about 50 per cent (as measured by capitalization) of the new wartime industry manufactured military-related and producers' goods. Another contrast with pre-war industry was the major role of state-owned enterprises in this wartime industrialization. While only 656 (17 per cent) of the factories recorded were 'public enterprises' (*kung-ying*), they represented 69 per cent of the total capitalization, were larger and employed more mechanical power than privately-owned factories, and dominated the producers' goods sector (especially chemicals, metals and machinery).[17]

The pattern of wartime industrialization in Nationalist areas, in particular the emphasis on military-related producers' goods such as chemicals, is apparent from table 5. After 1942 industrial activity in the interior began to slow down, the number of new firms declined sharply, and output not only ceased to rise but actually declined in certain capital goods lines. The principal reasons for this, apart from raw material shortages and inadequate transport, were uncertainty about the post-war fate of these inland industries (everyone was poised to return to Shanghai), and above all else the level of inflation. Hoarding and speculation in commodities became more profitable than manufacturing.

Industrial output in occupied China proper probably stagnated or declined during 1937–45. The evidence is inconclusive. There was apparently a general fall in production during 1937–9. In North China, from 1939 or 1940 to 1943 or 1944, the output of coal, iron and steel, cement, electric power, and chemicals showed an increase, but such consumers'

17 *Ibid.* 1.89–97; 4.93–6, excerpts from Directorate of Economic Statistics, 'Hou-fang kung-yeh kai-k'uang t'ung-chi' (Statistics on industry in the interior), May 1943.

TABLE 5

Relative quantities of output of selected industrial products,
electric power, and coal in Kuomintang-controlled areas, 1933, 1938–46 (1933=100)*

	1933	1938	1939	1940	1941	1942	1943	1944	1945	1946
Coal	100	47	55	57	60	63	66	55	52	182
Pig iron	100	153	182	130	184	278	203	116	140	90
Steel	100	3	4	5	7	10	23	45	61	52
Electric power	100	14	17	21	24	26	27	29	37	683
Cement	100	5	11	11	6	9	8	9	9	65
Alkalis	100	1	1	2	3	3	5	9	5	93
Sulphuric acid	100	3	2	8	10	13	12	15	5	138
Hydrochloric acid	100	8	6	12	10	32	29	32	26	233
Alcohol	100	—	241	1,362	1,605	2,340	2,289	2,180	4,814	3,673
Gasoline	100	1	1	12	35	316	537	675	718	842
Cotton yarn	100	1	2	2	7	7	7	7	4	95
Flour	100	2	3	5	7	7	6	4	3	117

* The geographic coverage differs significantly between 1933 and 1946, on the one hand, and the intervening years on the other; and also differs somewhat from year to year 1938–45.

Source: Yen Chung-p'ing, *Chung-kuo chin-tai ching-chi shih t'ung-chi tzu-liao hsuan-chi* (Selected statistical materials on modern Chinese economic history), 100–1.

goods industries as cotton and wool textiles and flour remained substantially below pre-war levels. After a sharp decline, the index of the gross value of factory output (in 1939 prices) in North China had returned to the 1933 level by 1942.[18] Shanghai cotton mills, China's most important industrial plants, however, fared badly during the war. Both yarn and cloth output in Chinese-owned mills fell sharply from 1937, recovered slightly in 1939–41, and then nearly expired.[19] It is still unclear whether or not Japanese-controlled firms performed any better.

Meanwhile Manchurian industry under Japanese control grew rapidly from 1936 to at least 1941. Prior to the mid 1930s Manchuria's economic growth was based mainly on the extension of the agricultural frontier. Small-scale Chinese-owned factories were in evidence, but the principal modern industries were a network of Japanese-controlled producers' goods enterprises intended to furnish raw and semi-finished materials to the Japanese economy. The Anshan and Pen-ch'i ironworks and the Fushun coal mines, large vertically integrated installations, were the most prominent among these units. Subsequent to the consolidation of the Manchukuo puppet state, Japanese interests sponsored a major effort to establish an integrated producers' goods sector. The rate of gross investment in fixed capital, financed largely by capital imports from Japan, which had been 9 per cent in 1924, reached 17 per cent in 1934 and 23 per cent in 1939. (The corresponding rate for China as a whole in 1933 was 5 per cent, a figure probably not exceeded before 1949.) Industry broadly defined (mining, manufacturing, public utilities, small-scale industry and construction) expanded at an annual rate of 9.9 per cent between 1936 and 1941 compared to 4.4 per cent in the years 1924–36. Factory industry grew even more rapidly, with the result that Manchuria, containing 8 to 9 per cent of China's total population, contributed almost a third of the total pre-1949 Chinese factory product. The rapid development of manufacturing came apparently at the expense of small-scale industry, that is, was accompanied by a 'modernization' of the industrial sector which as a whole expanded at the same rate as the Manchuria gross domestic product and did not gain in relative importance. This appears to be an important contrast with China proper. After 1941, as a consequence of the dwindling flow of equipment, financing and some critical raw materials from Japan, both the growth and the diversification

18 Yen Chung-p'ing, comp. *Chung-kuo chin-tai ching-chi-shih t'ung-chi tzu-liao hsuan-chi* (Selected statistics on modern Chinese economic history; hereafter *CKCTC*), 147–50; Wang Fu-sun, 'Chan-shih Hua-pei kung-yeh tzu-pen chiu-yeh yü sheng-ch'an' (Wartime industrial capital, employment and production in North China), *She-hui k'o-hsueh tsa-chih*, 9.2 (Dec. 1947) 48.
19 Wang Chi-shen, *Chan-shih Shang-hai ching-chi* (The economy of wartime Shanghai), 192, 194. I am grateful to Professor Thomas Rawski for this reference.

of Manchurian industry ground to a halt. Heavy wartime damage and the removal of the most modern plants and equipment by the Soviet armies in 1945–6 (losses amounting to U.S. $ one billion or more) seriously reduced the industrial capacity in Manchuria available to post-war China.[20]

The years 1946–9 were chaotic and soon dominated by spreading civil war and rampant inflation. Consumers' goods output had probably returned to pre-war levels by 1947, but the combination of crippled productive capacity in Manchurian heavy industry and mining, and the virtual abandonment of the 'hothouse' producers' goods factories of the wartime interior (which had depended on military and other government orders) after the Nationalist government returned to Nanking, resulted in a substantial decline in the volume of output and the relative importance of this sector. There was briefly, in other words, a return to the pre-war pattern of a heavily consumers' goods oriented industrial structure.

The Japanese surrender was accompanied by a partial breakdown in industrial output throughout China. In the formerly occupied areas Japanese technicians and managers were withdrawn and production came to a temporary standstill. There was no adequate planning for the take-over of Japanese industry and the restoration of industrial output. The recovered factories were treated like war booty as each civilian and military faction struggled to acquire a share of the loot. In the interior the plants established during the war were left to decay. The formerly Japanese-controlled plants and mines provided the basis for an expanding state-owned industrial sector. Through the auspices of the National Resources Commission significant parts of producers' goods output, electric power and mining came under government control.[21] At the end of 1947 the Commission supervised 291 plants and mines with a total of 223,770 employees. In the consumers' goods sector, 69 Japanese and 'puppet' textile plants (38 cotton mills, six woollen mills and 25 related enterprises) were confiscated in 1945 and turned over to a newly established China Textile Corporation (CTC), a joint-stock company dominated by government investment and operated under the direction of the Ministry of Economic Affairs. In 1947 CTC controlled 36.1 per cent of the cotton spindles in China and 59.4 per cent of the looms. Its plants produced 43.7 per cent of the yarn and 72.6 of the cotton cloth. Supplied

---

20 Alexander Eckstein, Kang Chao and John Chang, 'The economic development of Man-churia: the rise of a frontier economy', *Journal of Economic History*, 34.1 (March 1974) 251–60.

21 Substantial data on the relative positions of state-owned and private mining and producers' goods enterprises 1938–48 may be found in *CKCT*, 3. 1439–43, 873–9, 882–7.

with ample working capital by the Chinese government and receiving preferential treatment in the allocation of foreign exchange for the purchase of raw cotton, the CTC mills had a definite advantage over the private mills – a position analogous to that of the Japanese cotton mills in China whose heirs they were; except that the Japanese were more efficient. The CTC managements looked primarily for short-term profits, for themselves and for the Kuomintang government.[22]

From late 1948 both government and private factories and mines succumbed to the ravages of runaway inflation, communist sabotage of transport and the supply of raw materials, power shortages, labour unrest, and human frailty.

The critical measure of industrial development is the growth of production over time. John K. Chang's recent construction of an index of industrial production (excluding handicrafts) in mainland China, 1912–49, which supersedes all previous output estimates, provides a quantitative thread which ties together and confirms the scattered observations offered above. Based on 15 manufacturing and mining products, covering perhaps 50 per cent of industrial output and employing 1933 price weights, Chang's index is presented in table 6. Chinese- and foreign-owned firms, China proper and Manchuria are all included in his estimate. Starting from a very low base, to 1936 there was a steady rise in industrial production. Manufacturing and mining as a whole were apparently not adversely affected by the world depression, in spite of the substantial temporary difficulties experienced by many individual factories. Some upward bias is introduced for the depression years by combining China proper and Manchuria, in that Shanghai industry was more severely affected than was industrial enterprise in Manchuria. The outbreak of war brought a sharp decline in 1937–8, followed by a rise in output in both unoccupied China and Manchuria to a 1942 peak. From 1942 the picture is less clear: a fall in output through 1946, succeeded by a slight recovery in 1947–8, but not to the 1936 level.

Average annual growth rates for selected sub-periods (in net value-added) reflect substantial industrial expansion during and after the First World War (1912–20, 13.4 per cent) followed by a post-war recession in 1921–2. From 1923 to 1936 the average rate was 8.7 per cent; for 1912–42, 8.4 per cent; and for the whole period from 1912 to 1949 – because 1949 was a low year – 5.6 per cent. In a typical pre-war year, therefore,

22 State Statistical Bureau, Industrial Statistics Department, *Wo-kuo kang-t'ieh, tien-li, mei-t'an, chi-hsieh, fang-chih, tsao-chih kung-yeh ti chin-hsi* (Past and present of China's iron and steel, electric power, coal, machinery, textile and paper industries), 148–9; *CKCT*, 3. 1051–74.

TABLE 6

Index of industrial production of Mainland China, 1912–49

(15 commodities; 1933 = 100)

	Gross value of output	Net value-added
1912	11.9	15.7
1913	15.6	19.2
1914	20.1	24.0
1915	22.5	26.1
1916	24.0	27.7
1917	26.9	32.0
1918	27.8	32.2
1919	34.1	36.9
1920	40.2	42.9
1921	42.4	42.4
1922	34.7	39.0
1923	41.6	45.6
1924	46.9	50.5
1925	55.7	60.1
1926	59.0	61.0
1927	66.6	66.3
1928	72.1	70.5
1929	76.9	75.2
1930	81.6	80.1
1931	88.1	86.5
1932	91.6	90.3
1933	100.0	100.0
1934	103.6	106.8
1935	109.7	119.5
1936	122.0	135.0
1937	96.0	112.3
1938	76.2	104.1
1939	88.2	120.7
1940	94.1	137.6
1941	109.2	161.2
1942	115.7	176.1
1943	105.6	157.1
1944	91.8	140.9
1945	62.0	94.1
1946	90.7	93.6
1947	115.1	116.8
1948	96.7	101.1
1949	105.6	119.2

Source: John K. Chang, *Industrial development in pre-Communist China: a quantitative analysis*, 60–1.

the output of China's modern industry and mining as measured in 1933 prices was growing at an impressive rate of 8 to 9 per cent.[23]

Yet, as the Liu-Yeh national income estimate in table 2 (page 37) indicates, industry, including traditional industry, occupied a small place in the Chinese economy, and within the broadly defined industrial

23 John K. Chang, *Industrial development in pre-communist China: a quantitative analysis*, 70–4.

sector, modern factory production was overshadowed by handicraft manufacturing. In 1933 the combined output of factories, handicrafts, mining and utilities in China constituted only 10.5 per cent of net domestic product. The output of handicrafts accounted for 67.8 per cent of the industrial share; factories 20.9 per cent; mining, 7.0 per cent; and utilities, 4.3 per cent. Of a total non-agricultural working population estimated at 46.91 million, 12.13 million (25.9 per cent) were employed in handicraft industry, 1.13 million (2.4 per cent) in factories, 0.77 million (1.6 per cent) in mining, and 0.04 million (0.09 per cent) in utilities. In spite of the 8 to 9 per cent annual rate of growth estimated by Chang, the base from which this growth began was a very low one, with the consequence that the overall sectoral distribution of domestic product was not radically changed during the four decades of the republican era. China's modern industrial sector in the 1930s was small, however, only in relation to contemporary developed economies. As compared, for example, with Japan in 1895 it was neither inconsiderable nor without potential for further development.

There is no doubt that the relative share of handicrafts in the industrial sector as a whole was less in the 1930s than it had been in 1850 or 1912 (see table 3, page 39). In the mid nineteenth century, of course, there was no modern industry at all in China, and even in 1912 it was a tender shoot indeed. Table 7 summarizes the Liu-Yeh estimates of the identified handicraft share in the total output of various industries in 1933. Given the incomplete coverage of handicraft production in the available sources as compared to factory output, the average of 64.5 per cent for all industries is certainly too low.[24] Supplementary estimates by Liu and Yeh based on employment and value-added per handicraft worker suggest in fact that the handicraft share of gross value-added was close to 75 per cent in 1933.

Here the relatively hard data end. It has frequently been asserted that traditional handicraft manufacture in the century following the Opium War suffered a continuing decline as a result of competition from both imported foreign goods and the output of Chinese- and foreign-owned modern industry in China.[25] In Manchuria, as indicated above, it may have been the case that factory industry grew at the expense of 'small-

---

24 Ou, 'Chung-kuo kuo-min so-te i-chiu-san-san hsiu-cheng', 137–42, shows the net value added by handicrafts as 72% for all industries, based however on a definition of 'factory' which includes only firms employing 30 or more workers and using mechanical power.
25 This theme is implied in the arrangement of the materials in P'eng Tse-i, comp. *Chung-kuo chin-tai shou-kung-yeh shih tzu-liao, 1840–1949* (Source materials on the history of the handicraft industry in modern China, 1840–1949), valuable documentation that has not yet been adequately exploited.

TABLE 7

Handicraft production as percentage of gross value-added
in 14 product groups, 1933

Product	%
Lumber and wood products	95.5
Machinery, except electrical	31.3
Metal products	12.1
Electrical appliances	0.5
Transport equipment	69.4
Stone, clay and glass products	67.8
Chemical products	22.5
Textile goods	46.1
Clothing and knitted goods	66.5
Leather and allied products	56.2
Food products	90.1
Tobacco, wine and liquor	30.2
Paper and printing	55.9
Miscellaneous	63.7
All industries	64.5

Source: Liu Ta-chung and Yeh Kung-chia, *The economy of the Chinese mainland*, 142–3, table 38; and 512–13, table G-1.

scale' (that is, handicraft) industry. But was this equally true of China as a whole? The fragmentary information relating to this matter lends itself better to the conclusion that, in *absolute* terms, handicraft output as a whole held its own or even increased than it does to the melancholy view just noted.

The matter is complicated by which definition of 'handicraft' is used, the substantially different experiences among handicraft industries, and the timing of the several field surveys relied upon by most commentators to make their observations. Urban or semi-urban handicraft workshops or 'manufactories' (*shou-kung-yeh kung-ch'ang*) removed from the household unit have been present in the Chinese economy since at least the T'ang dynasty. Their importance, however, as measured both by employment and by output, before 1912 at least and to a lesser but unknown extent in the following four decades, was overshadowed by the handicraft production of individual rural and urban households.[26] Thus, for example, it is conceivable that the twentieth-century decline in the absolute output of handspun cotton yarn, which had been primarily a peasant household handicraft, was matched, wholly or in part, by new employment opportunities in the numerous handicraft workshops which sprang up under the impetus of growing foreign trade and factory production.

26 See Feuerwerker, 'Economic trends, 1870–1911', *CHOC*, vol. 11, ch. 1.

These small-scale factories, typically employing a handful of workers and without mechanical power, processed agricultural products for export (for example, cotton ginning and re-reeling of raw silk), or as sub-contractors supplied modern factories with simple parts and assemblies, or ventured to produce coarser and cheaper versions of factory-made goods (for example, textiles, cigarettes, matches and flour).[27] A significant part of China's early industrialization, therefore, like that of Japan, took the form not of a full-scale duplication of the foreign model, but of adaptations to China's factor endowment which were characterized by a high labour-capital ratio.

Some handicrafts did not survive the competition. Imported kerosene (paraffin) very nearly replaced vegetable oils for lighting purposes. Silk weaving, which had prospered in the first quarter of the century, declined from the late 1920s as a consequence of Japanese competition, the loss of such markets as Manchuria after 1931, the advent of rayon, and the general depression of the international market.[28] The fall in tea exports in the 1920s and 1930s probably indicates that that industry was in difficulty although we know little about changes in domestic demand. In neither the case of silk or tea, however, was there a simple linear decline from the nineteenth century onwards attributable to the displacement of handicrafts by factory products.

In the case of cotton textile handicrafts one can be more specific. Bruce Reynolds finds that the absolute output of handicraft yarn as well as the handicraft share in total yarn supply fell precipitously between 1875 and 1905, then more slowly to 1919, followed by another sharp drop to 1931 (table 8).[29] Handicraft weaving, in contrast, while its relative share dropped over the period 1875–1931, actually increased its total production in square yards during this half century. On the side of demand, this strong showing was due to the existence of partially discrete markets both for the handicraft cloth – typically woven with imported and domestic machine-spun warp threads and, until the enormous growth of domestic spinning mills in the 1920s, handspun woofs – and for machine-loomed cloths of a finer quality. From the side of supply, the survival and growth of handicraft weaving is attributable to its integral role in the family farm production system of pre-1949 China. The key was the availability

27 See P'eng Tse-i, *Chung-kuo chin-tai shou-kung-yeh shih tzu-liao, 1840–1949*, 2. 331–449.
28 See Lillian Ming-tse Li, 'Kiangnan and the silk export trade, 1842–1937', (Harvard University, Ph.D. dissertation 1975) 234–73.
29 Reynolds' results for 1875 and 1905, arrived at by a much different route, are very close to my estimates in 'Handicraft and manufactured cotton textiles in China, 1871–1910.' *Journal of Economic History*, 30.2 (June 1970) 338–78. I use his figures here rather than my own because they are part of a methodologically consistent estimate for the whole period 1875–1931.

TABLE 8

Sources of cotton cloth supply, 1875-1931 (million square yards)

	1875		1905		1919		1931	
		(%)		(%)		(%)		(%)
Manufactures	—	—	27	1.1	158	5.8	831	28.2
Imports	457	21.8	509	20.2	787	28.7	300	10.2
Handicrafts	1637	78.2	1981	78.7	1798	65.5	1815	61.6
Total	2094	100.0	2517	100.0	2743	100.0	2946	100.0
	1875		1905		1919		1931	
Manufactures	—	—	90.2	11.5	297.6	36.8	966.9	90.9
Imports	12.4	1.9	304.3	38.6	178.5	22.0	−76.0	−7.1
Handicrafts	632.3	98.1	393.2	49.9	333.6	41.2	173.3	16.3
Total	644.7	100.0	787.7	100.0	809.7	100.0	1064.2	100.0

Source: Bruce Lloyd Reynolds, 'The impact of trade and foreign investment on industrialization: Chinese textiles, 1875-1931', 31, table 2.4.

of 'surplus' labour, specifically household labour which had a claim to subsistence in any case and, unlike factory labour, would be employed in handicraft activities even if its marginal product was below the cost of subsistence. Household handicrafts, that is, could meet the competition of factory industry at almost any price so long as the modern firm had to pay subsistence wages to its workers while the craft workers had no income-earning alternatives. Rural families seeking to maximize income moved into and out of various activities supplementary to farming depending on their estimates of the relative advantages of each, which accounts in part for the variable fates of individual handicrafts. The technology of handicraft weaving improved significantly in the twentieth century with the diffusion of improved wooden looms, iron-gear looms and Jacquard looms, and this made possible a much higher labour productivity as compared to handicraft spinning. Inexpensive imported and domestic machine-spun yarn made handicraft spinning increasingly disadvantageous in relation to other side-line occupations. The combination of the availability and low cost of machine-spun yarn, the example of machine-loomed products, and the comparative advantage of weaving over spinning led to a shift into weaving by rural families. In such handicraft weaving centres as Ting-hsien, Pao-ti, and Kao-yang in Hopei, and Wei-hsien in Shantung, which experienced 'booms' at various times in the 1920s and 1930s, large numbers of peasant households were supplied with yarn from Tientsin, Tsingtao and Shanghai mills, and sometimes with looms by textile merchants who contracted for their output and distributed it throughout North China and Manchuria.[30]

It is of considerable importance to our received picture of the fate of handicrafts in the twentieth century that many of the better quality field surveys of rural China date from the 1930s, that is, from the brief hey-day of pre-war academic scholarship. After almost two decades of political disruption, this was seen as a hopeful time when China could at last embark on the journey to modern economic growth which had brought wealth and power to the West and Japan. To an impressively unanimous degree, China's economists and rural sociologists, even the majority who were not Marxist in outlook, tended to be as much concerned with the welfare implications of the functioning of the economic system as with analysing its interrelationships and measuring its performance. That agricultural production roughly kept up with population growth, or that the absolute output of handicrafts at least held its own, in no way compensated for the observable facts that: China's economy was 'backward', most Chinese were poor while a very few were rich, and even the low standard of living of the poor was subject to severe uncertainties and fluctuations. Prosperity, moreover, since the 'demonstration effect' was powerful, seemed achievable only through large-scale modern industrialization. In this context, there occurred both a disproportionate attention to the small modern sector and, even though the empirical data which were honestly presented frequently contradicted it, a tendency to draw conclusions from the declining phases of a cyclically fluctuating handicraft performance while ignoring the rising phases.[31] It was almost as if the more bankrupt the traditional sector could be shown to be, the more likely it was that a national effort to modernize and industrialize would be undertaken. The early 1930s were in all likelihood a relatively depressed period for the handicraft textile industry among others, but this does not appear to have been caused so much by the competition from modern mills as by the loss of the market in Manchuria and Jehol after 1931. To suggest that there was no recovery by 1936–7 as a result of the development of alternative markets goes beyond what we presently know and contradicts the upward trend of the Chinese economy as a whole in the two years before the outbreak of war in mid 1937. And for the long and bitter years of war and civil war between 1937 and 1949, is it believable that modern and urban consumers' goods factories suf-

---

30 See Kang Chao, 'The growth of a modern cotton textile industry and the competition with handicrafts', in Perkins, ed. *China's modern economy*, 167–201.
31 Chao, *ibid.*, 173–5, offers examples.

fered less destruction and curtailment of output than the vast and decentralized handicraft sector?

Given the growth of imports and of the output of domestic factories, the fate of handicraft production in absolute terms depended on two factors: the structure of imports and of factory production, and the size and composition of aggregate demand. In 1925, for example (see table 28, page 124), at most 50.5 per cent of imports were competitive with handicrafts (cotton goods, cotton yarn, wheat flour, sugar, tobacco, paper, chemicals, dyes and pigments). Apart from cotton goods and kerosene whose effects have already been noted, the largest remaining categories are sugar (whose importation was exceptionally high in 1925 and which includes unprocessed sugar not competitive with handicrafts), chemicals, dyes and pigments (only a small part of which replaced indigenous dyestuffs), and tobacco (the domestic processing of which increased in the 1920s and thus clearly was not swamped by imports). Other potentially competitive imports were minute and could not have seriously affected domestic handicrafts.

With respect to the impact of factory production, again excluding the case of cotton yarn in which handicraft output was sharply curtailed, the situation is similar. The most important handicraft products in 1933 were milled rice and wheat flour, which together accounted for 67 per cent of the identified gross output value of all handicrafts. Of the total production of milled rice and wheat flour plus wheat flour imports, 95 per cent came from the handicraft sector. If there had been any decline since the beginning of the century as a result of competition from modern food product factories or imports, it could not have been a very significant one.[32]

Knowing as little as we do about the domestic market for handicrafts, it is difficult to speak directly about the pattern of aggregate demand in the republican era. Three indirect indicators, however, may be useful. China's population increased at an average annual rate of almost 1 per cent between 1912 and 1949, while the growth rate of the urban population may have been as much as 2 per cent. Population increase alone, and especially the growth of the coastal commercial and manufacturing centres, was adequate to account for a large part of the consumption of imported or domestic factory-made commodities. A significant portion of modern manufactures consisted of urban consumption goods which had little value in rural China. Even for items in universal use such as

32 Ta-chung Liu and Kung-chia Yeh, *The economy of the Chinese mainland: national income and economic development, 1933–1959*, 142–3, 512–13; Hsiao Liang-lin, *China's foreign trade statistics, 1864–1949*, 32–3.

cotton textiles, product differentiation based on quality and cost was important. With respect to traditional demand, factory goods might be 'inferior' goods. And if this was not the case, the rural population continued to use the products of handicraft industry when, given low wage rates and the high price of capital, these were produced at a lower unit cost than by modern industry.

A second indicator is the persistence of external demand until the 1930s. One study reports that the value of handicraft exports in constant 1913 prices increased at a rate of about 2.6 per cent a year between 1875 and 1928. Another estimate suggests an annual increase of 1.1 per cent a year from 1912 to 1931 for a somewhat broader group of handicraft products.[33] Without more knowledge of domestic consumption, figures reporting increased exports are, of course, inconclusive. In the case of silk, however, which was China's largest single export in the 1920s, there are strong indications that in absolute terms the domestic market grew along with exports until 1930 while their relative shares were more or less constant.[34]

Finally, farm output, especially cash crops many of which required processing, increased at about the same rate as population – slightly below 1 per cent a year – between 1912 and 1949. Perkins estimates the annual gross value of farm output in 1914–18 at Ch.$16.01–17.03 billion, and in 1931–7 at Ch.$19.14–19.79 billion, a total increase of perhaps 16 to 19 per cent over two decades.[35] He also argues that 'no more than 5 or 6 percent of farm output could have been processed in modern factories in the 1930's, or less than half the percentage of *increase* in farm output between the 1910's and 1930's.'[36] At worst, in other words, handicraft processing of agricultural products held its own.

With respect to factory industry, in addition to its relatively small quantitative importance, several other general characteristics are worthy of attention:

1.   Modern manufacturing industry, as already noted, was concentrated in the coastal provinces, in particular in the treaty-port cities, and after 1931 in Manchuria. (In the all-important cotton textile industry, 87.0 per cent of all spindles in China and 91.1 per cent of all looms in 1924 were located in the provinces of Hopei, Liaoning, Shantung, Kiangsu, Chekiang, Fukien, and Kwangtung; the three cities of Shanghai, Tientsin and Tsingtao accounted for 67.7 per cent and 71.9 per cent of spindles

33 Chi-ming Hou, *Foreign investment and economic development in China, 1840–1937*, 169–70.
34 Li, 'Kiangnan and the silk export trade, 1842–1937', 266–73.
35 Perkins, *Agricultural development in China*, 29–30.
36 Perkins, 'Growth and changing structure of China's twentieth-century economy', 122–3.

TABLE 9

Output and number of workers in
Chinese- and foreign-owned factories, 1933

	Gross value of output (millions Chinese $)	%	Number of workers (1,000s)	%
China Proper				
Chinese-owned	1,771.4	66.9	783.2	72.8
Foreign-owned	497.4	18.8	163.1	15.2
Manchuria	376.7	14.3	129.5	12.0
Total	2,645.5	100.0	1,075.8	100.0

Source: table 4.

and looms respectively.) While there was some geographical dispersion of, for example, cotton spindles in the 1930s (in 1918, 61.8 per cent of the total spindles were located in Shanghai; 55.4 per cent in 1932; and 51.1 per cent in 1935), modern factory industry remained almost totally unknown in the interior provinces of China before the outbreak of the war with Japan.

2.   One reason for this geographical concentration was the very large share which foreign-owned factories occupied within the manufacturing sector. Foreign plants were restricted to the treaty ports. Between 1931 and 1945 the Manchurian economy was not linked to the rest of the Chinese economy, but it was precisely in Manchuria, if anywhere, that modern China experienced a degree of 'economic development', including the construction of a substantial base of heavy industry. While the prominence of foreign-owned factories in China's pre-war manufacturing industry is acknowledged by all sources, estimates of exactly how important they were in terms of their share of total output vary quite widely. Combining D. K. Lieu's survey data with other sources, Liu and Yeh have proposed the following figures for the gross value of output and number of workers in Chinese- and foreign-owned factories in China proper and Manchuria in 1933 (table 9).

For China proper, 78 per cent of the output of factory industry was accounted for by Chinese-owned firms. This is a substantially higher proportion than the Chinese-owned share of the capitalization of manufacturing industry in China which, according to one rather crude estimate, was only 37 per cent of the total in the 1930s.[37] The question arises as to

37 Ku Ch'un-fan (Koh Tso-fan), *Chung-kuo kung-yeh-hua t'ung-lun* (A general discussion of China's industrialization), 170.

whether the significance of foreign-owned industry in China is better measured by its share of output, or by the relative size of foreign capital investment as compared with Chinese. Excessive attention to capitalization tends to exaggerate the importance of foreign-owned industry. Capitalization is notoriously difficult to measure, and it slights the fact that Chinese-owned industry was primarily light manufacturing in which the problem of capital indivisibility was minimal and the degree to which labour could be substituted for capital was quite large. In other words, it implicitly assumes the same capital-output ratio in Chinese- and foreign-owned factories. Table 10 gives some indication of the output share of foreign enterprises in several branches of manufacturing industry in the 1920s and 1930s. (See also table 3, page 39, for 1933.) Data on coal mining are included here; in general, apart from the matter of concentration in the treaty ports, what is being said about factories applies as well to mining.

3. Factory industry in China exclusive of Manchuria was predominantly consumers' goods industry. In 1933 producers' goods accounted for 25 per cent of net value added by factories. The largest industries, as measured by the value of their output, were cotton textiles, flour milling, cigarettes and oil pressing. Among the 2,435 Chinese-owned factories investigated by D. K. Lieu, 50 per cent were engaged in the manufacture of textiles and foodstuffs. These 1,211 plants as a group accounted for 76 per cent of the value of output, 71 per cent of the employment, 60 per cent of the power installed, and 58 per cent of the capital investment of all Chinese-owned factories.

4. The average size of factories was small, and generally smaller for Chinese than foreign-owned firms in the same industry, but not very small as compared, for example, with Japanese plants in the Meiji era or with the early industrial experience of other countries. The 2,435 factories surveyed by D. K. Lieu had a total capitalization of Ch.$406 million, giving an average of Ch.$166,000 or about U.S.$50,000 at the prevailing exchange rate. These plants had a total motive power capacity of 507,300 horse-power or about 200 horse-power per factory. The average number of workers per factory was 202.

5. Of the Chinese-owned factories, even those located in the treaty ports, it may be said that the social context in which they existed and which impinged importantly on the 'modern' fact that they employed mechanical power and complex machinery, remained to a remarkable extent 'traditional'. Only 612 of D. K. Lieu's 2,435 factories were organized as joint-stock companies. The absence of a well-developed market for the transfer of equity shares contributed to a particular relationship between shareholders and management in which the demands of the

TABLE 10

Percentage of total output by Chinese and foreign† firms in selected industries

	Coal*		Cotton yarn		Cotton cloth		Cigarettes		Electric power		Matches	
	Chinese	Foreign	Chinese	Foreign	Chinese	Foreign	Chinese	Foreign	Chinese	Foreign	Chinese	Foreign
1913	7.0	93.0	57	43	41	59						
1919	24.4	75.6	67	33	50	50						
1923	21.1	78.9	62	38	44	56			23	77		
1928	22.0	78.0	71	29	39	61						
1933	16.7	83.3	71	29	36	64	43	57	37	63	89	11
1936	34.3	65.7					42‡	58‡	45	55	89‡	11‡

* 'Modern' mines only
† Foreign-owned or foreign-investment/control
‡ 1935

Sources: Yen Chung-p'ing, *Chung-kuo chin-tai ching-chi shih t'ung-chi shih tzu-liao hsuan-chi* (Selected statistical materials on modern Chinese economic history), 124, 130–1; Reynolds, 'The impact of trade and foreign investment on industrialization', 216, 221; Ch'en Chen *et al.*, comps. *Chung-kuo chin-tai kung-yeh shih tzu-liao* (Source materials on the history of modern industry in China), II. 971.

former for short-term profits often adversely affected long-term expansion and modernization through reinvestment. Such practices as guaranteed dividends frequently forced firms to borrow at high rates in order to obtain working capital. Financing for modern industry was never adequate in republican China. Investment in agricultural land and urban real estate continued to be attractive; to these were added in more recent times speculation in commodities, foreign exchange and government bonds. We shall see below how government fiscal policy tended to divert funds from productive investment.

Competent management was in short supply. Only 500 of some 4,000 technicians in 82 spinning mills in 1931 had received formal training. Higher management was not greatly different from what it had been in the *kuan-tu shang-pan* period (see volume 11). Such techniques as cost accounting were sparsely employed: two-storey factory buildings on cheap land were not uncommon, and the inadequacy of allowances for depreciation and the repair of equipment is noted by almost all observers. Such circumstances, however, have been characteristic of the early stages of industrialization throughout the world, and were not particularly worse in China than, say, in the American textile industry 50 years earlier.

Foremen in Chinese factories tended to retain a 'long-gown' attitude, disdained to engage in menial tasks, and left the actual supervision of workers to technically incompetent overseers who frequently were also 'contractors' who had recruited the workers by, for example, making arrangements with the parents of child operatives. While there were over a million factory workers by 1933, this was overall not a skilled, stable, disciplined labour force. Sectoral variations were probably significant, as in Japan. Where experience counted, it was rewarded. Highly skilled male workers were well-paid, well-trained and tended to stay with one employer. In the dominant textile industry, however, experience was not critically important, except for mechanics. Many workers retained their ties with the rural villages which, under force of necessity, they had left in order to supplement a meagre farming income with factory wages. This was especially true of the young women and children who formed a very high proportion of the labour force. The 493,257 workers in D. K. Lieu's 2,435 factories included 202,762 men, 243,435 women and 47,060 children under 16 years of age; for the textile industry, the comparable figures were 84,767, 187,847 and 29,758. With a labour force not fully committed to a lifetime in a factory, and with a potentially plentiful supply of workers available from the peasantry, industrial wages were low by international standards and hours were long. Chinese textile mills before 1937 typically operated on two 12-hour shifts; 11-hour shifts were general in Japanese-owned mills. The real income of the urban worker, however, was high by rural Chinese standards, a factor which sustained migration to the cities. In circumstances where capital was expensive and labour cheap, 'rationalization' of production in some Chinese firms took the form of more intensive use of labour by lowering wages and extending hours. The prevalence of low wage rates perpetuated a high labour turnover and made the worker reluctant to sever ties with his village, which continued to offer him a refuge in times of industrial slow-down. This then confirmed the employer's belief that the worker could live on a 'handful of rice'. The convention of low wages, moreover, partly justified itself by preventing a rise in labour efficiency.[38]

Probably it could not have been otherwise. One fundamental problem faced by Chinese industry was the weakness of demand. So long as outside of the treaty ports and their immediate environs the traditional society and impoverished peasant economy continued basically unchanged, what market could there be for new or improved (and costlier) goods produced with well-paid labour?

6. The concentration of modern industry in coastal cities, the large foreign-owned component, the predominance of consumers' goods, and the small size and technical backwardness of most factories – all of these are correlates of the very small share of modern industry in China's national product before 1949. But to estimate that the modern share of M+ (factory output, mining, utilities and modern transport) accounted for only 5 per cent (table 2, page 37) or 7 per cent (table 3, page 39) of total domestic product in the 1930s – that is, that China's economy was clearly an 'underdeveloped' one – should not lead to the conclusion that the modern industrial and transport sector was of no consequence for China's post-1949 economic development. If what the People's Republic of China inherited was quantitatively small, nevertheless over two-thirds of the increase in industrial production during 1953–7 was to come from the expanded output of existing factories.[39] In spite of the Soviet removal of industrial machinery and equipment from Manchuria, the new investment necessary to restore output in this major producers' goods base was less than would have been required for entirely new plant. If, taken as a whole, pre-1949 China was not industrialized, never-

---

38 On the origins, recruitment, wages and working conditions of labour in the 1920s, see Jean Chesneaux, *The Chinese labor movement, 1919–1927*, 48–112. The structure of industrial wages before 1949 is analysed in Christopher Howe, *Wage patterns and wage policy in modern China, 1919–1972*, 16–27. For an example of Japanese-style 'permanent' employment for skilled male workers, see *Andersen, Meyer and Company Limited of China*, 114. I am indebted to Professor Thomas Rawski for this last reference.

39 Kang Chao, 'Policies and performance in industry', in Alexander Eckstein, Walter Galenson, and Ta-chung Liu, eds. *Economic trends in communist China*, table 3, p. 579.

theless its cotton textile industry grew rapidly and steadily and was not monopolized by foreign-owned firms. Even in the 1930s China's cotton textile output was one of the largest in the world. After 1949, although new investment in consumers' goods industry lagged far behind producers' goods, the export of textile fabrics and clothing was – next to raw and processed agricultural products – a major source of the foreign exchange which paid for China's imports.[40]

Equally important, the small pre-1949 modern sector provided the People's Republic with skilled workers and technicians, experienced managers, and patterns of organized activity which, supplemented by Soviet advisers and training, made it possible to provide training and experience to the vastly expanded number of new managers and workers who were to staff the many new factories that began production in the late 1950s. And in the producers' goods sector, in particular, the dozens of relatively small Shanghai machine-building firms – many of which were inherited from the pre-1949 period – retained a qualitative flexibility to develop new products and techniques that allowed them to play a large role in overcoming the difficulties in the early 1960s stemming from the Great Leap Forward and the withdrawal of Soviet advisers and their blueprints.[41] 'Without this base, China's industrial development in the 1950's and 1960's would have been significantly slower or would have had to rely more heavily on foreign technicians, or both.'[42]

AGRICULTURE

China's economy in the republican era, as in the past, was overwhelmingly agricultural. Net value added by agriculture in 1933 was estimated at Ch.$18.76 billion or 65 per cent of the total net domestic product. This output was produced by 205 million agricultural workers, 79 per cent of the labour force. Only small changes in these percentages occurred between 1912 and 1933, although after 1933 the rapid industrial growth in Manchuria made the share of agriculture decline somewhat more rapidly than in earlier years (table 3, page 39). Plant products dominated, and within this category, food crops. Estimates shown in table 11 have been offered for 1933. By weight, certainly a rough measure, food crops (rice, wheat and other grains, potatoes, vegetables, fruits) accounted for 80 per cent of the plant products.

40 Feng-hwa Mah, *The foreign trade of mainland China*, app. C, pp. 194–200.
41 Thomas G. Rawski, 'The growth of producer industries, 1900–1971, in Perkins, ed. *China's modern economy*, 228–32.
42 Perkins, 'Growth and changing structure of China's twentieth-century economy', 125.

TABLE 11

Output of the several sectors of agriculture, 1933

	Gross value-added (billion Chinese $)
Plant products	15.73
Animal products	1.37
Forest products	0.60
Fishery products	0.41
Miscellaneous products	1.07
Total	19.18
Less depreciation	0.42
Net value-added	18.76

Source: Liu Ta-chung and Yeh Kung-chia, *The economy of the Chinese mainland*, 140, table 36.

TABLE 12

Gross value of farm output, 1914–57 (billions 1933 Chinese $)

	1914–18 (average year)	1931–7 (average year)	1957
Grain	9.15–10.17	10.31–10.96	12.32
Soy-beans	0.43	0.66	0.78
Oil-bearing crops	0.51	1.13	0.77
Cotton and other fibres	0.78	0.86	1.28
Tobacco, tea and silk	0.49	0.52	0.32
Sugar-cane and Sugar-beet	0.11	0.11	0.14
Animals	1.14	1.40	2.74
Sub-total	13.63	15.65	19.36
Other products	3.40	4.14	4.91
Total gross value	16.01–17.03	19.14–19.79	24.27
Per capita (Ch $)	36.1–38.4	38.1–39.4	37.5

Source: Perkins, *Agricultural development in China*, 30, table II.8.

Until 1937 the total output of agriculture approximately kept pace with the growth of population (from 430 million in 1912 to 500 million in the mid 1930s). The per capita value in constant prices of farm output in 1931–7 was about the same as it had been in 1914–18 (table 12), reflecting an output increase of slightly less than 1 per cent a year. In part this increment resulted from an expansion of cultivated land area which Perkins estimates at 1,356 million *shih mou* in 1918 and 1,471 million *shih mou* in 1933.[43] The balance came from increased output of grains and of cash

43 Perkins, *Agricultural development in China*, 233–40.

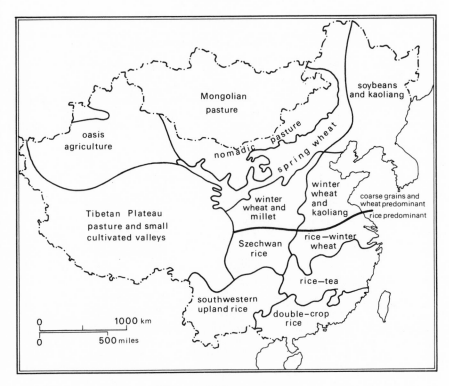

MAP 3. Major crop areas

crops on existing land. Grain output per capita remained unchanged at about Ch.$21 during this whole period while the per capita output of other products, including cash crops, increased from Ch.$15 to Ch.$17. Table 13 shows the changes in quantities of plant products 1914–57. From 1914–18 to 1931–7 all grains (in catties = 1.1 pounds) increased by 12.9 per cent. But rice output fell 5.8 per cent, while the production of potatoes and corn grew by 16.4 per cent and 39.2 per cent, respectively. These changes reflect a shift of cropping patterns to the production of plant products which yielded more calories per unit of land, thus releasing land for the increased cultivation of cash crops. Wheat, which grew by 16.8 per cent, was a cash crop in some areas of North China where it was marketed to buy rougher grains such as kaoliang and millet for farm consumption. In North and Central China wheat and cotton impinged on rice acreage, while in Central China oil seed-bearing crops were also augmented. Cash crop output accounted for approximately 14 per cent of farm output by value in 1914–18 and 17 per cent in 1931–7, while the physical output of individual industrial crops increased more rapidly than

TABLE 13

Physical output of plant products, 1914–57 (1,000,000 catties)

	1914–19 (average year)	1931–7 (average year)	1957
Rice	147,610	139,110	173,600
Wheat	39,570	46,200	47,100
Corn	14,680	20,440	37,470
Potatoes (grain equivalents)	7,060	15,280	43,800
Kaoliang	23,750	24,680	20,030
Millet	22,180	27,680	23,330
Barley	18,090	19,440	9,300
Other grain	10,370	10,940	15,170
Total grain	283,300	319,960	370,000
Soy-beans	10,970	16,860	20,100
Peanuts	4,540	5,250	5,142
Rapeseed	3,800	5,080	1,775
Sesame	670	1,810	625
Cotton	1,606	1,888	3,280
Fibres	1,410	1,350	1,290
Tobacco	1,590	1,830	1,220
Sugar-cane	18,720	18,720	20,785
Sugar-beet	—	—	3,002
Tea	445	399	223
Silk	406	420	225

Source: Perkins, *Agricultural development in China*, 266–89.

grains: sesame, 170.1 per cent; soy-beans, 53.7; rapeseed, 33.7; cotton, 17.6; peanuts, 15.6; and tobacco, 15.1.[44]

In addition to supporting a slowly growing rural population, in 'normal' times China's pre-war agriculture supplied part of the food and raw material needs of the urban areas which were growing somewhat more rapidly. Transport difficulties and other disruptions resulting from civil war in the 1920s required the increasing supplementation of urban consumption with imported grains. Imports then dropped off somewhat in the 1930s before rising again with the advent of war.[45] Agricultural commodities, moreover, accounted for the bulk of China's exports (see table 28, page 124). As a whole exports grew in value 3.5 per cent a year and in quantity terms 1.7 per cent a year during the period 1912–31.[46]

44 These are data for China as a whole, including Manchuria. For North China, see Myers, *The chinese peasant economy*, 177–206; many local studies are summarized in Amano Motonosuke, *Chūgoku nōgyō no shomondai* (Problems of Chinese agriculture), 1. 3–148.

45 For rice, wheat and wheat flour imports, see Hsiao, *China's foreign trade statistics, 1864–1949*, 32–4. Wu Pao-san, *Chung-kuo liang-shih tui-wai mao-i ch'i ti-wei ch'ü-shih chi pien-ch'ien chih yuan-yin, 1912–1931* (Causes of trends and fluctuations in China's foreign trade in food grains, 1912–1931).

46 Hsiao, *China's foreign trade statistics, 1864–1949*, 274–5.

All told, this was a creditable performance for an agricultural sector which experienced no significant technological improvements before 1949. For individual farm families or particular localities and regions, of course, the annual outcome was not so uniform during the four decades of the republican era. Output and income could fluctuate greatly due to weather, natural disasters, destructive warfare or unfavourable price trends.[47] Barely adequate overall production left no margin of protection against such all too frequent contingencies, nor against the frightening year-to-year uncertainty as to whether one's family would be fed. Even this 'creditable performance' requires some explanation.

Amano Motonosuke's magistral history of Chinese agriculture, which carefully examines the technology associated with each major crop as well as the development of farming implements, impressively demonstrates that the agricultural technology of the republican era was a continuation, with few improvements, of the farming practices of the Ch'ing period.[48] Sporadic efforts to improve seeds and develop better farm practices can be noted throughout the republican years. For example, 251 agricultural experimental stations were established in the provinces between 1912 and 1927.[49] The Nanking government's Bureau of Commerce and Industry, and later the Bureau of Agriculture and Mining and the National Economic Council, also encouraged agricultural research and the diffusion of agronomic knowledge.[50] These efforts, however, were small in scale and lacked the support of local government.

The slow growth of total farm production in the early decades of the twentieth century shown in tables 12 (page 64) and 13 (page 66) was not principally the result of improved seeds, and fertilizer, or increased irrigation and water control. Seventy per cent of the expansion in cultivated acreage between 1913 and the 1930s occurred in Manchuria, in particular through the growth of the soy-bean acreage as well as that for

47 Amano Motonosuke, *Shina nōgyō keizai ron* (On the Chinese agricultural economy; hereafter *Agricultural economy*), 2. 696–8 provides a listing of civil wars, floods, droughts, pestilence, and the provinces affected, 1912–31. See also Buck, *Land utilization in China. Statistics*, 13–20, for 'calamities' by locality during 1904–29.
48 Amano Motonosuke, *Chūgoku nōgyō shi kenkyū* (A study of the history of Chinese agriculture) 389–423, for example, on rice technology. F. H. King, *Farmers of forty centuries*, provides a vivid description of the 'permanent agriculture in China, Korea and Japan' in the early twentieth century.
49 Li Wen-chih and Chang Yu-i, comps. *Chung-kuo chin-tai nung-yeh shih tzu-liao* (Source materials on China's modern agricultural history; hereafter *Agricultural history*), 2. 182. The first volume in this collection, edited by Li, covers 1840–1911; the second and third, edited by Chang, cover 1912–27 and 1927–37 respectively.
50 Ramon H. Myers, 'Agrarian policy and agricultural transformation: mainland China and Taiwan, 1895–1954', *Hsiang-kang Chung-wen ta-hsueh Chung-kuo wen-hua yen-chiu-so hsueh-pao* (Journal of the Institute of Chinese Studies of the Chinese University of Hong Kong), 3.2 (1970) 532–5.

TABLE 14

Index numbers of agricultural prices, terms of trade, land values,
farm wages, land tax, 1913–37 (1926=100)

Year	(1) Agricultural products, wholesale prices Tientsin	Shanghai	China*	(2) Terms of Trade (1)÷Wholesale prices of all manufactured goods Tientsin	Shanghai	(1)÷Wholesale prices of consumers' goods Tientsin	Shanghai	(1)÷prices paid by farmers China*	(3) Land Values Buck	NARB	(4) Farm Wages	(5) Land Tax
1913	61		58	82		86		89	63		72	79
1914	58		59	78		83		92	66		74	80
1915	58		61	74		81		90	68		77	84
1916	61		65	72		81		92	72		80	86
1917	70		69	77		88		91	75		83	83
1918	64		69	67		74		87	77		86	84
1919	59		69	61		63		84	81		88	86
1920	77		80	76		79		94	83		89	86
1921	78	75	90	77	66	80	76	102	87		91	87
1922	75	86	92	78	83	78	90	101	89		93	86
1923	82	92	98	84	86	83	91	103	92		95	86
1924	89	92	97	90	92	90	94	96	95		95	88
1925	100	95	102	101	94	102	95	101	100		97	89
1926	100	100	100	100	100	100	100	100	100		100	92
1927	103	103	95	101	98	98	98	92	100		105	100
1928	103	95	106	97	92	94	92	97	96		112	109
1929	107	99	127	96	94	94	96	108	100		118	118
1930	107	113	125	90	98	81	101	99	99	(1931=100)	124	119
1931	96	106	116	72	80	70	82	86	103	100	126	140
1932	90	95	103	73	79	69	80	81	93	95		132
1933	73	94		64	84	61	86			89		

1934	64	86	60	83	59	84	82
1935	82	83	79	83	75	82	81
1936	102	102	87	91	82	91	84
1937		140		106		108	

* 37 localities in 36 hsien in 15 provinces

Sources: (1) and (2), Nan-k'ai ta hsueh ching-chi yen-chiu so (Nankai Institute of Economics), comp. *1913 nien–1952 nien Nan-k'ai chih-shu tzu-liao hui-pien* (Nankai price indexes 1913–52), 12–13; *Shanghai chieh-fang hou wu-chia tzu-liao hui-pien* (Shanghai prices before and after Liberation), 135; John Lossing Buck, *Land utilization in China: a study of 16,786 farms in 168 localities, and 38,256 farm families in twenty-two provinces in China, 1929–1933*, 149–50.

(3) Buck, *Land utilization in China, Statistics*, 168–9; *Nung-ch'ing pao-kao*, 7.4 (April 1939), 47, in Li Wen-chih and Chang Yu-i, comps. *Chung-kuo chin-tai nung-yeh shih tzu-liao* (Source materials on China's modern agricultural history), III. 708–10.

(4) Buck, *Land utilization in China, Statistics*, 151.

(5) Buck, *Land utilization in China, Statistics*, 167.

kaoliang and other grains consumed by a population which rose from about 18 million in 1910 to 38 million in 1940.[51] Thus, the extensive development of Manchurian agriculture employing 'traditional' technology, accounted for a large share of the increase in total farm output. There were also small acreage increases in Kiangsu, Hupei, Yunnan and Szechwan, but for the most part other increments to output were the result of the adoption of the best traditional farming practices in areas that had hitherto failed to use them. Part (perhaps most) of the increased yields on existing cropland came from the application of more labour.

Both the opening of the Manchurian frontier and the more intensive use of traditional practices were facilitated by the responsiveness of the Chinese farm family to rising export demand, favourable price trends, and the availability of urban off-farm employment opportunities, all of which persisted until the depression of the early 1930s. The increased agricultural output which resulted was adequate statistically to feed China's population because the rate of population growth was a very modest one – on the average less than 1 per cent a year. The slow growth rate, resulting from a relatively high birth rate in combination with a high but fluctuating death rate, reflected the generally low standard of living, poor public health conditions, and high susceptibility to the effects of natural and man-made disasters. Agricultural output was deemed adequate only because the average Chinese remained poor and population growth was subject to Malthusian controls. Within these dire limits, the demand for cash crops for export and by industries in the urban sector permitted some degree of shifting to the production of crops yielding a higher income per unit of land, especially on smaller farms.

Prices were favourable to the farmer until 1931 (see table 14). The general trend was upwards during the first three decades of the century – prices of agricultural products, goods purchased by the farmer for both production and consumption, land values, farm wages, and taxes all increased. While the terms of trade between agriculture and manufactured goods fluctuated in the 1910s, they were increasingly favourable to agriculture in the 1920s, indicating that prices received by the farmer rose even more rapidly than the prices he paid. Agricultural prices increased by 116 per cent (if one uses Buck's index in table 14) between 1913 and 1931, while prices paid by farmers rose by 108 per cent. In the same period land values increased by 63 per cent, farm wages by 75 per cent, and land taxes by 67 per cent. Wages tended to lag behind prices in North China but more nearly kept up with prices in the southern rice region, indicating

51 Eckstein, Chao and Chang, 'The economic development of Manchuria', 240–51.

a greater demand for labour and relatively more non-farm employment opportunities in South China. Where prices stayed ahead of wages, the farmer employing hired labour clearly profited more from the higher prices he received for his crops. Land values and land taxes increased least of all in these two decades. It appears that the real as opposed to the monetary burden of land taxes declined during these decades of generally rising prices.

From 1931 until the beginning of the recovery in 1935 and continuing into 1936, however, Chinese farmers experienced a sharp fall in income and a striking reversal in the terms of trade. These consequences were brought about by both the contraction of export markets resulting from the world depression (the effects were delayed in China as silver prices continued to fall until 1931), and by the outflow of silver from China as the gold price of silver rose from 1931, pushed upwards first by the abandonment of the gold standard in England, Japan and the United States, and then by the U. S. Silver Purchase Act of 1934. In this period of steeply falling prices, the farmer's fixed costs and the prices of manufactured goods tended to decline less than prices received for agricultural commodities which fell the first and most rapidly. There was a clear tendency for farmers to cut back on cash crop production and return to the cultivation of traditional grain crops in response to the depression.[52] Opportunities for off-farm employment, which had been essential to the family incomes of small farmers in particular, may also have declined temporarily after 1931, resulting in a flow of urban labour back to the rural areas.[53] Data on farm wages are sporadic, but wages probably fell less than agricultural prices. Land taxes on the average increased by 8 to 10 per cent during 1931–4 (and then declined in 1935 and 1936), while land values fell from 1931, indicating an increase in the farmer's real tax burden during the depression.[54] The outflow of silver from rural areas to Shanghai and other cities made it more difficult for farmers to obtain loans. In short, some of the gains made by the agricultural sector during the previous long inflationary phase were lost between 1931 and 1935. Recovery of both agricultural prices and cash crop output was underway by 1936, but very soon the Japanese invasion and full-scale war in mid 1937 introduced new problems.

The extent to which many farm families were affected, first, by the favourable rise in prices to 1931 and second, by their precipitous decline

---

52 Li Wen-chih and Chang Yu-i, comps. *Agricultural history*, 3. 476–80, 622–41.
53 *Ibid.* 3. 480–5.
54 *Nung-ch'ing pao-kao*, 7.4 (April 1939) 49–50, in Li Wen-chih and Chang Yu-i, comps. *Agricultural history*, 3. 708–10.

of almost 25 per cent between 1931 and 1936, depends on how far agriculture was commercialized and involved in market transactions. Perkins has estimated that in the 1920s and 1930s 20 to 30 per cent of farm output was sold locally, another 10 per cent shipped to urban areas, and 3 per cent exported. There was an increase in the last two categories mentioned, from 5 to 7 per cent and from 1 to 2 per cent, respectively, when compared with before 1910. Increasing commercialization in the twentieth century is attested also by qualitative data compiled by Chang Yu-i, even though his primary purpose is to illustrate the deleterious consequences for China's peasants of the activities of both indigenous and foreign imperialist merchants.[55] Yet outside of more commercialized regions like the Yangtze provinces and apart from commercially minded rich peasants, most farmers were still only marginally involved with markets. If we recall that cash crops (most of which were marketed) accounted for 17 per cent of farm output in the 1930s, Perkins' estimate of the extent of commercialization implies that less than a quarter of food crop output was sold by farmers and most of that in local markets little affected by international price trends. Even in Changsha, the major rice market in Hunan and one of the largest in China, prices in the 1930s fluctuated mainly with the provincial harvest and local political conditions. In the majority of farming communities a national average decline of prices by 25 per cent would have meant a much smaller drop in real income, maybe only by 5 per cent. That is, the effect of the depression – and of other price changes, up and down – in the interior provinces of China may have been no more calamitous than the inevitable fluctuations in the weather.

China's agriculture supported the Chinese people, even producing a small 'surplus' above minimum consumption levels. Over all, food consumption represented 60 per cent of domestic expenditure by end use, and total personal consumption accounted for over 90 per cent, leaving almost insignificant amounts for communal services, government consumption and investment.[56] As the average per capita farm output of Ch.$38–39 shown in table 12 (page 64) indicates, this plainly remained a 'poor' economy with minimal living standards for the mass of the population. China's grain yields per *mou* in the 1920s and 1930s were by no means low by international standards. Rice yields, for example, were slightly higher than those of early Meiji Japan – although 30 per cent lower

55 Perkins, *Agricultural development in China*, 136; Li Wen-chih and Chang Yu-i, comps. *Agricultural history*, 2. 131–300; Chang Jen-chia, *Konan no beikoku* (Rice in Hunan; trans. of 1936 report by Hunan provincial economic research institute), 87–113.
56 Liu Ta-chung and Yeh Kung-chia, *The economy of the Chinese mainland*, 68, table 10.

than Japan in the 1930s – and double or triple those of India and Thailand. Wheat yields were about the same as the United States. The average output of grain-equivalent per man-equivalent (one farmer working a full year) in China in the 1920s, however, was only 1,400 kilograms; the comparable figure for the United States was 20,000 kilograms – 14 times as large.[57] Here was the essential reason for China's poverty: four-fifths of the labour force was employed in agriculture, and the technical and organizational characteristics of this industry were such that the value added per worker was strikingly low both in comparison with developed economies and with the modern sector of China's economy.

The principal obstacle, probably, to overcoming China's economic 'backwardness' was the failure of either the private sector or the Peking and Nanking governments to marshal and allocate the funds, resources and technology required for significant and continued new investment. Annual gross investment in China proper probably never exceeded 5 per cent of national product before 1949. Due to the weakness of political leadership, China's continuing disunity, and the exigencies of war and civil war, the agricultural sector was unable to meet any greatly enhanced demands for urban food and raw materials or for exports to exchange for major new imports of industrial plants and machinery. This contributed to the slow rate of structural change. The alternative route of imposing drastic 'forced savings' on a slowly growing agricultural sector was not feasible for the weak governments of republican China.

Neither the 'distributionist' nor the 'technological' analysis of China's failure to industrialize before 1949, and in particular to achieve significant growth in agriculture, is by itself satisfactory. The technological or 'eclectic' approach rejects the notion that rural socio-economic relationships were the major problems of the agricultural sector, and concludes – as I have done above – that on the whole the performance of agriculture before 1937 was a creditable one. To the extent that growth was inhibited, this is attributed to the unavailability of appropriate inputs – especially technological improvements – and not to institutional rigidities.[58]

The emphasis of the distributionist approach is upon the contributions of unequal land ownership, tenancy, rural indebtedness, inequitable taxation and allegedly monopolistic and monopsonistic markets to supposed agricultural stagnation and increasing impoverishment. It concludes that 'lack of security of tenure, high rents and a one-sided relationship between landlord and tenant gave rise to a situation in which

57 Perkins, *Agricultural Development in China*, 35–6; Li Wen-chih and Chang Yu-i comps. *Agricultural history*, 2. 406–7; Buck, *Land utilization in China*, 281–2.
58 See Myers, *The Chinese peasant economy, passim.*

both the incentive and the material means to undertake net farm investment were lacking.'[59] At a more general level, the distributionist school
attributes China's 'continuing rural stagnation' to 'the siphoning off of
income from the tiller of the soil and its unproductive expenditure by a
variety of parasitic elements who lived on, but contributed nothing to,
the rural surplus.'[60]

There are at least two potential difficulties with a purely technological
analysis. It may ignore the extremely low absolute levels of per capita
output and income resulting from the modest expansion of agriculture
which it recounts, and thus underestimate the urgency of demands for
improvement. More important, it may be ahistorical in seeming to believe
that adjustments, say of the agricultural production function by introducing improved technology, could be made within the given equilibrium.
But it was problematic indeed in republican China, that within any reasonable time significant new inputs could be made without substantial
institutional change.

Likewise, a number of shortcomings weaken a purely distributionist
analysis. First, the progressive immiseration which is implied is not supported by any studies of the overall performance of the agricultural sector
during several decades. That individual farmers, localities and even
larger regions suffered severe difficulties of varying duration is beyond
doubt. This is not, however, evidence that, so long as population growth
remained low, the existing agricultural system could not sustain itself at
low and constant per capita output and income levels. For how long
may be a valid query – as is the ethical question of the desirability that it
should do so. But secular breakdown is not proven before the destructive
years between 1937 and 1949.

There is a problem, too, about the proportion of the 'surplus' produced
by agriculture that was potentially available for productive investment.
Following Victor Lippit, who identifies the rural surplus with the property income (mainly rents) received by landowners plus taxes paid by
owner-cultivators, Carl Riskin finds the actual total rural surplus in 1933
equal to 19 per cent of net domestic product. (The surplus produced by
the non-agricultural sectors he estimates at 8.2 per cent of NDP, giving a
total actual surplus of 27.2 per cent of NDP.) After deducting the proportion of investment, communal services and government consumption

59 Robert Ash, *Land tenure in pre-revolutionary China: Kiangsu province in the 1920s and 1930s,*
50. Ash himself also gives some weight to the more 'purely economic factors'. His study,
however, appears unconvincing in its evaluation of the degree and sources of agricultural
investment in twentieth-century Kiangsu.
60 Carl Riskin, 'Surplus and stagnation in modern China', in Perkins, ed. *China's modern
economy,* 57.

attributable to the rural surplus (four per cent out of a total of 5.8 per cent of NDP for these purposes in 1933), a further assumption is made that 15 per cent of NDP was utilized for luxury consumption by the rural elite.[61] Indeed some part was, but other parts were hoarded, 'invested' in real estate, or reloaned to peasant borrowers. The principal difficulty with assuming that a rural surplus above mass consumption equivalent to 15 per cent of NDP was available for redistribution is that neither Lippit, nor Riskin, nor I have any useful quantitative data with which to estimate the importance of these various alternative uses of the surplus. If, for example, net landlord purchases of agricultural land and urban real estate, hoarding of gold and silver, and consumption loans to farmers were large, this in effect led to a 'recirculation' of part of the landlords' income to peasant consumption. None of these was a direct burden on consumption in a given period, although in the longer run they may possibly have increased individual landlord claims to a share of national income. Only the conspicuous consumption of the wealthy, in particular their spending on imported luxuries, was an 'exhaustive' expenditure, a direct drain on the domestic product, because it thereby depleted the foreign exchange resources which might otherwise have been available for the purchase of capital goods.

And then, of course, the experience of China's agriculture in the first decade of the People's Republic should be evidence enough that while substantial social change may have been a necessary condition for sustained increases in output, it was far from being a sufficient one. Even with the post-1958 increased emphasis on investment in agriculture, China's farm output still lags behind. The problems of supplying better seed stock, adequate fertilizer and water, optimum cropping patterns, and mechanization at critical points of labour shortage have not been easily met. In sum, the whole experience of the first three-quarters of the twentieth century suggests that only with institutional reorganization *and* large doses of advanced technological inputs could China's agrarian problem be solved.

If the agrarian organization of the republican period cushioned rural China from the forced savings of an authoritarian regime, it did so by abandoning any hope that the lot of a farmer would ever be any better than that which his father, and his father before him, had experienced. In other words, if the redistributive effects of peasant-landlord-government relations in rural China before 1949 were perhaps not so onerous for the peasantry as is generally believed, their long-term output effects

61 *Ibid.* 68, 74, 77–81; Victor D. Lippit, *Land reform and economic development in China,* 36–94.

were debilitating for the economy as a whole. Land tenure, rural usury and regressive taxation were the natural issues around which sentiment could be mobilized for the overthrow of a social system which offered little prospect for betterment.

The estimates we have used for population (430 million in 1912, 500 million in the mid 1930s) and for cultivated acreage (1,356 million *mou* and 1,471 million *mou*), suggest that the area of cultivated land per capita decreased from 3.15 *mou* to 2.94 *mou* in the first decades of the twentieth century. Responses collected by Buck's investigators also indicate a decline from 1870 to 1933 in the size of the average farm operated.[62] Although derived from different sources and by different methods, the two estimates (1 *mou* = 0.167 acre) are very close – Buck: 1910, 2.62 acres (crop area) per farm family; 1933, 2.27 acres. Perkins (assuming an average household of five persons): 1913, 2.6 acres; 1930s, 2.4 acres. The size distribution of farms operated as of 1934–5 is shown in table 16(3) (page 82). In the southern provinces (Buck's 'rice region'), the average unit of cultivation tended to be substantially smaller than in the north (the 'wheat region'). In all regions there was a significant correlation between size of household and farm size, an indication that high population density had forced the price of land so high that peasants could afford to fill it only in a lavishly labour-using fashion. Therefore, farm size was small when household members were few.

The uneconomic aspects of miniature cultivation were aggravated by the fact that farms tended to be broken up into several non-adjacent parcels, a product in large part of the absence of primogeniture in the Chinese inheritance system. Considerable land was wasted in boundary strips, excessive labour time was used in travel from parcel to parcel, and irrigation was made more difficult. Buck's average was six parcels per farm; other writers mention from five to 40 parcels.

While the Chinese farmer had skilfully exploited the traditional agricultural technology to the very limits of possibility, few of the nineteenth- and twentieth-century advances in seeds, implements, fertilizers, insecticides and the like had found their way into rural China. Investment in agriculture was overwhelmingly investment in land. Human-power was more important than animal-power, and the farmer's implements – little changed over the centuries – were adapted to human-power. The utilization of human labour per acre of land was probably more intensive than in any other country of the world, while paradoxically the individual labourer was not intensively used except at peak periods such as planting

---

62 Buck, *Land utilization in China*, 269–70.

or harvesting. Only 35 per cent of rural men aged between 16 and 60 were engaged in full-time agricultural work, while 58 per cent worked only part-time. Part of the surplus labour power was devoted to subsidiary occupations, usually home industry, which provided 14 per cent of the income of farm families so engaged.[63]

The kind and quantity of agricultural output summarized at the beginning of this section were the results of the decisions as to the allocation of their human and material resources and the application of their farming skills by millions of peasant households. Nearly half of these family farms were less than 10 *mou* (1.6 acres) in size, and 80 per cent were smaller than 30 *mou* (5 acres). It is necessary, however, to distinguish between unit of cultivation and unit of ownership, and inquire into the effects of substantial tenancy upon agricultural output and the individual farm family.

How much land was rented in the 1930s? Buck, for example, estimated that 28.7 per cent of privately-owned farm land was rented to tenants [table 16(2)]. If the 6.7 per cent of farm land that was publicly owned (*kung-t'ien*, government land, school land, temple land, ancestral land, soldiers' land and charity land) and which was almost entirely rented out is added to this figure, it appears that a total of 35.5 per cent of agricultural land was rented to tenants.[64] This estimate is confirmed by data on the quantity of land that was redistributed in the course of land reform in the first years of the People's Republic – from 42 to 44 per cent of the cultivated area in 1952.[65] The proportion beyond 35.5 per cent is perhaps an indication of the zeal with which land owned by 'rich peasants' as well as landlords was confiscated during the land reform.

Land ownership in China was very unequal, but probably less so than in many other 'underdeveloped' countries. The best data for the 1930s were obtained by a land survey in 16 provinces excluding Manchuria conducted by the National Land Commission of the National Economic Council and the Ministries of Finance and Interior (shown in table 15). Some downward bias is present in these figures as a consequence of including information only about landlords actually resident in the areas surveyed. The average holding of the 1,295,001 owners covered by this 1934–5 survey was 15.17 *mou* (2.5 acres). But the 73 per cent of the families surveyed who owned 15 *mou* or less held only 28 per cent of the total land,

63 *Ibid.* 181–5, 294, 297.
64 *Ibid.* 193–6.
65 Perkins, *Agricultural development in China*, 87, 89; Lippit, *Land reform and economic development in China*, 95; Kenneth R. Walker, *Planning in Chinese agriculture: socialisation and the private sector, 1956–1962*, 5.

TABLE 15

Distribution of rural land ownership, 1934–5* (16 provinces)

Size classes of land owned (mou)	Number of families (hu) surveyed	% of families surveyed	Land owned (1,000 mou)	% of land owned	Average land per family (mou)
< 5	461,128	35.61	1,217	6.21	2.64
5–9.9	310,616	23.99	2,245	11.42	7.23
10–14.9	170,604	13.17	2,090	10.63	12.25
15–19.9	103,468	7.99	1,802	9.17	17.42
20–29.9	106,399	8.22	2,589	13.17	24.33
30–49.9	80,333	6.20	3,053	15.54	38.01
50–69.9	28,094	2.17	1,646	8.38	58.59
70–99.9	17,029	1.31	1,408	7.16	82.61
100–149.9	9,349	0.72	1,124	5.71	120.21
150–199.9	3,146	0.24	514	2.76	171.97
200–299.9	2,587	0.20	623	3.17	240.95
300–499.9	1,368	0.11	518	2.63	378.40
500–999.9	674	0.05	453	2.30	671.87
> 1,000	196	0.02	344	1.75	1,752.60
Total	1,295,001	100.00	19,650	100.00	15.17

* Provinces included: Chahar, Suiyuan, Shensi, Shansi, Hopei, Shantung, Honan, Kiangsu, Anhwei, Chekiang, Hupei, Hunan, Kiangsi, Fukien, Kwangtung, Kwangsi.

Source: National Land Commission, Ch'üan-kuo t'u-ti tiao-ch'a pao-kao kang-yao (Preliminary report of the national land survey), 33.

while the 5 per cent of families owning 50 *mou* or more held 34 per cent of the total land.

Few of the large holdings were farmed as such by their owners; commercial farming with hired labour was a rarity. In general the land was leased to tenants, or part was farmed by the landlord (using the labour of his family and/or hired labour depending on the size of his holding and his social status) with the balance being leased. In the twentieth century, with the breakdown of civil order in many parts of the interior, there was an increase of absentee landlords who abandoned the rural town for the protection of city walls. They ordinarily retained only a financial interest in their property, and entrusted the supervision of tenants and rent collection to local agents (*tsu-chan* or 'landlord bursaries' in the Yangtze valley, for example) who often stood to profit the more they were able to 'squeeze' their charges.[66] Particularly in the southern and eastern coastal provinces, this introduced an increasing harshness into rural class relations – never the subject for a pastoral idyll even under the best Confucian landlord, but possibly a little more personal and humane than under the inexorable pressure of the market.

Perkins suggests that in the 1930s three-quarters of rented-out land was owned by absentee landlords, most of whom attained their initial wealth from sources other than farming. Land, in other words, was an investment for rich merchants and others in those parts of China where rates of return were reasonable because well-established markets for grain were served by inexpensive water transport, namely in the more urbanized and commercialized Yangtze valley and in the south.[67] The data in table 16(5) show a rough correlation between rents as a percentage of land value and the incidence of tenancy in the several provinces. Kweichow is something of an anomaly in the south-west, as is Shantung in the north. In the former case, as perhaps in other relatively poor and backward areas, the basis for high rates of tenancy may have lain in the persistence of 'feudal' landlord-tenant relations (labour services, miscellaneous exactions, tighter controls) rather than in the strictly commercial return on the land.[68] High returns to land ownership in Shantung where the overall tenancy rate was low may result from the figure chosen by the National Agricultural

---

66 See Muramatsu Yūji, *Kindai Kōnan no sosan – Chūgoku jinushi seido no kenkyū* (Bursaries in modern Kiangnan – a study of the Chinese landlord system), 47–237, 391–636; and 'A documentary study of Chinese landlordism in late Ch'ing and early republican Kiangnan', *Bulletin of the School of Oriental and African Studies*, 29.3 (1966) 566–99.

67 Perkins, *Agricultural development in China*, 92–8.

68 Ch'en Cheng-mo, *Chung-kuo ko-sheng ti ti-tsu* (Land rents in China by province), 43, found the incidence of labour rents to be highest in Honan, Szechwan, Kweichow and Yunnan based on reports from 1,520 localities in 22 provinces excluding Manchuria.

Research Bureau's investigators for the 'average' value of a *mou* of land in Shantung.[69]

Estimates of the extent of tenancy in republican China vary considerably, and of course local differences were enormous, but overall about 50 per cent of the peasantry were involved in the landlord-tenant relationship – about 30 per cent as tenants who rented all of the land that they farmed, and 20 per cent more as owner-tenants who rented part of their land. Table 16(1) presents two estimates of the rates of tenancy by province in the 1930s, which, although they differ in detail, clearly indicate the much greater incidence of pure tenancy in the rice-growing provinces of the Yangtze valley and the southern coast than in the wheat-growing north.[70] These provincial data often obscure very considerable local variations within any province resulting from location, land quality, degree of commercialization and historical accretions.[71] It should also be noted that the categories owner, owner-tenant and tenant do not necessarily represent a descending order of economic well-being. The somewhat more complex categorization of the National Land Commission's 1934-5 survey shown in table 17, for example, is a warning that the rubric 'owner-tenant' in table 16(1) subsumes every case from a landlord who rents 1 per cent of his land to a poor peasant who rents 95 per cent. And the farmers of Shansi, Shantung, Hopei and Honan with less population pressure and larger farms, who were predominantly owner-cultivators, were not better off with respect to family income than their tenant brethren in Kwangtung. Nor is tenancy incompatible with economic progress: note that in the United States the percentage of farm operators who were tenants increased from 25.6 per cent in 1879 to 34.5 per cent in 1945.

Reliable historical data on the changing incidence of tenancy are nearly non-existent. A comparison of the estimates compiled by local observers, missionaries and others in the 1880s with those for the 1930s suggests considerable variation by locality but no significant change in the overall tenancy rate.[72] National Agricultural Bureau estimates show only a slight

69 National government, Directorate of Statistics, *Chung-hua min-kuo t'ung-chi t'i-yao, 1935* (Statistical abstract of the Republic of China, 1935), 462–3, shows land values in Shantung in 1933 as roughly the same as those in Chekiang; the NARB 1934 Shantung value, however, is one-third lower than Chekiang.

70 In table 16(1) I have used Buck's alternative estimate derived from his 'agricultural survey' rather than his 'farm survey' percentages which are usually cited. The latter are obviously too low both because his sample gives inadequate weight to the southern provinces, and because the nature of the survey dictated that relatively accessible localities dominated the data.

71 For regional variations in Kiangsu, see Ash, *Land tenure in pre-revolutionary China*, 11–22; for Shantung and Hopei, Myers, *The Chinese economy*, 234–40.

72 George Jamieson, 'Tenure of land in China and the condition of the rural population', *Journal of the North China Branch of the Royal Asiatic Society*, 23 (1889) 59–117.

TABLE 16

Tenancy, rented land, farm size, rent systems, and rental rates in the 1930s (22 provinces, excluding Manchuria)

	(1) Per cent farming families (*hu*) who are owners, owner-tenants, tenants						
	NARB, 1931–6 average				Buck, 1929–33		
Province	No. hsien reporting 1936	Owner	Owner-tenant	Tenant	No. localities surveyed	Owner	Owner-tenant	Tenant
NW								
Chahar	(10)	39	26	35	—	—	—	—
Suiyuan	(13)	56	18	26	—	—	—	—
Ninghsia	(5)	62	11	27	(1)	96	1	3
Tsinghai	(8)	55	24	21	(2)	20	8	72
Kansu	(29)	59	19	22	(6)	58	16	26
Shensi	(49)	55	22	23	(20)	68	15	17
N								
Shansi	(90)	62	21	17	(4)	38	38	24
Hopei	(126)	68	20	12	(6)	71	17	12
Shantung	(100)	71	17	12	(15)	72	18	10
Honan	(89)	56	22	22	(8)	58	23	19
E								
Kiangsu	(56)	41	26	33	(6)	31	23	46
Anhwei	(41)	34	22	44	(2)	35	13	52
Chekiang	(62)	21	32	47	(14)	29	20	51
C								
Hupei	(48)	31	29	40	(5)	35	31	34
Hunan	(41)	25	27	48	(13)	16	27	57
Kiangsi	(57)	28	31	41	(7)	33	35	32
SE								
Fukien	(42)	26	32	42	(1)	30	55	15
Kwangtung	(55)	21	27	52	(13)	16	35	49
Kwangsi	(50)	33	27	40	—	—	—	—
SW								
Kweichow	(23)	32	25	43	(6)	25	22	53
Yunnan	(39)	34	28	38	(8)	49	27	24
Szechwan	(87)	24	20	56	(3)	27	15	58
National average (excluding Manchuria)	(1,120)	46	24	30	(140)	44	23	33

TABLE 16 *(cont.)*

| Province | (2) Rented land as per cent farm area | | (3) Percentage distribution of size of farms operated, 1934-5 | | | | |
	National Land Commission	Buck	*(mou)* <10	10-29.9	30-49.9	50-99.9	>100
NW							
Chahar	10.2	—	1.4	7.9	2.2	8.9	79.6
Suiyuan	8.7	5.0	9.3	33.3	16.2	18.4	22.8
Ninghsia	—	0.5	—	—	—	—	—
Tsinghai	—	9.5	—	—	—	—	—
Kansu	—	9.1	—	—	—	—	—
Shensi	16.6	17.4	38.7	35.9	12.8	10.1	2.5
N							
Shansi	—	15.8	16.9	41.0	20.3	16.1	5.7
Hopei	12.9	9.8	40.0	41.4	10.8	6.1	1.7
Shantung	12.6	9.8	49.7	38.5	7.9	3.3	0.6
Honan	27.3	19.7	47.9	34.6	9.5	6.2	1.8
E							
Kiangsu	42.3	33.3	52.3	38.1	5.8	2.5	1.3
Anhwei	52.6	51.0	47.0	38.2	9.6	4.5	0.7
Chekiang	51.3	31.0	67.0	27.8	3.5	1.4	0.3
C							
Hupei	27.9	31.2	60.4	32.0	5.5	1.8	0.2
Hunan	47.8	36.6	56.5	33.4	6.3	3.1	0.8
Kiangsi	45.1	51.4	54.2	41.6	3.7	0.5	*
SE							
Fukien	39.3	55.7	71.8	24.8	2.5	0.8	0.1
Kwangtung	76.9	59.6	87.4	12.3	0.3	*	—
Kwangsi	21.2	26.0	51.1	37.7	7.2	3.0	0.9
SW							
Kweichow	—	25.8	—	—	—	—	—
Yunnan	—	27.6	—	—	—	—	—
Szechwan	—	52.4	—	—	—	—	—
National average (excluding Manchuria)	30.7	28.7	47.0	32.4	7.8	5.4	7.4

TABLE 16 (cont.)

Province	(4) Percentage distribution of types of rent, 1934			(5) Rents as per cent of land values, 1934			Fixed kind and share rents as per cent of value of crop, 1934
	Cash	Fixed kind (crop)	Share	Cash	Fixed kind (crop)	Share	
NW							
Chahar	19	51	30	2.9	4.4	6.9	37.5
Suiyuan	31	23	46	6.4	14.4	12.0	—
Ninghsia	46	19	35	—	—	—	⎫
Tsinghai	11	54	35	—	—	—	⎬ 30.9
Kansu	14	51	35	11.4	12.0	13.7	⎭
Shensi	15	9	26	10.1	13.0	12.6	41.1
N							
Shansi	27	45	27	6.2	5.9	6.2	50.1
Hopei	52	22	26	7.3	7.6	8.1	49.1
Shantung	30	31	39	16.0	18.8	20.8	46.5
Honan	17	39	44	—	—	—	49.5
E							
Kiangsu	28	53	19	8.7	7.8	12.8	40.3
Anhwei	14	53	33	9.4	9.4	16.4	40.4
Chekiang	27	66	7	9.6	10.3	13.2	42.4
C							
Hupei	20	58	22	8.3	6.8	13.6	38.6
Hunan	8	74	18	17.4	17.4	28.5	44.2
Kiangsi	7	80	13	19.2	18.1	36.8	42.6
SE							
Fukien	19	56	25	17.8	19.9	21.0	44.7
Kwangtung	24	58	18	17.0	19.0	15.4	42.5
Kwangsi	6	65	29	—	—	—	43.1
SW							
Kweichow	10	40	50	6.2	13.4	12.1	51.4
Yunnan	14	61	25	13.9	16.6	16.8	43.4
Szechwan	26	58	16	11.4	14.5	16.9	49.1
National average (excluding Manchuria)	21	51	28	11.0	12.9	14.1	43.3

* less than 0.05%

Sources: (1) *Nung-ch'ing pao-kao*, 5.12 (Dec. 1937) 330, in Li Wen-chih and Chang Yu-i, comps. *Chung-kuo chin-tai nung-yeh shih tzu-liao*, III. 728–30. Buck, *Land utilization in China, Statistics*, 57–9.
(2) Buck, *Land utilization in China, Statistics*, 55–6. National Land Commission, *Ch'üan-kuo t'u-ti tiao-ch'a pao-kao kang-yao*, 37.
(3) *Ch'üan-kuo t'u-ti tiao-ch'a pao-kao kang-yao*, 26–7.
(4) *Nung-ch'ing pao-kao*, 3.4 (April 1935) 90, in National Government, Directorate of Statistics, *Chung-kuo tsu-tien chih-tu chih t'ung-chi fen-hsi* (Statistical analysis of China's land rent system), 43.
(5) *Nung-ch'ing pao-kao*, 3.6 (June 1935), in *Chung-kuo tsu-tieh chih-tu chih t'ung-chi fen-h si*, 79. Ch'en Cheng-mo, *Chung-kuo ko-sheng ti ti-tsu* (Land rents in China by province) 94–5.

TABLE 17

Percentage of farm families in various ownership categories
(1,745,344 families in 16 provinces, 1934–5)

Landlord	2.05
Landlord-owner	3.15
Landlord-owner-tenant	0.47
Landlord-tenant	0.11
Owner	47.61
Owner-tenant	20.81
Tenant	15.78
Tenant-labourer	0.02
Labourer	1.57
Other	8.43

Source: *Ch'üan-kuo t'u-ti tiao-ch'a pao-kao kang-yao*, 35.

change (farmers who rented all of their land increased from 28 per cent in 1912 to 30 per cent of farm families in 1931–6), which is probably not significant since the 1931–6 data were obtained from regular mail questionnaires completed by thousands of volunteer crop reporters, many of whom were rural school teachers, while those for 1912 are only conjecture.[73] Ramon Myers' comparison of 22 counties in Shantung in the 1890s and 1930s discloses that the percentage of tenant households fell in 13 and rose in nine counties.[74] Comparative data from Honan, Anhwei, Kiangsi and Hupei for 1913, 1923 and 1934 show no significant changes: tenants increased from 39 to 41 per cent and owner-tenants from 27 to 28 per cent, while owner-cultivators declined from 34 to 31 per cent.[75]

The relatively slow rise of land values as compared with other prices shown in table 14 (page 68–69) may imply that the demand for land was comparatively weak in the relatively unsettled circumstances of the 1920s when, as Buck observed, 'agitation against landlords ... reduced the demand for land and even encouraged owners to sell their property.'[76] Finally, as indicated above, the amount of cultivated land distributed during land reform in the first years of the People's Republic was – even after a dozen very bad years of war and civil war – approximately the same as that controlled by landlords in the mid 1930s. One may perhaps conclude that while land was regularly bought and sold, the basic pattern of high tenancy in some areas and low tenancy in others – based primarily on the differential economic return to landlords, but also in the most

---

73 *Nung-ch'ing pao-kao*, 5.12 (December 1937) 330, in Li Wen-chih and Chang Yu-i, comps. *Agricultural history*, 3. 728–30.
74 Myers, *The Chinese peasant economy*, 223.
75 Amano Motonosuke, *Agricultural economy*, 1. 299.
76 Buck, *Land utilization in China*, 333.

backward areas on the persistence of 'extra-economic' labour service and other exactions – was not significantly altered in the republican era.

Was the tenant's position secure? Overall, it may have become slightly less so in the course of the twentieth century. A rough comparison of 93 counties in eight provinces between 1924 and 1934 shows a small increase in the percentage of annual rentals, no change in three- to 10-year contracts, and slight decreases in 10- to 20-year and permanent rentals.[77] That the 1930 Land Law, for example, contained a provision to the effect that the tenant had the right to extend his lease indefinitely unless the landlord took the land back at the expiration of the contract and farmed it himself, indicates recognition of the problem of insecure peasant holdings. No effort was made to enforce the law; hence insecurity of tenure undoubtedly continued to be a problem. As part of the process of modernization of property concepts in rural China the system of 'permanent terancy' (*yung-t'ien*) which had sharply differentiated the tenant's ownership of a 'surface right' from the landlord's 'bottom right', was gradually disappearing. Permanent tenure was replaced by less permanent contracts. The insecurity of the annual contract put the peasant at a considerable disadvantage and allowed the landlord to impose additional burdens in the form of land deposits (as security against non-payment of rents) and higher rents.

But these trends were occurring only very slowly. Of greater immediate significance for the productivity of China's agriculture is the continuing positive correlation in the eight provinces referred to above between the incidence of longer rent contracts, including permanent tenure, and the percentage of tenancy. The National Land Commission's 1934–5 survey also found 'permanent tenancy' to be most prevalent in Kiangsu, Anhwei and Chekiang – three provinces with high tenancy rates.[78] While tenants would have had an even greater incentive to improve their land if they had owned it outright, the long-run economic interests of both tenant and landlord appear to have resulted in sufficiently long rental contracts in areas of high tenancy so that tenant incentives to increase productivity by investing in the land they farmed were not completely discouraged.

A 1932 survey of 849 counties by the Ministry of Interior found that the rent deposit system (*ya-tsu*) was prevalent in 220 counties (26 per cent) and present in 60 others.[79] Land rents were paid in three principal forms:

---

77 National government, Directorate of Statistics, *Chung-kuo tsu-tien chih-tu chih t'ung-chi fen-hsi* (Statistical analysis of China's land rent system), 59.
78 National Land Commission, *Ch'üan-kuo t'u-ti tiao-ch'a pao-kao kang-yao* (Preliminary report of the national land survey), 46.
79 Ministry of the Interior, *Nei-cheng nien-chien* (Yearbook of the Interior Ministry), 3. *t'u-ti*, ch. 12, (D) 993–4. Ch'en Cheng-mo found *ya-tsu* widespread in 30% of reporting localities in 1933–4, and present in 6% more. Ch'en Cheng-mo, *Chung-kuo ko-sheng ti ti-tsu*, 61.

cash, crop and share rent. The National Agricultural Research Bureau's 1934 survey reported that 50.7 per cent of tenants paid a fixed amount of their principal crops, 28.1 per cent were share-croppers, and 21.2 per cent paid a fixed cash rent; see table 16 (4) (page 83). Comparable data in the 1934–5 land survey were: crop rent, 60.01 per cent; cash rent, 24.62 per cent; share rent, 14.99 per cent; labour rent, 0.24 per cent; and others, 0.14 per cent.[80] The incidence of cash rent was perhaps increasing very slowly in the twentieth century.[81]

In general, as shown in table 16 (5), the burden of share rent (which depended upon the extent to which the landlord provided seeds, tools and draught animals, and which on average equalled 14.1 per cent of land value) was slightly greater than crop rent (12.9 per cent), and crop rent greater than cash rent (11.0 per cent). Rents in kind, fixed and share, averaged 43.3 per cent of the value of the crop when the tenant supplied seeds, fertilizer and draught animals. The failure of the Kuomintang policy of limiting rents to 37.5 per cent of the main crops is evident.

In whatever form they were paid, rents were considerably higher, in absolute terms and in relation to the value of the land, in South China than they were in the north – but so too was the output per *mou* of land. A fixed rent in kind was the dominant system except for North China and Kweichow in the south-west, accounting for 62 per cent of rental arrangements in the five provinces with the highest incidence of tenancy (Anhwei, Chekiang, Hunan, Kwangtung and Szechwan) but only 39 per cent in the five provinces with the lowest tenancy rates (Shensi, Shansi, Hopei, Shantung and Honan). Under this arrangement, a tenant paid his landlord a fixed amount of grain whether he had a good harvest or bad (with possibly a reduction or postponement in catastrophically bad years). When combined with longer-term contracts, which were also more common in the high tenancy rice-growing provinces, a fixed rent in kind permitted the tenant to benefit from improvements in productivity resulting from his labour and investment, and thus provided a greater incentive for increased output than did share-cropping. Share rents were more common (32 per cent) in the five low tenancy North China provinces, where security of tenure was also less, than they were in the five high tenancy provinces (18 per cent). Contract terms were thus less encouraging to peasant investment in land improvements in the north than in the south, but tenancy was also less prevalent in the north.

80 National Land Commission, *Ch'üan-kuo t'u-ti tiao-ch'a pao-kao kang-yao*, 44.
81 National government, Directorate of Statistics, *Chung-kuo tsu-tien chih-tu shih t'ung-chi fen-hsi*, 43. The data, comparing 1924 and 1934, show such small changes that they may not be significant at all.

The province-level quantitative treatment offered above does not deal adequately with the fate of individual tenant families, or the rich variety of local practices, or the limits within which increased output could be furthered by these apparently rational aspects of the tenancy system. To what degree real peasant tenants in specific areas at specific times realized sufficient family income to make improvements which increased their total output can only be determined by detailed local studies such as those by Ramon Myers of Hopei and Shantung and by Robert Ash of Kiangsu; the former's finding is positive and the latter's negative.

The patterns of land tenure and cultivation described above were intimately connected with the structure of credit, marketing and taxation related to agriculture. Agriculture being an industry of slow turn-over, the small peasant in China, as in other countries, was often unable to survive the interval between sowing and harvesting without borrowing. Indebtedness was a major source of rural discontent. Buck reports that 39 per cent of the farms surveyed in 1929–33 were in debt. The National Agricultural Research Bureau estimated that, in 1933, 56 per cent of farms had borrowed cash and 48 per cent had borrowed grain for food. A third national estimate noted that 43.87 per cent of farm families were in debt in 1935.[82] All observers agree overwhelmingly that the rural debt had been incurred to meet household consumption needs rather than for investment in production, and that for the poorer peasants indebtedness was the rule.[83] Interest rates were high. This was a reflection of the desperate need of the peasant, the shortage of capital in rural China, the risk of default, and the absence of alternative modern lending facilities either government or cooperative. On small loans in kind, an annual rate of 100 to 200 per cent might be charged. The bulk of peasant loans, perhaps two-thirds, paid annual rates of 20 to 40 per cent; about one-tenth paid less than 20 per cent; and the rest, more than 40 per cent. About two-thirds of all loans were for periods of six months to one year.[84] Agricultural credit came largely from individuals – landlords, wealthier farmers, merchants – as the 1934 data in table 18 indicate.

There were few modern banks (government or private) in rural areas, and in any case such banks did not invest in consumption loans. The seven modern banks in Kiangsi, to give an example, had only 0.078 per

82 Buck, *Land utilization in China*, 462; *Nung-ch'ing pao-kao*, 2.4 (April 1934) 30, in *CKCTC*, 342; National Land Commission, *Ch'üan-kuo t'u-ti tiao-ch'a pao-kao kang-yao*, 51.

83 Buck, *Land utilization in China*, 462: 76% of farm credit was for 'non-productive purposes'; Amano Motonosuke, *Agricultural economy*, 2. 219–20, citing seven national and local studies.

84 *Nung-ch'ing pao-kao*, 2.11 (November 1934) 108–109, in *The Chinese Economic and Statistical Review*, 1.11 (November 1934) 7.

TABLE 18

Sources of farm credit, 1934

Source of farm credit	% of total number of loans
Banks	2.4
Cooperatives	2.6
Pawnshops	8.8
Native banks	5.5
Village stores and shops	13.1
Landlords	24.2
Well-to-do-farmers	18.4
Merchants	25.0

Source: National Agricultural Research Bureau, *Crop reporting in China, 1934*, 70.

cent of their outstanding loan funds in 1932 invested in farm loans.[85] Considerable attention has been directed to the rural cooperative movement which began in the 1920s, but the cooperatives even at their peak never involved more than a tiny fraction of Chinese farmers.[86] The moneylender, who was often the landlord or the grain merchant, performed the function of transferring part of the surplus of agriculture back to the peasant, thus allowing him to live beyond his means, but at the ultimate cost of preserving intact a landlord dominated rural society.

The Chinese village was not economically self-sufficient, although a larger unit, Skinner's 'standard marketing area', for many purposes can be considered so. To meet cash obligations such as rent and taxes, and to purchase many necessities, some part of the farmer's crop had to be disposed of on the market. About 15 per cent of the rice crop and 29 per cent of the wheat crop were sold by the peasants covered in Buck's survey, while the proportion for cash crops such as tobacco, opium, peanuts, rapeseed, and cotton was, of course, considerably higher.[87] In many cases the peasant had no choice but to sell in the local market. He was separated from more distant markets not only by inadequate and thus costly transport, but perhaps also by an information barrier – although the burden of rural illiteracy has probably been exaggerated. The market was subject to considerable price fluctuations, which might be unfavourable to the peasant as a result of the fact that supply would naturally be larger at harvest time when he wanted to sell and smaller in the spring

85 *The Chinese Economic and Statistical Review*, 1.11 (November 1934) 2.
86 See Li Wen-chih and Chang Yu-i, comps. *Agricultural history*, 3. 206–14; Amano Motonosuke, *Agricultural economy*, 2. 308–48.
87 Buck, *Land utilization in China*, 233.

when he wanted to buy. Moreover, in those areas near the major cities in eastern and southern coastal China where the commercialization of agriculture had made some headway, exploitative collection systems (such as that operated by the British and American Tobacco Company) put the farmer at the mercy of the buyer.

While as a small individual buyer and seller the peasant was unable to influence the markets in which he had to trade, to imply in crude Marxist (and Confucian) terms that all merchants were parasites who contributed nothing to the economy or to suggest that increased commercialization of agriculture in the twentieth century had a negative effect on rural production and income is absurd. In the atomistic rural sector there were no barriers to entry (other than the often exaggerated information barrier), virtually no government intervention, and low capital requirements for all businesses, so that most types of commerce were quite competitive. High profits quickly lured new entrants into existing markets. The richest merchants, in China as elsewhere, were those who did business in the more commercialized areas where almost everyone was informed, mobile and experienced in dealing with markets. They made their profits not by fleecing their customers, but by specialization, division of labour, and offering critical services at low unit prices. The local market has frequently been described as tending to monopsony for what the peasant sold and to monopoly for what he bought, but in fact there have been few studies to document this common assumption. If more than two-thirds of marketed crops were sold locally (as Perkins suggests; see page 72 above), then this trade may have involved few merchants at all; periodic markets were places where farmers bought and sold from and to each other. And if Perkins is also right that most rice marketings were by landlords (see page 79 above), who did not have to sell at harvest time and who had the information and connections which made it difficult to fleece them, then there is little support for monopsony.

I have noted above that the terms of trade between agriculture and industry were generally favourable to the farmer before 1931. The ability to grow and market cash crops was a major factor supporting the modest increase in total agricultural output that occurred between 1912 and the 1930s and which kept per capita rural incomes roughly constant over this period. Indeed, the agricultural market was fragmented, sometimes appeared to be stacked against the small peasant producer, and perhaps was burdened with excessive middlemen, all of which prevented greater increases in output and clearly detracted from rural welfare. But it did function well enough before 1937 to help keep the traditional economic system afloat.

Under both the Peking government until 1927 and the Nanking government which followed, agricultural taxation was probably inequitable in incidence, but the matter has never been carefully studied. The land tax was largely a provincial or local levy. Collusion between the local elite and the tax collector was common, with the result that a disproportionate share of the burden fell upon the small owner-farmer. Land taxes were also shifted onto tenants in the form of higher rents. And such additional abuses as forced collections in advance, the manipulation of exchange rates, and multiple surcharges were reported.[88] In the last decade of Kuomintang rule, the tax burden on the small owner and the tenant was increased by wartime tax collection in kind and compulsory grain purchases by the Chungking government.

If the incidence were inequitable, the most important economic characteristic of the pre-1949 land tax was its failure to recover a major share of the agricultural surplus appropriated by the landlord for redistribution to productive investment. The level of taxation in fact was low, reflecting the superficial penetration of the state into local society (see page 99 below). As in the cases of credit and marketing, the system of agricultural taxation reinforced a pattern of income distribution which allowed only a very modest overall growth of output with no increase at all in individual income and welfare.

Quantitative treatment of China's agriculture between 1937 and 1949 is nearly impossible. War and civil war put an end to even the modest collection of rural statistical data of the Nanking government decade. The principal scene of fighting was North China, and it is certain that physical damage to agricultural land, transport disruptions, conscription of manpower and draught animals, requisitions of grain for the armies, and mounting political conflict affected farmers in the north much more severely than in South and West China.[89] The pre-war process of increasing commercialization was reversed, agricultural productivity and output declined, and commodity trade between rural and urban areas was disrupted. Even by 1950, according to rural surveys made in the first two years of the People's Republic, some areas in North China had not returned to their peak pre-war output levels due to manpower and draught animal losses.[90] Both the harsh Japanese occupation and the

88 See Li Wen-chih and Chang Yu-i, comps. *Agricultural history*, 2. 559–80; 3. 9–65. Amano Motonosuke, *Agricultural ecomomy*, 2. 1–158.
89 Myers, *The Chinese peasant economy*, 278–87, briefly describes the damage and dislocations suffered by the North China rural economy during 1937–48.
90 Central Ministry of Agriculture, Planning Office, *Liang-nien-lai ti Chung-kuo nung-ts'un ching-chi tiao-ch'a hui-pien* (Collection of surveys of the rural economy of China during the past two years), 141–4, 149–51, 160, 162, 226–36.

great battles of 1948–9 left the south and west relatively unscathed, but here too manpower and grain requisitions by the military took their toll, and runaway inflation from 1947 undermined the supply of foodstuffs and industrial crops to the urban areas. The collapse of both the rural and the urban economy of China was a fact by mid 1948.

TRANSPORT

Poorly developed transport continued to be a major shortcoming of the Chinese economy throughout the republican period. This is apparent at both the microscopic and macroscopic levels. In 1919 the cost of production of a ton of pig iron at the Hanyang Ironworks in Hupei, China's major producer, was Ch.$48.50 while in 1915 the Japanese ironworks at Pen-ch'i in Manchuria produced pig iron at Ch.$22.00 per ton. Coke produced locally at Pen-ch'i cost Ch.$5.74 a ton, but high transport charges attributable to slow progress in building the Canton-Hankow railway and to inefficient handling by native boats for the river trip from P'inghsiang in Kiangsi 300 miles away, forced up the cost of coke at Hanyang to Ch.$24.54 a ton.[91] Since both firms obtained their raw materials from their own 'captive' mines, it is unlikely that the difference was due to market fluctuations between the two dates.

The wages of coolie labour were incredibly low, but the economic efficiency of the human carriers who dominated transport at the local level was even lower. One observer reported:

On the road from the Wei Basin to the Chengtu Plain, in Szechuan Province, one may meet coolies carrying on their backs loads of cotton weighing 160 pounds. They will carry these loads fifteen miles a day for 750 miles at a rate of seventeen cents (Mexican) a day, which is the equivalent of fourteen cents a ton mile. At this rate it costs $106.25 to transport one ton 750 miles. The railways should be able to haul this for $15, or one seventh the amount. The Peking-Mukden Railway carries coal for the Kailan Mining Company at less than 1½ cents a ton mile. With the coolie carriers the cotton spends fifty days on the road, whereas the railway would make the haul in two days, thereby saving forty-eight days interest on the money and landing the cotton in better condition.[92]

Comparative costs of transport in China by the principal modes of conveyance have been estimated (in Ch. cents per ton-kilometre) as follows: junks, 2 to 12; steamers and launches, 2 to 15; railways, 3.2 to 17;

91 D. K. Lieu, *China's industries and finance*, 197–219; Ku Lang, *Chung-kuo shih ta-k'uang tiao-ch'a chi* (Report of an investigation of the 10 largest mines in China), 3.49.
92 American Bankers Association. Commission on Commerce and Marine, *China, an economic survey, 1923*, 16.

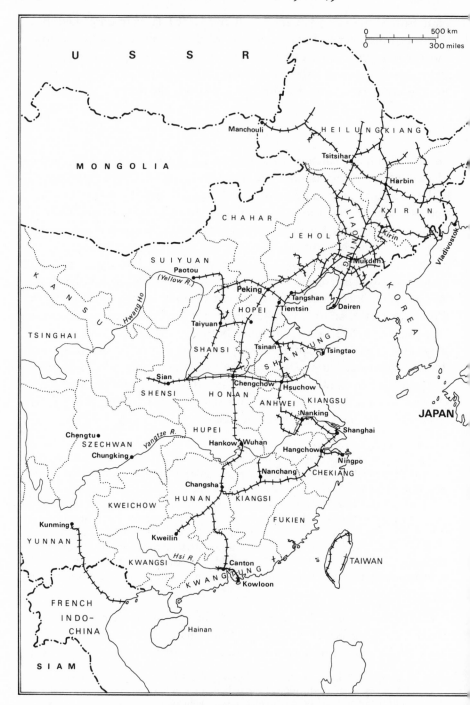

MAP 4.   Railways as of 1949

carts, 5 to 16.5; wheelbarrows, 10 to 14; camels, 10 to 20; motor trucks, 10 to 56; donkeys, mules and horses, 13.3 to 25; human porterage, 14 to 50; and rickshaw, 20 to 35.[93] Throughout the republican era, the bulk of goods continued to be carried by traditional modes of transport. The data for 1933, for example, which was not an atypical year, show that old-fashioned forms of transport contributed three times as much (Ch.$ 1.2 billion) to national income as did modern transport methods (Ch.$ 430 million).

An adequate railway network would have greatly reduced transport costs and facilitated the development of the interior. Among other things, goods carried by rail more often escaped likin (*li-chin*) and other local transit duties. And the presence of a railway tends to standardize weights, measures and currency along the line. But the example of British India should make it evident that a great railway network can coexist with a backward agricultural economy, that mere length does not lead automatically to economic development. In any case, the railways of republican China were inadequate in length, distribution and operation. At the end of the Second World War, China, including Manchuria and Taiwan, had a total of 24,945 kilometres of main and branch railway lines.[94] The amount built in each of the periods into which we may conventionally divide the republican era was as follows:

Before 1912	9,618.10 km
1912–27	3,422.38
1928–37	7,895.66
1938–45	3,909.38
Total	24,845.52 km

The first railway in China was an unauthorized 15-kilometre line running from Woosung to Shanghai built by Jardine, Matheson and Company and other foreigners. It was opened in 1876, but official and local antipathy was so violent that this line was purchased and scrapped by the Chinese government. Continued opposition from both the local population and conservative officials prevented any progress with railway construction until China's defeat by Japan in 1894-5. On the one hand, the 'self-strengtheners' were able to convince the imperial court of the necessity to build railways as a means of bolstering the dynasty against further foreign incursions. On the other hand, the exposure of China's weakness attracted foreign capital which saw the financing of railway construction as a means to promote foreign political influence and economic penetration. Only 364 kilometres of track had been laid by 1894.

93 National Economic Council. Bureau of Public Roads, *Highways in China*.
94 *CKCTC*, 172–80. Mileage estimates in other sources differ slightly.

In the first great wave of railway building, between 1895 and 1911, 9,253 kilometres of line were completed, for the most part with funds borrowed from foreign creditors. Of this total the Russian-built Chinese Eastern Railway across Manchuria and its southern extension from Harbin to Dairen accounted for 2,425 kilometres.

The failure of private railway projects undertaken by provincial gentry and merchants in the last decade of the Manchu dynasty inspired Peking's railway nationalization programme, an immediate cause of the overthrow of the dynasty. In the era of Yuan Shih-k'ai and the warlord regimes which followed until 1927, railway construction perceptibly slowed down. The several private lines were nationalized without the violent opposition which had been fatal to the Ch'ing dynasty, and for the most part in exchange for government bonds that were soon in default. While new loans were arranged with foreign lenders and some pre-1912 loans renegotiated, the First World War halted European investment in Chinese railways. When a new four-power consortium was assembled in 1920, the Peking government, contrary to American expectations, refused to transact business with it. Construction within China proper was limited to the completion of the Peking-Suiyuan line, and of sections of the Canton-Hankow and Lunghai railways, altogether totalling about 1,700 kilometres. An equal amount of new track was built in Manchuria, consisting on the one hand of Japanese financed feeder lines to the South Manchurian Railway and, on the other hand, of rival lines built by Chang Tso-lin in part with funds obtained from the revenue of the Peking-Mukden railway. Both the Chinese construction in North China and the new Manchurian lines were motivated as much by strategic as by economic considerations.

Between 1928 and 1937 approximately 3,400 kilometres of railway were constructed within China proper, including the completion of the Canton-Hankow line, the Chekiang-Kiangsi railway, and the T'ung-p'u line in Shansi. This was achieved without major foreign borrowing. The Chekiang-Kiangsi railway, for example, was financed mainly by loans from the Bank of China, and the Shansi railway out of provincial revenues. As in other areas, however, the demands of military spending and debt service left very few funds for the economic 'reconstruction' extensively discussed by the Nanking government. In the same period, some 4,500 kilometres were built in Manchuria, consisting mainly of new Japanese construction after 1931 as part of the planned development of Manchukuo into an industrial base. In spite of formidable obstacles during the Sino-Japanese war, the Chinese government claimed to have completed some 1,500 kilometres in unoccupied China which played an important part in supporting the economy and military effort. The Japanese, on their part, constructed a number of additional lines in Manchuria.

Of the railways built in these 50 years, approximately 40 per cent of the total track was located in Manchuria, 32 per cent in China proper north of the Yangtze River, 22 per cent in South China, and 4 per cent in Taiwan. The relatively small railway mileage in densely populated South China testifies to the persistence of an elaborate pre-modern (junk and sampan) and modern (steamboat and steam launch) network of water transport which continued to compete effectively with the steam train. In proportion to area and population, Manchuria was far better served than any other region in China, a circumstance underlying and reflecting Manchuria's more extensive industrialization. No railway had penetrated to the rich province of Szechwan or to such western areas as Kansu, Sinkiang and Tibet. In addition to the notoriously small total mileage in relation to the size of the country, the development of China's railways had been quite haphazard, and the distribution of lines was often uneconomic. For China proper a more desirable system might have been a radial network centring perhaps around Hankow. The actual system was a parallel network heavily concentrated in Northern and Eastern China. In Manchuria, a combined radial-parallel network had developed which was marred by the uneconomic duplication of lines resulting from Chinese-Japanese competition in the north-east in the 1920s.

The construction of the Chinese railway system had involved considerable borrowing from Great Britain, Belgium, Japan, Germany, France, the United States and the Netherlands, listed in the order of the total amount of railway loans extended by each country from 1898 to 1937. These loans (the terms of which often involved *de facto* foreign control of the lines constructed) were concentrated in the last years of the Ch'ing dynasty and first decade of the republic, and reflect the scramble for railway concessions and loan contracts by foreign syndicates whose rivalry and intrigues were as much political as financial. Repayment of the railway debt was to come from the operating revenue of the lines, but from about 1925 to 1935 most of the foreign railway loans were in default. On 31 December 1935 the total outstanding indebtedness, including principal and interest in arrears, amounted to approximately £53,827,443 or Ch.$891,920,730.[95] Railway bonds had fallen to as little as 11 per cent of their face value in the case of the Lunghai railway.

The earning power of the Chinese Government Railways was poten-

---

95 Chang Kia-ngau, *China's struggle for railroad development*, 170–1, table III.

tially just sufficient to pay the interest due to bondholders. Annual net operating revenue during 1916-39 averaged 7.4 per cent of the cost of track and equipment while interest rates on railway loans ranged from 5 to 8 per cent. That is, while their operation was apparently less efficient than that of the South Manchurian Railway, the government railways were economically viable enterprises which both contributed to such economic growth as the republican years saw and generally produced a small profit. On the average, however, only 35 per cent of the net operating revenue in these two decades was allocated to interest payments. Large portions of the net operating revenue – more than 50 per cent for example in the years 1926, 1927, and 1930-4 – were remitted to the Chinese government which utilized these funds for its general expenditures.[96] Remittances to the government during 1921-36 were double the amount appropriated for additions to railway equipment.

A principal cause of the low profitability of the Chinese Government Railways was the prolonged civil strife throughout the republic. Rival warlords not only commandeered railway lines for the movement of troops but at times diverted passenger and freight revenues to the maintenance of their armies. Of the passenger traffic (in passenger miles) carried on the Peking-Hankow railway between 1912 and 1925, for example, 21 per cent was military traffic; on the Peking-Mukden line between 1920 and 1931, 17 per cent of the passenger traffic was military.[97] Apart from direct war damage, which was perhaps minimal, repairs to the track and rolling stock were neglected. For more than two decades the Ministry of Railways could rely regularly only on the income of a few smaller lines: and the system as a whole became increasingly obsolescent and inefficient.

During the period 1912 to 1947, both passenger and freight traffic increased annually on the Chinese Government Railways until the mid 1920s (see table 19). The Northern Expedition and civil wars attendant upon the establishment of the Nanking regime affected both adversely, but in the relative calm of the 1930s railway traffic revived and exceeded previous levels. Japanese seizure of the bulk of China's railways as the Nationalist government was forced into the interior between 1937 and 1945 is reflected in the figures for that period.

About 40 per cent of the operating revenues of the Chinese Government Railways was realized from passenger service, of which a considerable part was troop movements. Minerals made up more than half of the

---

96 Hou, *Foreign investment and economic development in China*, 32, 39-42.
97 *CKCTC*, 210.

TABLE 15

Index numbers of passenger miles and freight ton miles carried on the Chinese Government Railways, 1912–47

Year	(1912 = 100)		(1917 = 100)					
	Passenger miles	Freight ton miles	Total freight ton miles	Manufactures	Mineral products	Agricultural products	Forest products	Animal products
1912	100.0	100.0						
1915	61.1	92.5						
1916	127.2	107.7						
1917	131.1	113.8	94.7	94.8	93.8	91.3	81.0	126.9
1918	143.0	140.8	100.0	100.0	100.0	100.0	100.0	100.0
1919	155.2	138.8	123.8	124.6	127.6	123.5	120.9	97.8
1920	194.8	186.7	139.6	132.6	159.0	114.3	147.3	104.1
1921	194.8	193.6	164.1	138.2	165.0	186.2	171.6	102.3
1922	204.6	165.7	170.2	138.9	175.7	168.8	198.2	92.1
1923	210.3	211.2	143.9	155.7	151.4	127.8	188.8	127.7
1924	220.7	187.9	185.7	183.3	240.8	135.6	264.8	144.1
1925	231.7	169.0	165.2	157.5	199.4	102.7	226.1	121.5
1926	159.9	99.6	148.6	152.5	132.6	97.0	220.6	105.9
1927	164.1	109.4						
1928	144.8	96.0						
1929	196.1	102.7	161.1	217.0	165.3	101.2	151.6	113.9
1931	267.4	183.3	161.1	197.3	189.2	89.2	110.6	82.9
1932	212.6	183.2	172.4	200.9	192.4	94.6	146.3	89.3
1933	248.3	196.1	226.5	237.9	273.4	149.4	169.7	110.4
1934–5	210.0	257.7	234.5	268.3	282.6	132.9	152.0	122.3
1935–6	267.9	266.8	83.4	79.0	111.9	37.5	34.1	37.4
1936–7	128.5	94.9	45.2	22.0	22.9	27.1	44.3	18.2
1937–8	56.3	51.4	21.9	10.7	11.1	13.1	21.5	8.8
1938–9	69.7	24.9	18.0	9.9	8.8	10.7	9.7	7.3
1939–40	88.6	20.5	18.7	10.2	10.6	8.4	16.0	8.8
1940–1	95.7	21.3	16.8	8.7	10.0	6.1	14.2	4.9
1941–2	90.7	19.1	19.7	7.8	12.0	5.8	15.3	4.6
1942–3	129.9	22.4	8.3	3.1	5.7	1.8	10.5	1.6
1943–4	62.1	9.4	13.2	8.0	10.4	4.1	32.1	10.8
1944–5	112.1	15.1	135.8	83.2	80.0	54.3	249.1	89.5
1945–6	765.1	154.4						
1946–7	524.7	112.5						

Source: Yen Chung-p'ing, Chung-kuo chin-tai ching-chi shih t'ung-chi tzu-liao hsuan-chi, 207–8, 217.

freight carried; second in importance were agricultural products. The general pattern of freight traffic was one in which agricultural products and minerals were carried from inland points to the coastal treaty ports, while manufactured goods flowed into the interior. Increased transport of agricultural products in the first decade of the republic reflects the growth of cash crop output suggested in my discussion of agricultural trends above. The railways in Manchuria in particular but also in North China facilitated the slow expansion of agricultural production shown in tables 12 (page 64) and 13 (page 66). Similarly both the adverse effects of the depression on cash crop output and the recovery just prior to the outbreak of war in 1937 are evident in table 19.

Little need be said about road mileage apart from indicating that no improved roads suitable for motor vehicles existed in 1912; before July 1937, about 116,000 kilometres had been completed, of which 40,000 kilometres were surfaced.[98] Most of this construction occurred after 1928, in which year there were perhaps 32,000 kilometres, and was undertaken for military as much as for commercial reasons by the Bureau of Public Roads of the National Economic Council. The Seven Provinces Project, for example, in which Honan, Hupei, Anhwei, Kiangsi, Kiangsu, Chekiang and Hunan cooperated, was conceived of as a means of tying together by a system of roads those provinces in which the Kuomintang government had its greatest strength. Sparse and primitive though they were, roads in 1937 tended to be better distributed within China proper than was the railway network.

The war led to additional road construction in the interior provinces including, of course, the famous Yunnan-Burma highway. But in 1949 as in 1912, inland China continued to depend much more on traditional means of transport, by water and land, for local and regional carriage than it did on motor vehicles or trains. By September 1941, for example, in the three provinces of Kiangsu, Chekiang and Anhwei, 118,292 native boats (*min-ch'uan*), totalling 850,705 tons and with crews totalling 459,178, had registered with the boatmen's associations established by the Wang Ching-wei government.[99] This was the principal means of short- and medium-distance bulk carriage in the lower Yangtze valley and elsewhere in South and Central China where a combination of rivers, lakes and centuries' accumulation of man-made canals had produced a complex and extensive network of water transport. Inter-port trade, in contrast to local carriage, even by the 1890s was already primarily carried by steamships, mainly foreign-owned. But the tonnage of Chinese junks entered and

98 Chinese Ministry of Information, *China handbook, 1937–1945*, 217.
99 Mantetsu Chōsabu, *Chū-shi no minsengyō* (The junk trade of central China), 134–5.

cleared by the Maritime Customs at the several treaty ports remained more or less constant from 1912 to 1922, and began to drop sharply only in the 1920s.[100] On China's major rivers steam shipping increased steadily in the first decades of the twentieth century as evidenced by the growth of registered tonnage of vessels under 1,000 tons from 42,577 in 1913 to 246,988 in 1933. But the river junk held its own in many places for a considerable period. Up-river from Ichang on the Yangtze, for example, junk tonnage increased slightly from the 1890s to 1917 before plunging downward in the 1920s. Between Nanning and Wuchow on the West River, junk traffic similarly gave way to steam ships only in the 1920s.[101]

In the transport sector as in others, the commonplace fact that China's economy changed only a little in the first half of the twentieth century has tended to be obscured, pushed out of sight by the disproportionate attention devoted to the small modern sector of the economy in official word and deed, in the writings of China's economists, in the yearbooks and reports intended for foreign consumption, and in the research which non-Chinese scholars have conducted on China's pre-1949 economy – apart from the Japanese, who in this matter, at least, had a more 'realistic' view of China. For the Nanking government, which had abandoned the land and drew its revenues overwhelmingly from the modern sector, this amounted to building paper castles.

GOVERNMENT AND THE ECONOMY

Both the Peking warlords and the Nanking regime which followed financed their governments primarily from the urban sector of the economy. Central government in republican China neither collected substantial revenue from the rural sector nor had very much influence over its collection and disbursal by semi-autonomous provincial and local interests. In other words, no national government before 1949 was able to channel a significant share of total national income through the central government treasury. And, as a result, government policies, while not without far-reaching consequences for the economy, were never realistically capable of pushing the Chinese economy forward on the path of modern economic growth.

During the years 1931–6, for example, total national expenditures of the central government varied between a low of 2.1 per cent and a high of 4.9 per cent of the gross national product, and averaged 3.5 per cent.

100 Yang Tuan-liu, *et al. Liu-shih-wu-nien-lai Chung-kuo kuo-chi mao-i t'ung-chi* (Statistics of China's foreign trade during the last 65 years), 140.
101 *CKCTC*, 228–9, 235–6.

(If the expenditures of all levels of local government were included, the percentage would perhaps be doubled.) Tax revenues were considerably less than this and reflected, on the one hand, the failure of the national government to mobilize the resources of the rural sector and, on the other, its inability or unwillingness to levy income taxes on society in general. Even this limited government revenue, moreover, was largely dissipated in maintaining a hypertrophic military establishment and financing continued civil war, or hypothecated to service the foreign and domestic debt. Neither the Peking nor the Nanking regime was able to finance any significant developmental investment out of its revenues, and the policies of neither were conducive to capital formation in the private sector of the economy.

Following the Revolution of 1911, the new republican government at first struggled along with the Ch'ing fiscal system. While nomenclature and bureaucratic structure were soon changed, the republican government was even less able to control the revenue sources of China than its predecessor had been. In 1913 an effort was made to demarcate the sources of central, provincial and local revenue, but the central government even under Yuan Shih-k'ai was too weak to enforce these regulations. After 1914, except for the maritime customs and the salt gabelle, the major taxes were administered by the provinces. Technically, the land tax (and several consumption taxes) still belonged to the central government, but in fact it was under provincial control and the proceeds were spent in and by the provinces albeit under the accounting rubric 'national expenditures of X province'. Yuan Shih-k'ai, until his death in 1916, was able to extract some land tax remittances from the provinces, and these continued fitfully and minimally until 1921 when the political situation dramatically worsened and civil warfare became so widespread that Peking's financial control all but evaporated.[102]

Maritime customs revenue was almost entirely committed to the service of foreign loans and indemnities. From 1912 through 1927 only 142,341,000 haikuan taels, or 20 per cent out of a total revenue net of first charges of 717,672,000 haikuan taels, was available to the Peking government for administrative and other expenditures.[103] In spite of the revision of specific duties in 1902 and 1918, due to rising prices the actual rate of duty collected on imports varied between 2.5 and 3.5 per cent until 1923, when a further revision brought the effective duty to 5 per cent. But no major increase of revenue under this heading was possible until China regained tariff autonomy in 1930.

102 Chia Shih-i, *Min-kuo ts'ai-cheng shih* (Fiscal history of the republic), 1. 45-77.
103 Stanley F. Wright, *China's customs revenue since the Revolution of 1911* (3rd edn, 1935), 440-1.

From 1913 through 1922, gross revenue from the salt gabelle exceeded gross maritime customs revenue. After 1922, however, only a part of the income from salt was available to the central government. In order to furnish security for the Reorganization Loan of 1913, without which the government of Yuan Shih-k'ai might not have survived, a foreign chief inspector was appointed to supervise and in effect control the Salt Administration. While national pride might be hurt, this measure resulted in an immediate jump in the revenues collected on the account of the central government. Actual payments on foreign loans secured on the salt revenues were small – from 1917 the Reorganization Loan, for example, was paid from the customs revenue. But this relatively happy situation was swept away by the continuous civil warfare. Provincial interference in the salt tax collection grew to serious proportions, salt funds were misappropriated, and smuggling increased. Total revenue fell markedly after 1922, as did the proportion of the collection that was actually remitted to Peking. Net collections, which had hit a peak of Ch.$86 million in 1922, fell to Ch.$71 million in 1924, Ch.$64 million in 1926, and down to Ch.$58 million in 1927. Even in 1922 only Ch.$47 million (or 55 per cent of the net collection) was actually remitted to Peking; Ch.$12 million was retained by the provinces with the central government's consent; but Ch.$20 million (23 per cent) was appropriated locally without consent. The total amount retained by provincial authorities and military commanders climbed to Ch.$37 million in 1926 while the amount actually remitted to Peking in that year was barely Ch.$9 million.[104]

Faced with a chronic state of financial embarrassment, the Peking government was forced to depend heavily on domestic and foreign borrowing. Between 1912 and 1926, 27 domestic bond issues were floated by the Ministry of Finance with a combined face value of Ch.$ 614,000,000.[105] Actual receipts to the government, however, were considerably smaller, for the bonds were always sold at a discount – in an extreme case as low as 20 per cent of the face value. Much is obscure about the details of domestic loan flotations in this period, and on into the period of the Nanking government as well. There seems to have been a close relationship between the establishment of new banks with the right of note issue and government domestic borrowing. A large part of these domestic bonds was taken up by the Chinese 'modern' banks who held government securities as investment and as reserves against note issue, while also making direct advances to the government.

104 P. T. Chen, 'Public finance', *The Chinese year book, 1935–1936*, 1298–9.
105 Ch'ien Chia-chü, *Chiu Chung-kuo kung-chai shih tzu-liao, 1894–1949* (Source materials on government bond issues in old China, 1894–1949), 366–9.

The Peking government transmitted a domestic indebtedness of only Ch.$241,000,000 to its successor, which would seem to indicate that its creditors, in spite of defaults, did not fare too badly with the discounted Peking government bonds. And Peking's domestic borrowing permitted warlord coffers to be replenished time and again. But the proceeds of these loans brought little benefit to the economy of the country. Debt service on domestic and foreign loans was the largest single expenditure of the Peking government; together with military expenditure it made up at least four-fifths of the total annual outlay.[106] After general administrative costs were met, there was nothing left for developmental investment. Provincial and local revenues, too, were drained by military and police outlays.[107] Nor were the foreign loans of the Peking regime usually undertaken with a view to furthering economic development.

New foreign loan obligations incurred in the period 1912–26 were smaller in amount than the indemnity and railway obligations of the last years of the Manchu dynasty. Total foreign holdings of Chinese government obligations (excluding the Boxer indemnity) increased from approximately U.S.$526,000,000 in 1913 to U.S.$696,000,000 in 1931.[108] The 1913 Reorganization Loan of £25,000,000 was the largest single new foreign debt. A further significant part of this foreign borrowing was represented by the so-called 'Nishihara loans' of 1918 – unsecured advances by Japanese interests to the Anfu warlord clique then in power in Peking, and to several provincial governments, the proceeds of which were used largely for civil war and political intrigue. Some of these advances were subsequently converted into legitimate railway or telegraph loans, but the largest part, perhaps Ch.$150,000,000, was never recognized by the Nanking government. Like the Japanese indemnity loans of the 1890s, Yuan Shih-k'ai's Reorganization Loan, and the domestic debt, this desperate borrowing by the Peking warlords, except for the several railway loans, contributed nothing to the development of the Chinese economy. In fact, there is reason to believe that China annually made greater out-payments on account of government debt (including the Boxer indemnity) than she received in new loans. C. F. Remer, for example, estimates that annual out-payments averaged Ch.$89.2 million during 1902–13, and Ch.$70.9 million during 1913–30, while average

106 Chia Te-huai, *Min-kuo ts'ai-cheng chien shih* (A short fiscal history of the republic), 697–8; Kashiwai Kisao, *Kindai Shina zaisei shi* (History of modern Chinese finance), 63–4.
107 C. M. Chang, 'Local government expenditure in China', *Monthly Bulletin of Economic China*, 7.6 (June 1934) 233–47.
108 C. F. Remer, *Foreign investments in China*, 123–47; Hsu I-sheng, *Chung-kuo chin-tai wai-chai shih t'ung-chi tzu-liao, 1853–1927* (Statistical materials on foreign loans in modern China, 1853–1927), 240–5.

in-payments in the two periods were Ch.$61.0 million and Ch.$23.8 million respectively. So large a 'drain' of capital must be counted as a net withdrawal from China's economic resources, the effect of which was probably to handicap economic growth.[109]

The establishment of the Nanking government in 1928 nominally brought political unity after a decade of civil war. In the nine years 1928–37, the central government probably achieved a greater degree of fiscal control over China proper than had existed at any time since the Ch'ing dynasty. Both revenues and the revenue system showed a remarkable improvement as compared with the warlord years of 1916–27. Tariff autonomy was recovered in 1929–30, and a new tariff with substantially higher rates gave a boost to the government finances. The shifting of import duties from a silver to a gold basis in 1930 through the instrumentality of customs gold units both preserved the real value of customs revenue and provided increased yields in terms of falling silver, thus facilitating service of the large foreign and domestic debt. Salt revenue, which before 1928 was largely appropriated locally, was integrated into the national fiscal system. Transfers to the provinces continued, but a substantial part of the salt tax became effectively available to the central government. Many, although not all, of the numerous central and local excises were combined into a nationwide consolidated tax collected for the central government in exchange for provincial appropriation of the land tax revenue. Likin was substantially although not completely abolished. The currency system was unified with the virtual elimination of the tael (the old silver unit of account) in 1933, and then the adoption in 1935 of a modern paper money system backed by foreign exchange reserves. This last was unintentionally facilitated by American silver purchases which drove up the price of silver and provided a substantial part of the required foreign currency reserves. In November 1935 silver was nationalized; the use of silver as currency forbidden; and the notes of the Central Bank of China, the Bank of China and the Bank of Communications made full legal tender. The government experimented with an annual budget, and greatly improved its collection and fiscal reporting services. Conferences were held and commissions appointed for the purpose of formulating and enforcing programmes of fiscal reform and economic development. A National Economic Council was established in 1931 to direct the economic 'reconstruction' of the country.

But however impressive these accomplishments appeared at the time in contrast to what had gone before, they were still largely superficial.

109 Remer, *Foreign investments in China*, 160.

Based as it was on indirect taxation applied to the modern sectors of the economy, national government revenue was severely limited by the slow growth of output. The inability to tax agriculture placed a formidable constraint on potential tax revenues – and thus on government programmes. Customs, salt and excise taxes probably bore heaviest on the small consumer, although the matter of the real incidence of taxation is a notably difficult one to trace; the well-to-do were not significantly taxed. The land tax in the hands of the provinces was neither reformed nor developed; it likewise burdened the small peasant farmer disproportionately. The economic policies of the Kuomintang government did not cope with the fundamental problems of agriculture, did not promote industrial growth, and did not effectively harness the political and psychological support of the populace in an attempt to raise the Chinese economy out of its stagnation.[110] Whatever small gains had been made by 1937 were swept away by the war and civil war which filled the next 12 years; and by the absence of governmental action to equalize in some measure the sacrifices which these years demanded of the Chinese people.

Table 20 shows the principal receipts and payments of the Nanking government for the nine fiscal years 1928-37. Provincial and local government expenditure remained important until 1938, after which in wartime it rapidly declined in relation to central expenditure. But even when provincial and local government expenditures are added to those of the central government, the total constituted a very small proportion of China's gross national product, only 3.2 to 6 per cent during 1931-6. Comparable figures for the United States are 8.2 per cent in 1929, 14.3 per cent in 1933, and 19.7 per cent in 1941.[111] The smallness of China's central government expenditures in relation to national income reflects both the narrowness of the national tax base and the limited size of the modern sector of the economy that in fact was called upon to shoulder the largest burden of national government taxation.

In early 1929 the Kuomintang government exercised some degree of fiscal control, apart from the Maritime Customs revenue, only in the five provinces of Chekiang, Kiangsu, Anhwei, Kiangsi and Honan. This situation later improved, but complete central government dominance over north, north-west and south-west China was never achieved before

110 Arthur N. Young, *China's nation-building effort, 1927–1937: the financial and economic record* provides a comprehensive account. Douglas S. Paauw, 'Chinese public finance during the Nanking government period' (Harvard University, Ph.D. dissertation 1950); 'Chinese national expenditure during the Nanking period', *FEQ*, 12.1 (Nov. 1952) 3–26; and 'The Kuomintang and economic stagnation', *JAS*, 16.2 (Feb. 1957) 213–20, are less sanguine than Young.
111 U.S. Bureau of the Census, *Historical statistics of the United States, 1789–1945*, 12.

1937. And soon after the outbreak of full-scale war, of course, the coastal and Yangtze provinces on which the government had principally based itself were lost to the Japanese.

The demarcation of central and provincial-local revenues at a National Economic Conference in June 1928, by which the central government formally ceded the land tax to the provinces, was then less a policy aimed at improving the admittedly chaotic financial administration inherited from the Peking regime than it was a recognition of political reality by the Nanking government. It meant, however, that in return for tenuous political support, the central government of China abandoned any fiscal claim on that part of the economy which produced 65 per cent of the national product. Abandoned too was any effort to overhaul an inequitable land tax system under which faulty land records and corrupt officials permitted the wealthy to escape a fair share of the burden. In consequence, a large part of the potential revenue of agriculture was withheld from community disposal for the general welfare.

In 1941, under the stress of war, the land-tax administration in unoccupied China was reclaimed from the provinces by the central government, which granted cash subsidies to the local governments to compensate for their loss of revenue. Collection of the land tax in kind and the forced borrowing of grains which accompanied it provided 11.8 per cent and 4.2 per cent of total central government receipts respectively in 1942–3 and 1943–4, but when the war with Japan ended central government taxation of agricultural land was quickly dropped. Wartime collection of the land tax in kind did provide the central government with the greater measure of control over food supplies which it sought, and at the same time it considerably dampened the wartime rate of increase in note issue by reducing the government's direct outlay on foodstuffs needed to supply the army, civil servants and city workers. It was carried out, however, without correcting any of the injustices of the antiquated land tax system, and individual small farmers were burdened with new inequities while other groups in the nation for the most part were exempted from or could avoid comparable direct taxation.[112]

Like almost all 'underdeveloped' countries – Meiji Japan and post-1949 China are the major exceptions – the pre-war Nanking government relied principally upon indirect taxation for its revenue. The three most important levies were customs duties (receipts from which rose rapidly after tariff autonomy was regained), the salt tax and commodity taxes. As table 20 indicates, revenue under these three headings provided 55.7

112 Shun-hsin Chou, *The Chinese inflation, 1937–1949*, 64–5; Chang, *The inflationary spiral*, 140–4.

TABLE 20

Reported receipts and expenditures of the Nanking government, 1928–37 (Millions Chinese $ and %)

Part 1

	1928–9 Ch$	%	1929–30 Ch$	%	1930–1 Ch$	%	1931–2 Ch$	%	1932–3 Ch$	%
Receipts*	434	100.0	585	100.0	774	100.0	749	100.0	699	100.0
a. Revenue*	334	77.0	484	82.7	557	72.0	619	82.6	614	87.8
i. Customs duty	179	41.2	276	47.2	313	40.4	357	47.7	326	46.6
ii. Salt tax	30	6.9	122	20.8	150	19.4	144	19.2	158	22.6
iii. Commodity taxes	33	7.6	47	8.0	62	8.0	96	12.8	89	12.7
iv. Other†	92‡	21.2	39	6.7	32	4.1	22	2.9	41	5.9
b. Deficit covered by borrowing	100	23.0	101	17.3	217	28.0	130	17.4	85	12.2
Expenditures*	434	100.0	585	100.0	774	100.0	749	100.0	699	100.0
a. Party	4	0.9	5	0.9	5	0.6	4	0.5	5	0.7
b. Civil*	28	6.4	97	16.6	120	15.5	122	16.3	131	18.7
c. Military	210	48.4	245	41.9	312	40.3	304	40.6	321	45.9
d. Loan and indemnity service	160	36.9	200	34.2	290	37.5	270	36.0	210	30.0
e. Other§	32‖	7.4	38	6.5	47	6.1	49	6.5	32	4.6

Part 2

	1933–4 Ch$	%	1934–5 Ch$	%	1935–6 Ch$	%	1936–7 Ch$	%
Receipts*	836	100.0	941	100.0	1072	100.0	1168	100.0
a. Revenue*	689	82.4	745	79.2	817	76.2	870	74.5
i. Customs duty	352	42.1	353	37.5	272	25.4	379	32.4
ii. Salt tax	177	21.2	167	17.7	184	17.2	197	16.9
iii. Commodity taxes	118	14.1	116	12.3	150	14.0	173	14.8
iv. Other†	42	5.0	109¶	11.6	211¶**	19.7	121	10.4
b. Deficit covered by borrowing	147	17.6	196	20.8	255	23.8	298	25.5
Expenditures*	836	100.0	941	100.0	1072	100.0	1168	100.0
a. Party	6	0.7	6	0.6	8	0.7	7	0.6

b. Civil*	160	19.1	151	16.1	163	15.2	160	13.7
c. Military	373	44.6	388	41.2	390	36.4	521	44.6
d. Loan and indemnity service	244††	29.2	238	25.3	294††	27.4	302	25.9
e. Other	53††	6.3	158‖††	16.8	217††	20.2	178††	15.2

* Includes cost of revenue collection, except 1928–9; excludes cash balances.
† Stamp tax, provincial remittances, profits of government enterprises, miscellaneous.
‡ Ch.$62.4 million = national revenue collected by provinces and directly disbursed for military expenses.
§ Largely transfers to provinces from salt revenue.
‖ Capital of Central Bank, Ch.$20 million, 1928–9; Ch.$74 million, 1934–5.
¶ Government enterprises receipts, 1934–5, Ch.$61 million; 1935–6, Ch.$67 million, mainly from railways, including value of transport services for military.
** Includes Ch.$78 million of various internal transfers.
†† Includes 'Reconstruction', 1933–4, Ch.$7 million; 1934–5, Ch.$26 million; 1935–6, Ch.$88 million; 1936–7, Ch.$54 million; in part this may have been investment in military-related industry.

Sources: Annual reports of the minister of finance, in P. T. Chen, 'Public Finance', The Chinese year book, 1935–1936, 1192–237; The Chinese year book, 1936–1937, 587–8; Arthur N. Young, China's nation-building effort, 1927–1937: the financial and economic record, 433–40.

per cent of total receipts/expenditures in the still unsettled 1928–9 fiscal year. During the next eight years this proportion varied between a high of 81.9 per cent in 1932–3 and a low of 56.6 per cent in 1935–6, and averaged 71.4 per cent. The balance came from various miscellaneous taxes, income from government enterprises, and above all from borrowing. Only in October 1936 were the first steps taken to introduce an income tax. The outbreak of the war in 1937 obstructed this programme; taxation on incomes, the inheritance tax and the wartime excess profits tax together never brought in more than 1 or 2 per cent of total government receipts. Speculative commercial and financial transactions which brought enormous profits to a few, including government 'insiders', during the war and civil war were never effectively taxed. Kuomintang fiscal policy depended on essentially regressive indirect taxation before the war, and although 1937–49 receipts were derived less and less from taxation, indirect taxes continued to dominate.

Foreign borrowing did not figure very largely in the finances of the Kuomintang government before the outbreak of the war. Several relatively small loans were made in the 1930s, including two American commodity loans totalling U.S.$26 million that was utilized and some borrowing for railway construction. Post-war United Nations (UNRRA) and American (ECA) aid funds (not loans of course) were used largely to meet China's large trade deficits, but without adequate plan or control and with little benefit to the economy. Wartime credits and Lend-Lease actually utilized between 1937 and 1945 amounted to approximately U.S.$2.15 billion (from the United States, $1.854 billion; Soviet Union, $173 million; Great Britain, $111 million; and France, $12 million). These were received in part in the form of military supplies and services, and in part were dissipated during and after the war along with accumulated government foreign-exchange holdings (obtained largely through American wartime purchases of local currency at an inflated exchange rate) in a vain effort to maintain the external value of the Chinese dollar.[113] In sum, foreign credits and aid helped the Kuomintang government survive the war; they contributed nothing to pre-war or post-war economic development.

The annual deficit between revenue and expenditures shown in table 20 was met principally by domestic borrowing, which in fact after 1931–2 annually exceeded the amount of the deficit itself, since some of the proceeds were held as cash balances in various accounts. Between 1927 and 1935, the Finance Ministry of the Nanking government floated 38

---

113 Arthur N. Young, *China and the helping hand, 1937–1945*, 440–2.

internal loan issues with a face value of Ch.$1,634 million.[114] This 'general purpose' borrowing was made necessary principally by the government's heavy military costs. These grew out of its political inability to 'break rice bowls' by reducing the swollen central and provincial armies, the mounting expenses of the campaigns against the communist-held Soviet areas, and after 1931 the modernization of Chiang Kai-shek's forces in the face of quickening Japanese aggression.

The troubled political and economic situation in 1931 and 1932 severely depressed the Shanghai bond market. Treasury issues secured on customs revenue fell, for example, from Ch.$62.90 in January 1931 to Ch.$26.60 in December. Scheduled payments on the domestic debt in January 1932 were about Ch.$200 million, a third of the revenue anticipated in the fiscal year 1931-2, and most of the internal debt was due to be repaid within five years. With further borrowing impossible and faced with the prospect of default, the banks and bondholders were reluctantly forced to accept a reorganization of the debt which reduced interest payments to a fixed 6 per cent and extended amortization periods to roughly double their former length. Beginning in 1933, as the effects of the world depression reached China, the pressure of deficits grew again. As table 20 shows, the amount of borrowing rose each year from fiscal 1933 to fiscal 1935 as military expenditures increased. In February 1936 a second reorganization of the internal debt was carried out by the issue of a consolidated loan of Ch.$1,460 million. This replaced 33 older issues of varying maturities and interest rates with five issues secured on the customs revenue which paid 6 per cent and matured in 12, 15, 18, 21 and 24 years. In addition a new loan of Ch.$340 million was floated, bringing the total of domestic bond issues through 1936 to nearly Ch.$2 billion.

The floating of this sizeable internal debt and its treatment reveals the interesting symbiotic relationship between the Kuomintang government and the Shanghai banking community, including the four large official banks. (The Farmers' Bank had been set up in 1933.) A very large part of the bond issues was absorbed by the banks. In February 1936, for example, they held two-thirds of the total outstanding issues. With few exceptions, at least before 1932, the practice of the Nanking government was to deposit bonds with the banks as collateral for cash advances of perhaps 50 to 60 per cent of face value. After the issue was publicly offered and a market price established, the banks purchased the bonds from the government for the difference between the original advances and the market

114 Ch'ien Chia-chü, *Chiu Chung-kuo kung-chai shih tzu-liao*, 370-5; Young, *China's nation-building effort*, 459-68.

price. While the issuing price of most bonds might be 98, maximum quotations on the market never exceeded 80 and at times fell to as low as 30 or 40. One informed estimate is that the cash yield to the Nanking government between 1927 and 1934 from loan issues with a face value of Ch.$1.2 billion was probably in the range of 60 to 75 per cent.[115] Nominal interest rates of 8.4 to 9.6 per cent, therefore, actually cost the Ministry of Finance 12 to 16 per cent, and if interest and amortization were duly paid bondholders might realize a 20 to 30 per cent return per annum. The burden of domestic borrowing improved somewhat after the loan reorganization of 1932. Average yields on domestic bonds ranged from 15 to 24 per cent through 1932, dropped to 16.8 per cent in 1933, and to 11.6 per cent in 1936.[116] Bonds were also purchased by the banks as reserves against note issues, which grew rapidly after the currency reform of 1935. Public demand for government bonds on the Shanghai market was largely for speculation rather than investment. The reorganization of the domestic debt in 1932 and 1936, which was forced upon the government by ever-mounting loan service costs, shook the market somewhat by reducing nominal interest rates and extending amortization schedules. Until wartime inflation in effect cancelled the domestic public debt – the only really 'progressive taxation' during the republican era – this providing of credit to the government remained highly profitable to the lenders.

Resort to this high-cost credit was linked to the fact that the principal creditors, the four government banks which dominated the modern banking system, were under the influence of individuals prominent in the government who utilized these institutions both in the political intrigues of the capital and to profit personally in the private sector of the economy. It was widely believed in the 1930s that the Central Bank of China was the preserve of K'ung Hsiang-hsi (H. H. Kung), the Bank of Communications of the 'C-C Clique', the Bank of China of Sung Tzu-wen (T. V. Soong), and the Farmers' Bank of China of the highest officers of the Chinese army. Personal corruption, however, is not easy to document. In any case it was probably less important in its economic consequences than the diversion of scarce capital resources, which might have been used for industrial or commercial investment, to the financing

115 Young, *China's nation-building effort*, 98, 509–10. Young, financial adviser to the Ministry of Finance, 1929–47, disagrees strongly with the lower estimate of a 50 to 60% net return which appears in Leonard G. Ting, 'Chinese modern banks and the finance of government and industry', *Nankai social and economic quarterly*, 8.3 (Oct. 1935) 591, and elsewhere and which originated with Chu Hsieh, *Chung-kuo ts'ai-cheng wen-t'i* (Problems of China's public finance), 231–2.
116 Young, *China's nation-building effort,* 98–9.

of current government military expenditures or to speculation in the bond market.

The Chinese banking system in the twentieth century failed lamentably to carry out the function of credit creation for the development of the economy as a whole. First, modern banking in China was undeveloped. While 128 new banks were established from 1928 to 1937, and in 1937 China had 164 modern banks with 1,597 branches, these were overwhelmingly concentrated in the major cities of the coastal provinces (Shanghai alone had 58 head offices and 130 branch offices in 1936). Modern banking facilities were meagre in the agricultural interior and never adapted themselves to the credit needs of a peasant economy. The cooperative societies which grew up in the 1920s and 1930s and which might have served as intermediaries between the banking system and the peasant farmer were in fact insignificant in number and tended to provide the bulk of their credit to those richer farmers who in any case could obtain loans at relatively low rates from other sources. The 'native' banks (*ch'ien-chuang*, etc.), which survived and sometimes thrived into the 1930s, tended to limit themselves to financing local trade. While the foreign banks in the treaty ports were amply supplied with funds, including large deposits by wealthy Chinese, their principal operations were the short-term financing of foreign trade and speculation in foreign exchange.

But beyond these considerations, the Chinese modern banking system that did develop in the decade before the war was distorted into an instrument primarily involved in financing a government which was continuously in debt. The capital and reserves of the principal modern banks increased from Ch.$186 million in 1928 to Ch.$447 million in 1935. Deposits during the same period increased from Ch.$1,123 million to Ch.$3,779 million. Much of the increment was accounted for by the growth of the 'big four' government banks. In 1928 the Central Bank of China, Bank of China, Bank of Communications, and Farmers' Bank of China had capital and reserves of Ch.$64 million or 34 per cent of the total; by 1935 the figure was Ch.$183 million or 41 per cent. Deposits of the four banks totalled Ch.$554 million or 49 per cent of all deposits in 1928; by 1935 they were Ch.$2,106 million or 56 per cent. At the end of 1935 the government held Ch.$146 million, or four-fifths, of the capital of 10 banks (including the four government banks). This represented 49 per cent of the total capital and 61 per cent of the combined resources of all modern banks. Other leading private banks were under the control or influence of the 'big four', and numerous interlocking directorates tied together the principal regional banking cliques, the government banks, native banking syndicates, and the insurance, commercial and industrial enterprises in which they invested. The largest provincial bank, that of Kwangtung which had 40 per cent of the total resources of all provincial and municipal banks, was closely linked with the Bank of China. Collaboration between the government and private banks facilitated meeting the needs of the Ministry of Finance for borrowed funds, but also diverted capital from private production and trade. The Central Bank of China, created in 1928, moreover did not become a true central bank with respect to the supply of money and credit; it was primarily a vehicle for the short-term financing of the government debt.[117]

In sum, this was a centralized banking structure dominated by the four government banks, and the concentration of banking resources which it represented was in line with the general goal of 'economic control' which characterized the economic thinking of the Kuomintang government. The purposes to which this control was directed, however, were not primarily economic reform and development. Credit made available by the banks to the government in the 1930s was devoted to financing the unification of China by force – the overriding priority in the eyes of the Nanking regime. Little was left for developmental expenditure despite the planmaking that kept numerous central and provincial government offices busy.

Even according to the published data for 1928–37, which may not reveal the full amount of government military allocations, from 40 to 48 per cent of annual expenditures were devoted to military purposes. Military appropriations together with loan and indemnity service – most of the borrowing was for army needs – annually accounted for 67 to 85 per cent of total outlays. An unduly large part of 'civil' expenditures represented the costs of tax collection – Ch.$60 million out of Ch.$120 million in 1930–1 and Ch.$66 million out of Ch.$122 million in 1931–2, for example. Appropriations for public works were small and welfare expenditures almost non-existent.

While total government spending was a relatively small part of national income, the pattern of income and expenditure described above tended

117 Frank M. Tamagna, *Banking and finance in China*, 121–96; Miyashita Tadao, *Shina ginkō seido ron* (A treatise on the Chinese banking system), 103–221; Tokunaga Kiyoyuki, *Shina chūō ginkō ron* (A treatise on central banking in China), 235–350; Andrea Lee McElderry, *Shanghai old-style banks (ch'ien-chuang), 1800–1935*, 131–85. Through 1934 only the Central Bank of China and the Farmers Bank of China were completely controlled by the government. Twenty per cent of the shares of the Bank of China and the Bank of Communications were owned by Nanking, which also had some influence on the appointment of key personnel; but the two banks exercised considerable independence and at times opposed government fiscal and monetary policies. In March 1935 the Bank of China and the Bank of Communications were 'nationalized' in a carefully planned coup executed by the minister of finance, H. H. Kung.

to have a negative effect on both economic development and the stability of the Kuomintang government. It is of course true that military outlays in the 1930s probably never exceeded 2 per cent of China's gross domestic product – the 1933 ratio was 1.2 per cent of the gross domestic product. And the looming Japanese threat was a real one. Furthermore, military expenditures may have had substantial economic side-effects: roads being built, peasant soldiers learning how to operate and repair simple machines, some industrial development (for example, chemicals for munitions), etc. The phrase 'hypertrophic military establishment' (page 100 above) may therefore in part reflect the bad press that the Nationalist government fully earned on other counts. But in terms of effectively available rather than potential financial resources, it remains true that Nanking's large military expenditures withdrew from the economy resources that alternatively could have been used for investment or consumption in the private sector of the economy, and yet did not conclusively provide either an end to internal disorder or protection against Japanese encroachment. Service of the domestic debt, given the prevalence of regressive indirect taxes, tended to transfer real purchasing power from lower income groups to a small number of wealthy speculators. Since the proceeds of the loans were spent largely for military purposes and debt service, and the bondholding classes preferred speculation to productive investment, domestic borrowing produced neither public nor private expenditure aimed at increasing the output of goods in a way to offset the burden on the Chinese population of the regressive national tax structure. In addition, for the private industrial entrepreneur credit was always short. A situation in which the banks in the 1930s paid 8 to 9 per cent on fixed deposits which were used to purchase government bonds, necessitated an interest rate on bank loans too high to permit extensive financing of private industry, commerce and agriculture.

In the last two years before the war a mild inflationary trend had already appeared, traceable in part to the ease with which the supply of money could be expanded following the currency reform of 1935. This was as nothing, however, compared with the inflation that began with the outbreak of hostilities in 1937 and ended in the complete collapse of the monetary system and of the Kuomintang government in 1948–9. China's runaway inflation was due principally to the continued fiscal deficit which was financed by ever-growing note issues. That ultimately it was caused by the Japanese seizure of China's richest provinces in the first year of the war and that it fed on eight years of war and three of civil war is undeniable. But it is equally of consequence that in the face of peril the Kuomintang government did little that was significant to stem the infla-

TABLE 21

Note issue and price index, 1937–48

Year*	Note Issue Outstanding[†] (million Ch. $)	Price Index[‡] (January-June 1937 = 100)
1937	2,060	100
1938	2,740	176
1939	4,770	323
1940	8,440	724
1941	15,810	1,980
1942	35,100	6,620
1943	75,400	22,800
1944	189,500	75,500
1945	1,031,900	249,100
1946	3,726,100	627,210
1947	33,188,500	10,340,000
1948	374,762,200	287,700,000

* At the end of each calendar year, except 1948 where the data are for June and July respectively.
[†] 1937–44: Arthur N. Young, *China and the helping hand, 1937–1945*, 435–6.
1946–8: Chang Kia-ngau, *The inflationary spiral: the experience of China, 1939–1950*, 374.
[‡] At the end of each year, except 1937 (January-June average) and 1948 (July). 1937–45: Index of average retail prices in main cities of unoccupied China (Young, *China and the helping hand*, 435–6); 1946–1947: all China; 1948: Shanghai (Chang, *The inflationary spiral*, 372–3).

tion, that the years 1937–49 saw a remarkable continuity of economic policies which had already been defective before 1937.[118]

Table 21 shows the growth of note issue and the soaring index of prices from 1937 to 1948. Until 1940 the inflation was still moderate and for the most part confined to the more sensitive urban sector of the economy. But the poor harvest of that year, the continued decline of food production through 1941, and the outbreak of the general Pacific war unleashed new inflationary pressures. From 1940 to 1946 annual price increases in unoccupied China averaged more than 300 per cent. Prices broke briefly after the Japanese surrender in the autumn of 1945, but from November to December 1945 the price index began to climb at an unprecedented rate. There was a momentary halt in August 1948, when new gold yuan notes were issued, and then onwards to catastrophe.

Real government revenue and expenditure both decreased drastically during the war, the former considerably more than the latter, however. The largest single source of pre-war revenue, the customs duty, was lost to the Chinese government as the Japanese quickly occupied China's coastal provinces. As the size of the territory under Kuomintang control

118 On wartime and post-war public finance and the inflation, see Chou, *The Chinese inflation*; Chang, *The inflationary spiral*; and Arthur N. Young, *China's wartime finance and inflation, 1937–1945*.

contracted, receipts from commodity taxes and other revenues naturally fell too. On the expenditure side, the real cost of servicing the domestic debt was reduced radically by the inflation, while by early 1939 payments on foreign loans secured on the customs and salt revenue were suspended. Military expenditure, as before 1937, dominated government outlays. Especially from 1940 a massive expansion of the army occurred as Chiang Kai-shek prepared both for a protracted resistance against Japan and a post-war denouement with the Communists. At the end of the war the Nationalist army was five million men strong, had consumed 70 to 80 per cent of government wartime expenditures, was inadequately equipped and poorly officered, and by its excessive recruitment of rural labour had probably contributed to a decline of agricultural production while by its concentration near the larger towns of unoccupied China it was adding enormously to the inflationary pressure. There is little to suggest, any more than before the war, that the size and cost of the military establishment contributed proportionately either to the defence of China or to the stability of the Kuomintang government. As the civil war grew in ferocity in 1947 and 1948, the demands of the military, supported by the leaders of the government, shattered all checks to runaway expenditure.

Again, following a pre-war pattern, insofar as the wartime Kuomintang government was financed by tax revenues, these were predominantly regressive indirect taxes. (One exception was the wartime land tax in kind discussed above; this, however, hit the poor farmer more heavily than it did the rich). In particular, no effort was made to tax the windfall gains of entrepreneurs and speculators who profited immensely by the inflation. The interlude, however brief, between war and civil war in 1945-6, as the government returned to formerly Japanese-occupied China, presented an opportunity to institute sweeping and equitable tax reforms to offset the expansion of money supply, but it was not taken.

Wartime and post-war government expenditures, however, were financed not by taxation but primarily by bank advances which generated continuous increases in the note issue. The sale of bonds, even with compulsory allocation, amounted to only 5 per cent of the cumulative deficit for the years 1937-45 and even less during 1946-8. After the exclusive right to note issue was given to the Central Bank of China in 1942, even the formality of depositing bonds with the banks as collateral for advances was dropped. Efforts to offset the inflationary effects of the note issue and to maintain the international value of the Chinese dollar by the sale of foreign exchange or gold and the post-war importation of commodities, served only to drain the country of accumulated foreign assets which might have been devoted to economic development after the defeat of Japan.

The inflation, of course, resulted from excessive monetary demand generated by the government deficit in circumstances of inadequate supply. To a limited extent the output of industrial consumer commodities in unoccupied China increased during the war, but the absolute magnitude was inconsequential in relieving the inflationary pressure. These commodities tended to be produced by small-scale private firms. In contrast, investments in producer goods industries were mainly by government or semi-official organs. In general, as in pre-war China, there was no effective policy channelling scarce resources to the most essential needs. In any case, the small industrial base which was developed in the interior in wartime was virtually abandoned as the government returned to coastal China.

Whatever hopes were held that the recovery of the industrially more developed provinces of China would solve the supply problem were rudely shattered by events: the Soviet removal of major industrial equipment from Manchuria; the communist control of important parts of the North China countryside which, for example, denied raw cotton supplies to the Shanghai mills; the incompetence and corruption of the National Resources Commission and China Textile Development Corporation which took over the operation of former Japanese and puppet firms; the absence of a rational and equitable plan to allocate the foreign exchange resources available at the war's end; and the same inability as in the pre-1937 period on the part of the Kuomintang government to control speculation, reform the tax structure, and give sufficient priority to developmental economic investment.

FOREIGN TRADE AND INVESTMENT

Foreign trade and investment played a relatively small role in the Chinese economy – even in the twentieth century. The effects of the Western and Japanese economic impact must be taken into account in a consideration of various distinct sectors, but most of the Chinese economy remained beyond the reach of the foreigner.

According to estimates by C. F. Remer and the Japanese East Asia Research Institute (Tōa Kenkyūjo), foreign investment in China had reached a total of U.S.$3,483 million by 1936, growing from U.S.$733 million in 1902, U.S.$1,610 million in 1914, and U.S.$3,243 million in 1931 (table 22). On a per capita basis – taking the Chinese population in 1914 as 430 million and in 1936 as 500 million – the figures for these two

TABLE 22

Foreign investments in China, 1902–36
(U.S.$ millions; % in parentheses)

Type of Investment	1902	1914	1931	1936
Direct investments	503.2 (64)	1,067.0 (66)	2,493.2 (77)	2,681.7 (77)
Obligations of Chinese Government	284.7 (36)	525.8 (33)	710.6 (22)	766.7 (22)
Loans to private parties	0.0	17.5 (1)	38.7 (1)	34.8 (1)
Total	787.9(100)	1,610.3(100)	3,242.5(100)	3,483.2(100)

Source: Chi-ming Hou, *Foreign investment and economic development in China, 1840–1937*, 13, which in turn is based on C. F. Remer, *Foreign investments in China*, and Tōa Kenkyūjo, *Rekkoku tai-Shi tōshi to Shina kokusai shūshi* (Foreign investments in China and China's balance of payments).

years are approximately U.S.$3.75 and U.S.$6.97 respectively. These per capita amounts are notably smaller than foreign investment in other 'underdeveloped' countries: for example, in 1938, India, U.S.$20; Latin America, U.S.$86; and Africa excluding the Union of South Africa, U.S.$23. Per capita foreign investment as of a given year may not be the most significant measure of the significance of that investment. Available data do not, however, permit any precise estimate of annual capital inflow figures which might be compared with national income and domestic capital formation. Very roughly, net private foreign investment in the early 1930s accounted for slightly less than one per cent of China's gross national product, and about 20 per cent of total investment.[119] That is, the aggregate was small, but not insignificant.

Remer's data indicate that, when the annual inflow of new investment capital is balanced against outpayments of interest and amortization on government loans and profits on foreign business investments, there was a substantial net outflow of capital in these accounts in the years 1902–31.[120] As table 27 indicates, however, overseas Chinese remittances to China more than balanced this outflow, so that overall there was an inflow of capital which, together with out-payments of specie, financed China's continued excess of imports over exports. The growth in the total value of foreign investment in these circumstances, apart from the effect of the upward movement of prices, seems to have been due to reinvestment of their profits by foreigners in China. Indeed, some of the 'foreign' remittances never left China, but were paid directly to foreign

119 Robert F. Dernberger, 'The role of the foreigner in China's economic development', in Perkins, ed. *China's modern economy*, 28–30
120 C. F. Remer, *Foreign investments in China*, 170–1.

TABLE 23

Foreign investment in China, 1902–36, by creditor country
(U.S.$ millions; % in parentheses)

	1902	1914	1931	1936
Great Britain	260.3 (33.0)	607.5 (37.7)	1,189.2 (36.7)	1,220.8 (35.0)
Japan	1.0 (0.1)	219.6 (13.6)	1,136.9 (35.1)	1,394.0 (40.0)
Russia	246.5 (31.3)	269.3 (16.7)	273.2 (8.4)	0.0
United States	19.7 (2.5)	49.3 (3.1)	196.8 (6.1)	298.8 (8.6)
France	91.1 (11.6)	171.4 (10.7)	192.4 (5.9)	234.1 (6.7)
Germany	164.3 (20.9)	263.6 (16.4)	87.0 (2.7)	148.5 (4.3)
Belgium	4.4 (0.6)	22.9 (1.4)	89.6 (2.7)	58.4 (1.7)
Netherlands	0.0	0.0	28.7 (0.9)	0.0
Italy	0.0	0.0	46.4 (1.4)	72.3 (2.1)
Scandinavia	0.0	0.0	2.9 (0.1)	0.0
Others	0.6 (0.1)	6.7 (0.4)	0.0	56.3 (1.6)
Total	787.9(100.0)	1,610.3(100.0)	3,242.5(100.0)	3,483.2(100.0)

Source: Chi-ming Hou, *Foreign investment and economic development in China*, 17.

creditors in Shanghai or Hong Kong who ploughed a substantial portion back into enterprises located in the several treaty ports. The growth of Jardine, Matheson and Company over the course of a century from a small agency house in the 1830s to the largest trading company in China with many industrial and financial interests illustrates this process quite well.

The largest foreign interest until 1931, when the Japanese seized Manchuria and began to invest heavily in its development, was that of Great Britain (see table 23). Of British direct investment, which accounted for 66 per cent and 81 per cent respectively of total British investments in 1914 and 1931, about half in 1931 was in fields directly associated with foreign trade, 21 per cent in real estate, 18 per cent in manufacturing, 5 per cent in public utilities, 2 per cent in mining, and 3 per cent miscellaneous. Japanese capital in China increased rapidly after 1905 when Japan became firmly entrenched in South Manchuria. Japanese direct investments, 77 per cent of the total in 1931, were mainly in transport (the South Manchurian Railway), import and export trade, manufacturing (chiefly cotton textiles) and mining. Russia's investment is accounted for almost entirely by the Chinese Eastern Railway which was sold to Japan in 1935.[121]

Direct business investment formed 66 per cent, 77 per cent, and 77 per cent of total foreign investments in the years 1914, 1931 and 1936

121 Hou, *Foreign investment and economic development in China*, 17–22.

TABLE 24

Foreign direct investments in China by industry
(U.S.$ millions; % in parentheses)

	1914	1931	1936
Import-export trade	142.6 (13.4)	483.7 (19.4)	450.2 (16.8)
Banking and finance	6.3 (0.6)	214.7 (8.6)	548.7 (20.5)
Transport (railways and shipping)	336.3 (31.5)	592.4 (23.8)	669.5 (25.0)
Manufacturing	110.6 (10.4)	372.4 (14.9)	526.6 (19.6)
Mining	34.1 (3.2)	108.9 (4.4)	41.9 (1.6)
Communications and public utilities	23.4 (2.2)	99.0 (4.0)	138.4 (5.1)
Property	105.5 (9.9)	339.2 (13.6)	241.1 (9.0)
Miscellaneous	308.2 (28.9)	282.9 (11.3)	65.3 (2.4)
Total	1,067.0(100.0)	2,493.2(100.0)	2,681.7(100.0)

Source: Chi-ming Hou, *Foreign investment and economic development in China*, 16.

respectively. The balance represented principally the borrowing of the Chinese government. Chi-ming Hou's recalculation of Remer's data and those of the East Asia Research Institute (table 24) indicates that in 1931 this direct investment was distributed as follows: import and export trade, 19.4 per cent; railways, 16.0 per cent; manufacturing, 14.9 per cent; property, 13.6 per cent; banking and finance, 8.6 per cent; shipping, 7.8 per cent; mining, 4.4 per cent; communications and public utilities, 4.0 per cent; and miscellaneous, 11.3 per cent. It is immediately evident from these figures that, in contrast to the typical pattern of foreign investment in many 'underdeveloped' countries, very little foreign capital in China had gone into export-oriented industries such as mining or plantation agriculture. Even in Manchuria, Japanese investment in agriculture was negligible.

In those countries – much of Latin America, for example, or Indonesia under the Dutch – where foreign capital was in fact concentrated in export industries, the result had been lop-sided development of the recipient economies which had come to specialize in one or more agricultural or mineral exports, the market for which was extremely sensitive to foreign business cycles. Foreign investment on this 'colonial' pattern, moreover, had allegedly reinforced the position of the native landowning class who were the chief beneficiaries of the commercialization of agriculture. Their increased income, however, was not invested in industrial development but was utilized in much the same way as in the past: in hoarding at home (land concentration, port real estate) and now also more safely abroad

TABLE 25

Geographical distribution of foreign investments in China, 1902, 1914, 1931
(U.S.$ millions; % in parentheses)

	1902	1914	1931
Shanghai	110.0 (14.0)	291.0 (18.1)	1,112.2 (34.3)
Manchuria	216.0 (27.4)	361.6 (22.4)	880.0 (27.1)
Rest of China	177.2 (22.5)	433.1 (26.9)	607.8 (18.8)
Undistributed	284.7 (36.1)	524.6 (32.6)	642.5 (19.8)
Total	787.9(100.0)	1,610.3(100.0)	3,242.5(100.0)

Source: Remer, *Foreign investments in China*, 73.

(in foreign banks and securities); and in luxury consumption (import surplus). The growth of export industries also had the further consequence of attracting native capital into intermediary tertiary activities, such as petty trade ancillary to the business of foreign firms, and as a consequence is alleged to have drawn off talent and the capital that might have been employed more productively. In very limited areas, as on the south-east coast and around Canton, some such process as the above may be discerned in China on a small scale. But the Chinese economy in the republican era was not significantly restructured by foreign capital so as to tie its fate to the vagaries of the world market.

Direct investment was heavily concentrated in the treaty ports, Shanghai in particular until 1931 as table 25 indicates. Japanese efforts to develop a Manchurian industrial base in the 1930s were discussed above, and the share of foreign-owned factories in the manufacturing sector which was located mainly in the treaty ports is suggested in tables 9 and 10, (pages 58 and 60 respectively). To many commentators, foreign-owned enterprises and foreign investment (which is often equated with control) in Chinese enterprises were primarily responsible for obstructing the development of Chinese modern industry. In this view Chinese firms simply could not compete successfully with foreign firms which had larger revenues, better technology and management, enjoyed the privileges of extraterritoriality and exemption from Chinese taxes, and were free from the depredations of Chinese officialdom. To counter this 'oppression argument' Chi-ming Hou has shown that, far from being overwhelmed, Chinese-owned modern enterprises maintained a 'remarkably stable' share of the modern sector over the years before 1937.[122] Although it might be argued that in the absence of foreign competition Chinese firms

122 *Ibid.* 138–41.

might have grown even faster, it is by no means certain that without the 'exogenous shock' of foreign trade and investment the pre-modern economy of nineteenth-century China would have been capable of embarking at all on the path of development.[123]

Apart from railway construction and industrial loans, it is doubtful whether Chinese government borrowing abroad was of any advantage to the Chinese economy. The relatively high service costs of these obligations (interest, discounts, commissions) was excessive considering the small benefit derived from them. An analysis of the indebtedness incurred during the period 1912–37 according to the purposes for which the borrowed funds were utilized seems to support the conclusion that foreign borrowing tended to be economically sterile.[124] Approximately 8.9 per cent (in constant 1913 prices) of the total was borrowed for military purposes and indemnity payments to foreigners. Another 43.3 per cent was earmarked for general administrative purposes, which meant largely for interest payments on the foreign debt itself. While the 36.9 per cent accounted for by railway loans was a potentially productive investment, its usefulness was limited by endemic civil wars and disturbances, and by provisions in the loan agreements which prevented efficient central management by establishing boundaries within which the several lines were treated as separate enterprises, and so could not pool their shop resources or gain other benefits of unified management. Telephone and telegraph loans constituted the largest part of the 10.8 per cent accounted for by industrial loans.

In view of the paucity of useful national income data, the ratio of total foreign trade turn-over to national product during the republican era can only be roughly estimated. In 1933, the one year for which an acceptable measure of domestic product is available, imports and exports together were valued at 7 per cent of gross domestic product. This was, however, after the loss of Manchuria whose foreign trade was not insubstantial and after the onset of the great depression. In the late 1920s China's foreign trade was probably equal to somewhat more than 10 per cent of national product. This is a relatively low proportion but not abnormally low in terms of international comparisons given China's size, level of development, distance from major maritime routes, abundant resources, and large domestic market. Values and index numbers of China's foreign trade for the years 1912–36 are given in table 26.

In current prices there was a slow growth of both imports and exports from the 1880s to 1900. Growth was more rapid from 1901 to 1918, and

123 Dernberger, 'The role of the foreigner in China's economic development.' 39–40.
124 Hou, *Foreign investment and economic development in China*, 29.

TABLE 26

Values and index numbers of foreign trade, 1912–36

| | Value in current prices* | | | Index of value of total trade 1913 = 100 | Indices of quantity 1913 = 100 | | Terms of trade (import price ÷ export price) 1913 = 100 |
	Net imports	Net exports	Import surplus		Imports	Exports	
1912	473	371	102	86.7	82.8	103.8	112.9
1913	570	403	167	100.0	100.0	100.0	100.0
1914	569	356	213	95.1	91.6	83.8	103.3
1915	454	419	35	89.7	70.3	96.5	104.8
1916	516	482	34	102.5	73.7	102.3	104.6
1917	550	463	87	104.0	73.4	108.3	123.4
1918	555	486	69	106.9	66.1	105.5	128.4
1919	647	631	16	131.3	75.4	140.0	134.1
1920	762	542	220	133.9	75.9	119.3	155.6
1921	906	601	305	154.8	94.7	126.9	142.3
1922	945	655	290	164.4	112.6	130.5	117.7
1923	923	753	170	172.2	108.5	137.3	109.1
1924	1,018	772	246	183.9	119.6	136.6	105.4
1925	948	776	172	177.1	109.9	132.9	103.5
1926	1,124	864	260	204.2	130.5	141.1	98.6
1927	1,013	919	94	198.4	109.8	154.1	108.6
1928	1,196	991	205	224.6	131.5	156.1	100.4
1929	1,266	1,016	250	234.4	139.9	149.2	93.1
1930	1,310	895	415	226.5	131.0	131.1	102.5
1931	1,433	909	524	240.7	129.9	136.5	116.0
1932	1,049	493	556	158.4	106.0	100.8	128.6
1933	864(1,346)	393(612)	471(734)	129.1	97.5	124.7	142.7
1934	661(1,030)	344(536)	317(494)	103.2	85.1	118.6	136.1
1935	590 (919)	370(576)	220(343)	98.6	83.6	126.7	122.9
1936	604 (942)	453(707)	151(235)	108.6	77.9	125.6	109.4

* in millions haikwan taels; from 1933 trade was valued in Ch.$ as shown in parentheses.

Sources: Hsiao Liang-lin, *China's foreign trade statistics, 1864–1949*, 23–4, 274–5; Yu-Kwei Cheng, *Foreign trade and industrial development of China*, 259.

TABLE 27

Balance of international payments, 1903, 1930, 1935
(millions Chinese $)

	1903	1930	1935
Current out-payments			
Merchandise imports	492	1,965	1,129
Specie imports	58	101	—
Service of foreign loans	69	111	108
Chinese expenditures abroad	7	3	55
Remittances of foreign enterprises			
and other profits	35	227	55
Total	661	2,417	1,347
Current in-payments			
Merchandise exports	374	1,476	662
Specie exports	51	48	357
Foreign expenditures in			
China	81	218	150
Overseas remittances	114	316	260
Total	620	2,058	1,429
Capital in-payments			
New foreign investments			
in China	42	202	140
Unaccounted for	− 1	− 157	222

Source: Li Choh-ming, 'International trade', in H. F. MacNair, ed. *China*, 501.

then noticeably accelerated from 1919 to 1931. Measured in terms of quantity rather than value, trade grew somewhat less rapidly. Imports were fairly steady in the last two decades of the nineteenth century; from 1900 there was a steady upward trend broken only by the disruptions resulting from the First World War which, we have noted, allowed some leeway for the growth of Chinese industry. Exports grew steadily from about 1907. Available data indicate that the trend in the simple terms of trade was against China (see table 26), but this would only be significant to the degree that the Chinese economy was linked to the world market as a result of expanding foreign trade. In the case of China that linkage was of less importance than in many other 'underdeveloped' countries.

In all the years of the republic, as had been the case since the 1880s, China's foreign trade was marked by an import surplus, and the current account balance was consistently unfavourable. China's ability to sustain merchandise imports in excess of merchandise exports to a large extent appears to have been due to remittances from Overseas Chinese, which year after year flowed back to the homeland, as well as to new foreign

TABLE 28

Composition of foreign trade (per cent current value)

	1913	1916	1920	1925	1928	1931	1936
Imports							
Cotton goods	19.3	14.1	21.8	16.3	14.2	7.6	1.5
Cotton yarn	12.7	12.4	10.6	4.4	1.6	0.3	0.2
Raw cotton	0.5	1.6	2.4	7.4	5.7	12.6	3.8
Rice and wheat	3.3	6.6	0.8	6.8	5.7	10.6	4.1
Wheat flour	1.8	0.2	0.3	1.6	2.6	2.0	0.5
Sugar	6.4	7.1	5.2	9.5	8.3	6.0	2.2
Tobacco	2.9	5.8	4.7	4.1	5.1	4.4	1.8
Paper	1.3	1.8	1.9	2.0	2.4	3.2	4.1
Kerosene	4.5	6.2	7.1	7.0	5.2	4.5	4.2
Petroleum	—	0.2	0.4	0.9	1.4	1.8	4.1
Transport materials	0.8	4.0	2.6	1.9	2.3	2.3	5.6
Chemicals, dyes and pigments	5.6	4.1	6.4	5.6	7.5	8.0	10.8
Iron, steel and other metals	5.3	5.1	8.3	4.7	5.4	6.2	13.2
Machinery	1.4	1.3	3.2	1.8	1.8	3.1	6.4
All others	34.2	29.5	24.3	26.0	30.8	27.4	37.5
	100.0	100.0	100.0	100.0	100.0	100.0	100.0
Exports							
Silk and silk goods	25.3	22.3	18.6	22.5	18.4	13.3	7.8
Tea	8.4	9.0	1.6	2.9	3.7	3.6	4.3
Beans and bean cake	12.0	9.3	13.0	15.9	20.5	21.4	1.3
Seeds and oil	7.8	8.4	9.1	7.9	5.8	8.4	18.7
Egg and egg products	1.4	2.6	4.0	4.3	4.4	4.1	5.9
Hides, leather and skins	6.0	6.0	4.3	4.0	5.4	4.1	5.7
Ores and metals	3.3	6.3	3.2	2.9	2.1	1.6	7.7
Coal	1.6	1.2	2.3	2.6	2.9	3.0	1.6
Cotton yarn and cotton goods	0.6	0.8	1.4	2.0	3.8	4.9	3.0
Raw cotton	4.0	3.6	1.7	3.8	3.4	2.9	4.0
All others	29.6	30.5	40.8	31.2	29.6	32.7	40.0
	100.0	100.0	100.0	100.0	100.0	100.0	100.0

Source: Yu-Kwei Cheng, *Foreign trade and industrial development of China*, 32, 34.

investment. All available estimates of China's balance of international payments, however, include a substantial amount 'unaccounted for' even after remittances and investment are considered. The estimates in table 27 for 1903, 1930, and 1935 are by H. B. Morse, C. F. Remer, and the Bank of China respectively.

In the mid nineteenth century China's principal exports had been silk and tea. They accounted for 92 per cent of the total in 1871, dropped to about 80 per cent during the 1880s, to approximately 50 per cent in 1898, and thereafter continued to decline as table 28 indicates. While they continued to be predominantly natural resource products, China's exports were considerably diversified in the course of the twentieth century. The principal new export was the soy-bean and its products, grown largely in Manchuria. Of increasing importance, too, were the export of iron ore and coal to Japan, and the shipment of cotton yarn to Japan by Japanese-owned spinning mills in China.

Until the 1890s when it was surpassed by cotton cloth and yarn, opium was the most important import into China. In about 1900 cotton cloth and yarn constituted 40 per cent of total imports. The growth of Chinese- and foreign-owned textile mills in China led to a decline in cotton textile imports. To supply these new mills, however, China became a significant importer of raw cotton. By 1936 domestic cotton output was almost able to meet the demand; but in the post-1945 period raw cotton was again critically short, testifying both to the decline of agricultural production and to the disruption of transport by the civil war. In general, the proportion of industrial raw materials and equipment in total imports grew steadily but very slowly, while such manufactured consumer goods as textiles, cigarettes and matches declined. In the late 1920s and early 1930s, rice, wheat and wheat flour climbed in importance among imports but then fell again with economic recovery in 1935 and 1936. Rural and especially urban population growth, lagging agricultural output, and poor transport made the task of feeding China's urban population always a difficult one.

Table 29 shows the proportions of China's trade with her leading suppliers and customers. There was a gradual diversification of trade between 1906 and 1936 as the growing percentage attributable to 'others' indicates (the apparent sharp drop in imports from Hong Kong is the result of a new invoice system, introduced in 1932, intended to identify the actual national origin of goods shipped to China through Hong Kong). Great Britain, Japan and the United States were China's principal trading partners. Japanese trade was predominant in Manchuria and North China and smallest in the south. The reverse was true of Great Britain. American trade, which exceeded that of all other countries in the mid 1930s, was concentrated in Central China. The decline in Japan's share after 1931 is to some degree a measure of the effectiveness of Chinese boycotts following the 'Mukden incident'.

The question remains of the overall consequences for China's economy of the patterns of foreign trade and investment just described. We have been categorical in stating that in aggregate terms they bulked much smaller than in many other 'underdeveloped' economies. Yet to many Chinese and foreign observers these were the most critical influences shaping the course of modern Chinese history. The difficulty here, we suggest, is one of precipitating out purely economic factors from the

TABLE 29

Distribution of foreign trade among trading partners
(per cent current value)

	1906	1913	1919	1927	1931	1936
Imports from:						
Great Britain	18.4	16.5	9.5	7.3	8.3	11.7
Hong Kong	33.8	29.3	22.6	20.6	15.3	1.9
Japan and Taiwan	14.3	20.4	36.3	28.4	20.0	16.3
United States	10.4	6.0	16.2	16.1	22.2	19.6
Russia	0.1	3.8	2.1	2.2	1.7	0.1
France	1.0	0.9	0.5	1.4	1.5	2.0
Germany	4.0	4.8	—	3.8	5.8	15.9
Others	18.0	18.3	12.8	20.2	25.2	32.5
	100.0	100.0	100.0	100.0	100.0	100.0
Exports to:						
Great Britain	5.6	4.1	9.1	6.3	7.1	9.2
Hong Kong	35.0	29.0	20.8	18.5	16.3	15.1
Japan and Taiwan	14.1	16.2	30.9	22.7	27.4	14.5
United States	10.9	9.3	16.0	13.3	13.2	26.4
Russia	7.9	11.1	3.4	8.4	6.0	0.6
France	10.7	10.1	5.4	5.6	3.8	4.3
Germany	2.4	4.2	—	2.2	2.5	5.5
Others	13.4	16.0	14.4	23.0	23.7	24.4
	100.0	100.0	100.0	100.0	100.0	100.0

Source: Yu-Kwei Cheng, *Foreign trade and industrial development of China*, 20, 48–9.

complex mixture that was the foreign impact upon twentieth-century China.[125] China was changed by her modern encounter with the West, and it was the hope of economic gain which first brought the foreigner and his ways to the Middle Kingdom. Foreign economic activity was largely responsible for calling forth a small modern sector of Chinese- and foreign-owned trading and manufacturing enterprises on the fringe of the Chinese empire. But the Chinese economy as a whole underwent no significant transformation; at best there occurred only a 'partial develop-ment'. The large foreign role in the modern sector of the economy was based on an artificially low tariff and the privileges of extraterritoriality, was supported by highly-developed industrial economies at home, and was abetted by the siphoning off of capital in indemnity and loan payments to foreign creditors. But all this cannot be made to bear more than a part of the obloquy for China's economic stagnation. To assert more than this is to obscure the ideological and political disequilibrium which was the most profound consequence of the impact of the West, and which for

125 See A. Feuerwerker, 'The foreign presence in China', ch. 3 of this volume.

decades obstructed the emergence of a new political integration capable of replacing the Confucian imperial pattern of the past and taking advantage of the possibilities of economic development inherent in modern industrial technology.

The Chinese economy, in the years covered by this chapter at least, did not occupy centre stage in the unfolding of the drama of Chinese history. It was only one of the supporting cast – with a few choice lines perhaps – waiting on the words of emperors, bureaucrats, diplomats, generals, propagandists, and party organizers.

CHAPTER 3

THE FOREIGN PRESENCE IN CHINA

The foreign establishment in early republican China had many facets:
territory, people, rights established by treaty or unilaterally asserted,
armed force, diplomacy, religion, commerce, journalism, freebooting
adventure, racial attitudes. The pages that follow describe briefly the dimensions of each of the principal guises in which the foreigner impinged
upon the polity, economy, society and mind of China. The physiological,
intellectual and spiritual results of the foreign presence are still beyond our
capacity to summarize.

THE FOREIGN NETWORK

Unlike India, South-East Asia (except Thailand) and most of Africa,
China was not partitioned and ruled by the alien powers which imposed
themselves upon the weakened Ch'ing empire in the last half of the
nineteenth century. China was too big for any one power to swallow, and
seemed too dazzling a prize for a satisfactory division of shares to be
worked out. Consequently China's sovereignty was impaired, but it never
came near to being vanquished. The foreigner had always to acknowledge
that there was a Chinese authority, central or local, with which he had to
contend. In some parts of China's territory, however, that authority was
formally reduced, even ceded, in the interests of foreign claimants and as
a consequence of demands to which China acceded only because she was
too weak to refuse. These were variously treaty ports, concessions,
leaseholds and spheres of influence.

Treaty ports

'Treaty port' is a protean term. The precise limits of the *chiang-k'ou*,
literally 'harbours' or 'anchorages', were matters of dispute because the
English text of the Treaty of Nanking (1842) granting foreigners the
rights of residence and trade read, more broadly, 'cities and towns'. But
there is no question that Shanghai, Canton, Foochow, Amoy and Ningpo

were sea ports. By 1893, 28 additional places had been opened to foreign trade, and during 1894–1917, 59 more, making a total of 92 by the latter date. Some were inland cities or places on China's land frontiers; others were coastal ports or railway junctions in Manchuria; many were river ports on the Yangtze or West Rivers. Collectively they were commonly called in Chinese *shang-pu* or *shang-fou*, 'trading ports'. Juridically, the ports that were open to foreign trade fell into three categories: 'treaty ports' proper, that is, ports opened as a consequence of an international treaty or agreement; 'open ports' voluntarily opened by the government of China though not obliged to by treaty; and 'ports of call' at which foreign steamers were permitted to land or take on board passengers and under certain restrictions goods, but at which foreign residence was prohibited. Maritime Customs stations were maintained at only 48 of these 92 various places as of 1915, which suggests that many played no significant role in China's international commerce.

At the 'treaty ports' proper China's sovereignty had been diminished in two important respects: first, foreign nationals could reside, own property and engage in business at these places under the extraterritorial jurisdiction of their consuls (and might travel inland with a passport, but could not legally, except for missionaries, reside in the interior); and second, foreign goods, having been landed at a treaty port, were upon one payment of the import duty (according to a tariff China did not control) exempt from all further levies if reshipped to other treaty ports. The treaty powers forced the Chinese government to extend this tariff privilege to the voluntarily-opened ports. However, these last were distinguished from those treaty ports in which foreign 'concessions' or 'settlements' existed in that Chinese local officials retained exclusive control of the municipal administration and police.

Foreign concessions or settlements were established in 16 treaty ports, that is, specific areas were set aside for foreign residence in which local administration (police, sanitation, roads, building regulations, and so forth) was in foreign hands and was financed by local taxes levied by the foreign authorities. The foreign residential areas at Tientsin, Hankow and Canton, for example, were 'concessions'. In these places entire areas were expropriated or purchased by the Chinese government and leased in perpetuity to particular powers (Great Britain, France, Germany, Japan, Russia, Belgium, Italy and Austria-Hungary at Tientsin; Great Britain, France, Germany, Japan and Russia at Hankow; Great Britain and France at Canton). The consul of the nation holding the concessional lease, aided sometimes by a municipal council, was the chief official of each concession through whom individual foreigners obtained sub-leases to particular pieces of property.

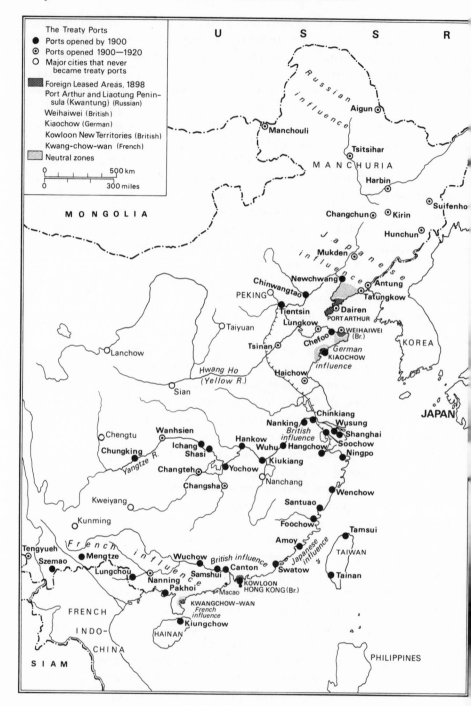

The Treaty Ports
● Ports opened by 1900
⊙ Ports opened 1900—1920
○ Major cities that never
   became treaty ports
▨ Foreign Leased Areas, 1898
Port Arthur and Liaotung Penin-
   sula (Kwantung) (Russian)
Weihaiwei (British)
Kiaochow (German)
Kowloon New Territories (British)
Kwang-chow-wan (French)
▦ Neutral zones

0   500 km
0   300 miles

MAP 5.   Foreign 'territory' in China about 1920

The International and French 'Settlements' in Shanghai consisted of areas set apart by treaty for foreign residence and trade but not leased to the powers concerned. The Chinese authorities issued title deeds to the foreigners who had purchased land from the original Chinese owners. The deeds were then registered in the foreign consulates, which in effect granted a title guarantee making the transfer of land more certain and enhancing the value of each property to the advantage of foreign lawyers, missionaries and others who realized considerable income, as trustee owners. No Chinese was legally permitted to hold land in a concession, although in fact many did through foreign proxy. In the Shanghai settlements substantial amounts of land were held directly by Chinese and never transferred to foreign ownership.

By means of pressure on the Tsungli Yamen by the Diplomatic Body in Peking – a formally legitimate means to obtain results in China – the limits of the International Settlement, originally an area of approximately one square mile for the combined British and American Settlements (see volume 10, pages 238–9), were extended to 2.75 square miles in 1893 and 8.35 square miles in 1899. The French Settlement, originally 0.26 square miles in area, grew by extensions in 1881, 1900 and 1914 to 3.9 square miles. Efforts in 1915 and later by the Municipal Council of the International Settlement and the British minister in Peking to obtain formal approval for the incorporation of additional territory into the International Settlement were resisted by the Chinese government, now beginning to respond to nationalist sentiments which demanded the rendition of all foreign concessions and settlements. But by the development and occupation of adjacent lands – the building of extra-concessional roads followed by the laying of water mains and electricity cables, and ultimately the exercising of taxation and policing powers – the 'external roads areas' under *de facto* foreign control grew considerably between 1916 and 1925.

Exclusively foreign municipal governments were elaborated in the Shanghai Settlements through the medium of successive 'land regulations' issued by the foreign consuls. The Chinese had not envisaged this municipal development when they assented to the 1842, 1843 and 1858 treaties, but the Peking government had to accept as *fait accompli* what the Diplomatic Body, which sometimes as in 1898 substantially modified Shanghai's proposals, presented for its formal sanction. The 1898 Land Regulations were the last revision of the 'constitution' of the International Settlement before 1928, when Chinese representatives were admitted to the Municipal Council. They provided the dominant 'taipan oligarchy' with less formal autonomy than it sought because decisions of the annual rate-payers' meeting remained subject to the approval of the Shanghai Consular

Body and the Diplomatic Body in Peking while the Shanghai Municipal Council's (SMC) powers were nominally restricted. Friction between the SMC and the Consular and Diplomatic Bodies was frequent and on occasion open. In practice, however, the latter might criticize but usually supported the more aggressive attitude of the Shanghai residents towards local Chinese authority.

The Municipal Council of the International Settlement, formally only an executive body of the ratepayers' meeting, extended its authority steadily and acquired wide powers of government, including the power to tax and police both foreign and Chinese residents. (No Chinese taxes were collected in the foreign settlements in Shanghai apart from a land tax – since the land remained Chinese territory – and the Maritime Customs duties.) The nine SMC members were chosen by an electorate limited to foreigners who owned land valued at not less than 500 taels or who paid a rental of at least 500 taels per annum. These numbered slightly more than 2,000 in the early republic, less than 10 per cent of the total foreign population. Ratepayers' meetings, in the absence of extraordinary issues, were often poorly attended. Election to the council was to a degree managed by a small inner circle, largely British, representing business interests. The municipal employees of the International Settlement were predominately British (965 out of 1,076 in the early 1920s not including 792 Sikhs in the police force) as were the heads of all the principal departments – Health, Public Works, Electricity, Sewage Disposal, Finance, the Fire Brigade, the Volunteer Corps and the Secretariat of the Municipal Council.

Chinese sovereignty was theoretically intact, but in practice the concessions and settlements were self-governing foreign enclaves. Within them, in addition to the extraterritorial rights and privileges extended to foreigners, the International Settlement authorities exercised *de facto* jurisdiction over Chinese residents who constituted the overwhelming majority of the population but who were not accorded the right of participation in the municipal governments. Chinese living in the concessions or settlements could be arrested by Chinese authorities only with the approval of the appropriate foreign consul. In the Shanghai International Settlement, civil or criminal cases between Chinese were tried before a mixed court often dominated in practice (not by treaty right) by foreign assessors. The right of Chinese troops to pass through the concessions or settlements was consistently denied by the foreign municipal authorities, who maintained that these were neutral territories with respect to China's civil wars.

Foreign life in Shanghai

The style of life for most foreign residents of the concessions and settlements may be caricatured with the observation that nothing other than ricksha hire (at five cents a mile) or sampan hire was ever paid for in cash, including the Sunday collection in church. The omnipresent 'chit' or handwritten note symbolized the largely self-contained world in which the commercial, diplomatic, military and religious representatives of the powers passed their sojourns in China. That some became knowledgeable observers of the changing Chinese scene, learned the language and something of the artistic and literary culture, even made Chinese friends, does not gainsay the fact that the daily 'diet', literally and figuratively, consisted of foreign ingredients transplanted to China's soil. 'It was the first of many hundreds of similar meals that I was to eat during the next few years', a new American employee recalled of the British-American Tobacco Company mess that he joined in August 1911, '– a thin consommé, breaded veal cutlet, rice, a boiled vegetable and a sticky pastry. English cooking – the flavour cooked out – with the inevitable Lea & Perrins sauce'.[1]

Rarely did a Shanghai resident set foot in the 'native city'. Before the more hectic 1920s and 1930s leisure time was spent entirely with other expatriates in a panoply of pursuits characteristic of treaty-port life. Wealthy citizens and their wives in their open carriages drove in the late afternoon up and down winding boulevards like Bubbling Well Road. The grand villas of the taipans (heads of firms) along this avenue, with their spacious gardens and tennis courts, were the scenes of lengthy afternoon teas in the English style. Abundant and inexpensive servants permitted for some a style of dining and entertainment more lavish than the BAT (British-American Tobacco Company) mess described above, but still reflecting the fact that foreign Shanghai was a British city – soup, fish, game, joint, savoury, dessert, followed by coffee, with port, liqueurs and cigars for the gentlemen. Bridge, accompanied by successive whisky-and-sodas, accounted for many of the hours after dinner. Before the films, cabarets, and nightclubs which multiplied in profusion after the First World War, 'night life' outside of the leading hotels[2] and social

---

1 James L. Hutchison, *China hand*, 20. But it was not only 'the good old L. & P.' that became standard fare in a country whose indigenous cuisine was matchless but undiscovered by many of the 'old China hands'.

2 The Astor House, first-class with sumptuous appointments, on Whangpoo Road; the Palace and the Grand; l'Hotel des Colonies in the French Settlement; the Japanese Hōyō-kwan and Banzai-kwan on Seward Road.

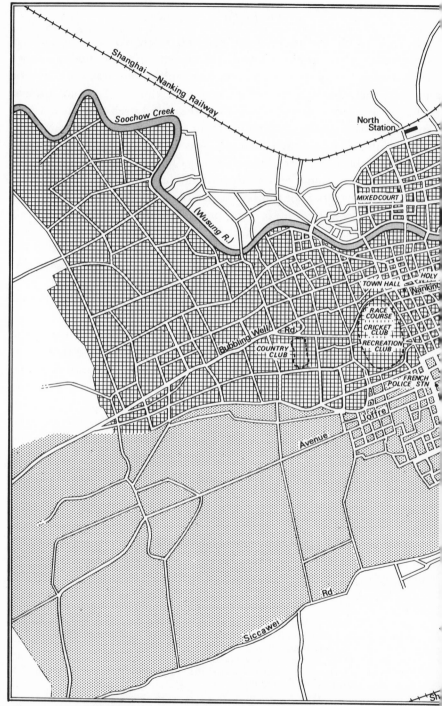

MAP 6. Treaty ports – Shanghai ca. 1915

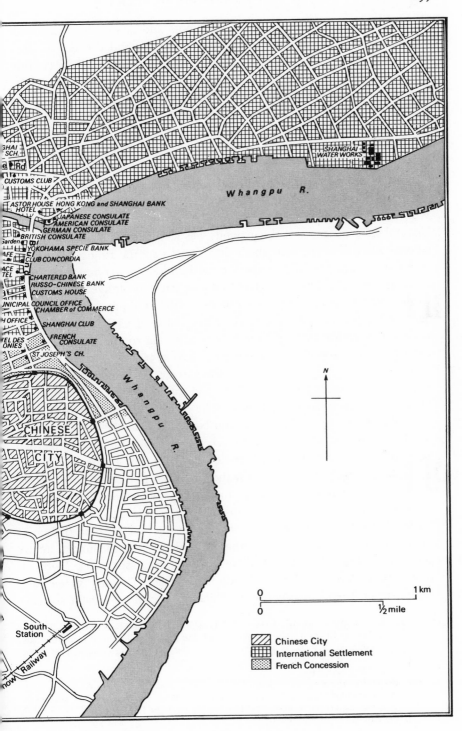

ASTOR HOUSE HONG KONG and SHANGHAI BANK
HOTEL
JAPANESE CONSULATE
AMERICAN CONSULATE
GERMAN CONSULATE
BRITISH CONSULATE
YOKOHAMA SPECIE BANK
CLUB CONCORDIA
CHARTERED BANK
RUSSO-CHINESE BANK
CUSTOMS HOUSE
MUNICIPAL COUNCIL OFFICE
CHAMBER of COMMERCE
SHANGHAI CLUB
FRENCH
CONSULATE
ST JOSEPH'S CH.

CUSTOMS CLUB

SHANGHAI
WATER WORKS

Whangpu R.

Whangpu R.

CHINESE
CITY

South
Station

Soochow Railway

N

0   1 km
0   ½ mile

▨ Chinese City
▦ International Settlement
▨ French Concession

clubs³ was limited to a few places like Louis Ladow's Carlton Café and Restaurant on Ningpo Road (see map 6) which provided excellent dinners with music for parties of the city's foreign society in full dress. 'But by ten o'clock the mixed dinner parties ended and only men were left. That was understood. From ten until bleak dawn other ladies of various nationalities, American, English, French and perhaps German, Russian, Italian and Spanish, from forbidding-looking grey stone houses in Kiangse and Soochow Streets, drifted in and out, shooting up the sales of champagnes and sparkling burgundies to enormous quantities'.⁴

The race-course, with impressive grandstand and club-house and covering an extensive area along Defence Creek at the east end of Bubbling Well Road, was the scene of three-day meets twice a year, in May and November. The centre of the grounds was laid out as a cricket field and tennis courts. Foreign Shanghai's devotion to sports, riding and tennis especially, compensated perhaps for the bibulousness common at most social gatherings. The Shanghai Club boasted 'the longest bar in the world'. The Cricket Club was equipped with 12 tennis courts and 18 nets for the practice of cricket. The Shanghai Golf Club was formed in 1894 and a handsome club-house with dressing-rooms for ladies and gentlemen, gear-room and bar was erected in 1898.⁵

Between rides or sets of tennis there were the productions of the Shanghai Amateur Dramatic Club and of the Société Dramatique Française in the French Settlement. The Municipal Band performed in the Public Gardens between May and November; in the winter months it played in the Town Hall. Each foreign community maintained its own association – the American Association of China, the Deutsche Vereinigung, St George's Association for the English, St Andrew's Society for the Scots, St Patrick's Society for the Irish – and national holidays and folk-days were celebrated with gusto. Energy was available for more serious literary and educational associations: the North China Branch of the Royal Asiatic Society, Photographic Society, Union Church Literary and Society Guild, American Women's Literary Association, Horticulture Society, American University Club, Deutscher Concert Verein, and Literarischer Abend, among others. Philanthropic and charitable societies

---

3 The British Shanghai Club, the German Club Concordia, and the Masonic Club, all on the Bund; the Country Club on Bubbling Well Road; the Japanese Club on Boone Road; and those, less exclusive, associated with the Seamen's Association, the Foreign YMCA, the customs service and the Volunteer Corps.

4 Hutchison, *China hand*, 236.

5 Also included in the array of athletic clubs were the Shanghai Rowing Club, the Yacht Club, the Paper Hunt Club ('fox' hunting in the countryside, in pursuit of riders wearing red cowls who scattered paper to mark a trail for the hunters), the Lawn Tennis Club, the Rifle Club, the Baseball Club, and others.

included the Shanghai Society for the Prevention of Cruelty to Animals, Benevolent Society, Seamen's Mission and First Aid Association. The international Chamber of Commerce was the most powerful of the professional and business associations, which included among others the Stockbrokers' Association, the Pilots' Association and the Society of Engineers and Architects with more than 100 members.

Schools for European children were the Shanghai Public School, l'Ecole Municipale in the French Settlement, and the Deutsche Schule in Whangpoo Road; there was also a Japanese Primary School. Hospitals were maintained by the Municipal Council of the International Settlement, by several mission societies and by the Japanese community. The Public Library had 15,000 Western-language volumes before the First World War. A dozen mission associations maintained establishments in Shanghai, making it the largest centre of missionary activity in China. Protestant churches included the very large Church of the Holy Trinity (in thirteenth-century Gothic style, the Cathedral Church of the Anglican Bishop of Mid China), the Union Church (early English style, in Soochow Road), the Baptist Church on the Bund, and the Deutsche Evangelische Kirche in Whangpoo Road. Catholic churches were located both in the French and International Settlements. A mosque, a synagogue and a Japanese Buddhist temple were also available. Weeks and Company, Lane, Crawford and Company, Hall and Haltz, Whiteaway, Laidlaw and Company for provisions, furniture, drapery, millinery; Kelly and Walsh for books and maps; Hope Brothers and Company, jewellers; the Shanghai Dispensary in Soochow Road; the *North-China Daily News, Shanghai Mercury, Shanghai Times,* and *China Press, l'Echo de Chine, Der Ostasiatische Lloyd,* the *Shanhai Nippō,* all foreign-language daily papers – anything could be bought or read in Shanghai.[6]

Shanghai set the style of the foreign presence in China, a style the other concessions and settlements sought to emulate. Tientsin, its concession area under seven different national administrations and including three separate British municipal districts, counted five churches, eight tennis clubs, five lodges, seven national associations, seven social clubs (the British Tientsin Club was the oldest, the Concordia Club for the Germans, the French Cercle d'Escrime, a Japanese Club, and so forth), swimming, hockey, baseball, cricket and golf clubs, and of course the Race Club with a fine new grandstand built in 1901 to replace an older structure destroyed by the Boxers. The Volunteer Corps dated from 1898;

---

6 Imperial Japanese Government Railways, *An official guide to Eastern Asia,* vol. 4, *China,* and C. E. Darwent, *Shanghai, a handbook for travellers and residents,* provide interesting details.

Central Station

West Station

Austro-Hungarian Settlement

CHINESE

N

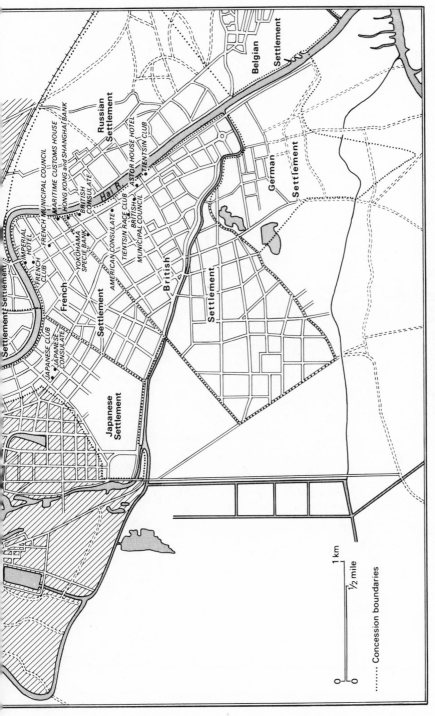

MAP 7. Treaty ports – Tientsin ca. 1915

Belgian Settlement

Russian Settlement

German Settlement

British Settlement

Japanese Settlement

French Settlement

Settlement

Hai R.

IMPERIAL HOTEL
FRENCH CLUB
FRENCH MUNICIPAL COUNCIL
MARITIME CUSTOMS HOUSE
HONG KONG and SHANGHAI BANK
BRITISH CONSULATE
YOKOHAMA SPECIE BANK
AMERICAN CONSULATE
TIENTSIN RACE CLUB
BRITISH MUNICIPAL COUNCIL
ASTOR HOUSE HOTEL
TIENTSIN CLUB
JAPANESE CLUB
JAPANESE CONSULATE

1 km
½ mile
0
0
······· Concession boundaries

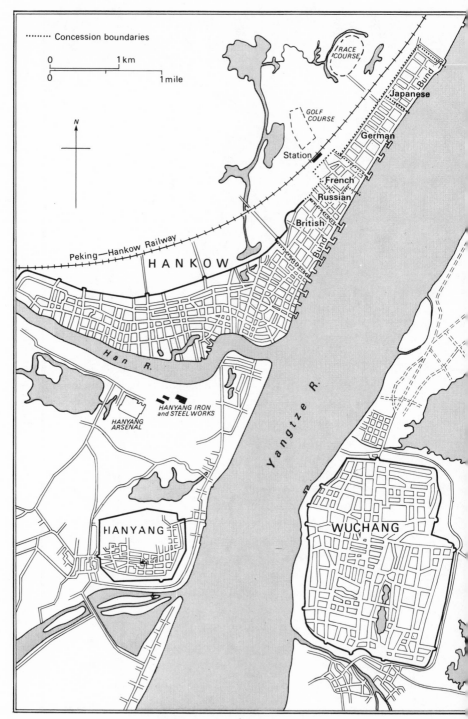

MAP 8.   Wuhan cities ca. 1915

the Municipal Library located in the British Concession held 7,000 volumes; and the *Peking and Tientsin Times,* edited from 1914 by H. G. W. Woodhead who was also editor and publisher of *The China Year Book,* competed with the *Tenshin Nichi-Nichi Shimbun, l'Echo de Tientsin,* and the *Tageblatt für Nord China.*

At Hankow the British, French, Russian, German and Japanese concessions stretched along the Yangtze River for several miles, miniature European cities tied together by the Bund, a fine boulevard with shade-trees and grass between the road and pavements. Each afternoon the foreign community gathered at the Race Club for tea followed by tennis or golf. Hankow's 18-hole course was the best in Asia. The verandaed club-house – containing a swimming pool, games rooms, lockers, a large tea-room – had a famous long bar, much frequented by the officers of the foreign gunboats which patrolled the Yangtze.

A glittering life, all things considered, which makes it easy to understand why 'old China hands' guarded their privileges. The 'Shanghai mentality' not only brooked no interference from the Chinese authorities, but typically considered the Diplomatic and Consular Bodies as nuisances which might sometimes be made use of but which were always excessively considerate of Chinese susceptibilities. While we have emphasized the glitter, following the more accessible sources, it was not all so simple. Life in treaty-port society in Shanghai and elsewhere was divided along sharp class lines. A man was known by his type of business, the clubs to which he belonged, and the number of ponies he owned. The Jewish, Portuguese and Eurasian populations lived segregated social lives. While the small Jewish commercial community in Shanghai was in general well-off, the Portuguese and Eurasians filled most of the routine and low-paid jobs, as clerks, book-keepers and secretaries, in the business houses. Each treaty port had its cohort of foreign drifters, stranded sailors and pitiful failures. The bottom of the foreign social pyramid and the underworld of vice and crime were rarely noticed in the glowing reminiscences of treaty-port life, but they were parts of the foreign establishment too.

Leased territories

Foreign 'leaseholds', five in number, were territories ceded by China in 1898 during the scramble for influence and strategic bases. Kiaochow Bay in Shantung and surrounding territory, a total of 552 square kilometres, was leased to Germany for 99 years in March 1898, and concessions were given to build three railway lines in Shantung and to operate mines within

10 miles on either side of the tracks. (Kiaochow was captured by Japan in November 1914 after heavy fighting in which the Japanese suffered casualties of 616 killed and 1,228 wounded, a side-show to the First World War. It was returned to China only in 1922.) The Russians obtained a 25 year lease of the Liaotung peninsula (including the harbours of Port Arthur and Talienwan [Dairen]) in Southern Manchuria in March 1898. The Russian-controlled Chinese Eastern Railway Company was, in addition, given permission to build a branch line from Harbin to Port Arthur and Talienwan, the South Manchurian Railway, and to exploit timber and mines within the railway zone. May 1898 saw the French extract a 99-year lease on the port of Kwangchou-wan, opposite Hainan Island in Kwangtung, as a naval station. In June, Great Britain obtained from China the lease for 99 years of a mainland extension to its Hong Kong colony, the 'New Territories'. Completing this series of raids on Chinese territory came the lease of Weihaiwei, a port in Shantung, to Great Britain in July 1898 'for as long a period as Port Arthur shall remain in the occupation of Russia'.[7]

In the leaseholds, in contrast to the concessions and settlements, China's sovereignty was explicitly extinguished for the duration of the several leases, as evidenced by the consensus among the treaty powers that their rights to extraterritorial consular jurisdiction which held in all other 'Chinese' territory did not extend into these areas. And two of them, in Shantung and Manchuria, were at the core of the more extensive 'spheres of influence' asserted by Germany, Russia and Japan – together with Great Britain and France whose 'spheres' were grounded on more diffuse claims – within Chinese territory.

The *de facto* basis for any power's claim to a sphere, including preferential or exclusive rights to make loans, construct and operate railways, open mines, have its nationals employed as 'advisers', or exercise some other form of territorial jurisdiction in particular parts of China, was the same one – China's weakness and the threat of alien force – which sustained the infringements of sovereignty described in the previous paragraphs. Formally the several spheres of influence had various bases: Chinese agreements with specified powers not to alienate certain areas to any third power; conventions or treaties to which China was a party but was in no position to reject; assertions by certain powers of rights due to contiguity; agreements among the powers to recognize each other's claims, to which China was not a party; and claims to further rights arising from the *fait accompli* of predominant financial and commercial interests.

7 The agreements covering these leases may be found in John V. A. MacMurray, *Treaties and agreements with and concerning China, 1894–1919*, I. 112–31, 152–8.

Russian rights in Manchuria derived from the secret treaty of alliance of May 1896, the construction of the Chinese Eastern Railway and its South Manchurian branch, and the lease of the Liaotung peninsula. From these bases, the Russian government proceeded to establish *de facto* political and military control within the railway zone, and strengthened its position through the occupation of Manchuria by Russian troops in 1900 consequent upon the Boxer uprising. Russian troops in Manchuria and increasing efforts to exert influence in Korea led to war with Japan in 1904–5 and an embarrassing defeat for Russia. The lease of the Liaotung peninsula was transferred to Japan, as well as the South Manchurian Railway between Ch'ang-ch'un and Port Arthur together with Russian 'rights, privileges and properties' in the railway zone. After 1905 Russia continued to exercise effective political jurisdiction within the zone of the Chinese Eastern Railway (CER) and in cities and towns (Harbin, for example) in North Manchuria on that line. The resulting division of Manchuria with Japan was formalized by Russo-Japanese conventions signed in 1907 and 1910. In 1914 the treaty powers, except for the United States, recognized Russian control over their nationals within the CER railway zone.[8] By virtue of a non-alienation declaration made by China in 1898, Japan claimed the province of Fukien as a sphere of influence, but this was of little practical consequence. It was in Manchuria, of course, that Japan's special status was progressively developed. China had no option but to give its consent to the assignment of Liaotung, and of Russian railway and mining rights in South Manchuria to Japan (Sino-Japanese treaty of December 1905), and by additional agreements to grant Japan 'settlements' at Yingkow, Antung, and Mukden as well as further railway concessions. The government-general of Kwantung was formally established in September 1906 to administer the leased territory (218 square miles) and the railway zones (108 square miles). Japan's sphere in Manchuria was implicitly acknowledged by France in 1907 (accompanied by a reciprocal Japanese recognition of the French sphere), by the United States in the Root-Takahira agreement of 1908, and by Russia as indicated above. And by Group II of the Twenty-one Demands, which Japan forced the Yuan Shih-k'ai government to accept in 1915, the Japanese position in Manchuria was further consolidated: the Liaotung lease and the South Manchurian Railway concessions were extended to 99 years; all of South Manchuria was opened to Japanese nationals for residence, commerce and manufacture; additional mining areas were made available to Japanese nationals; and commitments were made to give preference in the future

8 See B. A. Romanov, *Russia in Manchuria (1892–1906)*.

to Japanese capitalists for loans and to Japanese nationals in the employment of political, military and police advisers in South Manchuria and Eastern Inner Mongolia.

The Kwantung leased territory became an island of Japanese society and culture on the Chinese mainland. Japanese language publications, colourful kimono, Shinto festivals, and yen notes as the official currency became part of the life of the colony and its principal city Dairen. From Kwantung northwards through the economic heart of South Manchuria, the trunk line of the South Manchurian Railway ran 483 miles to Ch'ang-ch'un. It was served by feeder lines to the port of Yingkow, from Mukden (Shenyang) to Antung on the Korean border, and between Dairen and Port Arthur. In cities along the South Manchurian line and in the railway zones on either side of the tracks, Japan exercised *de facto* political jurisdiction in spite of Chinese protests. The Kwantung government-general was practically coterminous with the South Manchurian Railway Company: the majority of the shares were held by the Japanese government and the company was placed under the supervision of the governor-general of Kwantung. Japanese consuls in Manchuria were appointed by the company and many served simultaneously as secretaries of the government-general. In addition to the various railway lines, the South Manchurian Railway Company operated coal mines at Fushun (near Mukden) and Yentai (near Liaoyang), steamer lines and warehouses, and maintained schools, hospitals, experimental farms, public utilities and 'railway guards' within the railway zones.

Before 1931, however, Japanese political authority in Manchuria was restricted to the leased territory and the railway zones. Because of their favoured economic position which funnelled goods on the South Manchurian Railway from the key market centres of Fengtien province to Dairen and Port Arthur, from where they were carried by Japanese steamer to Tientsin, Shanghai, Yokohama and Osaka, the Japanese tended to over-estimate their influence over Chang Tso-lin, the warlord ruler of Manchuria. The authority of the Peking government was small in Chang's satrapy, but he was equally skilful and effective in limiting the Japanese, ignoring them or conciliating them as the case might be, but successfully playing off competing Japanese interests against each other so as to maintain an authentically Chinese semi-independent regime.[9]

From November 1914 until the restoration of Shantung to China by the Sino-Japanese Shantung Agreement of February 1922, concluded in connection with the Washington Conference, Japan occupied the

9 See Ronald S. Suleski, 'Manchuria Under Chang Tso-lin' (University of Michigan, Ph.D. dissertation, 1974).

former German Kiaochow leasehold; and in the face of strong Chinese protests, moved to control the Shantung railways and mines presumably with the object of linking the railways with those of Manchuria and thereby dominating North China. Between 1897 and 1914 Germany had administered its leasehold as a colony under the jurisdiction of the Ministry of the Navy and attempted to use its railway and mining concessions to extend its influence throughout the province of Shantung. Tsingtao, with a population of 55,000 Chinese and 5,000 Europeans and Japanese in 1913 (the total population of the Kiaochow leasehold was about 200,000), was known to the foreigners as the 'Brighton of the Far East'. Its climate and the marvellous east beach of the outer bay (Auguste Viktoria Bay), more than a mile in length on the Yellow Sea, made it a fashionable summer resort. The Strand Hotel accommodated 500 guests and, together with the race course, was situated near the beach. On the southern slope down to the bay there grew up the 'European town' of Tsingtao with its symmetrical plan, paved streets illuminated first by gas light and then electricity, lined with pavements and large trees, and the villas and gardens of the wealthy German inhabitants. Chinese servants lived in 'coolie houses' in the rear of the main buildings. The majority of the Chinese population resided in the 'Chinese town' which had been physically separated from the European sector by the demolition and removal of inconveniently proximate Chinese villages. Tsingtao was developed into a first-class port, and the municipality operated modern water and sewage systems, efficient hospitals, a German grammar school, and a German-Chinese high school founded in 1909 as a joint effort by the German government and Chinese officials. Industrial investment in the city itself was relatively small, the most famous enterprise being the Anglo-German Brewery Company established in 1904 which produced the still famous Tsingtao beer.

The Schantung Eisenbahn Gesellschaft and the Schantung Bergbau Gesellschaft, both formed in 1899 by a syndicate consisting of the financial houses which organized the Deutsch-Asiatische Bank in Shanghai together with German firms (for example, Carlowitz and Company) in China, were in theory Sino-German companies. In practice the capital and management of the railway built from Tsingtao to Tsinanfu were entirely German, as was also the case for the coal mines opened at Wei-hsien and Hung-shan. The German banking syndicate and British financial interests, both with the backing of their governments, agreed in 1898 (in connection with plans to build a railway from Tientsin to the Yangtze River) that the German sphere of influence would extend northwards into Hopei province while predominant British influence in the Yangtze valley and in Shansi province was recognized in return. Even in Shantung, however, the Germans found it increasingly difficult to realize the preferential treatment they claimed. A combination of German diplomatic isolation after 1900, fear of jeopardizing commercial interests elsewhere in China by exclusive claims in Shantung, and a concerted Chinese effort to limit the German sphere in Shantung effectively confined the Germans to their leasehold and to a narrow interpretation of the railway and mining concessions. Unlike Manchuria, Chinese and not German railway guards provided protection in the Tsingtao-Tsinan railway zone; efforts to take over the postal and telegraph services along the railway failed; only part of the mining concessions could be exploited; and even Tsingtao's status as a free port was ended in 1906.[10]

By virtue of their contiguity to French Indo-China, France claimed a sphere of influence in the southern Chinese provinces of Yunnan, Kweichow and Kwangsi. France was given a concession for a railway from Tongking across the border into Yunnan in 1898 (construction began in 1903 and was completed in 1910, entirely French financed and managed). France obtained assurances that none of the provinces bordering Indo-China would be alienated to a third power, and secured a leasehold of Kwangchou-wan as noted earlier. French commerce, especially in Yunnan, received preferential treatment by virtue of French ownership of the railway, but few other concessions were obtained or exploited. There was no local political control comparable to that of both Russia and Japan in Manchuria.

Great Britain, until the First World War, dominated foreign commerce in China, was China's leading foreign creditor, held the major railway and mining concessions, provided the majority of the foreign personnel in the Maritime Customs Service and the Salt Administration, and accounted for half of the Protestant missionaries. In a sense, its sphere of influence extended throughout the territory of China, and it would have preferred to keep things as they were before the international rivalries of the last part of the nineteenth century.[11] Apart from its Hong Kong colony, the New Territories leased in 1898, and Weihaiwei which was never developed as a strategic naval base, the British sphere lacked the specific territorial underpinnings and thus the temptation to develop a local political role comparable to the Japanese in Manchuria. In spite of vague promises to Great Britain, the concession for the Peking-Hankow trunkline was granted to a Belgian syndicate (the majority shares of which were held by the French Compagnie des Chemins de fer Chinois). The

10 See John E. Schrecker, *Imperialism and Chinese nationalism: Germany in Shantung.*
11 See L. K. Young, *British policy in China, 1895-1902.*

British government reacted with strong support in Peking for the British and Chinese Corporation (formed by the Hongkong and Shanghai Banking Corporation and Jardine, Matheson and Company) which resulted in railway concessions in the Yangtze valley (the Tientsin-Chinkiang line from the Shantung border southwards, and the Shanghai-Nanking and Soochow-Hangchow-Ningpo lines), between Canton and Kowloon, and in Manchuria (the line from Shanhaikuan to Newchwang), all granted in 1898. Simultaneously the Peking Syndicate, another British group backed by the financiers Carl Meyer and Lord Rothschild, obtained concessions to develop mines in Shansi and Honan, and for the construction of an east-west railway (Taokow-Chinghua line) connecting its mines in Honan to the Peking-Hankow main line. Political as much as financial reasons – that is, the broad political goal of preventing the consolidation of rival spheres of influence – underlay this British concession hunting. But direct control in the concession areas was neither envisaged nor achieved.

The substantial reshaping of the international system by the First World War, together with profound changes in China's domestic political situation, greatly reduced the significance of the foreign spheres of influence carved out at the turn of the century – except, a major exception, for the Japanese in Manchuria. While the continued existence of some foreign railway and mining rights, in various formats, did not make Chinese nationalists happy, by 1920 these were relatively minor facets of the foreign presence in China.

Foreign residents

No more than a rough estimate of the number of foreign nationals in China is possible. How many tens of thousands of Koreans, for example, had moved across the Yalu River into Manchuria? The Maritime Customs Service annually compiled estimates of the number of foreign 'firms' and residents at the open ports, which probably covered the majority of the places where there were any substantial concentrations of aliens other than the Koreans in Manchuria. Dairen, for example, in the Kwantung leased territory, was included, as was Harbin, from 1910, but not Tsingtao in the Kiaochow leasehold while it was under German control. Table 30 shows the customs estimates for selected years from 1903 to 1921.[12] The figures in this table are defective in several respects.[13]

12 China, Inspectorate General of Customs, *Decennial reports . . ., 1902–1911*, 2.354–5; *Decennial Reports . . ., 1912–1921*, 2. 450–1.
13 Before 1910 the bulk of the Russian population in Manchuria, which was heavily con-

TABLE 30

Estimated number of foreign 'firms' and residents in China*

	British		American		French		German		Russian		Japanese		Total†	
	Firms	Res	Firms	Res	Firms	Res	Firms	Res	Firms	Res	Firms	Res	Firms	Res
1903	420	5,662	114	2,542	71	1,213	159	1,658	24	361	361	5,287	1,292	20,404
1906	492	9,256	112	3,447	94	2,189	199	1,939	20	273	739	15,548	1,837	38,597
1909	502	9,499	113	3,168	84	1,818	232	2,341	83	336	1,492	55,401	2,801	88,310
1911	606	10,256	111	3,470	112	1,925	258	2,758	313	51,221	1,283	78,306	2,863	153,522
1913	590	8,966	131	5,340	106	2,292	296	2,949	1,229	56,765	1,269	80,219	3,805	113,827
1916	644	9,099	187	5,580	116	2,374	281	3,792	1,422	55,235	1,858	104,275	4,724	185,613
1918	606	7,953	234	5,766	156	2,580	75	2,651	1,154	59,779	4,483	159,950	6,930	244,527
1921	703	9,298	412	8,230	222	2,453	92	1,255	1,613	68,250	6,141	144,434	9,511	240,769

* Defects of the table are discussed in the text.
† Including other nationalities not separately listed.

Fairly accurately reflected is the fact of the large influx of Japanese into Manchuria after 1905, although the totals are too low. The Japanese government reported, for example, that 121,956 of its nationals were resident in China in 1914. After the capture of Kiaochow in 1914 and the movement of Japanese into Shantung, the main centres of Japanese residence were Dairen, Tsingtao, Shanghai, Antung and Amoy in that order. Nearly 40 per cent of the combined British, American, French and German populations was located in Shanghai. (Note the relatively large increase in the total number of American residents and the decrease in the German figures after the First World War.)[14]

Apart from Japanese and Russian civilians in Manchuria, the size of some of the major categories of foreigners in China in the second decade of the twentieth century can be estimated as follows: foreign employees of the Chinese central and local governments, 2,000 (including 1,300 in the Customs Service); diplomatic personnel, 500 (led in terms of numbers by Japan, Great Britain and the United States); missionaries, 9,100 (6,600 Protestants and 2,500 Catholics); military detachments and police, 26,000 (including 17,000 Japanese troops and 2,000 police in Manchuria); and businessmen in the thousands, the number being impossible to estimate, but – except for the Japanese who were engaged in more menial occupations – constituting most of the foreign residents of Shanghai and of the other major treaty ports.[15]

The customs data on foreign firms are especially misleading. It appears that the definition used was a highly elastic one. For Manchuria even the smallest shop serving the Russian and Japanese populations was included; in China proper the Shanghai head office and the branches of the same firm in other ports were separately enumerated. Of the 643 foreign firms in Shanghai in 1911, 40 per cent (258) were British, 16 per cent (103) German, 9 per cent (59) American, and 7 per cent (47) Japanese,

centrated in Harbin, was not included; the sudden increase of Russian nationals from 1909 to 1911 is only apparent. (Also, not yet reflected is the insurge from Siberia after 1920 of stateless 'White Russian' refugees without extraterritorial rights who eventually numbered more than 200,000.) Similarly, the largely German foreign population of Tsingtao, which was 4,084 of whom 2,275 were military and officials in 1910, was excluded. Not all of the missionaries resident in the interior were covered in the customs estimates, and foreign troops stationed in China were completely omitted.

14 Excluding Dairen and Harbin in Manchuria, the cities in China proper with the largest number of foreign residents were, in descending order with estimates for 1911 in parentheses, Shanghai (30,292), Tientsin (6,334), Hankow (2,862), Amoy (1,931) and Canton (1,324). Japanese nationals in Shanghai (17,682) formed the largest foreign contingent, followed by British (5,270), Portuguese (3,000), Americans (1,350), Germans (1,100), French (705) and Russians (275).

15 Carroll Lunt, ed. *The China who's who (foreign)*, published in Shanghai – I have seen editions for 1922 and 1925 – provides brief biographies based on questionnaires returned by foreign residents.

with the remainder scattered. After Shanghai, the cities in China proper with the largest number of foreign establishments in 1911 were Tientsin (260), Amoy (240), Hankow (125) and Canton (102).

Extraterritoriality

What these foreign nationals and firms of the several treaty powers – and also missionaries stationed in the interior – enjoyed in common were the rights and privileges of the extraterritorial system. Beginning with the basic concession of consular jurisdiction in the 1842–4 treaties, by the accumulation of formal agreements forced upon China or by unilateral assertions of privilege, the entire 'foreign establishment' was essentially exempted from the jurisdiction of the Chinese polity. All disputes in which the plaintiffs were Chinese, whether private individuals or agencies of the Chinese government, and the defendants nationals of treaty powers were adjudicated in the courts of the powers concerned and according to the laws of those powers. This was true for both criminal and civil cases. Controversies between nationals of the same treaty power, or between nationals of different powers, were likewise removed from Chinese purview. Extraterritorial jurisdiction was exercised primarily by consular officials in the ports and by diplomatic officials in Peking upon appeal. Both Great Britain and the United States, in addition, maintained national courts which sat in Shanghai: the British Supreme Court in China established in 1904 and the United States Court for China established in 1906.

It was undoubtedly offensive to the Chinese sense of nationalism that foreign criminal offenders on the whole received less harsh treatment in the consular courts than they would have done in their own countries. A more serious violation of sovereignty, with far-reaching consequences for China's economy and society, however, was the inability of Chinese authorities to restrict, regulate, license or tax directly foreign individuals or firms of the treaty powers who as 'legal persons' were subject only to the laws of their own consular courts. Because a foreigner carried his extraterritorial rights with him wherever he went, on business or for pleasure, in effect this freedom from regulation operated not merely in the treaty ports alone but elsewhere in China too. Foreign banks enjoyed extraterritorial rights; their issuance of currency could not be controlled, nor did they accept any other regulation. Individuals and corporations were immune from direct Chinese taxation not by any specific treaty right, but because tax officials accepted the futility of attempting enforcement through the foreign courts which only applied the laws of their own particular countries. Missionaries and other foreigners freely established schools which similarly enjoyed extraterritorial rights with regard to siting, curricula, teachers' qualifications and so forth. Behind the screen of extraterritoriality, an assertive foreign press subjected China and the Chinese to its frequently carping and malicious criticism without encumbrance. It was, moreover, a common abuse that foreign citizens or subjects of non-treaty powers were by agreement protected by those powers granted treaty rights, and thus also were removed from the jurisdiction of the Chinese courts. For example, when in China citizens of Memel, Monaco, Persia and Romania enjoyed French consular jurisdiction. One American diplomat summarized it as follows: 'The basic original right of freedom from Chinese court jurisdiction had been extended and broadened to include freedom from Chinese administrative control except in matters explicitly provided for in the treaties.'[16]

In the mixed courts of the foreign settlements in Shanghai, Amoy and Hankow the arm of extraterritoriality extended even into controversies in which the parties concerned were formally subject to Chinese law and procedure. The Mixed Court of the Shanghai International Settlement was established by agreement with the Shanghai taotai in 1864 to try Chinese offenders within the Settlement, and to settle civil claims by foreigners against Chinese, and claims by foreigners or Chinese against foreigners without consular representation, all of which according to the various treaties were matters within Chinese jurisdiction. A Chinese magistrate was delegated by the taotai to preside over the court. In those cases in which their nationals were plaintiffs, the treaty powers had the right (set up in Article 17 of the Treaty of Tientsin, 1858) to be represented by foreign 'assessors' who, together with the Chinese judges, would 'examine into the merits of the case, and decide it equitably'. Even before the Mixed Court was taken over in 1911 by the authorities of the International Settlement, the power of the Chinese magistrate had been much reduced while the influence of the foreign assessors, except in purely Chinese civil cases, had in practice become predominant. A test case in 1883 ended the magistrate's right to arrest Chinese residents of the Settlement; in the famous *Su-pao* case of 1903 the Chinese right to extradite 'political' offenders from the Settlement was restricted; and from 1905 the Settlement municipal police rather than Chinese 'runners' executed the writs and warrants of the Mixed Court. In the course of the Revolution of 1911, the Shanghai Municipal Council assumed control of the appointment and payment of the Chinese magistrates of the Court; and the foreign assessors now also formally heard Chinese civil cases. This

16 John Carter Vincent, *The extraterritorial system in China: final phase*, 26.

supposedly temporary measure, having no legal justification whatever and based entirely upon alleged foreign dissatisfaction with Chinese judicial practices, was ended only with the 'rendition' of the Mixed Court to Chinese control in 1926.

The extraterritorial rights of German and Austro-Hungarian nationals were lost when China entered the First World War on the Allied side in August 1917. Similarly, the October Revolution brought to an end the formal privileges extended to the Russians, first, through the closing of the moribund Tsarist consulates and the Russian concessions in Hankow and Tientsin by the Chinese government in September 1920, and second, by the voluntary renunciation of extraterritoriality (although not of its control of the Chinese Eastern Railway) by the Soviet government. Without force – that is, in the absence of the military support or at least the acquiescence of the treaty powers collectively – the extraterritorial system could not be maintained even against a weak China.

Armed forces

Military force had brought the foreign establishment in China into existence, and its continuous deployment on Chinese soil and in riverine and coastal waters constituted symbolically, and sometimes in practice, the effective sanction behind the formally correct diplomatic measures that were constantly exerted to maintain the treaty rights of the foreigners and to assure the protection of their persons and property. The basis for the presence of gunboats on the rivers and in the treaty ports and of larger naval vessels along China's coast was a very liberal interpretation of Article 52 of the 1858 Treaty of Tientsin which stated that 'British ships of war coming for no hostile purpose, or being engaged in the pursuit of pirates, shall be at liberty to visit all ports within the dominions of the Empire of China. . .'. In 1896 British naval tonnage on the China station totalled 59,000; Russia nearly the same; France 28,000; Germany 23,000; and the United States 18,000 tons. 'H. B. M. Squadron', now up to a total of 70,000 tons, numbered 33 vessels in 1908, of which four were armoured cruisers, two second-class cruisers, and the remaining 27 smaller vessels including river gunboats.

The use of or at least the threat of the use of foreign gunboats was a common occurrence in the 'missionary incidents' that punctuated the last half of the nineteenth century. Chungking was reached by British gunboats for the first time in 1900. French naval vessels carried out pioneer surveys of the upper Yangtze in the early 1900s seeking to discover routes for the extension of trade from their railway into Yunnan.

The Germans were active around Poyang Lake, much to the anxiety of the British who considered the Yangtze valley as their special preserve. At the end of the nineteenth century the strategic naval bases – Tsingtao, Port Arthur, Kwangchou-wan, Weihaiwei – that were ceded as leaseholds brought foreign cruisers and battleships to Chinese waters on a regular basis.

Before 1903 the United States unlike Great Britain did not maintain a fleet of gunboats regulary stationed at key points on the Yangtze. Perhaps once a year the occasional vessel from the Asiatic fleet steamed its way up and down that water-way. The American Yangtze Patrol – formally the Second Division, Third Squadron, Pacific Fleet from 1908 to 1919 – numbered six to eight antiquated gunboats at the time of the First World War as compared to 15 modern gunboats operated by the British. Patrols in the early republic were largely routine and most of the excitement for the sailors was on shore. But the vessels were there 'to keep peace on the river' and to leave no question about the willingness of the treaty powers to protect their interests.

Foreign troops and police guards were more conspicuous in the early twentieth century than they had been in the last decades of the nineteenth. Municipal police forces grew up in the several settlements and concessions as well as international militias ('volunteer corps'). The Shanghai Volunteer Corps, being the largest, in 1913 numbered 59 officers (mainly British) and about 1,000 rank and file (half British, the rest scattered among the companies of 15 nationalities). The leaseholds seized from China in 1898 and then the Boxer Protocol imposed by the powers in 1901 brought into being a permanent and more sizeable military presence.

By the terms of the protocol the powers were permitted to maintain armed detachments in Peking ('legation guards'), to occupy key points along the railway from Peking to the sea, and to station troops in Tientsin from which city Chinese troops were to be excluded.[17]

The British and French garrisons at Weihaiwei and Kwangchou-wan were minuscule, but German military and naval detachments in Tsingtao totalled 2,300. Four battalions of Japanese troops, 2,100 officers and men,

17 In 1913, the Peking Legation Guards totalled 2,075 (370 British, 329 American, 307 Japanese, 301 Russian, 288 French, 199 Italian, 151 German, 64 Austrian, 35 Dutch, and 31 Belgian). By 1922 the number had been reduced to 997, the German, Austrian and Russian contingents having disappeared as a consequence of the loss of extraterritorial rights by these powers, and the rest (except for the Americans who totalled 354) having decreased their forces somewhat. Foreign troops in Tientsin in 1913 numbered 6,219 (2,218 British, 1,021 French, 975 American, 883 Japanese, 808 Russian, 282 German, 21 Austrian and 11 Italian). The 1922 total was 2,720 (982 French, 762 Japanese, 504 American and 472 British). Elsewhere in North China, principally along the railway from Peking to Shanhaikuan adjacent to the foreign-run coal mines around T'ang-shan, there were 1,253 foreign troops stationed in 1913, and 602 in 1922.

replaced the Germans in Shantung in 1914, where they were stationed along the Tsingtao-Tsinanfu railway until 1922. They were supported by a substantial force of *gendarmerie*. The fighting at Hankow in 1911 led to the dispatch of British, German, Russian and Japanese troops to that port to protect their respective citizens. All but the Japanese were withdrawn in 1912; a Japanese batallion of 500 men together with detachments of special troops remained in Hankow until 1922. In South Manchuria, with headquarters in Liaoyang in the leased territory, Japan normally stationed a full infantry division with supporting cavalry and artillery. Some 16 batallions of railway guards totalling 10,000 Russian and Japanese troops were in place along the Chinese Eastern Railway and in the South Manchurian Railway zones in 1920. The presence of these railway guards was justified by provisions in the 1905 Portsmouth Peace Treaty between Japan and Russia, even though the Chinese asserted they had not assented to it in their agreement with Japan of December 1905 recognizing the transfer of Liaotung and the South Manchurian Railway from Russia to Japan. Japanese police in Manchuria in 1920 numbered 811 in the leased territory and 1,052 more in the South Manchurian and Antung-Mukden railway zones.[18]

Like the gunboats on the Yangtze, the total number of these foreign troops and police was perhaps not a particularly formidable military force. Even where their presence had some legal basis in China's forced consent to an international agreement such as the Boxer Protocol, they nevertheless were blatant infringements of China's sovereignty. This was even more unmistakable in the case of the railway zones in Manchuria and Shantung which the Japanese occupied despite repeated Chinese protests. More important than the formal legal basis of this foreign military occupation, which perhaps was arguable, was the understanding of what the stationing of foreign troops on Chinese soil implied – the ability and willingness of the extraterritorial powers to employ force if necessary in support of what they unilaterally considered to be their acquired rights.

DIPLOMATS

The Diplomatic Body in Peking met in the house of the doyen. . . . When we met in the British legation, in warm weather, the windows would be open on to a small inner courtyard, where the lilac blossomed in the spring. The legation parrot used to sit out there and join in our discussions (sometimes very aptly) with a hoarse guffaw, or a subdued chuckle, or a sudden screech. He was a talk-

18 *The China year book, 1919–20*, 333; *The China year book, 1923*, 603–4; *Conference on the limitation of armament, Washington, November 12, 1921–February 6, 1922*, 988–98.

ing parrot, but he only spoke Chinese, so that his remarks were unintelligible to most of the assembled diplomats.[19]

The diplomatic body

In the first years of the republic the most conspicuous component of the foreign establishment in China, the Diplomatic Body in Peking, consisted of envoys extraordinary and ministers plenipotentiary from 15 countries.[20] Peru, Norway (separated from Sweden in 1905) and Mexico also had treaty relations with China, making 18 nations in all who participated in the benefits of the 'most-favoured-nation' clause, but in 1913 these last-mentioned three did not have representatives resident in Peking. Within the Diplomatic Body, the 11 signatories to the Boxer Protocol of 1901 – Germany, Austria-Hungary, Belgium, Spain, the United States, France, Great Britain, Italy, Japan, Netherlands and Russia – formed a close-knit circle, and even more select were the countries that exerted the real influence in China as in the world: Great Britain, Japan, Russia, the United States, Germany and France.

Signor Varè, the Italian minister during the First World War, was largely correct in his observation upon the Chinese-speaking abilities of his colleagues. With the exception of Sir John Newell Jordan, G.C.I.E., K.C.B., K.C.M.G., who had first come to China as a student interpreter in 1876 and had served long and well in the British consular service in China and as Minister to Korea before his appointment in 1906 to Peking, the foreign ministers were typically professional 'diplomats' who moved from posting to posting (for example, as of 1913, Baron E. de Cartier de Marchienne of Belgium, Count P. Ahlefeldt-Laurvig of Denmark, Count Carlo Sforza of Italy, or M. Alexandre Conty of France). Of Jordan, who continued as minister until 1920, one of his Peking colleagues wrote:

'To him, China was not one post among many. It represented the beginning and the end of his career . . . it seemed to me that his world consisted of the British Empire and China, with Russia and Japan looming in the background (sometimes inconveniently near) and a lot of other powers fussing round and interfering in matters which did not really concern them and which they imperfectly understood.'[21]

Sir Ernest Mason Satow, Jordan's predecessor in Peking from 1900 to 1906, while more of a diplomatic professional than Sir John (he was the

19 Daniele Varè, *Laughing diplomat*, 128.
20 In the order in which treaty relations had been established: Great Britain, the United States, France, Belgium, Sweden, Russia, Germany, Portugal, Denmark, Netherlands, Spain, Italy, Austria-Hungary, Brazil and Japan.
21 Varè, *Laughing diplomat,* 120.

author of the much acclaimed *A Guide to Diplomatic Practice*, 1917 and
later editions), also began his career as a student interpreter, and reputedly
spoke some Chinese as well as excellent Japanese. Satow had spent long
years in the consular service in Japan, Siam, Peru and Morocco before
being appointed minister to Tokyo in 1895. Sir Ernest was described by
his private secretary as '. . . an austere man. He was very hard on his
staff and exacted a tremendous amount of work from them, but, as he
used to say, he had been brought up in a hard school – the school of Sir
Harry Parkes. . . . I learnt from Sir Ernest to follow Lord Elgin's maxim
for dealing with Chinese officials. Never make a demand which is not
absolutely just; when you make a just demand see that you get it.'[22]

The Japanese ministers were mostly professional diplomats (graduates
of the Law Faculty of Tokyo Imperial University) who had had considerable prior experience in consular posts in China and probably therefore
had some knowledge of the Chinese language.[23] The Japanese, together
with the British, as their diplomatic documents reveal, in these years had
the closest knowledge of any of the foreign powers concerning Chinese
political and economic affairs.

Former Republican congressman Edwin Hurd Conger, the American
minister 1898–1905, reached that office through his friendship with
President McKinley. However, his successor from 1905 to 1909, William
Woodville Rockhill, was a professional diplomat who in the 1880s had
been posted to Peking and Seoul. He was also a considerable linguist and
scholar (of Tibetan Buddhism, Central Asia and China's pre-modern
relations with the Western world, Korea and South-East Asia). William
James Calhoun, in Peking from 1909 to 1913, was President Taft's choice.
He had long been active in the Republican party in Illinois and had had
some experience as a special envoy for Presidents McKinley and Roosevelt
in Cuba and Venezuela. Paul Samuel Reinsch, minister during 1913 to

---

22 Sir Meyrick Hewlitt, *Forty years in China*, 35.
23 Uchida Yasuya, minister 1901–6, had been *chargé* in 1896 while first secretary of the legation.
   He later filled other major ambassadorial posts, and in 1911, 1918–23, and 1932 served as
   foreign minister, on the last occasion concurrently with the presidency of the South Manchurian Railway Company. His successor during 1906–8, and again in 1916–18, was Hayashi
   Gonsuke, educated in England as well as Tokyo, who at other times was ambassador to
   Great Britain and Russia, and briefly foreign minister. Ijuin Hikokichi, minister 1908–13,
   first came to China in 1893 as consul at Chefoo. During 1901–7 he was consul-general at
   Tientsin. He was later governor of the Kwantung leased territory, and foreign minister
   briefly in 1923. Yamaza Enjirō had been secretary of the Japanese legation in Seoul prior to
   his brief tenure as minister in Peking in 1913–14. Hikoi Eki, who transmitted Japan's
   Twenty-one Demands in 1915, had served in Korea during 1894–9, then in Peking as
   first secretary and *chargé* in 1900–2, before his appointment as minister in 1914. After several
   tours in Europe, he returned to China as Japan's representative at the 1925 Tariff Conference. Long service in Tientsin, Peking, and elsewhere as consul and *chargé* (in 1914, 1915,
   1916), culminated in the appointment of Obata Yūkichi as minister during the years
   1918–23.

1919, was again a political appointee, this time of President Wilson who was impressed by Reinsch's scholarly writings as professor of political science at the University of Wisconsin. Reinsch's memoirs, *An American diplomat in China* (1922) reveal a considerable if ineffectual sympathy with Chinese aspirations for greater international equality. Shortly after Shantung was awarded to Japan by the Paris Peace Conference, Reinsch resigned his post.

Much of the day-to-day contact with the Chinese Foreign Ministry was handled by the 'Chinese secretaries' of the principal legations, who in consequence frequently influenced the outlook of their mission chiefs. Sidney Barton, for example, a dominant figure in the British legation as its Chinese secretary from 1911 to 1922, had married the eldest daughter of a director of Jardine, Matheson and Company. He was a vigorous and at times insensitive defender of British interests, inclined to forceful measures which endeared him to the British community in China but made him disliked by the Chinese with whom he had to deal. From 1922 to 1929 he was consul-general at Shanghai. The United States legation selected its Chinese secretaries from American missionaries in China.[24]

The Legation Quarter

The Legation Quarter in Peking where the ministers and their staffs resided was an anomaly in international law. It was established by Article 7 of the Boxer Protocol of 1901 which stipulated: 'The Chinese Govern-

---

24 Edward T. Williams, Chinese secretary 1901–8, had served under the Foreign Christian Missionary Society from 1887 until 1896 when he left the ministry to accept an appointment as translator at the American consulate-general in Shanghai. He was first secretary of the American legation in Peking 1911–13, and served several months as *chargé*, between the departure of Calhoun and the arrival of Reinsch – a period which included the American recognition of the Republic of China and the 'Second Revolution'. During 1914–18 he was chief of the Far Eastern Division of the Department of State. Williams in 1918 became Agassiz Professor of Oriental Languages and Literature at the University of California at Berkeley. Succeeding Williams was Charles D. Tenney who had come to China in 1882 under the auspices of the American Board of Commissioners for Foreign Missions. Tenney had retired from missionary work in 1886 and spent the next two decades in educational activities in Tientsin blessed by the successive governors-general Li Hung-chang and Yuan Shih-k'ai. He served as principal of the Anglo-Chinese School from 1886 to 1895, and from 1895 to 1906 was president of the newly established government university at Tientsin (after 1900 known as Peiyang University). From 1902 to 1906 he was also superintendent of high and middle schools in Chihli. Except for a brief interval Tenney held the post of Chinese secretary to the American legation from 1908 until 1919, and served as *chargé* with the rank of first secretary in 1919–20. Since he was widely acquainted with Chinese officialdom, including President Yuan Shih-k'ai, Tenney's role in the legation was influential. Willys R. Peck, assistant Chinese secretary 1908–13, Chinese secretary 1913–14 and 1919–26, had been born in Tientsin to missionary parents. He was appointed a student interpreter in 1906 after graduation from the University of California, and between 1914 and 1919 held consular posts at Tsingtao, Hankow and Tientsin. Peck remained a prominent figure in the conduct of American relations with China until his retirement in 1945, serving as counselor of embassy during 1935–40.

ment has agreed that the quarter occupied by the legations shall be considered as one specially reserved for their use and placed under their exclusive control, in which Chinese shall not have the right to reside and which may be made defensible. . . .' The new Legation Quarter was some 10 times larger than it had been before 1900.[25] It was located just inside the massive south wall of the Tartar City, protected by a newly fortified perimeter wall (and permanent military guards), and bounded on the north and east by a 'glacis' – an open space intended for military protection and used for polo, football, exercising ponies and drilling legation guards, which in fact was the area formerly occupied by the imperial Hanlin Academy which had been razed to the ground during the Boxer uprising. The quarter extended most of the way between the central or 'front gate' (Ch'ien-men) in the south wall of the main, northern city to the Hatamen (or Ch'ung-wen men) on the east. (Sir Ernest Satow, among others, rebuked his colleagues in 1904 for their excessive appetites.)

In practice the Diplomatic Body extended its 'rights' considerably beyond the provisions of Article 7. Parts of the glacis were leased to hotels, bars frequented by legation soldiers, and a licensed brothel. Contrary to the theory that the glacis was the joint property of them all, building permits were issued by individual powers – at a consideration. Within the Legation Quarter itself were to be found commercial enterprises, shops, educational institutions and a large number of non-diplomatic personnel – although the Chinese had never intended to open Peking as another centre for foreign residence and trade. Among others, in the quarter or its immediate neighbourhood were the Hôtel du Nord, the Hôtel de Pékin, the Grand Hôtel des Wagon-Lits (often swarming with seekers after loan, railway and mining contracts); the Hongkong and Shanghai Bank, the Russo-Chinese Bank, the Deutsch-Asiatische Bank and the Yokohama Specie Bank; several large foreign stores; a soldiers' Y.M.C.A.; two Methodist episcopal hospitals; a Catholic church for the legation guards; the Methodist Mission church (with accommodation for 1,500 people), a Methodist girls' school, and 'Peking University' (also Methodist); the London Mission's Lockhart Medical College; the church and school of the American Board of Commissioners for Foreign Missions; and the Mission for the Blind. While *de jure* the only Chinese permitted in the quarter were the servants and employees of the legations in their special

25 H. B. Morse wrote, 'The Legation Quarter may be considered as the provision of a defensible fortress in the heart of the capital of a hostile Power – for which purpose it was much too large; or as the happy grasping of the opportunity to provide spacious quarters for the diplomatic representatives of the Powers, in park-like surroundings, free from the old-time insanitary conditions, and at the cost of China – and in that case it was not justified.' *The international relations of the Chinese empire*, 3. 355.

uniforms, in fact at times large numbers of Chinese lived in the Legation Quarter, frequently at the Wagon-Lits Hotel which was noted as a place of refuge for those ousted from the Peking government after 1911. The 'right of asylum' was claimed and enforced by the Diplomatic Body time and again: General Chang Hsun, for example, hid in the Netherlands legation after the collapse of his short-lived coup in 1917.

Joint administration of the Legation Quarter was achieved only in 1914, replacing the three distinct sections (western, British and eastern) which prior to that time each had its own administration and regulations. An Administrative Commission composed of three representatives of the legations of the Boxer Protocol powers and two representatives of the residents of the quarter oversaw the new general police regulations and road regulations. A land tax paid by the legations and private residents supported this minimal administration.

For the most part the Peking diplomats lived a life apart from the Chinese. This situation started to change in the last decade of the Ch'ing dynasty and even more so when the republic came into being. Nevertheless, the following observation by Charles Denby, the American minister from 1885 to 1898, still held more than a grain of truth:

Arriving at Peking, the first duty of the diplomatic stranger is to call on the Tsung-li-Yamen, foreign office, to pay his respects and be recognized in his official capacity.... The call on the Yamen is the only one the stranger is required to make.... The absence of the necessity of meeting each other socially was a great relief both to the Chinese and to the foreigners. Except on rare occasions, social intercourse would have been exceedingly tedious for both parties.[26]

During the halcyon days of the post-Boxer Manchu reforms, younger foreign-educated officials of the Foreign Ministry and the Ministry of Communications were known to pass evenings playing poker with staff members of the legations. But life in the Peking foreign community, diplomatic and private, was characteristically one of self-imposed isolation, of which the most dedicated exponents were probably the British who 'allayed their nostalgia with dinners and dancing, gossip and golf, happily ignorant of the customs or language or feelings of the people they lived among.'[27] The Italian minister, thinking back to 1918, described 'a sort of diplomatic mountain fastness. For the women and children, this was a good thing, if only from the point of view of hygiene. But

26 Charles Denby, *China and her people*, 1. 34–5.
27 Cyril Pearl, *Morrison of China*, 86, summarizing G. E. Morrison's impressions as noted in his unpublished diaries.

most of the diplomats were isolated from and out of sympathy with the
country they lived in.'[28]

However self-contained, life in Peking was hardly one of physical
deprivation for the diplomatic community. The British legation compound in 1900

> was an area covering just over three acres . . . formerly the residence of Duke
> Liang and was rented by Her Majesty's Government. The Main Building was
> the Minister's residence, a beautiful Chinese building with an imposing en-
> trance by a raised pathway passing under two stately porticos, known in Chinese
> as *t'ing'rh*. All these were covered with the official green tiles, permitted only
> to officials of high rank, yellow being reserved for the Imperial Palace. The
> Secretaries were housed in bungalows, with the exception of the First Secre-
> tary who had a foreign-style two-storeyed house. The students and chancery
> assistants were located in three sets of buildings. . . . There was also the chapel,
> a theatre and a bowling alley.[29]

The residence of the American minister was built in 'stately colonial
renaissance style . . . of imported American materials, . . . there is a
veritable hamlet of additional houses occupied by secretaries, attaches,
consular students, and the clerical staff. It is a picturesque Chinese village,
with an antique temple and many separate houses, each with its garden
enclosed within high walls.'[30]

The first secretary of the Italian legation in 1913 noted that he had
10 household servants, 'beginning with the number-one boy and ending
with the number-three coolie', and including 'the cook and the *marmiton*,
and two amahs, known respectively as the "wash-and-baby amah" and
the "sew-sew amah".' In addition, the legation servants included 'four
ma-fus, that is to say the old stableman and his three sons (there is also a
grandson who looks after the baby's donkey, but *I* pay him). Then there
is the washerman and his help; the head gardener, four garden coolies,
and the *k'ai-men-ti*, or gate porter, and the *t'ing-ch'ai*, or letter carrier.'[31]

There were few automobiles in Peking before the 1920s nor any motor
roads to speak of. The foreign community was largely dependent upon

28 Varè *Laughing diplomat*, 88.
29 Hewlitt, *Forty years in China*, 4. Even the politically unimportant Italian legation, besides
   the minister's residence and that of the first secretary, included 'a house each for the first
   and second "Chinese secretaries" (or interpreters) and for the legation chaplain. A chapel
   (as big as most churches) with a ceiling that had been sent out from Italy; stables for eight-
   een horses, with exercise ground and a large stable yard; a washhouse; a water tower;
   hothouses and two little buildings for the Chinese servants, the whole enclosed in a large
   shady garden. Besides all this, and connected with the legation compound, were barracks
   for the naval guard, with hospital, kitchens, houses for officers and petty officers; mess-
   rooms, offices, prison and munitions depot. Also a building for the apparatus to distil
   water, and more stables.' Varè, *Laughing diplomat*, 88.
30 Paul S. Reinsch, *An American diplomat in China*, 20.
31 Varè, *Laughing diplomat*, 92.

its ponies and carriages for trips to the race-course (some four miles west of Peking, burnt by the Boxers but rebuilt on a much grander scale), or to picnics at the Summer Palace, or to the Western Hills. Walking was also popular: the section of the south wall of the Tartar City between the Ch'ien-men and Ch'ung-wen men which had been handed over to the legations under the terms of the Boxer Protocol was extensively used by foreigners as a promenade. It was patrolled by legation troops and no Chinese were permitted to walk on it. In the summer months everyone, with the exception of the Maritime Customs officials, sought refuge from the heat of Peking in the Western Hills, 12 miles west of the capital, especially at Pa-ta-ch'u, a place noted for its temples which the foreigners (and some Chinese dignitaries) rented for the summer. The foreigner referred to the eight peaks with his own historical appellations: there was a 'Mount Bruce' and a 'Mount Burlingame'. The more formal etiquette of the endless rounds of dinners, balls and theatricals which filled the rest of the year was relaxed somewhat – although Sir John Jordan was known to dress for dinner even when he dined alone in a rented Chinese temple on a hot summer evening – and excursions to the surrounding villages brought these European visitors as near as most ever came to contact with the daily life of the Chinese populace.

There was of course work as well as play. Between October 1900 and May 1920, the Diplomatic Body held 219 formal meetings. Collectively, the diplomats considered *ad infinitum* stamp duties, currency circulation, monetary crises, and other financial matters; commerce, navigation and treaty ports; affairs of the concessions and settlements; the Shanghai Mixed Court; rights and privileges of diplomatic and consular staffs; the revolution of 1911 and its aftermath; and – conspicuously – the management of the Legation Quarter itself.

Diplomatic pressure

Under the regime of extraterritoriality and the 'unequal treaties', the Diplomatic Body and its consular subordinates in the treaty ports may be thought of, in effect, as integral parts of the government of China with exclusive civil and criminal jurisdiction over foreign nationals in China. The ministers were aggressively alert against all real or imagined violations of the treaties – not only to the letter but to the spirit as well, which in the accumulated precedents of the decades following the Treaty of Nanking had come to be one of loose and generous interpretation of the rights of the treaty powers. There was little reluctance about the application of sufficient pressure at the Foreign Ministry and elsewhere whenever the status of foreigners and their interests might be affected by some act of the Chinese government. Cases of direct damage were pursued sedulously and modest compensation infrequently accepted. Officials 'responsible' for these 'outrages' were denounced freely. Attempts were made to obtain the suppression of publications allegedly abusive to foreigners with little more hesitation than requests for the removal of obstructions to traffic on the Yangtze or Pearl Rivers. And much time and effort were spent in attacking the granting by the central or provincial governments, or the possibility thereof, of exclusive concessions or contracts to the representatives of some power other than one's own. 'In European countries', former American minister Denby wrote in 1906, 'his passport would be given him if he attempted to do a tithe of these things.'[32] Minister Denby also remarked that the minister to China (because of the pressure of opinion at home as expressed in the 'great newspapers') 'is bound to assume that in all cases his countrymen are in the right and the Chinese are in the wrong. It is considered a very strong proof of mental weakness, or moral obliquity, if the minister dares to look into the right or the wrong of any question which is alleged to involve the substantial rights of his countrymen.'[33]

However, the diplomatic representatives of the great powers probably were a good deal less effective than they thought they were in influencing the actions of Chinese governments central and local. There were too many ways in which late-Ch'ing and then republican officials could procrastinate, dissemble, or *in extremis* openly resist the importunities of a strong Western nation. This resistance was fed by the steady penetration of nationalist consciousness and aspirations for unconditional sovereignty first into the late-Ch'ing bureaucracy and then more explicitly among their republican successors. The several creditors in the case of the Reorganization Loan of 1913 might have believed that, by including a foreign director of the Bureau of National Loans into the disbursement process, they would be in a position to influence how President Yuan Shih-k'ai allocated the proceeds. Indeed, the final loan agreement had been delayed while the powers vied to have their nationals appointed as advisers and auditors. In practice, the foreign auditors and accountants learned only what Yuan found convenient.

The attitude reflected in the pursuance of certain claims often resting upon little more of than vague Chinese pronouncements, which in themselves were frequently made in response to foreign pressure, was fundamentally more harmful to Chinese sovereignty than were any practical

32 Denby, *China and her people*, 1. 91.   33 *Ibid.*, 1. 99.

gains that might accrue to the lucky concessionaires. One instructive example is the insistence of the United States that she participate in the projected Hukuang railway loan in 1909. Chang Chih-tung had just about wrapped up a loan agreement with German, British and French banking groups in June 1909 when (at the instigation of J. P. Morgan and Company, Kuhn, Loeb and Company, the First National Bank of New York and the National City Bank of New York) a personal telegram arrived from President Taft to Prince Ch'un, the regent, demanding a piece of the loan for the American banking group. The American case rested upon alleged promises by the Chinese government in 1903 and 1904 to Edwin Conger, the American minister, that if Chinese capital were unable to finance the railway from Hankow to Szechwan (now part of the proposed Hukuang system), United States and British capital would be given the first opportunity to bid for any foreign loan. On this basis, the Chinese were pressed relentlessly, and strong representations were made to Paris and London. But the pledges to Conger, which the Department of State described as 'solemn obligations', did not exist. In fact, in both 1903 and 1904 the Chinese Foreign Ministry had bluntly rejected requests by Conger on behalf of American firms. Its reply of 1903, for example, concluded with this statement: 'In short, when companies of various nationalities apply to China for railway concessions, it must always remain with China to decide the matter. It is not possible to regard an application not granted as conferring any rights or as being proof that thereafter application must first be made to the persons concerned.' Even the texts of the 1903 exchanges were not available in Washington. The Department of State asked Peking in July 1909 to transmit them forthwith to bolster negotiations in London. But, given their content, when they arrived, the texts were not shown to the British.[34]

China, in the end, acceded to the Taft telegram because of pressure, not because of the alleged 'pledges'. And the European banking group ultimately admitted the Americans to the loan consortium because they feared that it might be difficult to enforce their own quite shadowy loan guarantees in China if they denied similar American claims. No loan for the Hukuang railway system was ever made, but in the pursuit of economic advantage, however insubstantial, China was treated as an object and not as an equal partner in commerce.

One significant source of diplomatic arrogance was the language barrier. The principal foreign representatives in Peking seldom knew Chinese, nor did the leading foreign merchants in the treaty ports, with

34 John A. Moore, Jr. 'The Chinese consortiums and American-China policy, 1909–1917' (Claremont Graduate School, Ph.D. dissertation, 1972), 18–31.

honourable exceptions. At the consular level the language situation was somewhat better. In 1913 Great Britain maintained consulates at 28 ports as well as Peking. Eight of these were consulates-general with their more extensive staffs (Canton, Chengtu, Hankow, Kashgar, Mukden, Shanghai, Tientsin and Yunnan-fu). Seven student interpreters were attached to the Peking legation in that year. The British consular service, in contrast to the American before well into the twentieth century, was a highly professional body, recruited by competitive examination for those generally destined to a lifetime career in China. Upon appointment as a student interpreter, the prospective consul embarked upon two years of intensive study of the Chinese language in Peking, at the end of which the results of a language examination were important in determining his future placement within the service.

The United States, which in 1913 staffed five consulates-general (Canton, Hankow, Mukden, Shanghai and Tientsin) and nine consulates, appointed its first student interpreter only in 1902. This was Julean Arnold, later commercial attaché in Peking and the author of *China: a commercial and industrial handbook* (1926). In 1913 there were nine American student interpreters attached to the Peking legation, and among the consuls a number were clearly 'China specialists' including Nelson T. Johnson at Changsha and Clarence E. Gauss at Shanghai each of whom was later to serve as ambassador to China. This was clearly a change from the short-term political appointments and the system of consular agents employed on a fee basis typical of the era before the First World War.

The pre-1917 Russian consular service had an expertise on a par with that of the British, drawing on the skills of the Faculty of Oriental Languages at the University of St Petersburg and ultimately on the Russian ecclesiastical mission, which had enjoyed language training facilities in Peking since the eighteenth century. In 1913 eight consulates-general were maintained (Canton, Harbin, Kashgar, Mukden, Newchwang, Shanghai, Tientsin and Peking) and 11 consulates (of which nine were in Manchuria or Mongolia). Four student interpreters were attached to the legation in that year.[35]

35 The Sinological competence of many of the Russian consuls may be illustrated by the examples of the consul-general at Tientsin, Peter H. Tiedmann (P- G- Tideman), a graduate in 1894 of the St Petersburg Oriental Faculty and a student interpreter during 1896–9 before assuming consular posts; and A- T- Beltchenko, consul at Hankow and also a St Petersburg Oriental Faculty graduate who had first arrived in China in 1899. Beltchenko was the co-translator into English in 1912 of *Sovremennaia politicheskaia organizatziia Kitaia*, first published in Peking in 1910 by H. S. Brunnert (I- S- Brunnert), the Russian legation's assistant Chinese secretary, and V. V. Hagelstrom (V- V- Gagel'strom), secretary to the Shanghai consulate-general. The English version, revised and enlarged by N- Th- Kolessoff, consul-general and Chinese secretary at the Russian Peking legation, is that indispensable handbook of all later scholars of modern Chinese history, *Present day political organization of China*.

Japan in 1913 maintained eight consulates-general (Canton, Chientao, Hankow, Harbin, Mukden, Shanghai, Tientsin, and Hong Kong) and 22 consulates 10 of which were in Manchuria. Within the Japanese consular service, appointments to posts in China tended to be regarded as less desirable than service in European or American missions. Before the First World War, the language competence of Japanese consular officers who allegedly saw their Chinese service as stepping-stones to more attractive assignments elsewhere was often criticized in the Diet. On the whole, however, the Japanese consular contingent was highly professional (recruited through the higher civil service examination primarily from graduates of the prestigious Tokyo and Kyoto universities) and knowledgeable about the China in which it served.

For the rest, Germany in 1913 staffed one consulate-general and 16 consulates; France, three consulates-general and 10 consulates; Austria-Hungary, three in all; Belgium, six; Italy, seven; Mexico, four; Netherlands, nine; Portugal, seven; and Spain, seven, but usually in the charge of third-country nationals. Canton, Shanghai, Hankow and Tientsin were almost without exception consular posts for all the treaty powers, with the remainder of their consular offices distributed to reflect the 'spheres of influence' which each claimed, for example, Japan and Russia in Manchuria as already noted, Great Britain heavily represented in cities along the Yangtze River, and France in South-west China.

MISSIONARIES

After the turning point of 1900 when Christian missions were so widely attacked in North China and their attackers suppressed by a multi-power foreign invasion, the missionary movement saw itself entering a new era of opportunity. The right 'to rent and purchase land in all the provinces', secured by a ruse in the Sino-French Treaty of Tientsin of 1860, could be used increasingly to establish their mission stations far from the treaty ports to which other foreigners were restricted.[36]

The missionary establishment

In the early republic the missionaries were the largest single group among the European foreigners temporarily resident in China who were identified by a common purpose. Protected by general and specific extraterritorial provisions of the treaties, they reached into nearly every corner of the country. As of 1919 all but 106 out of 1,704 counties or hsien in China

36 See Paul A. Cohen, 'Christian missions and their impact to 1900', *CHOC*, vol. 10.

proper and Manchuria reported some Protestant missionary activity. The missionaries commonly learned Chinese and of necessity were in relatively close daily contact with those to whom their evangelical message was addressed. Their broadest goals stressed even-handedly individual salvation through conversion to Christ and the firm organization of a Chinese Christian church. By the early 1920s many (Protestants at least) had begun to see that the manifold activities of the foreign missionaries had failed to create a strong indigenous church, in fact that the very extent of the foreign presence might be a major obstacle to the achievement. The executive secretary of the interdenominational China Continuation Committee, E. C. Lobenstine, wrote in that Committee's magistral survey of Protestant activity in China:

The coming period is expected to be one of transition, during which the burden of the work and its control will increasingly shift from the foreigner to the Chinese. The rising tide of national consciousness within Christian circles is leading to a profound dissatisfaction with certain aspects of the present situation on the part of many of the ablest and most consecrated Chinese Christians. They have a very intense and rightful desire that Christianity shall be freed from the incubus of being regarded as a 'foreign religion' and that the denominational divisions of the West be not perpetuated permanently in China. They regard the predominance of foreign influence in the Church as one of the chief hindrances to a more rapid spread of Christianity in China.[37]

Only to a very limited extent was the task set by Dr Lobenstine accomplished before the suppression of the Christian church in China after 1949. Missionaries and communicants increased in number, more Chinese were recruited into the church leadership, the quality of educational and medical services was improved. But for the most part the Christian missionary component of the foreign establishment in China was not much different in character in the 25 years after 1922 from what it was in the first two decades of the twentieth century.

The flourishing of the missionary 'occupation' of China in the first quarter of the twentieth century, it may be said, was a brief interlude bounded at one end by the Boxer uprising and the other by the burgeoning of a virulent nationalism hostile to Christianity as an emanation of foreign imperialism. In the immediate post-Boxer years Protestant Christianity in China prospered because after more than a half-century of mediocre results it forged a temporary link with the domestic forces of reform which had a use for it. To the development of modern education in the last Ch'ing decade the expanding missionary schools contributed much at a

37 China Continuation Committee, *The Christian occupation of China: a general survey of the numerical strength and geographical distribution of the Christian forces in China made by the Special Committee on Survey and Occupation, China Continuation Committee, 1918–1921*, Introduction, p. 3.

time when indigenous facilities and teachers were in short supply; the same was true in the first decade of the republic, and not only in primary education. Modern Western medicine in China was to an important degree a consequence of missionary demonstration and instruction. Young China of the 1910s and 1920s was frequently the product of missionary schools – the new urban patriots and reformers, the leaders in such new professions as scientific agriculture, journalism and sociology. But the prosperity of the Protestant missionary enterprise depended on an ambiguous linkage with authority. It eventually became identified with the Kuomintang regime, since both were essentially urban-based and variations on the theme of bourgeois-style 'modernization'. Even conservative nationalism, as Lobenstine acknowledged, could accept for the long run only a truly indigenous church. And by being urban and non-political, in practice stressing the salvation of the individual within the existing political system, Christianity became increasingly distant from the growing rumblings of social revolution in the countryside which would in 1949 bring to an end the brief domination of China's revolution by the semi-Westernized urban elite to whom the missionary effort was wedded.

The period 1900–20 saw a substantial growth in all aspects of the 'Christian occupation of China', the unfortunate but telling phrase used in 1922.[38] Table 31 summarizes the data for the Protestant Missions.

Roman Catholic missions in China also expanded rapidly in the post-Boxer years. In 1901, 1,075 foreign and 500 Chinese priests served a Catholic community estimated at 721,000 communicants. By 1920 there were 1,500–2,000 European priests, approximately 1,000 Chinese priests, 1,000 foreign nuns, 1,900 Chinese nuns, a claimed 2,000,000 communicants, 13,000 Chinese catechists and teachers, and 180,000 students enrolled in Catholic schools. Among the 13 or more Catholic missionary societies, those of French origin (Lazarists, or Missions Etrangères, for example) were especially prominent, reflecting the French claim to a protectorate over the Catholic church in China based on the toleration clauses of the treaties. More than half of the foreign priests in China on the eve of the First World War were French nationals. The Catholic effort was formally organized into 51 'vicariats et préfectures apostoliques', which divided among themselves all of the provinces of China. Approximately 1,500 locations were staffed by foreign or Chinese priests, with the largest numbers of Catholics located in Chihli, Kiangsu, Szechwan and Shantung. While they were also present in the larger cities where

38 Most of the numerical data below are from the volume cited in the previous note. Information about the Roman Catholic 'occupation' is from Kenneth Scott Latourette, *A history of Christian missions in China.*

TABLE 31

Growth of the Protestant church in China

	1889	1906	1919
Foreign missionaries	1,296	3,833	6,636
Ordained Chinese	211	345	1,065
Total Chinese workers	1,657	9,961	24,732
Communicants claimed	37,287	178,251	345,853
Students enrolled in missionary schools	16,836	57,683	212,819

the Protestants were concentrated, the Catholics emphasized work in the more rural areas, sought the conversion of entire families or villages, attempted to build integrated local Catholic communities, and tended to restrict their educational efforts to the children of converts only. Prior to the 1920s the Catholic missions did not undergo a major expansion of educational and medical activities comparable to the post-Boxer Protestant effort. Any desire to have a broader impact on Chinese society was decidedly secondary to the saving of souls. Anti-Christian movements in the 1920s, in contrast to the nineteenth-century missionary cases, were directed almost exclusively against the Protestants, an indication that Catholicism remained apart from the main currents that were shaping twentieth-century China.

With the exception of the fundamentalist China Inland Mission and its associated societies, after 1900 Protestant missionaries gradually shifted their emphasis from a predominant concern with the conversion of individuals to the broadened goal of Christianizing all of Chinese society. This implied an increasing investment of personnel and funds in educational and medical work in order to realize, as one missionary leader wrote, 'the social implications' of the Gospel.

The 6,636 Protestant missionaries as of 1919 were resident in 693 locations in all the provinces of China where they staffed 1,037 separate mission stations. Of the 693 residential centres, 578 (83 per cent) were occupied by only one mission society, and 442 (65 per cent) had five or fewer missionaries in residence. These more sparsely settled locations tended to be in the interior provinces. Some 57 per cent of the missionaries were located in the coastal provinces, 26 per cent in the Yangtze valley provinces, and only 17 per cent away from the east coast and the Yangtze valley. The eight residential centres of Shanghai, Peking, Canton, Nanking, Foochow, Changsha, Chengtu, and Tsinan each had more than 100 missionaries and together accounted for 26 per cent of the total foreign personnel. Two-thirds of the Protestant missionaries and one-quarter of

TABLE 32

Relative strengths of Protestant denominations, 1919

	Societies	Number of missionaries	Stations	Communicants	Hospital
Anglican	4	635	79	19,114	39
Baptist	9	588	68	44,367	31
Congregational	4	345	34	25,816	32
Lutheran	18	590	116	32,209	23
Methodist	8	946	83	74,004	63
Presbyterian	12	1,080	96	79,199	92
China Inland Mission	12	960	246	50,541	17
Others	63	1,492	315	20,603	29
Total	130	6,636	1,037	345,853	326

the claimed communicants resided in 176 cities with estimated populations of 50,000 or more where perhaps 6 per cent of China's total population lived. In order of precedence, the seven coastal provinces of Kwangtung, Fukien, Chekiang, Kiangsu, Shantung, Chihli and Fengtien accounted for 71 per cent of the Protestant communicants, 63 per cent of lower primary students, and 77 per cent of middle school students. Evangelistic activity radiated out from the residential centres; 6,391 'congregations' and 8,886 'evangelistic centres' were claimed in 1919. Nevertheless, most were only a few *li* from an urban mission station.

In 1920 the number of separate Protestant missionary societies had increased from 61 as of 1900 to 130, to which must be added 36 Christian organizations such as the Y.M.C.A., the Salvation Army and the Yale-in-China mission, none of which was organized on a denominational basis. This increase was the consequence of the arrival in China after 1900 of many small sectarian societies, most of them American. The largest new mission to begin work in this period was that of the Seventh-Day Adventists. In 1905 one-half of the foreign force was part of the British Empire (including Great Britain, Canada, Australia and New Zealand), one-third American, and the rest from the European continent. By 1920 the British Empire and American proportions had been reversed, the Americans now accounting for one-half of the Protestant missionaries in China. The Catholic missionary effort was overwhelmingly European in personnel and control, American Catholic missionaries arriving in China mainly after 1920. Table 32 shows the strengths of the major denominations without regard to nationality.

From the first decade of the twentieth century, while denominational distinctions were continued and within them the separate identities of the individual societies, Protestant Christianity in China displayed tendencies towards formulating a common, basic theology and making substantial efforts to achieve organizational unity in certain spheres of activity. The irrelevance of confessional distinctions linked to a European past which was largely unknown in China furnished an incentive for modifying and simplifying theologies imported from abroad. The China Centenary Missionary Conference of 1907 adopted a collective theological stance which in later years continued to provide doctrinal guidelines for all but the more fundamentalist Protestant societies such as the China Inland Mission. Organizationally, the larger societies joined in publishing the major Protestant monthly magazine, the *Chinese Recorder*; supported non-denominational or interdenominational literature societies; participated in the China Christian Educational Association, the China Medical Missionary Association and the China Sunday School Union; founded union theological schools and interdenominational colleges and universities; and participated in all-China missionary conferences in 1877, 1890 and 1907, and in the National Christian Conference in 1922, which also formally included the Chinese church for the first time. A major expression of Protestant unity was the China Continuation Committee of 1913–22 which was succeeded by the National Christian Council in 1922, once more to enlarge the formal role of the Chinese church within the Christian establishment. Accommodation and cooperation were never, of course, completely effective. The conservative China Inland Mission, for example, withdrew from the National Christian Council in 1926.

The largest Protestant missionary societies, ranked by the number of missionaries maintained in the field as of 1919, are listed in Table 33, which also shows the number of mission stations and the geographical field of each major society.[39] These 18 societies together accounted for 4,350 (66 per cent of the total) missionaries and 611 (59 per cent of the total) mission stations. An 'average' mission station might be staffed by six or seven missionaries, but the actual distribution varied greatly from a frequent four or less for the China Inland Mission and the Christian and Missionary Alliance to averages of 14 or 15 for the Board of Foreign Missions of the Methodist Episcopal Church, the American Presbyterian Mission – North, and the American Board of Commissioners for Foreign Missions. In general, concentration of missionaries at one station was an indication of extensive educational and medical efforts as well as evan-

39 Of the number of 'missionaries' reported, at any one time as many as one sixth of the foreign workers might be out of China on furlough, approximately one twelfth newly arrived and engaged primarily in language study, and many of the married women occupied only part time with religious work. The number of full-time effectives, therefore, may be estimated at two thirds of the totals reported.

TABLE 33

The largest Protestant missionary societies, 1919

	Nationality	No. of missionaries	No. of stations	Location of mission stations
China Inland Mission and affiliates	Int.	960	246	An, Che, Chi, Ho, Hun, Hup, Kan, Ki, Ku, Kwei, Sha, She, Sung, Sze, Yun, Man, Sin
American Presbyterian Mission – North	U.S.	502	36	An, Che, Chi, Hun, Ku, Sung, Tung, Yun
Board of Foreign Missions of the Methodist Episcopal Church	U.S.	419	28	An, Chi, Fu, Ki, Ku, Sung, Sze
Church Missionary Society	G.B.	353	58	Che, Fu, Hun, Ku, Si, Tung, Sze, Yun
Protestant Episcopal Church, U.S.A.	U.S.	202	15	An, Hun, Hup, Ki, Ku
American Board of Commissioners for Foreign Missions	U.S.	198	14	Chi, Fu, Sha, Sung, Tung
Y.M.C.A.	Int.	192	24	major cities
American Baptist Foreign Mission Society (Northern Baptist)	U.S.	188	19	Che, Ki, Ku, Tung, Sze
Missionary Society of the Methodist Church of Canada	G.B.	184	10	Sze
Foreign Mission Board of the Southern Baptist Convention	U.S.	175	24	An, Ho, Ku, Si, Tung, Sung
American Presbyterian Mission – South	U.S.	146	15	Che, Ku, Sung
London Missionary Society	G.B.	145	17	Chi, Fu, Hup, Ku, Tung
Seventh-Day Adventist Missionary Board	U.S.	138	21	Che, Chi, Fu, Ho, Hun, Hup, Ku, She, Si, Sung, Sze, Tung, Man
Baptist Missionary Society (English)	G.B.	123	11	Sha, She, Sung
Methodist Episcopal Mission – South	U.S.	118	6	Che, Ku
Wesleyan Methodist Missionary Society	G.B.	118	19	Hun, Hup, Si, Tung
Christian and Missionary Alliance	U.S.	106	25	An, Hun, Hup, Kan, Ku, Si
Church Missions in Many Lands (Brethren)	G.B.	83	23	Ki, Sung, Mon

Key

An Anhwei	Fu Fukien	Hup Hupei	Ku Kiangsu	She Shensi	Sze Szechwan	Man Manchuria
Che Chekiang	Ho Hopei	Kan Kansu	Kwei Kweichou	Si Kwangsi	Tung Kwangtung	Mon Mongolia
Chi Chihli	Hun Hunan	Ki Kiangsi	Sha Shansi	Sung Shantung	Yun Yunnan	Sin Sinkiang

gelism, while dispersion to smaller stations reflected a primary if not exclusive emphasis on spreading the Gospel. As another indicator of the different emphases of the several societies, the China Inland Mission, for example, employed 66 per cent of its Chinese staff in evangelical work, 30 per cent in education, and 4 per cent in medical work, while the comparable figures for the American Board of Commissioners for Foreign Missions were 28 per cent in evangelism, 64 per cent in education and 8 per cent in medical work.

The introversion of the average Protestant missionary of the late Ch'ing persisted well into the republic. Paul Cohen has written of the former period,

The missionaries lived and worked in the highly organized structure of the mission compound, which resulted in their effective segregation – psychological as well as physical – from the surrounding Chinese society. . . . The missionaries really did not want to enter the Chinese world any more than they had to. Their whole purpose was to get the Chinese to enter theirs.[40]

With segregation went an absolute self-righteousness about their calling. This often overrode any moral qualms they may have had about the employment of gunboats by their own governments to settle the anti-missionary incidents punctuating their period of residence in China.[41]

Missions and Chinese society

Yet the two post-Boxer decades saw some changes both in the relationship of many Protestant missionaries to the society which surrounded them and in the degree to which they sought armed intervention to protect their special status. Their attitude of cultural superiority, galling even to Chinese Christians, remained, but increasing numbers of Protestant missionaries moved beyond the evangelical limits of the nineteenth-century mission compound to participate actively in educational, medical and philanthropic work, joining the reform currents of the early twentieth century. Education for women (Ginling College in Nanking was founded in 1915), the anti-footbinding movement, attention to urban and labour problems by the Y.M.C.A. and Y.W.C.A., famine relief, public health (to eradicate tuberculosis; campaigns against flies), public playgrounds and athletic and recreational programmes, the anti-opium movement, and the

40 'Foreword' to Sidney A. Forsythe, *An American missionary community in China, 1895–1905*, p. vii.
41 See Stuart Creighton Miller, 'Ends and means: missionary justification of force in nineteenth century China', in John K. Fairbank, ed. *The missionary enterprise in China and America*, 249–82.

scientific study of agriculture (by the School of Agriculture and Forestry of the University of Nanking) – these were some of the areas in which Protestant missionaries took the lead or were notably involved.

The mission station, a walled compound owned or leased by the missionary society and protected by extraterritoriality, remained the most typical feature of the missionary effort. Within the enclosure, which usually displayed a national flag, were the residences of the missionaries, the church, the school or classrooms and the hospital or dispensary. The typical station was located in an urban area. Street chapels were kept open for part of the day and staffed by a foreign missionary and his native helper. 'Out-station' communities of converts were served by native pastors and visited several times a year by the staff of the mission.

The station staff of two or three missionary families and a number of single women might on average in one station out of three include a physician or nurse, although the actual distribution of medical workers was uneven. Of the 6,636 Protestant missionaries reported in 1919, 2,495 (38 per cent) were men of whom 1,310 were ordained; 2,202 (33 per cent) were married women; and 1,939 (29 per cent) were single women. Physicians numbered 348 men and 116 women; and 206 of the women were trained nurses. The ordained men were responsible for the primary evangelical task of the mission and filled the vocal leadership roles. Many of the unordained men were teachers in the expanding network of missionary schools; the women were occupied in teaching and nursing, and carried out many of the visits to Chinese homes.

The principal medium for evangelization was preaching, in the mission church and in the street chapels, the success of which depended at least in part on a missionary's ability to speak colloquial Chinese. Before 1910 the only organized language schools for Protestant missionaries were run by the China Inland Mission at Yangchow and Anking, this last dating back to 1887. Language instruction was *ad hoc* at each mission station and poor command of Chinese continued to be a serious problem for many. By the early years of the republic, however, a number of substantial union (interdenominational) language schools were in operation employing modern 'phonetic inductive' methods and graded texts. The China Inland Mission maintained 'training homes' at Chinkiang and Yangchow which provided a six-month basic course using the Reverend F. W. Baller's primer and employing Chinese teachers. Approximately 150 students representing 20 different societies were enrolled annually in the Department of Missionary Training of the University of Nanking, which since 1912 offered a one-year residential course staffed by 51 Chinese teachers. A second year programme was available, but most students

TABLE 34

Protestant missionary schools and enrolments, 1919

	Number of mission schools	Enrolment in mission schools boys/girls/total	Enrolment in government schools 1916
Lower primary	5,637	103,232/48,350/151,582	3,752,982
Higher primary	962	23,490/ 9,409/ 32,899	388,941
Middle	291	12,644/ 2,569/ 15,213	179,621*
		199,694	

* Including equivalent technical and normal schools.

continued with correspondence courses in succeeding years. At Peking the North China Union Language School, formally organized in 1913 and affiliated with Yenching University in 1920, enrolled 147 students in 1921 and offered a programme similar to Nanking's. Other schools were the Union Missionary Training School in Chengtu, part of West China Union University; the Wu Dialect School of Soochow University in Shanghai; and the Canton Union Language School. Few missionaries, like few diplomats, ever attained a full proficiency in written Chinese, but some command of the vernacular was widespread.

Almost every mission station supported a lower primary school. Of the 693 Protestant residential centres, 306 reported higher primary schools and 141 middle schools. The number of schools at each level and the enrolments in 1919 are shown in table 34, which also gives the estimated enrolments in government schools in 1916. These figures may all be conjecture – the mission enrolments are fewer than those shown above in table 31 (page 168) – but the proportions are probably not a distortion. They indicate that mission lower primary school pupils were only four per cent as many as those in government schools, but that at the higher primary and middle school levels the proportion increased to over eight per cent. In the period 1907–20, the number of mission school students – perhaps one-half of whom came from Christian families – quadrupled while Protestant communicants only doubled in number, suggesting both a conscious missionary effort to reach China's youth and the lure of modern education. Protestant missionaries boasted that while overall only one in 75 of Chinese children of school age was receiving an education, one in three of all Christian youth was enrolled in a mission school.

The Protestant mission schools were staffed not only by foreign teachers, who were more in evidence at the higher primary and middle school levels, but also by around 8,000 male and 3,000 female Chinese teachers. Lower primary schools were often primitive one-room establishments sorely lacking in books and equipment. The upper schools had somewhat better facilities and frequently used English as a medium of instruction. First by choice and then from 1925 in order to qualify for government registration, missionary schools followed curricula similar to those established by the Ministry of Education for government schools. All the mission middle schools taught some religious subjects; Chinese language and literature courses employed the 'national readers' of the ministry; science teaching was poor in most schools, laboratory and demonstration equipment being expensive and in short supply; few offered any vocational training. They were probably no worse than the government middle schools, but the indications are that the mission middle-school effort in the early republic had over-extended itself given the resources it could readily finance.

In higher education 20 Protestant colleges and one Catholic college were in existence in 1920. The Protestant institutions through reorganization and amalgamation eventually formed the 13 Christian colleges whose hey-day was in the 1930s. Two additional Catholic colleges were organized in the closing years of the 1920s. In addition to these liberal arts schools, the Protestant missionary movement maintained a number of theological schools, some on a union basis, and several Christian medical colleges, and the Catholics a number of seminaries. Except for West China Union University in Chengtu, where Canadian and British personnel and organizational patterns prevailed, the Protestant liberal arts colleges were largely sponsored by American missionaries who sought to create in China replicas of the small denominational colleges of mid-western America from which they had themselves graduated. Most of these colleges had their beginnings in the secondary schools founded in the latter part of the nineteenth century, which were gradually expanded and upgraded academically with the intention of training a Chinese pastorate and teachers for the mission schools.

In 1920 the Protestant colleges together enrolled 2,017 students; after a period of rapid growth in the early 1920s that total reached 3,500 in 1925. Total college enrolment in China in 1925 was approximately 21,000, the Protestant schools therefore accounting for 12 per cent and the 34 government institutions for 88 per cent of the student body. Even the largest of the Christian colleges – Yenching University in Peking, St John's in Shanghai, the University of Nanking, Shantung Christian University in Tsinan – had no more than three or four hundred students. The size and disciplinary competence of the faculties were similarly limited. In 1920 foreign teachers totalled 265, and Chinese – most of them tutors – 229. But many also taught in the middle schools located on the same campuses.

Chartered in the United States, without any formal standing in China until forced to apply for official registration by the Nationalist government after 1928, controlled in fact by the absentee mission boards that supplied two-thirds of their finances and intervened in the selection of teachers, the Christian colleges were virtually self-contained foreign enclaves in the period here considered. Before the 1930s, probably only St John's, Yenching and the University of Nanking offered instruction at an academic level comparable to the better American undergraduate colleges. Of necessity most of their students came from graduates of the mission middle schools where alone sufficient English was taught to prepare students to follow the English-language instruction used in all courses except Chinese literature and philosophy. The attractiveness of some of the colleges (and of the mission middle schools) to Chinese students came to depend heavily on their excellent training in the English language, which provided for urban youth an entrée into the treaty-port world of business and finance, or access to government positions (in the telegraph, railway or customs administrations, for example) where knowledge of a foreign language was a significant asset. Of the 2,474 graduates as of 1920, 361 had become ministers or teachers, as the missionary founders had intended. However less than half of those enrolled in the first two decades of the twentieth century completed their courses. For most of the 'dropouts' it was evidently a command of English rather than a Christian liberal arts education that had been the lure.

The Christian colleges did not escape the nationalist torrent of the late 1920s.[42] In the 1930s they were increasingly secularized in their curricula and Sinified in their faculties and administration; but their foreign identity was inescapable.

Medical missionaries in the nineteenth century regarded themselves first and foremost as evangelists. Treatment in mission dispensaries and hospitals was designed also to give the patient exposure to the Gospel. Gradually medical professionalism developed, reflecting changes of outlook comparable to those which inspired educational professionalism. In 1919, 240 out of 693 Protestant residential centres reported the operation of a total of 326 hospitals. They averaged 51 beds apiece, the total number being 16,737. These hospitals were staffed by 464 foreign physicians, 206 foreign nurses and some 2,600 Chinese medical workers only a small number of whom were qualified. The hospitals, like other sections of the missionary establishment, were located in urban areas and concentrated in the eastern coastal provinces. As the above data indicate, trained medical personnel were very thinly spread among these facilities; few had more than one missionary doctor regularly in residence. With some outstanding exceptions, they were useful but fairly primitive institutions.

Western-type medical education in China began as an outgrowth of missionary medical work, developing from the informal training of assistants by overworked doctors. By 1913 there were 11 small, rudimentarily staffed and equipped medical colleges, eight for men and three for women. Only the Peking Union Medical College, which was taken over by the China Medical Board of the Rockefeller Foundation in 1915 when it formally ceased to be a missionary institution, approximated the standards of Western medical schools. The reorganized Union Medical College, small in size – only 166 students received M.D. degrees through 1936 – and attacked by its critics for its isolation from the medical needs of China's rural masses, did become a training and research institution of international calibre.

CHINESE GOVERNMENT AGENCIES

The foreign presence was highly visible in three departments of the central government which, while formally subordinated to Chinese authority, in many respects operated with *de facto* autonomy under the leadership of foreigners and with substantial foreign staffs in the more critical subordinate positions: the Maritime Customs Service, the Post Office and the Salt Administration.

Maritime Customs Service

Through 1900 the customs service was under the jurisdiction of the Tsungli Yamen with which agency the inspector-general, whose office was located in Peking from 1865 onwards, was in almost daily contact. The organizational structure, responsibilities and procedures, and the composition of service personnel as of the first years of the twentieth century were largely the creation of Robert Hart (1835–1911) who presided autocratically as inspector-general of maritime customs from 1863 to 1908.[43]

43 Hart left Peking for England in May 1908, but formally retained the title of I.G. until his death in September 1911. Robert E. Bredon (1846–1918) served as acting I.G. from April

In the course of 50 years in the service of China, Hart had accumulated a degree of personal power and independence that could not have been envisaged and certainly would not have been conceded to him by the Tsungli Yamen when he first took office. Far from doubting where his first loyalty lay, however, over the decades the inspector-general had repeatedly emphasized to his foreign staff that they and he were employees of the Chinese government. But by 1906 Hart was 71 years of age and in poor health; his retirement was imminent. To replace Hart with an equally powerful foreign successor was out of the question in the decade of the Manchu reform movement. The perhaps gentler 'imperialism of free trade' of the nineteenth century had given way to a fiercer international rivalry. By 1898 the whole of the then customs revenue had become pledged to the repayment of foreign loans contracted to finance the costs of the war with Japan and the large indemnity imposed by the Treaty of Shimonoseki, making the service in effect a debt-collecting agency for foreign bondholders. Nationalist resentment was given further grounds for seeing the customs service as a tool of foreign interests when in 1901 the unencumbered balance of the maritime customs revenue and the collections of the native customs within 50 *li* of the treaty ports – now placed under the control of the foreign inspectorate – were pledged for the service of the Boxer indemnity. The treaty powers were not timid in insisting that the service of these foreign debts, as much as the inspection and taxation of imports and exports in the facilitation of foreign trade with China, was the *raison d'être* of the customs service. The implication of the clauses sanctioned by imperial edict in the loan agreements of 1896 and 1898 was that during the currency of the loans the administration of the maritime customs should remain as then constituted, while under the terms of an exchange of notes in 1898 Britain bound China to agree that so long as British trade predominated the inspector-general would be a British subject. The customs, furthermore, administered the national Post Office with foreign nationals in the key executive positions, managed the lighthouse service, controlled the pilotage of China's harbours which in many ports was already almost entirely in foreign hands, and through its statistical, commercial and cultural publications was for the foreign world China's sole official information agency. And, after 50 years, no Chinese had yet been appointed to a responsible administra-

1908 to April 1910, to be succeeded in turn during 1910–11 by Francis A. Aglen (1869–1932) who became I.G. at Hart's death and served until 1927. See Stanley F. Wright, *Hart and the Chinese customs*; John King Fairbank, *et al.* eds. *The I.G. in Peking: letters of Robert Hart, Chinese Maritime Customs, 1868–1907*; and China, Inspectorate General of Customs, *Documents illustrative of the origin, development and activities of the Chinese Customs Service.*

tive position – not even as an assistant at any treaty port – within the service.

Transfer of the customs to the jurisdiction of the Ministry of Foreign Affairs which replaced the Tsungli Yamen in 1901 had been uneventful. But the establishment of a separate Revenue Bureau (Shui-wu Ch'u) in July 1906 – not at the ministry (*pu*) level, although headed at first by T'ieh Liang, the minister of finance, and T'ang Shao-i, the vice-minister of foreign affairs – to supervise the customs service was seen by foreign governments, customs staff and bondholders, whose securities were linked to the customs revenue, as a threat to the special foreign character of the service as it had evolved over half a century. The establishment of the Shui-wu Ch'u in 1906 was a mild attempt, as much as could be managed in the face of predictable foreign opposition, to downgrade somewhat the status of the Maritime Customs Service and to ensure that Hart's successor would not amass the influence or attain the independence that the circumstances of the maritime customs' first half century had bestowed on 'the I.G.'. Sir Francis Aglen's political role in Peking during his 18 years as inspector-general, in fact, never came near rivalling that of Hart. The new I.G. and his foreign staff were much less centrally involved in China's international relations than had been the case in the nineteenth century. Chinese began to appear in junior administrative positions in the elite Indoor Staff after 1911. But little significant Sinification of the customs occurred before the establishment of the Nanking government in 1928.

To all those Chinese who shared political power during the era of Yuan Shih-k'ai's presidency and the various Peking governments that succeeded it, the existence of a foreign-controlled customs service was one of the few constant and concrete manifestations of the unified and centralized China which each thought he could re-establish under his own aegis. It collected the revenues on foreign and coastal trade with maximum probity. While before 1917 there was no 'customs revenue surplus,' in the sense of an available balance after provision for loan service and the Boxer indemnity which could be released to the Peking government to use as it determined, the prospect thereafter was that this amount would increase – to the potential benefit of whoever was in power in Peking. Efficient service of the large foreign debt and the indemnity helped keep the treaty powers at bay, even if it did not significantly diminish their influence in China. And when cancelled indemnity obligations to Germany, Austria and Russia together with customs revenue surpluses were utilized to guarantee the domestic loans of the Peking government, the fact that the service of these loans was to be in the hands of the foreign inspector-general of customs – who was seen by investors as politically

neutral among the contending Chinese factions – substantially strengthened the government's credit.

The principal responsibilities of the Maritime Customs Service were,
of course, prevention of smuggling, examination of cargoes and assessment of the treaty tariff on imports, exports and coastal trade. Its jurisdiction extended to 'foreign-type vessels', whether owned by foreigners or
by Chinese, and to junks chartered by foreigners.[44] From the Treaty of
Nanking in 1842 until recovery of tariff autonomy in 1928–30, the tariff
for which the customs was responsible was set by agreement with the
treaty powers; in effect it was imposed upon China by its trading partners.
For the most part a fixed schedule vaguely intended to yield approximately
five per cent *ad valorem* on both imports and exports, the tariff was revised
upwards in 1858–60, 1902, 1919 and in 1922 with the stated purpose of
achieving an effective *ad valorem* return of five per cent on imports. The
1902 tariff, however, yielded only 3.2 per cent and that of 1919 only 3.6
per cent.[45]

The maritime customs house at each treaty port was a Sino-foreign
enterprise with jurisdiction shared by a Chinese superintendent of customs
(*chien-tu*) appointed by the Shui-wu Ch'u and a foreign commissioner
appointed by the inspector-general. (Only the I.G. himself was a direct
appointee of the Chinese government.) While sometimes deferring in
form to the superintendent, in practice the commissioner was *primus inter
pares*. The Indoor Staff (that is, the executive function) at the port was

44 By Article 6 of the Boxer Protocol, the revenues of the native customs at the treaty ports
and inside a 50-*li* radius were hypothecated to the service of the indemnity and these col-
lectorates placed under the administration of the Maritime Customs Service. Hart assumed
nominal control in November 1901, but in practice until 1911 the indemnity payments due
from the native customs were largely met from other provincial appropriations. Complete
control over the native customs within 50-*li* of the treaty ports was asserted only after the
Revolution of 1911 disrupted the remittance of provincial quotas for the indemnity service,
a circumstance which alarmed foreign bondholders. See Stanley F. Wright, *China's customs
revenue since the Revolution of 1911* (3rd edn), 181–2.
45 Foreign goods imported from abroad or from another Chinese treaty port (unless covered
by an exemption certificate certifying that duty had been paid at the original port of entry)
were assessed the full import duty. These goods could be carried inland exempt from likin
(transit tax) taxation *en route* to their destination under a transit pass obtained from the
customs by payment of one-half of the stated import duty. Chinese goods exported abroad
or to another Chinese treaty port were assessed the full export duty; if reshipped to a second
Chinese port, they paid an additional coast trade duty equal to one-half the export duty.
Chinese goods sent from the interior to a treaty port for shipment abroad under an outward
transit pass which freed them from likin *en route* were charged transit dues by the customs at
one-half the rate of the export duty. See Stanley F. Wright, *China's struggle for tariff autonomy:
1843–1938*.
    The inward transit pass privilege was extended to Chinese nationals by the Chefoo
Convention of 1876 (actually implemented from 1880) but Peking demurred until 1896
before conceding the outward transit pass to Chinese merchants. For a detailed guide to
Customs practices, see China, The Maritime Customs, *Handbook of customs procedure at
Shanghai*.

solely under the commissioner's orders. It was the commissioner and not the superintendent who dealt with the foreign consuls when disputes with foreign traders arose. The superintendent, however, appointed his own recording staff (called *shu-pan* until 1912 and *lu-shih* thereafter) through whom he was to be kept informed on a daily basis of the revenue collections. Native customs stations situated within a 50-*li* radius of the port were administered by the commissioners and their revenue remitted for payment of the indemnity, except that in matters of office staff and practice the commissioner was enjoined to act in conjunction with the superintendent. Native customs stations outside of the 50-*li* radius were under the sole jurisdiction of the superintendent.

Before October 1911 the inspector-general and his commissioners did not actually collect, bank and remit the customs revenue at the several treaty ports. The I.G. through the commissioners was responsible only for the correct assessment of the duties and an accurate accounting to the Chinese government of the amounts assessed. Foreign and Chinese traders paid their duties directly into the authorized customs bank(s) (*hai-kuan kuan-yin-hao*), entirely Chinese firms selected usually by the superintendents who were responsible to the imperial government for the security of the revenue and whose accounts were checked against the returns submitted by the foreign commissioners. In the wake of the Wuchang uprising in October 1911 and the collapse of central authority in much of China, including the departure of many of the Ch'ing-appointed superintendents who feared for their own personal safety, this system was radically altered. Fearing that the revolutionary leaders in the provinces would withhold the customs revenues that were pledged to the service of foreign loans and the Boxer indemnity, the commissioners at the ports in the provinces that had declared their independence from Peking, acting in the interests of the treaty powers, assumed direct control of the revenue and placed it in foreign banks. These arrangements were perforce accepted by the republican government which formally assumed power in February 1912, and were expressed in an agreement imposed upon the Chinese government by the foreign Diplomatic Body in Peking. The terms of the agreement provided for the formation of an International Commission of Bankers at Shanghai to superintend the payment of the foreign loans of the Chinese government secured on the customs revenue and of the Boxer indemnity; and entrusted the inspector-general with the collection of the revenue at the ports, its remittance to Shanghai for deposit in the foreign custodian banks 'for account of the loans concerned and indemnity payments', and responsibility for making loan payments as they fell due according to the priority determined by the Commission of Bankers.

Two implications of the 1912 agreement, which remained effective until the establishment of the Nanking government, should be noted. The treaty powers until 1921 assumed the right to determine whether or not there was a 'customs revenue surplus', after the foreign debt was serviced, and to give their approval before the release of any funds to the Peking government. Their estimates of the available surplus were conservative, to the ineffective displeasure of successive administrations in Peking. Moreover, large sums of Chinese government funds which formerly were at the disposal of Chinese banks were now deposited in three foreign banks in Shanghai – the Hongkong and Shanghai Banking Corporation, the Deutsch-Asiatische Bank (until 1917 when China declared war on Germany) and the Russo-Asiatic Bank (until its liquidation in 1926). While interest was duly paid, large balances were always available to these banks for their other commercial operations, and in the service of the foreign debt they profited substantially from handling the necessary currency exchange operations.

The first charge on the customs revenue was the office allowance to cover the salaries and operating expenses of the service. This allowance was negotiated directly between the Chinese government and the inspector-general, and in 1893 was set at Hk. Tls. (haikwan taels) 3,168,000 per annum, a figure not increased until 1920 when the allowance was raised to Hk. Tls. 5,700,000. In addition, the upkeep of the superintendents' offices annually consumed approximately Hk. Tls. 400,000. Total revenue in 1898 was reported at Hk.Tls. 22,503,000 and in 1920 at Hk.Tls. 49,820,000. The cost of collection – not including bankers' commissions and possible losses by exchange incurred in collecting and remitting the net revenue – amounted, therefore, to 15.9 per cent and 12.2 per cent of the total revenue in these two years. In 1898 the office allowance supported a staff of 895 foreigners and 4,223 Chinese (including 24 foreigners and 357 Chinese in the postal department) at an average cost of Hk.Tls. 619. By 1920 the customs staff numbered 1,228 foreigners and 6,246 Chinese (postal personnel were separated from the customs in 1911), reflecting the fact that many new ports had been opened to trade in the intervening years. The 1920 increase, which brought the average cost to Hk. Tls. 763, compensated for the strain on the finances of the service occasioned by this expansion.

The customs staff, Chinese and foreign, were assigned to one of the three branches of the service: the Revenue Department, the Marine Department (established in 1865) and the Works Department (established in 1912). Surveys of the coast and inland water-ways, the operation of lighthouses and lightships, the servicing of buoys and beacons, and the maintenance and policing of harbours, were the responsibilities of the Marine Department. By 1911 it had established and was maintaining 132 lights, 56 lightships, 138 buoys (many of which were whistling or gas-lighted), and 257 beacons (mainly on the Yangtze and West Rivers). The Works Department was charged with the erection and repair of Customs buildings and property. But the heart of the service, of course, was the Revenue Department.

Within the Revenue Department were three classes of personnel: Indoor, Outdoor and Coast Staffs, each of which in turn was divided into 'foreign' and 'native' sections. The Indoor Staff at each port was the executive arm of the customs responsible for administration and account-ing. It was headed by a commissioner who was assisted by a deputy commissioner and four grades of assistants, all appointed, promoted, assigned and transferred by the inspector-general who merely reported the appointments to the Shui-wu Ch'u. Hart, like the Reverend Lobenstine quoted earlier who envisaged the creation of a 'Church . . . truly indige-nous in China', repeated on more than one occasion the intention he had expressed in a memorandum of 1864 to the effect that the foreign inspec-torate 'will have finished its work when it shall have produced a native administration, as honest and as efficient to replace it.'[46] In fact, however, no Chinese attained even the lowest grade of assistant in the Indoor Staff during his tenure as I.G. He had once thought that the Chinese linguist-clerks (*t'ung-wen kung-shih*), who were required to have some knowledge of written and spoken English, might eventually furnish recruits into the class of assistants. Mainly graduates from mission schools, the Chinese education of these clerks was probably deficient; in any case it was a lacuna repeatedly alleged to be an obstacle to their appointment to higher official positions. Hart was also able to cite the opposition of higher officials in Peking to the promotion of the clerks, which is perhaps not surprising given their mission-school background and their largely South Chinese provenance. Many were Cantonese in origin, with the next largest contingents coming from Kiangsu, Chekiang and Fukien. They were usually recruited by examinations held by the commissioners at the largest ports and, in addition to competence in English, were selected in part for their knowledge of several local dialects. Originally mainly used as interpreters and translators, by the time of Hart's death many were performing the same office duties as the foreign assistants. The founding in 1908 of the Customs College (Shui-wu hsueh-t'ang) eventually provided a pool of well-trained graduates from whom, along

46 Quoted in Wright, *Hart and the Chinese customs*, 262.

TABLE 35

Indoor staff of the customs revenue department, 1915

	British	American	French	German	Russian	Other European	Japanese	Chinese	Total
Inspector-general	1	—	—	—	—	—	—	—	1
Commissioners	23	3	3	5	3	4	2	—	43
Deputy commissioners	11	1	3	4	—	3	—	—	22
Assistants	76	11	4	17	10	37*	32	60	247
Miscellaneous	10	1	2	2	—	2	—	—	17
Medical officers	31	5	5	2	—	3	3	9	58
Linguist clerks	—	—	—	—	—	—	—	627	627
Chien-hsi†	—	—	—	—	—	—	—	33	33
Lu-shih	—	—	—	—	—	—	—	350	350
Writers and copyists	—	—	—	—	—	—	—	110	110
Teachers	—	—	—	—	—	—	—	7	7
Shroffs	—	—	—	—	—	—	—	10	10
Totals	152	21	17	30	13	49	37	1,206	1,525
Total all non-Chinese				319					

* includes one Korean.
† graduates of Customs College, with provisional customs ranks.

with the most qualified of the clerks, Aglen began to appoint a number of Chinese assistants.

The *shu-pan* or *lu-shih* were the superintendent's accounting staff. The third group of Chinese employees in the Indoor Staff were the writers and copyists, skilled in the use of documentary Chinese and calligraphy, who prepared all the official Chinese correspondence between the commissioner or superintendent and local officials, as well as the documents forwarded to the inspectorate in Peking for transmission to the Shui-wu Ch'u.

In 1915 the personnel of the Indoor Staff of the Revenue Department, by position and nationality, were distributed as shown in table 35.[47] The foreign Indoor Staff was recruited either through the customs office in London, for the dominant British cohort, or through direct nomination to the I.G. by the several foreign legations in Peking. Many were young men with a university education who saw greater opportunities for themselves in China than appeared to be available in their own countries. There was some pressure on the inspectorate to make these appointments in proportion to the size of each treaty power's trade with China, which may account, for example, for why there were no Japanese at all in 1895, 16 – all assistants – in 1905, and 37 – including two commissioners – in 1915. British predominance reflects the fact that through 1911 the percentage of the total customs revenue accounted for by trade carried in British vessels never fell below 60 per cent. Even in 1915, in the midst of the First World War, British vessels carried 42 per cent of the total values of China's foreign and inter-port trade cleared through the customs.[48]

From the beginning of the service, Hart emphasized the importance of a competent knowledge of spoken and written Chinese by the commissioners and assistants. Newly arrived appointees to the Indoor Staff were expected to undertake language study in Peking before being assigned to a port. A compulsory annual language examination for all foreign Indoor employees was ordered in 1884, and from 1899 in principle no one could be promoted to deputy commissioner or commissioner without an adequate knowledge of Chinese. Assistants who failed to qualify in the spoken language at the end of their third year in rank or in written Chinese at the end of the fifth year were, again in principle, to be discharged. But on this matter Hart was more generous than on many others in his treatment of subordinates. The foreign Indoor Staff as a group were only moderately competent in Chinese; many never mastered it; a few became distinguished Sinologists. Aglen admonished the

47 *Ibid.* 903.   48 Hsiao Liang-lin, *China's foreign trade statistics, 1864–1949*, 201–23.

service in October 1910,[49] as a result of which stricter examinations and classification of assistants by language ability were immediately ordered and outlined again in great detail in 1915. Aglen appeared satisfied with the results, but proficiency in Chinese, among the customs staff as among other foreigners, was achieved by very few.

The Outdoor Staff of the Revenue Department in 1915 comprised 881 foreigners and 3,352 Chinese. Except for 14 Chinese tide-waiters (who checked cargo as it entered and left the port) out of a total of 490, all of the responsible positions – tide-surveyors and assistant tide-surveyors (the executives of the Outdoor Staff), boat officers, appraisers, chief examiners, assistant examiners, examiners, and tide-waiters – were filled by foreigners. Again British nationals dominated, accounting for 454 of the 881 foreigners and for 32 of the 57 top positions of tide-surveyor, assistant tide-surveyor and boat officer. The remaining 3,238 Chinese were weighers, watchers, boatmen, guards, messengers, office coolies, gatekeepers, watchmen and labourers. In the Coast Staff, also, the 40 commanders, officers, engineers and gunners were all foreigners – 29 of them British, while the 448 Chinese employees served as deck hands, engine hands and cabin hands. A handful of Chinese out of the 1,239 employed in the Marine Department held 'executive' posts, but these again were largely the preserve of the 117 foreigners. In the small Works Department, 14 of the 33 employees were Chinese. In sum, few of the 6,159 Chinese employees of the customs, as compared with the 1,376 foreigners, were in other than menial positions.

Foreign members of the Outdoor Staff, unlike the Indoor Staff of the Revenue Department, were recruited locally in the several treaty ports. In the early years of the service many were ex-sailors and adventurers who had tried to find success on the China coast. The distinction in social origin between the Indoor and Outdoor Staffs continued into the twentieth century and was reflected in the much better treatment with respect to salaries, housing, allowances and career opportunities enjoyed by the

---

49 'The reports received this year on the Chinese acquirements of the In-door Staff, while showing that, on the whole, Chinese study is not altogether neglected, make it quite evident that the standard of efficiency throughout the Service is too low and that, with a few brilliant exceptions, study of Chinese is not taken seriously.' The appearance of Chinese nationalism on the scene required something more. 'It is more than ever necessary in these times, for the reputation of the Service and for its continued usefulness, that the reproach now beginning to be heard, that its members do not take sufficient interest in the country which employs them to learn its language should be removed. . .'. I.G. Circular No. 1732 (Second Series), *Documents illustrative . . . of the Chinese customs service*, vol. 2: *Inspector general's circulars, 1893 to 1910*, 709.

Indoor Staff who were recognized by other foreigners as part of the treaty-port elite.[50]

The Maritime Customs Service, in fact, was seething with discontent by the time of Hart's departure, not only on the issue of elitism but as a general reaction to Hart's autocratic style. Aglen's official circulars as I.G. are hardly more modest in tone than those of his predecessor, but he did deal with some particular grievances, for example, establishing as of 1920 a superannuation and retirement scheme, a move that Hart had long resisted.

Post Office

Aside from the ancient official post that served the Ch'ing government, the Chinese public had sent mail through a multitude of private postal firms that served major centres by charging what the traffic would bear. The foreign powers had created their own postal services in China. In 1896, however, the Imperial Post was established. Yet in the first years of the Chinese republic, six of the treaty powers still maintained their own post offices and independent postal services: Great Britain at 12 large cities and in three locations in Tibet; France in 15 cities; Germany in 16 cities; Japan in 20 cities in China proper, six locations in its leased territory in Manchuria, and 23 elsewhere in Manchuria; Russia at 28 places, including many in Manchuria and Mongolia; and the United States at Shanghai only. The invariable justification for these foreign post offices, which were clear violations of China's sovereignty in that they had no basis in the treaties which otherwise limited that sovereignty, was that 'safety of communications in China was not assured'.[51] Although China's adherence to the Universal Postal Union in 1914 rendered void the special provisions of the Règlement d'Exécution of the 1906 Universal Postal Convention which had given some international legal basis to the continuance of foreign post offices on Chinese territory, it was not until the Washington Conference of 1921–2 that the treaty powers agreed to their

---

50 As late as 1919, a deputation representing the foreign Outdoor Staff complained to Aglen about 'the stigma attached to the word "Out-door", which extends beyond the Service and reacts on all social relation with the foreign community', and reported the 'prevalent feeling . . . that the In-door Staff goes out of its way to treat the Out-door Staff with contempt; that in disciplinary cases the Out-door Staff does not get a fair show, only one side of the case, and that the Commissioner's, being represented; . . . and that the private life of the Staff is unwarrantably interfered with by Tidesurveyors'. Semi-Official Circular No. 29, *Documents illustrative . . . of the Chinese customs service*, vol. 3: *Inspector general's circulars, 1911 to 1923*, 504.

51 Statement by Japanese delegation to the Washington Conference, quoted in Westel W. Willoughby, *Foreign rights and interests in China*, 887.

abolition as of January 1923. This concession to China's nationalist feelings did not, however, come without some strings attached: offices in foreign leased territories (which the Japanese claimed to understand as including their railway zones in Manchuria) were to continue, and the status of the foreign postmaster-general in the Chinese postal administration was not to be changed.

The foreign post offices competed with the Chinese post office in the major ports where the potential postal traffic was more lucrative without having any responsibility to serve less profitable outlying areas. They were notoriously lax in enforcing Chinese customs regulations, and on several occasions after 1914 had refused to handle mail from Chinese offices intended for overseas addresses. Of necessity, perhaps, in the 1860s when they first appeared, their continuance for any reason other than as a mark of the foreigner's special position in China had become redundant as China itself developed a modern postal system. This development had taken place under the aegis of the Maritime Customs Service.[52] From the customs post, which began in the 1860s as a service carrying the correspondence of the several foreign legations between Peking and the treaty ports, there evolved in the 1870s and 1880s a postal service operated on Western lines available to all users. It offered little competition to the native postal firms (*hsin-chü*) or the foreign postal establishments in the treaty ports before it was formally transformed into the Imperial Post Office in March 1896, but it expanded steadily thereafter.

Under the new arrangement, the management of the Imperial Post Office was vested in the inspector-general who operated it as a department of the Maritime Customs Service. The commissioners at the several ports were responsible also for the postal affairs of their districts. In 1898, 24 foreigners and 357 Chinese were detached from the customs for service in the Postal Department. Making good its claim to an official monopoly was accomplished in part by regulating and restricting the activities of the *hsin-chü*, in part by absorbing them. In 1906 specially designated postal commissioners were assigned to Shanghai, Canton and Hankow in order to relieve the more overburdened customs commissioners of their dual responsibilities. While the service and personnel of the post office grew (to 99 foreign and 11,885 Chinese employees in 1911), its revenues lagged somewhat behind. Until its separation from the customs, annual supplements from the customs revenue were required to keep the Postal Department afloat.

That separation came in May 1911 when the Imperial Post Office was

52 See Ying-wan Cheng, *Postal communication in China and its modernization, 1860–1896*.

transferred to the jurisdiction of the Ministry of Posts and Communications and its management conceded to T. Piry, the former postal secretary of the Customs Service, who was now to become postmaster-general. Piry, a Frenchman, had joined the Customs Service in 1874, was appointed postal secretary in 1901, and continued as postmaster-general until 1917. That he was a French national, as was his successor Henri Picard-Destelan, reflected China's commitment to France in 1898, during the 'scramble for concessions,' 'to take account of the recommendations of the French Government in respect to the selection of the staff' of its postal service. Piry's authority as postmaster-general, however, was more circumscribed than that of the inspector-general of customs had been, inasmuch as he was formally subordinated to a 'director-general' (*chü-chang*) of the Ministry, in line with China's growing nationalist sentiment. Although much more an authentic department of the Chinese government after 1911 than was the customs service even under Aglen, many of the leading postal administrative positions in Peking and the provinces continued to be filled by foreigners (transferred at first from the customs) during the next two decades. The typical pattern was to have a foreign commissioner head a postal district, seconded by Chinese or foreign deputy commissioners and Chinese and foreign assistants. A foreign staff of about 25 was attached to the postmaster-general's (officially he was styled 'co-director-general') office in Peking, and about 75 other foreigners were stationed in the provinces. In 1920 about half of the foreigners were British nationals, one-quarter French, and the rest scattered among a dozen other nationalities. Some 30,000 Chinese employees actually processed and delivered the mail.

Salt Administration

Imposed upon China in the twentieth century and not in the middle of the nineteenth, the Sino-foreign Inspectorate of Salt Revenues was something different from – and less than – the Maritime Customs Service.

Chinese opposition to foreign participation in the Salt Administration except in limited advisory and technical roles delayed completion of negotiations for the £25,000,000 Reorganization Loan to Yuan Shih-k'ai's new government from February 1912 until April 1913. The principal treaty powers – Great Britain, France, Russia, Germany, Japan and the United States (which withdrew from the consortium before the loan was concluded) – through the sextuple banking consortium sought to strengthen Yuan's government with the hope that it would be able to maintain China's unity and protect foreign interests. But the bankers would undertake a loan as large as £25,000,000 only upon adequate security. The customs revenue, completely hypothecated for the service of previous loans and the Boxer indemnity, for an undetermined time could be only a secondary guarantee; the Peking government therefore pledged the proceeds of the salt revenue. As a central condition for floating the loan, the consortium insisted upon a measure of control over the Salt Administration, not merely advice and audit, which the powers forced the increasingly bankrupt Yuan to accept. Accordingly, Article 5 of the 26 April 1913 Reorganization Loan agreement provided for the establishment, under the Ministry of Finance, of a Central Salt Administration to comprise a 'Chief Inspectorate of Salt Revenues under a Chinese Chief Inspector and a foreign Associate Chief Inspector'. In each salt-producing district there was to be a branch office 'under one Chinese and one foreign District Inspector who shall be jointly responsible for the collection and the deposit of the salt revenues.'

Patriotic sentiment was correct in seeing the insertion of an explicit foreign interest into the administration of China's salt revenues as a derogation of sovereignty, and the juxtaposition of Chinese and foreign district inspectors in the provinces looked very much like the customs arrangement in which foreign commissioners and Chinese superintendents nominally shared power at the treaty ports. Perhaps, too, because the Salt Administration was a more intimate part of the Chinese polity, one with delicate internal balances and long-standing interests, any foreign role at all was especially galling. The Salt Inspectorate, however, unlike the customs organization, which was a new creation expanding in tandem with the growth of foreign trade, represented at first only the interpolation of a new echelon of administration into a perennial Chinese fiscal complex comprising the manufacture, transportation, taxation and sale of salt. Superimposed upon these traditional arrangements to ensure that the revenues collected were in fact made available to the central government for the service of the Reorganization Loan, the inspectorate over time did acquire substantial *de facto* control over salt manufacture and marketing. But this control was not linked to any continuing and specifically foreign interest comparable to the growth and protection of international commerce – apart from meeting the instalments of principal and interest set forth in the amortization table of the Reorganization Loan. The benefits, such as they were, accrued mainly to whoever was in control of the Peking government, and after 1922 mainly to the provincial satraps.

The foreign associate chief inspector and his foreign subordinates, because they were representatives of the bankers of Europe, backed in turn by their respective governments, of course were more than the mere coadjutors that might be implied by a literal reading of Article 5. But no *imperium in imperio* resulted such as Robert Hart had erected for the Customs Service. Maximum foreign influence was exercised in the very first years of the inspectorate, when Yuan Shih-k'ai's centralization efforts looked as if they had some promise and the president gave his backing to Richard Dane, the first associate chief inspector. Dane (1854–1940), a former Indian civil servant who had served in turn as commissioner of salt revenue for Northern India and then as the first inspector-general of excise and salt for India, was responsible for some far-reaching reforms of the salt gabelle during his tenure in China from 1913 to 1917, but he was never a Hart.[53] The minister of finance and the Chinese chief inspector were not mere figureheads giving *pro forma* approval to whatever Dane might undertake, but on the contrary themselves represented a nationalist, albeit conservative, political current of bureaucratic centralization whose interests for a time paralleled those of the foreign syndicate and who gladly made use of such pressure against local, centrifugal forces as a foreign presence might provide.

There were, moreover, never more than 40 to 50 foreign employees of the Salt Administration (41 in 1917, 59 in 1922, and 41 in 1925 when Chinese employees totalled 5,363) while more than 1,300 served in the Maritime Customs Service of the early republic.[54] The large Chinese staff, in contrast to the customs service, was not under the control of the foreign chief inspector. Perhaps a dozen foreigners provided the administrative staff for the foreign chief inspector in Peking, while the remainder were stationed in the several salt districts as auditors, district inspectors, assistant district inspectors or assistants. Because what they, and their Chinese colleagues who occupied parallel ranks, were inspecting and auditing was not a *foreign* trade but a major component of China's *domestic* commerce and fiscal system, the Chinese colleagues could hardly be relegated to the largely supernumerary status of the customs superintendents. The foreign staff, as opposed to Chinese agents of a Salt Administration reformed with foreign assistance, did not penetrate to the base of the labyrinthian salt complex. In the case of the maritime customs, the foreigners were simultaneously the principal participants in the activity that was being regulated and taxed, the effective regulators and collectors, and before 1928 the final recipient in the form of loan and indemnity payments of the bulk of the revenue. But the specific foreign interest in

53 For Dane's reforms, see S. A. M. Adshead, *The modernization of the Chinese Salt Administration, 1900–1920.*
54 Japan, Gaimushō, Ajiya-kyoku, *Shina yōhei gaikokujin jimmeiroku* (List of foreign employees of China).

the Salt Administration extended only to ensuring that the revenues were paid on time to the foreign consortium banks. By July 1917 the customs revenue had grown to the point that it was able to carry the service of the Reorganization Loan as well as all previous foreign obligations directly charged on it. Thereafter, repayment of the Reorganization Loan was only indirectly linked to a foreign presence in the Salt Administration.

British influence in Peking and in the Yangtze valley was enhanced by the facts that the associate chief inspector was a British national and that almost half of the foreign staff were also British. (The Japanese were the second most numerous foreigners in the salt inspectorate.) The control exercised by the two chief inspectors over the 'salt surplus', that is, collections in excess of the instalments due on the Reorganization Loan, was based upon provisions of the loan agreement requiring that the gross salt revenue be deposited in the foreign banks without deductions and 'be drawn upon only under the joint signatures of the chief inspectors'. This gave Dane great leverage in Peking, provided, however, that the provincial authorities and military commanders continued to remit substantial salt revenues. After 1922 both the total reported collections and the proportion received by the central government fell precipitously. While the customs revenues remained centralized, even at the height of the warlord era, the Sino-foreign inspectorate could not and did not attempt to prevent the provinces from sequestering the salt revenue. Dane's successors – Reginald Gamble, also a former commissioner of salt revenue for Northern India, from 1918; and E. C. C. Wilton, a former British diplomat with long service in China, from 1923 – inevitably enjoyed much less influence than had Dane. The placement of a Russian national, R. A. Konovaloff, formerly of the customs service, in charge of the audit department supervising the expenditure of the Reorganization Loan, and of a German, C. Rump, at the head of a department concerned with future Chinese government borrowing produced little benefit to either of the two governments represented: Konovaloff was told only what the Chinese wanted him to know, and Rump was never consulted.

ECONOMIC INTERESTS

The foreign economic presence in China was very visible, but therein lay a paradox. Foreign firms, investments, loans and personnel dominated important parts of the modern sector of China's economy in the early republic. The modern sector, however, although prominently recorded in contemporary sources and retrospective studies, was only a minute portion of the Chinese economy as a whole. Foreign and Chinese modern enterprise both grew steadily, but neither bulked very large before 1949. As late as 1933, 63 to 65 per cent of gross domestic product originated in agriculture, entirely without direct foreign participation. The South Manchurian Railway Company operated a number of experimental farms in Manchuria, but in no part of China were there foreign-owned plantations producing even the major agricultural export items (tea, silk, vegetable oil and oil products, egg products, hides and skins and bristles), not to speak of the main crops of rice, wheat, vegetables and cotton. Handicraft production, again with no foreign participation, accounted for 7 per cent of GDP in 1933 compared to 2.2 per cent for modern industry, in which the foreign share was significant. Travel by junk, cart, animal and human carriers was three times as important (4 per cent of GDP) as the modern transport sector in which foreign-owned or operated railways and foreign steamships appeared so prominently. China's foreign trade and even her interport trade were carried mainly in foreign vessels, but total foreign trade turn-over certainly never exceeded (and probably never reached) 10 per cent of GDP. If all foreign owned, controlled, operated, or influenced enterprises could, hypothetically, have been nationalized in 1915, and all public and private indebtedness to foreign creditors cancelled, the overall effect in yielding a 'surplus' that could, again hypothetically, have been used for economic and social development would have been as nothing compared to the potential surplus of 37 per cent of net domestic product calculated by Carl Riskin as becoming available as a consequence of the redistribution of wealth and income after 1949.[55]

But the foreign businessmen and their capital were nevertheless present. Let us now look at what forms they took and what influence they exercised.[56]

Trade

Jardine, Matheson and Company, which dated from 1832, and Butterfield and Swire, which commenced business in Shanghai in 1867, were the most prominent of the British trading firms. Unlike many of the 'grand old China houses', both had survived the radical changes of the 1870s and

55 Carl Riskin, 'Surplus and stagnation in modern China', in Dwight H. Perkins, ed. *China's modern economy in historical perspective*, 49–84.
56 The statistical data cited below are derived mainly from the following sources: Yen Chung-p'ing, comp. *Chung-kuo chin-tai ching-chi shih t'ung-chi tzu-liao hsuan-chi* (Selected statistical materials on modern Chinese economic history); Chi-ming Hou, *Foreign investment and economic development in China, 1840–1937*; and Hsiao, *China's foreign trade statistics, 1864–1949*.

1880s when the merchant importing for the market on his own account was finally displaced by the 'commission merchant'. Jardine's head office was in Hong Kong, with branches in every major port. In addition to its general foreign trade department and numerous agencies, the firm controlled the Indo-China Steam Navigation Company (whose 41 steamers were a major presence along the coast and on the Yangtze) and the large Shanghai and Hongkew Wharf Company. It operated a major cotton mill (Ewo) and a silk filature in Shanghai; represented the Russian Bank for Foreign Trade and the Mercantile Bank of India, as well as numerous marine and fire insurance companies and several shipping lines; and had close ties with the Hongkong and Shanghai Banking Corporation. Butterfield was somewhat smaller, but in addition to its Shanghai headquarters also maintained branches in 14 other ports. It operated the China Navigation Company, with a fleet of more than 60 steamers on the Yangtze and along the coast; managed the Taikoo Sugar Refining Company and the Taikoo Dockyard and Engineering Company in Hong Kong; and had numerous shipping and insurance agencies. (More than 200 European insurance companies were represented by Shanghai firms before the First World War.) Gibb, Livingston and Company was also an old British firm in China that had earlier kept branches in Canton, Foochow, Tientsin and at various Yangtze ports. In the second decade of the twentieth century, however, it had offices only in Shanghai, Hong Kong and Foochow. Gibb devoted itself to the export of tea and silk, general commission business for which it had many agencies, Shanghai property, and shipping and insurance agencies. Founded in 1875, Ilbert and Company was one of the first British trading firms to operate exclusively as a 'commission merchant', importing goods that were bought on indentured terms by Chinese merchants. It also operated the Laou Kung Mao Spinning and Weaving Company in Shanghai. One could go on – Dodwell and Company, tea exports and cotton piece goods imports, shipping and insurance agencies, for example, and others – but the increase in German and Japanese competition facing British traders in the early republic should also be noted.

Siemssen and Company, in Shanghai since 1856, was that port's oldest German house and maintained offices also in Hong Kong, Canton, Hankow, Tientsin and Tsingtao. The firm was best known as engineers and contractors of complete equipment for factories and railways, for its insurance agencies, as well as for its extensive import-export business. Carlowitz and Company, which had commenced business in China in the 1840s, was perhaps the largest German firm. Shipping agents, managers of the Yangtze Wharf and Godown Company in Shanghai, exporters of wool, straw-braids, egg products and bristles – Carlowitz was especially prominent as the importer of German heavy machinery, railway and mining equipment (for the Han-Yeh-P'ing Iron and Steel Company and its P'ing-hsiang mines, for example), and weapons (as the exclusive agents in China for the Krupp works). Its main office in Shanghai in Kiukiang Road was the largest building in the International Settlement in 1908. Branches were located in Hong Kong and six treaty ports. A third important German trading firm, Melchers and Company, began business in Hong Kong in 1866 and opened its Shanghai office in 1877. It was the China agent for Norddeutscher Lloyd, and operated river steamers on the Yangtze and the Chang Kah Pang Wharf Company in Shanghai.

The China branches of Mitsui Bussan Kaisha, the largest Japanese trading company, were located at Shanghai and 10 other places. In addition to representing leading Japanese manufacturers and insurance companies, Mitsui held agencies for several well-known British, European and American firms. It operated its own steamer line, and owned and managed two spinning mills (Shanghai Cotton Spinning Company and Santai Cotton Spinning Company) in Shanghai.

In the export trade, foreign merchants had earlier been closely involved in establishing collecting organizations to obtain supplies from the scattered small producers and in making provisions for the grading, sorting and preliminary processing of materials for export. By the late nineteenth century, except for some processing operations (egg products, hides and brick tea by Russian merchants, for example), most of these functions had been taken over by Chinese merchants. In the case of tea, the foreign trader almost always bought in bulk from Chinese dealers at the ports. And although introduced by Europeans, the majority of modern silk filatures by the beginning of the twentieth century were Chinese owned (sometimes with European, usually Italian, managers). The role of the Chinese merchant in the import trade, once the goods had been landed at a treaty port, was even more prominent. With the development of steam shipping from the 1860s, Chinese dealers in imported cotton textiles or opium, for example, tended to by-pass the smaller ports and to purchase directly in Shanghai and Hong Kong. While the foreign houses were not ousted from the smaller ports, some branches were closed, and those that remained concentrated on the collection of export goods and the sale of more specialized imports rather than on the distribution of staples, which was largely in Chinese hands. In this way the business of the foreign trading firms in the early republic had become heavily concentrated in the major treaty ports – in the actual importation (typically as commission agents) of foreign goods for sale to Chinese dealers and in the exportation of Chinese goods (with some processing) from these same places.[57]

The Standard Oil Company of New York shipped its first kerosene to China in the 1880s where it was sold by firms such as Butterfield and Jardine. In 1894, after the failure of lengthy negotiations with Jardine, Matheson and Company to appoint the latter as Standard's permanent sales agent in Asia, including China, Standard Oil undertook to establish its own marketing organization. At first it sold its kerosene only in Shanghai to Chinese dealers who handled all the 'up-country' distribution. Standard Oil resident managers were, however, soon established in the major ports where bulk storage facilities were erected. They appointed and bonded Chinese 'consignees' and closely supervised the sales of these agents and their numerous sub-agents. 'In some places, as in Wuhu, for example, the hand of the New York company extended into street peddling.'[58] Specially prepared Chinese-language pamphlets and posters advertised Standard's premium 'Devoe' brand and the cheaper 'Eagle'. The free distribution or sale at a very low price of small tin lamps with glass chimneys (the famous 'Mei-foo' lamp) created a market for kerosene. By 1910 Standard Oil was shipping 15 per cent of its total exports of kerosene to China. (A 1935 rural survey found that 54 per cent of farming families regularly purchased kerosene.) American salesmen, many with college degrees, who came to China under three-year agreements guaranteeing return passage and offering the possibility of renewal, and Chinese assistants trained in American methods replaced the usual compradore staff of the foreign trading firm. Travelling constantly in the interior, required to learn the Chinese language, responsible for selecting dealers and ensuring supplies in large territories, in perpetual conflict with Chinese officials over local taxes, Standard's agents penetrated into Chinese society as deeply as some of the more enterprising missionaries. Few foreign careers in China were as colourful as that of Roy S. Anderson, son of the missionary president of Soochow University in Shanghai and manager of Standard Oil's Chinkiang office, who participated actively on the republican side in the siege of Nanking in 1911 and in later years was the trusted go-between of warlords.

Standard Oil's chief competitor in China, the Asiatic Petroleum Company (a subsidiary of Royal Dutch Shell, an Anglo-Dutch alliance), operated through a similar sales network under its own direct control. It also sent Western salesmen into the interior, erected storage facilities

57 G. C. Allen and Audrey G. Donnithorne, *Western enterprise in Far Eastern economic development: China and Japan* provides a detailed account.
58 Ralph W. Hidy and Muriel E. Hidy, *Pioneering in big business, 1882–1911*, 552.

in many Chinese cities, and maintained owership of the kerosene until the actual retail sale. But Standard Oil's and Asiatic Petroleum's success ultimately depended upon utilizing rather than replacing China's existing commercial system. Their Chinese 'consignees', that is, wholesalers or jobbers, were often established merchants who had other commercial interests as well. Even the retail proprietors of Standard Oil's distinctive yellow-fronted shops were usually prominent local dealers.

The Singer Sewing Machine Company, Imperial Chemical Industries, which sold chemicals based on alkalis, dyes and fertilizer, and the enormously successful British-American Tobacco Company also depended upon China's traditional marketing structure to reach the final consumer.[59] BAT was distinctive in that, in addition to importing cigarettes manufactured in Great Britain and America, it operated a half-dozen substantial factories of its own in China by 1915, which escaped significant direct taxation because of their claimed extraterritorial status. From 1913 BAT was actively involved in promoting the cultivation of tobacco grown from American seeds by Chinese peasants in Shantung – a foreign intrusion into agricultural production which was as rare in China as it was typical in the fully colonized Asian countries. But its system of distributors and dealers directed by a network of foreign agents was merely superimposed upon existing Chinese transport and local marketing facilities. And in the distribution of seed and fertilizer in Shantung – long a tobacco-growing area – as well as in its purchase of the crop, BAT relied primarily upon Chinese intermediaries.

Beyond the commercial structure itself, the overall poverty of the Chinese economy fundamentally limited the impact of foreign merchants and their goods. The large sales of kerosene, of cigarettes and of imported cotton piece goods (before these last were ousted by the competition of cloth woven in China) were important exceptions. Even in 1936 the per capita value of China's foreign trade, including Manchuria, was still smaller than that of any other country. If, as some analysts suggest, neither China's share of world trade nor its per capita foreign trade were 'abnormally' low for an 'underdeveloped' country of her size and resources, it is still true that foreign demand for China's agricultural and mining exports generated only very weak 'backward linkages' (that is, induced demand for the production of other products in the Chinese economy), while the imported manufactured or processed commodities went mainly to satisfy final demand and consequently generated only weak 'forward linkages' (that is, capital or raw material inputs into

59 See Sherman G. Cochran, 'Big business in China: Sino-American rivalry in the tobacco industry, 1890–1930' (Yale University, Ph.D. dissertation, 1975), on BAT in China.

Chinese production). The hope of economic gain had brought the foreigner to China, but it was less his specific economic influence than the political and psychological facts of his presence under privileged conditions that directly affected the course of China's modern history.

Banking

In the absence of modern financial institutions in China, the early foreign merchant houses undertook to provide for themselves many of the auxiliary services such as banking, foreign exchange and insurance essential to their import-export businesses. But by the second decade of the twentieth century, 12 foreign banks were operating in China.[60] These banks mainly financed the import and export trade of foreign firms. Some direct advances were also made to Chinese merchants, but their chief impact on the Chinese commercial structure took the form of short-term 'chop loans' to the native banks (*ch'ien-chuang*) who in turn lent to Chinese merchants. These credits to the *ch'ien-chuang*, which ceased with the Revolution of 1911, for a time gave the foreign banks considerable leverage over the entire money market in Shanghai.[61]

They practically controlled the foreign exchange market in China. Fluctuations in exchange between Chinese silver currency and gold (the world standard) were frequently large, and foreign exchange dealings and international arbitrage provided substantial profits to the foreign banks, especially the Hongkong Bank, whose daily exchange rates were accepted as official by the entire Shanghai market. The foreign banks used their extraterritorial position to issue bank-notes, a right which the Chinese government never conceded but which it was powerless to counteract. The total value of foreign notes in circulation in 1916 nearly equalled the note issue of Chinese public and private banks combined.[62] Wealthy Chinese deposited their liquid assets in foreign banks, providing one source of the steady silver income upon which the banks based their foreign exchange business. A more important source, however, was

60 Chartered Bank of India, Australia, and China, in China from 1858 (head office: London); Hongkong and Shanghai Banking Corporation, organized 1864 (head office: Hong Kong); Mercantile Bank of India (head office: London); Banque de l'Indo-Chine, in China from 1899 (head office: Paris); Banque Sino-Belge, from 1902 (head office: Brussels); Deutsch-Asiatische Bank, in China from 1889 (head office: Berlin); International Banking Corporation, from 1902 (head office: New York); Nederlandsche Handel-Maatschappij, from 1903 (head office: Amsterdam); Russo-Asiatic Bank, from 1895 (head office: St Petersburg); Yokohama Specie Bank, from 1893 (head office: Yokohama); and Bank of Taiwan (head office: Taihoku [now Taipei])
61 Andrea Lee McElderry, *Shanghai old-style banks (ch'ien-chuang), 1800–1935*, 21–2.
62 See Hsien K'o, *Chin pai-nien-lai ti-kuo-chu-i tsai-Hua yin-hang fa-hsing chih-pi kai-k'uang* (The issue of bank notes in China by imperialist banks in the past 100 years), *passim*.

the major banks' role in servicing China's foreign debt and indemnity payments, which brought an endless inflow of customs and salt receipts and of the working capital of many railways. The major banks, moreover, profited from the placement of indemnity and railway loans with European lenders. Foreign companies holding railway and mining concessions in China were frequently affiliates of the banks; the British and Chinese Corporation was closely linked to the Hongkong Bank, for example, as were the German Shantung railway and mining companies to the Deutsch-Asiatische Bank. One study of British bankers' profits in China from the issuance and service of foreign loans in the period 1895–1914 concludes that they averaged from 4.5 per cent (for non-railway loans) to 10 per cent (for railway loans which normally included provisions for profit-sharing and for the bank to act as purchasing agent) of the par value of the loans.[63]

The foreign banks lost some of their privileged position to the government-backed banks in the 1920s, especially after 1928 but they continued to be pre-eminent in financing foreign trade. At any time, however, their influence on the Chinese economy outside of the foreign trade and government finance sectors was negligible. Like the traders who were their chief customers, the foreign banks affected China most by being foreign, privileged and frequently arrogant. They of course had some links with China's small but widespread modernizing sector. Speculation in the Shanghai rubber market in 1910, for example, severely damaged the Szechwan Railway Company, and its demands that these losses be covered by the Peking government's scheme to nationalize the Canton-Hankow railway helped precipitate the Revolution of 1911. But, overall, while financial panics might make headlines, Shanghai and the other ports were only loosely tied to the economy of the vast hinterland. Domination of the modern sector, if it could be achieved by outsiders – or even by insiders – hardly constituted control of China.

Manufacturing and mining

In the second decade of the twentieth century foreigners had a dominant share in four industries which together accounted for 52 per cent of net value added by modern industry in 1933: these were cotton yarn and cloth, cigarettes, coal mining, and electric power.[64] In 1933 foreign-owned firms produced 35 per cent of the total value of production by

63 C. S. Chen, 'Profits of British bankers from Chinese loans, 1895–1914', *Tsing Hua Journal of Chinese studies*, N.S., 5.1 (July 1965) 107–20.
64 John K. Chang, *Industrial development in pre-communist China: a quantitative analysis*, 55.

TABLE 36

Foreign shares in coal mining and cotton textile industries

| | Coal mining (% total output in tons mined by modern methods) | | Cotton yarn and cloth (% spindles and looms in operation*) | | | |
| | | | Spindles | | Looms | |
	Foreign-owned mines	Sino-foreign mines	Foreign-owned	Chinese-owned	Foreign-owned	Chinese-owned
1910			30.3	69.7	—	100.0
1912	42.6	49.3				
1914			46.0	54.0	50.1	49.9
1915	35.2	54.5				
1918	34.1	43.2				
1919			43.6	56.4		
1920			41.9	58.1	49.0	51.0
1921	30.9	45.0				

* Spindles and looms in Sino-foreign mills are allocated equally to foreign and Chinese ownership.

manufacturing industries as a whole, but no comparable overall estimate can be made for 1910–20, at a time when 75 to 90 per cent of modern coal mining and nearly half of the cotton textile industry were in foreign hands. Estimates in table 36 show the foreign share in coal mining and cotton textiles. Production figures are not available, but the cigarette industry was dominated by foreigners too, judging by a comparison of BAT's sales of 12 billion cigarettes in 1919 (a large part manufactured in China) with the two billion sold by its chief Chinese competitor, the Nanyang Brothers Tobacco Company. And the generation of electric power in the major ports – again no output data are available for 1910–20 – was also largely a foreign preserve.

Yet the caveats already raised against reading too many conclusions into statistics about the modern sector, just because they are the only quantitative data available, need to be faced once more. Cigarette sales certainly boomed after BAT was launched in 1902, but there is little evidence that the predominant forms in which tobacco was consumed outside of urban areas did not continue to be in the peasant's long pipe, in water pipes, or as snuff – all of which had been widespread since the seventeenth century. Even as late as 1935 only 19 per cent of farm families purchased tobacco of any kind. In the case of cotton yarn, only 18 per cent of total consumption in 1905 (and 34 per cent in 1919) was produced in modern mills, Chinese- and foreign-owned, in China. The comparable figures for cotton cloth are 1 per cent and 5 per cent in 1905 and 1919, respectively. Handicraft production and imports together accounted for

82 per cent of the yarn consumed in 1905 and 66 per cent in 1919; and for 99 per cent and 95 per cent of the cloth. These proportions suggest that China's most developed modern industry, cotton textiles, in which the foreign share loomed so large, did not clothe a substantial majority of the Chinese population. The average annual production during the years 1912–21 of 10 million tons of coal by modern mining methods – or even the annual total of 16 million tons by modern and traditional mines together – provided only a meagre proportion of the total energy consumed by the 450–500 million Chinese who, as in the past, continued to depend upon wood, straw and vegetable wastes for their fuel. Even in 1933 China's total output of coal was only 28 million tons (compare 1973: 250 million metric tons), almost entirely consumed in the large cities, by railways and steamers, and by the small modern manufacturing sector. Similarly, the 1.42 billion kilowatt hours of electricity produced in 1933 (compare 1973: 101 billion), of which 63 per cent was accounted for by foreign-owned utilities, served exclusively the larger cities.

Of the 45 cotton mills in China in 1919, 15 were Japanese- and British-owned. On the average, the foreign mills spun yarn five to seven counts higher than the Chinese-owned mills. This difference had two important implications for the ability of the Chinese firms to withstand very strong foreign competition and to hold their share of the market in succeeding years. Low-count yarn was spun using a more labour-intensive technology than high-count yarn, and therefore fitted the circumstances of the Chinese producers for whom capital was more scarce and expensive and labour costs were somewhat lower. The lower-count yarn was also more readily marketed to handicraft weavers who used it as warp in combination with handspun weft to produce a coarse, long-wearing cloth much in demand in rural areas. There was a tendency, in other words, for Chinese and foreign manufacturing firms to operate in partially discrete markets, the bulk of the foreign output supplying consumers in the treaty ports and other large cities. The same pattern held in the cigarette industry where Nanyang Brothers concentrated on producing cheaper products for a different segment of consumers from those of BAT; in coal mining where foreign and Chinese mines did not usually operate in the same localities; and in banking where, as noted earlier, foreign banks specialized in financing international transactions.

Of course the modern manufacturing sector, foreign firms included, was neither stagnant nor unimportant as a base for later economic development. In fact the pre-1937 average annual rate of growth of China's industrial sector, Manchuria included, was 8 to 9 per cent.[65] These plants,

65 Ibid., 70–4.

moreover, made important contributions to China's post-1949 economic growth. Among the less obvious benefits, the inherited small-scale engineering plants in Shanghai and elsewhere contributed significantly to resolving the economic difficulties of the 1960s.[66]

What is questionable is the view that the conspicuous foreign role in the modern manufacturing sector was a primary cause of either China's overall economic backwardness or of the debilitating economic inequalities which characterized pre-1949 China. The *economic* consequences – with respect to both development and distribution – of whether a plant was foreign-owned or Chinese-owned were minuscule as compared with the primary political and psychological effects of the privileged, and in the case of modern industry sometimes dominant, foreign presence in China. Studies of pre-1949 industry show not only the impressive rate of growth cited above, but also strong evidence that Chinese-owned enterprises grew at least as fast as foreign manufacturing firms.[67] The long-term trend in the twentieth century, though imperfectly known, suggests a gradual increase in the Chinese share of capitalization and output in foreign trade and banking as well as in industry. To the extent that the traditional sector of the economy (handicraft manufacture, for example) was undermined by modern industry, the Chinese-owned modern sector was primarily responsible because it mainly served the geographically and technologically discrete rural market, whereas the foreign plants' customers were more likely to be relatively well-to-do urban residents. In the long run perhaps the most important aspect of foreign manufacturing was its transfer to China of modern industrial technology in the form of machinery, technical skills and organization. This 'demonstration effect' also operated in the financial and commercial sectors where Chinese modern banks and insurance companies became increasingly important after 1911 and Chinese foreign trading companies modelled on their foreign rivals began to be of some significance in the 1920s.

Foreign manufacturing firms benefited 'unfairly' from their extraterritorial status, from their ability to escape some direct taxation and the especially heavy hand of Chinese officialdom, from their access to foreign capital markets, and sometimes from better management or improved technology. This privileged status, as well as their conspicuousness and hauteur, fed the burgeoning nationalism of twentieth-century China which expressed itself in 'buy-Chinese' sentiments. Chinese-owned firms

66 See Thomas G. Rawski, 'The growth of producer industries, 1900–1971', in Perkins, ed. *China's Modern Economy*, 203–34.
67 Hou, *Foreign investment*, 138–41.

capitalized upon this through boycotts (for example, in 1905, 1908, 1909, 1915, 1919–21) both against goods produced by foreign plants in China and against imports, and probably also through more frequent labour disputes in foreign-owned than in Chinese-owned factories. Anti-imperialist sentiment was a growing reality, but it does not follow that, because nationalist propaganda pronounced it so, foreign industry in China in fact retarded China's modernization, undermined handicraft production (which contradicts the first assertion), prevented the growth of Chinese manufacturing, or exploited Chinese workers any more (or less) egregiously than native capitalists.

Transport

In the first two decades of the twentieth century, 85 to 90 per cent of China's foreign trade by value was carried in foreign flag vessels. Foreign-owned shipping also moved two-thirds of the coastal trade between open or treaty ports, insofar as this freight was carried in 'foreign-type vessels' and thus recorded in the Maritime Customs statistics. 'Inland waters navigation', that is steamer trade to or between places other than treaty or open ports, was recorded by the customs only to the extent that dutiable cargo entered or left such a port. In the absence of value data, we may judge from the number of foreign (1,125) and Chinese (211) vessels registered under the Inland Steam Navigation Regulations in 1914 that this traffic, too, was dominated by foreign shipping.

That China's overseas trade was carried primarily in foreign vessels is not surprising, but cabotage, that is, coastal and inland navigation, in international law is generally restricted to domestic carriers. Trade by foreign vessels between Chinese ports and navigation of China's rivers had been imposed upon China by the treaty powers; no reciprocal right, even in theory, was received by China.

It is impossible to assess the precise quantitative effects of foreign coastal and riverine steamer trade on traditional junks and their boatmen. Chinese government opposition to expansion of steam shipping reflected apprehension of disorders sparked by unemployed boatmen. On the other hand, Chinese junks probably benefited on balance from an expansion of total inland trade. There were countless places unreachable by steamer which were tied into the growing commerce by 500,000 junks which plied not only the rivers but also extensive networks of canals and creeks. All the qualitative indications as well as the scattered statistics available for the 1930s suggest that the junk was still the main means of transport in South China. Even in 1959 only 36 per cent of the total volume of goods transported in the People's Republic of China was carried by the modern transport sector; the rest primarily by junk.

Between 1903 and 1918 the major Yangtze River steamer route was shared in roughly equal proportions (with respect to both number of vessels and total tonnage) by four shipping companies: Butterfield and Swire's China Navigation Company, Jardine's Indo-China Steam Navigation Company, the Japanese Nisshin Kisen Kaisha, and the Chinese-government owned China Merchants' Steam Navigation Company. New England skippers and Scottish chief engineers predominated in the British and Chinese fleets. ('Tradition held that if you wanted the "chief", you just called "Mac" down the engine-hatch and he appeared'.[68]) To avoid price wars, these large lines frequently negotiated shipping rates among themselves. British and Japanese shipping dominated overall in the overseas and inter-port trade, the Japanese gradually drawing closer to their rival (38 per cent British and 21 per cent Japanese of the total tonnage entered and cleared by customs in 1910 compared to 38 per cent and 29 per cent respectively in 1919).

Transport accounted for nearly a third (31.5 per cent) of direct foreign investment in China in 1914. The bulk of this third was invested in railways, the capitalization of the steam shipping companies being relatively small. Foreign railway interests were a complex amalgam ranging from a fair number of unrealized railway concessions to several major lines directly controlled by foreign powers. Between these two extremes were lines built entirely or in part with foreign loans under contracts which generally granted the construction of the lines to the lenders (who profited as purchasing agents for imported materials) and, before the 1908 Tientsin-Pukow Railway Agreement, placed the management of the lines in the hands of the lenders during the period of the loan. In some cases before 1908 the foreign agencies were granted a share of the net profits until the loans were repaid. Even after 1908 most loan agreements provided for a foreign chief engineer which implied some participation by the creditors in the management of the lines.

As of 1918, out of an approximate total of 6,700 miles of railway lines in operation, including Manchuria, the lines built entirely with Chinese capital included only a few hundred miles of the incomplete Canton-Hankow line, the short Tientsin-Shanhaikwan section of the Peking-Mukden line, and 376 miles of the Peking-Suiyuan line. Only the last mentioned had been built by Chinese engineers. Foreign-owned railways

68 Esson M. Gale, *Salt for the dragon: a personal history of China, 1908–45*, 66.

totalled 2,487 miles: the Chinese Eastern Railway (Russia, 1,073 miles), the South Manchurian Railway and its branches (Japan, 841 miles), the Yunnan Railway (France, 289 miles), and the Kiaochow-Tsinan Railway (Germany, Japan from 1915, 284 miles). Between 1913 and 1915 the 4,000 miles of track constituting the Chinese Government Railways were welded into a national system, so far as accounts and statistics were concerned, with the assistance of Dr Henry Carter Adams (of the University of Michigan and the Interstate Commerce Commission) who served as adviser to the Chinese government on the standardization of railway accounts during 1913–17. Foreign financial interests, however, in varying degrees continued to have claims on much of this mileage. By the provisions of their several loan contracts British investors had substantial control of the Peking-Mukden line (600 miles) and the Shanghai-Nanking line (204 miles); and they participated in the management of the southern section of the Tientsin-Pukow line (237 miles), the Shanghai-Hangchow-Ningpo line (179 miles) and the Taokow-Chinghua line (95 miles) through the employment of British chief engineers and other personnel. A French chief engineer represented French creditors of the Cheng-T'ai (Shansi) railway (151 miles), and Belgian, Dutch, and French engineers and accountants supervised the 365 miles of the Lunghai line which had been completed by 1918.

The 'imperialist' purposes of the several powers was what brought foreign capital into China's railways. As glaring symbols of foreign violations of Chinese sovereignty and territorial integrity, both the concession lines and those with heavy foreign indebtedness drew the wrath of Chinese nationalism. Foreign political interests, too, contributed to the construction of a less than optimum network of parallel lines in Manchuria. While no study has yet been made of this question, it is probable that as a result of wars and political changes in China and abroad, a substantial part of the foreign capital invested in railways was never repaid. In any case, the enormous physical capital construction contributed by the foreigner played a crucial role in providing modern transport facilities in the northern half of China, where widely separated economic regions and the absence of substantial water routes were major barriers to economic development. The Government Railways of China, even after payment of their foreign debt service, showed a profit of Ch.$41 million on a total investment of Ch.$522 million in 1920. This Ch.$41 million is gross of any imputed interest on the Chinese government share of the total investment. If that return is calculated at 5 per cent, a net profit of Ch.$31 million still remained. In the warlord era, especially from 1922, profits fell and an increasingly smaller proportion came under the Peking government's control, yet these largely foreign-built and foreign-financed lines were an economic success.

Public finance

In the decade 1912–21, at least 70 mostly quite small unsecured loans and advances with a total outstanding balance of perhaps Ch.$200 million in 1921 were made to various central government or provincial agencies by a very wide variety of foreign lenders. The largest were the notorious 'Nishihara loans' of 1917–18, payments to Chinese officials by means of which Japanese interests sought to advance their claims in Manchuria and Mongolia. Given the deteriorating financial situation of the Peking government, these loans were mainly in default. The outstanding railway loan balance of about Ch.$300 million, in contrast was regularly serviced from the income of the several lines until about 1925. But the largest part of China's foreign public indebtedness was made up by the Japanese war and indemnity loans, the Boxer indemnity, the Crisp Loan of 1912, and the Reorganization Loan of 1913, which together represented an outstanding balance in 1921 of approximately Ch.$1,000 million.[69] These debts were all secured on either or both the Maritime Customs Service revenue and the Salt Administration revenue, and principal and interest were paid without interruption.

Apart from the railway loans, these foreign funds contributed nothing to the Chinese economy. The indemnity loans and the Boxer indebtedness represented a net drain while the rest were expended for the largely unproductive administrative and military needs of the Peking government. Foreign lenders saw themselves as propping up the central government or supporting some particular faction against its rivals. Their banks in Shanghai profited as the depositories of the customs and salt revenues earmarked for repayment of the secured loans, and from their control of the foreign exchange market on which Chinese silver was converted into the gold payments stipulated in the loan agreements. Perhaps some political influence with Peking was secured. Even excluding the Boxer indemnity, annual payments of interest and amortization on China's foreign debt in the second decade of the century amounted to at least a quarter or a third of the revenue of the impoverished Chinese central government. (Financial data for the early republic remain an unstudied morass.)

69 Hsu I-sheng, *Chung-kuo chin-tai wai-chai shih t'ung-chi tzu-liao, 1853–1927* (Statistical materials on foreign loans in modern China, 1853–1927); and *The China year book, 1923*, 713–27, 744–8.

About all that can be said in favour of China's foreign indebtedness in the early republic is that on a per capita basis – perhaps Ch.\$3 in 1921 – it was low by international standards.

Overall, the foreigner's economic gains, based in part on and multiplied by his privileged position, were not absolute deductions from China's economic welfare. On the contrary, China's indigenous economic modernization – the first ruptures of the 'high-level equilibrium trap' which ensnared the Chinese economy at a low level of total output – began only in response to the exogenous shock of imported foreign goods and foreign manufacturing in China.[70] Trade, foreign investment in manufacturing and transport, and the importation of technology produced absolute gains for the Chinese economy, albeit the growth of national product was slow and its social distribution questionable. In a different political context, that is, if China had been served by an effective central government, the backward and forward linkages of foreign trade and foreign manufacture with the Chinese-owned sector of the domestic economy could undoubtedly have been greater. The foreign economic presence, however, was only one factor – and not the major one – contributing to the debility of the Chinese polity.

70 See Robert F. Dernberger, 'The role of the foreigner in China's economic development, 1840–1949', in Perkins, ed. *China's modern economy*, 19–47.

CHAPTER 4

POLITICS IN THE AFTERMATH
OF REVOLUTION:
THE ERA OF YUAN SHIH-K'AI, 1912–16

The years immediately following the Revolution of 1911, when Yuan Shih-k'ai was president of the first Chinese republic (1912–16), can be approached in two quite different ways. One emphasizes the beginnings of warlordism: the breakdown of political unity, the emergence of military rule, and the spread of an amoral and treacherous spirit of *sauve qui peut* among those in authority. In this view, the triumph of the Revolution was rendered meaningless even at the very moment of victory. When the formal mandate to govern was passed from the child Manchu emperor and his court to Yuan Shih-k'ai in February 1912, China lost her powerful monarchical symbols of political integration with a history of over two thousand years. In exchange, an unscrupulous and reactionary militarist occupied the central post, with neither programme nor imperial potency; the new republican forms meant little. The result, according to this view, was a rapid slide into warlordism under Yuan Shih-k'ai's aegis.

The second approach stresses the continuities with the pre-revolutionary years and sees the Revolution of 1911 not as another episode in the weakening of China's polity, but as an early climax in a nationalist movement to invigorate politics and society. In this view, the aftermath of the revolution witnessed a testing in practice of the two competing ideas of self-government and administrative centralization, that had been winning adherents during the previous decade. It was a time of energetic political experimentation. Along with experiment went conflict, as the expansion of political participation collided with efforts to centralize authority. But it was only after these competing programmes had each had a period of vigorous life that the attributes of warlordism emerged. The Yuan Shih-k'ai presidency period is best understood, according to this interpretation, as the logical consequence of China's first wave of nationalism, embracing both its virtues and its fatal flaws.

Ample data can be marshalled on behalf of either approach. In this account the second approach is favoured, because it seems to make more sense of the leading political tendencies, among which Yuan's presidency was only one. But the first approach is a useful corrective to any inadvertent glorification of the politicians of the period. This first wave of nationalism, after all, came nowhere near attaining its essential objective of a strong and independent Chinese state. More thoroughgoing attempts were required before China's sovereignty was recovered. And meanwhile, warlordism and its special oppressions intervened.

THE AMBIGUOUS LEGACY OF THE REVOLUTION

Whichever approach is preferred, the ambiguity of the Revolution of 1911 must be acknowledged, hovering as it did between success and failure, with the unresolved tensions in the polity being passed on to the early republic. Our account of the period begins by noting these ambiguities or tensions and discussing their various sources.

The ambiguity of the revolutionary aftermath began with the negotiated settlement of the revolution itself. The first talks between imperial officials and representatives of the revolutionary forces took place in November 1911, about one month after the first republican successes. Formal negotiations began in December. The main issues were worked out during January 1912, and the abdication of the Ch'ing monarch was decreed on 12 February. Within three more months the institutions of a new national government were functioning in Peking. Who had won? Judging from the eruption of armed attacks on the government in 1913 and 1916 (sometimes called the Second and Third Revolutions), we can conclude that the settlement of 1912 was an unstable compromise.

On the one hand, the settlement consolidated an enormous revolutionary victory. The Ch'ing dynasty was overthrown, a feat that had eluded numerous previous attempts, including the massive Taiping Rebellion of the mid nineteenth century. Moreover, the Ch'ing was replaced by a new form of government; the imperial order, which had supported an immeasurable accumulation of attitudes and political habits, was abolished. Both these accomplishments proved to be irrevocable, despite attempts to rescind one or both of them in 1915–16 and 1917. The two irreducible aims of the republican revolutionaries had been permanently achieved: the overthrow of the Manchus and the establishment of a republic.

On the other hand, the new arrangements were far from ideal for those who had served the revolution the longest. Perhaps the generous settlement accorded the abdicating child emperor and his large household, including promise of a substantial stipend, was a harmless concession (though his survival allowed the Japanese to use him in the 1930s when establishing a subservient Manchu kingdom in the north-east). Revolutionary expectations were more seriously compromised by the new head of state, Yuan Shih-k'ai, a leading imperial official. The revolutionary spokesmen accepted the 52 year-old Yuan to lead the new order as the price for his arranging the Ch'ing abdication and in order to avoid a prolonged civil war. Some were even optimistic about his likely future role. He was capable and could be labelled a 'progressive' among the mandarins. After all his power was to be limited by constitutional arrangements, including a cabinet and a national legislature, designed by the revolutionaries themselves. But the resulting compromise of a constitutional president with no established revolutionary or republican commitments was to prove a source of great uneasiness. This uneasiness was heightened by Yuan's unwillingess to leave Peking in order to receive his presidential confirmation in Nanking, the centre of revolutionary power by early 1912. And it was further augmented by the limited role accorded veteran revolutionaries, who were excluded from the financial and army posts in the first republican cabinet in Peking. The question of who had won the revolution remained clouded.

Another ambiguity lay in the effect of the revolution on national unity. Conceived in nationalism, the revolution demanded the preservation of the territory of the Ch'ing dynasty as a basis for the new nation. Yuan's rise to the presidency stemmed from the urgency of this demand. In practice, however, the revolution severed most administrative ties between the provinces and the central government. In some provinces, ironically, distrust of Yuan as president increased the resistance to reconstituting administrative links between province and centre. Furthermore, the outlying areas of Outer Mongolia and Tibet had moved towards complete separation from any Chinese government.

In the case of Mongolia and Tibet, the set-back to Han Chinese nationalist goals had two aspects. Local non-Han elites took the occasion to escape from Peking's control, thereby shrinking the Ch'ing legacy to the republic. And foreign powers took the opportunity to expand their spheres of influence, thereby tightening the strategic encirclement of China. Begun in reaction to late Ch'ing programmes of intervention in these old dependencies, princely Mongolian and Tibetan movements to throw off Peking's authority succeeded in late 1911 and early 1912. But they consolidated their successes only under Russian protection in Outer Mongolia and British protection in Tibet. Peking's subsequent efforts to recover these lost territories had, of necessity, to take the form of negotiating with these European powers. Neither Russia nor Great Britain was insisting on full colonial absorption. But all that the early republican governments could salvage was a tenuous suzerainty in these outlying portions of the former Ch'ing empire.

Foreign governments took advantage of revolutionary disruption in a variety of ways. The degree of foreign participation in China's customs collection greatly increased, when foreign commissioners became not just assessors and accountants but also actual collectors of the revenue. Further, the proceeds were, by arrangements struck during the revolution, deposited in foreign banks before disbursement. The measure gave foreign financiers both heightened controls and profits. These and other augmentations of foreign privilege during the Revolution of 1911 betrayed Chinese nationalism and sullied the revolutionary banner.

A number of circumstances marking the revolution help to explain the ambiguities of the result. The revolutionary movement, whose broadest organization had been the T'ung-meng hui, had failed to preserve solidarity in the years preceding the revolution. Its national leaders often had little connection with revolutionary developments in the provinces and were unable to weld into a cohesive whole the forces that burgeoned there during the revolution. Such unified revolutionary determination as they were able to muster was blunted by the fear that continued disruption and warfare might lead to full-scale foreign intervention, for which they were strategically and psychologically quite unprepared. Hence, despite a loosely joined accumulation of revolutionary troops that quantitatively far surpassed those at the disposal of the Ch'ing court, compromise seemed necessary. Compromise included accepting the Ch'ing prime minister, Yuan Shih-k'ai, as president. Although 14 provinces established revolutionary governments, in the revolution's aftermath the old revolutionary organization could rely on committed adherents as chief executives in only three provinces (Kwangtung, Kiangsi and Anhwei). Revolutionaries had in fact never been completely in charge of the revolution and were not disposed to press the issue.

Another feature of the revolution that contributed to the ambiguity of the result was the social conservatism that accompanied its political radicalism. The revolution replaced a venerable system of government with the latest Western model. The constitution located sovereignty in the people. Sovereignty was to be exercised by a national assembly (or parliament) plus a president, cabinet and judiciary. But it soon became apparent that the new political system would not displace the prevailing social elites from their positions of dominance. On the contrary, the old ruling class emerged both unscathed and invigorated. Although secret societies with their lower class constituencies were active, notably in Szechwan and Shensi, they did not seriously challenge the political preeminence of army officers, republican revolutionary politicians, and the leaders of self-government bodies. All three of these dominant groups were socially elite, mainly gentry. Another possible threat to the received social order was the existence of mass armies, mobilized in support of the revolution in several provinces. But these too were contained and, where necessary, forcibly dispersed (Kwangtung was the most dramatic case).

The formal recognition of popular sovereignty was accompanied by the spread of political participation in the society, and this was radical. But at the same time the organized forces of the revolution, no matter how quarrelsome among themselves, were generally united in keeping political control in upper class hands, especially those of the gentry, and this was conservative. When Chiao Ta-feng as revolutionary military governor of Hunan appeared to be basing his power on secret societies in late October 1911, he was assassinated, and a more socially conservative grouping around the provincial assembly leader, T'an Yen-k'ai, took power. When the revolutionary government in Kweichow persisted in an alliance with lower class elements, it was overthrown in March 1912 by military force from a neighbouring revolutionary province (Yunnan). The Chinese social elite had become more variegated in its cultural styles and economic activity since the late nineteenth century. But in the aftermath of the 1911 Revolution it still acted with remarkable cohesion and determination in defence of its interests. The few defectors or waverers were easily deposed, without resort to assistance from Yuan Shih-k'ai in Peking.

While the gentry were successfully guarding against threats to their social power, they made two demands on the national and provincial leadership. The country should remain unified; and the localities should enjoy self-government. Here was another source of unresolved tension in the revolutionary aftermath. Chinese unity was both a treasured historical inheritance and, in the face of foreign designs, an urgent present necessity. There seemed to be no serious dissent from this fundamental proposition. But how was Chinese unity to be organized? In the wake of the revolution some important political leaders and groups urged a centralized administration. They included Yuan Shih-k'ai in Peking and Ts'ai O, military governor in the distant province of Yunnan. A centralized administration was a plank in some party platforms. But in the early months after the revolution, these voices were drowned out (and voted down in the national assembly) by the advocates of local self-government, who often espoused an extreme form of provincial autonomy.

The idea that autonomous provinces would better serve Chinese nationalism than would a centralized state had gained considerable currency in the last years of the Ch'ing. After most provinces emerged from the revolution fully autonomous, there was little disposition to surrender their accrued privileges, including command over provincial armies, the retention of tax revenues, and the selection of local and provincial officials. At the same time, local assemblies below the provincial level swelled greatly in incidence and assertiveness. To the minds of the provincialists, the two demands of unity and self-government could be wedded in federal structures. The early republic was at first a *de facto* confederation of provinces. But the continuing foreign pressure on Chinese sovereignty put a great strain on such a loose arrangement.

THE STRUCTURE OF THE NEW ORDER

The new political order had the task of establishing itself amidst these unresolved tensions. A brief description of its structure in the spring of 1912 is a necessary preliminary to tracing the main events.

As agreed in the negotiations concluding the revolution, Yuan Shih-k'ai was president. He swore to a republican oath composed, like the Provisional Constitution (Lin-shih yueh-fa) of 1912, by the revolutionary leadership. But the president was endowed by the new constitution with considerable executive power. Impeachment was not made easy; he was theoretically commander-in-chief of all China's army and navy; and, again theoretically, he possessed broad powers of appointment. He was to share responsibilities with a prime minister and cabinet, whom he appointed with the concurrence of the parliament or national assembly. The first prime minister was T'ang Shao-i, an old associate of Yuan's, whose sympathy for the revolutionary side unexpectedly persisted after the revolution.

The first provisional parliament of the republic consisted of representatives from the provinces, five delegates each. The parliament lacked any significant royalist group, but adherents of the main revolutionary party, the T'ung-meng hui, held less than one-third of the seats. This reflected the T'ung-meng hui's failure to dominate more than a minority of the governments even of those provinces that had joined the revolution. The other major parties represented either factions that had previously split from the T'ung-meng hui, or the reformist constitutional movement of officials and gentry that had adopted republicanism only during – and in some cases, after – the revolution. One principal achievement of this parliament was the legislation guiding the election of a more permanent, bicameral parliament and of new provincial assemblies. (The new assemblies actually were constituted in the first half of 1913.) Another achievement was the rejection of Yuan's efforts to establish administrative machinery for subordinating the provinces.

In most provinces, political leadership was drawn from two institutions: the army, especially the leaders of the modern New Army units formed around the country in the late Ch'ing, and the provincial assemblies. Although the precipitation of the revolution had often begun at lower levels, it was people from these two groups who had consolidated power as Ch'ing authority collapsed. The top executive was in every province the military governor (*tu-tu*). If we exclude the Manchurian provinces and Kansu, where conditions differed and comparison is difficult, then 12 of the remaining 17 'home' provinces had soldiers as military governors in the mid summer of 1912. (Of these 12, six were Chinese graduates of the Japanese Army Officers Academy.) There were five men without military backgrounds in this post, two of them in provinces that had not joined the revolution before the Ch'ing abdication. The balance between army and provincial assembly varied considerably from province to province. In Yunnan the New Army officers maintained rigid control over the provincial government. In Hunan they gave way to leaders out of the provincial assembly. In a few provinces the revolutionary party and its adherents were a third force and might even, as in Kwangtung, dominate the provincial government. In some cases, important sections of the army, not necessarily including the military governor, were adherents of the revolutionary party or shared its relative radicalism, as in Hupei and Kiangsu. The resulting politics was often quite confusing. Remarkably, sufficient cohesion was achieved in most of the formerly revolutionary provinces to prevent Peking from injecting its power locally. Only in the three northern provinces of Chihli, Honan and Shantung and, somewhat less confidently, in Manchuria could Yuan unilaterally appoint important officials.

Most provincial governments were not only immune to Peking's control; they were also able to muster sufficient energy to prevent lesser administrative units from splitting off. The consolidation of provincial authority was in several cases a difficult process. One pattern by which the revolution had spread was the establishment of sub-provincial revolutionary governments, often at the prefectural level. Their subordination to the provincial government was not always accomplished either swiftly or completely. But in comparison with Peking's authority in the formerly revolutionary provinces, the fiscal and appointive powers of provincial governments in their own domain were extensive by the end of 1912. This was due partly to the circumstances of the revolution – its primary act having been the destruction of central authority and its form being internally decentralized. It also owed much to the assertion that provinces could best serve China's interests by insisting on their autonomy in the face of the stifling centralization that was believed to have marked Ch'ing rule, especially in its final years.

Among the many presentations of the case for provincial autonomy was that written in 1912 by Tai Chi-t'ao, a young journalist in Shanghai. 'With respect to the localities, the role of the province is that of the highest administrative district. With respect to the centre, it is the largest sphere of self-government. To attain the goals of republicanism, one must seek to develop people's rights [*min-ch'üan*], and in seeking to develop people's rights, the scope of self-government must be enlarged.' Tai noted that advocates of centralization 'argue that the reason for China's not prospering is that localism is too ingrained, so that province is set off from province, and prefecture from prefecture. . .'. But Tai would reverse the argument. China was too large and its people too numerous to be ruled through centralized institutions, which had often caused decay and collapse under the empire. 'Seen in this light, the reason China has not prospered is that the ideas of centralization are too ingrained and the concept of self-government too weak.' Provincial autonomy and the popular election of provincial chiefs, Tai felt, were keys to national political progress and tranquillity.[1]

These sentiments were squarely opposed to those of Peking's bureaucrats, including the country's president. Tai's analysis also implied the need to check the attempt of sub-provincial districts to escape provincial power.

The actual success of provincial governments in extending their power throughout their provinces varied widely. The Ch'ing in its last few years had begun establishing self-government councils and assemblies at the hsien and lesser levels. After the revolution, the incidence of such bodies mounted rapidly. In the Ch'ing plan, these local representative organs were supposed to manage and finance a range of local reforms, particularly in education, under the guidance of centrally appointed officials. With the revolution, some local assemblies became politically aggressive and presumed to select their own executive authorities, including county magistrates. Such assertiveness harmonized with one persistent school of political thought over the centuries that urged a closer, more organic connection between local elites and their administrators. As a practical matter in 1912 and 1913, it not only violated the conceptions entertained for the Chinese polity by the centralizers in Peking; it also defied provincial authority. Generally speaking, provincial authority prevailed. But judging from provincial budgets in these years, the success

1 Tai Chi-t'ao, *Tai T'ien-ch'ou wen-chi* (Collected essays of Tai Chi-t'ao) (Taipei reprint edn, 1962), 187-95.

was often only partial, as more revenue seems to have been retained in the counties than had been the case in most provinces under the Ch'ing.

Meanwhile, the charge on provincial revenues was greatly increased by the expanded armies of the revolutionary aftermath. Despite some demobilization even before the Ch'ing abdication, the provinces that had joined the revolution were in most cases left with a large assortment of troops, some inherited from the Ch'ing and some conscripted during the revolution. The soldiers could not easily be dismissed without payment of the arrears that had commonly accumulated; but the longer they were retained, the greater was the amount owed and the more likely were they to take to rioting and looting. In Kiangsu, for example, a Japanese consul estimated that the province had 44,000 soldiers at the end of the Ch'ing rule there, that the numbers grew to 180,000 during the revolution, and that after strenuous efforts at disbandment, there were still over 100,000 in various military units in August 1912.[2] The precise numbers nationally were a matter of speculation. For purposes of negotiating loans with foreign banks, in part to pay for demobilization, the Peking government used a figure of over 800,000 men under arms throughout the country. As long as such locally financed troops remained, they both strengthened and weakened the provinces. They provided a potential defence against Peking authority; but they drained funds from provincial budgets that might otherwise have financed reforms and given vitality to provincial autonomy. Demobilization continued in 1912 and 1913, so that by the spring of 1913 there were perhaps half a million troops in fairly modernized or formal units.[3] But financing and command remained provincial responsibilities in most of the formerly revolutionary provinces, until Yuan's armed assault on provincial autonomy in the summer of 1913.

Despite numerous mutinies, which were characteristically directed against the actuality or threat of short wages, the armies did not turn against the social order or challenge the dominance of the existing elite groups. Nor did the countryside stay long in a turbulent state. Reports of banditry were common, and occasionally villages would rise up against extortionate taxes or malfeasant officials. But suppression was regularly applied and rural disturbances did not reach proportions worthy of national attention before the Second Revolution. The threat from below

2 Funatsu Shinichirō, consul in Nanking, to Uchida Yasuchika, foreign minister, secret despatch No. 38 (23 Aug. 1912), microfilms of the Japanese Foreign Ministry, MT 5.1.10.5-1.

3 Japanese General Staff, 'Kakumei-go ni okeru Shina kakushō zōgen ichi-ranbyō' (Table of changes in military strength of the various Chinese provinces after the revolution), 10 March 1913, microfilms of the Japanese Foreign Ministry, MT 5.1.10.5-1, reel 463, pp. 420-1.

preoccupied the local social and political leadership, even though it was diffuse and unorganized. It was successfully contained, while the national leadership experimented with liberal politics.

POLITICAL PARTIES AND CONSTITUTIONAL GOVERNMENT

The question of whether groups might properly band together outside the government in order to effect political ends has been a lively one in the course of Chinese history. The weight of orthodox opinion under the empire had been that such parties, cliques or factions were injurious to the proper working of government and were evil in themselves. Much of this critical view focused on the word *tang* or party. When the Ch'ing dynasty fell and the sanctions against parties vanished, it was as if the centuries of denial had produced an almost unquenchable thirst for political parties and associations. Within the first few months of the new republic, some dozen political groups emerged that were at least nominally in competition for political power through the representative system.

This proliferation of political organization was an important expression of the climate of the revolutionary aftermath, but it was also built upon pre-revolutionary experience. The leaders in party formation had more often than not spent time in Japan, where political parties had been developing for over three decades and were at the time of the 1911 Revolution entering a new stage of importance in Japanese politics. Chinese political parties had been appearing in clandestine and conspiratorial forms since Sun Yat-sen established branches of the Hsing-Chung hui in Honolulu and Hong Kong in 1894 and 1895. The establishment of provincial assemblies and the national consultative assembly in the last years of the Ch'ing stimulated the formation of open political groupings that hardly pretended to avoid the appearance of being *tang*. Liang Ch'i-ch'ao, prominent political writer and veteran activist, encouraged these developments, both in his widely-read essays and as practical adviser from his exile in Japan. When the revolution came, China's educated elite, particularly that portion which had absorbed Western notions of political organization, entered the political game with brash enthusiasm.

Interest first focuses naturally on the leading revolutionary group, of whom the most famous were Sun Yat-sen, Huang Hsing and Sung Chiao-jen. These national leaders had no disciplined organization at their disposal that effectively reached the local scene. Therefore they did not typically control the behaviour of even the most committed of local revolutionary activists. Recent scholarship has emphasized the autonomy of provincial politics after the 1911 Revolution. But national unity remained an ideal, and new national institutions, such as a parliament and a presidential office, were emerging and acquiring legitimacy. In this situation, the achievements of the national leadership – or their failures – were still important to all revolutionaries and affected the general political climate.

In the first year after the outbreak of the revolution, leading revolutionaries engaged sequentially in three political roles: as conspirators against Ch'ing rule, as office-holders and administrative authorities during and after the revolution, and as organizers of an open political party seeking victory in a national election.

The rapid spread of revolution under a republican banner owed much to the propaganda and diffuse conspiratorial network of the T'ung-meng hui and associated groups. The prestige of the veteran T'ung-meng hui leadership was greatly enhanced by revolutionary success. But, as already noted, the revolutionary provincial governments were in most cases swamped by the ready participation of gentry politicians and army officers. The local rewards of successful conspiracy were not monopolized by the prominent conspirators – far from it. Veteran revolutionaries did emerge as power-holders in some provinces, however, and the resulting access to funds and armies gave these men special weight in the T'ung-meng hui camp.

The transition from conspirator to administrator for the national (as distinct from provincial) leaders occurred first in the inter-provincial revolutionary capital established in Nanking in January 1912. Sun Yat-sen, for example, was president of the provisional revolutionary government in Nanking from January until that government disbanded in April. Later, like a few other prominent revolutionaries, he accepted an appointment in Yuan Shih-k'ai's new republican government in Peking. For Sun this meant becoming director of railway development, an office that carried little weight but apparently suited his intention of focusing on social concerns rather than politics. Huang Hsing was army minister in the Nanking government and then stayed on to be resident-general (*liu-shou*) of the southern armies by appointment from Yuan Shih-k'ai. He loyally disbanded soldiers in the Nanking area to the extent permitted by the money allotted him and then resigned in June 1912. Sung Chiao-jen, while in Nanking, drafted the constitution under which the new order was to be governed and, with some other T'ung-meng hui veterans, joined the new republican cabinet in Peking in the spring of 1912.

Neither the conspiratorial nor the administrative role provided the revolutionaries with lasting and predominant positions. Outside the few provinces where they were in charge or strongly represented, the tendency in the first year of the republic was towards a reduced proportion of administrative power in revolutionary hands. When T'ang Shao-i resigned as prime minister in late June 1912 over conflict with Yuan, the cabinet members who had come from Nanking soon followed T'ang out of the government. Yuan's domination of civil and military officialdom in Peking made withdrawal the only feasible course. Thereafter, the best prospect for the veteran revolutionaries' peaceful recovery of national political influence became party organization, not the perquisites of bureaucratic office.

The T'ung-meng hui had officially transformed itself from a revolutionary society into an open political party in March 1912. T'ang Shao-i, Yuan Shih-k'ai's choice for the premiership, had joined it as part of the negotiated arrangements between Peking and the revolutionaries. But it was a minority party in the provisional parliament, even though it could marshal a majority by alliance with other sympathetic groups. In August 1912, under Sung Chiao-jen's leadership, a new party was formed around the T'ung-meng hui core. Four smaller parties were absorbed and a new name was adopted: the Kuomintang (KMT), in its later incarnations usually translated as the Nationalist Party.

The reorganization was more than formal. The new party was the result of compromise. Its politics seemed significantly less radical than the old T'ung-meng hui. Mention of Sun Yat-sen's policy towards land taxation and ownership, which despite its moderation had disturbed those from socially elite backgrounds, was missing. Advocacy of equality for women was dropped from the party's platform. A reference to 'international equality', raising the issue of China's unequal treaties, was softened to 'maintaining international peace'. A call for 'administrative unity' in the T'ung-meng hui programme gave way to a more vague encouragement of 'political unity', while support for 'local self-government' was retained. The changes were conservative, but with a particular social and political bias quite different from that of Yuan Shih-k'ai. Sung Chiao-jen, against the wishes of some revolutionary veterans, was laying the basis for an approach to a socially conservative gentry constituency that had already developed a stake in local autonomy and participation in politics. The revolutionaries had adjusted their stance to the politically radical but socially conservative character of the revolution. Thus recast, the party was vastly successful in the national elections of the winter of 1912–13.

Viewed through the eyes of the revolutionary leaders, the first year of the republic could be seen as a series of retreats. During the revolution itself, force was not employed to its limits in a quest for total victory.

(Much revolutionary force was, in any case, not responsive primarily to the revolutionary party leaders.) Power seemed increasingly to slip from revolutionary hands as authority was reconstituted. Not until the winter elections of 1912–13 did the tide turn. Even then, some of the revolutionaries appeared sceptical about the electoral route to power and the dilution of revolutionary commitment that this entailed.[4] But when we view the year through other eyes, the T'ung-meng hui appears more formidable.

In the early months of the republic, some of the leading non-T'ung-meng hui parties attempted to amalgamate, without much success. One of them was the Min she, or Association of the People, organized around Li Yuan-hung, military governor of Hupei and national vice-president in the new republican order. This party, which emerged in January 1912, represented the alienation of the Hupei leadership from the T'ung-meng hui. It was important because of Li's prestige as chief of the first revolutionary government and his strength as commander of a sizeable army.

Another significant group was the T'ung-i tang, or Unity Party. Its dominant personality was the scholar Chang Ping-lin, who had been a republican for a decade and was once a leading member of the T'ung-meng hui. He broke with that organization in 1910 and was joined by some of his comrades from the Shanghai revolutionary organization, the Kuang-fu hui, or Restoration Society. After the revolution he was also joined by men prominent in Kiangsu and Chekiang affairs, who, though bureaucratic or 'monarchist' in background, had supported the revolution as it progressed. These included Chang Chien, the scholar-reformer who was a minister in Sun Yat-sen's Nanking cabinet, and Ch'eng Te-ch'üan, imperial governor and then republican military governor of Kiangsu. The Unity Party served as a vehicle for former officials and important gentry who hoped to make the transition to the new order with the help of Chang Ping-lin.[5] Its programme, like its name, stressed unity and spoke of the administrative reorganization of the country's regions in order to unify the national territory. It did not, in contrast to the T'ung-meng hui and KMT, specify the importance of local self-government.

Many who had played a prominent role in organizing for representative government under the monarchy, through provincial and national assemblies, formed another party that responded to Liang Ch'i-ch'ao's

---

4 Sun Yat-sen was one, at least retrospectively. Li Shou-k'ung, *Min-ch'u chih kuo-hui* (National assemblies in the early republic), 61–2. A major T'ung-meng hui contingent in Kwangtung held back from the new party for a time because of their critical view.

5 Ting Wen-chiang, *et al.* eds. *Liang Jen-kung hsien-sheng nien-p'u ch'ang-pien ch'u-kao* (Extended annals of Mr Liang Ch'i-ch'ao, First draft), 398, 400. Takeuchi Katsumi and Kashiwada Tenzan, *Shina seitō kessha shi* (A history of political parties and societies in China), 1.94.

leadership. By the fall of 1912 its name had become the Min-chu tang, or Democratic Party. This group had formed quasi-parties before the revolution and had worked together in a variety of projects, in particular the petition movement of 1909 and 1910 for the opening of a parliament. In its post-revolutionary form, this party was soon advocating the actual abolition of the provincial administrative unit as a step towards unifying the nation's authority and building a single strong government.[6]

These parties only begin the list of those that felt themselves the besieged minority before T'ung-meng hui strength. In May 1912 they came together in the Kung-ho tang, or Republican Party, in order, as Chang Ping-lin put it in a letter to Liang Ch'i-ch'ao, 'to fend off the power of a one-party dictatorship'.[7] The new party was unable for long to contain the different groups, and Chang Ping-lin's and Liang Ch'i-ch'ao's soon re-emerged as separate bodies. But the reasons had not to do with a changed estimate of T'ung-meng hui power. Rather, the split was partly attributable to excessive fear of that power. Liang was a particular object of revolutionary venom. Some party organizers in the first year of the republic were anxious to avoid the T'ung-meng hui onslaught that might be provoked by Liang's participation.

The T'ung-meng hui hostility to Liang Ch'i-ch'ao could be traced back to the competition for the loyalty of Overseas Chinese and Chinese students abroad during the previous decade, and to bitter debates between Liang and T'ung-meng hui spokesmen over the desirability of revolution, as well as numerous other issues.[8] Perhaps still caught in a reactive posture, Liang adhered unseasonably to the continuance of the Manchu throne, even as its imminent demise was apparent in late 1911 and early 1912. He publicly advocated at this time 'a republic with a figurehead monarch' (*hsu-chün kung-ho*). From his listening post in Japan, he commissioned emissaries in China to advance the proposition to, among others, Chang Ping-lin and Yuan Shih-k'ai. Liang's monarchical republic was the last gasp of the movement for a constitutional monarchy under the Ch'ing, which he had been organizing and agitating for over a decade. His final formulation was perhaps the movement's most radical statement of its case, with the monarch not only shorn of all power but consciously relegated to the role of symbol, like the post-1946 Japanese emperor. But Liang's efforts on its behalf, as well as specific plots during the revolution designed to frustrate the real republicans, did nothing to reconcile him to the T'ung-meng hui group.

6 Li Shou-k'ung, *Min-ch'u chih kuo-hui*, 72.
7 Ting Wen-chiang, *Liang Jen-kung hsien-sheng nien-p'u ch'ang-pien ch'u-kao*, 398.
8 For an excellent account of some of these debates, see Martin Bernal, *Chinese socialism to 1907*, 129–97.

Liang seems to have adopted the view of his associate Chang Chün-mai (Carsun Chang), who wrote him from China on the day of the Manchu abdication that, although the new political system the revolutionaries had designed was not what Liang's group had wanted, the country could not bear any further alterations, as it stood on the verge of disruption.[9] But attacks on Liang and his followers did not cease after his final abandonment of monarchy. A movement in Kwangtung advocated depriving him of his public rights as a Chinese citizen. In July 1912, reacting to an insulting article, some revolutionary editors organized the sacking of the offices of a reformist journal in Tientsin, and tried to effect the arrest of its managers, who were Liang's close associates. Party meetings were disrupted by T'ung-meng hui agents, Liang was told, and threats intimidated others from gathering.[10] Meanwhile, Yuan Shih-k'ai, who had unsuccessfully sought Liang's support during the revolution, apparently lost interest after concluding his negotiations with the revolutionaries in the early the spring of 1912. Even Yuan found Liang a liability in an atmosphere where the T'ung-meng hui set the political tone. Liang's representatives in China advised him that he should secure a formal invitation to Peking before returning from Japan.[11] Only after Yuan had received Sun Yat-sen and Huang Hsing in the capital could he be induced to extend the same invitation to Liang at the end of September 1912. The next month Liang was feted in Peking and shortly resumed his journalistic and political activities in China. But he was still unreconciled to the revolutionaries, who renewed their attack on him.[12]

This view of 1912 from other than T'ung-meng hui eyes shows that, although revolutionaries were deficient in administrative positions, they retained considerable political potential. Some of this potential was realized in the national elections that followed the founding of the KMT by three-and-a-half months and for which the new party was intended. These elections stand out as the only occasion when various Chinese political parties competed for the votes of a substantial nationwide electorate with considerable freedom from bureaucratic manipulation or coercion.

The formalities of the elections were these. Males over 21 years old, who either had the equivalent of an elementary schooling or were property owners and direct taxpayers at specified levels (the levels were

---

9 Ting Wen-chiang, *Liang Jen-kung hsien-sheng nien-p'u ch'ang-pien ch'u-kao*, 372.
10 *Ibid*. 395, 400–1. The continuing clashes between Liang Ch'i-ch'ao and the revolutionaries are described and analysed by Chang P'eng-yuan, *Liang Ch'i-ch'ao yü Min-kuo cheng-chih* (Liang Ch'i-ch'ao and republican politics), 42–58.
11 Ting Wen-chiang, *Liang Jen-kung hsien-sheng nien-p'u ch'ang-pien ch'u-kao*, 398.
12 For example, *Min-li pao* (Independent people's newspaper), 4 Nov. 1912.

modest but sufficient to exclude well over the majority of adult males) and who were two years' resident in their voting district (the hsien), were with few exceptions enfranchised. The proportion of population registered was probably in the range of 4 to 6 per cent. The electorate was thereby enormously enlarged over that in the late Ch'ing elections, when considerably less than 1 per cent qualified. Voting was for representatives to two new houses of the national parliament and to the provincial assemblies. The balloting was indirect: that is, the voters chose electors who later met to select the actual legislators. The process ran from December 1912 into January 1913 or beyond. The new provincial assemblies were constituted during the winter months. The new parliament (or national assembly) gathered in Peking in April 1913.

As a practical matter, some seats in the parliament, such as those designated for Tibet, Mongolia and Overseas Chinese, could not be filled by election and were effectively appointed by Yuan Shih-k'ai. In this manner, Ts'ao Ju-lin from Shanghai, practising law in Peking and soon to receive high office in the Foreign Ministry, became a delegate from Mongolia in the upper house.[13] If one leaves aside such anomalies (64 seats out of 274) and counts only those elected from the 21 'home' and Manchurian provinces, the KMT had won a clear majority in the upper house (123 seats out of 210). It was virtually the same in the lower house. In any case, since many representatives had no party affiliation or indulged in multiple membership, KMT members exceeded the combined total from the three other main competing parties in the lower house by 169 to 154. Liang Ch'i-ch'ao was very discouraged. The KMT was in an excellent position to press for a prime minister and cabinet selected from the predominant party in the parliament.

The explanation for the KMT's victory was, at the most general level, the political strength derived from being the party most closely identified with the revolution. Without predominance in the country's decentralized administrative structures, the KMT had to mobilize this strength by a direct appeal to the electorate, which was restricted to the educated and propertied classes. The party apparently relied both on whatever administrative authority it possessed and on an energetic campaign of persuasion in regions under hostile or indifferent governorship. In contrast to the other parties, the KMT espoused local self-government and accepted, at least under existing circumstances, a large amount of provincial autonomy. The position was popular with local and provincial elites. The KMT, then, constructed a winning strategy out of revolutionary prestige, organizational effectiveness, and a politically attractive programme.

13 Ts'ao Ju-lin, *I-sheng chih hui-i* (A lifetime's recollections), 79.

Although its scale has not been measured, the purchase of votes, particularly to influence the electoral colleges in their choice of members to the lower house, was widely reported. Thus China's liberal republic was no more immune to the influence of private and official money on its electoral process than other large representative systems as they developed. Neither the reports nor the electoral results, however, suggest that corruption was decisive nationally.

The leading architect of the KMT victory, Sung Chiao-jen, only 30 years old at the time, was emboldened to plan for his party the attainment of the national power that was denied the revolutionaries in 1912. The *entente* between Yuan Shih-k'ai and the revolutionaries had been damaged by the collapse of T'ang Shao-i's cabinet with its T'ung-meng hui participation and by instances of Yuan's arbitrary behaviour in the summer of 1912. But it had been revived in late August and early September by Sun Yat-sen and Huang Hsing. They visited Peking and joined Yuan in a celebration of unity, common purpose and mutual respect. As a result the KMT in the autumn of 1912 was cooperating with, though not significantly participating in, Peking's executive government. The KMT's electoral campaign of the following months was not overtly directed against Yuan Shih-k'ai. But as its success became apparent in January and February 1913 Sung Chiao-jen began to attack Yuan's government and its policies in his speeches.[14] He pressed more vigorously his assertion of the parliament as the progenitor of the cabinet, including the prime minister, and as being responsible for drafting a new more permanent constitution. He explicitly advocated the diminution of presidential powers. Indeed, Sung was seriously contemplating ousting Yuan from his post, despite Sun Yat-sen's continuing endorsement of Yuan's reconfirmation as president by the new assembly.[15]

Sung Chiao-jen's plans did not come to fruition. He was assassinated on 20 March 1913 by agents of Yuan's government. The relationship among elections, parties, the parliament and executive power that he had envisaged did not come to pass, either in that year or subsequently. Other political parties were later formed and reformed, but none came to power except at the head of armies.

The destruction of the parliamentary party movement, however, need not obscure the extraordinary vigour characterizing it in the first two years of the republic. It was built, after all, on the previous decade of ex-

14 K. S. Liew, *Struggle for democracy: Sung Chiao-jen and the 1911 Chinese Revolution*, 186–9.
15 *Ibid.* 189. Wu Hsiang-hsiang, *Sung Chiao-jen: Chung-kuo min-chu hsien-cheng ti hsien-ch'ü* (Sung Chiao-jen: precursor of Chinese democracy and constitutional government), 219–6. Ernest P. Young, *The presidency of Yuan Shih-k'ai: liberalism and dictatorship in early republican China*, 115–16, 282–3.

perience in political organization and movement outside the government and could draw on the intensive study and debate of those years. Moreover, party organization and contest were part of a period marked by liberal enthusiasms and liberating social tendencies. For example, reverence for officialdom dramatically diminished. A small but highly active and assertive women's movement, advocating female suffrage, universal education for women, and reform of marriage practices, drew national attention. Newspapers proliferated and national issues were strenuously debated. New hair and clothing styles prospered in the cities. Those of a conservative bent watched with growing concern the strain on the familiar social and political integument.

YUAN SHIH-K'AI ON THE ISSUES

No official of the late Ch'ing had achieved more for reform in as short a time as had Yuan Shih-k'ai. With the backing of Tz'u-hsi, the empress dowager, and the help of an ever growing entourage recruited on behalf of reform programmes, he had become involved in almost every aspect of institutional change and innovation sponsored by the empire in its last years.[16] His bent was practical rather than theoretical. He did not conceive the ideas for reform programmes or develop their rationale; rather, he implemented them and demonstrated their feasibility. Even allowing for this pragmatic emphasis, however, one is struck by Yuan's shift towards conservatism during his presidency.

As a pragmatist and politician, he had accepted the inevitability of a republic when the forces of the revolution showed their hold on the country. And during the first years of republicanism, he avoided a serious rupture with the revolutionary leaders by wooing them and by tactically retreating when confrontation threatened. But his unease with the political and social liberality of the revolutionary aftermath soon became evident. He thought students had become unruly. Advocates of women's equality, he felt, were attacking the family and hence the social order. The removal of Confucius from the primary school curriculum, in his view, went too far in the first year of the republic. Bureaucratic discipline

---

16 For research on aspects of Yuan's activities, while Chihli governor-general, see: Esther Morrison, 'The modernization of the Confucian bureaucracy: an historical study of public administration' (Radcliffe College, Ph.D. dissertation, 1959); Stephen R. MacKinnon, *Power and politics in late imperial China: Yuan Shi-kai in Beijing and Tianjin, 1901–1908*; John E. Schrecker, *Imperialism and Chinese nationalism: Germany in Shantung*; Watanabe Atsushi, 'En Seigai seiken no keizaiteki kiban – hokuyō-ha no kigyō katsudō' (The economic basis of the Yuan Shih-k'ai regime: the industrial activity of the Peiyang clique), in *Chūgoku kindaika no shakai kōzō: Shingai kakumei no shiteki ichi* (The social framework of China's modernization: the historical position of the 1911 Revolution).

had just about disappeared after the revolution, he complained, and taxes were being frittered away by local interests. The countryside was in disorder. In general, he was impressed by China's backwardness. Reforms were necessary, he often asserted, but too much had been attempted too quickly. Retrenchment was his keynote.

The domestic issues which most exercised Yuan in his first presidential years were the role of parties and representative assemblies and the relationship between the provinces and the centre.

Yuan had entered his presidency by swearing to uphold the constitution. The prominence of representative assemblies was intrinsic to the provisional constitution as drafted by the revolutionaries in 1912 and was a natural culmination of political movement and debate during the previous decade and more. Yuan contested neither the necessity of a constitution nor the appropriateness of some sort of representative system. But he was never happy with the forms developed in 1912, and he increasingly criticized their operations. One focus of complaint was the political parties. As early as July 1912 he warned, 'If the parties continue to maintain their own selfish ways and quarrel with each other without regard to the laws, the proclaimed republic will cease to exist.'[17] When the national elections began in December 1912, Yuan expressed concern that the winners might put the influence of party above concern for the general welfare.[18]

The KMT, with its electoral victory, became a particular enemy, but Yuan also showed little regard for the other parties. As Yuan turned to constructing his own arrangements for governance, he reflected that 'the government's hand has been tied by the provisional constitution. On the one hand the defects of this instrument have deprived the government of all liberty of action and on the other hand parliament has entirely failed to render its cooperation with the executive in promoting the common weal. The consequence has been complete disorganization of the administration and ever increasing ruin for the citizens.'[19] In this view, openly expressed only after Yuan had destroyed the KMT, the parliament had failed and a constitution more in accord with the needs of government was required. Yuan's assassination of Sung Chiao-jen in March 1913 was not simply the removal of a political enemy; it also expressed the gulf

---

17 *The China year book, 1913,* 514.
18 *Cheng-fu kung-pao* (Government gazette), 229 (16 Dec. 1912) 6–8.
19 'Inaugural address of president to the Council of Government', 15 Dec. 1913, British Foreign Office Archives, Public Record Office, London, FO 228/1852. This document purports to be a translation of a verbatim and unedited record of Yuan's speech; a comparison with the formal published text, *Cheng-fu kung-pao,* 585 (19 Dec. 1913) 1–6, tends to support its authenticity.

separating Yuan's and Sung's ideas about the proper organization of national government.

The second divisive domestic issue that preoccupied Yuan was the degree of centralization appropriate to China's polity. When Liang Ch'i-ch'ao publicly declined Yuan's offer of a post under the Ch'ing in November 1911, he identified the fundamental issues facing the country as two: whether the government should be monarchical or republican, and whether the organization of the polity should be federal or unitary.[20] The former question was resolved by the revolution but the latter was left unanswered. The first year of the republic was marked by the anomaly of a *de facto* federation presided over by a president increasingly committed to a unitary, centralized national structure.

Like the role of representative government and parties, the issue of centralization had emerged acutely in the previous decade. Many of the reforms sponsored by the Ch'ing court in its last years were dedicated to imposing a more centralized control over the country. The 1911 Revolution was in part a provincial reaction to Peking's pretensions to increased power. After the revolution those who still believed in a centralized unity were horrified at the extremes to which federalism had been taken. Bureaucratic, fiscal, legislative and even military autonomy were extensively assumed by most provincial governments. The argument persuaded some that federalism cut into the strength of the national government and that in a world of predatory imperialists, China could not afford anything less than a radical augmentation of power in the central government. (Those stressing the importance of parties and the national assembly did not necessarily favour federalism, although liberal centralizers, like Sung Chiao-jen, found it expedient tactically to ally with defenders of provincial autonomy and to sponsor some of their demands.)

Yuan, perforce, acquiesced in provincial autonomy during the early months of his presidency but showed growing impatience with it. In July 1912 he went through the motions of confirming in office all the provincial military governors who in no way owed him their positions. He piously pleaded for their 'cooperation with the government'.[21] In the autumn of that year, he tried with little success to assume the authority to appoint civil officials in the provinces. The effort was generally taken as interference in the internal affairs of the province and was frequently rejected, sometimes hotly. In late November, when asking the provincial authorities to submit to Peking for approval their appointments of county magistrates, he plaintively noted that the provisional constitution gave

20 Ting Wen-chiang, *Liang Jen-kung hsien-sheng nien-p'u ch'ang-pien ch'u-kao*, 346.
21 *Cheng-fu kung-pao*, 74 (13 July 1912) 2–3.

him the power to appoint and dismiss officials.[22] There was no detectable response. His legislative proposals for establishing a role for Peking in the provinces were unfavourably received by the provisional parliament. In January 1913 he took advantage of the *de facto* adjournment of the parliament for the elections to promulgate organizational rules for provincial government.[23] A storm of protest at the president's presumption ensued. Yuan's muted moves to reimpose central authority during his first year in republican office were largely frustrated. Peking's treasury correspondingly suffered from a scanty flow of revenue from the provinces.

The great reforming official of the Ch'ing was, as president, unable or unwilling to adjust to the decentralized liberal environment of the republic. He was offended by its social looseness and by the extreme limits it placed in practice on his central administration. The KMT electoral victory in early 1913 presented him with the prospect of further restraint on his power, even to the point of his removal. Constitutionalism, elections and provincial autonomy appeared to be forcing him back. Rather than retreat, he prepared for battle.

THE SECOND REVOLUTION

By the measurement of troops reliably responsive to his orders, Yuan Shih-k'ai did not command overwhelming force in the spring of 1913. His purely military advantage lay in the continuing cohesiveness and manoeuvrability of the units he did control, totalling perhaps about 80,000 men. The remainder of China's armies, several times as many, lay dispersed, geographically and politically. Yuan's exploitation of his military advantage depended on political success in acquiring allies and preventing adverse coalitions. The key to his victory over his enemies in 1913 was the degree to which he was able to isolate the radicals, get foreign support, and win at least the benevolent neutrality of power-holders in most provinces.

Armed civil conflict broke out in July 1913 and lasted for about two months. The underlying issues were the power of the national assembly to restructure the national government (an issue brought to a head by the KMT's electoral victory in early 1913) and Peking's authority in the provinces. The precipitating event that turned many KMT leaders towards armed resistance was the assassination of Sung Chiao-jen. Sung was shot in Shanghai on 20 March 1913, and died two days later. The chain of

22 *Ibid.* 210 (27 Nov. 1912) 4–5.   23 *Ibid.* 243 (9 Jan. 1913) 1–5.

evidence placed the planning of this assault in the offices of Yuan's government.

Sun Yat-sen had reiterated in the early weeks of 1913 the support for Yuan's presidency that he had so conspicuously affirmed in Peking the previous summer. Sung's murder, however, persuaded Sun that Yuan had to go. Further, Sung's electoral and parliamentary methods were now deemed inadequate. In late March 1913 major KMT figures, including Sun Yat-sen and Huang Hsing, attempted to line up sufficient military strength to defeat Yuan on the field. In blunting the parliamentary challenge to his power by murdering Sung Chiao-jen, Yuan had inspired a military challenge.

How could a military challenge be mounted? Virtually every province had its own armed forces. Three relatively large concentrations of troops had survived into the spring of 1913: around Peking in the north (the largest), in Hupei around Wuhan in Central China, and in Kiangsu around Nanking in the lower Yangtze region. Each occupied a corner of China's most developed communications triangle. Peking connected with Wuhan and Nanking by rail, and the Yangtze joined Wuhan to Nanking. Rapid large-scale troop movements were possible in either direction along each side of this triangle. Having no real hope of penetrating the core of Peking's forces, the KMT leaders tried to win allies in Hupei and Kiangsu. They tried to do this both from above and from below: that is, by seeking the adherence of the province's military governor, and by calling directly on subordinate army officers to respond to the anti-Yuan message.

In Hupei province, Li Yuan-hung, former Ch'ing officer and national vice-president, was in charge. Despite his early alienation from the veteran revolutionary leaders, he had been proposed as a presidential alternative to Yuan as part of Sung Chiao-jen's plan to cash in on the KMT's electoral victory. After Sung's death, he was asked to join the military revolt against Yuan.[24] Simultaneously, it would appear, efforts were made to conscript radical officers under Li into the anti-Yuan conspiracy.[25] Li spurned all overtures. And he interpreted the organization of dissidents in his army as a threat to himself. He had, after all, worked in alliance with Yuan since the beginning of the republic. Secretly and in small numbers, he invited troops from Peking to enter Hupei in early April. In May the secrecy was abandoned and the numbers swelled to over 10,000 of Peking's soldiers,

24 Gaimushō (Ministry of Foreign Affairs) comp. *Nihon gaikō bunsho*, 1913 (Documents on Japan's diplomacy), 2.350–1.
25 *Hsin-hai shou-i hui-i-lu* (Memoirs of the initial uprising of 1911), ed. Chung-kuo jen-min cheng-chih hsieh-shang hui-i Hu-pei-sheng wei-yuan-hui (Hupei committee of the Chinese People's Political Consultative Conference), 1.96–7.

garrisoned along the Yangtze in Hupei.[26] Long before a shot had been fired, Yuan possessed two of China's three critical military centres.

In Kiangsu, where Huang Hsing had close ties with the best forces, the military governor was not the dominating figure that Li Yuan-hung was in his own province. The issue of choice between Yuan and his enemies was not pressed until the Second Revolution actually broke out. But the early set-back in Hupei, as well as a widespread disinclination among the gentry and merchant elite for civil war, darkened prospects for any uprising. Some of the revolutionaries, especially Huang Hsing, reverted for a time to legal tactics of opposition, in the mode of the recently assassinated Sung Chiao-jen. But there were two remaining sources of strength in an anti-Yuan campaign. They were provincialistic resentment at Yuan's centralizing pretensions, and the network of KMT power-holders in the provinces.

Several provinces had come into conflict with Peking over issues of revenue and official appointment. When provincial resistance had been determined, Yuan had retreated. But he had come close to open hostilities with one province: Kiangsi, under the military governorship of Li Lieh-chün, a KMT adherent. Li brought to his job a background as a superbly educated Ch'ing army officer, a record of revolutionary activism in 1911, and an enthusiasm for the autonomy of Kiangsi, his native province. When Yuan unilaterally appointed a civil governor to share power in Kiangsi, the appointee was hounded out of the province soon after his arrival in December 1912. Then in January 1913 Yuan ordered the impoundment of a legal shipment of arms to Kiangsi. Despite Li Lieh-chün's objections, the commander of fortifications at Kiangsi's port on the Yangtze complied with Yuan's order. The issue then became one of the authority of the Kiangsi military governor over military officers in Kiangsi. Fighting was avoided in March only because Yuan backed off. In the period before Sung Chiao-jen's assassination, no leader had shown such open hostility towards Yuan. Li Lieh-chün had not shared Sung's emphasis on a national parliament and constitutional procedures. But he was keen for a movement to 'punish' Yuan with force.

The combination of KMT leanings and provincialist opposition to Peking, even if in a less volatile form than in Kiangsi, could also be found in Kwangtung and Hunan. Anhwei had a KMT provincial chief who joined the plotting. The anti-Yuan conspirators also had hopes for responses in Fukien, Szechwan and elsewhere.

26 W. H. Wilkinson, Hankow (11 April, 11 May, 22 May and 8 July 1913), FO 228/1873, Public Record Office, London. Diary of George Ernest Morrison (7 April 1913), item 97, G. E. Morrison Papers, Mitchell Library, Sydney.

The revolutionaries' position, then, was not without potential strength in the spring of 1913. But the contest with Yuan was not entered into out of overweening confidence in the result. Rather, it was forced by the president. Having chosen not to retreat before the KMT electoral victory, he went on the offensive.

Following the assassination of Sung (20 March) and the military invest-ment of Hupei (beginning in early April), Yuan's next major move was the conclusion of a large foreign loan. A consortium of foreign banks, guided by their home governments (Great Britain, France, Germany and the United States, soon joined by Japan and Russia), had been negotiating a large loan to the Peking government since the conclusion of the 1911 Revolution. The declared purposes were, chiefly, to refinance delinquent and imminently maturing payments on China's inherited debts, including foreign damage claims arising out of the 1911 Revolution, and to cover immediate governmental expenses. The consortium governments, led by Great Britain, set as a condition the injection of more foreign personnel into the Chinese government. Most dramatically, a foreign staff was for the first time to enter and thereby 'reorganize' the administration of the official salt monopoly, whose revenue was to guarantee the loan. Mean-while, the consortium governments worked, largely successfully, to prevent the Chinese from getting substantial loans outside the consortium. The Peking authorities faced a most unpleasant facet of China's semi-colonial condition: a solid front of the major capitalist nations, demanding a larger role in the Chinese polity in exchange for expensive loans. Even when Woodrow Wilson withdrew the United States from the consortium in March 1913, the Americans respected the consortium-enforced boycott of large lending to China until the consortium loan was concluded.

One need not have been a member of the KMT to see the dangers and to belabour Peking over the loan issue. In early 1913 K'ang Yu-wei, leader in the 1898 reform movement and veteran enemy of Sun Yat-sen, likened the proposed agreement to offering poisoned food to a starving man. K'ang argued that some way of avoiding the consortium's death-dealing bounty could surely be found. And what would the next step be after trading the salt administration for a £25,000,000 loan, which would in fact provide the Chinese government with little more than £10,000,000 after deductions for past debts and the expenses of floating the loan? Would not another government agency, or the land tax, have to be offered up for the next infusion of foreign money, K'ang asked. 'Truly, China would expire spontaneously, without foreign troops partitioning the country.' And how curious, he wrote, to be borrowing money from Russia and England at the very moment they are contending with Peking for Mongolia and Tibet: 'Who empowered the government to dare to parcel out to strangers the great expanse of our 5,000-year-old China?' Indignation at the contracting of foreign loans had helped bring down the Ch'ing. Noting this, K'ang hinted that, despite an observable atmosphere of public resignation to the necessity of a foreign loan, a rekindled indignation could repeat the performance in the republic.[27]

And yet in the early hours of 27 April 1913, Yuan went ahead and contracted for the so-called 'Reorganization Loan'. He needed financing for his anticipated showdown with the revolutionaries. Since the Peking government was not getting much revenue from the provinces, it was desperately in need of funds. K'ang Yu-wei's proposed remedy was to create a unified, national fiscal structure. Yuan agreed. But provincial and KMT opposition to centralizing initiatives meant that fiscal unification would come only with force, and force cost money. A foreign loan was the only recourse. Such was the logic of Yuan's course of action.

Yuan had decided, well before contracting the loan, not to submit it to the parliament for ratification. The provisional constitution, by which Yuan had agreed to rule, plainly required parliament's consent for this sort of agreement. Anger at the assassination of Sung and the unpopularity of the loan terms suggested ratification would be difficult. Meanwhile, the foreign signatories agreed in advance to accept illegal procedures. When the intention to conclude the agreement became known, the uproar in the parliament was enormous.

Yuan confided to the British minister in Peking that he regarded the parliament's proceedings as 'quite hopeless' and that he 'had a plan of dealing with them if they continued much longer'.[28] During the next month of May, at least parts of the plan were revealed. An effort to bring together all the non-KMT parties, which Yuan had been encouraging since the previous autumn, succeeded, in the form of the Progressive Party (Chin-pu tang). Liang Ch'i-ch'ao was a leading figure in this coalition. And much money was invested in bribing members of the parliament. As a result, impeachment of the government was aborted, and the parliamentary strength of the KMT was reduced. Later Yuan would resort to physical coercion and intimidation of parliamentary delegates.

By June Yuan's preparations were all but complete. He began ordering the dismissal of provincial chiefs most hostile to his plans. Li Lieh-chün, whose forces in Kiangsi had been on the brink of war in March, was the

---

27 K'ang Yu-wei, 'Ta-chieh-chai po-i' (A critique of the large loan), *Min-kuo ching-shih wen-pien* (Republican essays on public affairs), reprinted in Wu Hsiang-hsiang, ed. *Chung-kuo hsien-tai shih-liao ts'ung-shu* (Collected historical materials on contemporary China), 3.893–5.
28 John Jordan, Peking (30 April 1913), FO 228/1852.

first to go. Then Yuan ordered in succession the removal of the KMT military governors of Kwangtung and Anhwei. And on 8 July northern troops, dispatched from their camps nearby in Hupei, began to occupy stretches of Kiangsi along the Yangtze. Li Lieh-chün, who like the others had overtly accepted his dismissal for tactical reasons, returned to Kiangsi at about the same time to rally the troops. On 12 July 1913, Kiangsi formally declared itself independent of Peking, and the provincial assembly selected Li Lieh-chün to command a campaign to punish Yuan Shih-k'ai for his misdeeds.

The spring planning of the revolutionary leaders was then implemented. Nanking was seized for the anti-Yuan cause by revolutionary army officers, despite an unwilling military governor, Ch'eng Te-ch'üan, who departed. Huang Hsing came from Shanghai to lead. A brief sortie up the Tientsin-Pukow railway into Shantung took the war to Yuan's territory. And in Shanghai five intense assaults on the city's large arsenal were almost successful in overwhelming the defending garrison of northern troops, and would probably have taken this strategic point if the Chinese navy in Shanghai had not sided with Peking.

Varying degrees of favourable response to the rising came from a few other provinces, especially Hunan and Kwangtung. But the dispersion of Yuan's enemies highlighted the concentrated power of Yuan's own forces. The issue was decided in Kiangsi, Nanking and Shanghai, with no significant military contribution to the revolution from elsewhere. In a few weeks the anti-Yuan movement had collapsed. The leaders escaped, mostly to Japan.

Three years later, when Yuan seemed to control so much of China, he proved incapable of suppressing a movement against him. But in 1913 from a much more limited base he prevailed easily over his challengers. Yuan had in the Second Revolution two advantages that he subsequently lost: considerable support at home for his political stand and foreign help.

Yuan's domestic advantages over his opponents in 1913 were several. Even though his power did not then extend to much of the country, he emerged from the first year of the republic with a firm grip on the Peking bureaucracy, both civil and military. And this bureaucratic group in Peking was not the dispirited lot of later warlord years. A sense of mission lent cohesion to Yuan's political machine: to bring effective administrative unity to the country, a goal that seemed both possible and desirable.

On this point Yuan was publicly and privately emphatic. Shortly after fighting began in July 1913 he declared that the self-made military governors, whom the 1911 Revolution left in charge of civil and military matters, 'customarily disregarded the [higher] authorities. How were they to be held responsible for their performance? Later the division of [civil and military] administration was repeatedly planned, and civil affairs were to be placed under a separate top [provincial] post. But when the order of appointment was promulgated in the morning, the telegram of rejection was reported in the evening.' The first order of business was 'to restore the legal framework of governmental orders and build the prestige of the nation.'[29] As John Jordan, British minister, reported after a long conversation with the president in early June, 'Yuan was determined at all costs to secure the unification of the provinces under the Central Government. . .'.[30] The achievement of this goal would serve the interests of Yuan and his regime; but Yuan could and did persuasively argue that a loose federation left China weak and defenceless.

The attractiveness of this position reached beyond Yuan's entourage and helped isolate the radicals. The major non-KMT parties supported a policy of centralization. The minority of military governors who were not natives of the provinces they ruled had some interest in allies at the national level and hence might find common cause with Yuan as he battled against extreme versions of provincial autonomy. Ts'ai O, Hunanese military governor of Yunnan, seems to have been a case. Less than three years later Ts'ai would lead a successful assault on Yuan's regime. In 1913, however, espousing a centralized national administration, he co-operated with Yuan against the revolutionaries.[31] Military governors who were not of the KMT but presided over provinces where pro-KMT sentiment was considerable might at first also welcome Yuan's interventions. Examples include Li Yuan-hung in Hupei and Hu Ching-i in Szechwan. Only later, when it was too late, did they learn that Yuan's distaste for provincial autonomy would also sweep them out of power.

Meanwhile, the anti-Yuan movement was not adept at forging a broad coalition. The KMT itself was divided on the issue of provincial autonomy. The revolutionaries of 1913, though making use of accumulations of autonomous provincial power, did not, in contrast with Sung Chiao-jen's electoral campaign of the previous winter, clearly present themselves as defenders of provincial rights and local self-government. The assassination of Sung and Yuan's treatment of the parliament in Peking were by themselves remote issues for many whose preoccupations

29 Pai Chiao, *Yuan Shih-k'ai yü Chung-hua min-kuo* (Yuan Shih-k'ai and the Republic of China), reprinted in Shen Yun-lung, ed. *Yuan Shih-k'ai shih-liao hui-k'an hsu-pien* (Supplement to the serial publication of historical materials on Yuan Shih-k'ai), 68-9.
30 John Jordan, Peking (5 June 1913), FO 228/1852.
31 Hsieh Pen-shu, 'Lun Ts'ai O' (On Ts'ai O), *Li-shih yen-chiu* (Nov. 1979), 47-61; Donald S. Sutton, *Provincial militarism and the Chinese Republic: the Yunnan Army, 1905-1927*, 141-61.

were provincial and local. The impression of observers at the time was that the risings of 1913 did not win over the gentry and merchant elites. And massive popular mobilization was not attempted.

In addition to considerable domestic backing for his political stand against the leaders of the Second Revolution, Yuan enjoyed a second advantage: foreign support. The attention of the foreign powers was a mixed blessing, since it came with many strings attached. But Yuan's needs of the moment were served by a belief widely held among the powers that he could best preserve a Chinese order favourable to their interests. This conviction meant that Yuan could unconstitutionally contract the Reorganization Loan, in defiance of the national assembly. And the proceeds of the Reorganization Loan, while they lasted, gave Yuan an important edge over his opponents. He could purchase support, not only of defecting KMT members of the national assembly, but also of autonomous military commanders, like Chang Hsun in Shantung, who was also wooed, unsuccessfully, by Yuan's opponents. Further, with these funds Yuan's own forces were assured of solvency, a condition good for morale. The monetary and political price of the loan ran high, but the advantage of having lots of cash on the eve of a military campaign was ample compensation. One might fairly say that the consortium banks financed Yuan's victory over the KMT leaders.

The British belief that a unified and centralized China played to British strength in trade and could best protect foreigners and their interests in China was an old one. It was still held after the 1911 Revolution. Hence, the British diplomats and bankers in China, as well as the Foreign Office, were particularly keen in their support of Yuan, who was well-known to them. During the Second Revolution the bounds of neutrality and non-interference were frequently breached. Most dramatically, the British arranged to channel Reorganization Loan funds directly to Chinese naval vessels at Shanghai, to secure their adherence to Peking.[32] The remittance was timely. The following day a revolutionary attack on the Shanghai arsenal was frustrated by the guns of Chinese warships.

The revolutionaries in 1913 also had foreign friends. In the spring Sun Yat-sen and others among the conspirators had approached Japanese officials for support.[33] But the Japanese government was not yet ready to depart overtly from its cooperation with Britain in China, and no major assistance was provided the revolutionaries. Small amounts of money

32 Beilby Alston, chargé d'affaires, Peking, two telegrams (20 July 1913), FO 228/2498.
    Telegram from the Hongkong and Shanghai Banking Corporation, Peking, to the Group
    Banks at Shanghai (21 July 1913), enclosed in R. C. Allen, Peking, to Alston (21 July 1913),
    FO 228/2498.
33 Nihon gaikō bunsho, 1913, 2.340–41, 352.

probably reached them, and a handful of Japanese military advisers graced the rebel camps. Most usefully, the Japanese navy in China escorted many of the failed leaders to safety and eventual sanctuary in Japan. But this half-hearted Japanese assistance in no way matched what Yuan was getting – even from the Japanese, insofar as Japan participated in the Reorganization Loan.

Yuan's victory over the Second Revolution resolved some of the ambiguities of the first, 1911 Revolution. Revolutionary contribution to the overthrow of the Ch'ing dynasty would no longer serve as a credential for high office, although it was not by itself a disqualifying one. On the matter of the organization of national unity, the federalism of the first year and a half of the republic was to give way to a centralized administration. The curious conjunction of increased political participation and maintenance of the social hierarchy, which characterized the immediate aftermath of the 1911 Revolution and had produced the KMT electoral victory of 1913, was to be replaced by a polity conservative *both* socially *and* politically.

Two further, less obvious points about this turning-point should be made. First, the liberal style and the liberal institutions of the first two years of the republic failed to survive, but for rather particular reasons. Perhaps constitutionalism and representative, electoral forms of government would have eventually fallen of themselves, out of some incompatibility with Chinese preferences and political habits. But that is not what happened in 1913. Liberal politics were struck down with military force. The failure was in an inability to recognize the danger and mobilize the necessary defence. Although the conditions of 1912 and 1913 proved difficult to recapture, the *idea* of reviving the forms understandably lived on. The experiment had not been played out to its conclusion (whatever that might have been) but had been forcefully and prematurely terminated.

Second, the conservatism of the next few years was, in the main, not a reversion to 'traditional China' or to old views of Confucian politics. The nationalist definition of the aims of politics, which had been formulated in the 1890s and refined in the next decade, was still accepted. Yuan Shih-k'ai in his new role as dictator was still part of the modernizing movement that sought to fulfil nationalist aspirations. He and his supporters had reacted against what they saw as the extremes of political participation, self-government and liberal social attitudes. The proposition that China must change to survive was not rejected. Rather, Yuan thought he had a better idea of how to go about the necessary changes. China was to undergo another round of experimentation.

THE DICTATORSHIP

Yuan Shih-k'ai is remembered among Chinese for his treachery towards the reformers in 1898, towards the Ch'ing court in the 1911 Revolution, and towards the republic after becoming its president. The repeated opportunity to betray was provided, in this view, by control over strong military forces, known collectively as the Peiyang Army, and by skill at devious manipulation of people. He lied, cheated, manoeuvred, and murdered his way to predominance. In this quest for personal power, he represented the most reactionary social forces in his society and served the foreign imperialists. In short, he was just about everything morally despicable and politically backward that could be found in twentieth-century China. In later years one convenient way to vilify a Chinese leader was to suggest his similarities in these respects to Yuan Shih-k'ai, as was done to Chiang Kai-shek in the 1940s and to Lin Piao in the 1970s.[34]

As we turn to the period of Yuan's greatest power, it is worth considering Yuan's personality as an ingredient in his politics. Unlike Sun Yat-sen, but like most of the prominent figures of his generation, his personal life-style was firmly rooted in old ways, even as he laboured to adapt China to twentieth-century requirements as he saw them. He had more than a dozen wives and many children. He wore Chinese-style clothes, except on formal occasions, when he appeared in Western military dress. He knew no foreign languages, and he never travelled farther out of China than Korea. Although unsuccessful in the imperial examinations, he had been schooled in Confucian texts and seemed to believe in their moral efficacy.

On the other hand, his greatest prominence under the Ch'ing came to him as a leader in official reform, along Western and Japanese lines. He recruited into his entourage many with foreign education or experience. He carefully cultivated foreigners who might be useful to him. Some of his sons were sent abroad for their education. He seemed always to be searching for a blend between old and new, in the belief that this mixture would best serve China's conditions.

That, at least, is the better face than can be put on Yuan's career. His survival in positions of increasing status through the turbulence of 1898, the Boxer episode, and the 1911 Revolution indicates a talent for seizing the main chance. It can also be taken as an index of opportunism and

---

34 Ch'en Po-ta, *Ch'ieh-kuo ta-tao Yuan Shih-k'ai* (Yuan Shih-k'ai, the great thief who stole the country), Peking, 1949; first published in 1945. Sun K'o-fu and Fan Shu-sheng, *Yuan Shih-k'ai tsun-K'ung fu-pi ch'ou-chü* (The ugly drama of Yuan Shih-k'ai's veneration of Confucius and imperial restoration).

ambition. His cautious approach to change, blending the old and the new, though appropriate to his period as Chihli governor-general under the Ch'ing, appeared, in the exuberant aftermath of the 1911 Revolution, to lack purpose and firm direction. The one constant during the presidency – his push for a stronger central government – fits too well the hypothesis of a lust for personal power to be free of moral suspicion.

Although ambitious for himself and his ideas of how the Chinese polity should be organized, Yuan was not an egomaniac, demanding servility and flattery. He was ruthless and thought nothing of killing for political purposes. And yet his personal working relationships were genial and informal. He valued political loyalty among his subordinates but fostered no broad cult of his person. His excesses as president seemed inspired, not so much by self-aggrandizement, as by a rigidly bureaucratic outlook. He was entranced by regulations and procedural prescriptions. He preached bureaucratic discipline and valued administrative experience above all virtues. He distrusted spontaneity and uncontrolled political behaviour. Shaping governing structures and staffing them with 'reliable' officials were his nostrum for China's ills. What was most dangerous in his ruthlessness was its service to such formal notions of order. He might bide his time, but his urge to expunge the unpredictable and the irregular proved formidable.

After the summer of 1913 Yuan no longer had to bide his time. The liberal institutions and provincial autonomy of the previous months were swept away. The ensuing republican dictatorship was constructed around the principles of administrative centralization and bureaucratic order.

Yuan built his dictatorship in several stages. The first was the military occupation of large areas of China from which Yuan's troops had previously been excluded. The opportunity arose from victory over the Second Revolution. Not only did Yuan's conquering armies stay on after defeating the revolutionaries. They spread to some provinces where there had been no serious participation in the uprising. Eventually, all but six of the home provinces were so occupied, and the remaining six, mostly in the extreme south and containing less than a fourth of China's population, were intimidated to the extent that their leaders complied with Yuan's programmes. Military occupation, however, was merely the initial stroke in a grand scheme of reorganization. The second stage, therefore, was to root out the administrative expressions of provincial autonomy that had flourished since the 1911 Revolution. The power of official appointment in the provinces reverted to Peking. The old Ch'ing rule that one should not serve in one's own province – a rule that in 1912 had in practice been virtually reversed – was resurrected and gradually applied. The effect of these two changes was the extensive sacking of local officials. Even in Chekiang, which was one of the six home provinces not invested with Peiyang troops and which retained its previous, Chekiangese provincial chief, the proportion of Chiekiangese county magistrates declined dramatically under the dictatorship.[35] The centralized coherence of China's official system in 1914 and 1915 was not surpassed until 1949.

For a time in late 1913, it was the declared policy of the cabinet (in which Liang Ch'i-ch'ao played a leading role) to work for the complete abolition of the provincial administrative unit. Yuan finally proved unwilling to go so far. But in a major recasting of roles in the spring of 1914, Yuan promulgated regulations increasing the authority of civil provincial governors at the expense of the military. Titles were changed; rules of precedence were established favouring civil officials; and participation in civil affairs, including taxation and appointment of magistrates, was taken away from the military. To promulgate such regulations was not the same as effecting their underlying purpose – the recovery of civilian political predominance, eroded since the Taiping Rebellion in the mid nineteenth century and substantially lost in the 1911 Revolution. For example, Feng Kuo-chang at Nanking, a leading Peiyang general, could not easily be confined to the barracks. And yet the attempt was made; and his style was sufficiently cramped by Peking's controls for him to harbour grievances. Yuan's nationwide net of influence, initially established by military action, could not be converted overnight to a purely civilian administration. But the dictatorship was designed to move in that direction.

Much attention was devoted to the selection of proper civil officials. Examinations were instituted, particularly for aspirants to county magistracies. The new examinations tested, not the mastery of Confucian texts, but a range of bureaucratic skills and general knowledge. Thousands took them in Peking in 1914 and 1915, and performance in them became an important, though not universal, criterion for appointment.[36] Simultaneously, the prosecution of official corruption was publicly stressed. The censorate was revived, and, in an innovative move, a special court for judging official crimes was established (P'ing-cheng yuan). Accompanying the stick of punishment went the carrot of increased salaries and pension schemes.

35 Robert Keith Schoppa, 'Politics and society in Chekiang, 1907–1927: elite power, social control and the making of a province' (University of Michigan, Ph.D. dissertation, 1975), 296–8.
36 Odoric Y. K. Wou, 'The district magistrate profession in the early republican period: occupational recruitment, training and mobility', *Modern Asian Studies*, 8.2 (April 1974) 219–24.

Opinion about the local results of this campaign for an improved officialdom was mixed. Local responsiveness to central instructions was broadly achieved. The dignity of office, and its alienating distance from ordinary citizens, returned. Along with improved efficiency went the revival of mandarin airs and a bureaucratic conservatism that contradicted the heady, liberal spirit of 1912. In the words of one Chinese observer in the summer of 1914: 'I fear that, although the original intention was to stress experience, only old habits have been preserved; although the original intention was to systematize, there has only been a restoration of the defects in the system. . .'.[37]

One reason that the civilian structure neither fully subordinated the military nor won plaudits for its efficiency was the atmosphere of terror in which it was born. Not only was the initial military occupation of revolutionary areas often brutal. In all parts of the country Yuan, through military and police organs, conducted a campaign of repression against people linked with the 1913 uprising. An indirect or remote linkage was often sufficient to make one a target. The blood-letting, which lasted for more than a year, varied in dimension from province to province, but victims seem to have numbered in the several tens of thousands. The most prominent and more radical of the KMT leaders had escaped to Japan and elsewhere. The assault was out of all proportion to the amount and intensity of the remaining opposition to Yuan's regime in the immediate aftermath of the Second Revolution.

The severity of the terror presumably left an abiding distaste for Yuan in that substantial part of the electorate which had voted for the KMT the previous year. Further, it fed social disturbances that otherwise might have been easier to contain. The conspicuous case was the bandit force under Pai Lang, or White Wolf.

The man commonly known as White Wolf emerged after the 1911 Revolution as a successful bandit leader in southern Honan, with perhaps one thousand adherents by the summer of 1912.[38] White Wolf's constituency seems to have been like that of many other bandit groups: poor and landless peasants, and demobilized soldiers. The politics of his band in 1912 was anti-republican and pro-Ch'ing. One of their slogans was, 'Avenge the wrong done the great Ch'ing court in 1911.'[39] The social

---

37 Huang Yuan-yung, *Yuan-sheng i-chu* (Posthumous collection of writings of Huang Yuan-yung), reprinted in Wu Hsiang-hsiang, ed. *Chung-kuo hsien-tai shih-liao ts'ung-shu*, 2.246.
38 This account of White Wolf's band is based on Philip Richard Billingsley, 'Banditry in China, 1911 to 1928, with particular reference to Henan province' (University of Leeds, Ph.D. dissertation, April 1974). See also Edward Friedman, *Backward toward revolution: the Chinese Revolutionary Party*, 117–64.
39 Billingsley, 'Banditry in China', 373.

conservatism of the 1911 Revolution and the scope given to gentry power
in the new order make understandable such politics among those most
oppressed. But as the KMT faced off against Yuan Shih-k'ai in 1913,
contact between the revolutionaries and White Wolf began. Then, as
Yuan's victory was followed by such pervasive terror against the revolutionaries, many joined White Wolf's group, which was induced to participate in subsequent revolutionary strategies.

As a result of the accretion of refugees from Yuan's terror and of more
demobilized soldiers, White Wolf's band became formidable. As a purely
bandit group, it was a nuisance to the authorities but hardly different
from many such containable, if persistent, nuisances. Linkage with revolutionary, anti-Yuan politics changed the circumstances in two ways. The
suppression of this enlarged band became a special project of the central
government. And by venturing beyond its established base area in southern Honan, where there were local ties and protective assistance from
the population, the bandit army became vulnerable to being isolated and
destroyed piecemeal. In December 1913 and January 1914 the band
attacked into Anhwei and provoked an inter-provincial suppression
effort. In March 1914 major contingents from the group marched west,
apparently inspired at least in part by a request from Sun Yat-sen to
establish a base in Szechwan. A core force of three to ten thousand
fighters, multiplied several times by local groups joining for the duration
of White Wolf's presence in their area, crossed Shensi triumphantly. Cut
off from entering Szechwan, it met a hostile population in Kansu, where
localism was reinforced by ethnic and religious differences from the
White Wolf group. Dispirited remnants of the band were hunted down as
they attempted the return to Shensi and Honan. White Wolf himself died
in August 1914, either from wounds received in earlier fighting or through
betrayal to government troops, whose hundreds of thousands had taken
an embarrassingly long time to disperse his small force.

From White Wolf's saga, we can observe that the sources of social
upheaval and the desperation of portions of the population had not been
dissipated by the 1911 Revolution. So we might have guessed, since the
revolution had hardly taken cognizance of such problems. White Wolf's
success in winning adherents outside his home area, both from local bandit
groups and from the ranks of the government armies, testifies to this.
We can also observe the continuing struggle of the revolutionaries to
oppose Yuan. From his exile in Japan, Sun Yat-sen and a reduced cohort
strove to keep the fires lit at home. Striking ties with those, like White
Wolf's band, whose disaffection was primarily social rather than political,
formed one of several tactics.

If Yuan had limited his enemies to persevering revolutionaries and the socially oppressed who sought survival in banditry, his regime might have put down roots in the substantial remaining parts of the Chinese social order. But Yuan's vision of a smoothly functioning bureaucratic order was too grand to allow such modesty. As his indiscriminate campaign of terror implied, he worked on the assumption that much more was wrong with China than endemic banditry and revolutionary conspiracy. The whole phenomenon of political participation had got out of hand. The gentry and other socially elite parts of the population, including merchants, were made to surrender many of the political privileges accumulated since the beginnings of formal representative institutions about a decade before.

The campaign to restrict political participation began as an attack on the KMT and soon expanded its scope. The national assembly had survived the Second Revolution because the parliamentary wing of the KMT had dissociated itself from the armed uprising and because Yuan desired from it one further formality. That formality was his election as regular president (as distinct from the provisional post he already had), according to procedures specified in the provisional constitution of 1912 and subsequent legislation. Arbitrary arrest and even executions of assembly deputies had induced an atmosphere of extreme tension. Plied with bribes and intimidated by a threatening mob, the assembly assented on 6 October 1913. Even so, by prolonged balloting before confirming Yuan's presidency and by drafting a defiantly parliamentary constitution to replace the provisional one of 1912, the parliament demonstrated its alienation from Yuan's purposes. On 4 November 1913, citing guilt in the Second Revolution by political association, Yuan ordered the complete dissolution of the KMT and removed remaining KMT deputies from their seats. The KMT as a whole was defined as a rebel organization. This event marked a heightening of the terror throughout the country; and the parliament was crippled.

Not stopping there, Yuan in several quick strokes dismantled all elected assemblies in the first months of 1914. The remaining members of the parliament were told to go home. The thousands of local assemblies, introduced skeletally in the late Ch'ing and flourishing at the prefectural, county and sub-county level in the first year of the republic, were without exception dismissed. And the provincial assemblies, that had been so vociferous in the last two years of the Ch'ing and had been so important in the politics of the 1911 Revolution, were abolished. What an affront to the educated and propertied classes who had participated in building this structure of representation! The British minister in Peking, commenting on the dissolution of local self-government bodies, concluded that the order would 'affect, pecuniarily and from the point of view of their local prestige, a vast number of petty gentry and bourgeois throughout the country, and will range them on the side of his enemies.'[40] Though muffled by the terror, Chinese voices confirming this judgment were audible.

The pattern of Yuan's administration was an escalating effort to restrict areas of autonomy in the society. Press censorship was fortified and generalized by law in 1914, after two years of freedom from any central controls (though local governments had occasionally suppressed local press critics). Chinese chambers of commerce were put under new regulations, increasing their subservience to political authority. The Chinese Post Office submitted the mails to police surveillance. Thousands of plainclothesmen and informants sought out dissent. Railway passengers were carefully scrutinized and their luggage searched upon suspicions of treason. Within the rather severe technical limitations of staff and efficiency, Yuan's regime was acquiring the attributes of a singularly repressive police state.

By such means was the widespread movement towards an elite-based political liberalism dealt wounds from which it never fully recovered. In setting out the philosophical guidelines for the architecture of the dictatorship, Yuan spoke as follows in December 1913:

Nowadays, the word 'equality' is in all men's mouths, but equality only means that all men are equal in the sight of the law. It does not imply that distinctions of rank are to be obliterated and that each man may be a rule unto himself in negation of the law. . . . 'Liberty' is another beautiful modern expression, but it is limited to the bounds of the law, within which men are free. Such a thing as unrestricted liberty does not exist. Those who have advocated equality and liberty without enquiring whether sanction was extended to a reign of licence knew perfectly well that such things must not be: they made use of stately catch-words as a rallying cry for furthering rebellion. . . . Again, 'republic' is an elegant expression, but what foreigners understand by this term is merely the universal right to a voice in the country and not that the whole nation must needs interfere in the conduct of government. What possible result save the direst confusion could ensue from such interference? As to the term 'popular rights', it comprises the right of representation and the suffrage, besides the supreme privilege of electing the president; it must not be understood to include the conduct of administration.[41]

The tone is more familiar to modern Western experience than it is to

40 John Jordan, Peking (9 Feb. 1914), FO 228/1883.
41 'Inaugural address of president to the Council of Government.' See *Supra*, f.n. 19 for a comment on this source.

the Confucian conservatism of the nineteenth century. Yuan was resisting the consequences of a new, participatory, radicalizing nationalism – something with which Tseng Kuo-fan had not had to contend. At the same time, he was accepting some of its premises and goals. He was part of its conservative wing.

The dictatorship's programmes reflected this mixed reaction to twentieth-century Chinese nationalism. Existing elected assemblies were abolished, but the importance of popular representation was acknowledged. Yuan ordered planning for a new design, both locally and nationally. When Yuan died two-and-a-half years later, none of this plan had been put into effect. But from the numerous preparatory regulations, it was apparent that the emphasis was on subordination to official guidance and on an electorate much reduced from the number of voters in 1912 and 1913. A constitutional order, legal procedure, popular sovereignty and representative assemblies were all acknowledged as crucial for China's modernization, a much desired goal. In Yuan's view, however, they should be effected in ways that augmented, rather than diminished, the authority of the central state and the stability of the social order.

Elaborate efforts to revive the flow of revenue from the localities to Peking met with some success. By the time of the outbreak of the First World War in Europe, the Peking government had attained a bare fiscal self-sufficiency, obviating the need for further foreign loans (which in any case would be scarce in war-time). One could argue that Yuan's dangerous strategy of 1913 had worked: accepting foreign funds, with their humiliating conditions, to bring administrative unity to the country, thus laying the basis for fiscal independence. The fallacy in this scheme lay in the optimism that the domestic political price for all these outrageous acts need not be paid. When the bill was presented, the apparent fiscal achievement of 1914 and 1915 crumbled, leaving only the humiliating conditions Yuan had put his signature to in 1913.

Fiscal success was achieved by the dictatorship not just with the help of central bureaucratic control over the country, but also by the severe retrenchment of several expensive reforms. Various programmes, initiated through the official nationalism of the last years of the Ch'ing and greatly expanded under the liberal nationalism of the first two years of the republic, were either cut out or reduced. Among them were the self-government bodies, whose fate has just been discussed. The new judiciary, with its courts and judges separate from the executive organs of government, was pared down drastically, but not eliminated. The modern police lost much of their funding. Most dramatically, successor units of the late Ch'ing's modernized New Army, which ballooned after the 1911 Revolution, were reduced in size and budget in many parts of the country. Yuan's

Peiyang detachments were favoured, but not exempted. All this budget-cutting served the cause of eventual national independence from foreign creditors, but it also betrayed the reformist expectations of nationalists.

A partial exception to the rule of retrenchment was education. Yuan frequently delivered homilies on the importance of an educated citizenry. 'The prosperity and strength of a country hinges upon advancement in the virtue, knowledge and physical strength of the people. If we desire to improve the people's standards in these three respects, we must empha-size citizen education.'[42] The programmatic application of these thoughts was special attention to the spread of citizens' schools (*kuo-min hsueh-hsiao*), a four-year lower primary system, free of charge for all. Although universalization of education was only a distant goal, the incidence of such schools, which drew upon local financing, seems to have increased during the dictatorship.

The totality of Yuan's educational policies was complex and various. The Ministry of Education under T'ang Hua-lung, a veteran leader of Hupei's provincial assembly, wanted the teaching of classics at the pri-mary level limited to selections of passages, with the implication that the purpose was linguistic and literary, not moral, training. Yuan insisted on incorporating the whole of the *Mencius* into the lower primary school curriculum. He also authorized a pilot project of literacy instruction in romanized Chinese for adults. While the bottom rung was expanding, higher reaches of the school system suffered retrenchment during the dictatorship. Yuan was solicitous of elite needs by adding a small 'pre-paratory' channel upwards for the culturally privileged. Overall, his administration's approach to education was conservative but reformist, and less favourable to gentry aspirations (focused on the higher levels in the system) than had been the liberal republic of 1912 and 1913.

Since explanations of this period have often dwelt upon Yuan's evil character and the reactionary quality of his politics, discussion of the actual policies of the dictatorship is rarely to be found. One faces the revisionist's temptation to reverse all judgments. But that cannot be justified; the hostile characterizations have been based on certain irre-ducible facts. One could expatiate upon other reformist aspects of the dictatorship – the encouragement of economic development, for example, and the advantage taken of the natural protectionism afforded by the First World War.[43] Still, in the end, attention must return to the brutality

---

42 *Cheng-fu kung-pao*, 956 (6 Jan. 1915) 9.
43 An appreciation of Peiyang contributions to capitalist development under the dictatorship occurs in Kikuchi Takaharu, *Chūgoku minzoku undō no kihon kōzō – taigai boikotto no kenkyū* (Basic structure of the Chinese national movement: a study of anti-foreign boycotts), 154–78.

of the regime and its fundamental failure. Foolishly, Yuan tried to coerce responsiveness. This was foolish because it was an impossible task and because it evoked an opposite reaction, both from those elite sectors of the society most likely to support him and, eventually, from his own lieutenants and collaborators.

Yuan was sensible of the limits of coercion. He avowed the need for constitutionalism and representation. But instead of rapidly reviving the participatory aspects of the liberal republic, he tried to compensate by selected retrievals from imperial politics. The results were disastrous for him and his policies.

YUAN'S MONARCHICAL MOVEMENT

As President Yuan Shih-k'ai surveyed the results of the dictatorship, he had to contemplate the question: what was missing? Once the country's administration had been unified, why did people not jump when he clapped; rally when he called? Where was the strength that was supposed to accompany centralization? Why was China still so weak before foreign power? The crises in foreign affairs during Yuan's presidency ended uniformly in a Chinese retreat. Outer Mongolia and Tibet remained largely lost to European protection. He failed to effect any recovery, whether he signed agreements, as he did with Russia over Outer Mongolia in 1913 and 1915, or whether he refused to, as he did with Great Britain after the Simla Conference over Tibet in 1914. Meanwhile, a foreign hand had been inserted into the Salt Administration. Railway concessions proliferated. The foreign powers refused to renegotiate the tariff. The most humiliating result emerged from the Sino-Japanese negotiations begun in January 1915. In May, Yuan capitulated to Japan's modified, final version of her famous Twenty-one Demands. Yuan's implicit diagnosis of the disease behind these symptoms of inadequacy was imperial under-nourishment: the emperor was missing.

We may reasonably wonder how anyone could arrive at this conclusion so soon after the Ch'ing monarch had been so easily deposed. The ambiguity of the 1911 Revolution is one key to this line of thinking. One could after all take the revolution as anti-Manchu at the core, rather than anti-monarchical. From this point of view, the republic was merely a fortuitous consequence of the absence of an obvious Han replacement for the overthrown Manchu monarch. There were those in Yuan's entourage who had from the beginning desired the republic to be only a stopgap, until the time was ripe for Yuan's enthronement.

The most cogent rationale for a revived monarchy was the evident fact that the republic had failed to win the hearts of the masses. We have noted the pro-Ch'ing slogan of White Wolf's bandits in 1912. Although in some provinces the new revolutionary order had emerged with an important non-elite, popular engagement, within a few months these popular forces (such as secret societies) were cut off from the sources of power. When they resisted, they were brutally suppressed.

Perhaps more typical were the circumstances portrayed by Lu Hsun in his characterization of the 1911 Revolution in 'The true story of Ah Q' written a decade later. From his position at the lowest social level in his village, Ah Q is initially attracted by the vision of a possible upheaval. But his disappointment is profound as he observes instead how representatives of the old, classically-educated elite and the new, foreign-educated elite collaborate in taking over the revolution for themselves. When Ah Q tries to join, he is told to clear out. He angrily charges, 'So no rebellion for me, only for you, eh?' The accuracy of this analysis is underscored when Ah Q is executed by representatives of the revolution for robbery – a robbery he did not commit, though he had wanted to.[44]

The theme of popular exclusion from the revolution, and consequent alienation from the republic, is vividly stated in Lu Hsun's short story. In keeping with this genesis, the republic continued the exclusion of the masses from all the invigorating participatory institutions of its early liberal phase. Quite apart from formidable problems of communication and unfamiliarity with republican institutions, there was little reason even for those common folk who did glimpse the new order to see it favourably. Insofar as monarchical arguments rested on the strangeness or unpopularity of the republic among the masses, the arguments were probably sound.

The arguments weakened when they proposed the revival of the monarchy as a remedy – as an instrument to knit government and people together. There had been no determined popular defence of the monarchy when it fell during the 1911 Revolution. The occasional appearance of pro-Ch'ing slogans, such as those of White Wolf, before the Second Revolution seem better understood as complaints against the social leanings of the republic than as instant nostalgia for emperors. In any case, how were the people to be reached with a resuscitated monarchical message? The provincial and local elites, many of whom had learned to enjoy republican privilege, would be indispensable allies in the effort. Why should they cooperate?

A further argument for monarchism, particular to the time of the deci-

44 Gladys Yang, ed. and trans. *Silent China: selected writings of Lu Xun*, 42–58.

sion for it in mid 1915, had to do with foreign affairs and was, by its nature, not publicly presented. One of Yuan's intimates wrote of it at the time, and the British minister in Peking understood it to be a factor in the tenacity of the movement.[45] This was the use of the monarchy against Japan. After the conclusion of the Sino-Japanese treaty of May 1915, the fear of further Japanese demands on China remained lively in Peking. Japan had not got all she had asked, and the European war left China without the saving balance of avarice that kept any one power from grasping for the whole. It was apparently believed, at least by Yuan Shih-k'ai, that the switch to a monarchy would keep the Japanese, with their own monarchical proclivities, at bay until the war ended.

Ambition for himself and his descendants, the key to Yuan's monarchism in the view of his detractors, was surely present. Chinese history had bequeathed a compelling imperial tradition. There is no way comparatively to weigh the personal and the political components in Yuan's decision to tap that tradition. Similarly, his slowness in recognizing its futility can be attributed equally well to the blindness of ambition or a stubborn commitment to a particular analysis of China's condition.

Yuan's predisposition to revive traditional political ceremonies and symbols was evident from the beginning of his dictatorship. He seemed not to want merely to retreat into the past. Rather, he determinedly combined old and new, blending republican and imperial styles to accommodate, or beguile, a mixed constituency of the modernized and the benighted. In 1914 he celebrated both Confucius and the Wuchang uprising of 10 October 1911. He praised science and its purgation of superstition; and he led the country in the worship of Heaven, somewhat popularizing an ancient imperial prerogative by inviting all to participate. In August 1915 a campaign to declare Yuan emperor was launched, with the president's implied blessing. And yet the emperor was to be elected (the process turned out to be formalistic) and the monarchy was to be constitutional.

Perhaps as remarkable as Yuan's ill-fated lurch at dynastic immortality was its cool or hostile reception among the country's leading citizens. Hardly anyone seemed to be beguiled by Yuan's political blends of old and new. The centralized bureaucratic administration of the dictatorship was working well enough in 1915 so that power-holders everywhere followed instructions. Civilian and military provincial chiefs dutifully

---

45 Chang I-lin, *Hsin-t'ai-p'ing-shih chi* (Collection of Chang I-lin's works), reprinted in Shen Yun-lung, ed. *Chin-tai Chung-kuo shih-liao ts'ung-k'an* (Library of historical materials on modern China), vol. 8 (Taipei, n.d.), 38–42. John Jordan, Peking (20 October 1915), Jordan Papers, FO 350/13.

petitioned Yuan to ascend the throne. The appearance of general acceptance of the monarchy was, however, deceiving. Just beneath the surface
dissent was rampant.

Yuan's revolutionary enemies, of course, had long been warning that
the president had imperial intentions. The leaders of the Second Revolution, like Sun Yat-sen, were mostly in exile and politically divided. But
their opposition to the monarchy was automatic, a continuation of their
opposition to Yuan's rule.

Less predictable was the disaffection of political leaders who, though
not part of Yuan's entourage during his years as a Ch'ing official, had
worked with him in opposing the KMT and establishing the dictatorship.
Among them was Liang Ch'i-ch'ao, who had supported a reformed
Ch'ing monarchy before and during the 1911 Revolution and had served
in the cabinet during the first months of the dictatorship. He responded
to the announcement of Yuan's monarchical movement by publishing
forthwith a devastating broadside against it.

Even among the longest-standing of Yuan's associates there was substantial drawing back and foot-dragging at the beginning, followed eventually in a few cases by overt opposition. Conspicuous in this tendency
was Feng Kuo-chang, who had worked under Yuan's leadership since
the Sino-Japanese war in building the modernized Peiyang Army and in
1915 was military chief in Nanking. The most prominent of Yuan's
military associates from the 1890s was Tuan Ch'i-jui, who had been army
minister from the beginning of the republic. More than one policy difference with Yuan had led to Tuan's withdrawal in May 1915. He refused
various pleas for his return to office as long as Yuan persisted on his
monarchical course. Most military and civilian officials were preoccupied
as usual with covering their flanks, but active supporters of Yuan's
monarchy were fewer than members of his own political machine who
expressed their distaste for this *démarche*.

Why should those who had contributed their services to the dictatorship resist Yuan's monarchy to one degree or another? Some perhaps
felt that their own ambitions would suffer if the top were clogged by a
permanent court. But such considerations could count with only a very
few, if any. A more general source of unease was the injunction of Confucian morality that one should not serve two lords. For the former Ch'ing
official this prohibition applied more strongly to Yuan as emperor than
as president. At the other extreme, there were those who felt that the
imperial mode was out of style and were embarrassed by its reactionary
implications. Liang Ch'i-ch'ao argued that the monarchy was not necessary – it would add nothing to the president's existing powers – and that

it was in any case a dead institution, with no power to evoke awe and obedience.

Beneath this array of feelings and arguments against Yuan's monarchy one detects an underlying disillusionment with Yuan's leadership. For those who had supported the policies of the dictatorship it was difficult to admit that these policies had produced disappointing results. But those who left Yuan's camp to resist his monarchy found themselves espousing just those political forms that the dictatorship had condemned.

Liang Ch'i-ch'ao, for example, later testified that he had become disillusioned with Yuan's rule before the monarchical movement.[46] Although he had enthusiastically led the dictatorship's campaign to subordinate provincial authority to the centre, he found himself in 1916 as leader in a campaign explicitly calling for federalism. 'The province has long been the basic unit in Chinese politics', Liang noted in March 1916, and he might as well make the most of it.[47] Feng Kuo-chang and Ts'ai O (a collaborator in the dictatorship who became a leader in the armed campaign against Yuan) made similar political somersaults.

Yuan's centralizing policies had not worked. His substantial surrender before Japan's Twenty-one Demands was the latest and most persuasive evidence. In a curious way, Yuan's monarchical scheme was scapegoated for political failures in which many had shared. So when Yuan abandoned his monarchical scheme in March 1916 and resumed the presidency he did little to dampen the flames of opposition.

More speculatively, we may surmise that the mood of the elite in the country as a whole had turned against the dictatorship. Such a mood would at least be understandable in the light of Yuan's policies of harsh suppression of the favoured party of the restricted electorate of 1912 and 1913, and the dismantling of assemblies that gave the broad social elite a direct voice in the political process. The prevalence of this mood would, through its influence on administrators, help account for widespread official disaffection at an early stage in the monarchical moment. It would also explain why the movement against Yuan, led in part by defectors from the dictatorship, found it politic to champion programmes of constitutionalism, representative government, and federalism that harked back to the liberal phase of the republic.[48]

The armed effort to oppose Yuan's monarchy and then unseat him had several parts, which were never consolidated. Associates of Sun Yat-sen,

---

46 Liang Ch'i-ch'ao, 'Yuan Shih-k'ai chih chieh-p'ou' (An analysis of Yuan Shih-k'ai), *Ying-ping-shih wen-chi* (Collected essays from the Ice-drinker's Studio, Taipei, 1960), 12. 34.9.
47 Liang Ch'i-ch'ao, 'Ts'ung-chün jih-chi' (Diary of my military enlistment), in *Tun-pi chi*, 124–5.
48 Pai Chiao, *Yuan Shih-k'ai yü Chung-hua min-kuo*, 326.

notably Ch'en Ch'i-mei, Chü Cheng and Chiang Kai-shek, organized from their bases abroad various assaults along the coast. In November 1915 Yuan's military representative in Shanghai was assassinated. In early December a warship in the same city was temporarily seized in a failed attempt to win the navy for an uprising. Sun's largest project, under the aegis of his new, highly disciplined Chinese Revolutionary Party, was the creation of a small army in Shantung and an effort, with local allies, to take the provincial capital for the revolution in the spring of 1916. Obvious dependence on Japanese money and protection undermined the significance of the ability of this force to hold positions along the Japanese railway line in Shantung.

The central event in the anti-Yuan campaign was a concerted military uprising based in Yunnan, where no Peiyang troops were stationed. Sun Yat-sen's new party played no direct part in the Yunnan uprising, whose cohesiveness derived from a shared experience in building the Yunnan Army. This army was first formed in the last years of the Ch'ing as part of a national, modernized military force. The results in Yunnan were particularly good, and some of China's best trained young officers participated. One of them was Ts'ai O, originally from Hunan, who headed the post-revolutionary provincial government before accepting central government posts in late 1913. Ts'ai outspokenly advocated a centralized national polity and was prominently involved in the suspension of representative assemblies in 1914. But he became disillusioned with Yuan. After the monarchical movement was launched, he conspired with Liang Ch'i-ch'ao and others to defy Yuan's plans. They secretly left the north to take up their assignments.

Liang arrived in Shanghai in mid December 1915 and used his personal prestige and literary talent to enlist more adherents to the anti-Yuan cause. At about the same time, Ts'ai and other former officers of the Yunnan Army returned to that province, where they joined with local officers to lead the military campaign against Yuan. Among those returning was Li Lieh-chün of Kiangsi province, a veteran of the Yunnan Army and comrade with Sun Yat-sen against Yuan in the summer of 1913. Yunnan's military chief, T'ang Chi-yao, shared with this politically disparate group the same educational background and late Ch'ing experience in the Yunnan Army. He joined the revolt.

These events have been best known through the writings of Liang Ch'i-ch'ao, and something approaching a cult memorialized Ts'ai O in later years. The importance of both men at this time is uncontested, but the picture of a unique genesis of the Yunnan movement in Liang's lodgings in Tientsin in the fall of 1915 is a distortion. Yunnanese army officers on the spot had secretly been discussing resistance to the monarchy since September. The galvanizing effect of Ts'ai O's return to Yunnan in December depended upon the revolutionary leanings of a portion of the province's military leadership. His commanding presence served to bring around the waverers and accelerate the decision to strike at Yuan's forces.[49] Even if Ts'ai had never come, some sort of movement would likely have erupted in Yunnan.

The campaign took its name from a temple in the provincial capital and became known as the National Protection Army (Hu-kuo Chün). Yuan was delivered an ultimatum on 24 December 1915, which he ignored. The movement was formally launched on the next day. The planners counted on early support from the neighbouring provinces of Kweichow and Kwangsi. Invading expeditions were organized for Szechwan, Hunan and Kwangtung. The most important of these, the one into Szechwan, was under Ts'ai O's personal command. Among his officers was Chu Teh, later organizer with Mao Tse-tung of the Red Army. At first numbering about 3,000 men, this so-called First Army of the National Protection movement faced Szechwan's own divisions and well-armed Peiyang troops already present in Szechwan (one of the commanders was Feng Yü-hsiang of later warlord fame). When Yuan saw the seriousness of what was happening, he ordered large reinforcements up the Yangtze from Central China. The odds were formidably adverse for Ts'ai O's expedition, even as it acquired its own reinforcements.

And yet it persevered, demonstrating to the whole country Yuan's vulnerability. Ts'ai's force enjoyed the *esprit de corps* forged in the Yunnan Army in the late Ch'ing. Its command was well coordinated and skilful. Ts'ai's tactics were marked, according to Japanese military intelligence, by attacks initiated at night, sophisticated use of terrain, and effective political work with the Szechwan troops. A whole Szechwanese division defected to Ts'ai's side, and the Peiyang troops suffered unexpectedly large casualties.[50] In addition, the mobilization of 'bandit' forces in various

---

49 Sutton, *Provincial militarism*, 184-91 sifts the evidence regarding the initiation of the uprising in Yunnan in December 1915. For earlier challenges to Liang Ch'i-ch'ao's account see, Chin Ch'ung-chi, 'Yun-nan hu-kuo yun-tung ti chen-cheng fa-tung-che shih shui?' (Who was the true initiator of the Yunnan National Protection movement?), in Chou K'ang-hsieh, *et al.* eds. *Chin-erh-shih-nien Chung-kuo shih-hsueh lun-wen hui-pien, ch'u-pien: hsin-hai ko-ming yen-chiu lun-chi ti-i-chi (1895-1929)* (First collection of Chinese historical articles of the last 20 years: first volume of studies on the 1911 Revolution [1895-1929]), 261-86. Terahiro Teruo, 'Unnan gokokugun ni tsuite – kigi no shutai to undō no seishitsu' (The main constituents of the uprising of Yunnan's National Protection Army and the nature of the movement), *Tōyōshi kenkyū*, 17.3 (Dec. 1958) 27.

50 General Staff, 'Shina jiken sankō shiryō, sono hachi' (Reference materials on the China incident, no. 8). (March 1916), 'En Seigai teisei keikaku no ikken. Bessatsu: han En dōran oyobi kakuchi jōkyō' (The affair of Yuan Shih-k'ai's monarchical scheme. Supplement: anti-Yuan disturbances and conditions about the country), vol. 6, 1.6.1.75, Japanese Ministry of Foreign Affairs, Archives, Gaikō Shiryōkan, Tokyo.

parts of the province was encouraged by Szechwanese representatives of the National Protection Army, and was also stimulated by other, politically unrelated Szechwanese leaders who sought Szechwanese autonomy from Peking. The 'bandit' National Protection Army developed into a considerable guerrilla movement against the Peiyang occupation. Its development goes a long way in explaining Ts'ai O's successes.

Then, it turned out that even some of Yuan Shih-k'ai's own representatives in Szechwan – the officers of the occupation – were uncertain how far they would go in resisting the Yunnanese movement. Ts'ai soon established contact both with Yuan's proconsul in Szechwan, Ch'en I, and with Feng Yü-hsiang, the talented Peiyang commander. An accommodation was arrived at in March 1916. Although there had been tight moments, the National Protection Army prevailed over Yuan's influence in Szechwan.

From March onwards Yuan's power crumbled rapidly under a combination of foreign and domestic pressures. Externally, after an initial two months of apparent tolerance of the monarchical movement, the Japanese government had displayed a growing hostility to Yuan's monarchical intentions. The emerging policy of open disapproval was based less on an awareness of the monarchy's possible use as an impediment to Japanese aspirations than on a discovery of its enormous unpopularity among leading Chinese. In October 1915 Japan persuaded Great Britain and other foreign powers to warn Yuan of the risks. The outbreak of the Yunnan revolt in December, which justified these and subsequent warnings, increased Japanese opposition. Then in early March 1916 the Japanese cabinet formally adopted a policy of seeking Yuan's complete removal from power. One effect of this decision was a sizeable flow of Japanese funds to Yuan's opponents.[51]

Kwangsi's military chief, Lu Jung-t'ing, whose adherence to the revolution was expected earlier, finally acted in mid March 1916. Feng Kuo-chang at Nanking, who had expressed his disagreement with a revived monarchy the previous summer, now joined with other provincial military chiefs in calling for Yuan's abandonment of his imperial pretensions. On 22 March Yuan announced his return to presidential forms. But in April more provincial governments declared their break with Peking, and in May still others. In early June, when the only remaining question regarding Yuan was the manner of his departure, he died in Peking of uraemia at 56 years of age.

Meanwhile, the country had fallen into a state of the most remarkable

51 Albert A. Altman and Harold Z. Schiffrin, 'Sun Yat-sen and the Japanese: 1914–16', *Modern Asian Studies*, 6.4 (Oct. 1972) 385–400.

confusion. As Yuan's power was visibly fading, the opposition had no common organization nor any common vision of the post-Yuan order. Several clusters of power could be discerned. The southern tier of four provinces never occupied by Peiyang forces – Yunnan, Kweichow, Kwangsi and Kwangtung – formed for the moment a coordinated block, with extensions into Szechwan and Hunan as a result of the military campaigns. Some limited success was achieved in translating the cohesiveness of the Yunnan Army into a common political line, at least to the extent of holding out for Yuan's full overthrow and the revival of the 1912 constitution, which Yuan had replaced in 1914 by a document ratifying his dictatorship (see below, page 502). A second cluster centred on Feng Kuo-chang in the lower Yangtze area, as he summoned provincial chiefs for strategic discussions in the spring of 1916. He carved out for himself an intermediary position, generally opposing Yuan and the centralizing policies of the dictatorship but refusing to join forces with the southern revolutionaries.

In Peking, Tuan Ch'i-jui returned to office in April as prime minister and in effect supplanted Yuan as Peiyang leader and inheritor of the unifying aspirations of the dictatorship. But the aspirations could not be fulfilled. He represented in practice the centre of only a third cluster of power. This was dramatically illustrated when he tried to incorporate Hunan under Peking's administration in 1917. He found himself obstructed, not just by local Hunanese leaders, but also by an implicit coalition of the southern provinces and Feng Kuo-chang's allies along the Yangtze.

Another power cluster of future importance was beginning to emerge at the time of Yuan's death in the three north-eastern provinces of Manchuria under Chang Tso-lin. But Chang Tso-lin had not yet consolidated this vast area. None of these power clusters was in fact solid. They were constellations of military commanders and local officials, who pursued first of all their own survival in an exceedingly turbulent environment. The stage was set for instability and civil war. The warlord period had begun.

Another political tendency emerged as Yuan's star set. That was the resuscitation of the forms of the liberal phase of the republic. Even as Yuan clung to office, provincial and local assemblies were regathering beyond the reach of his power. With his death, both the 1912 constitution and the parliament of 1913 were revived. Perhaps the importance of this tendency in the late 1910s and the early 1920s has not been sufficiently appreciated. The linkage of provincial autonomy and self-government institutions lived on to influence early warlord politics, at least marginally.

But the vigour that representative government had had in the immediate aftermath of the 1911 Revolution never returned.

Retrospectively, it appears that the two failed political experiments of the early republic – liberal government and dictatorship – contributed to each other's destruction. Yuan Shih-k'ai found parliament and self-governed provinces debilitating to the nation-state, which, he believed, had to be centralized and strong in the age of imperialism. At his first opportunity he did away with both, as well as such auxilliary institutions as competing political parties and an uncensored press. But his own forms of rule inspired no general enthusiasm, though they were initially supported by some important independent figures like Liang Ch'i-ch'ao. Even its early advocates became disillusioned with Peking's authoritarian mode. Yuan's misguided monarchical gambit provided the occasion for this disillusionment to be mobilized. The dictatorship collapsed with the monarchy. But before a liberal consensus could re-emerge and gain an institutional edge, a decentralized military hegemony intervened. Both experimental forms of the early republic came to be recalled chiefly as negative political examples.

CHAPTER 5

A CONSTITUTIONAL REPUBLIC: THE PEKING GOVERNMENT, 1916–28

The death of Yuan Shih-k'ai in June 1916 ushered in the era of the warlords and yet throughout the ensuing decade or more of militarism, the Peking government remained the symbol of China's national sovereignty and hoped-for unity. In the absence of a dynasty, a dominant personality or a ruling party, the government at Peking still represented the idea of the state. In particular it was sustained by a widespread faith in constitutionalism, a belief that had grown up among Chinese patriots at the turn of the century along with the rise of nationalism.[1]

When China's newly-trained and -equipped navy was sunk by the Japanese in the war of 1894–5, many politically conscious Chinese concluded that 'self-strengthening' of an essentially technological and military nature was not enough to save China. At the same time, they were struck by the coincidence that all the most powerful countries in the world, including Japan, had more or less recently adopted constitutions. Furthermore, specialists in the new foreign discipline of political science asserted that a properly drafted constitution was the key to stable, effective government anywhere. It seemed clear that only a constitution could make China strong.

Despite disagreement over the form a Chinese constitution should take, most Chinese political thinkers agreed on two points. First, despite a basic unity of interests between government and people, the Chinese state was weak. This was due to the passivity of the people, which could be overcome by granting them a direct stake in government through such institutions of participation as study societies, elections and legislatures. As the reformer K'ang Yu-wei wrote in 1898, 'I have heard that the strength of nations east and west is due to the establishment of constitutions and the opening of parliaments. . . . How can a state be anything but strong when its ruler and its millions of citizens are united in a single body?'[2]

---

[1] This chapter draws heavily upon Andrew J. Nathan, *Peking politics, 1918–1923: factionalism and the failure of constitutionalism.*

[2] K'ang Yu-wei, 'Ch'ing t'ing li-hsien k'ai kuo-hui che', reprinted in Chien Po-tsan *et al.* comps. *Wu-hsu pien-fa* (1898 reforms), 2. 236.

Second, a major source of disorder in Chinese history had been the ambiguous definition of power relationships, resulting in struggles over the imperial succession, conflicts among ministers, and the overbearing behaviour of magistrates, which could be checked only by popular uprisings. But in a constitutional regime, as K'ang's disciple Liang Ch'i-ch'ao pointed out in 1900, 'the imperial succession is fixed, . . . the appointment of high ministers accords with legislative procedure and popular sentiment, . . . and any dissatisfaction among the people can be expressed to parliament. . . . Thus a constitutional form of government can never suffer from disorder.'[3]

Monarchists, among them K'ang and Liang, believed a period of tutelage was needed before the Chinese people could rule themselves. In this conception, influenced by the statecraft tradition of Chinese political thought, statesmen would combine education and sanctions to keep the public in order while gradually introducing institutions of popular participation. Republicans, on the other hand, led by Sun Yat-sen, argued that 'the future of China is like building a railroad. Thus if we were now building a railroad, would we use the first locomotive ever invented [constitutional monarchy] or today's improved and most efficient one [a republic]?'[4] The Ch'ing court put a price on the heads of K'ang and Liang but later accepted their arguments: in 1906 it ordered preparations for a monarchical constitution. But before the constitution was promulgated, the republicans won the day through revolution.

In some ways the edict of 1906 was more definitive than the Revolution of 1911. The idea of a republic was challenged at least three times by monarchists after 1911 – by Yuan Shih-k'ai's imperial venture, by Chang Hsun's 1917 restoration of the Hsuan-t'ung Emperor, and by the resurrection of the 'kingly way' in the Manchukuo of the 1930s. But at no point since 1906, even after 1949, has the necessity of one form or another of constitution been seriously questioned. Indeed, ever since the late Ch'ing a constitution has been considered necessary not only for the nation but for each political party, chamber of commerce and interest-group association.

Several sub-national units of government also adopted constitutions. The most important example of this trend was the so-called 'federalist movement' of the early 1920s (*lien-sheng tzu-chih yun-tung*, lit., 'movement for a federation of self-governing provinces'). Its leaders in Hunan, Szechwan, Kwangtung and several other southern provinces argued that

3 Liang Ch'i-ch'ao, 'Li hsien-fa i', in *Yin-ping shih wen-chi, ts'e* 2, *chüan* 5, pp. 3–4.
4 Quoted in Michael Gasster, *Chinese intellectuals and the Revolution of 1911: The birth of modern Chinese radicalism,* 138.

the nation would be stronger if each province could separate itself from the warlord melée to pursue stability and growth on its own. But when it came to mechanisms for achieving this goal, 'there were interminable discussions of the respective competence of the central power and the provincial authorities and of the structure of the latter, there were references to the German Bund of 1815, to the Swiss Confederation, to the United States of America, to Canada, to Australia, and comments on the various provincial constitutions promulgated or drafted at this time in China, but always from a technical, legal point of view rather [than] from that of Chinese realities.'⁵ Several provinces drafted constitutions and one (Hunan) briefly put its into effect. But the federalist movement did not rescue China from warlordism. Instead, several warlords cheerfully promulgated federalist constitutions of their own for tactical use in defying the central authorities.

What explains the persistence of the modern Chinese faith in constitutions despite so many disappointments? In the modern West, constitutions have been just as uncertain in their effectiveness and yet equally indispensable as in China. In both cases the idea draws vitality from basic national beliefs. In the individualist West constitutions are seen as rules for protecting personal rights and regulating inevitable conflicts of interest. In China, constitutions have been seen as basic statements of current community purpose around which to rally collective energies, as devices for promoting consensus and preventing error. As such, constitutions in China have been regarded as susceptible to change when community purpose changed.

There were pragmatic attractions as well. For a China struggling to achieve status in the world of nations, a constitution was part of the regalia of a modern state. Constitutions have afforded rulers a basis for claiming legitimacy. The early republican constitutions allowed a narrow community of factions to claim that their competition for power was legitimate while intrusions by revolutionary forces (the Kuomintang, the Communists, students, unions) were not. The factions could agree on the need for loyalty to the constitution, while permitting themselves to feud over the meaning of its provisions.

In short, the commitment to constitutionalism seemed to combine – in the early republic as well as later on, and in China as elsewhere – faith in a constitution's ability to strengthen the nation with pragmatic appreciation of its immediate convenience for the elite. The commitment was sufficiently real that a great deal of effort was devoted, in the years 1916

5 Jean Chesneaux, 'The federalist movement in China, 1920–3', in Jack Gray, ed. *Modern China's search for a political form*, 123.

to 1928, to writing constitutions, debating their provisions, denouncing opponents for breaching them, and congratulating allies for restoring them. On the other hand, with each cycle of factional conflict after 1916 there was a perceptible increase in the mendacity of the politicians' constitutional manoeuvres and a corresponding decline in public support for the republican regime. The eventual effect was to discredit the idea of a liberal republic and introduce the first of a series of authoritarian regimes, the national government of the Kuomintang. In a certain sense the constitutional monarchists of the late Ch'ing had won their point. The concept of tutelage, rather than monarchy as such, lay at the heart of their argument; and from 1928 until today Chinese governments have been supervised by one or another Leninist-style party, aiming to avoid repetition of the chaos of the early republic.

SOCIAL AND INTELLECTUAL ROOTS OF CONSTITUTIONALISM

Only a small proportion of the 400 million Chinese around 1920 knew or cared anything about constitutionalism, and of these a still smaller group was so placed as to be able to attempt to put the belief into practice. The interests and outlooks of the political elite go some way to explain the appeal of the constitutionalist faith.

The most influential portion of the national political elite were former Ch'ing bureaucrats. To such men, constitutionalism spelled modernization along Western lines. Most of them had not actively favoured the overthrow of the Manchu court, but they did not balk at it so long as their administrative predominance was preserved. Their overriding goal was a strong China, their models the Western nations and Japan, where constitutions and national power seemed conspicuously linked.

One can discern three roughly-divided age groups among the late Ch'ing bureaucrats who became leaders of the republic.[6] Men born in the 1860s belonged to the generation of Yuan Shih-k'ai (born 1859). Tutoring in the Confucian classics in preparation for government examinations was their normal training, but some of them experienced technical, foreign or new-style education. Most of this age-group accepted constitutionalism reluctantly after the defeat by Japan in 1895 and the Boxer fiasco of 1900, or accepted it as a *fait accompli* in 1911. Their commitment to the constitutional republic remained imperfect (their generation provided the main support for several Ch'ing-restoration schemes), and their leadership was autocratic and personalistic.

6 For examples to support the propositions that follow, see Nathan, *Peking politics*, 8–13.

The experience of new-style education became more common in the cohort born in the 1870s. But as with the earlier group, the new learning came relatively late in their lives after considerable classical tutoring. New-style education in China still had a high traditional content, especially with regard to fundamental social and political values. And students who went abroad tended to be from wealthy families with stakes in the *status quo*. For these reasons many in the 1870s cohort shared the political conservatism of their seniors. On the other hand, their greater exposure to both the technical and the political cultures of Japan and the West gave them greater facility in operating a republican form of government and providing administrative leadership in such fields as railway administration, finance and foreign relations. This age-group was a generous supplier of cabinet ministers to early republican governments.

For men born in the 1880s a pure classical education was no longer practical. Those who began their training with classical study aimed at the examinations had to change course when examinations based on the classical curriculum were abolished in 1905. Young men who aspired to government service now had to prepare themselves either through new-style domestic education or by study overseas, or both. Of those who studied abroad the vast majority went to Japan. Transplanted to a student community in a foreign country with other students from all over China, they formed clubs, journals and political parties, and conducted lively debates with half-understood jargon drawn from a wide range of Western and Japanese thought. They tended to reject Chinese traditions, to copy foreign intellectual and social fashions, and to adopt the view that 'nothing Chinese was good and everything Western was worth emulating.'[7]

Between the cohorts of the 1870s and the 1880s lay a major divide in elite political culture. It was the later generation that contributed the senior leadership of the May Fourth movement and provided the eldest sizeable group of Chinese Communist Party leaders. Of course, those younger men who elected to enter the Ch'ing bureaucracy under the patronage of elder bureaucrats were not so radical as their to-be-communist contemporaries. But because they better understood and were more committed than their seniors to the republican ideal, they became the major in-house critics of the republic's failings. If the 1880s cohort shared with that of the 1860s an ambivalence about the republic, in their case it came not from a feeling that the republic might be going too far but from a sense that it often did not go far enough.

The second major component of the early republican national political elite consisted of members of new professions – educators, lawyers, engineers, journalists, modern businessmen and bankers. Newspapers, colleges, courts, banks and other specialized new institutions required specially trained staff, and new-style and overseas education provided them (see volume 11, chapter 10). The late Ch'ing reforms gave a special impetus to the modernizing trend by requiring the establishment of professional associations (*fa-t'uan*) – chambers of commerce, lawyers' associations, bankers' associations – for self-regulation of the nascent professions. Because the professional associations were charged with quasi-governmental functions, the professions came to be regarded as a sector of the elite having a legitimate voice in public affairs. Their relationship of formal and informal cooperation with the national government was analogous to that traditionally enjoyed by the gentry. Indeed, to some degree they gradually replaced local landholding elites as the major recruitment pool and source of 'public opinion' for twentieth-century Chinese national governments. While *arriviste* landholding and military elites rivalled the old gentry on the local level, the professionals succeeded to its position at the national level. But less wealthy and less educated sectors of the newly-emerging urban middle classes – small merchants, artisans, students, clerks – were excluded from the elite's conception of the legitimate public.

Among the new professionals, the professional politicians played a particularly prominent role. From about 1900 onwards the Tokyo Chinese student community proved a rich recruiting ground. Here students read about nationalism and revolution and met actual party men and revolutionaries. Some chose to forgo bureaucratic careers to emulate these new models of political action. They chose between Liang Ch'i-ch'ao's path of agitation and propaganda for establishment of a constitution under the Ch'ing and Sun Yat-sen's programme of secret organization for a revolution to establish a republic.

The convening of the provincial assemblies in 1909 and of the national assembly in 1910 provided an opportunity for many politicians to pursue their careers within the establishment. The typical late Ch'ing provincial assemblyman was young (average age, 41), wealthy, of gentry class origin; one-third had received modern education in China or overseas.[8] Although these assemblies, like those in the republic, included bureaucrats, professionals, businessmen, landholders, and the like, the professional politicians dominated and set the tone.

The fact that the professional politicians had not served in the bu-

8 Chang P'eng-yuan, 'Ch'ing-chi tzu-i-chü i-yuan ti hsuan-chü chi ch'i ch'u-shen chih fen-hsi', *Ssu yü yen* 5. 6 (March 1968) 1439–42.

reaucracy tended to relegate them permanently to peripheral positions in early republican politics. The highest offices in the republic were achieved mainly by bureaucrats and ex-bureaucrats, often military men. Few cabinet ministers and no presidents (with the brief exception of Sun Yat-sen) were professional politicians in the sense just described. Between parliamentary sessions, the politicians were forced to serve as intermediaries, brokers and allies of the major bureaucratic factions. They took centre-stage only when parliament was in session and the struggle to expand its power could be pursued.

Constitutionalism served the interests of ex-bureaucrats and professionals because it offered them legitimate political roles without opening the political arena to the groups below them. But in addition, constitutionalism made intellectual sense to many Chinese at the turn of the century and into the 1920s. To begin with, they were impressed by the assurances of Western experts. 'The political troubles with which the Chinese have . . . been afflicted', wrote W. W. Willoughby, professor of political science at Johns Hopkins and for years a constitutional adviser to the Chinese government, 'have been due not so much to a general lack of capacity to maintain a self-governing or representative scheme of political control as that they have been attempting to govern themselves under an essentially defective constitution.'⁹

This view, characteristic of Western political science in the 1920s, fell on fertile Chinese intellectual soil. The prestige and self-confidence of the West, the desire in some Chinese circles to achieve world acceptance by becoming more like the Western nations, and the evident success of constitutional regimes in becoming world powers were only the more obvious motives for imitation. There was also the vogue of scientism in Chinese thought – the belief in the efficacy of a mechanistic version of modern science to solve human problems. Just as part of the attraction of 'scientific' Marxism in both the West and China was its claimed linkage with the nature-mastering powers of science, so modern 'political science' laid claim to the same second-hand charisma. Like Marxism a few years later, constitutionalism seemed to link what Ch'en Tu-hsiu was to call Mr Te (democracy) and Mr Sai (science) by providing for democracy to be scientifically engineered.

Even more fundamentally, the faith in constitutions fell in with a deep-seated Chinese belief in the dominant role of the conscious mind in the process of action. Confucius had argued that the ruler who would unify the empire must first 'be sincere in [his] thoughts'; the influential Ming Neo-Confucian Wang Yang-ming had stated that 'knowledge is the

9 W. W. Willoughby, *Constitutional government in China: present conditions and prospects*, 33.

beginning of practice; doing is the completion of knowledge.' As Sun Yat-sen succinctly put it, 'Whatever can be known can certainly be carried out.'[10] That is, if the conscious mind can be set straight as to how to do a thing, the actual doing of it will be relatively unproblematical. Correlatively, if a thing is being done wrong, the solution lies in correcting the conscious thoughts of the doer. Let the provisions of the constitution be regarded as the thing 'known' by the conscious national mind, and there is no reason a constitutional republic should not work. If it fails, the reason must be either imperfect mastery of and commitment to its principles, or flaws in the constitutional instrument itself.

If consistency with this 'voluntarist' tradition helped make constitutionalism plausible, its expected contribution to national wealth and power made it positively attractive. In Chinese eyes, a constitution's function was to connect the individual's interests with those of the state, thus arousing the people to greater effort and creativity on behalf of national goals. The trouble with old China, many Chinese thinkers believed, was the passivity and narrow selfishness of the people. In a modern state, on the other hand, because the people rule, they devote themselves wholeheartedly to the nation. When there are 'ten thousand eyes with one sight, ten thousand hands and feet with only one mind, ten thousand ears with one hearing, ten thousand powers with only one purpose of life; then the state is established ten-thousandfold strong. . . . When mind touches mind, when power is linked to power, cog to cog, strand around strand, and ten thousand roads meet in one center, this will be a state.'[11] This theme of constitution as energizer was linked with the Mencian notion that, in Paul Cohen's paraphrase, 'just policies and causes command popular support', and 'a ruler with popular support is invincible'.[12] Constitutionalism could be seen as such a just policy. The popular support it could command would provide the key to wealth and power for China.

THE PEKING GOVERNMENT

For most of the 1916–28 period, the Peking government operated on the basis of the Provisional Constitution of 1912. Although intended by its architects to lodge predominant power in the cabinet, the Provisional

10 Confucius quoted in Nathan, *Peking politics*, 21; Wang Yang-ming in David S. Nivison, 'The problem of "knowledge" and "action" in Chinese thought since Wang Yang-ming', in Arthur F. Wright, ed. *Studies in Chinese thought*, 120; Sun Yat-sen in Teng Ssu-yü and John K. Fairbank, comps. *China's response to the West: a documentary survey, 1839–1923*, 264.
11 Liang Ch'i-ch'ao, quoted in Hao Chang, *Liang Ch'i-ch'ao and intellectual transition in China, 1890–1907*, 100.
12 Paul A. Cohen, 'Wang T'ao's perspective on a changing world', in Albert Feuerwerker, Rhoads Murphey, and Mary C. Wright, eds. *Approaches to modern Chinese history*, 160.

Constitution was sufficiently ambiguous to encourage continuous conflict among president, prime minister and parliament.

The president, elected by parliament for a five-year term, had the symbolic functions and potentially the prestige of a head of state; his personality and factional backing determined whether he could translate these into real power. The cabinet was supposed to 'assist' the president by running ministries, co-signing presidential orders and enactments, and answering questions in parliament; usually composed by a division of spoils among factions, the cabinet in fact rarely functioned as a policy-making unit. The prime minister, despite a lack of specifically designated constitutional powers, could sometimes dominate government through his role in picking a cabinet and piloting its ratification through parliament, and by virtue of his control, through members of his own faction, of such crucial ministries as army, finance, communications and interior. Finally, parliament, composed of a house and senate whose members enjoyed three- and six-year terms respectively, had powers not only to elect the president and vice-president and to ratify the cabinet, but to approve budgets, declarations of war and treaties, and to interpellate and impeach. Often factionally disunified, and performing a relatively unfamiliar part in Chinese government, parliament was rarely able to act more than passively or obstructively. Table 37 lists the parliaments and other national-level legislative organs of the early republic.

Under the Provisional Constitution, parliament's major duty was to write a permanent constitution. Over the years successive legislatures worked at this task, returning to many of the issues raised in late Ch'ing debates and during the reign of Yuan Shih-k'ai – centralism versus local self-government, legislative versus executive power, and broad versus narrow political participation (see chapter 4). A good deal of time was spent in the 1913–14 session preparing a draft constitution, and the work was resumed in the 1916–17 session. In 1917 two governments came into existence, one in Peking and one in Canton, each claiming to carry out the Provisional Constitution, and each working on a constitutional draft. Finally, when the original (or so-called 'old') parliament reconvened in 1922, it produced the 'Ts'ao K'un Constitution' (so called because it was promulgated by President Ts'ao K'un) of 10 October 1923. After a *coup d'état* drove Ts'ao from office in 1924, a temporary document, the Regulations of the Chinese Republican Provisional Government, replaced the constitution, while a constitutional drafting commission was convened to try again. Chang Tso-lin's regime of 1927–28 provided itself with a document in lieu of a constitution, the Mandate on the Organization of the Marshal's Government.

TABLE 37

National-level legislative organs of the early republic

Name	Dates	Comments
Conference of Military Governors' Representatives (Ko-sheng tu-tu fu tai-piao lien-ho hui)	30 November 1911- 28 January 1912	Meeting first in Wuchang and then in Nanking, the military governors' representatives took the first steps to organize the new republic.
Provisional National Council [or assembly or senate] (Lin-shih ts'an-i yuan)	28 January 1912- 8 April 1913	Convened in Nanking, moved to Peking. Framed Provisional Constitution (*Lin-shih yueh-fa*).
First (or 'old') Parliament, first session (Kuo-hui)	8 April- 13 November 1913	Dissolved after Yuan Shih-k'ai expelled Kuomintang members.
Political Conference (Cheng-chih hui-i)	15 December 1913- 18 March 1914	Convened by Yuan Shih-k'ai to replace parliament. At first, called Administrative Conference (Hsing-cheng hui-i).
Constitutional Conference (Yueh-fa hui-i)	18 March- 5 June 1914	Summoned by Yuan to write the Constitutional Compact (*Hsin yueh-fa*).
National Council (Ts'an-cheng yuan)	26 May 1914- 29 June 1916	Temporarily performed legislative functions under Constitutional Compact.
First Parliament, second session	1 August 1916- 12 June 1917	The old parliament was recalled after Yuan's death; was dissolved in course of Chang Hsun's coup.
First Parliament 'extraordinary session' (Fei-ch'ang hui-i)	25 August 1917- 16 June 1922	In protest against the plan to elect a new parliament, many members of 'old' parliament reconvened in Canton. Later, this session met in Kunming and in Chungking.
Provisional National Council (Lin-shih ts'an-i yuan)	10 November 1917- 12 August 1918	Convened by Tuan Ch'i-jui to prepare laws for election of a new parliament.
Anfu Parliament (An-fu kuo-hui)	12 August 1918- 30 August 1920	Dissolved in aftermath of Chihli-Anfu war.
'New-New' Parliament (Hsin-hsin kuo-hui)	(summer, 1921)	At Hsu Shih-ch'ang's behest, 11 provinces carried out house elections, but the elections were not conducted elsewhere and this parliament never met.
First Parliament, third session	1 August 1922- 24 November 1924	Recall of the old parliament in its 1917 form, excluding new members elected to the 'extraordinary session' in 1919.
Reconstruction Conference (Shan-hou hui-i)	1 February- 21 April 1925	Summoned by Tuan Ch'i-jui's executive government to solve outstanding national issues.
Provisional National Council (Lin-shih ts'an-cheng yuan)	30 July 1925- 20 April 1926	An interim legislature; dissolved in a coup.
Constitutional Drafting Commission (Kuo-hsien ch'i-ts'ao wei-yuan hui)	3 August- 12 December 1925	Prepared a new constitutional draft which was never put into effect.

Sources: Liu Shou-lin, *Hsin-hai i-hou shih-ch'i nien chih-kuan nien-piao* (Tables of officials by year, 1911–28), 486–7; Nathan, *Peking Politics*, 183.

To the end of its life, the Peking government held a claim to legitimacy which made it important even in a nation increasingly dominated by contending warlords. Until 1923, if not later, many leaders of public opinion, while deploring the feuding and corruption of politicians, voiced hope in the ultimate success of the constitutional order. Each major warlord supported factional allies or followers in parliament, cabinet, or the political press, and if possible cultivated good relations with the prime minister and president. Often the aim was to gain official appointment (for example, as the governor of a province) to legitimize local rule.

A second reason for Peking's importance was foreign recognition. Against all evidence of fragmentation, the foreign powers insisted that there was only one China and – as late as 1928 – that its capital was Peking. The powers generally insisted that formal settlement of issues go through the central Ministry of Foreign Affairs, even if the case was essentially local in scope. The many appointments to lucrative posts in railway and treaty-port offices also needed Peking's acquiescence even if they were located in areas of warlord control, because they often involved foreign interests. Finally, the presence of the foreign legations afforded some physical protection to the city: although the privilege was not invoked during the period, the Boxer Protocol of 1901 provided in effect that warlord invasion of Peking or seizure of the Peking-Tientsin railway might bring foreign military intervention.

A third source of Peking's influence was financial. Taxes played but a small role in Peking's finances; remittances began to decline even before Yuan Shih-k'ai's death and shrivelled to insignificance thereafter. Far more significant was the financial consequence of foreign recognition: the ability to borrow. The government borrowed abroad on the pledge of China's natural resources, as in the 140 million yen 'Nishihara loans' of 1917–18. And it borrowed at home – Ch.$631 million in 27 bond issues from 1913 to 1926 – in part on the security of the salt gabelle and Maritime Customs Administration revenues which were shielded from warlord interference by the powers' involvement in their collection (more fully so in the case of customs than of salt revenues). Aside from major foreign loans and domestic bond issues, there were treasury notes (short- and long-term), bank advances, obligations contracted by specific ministries, salaries in arrears and other debts, whose total has never been calculated. Although money became increasingly difficult to raise, it is doubtful that a fraction of what the government borrowed domestically would have been available without the constant (if usually disappointed) expectation of large foreign loans and the security provided for some domestic bond issues by customs and salt revenues.

The borrowed money went into politics ('honorariums' to members of parliament and journalists) and the armies of militarists allied with Peking's rulers. Meanwhile, government offices were starved for funds. Salaries went unpaid and teachers, police and bureaucrats went on strike, demonstrated, and took bribes and second jobs to survive. Under the circumstances it is remarkable that any useful administrative work was performed. Yet there are indications that several ministries functioned fairly effectively throughout much of the period.

Elementary, secondary and higher educational institutions raised standards and expanded enrolments under the Ministry of Education's centralized leadership.[13] The court system under the Ministry of Justice remained incomplete and under-used but enjoyed a reputation for honesty, and there was progress in law codification and prison administration. Under the Ministry of Interior, Peking's modern police force kept its professional standards so high that Peking was described in 1928 as 'one of the best-policed cities in the world.'[14] The railways, telegraph and postal services of the Ministry of Communications functioned profitably and quite reliably despite occasional warlord attempts at interference. These surface impressions need to be followed up with careful research on the bureaucracy to see how the marriage of the indigenous tradition of bureaucratic service with Western technical and professional norms survived in such hostile political surroundings.

Perhaps the most effective of Peking's ministries – yet the most often attacked by contemporaries and posterity – was foreign affairs. Its cosmopolitan diplomats – men like V. K. Wellington Koo and W. W. Yen – doggedly pursued the task of rights recovery on behalf of a nation that lacked the military or financial capability to defend itself. By declaring war on Germany and Austria-Hungary in 1917, China cancelled their extraterritorial rights and terminated their Boxer indemnity payments, also winning a five-year suspension of Boxer payments to the Allies. Although purely nominal, China's entry into the war gave her the prestige of participating as a victor in the Paris Peace Conference of 1919. The Treaty of Versailles severely disappointed the Chinese by passing German rights in Shantung to Japan, but China's diplomats had gained points in the court of international opinion; in the Washington Conference of 1921–2 Japan was forced to agree to withdraw from Shantung. In addition, Great Britain agreed to return Weihaiwei; the nine powers declared they

13 H. G. W. Woodhead, ed. *The China year book 1926–7*, 407–10. For Justice, see 753–68; for Communications, 269–385.
14 *New York Times*, 30 Dec. 1928, quoted in David Strand, 'Peking in the 1920s: political order and popular protest' (Columbia University, Ph.D. dissertation, 1979), 43.

would respect China's sovereignty; the customs tariff was raised to 5 per cent; and provisions were made for eventual tariff autonomy and abolition of extraterritoriality. China gained further in the 1924 Sino-Soviet treaty: Russia gave up extraterritoriality, its concessions at Tientsin and Hankow, and Boxer indemnity payments. In 1926, even as the Peking government was on the brink of collapse, the Foreign Ministry persuaded the powers to send delegates to a Tariff Revision Conference. The conference disbanded inconclusively but the elaborate Chinese position papers formed the basis for the Nanking government's successful claim of tariff autonomy in 1928. The arduous negotiations behind all these achievements have yet to be studied, except for those leading to the 1924 Sino-Soviet treaty: the scholar of this event concludes that the Ministry of Foreign Affairs 'had more power and independence, more continuity, better personnel, more positive policies and nationalistic motivations than most people realize.'[15]

THE POLITICAL ROLE OF THE MODERN BANKS

An increasingly important feature of Peking politics in the early republic and into the 1920s was the political involvement of the modern treaty-port Chinese banks. Within the world of Chinese banking, these banks were flanked on one side by the treaty-port branches of the foreign banks, and on the other by the *ch'ien-chuang* (traditional money shops); both types of institutions were financially stronger than the Chinese modern banks. The 27 foreign banks with branches in China commanded three or four times the capital of the 119 (or more) Chinese banks. They virtually monopolized the lucrative foreign exchange and foreign trade markets, and enjoyed the privileges of issuing currency and of receiving several hundred million dollars per year in salt and customs receipts. They had the trust of Chinese and foreign businessmen alike and did the bulk of the banking business in the treaty ports. The innumerable money shops, on the other hand, were strongly entrenched in the fields of domestic currency exchange, securities speculation and short-term loans. While individually small, they had capital totalling more than that of the modern banks, and because they enjoyed established channels of activity they were more successful in maintaining liquidity than the modern banks. Indeed, the money shops served as a source of short-term capital for the modern banks.

The modern banks were financially weak in the early republic. With

15 Sow-theng Leong, *Sino-Soviet diplomatic relations, 1917–1926*, 294–95.

an aggregate authorized capital of Ch.$350 million, the 119 modern banks on which data are available were able to raise only Ch.$150 million in paid-up capital.[16] Because of low public confidence, they had to attract working funds, of which they were desperately short, by issuing paper money (if government authorization could be obtained), borrowing from the money shops at high interest, and accepting savings deposits at high interest. Then, in order to pay back the high-interest loans and deposits and support the value of their notes, the banks were forced to seek highly profitable, and therefore speculative, investments. Government bonds and treasury notes were an important part of such investment.

The government was driven increasingly into the domestic capital market as its other sources of revenue dried up. Domestic tax revenues started a precipitous decline in late 1915 when a number of provinces declared their independence of Peking in response to Yuan Shih-k'ai's imperial movement. In 1918 the new Hara Kei cabinet in Japan abandoned its predecessor's policy of granting generous, poorly-secured loans to China. A consortium of foreign bankers, organized in 1920, became the instrument of what was in effect a prolonged foreign financial boycott of the Chinese government (see chapter 2). As a result of these developments domestic credit became increasingly crucial to the revenue-raising activities of a series of desperate ministers of finance. Beginning with the Eighth-Year Bonds in 1919, however, bankers' enthusiasm for government securities waned. The government was deeply in debt, there was no reliable revenue left on which to secure the new bonds, and the political situation was insecure. Bankers were able to exact harsh terms from the government for small advances of cash. Left-over First-Year Bonds were sold by the government in Shanghai for Ch.$21.50 per $100 face-value; unsold Seventh-Year Bonds were sold for Ch.$54 per $100 bond. Banks made numerous short-term loans to the government at 16 to 25 per cent interest per month, with unsold bonds, valued at 20 per cent of face-value, used as security. From 1912 to 1924, Ch.$46,740,062 worth of treasury bills, payable in one or two years, were sold to banks at as little as 40 per cent of face-value, providing a handsome rate of return upon redemption.

The modern banks thus became the major holders of government bonds. The bonds could be bought at a fraction of face-value and often with the bank's own notes, but they might never be repaid and their value might continue to fall. On the other hand, the market value might leap at the news that a new security had been found for the issue, or that

16 For documentation see Nathan, *Peking politics*, 74–90.

a drawing would be held to redeem a portion of it, or that a new minister of finance was to be appointed. Bonds could prove a profitable investment because their market value rose and fell so violently. To speculate with success, however, it was necessary to anticipate or even influence the movements of the market. This required close political contacts.

The modern banks with headquarters in Peking and Tientsin were most closely involved in Peking politics. (The Shanghai banks also speculated in government bonds but did much of their business in exchange transactions and industrial investments; other treaty-port banks were more closely involved in local politics than in Peking politics.) The typical board of directors of a Peking or Tientsin bank was carefully composed. At its heart were a number of professional bankers with good contacts with a variety of political factions. To these were added men of banking or other financial experience who were more closely identified with one political group or another. The purpose of such balancing was to provide banks with intelligence on the political facts that determined fluctuations in the market price of bonds and with friends in government who could obtain and protect privileges, but to avoid a political one-sidedness in the bank's allegiances that might leave it defenceless when the political situation changed.

As the government became more and more impecunious after 1919, the political power of banks, and of political factions with influence in banking circles, increased. The Communications Clique (described below) emerged as an especially powerful arbiter of the fate of cabinets. At the same time, the ability of banks in general to enforce their interests on the government was strengthened. Meeting in Shanghai in December 1920, the Chinese Bankers' Association decided to refuse to buy any more government bonds until the government 'readjusted' the means of paying off the old ones. In response, by presidential mandate of 3 March 1921, the government committed its customs surplus to a sinking fund called the Consolidated Internal Loan Service, administered by the inspector-general of customs, Sir Francis Aglen. The First-, Fifth-, Seventh-Year Long-Term, Eighth-, and Ninth-Year Bonds (other issues were later added) were revalued at a portion of face-value and exchanged for two new bond issues, the service of which was guaranteed by the fund.

The establishment of the Consolidated Internal Loan Service was a boon to the bankers. The bonds had been revalued below face-value, but this did not matter because the banks had originally purchased them at large discounts. Now, by waiting for the loan service to redeem the bonds, the banks could receive twice what they had paid for them; or, if they wished to trade the bonds, they could sell them at a higher price than they had paid. The government's credit was also enhanced, although the blessing of Sir Francis Aglen now became necessary for the success of any new government-bond issue.

FACTIONALISM AND PERSONAL CONNECTIONS

The institutional façade of the Peking government was constitutional: legislative, executive and judicial functions parcelled out by law, policy decisions made by institutional procedures. The reality was factional: personal followings, cutting across the boundaries of official institutions, each faction centred on a particular leader and composed of his individually recruited, personally loyal followers.

In building such factions, political leaders kept alert for promising men who were able, politically active and trustworthy. The judgment of trustworthiness was heavily influenced by the idea of 'connections' (*kuan-hsi*). To most Chinese, society consisted of a web of defined role relationships such as father-son, ruler-minister, husband-wife and teacher-student. It was much safer to trust those with whom one had some definite connection than those who were merely acquaintances. Even if the connection was remote, it helped introduce stability into a relationship: it identified the senior and the junior member, and involved reliable rules about what one member had the right to ask or expect of the other.

Connections among blood relatives or in-laws, of course, were highly important, although where the relative in question was not politically skilful, he would be given a sinecure rather than a sensitive post. Another important kind of connection was between persons hailing from the same locality or region of China. Given the linguistic and cultural diversity of the nation, Cantonese or Anhweinese far from home in Peking tended to stick together. Other foci of loyalty grew out of the educational process: those who had studied together under the same teacher, graduated from the same school, or passed the pre-1905 civil service examinations in the same year considered one another fellow-students, a relationship which was often closer and more intimate than that between brothers. Such fellow-students also owed solemn and lifelong loyalty to their former teachers and examination supervisors. Similarly, ties to former colleagues and superiors grew out of bureaucratic service. In addition to, or instead of, such automatically-formed connections, one man might link himself to another in a master-disciple relationship, a patron-protégé relationship, or in sworn brotherhood.

On the basis of extensive networks of connections, outstanding political leaders gathered around themselves factions of able, well-placed, loyal followers. In the unfamiliar institutional world mandated by the republican constitutions, the leaders relied more and more on their factions to carry on political action.

One of the most influential and complex factions was headed by Tuan Ch'i-jui (1865–1936). Tuan graduated from the artillery course at the Peiyang Military Academy in 1887, and, after further study in Germany, he became commander of the artillery corps and supervisor and chief lecturer at the artillery school at Hsiao-chan, where Yuan Shih-k'ai was training his Newly Created Army (see volume 11, chapter 10). Because of his important role at Hsiao-chan, about half of the officers of the Newly Created Army, including many of the important North China militarists of the early republic, were his students. Tuan had access to another large pool of political talent as a native of Hofei, Anhwei, a city whose sons displayed strong localistic identification and uncommon political skill. Although he was an army general, Tuan did not have a warlord-style political base in the direct command of troops or the control of territory. His influence was based upon seniority, prestige and skill, and particularly upon his large personal following.

Through his followers Tuan's influence during the republican years was felt in many sectors of the government – the War Participation (later Border Defence) Army; the ministries of interior, finance, communications and others; the cabinet secretariat; the Peking-Hankow railway; the government-owned Lungyen Iron Mining Company; the Supreme Court. Of particular interest for this essay was the way in which Tuan projected his power into the parliament of 1918–20 through a parliamentary association called the Anfu Club, organized by two of his close associates, Wang I-t'ang and Hsu Shu-cheng. Wang was a native of Tuan's home city, Hofei, and a protégé of Tuan's. Hsu was a young army officer whom Tuan had selected during the late Ch'ing as an aide. (The Anfu Club is described below.)

Another leading republican faction was the Communications Clique. Its origins lay in the late Ch'ing Ministry of Posts and Communications (Yu-ch'uan pu, founded in 1906). As resources were poured into it for constructing or redeeming railways, extending the telegraph system, and founding the Bank of Communications, the ministry became an important locus of political and financial power. Followers of Yuan Shih-k'ai staffed the ministry and its agencies. One of them was Liang Shih-i (1869–1933), who from 1906 to 1911 held perhaps the most important post in the ministry, that of director-general of the Railway Bureau. According to a later description by American Minister Paul Reinsch, Liang 'was credited as being, next to Yuan Shih-k'ai, the ablest and most influential man in Peking. . . . Cantonese, short of stature and thickset, with a massive Napoleonic head, he speaks little, but his side remarks indicate that he is always ahead of the discussion, which is also shown by his searching questions. When directly questioned himself, he will always give a lucid and consecutive account of any matter.'[17] So great was Liang's financial influence that his contemporaries called him the 'god of Wealth'.

Liang served in a series of high government posts from 1906 to 1916. During this time he built a network of influence in the communications bureaucracy that survived his own retirement from government. For example, Liang's follower Yeh Kung-ch'o served as chief of the Railway Bureau, manager of the Bank of Communications, vice-minister of communications (1913–16, 1917–18), and minister of communications (1920–1, 1921–2, 1924–5). Another follower, Ch'üan Liang, served as director-general of the Kirin-Huining railway and managing director of the Kirin-Changchun railway, and several times as vice-minister and acting minister of communications. And there were many others.

A second dimension of the Communications Clique's power was its influence in the world of banking. The key was control over the Bank of Communications, which performed the functions of a government bank, yet was controlled by private investors. Liang had established the bank in 1908 as an organ of the ministry to handle the finances of the railway, post, telegraph and navigation administrations. In 1914 it was empowered to issue currency and to share the control of public finance with the Bank of China. Despite the bank's political power and special privileges, 70 per cent of the shares were held after 1914 by private shareholders. Liang often controlled the government shares, and he also controlled most of the private shares through his associates among the directors. In addition to the Bank of Communications, Liang founded a score or more of private banks, including some of the most important in China (among them the Kincheng Bank, Yien-yeh Bank, Ta-lu Bank and Peiyang pao-shang Bank). According to one source, Liang and his associates had an interest in 'a majority' of the domestic banks to which the government was in debt in the early 1920s.[18] As of approximately 1920 Liang was head of the Domestic Bond Bureau, an organ established to 'readjust' the domestic debt in order to re-establish the government's credit; his lieutenants Yeh Kung-ch'o and Chou Tzu-ch'i were ministers of communications and finance respectively; Liang himself held directorships not only on the Bank of Communications but on the boards of

17 Paul S. Reinsch, *An American diplomat in China*, 95–6.
18 *The North-China Herald and Supreme Court and Consular Gazette*, 4 Feb. 1922, 289.

six private banks (of which three were members of the Chinese banking group, a consortium that made loans to the government); and other members of the faction held directorships on the same and other important banks.

These examples suggest some of the diversity of factional activity in the early republic. Other factions were more heavily military (the Chihli Clique of Ts'ao K'un and Wu P'ei-fu; Chang Tso-lin's Fengtien Clique); still others were primarily composed of parliamentary politicians and journalists (the Research Clique, the Political Study Group). In any case, the most successful factions were large and diverse enough to survive changes of government and shifts of military and financial fortune.

A political system organized largely by factions could go through the outer motions of constitutionalism, but real political conflicts took on a logic that was factional. Based more on personal than on institutional loyalties, factions were limited in size to the few score men that the leader could cultivate personally or through immediate lieutenants. Masses of foot soldiers or ministry employees might in turn be commanded by these followers, but their utility was limited to the period when factional members were in office to command them. Factions could not generate the overwhelming institutional force to suppress rival groups and secure permanent control of the government. Even if one faction's leader managed to obtain the presidency or prime ministership, its rivals would retain their footholds in the ministries, parliament, the banks, or the regional armies. From these strongholds they would unite against the dominant faction or coalition, publishing diatribes, launching rumours, withholding funds, and blocking military consolidation, until the moment was ripe to use bribery or coup to force a change of government. Foreign contemporaries often saw the politics of the early republic as 'comic opera'. In fact, they were the politics of factionalism following its own logic, and destroying the constitutionalist fabric in the process.

ELECTION OF THE ANFU PARLIAMENT, 1918

A study of the parliamentary election of 1918 illustrates the inter-penetration of constitutional forms and factional realities, at a relatively early stage when it seemed the two might coexist. The first republican parliament, elected in 1913–14, had been dissolved for the second time on 13 June 1917, in the course of a short-lived attempt by a conservative general, Chang Hsun, to restore the Manchu emperor. Chang was driven from Peking by forces loyal to Tuan Ch'i-jui, who returned to his post as prime minister. In his earlier cabinet service, parliament had proved a thorn in Tuan's side, so now he determined to replace it. His pretext was that the defeat of Chang Hsun's coup was a second anti-Manchu revolution. It would be suitable to follow the precedent of the 1911 Revolution by convening a provisional national council to write a new parliamentary organic law and parliamentary election laws. The election of a new parliament would give the republic a fresh start. Of course, it was quite illogical to replace only parliament and not the prime minister, and five southern provinces refused to participate. Nonetheless, the Provisional National Council convened in Peking on 10 November 1917. Dominated by Tuan's followers and members of allied factions, it prepared regulations for election of a smaller, more pliable parliament.

The elections were conducted in two stages, the first one choosing each province's electors, who would meet later to select the members of parliament. In Kiangsu province, for example, the dates for the primary and final elections were set on 20 May and 10 June for the house, and on June 5 and 20 for the senate. The first-stage elections for the house were characterized by the British consul in Nanking, Bertram Giles, as 'a veritable orgie [sic] of corruption and rowdyism'. He wrote, 'The quotations for votes and the daily market fluctuations were chronicled in the native press as that of a marketable commodity, on the same footing as rice or beancake or other articles of commerce.' It was not unusual for an election supervisor to retain a large bloc of tickets that should have been handed out to registered voters, fill in the names of fictitious voters, and drop them into the ballot box or hire 'beggars, hawkers, fortune-tellers, peasants and such small fry' to cast the votes. Alternatively, the election deputy could sell a packet of tickets to a candidate who would proceed the same way. Some candidates, unable to buy enough tickets, hired toughs to seize them at the polling booth. In some cases, one candidate paid the others to withdraw. In the first-level senate elections, Giles reported, things went more smoothly since the smaller number of voters made it easier to buy up all the votes.[19]

In the second-stage elections the candidates 'began bidding against each other in earnest'. At this stage, votes for the house went for Ch.$ 150 to Ch.$500. The elections were repeatedly postponed as bargaining over the price of votes went on. If Kiangsu's cities were anything like Tientsin, from which we have a report, the business of teahouses, wine shops and brothels recovered from their annual post-Spring Festival lull as candidates entertained potential supporters and used the premises

---

19 F. O.228/3279, 'Nanking intelligence report for the quarter ended July 31st, 1918', Bertram Giles, n.d., pp. 15–23.

to close deals on votes. The Tientsin author asks: 'Who says elections don't benefit the little people?'[20]

Prime Minister Tuan's electoral machine, the Anfu Club, had a Kiangsu branch called the Ya-yuan (Elegant garden), probably after the name of the building in Nanking where Anfu emissaries entertained prospective supporters and exchanged money for ballots. Giles reported that as a result of the second-level elections for the house, the Anfu Club won about three-quarters of the house seats despite the fact 'that the bulk of the Province is strongly anti-Tuan.'[21] Anfu's main rival in Kiangsu was the Research Clique. After doing poorly in the house elections, the Research Clique made 'a great effort' to win some senate seats and, thanks to 'a vigorous if unobtrusive campaign' by an ally, Kiangsu Military Governor Li Ch'un, managed to buy several seats in the senate at the final elections.[22]

The cost of the election for one senatorial candidate was reported at Ch.$40,000. The Anfu Club's investment in Kiangsu was estimated by one observer as $100,000, by another as $160,000 for the senatorial election alone.[23] By providing financial support to candidates who could not afford to buy parliamentary seats, the club was able to ensure itself of more loyal support in the future parliament than it would have enjoyed if candidates of independent means had been elected under its banner.

Although the Anfu Club spent a good deal of money in other provinces, in few places was the outcome so much in doubt as in Kiangsu. British Minister Sir John Jordan exaggerated only slightly when he reported. 'The results in all cases comport with the views of the military leaders controlling the electoral area.'[24] Of course, parliamentary seats were sufficiently lucrative and honorific to stimulate competition even among the supporters of the dominant local warlord, with the concomitant buying and selling of votes. But in the majority of provinces only the precise composition of the provincial delegation was in doubt. Its political alignment was ensured in advance.

Of the 17 provinces that sent delegations to the new parliament, the warlords of 13 were allied with Tuan Ch'i-jui. The delegations of 11 of these 13 provinces joined the Anfu Club virtually as units and functioned within the club as one-, two-, or three-province blocs or delegations under

20 Nan-hai yin-tzu (pseud.), *An-fu huo-kuo chi* (How the Anfu Clique brought disaster on the country), 1.47.
21 F. O. 228/3279, 'Nanking intelligence report for the quarter ended July 31st, 1918', p. 24.
22 *Ibid.*
23 *Ibid.*; F. O. 228/2982, Dispatch 67, Giles to Jordan, 18 June 1918, p. 2; F. O. 228/2982, Dispatch 72, Giles to Jordan, 29 June 1918, p. 2.
24 F. O. 371/3184, 162951 (f 16666), Dispatch 351, Jordan to Balfour, Peking, 24 July 1918, confidential print.

leaders responsive to the wishes of the home warlords. Two of the provinces whose warlords were allied with Tuan produced substantial non-Anfu strength in their delegations. The three provinces whose warlords favoured Tuan's rival, Feng Kuo-chang, and neutral Chekiang also produced mixed delegations. The delegations of the special administrative regions, Mongolia, Tibet, Tsinghai, and the so-called 'central election assemblies' (six small groups of notables convened in Peking) produced strongly pro-Anfu delegations, because all were selected under direct central government influence.

In short, the Anfu Club won a major victory. In a parliament of 470 members, the club controlled 342 seats. Of the remaining 128 seats, the Research Clique controlled about 20, the Communications Clique perhaps 50 to 80, and the rest were held by non-party independents.

As the new members arrived in Peking in August 1918 the factions established clubs for liaison and mobilization. The clubs were to be the major organizations in parliament in the following two years. The largest, of course, was the Anfu Club. Headquarters were maintained at An-fu Lane in Peking, and a secretariat was established at roomier quarters where plenary meetings could be held. The secretariat was divided into five departments each of which was sub-divided into several sections. Each department was supervised by a leading member of the club, and each section was run by several designated club officials.

The club by-laws provided elaborate institutions for internal governance. There was a deliberative assembly, a members of parliament assembly and a political affairs research council. But in reality, the club was run autocratically by the small group who had organized it and who controlled its funds. Decisions about club policy were made in informal consultations among members of this group and between them and their political allies outside the club. Leaders of the provincial delegations then passed on the decision to informal meetings of the delegations held at provincial hostels scattered around Peking. Any problems were ironed out at these meetings, so that when the club formally assembled in caucus, the meeting usually consisted simply of speeches from the leadership and a nearly unanimous straw vote.

The leadership was so efficient that it deprived the members of a substantial portion of the income they had expected to reap in bribes from candidates for president, vice-president, speaker and vice-speaker, and from nominees to cabinet posts. In the absence of extensive bribes, the income of members of parliament came from their government salaries of $5,000 per year, supplemented by the $300 received each month as a gratuity from the club, paid in the form of a cheque cashable only at the club's accounting department. The club paid an extra $300 to $400 to leaders of provincial delegations and to members performing other important tasks. Income of prominent parliamentarians was further supplemented with salaries from government sinecures, such as advisory posts to ministries or seats on government advisory commissions. In addition, Anfu members of parliament often were able to place relatives and friends on the nepotism-swollen staff of the house secretariat. Since club members were unable to recoup their investments in their parliamentary seats by the usual method of taking bribes, they were forced to work to preserve the club's dominance in parliament so that its leaders could retain the influence and government posts that were the ultimate source of the monthly gratuities and the sinecures. The club's dominance in parliament thus helped to reinforce its internal discipline in parliamentary manoeuvres.[25]

The Anfu Club's discipline and its dominance of parliament made parliament function more smoothly, and in this sense helped constitutionalism to work. Election of the president was one of parliament's chief duties. On 4 September 1918, parliament nearly unanimously elected Tuan Ch'i-jui's favoured candidate, ex-Ch'ing bureaucrat Hsu Shih-ch'ang. This election was the only peaceful, constitutionally correct presidential succession of the early republic. After considerable bargaining, parliament also approved the nominations of a new prime minister and cabinet – one of the few cabinets of the early republic to go through the full process of parliamentary confirmation. The house and senate also provided themselves with speakers and vice-speakers. On the other hand, resourceful manoeuvres by the Communications and Research Cliques blocked the election of the vice-presidential candidate the Anfu Club promoted. Once questions of position were settled, parliament had fulfilled its essential role. Still, the Anfu Club was maintained and occasionally used by Tuan Ch'i-jui's faction until parliament disbanded in the aftermath of the Anfu-Chihli war of July 1920.

DECLINE OF THE CONSTITUTIONALIST IDEAL, 1922-28

It is hard to set the date when the liberal republic changed from a living ideal to a lost cause. Chinese expectations for the probity of politicians in a constitutional order were probably unrealistically high. Normal political compromises were seen as betrayals, tactical shifts as evidence of lack of principle. Still, a fresh start could produce a sense of renewed

25 On the Anfu Club's organization, see Nathan, *Peking politics*, 106–10.

hope. Li Yuan-hung's accession to the presidency after Yuan Shih-k'ai's death in 1916 was one example. The 1918 election of the Anfu parliament and its choice of Hsu Shih-ch'ang as president was another. But the third and fourth times the constitutional order was renewed and failed, disillusionment with constitutionalism was profound and widespread. Perhaps one reason was that the events of 1922–5 in Peking exposed more cruelly than ever before the realities of factional politics behind the constitutional sham.

The third cycle of constitutional renewal and decline started shortly after the first Chihli-Fengtien war in the spring of 1922 (see chapter 6). The Chihli Clique (led by Ts'ao K'un and Wu P'ei-fu) hoped to parlay its victory over Fengtien into national reunification under its auspices. They and their allies issued a series of public telegrams demanding the resignations of Hsu Shih-ch'ang from the Peking presidency and Sun Yat-sen from the Canton presidency, and promoting 'restoration of the constitution' under Li Yuan-hung. (Li had been driven from office by Chang Hsun in 1917, leading to the Anfu parliament election which the Chihli Clique now claimed was unconstitutional.) Before accepting office Li demanded that the warlords agree to a policy of 'reducing troops and abolishing tuchunships'. When this was agreed to, he came to Peking and issued a series of orders and appointments to this end. A number of warlords even changed their own titles from *tu-chün* (military governor) to *chün-wu shan-hou tu-pan* (military affairs reconstruction commissioner). Li also acted to remove superfluous officials, punish corruption and restore government credit.[26]

His most important achievement was the appointment of the so-called 'Able Men Cabinet' containing a number of prestigious, modern-minded lawyers, diplomats and educators. The new finance minister was Oxford-educated Lo Wen-kan, who resigned from the Supreme Court to join the cabinet. Lo quickly proved his ability by renegotiating the so-called Austrian Loans, reducing by some £200 million an existing government debt and gaining a cheque for £80,000 for immediate government use. It was a dramatic shock when Lo was arrested by presidential order in the middle of the night on 18 November 1922, on suspicion of illegal procedure and personal corruption.

The newspapers were filled with debate over Lo's guilt or innocence. It appeared that the speaker and vice-speaker of the House of Representatives had come to President Li on the evening of the 18th, made a number of charges against Lo, and presented circumstantial evidence of corrup-

26 Nathan, *Peking politics*, 189–93.

tion. Li had emotionally (and probably illegally) issued an immediate order for Lo's arrest. Although he soon regretted the act, he was unable to undo it; the cabinet resigned and Lo's case went to court, where, a year-and-a-half later, he was exonerated.

At the root of the incident lay the failure of the Able Men Cabinet to play parliamentary politics. (Li had recalled the 'old' parliament as soon as he returned to office.) Adopting an 'above-party' stance, the cabinet had failed to cultivate parliamentary factions and to channel sufficient funds to the members' of parliament warlord sponsors. Parliament had tried to harass the cabinet with interpellations and a bill of impeachment. The two speakers had probably not imagined that Li's naiveté would enable their ploy against Minister Lo to be as devastating as it was.

Li managed to instal a successor cabinet and continue as president. But Ts'ao K'un, Wu P'ei-fu's superior and leader of the Chihli Clique, was increasingly anxious to gain the presidency for himself. Even in late 1922 his agents had begun to set up political clubs to reserve parliamentary votes for an election.[27] The issue sharpened early in 1923, when Sun Yat-sen returned to Canton as the head of a new military government dedicated to freeing China from warlordism. Yet, despite serious doubts that there was any time left to serve in Li's term of office, neither he nor parliament took steps to call a presidential election.

On 6 June 1923, four cabinet members loyal to Ts'ao suddenly submitted their resignations, charging undue interference by President Li in cabinet responsibilities. This forced a general cabinet resignation. In the following days, Peking garrison officers and troops demonstrated at the presidential palace for back-pay; the police went on strike; organized demonstrations of 'citizens' surrounded the palace; and the garrison and police commanders submitted their resignations. On 13 June, the sixth anniversary of his submission to the Chang Hsun coup of 1917, the beleaguered Li fled the city, announcing his intention to continue to exercise presidential powers in Tientsin. But his train was intercepted at Yang-ts'un by a general of Ts'ao K'un's camp. In the middle of the night, some nine hours after his departure from Peking, Li signed a statement of resignation. Although he repudiated the statement as soon as he reached the security of Tientsin's British concession, in Peking a caretaker cabinet took over the presidential duties pending election of a successor.

A new obstacle faced Ts'ao K'un, however. During and after the coup, parliament's quorum melted away. Political leaders hostile to Ts'ao's ambitions – Chang Tso-lin in Manchuria, Lu Yung-hsiang in Chekiang,

Sun Yat-sen in the south, and others – had withdrawn their parliamentary supporters from the scene, while other members had fled in alarm. A decision was announced to move the parliament to Shanghai where an alternate government would be set up under the resilient Li Yuan-hung. Funds were provided to cover the travel and living expenses of members of parliament in Shanghai.

To rebuild their quorum in Peking, Ts'ao's lieutenants made a counter-offer. Peking would pay travel expenses back from Shanghai and a generous weekly fee for attendance at informal parliamentary 'discussion meetings'; the Parliamentary Organic Law would be revised to allow parliament to serve not for a limited period of time but indefinitely until a new parliament was elected; completion of the constitution would precede election of the president; on the occasion of the presidential election each member of parliament would receive an honorarium of Ch.$5,000. Attendance in Peking gradually climbed.

Meanwhile, Li Yuan-hung had set out from Tientsin. When he arrived in Shanghai, he found that the local warlords were unwilling to risk playing host to the controversial rival government, and he quickly left for Japan. With this, the Shanghai alternative collapsed. In Peking parliamentary attendance rose. On 5 October despite 'an almost complete lack of any visible signs of public interest',[28] the election was held. Ts'ao K'un assumed office on 10 October. On the same day China's new permanent constitution was promulgated. Although well drafted, its effectiveness was undermined by the sordid circumstances of its promulgation. Revelation in the newspapers of each pro-Ts'ao member of parliament's $5,000 bribe confirmed the public disgust with the 'piggish members of parliament' and the new regime.[29]

Ts'ao K'un had spent an estimated $13,560,000 to retire to the ceremonious languor of the presidential palace. He was not an activist president. In the absence of new parliamentary elections, the old parliament continued in session, its debates occasionally flowering into physical melees. But these were family squabbles. As the British minister, Sir Ronald Macleay, reported in June 1924, 'the political situation in Peking has been unusually quiet during the past five or six months, and . . . there have been no special developments tending either to weaken or strengthen the position of President Ts'ao K'un and the Central Government.'[30]

Meanwhile military events were maturing which would lead to still

28 F. O. 371/9812, Dispatch 586, Macleay to Curzon, 17 Oct. 1923.
29 For the 'piggish M.P.'s' quote and public reaction generally, see Liu Ch'u-hsiang, *Kuei-hai cheng-pien chi-lueh* (Brief record of the 1923 coup), 218ff.
30 F. O. 371/10243, F2665/19/10, Dispatch 400, Macleay to MacDonald, Peking, 23 June 1924. confidential print, p. 1.

another coup in Peking. Feng Yü-hsiang, a Chihli Clique militarist stationed near Peking, was ordered to march north to confront the Fengtien Clique. Instead, he entered the city, deposed President Ts'ao, and demanded an end to the hostilities (see chapter 6).

Feng's coup obviously rendered the Ts'ao K'un constitution inoperative. To patch together an acceptable political framework, Tuan Ch'i-jui was invited from retirement. Although more a political practitioner than a theorist, Tuan responded to the need of the day with an ideology of national *ralliement* and constitution-renewal. Tuan argued that there had been still another revolution; therefore, he took office 24 November as a 'provisional chief executive', temporarily combining the duties of president and prime minister until a constitution could be written. The procedures for writing the new constitution were unprecedentedly complex: first, a reconstruction conference representing major military and political interests would meet to make arrangements to unite the nation; second, a constitutional drafting commission would be convened under regulations determined by the reconstruction conference; and third, a national representative assembly would meet to enact the constitution.

Tuan's programme had little appeal to a weary public, but some politicians were willing to play along. The reconstruction conference convened 1 February 1925.

In three months of meetings, 160-odd delegates discussed over 30 resolutions covering military disbandment, political reorganization, taxation, educational finance, opium suppression, and other topics. Among the conference's enactments were regulations for convening the constitutional drafting commission (which opened on 3 August 1925, and completed a draft constitution in December) and those for electing the national representative assembly (these elections were never held). Meanwhile, Chief Executive Tuan convened a provisional national council to exercise interim legislative powers. The institutional arrangements were so complete, the discussions so sober, and the parliamentary manoeuvres so intense, that one might think the members of the executive government did not see the revolution exploding around them.

Constitutionalism could not restrain the brutal forces now ascending. Amid the turmoil of revolution, there was another coup in Peking: on 9 April 1926, Tuan Ch'i-jui's bodyguards were disarmed and he was deposed as chief executive.

Peking was to possess no real government for some weeks while the new ruling warlords debated whom to invite into office. Then a series of regency cabinets were formed 'to exercise the powers of the chief executive'. Finally, Chang Tso-lin dissolved the last regency cabinet and took office himself as marshal of the military government on 18 June 1927. He appointed a cabinet largely of his own followers. To the last, there were appointments to issue, funds to disburse, and the diplomatic corps to deal with. But when the National Government's troops entered the city 8 June 1928, China's experiment with parliamentary democracy was over.

The tide of change washed the wealthy and fortunate ashore in the foreign concessions of treaty ports. 'Socially', recalled one resident of Tientsin, 'life . . . was very charming and interesting.' The former Manchu emperor lived graciously in a large mansion in the Japanese Concession, and ex-President Hsu Shih-ch'ang enjoyed literature and gardening at a house in the British Concession. Ts'ao K'un was inclined to moroseness but received friends on his birthdays. 'Marshal Tuan [Ch'i-jui] was comparatively poor – in fact he had no house of his own, but lived in one provided by one of his loyal followers. He spent a part of his time studying Buddhism, but he also enjoyed a mild game of *mahjong*. . . . Sometimes on being asked the cause of China's internal dissensions, he would give the Buddhist interpretation, namely, that the country was suffering from the antics of wicked devils sent down to this earth, and until they had all been killed, the troubles would continue.'[31]

Later analysts have shared Tuan's bafflement that constitutions failed to regulate conflict and create consensus as many Chinese expected them to. It is still controversial why this was so. Some have explained it by saying that the politicians who ran the government were selfish, dishonest men who broke the law. Another view was that the Peking government was only a cover for a system of regional militarism. This chapter has argued that the constitutional system exhausted its own vitality through its members' absorption in factional struggles.

31 W. W. Yen, *East-West kaleidoscope 1877–1944: an autobiography*, 174–5.

CHAPTER 6

THE WARLORD ERA:
POLITICS AND MILITARISM UNDER
THE PEKING GOVERNMENT, 1916–28

The time between 1916 and 1928 is commonly called the 'warlord period,' and its politics can be analysed from two points of view. The view from the provinces requires a study of regional militarism, while the view from the centre calls for examination of constitutional and military struggles in Peking. These two views will help us appraise the place of warlordism in modern Chinese history.

THE VIEW FROM THE PROVINCES:
WARLORDS AND WARLORDISM

Most simply, a 'warlord' was one who commanded a personal army, controlled or sought to control territory, and acted more or less independently. The Chinese equivalent – *chün-fa* – is opprobrious, suggesting a selfish commander with little social consciousness or national spirit; some argue that 'regional militarist' is a more neutral term for the diverse personalities found among the military leaders of the time. Others argue that 'warlord' is more appropriate in its connotations of violence and usurpation of civil authority. In any event, it was 'the kind of authority he exercised and not his goals that distinguished the warlord.'[1] Since many leading warlords held the position of military governor of a province, the term *tu-chün* is used as a rough synonym for warlord or regional militarist.

The warlords were a diverse lot, and most generalizations about their character and policies suffer from a host of exceptions. Those prominent in the first two or three years after Yuan's death had been senior officers in the Ch'ing military establishment, and their values were set in a Confucianist mould. Tuan Ch'i-jui (1865–1936), for example, has been described in the preceding chapter as head of a widespread military faction (see page 272). He served as minister of war in Yuan's government, and was prime minister at the time of Yuan's death.[2]

1 Harold Z. Schiffrin, 'Military and politics in China: is the warlord model pertinent?' *Asia Quarterly: A Journal From Europe*, 3 (1975) 195.

Feng Kuo-chang's career (1859–1919) in some ways paralleled that of Tuan. Feng had also graduated from the Peiyang Military Academy and become one of Yuan Shih-k'ai's assistants in creating a modern army. During the 1911 Revolution, Feng used his troops to help Yuan in his political manoeuvres to force the Manchu abdication and become president. From 1913 he was military governor of Kiangsu. He was elected vice-president in 1916, but remained at his Nanking headquarters. Although Feng lacked Tuan's capacity to gather followers and inspire loyalty, he had extensive contacts and from 1917 increasingly emerged as a political rival.[3]

A more conspicuous traditionalist was Chang Hsun (1854–1923), who had spent his life in the service of the Manchus, and received special honours from the throne. He ordered his troops to retain their queues as symbols of loyalty to the court, and concerned himself with the fate of the fallen imperial house. Foreigners called him the 'pigtailed general'. In 1917 he briefly restored the Manchu emperor to the throne.[4]

By the early 1920s a second generation of warlords began to emerge, many from very humble status. Feng Yü-hsiang (1882–1948), for example, was an illiterate peasant boy when he joined the army in the 1890s. Through extreme diligence, a fortunate marriage to the niece of a Peiyang officer, and the ability to train soldiers, Feng moved steadily upward in the military hierarchy. He educated himself in a mixture of traditional Chinese and modern Western learning. He adopted Christianity in 1914, partly because it accorded with his own somewhat puritanical tendencies, partly because he appreciated the foreign support it might produce; at the height of his career he was widely known as the 'Christian general', and his troops were celebrated for their stirring renditions of Christian hymns for marching songs. Feng held very Confucian assumptions about the role of moral force in political leadership, and the obligations of government to the masses. He brought peace and order to the areas he ruled, and attempted to demonstrate his virtue.[5]

Chang Tsung-ch'ang (1881–1932) also came from a humble family, but his ambitions led him to petty crime and banditry before he became an army commander. His policies were the antithesis of reformist, and when

2 Strictly speaking, Tuan Ch'i-jui was not a warlord, because before 1916 he had relinquished direct control of troops in favour of high office in Peking. So many military commanders looked to him as teacher and leader, however, that he became the acknowledged head of one of the leading warlord factions. See Howard L. Boorman and Richard C. Howard, eds. *Biographical dictionary of Republican China*, 3. 330–5.

3 *Ibid*. 2. 24–8.

4 *Ibid*. 1. 68–72. Reginald Johnston, *Twilight in the Forbidden City*, 146–56, contains a translation of a brief autobiography Chang Hsun wrote in 1921.

5 James E. Sheridan, *Chinese warlord: the career of Feng Yü-hsiang*.

he became tuchun of Shantung in the mid-1920s he stripped that province of all the wealth that he could lay his hands on. His troops were widely known for their skill in 'opening melons', splitting the skulls of those with the temerity to challenge the 'dog-meat general'.[6]

Western-style education was a major influence on Ch'en Chiung-ming (1878–1933). Although he won the lowest degree in the traditional examinations about 1898, he increasingly turned to Western learning, edited a reform newspaper, and was active in the Kwangtung provincial assembly. During the 1911 Revolution Ch'en organized a military unit and captured Waichow, which launched his military career. Later, when he ruled Kwangtung, he attempted to initiate democratic political and educational reforms. But he was more committed to the independence of Kwangtung, and his own rule over it, than he was to Sun Yat-sen's cause; he split with the revolutionaries in 1922, and was finally driven out of the province by Sun's allies.[7]

Pragmatism seems to have been the salient trait of Li Tsung-jen (1891–1969) one of the leaders of Kwangsi. Coming from a once wealthy family he entered the Kwangsi Military Elementary School, and joined the Kwangsi army in 1916. By the early 1920s Kwangsi was in turmoil from the continual conflict among more than a dozen separate armies, each controlling a few counties. At the head of a small force, Li and two trusted partners joined the competition; by the end of 1925 they controlled the entire province. They joined the Kuomintang in 1926, and administered their province in an enlightened and practical fashion that gained fame throughout the country.[8]

Wu P'ei-fu (1874–1939), the 'scholar warlord', was a Confucian scholar turned militarist. He received a traditional education, in 1896 gained the first degree, and to the end of his life remained an articulate advocate of Confucian institutions and values. Wu graduated from Yuan Shih-k'ai's Paoting Military Academy in 1903, and two years later was assigned to the Peiyang Army Third Division. From 1906 the Third Division was commanded by Ts'ao K'un, one of the original group of officers gathered by Yuan to train the Peiyang Army. During Yuan's presidency, Ts'ao –

---

6 There is no thorough study of Chang Tsung-ch'ang. *Biographical dictionary of Republican China* in its bibliography lists a few insubstantial sources. The name 'dog-meat general' derived not from his diet but from his passion for gambling at *p'ai-chiu*, a high stakes game that in North China slang was known as 'eating dog meat'. (Compare 'roll those bones', 'snake-eyes', 'dead man's hand', in Western gambling games.) See Li Ch'uan, *Chün-fa i-wen* (Warlord anecdotes), 123.

7 Winston Hsieh, 'The ideas and ideals of a warlord: Ch'en Chiung-ming (1878–1933),' *Papers on China*, 16 (Dec. 1962) 198–252.

8 Diana Lary, *Region and nation: the Kwangsi Clique in Chinese politics, 1925–1937*. Te-kong Tong and Li Tsung-jen, *The memoirs of Li Tsung-jen*.

and Wu as his faithful adherent – used the Third Division to further Yuan's political goals. In 1916 Ts'ao became military governor of Chihli (Hopei), the metropolitan province, a position of great power. Wu P'ei-fu shared that power not only as Ts'ao's loyal lieutenant, but because Wu was himself a military commander of great talent and independent mind. Although he never repudiated Ts'ao's leadership, it was widely recognized that Wu was the effective military leader.[9]

Among the hundreds of warlords only a handful have been studied. Much remains to be done before we can generalize with confidence about their values, policies or character. But they all commanded personal armies, and controlled, or tried to control, territory.

Warlord armies

'Personal army' is imprecise, because warlord armies had an organizational autonomy that permitted them to be inherited intact by other commanders; they were not inextricably bound to a single individual by 'personal loyalty'. Indeed, a commander's closest supporters might abandon him when personal political advantage dictated. Nevertheless, the phrase 'personal army' is quite appropriate for two closely-related reasons. First, it was the commander himself, not his superiors, whose decision determined the use to which his army was put. The brigade commander who dutifully led his brigade where his superiors ordered was not usually a warlord; the brigade leader who personally decided what he would and would not do with his brigade was a warlord. The line was not always clear, but the difference was nonetheless real. Thus, in the sense that troops were employed independently by their commander, and were at his personal disposal, to be used even against his superiors, they formed a personal army.

Second, a commander was more likely to have such independent power when personal relations of affection, loyalty or obligation between him and some of his key officers overlapped their organizational relations. The hierarchy of authority and subordination, of discipline and obedience that is considered normal for military organizations existed in most Chinese armies. Indeed, the armies were perhaps the least disrupted organizations in early republican China. But in face of the omnipresent threat of conflict with other militarists, and in the context of weak government institutions and the questionable legitimacy of their own actions, warlords sought to strengthen their authority over their armies by exploiting the

9 Odoric Y. K. Wou, *Militarism in modern China: the career of Wu P'ei-fu, 1916–1939*. T'ao Chü-yin, *Wu P'ei-fu chiang-chün chuan* (Biography of General Wu P'ei-fu).

kinds of personal ties long hallowed by Chinese tradition. These included the lifelong bond of loyalty and mutual help between a teacher and his students. Anyone involved in the training of officers naturally established such relationships. Moreover, at times one could become another's 'student' or 'teacher' by mutual consent, without actually being involved in giving or receiving instruction. The strongest of all bonds in China was the family tie, and warlords sometimes appointed family members to key positions. Marriage relations were weaker, but were also used. Officers often cultivated talented young men and thus established a patron-protégé association. Graduation from the same school, and especially in the same class, established a bond between individuals, just as coming from the same locality formed the basis for a special affiliation.

While warlords used such personal ties to cultivate the loyalty of their officers, their subordinates often had similar relationships with their own juniors. Some commanders tried to minimize these secondary loyalties, and focus all allegiance directly on themselves, but it was difficult to eliminate them. Patterns of secondary loyalty constituted a weakness in army organization, for they allowed a defecting subordinate to take his followers and their men with him. That is why invitations to defect became an important tactic in warlord conflicts.

The rank and file of warlord armies was made up largely of peasants, recruited by poverty. The number under arms grew throughout the warlord period from about half a million in 1916 to two million or more in 1928.[10] Some viewed the army simply as a way of eating, others looked upon it as a chance for a poor and uneducated man to get ahead. Although formal regulations prescribed physical and other qualifications for recruits, as well as enlistment periods, pay and the like, in fact arrangements were highly informal. Most warlords took anyone they could get who seemed physically capable of work. For practical purposes enlistment seems to have been for an indefinite period, depending upon one's home circumstances, health and attitude. Some commanders found it difficult to pay their troops regularly. In the worst armies it was understood that pay would sometimes come in the form of loot. Warfare was a form of recruiting because victorious warlords customarily incorporated defeated troops into their own armies, where they generally seem to have functioned as well as in their original units. By the late 1920s it was not uncommon for Chinese soldiers to have served in three or four different warlord armies.

10 It is virtually impossible to establish with precision the number of men under arms during this tumultuous period. Ch'i Hsi-sheng discusses this problem in *Warlord politics in China 1916–1928*, 78, and constructs the estimate I have followed here.

These armies gave the Chinese military an extremely bad reputation. Chinese looked upon them as a plague: evil, destructive, merciless. Foreign journalists described them as hordes of undisciplined hoodlums. Books by old China hands spread the notion that Chinese armies normally settled matters by a mere display of force, and avoided real combat. Naturally, armies of peasant recruits, seeking a bit of pay and security, might well find quick retreat the better part of valour when a clear disparity of strength was apparent. A warlord might try to avoid battle by the use of 'silver bullets' or cash to persuade enemy officers to defect with their men. Moreover, warlords were normally not eager to put their armies into battle, for that opened the possibility of losing them. But they nevertheless did so, on myriad occasions, many of which were very bloody encounters. One retired warlord recalled that as a young officer he was assigned to command a unit that remained in the rear during battle, with orders to shoot any soldier from the front who retreated.[11] The wars of the time were made even gorier by the extreme dearth of medical facilities. The wounded often had to rely on their friends, or on volunteer Chinese or missionary doctors; most armies were not equipped to care for casualties.

Territorial control

An army was the essential ingredient for independence, but extremely difficult to maintain without territorial control. Territory provided a secure base plus revenue, materiel and men. A commander without territorial authority inevitably was a guest in someone else's domain. In this uncertain and dangerous position he would usually have to fight to win territorial rights, or else accept subordination or a disadvantageous alliance. Territorial control also conferred a kind of legitimacy on even the most independent and arbitrary warlord; a host of titles were employed for that purpose: pacification commissioner, inspecting supervisor, defence commissioner, and so forth, each designed to justify the activities of a particular militarist in a particular place. The officer who ruled the provincial capital was normally the tuchun, but in some instances he controlled only a small part of the province, and real power was divided among a number of petty warlords.

Control of territory involved responsibility for government, and there was a good deal of variation in the character and efficiency of warlord governments. Some militarists espoused 'progressive' political ideas.

---

11 'The reminiscences of General Chang Fa-k'uei as told to Julie Lien-ying How', the Chinese Oral History Project of the East Asian Institute, Columbia University.

Yen Hsi-shan, who ruled Shansi throughout the warlord era, was widely known as the 'model governor', a title which may have owed less to the exemplary quality of his administration than to the fact that he kept Shansi out of war for most of the period. Yen promoted a number of social reforms, including the abolition of footbinding, modest improvements in education for females, some measures to improve public health. On the other hand, he could not eliminate corruption in the provincial bureaucracy, and his administration generally ruled in accord with gentry interests, despite his occasional clashes with gentry groups.[12]

When Ch'en Chiung-ming ruled Kwangtung he established new schools, financed foreign study for over 80 students, restructured the Canton administration along more democratic lines, and promoted a provincial constitution with guarantees of civil rights and provisions against military interference with civil administration. In his provinces, Feng Yü-hsiang instituted reforms ranging from the abolition of footbinding and the prohibition of opium-smoking to road-building, tree-planting, and the arrest of corrupt officials. Neither Ch'en nor Feng was able to make permanent improvements in provincial administration, but their policies nevertheless reflected a 'progressive' orientation, a consciousness of their opportunities and responsibilities. On the other hand, Chang Ching-yao, tuchun of Hunan from 1918 to 1920, and Chang Tsung-ch'ang, warlord of Shantung from 1925 to 1927, were known for greed and extortion.

The most 'progressive' policies meant little if they were not carried out all the way down to the local level. Yet research on relations between warlords and local authorities is only now beginning, and most of our questions about the subject remain unanswered. In most provinces, a civil governor held office alongside the military governor, although in some cases the same man held both posts. In theory, a civil governor had authority over economic matters, education, judicial and financial affairs, and supervised the lower level bureaucrats. However, in fact the civil governor was usually completely subordinate to the tuchun.

Given the pre-eminence of the military during this era, it would not be surprising if army officers played an important role in local government, and that the lower levels of administration, like the higher, became militarized. There are indications that this happened. At the height of Wu P'ei-fu's control of Honan, in 1923, 86 of 144 local magistrates had seen army service. Twenty-four had been direct subordinates of Wu; another 37 had been on the staffs of his subordinates; 25 had served in other

---

12 Donald Gillin, *Warlord: Yen Hsi-shan in Shansi province 1911-1949.*

armies. Not all of these men had been line officers; many had served as advisers, secretaries, military judges, paymasters, or the like. Some held concurrent military posts even while serving as magistrates.[13]

There was evidently a high rate of turn-over among magistrates, especially in unstable regions. In Szechwan, for example, which was fragmented and in turmoil for the whole warlord era, the average tenure of district magistrates was extremely short; in one district, only two magistrates managed to hold office for a full year, and 22 maintained their positions for less than a month.[14] In contested areas, the situation could be particularly complicated; at one time in 1919 three rival magistrates set up headquarters in a single district of Kwangtung, and simultaneously asserted their right to rule.

The warlord period nullified the old system of avoidance whereby a magistrate was not permitted to serve in his home province. The number of provincial residents serving as magistrates in their own provinces apparently increased; in some cases, magistrates were residents of their own counties. For example, in one important county in Kwangsi, 15 of the 18 magistrates between 1912 and 1926 were natives of the province, and seven were from the district itself.[15]

Revenues

Warlord governments were intensely concerned to obtain funds for the personal aggrandizement of the warlord and his chief subordinates, and to provide the army with its weapons, supplies and pay. Because government at all levels was so often disrupted by the wars and rapid changes of personnel, and many warlords viewed their territorial ascendancy as probably transitory, they could not always rely on established revenue-producing procedures. They aggressively and imaginatively sought money in any way they could.

The basic source of revenue was the land tax, and some warlords collected it far in advance. A warlord might also set up government monopolies of important commodities. In Shansi, for example, Yen Hsi-shan controlled the manufacture of flour, matches, salt and other products. Monopolies were particularly appropriate for a militarist like Yen, who maintained a stable government for so many years. But there are instances of other warlords attempting similar monopolies. Warlords seized and

13 Wou, *Militarism in modern China*, 62.
14 Odoric Y. K. Wou, 'The district magistrate profession in the early republican period: occupational recruitment, training and mobility', *Modern Asian Studies*, 8.2 (April 1974) 237.
15 Lary, *Region and nation*, 30.

operated railways, ordered supplementary taxes on salt, and taxed goods in transit. Some warlords printed their own money: in at least two instances on a manual duplicating machine.

The sale of opium produced huge sums; tax centres for the drug proliferated under the guise of opium suppression bureaus. In some areas, legalized gambling provided a large income; in Kwangtung, for example, in 1928 gambling taxes produced $1,200,000 per month, and that was after various high officials had skimmed off large sums for their personal use. Prostitution and other rackets were encouraged and taxed by local warlords.

Warlords milked businessmen in a variety of ways in addition to normal taxation. In 1925 Shantung merchants were forced to purchase a new kind of revenue stamps from provincial offices, and use them on all vouchers and bills; merchants were presumably already using similar stamps required by the Peking government. Businessmen were invited to pay licence fees or taxes in advance and at a discount. For instance, pawnshops in Kwangtung were urged to pay their fees for two or three years ahead of time at a rate of 75 per cent of the normal amount. There are cases of landlords being forced to turn over a specified sum, usually one month's rental income, by a particular date. On occasion warlords simply declared that a city's merchants must produce a desired amount within a few days; a militarist about to be driven out of a city by enemy forces might try to gain a last golden egg before he lost his goose. Lu Yung-hsiang obtained Ch.$500,000 from Hangchow merchants as he left the city in 1924. Chang Ching-yao demanded $800,000 from the merchants of Changsha when Hunanese troops were approaching the city in 1920. He warned that his soldiers might loot the city, and he detained the chairman of the Chamber of Commerce as hostage. The merchants finally produced $110,000 which Chang accepted as he fled.

Despite this energetic pursuit of funds, provincial governments often were on the brink of bankruptcy. At least there was little money for government services, and there are instances of provincial payrolls being far in arrears, just as occurred in Peking by the early 1920s. The reason for this apparent paradox is, of course, that most of the money collected was not used for ordinary government purposes. Much was taken by the military chieftains for their own use. Many of them acquired personal fortunes. Moreover, military expenses were heavy; each province supported one or more armies. The percentage of public revenue actually devoted to public purposes evidently declined in most provinces through the warlord era.[16]

Warlord cliques

The leading warlords commonly belonged to factions or cliques, groups held together by a presumed identity of interests, much as the political factions were held together (see chapter 5). But cohesion among warlord groups varied from loose affiliation to tightly structured unity. The loosest cliques were essentially alliances concluded for the advantage envisaged by each participant. But bonds of personal association and obligation also played a role, particularly in the stronger cliques. The key relationship was that between each clique member and the clique leader; personal, lateral ties among clique members could be weak or non-existent. The personal bonds between the members and the leader were exactly those already discussed as supplementing the cohesion of warlord armies: family ties, teacher-student and patron-protégé relations, common provincial or local origins, friendship, academy or school ties.

Ch'i Hsi-sheng has ranked these personal associations from strongest (father-son) to weakest (schoolmate), and with that ranking in mind has examined the Anhwei, Chihli and Fengtien cliques, the three leading groups.[17] The Fengtien Clique was the simplest and strongest in internal organization, for virtually every member was bound to the clique leader by ties that Ch'i judged to be strong. The Chihli Clique, on the other hand, had an extremely complex structure. It involved a larger number of militarists, and a larger number of ties, but most of them of the sort Ch'i ranked as weak. Although Ch'i suggests that the very multiplicity of the ties reinforced them, and made for strong integration, the clique appears to have come much closer to an alliance of near equals than that of Fengtien. The Anhwei Clique was weaker than the other two because the commanders with most military strength were bound to the leader by the weakest ties. The Kwangsi Clique, which Ch'i did not analyse, differed from the three already mentioned in that it was, for most of the time, confined to a single province; it was essentially a single political-military organization in Kwangsi, with three leaders informally assuming different leadership roles, and surprisingly, maintaining an extraordinarily

16 The information about warlord revenues is culled from a wide range of sources: monographs on individual warlords, reports from diplomats and journalists, newspaper and periodical accounts. Some of the most interesting and revealing material is in 'The reminiscences of Chang Fa-k'uei, as told to Julie Lien-ying How', and Tong and Li, *The memoirs of Li Tsung-jen*. A concise and knowledgeable treatment of warlord revenues is Ch'i Hsi-sheng, *Warlord politics in China*, 150–78. Jerome Ch'en discusses the subject in *The military-gentry coalition: China under the warlords*, 130–45. Wou, *Militarism in modern China*, 55–80, examines in detail the sources of Wu P'ei-fu's finances. Chang Yu-i, *Chung-kuo chin-tai nung-yeh shih tzu-liao* (Source materials on China's modern agricultural history) emphasizes the range, diversity and extortionate nature of the warlords' quest for money.

17 Ch'i, *Warlord politics in China*, 36–76.

high degree of cohesion. A brief examination of the origins of the cliques will explain how they came to show such differences.

The Chihli and Anhwei cliques were based on relationships established among officers in the Peiyang Army under Yuan Shih-k'ai. Yuan cultivated various kinds of personal obligations among his subordinates to assure the unity and loyalty of the army. His followers did much the same with regard to their own subordinates. As long as Yuan lived, those networks of associations within the Peiyang Army were subordinated to the overall pattern of loyalty to Yuan. When he died, Peiyang officers had to adjust to a totally new situation. That adjustment required several years, as each officer made decisions about whose lead he would follow, what his geographic and military circumstances dictated, what his personal inclinations and aspirations were, how his personal interests would best be served, and how he judged the national political situation.

We have already noted (see chapter 5, page 272) how Tuan Ch'i-jui gradually built up the Anhwei Clique (Tuan was from Anhwei) and a political club to promote his interests, the Anfu Club. Officers not among Tuan's followers, and those who foresaw the day when they would become targets of his unification policy, were naturally hostile to Tuan. Moreover, Tuan's insistence on putting his own protégés in top positions left those who were passed over resentful. From that background of fear and resentment emerged an opposition group who looked for leadership to the only other Peiyang officer of Tuan's stature who also held high position in the government, Feng Kuo-chang.

Feng Kuo-chang had served in top-level Peiyang commands, as military governor of Chihli and, later, of Kiangsu, and became vice-president of the republic in 1916. In 1917 he became acting president, a post he would not assume until he was assured that his own protégés would retain control of three important Yangtze provinces. It is not completely clear why Feng should have come to head a group hostile to Tuan. Perhaps one reason was that Sun Yat-sen had set up a separate regime in the south, and Feng and Tuan disagreed about the proper policy for eliminating it and reunifying the country. Feng advocated negotiation, Tuan wanted to use force.

Feng retired from the presidency in 1918, but those who opposed Tuan continued to look upon him as leader. Because Feng was from Chihli, this developing group of militarists and politicians came to be known as the Chihli clique. At the end of 1919 Feng died, and there was nobody in a clear position to succeed him as head of the group. As Tuan Ch'i-jui attempted more vigorously than ever to establish his military and political superiority and so unify the nation, Ts'ao K'un, military governor of the metropolitan province, increasingly felt threatened by the Anhwei group. His relations with Tuan steadily cooled. Because of Ts'ao's leading role in the 1920 war that ultimately forced Tuan out of power, Ts'ao K'un finally emerged as the acknowledged leader of the Chihli Clique.[18]

The Fengtien Clique was created by Chang Tso-lin. Chang was one of the many militarists who rose from low estate. Born into a Manchurian peasant family, he started out as an enlisted soldier, and later organized a local defence force that became part of the regular Manchu military forces. As he went up the military ladder, he took the subordinates and associates of his youth with him, all bound by close personal ties. Chang supported the Ch'ing authorities during the 1911 Revolution, and when the dust had settled held the second spot among the Fengtien military. When the military governor retired in 1915, Chang used his strong local connections and his military following to make life impossible for the officer appointed by Peking. Finally, in April 1916, he was acknowledged as head of the Fengtien government.

Once in firm control of Fengtien, Chang moved to establish similar authority over the other two Manchurian provinces, using a combination of military threat and political influence. In 1917, Peking dismissed the Heilungkiang governor for supporting the Manchu restoration, and Chang's ready military force assured that the dismissal was effective. His influence in Peking obtained the appointment of his own choice as head of the province, and from that time Heilungkiang was run by men approved by Chang. The sequence of events in Kirin was similar, but Chang did not have the province fully under his subordinates until 1919. These three provinces were the core territory of the Fengtien Clique because of Chang's solid control over them, and, of course, because of their great wealth and geographic position. Later Chang extended his authority into North China, and other warlords became part of the Fengtien clique, though never as strongly bound to Chang as the militarists of Manchuria.[19]

The Kwangsi Clique remained for most of the time within a single province. Li Tsung-jen headed the clique, but it is more accurate to think of him as first among equals. Pai Ch'ung-hsi and Huang Shao-hung were the other two members of the clique at the outset, until Huang Hsu-ch'u replaced Huang Shao-hung. The clique emerged from the loose alliance

18 Andrew J. Nathan, *Peking politics 1918–1923: factionalism and the failure of constitutionalism*, 128–75, 232–9. Odoric Wou, 'A Chinese "Warlord" faction: The Chihli Clique, 1918–1924', in Andrew Cordier, ed. *Columbia essays in international affairs vol. III, the Dean's papers, 1967*, 249–74. See also Wou, *Militarism in modern China*.

19 Gavan McCormack, *Chang Tso-lin in Northeast China 1911–1928: China, Japan, and the Manchurian idea*.

established by Li, Pai and Huang in the early 1920s, aimed at unifying the highly fragmented province. By 1924 they had eliminated so many petty Kwangsi warlords that they faced the choice of fighting one another or making their cooperation permanent. Since they came from similar backgrounds and had developed a strong mutual respect, they decided to work together.[20]

Factions grew up within the warlord cliques. The Chihli Clique was split into two factions, one under Wu P'ei-fu, one under Ts'ao K'un. Ts'ao's faction, in turn, was divided in two. These factions wrangled over who should hold what office and control what revenues. Factions also existed in the Fengtien Clique, especially after Chang reorganized his army following a serious defeat in 1922. He advanced younger officers with modern military training, and yet continued to look for support to his old associates. This produced 'new' and 'old' factions in Fengtien.[21]

Wars

There were literally hundreds of armed conflicts, short and long, on local, regional and national scales. Many wars were waged for control of an administrative area, such as a province or county. Others were fought over control of local and regional economic networks that transcended administrative areas. For example, opium from Yunnan and Kweichow was shipped over a well-established trade route to Western Hunan, where it could be sent northward to the Yangtze Valley or southward to the Canton delta. The allegiance of the warlord controlling western Hunan determined which route would be selected, enriching the warlords of the Yangtze Valley or those in Kwangtung. Western Hunan was a prize because of its position on the trade route, and it was important to leaders in two different regions, thus directly and indirectly a source of conflict. Similar marketing networks existed throughout China and undoubtedly gave rise to warfare. Winston Hsieh has begun to open up this subject.[22]

The more or less formal wars between major cliques attracted most attention because they determined who controlled the national government in Peking, the symbol of legitimacy. When one clique gave promise of becoming so powerful as to restrain the other militarists, and create

20　Lary, *Region and nation.*
21　Nathan, *Peking politics*, discusses factions and his appendix provides profiles of seven important ones. For the leading officers in the military cliques, with their units see Wen Kung-chih, *Tsui-chin san-shih-nien Chung-kuo chün-shih shih* (Military history of China for the past thirty years), *passim.* but especially vol. 1, pt 2.
22　Winston W. Hsieh, 'The economics of warlordism', *Chinese Republican Studies Newsletter* 1.1 (Oct. 1975) 15–21.

a genuine centralized control, the other leading warlords temporarily combined their strength to bring it down. Thus, in 1920 the Chihli and Fengtien Cliques cooperated to eliminate the power of the Anhwei Clique in the Peking government, and transferred most of its provinces to the victors. In 1922 Fengtien allied with the remnants of Anhwei power, as well as with forces in South China, to try to overthrow Chihli. It failed but was saved from destruction because it had a strong, rich base that was removed from the cockpit of struggle in North China; Chihli was not prepared to invade Manchuria, so the Fengtien forces could go home, reorganize and prepare to try again. In 1924 Fengtien, again in alliance with Anhwei adherents in North China, and with southern forces as well, fought the Chihli Clique a second time, and successfully engineered the defection of one of the leading Chihli generals, Feng Yü-hsiang. Chihli militarists continued to control provinces in Central China, and in 1926 they allied with Chang Tso-lin to fight Feng Yü-hsiang, finally pushing his forces far to the west.[23] That left Chang Tso-lin as the major power in Peking when a new kind of armed force, the National Revolutionary Army, began its march northward to eliminate the warlords once and for all. The accompanying maps show the general changes in clique distribution of power as a result of these wars.[24]

Scholars have analysed these wars in terms of the balance of power, sometimes using a model from international relations.[25] Certainly the recurring coalitions of warlords against potential unifiers exemplifies the central process of the balance of power concept. In China, however, it was a highly unstable system. Warlord cliques did not seek balance as an end in itself; each sought hegemony until its imminent success moved the others to opposition. Moreover, it was a terminal system, and everybody knew it; each warlord took it for granted that warlordism would one day cease and the country be reunited. Each seems to have accepted reunification as inevitable, even desirable, but wanted it to take place without limiting his personal power. That was a contradiction which each major warlord hoped to resolve by effecting the reunification himself. Warlords who could not reasonably hope to head a national unification simply wanted to postpone it and make hay in the meantime. Warlords tended to think in very short term; they rarely thought about what things might be like in five or 10 years, but, rather, worked to reap next year's taxes this year.

23 See Wen, *Tsui-chin san-shih-nien Chung-kuo chün-shih shih*, vol. 2 for a straightforward account of the military aspects of these wars.
24 See maps pages 298–301.
25 Ch'i, *Warlord politics in China*, 201–39.

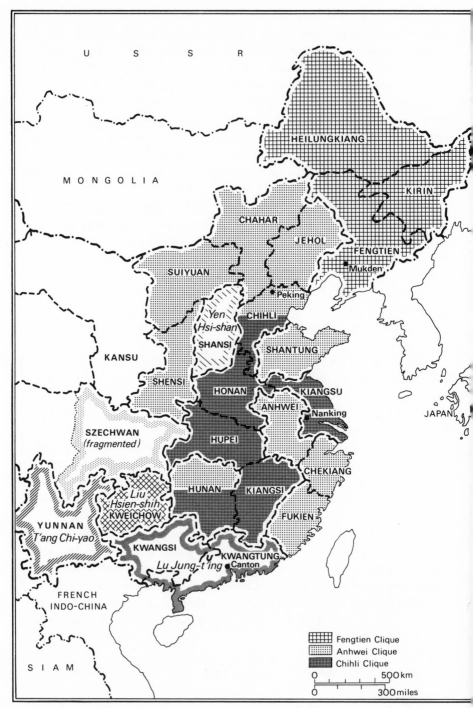

MAP 9. Distribution of warlord power on the eve of the Anhwei-
Chihli War, 1920

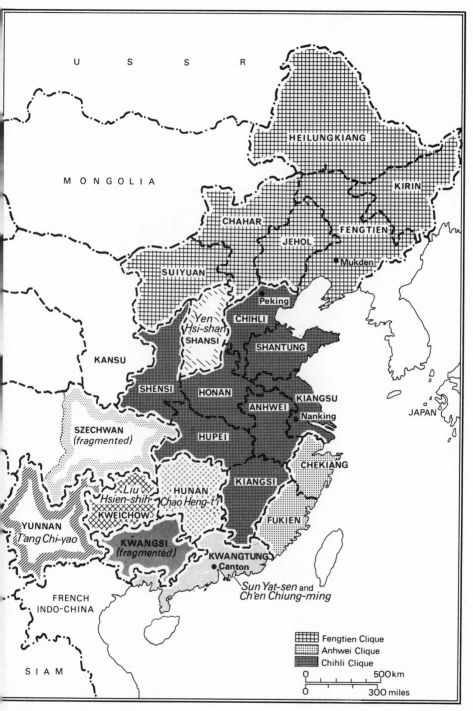

MAP 10. Distribution of warlord power on the eve of the First Chihli-Fengtien War, 1922

MAP 11. Distribution of warlord power on the eve of the Second
         Chihli-Fengtien War, 1924

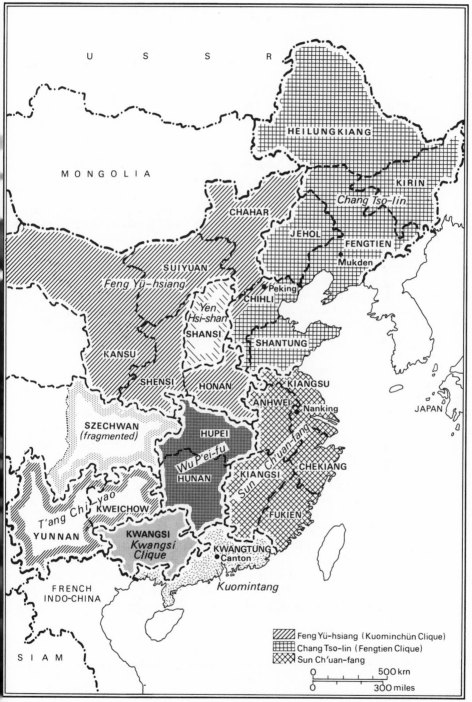

MAP 12.   Distribution of warlord power at the beginning of 1926

NOTE FOR MAPS 9 TO 12

These maps are based on biographies, government documents and announcements, chronologies, reports of foreign observers, and warlord studies. Ch'i, *Warlord politics in China*, 210, 212, presents similar maps of conditions before the Anhwei-Chihli War and before the First Chihli-Fengtien War.

These maps try to show the fragmented state of China in the early 1920s, and how the pattern of fragmentation changed, but they give an utterly false sense of precision and certainty. They are inaccurate in several ways: (1) Clique affiiliations largely follow the affiliation of the provincial tuchun, ignoring the existence of minor warlords, who often controlled important areas. (2) The maps do not show areas under contention, or where authority was non-existent or unclear. For example, maps 9 and 10 show Fukien as under the Anhwei Clique. During those years, Li Hou-chi was tuchun of Fukien, and he had strong ties with Tuan Ch'i-jui. Yet the southern part of the province was sometimes under Cantonese militarists, sometimes under rival northern commanders, and Li Hou-chi's authority was limited at the best of times. Shensi is shown in the Chihli camp on the eve of the Second Chihli-Fengtien War, yet in fact so many petty warlords contended for power in that province that it might just as well be labelled 'fragmented'. (3) The maps do not distinguish between strong clique affiliation and weak, questionable, or changing affiliation. For example, map 9 shows Honan in the Chihli camp. Yet Chao T'i, tuchun of Honan from the beginning of the warlord era, only moved towards some affiliation with the Chihli warlords when he thought Tuan Ch'i-jui was planning to replace him. Map 11 shows Shantung under Anhwei influence, although Chihli power in North China was then at its height. The reason is that T'ien Chung-yü, a Chihli adherent who had been tuchun since 1919, was relieved of his position in 1923, and succeeded by Cheng Shih-ch'i, who, all sources agree, leaned towards the Anhwei Clique; in 1923, that was not tantamount to being hostile to Wu P'ei-fu and Ts'ao K'un. (4) There is no correlation between the size of a clique's territory, as shown on the map, and its real power. For example, control of Suiyuan, Chahar, and Jehol makes for an impressive expanse of territory, but it was not particularly significant militarily, because those areas were poor, sparsely populated, and far from the main lines of communication. (5) Changes in the successive maps were not all due to the defeat or victory of this or that clique in the major wars to which the maps relate. For example, Li Hou-chi was ousted from Fukien in the late summer of 1922, and the map sequence inevitably implies that this was a consequence of the First Chihli-Fengtien War. Yet in fact he was ousted by Kuomintang troops from Kwangtung; that fact is not even suggested by the maps, because within a few months the Kuomintang forces had departed and Sun Ch'uan-fang was at the head of the province.

Although each of the wars produced a clear victor, in a more profound sense they were inconclusive, because none of the cliques had long-range plans for developing governmental political power. Each warlord's primary goals were individual and personal, the maximization of his power. Each man was a member of a clique not in order to contribute to goals of the group, but rather to contribute to a situation which would be to his personal advantage. The leader of a clique might hope to unify the country, but he stood alone, on quicksand. Not only did each clique leader have a simplistic notion of unity, but the attainment of his goal threatened his supporters as much as their enemies, for the fulfilment of his power-dreams would entail the loss of their independence, the very essence of their position as warlords. The temporary and short-range character of clique goals was a chief reason for the high instability of the period.

As military encounters, some major wars were very short, but the trend through the warlord era was for larger numbers of troops to be involved in larger, longer and bloodier wars. The Anhwei-Chihli war in 1920 was over in 10 days; it was dominated by Wu P'ei-fu's division, and did not involve massive troop movements or heavy casualties. The Chihli-Fengtien war of 1922 was even shorter – it lasted only seven days – but the number of troops was larger and the casualties more numerous. Following that war, the warlords involved expanded their armed forces. During the Second Chihli-Fengtien War, in 1924, there was fighting in North China, between Kiangsu and Chekiang, and at several places along the Manchurian border. Fighting lasted for just over two months. In 1926 Feng Yü-hsiang and Chang Tso-lin fought a very bitter war for about eight months, with heavy casualties.

Warlords and foreign powers

The chaos of warlordism, and the concomitant weakness of the Peking government, rendered China peculiarly vulnerable to foreign pressures and encroachments. But, at the same time, widespread disorder limited foreign activities and interfered with the economic exploitation of the country by foreign enterprises. Warlords on occasion arbitrarily increased taxation on foreign firms. Soldiers and bandits took a toll of foreign wealth and lives; to give one example, between 1917 and 1924, in a single consular district, 153 American individuals or firms were looted, incurring a total monetary loss of about Ch.$400,000.[26] Banditry and wars

26 Report from Consul J. C. Huston to the Department of State regarding political conditions in Hankow consular district, 4 April 1925. State Department documents relating to the internal affairs of China, 893.00/6206.

disrupted normal trade and business activities, as did warlord oppression of the Chinese trading partners of foreigners, the debasement of currency and the use of unsecured notes, and the destruction, military seizure and deterioration of railway facilities.

Foreigners responded to these conditions with fulminations and frustration. Foreign representatives delivered a steady stream of protests to the Chinese government in Peking, although the weakness of the central authorities precluded their taking effective action. Foreign powers were often reduced to dealing with local or regional military leaders about specific local matters. For example, in 1924, after the Russians reached agreement with Peking over the status and management of the Chinese Eastern Railway, they had to undertake four months of separate negotiations with Chang Tso-lin, in whose territory the railway lay.[27] In at least one instance, foreigners paid local authorities for protection and cooperation, and probably the practice existed on a broader scale.

Foreigners made their own contribution to the disorder of which they complained. Foreign soldiers of fortune played a small role in Chinese wars: an Englishman ran Chang Tso-lin's arsenal, three American pilots flew aircraft bombers for Ch'en Chiung-ming for a few months, and similar adventurers could be found here and there in other armies. Much more important was the fact that foreigners responded to the insatiable Chinese demand for guns by importing weapons in spite of the 1919 Arms Embargo Agreement signed by most of the powers. There was a grand impartiality in the arms trade; arms merchants sold to whoever had the means to meet the price, with no regard for political considerations. However, some foreign governments virtually sponsored selected warlords. Japan, for example, was conspicuously involved with Chinese militarists throughout the warlord era.

In 1916 the Japanese government launched a policy of full support to the government of Tuan Ch'i-jui, head of the Anhwei Clique, to establish close ties of political and economic cooperation, and financial obligation between China and Japan. During the following two years Japan supplied over 150 million yen to Tuan, ostensibly for purposes of national development but actually used by Tuan largely for his own political and military purposes. The two governments also concluded a military agreement which provided for Japanese aid, advisers and instructors to develop the Chinese War Participation Army to support the Allied cause in the First World War. The army never went to Europe, however, and served only to expand Tuan's military strength. While this financial and military

27 Peter S. H. Tang, *Russian and Soviet policy in Manchuria and Outer Mongolia 1911–1931*, 152–3.

assistance accrued to Tuan, Japanese businessmen initiated a number of ventures, formally in association with Chinese entrepreneurs, to exploit Chinese resources.

Japan had long shown special concern with events in Manchuria, and held a powerful position there since the Russo-Japanese war. Japanese had watched carefully the rise of Chang Tso-lin, and had actively intervened on occasion to see that personnel appointments and policies in Manchuria were not made in disregard of Japanese interests. With the defeat of the Anhwei Clique in the war of 1920, a defeat to which Chang Tso-lin contributed as an ally of the Chihli group, Chang emerged as a national figure; he controlled Manchuria and, as part of the spoils of war, Inner Mongolia. The Japanese government made a policy decision which formed the chief guideline for Japanese relations with Chang through the rest of his career: Japan would assist Chang directly and indirectly in organizing and developing Manchuria and in maintaining firm control there. However, Japan would not help Chang pursue his ambitions in the central government; they wanted Chang to stay at home and attend to the peace and order of Manchuria, not become involved in matters that might produce war and disorder and thus threaten Japanese interests.

The Japanese did not want to violate the Arms Embargo Act in a brazen fashion by supplying arms to Chang directly, so they helped him set up an arsenal to build his own weapons. Japanese described their attitude towards financial aid to Chang in these revealing terms:

While the imperial government is not unwilling to give friendly consideration to financial aid according to circumstances, it is important to do so by means of economic loans, especially by adopting the form of investment in joint enterprises, in order to avoid the suspicion of the powers and the jealousy of the central government. If Chang Tso-lin too will strive increasingly to promote the reality of Sino-Japanese cooperation, exerting himself, for example, in relation to the lease of land, the management of mines and forests, and other such promising enterprises, and if he will apply every effort to implementing the principles of so-called coexistence and coprosperity and devise methods of joint control both in already existing and in newly-to-be-set-up Sino-Japanese joint venture companies, then the finances of the Three Eastern Provinces can be made to flourish of their own accord and in an inconspicuous way.[28]

Japanese relations with Chang were by no means smooth. Chang continued to involve himself in national government affairs and in three wars in North China, despite the Japanese desire that he stay at home.

28 Gaimushō (Ministry of Foreign Affairs, Tokyo), *Nihon gaikō nempyō narabi ni shuyō monjo* (Important documents and chronological tables of Japanese diplomacy), 1 *Bunsho* (Documents), 525. For the quotation and some aspects of the preceding two paragraphs, see McCormack, *Chang Tso-lin in Northeast China*, 56–9.

He did not want to be a Japanese puppet, and tried to assert his independence wherever possible. Nevertheless, Japan continued to view Chang as the best available alternative in Manchuria, and did whatever was necessary to defend his position there. Japanese intervened against Wu P'ei-fu in peripheral but not unimportant ways during the Second Chihli-Fengtien War in 1924. They evidently supplied the money to buy Feng Yü-hsiang's defection in that war, and when one of Chang's generals rebelled and tried to seize Mukden in 1925 the Japanese interfered to rescue Chang from what seemed certain defeat. Ironically, the Japanese also killed Chang; in 1928, extremist Japanese army officers assassinated him in the hope of producing turmoil that could be exploited to Japan's advantage.

The Soviet Union actively helped Feng Yü-hsiang. After he brought the Chihli-Fengtien war to an end in late 1924 by turning against Wu P'ei-fu, Feng eagerly sought aid because he knew that he would soon have to go to war with Chang Tso-lin's formidable armies, trained and supported by the Japanese. From the Russian standpoint Feng's reformist views and revolutionary rhetoric made him seem a likely candidate to support the Kuomintang. Throughout 1925 the Russians provided Feng with weapons, money, personal advisers and instructors for his troops. In return, he was supposed to permit Kuomintang political education in his army, and generally cooperate with the Kuomintang. Feng accepted the aid, but did everything he could to prevent the politicization of his army by Russians or by Kuomintang agents because he knew that would mean loss of his personal control.

War with Chang finally came at the end of 1925, and quickly turned bad for Feng. Early in 1926, he resigned his command and departed for the Soviet Union, where he was to remain for about five months. Feng hoped that his absence would lessen the determination of Chang Tso-lin to destroy Feng's army, but he also wanted to broaden his knowledge of Russian leaders, their country and their communist ideology. Feng travelled with a Russian adviser who gave him a continuing education about Marxism, the Russian Revolution, political conditions in other parts of the world, problems of party organization, and the need for all Chinese to work in the Kuomintang-Communist coalition to effect genuine national unity and to expel imperialism from China. Feng seems to have been genuinely impressed with Soviet society and with the discipline and effectiveness of the Soviet Communist Party. At the same time, he maintained contact with his army in China, which was suffering a total defeat. In the early autumn, after negotiating four-and-a-half million roubles of additional military aid, Feng returned to his scattered and demoralized troops.

When Feng arrived in China, the Kuomintang-Communist military campaign to destroy warlordism and unite the country – the Northern Expedition – was already underway. Feng reorganized his army and co-operated with that campaign in the conquest of Honan. When Chiang Kai-shek attacked the Communists in 1927, Feng for a brief moment became the chief hope of Russian leaders; they wanted him to continue to support the left wing of the Kuomintang and the Communists and use his military power against Chiang. But Feng promptly came to an understanding with Chiang and advised the Russians to go home. It was the end of Russian involvement in warlord politics.[29]

Great Britain had long had the largest commercial and financial interests in China, and was therefore particularly concerned to encourage stable government. Stability appeared even more important after the First World War, when the British worked desperately to regain their pre-eminence in the China trade. Even when disorder seemed to augur the collapse of all central power, the British supported the government in Peking. Yet the British were never enthusiastic about Tuan Ch'i-jui's administration because of its pro-Japanese orientation. They welcomed Tuan's defeat by the Chihli Clique in 1920, because Chihli leaders had declared their opposition to further foreign obligations, and they were thought by the British to have the capacity to unite China. Many writers have asserted or implied that the British and Americans provided extensive and varied support to the Chihli leader, Wu P'ei-fu. But a recent thorough study concludes that while Wu assiduously cultivated the British and Americans to obtain financial and military aid, the British and American governments adhered to neutrality and refused aid despite the personal admiration that foreigners in China generally had for Wu. Wu received substantial sums from British companies in China – notably the British American Tobacco Company, and the Asiatic Petroleum Company – in return for prohibiting boycotts against them in areas under his control.[30]

THE VIEW FROM PEKING: MILITARISM AND INSTABILITY

The national government in Peking was bewilderingly unstable during the 12 years of the warlord era. Seven individuals served as president or

29 Sheridan, *Chinese warlord,* 163–9, 177–9, 197–202.
30 Odoric Wou, *Militarism in modern China,* 151–97. About Wu P'ei-fu's obtaining money from foreign companies see: F. P. Lockhart to MacMurray, 19 Sept. 1925, Department of State, Hankow File L, No. 2; F. P. Lockhart to secretary of state, 25 Sept. 1925, Department of State, Hankow File No. 8; *China Weekly Review,* 24 April 1926, 207; C. L'Estrange Malone, *New China: report of an investigation,* pt 1, *The political situation,* London, Independent Labour Party Publication, 1926; J. C. Huston to J. V. A. MacMurray, 1 July 1926, Department of State, Hankow File No. 63.

head of state, one of them twice, making in effect eight heads of state. In addition, four regent cabinets ran the government during short interim periods, and there was one brief restoration of the Manchu monarchy. Scholars have counted 24 cabinets, five parliaments or national assemblies, and at least four constitutions or basic laws (see chapter 5, page 265). This plethora of individuals, offices, and legal and political changes makes it very difficult to describe Peking politics in a clear and readable fashion. Chapter 5 above has summarized the efforts at constitutional government. Here we look at some of the same events to note how militarism supervened and finally supplanted the vestiges of constitutionalism.

Tuan Ch'i-jui had assumed the post of prime minister in the closing days of Yuan's regime, and he continued in that position under President Li Yuan-hung. From the outset, Tuan dominated Li's government. Under other circumstances, his leadership might have been seen as the emergence of a responsible prime minister, precisely what republican parliamentarians had wanted during Yuan's presidency. But many republican politicians did not support Tuan, and he looked to the senior military officers and military governors for his power base. Almost from the beginning, therefore, there was tension between Tuan, relying on military influence, and the parliament, seeking to check him.

The tension came to a head in the spring of 1917 over the issue of China's participation in the First World War. Liang Ch'i-ch'ao and Tuan Ch'i-jui argued that China should join the European war on the side of the Allies. Liang hoped that participation in the war and in the peace settlement to follow could be used to improve China's international position. In April Tuan convened a conference of military governors in Peking to generate pressure on the president, cabinet and especially parliament to approve a war policy. The militarists supported Tuan regarding a declaration of war. Parliament baulked at the pressure, and refused to act on the war issue as long as Tuan was premier. Provincial militarists urged Li to dissolve parliament. Instead, after some vacillation, Li dismissed Tuan from office. Tuan, in turn, called upon warlords for support, and the military governors of eight northern provinces declared their independence of the Li government. In the meantime, Li could find nobody willing to assume office as premier in face of the warlords' opposition.

In this impasse, Chang Hsun offered to mediate between Li and the militarists. Chang, the 'pigtailed general' who remained loyal to the Manchus, seemed to be in a good position to sway the militarists if he wished to, because a year earlier he had helped organize a number of tuchun into an association of military governors, and served as head of the group. However, Chang desired to mediate not in order to save Li or to protect the republic, but to further his personal plans. First, Chang demanded that Li dissolve parliament, precisely what the militarists had earlier wanted. Li, feeling that his options had run out, finally acceded, and issued the edict of dissolution in mid June. Chang Hsun then marched into the capital, and on 1 July 1917, declared the restoration of the Manchu emperor to the throne of China!

Chang had been discussing a restoration for some months, and many other militarists had approved or acquiesced. However, those presumed allies denounced the restoration almost as soon as it occurred. Some writers have argued that the tuchun changed their minds because Chang took too powerful a position in the restored court, and because differences among the warlords augured weaker support than had been anticipated. But the chief reason seems to be that the warlords had never seriously intended to restore the emperor; they were simply using Chang and his commitment to the throne as a means of striking against Li Yuan-hung's government.[31] Tuan Ch'i-jui immediately organized a military campaign against Chang, and announced that President Li had reappointed him premier. The struggle was brief; within two weeks the restoration was over, Chang Hsun had taken refuge in a foreign legation, and Tuan Ch'i-jui had re-entered the capital as the defender of the republic. Li Yuan-hung resigned the presidency, probably under pressure from Tuan, and Vice-president Feng Kuo-chang succeeded to that office to finish the remaining year of the five-year term begun by Yuan Shih-k'ai.[32]

The emergence of military-political cliques 1917–1920

Feng Kuo-chang was unwilling to accept the presidency if the constitution was to be the sole basis for his position. He agreed to assume the office only after he arranged for a protégé to succeed him as military governor of Kiangsu, and had supporters confirmed as military governors of two other Yangtze provinces, Kiangsi and Hupei. Thus he had the same kind of support enjoyed by Tuan, whose adherents were military governors of Anhwei, Chekiang and Fukien.

When Tuan resumed the post of premier, he decided not to recall the parliament that Li Yuan-hung had dismissed just prior to the restoration, for it had so often been in opposition to him. Instead Tuan Ch'i-jui

31 *Ko-ming wen-hsien* (Documents of the revolution), vol. 7, highlights the complicated plotting that preceded the restoration. See also T'ao Chü-yin, *Tu-chün-t'uan chuan* (Chronicle of the association of warlords).
32 Yuan's first regular term began on 10 Oct. 1913. Before that time, from March 1912, he had served as provisional president.

engineered the election of his Anfu parliament in 1918 (see chapter 5, pages 274–8). He then tried to increase his own military strength, subdue the dissident provinces by force, put his personal adherents into powerful positions, and in that way restore national unity. Other warlords, fearing they would be eliminated if Tuan should continue along those lines, gathered together to resist the dominance of Anhwei power, and in that fashion the Chihli Clique came into being.

Hunan's strategic position made it Tuan's first target; it was accessible by railway from the north, and it was contiguous with four of the secessionist southern provinces. In August 1917 Tuan appointed one of his followers to be tuchun of Hunan. The Hunanese resisted, and war broke out. They forced Tuan's appointee out of the province, and the war continued into the spring of 1918, when Wu P'ei-fu finally defeated the Hunanese armies and brought the province under the control of the north. Tuan appointed Chang Ching-yao, one of his own men, to be tuchun of the province, to the frustration of Wu, who had hoped for the appointment.

Until 1918, when Wu's army conquered Hunan, Wu's superior, Ts'ao K'un, had generally supported Tuan Ch'i-jui. From that time, however, the interests of the two men began to diverge. The deterioration of the relationship was partly due to Wu P'ei-fu. Wu had expected to be named military governor of Hunan after his victory there, but Tuan passed him over in favour of one of his own men. In response Wu stopped his military campaign against the south, and from this time voiced sharp criticisms of the Peking government. At the same time, Ts'ao K'un began to fear that Tuan planned to remove him from his position as military governor of Chihli. To militarists of independent ambitions, such as Ts'ao K'un and Wu P'ei-fu, there was an implicit threat in Tuan Ch'i-jui's steady accumulation of financial, military and political power. In August 1917 Tuan finally got his declaration of war against Germany. Early in 1918 Japan provided a series of very large loans to Tuan, and concluded military and naval agreements to provide a legal basis for helping Tuan to organize and arm a War Participation Army. Ostensibly for use in the European conflict, the army was really to serve Tuan's purposes in China, and after the armistice in Europe the army was renamed the National Defence Army.

In the face of Tuan's growing power, militarists who were not part of his group had looked to Feng Kuo-chang as the chief representative of their interests. Even more important, some of those who had followed Tuan's lead also recognized that his ultimate aim was to eliminate all warlords not obedient to the Anhwei government in Peking. It was certainly that consideration that, in conjunction with Tuan's failure to appoint Wu tuchun of Hunan, led Ts'ao K'un to abandon Tuan's camp. When Feng Kuo-chang left the presidency in 1918, and died a year later, Ts'ao gradually succeeded him as head of the opposition to Tuan, the Chihli Clique.

Chang Tso-lin in Manchuria was also concerned about the expansion of Tuan's power, and the implicit threat it held for Chang's independence. Indeed, Tuan was already spreading his authority into Inner Mongolia, a region that Chang considered his own sphere of influence. The Fengtien and Chihli Cliques therefore decided to cooperate against Anhwei.

Matters came to a head in the spring of 1920, after a series of events had focused harsh public criticism against the pro-Japanese orientation of Tuan's government. In 1919 the Paris Peace Conference turned over the former German concessions in Shantung to Japan, and justified that decision partly on the basis of agreements between Japan and Tuan's government. The decision produced passionate opposition among Chinese intellectuals and others, and also among Chihli militarists, notably Wu P'ei-fu. In 1920 the anti-Tuan militarists demanded that the government be reorganized to eliminate the monopoly of Anhwei power in Peking, that it reopen peace talks with the south, and reduce Tuan's military forces. Tuan refused those demands, and war broke out in July. The Chihli-Fengtien coalition quickly defeated the Anhwei warlords. Tuan, in the best tradition of the discarded Chinese official, retired to 'study Buddhism'.

Ascendancy and collapse of the Chihli government, 1920–4

During the warlord era, the personnel and policies of the Peking government reflected the wishes of the militarists who stood behind it. But one of the reasons for government instability was the difficulty of arranging offices and policies to reflect accurately the distribution of power among the militarists, especially when the generals themselves were unclear about their relative strength. After the 1920 war, when the Chihli and Fengtien Cliques shared power, they started by organizing the Peking government in a fashion acceptable to both, and then began pushing and pulling, using government officials and policies as pawns in their struggle, until finally they moved onto the battlefield.

The aged Hsu Shih-ch'ang, who had won the highest degree in 1886, continued as president. His seniority and prestige were appropriate to the office; he was not closely linked to either of the two factions. Chin Yun-p'eng was made prime minister. He was acceptable to Chang Tso-lin, to whom he was related by marriage, and to Wu P'ei-fu, who had once been his student and protégé. Chin walked on eggs for over a year, making important decisions only after consulting both camps.

When Tuan Ch'i-jui was driven out of the government his Anfu parliament had also been liquidated. President Hsu then issued an order for a new parliament to be elected in accord with the electoral laws of 1912, drawn up to implement the Provisional Constitution. However, this was unacceptable to the Constitution Protection Movement in Canton. In the Canton view new elections were superfluous since the original parliament had not served out its term. Moreover, President Hsu's orders were not legal, since he had been elected by the Anfu parliament, an illegal body. By this time the south had acquired a vested interest in separation, which justified the southern provinces remaining independent, and provided a career for many parliamentarians. Since only a minority of representatives had gone south, several hundred substitute members had been selected there in 1919. When despite southern protests Peking ordered the new elections, they were held in only 11 provinces, and the new members did not constitute a quorum, so the new parliament was never even called together.

The new government at Peking legalized the spoils of the victors by appointing them to various offices appropriate to their new power. Ts'ao K'un was named inspecting commissioner of Chihli, Shantung and Honan. In effect the inspecting commissioner (Hsun-yueh-shih) of several provinces – sometimes called 'super tuchun' – appointed their military governors. Chang Tso-lin, already inspecting commissioner of Manchuria, was appointed concurrently development commissioner of Mongolia and Sinkiang, which legitimized Chang's activities in Inner Mongolia.

Wu P'ei-fu was made assistant inspecting commissioner of Chihli, Shantung and Honan, appropriate for a subordinate of Ts'ao, but not enough for an independent militarist. Wu made his headquarters in Honan, and seems to have maintained complete control of that province. In addition, he acquired the province of Hupei in 1921 in a fashion that well illustrates the contradictions among warlords of the same camp. Wang Chan-yuan, identified with the Chihli faction for several years, was tuchun of Hupei. In the summer of 1921, when the federalist movement was near its peak, Hupei politicians demanded that the province set up its own constitution and institute democratic government. The tuchun of Hunan, where the federalist movement was far advanced, declared himself commander-in-chief of an army to 'rescue' Hupei from the grip of a non-federalist. Wang Chan-yuan turned to Wu P'ei-fu for help. However, Wu withheld his assistance until Wang was defeated, and then his army entered Hupei and drove the Hunanese out, so that Wu acquired Hupei for himself. Wu P'ei-fu increasingly emerged as the real military leader of the Chihli Clique.

Wu proceeded to organize an alliance of five Yangtze provinces against outside aggression and internal troubles. Chang Tso-lin in Manchuria and Sun Yat-sen in Kwangtung both felt threatened by this expansion of Chihli power, and came together in an alliance against Wu. Chang took advantage of a financial crisis in the Peking government at the end of 1921 to replace Prime Minister Chin Yun-p'eng with his own choice, Liang Shih-i. Wu P'ei-fu seized upon Liang's alleged pro-Japanese policies to attack him and, indirectly, Chang Tso-lin.

The first stage of most major warlord conflicts was a 'war of telegrams', in which each side denounced the policies and patriotism of the other and proclaimed the purity of its own motives. Chihli and Fengtien leaders exchanged such wires through the early months of 1922, and in the spring turned to the real war of troops and guns. The Chihli forces defeated the Manchurian armies with astonishing speed, particularly in view of the apparent superiority of Chang Tso-lin in numbers of troops and in weaponry. Chang retreated behind the Great Wall, where the Chihli armies were not prepared to go. The Peking government, now dominated by Chihli Clique militarists, dismissed Chang from all his official positions, but Chang simply proclaimed Manchuria independent of the central government, and continued to rule in grand isolation.

Chang's ally, Sun Yat-sen, was no more successful. After Sun sent a military expedition northward to cooperate with the Manchurian armies, his own ostensible subordinate, Ch'en Chiung-ming, attacked Sun's headquarters. Sun managed to escape, but his government was toppled and the expedition stopped. Although this move served Ch'en Chiung-ming's own ambitions as tuchun of Kwangtung, it was evidently taken in accord with an agreement with Wu P'ei-fu, still another example of the tangle of warlord alliances.

Although a single clique now dominated the capital, it had two major factions involved in Peking politics. Wu's conception of a soldier's duty and the Confucian principle of loyalty precluded his repudiating Ts'ao K'un publicly, but he had different ideas about government. Moreover, each man had followers who saw their own advancement in political schemes to promote their leader. The chief means by which the factions struggled, and revealed victory or loss, was by cabinet appointments and government policies.

Immediately after the war, the new rulers of Peking forced Hsu Shih-ch'ang to resign. Wu invited Li Yuan-hung to resume the presidency. At the same time, he recalled the old parliament, the body that had been first dissolved by Yuan Shih-k'ai in 1914, then by Li Yuan-hung in 1917, and a rump of which had ever since been in the south, mainly in Canton.

Li's second presidency lasted just a year, to June 1923, and proved to be a greater fiasco than the first. The Chihli militarists gave him no real power; his appointments and decisions were implemented only if the warlords approved, and he even had difficulty obtaining funds to support the presidential establishment. During the first half of Li's second presidency, Wu P'ei-fu very much dominated the government, and Ts'ao K'un found no way to pursue his aspiration to become president. Early in 1923, however, Ts'ao's followers succeeded in ousting the cabinet, composed of Wu's supporters, on grounds of corruption, and installed a government of Ts'ao's nominees. With the initiative in their hands, they decided to go all the way and elect Ts'ao president. Li had to be removed from office first, and that was achieved by literally running him out of town. Ts'ao was elected in October at a cost of five to seven thousand Chinese dollars for each member of parliament who voted for him.

Chang Tso-lin, still brooding behind the Great Wall, denounced Ts'ao's election as illegal, and proclaimed it his duty to rid the country of such traitors as Ts'ao and Wu. Since his defeat in 1922 Chang had retrained and reorganized his army. By 1924 he had renewed his alliance with Sun Yat-sen in the south and was ready to test Chihli's arms once again. Wu P'ei-fu, in the meantime, had given up earlier hopes of reuniting the country through representative conferences, and had concluded that unification could come only through military defeat of governors who did not acknowledge Peking's leadership. Chang Tso-lin, of course, was the most conspicuous example.

After the usual exchange of denunciatory telegrams fighting broke out in the autumn of 1924. A few weeks later, while Wu's campaign near the Great Wall seemed to be going successfully, one of his subordinates defected and brought the war to an unexpected conclusion. Feng Yü-hsiang, the Christian general, suddenly left the fighting zone and swiftly returned to Peking. On 23 October 1924 he seized the capital, imprisoned President Ts'ao, and declared peace. Wu rushed back to try to marshal other Chihli warlords against Feng, but they could not get aid to him before Wu's forces on all fronts were defeated, and he had to flee to central China.

Feng had been considered a member of the Chihli Clique since 1918, but had never been an intimate of Wu P'ei-fu. He had offended Wu by criticism of his personal behaviour and by refusing to send him the sums of money Wu requested when Feng was tuchun of Honan in 1922. Wu, on the other hand, had tried to limit the expansion of Feng's army, and had transferred Feng from his post as Honan governor to a far more vulnerable position in Peking. Feng, therefore, did not anticipate any personal gain in the event of a Chihli victory over Fengtien; on the contrary, Wu's expanded influence would make it easier for him to control Feng.

Against this background Feng was offered a huge bribe to turn against Wu. The money was provided by Japan, evidently in the form of a loan to Chang Tso-lin, perhaps with the promise of repayment by the new government to be installed in Peking. The amount has been variously estimated, but was probably about 1,500,000 yen.[33] For years Feng had suffered from an acute shortage of funds; he could expect little from a Wu victory, so he accepted the bribe. The Japanese had two goals: first, to prevent the defeat of their protégé, Chang Tso-lin; even more important, to reinstate Tuan Ch'i-jui as head of the Peking government and so renew the mutually profitable relations Japan had had with Tuan's regime in 1917-20.

Ascendancy of Chang Tso-lin, 1925-8

Feng's coup and the sudden defeat of Wu initiated widespread and complicated reshuffling of warlord relations that went on for about a year. At the outset the two victors gave themselves formal positions to correspond with the new distribution of power. Chang Tso-lin gained formal authority over the north-east: Fengtien, Kirin, Heilungkiang, Jehol and Chihli. Feng, in turn, was given charge of the north-west: Suiyuan, Chahar and Kansu. Warlords allied with Feng invaded Honan and Shensi, and assumed control of those provinces. Chang sent his armies into Shantung, Kiangsu and Anhwei, but a Yangtze militarist forced him out of the two last-named and added them to a five-province alliance he had formed among the Yangtze provinces. Wu P'ei-fu, after months of trying to parlay his seniority and prestige into another position of genuine power, acquired control of Hupei, was acknowledged as nominal leader of several provinces in Central China, and concluded an alliance with his long-time enemy Chang Tso-lin to fight his new-found enemy Feng Yü-hsiang.

The Chihli defeat in 1924 naturally had drastic repercussions in the formal organization of the Peking government. Tuan Ch'i-jui was finally recalled from retirement to head the new administration. In November 1924 he assumed the position of provisional chief executive, and issued

---

33 Sheridan, *Chinese warlord*, 138-48. McCormack has uncovered facts that confirm the central Japanese role; see his *Chang Tso-lin in Northeast China*, 131-45.

the Articles on the Organization of the Government of the Provisional Chief Executive (see chapter 5).

In the closing weeks of 1925, the expected war between Feng Yü-hsiang and Chang Tso-lin began. By the end of the year, it was clear to Feng that he could not win, and he resigned his post to leave the country, hoping that his subordinates could salvage something for him from the peace settlement to follow. Chang would have none of it; now in alliance with Wu P'ei-fu, who nursed a strong hatred for Feng, the Manchurian warlord continued to attack Feng's army with the intention of destroying it completely. He almost succeeded; by the middle of 1926 Feng's forces were in tattered and disorganized retreat in the west. They would be heard from again, but for the moment Chang and Wu emerged as the clear victors. Of course, their victory augured still another change for the bedraggled Peking government.

In April 1926 Feng's troops had tried to arrest Tuan Ch'i-jui, on the grounds that he was intriguing against them. Tuan took refuge in the Legation Quarter, although he was able quickly to return to his office when Feng's army was driven from Peking. However, Chang Tso-lin had decided against retaining Tuan in office, and thus devoid of support, Tuan resigned from his post on 20 April. For some weeks, no national government existed in Peking, while Chang Tso-lin and Wu P'ei-fu tried to decide what to do. Finally a 'regency cabinet' was organized, essentially a committee of politicans appointed by the ruling warlords. It underwent a number of changes through the remainder of 1926, and a new regency cabinet was organized at the beginning of 1927. The regency cabinets re-presented the culmination of the decline of the Peking government that had been going on for the preceding decade. From the middle of 1926 to mid 1927, the regency cabinets had 'no more substance than a ruler in a motion picture'. The minister of finance had no money. The minister of communications regulated no railways because they were all in the hands of military commanders. The minister of education presumably controlled government schools, but they were closed because utility bills had not been paid and teachers had received no salaries. The minister of interior 'could not name a single subordinate without first consulting the wishes of a warlord who happened to control the district in which the subordinate would act.' Provincial officials, working through local consulates, settled all disputes with foreign governments, so the minister of foreign affairs had nothing to do. The minister of the army had no authority over the troop units throughout the country; he took orders from the most powerful militarist.[34]

34 Franklin W. Houn, *Central government of China 1912-1928, an institutional study*, 158-9.

In these circumstances, it was to everyone's relief that the man with real power finally stepped forward to assume formal responsibility for the government. Chang Tso-lin, on 17 June 1927 proclaimed himself grand marshal, or generalissimo, and organized a military government. Although a cabinet was created, including a prime minister, in essence the government was staffed with Chang's subordinates, and he ruled as a military dictator. But, like all national governments since 1916, the authority of Chang's regime reached only as far as his bayonets, and that meant primarily Manchuria, Chihli and Shantung. Even that domain was soon challenged, because the dissidents in Canton had organized a revolutionary army, and had launched a Northern Expedition to seize China from the warlords. Chang's troops were finally defeated, and he fled from Peking in June 1928.

This sorry record of warlord politics in Peking suggests that the failure of constitutional government before 1928 should be understood not as a decline of effective government, but as an incapacity ever to create it. Tuan Ch'i-jui, Wu P'ei-fu and other national leaders at times established substantial military command over large portions of the country. But that achievement was primarily military; it was never followed by, or associated with, the creation of effective political institutions to provide a genuinely civil dimension to the government's power. There was no serious attempt to mobilize significant elements of the population in a fashion to strengthen the government's political institutions. Soldiers were the warlords' only constituency. When national officials could assert their power only through armies, that power could be nullified by larger armies. The weakness of the warlords was not that they sought power, but that they had such a narrow vision of what constituted power, and were unable to develop its non-military dimensions.

WARLORDISM AND CHINESE SOCIETY

As earlier pages have shown, the warlords who divided China among themselves differed greatly in abilities and social attitudes. The conditions they fostered therefore also varied from place to place, and through time as one commander followed another in local or regional office. No statement about specific forms of warlord exploitation, or the hardships warlords created, applies to all of China at any one time. But it is nonetheless correct to say that the warlords brought terror and exploitation, directly and indirectly, to millions of Chinese.[35]

35 Some scholars argue that the extent of warlord exactions and the hardships they caused have been much exaggerated because they assume an economy in which the state role was larger than it was in China, and they distort reality by ignoring the positive aspects of warlord

Warlord demand for money was insatiable, and the militarists wrung an astonishing array of taxes from the populace. They also printed worthless currency on a large scale and forced people to accept it, thus making commercial transactions a form of expropriation. In late 1924 it was estimated that in the single province of Kwangsi the military had issued five *billion* Chinese dollars in virtually unbacked notes. This enormous drain of wealth to military and other unproductive purposes inhibited orderly economic activity and planning, particularly for large-scale projects, and thus surely retarded China's economic development.[36]

Warlordism nurtured famine. In some provinces, warlords forced the cultivation of opium as a cash crop, thus reducing the acreage devoted to food crops. Diminishing government appropriations to maintain irrigation and flood control facilities helped to bring about several disastrous floods. Troops seized draught animals from peasants, not only imposing a direct economic loss but reducing the productivity of peasant farming. Devastating famines in North China during the mid and late 1920s were so clearly the product of warlord misgovernment that the China International Famine Relief Commission, which was chartered to aid victims of famine due to natural causes, had to change its definition of famine so that it could render aid to people who were starving from conditions caused by misgovernment and exploitation. In fact, the American Red Cross refused to participate in China famine relief at that time because the famine was created by political, not natural, phenomena.[37]

In many areas, the actions of organized armies were less serious than the hordes of uncontrolled and undisciplined soldiers who roamed the countryside preying on the peasantry. A study by the South Manchurian Railway in 1930 – two years after the warlord period was supposed to have ended – estimated that in the province of Shantung 310,000 unorganized troops and bandits, in addition to 192,000 regular troops, were living off the countryside.[38] Banditry flourished in all parts of the country, and robbery and violence were commonplace. Victorious troops looted whenever they could. Wars often destroyed civilian lives and property,

activity such as the development of industry, agriculture, transport and education. A good example of this view is Thomas G. Rawski, *China's republican economy: an introduction*. Virtually every student of warlordism acknowledges the constructive activities of some warlords. But, on balance, the consequences of warlordism can not reasonably be considered positive, and the notion that oppression and harshness were not widespread flies in the face of a large number of testimonials based on first-hand experience or observation.

36 For an attempt to calculate the funds diverted to military uses, away from possible use in economic modernization, see Jerome Ch'en, *The military-gentry coalition*, 189-90.

37 Nathan, Andrew James, *A history of the China International Famine Relief Commission*, 40-56.

38 Mantetsu Chōsabu, 'Shina no doran to Santō nōson' (Shantung villages and the upheaval in China) (Dairen, 1930), 20, 27, cited in Ramon H. Myers, *The Chinese peasant economy: agricultural development in Hopei and Shantung, 1890-1949*, 278.

government services were neglected or non-existent, and corruption, disorder and exploitation became the order of the day. The turmoil of the times drove thousands of individuals to leave their homes and travel to other parts of the country. One thoughtful writer concluded that the danger and disorder of warlordism during the 1920s produced 'one of the largest internal migrations of this century.'[39]

Warlordism influenced the shape of Chinese nationalism, the most powerful social movement in early twentieth-century China. Nationalism was partly a response to the disunity and international vulnerability fostered by warlordism. Moreover, many warlords disseminated patriotic, nationalistic slogans as means to legitimize their actions. Whatever their actual motives, in this way warlords nurtured the idea that Chinese should be concerned about national conditions, seeking national goals. For example, a Chinese general recalled that in 1912 he joined the army simply to make a living, but came to think of the military in national terms after hearing patriotic speeches by his commander, Feng Yü-hsiang.[40]

But warlord activity also helped produce a strong military dimension in Chinese nationalism. Although warlords proved unable to create national political power, they prevented non-military groups from doing so. In that way they contributed to the further militarization of Chinese politics; the heritage of militarism was more militarists. The Kuomintang had to develop a powerful military arm in order to compete with the warlords, and in the process the military came to dominate the party. The Communists, in turn, had to create a strong military in order to compete with the Kuomintang and also with the remnants of warlordism that persisted after 1928.

In the final analysis, however, this militarization was not profound or permanent. Warlord rule did not exemplify an enduring dynamic at the core of Chinese society that assures the military a uniquely powerful political role. It has been argued that 'warlords established the fact that in modern China political power cannot be divorced from military power. . . . And, so far, no one has been able to discover the secret of how to remove armies from the center of the Chinese political scene.'[41] The opposite is true: the failure of the warlords demonstrated that military power alone is an inadequate basis for political power in China.

The modern warlords had their counterparts in inter-dynastic periods throughout earlier centuries of Chinese history, but all ultimately made

39 Myers, *The Chinese peasant economy*, 278.
40 Liu Ju-ming, *Liu Ju-ming hui-i lu* (Recollections of Liu Ju-ming), 2–3.
41 Lucian W. Pye, *Warlord politics: conflict and coalition in the modernization of Republican China*, 169.

way for centralized civilian governments ruling over a united country. In the twentieth century, nationalism and communism for the first time played a role in that traditional process, but did not alter the result, civilian unity. Nationalism only emphasized the urgency of national unity, and all warlords accepted that fact, or at the very least paid lip service to it. Despite the independence – at times the formal secession – of provincial and regional military leaders, nobody ever proclaimed a new state or even indicated that his secession was intended to be permanent. The feeling of national unity was so profound that some leaders could argue that regionalism served the nation by strengthening its individual parts, an argument that only made sense on the assumption of ultimate reunification. The warlords also acknowledged the strong tradition of civilian rule by their public statements about the need for fealty to an effective civilian government. And despite the temporary militarization of Chinese politics to which the warlords contributed, the ultimate victor in the struggle for power in China, the Communist Party, held to a basic principle that the party should control the gun.

The regional power of the warlords did little to strengthen regional divisions in China. In fact, regionalism had traditionally flourished in China, even when central authority was strong. Geographic distinctiveness, economic interests, linguistic distinctions, ethnic and cultural patterns all fostered feelings of loyalty – of belonging – to regions. There was a system of 'layered loyalties': loyalties to the provinces, to multiprovincial regions, to intra-provincial regions, and to border-zone regions. But these were not normally political loyalties, which is why they could coexist with vigorous central power. Only when central authority collapsed did traditional regionalism acquire an important political dimension. The regional units that had cultural and economic importance in a unified China became the natural units into which the country disintegrated, and the natural territorial bases for warlords. But the very fact that the regions had a normal existence within a unified China meant that warlord regionalism was a less destructive force than it might otherwise have been. It was not regionalism that had to be destroyed to restore national unity, but the independent military power that fed on regionalism.[42]

Most warlords were conservative men, strongly attuned to traditional values. Paradoxically, the disunity and disorder they fostered provided rich opportunity for intellectual diversity and iconoclasm to flourish. Neither the central government nor the provincial warlords were capable

42 Lary, *Region and nation*, offers an acute analysis of regionalism and militarism in twentieth-century China. The phrase 'layered loyalties' is Lary's.

of efficiently controlling the universities, periodicals, publishing industries and other agencies of China's intellectual life. Chinese intellectuals in those years, partly in response to the evils of warlordism, engaged in the most intense discussion of ways in which China might be modernized and strengthened. The founding of the Communist Party in 1921 and the reorganization of the Kuomintang in 1924 stemmed partly from this intellectual flowering. Thus, on the one hand, the warlord years represented the low point of political unity and national strength in the twentieth century. On the other hand, they also represented the peak of intellectual and literary achievement, and out of that tumultuous and bloody era, partly in response to the warlords, flowed the intellectual and social movements that culminated in the reunification and rejuvenation of China.

CHAPTER 7

INTELLECTUAL CHANGE: FROM THE REFORM MOVEMENT TO THE MAY FOURTH MOVEMENT, 1895 – 1920

EVOLUTIONISM IN REFORM THOUGHT

The years 1898 and 1919 are usually thought of as two watersheds in the history of China's intellectual break with the values of Confucian civilization. The 1898 reform movement was an effort at institutional change on the part of ranking literati close to the throne. It began as a response to military defeat by Japan in 1895, but ended in the abandonment of the traditional Sinocentric world-view and a large-scale effort to assimilate the 'new learning' (*hsin-hsueh*) of the West. The movement bore fruit in the late Ch'ing modernization drive and in the collapse of the imperial system in 1911, bringing in its wake a wave of still more sweeping intellectual re-evaluation. Where the cutting edge of reform in 1898 had been directed at the inherited political order, the intellectual campaign for a totally 'new culture', which was symbolized by the May Fourth demonstrations of 1919, was seen as an attack upon the traditional moral and social orders as well. The leadership of the later movement came from China's newly modernized universities and schools. In addition to anti-imperialism, its goal was the establishment of a scientific and democratic 'new culture' purged of all relics of China's feudal past. In a generation China's intellectuals had apparently moved from the questioning of core traditional values to their total repudiation.

Moreover, in this same generation the intellectual elite as a class had undergone a number of important structural changes. It had created novel modes of communication and association, in the form of newspapers and periodical press on the one hand, and various types of study societies and political parties on the other. The classical examination system had ended, and had been replaced by a system of schools, leading to the erosion of traditional career opportunities in the civil service and the rapid professionalization and specialization of intellectual work. Centres of culture, historically urban to a degree in China, were subjected to the influence of a different kind of urbanism: that of the cosmopolitan industrializing city. If the intellectual class moulded by these shifts was developing a new cohesiveness, it was also threatened by a new estrangement from the rest of Chinese society. No longer educated for office, intellectuals more and more stood outside the mainstream of political power; educated more and more according to foreign models, they risked losing the inherited language which could form a bridge to the common people.

The discovery of the West: reformist evolutionary cosmology

Intellectual change after the 1890s must first of all be studied in the light of the Chinese 'discovery of the West' – not merely as the source of imperialist aggression or technological wizardry, but as a world civilization in its own right. At first this discovery was the result of the transmission to a broader elite of knowledge accumulated by a few pioneers after the 1800s. The important reform study societies of the years 1895–8 began by propagating the works of treaty-port publicists and compradores like Wang T'ao and Cheng Kuan-ying, or of early envoys to Europe like Hsueh Fu-ch'eng and Kuo Sung-tao; or of Christian missionary education societies and the early Chinese arsenal schools for technological 'self-strengthening'. However, compared with the flood of energy aroused by the reform movement itself, these early explorations of Western learning soon seemed limited indeed. Pushed by political exile and pulled by the lure of the new education, thousands lived and studied abroad after 1900, and returned to China to claim positions as intellectual leaders. For those who remained at home, translations – especially of works on world history, geography, politics and law – were increasingly available, at first mainly from Japanese but later from European languages as well. Pioneer Chinese translators like Yen Fu, who specialized in British and French social and political philosophers, and Lin Shu, who was famous for European romantic fiction, were among the most popular authors of their generation. In Peking in 1895 members of the radical Study Society for Self-Strengthening (Ch'iang-hsueh hui) organized by K'ang Yu-wei had not been able to find a world map in any bookshop in the city. By 1919 the capital's reorganized Peking University under the chancellorship of Ts'ai Yuan-p'ei (trained both at the Hanlin Academy and at Leipzig University) employed graduates of Western universities, and included courses in European literature, history, science and philosophy.

Facts like these have led to a widespread assumption that the reform generation was stamped by the Chinese 'response to the West', and must be analysed in terms of the impact of foreign ideas upon native systems of thought. Fung Yu-lan, a leading neo-traditional scholar, has typically characterized the period between the 1890s and the 1920s as one of Chinese infatuation with the 'spiritual civilization of the West' – to be distin-

guished from both the Sinocentrism of the dynastic era and the critical
neo-traditionalism of the 1920s and 1930s.[1] Chinese Marxist historians
like Hou Wai-lu have linked this presumed infatuation with the West to
structural changes in the society – the drive for industrialization of an
emerging bourgeoisie, which, like its European counterpart, found the
scientific and democratic ideology of the Enlightenment a fit form to
express their socio-economic aspirations.[2] The American scholar Joseph
Levenson was more impressed with evidence suggesting that Chinese
reformers viewed the West and its intellectual claims with a good deal
of ambivalence, but interpreted the latter as an expression of tension
between their commitment to universal values – which dictated the
necessity of adopting new beliefs from abroad – and their particularistic
sense of national cultural identity, which tugged them towards the comforts of tradition.[3]

The notion of 'response to the West' does indeed call attention to the
critical importance of Western imperialism as an external force motivat-
ing the desire to change, and to the enormous stimulus, both positive and
negative, generated by this first serious Chinese exploration of dominant
nineteenth-century Western traditions of science and socio-political
thought. One danger in the concept, however, is its tendency to suggest
that the process was one of linear substitution of 'Western' ideas for native ones; and that Chinese played an intellectually passive role. Another
is to foster the assumption that once the process of Westernization had
occurred, it was impossible for Chinese thereafter to maintain any authentic commitment to traditional values. The notion that the Chinese moved
reactively from the assertion of traditional values before 1890 to their
denial in the course of the campaign for a 'new culture' in 1919 has been
a consequence of this explanatory model.

An alternative perspective is first suggested when one distinguishes the
political occasion behind the reform movement from its intellectual
content, and so can recognize native sources of inspiration for the latter.
Increasingly scholars have noted that comparatively heterodox movements of traditional thought – whether the anti-despotism of the late
Ming loyalists of the seventeenth century, the individualism of the Lu-
Wang tradition of Neo-Confucianism, the social humanitarianism of
Mahayana Buddhism, the libertarian strands in Taoism, or the pragmatic
and utilitarian approach to statecraft of a Mo-tzu, a Yen Yuan, or even the

---

1 Fung Yu-lan, *Hsin shih lun* (New culture and society).
2 Hou Wai-lu, *Chin-tai Chung-kuo ssu-hsiang hsueh-shuo shih* (Interpretive history of modern
  Chinese thought).
3 Joseph R. Levenson, *Confucian China and its Modern Fate*.

Legalists – were all *points d'appui* upon which many reformers built their cases. The imperial orthodoxy had concealed the diversity of the Chinese tradition more than it had destroyed it, and not all native traditions – elite or popular – were conservative ones. On the other hand, it is also increasingly understood that China's own neo-traditional philosophers and their Maoist adversaries alike have been correct in saying that commitment to Confucian values survived the iconoclastic onslaught of the 'New Culture' and May Fourth movements, and has continued to guide the social behaviour and spiritual life of many Chinese down to post-Liberation times.

Nonetheless, the 'response to the West' model of intellectual change is only partially challenged by an analysis which perceives continuities, like discontinuities, as historically linear. A more fruitful approach may be to recognize that the leading thinkers of the reform generation were trying to understand how both continuities and discontinuities fit into significantly altered structures of meaning. The socio-political struggle for reform was not articulated in isolation, but within the framework of a new evolutionary cosmology. This was a systemic conception of the universe, in which natural, spiritual and social phenomena were perceived as manifestations of a single cosmic reality. The external source of this new cosmology lay in the Chinese discovery of what they took to be new truths of nature and facts of history revealed by the West. On the one hand there was the discovery of a world history encompassing a plurality of high civilizations in dynamic interaction with one another as well as with a 'barbarian' perimeter; on the other, there was the exploration of the implications of Western scientific law – particularly the laws of evolution based upon Darwinian biology, but also those of Newtonian physics as well. Internally the cosmology relied upon the Confucian-Taoist tradition which taught that socio-political phenomena and natural cosmic patterns are linked in a process of interdependent causation. There resulted from the new cosmology a world-view which took away from Chinese their self-image as the sole source of world civilization, and exposed them as members of one culture and one nation among many. But at the same time the consequent relativization of China was no simple cutting down to size – rather it implied the relativization of all cultures, all social stages, and all points in historical time. It resulted in a new faith in world-historical progress among Chinese, but one which stressed both the moral teleology of the historical process and its relative incompleteness at any given temporal stage. This in turn led to a reemphasis upon time itself, in the classic sense of 'change' (*i*) as a metaphysical reality – the cosmic energies at work directing all the structures of existence in their ultimately interacting motions. Finally, it created a heightened sense of certain problems of human moral action in a cosmos now considered remarkable for its dynamism – which would have either to create human beings in its own Faustian image, or leave them helpless before an externally determinative process.

Not surprisingly, the first to express the new affirmation of change in a relativized world were a few men whose early personal contact with Europe had been relatively sustained. Hsueh Fu-ch'eng, a member of the Chinese diplomatic mission to London between 1890 and 1894, his writings on reform first stimulated by the Japanese seizure of the Ryūkyūs in 1879, offered a typical early sketch of the new world history. Between the dawn of humanity and today 10,000 years have elapsed, he believed, a fact known by the inherent law of alternation which governs the speed of world change. Hsueh's internal periodization of that 10,000 years followed standard traditional historiography, but he assessed the present as a fundamental turning-point: the end of the era of separation between Chinese and barbarian and the coming of an age of association among states. Importantly, Hsueh saw these transformations as simply necessary, independent of human desire: 'The reason for its happening is not that people love change; it is time and circumstance'.[4]

This sense of necessity was more subtly and affirmatively underscored by Yen Fu, the great translator of European social classics, in his famous essay of 1895, 'On the speed of world change', which offered the first definitive reform analysis of the idea of progress. Yen Fu was also impressed by parallels between the present and the Ch'in-Han era, the great watershed in traditional Chinese institutional history, but he confessed that the causes behind such historical transformations remained mysterious:

Using forced language we speak of a cosmic-historical process of Change [*yun hui*]. When such a process is at work, even sages have no power over it. . . . To say they can take hold of it and move it is false. The sage's role is merely to know its origins and foresee its movements.[5]

Convinced that their moment in history was a turning-point so basic it could only be the result of some cosmic principle at work, reformers first saw evolutionary time as patterned according to deeply satisfying

---

4 Hsueh Fu-ch'eng, *Ch'ou-yang ch'u-i* (Preliminary proposals on foreign affairs, 1886), reprinted in Yang Chia-lo, ed. *Wu-hsu pien-fa wen-hsien hui-pien* (Documentary collection of the literature of the 1898 reform movement), 1. 159–61.
5 Yen Fu, 'Lun shih-pien chih chi' (On the speed of world change), reprinted in *Yen Chi-tao shih wen-ch'ao* (Essays and poems of Yen Fu, preface 1916), *ch'üan* 1.1.
6 Wang T'ao, 'Pien fa' (Reform), reprinted in Yang Chia-lo, *Wu-hsu pien-fa wen-hsien hui-pien*, 1.133–5.

traditional beliefs, and their own role in 'serving the times' as that of regulators of cosmic order. In the words of the pioneer treaty-port journalist Wang T'ao, 'The Way honours institutions which suit the times, and no more'.[6] In this context the political reform movement in China was less an end in itself than an accommodation to a new stage in world historical development; and the known institutions of the industrialized Western world provided intimations, the more exciting because dimly outlined, of utopian future possibilities for human society as a whole.[7]

As the foregoing suggests, evolutionary cosmology took shape less as the insight of one individual than as a set of common conceptions arrived at among many. Nonetheless, in its mature form it is best examined here through the thought of the major reform intellectuals who were in part its creators. The senior partner of the group was certainly K'ang Yu-wei, whose works, *The false classics of the Hsin period (Hsin hsueh wei-ching k'ao*; 1891), and *Confucius as a reformer (K'ung-tzu kai-chih k'ao*; 1897) had supported the canonical claims of the long submerged New Text School of Confucianism in a provocative effort to make tradition serve reform. Shortly after the collapse of the imperially sponsored Hundred Days reform effort of 1898, which K'ang had personally led, he put together his major utopian synthesis, *The book of the great commonwealth (Ta-t'ung shu)* – a work which although never completely published in his lifetime was known in draft and outline among his more influential disciples.[8]

Of these, T'an Ssu-t'ung was certainly the boldest and most provocative thinker, whose philosophical originality rivalled that of K'ang himself. His execution at the age of 33 by the Ch'ing authorities after the counter coup of September 1898 was a martyrdom deliberately sought on his own part, and it canonized his spirit in the minds of his surviving comrades, making his posthumously published book, *On humanity (Jen hsueh*; 1901) a talismanic legacy.[9] Liang Ch'i-ch'ao, who served as K'ang's close political ally, together with K'ang virtually created the study society movement through which reform ideas swept the country after 1895. Already a pioneer journalist as editor of the study society vehicle, *Shih wu pao* (Current affairs; The China progress), in 1896 and 1897, he attained

---

7 The new optimism has been analysed against the background of Neo-Confucian political culture in Thomas Metzger, *Escape from predicament: Neo-Confucianism and China's evolving political culture.*

8 K'ang Yu-wei, *Ta-t'ung shu* (Book of the great commonwealth). English translation by Laurence G. Thompson, *Ta Tung Shu: book of the great commonwealth.*

9 T'an Ssu-t'ung, *Jen hsueh* (On humanity), first published in *Ch'ing-i pao* (1899), and reprinted four times in the next 15 years. My study of T'an has been greatly aided by David Wile, 'T'an Ssu-t'ung: his Life and Major Work, the Jen Hsueh' (University of Wisconsin, Ph.D. dissertation, 1972).

the peak of his influence as the editorial voice of the reform opposition in Japanese exile after 1899.

If the foregoing three men had all staked their careers upon winning reform under the monarchy in 1898, paying for their failure with exile or death, Yen Fu, the fourth great inspirer of the movement, maintained a more temperate stand on the edge of events. Ostensibly the superintendent of a naval academy in Tientsin, he was a rare British-trained 'foreign expert' in engineering. Rarer still, and unique to his generation, was his synthetic view of contemporary Anglo-European civilization, which he developed in a series of remarkable translations of major works of Herbert Spencer, T. H. Huxley, J. S. Mill, Adam Smith, Montesquieu, and others. Here he utilized the scholar's traditional convention of commentary and the resources of the classical Chinese philosophical vocabulary to present a dazzlingly interpretive rendition of his originals.

The complex intellectual relations among these four may be represented by seeing K'ang and T'an as drawing most deeply upon native roots for their philosophical synthesis, by contrast with the Western inspired Social Darwinism of Yen Fu and Liang Ch'i-ch'ao. Such an analysis sees K'ang and T'an tending to internationalism, reminiscent of the *t'ien-hsia* ideal of a Sinocentric cosmos; to utopianism, as they projected the canonical golden age on to the future, and to faith in the Confucian idea of *jen* (goodness) as a cosmic-moral principle. By contrast Yen Fu and Liang Ch'i-ch'ao appear encouraged by their Social Darwinist orientation to take more nationalistic, pragmatic and secular perspectives. However, before 1903 or 1904 the writings of all four displayed an underlying optimism about China's long-range prospects which belied the indignant and anxious tones of their anti-imperialist, anti-court polemics, and which is best understood as based upon a shared belief in the benign nature of the metahistorical process as a whole, leading to a progressively realized world community.

The major contribution of both the *Ta-t'ung shu* and the *Jen-hsueh* was to present the idea of evolution integrated into a cosmology which linked the process of evolutionary unfolding with social change. Both works recognized the transvaluation of social values which the new stage of world history portended, while remaining confident that Confucian spiritual truth would continue to be the metaphysical source of the pattern of change.

Originally New Text Confucianism had provided K'ang Yu-wei with a Chinese *schema* of advancing historical stages which could be accommodated to a full-scale Western theory of progress. By means of this he embraced unilinear historical change with the enthusiasm of a discoverer. However, a parallel – although in a formal sense devolutionary – analysis of the metahistorical process found in a text attributed to the classic Confucian school was even more important as a source of the *Ta-t'ung shu*. This text, *Evolution of the Rites* (*Li yun*), described the doctrine of the 'three ages', beginning with the golden age of antiquity 'when the great Tao prevailed' – an era of 'Great Peace' (*Ta-t'ung*) unsullied by the institutions of familism or private property. According to the *Li yun* the historical sage rulers of the Three Dynasties had presided over a second era of 'lesser tranquility', a devolution away from the golden age to a world marked by both military power and ritual morality: 'the empire became a world of families where people love only their own parents and their own children [and] goods and labor are used only for private advantage'.[10] When K'ang located the present as transitional between the third 'age of disorder' which had begun in the times of Confucius, and a coming 'age of rising peace' which would lead the world back towards Great Peace, he was prophesying a transition away from a social system based on patriarchal clans and tribes and a corresponding political system based on the despotic authority of rulers over people or nobles over commoners. Instead would emerge a world where the hierarchical distance between peoples and their rulers and between different individuals in their social relations would be markedly diminished. The political form embodying this new relationship among people would be the nation-state and constitutional monarchy. In the immediate sense, these were the 'institutional reforms' (*pien-fa*) which would bring China to a level of parity with Japan and Europe and effect her transition to the social system of rising peace. The final stage of Great Peace was still several centuries distant, K'ang believed, although the political systems of Switzerland and the United States, as republican nations, already exhibited in embryo the egalitarianism which would then permeate all social relationships. Such a world, sketched in the *Ta-t'ung shu*, would be without any social distinctions based on property, class, race or sex. Here the nation-state itself would be superseded by a global parliamentary government, and all people would accept common customs and be united in common faith.

K'ang's *ta-t'ung* seemed to break with the fundamentals of Confucian belief by its assertion that the perfectly moral society should have no hierarchical social distinctions; it arrived at this position through a development of the classic Mencian idea that the 'extension' of benevolence in the world springs from the nurture of natural human capacities for sympathy with others. Thus, extended and universalized human goodness

10 Quoted in Fung Yu-lan, *A history of Chinese philosophy*, 1.378.

becomes 'love' (*jen*), which in K'ang's version was conceived as a dynamic cosmic-moral energy. As such, it evinced itself in what he saw as the power of attraction and repulsion inherent in the motions of the external cosmos as well as in the surges of spontaneous 'attractive' sentiment which underlie the moral life of conscious beings. During the age of rising peace social norms, or *li*, still permitted a limited or 'partial' expression of human solidarity, by allowing for ethical distinctions between near and far, or high and low; in the age of the great community social customs would have cast off all such 'selfishness', and would perfectly reflect a spirit of undifferentiated universal love (*jen*).

Thus K'ang's model of natural and social evolution took off from the historical transition from barbarism to civilization, and included a secular vision of advanced democratic and affluent societies suggested by Western examples. Yet fundamentally he believed that the whole process was an odyssey of human spiritual perfection. Underpinning his prophecy of a utopia through modernization lay the traditional Neo-Confucian vision of an organismic cosmos transformed through the self-actualization of the sage's sincere mind. Yet K'ang's version suggested a novel relationship between the poles of that organism: that is, between the sage on the one hand and the external cosmos of 'Heaven and Earth' on the other. Rather than placing sages in the centre as the source of cosmic transformations, K'ang imagined them almost as spectators before the awesome panorama of the universe. *Jen*, though still playing its role as the source of the moral consciousness of the individual, manifested itself most potently in the external sphere – in the starry heavens, in the dynamism of change itself. From this came his orientation towards materialism, the seeds of cosmological determinism, and a radical moral optimism. Gone was the common Neo-Confucian tendency to anxiety over cosmic deficiency and moral failure; instead K'ang breathed confidence that spontaneous human desires are in harmony with *jen*, and that personal enjoyment, pleasure, abundance – all these as well as enlightenment were to be expected bounties of the utopia of the future. The sage would not create social utopia; history itself would. If the attainment of spiritual perfection would come through the collapse of social barriers to human community, K'ang imagined this less as the result of human struggle than as a gift of liberation.

Therefore, this dream of the human conquest of selfishness appeared devoid of any strong sense of the necessity of internal struggle to overcome it. Indeed K'ang usually explained the obstacles to moral success as arising from environmental and ritual 'barriers' external to the self. But he also defined moral action in practice as requiring in fact acceptance of these barriers, that is, as action suited to the times in which one happens to live. As such the evolution of the spirit becomes a deterministic cosmic unfolding: 'When the proper time arrives, the changes suited to it take place of themselves'. Only a seer's foreknowledge might be said in part to determine the future even in reflecting it; the true moral action of the sage, then, lies in prophecy.

Presented in this context, K'ang's specific social ideals, though modern and even 'Westernized' in detail, still lacked a truly secular autonomy within his system of belief. The imagery he preferred (that of the 'nine barriers' to human community) echoed that of classic statements of the mystical experience – Confucian and otherwise – where the ordinary boundaries between the self, the external world and the numinous are at least fluid, at most obliterated entirely. K'ang's social ideal emphasized the elimination of political, racial, sexual and national barriers, not so much because such hierarchies were evil as because all differentiation of phenomena obscures the truth that on the level of philosophic truth 'reality' is 'one'. On the psychosocial level, the *Ta-t'ung shu* did express K'ang's own protest against the constraints of familism. These barriers he indeed keenly felt as evils, but here too K'ang was bypassing the intermediate sphere of social relations. For him barriers were seen as either concrete constraints upon individuals in their personal lives, or as abstract illusions due to an imperfect metaphysical understanding.

In this way K'ang's adaptation of Confucian metaphysics shifted the balance between sage and cosmos: as a teleological force K'ang's external cosmos had more purposeful dynamism than the traditional view easily allowed; as a limited foreknower of the process of change, the sage had correspondingly less. T'an Ssu-t'ung's work redressed the balance. In reasserting the ideal of the sages' power, he created a politicized sage as secular hero. He offered a dialectical model of external cosmic forces of enlightenment and resistance as the necessary theatre for the drama of sagely self-actualization. Put together, the two views made evolutionary cosmology evoke both cosmic mechanisms and human powers at play in an expanding universe.

If K'ang's book reflected its author's self-image as a prophet T'an's might be said to suggest his finally chosen destiny as a martyr. In its moral activism religious saviours were seen as the key agents of world historical change; at the same time T'an imagined the final culmination of that change would be the transcendence of selfhood itself. Where K'ang did not look far beyond an earthly paradise, T'an made the final goal of evolution secondary to a stage when even human consciousness as presently conceived would cease to exist.

Like K'ang, T'an posited cosmic-moral energies which, by regulating their own motions, are presumed to create the structures of the 'things' in which they inhere. This view implied a criticism of the Neo-Confucian dualism of 'principle' (*li*) and 'material force' (*ch'i*), and was bolstered by physical notions borrowed from Western science; but his model of the motions of 'matter' was more heavily indebted to Buddhist-Taoist pheno-menology. Where K'ang identified *ch'i* (material force) with 'electricity', T'an started with the idea that 'ether' was the unitary material substance permeating, inhering and connecting all the realms of phenomena, space and living things. But while the basic substance was defined as material, the all-important mode of its active functioning was moral: '*jen* is the function of ether'. Thus, the transformations of ether are generated through the activity of moral energy, and the identifying characteristic of this activity, T'an called *t'ung*.

'Pervasiveness', 'communication', 'permeability', 'circulation': *t'ung* eludes translation least when juxtaposed with its opposite, *sai* or 'obstruc-tion', 'stoppage'. By means of this key concept T'an achieved a comple-mentarity K'ang had missed between the structure of his cosmology and the structure of his ideal social relations. The moral functioning of ether is most apparent when the boundaries of things are permeable. In the realm of society they may be boundaries of culture, nationality, custom; or the economic boundaries which inhibit trade and communication among peoples. In the realm of interpersonal relations they are the bar-riers of selfishness which prevent moral community. On the natural level they are boundaries which organize the psycho-physical continuum into discrete phenomena bounded by time and space, distinguished relationally in terms of their opposites, defined imperfectly as 'objects' by individuated human egos. In its most truly perfected form, then, the moral activity of ether in its unimpeded flow would reveal the interconnected unity of everything: the truth of the Confucian metaphysical axiom, 'the great man regards Heaven, Earth, and the myriad things as one body.'

In this way, T'an derived the socially revolutionary prescription to 'break through the nets' of the existing Confucian order. T'an saw tradi-tional Chinese as enslaved to the 'doctrine of names' (*ming-chiao*). Lin-guistic 'naming' – a primary human tool used to identify phenomena of experience according to their discrete characteristics – historically had been understood in China as Confucius' method of rendering moral judgments and so defining moral norms. Therefore, for T'an, it became the symbol for the formal hierarchical norms of personal and political conduct prescribed as the *li* or 'five relationships'. T'an's theory of pro-gress envisaged the overthrow of the current social system based upon *li* under the influence of the quickening activity of *jen*. This can be interpreted as the inner message of the book's title: as the human 'learning of love' is perfected, human beings will come to enjoy a more lively and abundant material life, quicker, more natural and spontaneous emotional experience, more egalitarian political and personal relationships, and an ever broadening spiritual consciousness.

T'an's projection of evolution extended from the original generation of the cosmos to a final age of 'Great Peace'. He combined the New Text *schema* of the 'three ages', the facts of geological and biological evolution as he understood them, and aspects of traditional Taoist cosmology. Thus he proceeded from the primary differentiation of existence from non-existence, through the formation of the solar system and the presumed march of the Darwinian evolutionary process towards higher and higher forms of organic life. For the future he predicted the eventual uniform distribution over the globe of a human population hundreds of times its present size, yet protected from threats to health and sustenance by the achievements of science and medicine. The advance of science would be aided by an innate evolutionary tendency of successive generations of living beings to assume ever more refined and spiritual forms, leading eventually to a race of 'pure intelligences', able to live on air and water, and to escape the confines of the earth itself.

However, at the most general level, T'an believed that the pattern of all these changes was to be discerned, fittingly, in the *I ching* or *Book of changes* itself. T'an's final cosmic myth of evolution depended for its logic on the numerological symbolism of the primary *I ching* hexagram, *ch'ien*, and on a biological metaphor of stages of the life-cycle as traditionally associated with the spiritual development of Confucius. He envisaged six stages, the first three a devolution from the primitive 'great peace' of archaic tribal society to Confucius' own 'world of disorder'; the second three an ascension through the disorder of the later empire to the 'ascending peace' of the near future, culminating in the final 'great peace' where, like Confucius in his old age, people would 'follow [their] heart's desire without transgressing what is right'. For T'an the structure of each age was determined by the role of political rulers and religious teachers in society – proceeding from the gradual emergence of these forms of leadership to their unification on a global scale, which in turn would prepare the way for a world in which 'everyone possesses the virtue of a religious teacher and so the religious teacher is eliminated; everyone possesses the power of a ruler and so the ruler is eliminated'.[11]

11 T'an Ssu-t'ung, *Jen hsueh*, reprinted in *T'an Ssu-t'ung ch'üan chi* (The complete works of T'an Ssu-t'ung, 1966), 88.

Unlike K'ang Yu-wei, T'an Ssu-t'ung was not content with a teleology devoid of any central human mechanism, and his theory included a model of the role of moral action in the cosmic process. This model formed a bridge between conventional Neo-Confucian models of self-cultivation and an ethic which defined the good both instrumentally in terms of future goals, and subjectively by the psyche's experience of internal struggle to attain them. At the beginning of the reform movement T'an had spoken of the commitment to change as requiring 'daily renewal'. However, in the *Jen hsueh* he introduced another, more original concept, 'psychic energy' (*hsin-li*) with the message that the psyche capable of working in tandem with the energies of the cosmos moves in an open-ended, developmental direction, and finds its expression in active struggle to change the world. Fully developed, 'psychic energy' would be expressed in actions combining the spontaneous empathy of Mencian mind (*hsin*) with the salvationist compassion of the Bodhisattva. Here of course T'an was constructing a theory of the self which could correspond to his cosmology of circulating ether. However, it was critical to his conception that psychic energy, as a form of ether in motion, was seen as stimulated to its characteristic activity in proportion as it met forces of resistance. For its own self-perfection, sincere mind required obstacles to overcome. 'The more we progress, the greater the obstacles, and this continues ceaselessly without rest'.[12] Further, psychic energy is 'what people rely upon to perform tasks',[13] that is, an instrument used to attain goals analytically separable from its own activity, and so containing a morally ambiguous potential. In the final pages of the *Jen hsueh*, T'an chose to return to the religious saviour as his preferred human agent of evolutionary change. But his sensitivity to the Faustian ideal of human action in a progress-oriented cosmos linked his own philosophy and that of the Social Darwinian, Yen Fu.

Yen Fu advocated the infusion of Anglo-Saxon liberalism into Chinese politics, because he saw its characteristic 'individualism' as the 'psychic energy' driving the movements of advanced scientific and industrial civilization. Since that civilization took its shape from these Faustian energies of striving individuals acting in and upon the world, the key to his underlying cosmology lay in the theories of Herbert Spencer. 'He has explained all transformations in terms of evolution. He has written books and composed treatises which embrace Heaven, earth and humanity under one principle'.[14]

12 *Ibid.* 74.
13 *Ibid.* 80.
14 The basic study of Yen Fu in English is Benjamin Schwartz, *In search of wealth and power: Yen Fu and the West*. The excerpted quotation is on p. 111.

Most deeply satisfying in Spencer's philosophy was its underlying monistic view of natural and social evolution as a unilinear progression from the simple and homogeneous to the heterogeneous and complex. The agent of evolution was the Darwinian mechanism of struggle for survival among species and the elimination of the weak by the strong. In Yen Fu's view this process was benign both because it served the ends of civilization, and because the 'strength, intelligence and morality'[15] of successful competitors in the social evolutionary process was itself in his eyes an admirable thing. Successful human groups 'begin in mutual antagonism; they end by completing one another.'[16] His major book on Darwinism, the translation of Huxley's *Evolution and ethics* (published in Chinese as *T'ien-yen lun*), argues in favour of Spencer as opposed to Huxley in that human ethics and the natural forces of evolutionary selection are seen as complementary parts of an overall cosmic process. *Ch'ün hsueh*, Yen Fu's term for Spencer's sociology, is an allusion to the idea of 'groups' in the naturalistic philosophy of Hsun-tzu, in which it is claimed that human beings owe their position at the top of the hierarchy of living things to their social 'grouping' instinct. Yen Fu believed that human groups which excel in ever more complex forms of social organization would create the culture that eventually inherits the earth.

In his selection of European classics which would acquaint his compatriots with nineteenth-century liberalism – in his view the Western value system *par excellence* – Yen Fu proved most sensitive to the historicist and sociological themes of his originals. Looking at Adam Smith, he stressed the utilitarian 'invisible hand' by which the action of individual enlightened self-interest worked to serve the long-term economic needs of society. In Mill's *On Liberty* he was impressed with the role of freedom in providing an arena for impartial truth-seeking, so that in the long run society might be united on the basis of correct commonly-held principles. To explain the importance of law in European politics, Yen Fu turned to Montesquieu, yet even here his affinity lay with Montesquieu's doubts about legislated 'natural rights', and with his contrasting sense that strong social determinants shape political institutions. Throughout, Yen Fu interpreted the European liberal tradition in ways which pointed to a natural complementarity between self-assertive individual action and the needs of the social organism.

Like the evolutionary theorists of the New Text School, Yen Fu had an overview of human history, which envisaged a unilinear march of progress to a future democratic and industrial world marked by abundance

15 Yen Fu, 'Yuan ch'iang' (On strength). For reprint see *Yen Chi-t'ao hsien-sheng i-chu* (Posthumous works of Yen Fu), 101.
16 *Ibid.* 107.

and enlightenment. However, in analysing its stages, he focused less on the utopian distance and more on the present national task of transition to a level of parity with the West in 'wealth and power'. Spencer had laid down the path of progress as moving from tribal and patriarchal forms of society to the 'military state' of early modern nationhood, and beyond. Yen Fu believed the Chinese present represented an uneasy turning-point between these first two. As the pioneer modern theorist of Chinese backwardness, he argued China had enjoyed the political form of the military state since Ch'in, but that its natural development had been stunted by the continuing influence of 'patriarchal' Confucian cultural norms, absolutized as a code of ritual morality (*li*). Progress would come through the psychological transformation of great numbers of individual Chinese who were to cultivate in themselves the 'strength, intelligence and morality' the nation needed to build a powerful enlightened modern culture. Here Yen Fu's belief in the determining power of culture, which is of human making, counterbalanced much of his pessimism concerning China's backwardness. Dependent upon an effort of national spirit rather than upon material constraints, China's prospects were directly correlated with the people's capacity for self-transformation.

If to be a Confucianist one must embrace its humanistic metaphysics, Yen Fu would scarcely qualify, even in the unconventional manner in which K'ang Yu-wei and T'an Ssu-t'ung did. His method of moralizing the cosmos was otherwise: it was not some inner altruistic core of sincere mind which defined those human actions which truly led to progress, but rather the capacity of such action impersonally to serve the times itself. In this way Yen Fu shifted the balance even further from the transforming power of virtue as an internal quality of the sage personality and towards the adaptive power of the insightful intelligence as a response to socio-historical forces. Yet even this seemingly more deterministic ideal of human action in an evolutionary cosmos was substantially counterbalanced by another consequence of Yen Fu's detachment from the Confucian sage personality ideal in ethics. His emphasis upon individualism was inextricably linked with a belief that 'the people are true lords of the world'. His conception of nationalism was built upon this conviction that the collective energy of a whole people constitutes the critical mass which makes cultural development possible. When K'ang and T'an spoke of universal moral ends for which the nation state could only be a transient vehicle, they pointed inwards to personal salvation as the means embracing the paradox – in T'an's words – that 'in saving the world one may fail to save oneself; in saving only oneself one may yet save the world'.[17]

17 *T'an Ssu-t'ung ch'üan chi*, 89.

In solidly resting his hopes on a progressive enlightened people, Yen Fu was a pioneer of the populist interpretation of Chinese nationalism.

However, in spite of these differences all three saw evolution organically as a total process linking natural, social and spiritual forces in an inter-dependent whole. All believed that this interdependence extended over time as well, enabling the mind of the philosopher to encompass the whole from the experience of any one of its stages. Most important, all were equally convinced that an ineffable metaphysical 'unknowable', itself lying outside the process, still constituted the ground against which it developed. Where the first two grounded their theories in the Confucian humanist's faith in *jen* as a cosmic force, Yen Fu's metaphysics was more Taoist. He identified Spencer's 'unimaginable' with the mystical scep-ticism of Lao-tzu, and his acceptance of evolutionary necessity was deeply informed by that sage's anti-anthropomorphic mystical naturalism. Above all, the cosmos envisaged by all these reformers possessed an open-ended dynamism which implied fundamental social change, and which in the case of T'an and Yen, incorporated the idea of struggle in and of itself as the characteristic function of virtuous 'mind'. This introduced into Chinese cosmological thought a sense that the expanding universe of scientific law was matched in the Faustian energies of human actions. Such in sum were the evolutionary laws constantly referred to in reform literature as '*kung-li*' – the 'universal principles of nature and society'.

Of the four great reform leaders, Liang Ch'i-ch'ao strayed least from the political issues of the immediate present, and the imperatives for action these created. His journalistic immediacy was an important source of his enormous popularity and influence, even as the variability of mood and opinion it entailed aroused criticism as well. But it was his historical perspective, in fact, which made him look for the key to broad patterns of evolutionary change in contemporary events. Yen Fu and the Japanese thinker Katō Hiroyuki were the sources of Liang's knowledge of Social Darwinism, in the latter's hands given a heightened nationalist and racialist interpretation. However, even as he analysed the modern era of imperialism in which Asians and Westerners were locked in struggle for hegemony, he was sketching out a philosophy of history and a theory of human action whose cosmological underpinnings recall T'an Ssu-t'ung, and which developed the Faustian implications of Yen Fu's inter-pretation of Western individualism.

Cosmologically, Liang's structures were comparatively simple. He coalesced T'an's 'ether' and 'psychic energy' into a single concept: 'dynamism' (*tung-li*), or the kinetic energy in material and spiritual phe-nomena. 'Where there is dynamism [*tung*] there is interpenetration [*t'ung*];

where there is interpenetration there is *jen*, so all mutually sympathetic things cannot remain apart like Ch'in and Yueh, but must be activated by consciousness and create the new without end.'[18] However, by introducing a 'dialectic' element into this framework Liang suggested that the socio-historical pattern of change is based on the alternation of cosmic 'motive forces' of action and resistance In concrete terms, the recent past in Europe and China was one in which repressive forces of autocracy had given rise to an inevitable counter-movement of resistance in the form of a rising social demand for people's rights.

By linking historical movements with an account of the metahistorical forces presumed to be responsible for them, Liang presented both a moralized version of Darwinian evolution, and a conception of liberty as the attribute of those found 'fit' in the Darwinian struggle. By people's rights (*min-ch'üan*), Liang was explicit that he did not mean the 'natural rights' of Western Enlightenment political theory, but rather something closer to effective capabilities, won by striving individuals through the successful exertion of their energies. 'Rights' are really a kind of 'power' (*ch'üan-li*), Liang declared, though insisting that this did not invalidate the moral basis of the political ideal. 'This doctrine [of *ch'üan-li*] seems the negation [of people's rights] but actually is the perfection of it'.[19] Implicitly then, 'rights' are a manifestation of the psychic energies of the self maximally extended beyond the mind to the outside world. Histori-cally, Europe's ancient liberties had been aristocratic privileges forcibly preserved, while modern democratic liberties had been won through popular struggle and revolution. Further, since the psychic energies of individuals are characterized by inherent powers of mutual attraction, an ever broader consolidation of 'groups' would appear the natural result of evolutionary struggle. Liang's famous call for the emergence of a 'new people' (*hsin min*) in China pointed the liberated individual in this same collectivist direction. Thus, the progress of human liberty was described as the spread of the collective human power of dynamism to wider and wider groups of humanity – a process exhibited in primitive times through the struggle between tribes, and expected to culminate in the distant future as a result of the successful assertion of 'rights' by the weakest members of the human race – the common people (*p'ing-min*) and women.

As in T'an Ssu-t'ung, Liang's theory of human action in the historical

18 Liang Ch'i-ch'ao, 'Shuo tung' (On dynamism), first published 1898, reprinted in *Yin-ping-shih wen-chi* (Collection from the ice drinker's studio; hereafter *YPSWC*), *ts'e* 2. 37–40. See also Chang Hao, *Liang Ch'i-ch'ao and intellectual transition in China, 1890–1907*.
19 Jen-kung [Liang Ch'i-ch'ao], 'Lun ch'iang ch'üan' (On power), *Ch'ing-i pao*, no. 31 (1899).

process assigned a positive value to reactionary forces (such as autocracy and imperialism) – as necessary to motivate the reactive dynamism of the generators of progress. He also asserted that the psyche's inborn power of movement in struggle itself led to more human self-actualization through the creation of higher forms of social 'grouping'. From the cosmic perspective the dynamism which generated historical change exhibited something like a principle of entropy. Liang believed that human equality would finally be achieved when the energies of domination and those of resistance were evenly balanced throughout the world. The utopian great community (ta-t'ung) would be undifferentiated – its social manifestation would be equally shared power; its historical manifestation, stasis or the end of history.[20]

Unlike T'an Ssu-t'ung, Liang Ch'i-ch'ao in 1902 specifically denied that his philosophy of historical evolution had a Confucian core. Jen, he said, was too 'yielding' a virtue to be the motive force of the self-development of a modern nation. Nonetheless the definitive statement of his philosophy of history written the same year remained rooted in assumptions about the evolutionary process itself which substantially overlapped those of the others. He asserted that 'humanity is the pivot [chi-tse] of evolution, the inexhaustible source of its transformations.' When he asked that his 'new history' be based upon study of the evolution of social 'groups' (ch'ün), he acknowledged their common organicism. He saw race as a key source of group cohesion and therefore a basis for competition between contemporary 'groups' or nations. But nonetheless Liang believed that the psychic energies expressed through the total manifestations of a culture were the dominant agents of change in individual social systems. In claiming that history would serve the nation by disclosing the directions of social change, he was making a common claim for the existence of a historical teleology known to scholars through their intuition of the metahistorical 'spirit' (ching-shen) presumed to inform and guide it. In claiming a legitimate place for the 'subjective' in historical writing, he was not simply giving licence to interpretive opinion, but pointing to the creative contribution of those with foresight whose subjective mind is capable of grasping the total historical continuum in a synthesis.[21]

All in all, the evolutionary cosmologies of the major reform thinkers form a spectrum: from a more cosmic to a more human-centred concept of the forces underlying world change, from comparatively static to more

20 Liang Ch'i-ch'ao, 'Shuo ch'ün hsu' (Preface to 'groups'), YPSWC, ts'e 2. 3–4.
21 See the following essays by Liang Ch'i-ch'ao: 'Chung-kuo shih hsu-lun' (Sketch of Chinese history), YPSWC, ts'e 3. 1–12; 'Kuo-chia ssu-hsiang pien-ch'ien i-t'ung lun' (On similarity and difference in alterations in national thought), ibid. ts'e 3. 12–22; 'Kuo-tu shih-tai' (A transitional age), ibid. ts'e 3. 27–32.

dialectical models of them, and from less to more emphasis upon the modern nation as a positive factor in the evolutionary process. All of these marked a shift away from Confucian-Taoist metaphysics towards a more naturalistic, historicized and secular model of the evolutionary process. Liang Ch'i-ch'ao demonstrated both his understanding of this spectrum and the limits he set on it when he offered his view of the function of the philosophy of history in the modern world. It should, he said, provide a substitute for religious dogma: by which he meant a complete explanatory system concerning human society, the causal patterns underlying events, and the moral purposes implicit in them. For Liang, as for the other reformers, evolutionism provided for a new ethic of personal striving in association with a philosophy of modernization. At the same time, evolutionism endowed the future with cosmically grounded moral purposes, allowing him like the other reformers to hope their innovations would serve to perfect a traditionally recognized kingdom of ends.

Ta-t'ung and Western models for institutional change

Evolutionary cosmology supplied the framework for the Chinese reformers' interpretation of the strengths of Western civilization, powerfully influencing the way European and American nations were taken as models of progress. Western accounts too often assume that Asian reformers' admiration of the West was simply a belated appreciation of the West's true achievements. This neglects both the limits and biases in reformers' sources of information, and the implications given to that information at Chinese disposal by the overarching value system within which it was assimilated. Both the Protestant missionaries and the anglicized Chinese of the treaty ports, who were the early tutors of the reform leadership, certainly spoke as apostles and apologists for Victorian civilization. In Meiji Japan, Chinese reformers had an alternate model for successful Westernization already filtered through East Asian cultural adaptations. However, in responding to the optimistic picture of Western economic and political institutions these accounts suggested, Chinese were combining a genuine sense of discovery with their own utopian projections. The 'West' in this sense served not only as a 'real' model of civilized alternatives, but also as a repository for ideal images projected out of the historical imagination of the Chinese themselves. Filtered through the interpretive matrix of reform cosmology, science and democracy appeared to be the material and social manifestations of a total cosmic order linked to the ultimate ends of ta-t'ung. Science and technology offered a vision of a materialist universe whose secrets would yield wealth and power such as had eluded generations of imperial rulers. Democracy suggested institutions by which Chinese might revitalize their political community, bringing it closer to the perennial ideal of 'public-mindedness'.

The first major contribution of Western science to Chinese reform thought was as the theoretical underpinning of evolutionary cosmology itself. In using concepts of physics as building blocks for their philosophy, both K'ang Yu-wei and T'an Ssu-t'ung communicated a new kind of certainty that truths of nature were reliably known. They thought that science demonstrated the relativity of all phenomena, an ideal more revolutionary to them in its cultural and social application than in its theoretical essentials. Confucian philosophy did not make humanistic values dependent upon a cosmological divide between spirit and matter. Nor had these values historically been associated with the notion of a spatially fixed, anthropocentric world, or a taxonomically fixed human species marked off from nature by a unique capacity for transcendence.

Because of this – and all the more because nineteenth-century missionaries themselves typically taught science as a kind of natural theology, proof of Heavenly Design – the reformers found in science a confirmation of Buddhist-Taoist phenomenology untainted by the corrosion of scepticism. For K'ang the instruments of scientific measurement showed the relativity of our ordinary perceptions: we 'see' the light of a dead star but do not see the swirling molecules which make up a drop of water. For T'an scientific theories of the underlying construction of matter 'come close to destroying relativity' as a final – as opposed to an initial – truth of experience. Both drew the analogy with Buddhist cosmology, and exuberantly gave way to a Mahayana sense of possible worlds – of 'world seas' beyond the galaxies, and 'lotus seas' beyond the 'world seas'; of 'unimaginable realms' where the 'divine sages play'. Thus science reinforced their belief in an external, determinative cosmos which was in and of itself a source of God-like power relatively independent of human will.

Obviously neither K'ang nor T'an understood how definitions of scientific truth must be controlled by experimental verification. They felt free to incorporate into their cosmologies as science the traditional constructs of speculative reason. Nonetheless, they believed in scientific truth the more because empirical observation on the one hand, and mathematics on the other appeared to support it. K'ang was a keen astronomical observer, and T'an experimented with classical mechanics; both were fascinated by mathematics as a kind of deductive reasoning capable of expressing the truths of nature they thought they discerned. For T'an algebra supplied an abstract method of stating the universal cosmological relationships of relatives and the constant. K'ang, an ethical relativist in the sense that he saw social morality as historically conditioned, tried to prove that final moral truths are best expressed in the axioms of Euclidian geometry.

By contrast Yen Fu's appreciation of science rested more on a belief in a methodology of verification. This led him to translate first J. S. Mill's *Logic*, and then Stanley Jevons, in an effort to introduce to China principles of induction as the foundation of all solid truth-seeking. Even so, in spite of this pioneering role in introducing positivistic philosophy of science, as a 'social scientist' Yen Fu was like the others in his belief that the facts of science – here in particular Darwinian biology – confirmed the authority of his entire evolutionary cosmology.

A keen practical appreciation of Western technology had been commonplace in statecraft circles since the early days of the 'self-strengthening' movement in the 1860s; however, the reformers' new faith in science as a kind of true cosmology made it easier for them to welcome the coming of technological civilization. The 1898 reform leaders took the basic step of accepting the socially transformative potential of industrialization. Almost equally important, they came to see that technological change is open-ended, both necessitating a continued flow of invention, and holding open the possibility that problems of human health and welfare deemed intractable today might be solved by methods to be developed in the future. The view that economic development and scientific progress were valuable as a means to the nationalist ends of independence and state power was a staple of reform propaganda, but the leaders went significantly beyond this to present the fruits of development as human goods in their own right.

They not only submitted plans for developing strategic industries like railways and mines; they also offered classic meliorative arguments for the mechanization of production: it would create jobs and increase leisure too; scientific agriculture would augment the food supply; modern communications would facilitate the world-wide spread of enlightenment. If these views suggest a Chinese version of a classic nineteenth-century faith in industrial progress, equally typical of such a faith was the Chinese reformers' conviction that they did not face any insurmountable material obstacles to success. To Western scepticism about China's ability to modernize, Liang Ch'i-ch'ao replied by echoing the Europeans' own confidence in the resources of science and invention to overcome problems of population and food supply. He and others imitated Europe's own confidence in the inexhaustible resources of nature by assuming that a nation of China's size and diversity must enjoy a full measure of these waiting

to be exploited. Consciousness of backwardness was there, but counterbalanced by a 'great leap' mentality which showed up most strikingly
in the summer of 1898. All reformers, even the sober Yen Fu, spoke of
overtaking Europe in decades at the most, observing that Europe's own
economic pre-eminence was recent, and that latecomers to development
have the advantage of being able to learn from their precursors' mistakes.

The social costs of industrialism, so visible in Europe itself, were
little discussed in the early years of reform. When K'ang Yu-wei or
Liang Ch'i-ch'ao noted in passing that the growth of industrial capitalism
in Europe so far had not eliminated, and might even have widened, the
gap between the rich and the poor, they saw this as Europe's moral failure,
but neither an inevitable nor a permanent feature of the development
process. T'an Ssu-t'ung offered an arresting ethical defence of capitalist
behaviour by comparing the liberality of extravagance with the stinginess
of thrift. His conclusion was that by contrast with traditional agrarian
habits of frugality – hoarding and saving – the capitalist modes of spending
and investing expressed the spirit of 'permeability' (*t'ung*) in the economic
sphere. This does not mean that he or the other reformers understood
consumer capitalism as the end of development. T'an rather believed that
the attainment of material abundance would liberate people from enslave-
ment to their desires for things; while K'ang prophesied that in the
world of the 'great community' wealth would be shared publicly by all.
Capitalist development represented the inevitable, indeed the only model
at hand, but in light of the altruistic moral ideal of *ta-t'ung* it was perceived as only a stage. From the other end, Liang Ch'i-ch'ao, on being
exposed to the ideal of socialism in 1902, heartily approved of it, seeing
it as the natural direction for advanced economic systems to take towards
a pre-established goal.

While Western science and technology promised to transform society
materially, democracy aroused hopes for political renewal. Here the
reformers had both an immediate target of criticism in the imperial
autocracy, and a long-term ideal of 'public' government which had eluded
centuries of bureaucratic practice.

Historically, Chinese practitioners of statecraft had seen the goal of
'public' government as a moral spirit of politics. In organizing public
administration and recruiting leaders they had posed two broad alternatives, each with unacceptable costs. One was a 'feudal' model of hereditary
local self-government, which was believed to foster a commonality
(*kung*) of ties between the ruling group and the people at the grass-roots
level, but at the cost of privatizing rulership in local hereditary families.
The other was a 'bureaucratic' model of an impersonal centralized civil

service, which was more effective in enforcing a commonality (*kung*) of impartial regulation, but at the cost of estranging the governing elite from the people. Exposure to Anglo-Saxon politics and the 'spirit of public morality' widely believed to prevail among the citizens of parliamentary democracies gave reformers hope for a resolution of this ancient dilemma. 'Public assemblies' (*i-yuan*) seemed capable of resolving the tension between the values of community and those of impartiality, and so realizing the Confucian-Legalist synthesis in the political ideal of 'public mindedness'.

Since reformers contrasted the 'public' rule of constitutional assemblies with the 'private' rule of imperial autocrats, people looked to parliamentary politics as a corrective to typically bureaucratic evils, tipping their interpretation of the ideal in the 'feudal' communitarian direction. Some in the K'ang-Liang group felt that public assemblies would rectify just about every widely recognized defect of the imperial administrative system, from its over-centralization to its stress on seniority or duplication of office. As an alternative to bureaucracy, rather than, as in the West, to hereditary class rule, parliaments were imagined to provide a finely articulated system of *communication* among all levels of participation in the political process. Confucianism assumed that correct political action must be based upon commonly recognized principles, and so assemblies were valued not for mediating among a plurality of interests, but rather as educative and expressive instruments for achieving a common consensus. Thus they were conceived as a corrective to the moral evils of officialism: estrangement papered over by commandism on high; submission accompanied by covert criticism from below. The goal was less to create a formal equality of status between rulers and ruled than to create a community of understanding and purpose among them.

Thus idealized, the Chinese reformers viewed constitutional systems as the political form naturally appropriate to highly evolved social groups. T'an Ssu-t'ung stated the organic collectivist interpretation of such democratic political forms in a particularly forceful way. Instead of having purely political assemblies, he proposed that the problems of the reform agenda be attacked by a network of voluntary 'study societies' (*hsueh-hui*), representing functional groupings in society: farmers, artisans, merchants, students, officials, and so forth. These would provide a forum for the common pursuit of enlightenment among persons with a natural unity of purpose in a context linking learning with action. 'In this way,' he dreamed, 'people who are distant will be brought close, what is bogged down will move forward; the stopped-up will flow, the separate will unite, the obscure become clear, and the weak strong; moreover, broad publicity will lead people to speak, allowing no concealment'.[22]

Viewed in this harmonious light, democracy suggested to the reformers analogies with utopian models of politics drawn from antiquity. K'ang and T'an believed that Confucius was a reformer not only because he understood the principle of adaptation to change, but also because he upheld a 'democratic' ideal of rule by the virtuous, exemplified in the ancient sage kings Yao, Shun and the Duke of Chou. Liang Ch'i-ch'ao made still more forceful claims for a 'democratic spirit' in Mencius' view that the mandate of Heaven finally lay with the people; while some others even conjectured that public assemblies had actually existed in the Chou dynasty. For Yen Fu, Lao-tzu was the antique source of a democratic spirit of personal independence and social 'yielding'.

Western scholars have commonly viewed such analogies as inspired by cultural nationalism: the desire to find native Chinese 'equivalents' for admired aspects of Western culture. Among conservative Chinese at the time they were denounced as efforts to gain respectability for new ideas by cloaking them in native dress, while later Chinese radicals dismissed them as disguised traditionalism. However, within the K'ang-Liang group itself there was recognition of evolution even as reformers found these classical analogies compelling. What they admired in antiquity, they said, was the latent essence in incipient form of an essential moral ideal that history would realize and complete. Yen Fu and Liang Ch'i-ch'ao combined explicit recognition that Mencius' populism, for example, was more paternalistic than participatory with the conviction that whatever the 'germs' of 'ancient democracy' may have been in China or in Greece, they were organically linked by the logic of historical evolution with the full-blown democratic political systems only just presently coming into being in the modern world.

The original Chinese discovery of the West had led to the emergence of evolutionism as a reform philosophy in China. Evolutionism itself, by identifying the West with the future and the teleology of moral ends that symbolized, encouraged utopian thinking about Western institutions. Science and democracy remained the most admired aspects of Western civilization for most Chinese down through the May Fourth movement of 1919. At the same time the goals of development continued to be associated with the native utopian ideal of *ta-t'ung*: as entailing not only the creation but also the common sharing of wealth; as bringing the

22 T'an Ssu-t'ung, 'Chih shih p'ien' (Essay on public affairs), reprinted in Yang Chia-lo, ed. 3. 83–92. See p. 86.

elimination of status hierarchies, if not literally, then through the formation of new psychological bonds of community; as making possible the moral self-actualization of the individual.

It was a paradox that the 'West' as a total civilization was the object of this admiration during a period of its unprecedented imperialist encroachments on China. The same reform journals which sketched out the new cosmopolitan world-view also analysed the dangerous shifts in the Far Eastern power balance since 1895. Here the 'West' stood for the expansionist 'scramble for concessions' – in anything but a friendly light – and the K'ang-Liang group was deeply involved in the politics of national resistance.

Nonetheless reformers' accounts of imperialism were more self-critical than anti-Western. Domestically, the reformers wished to discredit the militant 'expel the barbarian' policies of the conservative '*ch'ing-i*' faction at court, which were held responsible for the recent military defeats. Even beyond this, however, there was no way to avoid the logical connection between pro-Westernism in culture and appeasement in foreign affairs, holding Chinese rather than foreigners as basically responsible for the crisis. Reform nationalist propaganda hammered away at the object lessons to be drawn from the history of fallen empires like Persia or Turkey, and of 'lost' peoples like the Poles, the Irish or the American Indians – all social organisms seen as having failed in the evolutionary struggle. The underlying message was that China's problems lay within.

In 1895 Yen Fu said simply that Westerners had not originally come to China with an intent to do harm. T'an Ssu-t'ung offered a subtle contamination theory of imperialism, pointing out that the 'strong and righteous' nations of the West, in their impatience to cure an ailing China, were resorting to methods of fraud and coercion which risked becoming their habitual mode of conduct, first abroad, but then also at home. Yet even this penetrating account of the dynamics of power's corruption was offered along with criticism of the weak, who, as targets of opportunity, had to acknowledge their own complicity in the occasion of crime. If the union of 'strength, morality and intelligence' which Yen Fu saw as the mark of powerful peoples was recognized as a synthesis subject to internal fluctuation, still to most reformers the interdependence of all parts was axiomatic. Confucianism taught that virtue and power come from a single source. Western strength was linked to the level of culture presumably attained by Western peoples. Blaming themselves for their powerlessness, Chinese reformers sought the remedy in the inherent momentum of evolution on the one hand, and on the other in their own efforts of psychological self-renewal.

Furthermore, after the 1898 'scramble for concessions' and the 1900 Boxer catastrophe had passed, the empress dowager finally committed the court to reform in 1901, making the prospects for internal development appear hopeful at long last. In spite of continued dangers from the Western powers, the nation appeared embarked upon the serious pursuit of its own modernization along lines pioneered in Meiji Japan. While the reading public was always more or less impatient with the pace of change as directed by the Manchu court, it exhibited through the new popular press growing enthusiasm for modern 'enlightenment' (wen-ming). A widely read serialized novel of 1903 affirmed the spirit of 'modern times':

Just look at what has happened over the past few years . . . people's minds have been stimulated and all levels of society have been roused to action. Are these not indications, like the sea and the wind, that the sun is about to rise and the rain to fall? Whether these people have succeeded or failed, flourished or declined, been public-minded or selfish, genuine or false, they eventually will be recognized as men of merit in a civilized world. . . . 'The vile and the beautiful are mutually transformed by change'. With these words I felicitate the future.[23]

And so the continued political disgrace and exile of Liang Ch'i-ch'ao, K'ang Yu-wei and many of their followers did not prevent the ideas they had pioneered from acquiring an influential constituency. By 1903 or 1904 evolutionism as a 'bland religion of modernization' was rapidly passing into the mainstream of elite culture.

The erosion of reformist evolutionary optimism

However, even as the reform consensus hardened, it began to be exposed to a new kind of attack. After 1905 reform gradualism was attacked by the revolutionary T'ung-meng hui. Reformers' appeasement of the West and of the court was now challenged by a new anti-imperialist and anti-Manchu militancy. Reform pro-Westernism in culture had to face a nativist backlash, the 'national essence' movement visible from about 1904. Finally, reform utopianism was vulnerable to the inevitable fear of failure – as evidence mounted suggesting Chinese backwardness was a more intractable burden than originally hoped.

The attitudes of Liang Ch'i-ch'ao, who abandoned 'revolution' for 'reform' between 1903 and 1911, display an underlying consistency when

---

23 Li Po-yuan, *Wen-ming hsiao-shih* (A little history of modern times), translated by Douglas Lancashire, *Renditions: a Chinese-English translation magazine*, 2 (Spring 1974) 128.

seen in this context.[24] Like Yen Fu, Liang had always tied the progressive evolution of Chinese politics to the spread of modern cultural enlightenment among the people. For this reason his populist ideal of 'the new citizen' was less organically holistic than it seemed. It incorporated a social distinction quite traditional in China between the civilized and the barbarian, the educated and the ignorant, and made confidence in progress depend upon the triumph of the former over the latter. Again like Yen Fu, Liang was from his first exposure to the Enlightenment concept of 'natural rights' generally sceptical of it. That the people might be sovereign through some form of abstractly legislated *a priori* rights was an idea incompatible with his own belief that political utopia would be arrived at through a historical process of human self-actualization.

With these assumptions, Liang's faith in the populist politics of the 'new citizen' was steadily undermined by what he took as evidence of continued moral backwardness in Chinese society. In practice these evils were identified more with the activities of the emerging revolutionary left after 1903 than with the traditional masses, as the new spirit of politics seemed to be leading to the 'backward' phenomenon of an anarchic breakdown of order.

In accommodating his belief system to the new requirements of gradualism, Liang simply adjusted evolutionary cosmology to a distopian interpretation. Instead of rapid advance, such an interpretation stressed cosmic reversals. Instead of emphasizing voluntarism – that success in the evolutionary struggle is the direct consequence of the exercise of human psychic powers – it stressed all of the historical determinants inhibiting people from changing themselves or society. Instead of holding out hope of moral success, it was haunted by the spectre of moral failure. This distopian version of evolutionary cosmology did not require a basic shift in assumptions, only a more pessimistic appraisal of the 'times' themselves, since evolutionism made events themselves the only source of interpretation.

Ironically, though evolutionary cosmology had explained the Chinese historical situation during a great political reform movement, it eventually came to suggest a sharply diminished role for 'politics' as an autonomous source of change. In the culminating event of the generation – the Revolution of 1911 – Chinese intellectuals had a powerful lesson in the impotence of groups of conscious political actors to accomplish their desired goals, a lesson which helped distopian evolutionism achieve wide currency. As the respected Shanghai organ of the constitutionalist movement, *Tung-fang tsa-chih* (Eastern miscellany), noted in 1914, a prin-

24 For Liang's political career see Philip Huang, *Liang Ch'i-ch'ao and modern Chinese liberalism*.

ciple of Spencerian sociology is that 'living organisms and social systems gradually change in order to maintain forms in harmony with their environment and circumstances'.[25] Their conclusion was that the Chinese national psychology must be recognized as ill-adapted to modern political forms. To Yen Fu the lesson of the new democracy was that 'the level of civilization of our masses cannot be forced'.[26] Liang Ch'i-ch'ao acknowledged that the revolution as an event was irreversible, but drew the lessons of a conservative historicism: 'the [imperial] political authority, once trampled, cannot recover its mystery'.[27]

If after 1911 a deterministic emphasis upon China's historical situation meant resignation to backwardness, stress on the human factor spelled acceptance of moral responsibility for failure. Evolutionary cosmology had balanced the determinism of cosmic forces with a complementary emphasis upon the Faustian human spirit as contributing to the process of change. Consequently the failure of the republic implied not merely fate but also moral blame. In the mood of disillusionment that swept the country, intellectuals freely castigated new republican office-holders, but their overall focus was not just on corruption of leadership, but on the cultural backwardness of the race which they thought it illustrated. Even as indignation poured forth, with it seeped the poison of self-accusation. Critical evaluations of the Chinese 'national character', and of 'national psychology' became stock essay themes after 1912. Inasmuch as these assumed that the people as a whole are the activating agents in the social organism, they carried on the voluntaristic tradition of reform thought, but in a context which inescapably compromised the reformers themselves.

Liang Ch'i-ch'ao's historiographical principles did not change, but the lessons he drew from history did. When in 1916 he looked back over the first five years of the republic, he still saw his own generation as a 'transitional age' whose 'motive force' had been the external stimulus of the West, causing the old doctrines to lose their credibility. The problem was, he thought, that China's 'reactive force' had dissipated itself in a single violent spasm of revolution and restorationist backlash. He still believed that human psychic energies move history in a long-term arc of progress, but for the present time in China he saw these as depleted by habituation to novelty, and feared that in the immediate future 'there will be no more thunder and lightning available for use'. Such exhaustion of

25 Ch'ien Chih-hsiu, 'Shuo t'i-ho' (On adaptation), *Tung-fang tsa-chih*, 10. 10 (1 Jan. 1914).
26 Quoted in Schwartz, *In search of wealth and power*, 218–19.
27 Liang Ch'i-ch'ao, 'Fu-ku ssu-ch'ao p'ing-i' (Critique of the restorationist thought tide), *Ta Chung-hua*, 1. 7 (20 July 1915).

spirit was seen as both cause and consequence of the fact that 'we are not in accord with the pattern of world cultural progress'.[28]

With such a conclusion, evolutionary cosmology among the reformers reached the end of the road. Reform discovery of the West – of the ideas of natural science and historical progress – had first stimulated what almost might be called a resurgence of organismic metaphysical theory. Evolution came to be imagined as a self-generating cosmic process, its dynamism and direction guided by 'dialectical' forces inherent within it. Then, as its teleology of moral ends was envisaged in the form of a social utopia identified with modernization, it became necessary for reformers to judge the system by the achievements of their own history itself. As the power of the cosmos was imagined in ways that dwarfed the role of the traditional sage, reformers tried to recreate him as a Faustian hero, or to collectivize human psychic energy as the 'spirit' (ching-shen) of the people. Each step constituted a de facto secularization, as the metaphysically grounded moral purposes which presumably constituted the 'motive force' of change were tested by people and events themselves. When moral teleology was no longer credibly perceived as at work in the world, evolutionary cosmology became a purely naturalistic system of belief, which maintained the integration of the social and cosmic orders at the cost of, in the Confucian sense, 'dehumanizing' men and women themselves. Beyond the resulting crisis of faith, which by the time of the May Fourth movement had touched all the surviving reform leaders, there had to emerge a different conceptual framework for understanding the relationship of historical process and spiritual value.

NATIONAL ESSENCE AND THE FUTURE OF CONFUCIANISM: THE EMERGENCE OF NEO-TRADITIONAL ALTERNATIVES

In the thinking of the original reform generation, evolutionary cosmology had first embraced change's possibilities and then increasingly justified adaptation to its necessities. However, whether a thinker stressed the moral ends embodied in the movements of the cosmos, or, alternatively, thought primarily of the naturalistic and social processes of history, neither pole of emphasis implied denial of linkage with the other. As the dissolution of China's traditional political order, anticipated since the 1890s, became a fact of revolutionary politics in 1911, these organicist assumptions became increasingly burdensome to their adherents. However much the monarchy may have been castigated for its political failures,

28 Liang Ch'i-ch'ao, 'Wu-nien-lai chih chiao-hsun' (Lessons of the past five years), Ta Chung-hua, 2. 10 (20 Oct. 1916).

it had been a sacred institution, symbolizing the interdependence of the Chinese value system and the socio-political order. The break-up of this unitary institution, and even more its apparent sequel in a rudderless, unprincipled and ineffective republic, was profoundly dispiriting.

As the links between the Confucian spiritual order and the socio-political system were thus seen to weaken, many intellectuals shifted from a philosophical language based upon the assumptions of evolutionary cosmology to one which more resembled evolutionary naturalism. The first was syncretic: it embraced science but also assumed Confucian-Taoist processes underlying nature were metaphysically prior and fundamental to science's functioning. The second was Westernized: it opted for contemporary physical models of the universe. The first saw consciousness as linked to the human spirit, and imagined it microcosmically – embodying the same forces that move the cosmos at large and capable, because of this, of interacting harmoniously with them. The second saw consciousness as psychology, and imagined human beings as purely biological and social organisms, so denying that human history can reflect ontology. Where the first balanced determinative cosmic processes against human heroes able to save society by activating the spirit of a 'new people', the second saw individuals and the realm of politics itself as determined by underlying sociological forces. Although the pull of such a naturalistic and sociological view of evolution was powerfully felt by men like Liang Ch'i-ch'ao, its secularist implications were in the final analysis unacceptable to surviving reformers.

Rather, evolutionary naturalism became the preserve of more radical thinkers. These included the extremist fringe among the republican revolutionaries, the anarchists. Their ideology, developed in the years immediately preceding the 1911 Revolution, glorified the institutional destabilization accompanying revolutionary moments in history, and also identified social revolution as the fundamental agent of progress. They also included the Westernizers of the emerging New Culture movement after 1911,[29] who began to construct a Marxist-derived critique of the 'feudal' social institutions responsible for China's backwardness. Such radicals did not entirely abandon metaphysical thinking about change based on traditional cosmological notions. But their debts to Confucianism were unacknowledged, papered over by a programmatic embrace of science not only as a naturalistic cosmology, but also as a positivist method of verification justifying the rejection of all tradition. The cumulative effect of these radical departures was to make their opponents identify

29 The classic study of intellectual radicalism in the May Fourth period is Chow Tse-tsung, *The May Fourth movement*.

the negative direction of republican politics and society squarely with an amoral secular rationalism of Western origin.

In this way, the erosion of the Confucian spiritual order and its invasion by the West could be seen as a secular erosion of all value. Those who thought this could not help being stirred by deep feelings of spiritual crisis. Born of this crisis, neo-traditionalism eventually forged an alliance between those who had been suspicious of late Ch'ing modernization from a very early stage, and those original reformers like Liang Ch'i-ch'ao and K'ang Yu-wei who were increasingly depressed by the distopian evolutionism which seemed to offer the only consistent explanation of the moral failures of the revolution.

In seeking a way out, however, neither K'ang-Liang nor any other neo-traditionalists began with a wholesale repudiation of evolutionary principles. In seeking to adapt tradition to contemporary needs, all assumed that traditions do change. In the effort to explain the relationship between 'essential' traditional values and contemporary cultural expression of them, all took advantage of the fact that Confucian-Taoist cosmology had not analytically distinguished the essential Way from the process of Change. Nonetheless, their philosophical assertion of organic unity was continually juxtaposed with an analysis of contemporary socio-political conditions that belied it. As a result two alien philosophical vocabularies coexisted uneasily in neo-traditionalist writings. One was based on the old assumptions of the interdependence of society and value in a dynamic cosmos; the other vocabulary reflected a newly perceived discontinuity between the socio-political realm on the one hand, where modernization was generally accepted as necessary, and the spiritual-moral realm of value on the other. 'Spiritual East' and 'materialist West': these commonplaces of neo-traditionalist rhetoric owed their vast popularity to the double and contradictory message conveyed. On the one hand they suggested a seemingly organicist evaluation of total cosmic and world orders; on the other they did not suggest two parallel entities, but metaphorically or symbolically mapped a dualistic universe in which spiritual values must abide above and apart from socio-political fact. The history of neo-traditionalism down through the May Fourth period saw the gradual supplanting of the first connotation by the second.

Between the 1898 reform and the May Fourth movement three neo-traditional currents may be discerned, each with its own strategy for adapting Confucianism and the classical heritage to modern conditions.[30] One was the National Essence (*kuo-ts'ui*) movement among classical

30 See Wing-tsit Chan, *Religious trends in modern China*, and Charlotte Furth, ed. *The limits of change: essays on conservative alternatives in republican China*.

scholars and political activists. Well before the Revolution of 1911, they were interested in an analysis of Chinese history which explored the origins and development of national traditions from archaic roots in land, race and culture – and which would validate the current struggle for sovereignty and independence. Since they made history serve nationalist ideology, and justified nationalism as the essential means for the survival of the Chinese cultural heritage, the National Essence group gravitated toward the anti-Manchu, anti-imperialist political movement. However, their effort to recast the Confucian classical canon as national history also reflected late Ch'ing educational change which had disassociated classical knowledge and office-holding, necessitating new roles for learning and new social functions for the learned.

The second neo-traditional current was led by Liang Ch'i-ch'ao upon his return to the mainland as a prestigious elder statesman after the 1911 Revolution. Liang still focused on the collective psychology of the Chinese people as he had in his call for a 'new people' in 1902. Now, however, he attempted to define and defend a historically rooted 'national character' (*kuo-hsing*) – a presumably still vital social morality to be found in unique Chinese norms of interpersonal relations and spiritual self-cultivation. Like 'national essence' history, the 'national character' was subject to evolutionary law, but its value derived from its organic links with the past, and change was now to be judged by compatibility with its temper. His post-revolutionary journals, *Yung-yen* (Justice) and *Ta Chung-hua* (Great China) became forums for debate in which admirable and faulty qualities of the national psychology were extrapolated from contemporary social evidence.

Third, a concern for the modern relevance of the central spiritual symbols of Confucianism still preoccupied many. Some of these followed K'ang Yu-wei who had advocated since the original 1898 reform period that Confucianism become institutionalized as a state cult. During the first years of the republic this idea attracted an organized following which lobbied for a 'religion clause' in the constitution. More philosophically inclined Confucianists looked for support in an evolutionary sociology of religion – defending the faith as an historically advanced one, free of the superstition and super-naturalism of more primitive beliefs. In this debate, of course, both sides shared a common goal: to see Confucianism as a functionally modern belief system.

All three of these neo-traditional currents shared some underlying characteristics. All were suspicious of dominant Western values – identified as competitive individualism, materialist profit seeking and utilitarianism. All implicitly defined core Chinese values reactively as the antitheses of these. Since they opposed 'Westernization' in culture, neo-traditionalists made a special contribution to anti-imperialist and nationalist sentiment. Second, in each movement evolutionism was balanced by a revisionist essentialism, as the presumed dross of heritage was dismissed in favour of some core of truth. Sometimes the criteria for such truth were historically fundamentalist, as when National Essence scholars pruned the classics of the accumulation of 2,000 years of imperially-sponsored commentaries. Sometimes the criteria were evolutionary, as when the present 'national character' was detached from the ritual morality of the recent past and presented as functionally compatible with modernization. In this way neo-traditionalists shared in the contemporary penchant for sociological reasoning, making the functional utility of traditional systems of belief the basis for justifying faith. But they also felt a need to see contemporary Confucian value from a perspective outside history, as immune to its fluctuations. So where imperial Confucianism had merged sacred and secular institutions, diffusing religious and moral sentiment in the practices of daily life, neo-traditionalists were gradually forced to regard value as a distinctly autonomous sphere.

When at the height of the May Fourth movement two 'choice souls' in the younger generation, the philosophers Liang Sou-ming (Liang Shu-ming) and Hsiung Shih-li, experienced emblematic conversions to Confucianism, the sacred-secular polarization was at last explicitly acknowledged by Confucianists themselves. Rather than justifying their new belief on evolutionary or utilitarian grounds, Liang and Hsiung said they valued Confucianism for its capacity to order and express the uniquely spiritual side of their personal experience, and to answer questions about the meaning of existence as a whole. This, then, was a classic modernist defence of the special genius of 'religion': its capacity to provide symbolic resources for dealing with aspects of the human condition for which secular philosophy has no answer. Following this, evolutionist and functionalist defences of faith, always ambiguous, rapidly gave way to 'intuitionist' ones.

National essence

A Japanese neologism of the Meiji period, the term '*kuo ts'ui*' (national essence) began to appear in the writings of Chinese intellectuals around 1903, when the reform of the educational system and the secularization, if not abolition, of the monarchy were first clearly delineated as goals of the Ch'ing reform movement. In the broadest sense, 'national essence' was the slogan of scholars who were looking for an alternative to Confucian learning in the service of the imperial orthodoxy and examination system.[31] Interest in a modern 'national learning' (*kuo-hsueh*) first surfaced among Chang Chih-tung, Lo Chen-yü and other central government bureaucrats in charge of new educational policies, who wanted to limit foreign influence on curriculum and establish Chinese ethics as a stream-lined department of study in the new school system.[32] However, many classical scholars saw the issue as not merely one of adapting to new condi-tions, but in a spirit of resistance to Western-oriented change, making the movement to 'preserve the national essence' a vehicle for militant nationalists and critics of the reform movement.

Beginning about 1904 leadership gravitated to a clique of brilliant eccentrics who found in anti-Manchu politics a strategy for revolution as the restoration of the spirit of the Ming, T'ang or even pre-Han era, and also a rationale for a Darwinist influenced historiography glorifying the unique Han race and culture. The Association for the Preservation of Classical Chinese Learning (Kuo-hsueh pao-ts'un hui), founded in Shanghai in January 1905 by Teng Shih, Huang Chieh and Liu Shih-p'ei, preached anti-Manchu revolution as an attractive alternative to reform modernism and accommodation with the West. Although national essence advocates acknowledged that the West was a source of world civilization in its own right, and that some interrelation between centres of civiliza-tion was a necessary pattern of world history, much of their scholarship, in fact, appeared motivated by a search for historically rooted native alternatives to the crumbling imperial Confucian orthodoxy. Here they drew primarily on the Confucian and non-Confucian 'one hundred schools' (*chu-tzu pai-chia*) of the classical Chou era, but also on the Ming loyalists, Buddhism, and on the 'knight errant' tradition of heroic vio-lence.[33] Finally, within the movement there was a strong undercurrent of solidarity with China's common people, who were like these neo-traditionalists in being the natural victims, rather than beneficiaries, of modernization programmes dominated by the court and provincial elite. The archaic populist rhetoric of secret societies and dynastic revolts, basic to anti-Manchu polemic, was well suited to inspire cultural conserva-tives to support political strategies based on violence, and to express sympathy with the more backward common people against the so-called 'enlightened' and pro-Western privileged.[34]

Initial efforts at revisionist history by 'national essence' historians were

31 'Pei-ching ta-hsueh t'ang chih kuo-hsueh wen-t'i' (The problem of national learning at Peking University), *Hsin-min ts'ung-pao* 34 (July 1903) 61–2.
32 Marianne Bastid, *Aspects de la réforme de l'enseignement en Chine au début du 20e siècle*, 64–5.
33 Furth, *Limits of change*, pt 2, 'National Essence', 57–168.
34 See Joseph Esherick, *Reform and revolution in China: the 1911 Revolution in Hunan and Hupeh*.

heavily influenced by political anti-Manchuism. Chang Ping-lin's *Book of raillery*, Liu Shih-p'ei's *Book of the expulsion* and Huang Chieh's *Yellow history*, all published between 1901 and 1906,[35] constituted a scholarly attack on the legitimacy of Manchu rule. All of these works defined the Chinese nation (*min-tsu*) in terms of racial myth: the presumed common descent of the Chinese people from the legendary Yellow Emperor (2697–2597 BC). The implication was that on racial grounds the Manchus should be excluded from the national community. These works broke decisively with canonical tradition by emphasizing the primitive and archaic nature of the earliest stages of Chinese history. Chang and Liu drew upon the Darwinist sociology of Herbert Spencer for a comparatively based evaluation of ancient China and other cradle civilizations and so-called savage peoples. For a time they were even impressed with the ideas of the Belgian Sinologist Terrien de la Couperie, who had posited a common 'cradle' for both Chinese and Middle Eastern antiquity.[36] Nonetheless, the strongest single influence upon these works remained the *Yellow book* (*Huang shu*) of the seventeenth-century Ming loyalist historian, Wang Fu-chih.

As 'national history', these works transcended their anti-Manchu polemical purpose. They offered a definition of the Chinese people as a 'nation' (*min-tsu*) – an organic collectivity based upon common ties of place, blood, custom and culture. All of them pointed to some antique point of origin for the complex of national values which might provide a key to the restoration of polity and culture today. Melding Rousseau and Wang Fu-chih, Liu Shih-p'ei hypothesized that an original social contract between sage ruler and people had led to the creation of unique, Confucian social and ritual forms by the early sage kings. For Chang Ping-lin, the family system and its formal genealogical lines established China's racial unity, while language itself concentrated the essence of Chinese thought, and legalist statecraft of the Ch'in-Han era had shown the way to serve the needs of national wealth and power. None denied the existence of an evolutionary pattern in history, but as organicists all stressed origin over development, affirming essential identity over evolutionary continuity between past and present values.

In their message concerning value, 'national essence' scholars had signi-

---

35 *Ch'iu shu* (Book of raillery), reprinted in Lo Chia-lun, ed. *Chung-hua min-kuo shih-liao ts'ung pien* (Collection on the history of the Chinese republic); *Jang shu* (Book of expulsion), first published 1903, reprinted in *Liu Shen-shu hsien-sheng i-shu* (Collected works of Mr Liu Shen-shu [Liu Shih-p'ei]), 1. 762 ff.; *Huang shih* (Yellow history), first published in *Kuo-ts'ui hsueh-pao* (National essence journal) (1905), 1–9.

36 Selections from de la Couperie's *Western origins of Chinese civilization* were published in *Hsin-min ts'ung-pao* between Sept. 1903 and Jan. 1905.

ficantly shifted their focus from the Confucian classical tradition, to a more abstract idea of the totality of the culture as essence – the accumulated spiritual legacy of a particular people. Moreover, this new view of the inherited classical culture went hand in hand with a distinctive critique of earlier forms of classicism, which built upon the established 'school of Han learning' (*Han-hsueh*). Since the seventeenth century this school had promoted understanding of the classics through careful philological and textual analysis of surviving documents, and in the nineteenth century had led to a revival of interest in long buried and heterodox systems of thought. However, 'national essence' scholars transcended these traditional approaches to strip the classics of their authority as the sacred repositories of normative ideals, re-evaluating them as a section of the vast, heterogeneous corpus of ancient Chinese literature, now seen simply as documents for the study of history. This also made possible a historical methodology which established a bridge between the traditions of careful evidentiary analysis of Ch'ing dynasty textual scholars of 'Han learning' and a twentieth-century critical approach to evidence identified with the Western scientific method.

At the same time the 'national essence' approach to learning took shape not just as an alternative to both canonical Confucianism and straight-arrow 'Westernization'. A basic concern of the greatest 'national essence' historian, Chang Ping-lin, was to criticize the cultural programme of K'ang Yu-wei's reform group. Opposing what he saw as reform evolutionary modernism with anti-Western, anti-imperialist cultural essentialism, Chang popularized his ideas between 1906 and 1908 as editor of the T'ung-meng hui's revolutionary *People's Journal* (*Min pao*), and presented them in more academic form in his acclaimed *Critical essays on antiquity* (*Kuo-ku lun-heng*) published in 1910.[37] Politically the Chang-K'ang polemic was associated with the rivalry of 'reform' and 'revolutionary' factions of politicians; intellectually, it was identified as the Old Text–New Text controversy over the classics, pitting rival versions of the Confucian legacy. The result was two contrasting modern ways of looking at the sage, both of which, by the standards of neo-Confucian and imperial orthodoxy, were equally heterodox, since neither allowed the traditionally received texts to be taken as a canonical legacy of a true Golden Age of antiquity.[38]

In the hands of K'ang Yu-wei, the early Han New Text tradition of oral transmission of the classics had suggested a radical interpretation of Confucius as a religious founder who had literally created the canon bet-

37 Chang Ping-lin, *Kuo-ku lun-heng* (Critical essays on antiquity).
38 Chou Yü-t'ung, *Ching ku-chin wen-hsueh* (Old and new text classical learning).

ween the sixth and fifth centuries BC as a vehicle for his own prophetic visions of *ta-t'ung*. K'ang's argument was technically complex, depending upon finding philological bases for thinking that the versions established as authoritative by Liu Hsin in the first century AD were politically inspired forgeries, and that their originals did not date earlier than Confucius' own lifetime. However, to say that the classics were prophecy made it impossible to believe in them as containing an objective core of historical truth concerning high antiquity. As K'ang's critics noted, 'if Liu Hsin was a forger, Confucius was also a forger'.[39] K'ang had posed a choice unprecedented in Confucian tradition between either a mystical faith in Confucius as a being transcending history, or doubt that there was any historical base for the Confucian Golden Age the classics recorded.

Moreover, this scepticism had a corollary: dethroned as canon, the classics would have to be understood in the historical context of the ages in which they were now thought to have been created, that is, as politically motivated inventions designed to bolster the legitimacy of the Chou dynasty 'later kings' or of their successors, the Western Han emperors. To his critics, K'ang Yu-wei's theories suggested both a false portrait of Confucius as a divine religious founder, and a true and lamentable evaluation of Confucian scholarship as the tool of state power throughout imperial history. Rather than interpret such scholarship as ideology, reflecting the values and priorities of an age, they saw it as distortion, revealing the compromised morality of generations of literati statesmen whose learning advanced careers more than truth, contributing ultimately to imperial decline. In this way, K'ang's philosophical and historical theses were turned against their author, to condemn the K'ang-Liang reform movement as a contemporary manifestation of the careerist 'practical statecraft' (*ching-shih*) tradition in Confucianism.[40]

In orchestrating this attack upon New Text Confucianism, Chang Ping-lin relied upon the more conventional 'Han learning' tradition that Confucius had been 'a transmitter, not a creator', and that 'the six classics are history' – that is, surviving remnants of the public records of the early Chou court. However, Chang used these precedents both to ridicule the idea that Confucianism could be a religion on the model of Christianity, and by extension to claim the Confucian school had no privileged message to convey concerning social morality. In denying Confucianism its historic role of ordering society, he rejected both its basic model of sagehood as linking 'sage within and king without', and the scholar-

39 Quoted in Hou Wai-lu, *Chin-tai Chung-kuo ssu-hsiang hsueh-shuo shih*, 789.
40 The impact of the New Text-Old Text controversy on early republican historiography is analysed in Laurence A. Schneider, *Ku Chieh-kang and China's new history*.

statecraft symbiosis which had characterized the traditional political culture. His own Confucius, instead, was a scholar who had created the first private, as opposed to court-sponsored, school of thought in Chinese history – a pioneer both of 'scientific' fidelity to facts in scholarly work, and of an admirable detachment of the intellectual vocation from the corruptions of power.

In their opposition to New Text utopian reformism, most early 'national essence' partisans did not follow Chang Ping-lin all the way to rejecting the idea of Confucius as China's foremost moralist. Rather, while branding K'ang as a fame-seeking corruptor of the sagely ideal, they remained within the more standard anti-superstition pole of Confucian humanism. Chang Ping-lin's thought went beyond such superficial rationalism and moralism, leading to the first fundamental neo-traditional criticism of the evolutionary principles underlying reform cosmology as a whole. In his repeated attacks on the reformers, published in a variety of anti-Manchu revolutionary periodicals between 1903 and 1908, Chang castigated the speculative New Text historical reasoning not only because K'ang did not 'seek truth from fact' and 'hid the failings of the ancients'[41] but also because the reform model of the cosmological process imposed a fixed law of natural and social evolution upon events which in fact defy such a deterministic analysis.[42]

In Chang's cosmos, change, rather than being predictable and regular, is marked by discontinuity, randomness and chance. Time, rather than presenting itself as a linear sequence of events towards a teleologically predetermined goal, appears without beginning or end, as 'movement and stasis in mutual opposition'.[43] Matter, when analysed philosophically, leads to epistemological scepticism concerning its own nature, and thus to the negation of 'materialism'. From Taoism Chang drew cosmological constructs which portrayed the universe as an undetermined flux, in which phenomenal forms continually take shape free from any external coercion or direction. From Wei-shih Buddhism he took the belief that this flow of phenomena itself must be acknowledged the creation of mind, 'perfuming' a monistic 'storehouse consciousness' with an unstable succession of dharmas in motion. In light of such a model of cosmic truth, Chang believed that reform evolutionists and their faith in *kung-li*, or

41 Quoted in Hou Wai-lu, *Chin-tai Chung-kuo ssu-hsiang hsueh-shuo shih*, 801–2.
42 See the following by T'ai-yen [Chang Ping-lin]: 'Chü-fen chin-hua lun' (Progress as differentiation), *Min-pao*, 7 (5 Sept. 1906) 1–13; 'She-hui t'ung-ch'üan shang-tui' (Discussion of the 'History of politics'), *Min-pao*, 12 (6 March 1907) 1–24; 'Wu-wu lun' (The five negatives), *Min-pao*, 16 (25 Sept. 1907) 1–22; 'Po shen-wo hsien-cheng shuo' (Against 'soul' as a foundation for constitutional government), *Min-pao*, 21 (10 June 1908) 1–11; 'Ssu-huo lun' (On four delusions), *Min-pao* 22 (Sept. 1906–July 1908) 1–22.
43 Chang Ping-lin, 'Ssu-huo lun', 10.

natural laws of progress, were absurd. When Yen Fu as a Spencerian out-lined a world pattern of historical development from patriarchal to mili-tary state, he betrayed his ignorance of China's institutional history, a subject in which Chang was an expert. But more important he showed his insensitivity to the unique nature of any particular historical or human experience, and to the elusive nature of causal processes. When K'ang and Liang said that the human grouping instinct would lead to higher, more successful forms of material and moral community, they were im-posing Darwinian laws of social cooperation on human beings whose life ideal should rather be the autonomous, detached and spontaneous 'natural' existence dictated by Chuang-tzu's doctrine of the 'equality of things' (*ch'i wu*).

In seeing reform cosmology as materialistic and deterministic Chang was responding to the established association between reform thought and Westernization, and also to the place of science in the cosmology itself, suggestive as it was of powerful external cosmic processes of nature and machine overshadowing human effort. But in his protest against determinism Chang mostly returned to an old debate on nature and society which had historically divided Warring States Confucianists and Taoists. In saying that human beings have no natural ties with others and that no social laws bind them as moral absolutes, he uttered the classic Taoist cry of individualist protest against Confucian social values – a cry which did not imply an assertion of the right to socially defined freedom, but rather the desire to align the self with the a-social, self-generating, spontaneous rhythms of the natural universe.

Chang Ping-lin, like the reform cosmologists, philosophized as if metaphysics maps out structures which harmonize with socio-historic processes; but given the nature of his cosmology, the linkages of inter-dependence were extremely difficult to maintain. Like the reformers, Chang turned to the traditional symbolism of cosmic 'barriers', which could express either external social and natural obstacles to human com-munity, or internal psychological and spiritual barriers obstructing the true self's experienced identity with the cosmos as a whole. Yet where reform utopians imagined the breaking of barriers to lead to the moral community of *ta-t'ung*, Chang wanted to 'end the triple fusion of human kind, living things and the world'.[44] With the destruction of consciousness the world itself, product of the defective perceptions of living beings, would be obliterated. Tan Ssu-t'ung had employed very similar Buddhistic constructs to express a vision of the transcendence of consciousness; Chang Ping-lin's version saw annihilation.

44 Chang Ping-lin, 'Wu-wu lun', 22.

Buddhism as a 'life-negating' cosmology traditionally had the potential to be this kind of metaphysical alternative to Confucianism. In the reform generation, however, the appeal to such an alternative reflected something new – the emerging sacred-secular polarization which accompanied the broader revolution. In the Old Text–New Text controversy Chang maintained, as against K'ang Yu-wei, that Confucianism is not a religion – a surface formulation of his underlying assumption that socio-political order and cosmic truth occupy separate spheres. However, in this case rejecting Confucian spirituality was not a choice for secularism; it was a neo-traditionalist's search for spiritual alternatives to the old comforts of the moralized Confucian universe. On the level of private belief Chang turned to Buddhism and Taoism both for a native critique of Confucian errors, and for a harsh kind of existential understanding. In life as a 'national essence' man of learning he opted for the vocation of 'disinterested scholarship', implying that pure knowledge is a value outside society and in essence superior to it. In this way his personal cosmological beliefs complemented the more widespread national essence idealization of the spirit of Chinese culture, preserved in the classical legacy.

Moreover, as a critical theory, Chang Ping-lin's beliefs were adaptable to the emerging neo-traditional analysis of Eastern versus Western cultures. Staples of this analysis included such views as: that progress is an illusion and belief in it a kind of modern superstition; that pursuit of wealth and power in a Darwinian struggle for existence leads to perilous reliance upon externals at the expense of inner life; and that Chinese culture will perish if it does not rely upon its own internal spiritual powers of renewal.

During the May Fourth movement of 1919 the slogan 'national essence' was identified with opponents of vernacular language reform, and the movement appeared a clear loser in the battle over China's New Culture. Nonetheless, the national essence critique of Westernization and its model of national history focusing on the ethnic and territorial roots of a uniquely Chinese culture were carried on by Kuomintang scholars. The 'national essence' concept of a politically disinterested scholarly vocation found ready acceptance among many later republican academics. More important, the movement introduced a new way of looking at the concept of 'culture' itself, seeing it as an absolute, a repository of values which stands outside the socio-political processes of modernization, yet constitutes an evaluative standard against which that process must be measured. This concept, and the critique of evolutionary cosmology which complemented it, broke ground for a new style dualistic metaphysics based on the opposition of spirit to matter.

The national character

As might be expected, Liang Ch'i-ch'ao's post-1911 defence of tradition was the one which went furthest in accommodating evolutionism, a secularist approach to value, and concern for reforming social morality. As if the fall of the Manchu dynasty itself was a signal that protracted upheaval contains perils of social dissolution, Liang started the new journal *Yung-yen* (Justice) on his return to the mainland in 1912, and presented in the leading article of the first issue an affirmation of the 'national character' (*kuo-hsing*).[45]

Ever since his first call for a 'new people' in 1902 Liang's reformism had been based upon the assumption that the key to progress and social well-being lay in the health and vitality of an organically conceived spirit, expressed through the collective national psychology. Liang now renewed his hopes for the national psyche. The virtues of this 'national character' were relatively modest: it was neither eternally valid, nor directly in touch with the ontologically true. It was simply historically suitable. Yet in making his claim for suitability, Liang was here no longer making a concession to Chinese backwardness, but saying that certain fundamental features of Confucian social morality could and must outlive the old absolutized norms of the 'five relationships' to provide a basis for healthy, and therefore gradual, national development. He stated that nations have a nature (*hsing*) like people, and that their fate depends upon this intangible quality, visible in religion, customs and language. The 'nature' can change, but only gradually, as a body may alter its physical composition but cannot be totally overhauled without killing the organism. 'A gardener in pruning trees trims branches, and gets rid of leaves, but he is never willing to damage the trunk or root'. A nation's 'nature' is killed when not one of its traditions is sacred.[46]

In this way Liang came to idealize not an abstract historical 'objective geist' of culture, but a presumably living 'national character' (*kuo-hsing*), an attainable moral property of those millions of ordinary Chinese who he thought had not been spoiled by the events of the past 20 years. As against Western 'individualism' and 'hedonism', Liang offered the antidote of 'familism' (*chia-tsu chu-i*), identifying the fundamental familistic values as 'reciprocity' (*shu*), 'respect for rank' (*ming-fen*), and 'concern for posterity' (*lü hou*).[47] Of these three virtues the last two were seen as par-

---

45 Liang Ch'i-ch'ao, 'Kuo-hsing p'ien' (Essay on the national character), *Yung yen*, 1. 1 (Jan. 1913), 1–6 (sep. pag.).
46 *Ibid.*
47 Liang Ch'i-ch'ao, 'Chung-kuo tao-te chih ta-yuan' (Fundamentals of Chinese morality), *Yung-yen* 1. 2 (Dec. 1912) 1–8; 1. 4 (Feb. 1913) 1–8 (sep. pag.).

ticularly functional for modern nationalism. They encouraged a spirit of collective solidarity and self-sacrifice in building the future and confirmed the moral legitimacy of a political elite based on talent as against democratic levelling. In making 'reciprocity' the cardinal virtue of interpersonal relations, Liang opted for a moderate liberalization of generational and sexual relationships which would not threaten the underlying solidarity of the family. As against the unilateral virtue of 'filiality', 'reciprocity' had always called attention to the moral claims of inferiors without, however, fundamentally challenging the hierarchy of interpersonal roles.

This clear-cut revisionist interpretation of the Confucian social ethic did not break with the underlying concepts of evolutionary cosmology, but merely underscored reform evolutionism's assumption that core values shape and inform social change. 'I have advocated preserving the "national essence" all of my life', Liang said in 1916, 'but I mean by it something different from the common interpretation.'[48] His position was simply that if any particular historical Confucian customs were relative and partial, the Confucian idea of the moral personality (*jen-ko*) in itself was an intrinsic, not a contingent value, which would survive the era of nationalism in world politics.[49]

If Liang's theory of the 'national character' was in keeping with his underlying evolutionary beliefs, it also carried his stress on the priority of society and culture over politics. Concurrent with the discussion of the 'national character', *Yung-yen's* political analyses of the controversy over a monarchical restoration argued against it, but on relativistic grounds. Liang declared that the form of government (*cheng-t'i*) – that is, its actual system of representative and administrative organization – is a more fundamental index to the functioning of a political system than the form of the state (*kuo-t'i*) – that is, its seat of formal sovereignty. The implication was that, while China's 'state form' should now remain republican in recognition of the simple facts of recent history, its future 'form of government' properly ought to evolve compatibly with native norms of social relations.[50]

Both because it dealt with concrete norms of social ethics and because of the evolutionary model of change it entailed, Liang's theory of the 'national character' confronted the New Culture movement on common ground. While giving sharply different answers, the two sides asked the same kind of questions: given that the norms of interpersonal relations

48 Liang Ch'i-ch'ao in *Ta Chung-hua*, 1. 2 (Feb. 1915) 7.
49 *Ibid.*
50 See *Yung-yen*, 1. 3 (1913) 3–4 and *Ta Churg-hua*, 1. 8 (Aug. 1915) 13.

are cultural forces determining the evolution of political order, how do China's historical models serve, and do they need to be changed fundamentally? Answers took a common turn: for every article that praised a Chinese devotion to peace, inner contentment, familistic emotions, another savaged the presumed national predilections for passivity, conformity, dependency and slavishness to authority. The argument for the functional modernity of Chinese traditions of collectivism and public-mindedness was matched by the example of the functioning modernity of Western individualism, competitiveness and scientific rationality.

Not surprisingly, then, Liang's defence of the evolutionarily modernized 'national character' eventually met the same fate as his advocacy of the evolutionarily advanced 'rational' Confucius. Even during the early republican years, disappointments with republican politics had caused Liang to alternate his neo-traditional assertions of value with occasional outbursts of distopian pessimism.[51] Finally the experience of the First World War, which so gravely damaged the prestige of Western civilization in the eyes of Chinese intellectuals in general, taught Liang one final lesson of the times – that the assumptions of evolutionary cosmology itself must be abandoned. Returning from a humiliating, dispiriting assignment as a Chinese observer at the Paris Peace Conference which ignored China's national rights, Liang wrote his 'Reflections on a trip to Europe'.[52] It condemned contemporary Western civilization *in toto*. Liang no longer saw an organic vision of human historical progress, even if with twists and turns, but two starkly diametrical metahistorical systems. The first was a Western one dominated by the iron laws of a 'scientific view of humanity', generating an economic and social system based on the machine and given over to the pursuit of power and wealth, and to the corruptions of hedonism and greed. The contrasting Eastern civilization was now at a turning point, risking disaster if she followed Europe in infatuation with the idea of an omnipotent science. The limits of Liang's accommodation with a secular evolutionism had been reached. Once it appeared finally inhospitable to symbols of Confucian moral value, he abandoned evolutionary theory. Liang Ch'i-ch'ao's last cosmic myth of total civilizations was not a true organic cosmology, but a metaphor for a dualistic metaphysics of matter and spirit. Chinese spirit could be seen as embodied in a civilization only if that civilization stood apart from the process of modernization apparently engulfing the planet as a whole.

51 See supra, fn. 26.
52 Liang Ch'i-ch'ao, 'Ou yu hsin-ying lu chieh-lu' (Reflections on a trip to Europe), 1919 reprinted in *Yin-ping-shih ho-chi* (Combined writings), *chuan-chi, ts'e* 5. 1–152.

Confucianism as a religion

Historically Confucianism was a *'chiao'* (doctrine or teaching) and the English word 'religion' had no exact classical Chinese translation. As it was brought in by nineteenth-century missionaries, the concept itself was linked to Christian assumptions of a spirit-matter dualism which Confucianists did not share; institutionally it evoked the Christian separation of church and state which was irrelevant in a patriarchal society. Therefore when in the 1890s the New Text reform intellectuals began to raise the question whether Confucianism was, or should be considered as a religion, they had to import new language (beginning with the Japanese neologism for religion, *tsung-chiao*), propose new institutional structures and eventually suggest an altered definition of Confucianism's central meaning. At each step, however, the syncretic Confucian heritage, in which neither Confucian humanistic rationalists at one pole nor Confucian mystics at the other traditionally felt required to repudiate the other, provided a reservoir of symbols and concepts that could blur the sacred-secular polarization which the idea of 'religion' here implied. The notion that Confucianism was a 'religion' at all, then, was controversial, attacked by those who considered themselves within the tradition perhaps even more hotly than by secularists without.

The New Text Confucianism of K'ang Yu-wei and T'an Ssu-t'ung introduced the religion issue first of all in the form of a doctrinal influence. As self-styled syncretists, both K'ang and T'an held that all three of the world's great historic religions had a common core of truth – a position which gave Christianity an explicit contribution to make to ontology. To make Confucius a religious founder, to speak of *jen* as encompassing fraternal love, to exalt prophecy and martyrdom, and express hope for religious Messiahs to come and save the world – these things certainly bespoke syncretists who had been touched by the Christian drama even as they denied the exclusively Christian origin of such ideas. K'ang was further impressed with the Protestant ideal of an inner spiritual voice overriding doctrinal convention, and liked to compare his own role in China to Luther's leadership of the Reformation.[53] In T'an Ssu-t'ung's work Christian influence is suggested most directly in those passages of the *Jen hsueh* which see fundamental tension between the human spirit and body, and assert that the Confucian tradition had its own form of a doctrine of immortality.[54]

New Text reformers were led by this doctrinal syncretism to make their

53 See Hou Wai-lu, *Chin-tai Chung-kuo ssu-hsiang hsueh-shuo shih,* 704–27.
54 T'an Ssu-t'ung, *Ch'üan chi,* 24–35.

first claim that Confucianism has a 'religious' character. But the Christian theological impact upon reform cosmology probably had less to do with this claim in the short run than the example of the Christian church as an institution. K'ang Yu-wei's famous campaign to make Confucianism into a state religion, inaugurated in 1895 and doggedly pursued by him and others until the death of Yuan Shih-k'ai in 1916, in fact was a reflection of socio-political more than spiritual concerns.[55] Recognizing the extent to which a constitutional monarchy and new school system meant the secularization of politics, K'ang hoped to create a corps of religious specialists who would preside over a formal state cult. Separation of church and state appeared to him a key to the ability of strong nations of the West to 'drive a cart on two wheels', upholding social morality in a pluralistic polity. In this way, he said, 'religion maintains its awesome power, morality is honoured, even as dissension rages'.[56] K'ang's blue-print for Confucian religion was an accommodation to the break-up of the imperial Confucian synthesis and accompanying scholar-official rule. Nonetheless, it was only a social accommodation to China's contemporary needs, not a strategy conceived out of the conviction that Confucian truth required such forms of expression.

The utilitarian argument for faith as a prop to social morality attracted a certain kind of support. Gentry dismayed by what they saw as the moral collapse accompanying the revolution were ready recruits to the network of provincial Confucian societies which sprang up after 1911, and which campaigned heavily between 1912 and 1914 for a religious clause in the republican constitution. This movement had K'ang's blessing, and was formally led by his disciple, the Columbia educated economist Ch'en Huan-chang. However, officials under Yuan Shih-k'ai saw to it that changes in the republican government's official sacrifices tended towards civic plainness more than ritual elaboration, while Yuan disavowed that any of his regime's ceremonials constituted the establish-ment of a state religion. Here Yuan was adjusting his manipulation of traditional symbols to an educated public opinion which argued that a state cult was an historically regressive idea, since it substituted a more primitive Western style supernaturalism for the native humanistic faith which in fact marked China as an advanced civilization.

As a utilitarian proposal justified as suitable to the times, the state cult idea was vulnerable to alternatives whose claim to a suitable modernity

55 See Hsiao Kung-chuan, *A modern China and a new world: K'ang Yu-wei, reformer and utopian 1858–1927*, ch. 4, pp. 97–136.
56 K'ang Yu-wei, 'Chung-hua chiu-kuo lun' (On China's salvation), *Pu-jen tsa-chih*, 1 (March 1913) 21–2.

could be called superior. A more attractive intellectual defence of Confucianism, then, used the idea of the evolution of religion to evaluate China's lack of a Confucian church as the mark of advance, not regression. An early republican history of Chinese religion from such an evolutionary perspective was in Hsia Tseng-yu's *Textbook on Chinese History* (*Chung-kuo li-shih chiao-k'o shu*).[57] Hsia argued that China had moved from a primitive belief in the power of spirits to a higher level of religious consciousness with the emergence of Confucianism and Taoism in the 'Spring and Autumn' era. But, he continued with an indirect slap at the New Text movement, for political reasons superstitious elements were revived by the architects of the imperial cult in the Western Han. Hsia argued that the mystical content in an originally ethical Confucianism was the result of Taoist influence, leaving open the possibility that contemporary Chinese might follow Chang Ping-lin in looking to Taoism for ontological doctrine, while honouring Confucian morality. The more standard approach, however, was to reject this Taoist influence as also a 'superstitious' and negative one, and to agree with Liang Ch'i-ch'ao's original argument against K'ang in 1902 that 'to make Confucianism a religion is to distort the true spirit of Confucius.'[58] The Christian concept of 'religion' applied to the Confucian tradition had bred its opposite, a rationalistic model of the sage. Secular values such as intellectual tolerance, acceptance of the body and rejection of an after-life became, by such reasoning, hallmarks of the Confucian consciousness, and defence of faith rested upon its compatibility with the truths of science.

In 1913 a sophisticated compromise was suggested by the philosopher Chang Tung-sun in the form of a mild criticism of the early republican proliferation of Confucian societies.[59] Turning from analysis of Chinese doctrine to Western philosophy of religion in the abstract, Chang suggested that William James' definition of 'religion' left no doubt that Confucianism, having both ontology and ethics, should be included under the concept. At the same time he argued for the scientific rationality of advanced forms of religious belief, noting that the *I ching* teaches that the supraphenomenal world of the Great Ultimate (*t'ai-chi*) is unknowable, and that Tao is an evolutionary principle of the cosmos. As a corollary,

57 Hsia Tseng-yu, *Chung-kuo li-shih chiao-k'o-shu* (Textbook of the history of China). See the analysis in Ts'ai Yuan-p'ei, 'Wu-shih nien-lai Chung-kuo chih che-hsueh' (Chinese philosophy in the last fifty years), *Shen-pao* anniversary issue, *Tsui-chin wu-shih nien* (The last fifty years).

58 Liang Ch'i-ch'ao, 'Pao-chiao fei so-i tsun K'ung lun' (To 'save the faith' is not the way to honour Confucius), *Hsin-min ts'ung-pao*, 2 (22 Feb. 1902) 59–72.

59 Chang Tung-sun, 'Yü chih K'ung-chiao kuan' (My view of Confucianism), *Yung-yen*, 1. 15 (July 1913) 1–12.

Chang praised Confucian ethics as in harmony with the modern moral ideal of socialism.

These Confucian modernizers, then, whether they spoke for a state cult, for Confucius as a rationalist, or for 'rational religion', all used styles of reasoning that depended upon an evolutionary framework but paid the price of appearing utilitarian in nature. Even if their arguments lacked the crude instrumentalism of appeals to faith as a guarantee of social order, they all broadly viewed it as functional to evolving social systems, and so had to prove this functionality, not in terms of some distant world of *ta-t'ung*, but in the present. But to support Confucian humanism detached from Confucian mysticism or ritual was to make the core of faith rest in a socio-political morality already deeply compromised by change, and whose ethical norms Confucian reformers had themselves been early to attack. On the other hand, to identify Confucianism with contemporary ideals of scientific rationalism made faith vulnerable to challenge from the more thoroughgoing rationalism of science itself – from views of the cosmos based on atomic physics more than on the *I ching* and from models of truth derived from laboratory experiment more than traditionally validated belief. The sacred-secular polarization which had created the 'religious' and 'rational' versions of the sage in the first place, ended by rendering the 'rational' sage obsolete.

By the May Fourth period the debate over a modern form for Confucianism had led neo-traditionalists to a new consciousness of a 'problem of religion' in human life which the discussions of the previous decade had not adequately explored. In its light, all previous strategies for an evolved, modernized Confucianism were seen as equally tainted with utilitarianism. In the May Fourth discussions of the 'problem of religion', evolutionary assumptions became the monopoly of secularists, who argued that with the march of progress and gradual perfection of scientific knowledge, 'religion' would become socially obsolete. Western science, which suggested to earlier reformers a speculative model of the natural world's functioning in harmony with ideal values, now was recast as a positivistic method of verification challenging them. With this shift, the defence of faith also shifted ground. There was not only a retreat from evolutionism but also a new preoccupation with a Western-derived epistemological issue, in which scientific rationalist theories of verification would be countered by 'intuitive' models of truth.[60]

A leading intuitionist metaphysician was Liang Shu-ming, a young

60 Yen Chi-ch'eng, '"Shao-nien Chung-kuo" tsung-chiao wen-t'i hao p'i-p'ing' (Critique of the special issue on the religious question of *Young China Magazine*), *Min to* (People's tocsin), 3.2 (1 Feb. 1922) 1–12. See also Chow, *May Fourth movement*, 322–3.

Peking University philosopher, himself the product of the most advanced education the reform generation had to offer. He had experienced a crisis of faith in the first years of the republic which led him initially to a Buddhist and then increasingly to a Confucian commitment.[61] When members of the Young China Association, led by a group studying abroad in France, inaugurated a public debate on the 'problem of religion' in 1921, Liang spoke in the spirit of his own conversion, which had been preceded by bouts of suicidal depression, and had taken place in a mood of protest against all nationalistic or other utilitarian impulses to belief. Religion, Liang said, will always be humanly relevant because it alone deals with issues which 'lie outside the particular universe, if not outside its extension.'[62] In focusing upon death and suffering as the perennial human realities to which religion alone can give satisfactory meaning, Liang leaned heavily towards Buddhism – 'Indian religion' – as the model for a true religion of 'transcendence' (*ch'ao-chueh*). However, his own Confucian view, developed in the debate of 1921 and published in a book the next year, was concerned with the same fundamental issue in its central claim that Confucianism is an affirmation of the ontological reality of 'life' (*sheng*) itself.

Liang's book, *Eastern and Western civilizations and their philosophies* (*Tung Hsi wen-hua chi ch'i che-hsueh*) made him perhaps the most popular single neo-traditional thinker of the May Fourth period.[63] The book's success may be attributed to the fact that with remarkable emotional effect if not logical clarity it blended the neo-traditional thinker's rival impulses – on the one hand to continue the now familiar traditions of evolutionary cosmology, and on the other hand to express the new sense of estrangement between an a-historical world of value, understood through the intuitive human knowledge of the good, and natural and sociopolitical processes governed by science.

Eastern and Western civilizations first of all sketched an outline of human civilization evolving through metahistorical stages, each, according to Liang's vocabulary (which here was indebted to Schopenhauer), the product of the direction of a spiritual Will (*ta i-yü*). Liang identified the Will with life itself (*sheng*) and also with *jen*. Like T'an Ssu-t'ung Liang found in Wei-shih Buddhism and in Neo-Confucian cosmology based on the *I ching* the inspiration for a view of the total cosmos as a mind-created ceaseless flux of existence, taking shifting phenomenal form through the

61 See Guy Alitto, *Liang Shu-ming*.
62 Quoted in Yen Chi-ch'eng, 'Shao-nien Chung-kuo tsung-chiao wen-t'i'.
63 Liang Shu-ming, *Tung Hsi wen-hua chi ch'i che-hsueh* (Eastern and Western civilizations and their philosophies).

mediation of *yin* and *yang* forces. However, biology, as transmitted through the vitalism of Henri Bergson, let Liang assert that the universe is literally organic, a living structure. Where for an earlier reform-generation philosopher like T'an life and death were metaphors for a finally undifferentiated continuum, in Liang Shu-ming's cosmic myth they were sharply polarized. Where T'an blended physics, ethics and ontology in his concept of interpenetrating ether, Liang, in reaction against the science-inspired naturalistic models of causation, divided 'causal relationships' (*yuan*) from true 'causes' (*yin*). The first, he said, could be understood in terms of material forces like history or environment, while the second must be seen as proceeding from spirit (*ching-shen*).

Formally speaking, Liang's vision of human destiny presented an 'evolution' of humanity from a 'Western'-style world civilization where the Will's animating direction is towards mastery of the external environment, to a 'Chinese'-style civilization in which the Will moves to adjust and harmonize with the world, coming finally to rest in an 'Indian' civilization of the Will's mystical self-abnegation and rejection of life itself. Formally also, each stage of the metahistorical movement of cosmic Will was seen as giving rise to typical historical patterns of culture. First was a Western culture characterized since the Greeks by philosophical scepticism and utilitarianism, leading to science, democracy and industrial capitalism as the social and material manifestations of a spirit of rationalist self-seeking. By contrast, Chinese civilization since Confucius had been spiritually shaped by the living force of *jen*, and so in its social arrangements had been tolerant and flexible, frugal and agrarian, cooperative and nourishing of human sentiments.

However, this 'evolutionary' scheme was presented more as a set of autonomous ideal alternatives than as a literal temporal sequence. Basically, he presented China's as the only kind of civilization which could be seen as in harmony with the true nature of the cosmos, as 'life' itself. The heart of Liang's message was a defence of Confucian metaphysical values because they alone recognize that the living cosmos cannot be grasped by fixed categories of rationalist analysis, but dictate instead human acceptance of the fluid, intuitive (*chih-chueh*) nature of experience. Only the Confucianist doctrines of *jen* and of the mean (*chung-yung*) allow human life to move with, rather than against, these cosmic rhythms, making possible a truly living life, free and unimpeded in the flow of the inner spirit's intuitions, emotions and joy.

In Liang Shu-ming as in the original reformers there survived a Confucian metaphysical pathos: a traditional rendering of the true self as weakly bounded, capable of extending and transforming the world through mind, and also subject to invasion and loss at the hands of bad external cosmic forces. In terms of moral psychology, the movements of authentic inner mind are recognizable because these alone are truly spontaneous and so free; as opposed to the external calculating mind of self-interest. However, superimposed upon this moral metaphysic, and shifting its direction and meaning, was a new polarization derived not from Chinese tradition, but from the Western philosophical clash of science and metaphysics. Liang identified scientific rationalism with the amoral rationalism of the calculating mind. The deterministic universe, that he presumed was dictated by Western scientific law, was linked to the externally threatening cosmic forces which obstruct the work of potentially transforming mind. In this way the fluid inner-outer dualisms of the older metaphysics were now associated with structurally distinct spheres: matter versus spirit, rationality versus intuition, intellect versus emotion. Such spirit, intuition, emotion cannot gradually infuse and transform their opposites; they can only, if possible, displace them. The implication of this, if it does not lead the philosopher to a radical monism, must be dualistic: if through intuitive forms of consciousness one may be in touch with the structures of the cosmos, it will be with those of a special transcendent kind, operating above other more mundane processes of nature and thought. Liang acknowledged this clearly in his later work, where he dropped all preoccupation with the idea of a metahistorical cosmic continuum for a philosophy of '*li-hsing*', a Mencian kind of intuitive reason. But the direction of his new Confucianist defence of faith was already evident in 1921 and 1922, and later 'new Confucianists' of the 1920s and 1930s, like Chang Chün-mai and Fung Yu-lan, followed the same path.

In this way by 1919 neo-traditionalists who had seen evolutionary theory as maintaining the links between core Confucian values and socio-political change were in disarray. Liang Ch'i-ch'ao had abandoned his vision of a global modernization process compatible with China's moral revival; K'ang Yu-wei lost his bid for the institutionalization of Confucian religion in a republic; functionalist arguments for Confucian ethics and 'national essence' arguments for classical language and canon were alike on the defensive. Confucianists, to be persuaded, sought a new path. Here Confucian truth was seen as metaphysically detached from history, validated finally only by direct intuitive experience, and able to speak to theological problems of meaning more than social problems of choice. The 'spiritual East' had become a country of the heart.

Science and metaphysics

Ironically it might be said that the development of neo-traditionalism in early twentieth-century China is a story of the gradual 'Westernization' of Confucian philosophy. By 1919, even as the various movements to 'save the faith', 'preserve the national essence' and speak in favour of the 'national character' expressed increasingly urgent anti-Western views, the conceptual language they used reflected the impact of the secularist and scientific intellectual revolutions brought by the West. However, by 1919 the West had also provided ammunition to counter the programmatic scientism and secularism of new culture radicals. It presented stunning examples of the failure of its own liberal democratic institutions: the farce that was the constitutional republic of China at home and the catastrophe of the First World War abroad. Liang Shu-ming's *Eastern and Western civilization* and Liang Ch'i-ch'ao's *Reflections*, both bore the stamp of these events. They were the opening statement of a response to the high tide of intellectual radicalism of that year which fully utilized the resources of the new neo-traditional dualistic framework.

This response culminated in a sprawling debate on the subject of 'science and metaphysics', sparked by Liang's associate, the philosopher Chang Chün-mai, which took place in 1923, eventually drawing in dozens of partisans of metaphysics, including Liang himself, Chang Tung-sun, Lin Tsai-p'ing and Fan Shou-k'ang.[64] In that debate defenders of Confucian spiritual truth condemned Darwinian evolutionism, the idea of an authoritative social science, physiological models of psychology, and all positivistic theories of knowledge. In his lead article setting off the controversy, Chang Chün-mai contrasted naturalistic knowledge, governed by science, with 'a point of view based on living experience' (*jen-sheng kuan*). This latter he summarized as 'subjective, intuitive, synthetic, freely willed and unique to the individual.'[65] Like Liang Shu-ming, Chang associated the sphere of 'life' with the inner spirit's experiential consciousness of value, and he saw it threatened by the bad cosmic forces of the 'deterministic universe'. However he opposed the fluid inner sphere to a fixed and static outer sphere of experience. Then, he went on explicitly to identify this inner spiritual consciousness with the idea of 'intuitive knowledge' (*liang-chih*) in the doctrine of mind of the Lu-Wang school of Neo-Confucianism.

The choice of Lu-Wang doctrine marked a shift of emphasis among

---

64 *K'o-hsüeh yü jen-sheng kuan* (Science and philosophy of life), prefaces by Hu Shih and Ch'en Tu-hsiu.

65 Chang Chün-mai, 'Jen-sheng kuan' (Philosophy of life), in *K'o-hsüeh yü jen-sheng kuan*.

Confucian reformers and neo-traditionalists – away from the fundamentalist 'five classics' or the speculative cosmologists of the early Sung, and towards a central focus on the classical Neo-Confucian school which had stressed a metaphysic based on moral experience. Not only was this school potentially more adaptable to the needs of the new neo-traditional philosophical dualism, but also its preoccupation with understanding moral experience or moral knowledge suggested linkages with the alien Western epistemological issues in which the debaters quickly became embroiled, once scientific models of verification had to be challenged on their own philosophical ground. However, in spite of substantial debts to Kant, Bergson, Rudolph Eucken and Hans Dreisch, Chang and his supporters were less adept epistemologists than they were emotionally eloquent metaphysicians. On the subject of the moral sentiments, although Chang and others spoke in passing of their aim through the development of inner life to create a spiritual culture, by and large they neglected metahistorical system building for attempts to characterize subjective moral experience.

The liberal and radical partisans of science in the debate were the ones who embraced evolutionism in its naturalistic form, and did so moreover with a utopian optimism and speculative exuberance reminiscent of the old K'ang Yu-wei. Hu Shih, with a bow to Dewey and Russell, offered a prose poem of praise to the 'naturalistic universe', where human life, however frail, has a purpose and will succeed, through the action of 'creative intelligence' in constructing an affluent and rational world culture. Wu Chih-hui, the veteran anarchist, even conjured up the entire Confucian-Taoist cosmological continuum of the reformers – that ceaseless flow of Change carrying mankind in its bosom into the mists of an evolutionary future. In these presentations, the original reform conception of science as a kind of true cosmology, reliably mapping the natural universe while offering technological liberation that empowers human beings to work successfully for moral and material utopia, remained virtually unaltered.

As a full dress polemic (*lun-chan*) among intelligentsia, the 'science and metaphysics' debate could not end without the public's verdict on winners and losers. When metaphysicians were declared to have reaped the worst of it, this reflected the size of their following but not necessarily its staying power. In fact the first to fade from China's intellectual centre stage were the scientists, whose evolutionary naturalism had lost out to Marxism by the late 1920s. Since neo-traditionalism now offered intellectuals a well-defined modern alternative to the secularization of Chinese values, it had persistent powers of renewal. As an attitude of cultural resistance to the West, it had substantial social appeal in the succeeding two decades.

SOCIAL UTOPIA AND THE BACKGROUND OF THE MAY FOURTH MOVEMENT

Reform and revolution

Neo-traditionalism as a reaction against reform modernization began in China with the 'national essence' movement which gained a following between 1904 and 1907. A clearcut revolutionary movement, aimed at the overthrow of the Manchu dynasty and the establishment of a republic, emerged clearly around the same time. As part of a single historical trend the two currents quite naturally mingled for a while, particularly through the persons of anti-Manchu classical scholars who shared with revolutionary radicals a common hatred of the present. One such, Chang Ping-lin, was even the chief defendant at a political trial in Shanghai in 1903 which is often identified as the opening cannonade in the revolutionary faction's campaign.

In 1905 the radicals achieved a consolidation of sorts with the formation of the T'ung-meng hui (Revolutionary Alliance) under Sun Yat-sen, which based itself on a student constituency, while seeking allies among Overseas Chinese, secret societies and new army units on the mainland. Between 1905 and 1908 the Revolutionary Alliance's Tokyo-based periodical, *Min pao*, enjoyed wide attention as the voice of the Chinese revolutionary movement, engaged in a dramatic polemic with the reformers, personified by Liang Ch'i-ch'ao's *Hsin-min ts'ung-pao* (Journal of the new people). Yet even as the Alliance claimed victory in this polemic, dissatisfied voices from its own left criticized its ideology of political revolution as offering no important social alternatives to constitutionalist reformism. These were China's anarchists, a radical fringe intellectually significant out of all proportion to their tiny numbers. All revolutionaries were identified by their faith in political revolution itself as a necessary catalyst of institutional change. But the anarchists went on beyond politics to define revolution as the realization of utopian social alternatives associated with the ideal of *ta-t'ung*, not just as the eventual gift of the evolutionary process but as the right of youth today. Anarchist social utopianism, therefore, survived the political Revolution of 1911 to inspire the iconoclastic spirit of rebellion among a republican 'new youth' at war with the old social system.

Since reformers and revolutionaries all had assumed that social change is integral to the evolutionary process, between 1903 and 1907 when the distinction between the two groups was first coming into general use, their differences were not always easy to discern. While literary war raged in the pages of *Min pao* and *Hsin-min ts'ung-pao*, the questions dividing the two sides often appeared more tactical than strategic. The basic issue was the ability of the Ch'ing court to advance the nation towards common goals of modernization and national independence.[66] On potentially significant social issues the reformers, led by Liang Ch'i-ch'ao, did oppose Sun Yat-sen's principle of 'land nationalization' (part of his *min-sheng chu-i*) as economically irrational and a device for stirring up 'barbarous' elements among the common people against the more prosperous 'enlightened'. But social policy received limited attention in a politically oriented controversy, while Sun and Liang accepted a common overview of social evolution: imperial China had been spared the 'feudal' class divisions of Europe, while contemporary China would need a mixed economy accommodating some forms of capitalist enterprise in order to develop, yet happily might build upon native traditions of social harmony in a transition to a cooperative mode of industrialism in the future.[67]

In its earliest stage of development between 1903 and 1907 then, the revolutionary outlook appeared rather as an exaggeration of reform views than a repudiation of them – no more than a call for the speeding up of history, casting the new Faustian personality in the guise of a revolutionary hero. Revolutionaries were simply the latest mouthpieces for the original reform utopianism. Revolution was not only Chinese, but harbinger of a new world order of science and democracy. Moral progress goes hand in hand with material development: in casting off the old society, revolutionaries are abandoning a stifling and outmoded autocracy in politics, and the social forms that inhibit the development of wealth and power, the realization of the self and the attainment of *ta-t'ung*. Such attainment depends upon the moral success of the revolutionary person, whose activities must be free of all taint of utilitarian self-interest if they are to complement the forces of progress. These were staples of revolutionary faith as earlier they had been of reform faith.

By 1905 what separated Liang Ch'i-ch'ao and the reform faction from a truly revolutionary mentality was their unwillingness to believe in revolution as an inevitably progressive movement, a necessary agent of history. As a reformer Liang had been among the first to introduce the newly awakened Chinese public opinion to the idea that modern revolution (*ko-ming*) involves institutional change, as opposed to the mere re-

66 For analysis of the debate see Michael Gasster, *Chinese intellectuals and the Revolution of 1911.*
67 Martin Bernal, *Chinese socialism to 1907.*

moval of Heaven's mandate (the original meaning of *ko-ming*) from ruling houses as in past Chinese crises of dynastic succession. Further, Western history showed the revolutions of 1776 and 1789 as historical facts, climactic flashpoints in the clash of forces of action and resistance which drive history forward. Nonetheless, after 1905 Liang's own evaluation was that the spirit of the contemporary age of 'national imperialism' mandated Chinese adherence to strong government – either 'enlightened despotism' or constitutional monarchy.[68] For Liang, such political arrangements were the price to be paid for Chinese backwardness. With such a conclusion the reformers' evaluation of the primary agents of change implicitly shifted from the political to the cultural and social realms. Political leaders do not order culture and society; rather these in their lava-like flow slowly mould politics along channels grooved to withstand radical shifts of direction. So Liang began to contrast 'social reform, which recognizes present social organization and corrects it' and 'social revolutionism . . . [which] cannot be practised; or, if it can, only after a millennium.'[69] However, this conservatism did not imply a rejection of political violence, which Liang did not in principle condemn. Violence was a tactic like any other, adaptable to gradualist ends. In this way Liang's disagreement with the revolutionaries over the nature of the times came close to the classic division between radical as stage-leaper and conservative as guardian of existing arrangements.

If radicals first broke with reformers over the speeding up of history, this acceleration not only led to a theoretical celebration of socio-political struggle, but also forced the social goals of that struggle into the foreground of radical thought. *Ta-t'ung*, telescoped in time, was instead extended in space, inspiring in the anarchists an internationalism that sometimes literally took the present 'streets of Paris, markets of London, skyscrapers of New York'[70] as the reification of progress. Where K'ang Yu-wei dreamed of a future world parliament, Chinese anarchists linked their working organizations with European radical parties, chiefly the anarcho-communists, and associated *ta-t'ung* directly with the theory and practice of Western revolutionary socialism. Looking at China, anarchists were specially sensitive to social conflicts there, and offered a sharpened social criticism both of the feudal past and of the reformist present. Finally the anarchists took over the call for personal liberation from the constraints of Confucian social roles – a call that had first come from

68 Liang Ch'i-ch'ao, 'K'ai-ming chuan-chih lun' (On enlightened despotism), *Hsin-min ts'ung-pao* (1906), reprinted in YPSWC, *ts'e* 6. 13–83.
69 Quoted in Bernal, *Chinese socialism*, 158–9.
70 Min [Ch'u Min-i], 'Wu-cheng-fu shuo' (On anarchism), *Hsin shih-chi*, 40 (28 March 1908) 158. Pagination according to 1966 Tokyo reprint.

K'ang Yu-wei and T'an Ssu-t'ung – and made it the focal point of their social programme. Where K'ang and T'an had finally subordinated social emancipation to political reform in the present and to spiritual liberation in the future, the anarchists judged all other issues by this one. For them the emancipation of the individual from the 'net' of ritualism was the test by which the revolution should ultimately be judged.

If the first hallmark of a distinctly radical outlook was a focus on individual liberation and on revolutionary 'moments' as evolution's catalyst, the second was a scientism which associated utopia with the naturalistic version of evolutionary cosmology. Taking up from the original reformers the faltering banners of progress, the anarchists and later the group around the *New Youth* magazine (*Hsin ch'ing-nien*) proudly inscribed these with secular mottoes affirming the material bases of consciousness, the biological nature of life forces, and the sociological foundations of causal mechanisms in history. Their real intellectual debts to Confucian humanism and Confucian metaphysics went largely unacknowledged, as they reduced the tradition to a reactionary system of social ethics.

However, radical scientism did not provide an unbroken path to utopia. Distressed like everyone else by republican disorder, radicals turned to sociological analyses of the historical forces deemed responsible for China's backwardness: feudal customs which were a drag on politics; feudal cultural values underlying feudal customs; the economics of agrarianism interdependent with both of these. But by embracing a scientific world-view, they were paradoxically less paralysed than neo-traditionalists were by the spectre of sociological determinism. Liang Ch'i-ch'ao's 1902 call for a 'new people' was revived by *New Youth* in 1915 as a summons to cultural revolution. This time a personality ideal of individual autonomy and scientific intelligence was consciously opposed to a 'metaphysical' outlook, yet still seen as a moral agent of progress. Secularism and evolutionary cosmology were harmonized in a radical vision of social utopia.

Early anarchism: revolutionary nihilism

Chinese were interested in Western anarchism as early as 1902, but the first phase of this interest was in keeping with the early radicals' focus on political revolution.[71] The term 'anarchism' (*wu-cheng-fu chu-i*) referred to the 'nihilists' of Europe's 'extreme revolutionary' party – an ideology noteworthy for its use of terrorism as a political tactic. Its immediate foreign

71 For discussion of the nihilists see Don C. Price, *Russia and the roots of the Chinese revolution*, ch. 7; and Bernal, *Chinese socialism*, 198–226.

inspiration was the conspiratorial fellowships of the Russian revolutionary movement, which had carried out such spectacular assassination attempts against Czarist officials in the late nineteenth century, leading up to the revolution of 1905. In China the native popular tradition of 'knight errantry' supplied complementary models of idealistic outlaws like the Liang mountain band, or of sworn brotherhoods who, like the heroes of the Peach Garden Oath, took up arms for justice in an age of chaos.

Nonetheless, for Chinese radicals the essential fascination of the terrorist act was as an instrument of progress. Revolutionary violence was imagined as a kind of 'reactive force' – the only response to autocracy strong enough to outmatch its heavy weight of oppression. In the words of one student pamphleteer, 'revolutions in all nations stem from uprisings and assassinations, but the impact of assassinations is even greater than that of uprisings. . . . As the power of heroes grows, the power of monarchs must come to an end.'[72] The terrorist could thus be called a radicalized compatriot of the new citizen – one who makes the utmost possible outward assertion of personal powers and so stands for the most emphatic rejection of the passive psychology of tradition and the historical stagnation it complemented. The young hotheads who attempted political assassinations beteen 1904 and 1907 acted as if, by some supremely self-disregarding history-making act, they could become both instruments of progress and the conscious embodiment of its moral goal of public community.

The terrorist's path, then, was an individualistic one, but those who thought of following it were perhaps even more concerned than the ordinary new citizen to moralize their self-assertion into conformity with the metahistorical process it was designed to serve. Here the enormity of violence directed against others could be balanced only by the risks it presented to the self. In demanding absolute 'sincerity' of the revolutionary, the nihilists put to new uses the neo-Confucian concept that the sage's power must be linked to the flow of 'sincere mind' pervading the self unimpeded. If 'sincerity' both sharpened the assassin's knife and validated its use, the best proof of this in practice would be the spontaneous ego-abandonment of one whose risk of life is total.

This heavy reliance on internalized neo-Confucian moral norms, while necessary to legitimize the revolutionary vocation, was also perhaps partly responsible for the ineptitude of nihilist attempts. Chang Chi, Yang Tu-sheng, Liu Shih-fu and Wang Ching-wei were all prominent radicals implicated in assassination plots, none of which succeeded in killing its

72 Quoted in Price, *Russia and the roots of the Chinese revolution*, 148.

intended victim. The movement's true heroes and heroines were less killers than martyrs: Ch'iu Chin, the woman warrior who allowed herself to be captured and executed after being implicated in an abortive rising in Anhwei in 1907;[73] or Wu Yueh, the high-school student who was killed in 1905 by the bomb he was trying to throw at a group of imperial ministers at the Peking railway station.

Ch'iu Chin's message to the world was that an exemplary self-sacrificing act can change society; Wu Yueh saw his nihilist's mission in terms of evolutionary cosmology. His 'testament', which with a photo of his shattered body was published in a memorial issue of *Min pao*, explained his act as part of an 'age of assassinations' historically necessary to activate the forces of repression, and so move the pendulum of revolution's dialectical advance. Where Ch'iu Chin saw the task of revolution as society's moral regeneration and so chose martyrdom in the style of T'an Ssu-t'ung, Wu Yueh intended his act to embody a 'reactive force' of change equal to autocratic 'motive force' which had provoked it.[74] Both showed the nihilist's debt to traditional Chinese ideals of moral heroism, but their acts were also an effort to balance the claims of social duty and those of self assertion. They offered an early and extreme solution to the problems lying in wait for radical Chinese who sought to develop the individualist potential of the new personality ideals in defiance of Confucian ideals of group interdependence. Thus the nihilists, while more political than social revolutionaries, raised moral problems of individualism which the later anarchist social utopians would have to face.

The Paris group and the Tokyo group

Two widely separated yet intellectually kindred anarchist groups appeared among overseas Chinese students in Paris and in Tokyo at almost the same time, the summer of 1907. Each grew out of a preliminary study society organized under the stimulus of direct contact between Chinese and foreign radicals – French and Japanese – who advocated anarcho-communism, then at the height of its pre-1914 European influence. Each group published a journal, the work of a small coterie of students clustered around one or two older, more prestigious scholars. Though half a world apart, the Paris and Tokyo anarchists kept in touch with each

73 Mary Backus Rankin, 'The emergence of women at the end of the Ch'ing: the case of Ch'iu Chin', in Marjorie Wolf and Roxane Witke, eds. *Women in Chinese society*, 39–66.
74 Wu Yueh, 'Wu Yueh i-shu' (Wu Yueh's testament), *T'ien t'ao: Min-pao lin-shih tseng-k'an* (Demand of heaven; Min-pao special issue), 25 April 1907. See also Price, *Russia and the roots of the Chinese revolution*, 150–1.

other's work, as well as with the activities of the T'ung-meng hui, which they considered at least temporarily allied to their own cause.[75]

In the nineteenth-century West, anarchist utopians were of two classic types: those looking to liberation through technological progress, evoking utopia through scientistic fantasies of the future in the manner of Saint Simon; and those more like Charles Fourier who sought happiness in the unspoiled simplicity and intimate community of arcadia. The two Chinese groups included both these imaginative poles.

As their journal's name of *New Century* (*Hsin shih-chi*) implied, the Paris group believed themselves on the most advanced frontier of modernism, in touch with industrial civilization, and with its social and moral vanguard in the anarcho-communist movement led by Peter Kropotkin, Elisee Reclus and Errico Malatesta. Li Shih-tseng, a founder of the group, was a student of biology at the Pasteur Institute and a friend of Paul Reclus, Elisee's nephew. *New Century*'s senior editor, Wu Chih-hui, had some training in paleontology and preached Kropotkin's 'mutual aid' as a scientific sociology superior to Yen Fu's Spencerian evolutionism, which dictated the support of rationalism versus superstition in culture, and internationalism and pacifism in politics. As self-styled scientific materialists, the Paris group captured some of the prophetic *élan* of the 1898 visionaries of *ta-t'ung*. Wu Chih-hui showed particular exuberance as a technological utopian. Praising the inventive, tool-making faculty as the root of human genius, he called for 'saving the world through machines' in a spirit of inspired play – half cosmological fantasy, half science fiction:

At that time of the most broadly developed [scientific] learning, engineering for the convenience of communication will be preeminent, seeking to facilitate free travel under sea and in the air. Further, there will be [substitute] materials to reform the barbaric habit of meat eating; while the refinement of health and medicine will prolong our years of life. As to chemistry, physics and all the progressive natural sciences . . . at that time due to the simplification and unification of written language . . . a hundred new methods will make them easy to learn and easy to understand. When travelling through parks and forests we may sit at ease among the flowers and beneath the trees, chatting and drawing, conversing with strangers met along the road, and drawing our study materials from our knapsacks. When difficult problems are solved like this, adolescent youngsters will be able to master all today's total of scientific knowledge.[76]

However, unlike K'ang Yu-wei, Wu's scientism took the Westernized

75 English language treatments of these two groups may be found in Robert A. Scalapino and George Yu, *The Chinese anarchist movement*, and in Agnes Chan, 'The Chinese anarchists' (University of California, Berkeley, Ph.D. dissertation, 1977).

76 X yü X [Wu Chih-hui], 'T'an wu-cheng-fu chih hsien-t'ien' (Casual talk on anarchism), *Hsin shih-chi*, 49 (30 June 1908) 191-2.

form of setting rationalism against religion. Insisting quaintly that his was a naturalistic view of the universe purged of metaphysical ghosts, Wu refused to acknowledge that his vision of 'the process of evolutionary purification' through 'benevolence'[77] owed any debt to Confucian spiritual symbolism. Following his lead, *New Century* insisted upon the sacred-secular polarization, and used it to condemn Confucianism as no more than reactionary superstition. In place of the reform tendency to see modern ethics as a steady development of germs incipient from ancient times, *New Century*'s account of the process of ethical change often relied upon images of purgation, whereby in the catharsis of a revolutionary 'moment' an originally good state of nature is rid of accumulated impurities.

By contrast with the scientistic *New Century*, *Natural Morality* (*T'ien-i*), the anarchist journal published in Tokyo, reflected the humanistic bent of its editors, the classical scholar Liu Shih-p'ei and his wife Ho Chen.[78] A founding member of the National Essence Preservation Association and scion of a famous scholarly family, Liu found that his anti-Manchu opinions made a sojourn abroad advisable in 1907. In Tokyo an acquaintance with the Japanese radicals Kōtoku Shūshui and Kita Ikki just as they were abandoning reform socialism to become anarcho-syndicalists led Liu to his two-year experiment with anarchism. Ho Chen, apparently equally affected by the Tokyo milieu, formed a Society for the Recovery of Women's Rights and, as formal editor and publisher of *Natural Morality*, made radical feminism an integral part of the anarchist message.

Natural Morality, then, blended an iconoclastic attack upon existing institutions with a curious cultural conservatism. Rather than asserting that modern Europe is closest to *ta-t'ung*, Liu Shih-p'ei and Ho Chen argued that 'Europe, America and Japan have only pseudo-civilizations.'[79] They imagined a utopia of farmer-scholars dwelling in small autarchic agrarian communities, where 'none shall depend upon another nor be the servant of another', and all would live in a state of 'non-interference' (*fang jen*).[80] Although *Natural Morality* published the first Chinese translation of *The communist manifesto*, Liu Shih-p'ei gave equal place as precursors of anarchism to the fourth century A.D. Taoist philosopher Pao

77 Lai kao [Wu Chih-hui], 'T'ui-kuang jen-shu i i shih-chieh kuan' (On curing the world through the extension of the benevolent arts), *Hsin shih-chi*, 37 (7 March 1908), 147–8.

78 *T'ien-i* (Natural morality), nos. 3–19 (10 July 1907–15 March 1908). Pagination according to the 1966 Tokyo reprint.

79 Liu Shih-p'ei and Ho Chen, 'Lun chung-tsu ko-ming yü wu-cheng-fu ko-ming chih te-shih' (On the strengths and weaknesses of racial revolution as opposed to anarchist revolution), *T'ien-i*, 6 (1 Sept. 1907) 135–44.

80 Liu Shih-p'ei, 'Jen-lei chün-li lun' (On the equalization of human powers), *ibid.* 3 (10 July 1907) 24–36.

Ching-yen (Pao P'u-tzu), and to the Warring States agronomist Hsu Hsing. Pao P'u-tzu was the author of a classic tract denouncing all government, while Hsu Hsing rejected Mencius' division of society into functional hierarchies of mental and manual labourers, and insisted instead that all without exception till the soil. Where *New Century* chose Kropotkin as their Western sage, *Natural Morality* especially revered Tolstoy, publishing his 'letter to the Chinese', which praised traditional China as the freest society in the world, and warned against the oppressive consequences of constitutional government, industrialism and military power.[81]

Both as a traditionalist and as an anarchist, Liu Shih-p'ei hated the modernizing direction of the late Ch'ing reforms, which he saw as leading to a society infected with evils of the contemporary West: the growth of militarism and the coercive apparatus of the state, the creation of new and deeper class divisions, and of a commercialized culture stained by materialism and greed.[82] For Ho Chen modernization programmes to end female seclusion and to foster women's education offered the same false illusion of reform, denying women the possibility of true economic and personal independence, while furthering new libertarian forms of male sexual exploitation.[83] Faced with the possibility that the coming political revolution might not lead to the abolition of all government, Liu and Ho made unfavourable comparisons of China's future with its past. If *ta-t'ung* is closer when there are few status barriers of wealth and rank, then traditional China was both post-feudal and pre-capitalist; its vaunted political despotism had been a facade, whose structural weaknesses had been successfully manipulated by the people 'to cast off the sphere of human government and guard their formless liberty.'[84] Although Liu Shih-p'ei did not mistake this nostalgic characterization of historical China for his utopian ideal itself, his revolt from modernity both inspired his radical thought and also motivated him in deciding to abandon the revolutionary cause late in 1908.

Like the reformers of 1898, both groups of anarchists saw themselves as internationalists. However, by 1907 internationalism was less simply a development of the traditional East Asian cosmopolitan ideal of 'all under heaven' (*t'ien-hsia*) and more a contemporary protest against both the anti-Manchu and anti-imperialist nationalist movements which had

81 *T'ien-i*, 11–12 and 16–19 (30 Nov. 1907 and 15 March 1908).
82 Liu Shih-p'ei, 'Lun hsin-cheng wei ping-min chih-ken' (On why the new politics injures the people), *T'ien-i*, 8–10 (30 Oct. 1907) 193–203.
83 Chih Ta, 'Nan-tao nü-ch'ang chih Shang-hai' (Shanghai, where men are robbers and women are whores), *T'ien-i*, 5 (19 Aug. 1907) 95–8.
84 Liu Shih-p'ei and Ho Chen, 'Lun chung-tsu ko-ming', 138.

grown up so powerfully since the 1890s. The anarchist rejection of 'wealth and power' as national defence priorities in the face of imperialism, more than any other single issue, provoked criticism from readers of both magazines. To answer, the anarchists drew upon Kropotkin against Darwin and Spencer, arguing that analogies from the group life of animals show that human social evolution is propelled by intra-species cooperation rather than by strife.

Yet a contrasting implication of their internationalism was that national enmities obscure other, deeper social cleavages. Where reformers saw class conflict, if at all, as largely external to China, the anarchists repeatedly discussed contradictions between rich and poor, bureaucrats and the people, the educated and the ignorant, city dwellers and country folk, and males and females. These deep-rooted antagonisms marring the past and present social orders were caused, they said, by the 'coercive power' of inherited systems of political authority.

On the theory that every political system serves the power interests of some elite group, *New Century* argued that the common people of China should recognize that a constitutionalist government would become the instrument of the gentry, just as abroad such governments served the capitalists. Ho Chen attributed female subordination to women's economic dependence on men, and saw female productive labour as the most menial in a general hierarchy of labour exploitation. Liu Shih-p'ei criticized the social costs of the Ch'ing reform programme: it was taxing the peasants in order to create schools, security organizations and 'self-government' assemblies for the political aggrandizement of the local elite. Analyses like these showed a class consciousness adaptable to Marxist perspectives, and so paved the way for the populist mass movements of the May Fourth period.

Sensitivity to the reality of social conflict was a function of the anarchist passion for equality. Class and status hierarchies were seen as imposed by the 'boundaries' (*chieh*) of all social distinctions, whether race, nationality, wealth, occupation, place of residence, or sex. Many extreme features of anarchist utopian blueprints were in fact strategies to overcome the subtlest differentials in the life situation of different individual human beings. Both *Natural Morality* and *New Century* proposed the rotation of sexual partners and of places of residence. Liu Shih-p'ei, following Hsu Hsing's criticism of Mencius, saw all functional divisions of labour as sources of social hierarchy. Trying to adapt Hsu Hsing's remedy of individual economic self-sufficiency to the modern scene, he proposed that each person in the course of a lifetime follow all the basic occupations seriatim:

road construction at age 21, mining and lumbering at age 22, manufacturing between 23 and 30, and so on.[85]

However, since group differences stratify even more sharply than individual ones do, the anarchists also saw 'boundaries' blocking equality in the existence of all social groups – whether family, clan, tribe, province or nation. All these create bonds of privatized attachment which pit one group collectively against all others. European anarcho-communists constantly spoke of how voluntary associations would provide a healthy structure of social organization once governments had vanished. But the Chinese anarchists were more likely to imagine either the autarchy of small, self-sufficient communities or a unitary world – in either case a system which locates the autonomous individual in a single undifferentiated collectivity. Only this could preserve the public character of utopian institutions from the corruption of private group or individual interests. Therefore it is not surprising to find that in their more original writings – those not directly abstracted from a Western model – the anarchists focused on the emancipation of the individual from all group attachment, and in particular from the most primary attachment of the family.

In the final analysis, for every anarchist the restructuring of family life was the most fundamental issue. Formulations varied: most saw the family as the root political structure that undergirds all other systems of authority. Others stressed that the family's special personal immediacy made it the place in the social system where change must begin. Others located the moral root of selfishness in the particularistic ties families create. All made clear the family's centrality to their own experience, and therefore to any utopian vision of an alternative mode of human happiness.

In asking for revolution in interpersonal relations the anarchists in fact were following K'ang Yu-wei and T'an Ssu-t'ung who had predicted the eventual 'breaking of the nets' of Confucian ritualism. K'ang Yu-wei's earliest philosophical manuscripts, which predated his evolutionary system of *ta-t'ung* by at least a decade, stressed personal 'autonomy' (*tzu-chu*) as an essential dimension of human nature which could find outer expression only within the framework of egalitarian interpersonal relationships.[86] In the chapters on the family in the *Ta-t'ung shu*, for which these manuscripts were a primary source, K'ang never denied that filial piety imposed upon children an absolute moral obligation to repay parents for their nurture. But he saw this obligation as the source of such

---

85 Liu Shih-p'ei, 'Jen-lei chün-li lun', 27-8.
86 Li San-pao, 'K'ang Yu-wei's iconoclasm: interpretation and translation of his earliest writings, 1884-87', (University of California at Davis, Ph.D. dissertation, 1978).

deep psychic pain as could be eased only when 'men will have the happiness of having abolished family, without the suffering of leaving the family.'[87] Many key institutions of K'ang's utopia, such as its public nurseries, hospitals, schools and old age homes, were substitute structures where services historically performed by the family would be provided in a way that would bypass private dependence, and therefore leave only a generalized public sense of debt. 'Having neither given favors nor received favors, there will naturally be no ingratitude.'[88]

K'ang Yu-wei believed that hierarchy in interpersonal relations came from morally binding if psychologically intolerable asymmetrical relations of owing and being owed. This was the meaning behind his condemnation of the Confucian cardinal virtue of 'duty' (*i*) as the source of all inequality.[89] T'an Ssu-t'ung, on the other hand, described the Confucian family simply as a system of oppression where 'those above . . . control those below'.[90] Both saw the interdependence of high and low within the family as morally corrupt, but for K'ang that corruption was based on guilt, while for T'an its source was tyranny. Between K'ang's appeal, which was for freedom from the burdens of reciprocal obligation, and T'an's, which was for emancipation from the dependency of slavery, there was the potential difference between psychological rebellion and political revolt.

Although both these elements were present in anarchist attacks on the family system, the later utopians tended to follow T'an's political model of family relationships. They claimed that family relationships, rather than being based on legitimate moral feelings, were purely practical arrangements. 'The father wishes his son to be filial and exacts this by fear and force, and the son becomes a slave and beast. So filial devotion is the father's personal gain. . . . The son wishes the father's benevolence only for his own benefit, . . . and parents become "ox and horse to posterity". . . . So parental benevolence is the son's personal gain.'[91] Such, according to Li Shih-tseng, was the utilitarian essence of relations that Confucianists habitually glossed over with sayings about 'reciprocity' (*shu*) and 'human sentiments' (*jen-ch'ing*). Moreover, these utilitarian arrangements of mutual dependence and servitude were based on 'fear and force'. So the politicized model of familism as a crucible of oppression had to be matched by a call for revolt, and by an assertion of faith

87 *Ta-t'ung shu*, Thompson trans., 184.
88 *Ibid*. 186.
89 Li San-pao, 'K'ang Yu-wei's iconoclasm', ch. 2.
90 T'an Ssu-t'ung, *Ch'üan-chi*, 14.
91 Chen [Li Shih-tseng], 'San-kang ko-ming' (Revolution against the three bonds), *Hsin shih-chi* 11 (31 Aug. 1907) 42.

that this 'coercive power' (*ch'iang-ch'üan*) is external and artificially imposed. In this way the present Hobbesian society where strong and weak are locked in a mutually brutalizing struggle for supremacy was seen as only the prelude to a time when 'human sentiments' might flower once more in a world irradiated by 'natural morality' (*kung-tao chen-li*) alone.

Every utopian who saw the transformation of the family as the most basic social goal was driven by the logic of this concern to advocate some feminism. Some like Li Shih-tseng followed T'an Ssu-t'ung, who had considered women the weakest of all persons in the familistic hierarchy, and so the purest victims of the system. As male radicals they wrote of women's sufferings as surrogates for their own as youth before the elders. They lectured upon women's need for self-improvement to overcome dependency with a paternalism tempered by their own sense of only relative superiority. Others in thinking of the problems of women were more affected by K'ang Yu-wei's reasoning: if the family as a biological continuum is to be abolished, its greatest vulnerability is in the marriage relationship. Preparing women for autonomy through education and work became the essential prerequisite to the detachment of childbearing from the nexus of family relationships. For Liu Shih-p'ei and Ho Chen, however, utopia most fundamentally required the abolition of the division of labour, a theoretical position which made the equality of the sexes the last and most difficult of uniformities to obtain, limited as it must be by irreducible differences in biological function. For this reason Ho Chen argued that women who did not wish to be servants of men must choose to work for a communist society where alone all forms of servitude can be eliminated.[92]

However, male utopians and women radicals differed significantly on the role of sexuality in the transvaluation of family values. From K'ang Yu-wei to the *New Century* group, a typical male utopian ideal was a world where men and women would enjoy free sexual relations unburdened by obligation. Intellectually this was a quite natural extension of their defence of spontaneous human sentiment against ritualized morality, and their suspicion that all kinds of exclusive personal relationships are inherently selfish. But Ho Chen, like most other Chinese women feminists, was more puritan than libertarian about sexuality – her ideal being an end to polygamy and to women's oppression as sexual 'playthings'.[93]

---

92 Ho Chen, 'Lun nü-tzu tang chih kung-ch'an chu-i' (On how women should know about communism), *T'ien-i*, 8–10 (30 Oct. 1907) 229–37.
93 Ho Chen, 'Nü-tzu fu-ch'ou lun' (On women's revenge), *T'ien-i*, 3 (10 July 1907) 7–17. See also Rankin, 'The emergence of women at the end of the Ch'ing'.

Anarchist rhetoric was at its most militant when the social institutions of marriage and the family were being analysed as political systems, based on raw power. However, this political model of family relations was difficult to sustain when anarchists dwelt at any length upon the subjective feelings of individuals as family members. In Chinese funeral ceremonies pious Confucian children ritually blame themselves for their parent's death. 'How can the children be to blame?' cried Li Shih-tseng,[94] intending to lay blame for false social attitudes on a corrupt environment. But in the family slaves are also dependants; and the parents' external power is matched by the child's docile acceptance of weakness and need. Belief in false Confucian values, the 'superstition' that chains an individual to accept dependency became, then, an internal failure of the self, to be overcome by moral effort. In this way the anarchists' desire to revolutionize the Confucian family system led them to reaffirm the earlier reform belief in the human being's responsibility as a moral agent in the furtherance of progress.

Yet within this new individualist framework, the question of the nature of moral success posed ambiguities earlier reformers had not faced. 'Without autonomy (*tu-li*), one naturally loses the power of liberty (*tzu-yu*); without liberty one naturally loses the power of equality (*p'ing-teng*),'[95] said Liu Shih-p'ei. The Western neologism 'liberty', used here to refer to formal civil rights in a political community, is merely a link in the natural process which begins with the individual's inner self-definition (autonomy) and ends with his or her ideal experience of human relationships (equality). Yet in this sense the enemies of autonomy and equality are not the impersonal structures of the state, which threaten liberty, but those other individuals who in actual life are the usual source of the most intimate human ties. In opposing autonomy and equality to kinship, the anarchists suggested not a political ideal of the free citizen, but a moral ideal of the self-sufficient person. Its realization carried new psychic costs: rejection of the network of relationships which were both conventionally venerated and a primary source of security and gratification. The struggle for autonomy became not a straightforward search for personal liberation, but an arduous self-discipline where there was a heavy burden of responsibility for self and all too easily also a burden of guilt.

The demand for individual liberation from the constraints of Confucian ritualism was at the heart of what may be called the existential liberalism of the reform generation. The attack on the family swelled this movement, but it also showed the psychic costs of individualism when

94 Li Shih-tseng, 'San-kang ko-ming', 41-2.
95 Liu Shih-p'ei, 'Jen-lei chün-li lun', 25.

it was defined as detachment from all social relationships. Such detach-ment could be imagined as leading to happiness only on a mystical level where the individual as a discrete atom in equal relations with others, dissolves into the undifferentiated.

Individual liberation, then, was finally imagined in the utopian language of K'ang and T'an's evolutionary cosmology: a process whereby a whole complex system of 'boundaries' (*chieh*) would be broken. In New Text Confucianism, the idea of boundaries had evoked geographical, cultural and ethnic obstacles to unified human fraternity. Buddhist-Taoist meta-physics saw boundaries as the artificial grid of things imposed upon an undifferentiated continuum of reality; while Neo-Confucian tradition gave the concept a moral basis, stressing the multiple layers dividing the inner moral mind and bad external forces of the world – the permeable membranes, as it were, which form the battleground of moral effort.

So for the anarchists the symbolism of boundaries dissolved became a way of suggesting a possible human happiness transcending social utopia. *New Century* discussions of utopian liberation commonly drifted into metaphysical reflection on a self-forgetting which can lead to harmony with the unbounded cosmic flux:

When people lack the mind that distinguishes this from that, all living things in the world are equal. There is no means for creatures to struggle, no basis for nature to select . . . in mutual succour and mutual aid all trace a path towards peace. Such love is not born of feelings, but is the extreme of non-feeling.[96]

This is how Wu Chih-hui attempted to reconcile the humanly involving love of Christians (and Confucians) with the metaphysical detachment of the Buddhist-Taoist sage.

Even in his discussions of technology and utopia, Wu Chih-hui, like K'ang Yu-wei before him, described science's greatest gifts as fostering a life like Chuang-tzu's 'free and easy wandering', where everywhere becomes nowhere. Freed by science from laborious work and disease, the men and women in utopia are above all students and travellers. In study the goal is universal knowledge – an omnivorous grasping of the world in imagination. In travel, there are movable dwellings, inns and hostels, great ships, trains, balloons and sea diving bells, even mechanical con-veyor belts between settlements. Such picturesque fantasies sketched out a style of living in which the loving permeability of one's effortless communication with the whole world implies also its opposite: detach-ment from any particular ties in that world.

96 Wu Chih-hui, 'T'ui-kuang jen-shu', 148.

If *New Century* writers symbolically represented liberation of the self as the individual's merging with the whole, Liu Shih-p'ei in *Natural Morality* imagined self-liberation through the play of cosmic forces leading humanity from autonomy to equality. The moral energies of self-assertion present in each individual would eventually be balanced constantly by exactly equivalent energies in all others, making the stasis of utopia dependent upon the fine tuning of a 'uniform distribution of power' (*chün li*). But in both cases the process of liberation begins with the self-assertion of the individual seeking to realize emancipation and ends with the nullification of social individuality.

A basic philosophical conflict between Confucianism and Taoism had revolved around the irreconcilability of Taoist individualist mystical detachment and Confucian humanistic social involvement. In refusing to choose between these alternatives the anarchists were saying that there should not be any deep-rooted contradictions between the psyche's search for spiritual enlightenment and its participation in the work of saving society. In this way, in spite of their affinity for Taoist-style egalitarian criticism of Confucian social ethics, the anarchists opted for a morally affirmative metaphysics more in harmony with Confucian myths of cosmic-human interdependence. Still, their denial that moral feelings can truly be expressed in particular human relationships allowed a Taoist spirit of detachment to infuse their discussion of social utopia. In this situation they could resolve the conflict between individual freedom and social community only by presenting the social equality (*p'ing*) of inter-related persons as an illusionary reflection of the cosmological equality (*p'ing*) of an undifferentiated ego-dissolving continuum of experience.

The social utopians had raised, if they did not answer, the question of whether individual emancipation ought to be considered an ultimate end, in light of a morality detached from all consideration of social involvement. When they were not engaged in mystical leaps, most social utopians drew back from this brink; the anarchists insisted that the realization of equality establishes public social relationships characterized by mutual aid. But such claims, tested in experience by those who followed the summons to struggle against the political authority of elders, left the youth of the early republican family revolution to consider in personal terms the rewards and the costs of autonomy. Though most New Youth later hastened as far as they could to justify their personal rebellion as furthering progress, by 1919 a few hardy souls were taking the stand that the only alternative to ritual culture is the unchecked assertion of a socially amoral self. Some were liberal academic scholars, like the historian Fu

Ssu-nien who chose personal 'spontaneity' over social 'obligation' as a private right.[97] Some were literary romantics, like the bohemians of the Creation Society, who pronounced their art to be a form of pure self-expression, requiring no social justification beyond its own beauty and interest. Even Lu Hsun told the New Youth that the 'way of the viper' was preferable to that of the sage, and proposed as a new culture hero the Nietzschian 'superman'.[98] All these rebels were expressing a desire to root action in a subjectivity that is a law unto itself, even if it brands its possessors with the status of madmen. In this way the anarchist call for personal emancipation contained the potential for a kind of pure individualism, but one which its followers themselves saw as demonic. Under the circumstances it is not surprising that few Chinese followed the utopian individualist path to the end.

In their commitment to social equality, which underlay both their call for the emancipation of the individual and their critique of familism, the anarchists broke new ground in Chinese social thought. Nonetheless this radical content was largely presented within the theoretical framework of reform evolutionary cosmology. The anarchists' emphasis upon the catalytic agency of revolutionary 'moments' was easily incorporated within an overall view of nature as the scientifically 'material', morally charged and dynamically developing cosmos of the reformers. Their reductionistic definition of Confucianism as a system of reactionary social practice simply left them with an unacknowledged debt to the Confucian metaphysical symbolism pervading their models of a slowly humanizing universe. Ch'u Min-i's formulation of these themes in *New Century* was particularly striking.[99] He saw a struggle between 'coercive power' and moral enlightenment pervading the world, in which the forces of creation and destruction acting on matter are interdependent, generating the 'negative power of progress' or 'revolution' hand in hand with the 'positive power of progress' or 'education'.[100] In this way, Ch'u said, the cosmos would progress in an open-ended cumulative fashion from the condition of 'existence' (*yu*) to one of 'non-existence' (*wu*): the first qualitatively enforced, seeming, ritualistic, false; the second spontaneous, genuine, benevolent, true. Belief in Kropotkin's mutual aid reinforced

97 David Reynolds, 'Iconoclasm, activism and scholarship: the tension between "spontaneity" and "obligation" in the thought of Fu Ssu-nien', paper presented at the Regional Seminar on Confucian Studies, University of California, Berkeley, 4 June 1976.
98 Lu Hsun, 'Wen-hua p'ien-chih lun' (On the pendulum movement of culture), and 'Mo-lo shih li shuo' (On the power of Mara poetry), in *Fen* (Graves). First published in *Honan* (Honan magazine), 1907.
99 Min [Ch'u Min-i], 'Wu-cheng-fu shuo' (On anarchism), *Hsin shih-chi*, 31–48 (21 Jan.–16 May 1908).
100 *Ibid*. 158.

Mencian teachings on human nature to produce in Ch'u an extravagant moral optimism that today a 'truly human world' is coming into being, and a faith in the prophetic role of those with a morally pure 'discerning mind' who alone can grasp the idea of revolution in its totality.

As a secularist scientific philosophy, the ideas of a Ch'u Min-i or a Wu Chih-hui were imperfect at best, distinguishable from reform versions of scientism only in the explicit claims that the sacred and the secular belong to distinct incompatible spheres of meaning. Their resulting commitment to scientific models of truth, derived as it was from alien Western controversies opposing science against religion, became an anarchist dogma without having much impact upon their actual cosmological thought. Rather, the latter continued along the reform path in its metaphysical assumptions of cosmic-human interdependence.

As theorists of revolution the anarchists followed T'an Ssu-t'ung and Liang Ch'i-ch'ao in developing the most dialectical of reform descriptions of the forces of change. Here, however, anarchist versions of evolutionary cosmology were linked to the significantly new elements in their social thought. Believing that human society is basically divided between oppressed and oppressing social groups, anarchists envisioned progress through the clash of these rather than simply via the harmonious spread of enlightenment from advanced to backward sections of the human community. Although they saw the gradualist processes of education and revolutionary flashpoints as interdependent in the historical process, they sought to educate oppressed groups, making the educative function a dialectical one: generator of resistance, not collaboration. In these ways anarchists did not simply develop a socially utopian vision of the future, but contributed to a socially revolutionary model of the political process.

Post-revolutionary anarchism and socialism

The founding of the republic in 1911 opened the way both for the free dissemination of anarchist ideas on the Chinese mainland and for new experiments in radical organization. Even in pre-revolutionary exile, the Paris and Tokyo groups had downgraded the sphere of politics but had looked upon agitational activities as education for social revolution. At the time of the 1911 Revolution, anarchists drew upon European radical experience to advocate all sorts of activities – from study societies to rallies, clubs, assassinations, strikes and tax boycotts – as propaganda, designed to raise Chinese public consciousness to the level of the European *avant-garde*. In this way China could be ready for the world-wide 'age of revolution' which they expected would be launched in Europe some time in the next generation.

Two groups led the way in propagandizing activity as soon as the old government had been overthrown. The first was the Conscience Society (Hsin she) of Liu Shih-fu, the second, Chiang K'ang-hu's Chinese Socialist Party (Chung-kuo she-hui tang).[101] Liu Shih-fu had been politically awakened in 1907 by reading *New Century* while serving a prison term in Canton for an anarchist assassination attempt, an ordeal which resulted in his declaring himself a disciple of Kropotkin. In February 1912, gathered with a few close followers on a retreat at the Buddhist White Cloud monastery near Hangchow, he dedicated his life to the propagation of the anarchist cause, and the Conscience Society was born. Chiang K'ang-hu had been exposed to anarchism and socialism on travels to Japan and Europe in 1907 and again in 1909, which had brought him into contact both with the Tokyo radicals and with the Paris *New Century* group. Back in China as administrator of several schools for women's education, he began to make speeches advocating socialism for China in the summer of 1911, and immediately took advantage of the revolution to organize a network of educational clubs for the dissemination of his ideas.

Both these movements saw their key programme as based on the abolition of the family and the creation of universal public institutions in its place, and on universal equal education. Together these were expected to end all class division and status hierarchies, and create a society of socially uniform individuals. Nonetheless, Chiang and Liu Shih-fu soon became adversaries, predictably reflecting their respective alliances with the European socialist Second International and with the International Anarchist Congress.

In the ensuing debate between them over the proper meaning of 'socialism', Liu Shih-fu objected both to Chiang K'ang-hu's acceptance of a role for state power in socialist society, and his tolerance of a degree of private enterprise in a socialist economy. With a purity of vision uncompromised by any utilitarian considerations, Liu Shih-fu projected a harmonious and atemporal total communism, where consumer as well as producer goods would be publicly owned, where money would be abolished and work rendered easy and enjoyable through the progress of science. Moreover, he insisted that anarcho-communism, based on the

101 For Liu Ssu-fu, in addition to Chan, 'Chinese anarchists', see also Edward Krebs, 'Liu Ssu-fu and Chinese anarchism 1905–15', (University of Washington, Ph.D. dissertation, 1977). For a discussion of Chiang and his party see Martin Bernal, 'Chinese socialism before 1913', in Jack Gray, ed. *Modern China's search for a political form*, 89–95; and Frederic Wakeman, *History and will: philosophical perspectives on Mao Tse-tung's thought*, 207–10.

principles of mutual aid innate in human nature, had nothing in common with any individualist interpretation of anarchism.[102]

Chiang K'ang-hu, on the other hand, remained a nationalist and a Darwinian of the Spencerian mould, believing that economic progress depends upon the utilization of human beings' natural competitive instincts in productive activities. As the means for achieving human equality, he advocated the abolition of the family, a transformation which he said centrally depended upon the complete emancipation of women; and the abolition of inherited wealth, which he thought would foster healthy economic competition and specialization of labour while ensuring that individuals nurtured by public institutions would repay these on their death.[103] Among Western social thinkers Chiang was particularly attracted by the ideas of August Bebel in *Women and socialism*, and by the Scottish Presbyterian evolutionary socialist, Thomas Kirkup, whose *History of socialism* he translated into Chinese.

Organizational as well as doctrinal differences separated the two groups. An energetic promoter, Chiang K'ang-hu saw his network of socialist clubs as preparatory to the organization of a political party. Although his claim that by 1913 the Chinese Socialist Party had 400,000 members and 400 branches was doubtless exaggerated, it reflected his hope to achieve a mass base. It also explains the Peking government proscription which resulted in his retirement to the United States late in 1913 and the movement's immediate decline thereafter.[104] Liu Shih-fu's Conscience Society, on the other hand, was built on close-knit, organic principles whose very personalism and intimacy made its suppression more difficult. It was the most devoted of a number of similar anarchist-inspired fellowships established right after the revolution when the symbolism of renewal inherent in that event suggested innovations in living to further the ideals of *ta-t'ung* in social practice. The dream of establishing an experimental rural community, harboured by Liu Shih-fu, Chang Chi and others, was never realized by any of these associations. However, the Conscience Society followed a pattern of collective self-help pioneered by the *New Century* group in Paris: members supported themselves out of a common fund raised in part from contributions and group-owned

---

102 Shang-hai wu-cheng-fu chu-i kung-ch'an t'ung-chih she kung-pu [Shih Fu], 'Wu-cheng-fu kung-ch'an-tang chih mu-ti yü shou-tuan' (Goals and methods of the anarchist-communist party), *Min-sheng* (Voice of the people), 19 (18 July 1914) (reprint edn by Lung-men shu-tien, Hong Kong, 1967), 222–225.
103 Chiang K'ang-hu, *Hung-shui chi: Chiang K'ang-hu san-shih sui i-ch'ien tso* (Flood tide: collection of writings by Chiang K'ang-hu before the age of thirty).
104 Bernal, 'Chinese socialism before 1907', 91.

productive enterprise, such as a restaurant or print shop, and shared a common residence.

More important than these tentative experiments in communal living, the association of utopia with the ideal of a morally perfected self bore fruit in ascetic and self-denying codes of personal conduct. A pledge to uphold the code in fact constituted the normal ritual establishing one's membership in an anarchist fellowship. The Conscience Society code showed a classic religious association of evil with pollution in its strictures against alcohol, tobacco and meat-eating; specifically anarchist goals were reflected in the rules against contracting a marriage, affiliating with a religion, or holding any kind of political office; while the emancipated personality ideals of autonomy and equality dictated prohibitions against employing servants or riding in rickshaws or sedan chairs. Other anarchist fellowships had more lenient codes than the Conscience Society. The largest, the Society to Advance Morality (*Chin-te hui*), founded in 1912 by the original *New Century* leadership, even allowed for degrees of membership according to the level of personal commitment. Such concessions to human weakness and the demands of existing social institutions were perhaps inevitable.

The Conscience Society's decline after 1915 was largely due to external events: Liu Shih-fu's premature death from tuberculosis that year, shortly after the group had been rocked by the outbreak of the First World War, which fatally tested the internationalist principles of the European parent organization led by Kropotkin. However, between 1912 and 1915, the Society published four anthologies of selections from *New Century*, a number of pamphlets and broadsheets, and a journal, *Min sheng* (Voice of the People), printed in Chinese and Esperanto;[105] and it had spawned affiliates in several cities. It was claimed that as late as 1919 loose successors of the Conscience Society were active in Peking, Shanghai, Nanking, Tientsin and in the province of Shansi, bearing such names as The Collective (Ch'ün she), Society of Anarchist Comrades (Wu-cheng-fu chu-i t'ung-chih she), Truth Society (Shih she), and Equality Society (P'ing-she).[106] The original *New Century* group also continued to be active after 1915. Although its leaders Li Shih-tseng and Wu Chih-hui remained based in Europe, it had a significant impact upon the Chinese student movement through its sponsorship of a series of innovative work-study programmes in France, where wartime mobilization had created a

105 *Min sheng* (Voice of the people) 1-33 (20 Aug. 1913-15 June 1921).
106 Yang Ch'üan, 'Chung-kuo chin san-shih nien lai chih she-hui kai-tsao ssu-hsiang' (Social reform thought in China in the last thirty years), *Tung-fang tsa-chih*, 21. 17 (10 Sept. 1924) 53.

labour shortage. By this means between 1912 and 1920 several hundred Chinese students pooled earnings to support themselves and their fellows while learning abroad.

After 1912 these groups of revolutionary socialists contributed to Chinese radicalism more through educational propaganda and social experiment than through doctrinal innovation. Compared with their predecessors, the post 1911 groups showed a heightened concern with social practice which stimulated closer attention to the organizational work of their European prototypes. This in turn produced, in addition to the native style anarchist fellowships, efforts at political party-building and popular education, and in Shanghai, attempts to organize urban workers. Expressions of sympathy for anarchism as the modern doctrine of *ta-t'ung* were commonplace among Chinese of radical temper in the years between the revolution and the May Fourth movement. After 1917 this sympathy extended to Peking University under the presidency of Ts'ai Yuan-p'ei, who encouraged free thought, revival of the Advance Morality Society and work-study programmes on the *New Century* model. A substantial number of the founding members of the Chinese Communist Party, including Mao Tse-tung, recalled that it was anarchism which had attracted them politically before their conversion to Marxism-Leninism after 1920. The very word 'communism' (*kung-ch'an chu-i*) was generally understood as an anarchist, not a Marxist term down to this time.[107]

Thus, before 1919 the Western socialist tradition was known to China chiefly in anarchist rather than Marxist guise. This exposure made Chinese familiar with the broad outlines of the history of the socialist movement in Europe and America, but with only a tiny corpus of original socialist literature, and that overwhelmingly from Kropotkin and his associates. Marxism, where it had been discussed in passing by reformers and revolutionaries alike before 1917, was associated with the European social democratic and labour movements in a context of parliamentary democracy and industrial production alien to the Chinese environment. The Chinese social-utopian stress on the revolution in family relationships made an un-Marxist claim for the transformation of personal life as a cause, rather than merely an effect, of other changes in the revolutionary process. Still, the anarchist exposure in some ways prepared Chinese for orthodox Marxism-Leninism later on. It acquainted people with a Marxist-style periodization of history to compete with the Spencerian one; and also with a dialectical view of change operating through a revolutionary process. It fostered a naïve but intensely felt class conscious-

107 Chow, *The May Fourth movement*, pp. 97–8, 224–5.

ness and a sympathetic concern for the common people as the agents of progress. In addition, certain persistent strands in later Chinese communist theory and practice may be better understood in light of the indigenous radical vision that the Chinese social utopians mobilized and developed. These include the Maoists' stress on cultural remoulding and rectification of personality as autonomous sources of revolutionary change; their dislike of urban-industrial economic rationalization in favour of rural-communal social mobilization; their suspicion that functional 'boundaries' create class differences; their cult of 'self-reliance'; and last but not least their need to rely on moralized human energy as the dynamo of change, which has produced both moments of utopian effort to leap forward into the millennium and recurrent haunting fears of historical reversal.

New youth

In September 1915 a magazine, New Youth (Hsin ch'ing-nien), was founded in Shanghai under the editorship of Ch'en Tu-hsiu, a well-known radical and professor of the humanities.[108] This publication, which officially inaugurated China's New Culture movement, drew together ideas which formed the third stage of thinking about evolutionary cosmology since the original reform movement of the 1890s. The original reformers had set forth the new progress-oriented world view between 1895 and 1905. The anarchists had then developed the reform utopian vision to stress revolutionary struggle to destroy social inequality and Confucian ritualism as the means to personal happiness and social utopia. Writers in New Youth described evolution in naturalistic scientific language, devoid of Confucian moral meaning. But at the same time they saw the energies of 'youth' itself propelling the process of change, infusing the universe with a new kind of moral optimism based on vitalist biology.

However, New Youth did not begin in 1915 with a straightforward affirmation of this optimistic philosophy of progress. Rather at first it was a vehicle for radical intellectuals anxious to counteract what they saw as retrogressive forces in politics and culture which were growing stronger as the experiment in republicanism faltered under the presidency of Yuan Shih-k'ai, and then fell hostage to contending militarists after his death. Still, the venture that opened as a defensive counter-thrust by beleaguered radical modernists gained momentum as large numbers of actual 'new youth', educated in the post-imperial environment, gathered

108 Hsin ch'ing-nien (New youth), Sept. 1915–July 1926, reprint edn in 14 vols. (Tokyo, 1962).

behind *New Youth*'s slogans advocating science, democracy, literary revolution, and the revolt of youth and women. By 1919 the militancy of the student movement and the apparent rout of conservatives from academic leadership at Peking and other universities gave grounds for belief that the New Culture was becoming a reality. The student-led May Fourth demonstrations of that year against foreign imperialism and the warlord government in Peking suggested the complementary appearance at last of a mobilized and awakened people as a progressive political force. This quickening of change at home had counterparts abroad in the end of the First World War, and above all in the Russian Revolution. By 1920 Ch'en Tu-hsiu and his close collaborator on *New Youth*, the philosopher and Peking University librarian Li Ta-chao, announced their conversions to Marxism and turned the magazine into a vehicle for the new Chinese communist movement. Utopian perspectives on Chinese and world history were now rekindled in a new ideology, and ground was laid for the Chinese communist revolution itself to give a retrospective imprimatur to the idea that the New Youth movement had in fact marked another great transformation of the times.

At *New Youth*'s inception in September 1915, Ch'en Tu-hsiu and his associates largely shared the pessimism about evolution that oppressed emerging neo-traditionalists and constitutionalists in the early years of the republic. Far from conjuring up anarchist-style ideal alternatives by leaps of pure imagination, *New Youth* was soberly preoccupied with the problem of China's cultural backwardness, and the dangers this posed to contemporary politics. Sharing the by then common sociological perspective on evolution, they reasoned that social custom, ethics and national psychology exercise a determinative influence upon political change. Like Liang Ch'i-ch'ao and other analysts of the 'national character', they were concerned how to overcome maladaptive disjunctions between parts of the social organism. So *New Youth*'s campaign against cultural backwardness was presented first of all instrumentally, as the way to combat a monarchic restoration in politics. Wu Yu, the magazine's best-known critic of familism, argued that China's historic inability to escape despotism was due to patriarchal mores, while Ch'en Tu-hsiu himself, in a running polemic with K'ang Yu-wei, lodged similar arguments against Confucian ethics as the tool of conservative political control under Yuan Shih-k'ai's dictatorship.[109]

However, this instrumentalist argument, which by 1915 was central

---

109 Siu-tong E. Kwok, 'The two faces of Confucianism: a comparative study of anti-restorationism of the 1910s and 1970s', paper presented to the Regional Seminar in Confucian Studies, University of California, Berkeley, 4 June 1976.

to the moderates' case for cultural reform, played only a secondary role in Ch'en Tu-hsiu's thinking. His point of departure was a new faith in science, not only in the reform manner as a form of natural philosophy, but as a positivistic method of verification controlling standards of truth about nature and society. Liang Ch'i-ch'ao in defending the 'national character' advocated cultural adaptation within the parameters of what he saw as Confucian ideals of moral personality, and viewed the naturalistic interpretation of evolution with increasing unhappiness. But Ch'en took science as a verification procedure which mandates accepting the naturalistic universe as both fact and value. Unlike most of the anarchists, who still saw consciousness as linked to an authentic 'mind' reflecting a spiritual dimension of experience, Ch'en Tu-hsiu spoke of consciousness as based on physiological psychology and imagined human beings as purely biological and social organisms. This denial that historical evolution is linked to cosmological process meant that Ch'en Tu-hsiu represented the extreme of his generation in secularism and detachment from the sage personality ideal. In consequence he and *New Youth* had the reputation of standing for 'total Westernization'.[110]

Of course Ch'en Tu-hsiu's scientistic world view was not as totally uprooted from inherited beliefs and mores as he would have had his audience believe. True, he was among the first to present his ideas in a vernacular vocabulary almost free of traditional philosophical concepts, thus avoiding the frequent reform and anarchist tactic of presenting traditional metaphysical beliefs in new rationalistic dress. Still, the personality ideal he offered to youth in 1915, for all its heightened secularism, remained in many ways a direct descendant of the 'new citizen' of 1902.

The reformers' 'new citizen' had been asked to be progress-oriented, self-assertive, dynamic and independent. K'ang Yu-wei had posited a cosmic base for the independent self, in that each individual partakes of the primordial essence of the universe. T'an Ssu-t'ung had made struggle an experiential dimension of moral personality, and Liang Ch'i-ch'ao had said that the striving individual as an agent of progress embodies the morality of its goals in the literal sense that combativeness, seen as refusal to yield to others' superior power, must contribute to the moral end of equality. Such Social Darwinism from the perspective of the weak reconciled the interests of the individual and the collective with relative ease, and allowed pragmatic, productive effort to claim moral value.

In Ch'en Tu-hsiu's lead essay, 'A call to youth', the animating energy in the human personality was seen as youth itself, not as a function of

110 For Ch'en Tu-hsiu's scientism see D. W. Y. Kwok, *Scientism in Chinese thought 1900–1950*, 59–81.

years but as the psychic attribute that makes individuals truly self-aware, and so capable of the powers of renewal that serve progress. 'Youth is like early spring, like the rising sun, like trees and grass in bud, like a newly sharpened blade!'[111] In this way naturalistic metaphors replaced cosmological ones as the thematic framework for a summons to adopt the attitudes of a modern person. 'Be progressive, not conservative'; 'Be aggressive, not retiring'; 'Be cosmopolitan, not isolationist'; these injunctions reflected basic goals of cultural renovation since the 1890s. 'Be autonomous, not servile' incorporated the social-utopian demand for radical emancipation from ritual personal relationships, but also in Ch'en's interpretation suggested the use of scientific reason as the criterion for independent thought and action. Here and in his call to 'Be practical, not formalistic,' and to 'Be scientific, not speculative,' Ch'en developed the pragmatic, task-oriented potential of the original 'new citizen' ideal in the light of his own advocacy of experimental models of verification and social decision-making.

Therefore, in accounts of the emancipated individual in *New Youth*, this scientistic secularism fostered a further shift towards defining self-realization through external social practice and away from the earlier model of personal liberation conceived of as an aspect of moral self-actualization. The individualist virtues – independence, self-reliance – were not associated in social-utopian style with a radical and essentially mystical emancipation from all entangling social relationships. Instead they suited a European model family system based upon free choice of marriage partner, the nuclear family and the economic independence of all adults. More important, these virtues were seen as functionally related to economic productivity: 'The pulse of modern life is economic and the basic principle of economic production is individual independence.... The independent individual in ethics and private property in economics bear witness to each other: this is unassailable. Social mores and material culture have advanced greatly because of it.'[112]

The same belief in the functional interrelationship of psychological attitudes and social consequences informed *New Youth* discussions of the problem of suicide, which had fascinated so many Chinese of the reform generation as they sought to understand and internalize new personality ideals. Nihilists earlier had condemned 'escapist suicide' in favour of 'suicidal assassination' on the grounds that only the second 'not only

111 Ch'en Tu-hsiu, 'Ching-kao ch'ing-nien' (A call to youth), *Hsin ch'ing-nien*, 1. 1 (September 1915).
112 Ch'en Tu-hsiu, 'K'ung-tzu chih tao yü hsien-tai sheng-huo' (Confucianism and modern life), *Hsin ch'ing-nien*, 2. 4 (1 Dec. 1916) 297.

saves oneself but also improves the world'.[113] When supporters of the New Youth movement denied the act of suicide its traditionally recognized message of moral affirmation or protest, their own withdrawal of the power to be moved in fact altered suicide's effective social meaning. But their intent was also to go beyond the nihilists' simple rejection of passivity in order to question the validity of any act based upon a Confucian moral ideal of exemplary inner self-abnegation, as well as the Confucian presumption of its resonance in a cosmic continuum extending beyond mortality. In the light of these beliefs, T'an Ssu-t'ung had chosen martyrdom, but 20 years later in the secular world of *New Youth*, the choice of death however nobly intended was seen simply as an evasion of social responsibility: 'Only the living can struggle.'[114]

For the evolutionary naturalists of *New Youth* life itself was both the source of human value and proof of evolution's moral teleology. During the May Fourth period the French philosopher Henri Bergson attracted attention from neo-traditional Confucianists as a Western sage whose doctrine of '*élan vital*' showed he understood the intuitive roots of moral experience inaccessible to scientific reason. But Bergson's 'creative evolution' made Ch'en and his associates think they had found a scientifically valid philosophical language that reaffirmed an evolutionary vision of natural human interdependence in a developing universe suffused with humanist purposes. Youth, by virtue of its comparative freedom from the backward drag of the inherited environment and its 'class' hostility to gerontocracy, was the social group most fit to act as the cutting edge of progressive change. Youth was also the symbol of the biological energies presumed to animate the forces of the universe as a whole.

By this route the scientific, pragmatic modernists of the New Youth movement came back to cosmological theories of the metahistorical process. In Li Ta-chao[115] the magazine had a metaphysician of youth who drew on Confucian-Taoist cosmic symbolism unaccompanied by Confucian moral symbolism to celebrate all the movements of the naturalistic universe as having the inherent value of life itself: 'The cascade of the great actuality continually arises from actuality without beginning and flows towards actuality without end. My own "I", my own life also is endlessly part of the flow of life in compliance with the flow of great actuality, and with its increase, continued movement, onward revolution

113 Quoted in Bauer, *China and the search for happiness*, 354.
114 T'ao Meng-ho, 'Lun tzu-sha' (On suicide), *Hsin ch'ing-nien*, 6. 1 (15 Jan. 1918) 22. See also Ch'en Tu-hsiu, 'Tui-yü Liang Chü-ch'uan [Liang Chi] hsien-sheng tzu-sha chih kan-hsiang' (Impressions of the suicide of Mr Liang Chü-ch'uan), *ibid.* pp. 25–26.
115 For a full-scale study of Li Ta-chao see Maurice Meisner, *Li Ta-chao and the origins of Chinese Marxism*.

and advance. Actuality is energy; life is its onward revolution.'[116] Li selected the moment of creation as the primary aspect of the metahistorical process. Within the universe of phenomena characterized by bipolar pairs of qualitative forces, youth, spring, birth, creation have existence only thanks to their relativistic dependence upon their opposites – death, winter, age and destruction. But beyond phenomena the universe as a whole must be seen under the aspect of time itself. Here time's phenomenal characteristics – differentiation, relativity and change – must be contrasted with its numinous aspects – the absolute, uniformity and constancy. Therefore 'youth', 'spring', 'now', are numinous reality: the energies of these moments vibrate through all others. 'Use the springlike self of today to kill the white-haired self of yesterday; . . . use the springlike self of today to prepare to kill the white-haired self who is coming.'[117] For Li Ta-chao the social message implied by such transcendent images was that conservatives must be recognized as out of tune with the energies of the cosmos, and that the only authentic human use of the present is to struggle to create the future. The biological and emotional lesson was the denial of death – either of the self, the nation, or the physical universe.

An euphoric impulse towards a poetry of celebration was basic to Li Ta-chao's temperament, visible as early as 1915 when in a widely read literary exchange he reproached his friend Ch'en Tu-hsiu for pessimism and misanthropy in face of the nation's difficulties.[118] But the spread of the New Culture movement at home and the quickening pace of world change in the closing years of the European war raised expectations in both men. Ch'en Tu-hsiu saw events confirming his belief in the power of acceleration in history generated by the complex interplay of cultural and institutional causes and effects: 'A kind of theory gives rise to a form of society; a form of society gives rise to a kind of theory. Complex influences shift with the times; the more complex the shifts and the shorter the time in which they occur, the higher the level of progress.'[119] So intent became their focus on contemporary affairs that in 1918 Li and Ch'en started a second magazine, *Weekly Critic* (*Mei-chou p'ing-lun*), devoted exclusively to the discussion of national and world politics.

At first it seemed as if the Allied victory in the world war was the climactic event which defined this great turning point in the times. Not only *New Youth*, which had identified history's goals with the advance of

116 Li Ta-chao, 'Chin' (Now), *Hsin ch'ing-nien*, 4. 4 (15 April 1918) 337.
117 Li Ta-ch'ao 'Ch'ing-ch'un' (Spring), *Hsin ch'ing-nien*, 2. 1 (1 Sept. 1916) 16.
118 Li Ta-chao, 'Yen-shih hsin yü tzu-chueh hsin' (On misanthropy and self awareness), *Chia-yin* (Tiger magazine), 1. 8 (10 Aug. 1915).
119 Ch'en Tu-hsiu, 'K'ung-tzu chih tao yü hsien-tai sheng-huo' *Hsin ch'ing-nien*, 296.

Western democracy and science, but all Chinese aware of the Wilsonian programme of self-determination expected the Allied victory to reverse the recent course of imperialist encroachments on China's sovereignty. But Li Ta-chao's 1918 salute to the Bolshevik Revolution turned out to be more significant. When he greeted the new year of 1919 as the dawn of a 'new era' (*hsin chi-yüan*), drawing upon the historical symbolism of renewal implied by a change of reign titles, Li made clear that the pattern of progress he now foresaw would be generated by systems of economic production as Marx foretold:

From now on all know that productive systems can be reformed, national boundaries can be as if struck down, and human kind can all enjoy opportunities for work, and that all kinds of sorrow, hardship, anxiety, strife, can all naturally vanish.... Now the productive system is giving rise to a great movement. The united working class and their comrades all over the world will make rational production unions, break down national barriers and overthrow the world capitalist class ... these are the glories of our new era! Like ice exposed to spring sun, in the light of these glories the evils of the past will gradually melt away, the residues of history will as leaves blown by autumn wind fall to the ground.[120]

The interest in Marxism which spread rapidly among radical Chinese in 1919 and 1920 was stimulated by the same disillusionment with the victorious liberal democracies that prompted neo-traditionalists to unite behind a post-war critique of the 'materialistic West'. The Versailles Treaty, then, on all sides became a catalyst stimulating re-evaluation of the reform model of the West which had so powerfully influenced a whole generation's vision of Chinese and world progress. The trauma of republican politics, the First World War and China's betrayal at the Peace Conference made Liang Ch'i-ch'ao abandon faith in the moral teleology of evolution. Ch'en Tu-hsiu, who (through the war) had identified the Allied cause with the ideals of justice, in 1919 found the shock of the Versailles Treaty compounded by a five-month stay in prison for his role in the May Fourth demonstrations against it. By the middle of 1920 Ch'en was totally committed to the new revolutionary social science of Marxism. From all sides of the ideological spectrum many followed the direction of either Liang or Ch'en, giving vent to a criticism of the liberal West all the stronger for having been so long unexpressed. For a whole generation Chinese committed to their own national revival according to a pattern of world progress had tended to mask one of the two Janus faces the West presented to China. Either they had compartmentalized their anger at violations of Chinese sovereignty, dealing with these on a

120 Li Ta-chao, 'Hsin chi-yüan' (A new era), *Mei-chou p'ing-lun* (15 Jan. 1919).

purely non-theoretical practical level, or they had maintained belief in the unity of enlightenment and power at the price of blaming themselves for Chinese weakness. The Marxist perspective, like the neo-traditional one, permitted a release from the bitterness of silent humiliation, as the balance shifted back toward belief that external evils were responsible for many of China's problems.

The reform model of the liberal West never recovered its original lustre. In the immediate atmosphere of the May Fourth anti-imperialist movement, the liberal reform belief which suffered most in radical circles was that in gradualism itself. Instead, evolutionary and revolutionary methods of change were seen as increasingly incompatible alternatives. Where the earlier anarchists had argued that a long-range historical perspective united these two in a complementary dialectic, young Mao Tse-tung, as a student radical in the provincial capital of Changsha, was an opponent of those he called evolutionary believers in *ta-t'ung*. Rather, he called for a mobilization of 'a great union of the popular masses' which he claimed could quickly achieve a total transformation of Chinese society.[121] Hu Shih, a popular Peking University professor who had become a follower of John Dewey in the course of his American education, found in the fall of 1919 that his advocacy of a scientistic, problem-oriented approach to reform was now sharply challenged. In a polemic dubbed the 'problems versus isms' debate, his claim that change comes 'in inches and drops' was countered by Li Ta-chao, who replied that each age is characterized by a fundamental orientation of the times derived from its system of economic relations. In the light of this, Li said, all of its problems may be shown to be interrelated, the people's consciousness can achieve a common foundation, and a direction can be set for total change. Both sides understood the arguments for a 'problems' approach as an attempt to challenge revolutionary socialist ideology.[122]

By the end of the May Fourth period, in radical circles the concept of *ta-t'ung* was increasingly associated with the previous generation's reform ideology and with a passive, apolitical and elitist approach to change. Nonetheless, as the foregoing suggests, at least one factor in the intellectual appeal of Marxism for Chinese at this time was that, side by side with the model of political action the Bolshevik revolution supplied, it was possible to see in early Marxist interpretations of history and society a final revision of evolutionary cosmology. While Chinese disillusionment

121 Mao Tse-tung, 'Min-chung ti ta-lien-ho', first published in *Hsiang-chiang p'ing-lun* (Hsiang River review), 21 July–4 Aug. 1919. See annotated translation by Stuart Schram, 'The great union of the popular masses', *The China Quarterly*, 49 (Jan.–March 1972) 88–105.
122 Chow, *May Fourth movement*, 218–22; Meisner, *Li Ta-chao*, 105–12.

with the liberal democracies proved irreversible, the Chinese faith in 'democracy' and 'science' as reform utopians originally interpreted them could survive uprooting from the soil of contemporary Europe and America to be projected yet again onto the world's distant future. Li Ta-chao, as the first major Chinese Marxist theorist and Mao's early teacher, not only believed that Marxism was the true carrier of the Western scientific and democratic heritage, but also took up social-utopian themes of personal liberation and the natural ethic of mutual aid as part of his Marxist creed.[123]

As a Marxist, Li Ta-chao portrayed the class system as operating on a world-wide scale to make the labouring people the motive force of world progress, and their struggle an inevitable manifestation of the development of natural and social phenomena. Moreover, he believed that the common people's power to make revolution was derived from their autonomy: from their self-consciousness of their own power, and their knowledge that those who belong to themselves are those who can rise up to be useful to society. Li saw in the labouring masses a human agent of change dynamic enough to complement the impersonal forces of production without being overwhelmed by them. In this way even without developing a sophisticated Marxist theory of social practice, Li found the balance that evolutionary cosmologists had sought between the 'voluntarism' of inner human conscious activity and the 'determinism' of external metahistorical processes. Finally, just as evolutionary cosmologists had sought to harmonize Darwinian means of competitive struggle and Confucian ends of moral community, Li considered mutual aid to be a complement to class struggle: as the ethical goal of socialism mutual aid could not, he thought, be disassociated from the processes of class struggle to attain that goal.

Throughout the reform generation, those who took their intellectual orientation from evolutionary cosmology, whether in its more sacred or more secularized forms, had depended upon a few essential ideals. They had assumed that traditional Confucian-Taoist cosmological categories complemented rather than contradicted Western models of the natural universe. They had maintained an organicist assumption of the interdependence, above, of the natural-historical and the cosmic-spiritual spheres, and, below, of the social, cultural and political orders: even as all these parts were increasingly perceived as analytically distinct. They projected a utopian portrait of world-wide progress, leading, with whatever twists and turns, to the ideal world of *ta-t'ung*. And, while they

<hr />

123 Meisner, *ibid.* 140–54.

had dethroned politics and political leaders as the primary agents of change, they had resisted deterministic alternatives which made progress subject to impersonal social and historical forces alone. Instead, they looked within humanity, first for moral energy conceptualized as a subjective spiritual force, then as an organic collective spirit of a whole people, and finally objectified in mass political movements. When Chinese Marxists no longer relied upon any Confucian-Taoist symbols to describe the universe at large, when they no longer linked the energies of the revolutionary working classes to a spirit of universal humanistic enlightenment developing within the people, and when they portrayed themselves as strict, secular scientific materialists, they had stepped outside the boundaries of evolutionary cosmology as a belief system. To the extent that the Marxist focus on mass political movements as agents of change demanded attention to social action, the intellectual energies of Chinese Marxists no longer went to evolutionary myth-making. Yet as the case of Li Ta-chao illustrates, this break was by no means always immediate or sharp, and evolutionary cosmology has left its imprint upon the structure of Chinese Marxist dialectics.

CHAPTER 8

THEMES IN INTELLECTUAL HISTORY: MAY FOURTH AND AFTER

THE MAY FOURTH INCIDENT

It goes without saying that many factors combined to create the great intellectual upsurge of 1919 and the early 1920s that in the Chinese fashion has been given a neutral numerical designation as the 'Five-four' (*Wu-ssu*, that is, fifth month, fourth day) movement. There were several necessary developments behind this phase of China's intellectual transformation, the first and foremost being the creation of Peking University (generally abbreviated as Peita) as a modern institution of higher learning. From 1917 it was under the leadership of a new president, Ts'ai Yuan-p'ei (1867–1940). Ts'ai's career spanned the old and the new eras. By the age of 25 he had distinguished himself in classical studies at the Hanlin Academy but he subsequently became a revolutionary in the T'ung-meng hui, studied Western philosophy in Germany for four years, and served as the Chinese Republic's first minister of education for six months in 1912. Taking control at Peita, he welcomed ideas from all over the world and collected a faculty of brilliant young men of diverse backgrounds.

This institutional development soon brought forth a major linguistic reform, namely *pai-hua*, the written vernacular. Ch'en Tu-hsiu (1879–1942), who became dean of letters, had studied in Japan and France, participated in the Revolutions of 1911 and 1913, and founded several magazines including *Hsin ch'ing-nien* (New youth) in 1915, which he continued to edit after becoming dean. Another classically-trained young scholar, Hu Shih (1891–1962) returned to Peita from study between 1910 and 1917 at Cornell and Columbia. Hu Shih soon had Ch'en Tu-hsiu's support in the promotion of *pai-hua*, as an essential tool both for modern thinking and for bringing education to the common people. The esoteric classical writing intelligible only to scholars was abandoned in favour of the expressions and vocabulary of everyday speech – the change made when Latin gave way to the national languages in the European Renaissance. By 1920 the Ministry of Education prescribed the use of *pai-hua* in the schools.

Meanwhile patriotic public concern over the fate of the country, although still superficial in numerical terms, had been increasingly exercised by Japanese encroachment. It was epitomized in the Twenty-one Demands of 1915 and by the tendency of warlords, especially of the Anfu Clique dominant in Peking, to conspire for their own gain with Japan's imperialists. In 1919 Chinese nationalism was at a new height of concern over the Shantung issue. At the Paris Peace Conference it was finally decided to honour the secret wartime agreements made by Japan with Great Britain, France and Italy by which Japan would retain the entitlements of Germany in Shantung province, from which the Japanese had expelled the Germans in 1914. This flagrant denial of the new Wilsonian principles of open diplomacy and self-determination touched off the May Fourth incident.

On that afternoon over 3,000 students from a dozen Peking institutions rallied at the Gate of Heavenly Peace (T'ien-an men) at the entrance to the palace to protest at the Paris decision and the complicity of the Anfu government that had itself in 1918 secretly agreed to let Japan remain in Shantung. Beginning peaceably, the demonstrators eventually beat a pro-Japanese official and burned a cabinet minister's residence. The Peking government used force to imprison hundreds of students, whose fellow students then became all the more active. The whole patriotic public was aroused. Student disturbances erupted in at least 200 other localities. Shanghai merchants closed their shops for a week and workers went on strike in some 40 factories. A student movement was born in which women participated, broad public support was enlisted, and the sanction of saving China was invoked to achieve an unprecedented degree of student organization and activism. This was a new political expression of nationalism, all the more significant because it was unpremeditated. Of the many consequences that flowed from the incident, the Peking government was obliged to give in, and some 1,150 students marched victoriously out of jail – a victory that was to be felt for a long time afterwards.

Because May Four as an incident occurred at a time when major developments in politics, thought and society were already under way, it was neither a beginning nor a culmination, even though its name is now used to cover an era. It follows that we must look before and after if we are to see the long-term trends of the time. We must also accept the fact that so broad and protean a period of China's history is most feasibly approached on one level at a time. Even on the plane of thought and culture, moreover, we must recognize limits.

The contributions to this volume concerned with modern China's intellectual history focus their attention for the most part on the intellectuals themselves. It is a focus which requires no apologies, for this stratum, small as it was, concerned itself with themes and issues of enormous, intrinsic significance for China and for the modern world in general. Yet the fact remains that in so directing our attention, we are not dealing with the conscious life of the vast majority of the Chinese population who, for the most part, continued at least until 1949 to live in a world still dominated by the categories of the traditional popular (and high) culture. To be sure, China in the twentieth century sees the emergence of a large urban population exposed to the world of the new popular press, new kinds of Western-influenced literature and even cinema; a population which participates in political events, and shares new ideas – and yet, a population which also continues to live deeply within the older traditions. Indeed, the world of popular religion and of 'superstition', the world of secret societies and religio-political sects, the world of Buddhist monks, Taoist priests and sect leaders, is a world which still lives on even now in Taiwan and other sectors of the Chinese cultural world outside of the People's Republic. There its fate still remains uncertain in spite of official suppression. It is a world which is only now beginning to receive serious scholarly attention in the West. Its twentieth-century history has yet to be written.

Within the Chinese intelligentsia itself, there have been scholars, politicians and novelists – men such as Ku Chieh-kang, Cheng Chen-to, Ch'ü Ch'iu-pai, Lu Hsun, and Shen Ts'ung-wen among others – who have concerned themselves with the world of popular culture. As we shall indicate below, they have tended to view that world in terms of particular concerns and preoccupations of their own, but their writings taken together with the work of pioneer Japanese scholars and some Western anthropologists will facilitate future work on this subject.

The main focus of this chapter is on themes and issues which were to dominate the discourse of the intellectual stratum during the May Fourth period (loosely defined) and after. Yet to begin our account with 4 May 1919, would be to begin *in medias res*. It is now clear to all students of twentieth-century intellectual history that some of the overarching themes which were to dominate the first half of our century (and beyond) in China were in fact already posed at the end of the nineteenth and beginning of the twentieth centuries. Since many of these themes have been analysed in the contributions to this volume of Charlotte Furth and Leo Ou-fan Lee, we can begin here with a brief recapitulation.

PROGRESS AND NATIONALISM

As the preceding chapter points out, the grandest and most enduring theme of all is the theme of historical or evolutionary progress as first interpreted in the writings of the great pioneers like K'ang Yu-wei, Yen Fu, and T'an Ssu-t'ung. It is in their writings that we meet the notion of a vast cosmic-social process leading mankind eventually to the realization of unimagined possibilities of human achievement or even to a utopian resolution of all human problems. Whether the idea was frankly accepted as Western or whether, as in the case of K'ang Yu-wei, one sought Chinese roots for it, it remained profoundly subversive in its implications for the conventional Confucian socio-political order which had prevailed for so many centuries.

While the idea itself is universalistic in its implications, its acceptance in China can be related to certain immediate pressing concerns of the last decade of the nineteenth century. The prospect of the possible imminent collapse of the polity was one which Chinese literati such as Yen Fu, K'ang Yu-wei, and Liang Ch'i-ch'ao could not accept. Their deeply ingrained sense of themselves as custodians and political leaders of the society made it unthinkable for them to accept the notion of the demise of China as an independent socio-political entity.

By the end of the century they finally confronted the crucial question of whether the survival of the established conventional Confucian order as a total system was any longer compatible with the survival of China as a socio-political entity (what Liang Ch'i-ch'ao called the 'ch'ün'). Having opted for the latter they had in effect opted for nationalism as the demand of the immediate future. Once the survival and prosperity of the nation was established as a paramount goal, the theme of nationalism was to remain dominant in spite of its involvement from the very outset with ideologies like social Darwinism which posited more universalistic goals. It was a burning question of national survival, which in the first instance led to an uninhibited examination of all those technologies, institutions, systems and ideas that had promoted the ascendancy of the Western nation-state. The revitalization of China as a socio-political entity was – at least in the short range – to remain a major object of progress.

Yet the idea of progressive evolution itself had a significance which went beyond this goal. What Yen Fu learned in the West was not simply the fact that new unimagined human possibilities had been realized in the West and might be emulated in China. What he had acquired was a new faith in the idea of progressive cosmic evolution. The West had progressed by somehow being in line with the soaring energies of the cosmic processes of evolution – a universal process which must somehow also be at work in China itself.

The notion of impersonal forces and configurations of history beyond the control of individual men was itself not a new idea in China. History had often been described in terms of the mysterious workings of Heaven or the 'Tao' within the cosmic-social 'outer realm' over which men exercised the most limited control. There was in fact a strand of Chinese thought represented by Shao Yung, Chang Hsueh-ch'eng and others which was much preoccupied with such historical patterns. On the whole, it was not one of the more sanguine strains in Chinese thought since it tended to stress the constraints imposed on human hopes by historical fate. What was new in Western nineteenth-century doctrines of progressive evolutionism and historicism was not the notion of the impersonal forces of history as such – but the notion that such forces inevitably tended in a direction favourable to human hopes. This idea itself – quite apart from the particular conception of the dynamic forces involved – was what united K'ang Yu-wei, who still employed traditional terminology, with Yen Fu, who used the language of social Darwinism.

What this implied on the negative side was nothing less than the historical relativization of the established conventional Confucian order. The kingship, the examination system, the immemorial structures of bureaucracy and the rituals of human relations, which had seemed to be part of an eternal order (even when the actual functioning of the order was subject to severe criticism), now belonged to their place in time. To be sure, Yen Fu, K'ang Yu-wei and Liang Ch'i-ch'ao remained monarchists throughout the first decade of the century, but this was now an instrumental monarchism. The Chinese people were woefully unprepared for a republic. Yet it was they who at one stroke had reduced the kingship to the humble status of a passing human institution.

What one perceives here is a radical sense of release from all prevailing structures – a 'breaking out of all the networks' in the vivid phrase of T'an Ssu-t'ung. On this level, we have something like a radical critique of the past. Why had the forces of history which had moved inexorably forward in the West been paralysed in China? To K'ang Yu-wei, Confucius' true message had been distorted by centuries of Old Text Confucianism. To Yen Fu, the sages and sage-kings had almost systematically repressed the creative energies of the people. Such explanations seem hardly consonant with a determinist doctrine of progressive evolution. They seem to suggest the power of the conscious will to retard the evolutionary forces. It is this theme, in fact, which already prefigures the 'unmasking' view later found in the writings of the New Culture and more vulgar Marxists – namely, the view that China's traditional elite culture had been a kind of deliberate device for suppressing the forces of progress. Whatever the inconsistencies of these doctrines, however, one could now hope that the forces of evolution or history would finally break through all the barriers, structures, and the negative repressive authoritarianism of the past. In all of this one perceives a pervasive mood of 'anti-structuralism' – a preference for reality conceived of in terms of a continuum of energy and transcendent formless forces rather than in terms of eternal orders and structures.

We have spoken here of the conventional Confucian order rather than of the entire heritage of the past, for the fact is that the pre-1911 generation did not carry out a 'totalistic' rejection of that heritage. It was deeply enough immersed in the culture to be acutely aware of its rich variety and inner conflicts. Alternative traditions were often invoked in order to find Chinese equivalents of Western ideas, and here the motives involved may well have been the need to salvage national pride at a time when what was 'valuable' no longer corresponded to history, as has been suggested by Joseph Levenson.[1] Yet the revival of Mahayana Buddhist philosophy[2] and 'philosophic' Taoism at the end of the century (and even before) cannot be completely disposed of in this way. The fact is that Buddhism and Taoism brought to bear a perspective which relativized and devalued Confucian concepts of eternal structures from the point of view of a transcendental realm of being beyond all forms and structures.

In the past this transcendance had not been subversive in any sociopolitical sense. The 'Buddha mind' of Yogacara Buddhism, the realm of non-being (*wu*) of Taoism, had provided places of refuge into which one could 'sink back' from all the sufferings of a corrupt world. To some of those involved in the Buddhist revival such as Yang Wen-hui, Ou-Yang Ching-wu and even the revolutionary Chang Ping-lin, the basic attraction of Buddhism still lay here. Yet what we note now is a kind of inversion in which the ultimate source of being is no longer viewed as a refuge but as the source of a kind of infinite propulsive energy breaking through all the confining structures of human history and finally leading men to an ultimate deliverance on both the societal and individual levels.[3] On the individual level, in the form of a quasi-Buddhist-Taoist pantheism,

1 See Levenson, Joseph R., *Liang Ch'i-ch'ao and the mind of modern China*; and also *Confucian China and its modern fate*.
2 See Chan Wing-tsit, *Religious trends in modern China*, for an English source on this subject.
3 This inversion was not entirely without historical precedent. The theme of the world-saving Bodhisattva who saves men not through religious compassion but through sociopolitical transformation can be found in Wang An-shih and others.

it could even become the inspiration of the variety of romanticism which would eventually lead to Kuo Mo-jo's rhapsodic cry, 'All nature is a manifestation of God. I am also a manifestation of God. Therefore I am God. All nature is a manifestation of myself.'[4] The invocation of these traditional strains meant that the kind of abyss between the human realm and the cosmic realm presupposed by so many modern Western versions of the idea of progress did not emerge as a major issue to these pioneer thinkers.

In all of this the pioneers confronted what might be called the Leninist dilemma. Like Lenin they had enthusiastically embraced the concept of a linear development of the 'objective forces' of history leading to a predictable future. Yet like Lenin, they also were exasperated by the failure of these forces to operate in China's living present. If history in the past could be ascribed to objective organic forces, the metaphor more applicable to the present was that of history as a kind of pre-existent path or ladder. The faith that the goal is pre-ordained remains an inspiring faith yet the responsibility for leading China along this path would fall to a new stratum of 'sages', 'foreknowers' and 'vanguards'.

Despite the common spirit of radical negation towards the immediate past, when we turn to the pioneer thinkers' positive visions of the future we note significant differences among them. They seem roughly in agreement concerning the requirements of the next historical stage – some programme of modernization pivoted on the monarchy roughly along the lines of Meiji Japan. Yet the orientations of K'ang Yu-wei and Yen Fu were profoundly different. Yen Fu was prepared to discern the universal republic of man in the distant future, but his present attention was firmly fixed on the concrete study of those mechanisms of material and social technology which had led the West – Great Britain in particular – to its present high estate. The tasks of the intellectual vanguard in China would be the sober scientific tasks of mastering the knowledge of those technologies, institutions and infrastructures which would lead to the release of the physical, intellectual and moral energies of the individual and the consolidation of these energies in the service of the nation-society. Involved in all this was the actual appropriation of many of the doctrines of Anglo-American liberalism. What was required was the creation of rationalized bureaucratic, legal, economic and educational systems which would create a 'new individual' (Liang Ch'i-ch'ao's 'new citizen') all of whose constructive energies and capacities would be developed in the service of the nation. By his translation of Adam Smith's *Wealth of nations*

4 Cited by Leo Ou-fan Lee, *The romantic generation of modern Chinese writers*, 183, from Kuo's preface to his translation of Goethe's *Sorrows of the young Werther*.

Yen even indicated that a capitalist economy would be an essential component of such a programme. The essential pathos is that of rational technocracy despite the fact that the pleas for liberty often take on a genuinely emotional tone.

When we turn to K'ang Yu-wei we find that his sweeping spiritual-moral imagination led him to quite a different pathos in spite of his acceptance of a programme of modernization for the next stage of history close to that just described. His utopian imagination quickly led him to leap beyond the model of the future provided by the contemporary West to his own quite different apocalyptic vision. When we now examine his utopian work (*Ta-t'ung shu*) (The book of the great harmony) we note that while it may well have been influenced by nineteenth-century Western socialist literature, there is a distinctly Buddhist-Taoist dimension in the text. The utopia of the future will be a universal republic of mankind in which all the structures of family, class and nation which divide men from each other will have been dissolved and along with them all the obligations which had burdened men's lives. Yet these structures are not dissolved in order to liberate the 'individual' from society. They are rather dissolved in order to fuse men into a common humanity no longer separated by obstacles and barriers. On an even more mystical level, this sinking into the ocean of humanity may ultimately involve a more cosmic liberation of suffering mankind from the trammels of individual existence as such. While K'ang Yu-wei and his disciple T'an Ssu-t'ung interested themselves in science and technology, their ultimate vision of history was that of a spiritual-moral drama leading to a spiritual-moral resolution. It is a theme which stands in striking contrast to Yen Fu's 'technocratic' vision of the foreseeable future.[5] The two contrasting visions are fraught with implications for the future.

It was, of course, Yen Fu and Liang Ch'i-ch'ao who introduced a striking new view of the dynamic principles of evolution – the gospel of social Darwinism. However questionable its relation to Darwinism as biological science, this new, shocking and exciting doctrine was now destined to become the source of a transformation of Chinese values. The processes of natural selection and the survival of the fittest, whether applied to the interactions of individuals or of national societies, required a new conception of man. Dynamism, aggressiveness, self-assertion, the realization of capacities – all the vitalities which had been suppressed by a morality which had fostered peace, harmony, passivity and resignation –

5 There is, to be sure, a somewhat different Taoist-Buddhist dimension in Yen Fu's own thought. See Benjamin Schwartz, *In search of wealth and power: Yen Fu and the West,* particularly ch. 10.

must now be exalted. Above all, what was required was the kind of economic competition and 'struggle for survival' among men of capacity and talent which seemed so compatible with liberal ideas. The idea assumed its more radical and lurid aspect when applied to the conflicts of nations. The theme of the struggle of collectivities as an engine of progress would, of course, eventually find a new and different embodiment in Marxism-Leninism.

Social Darwinism in China was by no means as favourable to the cause of economic individualism as one might suppose from its contemporary Western context. It did not inhibit an interest from the very outset in contemporary Western doctrines of socialism or the socialist critique of capitalism. K'ang Yu-wei's vision of utopia was certainly 'socialistic' in spirit. Liang Ch'i-ch'ao, who was to become the somewhat inconsistent spokesman of both his earlier master K'ang Yu-wei and of Yen Fu, was to be the first in China to discuss socialism and the socialist critique of capitalism. Yen Fu's own advocacy of Adam Smith's doctrine was not based on any passionate acceptance of the gospel of classical economics, but on a 'realistic' assumption that capitalism was evolution's engine for achieving industrial development. Liang Ch'i-ch'ao, who was eventually won back to this view after 1905 in the course of his debates with the revolutionaries, nevertheless entertained the idea that in the future a state socialism which controlled and consolidated the economy while diminishing economic inequality might make China a more effective combatant in the jungle of international affairs than a liberalism which in the end could only weaken the state by its emphasis on divisive individual and group interests.

One of the concomitants of the interest in socialism – whether combined or not combined with social Darwinism – was, in fact, to be the emergence of a somewhat more benign attitude towards the Chinese past – an attitude which seemed to run directly counter to the indictment of that past discussed above – coupled with the beginnings of the anti-capitalist critique of the contemporary West from a 'higher' standpoint. In China, as both Liang Ch'i-ch'ao and Sun Yat-sen insisted, it had always been assumed that the ruling class would concern itself with the people's livelihood. China had never known the sharp divisions of class which marked the truly Darwinian history of the West. China might in the future use 'the advantages of backwardness' (later echoed in Mao's conception of China's 'poverty and blankness') to avoid some of the most dire consequences of Western capitalism. Yen Fu, who remained more faithful to his Spencerian source of inspiration continued to insist that the harsher conflicts which had supposedly marked the history of the West, and even the individualistic competition of capitalism, were all proofs of that civilization's superior fitness. China required individual as well as collective dynamism.

REVOLUTION

The first decade of the twentieth century was also to witness the powerful impact of yet another theme – that of revolution. The concept of revolution as a kind of collective act marking a total qualitative break with the established socio-political order is, of course, based on the idea of progress, yet in some ways it seems more easily linked to Western eighteenth-century ideas than to nineteenth-century concepts of an incremental evolutionary or historical growth. Chinese revolutionaries such as Sun Yat-sen and the revolutionary students in Japan at the beginning of the century would speak in a rhetoric which mingled eighteenth-century Western ideas with the rhetoric of social Darwinism.

In dealing with the past Yen Fu and Liang Ch'i-ch'ao (who again is less consistent in his rhetoric) had evidenced a certain variety of populism. They had indignantly deplored the way in which the traditional culture had inhibited the creative energies and capacities of the people. Yet having been inhibited, the potentialities of the people could be cultivated only by a long and ordered process of evolutionary development under the guidance of a vanguard. There was no reason to believe that there was some latent popular wisdom just below the surface which would make itself manifest once the obstacle of the old society had been eliminated by a revolutionary transformation. The revolutionaries as a whole used a variety of arguments. Sun Yat-sen was prepared on one level to argue that the Chinese people had in fact developed roots of 'village democracy' which would provide a firm foundation of democracy once the incubus of the Manchus had been removed. Others argued that the forces of evolution could only be released by revolution. 'Revolution', states Tsou Jung in his *Ko ming chün* (Revolutionary army), 'is the law of evolution'. For them, the dichotomy perceived by later Marxists in both China and the West between 'positivistic evolutionism' and 'dialectic revolutionism' was quite blurred. It should be added that the outcome of the revolution was envisioned as a democratic republic – although very often as a democratic republic with a 'socialistic' dimension.

From the outset the Chinese revolutionaries confronted the same Leninist dilemma. Was a revolution an objective event which would simply happen when its time had come or did it require a vanguard of revolutionary activists and heroes? Like most of their revolutionary contemporaries in Russia and to some extent under their influence, they were, of course, speedily convinced that the revolution required revolutionary leaders. It was on this level that the young revolutionaries were to seek not only an answer to the needs of the nation but also a new image of themselves as individuals. The new individual of Yen Fu and Liang Ch'i-ch'ao would be a productive and disciplined 'modern man' – the self-confident engineer, industrialist and professional of the new society. Yet the same negation of the existing order which had made possible this image also made possible a more romantic view of individuality which emphasized the liberation of man's capacities for emotional experience. Lin Shu's translations of Western literature at the beginning of the century opened up new vistas of rich emotional experience – new images of love, adventure and heroism.[6] The assimilation of this new sensibility to the image of revolutionary heroism as a mode of self-realization can be readily seen in individuals such as the famous revolutionary martyrs Ch'iu Chin, Wu Yueh and Ch'en T'ien-hua.

As noted above, in the case of the revolutionaries as well as in the case of the reformers, this new ideal by no means involved a 'totalistic' rejection of the entire cultural heritage. The young revolutionaries still had strong roots in the broader heritage even as they rejected the established conventional Confucian order. The tradition of warrior heroes (*yu-hsia*), of the heroic martyrs of the Ming dynasty and non-collaborators of the early Ch'ing, blended in their minds with the examples of Russian populist terrorists and the image of poet-rebels like Lord Byron. One need not doubt their sincere devotion to the cause of revolution, but revolution had also become a mode of individual self-realization.

Not only do we find strong traditional elements in the outlooks of the revolutionaries. We even find that the revolutionary movement as a whole was to become the centre (although reformers also participated) of a movement of integral cultural nationalism which stood in marked contrast to the essentially iconoclastic nationalism of Yen Fu. Here we find the ubiquitous dilemma of modern nationalism. On the one hand, the achievement of national wealth and power may require a radical break with the constraints of tradition. On the other hand, a vital sense of national identity seems to require faith in the intrinsic worth of the nation's cultural accomplishments of the past.

In China the theme of anti-Manchuism as preached by the fiery scholar Chang Ping-lin seemed to provide an extraordinarily effective basis for an organic sense of nationhood. The Ch'ing dynasty was, in his view,

6 See Lee, *The romantic generation.*

not simply a dynasty in decline. It was the representative of an inferior 'race' which had for centuries kept in thrall the Han people which was in every way its superior. The revolution, once accomplished, would finally liberate the high creative powers of the Han race. The Han people is an organic entity with its own history, its own 'national essence', and its own path into the future. As in the case of the European organic notions of nationalism, with which he was certainly familiar, Chang vehemently insists that Chinese derive their categories of thought from their own tradition. Yet, paradoxically, this emphasis on the Chinese spirit does not seem to require a particular loyalty to any specific manifestation of that spirit as the embodiment of universal truth. As a famous scholar in the Ch'ing tradition, Chang Ping-lin was above all insistent that Chinese youth acquire a knowledge of and pride in their entire cultural heritage. Yet at another level, he himself had his own particular commitments within the heritage. This was equally true of other revolutionary cultural nationalists such as Liu Shih-p'ei, Liu Ya-tzu and others whose predilections within the national heritage tended to its more literary and aesthetic aspects. Organic 'cultural' nationalism was, to be sure, only one tendency within the revolutionary camp. Sun Yat-sen, whose personal life experience had been far removed from that of literati such as Liu Shih-p'ei and Chang Ping-lin, was indeed able to incorporate strong components of organic nationalism into the eclectic body of his Three People's Principles, but his fundamental orientation remained Western as did that of many in his entourage. Yet 'organic nationalism' as a theme was to play a significant role in the future history of the Kuomintang movement.

One more strain to be noted within the revolutionary camp is the strain of anarchism. Anarcho-syndicalism at the turn of the twentieth century was a dominant influence in the more radical wing of the European and American left. At the time, it was indeed the anarchists rather than the European socialists in general or Marxists in particular who represented the 'revolutionary left'. In this as in many other matters, translations from the Japanese and contacts with Japanese radicals were the main channel of communication.[7]

The acceptance of anarchism by some of the revolutionaries can be related to the vehement attack on the repressive, negative authority of the past which we already find in the pioneer thinkers. To be sure, they (as well as many of the revolutionaries) by no means drew the conclusion that all authority as such is inherently evil or dispensable. What China

7 Martin Bernal, 'The triumph of anarchism over Marxism 1906–1907', in Mary Wright, ed. *China in revolution, the first phase 1900–1913*. See also above, pages 391–6.

required in their view was a new type of constructive, nurturant authority which would foster the powers of the people. Some more apocalyptic minds were able to leap precisely to that conclusion, fortified by a faith nourished from abroad that a world anarchist revolution was imminent in the West. It is indicative of the kaleidoscopic interweavings of doctrine at this time that Liu Shih-p'ei, an enthusiastic advocate of 'national essence', was able to find in the book of Lao-tzu warrant for his belief that an anarchist revolution in China would restore the primeval state of a Taoist society of 'non-action'. Others, however, sought cosmological support in Kropotkin's benign 'mutual aid' version of Darwinian doctrine. Here one could find a cosmology more congenial to Chinese tradition allied to a doctrine of extreme political radicalism.

It should be added at this point that both before and after 1911 we find certain idiosyncratic temperaments who do not respond to the same drummer as most of the new literati. For whatever reason, they prove highly resistant to the overwhelmingly socio-political preoccupations of the twentieth century.

The complex figure of Chang Ping-lin, who was, on one level, deeply and passionately involved in socio-political conflicts and the rise of cultural nationalism, was on another 'existential' level deeply influenced by the revival of Mahayana Buddhist philosophy (particularly the consciousness-only, 'Vijnanavada' school) and the thought of Chuang-tzu. On this level, he found his ultimate solace in a mystic perspective which denied the intrinsic value of the entire phenomenal world. Freely accepting Darwinism as a paradigm of the world of fluctuating forms, he simply denied that it bore with it any hope of ultimate redemption. In effect he negated progress.

Another interesting instance is that of Wang Kuo-wei, whose personal temper and life experience led him to disclaim what he regarded as the shallow concerns with national 'wealth and power' or with any doctrine of political salvation. Having come into contact with the thought of Schopenhauer, he found a Western confirmation for his basic feeling that life itself is the problem, quite apart from the particular miseries of specific conditions. Having eventually been convinced, evidently by Nietzsche and the positivists, that Schopenhauer's metaphysics 'could not be believed' in spite of the promise it held for release from life's miseries, he then found solace in a kind of philosophically inspired literary criticism (as in his interpretation of the novel The dream of the red chamber) and finally in a life of creative scholarship which blended the Ch'ing and Western philological traditions.

THE 1911 REVOLUTION AND THE 'NEW CULTURE'

The Chinese Revolution of 1911 has often been considered 'superficial'. It produced no social revolution. Yet the fact remains that the end of the universal kingship and the collapse of the entire cosmology which legitimized it; the fragmentation and militarization of power and authority throughout the society often down to the local level; the loss of moral authority on many levels of that society; the convulsive insecurity of local holders of power and wealth both old and new; the failure of the new republic to establish its own bases of legitimacy – were all to have a traumatic impact on the intellectuals' perceptions of the themes treated above. Many of these trends had been underway before 1911. The end of the examination system had itself had an enormous effect on the social role of the literati. The cosmology of kingship had already been undermined by the evolutionary doctrines of K'ang Yu-wei, Yen Fu, Liang Ch'i-ch'ao and others, but in the apt words of Lin Yü-sheng, 'Over a long period the gate of the dike may be eroded; when it finally bursts nothing can hinder the thrust of the flood that spreads ruin and destruction in the natural order beyond.'[8] No doubt, an objective study of Chinese society in all its regional variations between 1911 and 1919 would reveal a variety of conditions and even some positive developments. Yet in the perception of most of the 'high' intellectuals, the total scene was one of deterioration, fragmentation, corruption and brutality. Somehow the stream of evolution in China seemed to have sunk into a slough of despond.

Yen Fu and K'ang Yu-wei now both felt confirmed in their conviction that 'evolution cannot be forced', and that a republican revolution at this stage of China's evolution was an enormous mistake. Liang Ch'i-ch'ao accepted the revolution and the irreversibility of the demise of monarchy as the decree of History. He was at first, on thoroughly consistent grounds, in favour of Yuan Shih-k'ai's efforts to create a 'republican' dictatorship which would be able to carry through the tasks of modernization. K'ang Yu-wei, again on thoroughly consistent evolutionary grounds, continued to believe that at this point only the symbols of monarchy could restore the centre that had collapsed.[9] A common tendency among all three during this period was a greater inclination to accept the premises of cultural nationalism. K'ang Yu-wei had of course long ad-

---

8 Lin Yü-sheng, *The crisis of Chinese consciousness: radical anti-traditionalism in the May Fourth era*, 17.

9 This was to lead to his support of the efforts of the queue-wearing warlord Chang Hsun to restore the Ch'ing dynasty in 1917.

vocated the need for his own version of a Confucian religion during the middle historical stage of 'lesser order' (*hsiao-k'ang*). Yen Fu and Liang Ch'i-ch'iao, in an environment of growing disintegration, were now increasingly convinced that China required minimal elements of a stabilizing common faith. It is in such circumstances that we find Yen Fu signing the petition of the 'society for Confucianism' that Confucianism be recognized as a state religion.[10] China, he argued, was still, alas, in a period of transition from a 'patriarchal' to a 'military' stage of society[11] and it still required a patriarchal faith.

The responses of the active revolutionaries were diverse. Many quickly demonstrated that their ideological commitments had been emphatic rather than profound. Soon they became embroiled with the politics of the unsavoury warlord era. Sun Yat-sen continued (actively, but without much effect) during the bleak years after the Second and Third Revolutions to seek for a base of political power. The adherents of the 'national essence' school soon found that the Han race did not automatically achieve a full 'restoration' once the corrupt Manchus had been removed. In the case of men such as Liu Shih-p'ei the preoccupation with the preservation of national cultural identity continued but the faith that it might be preserved through political means now faded. In the words of Laurence Schneider, 'the cultural mission of the group was now its sole source of solidarity.'[12] Its concept of culture tended to focus on literature and traditional scholarship, leading it to become a vehement source of opposition to both the linguistic and literary revolutions of the May Fourth period.

The most significance response to the discouragement of the post-revolutionary period was, however, to be the New Culture movement most prominently represented by the journal *New Youth*, founded by Ch'en Tu-hsiu in 1915. Characterizing this movement as a whole, what we find on the negative side is a much more radical – more 'totalistic' – attack on the entire cultural heritage. There is little novelty in Ch'en's exhortations 'be independent not servile, progressive not conservative, aggressive not passive',[13] but now these attacks are directed not simply against the conventional Confucian socio-political order but against the entire tradition with all its 'three teachings of Confucianism, Taoism and Buddhism' (not to speak of the superstitious culture of the masses).

10 Yen Fu *et al.* 'K'ung-chiao-hui chang-ch'eng' (The programme of the Society for Confucianism), *Yung-yen* (*Justice*), 1. 14 (June 1913) 1–8.
11 Schwartz, *In search of wealth and power*, 234.
12 Laurence A. Schneider, 'National essence and the new intelligentsia' in C. Furth, ed. *The limits of change: essays on conservative alternatives in Republican China*, 71.
13 Ch'en Tu-hsiu, 'Ching-kao ch'ing-nien' (A call to youth), *Hsin ch'ing-nien* (New youth), 1. 1 (Sept 1915) 7.

The language of social Darwinist evolutionism is still invoked but in some sense the 'old society' and the 'old culture' are now treated as a kind of vast, inert incubus which had paralysed the soul of the nation. The revolution had proven that one could, after all, remove the entire traditional political structure without affecting the rot which permeated the whole society. Indeed, not only did the dead weight of the past have the power to persist. It seemed (as in the case of Yuan Shih-k'ai's attempts to restore the monarchy) to have the power to reconstitute itself. The task which lay ahead was thus nothing less than to transform the entire conscious life of a nation. The 'new cultural' leaders felt that this task was the absolutely necessary precondition of any political action or institutional reform. The resolve expressed by the young Hu Shih in 1917 upon his return from the United States 'not to talk about politics for twenty years' seemed to express the common sentiment of the entire New Culture group. As the title of their main organ indicated, they regarded their first and primary audience to be the educated youth who had not yet been entirely corrupted by 'the old and the rotten'.[14]

Here too there seems to be only a difference of degree between the New Youth outlook and that of the pioneer thinkers. In confronting what I have called the Leninist dilemma, the pioneers had come to stress the role of conscious ideas in changing society. Yet their educational approach was supported by the sense that changes were actually taking place or about to take place in the institutional infrastructure of society during the course of the Manchu reform movement. Evolution – with some conscious help – then seemed to be on the move. Similarly, the diagnosis of the New Culture group before 1919 led them to feel that nothing but a change of consciousness could move the society.

One aspect of the new cultural movement before 1919 which was to have continuing implications for the future was the sharp line it drew between politicians and intellectuals. This disassociation had been prefigured in the abolition of the examination system in 1905. It is also clear that in the past, in spite of the 'scholar-official' cliché, there had always been literati who were primarily intellectuals and others who were primarily politicians. Also, in the period after 1919, many intellectuals were to immerse themselves once more in political life. Yet the self-perception of the intellectuals (particularly the academic and literary intellectuals) as a separate stratum was to persist even after 1949 and was even to carry with itself a certain ongoing sense of the 'right' to autonomy in intellectual life.

Another vital aspect of the New Culture movement was the emergence

14 *Ibid.* 1–2.

of the 'New Literature' so ably treated elsewhere in this volume (see chapter 9). Here also we see the emergence of literature[15] as a major, autonomous area of human experience. Although poetry and belles-lettres had long been an organic part of the high culture of the literati ideally they had never been separated from the entire programme of self-cultivation. There had always been figures such as Ou-yang Hsiu who had been very 'literary' in orientation (*wen-jen*), but the notion of literature (in the sense of belles-lettres) as a high, autonomous vocation had not prevailed. Above all, the writing of fiction as a department of literature had not been a respected high cultural activity. Here, as in so many other areas, Liang Ch'i-ch'ao had been a pioneer in his advocacy of the employment of fiction as a powerful emotional medium for promoting his socio-political ideas. The young brothers Chou Shu-jen (Lu Hsun) and Chou Tso-jen had also been pioneers during their days in Japan before 1911 in their aspiration to use literature as a means of curing the deep spiritual ailments of the Chinese people. It was, however, the New Culture movement which effectively launched the new vernacular 'high cultural' literature. Yet if the new culture elevated the genre of fiction to a high cultural status, it did so for the most part by wedding it to the view that fiction must 'serve life'. To this extent, the new literature in China was in the main oriented from the outset to the view that literature must serve social ethical goals. This general orientation does not, of course, preclude an absorption of some of the greater writers in purely literary concerns, but the general goals were to retain their hold.

Even the romantic 'Creation' group of Kuo Mo-jo, Yü Ta-fu and others which had ostensibly adopted the slogan of 'art for art's sake' was deeply moved by concerns which were not strictly artistic.[16] Romanticism as a release from the repressive structures of traditional life had, as we have seen, emerged before 1911 and even then had been as much related to the search for individual meaning in life as to the romance of revolution. In the years after 1911 when the promise of political salvation dramatically receded, the concern of the younger intellectuals with the meaning of their own personal lives, in a world where faith in traditional values both public and private had sharply declined, was to become an important dimension of the new culture. In a sense, 'individualism' in both its liberal and romantic senses now seems to have had a direct impact on personal life to a degree which was certainly not true for the pioneer generation, who still lived quite comfortably within the confines of conventional Confucian family values. For a time, at least, the concern with individ-

15 See Lee, *The romantic generation* ch. 2.
16 Discussed in Lee, *The romantic generation*; also in David Roy, *Kuo Mo-jo: the early years*.

ualism as such seemed not to be entirely instrumental to socio-political goals. The translation of Ibsen's *A doll's house* in the Ibsen issue of *New Youth* sponsored by Hu Shih is symbolic of this concern. Similarly the rapt absorption of the romantic 'Creation Society' authors in their own unfulfilled emotional yearnings was anything but a concern for 'art for art's sake'. In the words of Leo Lee, 'Far from the French symbolist notion that art not only restructures life but also constructs a new edifice into which the artist can escape life, Ch'eng's (Fang-wu) arguments point in the other direction',[17] towards an overriding concern with 'life' whether this concern took the form of Yü Ta-fu's melancholy self-indulgence or Kuo Mo-jo's soaring narcissism.

Another development clearly associated with the New Culture movement is what might be called the 'higher criticism' of the traditional heritage represented by figures such as Hu Shih, Ku Chieh-kang, Ch'ien Hsuan-t'ung and others.

Conflicts regarding the validity and authenticity of various traditions and scriptures had been a feature of Chinese thought for ages. The great philological scholars of the empirical research (*k'ao-cheng*) school of the Ch'ing dynasty had also fostered the critical treatment of the great texts, although it is much to be doubted that their work had the sceptical-iconoclastic connotations ascribed to it by their twentieth-century admirers. K'ang Yu-wei – by no means a critical scholar – had attempted at the beginning of the century to use a systematic attack on the orthodoxy of certain Old Text scriptures to support his own New Text version of Confucianism.

Like the scholarship of K'ang Yu-wei the movement to 'reorganize the national heritage' (*cheng-li kuo-ku*), as it was designated by Hu Shih, had a deep ideological motive. The methods of 'science' could, in the words of Laurence Schneider, be used 'to undermine the credibility of orthodox histories and the historical foundations of scripture.'[18] One of the most effective ways of removing the dead hand of tradition was to dissolve the factual claims of the myths which supported that tradition. In the end this critical liberation of historical studies from the burden of certain fundamentalistic and conventional ways of viewing the past was to be taken up by many other scholars of 'national studies' – even by 'neo-traditionalist' scholars who did not necessarily share the iconoclastic preoccupations of Hu Shih and Ku Chieh-kang.

Even in the case of the iconoclastic 'new cultural' scholars, their intentions were not entirely destructive. Although Hu Shih, Ku Chieh-kang

17 Lee, *The romantic generation*, 22.
18 Laurence Schneider, *Ku Chieh-kang and China's new history*.

and Fu Ssu-nien committed themselves to a future whose model was to be found in the contemporary West, as Chinese nationalists they were by no means entirely free of the desire to find what Hu Shih called 'congenial stocks' in the Chinese past from which a modern culture might grow. The view of science advocated by Hu Shih's teacher John Dewey, with its notion of gradual, incremental evolution, encouraged the idea that the present must somehow grow out of the past. Both Ku Chieh-kang and Hu Shih were indeed able to find to their own satisfaction strands of Chinese thought which pointed towards modernity. There was the presumed 'scientific' method of Ch'ing scholarship, the beginnings of logic in China's ancient thought, and in the case of Hu Shih, the vital vernacular literature of the past which was in such striking contrast to the decadent, formalistic classical literature of the elite. This populist theme which contrasted the discredited and oppressive 'high culture' of the elite with the vital energy of the folk was eventually to lead Ku Chieh-kang to his extensive studies of folklore (see below). Hu Shih, who was equally concerned with both the new literature and the new scholarship, was later able to combine both interests in his scholarly investigations of the vernacular fiction of the past. All of these endeavours, whether literary, scholarly or simply publicistic, were thoroughly infused with the common premises of the New Culture movement.

Despite the shared premises of the movement, when we juxtapose the names of some of its major protagonists – Hu Shih, Ch'en Tu-hsiu, and Lu Hsun – we become acutely conscious of the profound differences among them. As a young student before 1911, Hu Shih had already been profoundly influenced by the social Darwinist ideas of Yen Fu and Liang Ch'i-ch'ao. His happy experiences as a student in the United States and his contacts with the philosophy of the earlier John Dewey then seem to have led him by a kind of smooth evolution to his own version of Ch'en Tu-hsiu's famous formula 'Mr Science and Mr Democracy', a formula which once it had been set forth was to remain essentially unchanged. Yen Fu's Bacon-Mill conception of science as a kind of simple inductionism was to provide a bridge to Dewey's experimentalistic concept, and Hu Shih's own life experience in early twentieth-century America was to provide him with a happy image of democracy in operation even though he also enthusiastically accepted Dewey's more advanced, critical view of true democracy.

In John Dewey, science and democracy were inseparable values. The experimental method of science in its reliance on tentative hypotheses applied to the study of 'problematic situations' represented a rejection of all spiritual authority and all pre-established dogma – whether religious, political or metaphysical. It thus was the very basis for the assertion of freedom. If men would cooperate together to apply the methods of science, which had been so successfully applied to nature, to the study of human social and cultural problems – an area still subjugated to the empire of dogma – the ends of true liberty and equality would be brought close to realization. The spread of scientific intelligence, thus conceived, through the whole society by education, would lead men to analyse and deal effectively with their collective problems and even to reconcile their clashing interests. In spite of Dewey's sharp criticism of mere formal 'political democracy' and constitutionalism, there seems little doubt that his whole outlook presupposed a common acceptance of constitutional democracy as 'the rules of the game'.

While Hu Shih seems to have accepted Dewey's view of science as methodology, the subtle epistemological issues raised by Dewey as a philosopher seem to have escaped him entirely, and he found it quite possible to combine Dewey's pragmatism with a simple dogmatic mechanistic-naturalistic metaphysics.[19] In this area he remained very much in the tradition of Yen Fu and Liang Ch'i-ch'ao, even though his naturalism is unencumbered by Taoist-Buddhist overtones. Again, Dewey's emphasis on 'scientific inquiry' and education in dealing with socio-political problems; his deprecation of 'mere politics' seems to have reinforced a preexistent tendency in Hu Shih to regard the disorderly and 'irrational' political conflicts of China as irrelevant to China's true progress.

Dewey's emphasis on scientific intelligence and education was entirely in keeping with the whole new cultural emphasis on the transformation of conscious life. It was thus entirely appropriate that when Hu Shih returned to China in 1917 he should have become closely associated with the movement. His deep interest in language reform was entirely in keeping with the broad educational goals of the movement. His interest in the New Literature reflected both a deep personal fondness for literature and a conviction that the affective power of literature provided a most powerful vehicle for communicating new ideas. When one surveys his life in retrospect, one cannot but feel that Hu's pronounced literary and scholarly concerns reflected personal inclinations as well as the no doubt sincere belief that 'reorganizing the national heritage' was a crucial cultural task. This does not mean that he did not devote a good deal of attention to social and political questions in his writings over the years, but, unable as he was for the most part to affect the actual course of poli-

---

19 Hu Shih's staunch support of this kind of metaphysics seems to have shielded him from any response to Dewey's later subtle discussions of religious and aesthetic experience.

tical affairs, he found that it was much more feasible to apply 'scientific intelligence' to the critique of the cultural heritage.

When we turn to Ch'en Tu-hsiu we find that while he actually created the formula 'Mr Science and Mr Democracy', his view of both these categories was different in subtle ways from that of Hu Shih. His temperament, unlike that of Hu, was passionate and impatient. The fact that the Western influence which had been predominant in his case had been French rather than Anglo-American was not insignificant. His view of science was basically that of a crude Darwinian metaphysic. Science was a corrosive which could be used to undermine traditional values. The fact that the forces of evolution seemed to have completely bogged down in China led him to moments of deep depression, yet like Hu Shih, he was basically able to combine his 'scientific' determinism with a strong faith in the powers of an intellectual elite. Unlike Hu Shih, the positive doctrine of science as a piece-meal experimental methodology did not penetrate the centre of Ch'en's consciousness and he was later able to transfer the use of the word science from Darwinism to Marxism without losing any sense of its apodictic certainty.

Similarly, Hu Shih's conception of scientific method seems to have rendered him impervious to the appeal of the notion of total revolutionary transformation, while Ch'en Tu-hsiu, who greatly admired the French Revolution as a fountainhead of modern democracy, was probably inherently more vulnerable to the appeal of revolutionary transformation in spite of his thoroughly anti-political 'cultural' approach during the period before 1919. Yet during the period of close collaboration between the two (1917–19) there was nevertheless a great resemblance in their views on the individual and on the ingredients of democracy.

Lu Hsun (Chou Shu-jen), who was to become modern China's most distinguished literary giant, was a man of quite different sensibilities. Throughout his life in his more literary persona, he seems to have had a peculiar sensitivity to the 'powers of darkness'. In his youth, he was easily converted to the evolutionary creed and yet his dark doubts began to emerge even before 1911. His own personal family experiences, his deep sense of the corruption and 'slave mentality' of the Chinese people, seem even before 1911 to have diminished his faith in the effectiveness of the forces of evolution in China. His contacts with Nietzsche's writings did not turn him into a true Nietzschean but provided him with the vivid image of the free, heroic, defiant spirit who sets himself against the 'slave mentality' of the mass of mankind. For a time, he indulged in the youthful dream of the Nietzschean-Byronic poetic hero who would be able to rouse mankind out of its spiritual slumbers. It may also have been Nietzsche and Byron who led him very early to a certain lack of sympathy for the prosaic, 'bourgeois' culture of Western Europe and America. In spite of Yen Fu's influence, Lu Hsun was to remain cool to the Western technocratic strain of thought as well as to the detached 'realism' of much Western literature with its over-complicated view of man's moral life.

The post-1911 revolutionary situation was to lead Lu Hsun to a blank wall of despair. His vision of the capacity of Nietzschean literary heroes to mould society seems to have faded rapidly. His 'totalistic' image of China's bad past and present was if anything more sombre than that of his 'new cultural' colleagues. The cruelty, corruption, servility and hypocrisy of contemporary China did not represent a decline of traditional values, but in some sense were actually a manifestation of those destructive values. In his 'Diary of a madman', he makes it clear that it is not only the actuality of Chinese society which makes it 'man-eating'. Its ideals are also 'man-eating' ideals. Even the young revolutionaries of the pre-1911 period had speedily succumbed to the poisonous influence of this incubus. Lu Hsun's decision to take up writing once more was a response to the 'educational' aims of the New Culture movement but it seems to have been a highly sceptical response.

In spite of his 'totalistic iconoclasm' it is nevertheless important to point out that on the level of his literary imagination, Lu Hsun continued to be fascinated by certain 'counter-traditional' aspects of the Chinese past. The past to which he looked was, however, entirely different from the past in which Hu Shih sought his 'congenial stocks'. It was the past of 'neo-Taoist' bohemians of the southern dynasties, of popular fantasy and fable and even the past of certain intimate personal values. Yet none of these attractions seems to have wrenched Lu Hsun from his rejection of the heritage as a whole.

MAY FOURTH AND ITS CONSEQUENCES

In dealing with the consequences of the events of May 1919, we shall not here dwell on the multiplicity of doctrines which were to find expression in a myriad of new periodicals. May Fourth simply marked an explosive stage in the expansion (already under way) of the audience for the themes of the New Culture – particularly its 'totalistic' rejection of the cultural heritage. It is now, however, quite clear that most of the doctrines embraced were not new.

One of the main consequences of these events for our purposes here is their implications for the purely cultural diagnosis of China's ills. May Fourth was a political act, a seemingly effective act of political protest against foreign imperialism. It even led for a time to a kind of mass movement (albeit of students and urban strata only). The new cultural leaders had in the past been mainly concerned with China's domestic ills. The social Darwinist coloration of their thought had not on the whole led them to moralistic judgments of the behaviour of the imperialist powers or to attribute China's ills primarily to foreign causes. Yet the nationalistic impatience and sense of urgency of the students forced some of their intellectual elders to turn their attention away for the moment from their long-term cultural effort, to face the sad state of contemporary politics in China.

Even the antipolitical Hu Shih was forced by the events of May Fourth to reassess his posture. The immediate effect was to raise his hopes that the cultural transformation which, to his delight, already seemed to have taken place among young intellectuals, would flow not into politics but into a 'social movement'. John Dewey, who was himself present in China in 1919, encouraged this hope by his own observation that 'the students' organizations have gone into popular education, social and philanthropic service and vigorous intellectual discussion.'[20] Hu Shih spoke of 'masses to educate, women to emancipate, schools to reform'.[21] The assumption seems to have been at the outset that all these goals might be pursued while by-passing the intractable facts of political-military power as they existed in the China of 1919. Yet by the summer of 1922, Hu Shih, under the proddings of his friend Ting Wen-chiang, was himself induced to help found the journal *Nu-li chou-pao* (Endeavour), which was frankly dedicated to political action.

Ting Wen-chiang, who, as an able geologist was one of the few actual scientists among the new culture's 'scientific' intellectuals, had been trained not in America but in Scotland.[22] There he had acquired a thoroughly British empiricist view of science (like Hu Shih he was an admirer of the Ch'ing 'empiricists') but a type of empiricism not as implicated with the gospel of democracy as was Dewey's version of experimentalism. Accordingly, Ting was less inclined to indulge in the moralistic judgments of militarists and politicians that figured so strongly in Hu Shih's outlook. His attitude towards established power seemed to be – is it usable for our purposes? Hu Shih had in the interim himself become painfully aware of the power of political forces to interfere with the intellectuals' rights of freedom of speech and action. He had also become aware of the rise of new authoritarian '-isms' – prepared to pre-empt the arena of political

20 Jerome B. Grieder, *Hu Shih and the Chinese renaissance*, 179.
21 *Ibid.* 177.
22 On Ting see Charlotte Furth's study *Ting Wen-chiang: science and China's new culture.*

action. Hence one aspect of his political action was the liberal call for 'civil rights' as against the arbitrary acts of government. This was a cause to which he remained faithful ever after.

The other side of Hu Shih's political proposals – his call for a government of 'good men' and a 'government with a plan' – already pointed to the grave problem of how to relate 'science' to 'democracy' in China. Given his 'common-sensical' definition of science, Dewey allowed himself to hope that the methods of scientific inquiry would rapidly be propagated throughout American society, making science a weapon of an enlightened people through the new education. Given China's situation, Hu Shih could only hope that men of scientific enlightenment (who were 'good' by definition but also few in number) might bring their influence to bear on established centres of power. Hu Shih no less than the Communists and Nationalists felt himself forced to believe in an enlightened elite. The hope of being able to work with Wu P'ei-fu's government was of course to be short-lived, and Hu Shih was soon to return to his cultural view of China's problems.

One of the groups better able to take advantage of the nationalist political fervour which pervaded the young during May Fourth (a fervour which overrode all ideological differences) was Sun Yat-sen and his entourage. Whatever one may think of Sun's merits as a thinker or statesman, the fact is that during the whole bleak period from 1911 to 1919 he had not been diverted from his political goal of establishing a strong central government, however ineffective his methods. He did not succumb to the 'new cultural' obsession with the sickness of China's culture. On the contrary, even before 1911 his contacts with 'national essence' thinking had convinced him that national pride in the achievements of the past must be fostered and he had even developed definite ideas of what was to be prized.

One of the traditional values to be prized was the old stress on 'people's livelihood' which Sun had long since been able to link (like Liang Ch'i-ch'ao) to the 'socialist' critique of the sharp class antagonism in Western society. Like Liang he constantly stressed the relative lack of class antagonism, as he defined it, in traditional Chinese society. Also during the years of growing bitterness after 1911, he had devoted a good deal of attention to the problem of how to create a disciplined, unified vanguard party in China. In general his faith in constitutional democracy of the Western type gradually declined. It is thus not surprising that Sun and some of his closest disciples expressed an immediate and keen interest after the October Revolution in Lenin's views on party organization as well as in the Bolshevik formula for dealing with military power. Some of the younger men in Sun's entourage – such as Hu Han-min, Tai Chi-t'ao, Chu Chih-hsin – were indeed to prove remarkably receptive to the Leninist theory of imperialism as an analysis of Western behaviour.[23]

INTRODUCTION OF MARXISM-LENINISM

The doctrine of the Bolshevik revolution was to be one of the newer additions to the doctrinal storehouse of the May Fourth period which otherwise drew on older themes. The phraseology of the Leninist theory of imperialism very quickly became popular among many circles after the 'betrayal of Versailles', but the acceptance of Soviet communism as a total doctrine was to prove a much slower process as is amply proven by the small number of immediate converts. Thus in dealing with the appeals of Marxism-Leninism we must by no means confine ourselves to the early beginnings of the communist movement.

The first appeal of the October Revolution lay perhaps in the fact of revolution itself. The lively faith in a progressive evolutionary cosmology which had been the central creed of the pre-revolutionary period had lost its vigour. The new cultural leaders who still thought of the present West as China's future had felt obliged to fall back on their own resources as educators. Even those prepared to call themselves socialists and anarchists who had accepted the anti-capitalist image of the West could discern little sign of dramatic historic movement in what appeared to be an increasingly stable West.

The man who most vividly symbolized the response to the Bolshevik Revolution as a sign that world history was again on the move was Li Ta-chao.[24] One of the more idiosyncratic members of the new culture group, he had somehow managed to maintain a buoyant faith in his own poetic version of historical progress even during the bleak years. His own conception differed from the prevailing social Darwinist creed. Inspired by sources as diverse as Emerson, Bergson, Hegel, and a Taoist-Buddhist strain, he had conceived of history as a kind of unified, ever youthful World Spirit ever able to break through the static structures to which it gives rise. His readiness for a cosmic act of liberation thus made him extraordinarily responsive to the apocalyptic message of the Bolshevik Revolution as the harbinger of a new historic movement which would sweep away 'all national boundaries, all differences of classes, all barriers.' As Maurice Meisner points out, this more universal vision was combined in Li with a bone-deep Chinese nationalism which seemed to envisage

23 Their ideas found expression in the journal *Chien she* (Construction), 1920.
24 For a study of Li see Maurice Meisner, *Li Ta-chao and the origins of Chinese Marxism.*

the possibility that China would somehow be able to participate in this world drama as a 'people-nation'. The Leninist doctrine of imperialism with its positive attitude towards the provisional role of nationalism in the 'backward' world during a bourgeois democratic stage, provided a space for Li Ta-chao's vision although it is by no means clear that Li truly accepted the provisional nature of the nationalist component. As Joseph Levenson has, however, pointed out, this new vision of history – even before it involved any deep knowledge of the dynamics of Marxism – now would place China itself in the vanguard of an historic movement which would lead beyond the corrupt contemporary West. The West could be rejected from a higher yet iconoclastic point of view.

As has often been pointed out, the Marxist-Leninist revolution was also responsive to a problem we have met before and already described as the Leninist dilemma. The problem involved both a deep belief that History is 'on our side' and deep doubts whether the movement from the present into the future can be entrusted to impersonal forces. Lenin had faced the problem of the conscious vanguard – a problem faced not only by Yen Fu and Liang Ch'i-ch'ao in the past but by Sun Yat-sen and even Hu Shih and Ting Wen-chiang in the May Fourth era. But he had done so in a new way. The model of the communist party as the concentration of the general will of the industrial proletariat, the military metaphor of the party as a general staff of highly disciplined, monolithically united 'professional revolutionaries', who could analyse the temporal terrain of emerging objective historical situations just as generals can interpret the spatial terrain in which they operate – these notions were to become indispensable components of the Marxist-Leninist message.

In retrospect, however, it would appear that an even more important aspect of Leninism as a political strategy was another side of the military metaphor – its emphasis on mass mobilization as a source of political power. The organizational philosophy of the party could be borrowed by others (as the Kuomintang did after 1923). The essential, however, was the combination of the concept of the vanguard party with a concern for mass mobilization. Lenin no doubt sincerely believed that the Bolshevik party was the incarnation of the general will of the industrial proletariat, and this belief led him to relate himself aggressively (but not always successfully) to the organization of the party's 'class basis'. But beyond that he had a deep appreciation of the power to be derived from a linkage to immediately felt mass needs, as in his adoption of the slogan 'peace and land' in 1917. None of this implies that individuals who enter the movement are not directly moved in their organizational activities by immediate sentiments of compassion and indignation. It does mean that the leadership remains a 'general staff' whose strategies and perspectives are not in theory confused by the 'limited', short-term perspectives of the masses. The leadership is confident that it operates from a long-term historical perspective. Again the military metaphor also implies a determination to relate oneself not only to mass mobilization but to a constant realistic and detached assessment of the strength and disposition of political forces in the environment. By constantly interpreting these political forces as reflections of 'class relations' in the Marxist sense, one could maintain one's faith that one was relating practice to Marxist theory.

One should hasten to add that none of these abstract propositions guaranteed an ultimate communist victory in China. The question of how one was to acquire a mass base was not itself answered by the bare formula. The question of whether an effective party could be created without great leaders remained to be resolved. The emphasis on a 'realistic' political strategy provided no guarantees of the correctness of the strategies pursued either in China or in Moscow, nor could one ever discount the crucial decisiveness of unforeseen contingencies such as the Japanese intervention of later decades.

A word should be said at this point about the relative lack of attention to the political potential of mobilized mass energy before 1919. Certainly China had known the power of mass mobilization in the rebellions of the past. Yet despite the widespread older assumption that 'the people' would be the beneficiaries of progress, even the revolutionaries before 1911 did not, on the whole, think of mass organization as a source of political power[25] (with the somewhat questionable exception of their cooperation with secret societies[26]). One may speculate that in some sense the new Western ideas of the literati increased rather than diminished their distance from the masses, intensifying their perception of the people as a helpless entity sunk in ignorance and passivity.

Despite the fascination of the pre-1911 revolutionaries with Russian 'revolutionary heroism' the idea of 'going to the people' did not truly emerge until the May Fourth period in the 'social movement' of the times. The notion of direct contact between intellectuals and masses was to have a considerable future in the work of Yen Yang-ch'u, T'ao Hsing-chih, Liang Shu-ming and others, but again this was not to involve the

---

25 Edward Friedman in his book *Backward toward revolution: the Chinese Revolutionary Party* speaks of the 'mass' organizational activities of some of Sun's followers such as Chu Chih-hsin after 1911.

26 For a discussion of this cooperation see Mary Backus Rankin, *Early Chinese revolutionaries: radical intellectuals in Shanghai and Chekiang, 1902–1911.*

idea of mass mobilization as a source of political and military power. It need hardly be added that the 'new cultural' perspective of the period before 1919 was hardly oriented to mass political mobilization, however sincere its ultimate commitment to mass education.

PROBLEMS AND '-ISMS'

One of the more significant conflicts which emerged out of the winds of doctrine of the May Fourth period was the debate between Hu Shih, Li Ta-chao and others concerning the question of 'problems versus -isms'. In the textbook accounts of the intellectual history of China after the May Fourth period, often written under Marxist inspiration, one finds a series of debates, each leading to the clear victory of one side and gradually leading by a progressive ascent to the victory of Marxism and then within the Marxist camp to a victory of 'true' Marxism. A less triumphalist view of these debates does not lead to such confidence concerning the designation of clear winners and clear losers.

Hu Shih's articles in *Mei-chou p'ing-lun* (Weekly critic) of July and August 1919 on 'Problems and -isms' reflect his disturbance over the drift of his friends Ch'en Tu-hsiu, Li Ta-chao and others into the communist camp. As he was later to remark, 'Though the slaves of Confucius and Chu Hsi are fewer now, a new breed of slaves of Marx and Kropotkin has sprung up.'[27] In these articles Hu draws a sharp contrast between Dewey's scientific approach to society which directs its attention to concrete situations and problem areas, analyses them and provides concrete solutions for specific problems, on the one hand, and totalistic '-isms' which claim to provide total and 'fundamental solutions' for all the problems of a society on the other. As one might have expected, his opponents reply that all the separate problems of a society are related to a total structure or system and can be solved fundamentally only when the 'system' is changed as a whole. It is interesting to note that at this time Ch'en Tu-hsiu, who had not yet been won over to the communist camp, still tended to support Hu Shih's point of view. Yet Li Ta-chao and many of the students were yearning to find in anarchism and Marxism warrant for their ardent hopes that there might indeed be a 'fundamental solution' to China's overwhelming problems and that History would lead to such solutions. In post-1949 China, Hu Shih has, of course, been treated as the decisive loser of the debate.

One need not be a follower of John Dewey's 'scientific methodology'

27 Grieder, *Hu Shih and the Chinese renaissance* 189, cited from 'Wo ti ch'i-lu' (My crossroads), *Hu Shih wen-ts'un* (Collected works of Hu Shih), 3. 99–102.

to assert that any society, whatever its socio-political structure, tends to confront separate problems which must be considered separately no matter how much they may be enmeshed with other problems. While the rise of the People's Republic may indeed have solved some fundamental problems (among them the creation of a political order which seems to maintain its general legitimacy), it has, even in the view of its leadership, continued to be confronted by serious – even fundamental – problems, some old and some new, many of which are by no means easy to solve.

The fatal weakness of Hu Shih and the ultimate strength of his opponents was his notion that one could proceed to the solution of social-educational problems without confronting the tragic problems of political power. To involve oneself in an effort to create one's own base of political power in the current Chinese environment was, in his view, to become embroiled with all the irrational passions and selfish intrigues and violence of warlord politics. All this had little to do with the attitude of 'scientific' rationality required for the solution of these problems. To the extent that he did relate himself to politics he, like his scientist friend Ting Wen-chiang, could only hope to influence incumbent holders of power to accept his recommendations.

What is involved here is not the abstract question of whether those who possess social and political power can ever under any circumstances be persuaded to implement reforms. For a time, Ting Wen-chiang, who did not share Hu Shih's moralistic diffidence towards militarists, was actually able to influence the Kiangsu warlord Sun Ch'uan-fang to carry out certain judicious urban reforms in the Shanghai area.[28] In the brutal and desperately insecure political environment of this period in China, however, holders of power and privilege were not easily to be diverted from their narrow obsessions with political survival.

The communists (although not notably Li Ta-chao) were, on the other hand, prepared to address themselves to the problem of creating political (and ultimately) military power and to act in terms of existing intractable power realities, whether these realities did or did not ultimately conform to the class categories of Marxist analysis. This did not mean that in 1919 Li Ta-chao or any other self-professed communist had access to some 'fundamental solution' of all the current problems of China or even that the slogan 'revolution' had any immediate consequences for Chinese politics. The French and Russian Revolutions have been called social rather than simply political yet at their core lay the destruction of an established *ancien régime*. The destruction of the Peking government in the fragmented

28 See Charlotte Furth, ch. 7 of this volume.

China of 1919 would have had little consequence, and both Nationalists and Communists were to see their task in the next few years as that of dealing with the 'problem' of how one constructs the bases of a new political authority in China rather than the problem of destroying an *ancien régime*. The social could not be divorced from the political and the political task was one of building a new political order rather than that of destroying a firmly established old political order.

THE THEME OF POPULAR CULTURE

The May Fourth episode did not lead to immediate political results, and there were many in the intellectual stratum including Lu Hsun who were not particularly impressed with its significance. There were those such as Hu Shih, Ku Chieh-kang, Fu Ssu-nien and others who were to continue in their belief that the root of China's problem was cultural, and they must therefore 'reorganize the national heritage'.

One new tendency within this enterprise was the emergence of a positive attitude towards the study of popular culture. Even Hu Shih, in his insistence that the vernacular literature of the past had been much more vital and alive than the sterile 'classical' works of the high culture, had introduced a kind of populist theme into his outlook. He seemed willing to include the 'vernacular literature' of the past among the 'congenial stocks' to be preserved. None of this would involve interest in any aspect of the religious culture of the masses. Yet the theme of the greater vitality of popular culture led him to encourage Ku Chieh-kang and others in their efforts to explore folkways and regional customs and collect folktales and folksongs. Ku Chieh-kang had himself been touched by the new movement which had emerged among students since 1919 to 'go to the people' and he was able to relate this movement to his own thesis that while intellectuals in the past had allied themselves to the old aristocracy, they should now take advantage of their new found autonomy as intellectuals to relate themselves to the common people. To do this, one would, however, have to study the conscious life of the masses – their folklore, their customs and folksongs, always employing the methods of scientific inquiry.[29]

From the very outset of this effort there emerged the idea of using popular forms to convey new messages of enlightenment, such as the notion of composing popular ballads with new educational content. In the case of Ku Chieh-kang, however, his interest in folksongs, temples and

29 See Schneider, *Ku Chieh-kang and China's new history*, ch. 4.

festivals gradually took on a more positive aspect. He gradually came to find in the forms of popular culture the embodiment of aesthetic values. In an attack on the anti-superstition policies of the Nationalist Government in 1929 (which was, on the whole, fundamentally hostile to popular culture) Ku was to complain that 'the superstitions are not necessarily overthrown while the artistic legacy of earlier men is indeed overthrown.'[30] Appreciation of the positive aspects of the vital, creative popular culture went hand in hand with the growing bitterness of Ku's 'scientific' assault on the orthodoxy of the high culture. Here he again took up the 'unmasking' theme of the pioneer thinkers – that, from Ch'in to Ch'ing, this culture had been used to suppress the creative life of the people. In the course of his scholarly activity over the years in such journals as the *Ke-yao chou-k'an* (Folksong weekly) and *Min-su chou-k'an* (Folklore), Ku and other students of popular culture such as Cheng Chen-to and Chung Ching-wen were to produce an impressive corpus of research.

The interest in the 'creative, original' aspects of popular culture was not confined to the scholars. Lu Hsun's ambivalence towards various aspects of Chinese popular culture such as graphic arts and the folk theatre continued to colour all of his fictional writings, while Shen Ts'ung-wen, who had spent his youth in the frontier areas of West Hunan, wrote at great length about the life and customs of an area in which Chinese and Miao peoples lived side by side, again finding in this popular culture a source of unreflective vitality.

In all of this one finds little inclination on the part of intellectuals to regard with any sympathy the current 'action' movements among the non-Westernized population such as Buddhist or syncretic sectarian movements or secret societies. Political enlightenment it was felt must come from elsewhere.

This view is particularly marked in the case of the communist Ch'ü Ch'iu-pai who harshly criticized his fellow Marxist literateurs for their 'Western classicism'. His point was simple. If a revolutionary literature were to be written in China which would rouse the masses (and here his mind was focused mainly on the urban proletariat), it must be written in a language and using the forms of life which the masses understood. These popular forms were, however, to be used basically to serve a new content and not because of any intrinsic value of their own. In concentrating on urban working people, Ch'ü was quite convinced that he would be dealing with basically 'modern' common men. His criticism of the

30 *Ibid.* 152.

effort of the 'popular culture' scholars was, on the whole, harsh. The vernacular literature so highly praised by Hu Shih was in essence the work of literati, and the culture of the masses contained a mass of superstitions designed to keep the people in bondage. In the Yenan period Mao Tse-tung would later take up the theme of using the forms of popular culture (now that of the peasant masses) for strictly modern political purposes. Yet the nationalistic emphasis in the Mao of Yenan was to lead him to a somewhat more favourable assessment of the value of popular culture of the past and to a broader sense of its contents. Like Hu Shih, he was prepared to admit vernacular Chinese fiction into the precincts of the people's culture, however suspicious the 'popular' credentials of its authors.

'NEO-TRADITIONALISM' – FINDING TRUTH IN THE HERITAGE

Another outcome of the May Fourth movement which until recently has received comparatively little attention in Western literature was the whole 'neo-traditionalist' reaction against the 'totalistic iconoclasm' of the movement. The neglect of the figures associated with this tendency has again been based on the premise that its presumed defeat in 1949 renders its ideas completely uninteresting. Let us note first that the figures to be dealt with here have little to do with the popular culture orientation just discussed. They were unabashedly oriented towards the high culture of the past even when they tended to identify this high culture with the 'Chinese spirit' in general. Also they were acquainted in varying degrees with modern Western thought and did not hesitate to employ Western ideas to support their positions. In the view of Joseph Levenson this search for support from the sages of the West indicated anew the 'tradi-tionalistic' nature of their thought. It betrayed a lack of confidence that traditional Chinese thought could stand on its own merits. It was again a case of salvaging national pride by finding Chinese equivalents of Western ideas. However, while this kind of 'romantic' cultural nationalism is often present (most notably in the case of Kuomintang ideology after 1927), one cannot make the a priori assertion that this is inevitably the case.

Levenson's view probably holds true for the revolutionary 'national essence' circle of Liu Shih-p'ei, Liu Ya-tzu and others before the May Fourth period. Yet the successors of this older 'national essence' group after May Fourth represented an entirely different breed. Men such as Mei Kuang-ti and Wu Mi, who had studied at Harvard University under the eminent Irving Babbitt and who still continued their affiliations with the older 'national essence' group, adopted an entirely different approach which found expression in their periodical the *Hsueh heng* (Critical review). Through Irving Babbitt they came in contact with the Western tradition of the literary critic as the critic of life. Babbitt had erected the categories 'classical' and 'romantic' into the status of major life attitudes. The 'classical' represented metahistorical aesthetic and ethical standards, as well as the 'inner check' in the moral life of the individual. It represented order and structure. The 'romantic' represented the dissolution of all standards, the unbridled domination of passions in individual and collective life, and so forth. The *Critical Review* leaders were convinced that these were categories which cut across cultural differences and they were much encouraged by Babbitt himself to believe that the Confucian values and classical Chinese literature represented that which was most classical in China. Whether this represents 'cultural nationalism' or a genuine perception of spiritual affinities across cultures is a matter which cannot be clearly decided. The fact remains that this particular brand of 'neo-traditionalism' was not to prove very vital. Liang Shu-ming, who regarded himself as the bearer of authentic Confucianism, dismissed the scholastic and aesthetic focus of the whole 'national essence' group as representing the 'picking up of stiff rotten goods'.[31]

It is noteworthy that the man who points out the main line of 'neo-traditional' thought after the May Fourth period is again the ever voluble Liang Ch'i-ch'ao. Having made a trip to Europe as a non-official member of the Chinese delegation to the Paris Peace Conference, he felt the genuine sense of gloom and dismay among many European thinkers on the continent after the catastrophe of the First World War. These contacts led him to write his 'Reflections on a European journey' which is nothing less than a total reassessment of the essence of 'Eastern and Western civilizations'. Discussions of this type which had gone on before in the writings of Yen Fu, Ch'en Tu-hsiu and others had always led to the drastic reduction of those vast complexes called civilizations to simple, manageable dichotomies. The essence of Western civilization was to Liang essentially what it had been in the past – a 'materialistic' civilization (as he now called it) bent on the subjugation of nature through science and technology, a Darwinian universe of inexorable conflict among individuals, classes and nations. What was drastically reversed was his evaluation of this civilization. In the past he had enthusiastically accepted social Darwinism as a positive prescriptive ethic. Now it was the ethic which in the opinion of critical Western thinkers themselves had led to the

31 See Guy Alitto, *The last Confucian: Liang Shu-ming and the Chinese dilemma of modernity*, 118.

holocaust of the First World War. Since this was the essence of Western civilization (for its aggressive, belligerent nature had even earlier historical roots), wherever he now found in the West more spiritually oriented critics such as Eucken or Bergson, he now tended to detect the influence of the East.

More pertinent to our theme, however, is the question of where Liang now finds the locus of the Chinese spirit. He finds it not in those doctrines which had dwelt in the past on the so-called 'outer realm' – doctrines concerning rules of proper behaviour (*li*), institutions and social organization and doctrines concerning the structure of the natural world. Here China would have to continue to learn much from the material and social technology of the West. He rather finds it precisely in those modes of thought which had stressed the 'inner realm' – in the Sung-Ming Neo-Confucianism of Chu Hsi and Wang Yang-ming, and beyond that in the Mahayana Buddhistic philosophy to which he had been attracted as a youth. The core of China's unique culture lies in its faith that man has an inner intuition which unites him to the cosmic, ineffable source of all being, a source from which he derives the power of spiritual and moral self-transformation. The West thought of freedom only in terms of the satisfaction of creaturely needs – not in terms of a cosmically based moral autonomy.

In the case of Liang Ch'i-Ch'ao – man of many transformations – one can never be entirely sure of the springs of his thought. Joseph Levenson may be quite right to assume that he derived a good deal of ordinary nationalistic gratification from his new-found sense of China's spiritual superiority. Yet Liang's finding the core of Chinese thought in Neo-Confucianism prefigured the central tendency of the whole neo-traditional movement of the following period.

THE DEBATE ON SCIENCE AND HUMAN LIFE

Another important moment in the emergence of the new traditionalism, as well as in the clarification of the meaning of the term science in China, was provided by the 'debate on science and human life'[32] launched by Liang's young associate and student of German philosophy, Chang Chün-mai, in 1923. His contention that science could not explain man because human life was 'subjective, intuitive, freely willed and unique to the individual' reflected his neo-Kantian studies as well as the German debates on 'natural sciences and spiritual sciences' (Naturwissenschaft

32 See *K'o-hsueh yü jen-sheng-kuan* (Science and the philosophy of life), prefaces by Hu Shih and Ch'en Tu-hsiu. See also above, pages 372–3.

und Geisteswissenschaft). Unlike Liang, Chang was acutely aware of the German counter to the tradition of Anglo-American empiricism. Nevertheless, he seemed able to make a quick transition from Kant's epistemological scepticism to the cosmic intuitionism of Wang Yang-ming.

Ting Wen-chiang, who most concretely represented science among the intelligentsia, took up the challenge of Chang's attack on the universal claims of science. From the first discussions in the writings of Yen Fu the word 'science' in China had conveyed a sense of apodictic certainty. From the outset the prevailing concept of science was that of a Baconian inductionism which finds its most complete expression in Mill's *Logic* (translated by Yen Fu). John Dewey's scientific methodology with its focus on experience and experiment was clearly in this tradition in spite of his deep reservations concerning British sensationalist empiricism. From Yen Fu to Mao Tse-tung, however, there also seemed to be little questioning of the faith that systems such as Herbert Spencer's social Darwinism and Marxism were based on concepts derived by inductive observation. The recognition that the cutting edge of the natural sciences lay more in the power of mathematico-deductive hypotheses, rather than in simple procedures of observation and experiment, was not to gain many adherents in China.

Ting Wen-chiang's outlook was based on the positivist epistemology of Karl Pearson's *Grammar of science*, which insisted that science provides the only way man has of organizing and classifying the sense data which are the only link between him and a world beyond that he can never know 'in itself'. While this introduces a rare concern with Western epistemological scepticism, its view of science does not stray from the inductionist tradition. As Charlotte Furth has pointed out in chapter 7, Ting's science of geology was precisely an observational-classifying science. The other participants in the debate, such as Wu Chih-hui, Hu Shih and ultimately Ch'en Tu-hsiu, who was by now a Communist, tended to ignore Ting's epistemology (as well as Dewey's) and to maintain staunchly that science supported either the kind of fanciful mechanistic materialism interlaced with Taoist-Buddhist overtones advocated by Wu Chih-hui or the new true social science of Marxism. Hu Shih and Ch'en Tu-hsiu were to agree that science was a tool for controlling the world of nature and society and that it undermined Chang's faith in the 'inner' transformative spiritual and moral power of the individual. Beyond this, the debate simply laid bare the fact that the word science itself no longer provided any common ground of solidarity.

Chang Chün-mai's argument and his subsequent development demonstrated once more that the heart of the more vital new traditionalism would be Neo-Confucian thought in general and Wang Yang-ming in particular.

A word should be said at this point about the centrality of Wang Yang-ming in traditional thought after May Fourth. Without attempting an analysis of the Ming sage and his followers something must be said about his appeal to figures as diverse as Liang Shu-ming, Hsiung Shih-li and even Chiang Kai-shek. There is first of all the faith in the spiritual-moral inner intuition which links man to an ultimate ground of cosmic being as a source of spiritual-moral life. What we have here is a defiant rejection on intuitive grounds of Western post-Cartesian epistemological scepticism and the concept of a 'valueless' universe. While Wang's intuition led him to conclusions which were in harmony with Confucian moral-political values, his reliance on the 'inner light' bore within itself the possibility of a detachment from traditional Confucian views of the 'outer realm'. By contrast, Chu Hsi's insistence on the need to derive truths by the 'investigation of things' seemed to bind him irrevocably to the 'things' of the traditional order. Finally, Wang's insistence that intuitive moral insight could be gained only in the course of individual action in the world of concrete social situations gave some at least a strong motivation for action in the world.

One of the most notable figures in the neo-traditional movement has been Liang Shu-ming (still alive and flourishing at this writing). Having been exposed in his childhood to a thoroughly Westernized education on the lines proposed by Yen Fu and Liang Ch'i-ch'ao, Liang was not driven in the discouraging years after 1911 into the 'new culture' camp. The sterling example of his father, Liang Chi, who was a kind of living paradigm of Confucian virtue, would have been enough to make him reject Lu Hsun's totalistic negative view of tradition. Instead he sought solace first in Buddhism and then in the Neo-Confucian outlook of the Wang Yang-ming school.

We shall not dwell here on his famous work of 1921, *Eastern and Western cultures and their philosophies*,[33] except to remark that its image of the West was in broad strokes very much that of Liang Ch'i-ch'ao. The essence of Chinese culture lay in its early discovery that what is essentially human in man is his spiritual-moral nature which, when unimpeded, leads both to inner harmony and to unobstructed empathy among men. The achievement by Chinese culture of this insight so early in its history had had its costs. While the West's dynamic civilization had led it to what he saw as a monstrous capitalist-consumer society, it had also led it to

33 All these matters are superbly covered in *The last Confucian* by Guy Alitto.

discover the methods for coping with man's elemental needs. China required the benefit of these methods but not at the cost of losing its spiritual base. Liang fully accepted the activist implications of Wang Yang-ming's philosophy and also seemed to share Wang's conviction that Confucianism had definite implications for social as well as personal reality, that is, Confucianism had implications for the 'outer' as well as the 'inner' realm. It was this conviction which gradually led him to his interest in the 'rural reconstruction' movement already underway and supported by 'Westernizers' such as James Yen and T'ao Hsing-chih. The vast masses of China's countryside had in his view not yet been corrupted by the corrosive effects of urban capitalism but were nevertheless suffering from the myriad evils of poverty, corruption and instability.

Liang's educational and reform activities in Tsou-p'ing county, Shantung, after 1930 were based on a rejection of the political bureaucratic path. Chiang Kai-shek's effort to combine Wang Yang-ming notions of 'self-cultivation' with his own dream of a rationalized, modern bureaucratic-militarized state seemed to Liang to provide no solution. In the conditions of corruption, military coercion and violence which prevailed the sage could bring his moral influence to bear only through direct contact with the rural masses. In one respect there was some resemblance between Liang's ideas and those of Mao Tse-tung during the Yenan period. Guy Alitto has indeed argued that some of Liang's ideas on moral self-scrutiny or small group confessionals, and on the reorientation of rural education may indeed have significantly influenced his friend Mao after their famous interview of 1938.[34] Yet the differences were to remain significant. Liang's programme was based either on the by-passing of the established political structure or, *faute de mieux*, on the support of favourably inclined power-holders (in this but in no other way he resembled Hu Shih). Mao's was premised on the Marxist-Leninist whole-hearted acceptance of the brutal game of power. To Liang any effort to construct a political organization of his own would negate his own Confucian conception of the moral bases of authority. In this, of course, he was like Mencius before him who managed to disguise the fact of the violent origins of the 'sacred three dynasties' themselves. The Maoist use of 'rural reconstruction' as instrumental to the ulterior purpose of building a base of military and political power no doubt already suggested to Liang the possibilities of the future corruption of the communist effort in spite of his admiration of it. In 1953 he was indeed to charge that the adoption of a Stalinist model

34 *Ibid*. 283–92.

of development by the People's Republic was the expression of such a bureaucratic perversion. Yet he himself discovered no way of insulating his rural reconstructional activities from the vicissitudes of the political environment.

While Liang Shu-ming's Confucianism led him directly to the realms of action, the same was not true of Hsiung Shih-li and his disciples T'ang Chün-i, Mou Tsung-san, and others. Hsiung Shih-li (1885–1968) was a somewhat idiosyncratic 'marginal' personality whose educational formation had been largely within the framework of the traditional culture although he had briefly become involved in revolutionary politics. Like others before him he had first been attracted by 'consciousness-only' Buddhism and then was won back by Wang Yang-ming to a Confucian belief in the significance of man's moral life. Unlike Liang Shu-ming, neither he nor his disciples became committed to an immediate programme of action, even though they acknowledged the social implications of their doctrines. The defence and elucidation of the foundations of their intuitionist philosophy seemed to them to require all of their attention, unlike Liang Shu-ming, who seemed quite secure in his own 'sageliness'. Thomas Metzger has argued that the kind of religio-ethical optimism and faith in 'sagely' power found in the writings of T'ang Chün-i, when detached from the older external Confucian order, could become the basis of an ebullient faith in the possibility of a total social transformation.[35] He argues that on an unacknowledged level Mao Tsetung himself shared in this 'traditional' faith. Yet the fact remains that T'ang Chün-i, Mou Tsung-san and Hsiung Shih-li (who lived on in the People's Republic until his death in 1968) did not accept the People's Republic as the realization of their vision and continued to be deeply preoccupied with the relevance of their faith to the existential problems of personal life.

Quite another version of Neo-Confucianism is that represented by Fung Yu-lan who was trained as a philosopher in the United States. Like Mei Kuang-ti, he found his philosophic inspiration in the Anglo-Saxon West. If he is a 'neo-traditionalist' at all, his traditionalism is of a distinctly cosmopolitan variety. Having committed himself to the kind of Platonic 'neo-realism' which flourished for a time in early twentieth-century America and England, he felt confident that its categories could be applied to Chu Hsi's thought. Significantly, neo-realism represents a sharp reaction in the West against the dominant tradition of epistemological scepticism. Some of its adherents were indeed prepared to accept a Platonic

35 Thomas A. Metzger, *Escape from predicament: Neo-Confucianism and China's evolving political culture.*

account of mathematical and logical truth as objective, eternal forms. Fung seems to have been deeply impressed by the ancient Greek ideal of intellectual contemplation as the way to achieve a sense of sublimity and of detachment from the disorders of man's daily existence. Science, in this view, does not merely involve an effort to apply logico-mathematical ideas to an achievement of the mastery of the physical world. To the 'sagely' man science involves the contemplation of the beauty of mathematical and logical 'forms'. In Fung's view this involved intellectual contemplation but not mysticism. Thus, in seeking a Chinese equivalent of his outlook Fung was attracted precisely to what he perceived to be the intellectualism of Chu Hsi rather than to the 'anti-intellectual' intuitionism of Wang Yang-ming. Whether his interpretation of Chu Hsi's *li* as Platonic forms is valid remains a matter of great dispute. Yet one need not doubt that Fung believed he had found here a Chinese framework for his basic outlook.

None of this implied a rejection of the social and nationalistic concerns of his contemporaries. On the contrary Fung was quite ready in the 1930s to accept a quasi-Marxist determinist view of history. History like nature has its own presiding configurations – its own 'forms' of growth and Fung is quite prepared to think of these forms in terms of necessary stages of historical process based on a conception of economic determinism. Moral behaviour in this view means behaviour which conforms to the requirements of a given socio-historical stage of development. On the contemplative level of his being the 'sage' is above the vicissitudes of history. In his moral-practical life he is able to adjust to the requirements of history. This philosophy led him to a willing acceptance of the People's Republic but it did not shield him against future troubles.[36]

It should be added that all these varieties of traditional thought have continued to exercise their influence in Hong Kong, Taiwan and even among Chinese intellectuals abroad. They remain part of the larger intellectual scene of twentieth-century China.

THE ASCENDANCY OF MARXISM

Before we deal with the rise of Marxism to a position of dominance in the Chinese intellectual world, something should be said about those tendencies which are labelled liberal – often on doubtful grounds. Hu Shih continued after May Fourth to cling staunchly to his basic positions even though he was now assailed by enemies on all sides. The spectacular

36 See the unpublished dissertation of Michel Masson, 'The idea of Chinese tradition: Fung Yu-lan, 1939–1949', (Harvard University, Ph.D. dissertation, 1978).

events of the years 1924–7 and the passionate emotions which accompanied them did not sway him. Irrational political passion as ever remained irrelevant to truth. Although he, like his mentor Dewey, was by no means committed to capitalism, he remained convinced that China's basic ills were not due to foreign imperialism. He continued to attack the 'dogmas' of both Sun Yat-sen and the Marxists.

After the establishment of the Nationalist government, Hu continued to attack the traditionalistic components of the Kuomintang ideology, continued to call for the application of 'scientific intelligence' to national policies, continued to call for constitutionalism and civil rights and to advocate a 'modern' system of education which would create a new elite of enlightened and modern men. In the *Tu-li p'ing-lun* (Independent critic) published during the years 1932–7 under the shadow of the growing Japanese threat, Hu Shih was joined by such figures as Ting Wen-chiang and the historian Chiang T'ing-fu in their effort to influence the policies of the Nationalist government. It was soon to become apparent, however, that what they shared with Hu Shih was more his commitment to 'science' than his commitment to democracy.

Ting Wen-chiang had never been as committed to liberal values as Hu Shih and in the sombre decade of the 1930s he, like Chiang T'ing-fu, had come to feel (like Yen Fu and Liang Ch'i-ch'ao before them) that what China needed was a 'scientific' dictatorship – a technocracy which would modernize the bureaucratic, industrial and educational systems of the country. Ting had even been much impressed by Stalin's Russia as a model. They both had a rather poor opinion of the competence of the Kuomintang leadership despite the Nationalist government's professed commitment to the same goals. Yet they could only continue to hope that the Nationalist government, the only centre of organized power, would heed their advice. The rural revolutionary drama of the Chinese Communists in Hunan and Kiangsi and later in Yenan seemed to them utterly irrelevant to the nation's needs and further enfeebled the central power of the state. Hu Shih himself was torn between his attraction to their vision of a scientific elite and his faith in constitutional democracy. Like the others, however, he could only hope to bring his influence to bear on established power. In the end, with the polarization between what he regarded as totalitarian communism and the more limited albeit corrupt authoritarianism of the Kuomintang, which might eventually be pushed in a more liberal direction, he felt that he had to choose the lesser evil. To the end he proved unable as the spiritual leader of a political cause to cope with the tragic and intractable realities of political power in twentieth-century China.

The years between 1924 and 1927 were however, marked above all by the spectacular spread among the urban intelligentsia of certain versions of Marxism as a dominant intellectual outlook. It should nevertheless be noted that the spread of Marxism and the ultimate victory of the Chinese Communists remain two related but separable facts.

In the stormy years 1924-7, many of the younger generation of the May Fourth era, who had thoroughly internalized its totalistic anti-traditionalism, now had a concrete opportunity to participate in the dynamic political drama made possible by the Kuomintang-Communist alliance. From the very outset, the Leninist theory of imperialism and its image of the Western world was to win wide acceptance not only among those close to the Communist Party but even among Kuomintang-affiliated intellectuals and politicians. The events of 30 May 1925 seemed to confirm most graphically the link between foreign imperialism and the exploitation of China's new industrial proletariat. The activism of the urban population and the Communist Party's actual success in establishing a link to the urban working class seemed to confirm Marxist-Leninist views regarding the role of that class in history. The ability of P'eng P'ai, Mao Tse-tung[37] and others to create a link to the peasantry was again not inconsistent with Lenin's view of the role of the peasantry in a bourgeois democratic revolution. During the northern expedition of 1926-7 many intellectuals found themselves participants either in mass organization activities or in the organs of the newly founded Wuhan government. The experience kindled both their nationalist rage and their more universal hopes for the transformation of the world. The revolution would achieve both national unification and the transformation of China into a radically new society. To be sure, bitter conflicts in Moscow showed that Marxism-Leninism yielded no automatic illumination, but so long as the trajectory of revolution moved forward, the desire to believe that Moscow was the source of a higher universal wisdom remained strong.

Among the Marxist intellectuals the members of the romantic Creation Society (see page 474) and of the newly formed 'Sun' (T'ai-yang) Society were to play a prominent role. Having explored the ecstasies and despairs of romantic love and the expressive experience of the writer, Kuo Mo-jo, Chiang Kuang-tz'u and others felt that they now had significant heroic roles to play as revolutionary leaders. Their self-image was thus very similar to that of the romantic revolutionaries before 1911. They would inspire the ardour of the revolutionary masses through the vehicle of a new proletarian literature.

37 For a study of the beginnings of the communist peasant movement see Roy Hofheinz, Jr. *The broken wave: the Chinese communist peasant movement, 1922–1928.*

Lu Hsun's gravitation to Marxism-Leninism was much more painful and arduous. His deep despondency concerning the 'man-eating' power of the old culture had not really been shaken by the events of May Fourth.[38] His mordant reflections on what had happened to many of the young idealists of the pre-1911 period was, perhaps, a factor of some importance in his failure to respond. His hesitancy to accept the new theory of human progress may also have stemmed from his hostility to what he regarded as the romantic revolutionary posturings of his enemies in the Creation Society, who fancied that they could influence the course of history through their proletarian rhetoric. Even when he moved into the Marxist camp, he was to seek theoretical support from Plekhanov and others for his attack on their wild exaggeration of the causative role of literature in social revolution. His use of Marxist categories began before 1927, but it is characteristic of him that what finally drove him close to the Communist Party was the bitter rage roused by the Nationalist government's execution of young people in his immediate entourage. This was no doubt reinforced by a more positive and yet hesitant hope that the Marxist-Leninist analysis of history would prove more accurate than the evolutionary doctrines of the past.

An important element in the polarization of the urban intelligentsia towards Marxism was the abyss which arose between them and the faction within the Kuomintang led by Chiang Kai-shek. While Chiang had been influenced by the anti-imperialist aspect of Leninist rhetoric, his education in both Chekiang and Japan had early led him to the kind of cultural nationalism that rendered him immune to the totalistic iconoclasm of May Fourth. The military basis of his rise to power may have led him further to deprecate the usefulness and trustworthiness of urban intellectuals. It also gave him even after 1927 an unswerving conviction that the task of first priority in China was military unification. In all of these convictions, he seemed to feel that he remained a faithful disciple of Sun Yat-sen. By the same token, all his opponents both within the Kuomintang and outside the party saw in him the recrudescence of the older militarism. He was the symbol of the melancholy fact that the subordination of military to civil power had not yet taken place. Also, the gap between his cultural nationalism and 'totalistic iconoclasm' remained.

The débâcle of 1927 did not lead to a decline in the prestige of Marxism. The Leninist notion that a wrong political strategy basically reflects a wrong 'revolutionary theory' encouraged the view that with a correct theory the revolution would forge ahead. For many (but not for all) the

---

38 See Harriet C. Mills, 'Lu Xun: literature and revolution – from Mara to Marx' in Merle Goldman, ed. *Modern Chinese literature in the May Fourth era.*

continued existence of the Soviet Union as the headquarters of revolution provided valid reassurance that history would ultimately follow a Marxist-Leninist trajectory.

It is thus no accident that a major concern of many Marxist intellectuals during the next decade was to understand Chinese society in Marxist terms. The Leninist use of theory as 'a guide to action' encouraged the belief that the 'party line' of a given period must be based on a Marxist analysis of the disposition of class forces and on the determination of the historical stage. The 'debate on the social history of China'[39] was to be an expression of this concern. However, the determination of China's present 'mode of production' in Marxist terms was to prove to be no easy matter. Quite logically it led to a concern with the periodization of China's long social history. In probing all these questions the participants imperceptibly were driven from a consideration of 'theory as a guide to action' to the more deterministic aspects of Marxist doctrines as applied to the past. Some who participated in the debate were fundamentally interested in Marxism as social science *par excellence*. Thus T'ao Hsi-sheng, a leading figure in the debates, like some other participants was an adherent of the Kuomintang. He found no difficulty in placing his Three People's Principles ideology within the framework of Marxist categories or in drawing non-communist conclusions from his analyses. Other participants, however, represented Stalinist and Trotskyist factions.

At this point we can only note certain features of the debate. On the whole, it would appear that in attempting to use the Marxist concepts of capitalism and feudalism in the analysis of Chinese society, the participants simply illuminated certain unresolved obscurities in Marx's own doctrines on these matters. Is feudal society any agrarian society dominated by a ruling class which rules by 'extra-economic' power? Or do different 'relations of property' reflect different 'relations of production'? Is any type of landlord class feudal? Can the prevalence of commercial relations define the nature of society or is the role of the 'mode of production' crucial? Texts could be found supporting divergent answers to these and many other questions.

The Marxist concept of the 'Asiatic mode of production' was largely rejected by most of the participants, who opted for some version of the unilinear scheme of historical periodization which Marx had prescribed for the West. It was, after all, only within the framework of this scheme that he had actually described the dynamic dialectic of history. There

39 For a study of the debate see Arif Dirlik, *Revolution and history: origins of Marxist historiography in China 1919–1937*; also Benjamin Schwartz, 'Some stereotypes in the periodization of Chinese history', *Philosophic Forum*, 1. 11 (Winter 1968) 219–30.

were some participants such as T'ao Hsi-sheng who envisioned other ways of describing and periodizing the unilinear view, but to accept for China Marx's view of a static 'Asian mode of production' was virtually to deny that Chinese social history had a dynamic of its own.

If the debate was won, it was won by fiat rather than by argument. The Mao Tse-tung of the Yenan period made no 'theoretical' contribution whatsoever to the debate. His own interest in high theory led him to another debate less prominent in Marxist circles concerning the philosophic interpretation of the dialectic and questions of Marxist epistemology.

In the 1930s Marxism was also to become a dominant force on the literary front. In the League of Left-wing Writers formed by Lu Hsun, Ch'ü Ch'iu-pai and others we find the emergence of stormy unresolved debates concerning the Marxist view of the role of literature as a 'superstructural' phenomenon. While Marxism seemed to be the culmination of the tendency to stress the moral-political function of literature, it by no means logically led all the participants to accept the subordination of the writer to the authority of shifting party lines. It was thus quite clear that Lu Hsun himself had not accepted the claim of such authority.

The decade of the 1940s was, of course, to witness the full assault of the Japanese war-machine. The vast disruption produced by the war and the emotional engagement of all allowed little energy for new intellectual trends. The pressures of the war did, it is true, tend to politicize even those who were least political such as Liang Shu-ming, who was to become a founder of the Democratic League. One noteworthy feature of this politicization, however, was that it revealed a kind of 'liberal' strain within the intellectual stratum as a whole, even though most of them were by no means liberals in some of their basic commitments. Over the course of the first half of the century, the intellectual stratum had, for better or worse, achieved a sense of its own autonomy as a separate intellectual (rather than political) element. The 'scholar' had up to a point been sundered from the 'official'. They had also grown accustomed to the free exchange of ideas. Often in responding to the claims of the nationalist and communist governing elites, they had perforce tended to stand on the grounds of civil rights. In the polarized world of civil war after 1945 a large part of the intelligentsia was drawn to the communist side. Yet subsequent events were to demonstrate that this 'liberal' strain would remain a problem.

Another significant development of the 1940s was, of course, the Yenan 'thought of Mao Tse-tung'. Without in any way derogating his political genius, we can be quite clear that many of the subjects with which he dealt were part of the general intellectual discourse of the period covered in these pages. The problems Mao considered had been considered by others before him.

Have all the issues raised by the intellectuals during the first half of the century been resolved since 1949? Some have undoubtedly been resolved, at least for our segment of time. A powerful centre of political authority has been created (some would say all too powerful). In spite of recurrent political causes, law and order has been re-established. A relatively equitable distribution of goods has been achieved within a very poor economy. Nationalist passions have been somewhat appeased. Public health has advanced and the status of women has been improved. Yet in spite of the claims of the '-ism,' many of the fundamental 'problems' considered above remain. What will be China's future relationship to its cultural heritage? Can one avoid the 'technocratic' approaches envisioned by Yen Fu and Ting Wen-chiang if one's aim is to achieve 'modernization'? Have the questions of bureaucracy and power been resolved? What about literature, art and the meaning of personal existence? Chinese must grope their way into the future like all the rest of us.

CHAPTER 9

LITERARY TRENDS I:
THE QUEST FOR MODERNITY, 1895–1927

In a seminal essay on modern Chinese literature, Professor C. T. Hsia delineates a 'moral burden' which tends to overhang the entire corpus of literary creation in the first half of the twentieth century. 'What distinguishes this modern phase of Chinese literature', Professor Hsia remarks, is its 'obsessive concern with China as a nation afflicted with a spiritual disease and therefore unable to strengthen itself or change its set ways of inhumanity.' This 'patriotic passion', which enkindles all the major writers of the period, also produces in Hsia's view, 'a certain patriotic provinciality': 'the Chinese writer sees the conditions of China as peculiarly Chinese and not applicable elsewhere.'[1] It is this obsession that dictates, in turn, a general preoccupation with content, rather than form, and a preponderance of 'realism' – as the modern Chinese writer's effort to make some sense of the socio-political chaos in his immediate environment. The study of modern Chinese literature is, therefore, burdened with China's modern history, and a generally historical approach – with due regard to intrinsic literary concerns – is both imperative and inevitable.

From a historical perspective, the theme of 'obsession with China' contains at least three major variations which may be regarded as further hallmarks of modern Chinese literature. First, the moral vision of China 'as a nation afflicted with spiritual disease' creates a sharp polarity between tradition and modernity: the disease is rooted in Chinese tradition, whereas modernity means essentially an iconoclastic revolt against this tradition and an intellectual quest for new solutions. In this sense, the rise of modern Chinese literature represents an integral part of the New Culture movement, as most students of the May Fourth movement have pointed out.[2] Second, this anti-traditional stance in modern Chinese literature is derived not so much from spiritual or artistic considerations (as

---

1 C. T. Hsia, 'Obsession with China: the moral burden of modern Chinese literature', in his *A history of modern Chinese fiction*, 2nd edn, 533–6.
2 See, for instance, Chow Tse-tsung, *The May Fourth movement: intellectual revolution in modern China*. See also Benjamin Schwartz, ed. *Reflections on the May fourth movement: a symposium*, esp. the Introduction.

in Western modernistic literature) as from China's socio-political conditions. It may be argued that modern Chinese literature arose as a result of the increasing gap between state and society: as the intellectuals became more and more frustrated with the state's failure to take initiatives, they turned away from the state to become radical spokesmen of Chinese society. Modern literature thus became a vehicle through which to voice social discontent. The bulk of modern Chinese literature is anchored in contemporary society and evinces a critical spirit vis-à-vis the writer's political environment. This critical stance has been the most enduring May Fourth legacy; its repercussions have been persistently felt down to the present day.

A third hallmark of modern Chinese literature is that, much as it reflects an overpowering sense of socio-political anguish, its critical vision is intensely subjective. Reality is perceived from the writer's individual point of view, which betrays, at the same time, an obsession with self. This prevalent tendency of what Professor Jaroslav Průšek calls 'subjectivism and individualism' – an 'orientation toward the author's own fate and own life', his 'own person and character' which is set 'in opposition to the whole society'[3] – thus gives rise to an aggravated ambivalence in the modern Chinese writer's conception of self and society. His obsessions with China are coupled with a feeling of personal disgust with her ills; he yearns for hope and commitment, while at the same time he suffers from a sense of loss and alienation. It is this subjective tension, born of largely unresolved ambivalence, which provides the basic impetus for three decades of literary creativity and movements and which marks off the 'modern' phase of Chinese literature from its traditional and communist phases.

LATE CH'ING LITERATURE, 1895–1911

The origins of modern Chinese literature can be traced to the late Ch'ing period, more specifically to the last decade and a half from 1895 to 1911, in which some of the 'modern' symptoms became increasingly noticeable. It is to this period that we shall first direct our attention.

The growth of literary journalism

The emergence of late Ch'ing literature – particularly fiction – was a by-product of journalism, which evolved out of a societal reaction to a series

3 Jaroslav Průšek, 'Subjectivism and individualism in modern Chinese literature', *Archiv Orientalni*, 25. 2 (1957) 266–70.

of deepening political crises.[4] China's humiliating defeat in the first Sino-Japanese war of 1894–5 finally shocked the intellectual elite into action. But their demands for change culminated only in the unsuccessful reform movement in 1898. Disillusioned with the prospect of change from above, the reform-minded of the literati turned away from the ineffectual state to become the radical spokesmen for Chinese society. Their efforts were concentrated on generating 'public opinion' with which to bring pressure to bear on the central government. And they found in treaty-port journalism a useful medium for their purposes.

Non-official newspapers had already appeared by the second half of the nineteenth century, mainly under the sponsorship of Western missionaries. But the rapid proliferation of such newspapers was led by the reform-minded of the intellectual elite. Liang Ch'i-ch'ao's *Ch'iang-hsueh pao* (Self-strengthening news) and *Shih-wu pao* (Current affairs) were founded in 1895 and 1896 as organs of K'ang Yu-wei's reform party. After their failure in 1898 Liang escaped to Japan where he continued his journalistic career by founding two newspapers, *Ch'ing-i pao* (Political commentary; 1898–) and *Hsin-min ts'ung-pao* (New People miscellany; 1901–), both of which were quickly to become authoritative. Liang's example was followed by Yen Fu, who helped publish *Kuo-wen pao* (National news; 1897–), and Ti Ch'u-ch'ing, who founded *Shih-pao* (The times; 1904–). The journalistic ranks were soon joined by revolutionaries with their own newspapers, notably Chang Ping-lin's *Su-pao* (Kiangsu tribune; 1897–) and *Kuo-min jih-jih pao* (National people's daily; 1903–). By 1906, according to two tabulations, a total of 66 newspapers had been published at Shanghai alone, and the total number of newspapers published in the entire period came to 239.[5]

In order to popularize their cause, it was standard practice for these newspapers to write trenchant news items, but also include poems and articles of an entertaining nature, which were later allocated to a special 'supplement' (*fu-k'an*). As the demand for these supplements increased they were expanded and published separately as independent magazines. Thus literary journalism was born. Edited by a hybrid group of journalist-littérateurs – men who had some knowledge of Western literature and foreign languages but a more solid background in traditional Chinese

4 Leo Ou-fan Lee, *The romantic generation of modern Chinese writers*, 3–7.
5 The figure of 66 was given by Li Pao-chia. Of these at least 32 are what A Ying calls 'little newspapers', which are less overtly political but more attuned to the leisurely amusements of the urban middle class. See A Ying, *Wan-Ch'ing wen-i pao-k'an shu-lueh* (A brief account of late Ch'ing literary journals and newspapers), 51. The figure of 239 is given in an article, 'Ch'ing-chi chung-yao pao-k'an mu-lu' (A catalogue of important newspapers and periodicals), in Chang Ching-lu, ed. *Chung-kuo chin-tai ch'u-pan shih-liao ch'u-pien* (Historical materials on modern Chinese publications, first collection), 77–92.

literature – these publications featured a plethora of pseudo-translations, poetry, essays and serialized fiction which, although claiming to awaken the social and political consciousness of the people, served also as mass entertainment. By the end of the period, four major magazines had formed the top rank of Shanghai literary journalism: *Hsin hsiao-shuo* (New fiction; 1902–), founded by Liang Ch'i-ch'ao; *Hsiu-hsiang hsiao-shuo* (Illustrated fiction; 1903–), edited by Li Pao-chia (Po-yuan); *Yueh-yueh hsiao-shuo* (Monthly fiction; 1906–), edited by Wu Wo-yao (Yen-jen) and Chou Kuei-sheng; and *Hsiao-shuo lin* (Forest of fiction; 1907–), edited by Huang Mo-hsi.

For at least two decades before the 'literary revolution' of 1917, urban literary journalism – a half-modernized form of 'mass literature' – had already established the market and the readership for the latter-day practitioners of New Literature. The editors and writers of these magazines wrote feverishly to meet deadlines, and profusely to make money. Their arduous efforts resulted in the establishment of a new profession: the commercial success of their works proved that the practice of literature could be an independent and potentially lucrative vocation. It remained, however, for their May Fourth successors to lend an aura of social prestige to the new profession.

A noteworthy feature of late Ch'ing literary journalism was the dominant position accorded to 'fiction' (*hsiao-shuo*) both in magazine titles and as an important genre of literature. The term *hsiao-shuo* still retained from traditional times its broad connotations of miscellaneous writings falling outside the domains of classical prose and poetry. Thus *hsiao-shuo*, as understood by the late Ch'ing practitioners, comprised all forms of popular narrative literature – the classical tale, the novel, the *t'an-tz'u*, (a form of oral story-telling), and even drama. But of these variegated forms, the serialized novel emerged as definitely the major form of late Ch'ing literature. This was due especially to the pioneering efforts of Liang Ch'i-ch'ao and other members of the literary elite to infuse this traditionally 'debased' literary genre with new intellectual vitality and political significance.

Theories of 'new fiction'

The crucial relationship between fiction and society – the socio-political function of *hsiao-shuo* – was articulated in three important manifestos. In the first issue of the Tientsin newspaper *Kuo-wen pao*, Yen Fu and Hsia Tseng-yu wrote an article entitled, 'Announcing our policy to publish a fiction supplement', in which the two men took pains to demonstrate the power of fiction among the masses in the past in order to underscore its vast potential as an educational instrument in the present. But traditional Chinese fiction, Yen warned with a touch of condescension typical of traditional literati, was also full of 'poison'. 'And because people of shallow learning are addicted to fiction, the world has suffered incalculably from the poison of fiction and it is difficult to speak of its benefit.' Thus, the Chinese people had to be re-educated with a new kind of fiction which had worked wonders in the West and in Japan.

Liang Ch'i-ch'ao followed basically this line of argument in his 1898 essay, 'A preface to our published series of translations of political fiction'. He agreed with Yen Fu on the educational potential of fiction but showed even greater contempt for the traditional product. Since most Chinese novels were imitations of either *Shui-hu chuan* (The water margin) or *Hung-lou meng* (Dream of the red chamber), Liang argued, they had earned the disapprobation of scholars for their 'incitement to robbery and lust'. What was urgently needed, then, was a 'revolution in the novel' whereby public interest in old fiction could be switched to translations of 'political fiction'. Inspired mainly by the Japanese example (the preface served as introduction to the Chinese translation of Shiba Shiro's *Kajin-no-kigu* or 'Strange adventures of a beauty'), Liang gave a fanciful, yet forceful, account of the genesis and prestige of political novels in foreign countries:[6]

Formerly, at the start of reform or revolution in European countries, their leading scholars and men of great learning, their men of compassion and patriotism, would frequently record their personal experiences and their cherished views and ideas concerning politics in the form of fiction. Thus, among the population, teachers would read these works in their spare time, and even soldiers, businessmen, farmers, artisans, cabmen and grooms, and schoolchildren would all read them. It often happened that upon the appearance of a book a whole nation would change its views on current affairs. The political novel has been most instrumental in making the governments of America, England, Germany, France, Austria, Italy, and Japan daily more progressive or enlightened.

The *locus classicus* of the argument for political fiction in the late Ch'ing was Liang's most celebrated essay, 'On the relationship between fiction and people's rule', published in *Hsin hsiao-shuo* in 1902. Drawing again upon foreign examples, Liang asserted that renovating fiction was crucial to renovating the people of a nation. Creating a new fiction could exert a decisive influence in all spheres of a nation's life – morality, religion,

---

6 This and the preceding quotes are translated by C. T. Hsia in his 'Yen Fu and Liang Ch'i-ch'ao as advocates of new fiction', in Adele A. Rickett, ed. *Chinese approaches to literature from Confucius to Liang Ch'i-ch'ao*, 230–2.

manners, mores, learning and the arts, even the character of its people. Besides listing the wide-ranging impact of fiction on society, Liang also attempted in this essay to pinpoint the four basic emotive powers of fiction: the power to 'incense' (*hsun*), to 'immerse' (*ch'in*), to 'prick' (*tz'u*) and to 'uplift' (*t'i*) the reader. Liang attached the greatest importance to the last virtue – its power to lift the reader to the level of the fictional hero and to imitate him. But the heroes worthy of Chinese emulation were to be drawn from Western, rather than Chinese, history: the real paragons of national virtue for Chinese were Washington, Napoleon, Mazzini, Garibaldi, and many other modern patriots, revolutionaries, and statesmen whose biographies Liang had described in his other works.

Strictly speaking, neither Yen Fu nor Liang Ch'i-ch'ao can be regarded as literary men. For them literature – especially fiction – served an ulterior purpose: the enlightenment of the Chinese people. Liang dabbled in fiction but never completed any of the several novels he had started. Their views on the function of fiction should not be seen as literary criticism, for which they were obviously unqualified, but rather as documents of social and intellectual history.

While both Yen and Liang were deeply steeped in the 'great tradition', they were also reacting against the recent degeneration of that tradition: eight-legged essays, the formalized but meaningless exercises of much of mid- and late-Ch'ing prose writing, resounding phrases of 'statecraft' which on closer scrutiny were but shallow clichés. With the ossification of the 'high' forms of culture, an effort to revitalize a 'lower' popular genre was highly opportune. But in this area of popularization Yen Fu's contribution was more limited than Liang's. Yen's translations of Spencer, Huxley and J. S. Mill were rendered still in elegant, often erudite, classical prose. He refused to compromise with 'popular tastes' in spite of his advocacy of fiction. Liang, on the other hand, proved far more receptive to both popular and foreign expressions. His essays were written definitely

---

7 Liang still used a *wen-yen* (classical style) syntax but suffused it with vernacular expressions. Many of his followers went a step further by experimenting boldly with the spoken vernacular – including both the Mandarin and the various local dialects (especially of the Kiangsu and Chekiang regions). One of the earliest newspapers written entirely in the vernacular was *Yen-i pai-hua pao* (Paraphrased news in vernacular), first published in 1897, which aimed to bring news – especially concerning foreign powers – to the general public in a more easily comprehensible form and to 'paraphrase various useful books, newspapers, and journals into vernacular with the expectation that they may prove beneficial to read' (A Ying, *Wan-Ch'ing wen-i pao-k'an shu-lueh*, 64) The resulting effect on literary journalism was a gradual blurring of the demarcation between *wen-yen* and *pai-hua* and the increasing importance of *pai-hua*. At the turn of the century, the vernacular was used not only in journalism and literature but also increasingly in works on history, geography, education, industry, and science. See Milena Doleželová-Velingerová, 'The origins of modern Chinese literature', in Merle Goldman, ed. *Modern Chinese literature in the May Fourth era*, 13.

to reach a wide audience.[7] Thus in a way Liang Ch'i-ch'ao's works managed to bridge the gap between the reformist elite – men like K'ang Yu-wei, T'an Ssu-t'ung and Yen Fu – and the urban populace. Without Liang's pioneering achievements in popular journalism, the impact of Yen Fu's translations and reformist thought in general would not have been so far-reaching.

Liang's championship of new fiction also represented a significant shift in political perspective. After the failure of the Hundred Days reform, Liang had turned his attention almost entirely to Chinese society; he tried to construct the blueprint of a new communal group (*ch'ün*) which would then constitute the modern Chinese nation. In spite of its many elitist implications, Liang's celebrated concept of *Hsin-min* (New People) was popular in intent and aimed at renovating the entire Chinese people. With this new orientation, Liang's advocacy of the power of fiction was both natural and inevitable, with or without his knowledge of the Meiji experience. And given his manifest socio-political purpose, Liang was not interested, as Hu Shih was later, in the problems of language *per se*, but in audience impact. His four characteristics of fiction were concerned not with the writer, nor with the intrinsic 'world' of literature, but solely with the reader.

While Liang took the credit for making fiction an important medium, he had little to do with the literary qualities of late Ch'ing fiction. In this respect, credit must go to the less well-educated but more literarily gifted treaty-port journalist-littérateurs.

The practice of new fiction

Two prevalent forms of fiction writing can easily be discerned on the late Ch'ing literary scene: the social novel (or, to use Lu Hsun's term, 'fiction of social criticism', *ch'ien-tse hsiao-shuo*) and the sentimental novel (*hsieh-ch'ing hsiao-shuo*), in which the central focus is on human emotions.

In Hu Shih's opinion, the majority of late Ch'ing social fiction was modelled on one seminal work, the eighteenth-century novel, *Ju-lin wai-shih* (The scholars).[8] Given the socio-political orientation of 'new fiction', as advocated with great impact by Liang Ch'i-ch'ao and Yen Fu, it was natural for the practitioners to find in *The scholars* a glorious precedent for social fiction. But Chinese society of the late nineteenth century was more crisis-ridden than the eighteenth-century world depicted in Wu Ching-tzu's celebrated novel. Thus, besides the obvious similarities of

8 Hu Shih, 'Wu-shih-nien-lai Chung-kuo chih wen-hsueh' (Chinese literature of the past fifty years), in *Hu Shih wen-ts'un* (Collected works of Hu Shih), 2. 233–4.

form and content, late Ch'ing fiction evinced a more strident tone of urgency and a more sombre mood of catastrophe. Often this sense of urgency is conveyed by heavy caricature: Wu Ching-tzu's gentle satire is carried to excess. In Wu Wo-yao's novel, *Erh-shih-nien mu-tu chih kuai-hsien-chuang* (Bizarre phenomena witnessed in the past twenty years),[9] light-hearted humour is so intertwined with revelations of the horrible and the ludicrous that the effect becomes more pathetic than funny. Li Pao-chia's *Kuan-ch'ang hsien-hsing chi* (Exposés of officialdom) is more morbid. One detects almost a conscious desire on Li's part to magnify the dark, grim aspects of life (perhaps an unintentional effect of the author's own suffering from tuberculosis). The abundance of burlesque and distortion in *Kuan-ch'ang hsien-hsing chi* seems to indicate the author's utter disgust with what took place around him. The novel is peopled with negative characters – all greedy, amorally ambitious, addicted to office-seeking and money-grabbing, and eager to bribe and to be bribed. Even reform programmes and the reform-minded of the officials were not spared Li's scathing satire, as can be noted in another novel by Li, *Wen-ming hsiao-shih* (A short history of civilization). What Professor Průšek calls the 'tragic' outlook of these authors is essentially a manifestation of personal exasperation: it was difficult to see hope for a country so permeated with ineptitude and hopelessness.[10]

In order to dramatize this feeling of near-despair, Li and Wu often resorted to striking epithets. The narrator of *Erh-shih-nien mu-tu chih kuai-hsien-chuang* called himself 'a lone survivor after nine deaths' (*chiu-ssu i-sheng*) who managed to escape from three types of 'creatures': snakes, wolves and tigers, and demons. Tseng P'u, author of the famous novel, *Nieh-hai hua* (A flower in a sea of retribution), adopted the pen-name of 'the sick man of East Asia' (*Tung-Ya ping-fu*). Two other authors wrote under the pseudonyms respectively of 'the foremost man of sorrow under Heaven' (T'ien-hsia ti-i shang-hsin jen) and 'the misanthrope of a Han country' (Han-kuo yen-shih che). Liu E (T'ieh-yun), the author of perhaps the best novel of the late Ch'ing period, *Lao Ts'an yu-chi* (Travels of Lao Ts'an), imparted in his chosen *nom de plume* the saddened metaphor of an 'old derelict' making the last few moves on a beleaguered chessboard. Novels bearing such titles as *T'ung shih* (Painful history), *Hen hai* (Sea of sorrow), *Chieh-yu hui* (Ashes after calamity), *K'u she-hui* (Miserable society) have given late Ch'ing fiction a dimension of unprecedented gloom

---

9 An abridged translation in English appeared under the title of *Vignettes from the late Ch'ing: bizarre happenings eyewitnessed over two decades*, trans. by Shih Shun Liu.

10 Some of this discussion is based on notes taken from Professor Průšek's lectures at Harvard in 1967. For a comprehensive analysis of late Ch'ing fiction, see the collection of scholarly articles in Milena Doleželová-Velingerová, ed. *The Chinese novel at the turn of the century*.

and a pervasive feeling of sad exasperation. Their accumulated depth of
disturbed emotion is unmatched by the relatively more serene *The scholars*.

The overall debt of late Ch'ing social fiction to *The scholars* should
not blind us to some of its more original features: foreign terms and ideas
are freely mixed with native scenes and indigenous characters. *Kuan-ch'ang
hsien-hsing chi* contains references to Rousseau's *Social Contract* and Montesquieu's *Esprit des lois*. In *Nieh-hai hua* even foreign characters – John
Fryer, Thomas Wade, a Russian nihilist, and a German general (Wal-
dersee) – make their appearance. Moreover, part of the action takes place
in Europe. Discussions of 'foreign affairs' (*yang-wu*) and the influx of
foreign fashions can also be found in many late Ch'ing novels. While
most writers were eager to incorporate foreign ideas, they were notably
uninterested in emulating Western literary technique, in spite of the increasing availablity of Western translations.[11] Rather, the extent of their
literary borrowing was confined to some Western fictional heroes and
heroines. Conan Doyle's Sherlock Holmes became an immensely popular
figure and helped trigger a series of imitative Chinese detective heroes.
The popularity of detective fiction was both a vulgarized extension of
social fiction and the result of Western influence.

Political fantasies were another new feature of late Ch'ing fiction.
The inspiration may have come from Liang Ch'i-ch'ao's uncompleted
novel, *Hsin Chung-kuo wei-lai chi* (The future of new China) which begins
fifty years after the founding of a utopian Chinese republic. Another
popular novel, *Ch'ih-jen shuo-meng chi* (An idiot's dream tale) by Lü-sheng,
ends with a dream of future Shanghai in which there are no more foreigners, foreign policemen, foreign signs on buildings or foreign debts
but, instead, an abundance of railways and schools built by Chinese. In
Ch'en T'ien-hua's novel, *Shih-tzu hou* (The lion's roar), the story takes
place on the island of Chusan, which is turned by the offspring of some
Ming loyalists into a political paradise. On the island there is a 'people's
rights village' complete with 'assembly hall, hospital, post office, park,
library, gymnasium', three factories, a steamship company and many
modern schools – all run in an orderly fashion for the benefit of some three
thousand families of the village.[12] Obviously, these novels owe much to
the conventions of fantasy used in traditional Chinese literature. But
their future-orientation and modern content are further indication of the
general social temper for accelerated change. The utopias of new China

11 Hu Shih argues, however, that Wu Wo-yao's novel, *Chiu-ming ch'i yuan* (The scandalous
   murder case of nine lives), was influenced by Western fiction in its use of the flashback
   technique and in its structural unity. See Hu Shih, 'Wu-shih-nien-lai Chung-kuo chih wen-
   hsueh', 239.
12 A Ying, *Wan-Ch'ing hsiao-shuo shih* (A history of late Ch'ing fiction), 97.

offered to writers and readers alike both an ebullient political vision – the wish-fulfilment of their shared obsession with the fate of China – and a romantic escape from the problems of the contemporary scene.

While these utopian variations on the fate of China all pointed to the urgency for reform, by the turn of the century reformism itself had become a hackneyed style shorn of intellectual substance and political gravity. As depicted in the works of Li Pao-chia, Wu Wo-yao and Tseng P'u the reform ideology had degenerated into a set of clichés, parroted by a string of 'foreign affairs (*yang-wu*) experts' – products of the regional efforts at 'self-strengthening' – who were no more than clever dandies roaming in the glitter of the compradorial 'foreign mall' (*yang-ch'ang*) in such treaty-port cities as Shanghai, Canton and Tientsin. The landscape of late Ch'ing fiction is dotted with such figures who, moving in the twilight zone between East and West, mixed with greedy merchants, status-hungry *nouveaux riches*, and decadent scions of rural landlords who migrated into the cities for fun and pleasure. Reading through these satirical vignettes – the lighter side of an otherwise grim picture – we cannot fail to perceive the authors' self-mockery and ambivalence. As saddened commentators on the contemporary scene, these journalist-littérateurs nevertheless realized that their own livelihood depended on the very people they satirized; they, too, could be taken as indirect descendants of *yang-wu* and *wei-hsin* (reformism). The modish trend of reformism which they abhorred also served to make their works popular. Thus, in spite of their parasitical existence few were in favour of outright revolution which might destroy the very world in which they felt both at war and at ease.

While the major theme of late Ch'ing fiction is social satire, the critical perception of society and politics also involves a subjective awareness of the author's own sentiments. Often, the social and sentimental strains are combined to attain an emotional height and to justify the author's seriousness of purpose. In an essay published in *Hsin hsiao-shuo* under the title of 'The relationship between society and fiction of sentiment', Wu Wo-yao, who supposedly launched the 'novel of sentiment' with *Hen hai* (Sea of sorrow), made the following declaration:

I commonly hold the opinion that human beings are born with sentiment. . . . The common notion of sentiment refers not merely to the private emotions between man and woman. Sentiment, which is born in the human heart, can be applied everywhere as a human being grows up. . . . When applied to the emperor and the country, it is loyalty; when applied to parents, it is filial piety; when applied to children, it is kindness; when applied to friends, it is righteousness. Thus the cardinal virtues of loyalty and righteousness are all derived from sentiment. As for the kind of sentiment between man and woman, it can only be called idiotic madness [*ch'ih*]. And in cases where sentiments need not or should not be applied but are nevertheless squandered, we can only call it bewitchedness [*mo*]. . . . Many novels that pretend to describe sentiment describe in fact this bewitched fascination. . . .'[13]

In this lofty justification Wu wished to give subjective sentiments a broad social and ethical basis, much in the same way that Lin Shu (Ch'in-nan), the translator, sought to justify his emotions in moral terms. However, the Confucian contours of this manifesto do not prescribe the real content of late Ch'ing sentimental fiction. Most of it deals in fact with the 'idiotic madness' between man and woman and the 'bedevilled' excesses of sentimentality. As Lin Shu gradually came to realize, personal sentiments, if genuinely expressed, could be the central *weltanschauung* of a man, whether or not they reflected the established ethical norms.[14] The popular writers of sentimental fiction further diluted this ethical seriousness when they became aware that the portrait of sentiment, especially in its *ch'ih* or *mo* forms, fell on enthusiastic ears among their urban audience. Thus, this sentimental genre has been regarded by Chinese literary historians as representing a more trivial strain of late Ch'ing fiction.[15] While the model was clearly the great *Dream of the red chamber*, much of it had more in common with the mid nineteenth century 'talent-beauty' (*ts'ai-tzu chia-jen*) novels such as *Liu ts'ai-tzu* (Six talented men), and *Hua-yueh hen* (Vestiges of flowers and moonlight). The most popular ones catered, in fact, to prurient interests and came to be known as 'guides to brothels', since the 'beauties' in these works with whom the talented dandies become infatuated are invariably courtesans. Hu Shih has singled out two notable titles – *Hai-shang fan-hua meng* (Dream of the splendour at the seaside) and *Chiu-wei kuei* (Nine-tailed turtle) – for special reproach for their lack of intellectual insight and literary value. Consequently, the underside of the 'fiction of sentiment' seems to be an adulteration of sentiment – a practice which, according to the literary historian, A Ying, soon ushered in the more debased fiction of the 'Mandarin Duck and Butterfly' variety.[16]

BUTTERFLY FICTION AND THE TRANSITION
TO MAY FOURTH, 1911–17

The term, 'Mandarin Duck and Butterfly School' (*Yuan-yang hu-tieh p'ai*) has been traced to one of the best sellers of this type, Hsu Chen-ya's

13 *Ibid.* 173–4.
14 See Lee, *The romantic generation*, ch. 3. Lin's translation work is discussed in the second part of this chapter.
15 See A Ying, *Wan-Ch'ing hsiao-shuo shih*, ch. 13.
16 *Ibid.* 169, 176.

Yü-li hun (Jade pear spirit), first published in 1912 – a sentimental novel padded with poems comparing lovers to pairs of butterflies and mandarin ducks.[17] The label, initially pejorative, was applied in the era from about 1910 to about 1930 to an increasing crop of some 2,215 novels, 113 magazines and 49 newspapers. The label is also interchangeable with the title of the best-known magazine, *Li-pai-liu* (Saturday), which explicitly declared its purpose to 'help pass the time'.

The immense popularity of Butterfly fiction is one of the supreme ironies in modern China's literary history. It seems that the reformist thrust and serious intent of late Ch'ing fiction had gradually been dissipated as the dynasty came to an end. Just as sentimental fiction degenerated into 'courtesan' and Butterfly literature, the mainstream of social fiction also changed its basic orientation from conscientious criticism and exposé of socio-political ills to sensationalism for its own sake: the few respected masterpieces of 'social criticism' were replaced by a host of the so-called 'black screen' (*hei-mu*) novels of social scandal and crime. By the first decade of the republic, both types of mass literature – vulgarized modes of social and sentimental fiction – reached their hey-day of popularity. They commanded a readership and a sales record unsurpassed by works of either earlier or later periods.[18] In Perry Link's pioneering study of the Butterfly School, one confronts the striking conclusion that the genuine 'popular literature' before the 1930s – in the sense that it appealed to middle and lower class tastes and reflected their value system – is neither the 'new fiction' as advocated by Liang Ch'i-ch'ao nor the New Literature of the May Fourth era but these works of 'idle amusement'.

In Link's analysis, the rise of this type of urban popular fiction mirrored the psychological *angst* of urban dwellers as they experienced rapid change in a 'modernizing environment'. As the new urban life – especially in Shanghai – became burdensome, 'the reader's desire to keep up with the world gave way to the desire to forget that he could not keep up.'[19] Aside from fulfilling a need for escape from the realities of an urban world in transition, Link also implies that the successive waves of popular themes in Butterfly fiction can be correlated with specific socio-political developments. The first wave of love stories in the early part of

17 E. Perry Link, 'Traditional-style popular urban fiction in the teens and twenties', in Goldman, ed. *Modern Chinese literature*, 327–8. See also his Ph.D. dissertation, 'The rise of modern popular fiction in Shanghai' (Harvard University, 1976).

18 According to Link, the most popular works of this genre 'must have reached between four hundred thousand to a million people in Shanghai.' See Link, 'Traditional-style popular urban fiction', 338. The sales record of Butterfly fiction remained unsurpassed until the late 1930s, when it gradually declined. Circulation figures of communist fiction in the period after 1949 are, of course, much larger.

19 *Ibid.* 330.

the first decade of the 1900s took freedom of marriage as their common theme, as the issues of women's emancipation and women's education drew much attention within the ferment of late Ch'ing reforms. The subsequent waves of detective stories, scandal fiction and 'knight-errant' novels of the latter part of the 1910 decade and the early 1920s coincided with the political chaos created by Yuan Shih-k'ai and the warlord governments. In each of these waves, the keynote underlying all fictional escapism was one of reactionism and disillusionment. Writers had lost the faith in reform, modernization and progress towards new China which most of their predecessors – the late Ch'ing journalist-littérateurs – had espoused. Instead, they evinced a 'conservative attitude towards popular Chinese values'.[20] They considered the Westernization trend to be out of all proportion and reacted to native Chinese problems, not in the spirit of radical protest that favoured an alternative social order, but in the traditional manner of 'remedial protest' – against certain abuses and excesses of the Confucian value system.

Link's findings throw considerable light, by contrast, on the nature of popular literature during the period which immediately preceded Butterfly fiction and on the 'literary revolution' that was to follow. It seems apparent that late Ch'ing literature underwent a paradoxical process of popularization. It began as a conscious effort by members of the intellectual elite to enlighten the lower-class masses in Chinese society about China's precarious state and the urgency of reform. Thus, 'new fiction' emerged more as an ideological imperative than as a purely literary concern. But the seriousness of this ideological purpose became diluted by the commercial necessity of 'audience appeal' as the practice of fiction writing became lucrative. Popularization set the late Ch'ing writer the dual task to educate and entertain his reader. As it developed from an elitist design to a popular product, 'new fiction' also gradually lost the enlightened ethos with which it had been infused and which, in some cases, had given it its enduring literary worth. From a commercial viewpoint late Ch'ing popular fiction achieved unprecedented success; from an intellectual and artistic perspective, however, its development ended in failure, despite its initial promise. The reformist, progressive outlook in the fictional output of 1900–1910 was replaced in the next decade by conservatism and escapism. In *Lao Ts'an yu-chi*, written between 1904 and 1907, the reader could be moved by that memorable scene of distilled emotional intensity and lyrical beauty as the solitary hero, pondering the sad fate of his country and his life against the wintry landscape of the Yellow

20 *Ibid.* 339.

River in frozen grandeur, suddenly realizes that the tears on his face are also frozen. But the average urban reader in 1913 would only shed his tears on the fate of a pair of love-torn 'mandarin ducks' in Hsu Chen-ya's bestseller, *Yü-li hun*.

The phenomenon of Butterfly fiction's popularity therefore testified to the strongly felt need, on the part of a new and even more radical generation, to begin anew, to create a different type of popular literature as part of an overall intellectual revolution. From the 'new' perspective of the May Fourth writers, the 'new fiction' of the late Ch'ing, together with its Butterfly vulgarization, already looked 'old' and had to be relegated to the corrupt world of 'tradition', despite the considerable advances made by their late Ch'ing predecessors in establishing a vernacular style, a popular readership and a viable profession.

THE MAY FOURTH ERA, 1917–27

The early years of the republic have been perceived by most Chinese literary historians as a 'low' period in modern Chinese literature. A decade of dynamic creativity, which produced, among many others, the four great novelists of late Ch'ing literature – Wu Wo-yao, Li Pao-chia, Tseng P'u, and Liu E – had suddenly come to an end. Of these four gifted writers, Li Pao-chia died in 1906, having completed less than half of his projected 120-chapter masterpiece. The prolific Wu Wo-yao (15 novels) also died in 1910. Liu E, perhaps the most literary of the four, wrote only one novel, which did not receive its full popularity until it was reissued in the 1930s. Tseng P'u, the most revolutionary in his political convictions, was too busy with his many other activities to complete his novel which, like *Lao Ts'an yu-chi*, was not fully appreciated until the 1920s.[21]

The unexpected victory of the 1911 Revolution did not bring about an immediate literary renaissance. Rather, chaos on the political scene made the escapist Butterfly fiction the most popular type of reading. The only rival school of note was the *Nan she* (Southern Society), a loose grouping of revolutionary politicians and journalists who dabbled in literature. The Society, founded in 1903 by three journalists and members of the T'ung-meng hui (Revolutionary Alliance) – Liu Ya-tzu, Kao T'ien-mei, and Ch'en Ch'ao-nan – published periodically collections of poetry

---

21 For two recent scholarly studies of these two authors, see Peter Li, *Tseng P'u* and C. T. Hsia, 'The travels of Lao Ts'an: an exploration of its art and meaning', *Tsing Hua Journal of Chinese Studies*, 7. 2 (Aug. 1969) 40–66. See also Harold Shadick's masterful translation, with annotations, of *The travels of Lao Ts'an*.

and prose by its members, often the product of their social gatherings. Revolutionaries and young men in the early years of the republic are said to have received these works with enthusiasm. But as one reads samples of the Society's poetry half a century later, the mood and imagery seem generally traditional. Hu Shih went so far as to brand it 'debauched and extravagant'.[22] It seems that, in retrospect, the function of the Southern Society was not so much to echo the revolution as to provide an arena for the revolutionaries to display their literary talents.

Like the treaty-port journalist-littérateurs, most members of the Southern Society were men steeped in classical learning. But their style and diction proved even more elegantly classical than those of their late Ch'ing counterparts. If treaty-port literary journalism can be regarded as the literary side of late Ch'ing reformism, it was surely more radical in its thematic and stylistic aspects than the poetry of the Southern Society, in which 'rich and elegant diction' tended to overshadow its alleged 'emotions of patriotism, of grieved concern for the people, and of national regeneration.'[23] The Society, which at one time boasted a membership of more than 1,000, declined gradually after its last 'revolutionary' act against Yuan Shih-k'ai. Most of the prominent members plunged into the cauldron of warlord politics; others, like Liu Ya-tzu, after brief terms of governmental service, returned to journalism.

The Southern Society episode had been half forgotten when the May Fourth movement ushered in a changed socio-intellectual mood. Although an ideological gap was clearly visible, we can also find some institutional links between the May Fourth leaders and members of the two transitional groups. When Ch'en Tu-hsiu persuaded a Shanghai publisher to fund his new journal, Ch'ing-nien (soon retitled Hsin ch'ing-nien, or 'New youth') in 1915, members of the Southern Society and some powerful treaty-port journalist-littérateurs were still in control of the major newspapers. The literary supplements of the three major newspapers in Shanghai – Shen-pao (Shanghai times), Hsin-wen pao (News tribune), and Shih-pao – were under the editorship of such master craftsmen of Butterfly fiction as Chou Shou-chüan, Chang Hen-shui, Yen Tu-ho, Hsu Chen-ya, and Pao T'ien-hsiao, who was also an active member of the Southern Society. The May Fourth intellectuals were fortunate in being able to publicize their cause in some of the newspapers controlled by the Southern Society, and also in winning the support of other re-

22 Ts'ao Chü-jen, Wen-t'an san i (Three reminiscences of the literary scene), 150–1. For a general account of the Southern Society, see Liu Ya-tzu, Nan-she chi lueh (A brief account of the Southern Society).
23 Wang P'ing-ling, San-shih-nien wen-t'an ts'ang-sang lu (Changes on the literary scene in thirty years), 5.

volutionary journalists and followers of Liang Ch'i-ch'ao. Gradually, they also managed to wrest editorship of newspaper supplements and magazines away from the Butterfly writers. The most celebrated case was the change-over of format and content of the *Hsiao-shuo yueh-pao* (Short story monthly), published by the august Commercial Press, which had been a bastion of Butterfly literature until Mao Tun assumed the editorship in 1921 and turned it into a major organ for New Literature.

The literary revolution

As the *New Youth* gained increasing attention in journalistic and academic circles, a climate of intellectual revolution had already been fostered before the literary revolution was formally launched in February 1917. From 1915 to 1917 Ch'en Tu-hsiu's magazine published an increasing number of articles, by Wu Yü, I Pai-sha, Kao I-han, and Ch'en himself, which assailed Confucianism and extolled Western thought. The idea of a literary revolution, first conceived by Hu Shih in America, was welcomed enthusiastically by Ch'en Tu-hsiu as part of the movement of iconoclastic anti-traditionalism. This well-known story has been told with zest by Hu Shih himself, who also inadvertently perpetuated his 'version' of this important event.[24] The ensuing analysis may not agree entirely with Hu Shih's recapitulation, though it inevitably draws upon it.

When Hu Shih first used the term 'literary revolution' (*wen-hsueh ko-ming*) in a poem he wrote at Cornell University in 1915, his intention was initially confined to largely academic discussions with his friends on the Chinese language. He was eager to argue and to demonstrate the feasibility of *pai-hua* (vernacular language) as a viable literary tool. The significance of the vernacular had been recognized long before him; its function of popular enlightenment had been advocated and practised by a host of late Ch'ing thinkers and journalist-littérateurs. Aware of these precedents Hu Shih nevertheless made a truly 'revolutionary' observation – something his predecessors had failed either to notice or to argue with conviction. While the late Ch'ing advocates of *pai-hua* recognized it as a medium of popularization and political education, they

24 See Hu Shih's celebrated essay, 'Pi-shang Liang-shan' (Forced to the Liang mountain), appended to his *Ssu-shih tzu-shu* (Autobiography at forty), 91-122. See also his lectures in English at the University of Chicago, *The Chinese renaissance* and his 1958 speech in Taiwan, 'Chung-kuo wen-i fu-hsing yun-tung' (The Chinese renaissance movement), included in Liu Hsin-huang, *Hsien-tai Chung-kuo wen-hsueh shih-hua* (Discourse on the history of modern Chinese literature), 1-15. For secondary sources, see Jerome B. Grieder, *Hu Shih and the Chinese renaissance*, ch. 3; Yü-sheng Lin, *The crisis of Chinese consciousness: radical anti-traditionalism in the May Fourth era*, chap. on Hu Shih. Most of Hu's articles written during the period of the Literary Revolution are included in *Hu Shih wen-ts'un*, vol. 1.

stopped short of accepting it as *the* major form of literary expression. Hu Shih went much further than Yen Fu and Liang Ch'i-ch'ao by stating categorically that in the past millennium the mainstream of Chinese literature was to be found, not in poetry and prose written in the classical style, but in vernacular literature. In Hu's view, *wen-yen* had been a 'half dead' language which contributed to much ornamentation of form and ossification of substance in traditional Chinese literature, poetry in particular. *Pai-hua*, on the other hand, had been the natural result of literary revolution; its vitality as a living language had been demonstrated by the *yü-lu* (records of conversations) of Sung Neo-Confucianists and by drama and fiction in the Yuan and Ming periods. According to Hu Shih, the trend towards identification between the written and spoken language reached a peak during the Yuan. Had this tendency not been checked by the regressive practices of the 'eight-legged' essay and the restoration of the ancient style since the Ming, Chinese literature would have developed into a vernacular literature of the spoken language – a phenomenon which Hu Shih compared to Italian literature since Dante, English literature since Chaucer, and German literature since Luther. (Accordingly, in his subsequent lectures at the University of Chicago, Hu Shih considered the literary revolution to be a 'Chinese renaissance'.) He was therefore convinced that a living language was the prerequisite to modern intellectual movements, and the primary task for a literary revolution in China was to 'replace the classical style with the vernacular' – to restore, in other words, the natural sequence of literary evolution since the Sung dynasty.

Hu Shih was aware that vernacular literature did not itself constitute a new literature; 'a new literature must have new ideas and new spirit.' But he insisted on the priority of linguistic tools:

A dead language can never produce a living literature; if a living literature is to be produced, there must be a living tool. . . . We must first of all elevate this [vernacular] tool and make it the acknowledged tool of Chinese literature that totally replaces that half-dead or fully dead old tool. Only with a new tool can we talk about such other aspects as new ideas and new spirit.[25]

This preoccupation with what he later conceded to be purely a 'stylistic revolution' (*wen-t'i ko-ming*) was clearly evidenced in his letter to Ch'en Tu-hsiu in October 1916 in which he listed eight principles for the new literature:

(1) Avoid the use of classical allusions.
(2) Discard stale, time-worn literary phrases.

25 Hu Shih, 'Pi-shang Liang-shan', 112.

(3) Discard the parallel construction of sentences.

(4) Do not avoid using vernacular words and speech.

(5) Follow literary grammar.

(The above are suggestions for a revolution in literary form.)

(6) Do not write that you are sick or sad when you do not feel sick or sad.

(7) Do not imitate the writings of the ancients; what you write should reflect your own personality.

(8) What you write should have meaning or real substance.

(The above are suggestions for a revolution in content.)

In this initial formulation, Hu Shih's suggestions for literary form are obviously more detailed and concrete than his suggestions for content. Ch'en Tu-hsiu, while supporting Hu Shih with enthusiasm, was nevertheless wary that Hu's eighth principle might lend itself to a traditional interpretation of 'wen i tsai-tao' (literature to convey the Confucian way). Thus in Hu's subsequent article, 'Some Tentative Suggestions for the reform of Chinese Literature', published in New Youth in January 1917 (and The Chinese Students Quarterly in March) he had seen fit to change the order of his eight principles (the new sequence became 8, 7, 5, 6, 2, 1, 3, 4) and attempted to pay more attention to the 'substance' of new literature. Hu differentiated the new 'substance' from the Confucian 'way' by insisting on two basic components – 'feeling' and 'thinking' – which nevertheless remained vague generalities. He was considerably more at pains to explain the importance of three other principles: (2) do not imitate the ancients (he argued for an evolutionary view of literature and concluded with high praise for late Ch'ing fiction); (6) avoid the use of classical allusions (he tried to distinguish a broader category of allusions which still carried contemporary meaning and a narrow category of outmoded allusions whose use he rejected); and (8) do not avoid vernacular words and speech. The last point was obviously most central to his concerns and represented the crux of his earlier debates with friends.

Still, the tentative tone and scholastic approach in Hu Shih's article proved too moderate for the radical temper of the New Youth editors. Ch'ien Hsuan-t'ung took issue with Hu Shih's liberal view on classical allusions and argued for the rejection of all allusions. For Ch'en Tu-hsiu the need to substitute the vernacular for the classical language was self-evident; he had no patience for free academic discussions. Thus in the very next issue of New Youth, published on 1 February 1917, Ch'en simply brushed aside Hu Shih's modest reform intentions and proclaimed the coming of the literary revolution:

I am willing to brave the enmity of all the pedantic scholars of the country, and hoist the great banner of the 'Army of the Literary Revolution' in support of my friend [Hu Shih]. On this banner shall be written in big, clear characters my three great principles of the Revolutionary Army:

(1)   To overthrow the painted, powdered and obsequious literature of the aristocratic few, and to create the plain, simple, and expressive literature of the people;

(2)   To overthrow the stereotyped and over-ornamental literature of classicism, and to create the fresh and sincere literature of realism;

(3)   To overthrow the pedantic, unintelligible, and obscurantist literature of the hermit and recluse, and to create the plain-speaking and popular literature of society in general.[26]

As Professor Chow Tse-tsung has pointed out, the targets of Ch'en's attack were the prevalent trends dominated by three literary schools – the T'ung-ch'eng and Wen-hsuan schools of prose, and the Kiangsi school of poetry.[27] But the constructive part of Ch'en's three principles, though it incorporated Hu Shih's plans for the *pai-hua* style, was more oriented towards matters of literary content. Ch'en had argued in earlier articles for the introduction of realism in China, because he was convinced that modern European literature had progressed from classicism and romanticism to realism and naturalism, and realism was more suitable for China than naturalism.[28] His other two principles seem to have transformed Hu Shih's stylistic concern for the vernacular language into a more politicized demand for the creation of a new literature which should be more 'popular' and 'social' in content.

But in spite of Ch'en's distaste for the elitism of traditional literature, his populist sympathies remained vague. The kind of new literature he might have conceived could at best be called 'social realism', but not necessarily socialist or proletarian literature. He would probably welcome new literary works that depicted, realistically and honestly, different aspects of the lives of all kinds of people so long as they did not belong to the 'aristocratic few'. A more class-conscious orientation towards the workers and peasants was not his exclusive concern at this early stage. While he envisaged a more expanded scope for the new literature, Ch'en offered no concrete proposals as to how to create such a literature. The task was taken up by Hu Shih in a long article published in the spring of 1918 entitled, more aggressively than before, 'On a constructive literary revolution'.

Hu's article carried a resounding slogan; 'a literature in the national

26 Chow Tse-tsung, *The May Fourth movement*, 275–6.
27 *Ibid.* 266–70.
28 *Ibid.* 272.

language, a literary national language (*Kuo-yü ti wen-hsueh, wen-hsueh ti kuo-yü*)'. The constructive goal of the literary revolution, he stated, was to create a new national literature in the vernacular language. But how could such a literature be created when there was no standard 'national language' to speak of? Hu Shih's response was characteristically experimental: new writers should try to write by employing all available vernacular possibilities. They could use the language of traditional popular fiction, supplemented by present-day spoken expressions and, if need be, even a few *wen-yen* words. They should practise using only the vernacular in all types of writing – poetry, letters, notes, translations, journalistic articles and even tombstone inscriptions. With constant practice, writing in the vernacular would gradually become easy. Concerning the 'methods' of literary creation, Hu Shih argued that the subject matter of New Literature should be broadened to include people in all walks of life, and that on-the-spot observation and personal experience, reinforced by vivid imagination, should be the prerequisites for writing.

Although Hu Shih went to great lengths to expound on linguistic tools and literary techniques, he was silent on what should have been the most crucial component of his constructive proposal: the intellectual substance of New Literature. Unlike Ch'en Tu-hsiu, Hu Shih was rather reluctant to specify the type of new literature (however vaguely defined) which he deemed most desirable for modern Chinese readers. It may have been that Hu Shih was more open-minded and less dogmatic than Ch'en Tu-hsiu.[29] More likely, however, he was simply not interested, since the literary revolution was for him essentially a revolution in language. But the intellectual revolution which had already begun dictated nothing less than a total change in the *content* of Chinese culture, of which literature formed an integral part. Ch'en Tu-hsiu had grasped this crucial link between the two revolutions – intellectual and literary – and effected its success. Hu Shih, on the other hand, had never been as committed as the other *New Youth* leaders to the cause of anti-traditionalism. His academic preoccupation with language, therefore, made him curiously unaware of its ideological implications.

Insofar as Hu Shih's personal objective was concerned, the literary revolution was a resounding success. The vernacular language came to be used in all the new literary journals which mushroomed. And by 1921 the Ministry of Education decreed that *pai-hua* would henceforth be used exclusively in primary school texts. The opposition was weak and belated, and easily crushed by the 'army of the literary revolution'. Lin Shu's

29 Hou Chien, *Ts'ung wen-hsueh ko-ming tao ko-ming wen-hsueh* (From literary revolution to revolutionary literature), 32.

famous long letter to Ts'ai Yuan-p'ei was written almost two years after the launching of the literary revolution in 1917. The magazine *Hsueh-heng* (Critical review), edited by Hu Shih's old friends and foes Mei Kuang-ti, Wu Mi and Hu Hsien-su, was not published until 1921 when the vernacular had already become a 'national language'. When Chang Shih-chao, then minister of education under the warlord government, fired a last shot in his *Chia-yin chou-k'an* (Tiger magazine) in 1925, Hu Shih and Wu Chih-hui in their rejoinder did not even take him seriously; the New Literature had advanced to such a point that they could afford to mourn facetiously the 'demise' of Old Chang and of old literature.

Aside from personal attacks, the arguments of the opposition groups centred around a few related themes. The *Critical Review* group took issue with Hu Shih's evolutionary justification by maintaining that the types of literature which emerged at the end of the evolutionary scale – such as realism, symbolism and futurism – were not necessarily better than earlier literature, nor would they take the place of earlier literature.[30] In a related sense, the classical heritage of every culture, they argued, had to be treasured, for it provided the foundation on which changes and reforms could be made. As the major vehicle of China's classical heritage, *wen-yen* could not be replaced entirely by *pai-hua*. Moreover, as Lin Shu argued, without comprehensive knowledge of *wen-yen* writings, writers could never create a vernacular literature.

These arguments clearly betray a classical bent and, in the case of the *Critical Review* group, the intellectual imprint of their teacher, Irving Babbitt, who had urged his Chinese disciples to 'retain the soul of truth that is contained in its great traditions'.[31] But in this new era of effusive iconoclasm, this rational defence of tradition, however well thought out, was doomed to failure, for it ran counter to the radical thrust for revolutionary change. The concept of literary evolutionism, which characterized not only Hu Shih but many members of this radical generation, was a direct expression of their future and Western orientation – that new ideas from the West had to replace old tradition in order to transform China into a modern nation. Even the opposition groups were not against change; they were only against certain excesses. The weakest link in their cultural conservatism was their condescending distrust of the vernacular language. They were worried that since spoken language changed too often, it was inadequate as a language of the 'classics', of literary masterpieces which could last to eternity or at least be comprehensible to posterity. Neither the advocates nor the opponents of vernacular literature

---

30 Hou Chien gives a sympathetic analysis of their views, see *ibid.* 57–95.
31 Chow Tse-tsung, *The May Fourth movement*, 282.

seem to have realized that the kind of 'national language' which finally emerged in May Fourth literature contained a mixture of spoken idioms, Europeanized phrases and classical allusions. The elitist worries of the conservative critics were misplaced, for the use of the vernacular in literature did not necessarily degrade quality; and premature, for the *pai-hua* literature of the May Fourth period itself was to come under attack in the 1930s by leftist critics like Ch'ü Ch'iu-pai for its aristocratic elitism under a modern garb.

The emergence of new writers

While the destructive task of the literary revolution was easily accomplished despite scattered rear-guard actions by a none-too-formidable enemy, the constructive phase proved to be more difficult.

The immediate and enthusiastic response of the 'new youth' of China went perhaps beyond the wildest expectations of the leaders of the literary revolution. In a few years, new literary magazines mushroomed, and more than a hundred literary societies were formed in the major cities.[32] All these spontaneous developments testified to the effusive mood generated by the May Fourth movement, particularly the student demonstrations in 1919.

The leadership of this emergent literary scene rested, initially, with the professors in the Peking area: Ch'en Tu-hsiu, Hu Shih, Ch'ien Hsuan-t'ung, Li Ta-chao, Shen Yin-mo, Lu Hsun (pen name of Chou Shu-jen), and Chou Tso-jen. Some of their students – Fu Ssu-nien, Lo Chia-lun, Chu Tzu-ch'ing, and Yeh Shao-chün – established the Hsin-ch'ao (New Tide) society and published a journal under the same name. A learned and enterprising editor, Sun Fu-yuan, took over the literary supplements of first the *Ch'en-pao* (Morning news) of Peking and then the *Ching pao* (Capital news) of Tientsin and turned them into prominent showcases of New Literature which featured the works of many new talents. These scholars, students, editors and contributors constituted a very loose grouping centred in Peking. Most of them evinced an urbane, scholarly outlook which contrasted with the Bohemian abandon of the literary upstarts in Shanghai. The older members of this 'Peking aggregate' – the Chou brothers, Sun Fu-yuan, Ch'ien Hsuan-t'ung and the publisher Li Hsiao-feng – subsequently founded the *Yü-ssu* (Threads of talk) weekly (1924–30) in which they further practised the celebrated *Yü-ssu* style of cultured criticism while shunning excessively radical stances. With the

32 Lee, *The romantic generation*, 9.

split of the New Youth leadership in 1921, Hu Shih soon branched off and joined hands with a group of mainly Anglo-American educated scholars – notably Ch'en Yuan and Hsu Chih-mo. Ch'en founded the *Hsien-tai p'ing-lun* (Contemporary review), and Hsu was the prime mover behind the Hsin-yueh (Crescent Moon) society, which later published the *Hsin-yueh* magazine (1928–33) and played a prominent role in literary polemics by defending its basically liberal outlook in literature and politics against the assaults from the left and Lu Hsun. But in the early 1920s, after the *New Youth* changed into a political magazine, thus forfeiting its leadership in New Literature, and before the *Yü-ssu* and *Hsin-yueh* journals were able to exert any impact, the literary scene was dominated by two major organizations: The Association for Literary Studies (Wen-hsueh yen-chiu hui) and the Creation Society (Ch'uang-tsao she).

The Association for Literary Studies was officially founded in January 1921 in Peking, with an initial membership of 21 drawn mostly from the 'Peking aggregate', such as Chou Tso-jen, Cheng Chen-to, Sun Fu-yuan, Yeh Shao-chün, Hsu Ti-shan, Wang T'ung-chao, and Kuo Shao-yü. Its formation was made possible by Mao Tun, one of the few non-Peking-related founders, who had just been appointed editor of the influential *Short Story Monthly*, thereby offering them a golden opportunity to renovate this established journal of Butterfly fiction for purposes of New Literature. The first issue of this refashioned magazine (volume 12, number 1) published the Association's manifesto which stipulated three fundamental principles: (1) 'To unite in fellowship' the practitioners of New Literature for 'mutual understanding' and to form 'a unified organization of writers'; (2) 'To advance knowledge', especially in foreign literature; (3) 'To establish a foundation' for a professional union of writers so as to promote the literary endeavour not as a form of amusement or diversion but as 'a life-time occupation'.[33]

This manifesto, issued in January 1921, marked a milestone in the history of modern Chinese literature, for it was the first proclamation by the new writers as a professional group dedicated to the practice of literature as an independent and honourable vocation. It legitimized two decades of efforts by their late Ch'ing predecessors towards literary professionalism, but invested it with a new aura of social prestige and self-esteem. By expanding its membership, establishing branch offices in many other cities, and publishing several new journals – besides *Hsiao-shuo yueh-pao*, notably *Wen-hsueh hsun-k'an* (Literature thrice-monthly), *Wen-hsueh chou-pao* (Literature weekly), and *Shih* (Poetry) – the Association was

33 *Ibid.* 12.

able to solidify and broaden the literary arena so that more and more young novices could develop their potential and build up their reputation as professional writers. In addition to Yeh Shao-chün, Mao Tun, Wang T'ung-chao, and Hsu Ti-shan, the Association also nurtured such diverse talents as Hsieh Ping-hsin, Hsu Ch'in-wen, Huang Lu-yin, and Ting Ling. The Association also sponsored massive translations of European literature. Special issues of the *Hsiao-shuo yueh-pao* were devoted to Tolstoy, Tagore, Byron, Hans Christian Andersen, Romain Rolland, the literature of 'oppressed nations', 'anti-war literature', French literature and Russian literature. The Association reached its peak of activity by 1925 and thereafter declined until its quiet demise in 1930.

The second major literary group, the Creation Society, emerged almost concurrently with the Association for Literary Studies. It first grew out of a small circle of close friends consisting initially of Kuo Mo-jo, Yü Ta-fu, Ch'eng Fang-wu, and Chang Tzu-p'ing – all of whom had been students at the Tokyo Imperial University. After a series of informal discussions they decided to publish a magazine for New Literature. When they returned to China, the manager of a small Shanghai publishing firm, T'ai-tung, was the first to capitalize on their talents. In July 1921 the Society was formally established in Shanghai with an initial membership of eight. At the suggestion of Kuo Mo-jo, they decided to publish a journal, *Ch'uang-tsao chi-k'an* (Creation quarterly, 1922–4). Two other periodicals followed: *Ch'uang-tsao chou-pao* (Creation weekly, May 1923–May 1924), and *Ch'uang-tsao jih* (Creation day, one hundred issues, 21 July–31 October 1923, attached to the newspaper *Chung-hua jih-pao* or *China Daily*). A group of younger writers joined the Society in 1924 and began to publish a new fortnightly newspaper, *Hung-shui* (Deluge). In 1926, when most of the veteran members of the Society went to Canton, Chou Ch'üan-p'ing was put in charge of the publications department and brought in his more radical friends. A widening chasm began to extend between the old and the new Creationists. The old members founded another new journal in 1926, *Ch'uang-tsao yueh-k'an* (Creation monthly) which lásted until January 1929. But the 'junior partners' who gained firm control in Shanghai, evicted Yü Ta-fu from membership and persuaded Ch'eng Fang-wu and Kuo Mo-jo to use the society publications as an 'ideological stronghold' of Marxism. Thus the Society is said to have undergone two phases: an early 'romantic period' from 1921 to 1925 and, after Kuo Mo-jo's conversion to Marxism in 1924, a gradual shift to the left – in their own well-known phrase, 'from literary revolution to revolutionary literature'.

Most literary historians have approached the differences between these two organizations in terms of a dichotomy between two slogans: 'art for life' versus 'art for art'.[34] The former stance was supposedly advocated by the Association, whose members favoured 'realism', while the latter position was assumed by the Creationists, who practised 'romanticism'. But on closer examination, this theoretical antagonsim is more apparent than real. The two groups represent, in fact, two related facets of a prevailing ethos which characterized most new writers of the May Fourth period. It is an ethos anchored in a humanistic matrix of self and society but often expressed in strong emotionalism. In the writings of the Associationists, this humanistic ethos was couched in more social and humanitarian terms than can be found in the early works of the Creation leaders, who tended to centre on the individual self. But the two types of propensities are not mutually exclusive. Thus, in Chou Tso-jen's two important articles – 'Humane literature' and 'The demands of literature' – he argued that literature should have close 'contact with life' through the writer's *own* feelings and thoughts. The expression of self, in other words, was invariably bound up with humanity, since Chou defined the individual as a 'rational' being and 'a member of humanity'.[35] In giving New Literature a more social focus, Mao Tun also reminded his readers that the genuine kind of self-assertion was not incompatible with 'social sympathies'.[36] In the Creationists' more 'romantic' formulations, glorifications of 'beauty', 'perfection' and the creative act were frequent. But their so-called 'art for art' slogan had little in common with what the phrase implied in European literature, which opposed an artistic world of deeper reality to the philistinism of external life and reality. Rather, the function of artistic 'beauty', in Ch'eng Fang-wu's view, was to 'nourish' and 'cleanse' life: 'Literature is the food for our spiritual life. How much joy of life, how much vibration of life can we feel!'[37] Kuo Mo-jo

34 Almost all standard Chinese secondary sources adopt this bifurcation. See, for instance, Li Ho-lin, *Chin-erh-shih-nien Chung-kuo wen-i ssu-ch'ao lun* (Chinese literary trends in the recent twenty years), ch. 4; Wang Yao, *Chung-kuo hsin-wen-hsueh shih-kao* (A draft history of China's new literature), 40–53; Liu Shou-sung, *Chung-kuo hsin wen-hsueh shih ch'u-kao* (A preliminary draft history of China's new literature), ch. 3.

35 Quoted in Lee, *The romantic generation*, 20. Chou Tso-jen's article, 'Jen ti wen-hsueh' (A humane literature), first appeared in *Hsin ch'ing-nien*, 5. 6 (Dec. 1918) 575–84, before the Association was founded and was, strictly speaking, not intended as a position piece for the Association.

36 Mao Tun, 'Shen-mo shih wen-hsueh?' (What is literature?), in Chang Jo-ying, ed. *Hsin wen-hsueh yun-tung shih tzu-liao* (Materials concerning the new literary movement), 312–3.

37 Quoted in Lee, *The romantic generation*, 21. For a balanced summary of literary polemics, see Cheng Chen-to, 'Wu-ssu i-lai wen-hsueh shang ti lun-cheng' (Literary controversies since the May Fourth period), which serves as an introduction to vol. 2 of Chao Chia-pi, ed. *Chung-kuo hsin-wen-hsueh ta-hsi* (Comprehensive compendium of China's new literature). The eight introductory essays of this compendium have been collected in Cheng Chen-to *et al. Chung-kuo hsin wen-hsueh ta-hsi tao-lun hsuan-chi* (Selected introductory essays to *Comprehensive compendium of China's new literature*; hereafter *Ta-hsi tao-lun hsuan-chi*).

had further turned this 'vibration of life' into a rebellious act of social discontent.

The Creationists in their pre-Marxist phase were more ecstatic about their 'life' than the more sedate Associationists. The differences between the two groups are, therefore, more of emphasis and predilection than of basic aesthetic theory. In varying degrees writers of both schools had lent strong support to one of Hu Shih's principles of literary reform: 'What you write should reflect your own personality.' But within this humanistic spectrum of self and society, the majority of modern Chinese writers in the early 1920s were more preoccupied with the former.

Romanticism and emancipation

Yü Ta-fu once wrote that 'the greatest success of the May Fourth movement lay, first of all, in the discovery of individual personality.'[38] In the first few years following the literary revolution, the literary market was congested with diaries, letters and heavily autobiographical works – all filled with youthful self-pity and self-glorification and written with an ebullient flair of youthful abandon. The literary revolution had ushered into prominence men and women who were still in their twenties. Their emotional effusions were partly a manifestation of their youth. In many ways, they truly embodied the qualities which Ch'en Tu-hsiu called for in his New Youth manifesto: they were progressive, adventurous, scientific and individualistic. Their lives and works brought, in Ch'en's metaphor, fresh and vital cells to the stale, decaying body of Chinese culture.

What characterized the May Fourth intellectuals in general and the writers in particular was a marked degree of dynamism which gave the May Fourth man of letters (wen-jen) a more positive stature and distinguished him from his frail and effete traditional counterpart. Much of this youthful energy was, of course, directed towards the destruction of tradition. As the theme of Kuo Mo-jo's long poem, 'The resurrection of the phoenixes', puts it most vividly: the fire of individual and collective passion would burn up all the remnants of the past and, out of their ashes, the phoenix of New China would be reborn. In this respect, as C. T. Hsia remarks, 'the optimism and enthusiasm with which the young Chinese greeted the May Fourth Movement are essentially of the kind that enkindled a generation of Romantic poets after the French Revolution.'[39]

But the vision of a rejuvenated China took much longer to realize than the May Fourth iconoclasts had expected. Having dislocated all

---

38 See *Ta-hsi tao-lun hsuan-chi*, 150.   39 Hsia, *A history*, 19.

traditional ways and values, destroyed all faith and proper orientation, the May Fourth writers found themselves in a cultural vacuum of a transitional period before a new system – the Thought of Mao Tse-tung – was evolved. The political chaos of warlordism further exacerbated the situation by enhancing their sense of alienation. Cut off from political power and lacking an organic contact with any social classes, the May Fourth writer was compelled to fall back upon himself and to impose the values of his own ego on the rest of society – all in the name of intellectual and literary revolution.

For almost a decade, the keynote of this youthful emotional outburst was summarized in the amorphous word, love. For the May Fourth youths 'riding on the tempestuous storm of romanticism',[40] love had become the central focus of their lives. The writers themselves were leaders of this trend. It was considered *de rigueur* to produce some confessional love pieces and to evolve a 'modern' (or *mo-teng*, in its chic Chinese transliteration) lifestyle based on love. Thus the popular image of the May Fourth writers was often that of a couple or even triangle bound and complicated by love. The importance of the individual personality was given wide recognition by the amorous acts and styles of such love-torn figures as Yü Ta-fu and Wang Ying-hsia, Hsu Chih-mo and Lu Hsiao-man, Ting Ling and Hu Yeh-p'in. Love had become an overall symbol of new morality, an easy substitute for the traditional ethos of propriety which was now equated with conformist restraint. In the general wave of emancipation, love was identified with freedom, in the sense that by loving and by releasing one's passions and energies the individual could become truly a full and free man – or woman. To love was also considered an act of defiance and sincerity, of renouncing all the artificial restraints of hypocritical society so as to find one's true self and expose it to one's beloved. In this sense, the romantic mood of the 1920s was completely secular and, in C. T. Hsia's criticism, 'philosophically unambitious and psychologically crude': it failed 'to explore the deeper reaches of the mind and to give allegiance to a higher transcendental or immanent reality.'[41]

But as an activistic ethos, romantic love had a particular bearing on social movements. This was especially true of the movement for women's liberation, which began at the turn of the century and reached a peak in the 1920s. Again, new writers played a crucial role. The 'godfather' of this movement was Hu Shih (who in his personal life was perhaps one of

---

40 This is the Creationist Cheng Po-ch'i's observation about the early May Fourth period. See *Ta-hsi tao-lun hsuan-chi*, 94.
41 Hsia *A history*, 18.

the least liberated of men). Introducing Ibsenism to China by translating *A doll's house* in 1918, Hu Shih had unwittingly propelled the play's heroine, Nora, to unsurpassed popularity as the symbol of women's liberation on the May Fourth scene. Countless young women who began to break away from the confines of their families and their childhood milieu justified their action with the example of Nora, whose final act of slamming the door on a family and a society that bred selfishness, slavishness, hypocrisy and cowardice (the four evils in Hu Shih's analysis) was, for them, the crux of her significance as a liberated woman. And they quoted with approval Nora's assertion, in response to her husband's accusation: 'My sacred duty is to myself.'[42] In the prevalent interpretation of the time, a Chinese Nora's primary duty to herself was her ability to love. In the name of love, traditional marriages were broken and new relationships were formed. *Lien-ai tzu-yu*, freedom to love, became the reigning slogan which was almost coterminous with women's liberation.

But this romantic credo for individual emancipation is also fraught with problems which, especially for modern Chinese women writers, served to accentuate in a poignant way the limitations of this all-embracing value. For the many Noras of the May Fourth generation, the crucial point of Ibsenism was the initial act of 'going away' (*ch'u-tsou*). As Nora slammed the door to 'a doll's house', her emancipation was considered complete. Very few of them gave serious thought to the question, first raised by Lu Hsun in 1923, 'What happens after Nora goes away?' As Yi-tsi Feuerwerker observes in her perceptive essay on women as writers in the 1920s and 1930s, the modern Chinese woman writer, 'having broken so drastically with authority, both literary and social, and with the old order and values that would have regulated her life, . . . was suddenly on her own, with nothing to fall back on but her feelings or uncertain new relationships, which were also dependent on tenuous feelings. The right to self-affirmation when finally won proved to be but a precarious thing, and the reliance on love and sensitivity for the management of her life only made a woman all the more vulnerable to other kinds of suffering.'[43]

The works of some notable women writers of the period – Huang Lu-yin, Feng Yuan-chün and Ting Ling – gave moving testimony to this mixed feeling of courage and vulnerability, defiance and disillusionment. In her celebrated story, 'Separation' (*Ke-chueh*), Feng Yuan-chün depicted the trials and tribulations of an inexperienced romantic couple as they journeyed away from home following a 'break-up' with their families. In

42 Hu Shih, 'I-pu-sheng chu-i' (Ibsenism), in *Hu Shih wen-ts'un*, 1. 643.
43 Yi-tsi Feuerwerker, 'Women as writers in the 1920s and 1930s', in Margery Wolf and Roxanne Witke, eds. *Women in Chinese society*, 161–2.

the works of Huang Lu-yin, a member of the Association, one finds a persistent theme of deceit and victimization: her emancipated heroines, with their images of love nourished by the traditional sentimental novels they had read at home, are singularly unprepared for a society still dominated by men. Their initial rebellion soon leads to their 'fall', as the Nora-figures become debutantes in the world of 'debauchery' led by the fashion-conscious dandies who, with their smooth speech and self-proclaimed literary gifts, play adeptly the game of 'free love' and exploit the naive idealism of their inexperienced victims.

The early stories of Ting Ling, perhaps the foremost modern Chinese woman writer, provide the most daring case of this emotional confusion. 'The diary of Miss Sophie' (Sa-fei nü-shih jih-chi) her most celebrated story, portrays a 'modern girl' involved with two men: she is not satisfied with the weak and sentimental youth but finds herself attracted to a rich playboy from Singapore. Unlike Lu-yin's 'play with life' heroines, Miss Sophie manages to conquer both men, but her desire for conquest, which on the surface seems to demonstrate her strong personality, veils a complex inner agony of yearning and guilt. The story of Miss Sophie can be read as a story of a modern girl in conflict and confusion over the differences between physical and spiritual love; in her turbulent psyche, she fails to integrate them.[44]

For both Huang Lu-yin and Ting Ling the enduring quality of love was primarily spiritual. In reaction against the traditional practice of eroticism as a man's hobby, the May Fourth followers of Ibsenism, who sought to restore love to marriage, objected to China's customary polygamy on the grounds that its active element was carnal, not spiritual. Since love was regarded as a new morality, and the moral implications of love tended to be more spiritual, the emotional experience of the Chinese Noras often engendered a new irony. Although they could easily reject the traditional marriage system in the name of love, they found it difficult to form new relationships or marriages based on their conception of love. With their 'spiritual' propensities they were at a loss to 'clarify and interpret to themselves the rush of impetuous, unsettling experiences they were living through.' Thus, they wrote with excessive self-absorption, in order to justify their existence as emancipated women, and at the same time 'to discover what they were through self-expression.'[45]

The intensely subjective quality of women's writings brings a new

44 For a different interpretation of Ting Ling, see Yi-tsi Feuerwerker, 'The changing relationship between literature and life: aspects of the writer's role in Ding Ling', in Goldman, ed. Modern Chinese literature, 281–308.
45 Feuerwerker, 'Women as writers', 108.

depth, and a new range of psychological complexity, to May Fourth literature. But it also betrays the limited nature of their art. As Yi-tsi Feuerwerker remarks, 'Whereas many male writers managed to move beyond self-indulgent, confessional writing, no women of the post-May Fourth period painted the broad social canvases of Mao Tun or achieved the ironic perspective of Lu Hsun or the satiric force of Chang T'ien-i.' The reason may be that 'the creative phase in the lives of most women writers was mainly coterminous with, and often did not outlast, the period following emergence from adolescence.'[46] Once they outlived this phase and their youthful search for self-definition and self-affirmation was over, their impetus to write also seems to have been lost. With the exception of Ting Ling most women writers settled down to more conventional lives after a period of wild indulgence in love. The euphoria of the 1920s was dissipated in the 1930s and most of the romantic Noras gave up their writing careers by becoming teachers, scholars or, as in the case of Ling Shu-hua and Ping Hsin, housewives. It seems that Lu Hsun's answer to his own question – 'What happens after Nora goes away?' – proved quite prophetic: Nora would either 'fall into debauchery' or 'return home'.[47] The implication of Lu Hsun's question and answer seems to be that without economic independence from and equal status with men Nora's emancipation can be at best a fashionable style, a romantic outlook and ultimately an illusion. Without a fundamental transformation of all segments of the Chinese people, the Chinese Noras will never attain complete emancipation.

In spite of his strong reservations about the feasibility of women's liberation in early twentieth-century China, the middle-aged Lu Hsun was sympathetic and even solicitous towards young women writers. For some of their male colleagues, however, he had nothing but cynical disdain. The term 'dilettantes plus rogues' was his pithy epithet, levelled especially against the Creationists. But he would have gladly extended it to a host of literary upstarts, each flaunting a story or a poem which had just been published in one of the new magazines and clamouring for immediate recognition. Their reputation was measured not so much by the quality of their works as by the style of their romantic behaviour. For many May Fourth writers, life was art and art, life. This exaltation of the writer's personality and life experience – the excessive preoccupation with self – had a crucial impact on the nature and quality of literary creativity during the May Fourth period.

46 *Ibid.* 108.
47 Lu Hsun, 'No-la ch'u-tsou hou tsen-yang' (What happens after Nora goes away), in his *Fen* (Graves), 141–50.

Lu Hsun and the modern short story

The most noteworthy feature of May Fourth literature is its intense subjectivism. The emergent strain in late Ch'ing fiction, in which the author's personal perception was given increasing prominence in his works, reached a full flowering in the May Fourth period. Whereas a few late Ch'ing writers still experimented with thinly disguised authorial protagonists (Liu E) or with the first-person narrator as conventional story-teller (Wu Wo-yao), the May Fourth writers dropped the story-telling pose altogether, 'and the narrator became one with the implied author and often with the author himself.'[48] In many cases, the author, undisguised, figured also as the 'fictional' protagonist. This 'emergence of a new authorial persona' is evidenced most frequently in the short story, which was undoubtedly the predominant literary form in the first decade after the literary revolution. It seems as if the May Fourth writers were too involved in the rush of their own impetuous, unsettling experiences to devote much time to writing long novels.[49]

According to Professor Průšek, this choice of the short story is also related to the dual impact of Western literature and China's literary tradition. In reacting against the dominant classical forms of Chinese literature, the May Fourth writers were naturally attracted to genres least bound by traditional conventions. Since the short story and the novel were 'forms which with certain exceptions were traditionally excluded from classical literature', they became the favourites of the new authors.[50] Poetry, which had an exalted position in classical literature, was demoted to a subordinate place. Of the two forms of prose narrative, the novel did not become prevalent until the late 1920s and early 1930s. The reason may be, as pointed out by Průšek, that the nineteenth-century European novel, which the May Fourth writers tried to imitate, is more unified in thematic plan, less loosely structured than the classic Chinese novel, and therefore more difficult for the modern Chinese writers to master. And in spite of its considerable artistic advances, the late Ch'ing novel was still too 'traditional' to be a feasible vehicle for the fervently iconoclastic new writers.

In the short-story genre, one of the most famous practitioners in the

48 Cyril Birch, 'Change and continuity in Chinese fiction', in Goldman, ed. *Modern Chinese literature*, 390.
49 For a few less emotional writers, the most coveted short literary form was the personal essay, a traditional genre developed to new heights by Chou Tso-jen and Lu Hsun. For an insightful discussion of Chou Tso-jen's art of essay-writing, see David E. Pollard, *A Chinese look at literature: the literary values of Chou Tso-jen in relation to the tradition*.
50 Jaroslav Průšek, 'A confrontation of traditional oriental literature with modern European literature in the context of the Chinese literary revolution', *Archiv Orientalni*, 32 (1964) 370.

early 1920s was Yü Ta-fu. The stories in his first collection – 'Sinking', 'Moving south', and 'Silver-grey death' – created a sensation by their unprecedentedly frank portrayal of 'sexual depravity'. But a more significant feature of Yü's early stories is his quest for emotional fulfilment, of which sexual frustration becomes a 'hypochondriac' expression. Life for this self-styled 'superfluous' loner is a sentimental journey in which the solitary hero wanders aimlessly in search of its meaning. Consequently Yü's stories are marked by a spontaneous flow of feelings, observations, and incidents which are not, however, compressed into a coherent structure. Layers of past and present are woven impressionistically, almost at the mental caprice of the autobiographical hero. Invocations of mood and memory are made not to forward the progression of the plot but to achieve a certain emotional intensity. At his best Yü imparts both an intensity and an authenticity of feeling; at his worst he leaves the reader with an impression of carelessness, fragmentation and incompleteness.[51]

In spite of his considerable talent Yü Ta-fu must be regarded as a novice writer who gropes, through imitation and experimentation, towards a novelist's technique. Some of his stories read, in fact, more like lyrical essays than well-wrought fiction. Compared with Yü Ta-fu's works the fictional output of other members of the Creation Society is crude (Ch'eng Fang-wu), unabashedly maudlin (Wang Tu-ch'ing), or downright exploitative (Chang Tzu-p'ing). The only exception may be Kuo Mo-jo, but his creativity is manifested, however, more in poetry than in fiction. The works of the Association writers, on the other hand, seem to fare slightly better. While a strongly autobiographical impulse likewise informs their fiction, the Association writers are, in general, less exaggeratedly self-glorifying than their colleagues in the Creation Society. The theme of emotional search for life's meaning is depicted with less self-indulgence and more humanitarianism. In Huang Lu-yin's works, as analysed earlier, this search takes the form of the heroine's progression from idealism to disillusionment. In Ping Hsin, the treatment of 'the dilemmas of the younger generation in a period of agonizing transition'[52] is more idealistic and 'philosophical'. Celebrated especially for her *Chi hsiao-tu-che* (Letters to my little readers), Ping Hsin, contrary to Huang Lu-yin, tends to sentimentalize mother love and idealize the world in the image of the author's own childhood happiness. The best specimens of creative writings from the Association are provided by Yeh Shao-chün.

51 For analyses of Yü Ta-fu's art, see Lee, *The romantic generation*, ch. 6; Anna Doležlová, *Yü Ta-fu: specific traits of literary creation*; Michael Egan, 'Yü Dafu and the transition to modern Chinese literature', in Goldman, ed. *Modern Chinese literature*, 309–24.
52 Hsia, *A history*, 73.

In the opinion of C. T. Hsia, of all the early writers who published articles in *Hsiao-shuo yueh-pao*, Yeh Shao-chün 'has best stood the test of time'. In his voluminous output of short stories he has maintained a 'standard of competence' and 'a civilized sensibility' rivalled by few of his contemporaries.[53] Most of Yeh's early stories deal with the theme of education, which reflects his own experience as a dedicated teacher. The pathos of these stories is derived not so much from the hero's personal suffering (as in Yü Ta-fu) as from a passionate concern with the social environment in which the hero attempts to realize his objectives. In story after story Yeh delineates a pattern of thwarted idealism: the zealous and idealistic teachers meet only with difficulty and frustration. In his novel entitled *Ni Huan-chih*, Yeh Shao-chün gives a summary portrait of the May Fourth intellectual as educational reformer. Largely autobiographical, the novel – one of the first of considerable merit to appear (1927) – depicts the experience of an elementary-school teacher whose rosy visions for educational and social reform, first nourished by his school principal and the love of his girlfriend, are crushed by the sombre realities of the political environment. The protagonist finally dies of typhoid fever.

Ni Huan-chih was hailed by Mao Tun as a notable achievement for the freshness of its realism, though Mao Tun also pointed out that despite the final tone of disillusionment Yeh Shao-chün was still something of an immature idealist. While he depicted the 'greyness' of urban intellectual life, he was not averse to giving a few touches of 'brightness'. For him, 'beauty' and 'love' were the essence of life's meaning and 'the essential requirements which transform a grey life into a bright one'.[54] For all his honesty, his sure craftsmanship, and his civilized sensibility, Yeh-Shao-chün is still no match for Lu Hsun, the most mature and profound writer in the May Fourth period. Although Lu Hsun has written only two collections of stories (as compared to Yeh Shao-chün's half a dozen), he has left behind a fictional legacy which gives both intellectual and artistic depth to an otherwise shallow corpus of early May Fourth literature. Accordingly, it deserves a more careful analysis.

Lu Hsun's genius as a creative writer was unique among his contemporaries; his first short story, 'Recollections of the past' (*Huai chiu*), which predated the literary revolution, already demonstrated an original sensibility and a masterful technique, although it was written in the *wen-yen* style.[55] Lu Hsun's subsequent stories, which were mostly cast in

---

53 *Ibid.* 57–8.
54 Quoted in Wang Yao, *Chung-kuo hsin-wen-hsueh shih-kao*, 89.
55 For an analysis of the story's importance, see Jaroslav Průšek, 'Lu Hsun's "Huai-chiu":
   a precursor of modern Chinese literature', *Harvard Journal of Asiatic Studies*, 29 (1969) 169–76.

the traditional milieu of his native place, Shao-hsing, were infused with a subjective lyricism which revealed his complex and ambiguous reactions to the problem of self and society. Although they were well received as anti-traditional literature, Lu Hsun's stories were rather atypical of the early crop of creative writing as represented by the two major literary groups.

Lu Hsun himself acknowledged at different times that two significant impulses lay behind his fictional writing. He declared that its purpose was to enlighten his people and to reform society: 'My themes were usually the unfortunates in this abnormal society. My aim was to expose the disease so as to draw attention to its cure.'[56] But he also admitted that his stories were products of personal memory: he wrote because he had been unable to erase from memory certain aspects of his past which continued to haunt him. Thus, in his fictional output he endeavoured to combine artistically a private act of remembrance of things past with a public concern for intellectual enlightenment. He attempted to rearrange recollections of personal experience in such a way as to fit them into a larger picture of China's national experience, thereby making it less ego-centred, as in most early May Fourth literature, and more significant to his readers. To some extent, Lu Hsun succeeded in blending expertly these two impulses into an artistic whole. But this creative interaction between the public and personal sides does not always result in harmony.

When Lu Hsun was first asked by Ch'ien Hsuan-t'ung to contribute to the *New Youth* magazine, he countered with a laden metaphor.

Imagine an iron house without windows, absolutely indestructible, with many people fast asleep inside who will soon die of suffocation. But you know since they will die in their sleep, they will not feel any of the pain of death. Now if you cry aloud to wake a few of the lighter sleepers, making those unfortunate few suffer the agony of irrevocable death, do you think you are doing them a good turn?[57]

To conceive such a gloomy image in an era of unbridled enthusiasm and optimism bespeaks the uniqueness of Lu Hsun's frame of mind. An iron house with no windows to usher in the light – certainly a dark image of enclosure – was what he considered to be a fitting symbol of Chinese culture and society. The obvious message, of course, calls for intellectual enlightenment. But implicit in this paradoxical metaphor is also an ominous inkling of tragedy: the 'lighter sleepers', when awakened, would

---

56 Lu Hsun, *Lu Hsun ch'üan-chi* (The complete works of Lu Hsun), 3. 230. See also, William Lyell, *Lu Hsun's vision of reality*.
57 Lu Hsun, 'Na-han tzu-hsu' (Preface to *A call to arms*), in *Na-han*, 10; English translation in Yang Hsien-yi and Gladys Yang *Selected stories of Lu Hsun*, 24.

eventually come to the same end as the 'sound sleepers', and Lu Hsun offered no clue for the destruction of the iron house. As his stories unfolded the 'iron house' theme was developed in a series of tragic confrontations between a few awakened or half-awakened individuals and the slumbering majority whose singular lack of consciousness is often exacerbated by acts of senseless cruelty. This central image of the loner versus the crowd thus discloses a profound sense of ambivalence in Lu Hsun's 'nationalism' and an unresolved mental paradox between what he called 'individualism' and 'humanitarianism': he was torn, in other words, between his public ideological commitment to enlightenment and a private pessimism he could not overcome.

Lu Hsun depicted the 'crowd' in several of his stories: the customers at the Prosperity Tavern in 'K'ung I-chi', the neighbours in 'A madman's diary' and 'Tomorrow', the villagers in 'New Year's sacrifice' and 'Storm in a teacup' and, the most graphic of all, in the relatively unappreciated piece, 'Peking street scene' ('*Shih chung*'). He is at his satirical best in castigating some of the crowd's older members in such stories as 'Master Kao', 'Soap', and 'Divorce'. Through these individual or collective sketches, Lu Hsun has pieced together a composite portrait of his countrymen – a people living in a world of 'sloth, superstition, cruelty, and hypocrisy.'[58] He has laid bare, in all its gloomy reality, a 'diseased' society in dire need of a cure. The essential cause of this 'disease', in Lu Hsun's view, was not physical or even environmental, but spiritual. His conception of the crowd was guided by a persistent effort, ever since he made the decision to forsake medicine for literature in 1906, to investigate its 'spiritual' content and to explore the depths of the Chinese 'national character' by means of literature. The result of his findings, which can be found in his many writings, was presented conclusively in the longest story Lu Hsun ever wrote, 'The true story of Ah Q'.

In this his most famous work Lu Hsun has not brought forth a powerful individual hero; instead, he has created, most impressively, a mediocrity – Ah Q, the most common of commoners, a face in the crowd. The biography of Ah Q can therefore be read as a summary portrait of the Chinese crowd. Ah Q's many flaws, which are also those of the Chinese as a people, can be grouped under two overriding negative qualities: his attitude of 'spiritual victory', a self-deluding way of rationalization to turn setbacks into apparent victories; and his 'slave mentality', which renders him a willing victim of oppression. These two traits, in turn, lie at the root of China's illness – the legacies of past history. Lu Hsun

58 Hsia, *A history*, 32. Hsia also gives a perceptive analysis of 'Soap' and 'Divorce' in 42–6.

implies that the historical experience of repeated humiliations, especially in the recent past, by stronger groups of barbarians has instilled in the Chinese mentality a passive, unreflective attitude of resignation. Thus the spirit of Ah Q is, ironically, a total lack of spirit.

Although Ah Q stands as the mirror image of the crowd, he is also alienated by the crowd – a labourer turned social outcast. In the last three chapters of the story Ah Q finds himself becoming first a 'revolutionary', then a robber, and finally an alleged criminal. In the 'grand finale' he is paraded in front of the crowd and executed. This final experience of his life thus offers a sad comment on the futility of the 1911 Revolution.[59] In his last moments, Ah Q does attain, albeit belatedly, a certain awareness – not of his own nature or of the meaning of revolution, but of the true character of the Chinese crowd: he realizes that the crowd of spectators – who seem eager to devour his flesh and blood and 'bite into his soul' – have been persecuting him: he has unknowingly allowed himself to become their victim and sacrificial lamb.

As a 'sound sleeper' Ah Q has not suffered the pain of death, in spite of his partial awakening by the end of his life. But when it comes to the 'lighter sleepers' – those unfortunate individuals, mostly intellectuals, who, unlike Ah Q, cry out in their alienated existence amidst the slumbering crowd – Lu Hsun's public didacticism is often tempered by a more personal feeling of sympathy and embittered hopelessness. These figures seem to emerge from a nightmare of memory, the result of Lu Hsun's painful *'recherche du temps perdu'*; they embody Lu Hsun's own confrontations with his inner psyche. Above all, they represent a central philosophical dilemma which Lu Hsun attributes to all the 'lighter sleepers', particularly himself: having awakened with a gift of sensitivity and perception, how do these unfortunate few find any meaning in suffering the 'agony of irrevocable death'?

The protagonist of 'A madman's diary' (the first modern Chinese short story) is the earliest and most dramatic of Lu Hsun's awakened intellectuals. He can be seen, to some extent, as a 'psychotic' descendant of the 'Mara poet' whom Lu Hsun so admired in his Japan years – a rebel and an originator of new ideas with which all political, religious and moral reforms begin. But this heroic stance is significantly modified by his total alienation, which makes his impact on society almost nil. His ex-

---

59 In Lin Yü-sheng's insightful analysis of this story, the 1911 Revolution not only failed to accomplish anything positive but, on the contrary, unleashed the evil forces of Chinese society from its conventional restraints. Ah Q's death as an unthinking 'revolutionary' points to the inevitable lesson that an intellectual revolution must be the precondition of change in China; see the chapter on Lu Hsun in his *The Crisis of Chinese Consciousness*.

cessively keen and probing consciousness is the hallmark of his madness and the curse of his existence. Because of it, he stands alone, victimized and alienated by the crowd of 'sound sleepers' around him.

Although his warnings about the cannibalistic nature of Chinese society are taken as the ravings of a madman, Lu Hsun's intellectual hero nevertheless utters a sober message at the end of his diary: 'Save the children.' In some of Lu Hsun's subsequent portraits of modern intellectuals, however, this didactic thrust gradually gives way to a more melancholy bent; the angry rebel is replaced by the pensive loner, the embittered sentimentalist, and the suicidal misanthrope. In three typical stories with strong autobiographical overtones, Lu Hsun's depiction of the 'light sleepers' also becomes progressively pessimistic, even verging on total despair.

In 'My old home', the intellectual narrator, Lu Hsun's fictional *alter ego*, encounters his childhood companion, Jun-tu, who has changed from a lively rustic youth into a weather-beaten man burdened with children. The narrator feels a profound sense of alienation, caused not only by the gap of social status between him and Jun-tu, but also by the ironies of time which transform the pleasures of his past into present miseries. He sees clearly Jun-tu's entrapment in a world which he can no longer re-enter and from which he has no way to extricate his former friend. His loneliness is, therefore, the result of a feeling of empathy stifled in hopelessness. Again it is the intellectual's power of perception that makes this confrontation between past and present all the more unbearable.

The narrator in 'In the wine shop' similarly interacts with an old friend he encounters in the wine shop. The two friends share a past of radical idealism and a more recent experience of deflated ambitions. Thus when the narrator listens to his friend's account of his recent visits to his little brother's grave and to his neighbour's family, their mutual understanding is akin to identification: the narrator and protagonist in the story can be seen, in fact, as two artistic representations of Lu Hsun himself. By cleverly manipulating the conversations of the two characters, Lu Hsun is adroitly conducting a kind of inner dialogue in fiction.

Lu Hsun's inner conflict in this story is not resolved positively. The central theme of both 'In the wine shop' and 'My old home' is, as Professor Patrick Hanan has suggested, the 'failure to live up to the ideals of social service and morality which Lu Hsun's generation espoused'; it involves 'matters of personal conscience and even guilt.'[60]

60 Patrick Hanan, 'The technique of Lu Hsun's fiction', *Harvard Journal of Asiatic Studies*, 34 (1975) 92–3.

In the most maudlin of Lu Hsun's stories, 'The misanthrope', guilt and disillusionment further deteriorate into utter self-disgust and self-defeatism. Having suffered a series of setbacks and having attended the funeral of his grandmother, the last kindred spirit in his life, Wei Lien-shu, the story's protagonist, is confronted with the central problem that afflicts all misanthropes: what is left in life that is worth living? Wei Lien-shu's answer, as evidenced in his final farewell letter, is revealing:

I have failed, I thought I had failed before, but I was wrong then; now, however, I am really a failure. Formerly there was someone who wanted me to live a little longer, and I wished it too, but found it difficult. Now, there is no need, yet I must go on living. . . .

I am now doing what I formerly detested and opposed. I am now giving up all I formerly believed in and upheld. I have really failed – but I have won.

Do you think I am mad? Do you think I have become a hero or a great man? No, it is not that. It is very simple: I have become adviser to General Tu. . . .[61]

The final ironical note thus brings Lu Hsun's image of the awakened loner facing a bitter end. He has lost the air of gifted madness, of lone heroism, and even of eccentricity and cynical arrogance. His disgust with himself, with a life of alienation and unappreciation, leads to a pessimistic end: by a suicidal act of compromise – the 'irrevocable death' – he has joined the mundane crowd.

'The misanthrope' was written in October 1925, at a time when Lu Hsun had reached the nadir of his depression. But he did not follow the example of his protagonist; rather, he was to bring himself gradually out of it in the next few years and embark upon a path of political commitment to 'leftist' literature. This phase in his life has come to be known as his Shanghai years (1928–36). The two collections of his short stories, which represent his initial 'outcry' in the May Fourth movement and his ensuing 'wandering' after its 'high tide' was over, provide a most profound testimony to his mental state as a May Fourth intellectual, which is qualitatively different from that of his younger contemporaries. With his mature perspective – the seasoned insight of a middle-aged man – he was able to see through the romantic glitter of May Fourth iconoclasm and locate the problems and conflicts which lurked behind it. He offered no solutions to the problems; in fact, his didactic intent of exposing the disease did not result in any definite prescription. The destruction of the 'iron house' was nowhere in sight. But, more than any other writer, Lu Hsun succeeded in subjecting some 'sound sleepers' inside it to scathing satire. He also succeeded in showing, in all its pathos and intensity, the tragic fate of the awakened intellectual in an era of turbulent transition. For

61 Lu Hsun, *P'ang-huang* (Wandering), 134.

this alone, Lu Hsun's importance in the history of modern Chinese literature is assured.

Impact of foreign literature

Aside from being the foremost short-story writer, Lu Hsun was also one of the most indefatigable translators of foreign literature. Together with his brother, Chou Tso-jen, he pioneered the first translations of some Russian and East European stories which were published in two volumes in 1909 under the title of *Yü-wai hsiao-shuo chi* (Stories from abroad). But the work proved a dismal commercial failure: the two volumes sold only about 20 copies each.[62]

A far more successful translator than the Chou brothers was Lin Shu, a late Ch'ing scholar who had never been abroad and knew no foreign languages. But by the time the Chou brothers' translation appeared, Lin had already published 54 titles. In an impressive career spanning more than 20 years, Lin had translated some 180 titles of which more than a third were completed in the last 13 years of the Ch'ing period and the rest during the first 24 years of the republic.[63] It is an unprecedented as well as unsurpassed record in modern China's literary history.

Lin Shu's popularity had to do first of all with his native literary sensibility and his command of an elegant classical style: aided by oral assistants, he was able to capture the mood and tone of a foreign novel with apparent ease. He once stated that he had acquired the ability to differentiate the nuances of one novel from another in the same way he grew accustomed to listening to the footsteps of his family members.[64] As an accomplished classical scholar steeped in the tradition of T'ang and Sung prose, Lin developed an uncanny sense of judging Western literature: he considered Charles Dickens to be a much better writer than Rider Haggard, and compared the various techniques of this English master to those of Ssu-ma Ch'ien, the great historian, and Han Yü, the 'ancient prose' master of the T'ang. His learned prefaces (which may have been no more than intellectual rationalizations of his translation efforts) must have

62 For Lu Hsun's early literary endeavour during his Japanese years, see Leo Ou-fan Lee, 'Genesis of a writer: notes on Lu Xun's educational experience, 1881-1909', in Goldman, ed. *Modern Chinese literature*, 179-86.

63 Chu Hsi-chou, Lin's disciple, gives the total figure of Lin's translations as 206. See Chu Hsi-chou, ed. *Lin Ch'in-nan hsien-sheng hsueh-hsing p'u-chi ssu-chung* (The life and works of Mr Lin Shu, four records), 'Ch'un-chueh chai chu-shu chi' (Works from the Ch'un-chueh study), 1.17. The number of 180 is based on Chow Tse-tsung, *The May Fourth movement*, 65. For a thematic account of Lin Shu's life and work, see Lee, *The romantic generation*, ch. 3.

64 See Lin's preface to his translation of Charles Dickens' *The old curiosity shop* in Ch'un-chueh chai chu-shu chi, 3.5.

appealed to readers of both elite and non-elite backgrounds. But Lin's commercial success may be more closely connected with his ability, and good fortune, to capitalize on the prosperous business of literary journalism and fit his translations into the prevailing modes of late Ch'ing fiction. For the largest number of his translations fell into the two popular categories of social and sentimental fiction; in addition, a sizeable number were detective stories and novels of adventure. (Haggard's works alone constituted 25 titles.)

It was Lin Shu, master of *wen-yen* and opponent of the literary revolution, who provided the essential nourishment that fed the imaginations of a younger generation: there was hardly any May Fourth writer who did not first come into contact with Western literature through Lin's translations. His renditions of the novels of Dickens, Walter Scott, Washington Irving, Rider Haggard, and, in particular, *La dame aux camélias* (*Ch'a-hua nü*) by Dumas *fils* have been perennial favourites. While Lin Shu made Western literature accessible to modern Chinese writers and readers, it remained for Lin's contemporary, Su Man-shu, to transform Western authors into glamorous legends.[65] With the publication of his *Selected poems of Byron* (1909) – especially his translation of Byron's 'Isles of Greece' – Su Man-shu made this English romantic poet a hero *par excellence* and perhaps the most glorified Western writer in modern Chinese literature. Su's idolization of and identification with Byron also set an interesting precedent for the Chinese reception of Western literature: just as Byron was worshipped by Su in the glittering image of the Byronic hero, the stature of a foreign author in China was henceforth measured by the legend of his life and personality; the literary worth of his work hardly mattered.

By the May Fourth period Su Man-shu's legacy, as perpetuated by Hsu Chih-mo and Yü Ta-fu and other Creationists, had become a new convention: foreign literature was used to bolster the new Chinese writer's own image and lifestyle. With their own inflated egos and mania for hero-worship, these leading men of letters established a fetish of personal identification: Yü Ta-fu with Ernest Dowson, Kuo Mo-jo with Shelley and Goethe, Chiang Kuang-tz'u with Byron, Hsu Chih-mo with Hardy and Tagore (two figures whom he met and became friends with); T'ien Han as a 'budding Ibsen', and Wang Tu-ch'ing as a second Hugo. To be '*à la mode*' on the literary scene required that a literary man display not only his new poem or story but also his pantheon of foreign masters: Byron, Shelley, Keats, Goethe, Romain Rolland, Tolstoy, Ibsen, Hugo

65 Lee, *The romantic generation*, ch. 4.

and Rousseau were among the favourites on almost everyone's list. Most of these 'heroes' are, of course, outstanding figures of European romanticism; even those who do not summarily fit into the romantic category – Tolstoy, Nietzsche, Hardy, Maupassant, Turgenev, to mention a few – were worshipped by their adulators in a romantic perspective as towering figures of 'crusading idealism' with superhuman vitality.

This emotional idolization of Western writers also led to a related tendency to regard foreign literature as a source of ideology. Terms like romanticism, realism, naturalism and neo-romanticism were bandied about in the same fervent spirit as were socialism, anarchism, Marxism, humanism, science and democracy. A superficial knowledge of these big '-isms', as with the big 'names' of foreign authors, served to bestow immediate status. For a historian of modern Chinese literature, one of the most thorny problems is to clarify, compare and evaluate the various literary '-isms' that originated from other countries and to gauge the true nature of this 'foreign impact'.

The sheer volume of translations presents the first Sisyphean task of classification and analysis. The section on translations in *Chung-kuo hsin wen-hsueh ta-hsi* (A comprehensive compendium of China's new literature), volume 10, lists a grand total of 451 titles of individual works and collections published in the period from 1917 to 1927. Another list, included in *Chung-kuo hsien-tai ch'u-pan shih-liao* (Historical materials on contemporary Chinese publications) and updated to 1929, gives the figure as 577.[66] Of these, translations from French literature led with 128 titles, followed by Russian (120), English (102), German (45) and Japanese (38). Multi-author and multi-nation collections (31) are not counted. And translated poems, stories, plays and articles which appeared in literary journals were too numerous to tabulate. Aided by a thriving publishing industry, translations of foreign literary works had reached immense proportions by the end of the decade following the literary revolution.

The popularity of a foreign author is hard to gauge, for it rested on a combination of his translations and his personal appeal. The more glamorous writers – Byron, Shelley, Keats, Dumas *fils*, and other romantics – became household names, however, in spite of the limited amount of their translated work. Other writers who were represented by extensive translations – Haggard, Andreev, Galsworthy, Hauptmann – nevertheless failed to achieve much popularity. Instances of a good balance between volume and popularity – Dickens, Maupassant – are rare.

66 *Chung-kuo hsin-wen-hsueh ta-hsi*, 355–79; Chang Ching-lu, ed. *Chung-kuo hsien-tai ch'u-pan shih-liao* (Historical materials on contemporary Chinese publications), *chia-pien*, 1st Series, 272–323.

The lists of translations encompassed authors from more than 20 countries and different historical periods. In general, however, the overwhelming majority of the works introduced belong to nineteenth-century European literature, of which two major trends held sway in China: realism and romanticism.

From the viewpoint of literary history it can be said that the mania in China for things Western represented a zestful effort to squeeze the entire nineteenth century into one decade. Almost all the May Fourth writers were scornful of Western classicism, because in their iconoclastic fervour they equated classicism with tradition. Only Chou Tso-jen professed an interest in the Hellenistic heritage. And only a handful of Chinese critics – most of them disciples of Irving Babbitt – seemed to share the views of Matthew Arnold. Of the pre-nineteenth-century authors, only Aristotle, Dante, Shakespeare and Goethe enjoyed some degree of recognition.[67] And what came to be known as 'modernism', which emerged in Europe following the First World War, did not interest the Chinese men of letters until the 1930s and 1940s – and then only a small coterie of writers and critics.

The main reason for this phenomenon may be traced to a prevalent conception of literary evolution. As Bonnie McDougall has shown in her valuable study of the introduction of Western literary theories into China, the Chinese writers, influenced by a host of textbooks in English and Japanese, apparently believed that European literature developed organically through the stages of classicism, romanticism, realism, naturalism and neo-romanticism.[68] While this scheme is not a gross misrepresentation of European literary history, the Chinese cast it as a *progressive* sequence of literary evolution: new forms were believed to be a definite improvement on the old. This conviction of the forward progress of literature led many Chinese followers not only to a general lack of interest in the classical, medieval and neo-classical literatures of the West but also to an over-eagerness to compress modern Chinese literature into these deterministic categories. Convinced that traditional Chinese literature stopped somewhere between the stages of classicism and romanticism, they decided that modern Chinese literature had to go through the stages of realism and naturalism, whether or not they might be personally attracted to them.

This evolutionary commitment to realism, in spite of a romantic temper,

---

67 Bonnie S. McDougall, *The introduction of Western literary theories into modern China, 1919–1925*, 256. For a study of Chou Tso-jen's interest in ancient Greek culture, see C. H. Wang, 'Chou Tso-jen's Hellenism', *Renditions* 7 (Spring 1977) 5–28.
68 McDougall, 254–5.

gave rise to a great deal of interpretive confusion. As mentioned earlier, Western realistic authors were often received 'romantically' in China. The anti-romantic stance of French masters of realism – Flaubert and Maupassant – was given an ideological twist as exposing bourgeois decadence. Tolstoy was admired for his moralism and humanism, in addition to his titanic stature as a 'superhuman' hero. Conversely, romantically-inclined Chinese writers tended to focus on the 'realistic' aspects of European romanticism: the mystical and transcendent dimensions of the romantic aesthetic were largely ignored in favour of a humanistic, socio-political interpretion. Emphasis was placed on self-expression, individual emancipation, and anti-establishment rebellion. T'ien Han even went so far as to equate romanticism with freedom, democracy, revolution and socialism.[69]

A typical May Fourth man of letters may be characterized, therefore, as a composite of three elements: romantic in temperament, 'realistic' in professed literary doctrine, and humanistic in general outlook. This peculiar synthesis was the product of two interrelated factors: the native predispositions of the May Fourth writers and the historical circumstance in which New Literature was created. Few of the modern Chinese 'theorists' and practitioners were interested in literary theory *qua* theory: in a heady decade of restless activism, they were in no mood to sort out the theoretical intricacies of an amorphous body of foreign doctrine – be it romanticism or realism. Rather, literary theories were employed for argument in order to attack or defend an extra-literary cause. The new-style intellectuals had nevertheless inherited their fundamental mode of thinking from the scholar-officials; the concern with contemporary society was deeply ingrained in their consciousness, even at a time when the majority of them felt politically powerless and alienated.

Beginning with Ch'en Tu-hsiu, the concept of 'realism' contained a strong dose of this socio-political obsession. As implied in his manifesto on the literary revolution, realism meant basically the combination of a humanistic concern for society with a simple, lively, vernacular style. It was used primarily as an ideological weapon to break the hold of past conventions in Chinese literature and to redefine the nature and task of New Literature. The new demand, as exemplified in the slogan of 'art for life', was for creative writing to reflect immediate social reality – to deal with the actual life experience without the artificial mediation of literary or cultural conventions. Given this utilitarian purpose, the principle of realism was, therefore, never intended by its May Fourth advocates as a

69 McDougall, 97.

pure canon of artistic theory which decrees a particular approach to literary creation or analysis. The 'realistic' literature produced in the early 1920s was a far cry from Balzac or Flaubert; it yielded not so much an objective representation of reality as 'reality refracted through a very subjective consciousness.'[70]

Subjectivism likewise seemed to characterize the Chinese reception of naturalism (it was often used interchangeably for realism). In this case, the May Fourth writers may have inherited a more immediate legacy from Japan where naturalism was particularly popular at the turn of the century. But the Zolaesque emphasis on social determinism and scientific objectivity proved too brutal for the Japanese writers to handle. Thus, by a clever twist in the implication of the word 'nature' (*shizen*), naturalism 'was given a new dimension of meaning: the principle of inward reflection and the subjective expression of human "nature" in isolation from objective realities.'[71] As the concept was introduced, with much intellectual sophistication, by Mao Tun in his famous 1922 article, 'Naturalism and modern Chinese fiction', this subjective 'bias' was preserved; between the 'absolute objectivity' of Zola and the 'partly subjective naturalism' of the Goncourts, Mao Tun favoured the latter.[72]

Mao Tun's original target for writing this article (published in the newly refurbished *Hsiao-shuo yueh-pao*) was the Butterfly School of fiction, whose mawkish sentimentality he detested; naturalism would therefore provide a necessary antidote. Mao Tun was fully aware that naturalism had a 'bad' tendency to exaggerate evils and to connote fatalism and despair. Nevertheless he argued on the basis of literary evolutionism that 'Chinese writers must first undergo the baptism of naturalism', at least for a brief period.[73]

Mao Tun did not practise what he preached until a decade later, when he finally wrote a long naturalistic novel, *Tzu-yeh* (Midnight), in which he paid the utmost attention to such 'objective' details as the Shanghai stock market and industrial management (the result of his painstaking research). But by the early 1930s realism and naturalism had also undergone a notable transformation. The overtly subjective trend of self-centred confessionalism in the early 1920s gradually gave way to a broader societal orientation. As Cyril Birch has pointed out, the good works were written by those writers who 'largely eschewed the autobiographical':[74] Lao She, Chang T'ien-i, Wu Tsu-hsiang, Shen Ts'ung-wen and Mao

---

70 Feuerwerker, 'Women writers', 159.
71 Cheng Ch'ing-mao, 'The impact of Japanese literary trends on modern Chinese writers', in Goldman, ed. *Modern Chinese literature*, 78.
72 McDougall, *Introduction of Western literary theories*, 177.
73 *Ibid.* 1895.
74 Birch, 'Change and continuity', 391.

Tun. In their fiction, which contained an artistic vision no less individual than that of the early May Fourth writers, we find a descriptive mode which embraced the larger reality: realism in the early 1930s was no longer 'romantic', but 'social' and 'critical' in its unadorned revelation of the dark side of urban and rural life. It was but one more radical step for Mao Tse-tung to politicize totally this new tradition of 'social realism' into 'socialist realism'.

According to the evolutionary scheme, the next stage after realism and naturalism should be symbolism or 'neo-romanticism'. Curiously, despite certain personal preferences, the two terms never seemed to catch on in the Chinese literary scene. This was due, partly, to changed socio-political circumstances: by the early 1930s the majority of modern Chinese writers had already leaned towards the left and begun to embrace such political slogans as 'revolutionary literature' and 'proletarian literature'. Symbolism was advocated and practised only by a few individual poets, most of them apolitical and associated with the *Hsien-tai* (Contemporary) magazine. But aside from political considerations, the issues involved had as much to do with definition as with application.

From the documentary evidence marshalled by Bonnie McDougall it is apparent that when the terms 'symbolism' and 'neo-romanticism' were discussed, they were treated in a tentative and perplexed manner, perhaps due to the lack of adequate information and perspective. Symbolism, as normally understood today, refers to a poetic movement that originated in France at the end of the nineteenth century and comprised such figures as Baudelaire, Verlaine, Rimbaud, Mallarmé and Valéry. 'Neo-romanticism', on the other hand, is a much more amorphous term which, for those who still prefer to use it, refers to the briefly resurgent literature of new idealism as represented by Romain Rolland, Henri Barbusse, Anatole France and Vincente Blasco Ibanez, among others.[75] The names of all these Western authors were known to the Chinese: some, like Romain Rolland, Baudelaire and Verlaine, were worshipped as romantic heroes. But the literary significance of French symbolist poetry was not appreciated by these early hero-worshippers until the 1930s, when Tai Wang-shu and Shao Hsun-mei began to translate Baudelaire's *Les fleurs du mal* into Chinese and to adapt his poetic imagery in their own works.[76]

75 The term 'neo-romanticism' has been used by Průšek and McDougall, but it is not found in such standard works as René Wellek, *Concepts of criticism*, or M. H. Abrams, *A glossary of literary terms*.
76 For a study of Baudelaire's influence in China, see the papers by Gloria Bien, 'Baudelaire and the Han Garden' (read at the Chinese Language Teachers Association panel at the Modern Languages Association annual meeting, New York, Dec., 1976); and 'Shao Hsun-mei and the Flowers of Evil' (read at the Association for Asian Studies annual meeting, Chicago, April, 1978).

The reigning theoretician of symbolism in China in the 1920s was Kuriyagawa Hakuson, whose book, *The symbol of suffering* (*Kumon no shōchō*) was translated three times into Chinese. But Kuriyagawa's theory is fraught with contradictions and inconsistencies which resulted from his own undigested borrowings from European sources. Following him, Chinese writers added more confusion. The otherwise astute Mao Tun at one point lumped together symbolism and neo-romanticism but, at another, considered neo-romanticism to be a brand-new wave which would replace symbolism. Yü Ta-fu divided neo-romanticism into two categories: the positive kind of neo-heroic and neo-idealistic literature (represented by Rolland, Barbusse, and Anatole France); and the negative type of symbolist poets who followed the decadent nihilism and moral anarchism of Baudelaire and Verlaine.[77] Although Yü professed public enthusiasm for the former, it is apparent that in his creative writing he was probably more sympathetic to the latter.

Despite their impressive knowledge of European literature, Yü Ta-fu and Mao Tun seemed as inclined to ideological posturing as their less well-informed colleagues. (This early tendency soon led to a series of literary polemics, to be discussed in a later chapter.) It is remarkable that very few May Fourth writers were able to apply the considerable corpus of Western literary theory to their own creative writing. The prevalent mode of realistic fiction of this period was singularly unconcerned with technique. The early crop of new-style poetry (Hu Shih, K'ang Pai-ch'ing, Liu Ta-pai *et al.*) shared a crudity of form, not to mention the shallowness of content. The most gifted poet of the early 1920s was Kuo Mo-jo, whose works were influenced by the Imagist School and Walt Whitman.[78] The uninhibited vitality of Kuo's poetry was, however, expressed in an intentionally crude form, and it was not until Hsu Chih-mo returned from England and inaugurated his *Poetry Journal* (*Shih-k'an*) in 1926 that serious efforts of reform – especially in matters of poetic metre – were underway, mainly under the influence of English Romantic poetry.[79] Several *avant-garde* schools of the early twentieth century – expressionism, futurism, Dadaism, and so forth – were likewise known and discussed in the 1920s, but few made much use of their new artistic offerings. The literary situation of this first decade thus had a certain historical irony: although the literary revolution, which had abolished old

77 McDougall, *Introduction of Western literary theories*, 202–3.
78 See Achilles Fang, 'From imagism to Whitmanism in recent Chinese poetry: a search for poetics that failed', in Horst Frenz and G. A. Anderson, eds. *Indiana University conference on Oriental-Western literary relations*.
79 See Cyril Birch, 'English and Chinese Meters in Hsu Chih-mo', *Asia major*, N.S. 8. 2 (1961) 258–93.

forms, compelled *all* modern Chinese writers to be formal experimentalists and borrowers from abroad, their actual literary practice showed an amazing lack of technical adaptation. The major exception in this regard was Lu Hsun and, to a lesser extent, Yü Ta-fu.

In his early stories Yü Ta-fu himself acknowledged his heavy debt to foreign literature. The setting in 'Silver-grey death' was taken from Robert Louis Stevenson's 'A lodging for the night', and the theme of a young man in love with a waitress from the life of Ernest Dowson. Though he did not mention it, the pastoral landscape in 'Sinking' was imitative of the Japanese romantic writer, Satō Haruo.[80] But as literary imitations these stories are definite failures, for their 'exotic' setting, laden with numerous quotations of European romantic poetry, presents a fictional landscape rather incongruous with the autobiographical content of the stories.

The case of Lu Hsun was truly exceptional on two accounts. First, as Patrick Hanan has demonstrated, he was uncommonly concerned with literary technique. His early stories showed a conscientious effort to incorporate some of the themes and conventions of Russian and East European fiction. Second, more intriguing than his technical adaptations was the fact that, unlike his fellow Chinese novelists, Lu Hsun was simply not interested in the theory and technique of realism.[81] He had no interest in French realists or naturalists, or Japanese naturalists. His early literary tastes tended rather to favour either 'pre-realists' like Gogol, Lermontov, Sienkiewicz, and Petofi, or 'post-realists' like Andreev, Artzybashev and Garshin. The title of his first story, 'The diary of a madman', is taken from Gogol, but the symbolic conception and the atmosphere of 'metaphysical horror' in this work and in 'Medicine' are indebted to Andreev (especially to such stories as 'Silence' and 'Red Laugh', as demonstrated convincingly by Professor Hanan).[82] Moreover, as Professor D. W. Fokkema has indicated, Lu Hsun's penchant for the outcast and underdog as well as the madman and the alienated intellectual, who speak the truth in a perpetual state of humiliation and oppression, may have been inspired by the Russian romanticist convention. As Fokkema concludes: 'Lu Hsun was attracted by romanticist and symbolist values. Of realist values, only the didacticism and the typicalness of characters attracted him.'[83] One might add that even his typical characters are impregnated with symbolic layers of meaning.

80 Lee, *The romantic generation*, 112–3.
81 Hanan, 'Lu Hsun's fiction', 61.
82 *Ibid.* 61–8.
83 Douwe W. Fokkema, 'Lu Xun: the impact of Russian literature', in Goldman, ed. *Modern Chinese literature*, 98.

The intriguing implication of this foreign literary impact on Lu Hsun is that almost alone in modern Chinese fiction, Lu Hsun had 'progressed' to the symbolist stage, though none of his contemporaries (with the exception of his brother, Chou Tso-jen) acknowledged it. This symbolist tendency is particularly noteworthy in his collection of prose poetry, *Yeh-ts'ao* (Wild grass), written between 1924 and 1926. Compared by Průšek to Baudelaire's *Petits poëmes en prose* in mood and tone, these 23 pieces evoke a nightmarish world suffused with such darkly glowing and oddly lyrical images as dilapidated tombstones, frozen flames of fire, ghost-infested 'hells', a beggar-like traveller journeying to the grave, a tormented Jesus in the last throes of the crucifixion, and a javelin-throwing fighter combating, single-handed, the throng of 'nothingness'.[84] As a symbolic representation of Lu Hsun's private psyche and a metaphorical record of his search for meaning, the collection is the most difficult of all his works and is, consequently, the least understood among Chinese readers. It seems as if in his prose poetry Lu Hsun had gone beyond the familiar sensibilities of his generation to the threshold of Western modernistic literature.

However, references to Nietzsche, Kierkegaard and Christian martyrdom notwithstanding, the basic ethos which informs this collection is nevertheless qualitatively different from that in Western modernistic literature. Rather than revealing the 'universal' human condition of absurdity – of the individual man trapped in the impasse of meaninglessness – this most 'surrealistic' of Lu Hsun's works still carries a humanistic compulsion to find meaning. While burdened with many paradoxes – of life and death, past and future, hope and despair – Lu Hsun's wandering spirit is not entirely lost in nihilism. On the contrary, several pieces of the collection seem to suggest that there is, indeed, a way out of the impasse: the frozen 'dead fire' finally opts to fling itself out of the icy valley, and the weary traveller, pausing on the road of life, finally decides to walk on. Although Lu Hsun never specifies it clearly, the message at the end seems to point to the possibility that an ethical act of human will can still impose a certain meaning on this existential condition of meaninglessness. Accordingly, Lu Hsun's artistic and 'metaphysical' flirtation with Western symbolism and modernism in this collection has not led him to Eliot's 'wasteland' or to the absurd world of Beckett or Ionesco. Instead, it compels him to return to humanity. At the end of a piece describing the last moments of Christ's crucifixion, Lu Hsun enters the closing comment: 'God has forsaken him, and so he is the son of man after all.'

84 Lu Hsun, *Yeh-ts'ao* (Wild grass).

After 1927 Lu Hsun himself had put an end to his inner torment and chose to confront the concrete realities of Chinese society by taking up his essay-writing on behalf of the 'leftist' cause. From a purely aesthetic point of view, this apparent volte-face spelled the end of Lu Hsun's career as a creative artist,[85] but from an ideological standpoint it was simply a case of political commitment overriding artistic interest. However, these two extremes of interpretation tend to obscure some of the more profound implications not only of Lu Hsun's relationship to Western literature but also of the true nature of modern Chinese literature when viewed in the comparative perspective of 'modernity'.

The quest for modernity

From the foregoing analysis of Lu Hsun it can be concluded that the Chinese preoccupation with the predominant trends of nineteenth-century European literature and their hesitant dallying with early twentieth-century developments reveal not merely the problem of 'natural time-lag' in any situation of inter-cultural contact but the inherent ambiguities of the term 'modernity'.

Viewed in a Western perspective the term 'modern' – defined as a temporal consciousness of the present in reaction against the past – had by the nineteenth century acquired two different kinds of connotations. According to Professor Matei Calinescu, since the first half of the nineteenth century, 'an irreversible split occurred between modernity as a stage in the history of Western civilization – a product of scientific and technological progress, of the industrial revolution, of the sweeping economic and social changes brought about by capitalism – and modernity as an aesthetic concept.'[86] This latter concept, which brought into being such new trends as symbolism and *avant-gardism*, represented a strong and radical reaction against the former modernity, which was characterized by the new rebels as the modernity of the middle class and of the philistine – 'with its terre-à-terre outlook, utilitarian preconceptions, mediocre conformity, and debasement of taste.'[87] The beginnings of this reaction can, in fact, be traced to certain strains of the Romantic movement which were opposed both to the classic notions of permanence and perfection

---

85 This is the view adopted by William Schultz and the late Tsi-an Hsia. See Schultz, 'Lu Hsun: the creative years' (University of Washington, Ph.D. dissertation, 1955); Tsi-an Hsia, 'Aspects of the power of darkness in Lu Hsun', in his *The gate of darkness: studies on the leftist literary movement in China*, 146–62. This article presents a brilliant study of Lu Hsun's literary mentality as exemplified mainly by his 'Wild Grass' collection.
86 Matei Calinescu, *Faces of modernity: avant-garde, decadence, kitsch*, 41.
87 *Ibid.* 45.

and to the hypocrisy and vulgarity embodied in the increasingly materialistic civilization of the nineteenth century. By the turn of the century, however, this new modernism had taken on some definite polemical positions. It was anti-traditional, anti-utilitarian and 'anti-humanist' in the sense of seeking artistic 'dehumanization' (in Ortega y Gasset's famous phrase). The new artistic rebels had become weary of empty romantic humanitarianism; the human content of nineteenth-century life, with its 'bourgeois mercantilism and vulgar utilitarianism' had generated in them 'a real loathing of living forms or forms of living beings' and led to a progressive elimination of the human elements which had been predominant in romantic and realistic art.[88] The new modernism was also anti-rationalistic and anti-historical: as Georg Lukacs has charged, 'modernism despairs of human history, abandons the idea of linear historical development.'[89] This sense of despair, the result of a disillusionment with the positivist notion of progress and the Enlightenment idea of rationality, had caused the modernist writers and artists to lose their interest in the outside world, by now seen as hopelessly recalcitrant and alienating; rather, they took upon themselves, in an extreme gesture of subjectivism and iconoclasm, to reinvent the terms of reality through their own artistic creativity.

Viewed against this perspective, the Chinese concept of modernity shows some striking differences. Since the late Ch'ing, the increasingly 'present-oriented' ideologies (as opposed to the general past orientation of classic Confucianism) were filled, both literally and figuratively, with a 'new' content: from the 'reform anew' (wei-hsin) movement of 1898 to Liang Ch'i-ch'ao's concept of the New People (Hsin-min), to the May Fourth manifestations of New Youth, New Culture and New Literature, the epithet hsin ('new') had accompanied almost all the social and intellectual movements to free China from the shackles of the past so as to become a 'modern' nation. 'Modernity' in China thus connotes not only a preoccupation with the present but a forward-looking search for 'newness', for the 'novelties' from the West.[90] Accordingly, this new concept of modernity in China seems to have inherited, in varying degrees, several familiar notions of Western 'bourgeois' modernity: the idea of evolutionism and progress, the positivist belief in the forward movement of history, the confidence in the beneficial possibilities of science and tech-

---

88 José Ortega y Gasset, 'The dehumanization of art', in Irving Howe, ed. The idea of the modern in literature and the arts, 85, 92.
89 Howe, The idea of the modern, 17.
90 One literary historian considers this quest for 'newness', rather than the use of vernacular language, to be the central hallmark of modern Chinese literature. See Wang Che-fu, Chung-kuo hsin wen-hsueh yun-tung shih (A history of the new literary movement in China), 1–13.

nology, and the ideal of freedom and democracy defined within the framework of a broad humanism. As Professor Benjamin Schwartz has noted, some of these liberal values received a very 'Chinese' reinterpretation in the works of Yen Fu and his contemporaries: the faith in the individual was combined with a fervent nationalism in an envisioned effort to achieve the goals of national wealth and power.[91] Thus, this Chinese view foresaw no necessary split between the individual and the collective.

When the May Fourth iconoclasts launched a totalistic attack on tradition, their emotive ethos brought about a romantic assertion of the self which was opposed to the 'philistine' society of early twentieth-century China. While sharing, to some degree, the sense of artistic revolt of Western aesthetic modernism, the May Fourth writers did not give up their faith in science, rationality and progress. In literature, the demand for 'realism', in fact, echoed Ortega y Gasset's summation of nineteenth-century European artists as a whole – that they 'reduced the strictly aesthetic elements to a minimum and let the work consist almost entirely in a fiction of human realities. In this sense all normal art of the last century must be called realistic.'[92]

In his otherwise perceptive assessment of the Chinese literary revolution, Průšek acknowledges this nineteenth-century impact but then goes on to state that the subjectivism and lyricism of May Fourth literature 'was certainly in essence closer to modern European literature after the First World War than to the literature of the nineteenth century' – the result, according to Průšek, of a 'convergence of the old Chinese tradition with contemporary European moods.'[93] In basic agreement with Průšek, McDougall likewise stresses the Chinese interest in *avant-gardist* trends. But as we examine closely McDougall's own evidence, the Chinese writers' sense of the *'avant-garde'*, although springing from an artistic revolt against tradition, was still confined to the realm of 'life': in other words, their feelings of anger, frustration and loathing of contemporary reality propelled them to a stance of rebellion which, however, was rooted in a socio-political nexus. The Creationists' slogan of 'Art for art's sake' neither followed Gautier's idea of the gratuitousness of art nor echoed the Symbolists' polemical assertion of the superiority of a transcendental reality – not to mention the characteristic modernist claim of creating a new aesthetic world more 'authentic' than the shallow external world of contemporary life and society. Even the mood of flux and impermanence

91 See Benjamin Schwartz, *In search of wealth and power: Yen Fu and the West.*
92 José Ortega y Gasset, 'The dehumanization of art', 85.
93 Cited in McDougall, *Introduction of Western literary theories*, 262.

found in such works as Yü Ta-fu's early stories is connected with China's historical situation and not with the more abstract and ahistorical notions of 'the transitory, the fugitive, the contingent' (in Baudelaire's phrase). Finally, nowhere in May Fourth literature can we find any evidence of modernism mocking and turning against itself (as in 'decadence' and 'kitsch'). Yü Ta-fu's 'decadence' remained essentially a glamorous style that barely veiled his frustrations as a 'superfluous' intellectual afflicted with a sense of socio-political impotence.[94]

The most salient feature of the 'modernism' of May Fourth literature is that, instead of turning within himself and the realm of art, the modern Chinese writer displays his individuality most prominently and imposes it on external reality. In this sense, May Fourth literature resembles to some extent the first phase of Western modernism, according to Irving Howe, when modernism, not disguising its romantic origins, 'declares itself as an inflation of the self, a transcendental and orgiastic aggrandizement of matter and even in behalf of personal vitality.'[95] The epitome of this first stage is Whitman, an idol of the early Kuo Mo-jo. But modern Chinese literature has largely eschewed (until the 1960s in Taiwan) the middle and late stages of Western modernism: 'In the middle stages, the self begins to recoil from externality and devotes itself, almost as if it were the world's body, to a minute examination of its own inner dynamic: freedom, compulsion, caprice. In the late stages, there occurs an emptying-out of self, a revulsion from the weariness of individuality and psychological gain.' The exemplars of these stages are, respectively, Virginia Woolf and Beckett. As argued above, only Lu Hsun brought himself fortuitously into a Beckett-like landscape in his prose poetry; and the Virginia Woolf legacy was known only to two later women writers: Ling Shu-hua and Chang Ai-ling (Eileen Chang).[96]

Lu Hsun's 'return' from the frontiers of a Western type of modernism to Chinese reality is, therefore, indicative of the 'modernizing process' of his contemporaries. To be 'modern' in the May Fourth period means, on the superficial level, to be 'chic' (*mo-teng*), *à la mode*, to be abreast with the latest fashions from the West – from styles of clothing and hair to trends in literature. But on a deeper level, as represented by Lu Hsun, it implies a subjectivism in profound tension with the forward journey

94 Lee, *The romantic generation*, 250.
95 Howe, *The idea of the modern*, 14.
96 In an interview in London in 1968, Ling Shu-hua stated that her favourite Western author was Virginia Woolf. But nowhere in modern Chinese literature can we find better examples of the self recoiling from external reality and entering into a 'minute examination of its own inner dynamic' than in Eileen Chang's stories. For an analysis of Chang's works, see Hsia, *A history*, ch. 15.

towards a national modernity – to build a new China in a new and better world of the future. C. T. Hsia's judgment is therefore precisely on target:

He [the modern Chinese writer] shares with the modern Western writer a vision of disgust if not despair, but since his vision does not extend beyond China, at the same time he leaves the door open for hope, for the importation of modern Western or Soviet systems that would transform his country from its present state of decadence. If he had the courage or insight to equate the Chinese scene with the condition of modern man, he would have been in the mainstream of modern literature. But he dared not do so, since to do so would have blotted out hope for the betterment of life, for the restoration of human dignity.[97]

It seems that even the most profound modern Chinese writer – Lu Hsun – has been unable to transcend this obsession with China.

Lu Hsun's own journey to the left also typified the trend of literary politicization which began in the late 1920s. This further 'outward' drift eventually led to an end of subjectivism and individualism. Thus in historical hindsight, it can be said that the May Fourth era marked an unparalleled height in the development of these two varieties of the modern temper. At its best, May Fourth literature conveys a mode of mental conflict and agony perhaps even sharper than its Western counterparts, in the sense that the threat of outside reality did not retreat from the writer's consciousness but remained: the problem posed by a stagnant, philistine society intruded upon the writer's conscience with aggravating force. The modern Chinese writer, unlike his Western contemporary, could not afford to dismiss 'reality'; the price he paid for his 'patriotic provinciality' was, therefore, a deepened sense of spiritual torment which carries the 'realistic' force of imminent crisis. From a less aesthetic point of view, the quest for modernity in Chinese literature yielded a tragically human meaning. It never became 'inverted' to the *cul-de-sac* of 'pure aestheticism'. Nor was it confronted with the self-defeatist dilemma in which Western modernism defines itself: obsessed with the impermanence of time, modernism can never succeed, for if it does, it, too, becomes 'old', thereby ceasing to be modern. In Irving Howe's subtle summation, 'modernism must always struggle but never quite triumph, and then, after a time, must struggle in order not to triumph.'[98]

In his search for the 'betterment of life' and the 'restoration of human dignity' to himself and his country, the modern Chinese writer kept on hoping for a bright future as he agonized over the gloomy reality of worsening social crisis. This conflict between ideal and reality provided

97 Hsia, *A history*, 536.   98 Howe, *The idea of the modern*, 13.

the source for some of the most mature works in the early 1930s. But modernity never really triumphed in the history of Chinese literature. After the outbreak of the Sino-Japanese war, the artistic side of this modern quest was overshadowed by political exigency. The value of creative literature was reduced to a position subservient to politics, in spite of its constant socio-political dimension. And with the canonization of Mao Tse-tung's Yenan 'Talks on literature and art', the very concept of artistic reality has been prescribed by political ideology; modernity, whether in its Western or Chinese connotations, thus ceased to be a central hallmark of Chinese Communist literature, as modern Chinese literature entered into its contemporary phase.

CHAPTER 10

THE CHINESE COMMUNIST
MOVEMENT TO 1927

There is nothing intrinsically wrong in committing oneself to a political doctrine initially on emotional grounds. 'How many Parisians had read Rousseau and how many St Petersburgers had read Marx before they plunged into their revolutionary movements? The point is that in their minds the ideas of Rousseau and Marx had already existed; Rousseau and Marx did no more than articulate these ideas.'[1] Revolution is a mass phenomenon which, however, achieves mass action only through the contemplation and planning of its leading elite. When the record comes under scholarly scrutiny, undue emphasis on the intellectual process of the leadership, which to some extent shapes the fast moving events, tends to downplay the role of mass emotions and mass demands. However inarticulate these emotions and demands may be, they are understood by the revolutionary leaders of the time, who are themselves guided by their own emotions and intellect, their own spontaneity and consciousness. Neither Lenin nor Trotsky was an exception to this. The interaction of emotion and intellect, instead of simplifying, makes the conversion to a political doctrine even more complicated. In the case of China between 1917 and 1921 the conversion to Marxism involved the perception of Chinese reality on the part of the converts, their personal temperament and traits, and their understanding of the doctrine itself.[2]

CONVERSION TO THE DOCTRINE

The military weakness and economic misery of China had been clear to politically conscious Chinese long before the advent of Marxism; hence the call for national power and wealth. But it was not until the rise of reformist thought, including its more conservative t'i-yung school (see chapter 7), that the concept of 'a China worthy of devotion' began to

1 Ch'en Tu-hsiu in *Kung-ch'an-tang* (The Communist Party), 2 (7 Dec. 1920) 2–9.
2 So far, systematic treatments of the conversion of early Chinese Marxists can be found in Benjamin I. Schwartz, *Chinese communism and the rise of Mao* and Maurice Meisner, *Li Ta-chao and the origins of Chinese Marxism*.

emerge. The very term 'reform' (either *kai-liang* or *wei-hsin*) implies an undesirable component in the nation's inseparable culture and polity which must be removed or remoulded. From the reformers' perspective, those who opposed such changes were defending China's undesirable qualities, and so were responsible for their continuation. In the first stage of the development of reformist thought, there was hardly any guiding philosophy except piecemeal observation and comparison at both the individual and societal levels; the admirable qualities of the West – its strength, affluence, education, and good social order – were observed and compared with the unworthiness of China. The coincidence of K'ang Yu-wei's revision of Confucianism and the translation of Thomas Huxley's essays on evolution and ethics by Yen Fu carried reform into its second stage by furnishing it with a philosophical basis, Confucianized social Darwinism. This eclectic philosophy had great appeal for a considerable period of time. Within its framework China and her people were treated as an indivisible entity; thus no social group was perceived as alienable from her political society. Even after the failure of the reform of 1898, the revolutionaries who rose to replace the reformers on the political stage deemed it unnecessary to alienate anyone from political power except the ruling Manchus, on grounds of their racial inferiority. In spite of its philosophical sophistication, Chinese reform or revolution had no other empirical frame of reference than the decaying model of China and the successful model of the West, including Meiji Japan.

China's continued moral degeneration, political instability and economic deterioration provided the context for the repeated attempts at imperial restoration and foreign encroachment. In a wide context, the war in Europe revealed the inherent weaknesses of the much admired Western civilization, and the triumph of the Bolsheviks with its consequent abrogation of the Czarist privileges in China pointed a new way to China's emancipation. As if these epochal events were not enough, the Paris Peace Conference decided to hand the former German possessions in Shantung to Japan, instead of their just rendition to China. Under the combined impact of these events and decisions the intellectual and political climate of China suddenly was transformed – the hegemony of Confucianized social Darwinism was shattered. In its wake there was intellectual confusion in which Chinese scholars were open to persuasion and conversion by the views of Russell or Bergson, Nietzsche or Comte, Kropotkin or Marx.

Who were the Chinese Marxist converts? What was their understanding of the reality of their country? What were their personal experiences in social and political activities? Why did they give their faith to such a doctrine?

Among the converts to Marxism in the five years following the May Fourth movement only a dozen are known to be of proletarian origin.[3] All the rest were educated and some were from fairly well-off petty bourgeois backgrounds. Geographically they were distributed in Peking (around Peking University where Ch'en Tu-hsiu and Li Ta-chao were leading figures), Shanghai (around the left-wing Shanghai University founded in 1923 and the labour unions Ch'en Tu-hsiu helped found in 1919–20), the Wuhan cities (around the Chung-hua University (see map 8) and its affiliated high school where Li Han-chün and Yun Tai-ying were teachers), Changsha (around the New Citizens' Society organized by Mao Tse-tung, Ts'ai Ho-sen, and others), Canton (around a number of colleges where Ch'en Kung-po, T'an P'ing-shan and others taught), Hai-feng-Lu-feng in Kwangtung (around the peasant organizations of P'eng P'ai), Inner Mongolia (with its easy access to the Soviet Union and Peking), Yü-lin in Shensi (around the normal school taught by Li Ta-chao's students like Wei Yeh-ch'ou), Chengtu (around the senior normal school where Wu Yü-chang and Yun Tai-ying were teachers), as well as in Japan, France and Russia where many Chinese students came under Marxist influence. The fountainheads of intellectual influence were predominantly Peking through its widely-circulated magazine *Hsin ch'ing-nien* (New youth), together with Japanese translations of works by Marx and Engels, Lenin and Kautsky, and the contacts with Marxists and Marxism in France. These radical ideas could be verified against social conditions and given voice in metropolitan cities like Shanghai and Peking, to be echoed far into the interior of the country in places like Chengtu and Yü-lin.

There were only a handful of early converts to Marxism and Leninism in China; among them, a few were old enough to have participated in the Revolution of 1911 and a few more were aware of the political significance of the upheavals of the 1913 civil war and the 1915 and 1917 monarchical attempts. Although most of them had had at least a high school education, none of them can be described as academic research scholars. To most of them knowledge always entailed an action consequence; otherwise it would be a pointless acquisition. Its validity, in

3 Ch'en Yü, Su Chao-cheng, Hsiang Chung-fa, Hsiang Ying, Teng Fa, and Liu Ning. See Donald W. Klein and Ann B. Clark, *Biographic dictionary of Chinese communism, 1921–1965*. Also Teng P'ei, Chu Pao-t'ing, Hsi Pai-hao, Liu Wen-sung, Liu Hua, and Ma Ch'ao-fan. See Jean Chesneaux, *The Chinese labor movement*, 400–2. Chinese characters not always available.

their view, could be established only through practice. A theory once proved to be wrong through practice was to be modified or abandoned while the search for another began.[4] Politically involved and concerned, they voluntarily (or involuntarily) avoided an academic life; Dr Hu Shih was an exception. This is not to say, however, that they were in any sense less studious or less meticulous in seeking knowledge, even though their common predilection was to study collectively in small groups or societies. They were iconoclastic, conscious of tradition being obsolescent and seeking a totalistic way to eradicate it. Their cultural alienation resulted in their political alienation either by their own choice or because of a lack of prestigious social status.

They were all nationalists in the sense that they were concerned with the backwardness of their country, looking for a means to make it worthy of their devotion. This made their nationalism conditional – one loved China because she could be made worthy,[5] not simply because one was born a Chinese citizen.[6] The backwardness was epitomized by her economic stagnation, as Ch'en Tu-hsiu pointed out in 1918, or as Mao Tse-tung wrote in the same vein in his inaugural essay of the *Hsiang-chiang p'ing-lun* (Hsiang River review) some 10 months later.[7] Others such as Hsiang Ching-yü arrived at the same conclusion but by different routes. In her search for the liberation of women, Hsiang came across Marxism, to become one of the first female Marxists in China. She came to believe that 'all that which lay in the past was wrong and evil'.[8]

4 For this point, I am indebted to Adrian Chan, 'Development and nature of Chinese communism to 1925' (Australian National University, Ph.D. dissertation, 1974), 39–40. Chan, however, confined his studies in this section to Ch'en Tu-hsiu only, whereas I have no doubt that Li Ta-chao, Tung Pi-wu, Wu Yü-chang, Lin Tsu-han, not to mention Mao Tse-tung, were all of the same bent. See also Meisner, *Li Ta-chao*, 106.

5 The most complete statement on 'Love of country' is to be found in the manifesto of the *Hsin ch'ing-nien* (New youth) by Ch'en Tu-hsiu, 7 (1 Dec. 1919) 1.

6 Li Ta-chao's approach to this problem was more complicated. In 1915 he said: 'The meaning of self-consciousness lies in the spirit of changing the nation in order to make the country lovable and not refusing to love it because the country has deficiencies,' Obviously Li did not defend the deficiencies; nor did he attempt to be apologetic for them. His dilemma lay in the fact that the deficiencies would ultimately render a patriot ineffectual in his endeavour and his love would remain unrequited as long as the deficiencies existed. To free him from the horns of this dilemma, he toyed with the idea of a rebirth of China in the fashion of the proverbial phoenix, but later, during the process of his conversion to Marxism after the First World War, he turned away from his narrow, *a priori* nationalism to the whole history of humanity and the great mission of mankind by linking China to the future of the world. Meisner, *Li Ta-chao*, 22–3, 27 and 180.

7 Ch'en Tu-hsiu, *Wen-ts'un* (Collected essays), 2 (15 Sept. 1918) 275, and Takeuchi Minoru, ed. *Mao Tse-tung chi* (Collected writings of Mao Tse-tung; hereafter Takeuchi edn) 1 (7 July 1919) 53.

8 See Li Li-san's essay in *Hung-ch'i p'iao-p'iao* (Red flags flying), 5. 28–31; *Hsin-min-hsueh-hui hui-yuan t'ung-hsin-chi* (Correspondence of members of the New Citizens' Society), 2, in the *Wu-ssu shih-ch'i ch'i-k'an chieh-shao* (Introduction to the periodicals of the May Fourth period), 1, 154–5.

The general backwardness of China was regarded by Ch'en Tu-hsiu and Li Ta-chao to be the result of spiritual gloom, moral bankruptcy[9] and unruly militarism abetted by a retinue of corrupt bureaucrats and unprincipled politicians.[10] These militarists and their supporters were what Mao vaguely called 'possessors of power and evil-doers' (*ch'iang-ch'üan-che, hai-jen-che*).[11] It came as a further, immensely significant revelation to these radical thinkers that the mighty evil-doers in China were all backed by the 'imperialists'.[12] This opened the gate to later application of such concepts as class struggle, exploitation of surplus value, international alliance of the oppressed, and organization of the vanguard of the proletariat. Thus far, the changes in the radical perception of Chinese reality had been gradual, although the groundwork was laid for the acceptance of the basic elements of Marxism. The October Revolution and the rude awakening over the Shantung decision at the Paris Peace Conference hastened the transformation.

As Ch'en Tu-hsiu recalled in his own defence at his trial for subversion, the May Fourth movement marked a turning-point in his intellectual development. Before that date he had addressed his plea for the reconstruction of China to the intelligentsia; thereafter, he shifted his attention to the labouring people. 'Since the revolutionary situation of the world and the domestic conditions of China indicated [the way] so clearly, my change of view was inevitable.' Earlier in 1919 the image of his ideal China no longer conformed to the model of Anglo-Saxon democracy because of his increasing antagonism towards capitalism and the imperialist exploitation of China. Concurrently, Li Ta-chao voiced his objection to capitalist exploitation while regarding democracy as having already lost out in the United States.[13] True, both Li and Ch'en still lingered over the

---

9 Ch'en Tu-hsiu, *Wen-ts'un*, 2 (1 Oct. 1916) 85–6 and 4 (1 March 1917) 52; Shih Chün, *Chung-kuo chin-tai ssu-hsiang-shih tzu-liao – wu ssu shih-ch'i chu-yao lun-wen-chi* (Materials of modern Chinese intellectual history – Selected important essays of the May Fourth period; hereafter *Ssu-hsiang-shih tzu-liao*), 1 Feb. 1917, 1906; see Meisner, *Li Ta-chao*, 24 and 34 for Li's views on this subject in 1915–17.

10 Li Ta-chao, *Hsuan-chi* (Selected works), 81–2, which was originally published in the *Chia-yin jih-k'an* (1914 daily), 29 March 1917; Ch'en Tu-hsiu, *Wen-ts'un*, 1 (15 Feb. 1916) 53–4; *Hsin ch'ing-nien*, 3: 4 (June 1917); and Ch'en Tu-hsiu, *ibid.* 1 (15 July 1918) 222, and 2 (2 Nov. 1919) 387.

11 'Min-chung ti ta-lien-ho,' (The great union of the popular masses), 1919, Takeuchi edn, 1. 61–4.

12 Ch'en Tu-hsiu's articles in the *Mei-chou p'ing-lun* (Weekly review), no. 4 (12 Jan. 1919) and no. 8 (7 Feb. 1919). Meanwhile Li Ta-chao developed from his Darwinian introspective nationalism of 1915–16 to a firm anti-imperialist stance in January 1919, see Meisner, *Li Ta-chao*, 24 and Li's editorial, 'The new era', in the *Mei-chou p'ing-lun*, no. 3.

13 Ch'en Tu-hsiu, *Pien-shu-chuang* (My defence, n.p.) dated 20 Feb. 1933, p. 1. See also Ch'en's essays in the *Mei-chou p'ing-lun* in March and April 1919 which heralded the often quoted article, 'The basis for the realization of democracy', on 2 Nov. 1919. I am aware of the view that Ch'en's conversion to Marxism dates from a year or two after Li Ta-chao, as maintained

idea of democracy, but in a different sense. Their 'democracy' required a much broader mass participation than the Anglo-Saxon model, as they understood it. In January of that year Ch'en, writing in *Mei-chou p'ing-lun* (Weekly review) – a radical periodical – advocated the need of a party with a mass following; by March, in a further article his ideas reached as far as something akin to a people's dictatorship.[14] Between these two articles, the paper carried an editorial under the title of 'The crimes of the Chinese elite class', calling for a social revolution of the workers and peasants to overthrow the rule of the elite. The editorial was probably penned by Ch'en and Li whose concept of democracy was indeed changing, but in a progression from a popular democracy through a popular revolution to a popular dictatorship. Towards the end of the year Ch'en launched a fierce attack on the moral decay of the system based on private ownership – 'In the West, men are lazy and profitseeking while women are extravagant and licentious. Wars, strikes and all sorts of lamentable unrest, which of these is not caused by the moral decay of the system of private property?' Six months later Ch'en wrote in a definitive tone that the profit sought by Western man was the surplus value produced by workers but stolen from them by capitalists.[15]

The shift of the radicals' focus from oppressed youth and oppressed women – subjects they had treated in full detail in their periodicals – to the oppressed labouring masses amounted to a new identification with them. Their scope of view being wider, their sympathies now extended to all the under-privileged. Externally they ceased to be chauvinistic, following the example of the *Mei-chou p'ing-lun* which published a series of articles on the struggles for independence in Ireland, the Philippines and Korea two months before the May Fourth movement; internally, a spate of articles based on social surveys, covering a wide range of topics on the working and living conditions of workers in Shanghai, Hankow and T'ang-shan and the miseries of the peasants in Shantung, Kiangsu and Fukien, appeared in the *New Youth*, the *Weekly Review*, and the *Morning Post (Ch'en-pao)*. Before the founding of the Chinese Communist Party (CCP) there were even special magazines for or about the working man which provided information on workers and peasants, fostered a new attitude towards labour, and drew attention to some of the most serious

by Schwartz, *Chinese communism*, 22 and Meisner, *Li Ta-chao*, 112–13. However, in spite of his courteous treatment of J. Dewey, Ch'en's November article not only criticized the Deweyan concept of democracy as being 'not thorough enough', but also unambiguously laid the political superstructure of a society on its economic foundation. *Cf. Wen-ts'un*, 1. 375. For Li Ta-chao's view, see *Ch'en-pao* (Morning post), 7–8 Feb. 1919.

14 *Wen-ts'un*, 3 (19 Jan. 1919) 589–91 and 4 (26 March 1919) 646.
15 *Ibid.* 2 (1 Dec. 1919) 72. Also *ibid.* 4. 216–17.

social problems. Soon young radicals were exhorted to work among the working people and some of them did so – P'eng P'ai among the peasants in Haifeng, Chang Kuo-t'ao and Teng Chung-hsia among the railway workers in the north, Mao Tse-tung among the workers in Changsha, and Yun Tai-ying among the workers in Wuhan.

One must ask: could China's national aspirations have been fulfilled and social justice been achieved without recourse to a violent revolution? Would the ruling elite have allowed these purposes to be served through a process of peaceful transformation? By the time of the May Fourth movement the perceived enemies of the nation – the imperialists, militarists, and corrupt bureaucrats, had been identified, but they could not be driven from positions of power merely 'by a few citizens' meetings', as Li Ta-chao put it.[16] Here the experiences of the 1911 (Chinese) and 1917 (Russian) Revolutions furnished indubitable evidence. In the mind of Ch'en, the glory of Europe resulted from her revolutions; in the mind of Li, the greatest achievement could only follow the greatest suffering and sacrifice.[17] As the famous editorial of the *Weekly Review* on 'The new era' (in numbers 3 and 5, January 1919) explained, evolution was based on cooperation rather than competition. Since the greed of the few that drove man to exploit man created a competitive instead of a cooperative situation, social injustice was the outcome. This injustice could not be eliminated by means other than revolution. To both Li and Ch'en, revolution was not a simple act of violence, for it encompassed both the destruction of the old and the birth of the new. In Marxist thinking the solutions to all social problems had to come after the victory of the revolution. Thus, when discussing the question of women's liberation, Li Ta-chao linked it to the destruction of a social system under the dictatorship of the property-owning class while Ch'en Tu-hsiu put it succinctly: 'Problems concerning women, youth and workers can be solved only by a class war'.[18] Other radicals such as the contributors to the *Chueh-wu* (Enlightenment), a supplement of the *Min-kuo jih-pao* (National daily), drew similar conclusions. Moreover, they accepted the materialist interpretation of history and the dictatorship of the proletariat.[19] In France, Chinese students had the *Manifesto of the communist party* translated into Chinese and involved themselves in sessions of serious Marxist studies.[20]

16 *Mei-chou p'ing-lun*, 22 (18 May 1919) 22 in his *Hsuan-chi*, 214.
17 *Ssu-hsiang-shih tzu-liao*, 1906 and 1201.
18 *Ibid.* (15 Oct. 1918) 1207; *Hsin ch'ing-nien*, 6 (15 Feb. 1919) 2; Ch'en, *Wen-ts'un*, 4 (1 Sept. 1920) 224.
19 *Wu-ssu ch'i-k'an*, 1. 193–4, and 198.
20 Ho Ch'ang-kung, *Ch'in-kung chien-hsueh sheng-huo hui-i* (Memoirs of the work-study programme), 61 and *Hsin-min hsueh-hui hui-yuan t'ung-hsin-chi*, in *Wu-ssu ch'i-k'an*, 1. 154.

It was through the influence of one of these students, Ts'ai Ho-sen, that Mao Tse-tung exchanged his earlier admiration for Kropotkin for that of Marx.[21] The emotional defiance in all these cases of personal transformation was apparent. Without it they would not have been fervent revolutionaries, as they were to be.

But why Marxism? What did the radicals know about it before taking the plunge into organized political action? Prior to the founding of the CCP several translations of the *Communist manifesto* were available; there were also essays introducing historical materialism in the *New Youth* and the supplement of the *Morning Post* (by Kawakami Hajime). Kautsky's *Karl Marx's ökonomische Lehren* received two translations, one by the Kuomintang (KMT) theorist, Tai Chi-t'ao, but *Das Kapital* itself was available in Chinese only in drastically abridged forms. Also in Chinese were *Wages, labour and capital; Critique of the Gotha programme; Civil war in France; On the Jewish question; The holy family; The poverty of philosophy; A contribution to the critique of political economy;* and *Socialism: utopian and scientific*. In the library of Peking University there was a considerable collection of communist literature in English, German, French and Japanese which Li Ta-chao used in the discussions with his group of socialist youths. Apart from these, the October Revolution naturally drew the attention of the radicals to Russia under the Bolshevik leaders. Lenin's *State and revolution, Imperialism: the highest stage of capitalism*, and *Left-wing communism: an infantile disorder*; and Trotsky's *Communism and terrorism* and *Bolshevism and world peace* were translated into Chinese. The Chinese version of Lenin's report on the constitution of the Communist Party of the Soviet Union at the party's Eighth Congress in December 1919 found space in the *New Youth* (volume 8, numbers 3 and 4) in two instalments – 'National self-determination' and 'The economy in the period of transition'. The work of introducing Marxism-Leninism gained momentum with the founding of the monthly, *Kung-ch'an-tang* (The communist party), in Shanghai in November 1920 while various aspects of the party, state and society of Russia, together with Russia's new arts and literature were reported in several radical periodicals.[22] Not satisfied with the translated reports on the new Russia, Chinese either went to Russia for first-hand observation or sent correspondents to reside in Moscow. Among them was Ch'ü Ch'iu-pai whose motive was 'to search for the key to China's

---

21 Takeuchi edn, 1. 58 and *Hsin-min hsueh-hui hui-yuan t'ung-hsin-chi,* 3 quoted in the *Hu-nan li-shih tzu-liao* (Historical materials of Hunan), 4 (1959) 80.

22 The best sources on this subject are *Wu-ssu ch'i-k'an,* vols. 1 and 3; Chang Ching-lu, *Chung-kuo chin-tai ch'u-pan shih-liao* (Historical materials on modern Chinese publications), pt 1, 68 and 75; an advertisement in *Hsin ch'ing-nien,* 9 (1 Sept. 1921) 5; and *Chin-tai-shih tzu-liao* (Materials of modern history), 2 (1955) 161–73.

reconstruction'.[23] Through their reportage, abstract theories turned into concrete reality. In the interior of the country, these publications were distributed by such bookshops as the Mass Welfare (Li-ch'ün shu-she) in Wuch'ang founded by Yun Tai-ying and the Culture Bookshop (Wen-hua shu-she) in Changsha founded by Mao Tse-tung with its branches in several counties in Hunan, and also by *Hsin Shu-pao* (New Szechwan daily) in Chungking edited by Hsiao Ch'u-nü.[24]

With these publications, the main analytical tools of Marxism-Leninism – dialectical materialism, class struggle, surplus value, and so forth – were within the grasp of the early converts. The ugly aspects of their country, the suffering of the working people, were seen as the outcome of imperialist, capitalist and landlord exploitation, and their monopoly of state power. In this perspective Chinese society was viewed as being composed of the oppressors and the oppressed classes and its nature was semi-colonial and semi-feudal, a far cry from the proud empire of only a couple of decades before. Admittedly its transformation required a revolution, but why a revolution guided by Marxism-Leninism and led by a communist party when it had neither a developed bourgeoisie nor a massive proletariat? Li Ta-chao's answer to this question in an editorial of the *Weekly Review* on 4 May 1919 was a simple one – since the Chinese bourgeoisie was underdeveloped, the Chinese revolution could be easier than those in Russia, Germany, Austria and Hungary. On the eve of the founding of the CCP, he argued that in a world of rising labour movements, it would be theoretically as well as practically untenable for China to develop her own capitalism. 'Let us look at China's position among the nations. While the others have already advanced from free competition to socialist collective society, we are about to make our own start, meaning to follow in the footsteps of the others. . . . Under these circumstances, if we wish to adapt ourselves and co-exist with the others, we must cut short the process by leaping to a socialist economy in order to ensure a measure of success.'[25] Ch'en Tu-hsiu subscribed to this leap-frog theory, also on practical grounds, although unlike Trotsky he did not develop a strategy of permanent revolution. In his view, an embryonic capitalism was no less developed in China in 1920 than it had been in Germany in 1848 or Russia in 1917. Since Russia had successfully

23 *Wu-ssu ch'i-k'an*, 1. 135–6.
24 *She-hui hsin-wen* (The social mercury), 1. 8 (25 Oct. 1932) 176–8; Lo-fu (Chang Wen-t'ien), *Ch'ing-nien hsueh-hsi wen-t'i* (Problems of young people's study), 95–107; and Takeuchi edn, 1. 71–3.
25 *Shou-ch'ang wen-chi* (Collected essays of Li Ta-chao), Shanghai, 1952 (20 March 1921), p. 189.

made the jump, why not China?[26] The leap-frog theory may not be strict-ly speaking dialectical; to Ch'en, Li and their followers like Chou Fu-hai, Ch'ü Ch'iu-pai and Ts'ai Ho-sen, socialism represented all that was wor-thy. It was a society without class antagonism, affording opportunity for all men to develop themselves to the limits of their abilities.[27] As Ch'ü Ch'iu-pai put it before his journey to Moscow, what he and his fellow sponsors of the magazine, *Hsin she-hui* (New society), wanted to bring about was a democratic new society which was free, equal, without class distinction, without the threat of war.[28] The prospect of a long and dreary 'capitalist stage' was too repulsive for them to contemplate. At this stage of the understanding of Marxism in China, Lenin's theses on the agrarian and national and colonial questions presented before and at the Second Congress of the Communist International (CI) in July 1920 probably remained unknown to the early Chinese Marxists. For that they had to depend on their conversations with the representatives of the CI, prin-cipally Sneevliet (Maring) and Voitinsky.

FOUNDATION OF THE PARTY

China's fascination with Russia was reciprocated by the Bolsheviks' interest in China – due to the long common frontiers, the Chinese com-munities in Russia (not to mention that Chinese had fought for the revolu-tion in the civil war), the Russian position in China, and the ideological commitment to promote the world revolution. A Chinese state founded on the same principles as those of the communist state in Russia would serve both national and revolutionary purposes.

The Boxer uprising and Russia's role in it drew Lenin's attention to China, but it was the Chinese and other Asian revolutions that made him realize the new awakening of Asian nations[29] and condemn the savagery of the Europeans in Asia in his article, 'Backward Europe and advanced Asia', published in *Pravda* on 18 May 1913. His theory on imperialism as the highest, also the last, stage of capitalism was not hammered into a global revolutionary strategy until the Second Congress of the CI in 1920.[30] Thus were forged the links between the class struggle in the West and the national struggle in the East. The foundation was laid for the strat-

---

26 *Hsin ch'ing-nien*, 8 (1 Nov. 1920) 3.
27 See Chou's article in *ibid.* 8 (1 Jan. 1921) 5 and Ts'ai's correspondence in the *Hsin-min hsueh-hui hui-yuan t'ung-hsin-chi*, quoted in the *Wu-ssu ch'i-k'an*, 1. 158–9. Also Ch'en's article in the *Hsin ch'ing-nien*, 1 Sept. 1920.
28 *Hsin she-hui* (New society), inaugural essay, 1 Nov. 1919.
29 *Pravda*, no. 103 (18 May 1913), *Lieh-ning Ssu-ta-lin lun Chung-kuo* (Lenin and Stalin on China), 20.
30 *Ibid.* 43–63; H. d'Encausse and S.R. Schram eds. *Marxism and Asia: an introduction*, 153–69.

egy of a two-phased revolution, which would move from the bourgeois-democratic stage to the socialist stage. This necessitated an alliance between the incipient communist movement and the bourgeoisie in colonial and semi-colonial countries, and pointed to the possibility of forming peasants' soviets at an appropriate moment in such countries. Lenin ascribed a leadership role to the Western proletariat over the backward masses of the East, a thesis that bestowed authority on the CI to instruct and guide the inexperienced oriental revolutions.

Such then was the background for sending Voitinsky and Maring to China. In the six or seven months of his sojourn in China, Voitinsky helped impress upon the Chinese radicals – a motley group of people of various socialist persuasions – the need for a party, along the Leninist organization line as embodied in *What is to be done?* The scattered nuclei of socialist studies and the loosely structured Socialist Youth Corps established by Ch'en Tu-hsiu in August 1920 were tightened up to lay the foundation of the CCP, which came into being late in 1920 and was formally constituted at the First Congress in early July 1921. This was a meeting of a dozen or so young men in their twenties. Beginning in a girls' school in the French concession (empty in the summer), the members feared police surveillance and adjourned by train to continue their discussion in a pleasure boat on a lake. The details are murky and differ according to different witnesses.

According to Ch'en Kung-po, a participant of the First Congress, the first constitution of the CCP defined the tasks of the party as organizing and educating the working masses to carry on class struggle and socialist revolution and ultimately realize the proletarian dictatorship. Although it did not spell out the principle of democratic centralism, the party was to have a systematic, pure and secret organization from the cells to the centre so that it could lead the masses of workers, peasants and soldiers to the fulfilment of its revolutionary tasks. Implicitly assuming that the party must represent the interest of a class, the CCP adopted a hostile, uncooperative attitude towards other existing parties in China, including the KMT. However, to the CI, the CCP was to send monthly reports and to keep in close contact with it. By these stipulations, the CCP became, instead of merely a study group, a revolutionary party right from its inauguration, much to the chagrin of some of its founder members who were to leave the party for this reason. The centre consisted of a triumvirate – Ch'en Tu-hsiu was the secretary, Chang Kuo-t'ao headed the Orgburo, and Li Ta led the Agitburo.[31]

31 Ch'en Kung-po, *The communist movement in China: an essay written in 1924*, 79–82, 102–105; C. Martin Wilbur and Julie Lien-ying How eds. *Documents on communism, nationalism, and*

The election of Ch'en *in absentia* to the secretaryship and his continued dominance of the centre till his resignation on 15 July 1927 was a matter of great importance to the growth of this young party. Of the two highly admired Marxist pioneers – Li Ta-chao and Ch'en Tu-hsiu – why was Ch'en preferred to Li, who acquired merely the position of an alternate member of the centre? Li was giving lectures in Szechwan whereas Ch'en was working to reform the educational system of Kwangtung. There was little to choose between their intellectual standing, social prestige and contribution to the spread of Marxism. Practical considerations may have decided the issue. Since his resignation from Peking University, Ch'en was without a regular job, and was thus able to devote more time to editing a radical periodical, for example, *Kung-ch'an-tang*, running a Russian language school in Shanghai, and agitating among Shanghai workers.[32] His practical political experience suggested that he might be the right man for day-to-day organization work.[33] The choice was by no means easy, for Ch'en was noted for his strong personality, as Chou Fo-hai, another participant of the First Congress remarked: '[Ch'en Tu-hsiu] Chung-fu was a tough man.'[34] He also had an antipathy towards militarism and an aversion to other political parties. These personal attributes were at odds with the CI's China policy.

At the Second Congress (at Hangchow in May 1922) the characteristic of the party as the vanguard of the proletariat in its revolutionary struggle was reaffirmed. In theory at least, the principle of democratic centralism was enshrined in the second constitution as the party adopted a three-tier system of local, regional and central executive committees with the cells (*hsiao-tsu*), whose monthly (or weekly) meetings were compulsory for all members, lying at the basic level. That the representatives at the national congress were to be appointed by the central executive committee, instead of being elected, ensured that power would be in the hands of the leaders. This centralization was strengthened by the most distinctive feature of the new constitution, a full chapter on discipline, which required the local and regional committees to obey the policy decisions of the cen-

---

Soviet advisers in China, 1918–1927, 100–9; Kuo Hua-lun (Warren Kuo), *Chung-kung shih-lun* (Analytical history of the CCP; hereafter Analytical history), 1. 26–7, 31; Chang Kuo-t'ao, 'Wo-ti hui-i' (My recollections), in *Ming-pao yueh-k'an* (Ming Pao monthly; hereafter *Ming-pao*), 6. 6; or see in English Chang Kuo-t'ao, *The rise of the Chinese Communist Party*, 1. 136–52.

32 Richard C. Kagan, 'Ch'en Tu-hsiu's unfinished autobiography', *CQ*, 50. 295–314; Chan, 'Development', 45; Schwartz, *Chinese communism*, 10ff.

33 Meisner, *Li Ta-chao*, 204–5, for instance, points out that Li's call to youth to work in the countryside had nothing to say on organization.

34 Warren Kuo, *Analytical history*, 1. 95.

tre. Disobedience could be punished by either the local or the central committees.[35]

As the party grew in size to some 20,000 after the May Thirtieth movement in 1925, the structure of the centre was augmented by the addition of women's, labour, peasant and military affairs departments.[36] At the Fifth Congress in April-May 1927 the central executive committee was enlarged from its original three members to 29, too big to act efficiently and react swiftly in the tense and rapidly changing situation of 1927. Probably because of this, the political bureau (Politburo) was instituted.

Being an apparatus of class struggle to fulfil the long- and short-term goals of the class it represented, the party's political line and organization line, and to a lesser extent its political style too, could not be incompatible with each other without causing serious internal difficulties. Under Ch'en Tu-hsiu, the party's goals in 1923-27 – the elimination of imperialist and 'feudal' control of China – impelled the party to strengthen its power base among the proletariat, peasantry and soldiery, together with its petty bourgeois mass organizations of women and youth, in a time sequence determined by the needs of circumstance. But the party had to retain its centralism; otherwise it would sooner or later find itself impotent vis-à-vis the reactionaries. Although history records little of party life under Ch'en's leadership, what few pieces of information there are depict a patriarch presiding over a loosely organized party with a more smoothly functioning channel of communication from the top down than from the bottom up. At the top and in the middle echelons, the CCP depended more on personal ties with Ch'en and Li Ta-chao, in most cases the ties between a master and his disciples, than on impersonal discipline. In fact, whenever these ties were weakened by other considerations, the members concerned showed a tendency to leave the organization.[37] Li Ta-chao and the northern branch of the party had scarcely any recorded contact with the centre in Shanghai, being more or less independent. Even such a seminally important action as the overrunning of

35 Full text of the second constitution in Ch'en Kung-po, *The communist movement in China*, 131–5; translated back into Chinese in Wang Chien-min, *Chung-kuo Kung-ch'an-tang shih kao* (A draft history of the CCP), 1. 52–5; Wilbur and How, *Documents*, 104–9.

36 James Pinckney Harrison, *The long march to power: a history of the Chinese Communist Party, 1921–72*, 67–8. Chang Kuo-t'ao lists slightly differently the following structural changes: the centre after the Fourth Congress consisted of a secretariat, departments of organization and propaganda, and the editor of the weekly, *Guide*; a labour department came into being after the May 30th movement and the peasant department in the spring of 1926. *Ming-pao*, 13. 89.

37 Ch'en Kung-po, *Han-feng chi* (Cold wind), 226; Ch'i-wu lao-jen, 'Chung-kuo Kung-ch'an-tang ch'eng-li ch'ien-hou ti chien-wen' (My impressions before and after the founding of the CCP), *Hsin-kuan-ch'a* (New observer), no. 13 (1 July 1957); Thomas C. Kuo, *Ch'en Tu-hsiu (1879–1942) and the Chinese communist movement*, 255.

the British Settlement in Hankow at the beginning of 1927 was neither planned nor directed by the centre.[38] Only four months before that an enlarged conference of the central executive committee expressed its grave concern over the organizational deficiencies of the much expanded party. The leadership demonstrated a bureaucratic tendency while some comrades even committed embezzlement and corruption.[39]

The party wanted to see at the basic level, among the cells, the growth of a new philosophy of life which was to be collectivistic instead of individualistic in style, objective instead of subjective in the members' outlook, and absolutely confident instead of being sceptical about the party. In practice, the cells dealt mostly with practical work at the expense of theoretical training.[40] Life at that level remained in many instances unorganized and easygoing. Ch'en's views on a rigorous party organization seem to have been more akin to those of Rosa Luxemburg than to Lenin's. For instance, according to available documents, nowhere under Ch'en's secretaryship was the practice of criticism and self-criticism mentioned.[41] The major policy decisions were taken by the regularly convened congresses and executive committee plenums while Ch'en and his comrades in the secretariat carried out the daily work of the centre. The conference held on 7 August 1927 after Ch'en's resignation, criticized his leadership-style as being 'patriarchal' and 'peremptory' and his organization line as being 'undemocratic'. This represented the view of a new generation of Moscow-trained leaders whose experience in party life, particularly with respect to criticism and self-criticism, had been vastly different.

TENSION IN THE FIRST UNITED FRONT

The most important single political problem for the CCP as led by Ch'en Tu-hsiu was its relationship with the KMT as led by Sun Yat-sen. The complexity of the problem was such that the CCP had no wish initially to become enmeshed. At its First Congress its attitude to the other parties of China was either hostile, as Ch'en Kung-po reported, or supportive of

---

38 Meisner, Li Ta-chao, 119; 'Chung-kung "pa-ch'i" hui-i kao ch'üan-tang tang-yuan shu,' (Letter from the August 7th conference to all the members of the party), Hung-se wen-hsien (Red documents), 108.
39 Full text of the resolutions of this plenum, 12–18 July 1926, is in Warren Kuo, Analytical history, 1. 224–30 and trans. in Wilbur and How, Documents, 271–81, 288–317, see 276.
40 Wilbur and How, Documents, 95, 106 and 137. The party life in a cell contrasted sharply with the practice of criticism and self-criticism among the members of the CCP in Moscow. The return of the Moscow-trained CCP members may have been responsible for the acute criticism of Ch'en's organization line in 1926 and later.
41 Harrison, The long march, 126.

the KMT's forward-looking policies, but in a non-party collaboration, as Ch'en T'an-ch'iu recalled.[42] It must be remembered that Ch'en Tu-hsiu was then working with the Kwangtung warlord, Ch'en Chiung-ming, while Li Ta-chao contemplated a parley with the northern warlord, Wu P'ei-fu – both Sun Yat-sen's enemies.[43] By the time of the Second Congress of the CCP, however, the Ch'en Chiung-ming episode had ended and Wu P'ei-fu was severely censured by Maring and by the party's statement on current affairs. The statement concluded with the invitation to the KMT and other democratic and socialist bodies to join in forming 'a democratic united front' for the liberation of China from the two-fold oppression of imperialism and the warlords.[44]

This overriding goal of the united front was beyond question; what committed the CCP to subsequent doctrinal and organizational difficulties was the 'bloc within' policy – by which the individual members of the CCP joined the KMT while preserving the independence of the party structure of the CCP – adopted in June 1923.[45] In the first place, the strategy of cooperation with the Chinese bourgeoisie contradicted the party's ideological commitment to eradicate it; on the other hand, the corporate action of party members is part of the very essence of the Leninist conception of a communist party.[46] The premise that a united front must precede the struggle for power seemed validated by the numerical weakness of the CCP, but it sowed the seeds for the eventual split of the united front when the national revolution appeared to be winning and the weaker ally could be jettisoned by the stronger. The alliance had to be, therefore, a temporary one, for the transition from one phase of the revolution to the other was unlikely to be peaceful. Following Lenin's *Two tactics*, Ch'ü Ch'iu-pai's significant article, 'From democracy to socialism',[47] seems to have suggested this precisely. But the CI was more sanguine, seeking to control and transform the KMT from within.[48]

The KMT did change through accepting the two-fold goal of anti-

---

42 North, *Moscow and Chinese communists,* 59. See Chen Pan-tsu (Ch'en T'an-ch'iu), 'Reminiscences of the First Congress of the Communist Party of China', *Communist International,* American edn 14. 10 (Oct. 1936) 1361–6; British edn 13. 9 (Sept.–Oct. 1936) 593–6.

43 The *Hua-tzu jih-pao* (The Chinese mail) carried many reports on Ch'en Tu-hsiu's activities in Canton since March 1921, especially on 10 Sept. 1921; Warren Kuo, *Analytical history,* 1. 31.

44 *Hung-se wen-hsien,* 28 and 34. Scholars generally agree that the idea of a united front came from Moscow and the CCP was cajoled into accepting it. For an opposing view, see H.R. Isaacs's interview with H. Sneevliet in 'Documents on the Comintern and the Chinese Revolution', *CQ,* 45 (Jan.–Mar. 1971).

45 Brandt, *et al. A documentary history of Chinese communism,* 68.

46 Schwartz, *Chinese communism,* 52.

47 *Hsin ch'ing-nien,* 2 (20 Dec. 1923) 79–102, signed Ch'ü Wei-t'o.

48 Schwartz, *Chinese communism,* 52; C. Martin Wilbur, *Sun Yat-sen, frustrated patriot,* 148–50.

imperialism and anti-feudalism as enunciated in its manifesto of 1924 and through its reorganization to don a Leninist mantle.[49] After the inauguration of the united front, the CCP sought to influence the KMT by introducing its members into the mass movement departments of the KMT centre and into the Whampoa Military Academy. The fact that KMT members showed a greater interest in the departments traditionally regarded as prestigious and substantive, for example, finance and foreign affairs, instead of organization, propaganda, labour, or peasants, indicated an unchanged KMT view of party organization and revolution. The conservatives struggled for positions in the government or the generalissimo's headquarters, where there were power and money. Meanwhile the CCP official organs, *Hsiang-tao chou-pao* (Guide weekly) *Hsin ch'ing-nien* and *Ch'ien-feng* (Vanguard) never ceased to criticize the organizational deficiencies and compromising tendencies of the KMT. These efforts, together with Russian aid and the presence of Russian advisers, contributed to the emergence of a left wing in the KMT, thus gradually splitting the party after the death of its founder, Sun Yat-sen, in the spring of 1925 (see chapter 11).[50] With the KMT party structure falling into the hands of the left while the government remained in the grasp of the right, Borodin, Stalin's envoy who was the political adviser to the KMT, hoped for the formation of a central faction to unite and dominate the party.[51]

The schism within the KMT caused the CCP to reformulate its theory of the united front, from which the right-wing KMT, characterized by Ch'en Tu-hsiu as 'counter-revolutionary',[52] had departed while the central faction kept its inscrutability and the KMT left wing had 'revolutionary tendencies but [was] prone to compromise'. Ch'en, consequently, switched from his earlier position that only the bourgeoisie had the ability to lead the bourgeois democratic revolution to a position that only the proletariat could assume the hegemony. In Moscow at about the same time, Stalin presented his view that the KMT was in fact a bloc of four classes – workers, peasants, urban petty bourgeoisie and grande (national) bourgeoisie;[53] hence theoretically it was possible for the CCP to remain in it so as to preserve the 'bloc within' alliance and to work for the transformation of the KMT.

In more pragmatic terms, the CCP reaped the benefit of the KMT's

---

49 The KMT Department of Organization, *Ti-i-tz'u ch'üan-kuo ta-hui hsuan-yen* (Manifesto of the First National Congress), n.p. Aug. 1927. See also Wilbur, *ibid.* 172–4.
50 Jerome Ch'en, 'The left-wing Kuomintang – a definition', *Bulletin of the School of Oriental and African Studies*, 25. 3 (1962).
51 Harrison, *The long march*, 58.
52 *Hsiang-tao chou-pao* (The guide weekly), 101 (7 Nov. 1925) 844–5.
53 d'Encausse and Schram, *Marxism*, 228.

banner of legitimacy for propagandizing and organizing the masses,[54] scoring spectacular successes in the May Thirtieth movement of 1925 and its subsequent boycott of the Canton-Hong Kong trade in 1925–6 and the rendition of the British settlements in Hankow and Kiukiang in January 1927. These successes were attributable to the party's work among urban labour.[55] Towards the end of the first united front, the party could perhaps influence some three million factory, mining and railway workers. Compared with a mere 385,000 in 1920,[56] this phenomenal increase was due to the measures for the expansion of labour-union work adopted by the party at its Fourth Congress in January 1925 at Canton and to the May Thirtieth movement itself. Industrial disputes increased in frequency – from 348 in 1925 to 435 in 1926, though mostly for economic causes.[57] During the Northern Expedition (see below, page 589) workers in Hunan helped deliver army supplies while they disrupted the railway system under the control of the northern armies,[58] and their comrades in the Hanyang Arsenal went on strike to interrupt the production of munitions for Wu P'ei-fu's troops.[59] Rapid expansion may have resulted in fragile union organizations. In Canton both the leadership and the discipline of the unions were disappointing as the unions themselves were bitterly divided along communist and anti-communist lines.[60] In Wuhan a then prominent leader of the union movement, Liu Shao-ch'i, admitted the feeble mass base, disunited organization, and vague political consciousness of the unions.[61]

Without disavowing the orthodox Marxist stance on the peasantry, the Second Congress of the CI drew the attention of Asian revolutionaries to the agrarian problems in their home countries. At its Fourth Congress in 1922, the CI exhorted emphatically:

54 Jerome Ch'en, *Mao and the Chinese revolution*, 119; Harrison, *The long march*, 50.
55 *Ti-i-tz'u kuo-nei ko-ming chan-cheng shih-ch'i ti kung-jen yun-tung* (The labour movement during the first revolutionary war period; hereafter *Kung-jen*), ed. Chung-kuo hsien-tai-shih tzu-liao ts'ung-k'an (Peking, 1954), 546–9.
56 Ta Chen, 'Labour unrest in China', *Monthly labour review*, 6 (Dec. 1920) 23.
57 Harold R. Isaacs, *The tragedy of the Chinese revolution*, 2nd rev. edn, 123; *Hsiang-tao chou-pao*, no. 159 (23 June 1926); no. 167 (15 Aug. 1926); and no. 168 (22 Aug. 1926).
58 *Kung-jen*, 319–28
59 The *Min-kuo jih-pao* (National daily), Canton, 21–25 Sept. 1926 in Hua Kang, *Chung-kuo min-tsu chieh-fang yun-tung-shih* (A history of the Chinese national liberation movement), Shanghai, 1947, 2. B149.
60 *Lao-tung chou-pao* (Labour weekly), nos. 5–8 (May and June 1923) quoted in Li Jui, *Mao Tse-tung t'ung-chih ti ch'u-ch'i ko-ming huo-tung* (Comrade Mao Tse-tung's early revolutionary activities), 172, f.n. 12; *The Times*, 1 Dec. 1926; Tsou Lu, *Hui-ku-lu* (Reminiscences), Shanghai, 1943, 1. 166.
61 See the report at the First Congress of the Hupei General Labour Union, Jan. 1927, in *Kung-jen*, 407–8 and 413.

The revolutionary movement in the backward countries of the East cannot be successful unless it relies on the action of the broad peasant masses. Therefore the revolutionary parties of all oriental countries must formulate a clear agrarian programme, putting forward the demand for the complete abolition of the feudal system and survivals of it in the form of large landownership and tax farming.[62]

The sixth CI plenum (February-March 1926) and the seventh too (November-December 1926) made the same appeal.[63] The CCP leaders, prominently Ch'en Tu-hsiu and Chang Kuo-t'ao, tended to underestimate the peasants' interest in political issues and capacity for organized action.[64] The Fourth Congress of the CCP in 1925 had shown only a marginal interest in agrarian revolution. This is, however, not to deny that some individual members of the party devoted themselves to rural work of considerable importance later: Shen Hsuan-lu's peasant association in Hsiao-shan, Chekiang, which fought for rent reduction; and P'eng P'ai's peasant associations in Hai-feng and Lu-feng which began in 1921, and had a membership of over 100,000 in 1923. Later, under KMT auspices but with CCP leadership, the movement spread to the whole province of Kwangtung involving some 700,000 people. In a less systematic manner, Yun Tai-ying, the Youth Corps leader, advised members of the corps to go and work in the countryside.[65] Because of its enormous size and Mao's role in it the Hunan peasant movement was *sui generis*. It began in 1923 and received a strong boost when the province was captured by the KMT army in 1926. According to Mao, the association there had a membership of two million at the beginning of 1927.[66] When the KMT armies reached Hupei the peasant movement flared up there too. By May 1927 it claimed 2.5 million members, while Kiangsi was said to have 83,000 in its peasant associations.[67] The organized peasants sought to destroy or weaken the rule of 'local bullies and bad gentry', attack irrational

62 Jane Degras, *The Communist International 1919–1943: documents*, 1. 387.
63 *Ibid.* 2. 279; *Hung-se wen-hsien*, 254–5.
64 Ch'en Tu-hsiu in *Hsin ch'ing-nien*, 12. 4 (1924); Chang Kuo-t'ao in *Hsiang-tao chou-pao*, no. 12 (Dec. 1922).
65 *Hsin ch'ing-nien*, 9. 4 (1 Aug. 1921); 9. 5 (1 Sept. 1921); 10. 6 (1 July 1922). See also Nym Wales, *Red dust*, 199–200; *Ti-i-tz'u kuo-nei ko-ming chan-cheng shih-ch'i ti nung-min yun-tung* (The farmers movement in the first revolutionary civil war period; hereafter *Nung-min*), ed. Chung-kuo hsien-tai-shih tzu-liao ts'ung-k'an, Peking, 1953, 35–9. About P'eng P'ai's style of work see *Hung-ch'i p'iao-p'iao*, 5. 38–42. On P'eng and Hai-lu-feng see Etō Shinkichi, 'Hai-lu-feng – the first Chinese soviet government', *CQ*, nos. 8 and 9 (1961); and particularly Roy Hofheinz, *The broken wave*. On Yun's work, see also *Chung-kuo ch'ing-nien* (The Chinese youth), no. 32, 24 May 1924.
66 Hu Hua, *Chung-kuo hsin-min-chu-chu-i ko-ming-shih ts'an-k'ao tzu-liao* (Historical material on the Chinese new democratic revolution), 63; Mao, *SW*, 1. 14. Li Jui, however, gives the figure of 5,180,000 in April 1927. See *Nung-min*, 288.
67 *Nung-min*, 391, 410 and 413.

customs and habits, and eliminate corruption.[68] In Hunan, they went beyond the reduction in rent and interest to raise the demand for land redistribution.[69] They also gave aid to the KMT troops by supplying military intelligence and acting as guides.[70]

By June 1927 the peasant department of the Wuhan KMT (see below, page 644) claimed the staggering figure of over nine million members in the peasant associations in six provinces.[71] Like the labour unions, their rapid growth also resulted in loose organization and discipline.[72] T'an P'ing-shan, who had been the communist head of the KMT peasant department, publicly conceded his failures in strengthening the peasant movement.[73] What was worse was the vagueness and uncertainty of the policy decisions above that influenced irresolute action below. As one leader put it:

What about ourselves? [We] were then in a quandary. On the one hand, we had to fight against the feudal forces of local bullies and bad gentry and the bourgeoisie; on the other, we had to cooperate with the KMT which represented them. We had to make friends and come to terms with the remnants of feudalism, landlords and capitalists. We had to prevent workers and peasants from solving their problems by themselves. We told them to wait for orders from the headquarters of the KMT. But the wait was as endless as that for the waters of the Yellow River to become clear.[74]

Indeed, Wang Ching-wei, the left-wing KMT leader, condemned the excesses of the peasant movement.[75] Stalin's assertion that the left KMT was essentially petty bourgeois proved to be only a mirage; the confiscation of land and the organization of peasants' self-defence forces pared the interests of the left-wing KMT to the quick and exposed the fundamental irreconcilibility of the 'bloc within' policy with a revolution from below.

The CCP did not have a land policy until the momentous Fifth Congress in April 1927. Immediately before that, Mao's draft resolution submitted to the KMT Land Committee meetings advocated both political

68 Mao's Hunan report in Takeuchi edn, 1. 209.
69 Nung-min, 289.
70 Hollington K. Tong, Chiang Tsung-t'ung chuan (A biography of President Chiang), Taipei, 1954, 1. 78–9; the Hua-ch'iao jih-pao (Overseas Chinese daily), Hong Kong, 7 Sept. 1926.
71 Nung-min, 18–9. An exaggerated picture of the peasant movement may have been due to the inclusion of nung-hui (the gentry-led agrarian societies) in the nung-min hsieh-hui (peasant-led peasant associations).
72 Mao, 'Ch'uan-kuo nung-hsieh tsu-chih ming-ling' (A recent decree of the National Peasant Association), 3 June 1927, Takeuchi edn, 2. 9.
73 Harrison, The long march, 113.
74 Liu Chih-hsun, 'Ma-jih shih-pien hui-i,' (Reminiscences of the Horse-day [21 May 1927] Incident), Pu-erh-sai-wei-k'e, no. 20 (30 May 1928).
75 Wang Ching-wei chi (Collected works of Wang Ching-wei), Shanghai, 1929, 3 (5 July 1927) 141.

confiscation of the land of 'local bullies and bad gentry', and warlords, and the economic confiscation of all land for rent.[76] The land resolution of the congress itself was much milder – confiscating only communal and landlords' land while excluding small landlords and revolutionary officers from this tribulation.[77] The congress did not insist upon collective ownership after confiscation, but deemed it advisable to disarm landlords' armed forces while helping peasants organize village self-defence forces to safeguard the fruit of land redistribution.[78] Under conditions of a military preponderance of warlords and landlords, it was doubtful that both confiscation and armament could be carried out as expected. The purchase of arms by peasant associations was forbidden by the Wuhan government of the KMT.[79] This had the same effect as disarming the workers' pickets in the cities. Without armed peasants, the agrarian movement in the countryside was exposed to merciless suppression, for example, the 'horse day' (21 May 1927) incident near Changsha. Later this was to affect the setting up of the first soviets during the Autumn Harvest Uprisings (see below, page 676–81).

As mentioned before, Ch'en Tu-hsiu was against militarism; this, however, does not mean that he was a pacifist. In an article in *Hsiangtao chou-pao* on 18 April 1923 he clarified his position, making it compatible with his Marxism, by outlining a revolution of armed people versus armed warlords, a perfectly Leninist vision of people's militia pitched against the regular troops of the reaction. What Ch'en failed to envisage was a politicized army that could fight and conquer. Soon after the Fourth Congress of the CCP, the Young Servicemen's Club, a communist front-organization, was founded among the Whampoa Academy cadets[80] and a little later, a rival body, the Sun Yat-senism Society came into being. With the establishment of the General Political Department in the KMT armies in September 1925, members of the CCP (for example, Li Fu-ch'un in the Second Army and Lin Tsu-han in the Sixth) devoted themselves to political work among the fighting forces.[81] But it was questionable whether these officers had power and influence comparable to their equivalents in the Russian Red Army. The CCP's weakness in military work became manifest when Chiang Kai-shek staged his coup on 20 March 1926 which ended, among other things, in the dissolution of both

76 Chiang Yung-ching, *Pao-lo-t'ing yü Wu-han cheng-ch'üan* (Borodin and the Wuhan regime), 289–90.
77 Warren Kuo, *Analytical history*, 1. 240; Etō Shinkichi, 'Hai-lu-Feng', *CQ*, 9. 162; Stuart R. Schram, *Political leaders in the twentieth century: Mao Tse-tung*, 98–9.
78 Warren Kuo, *Analytical history*, 1. 241.
79 *Nung-min*, 400–1.
80 Chiang Kai-shek, *Soviet Russia in China*, 35–6.
81 *She-hui hsin-wen*, 1. 14 (12 Nov. 1932) 308–9.

the left- and right-wing organizations among the Whampoa cadets. On that occasion, P'eng Shu-chih lamented the relaxation of the KMT's control over its own army,[82] which was symbolized by Wang Ching-wei's departure for France and Chiang Kai-shek's proposal to the second plenum of the KMT central executive committee to restrict communists from appointment to the army as political commissars. Finally, in June 1927, both the Political Department of the armies and the commissars were abolished by Chiang.[83]

Equally ineffective was the CCP's attempt to delay the Northern Expedition actually launched in July 1926. P'eng Shu-chih and Ch'en Tu-hsiu argued on political, economic, and even strategic grounds for its postponement, to no avail. Even Borodin's objection was overruled.[84] When the end of the united front came, however impressive were the figures of the CCP's mass work on paper they were evidently no match for the armed forces of Chiang and other military leaders in the field, as Wang Ching-wei bitterly complained. Without consolidated mass organizations, without armed forces, and without a sound economic base, the revolution from below buckled under the crumbling revolution from above. While the writing was already on the wall after Chiang's coup of March 1926, Stalin over a year later remained confident enough to use the emotional appeal of the simile of squeezing the lemon[85] of the right-wing KMT to persuade the CCP that its alliance with the KMT was still the best course to take. The Executive Committee of the CI gave the same advice on the ground that the left KMT was a coalition of the proletariat, peasantry and petty bourgeoisie. If the CCP 'does not play a leading role' in this simplified united front,[86] 'it will not fulfil its leadership functions in the country at large'. Therefore it would be wrong to withdraw from the alliance at once; it would also be wrong 'not to withdraw from it at all'.[87] The CI's exhortation at this critical moment was therefore to compromise with the Wuhan KMT while refraining from 'playing with insurrection'.

The CI's resolutions practically vetoed Ch'en Tu-hsiu's proposal at the Fifth Congress in April 1927, which he had put forward several times,

---

82 *Hsiang-tao chou-pao*, 167 (8 Aug. 1926) 20–1.

83 *Chiang wei-yuan-chang ch'üan-chi* (Complete works of Generalissimo Chiang), ed. Shen Feng-kang, 5. 12; *Hua-tzu jih-pao*, 13 June 1927.

84 *Hsiang-tao chou-pao*, no. 161 (7 July 1926) and no. 165 (28 July 1926); Louis Fischer, *The soviets in world affairs: a history of the relations between the Soviet Union and the rest of the world*, 2. 648.

85 Isaacs, *The tragedy of the Chinese revolution*, 162.

86 Harrison's terminology, *The long march*, 96.

87 The ECCI's resolution on China at its eighth plenum, May 1927, in *Hung-se wen-hsien*, 277. English translation in Xenia Joukoff Eudin and Robert C. North, *Soviet Russia and the East, 1920–1927: a documentary survey*, 369–76.

to turn the alliance into a 'bloc without' one.[88] What alternatives were there, now that Chiang had begun his deadly suppression of the Communists in Shanghai and Nanking in the spring of 1927? At the congress, there was only confusion, compounded by contradictory policy proposals. Unwilling to leave the united front and yet too weak to carry the ally with it, the CCP could only watch the situation deteriorate. That was right opportunism in the communist or any other parlance.

Once the party committed itself to the strategy of a violent revolution, it had to face the possibility of violent persecution either in 1922 or in 1927. The naked truth was that in a China dismembered by warlords, political power could come only from the barrel of a gun. The difference that the first united front had made was that instead of possessing only about 130 members as in 1922, the CCP had grown by mid 1927 to be a mass party of nearly 60,000 which in spite of its subsequent losses could withstand the KMT's ruthless but often inefficient persecution. It could have done worse had it chosen to fight alone without the alliance with the KMT in 1922 and 1923; it might have done better had it girded itself sooner for the eventual break. In any case, the situation in July and August 1927 was inevitable – the CCP had to have an army, a territory and a government. In other words, it had to make a state within the state.

88 Degras, *International Documents*, 2. 276–77. See Ch'en Tu-hsiu's 'A Letter to all comrades of the Party,' trans. in *Chinese Studies in History* 2. 3 (Spring 1970) 224–50. The position taken by the CCP leaders at this Congress is far from clear. A monographic study of this Congress is obviously overdue.

CHAPTER 11

THE NATIONALIST REVOLUTION: FROM CANTON TO NANKING, 1923–28

CREATING A REVOLUTIONARY MOVEMENT

The Nationalist Revolution of the 1920s, one of the most interesting episodes in modern Chinese history, succeeded because of a remarkable mobilization of human energy and material resources in the service of patriotic and revolutionary goals. An organizational phase lasted from late 1923 until mid 1926 during which time a group of determined Chinese, starting with very little, created a revolutionary movement aimed at uniting the country, overcoming foreign privilege, and reforming a variety of social inequities. They were advised and aided by a group of Russian experts, who provided revolutionary doctrine, organizational know-how, money, military training and weapons. Next came the conquest phase, lasting until mid 1928, when armies originally based in the extreme south fought their way to Peking in the north. This campaign combined military prowess, effective propaganda, and subversive activity in the enemy's rear. There was also a great tragedy. Part way through the campaign the leadership split over the issue of violent social revolution – inter-class warfare within the revolutionary camp – during the course of a national unification war. In the eight months of internecine struggles thousands of revolutionaries lost their lives. Thereafter the civil war between the more radical and more conservative Chinese nationalists never really ceased.

China's political and social environment provided the revolutionary potential, but this potential had to be converted into a revolutionary situation. The cradle of the revolution was Canton, one of the largest, richest and most progressive Chinese cities, set in a fertile and densely populated delta where three important rivers merge. The chief inspirer of the national revolution was the indomitable Sun Yat-sen. He had devoted most of his adult life to advocating constitutional republicanism and opposing regimes in Peking which obstructed his ideal. Twice he had set up governments in Canton, once in 1917 in opposition to the Peking government dominated by Tuan Ch'i-jui and the Anfu Clique, and again late in 1920 in opposition to the government dominated by the Chihli Clique. During the second regime he arranged for a rump parliament to elect him 'Extraordinary President' of what he proclaimed to be the Chinese Republic. In the spring of 1922, in alliance with several military factions, he attempted a campaign against the Peking government, but Wu P'ei-fu defeated his major ally, Chang Tso-lin, while troops of his own theoretical subordinate, Ch'en Chiung-ming, drove Dr Sun from his presidential residence in Canton on the night of 15/16 June. By mid August 1922 he was back in Shanghai scheming to acquire the presidency in Peking by political means and to recover his base in the south by military force.

Sun Yat-sen's weak position in 1923

Dr Sun was unsuccessful in the first aim, but by 15 January 1923 troops in his pay had driven Ch'en Chiung-ming from Canton, and he returned there in triumph on 21 February. He was then 56 years old, but in less than two years he would be struck down by cancer. In this brief period he launched the organizational phase of the Nationalist Revolution in the face of great initial difficulties.

The difficulties may be summarized as follows. Upon his return to Canton, Sun's hold on the southern base was precarious, for he lacked the substance of power. He was not really master of the armies which had captured the base for him nor did he control the purse strings of its government. His Nationalist Party, the Chung-kuo Kuo-min-tang, had only a few thousand members in China, was loosely organized, and had no well-devised strategy for achieving its reformist goals, which aroused little enthusiasm from the articulate public. The goals were stated in a Kuomintang manifesto on 1 January 1923, which gave some detail to Sun's famous Three People's Principles – nationalism, democracy and people's livelihood.[1] His problem was to create a dynamic revolutionary movement, to gain control over sources of substantial revenue, and to create a subservient and reliable military force that could protect and enlarge the southern base.

The military problem had two aspects, internal and external. A miscellany of essentially autonomous divisions, brigades and regiments had taken Canton when their commanders were bought over by Dr Sun's associates in Hong Kong. Those from Yunnan were headed by General Yang Hsi-min but there were several independent Yunnanese forces,

---

1 See Milton J. T. Shieh, *The Kuomintang: selected historical documents, 1894–1966*, 65–70.

including one led by Chu P'ei-te, one of Dr Sun's more loyal military followers. Generals Liu Chen-huan and Shen Hung-ying headed the Kwangsi units. There were also divisions and regiments of the politically-divided Kwangtung Army, and several local 'people's corps' which entered the fray at the last moment. On arrival in the delta the commanders of these units scrambled to establish lucrative bases in the cities and towns, seizing most of the revenue-producing agencies. The troops, which numbered some 35,000 (by a well-informed contemporary estimate), were poorly equipped and most of them badly trained. There was rivalry between them, and they faced other military forces associated with Ch'en Chiung-ming that were eager to take Canton. General Ch'en seemed to be in alliance with Dr Sun's foe, Wu P'ei-fu. To get Generalissimo Sun Yat-sen's armies into battle required large amounts of extra cash, most of which was extracted from the Canton population by the municipal government imposing extra tax levies that were collected by the efficient Canton police.

During the spring and summer of 1923 Sun's military supporters defended his base from attacks by General Shen Hung-ying, who had support from Wu P'ei-fu, as well as from armies backing Ch'en Chiung-ming. Through these wars the base area was extended west and north to the borders of Kwangtung, but Canton was still exposed to attack from Ch'en's adherents nearby on the east. By autumn Dr Sun had not been able to bring his forces under more than nominal control, and there was very little improvement in their quality. The 'guest armies' were virtually armies of occupation.[2]

Dr Sun's financial problems were serious. Essentially there were three sources of revenue – contributions, loans and taxes. In the autumn of 1922 his party had raised more than half a million dollars (Shanghai and Hong Kong currency) in gifts and loans from his Chinese supporters to finance the recapture of Canton. Now it was difficult to raise more. In the spring of 1923 he tried unsuccessfully to negotiate a six-million-dollar loan from Hong Kong merchants and a million from the Canton Chamber of Commerce. He also hoped for a large concessionary loan from British business interests, but his precarious military position made this impossible. In order to realize the tax potential of his base it was necessary to get the administrative apparatus under the control of his own appointees.

Sun's government was organized on three levels – the generalissimo's

---

2 This discussion and what follows in the next few paragraphs is based upon C. Martin Wilbur, 'Problems of starting a revolutionary base: Sun Yat-sen and Canton, 1923', in *Bulletin of the Institute of Modern History, Academia Sinica*, 4.2 (Dec. 1974) 665–727.

headquarters (set up like a national administration), the provincial government and the Canton municipal government, the last mentioned being the most substantial. Canton was a wealthy city. It had a relatively efficient government under Sun Fo, Dr Sun's 31-year-old son, who returned to the job as mayor near the end of February. The city also had a fine police force, and Dr Sun appointed an old associate, Wu T'ieh-ch'eng, as commissioner of public safety for Canton. Mayor Sun and his six Western-educated commissioners pushed forward Canton's modernization during the following months, and also made the city the chief source for military financing.

According to the official municipal report for 1923 the city provided the generalissimo's headquarters with more than six million dollars (Cantonese) for military rations, in addition to the city's operating expenses. By contrast provincial revenues declined by nearly nine million from the previous year because only parts of the province could be tapped by the Provincial Finance Office. Dr Sun was able to seize control of the local salt tax revenues, netting nearly three million from May through December 1923, although the foreign-managed salt gabelle was supposed to be a collecting agency for the Peking government to assure payment of a foreign debt contracted in 1913. The interested powers protested but did not prevent this 'misappropriation'; although when Dr Sun threatened at the end of the year to seize the most stable source of revenue, that collected by the Maritime Customs Service at Canton, they intervened by force to prevent it.

The picture is one of crisis finance, with Sun's government competing with the military to collect tax revenues, and both laying heavy burdens on the populace. Yet during the first eight months after Sun's return the southern government gradually increased its income, which was necessary for its survival, and extended its territorial base.

The Nationalist Party had a history of nearly three decades, counting as its antecedents revolutionary parties organized and headed by Sun Yat-sen. Central headquarters in Shanghai had five bureaus and a small staff engaged in fund-raising and publicity. Apparently in 1923 there were no active branches in other cities except Canton, though there were many lodges among Chinese communities overseas. Total membership was unknown because records of local branches in Kwangtung had been lost as a result of Ch'en Chiung-ming's revolt of June 1922. In any case, membership figures were deceptive because of Dr Sun's practice of enrolling entire organizations such as armies, unions and student organizations – or of claiming them as members.

Nevertheless, the party had a potential for national influence because of its experienced leaders and its reputation for crusading against the Manchus, opposing Yuan Shih-k'ai, denouncing foreign privilege, and advocating governmental reform. The leaders came from various strata of society. Many had a good classical education and some had been officials under the imperial regime. Some had degrees from universities in America and Europe, and many had studied in Japanese colleges and military schools. Now mostly of middle age, these leaders had formed student friendships abroad, and variously had conspired to overthrow governments, gathered and dispensed funds for revolution, smuggled arms, spread propaganda among troops, worked with underworld secret societies, participated in parliamentary struggles, established literary and political journals, taught in colleges, organized trade unions, commanded armies, governed provinces, and engaged in business ventures. They came from all regions of China and had their local ties, though most of them were from Kwangtung and the Yangtze valley provinces. They formed a network of relationships with the traditional and the more modern sectors of Chinese society.

The party needed to be galvanized into action. Apparently Dr Sun was too engrossed in financial and military problems to pay much attention to the Kuomintang, though he called upon the Shanghai office from time to time to execute diplomatic missions or propaganda campaigns, and doubtless to forward money. In October 1923 Sun turned his attention to revitalizing the party. Michael Borodin, the chief adviser sent to him by Soviet Russia, arrived in Canton on 6 October, and for the next seven weeks the two men regularly consulted on plans for party reorganization.

Background of Soviet interest in the Kuomintang

In the early 1920s Soviet Russia had national strategic interests in China as well as revolutionary ones. Russia and China shared a long border, and the Soviet government desired to establish diplomatic relations with the Peking government for the many advantages this would bring. An important Russian strategic objective was to acquire control over the Chinese Eastern Railway (formerly a Russian state enterprise), which traversed Manchuria and was a vital link in the Trans-Siberian Railway that joined the Russian maritime provinces with Central Siberia. Russia and China were rivals for dominance in Outer Mongolia, which China considered its own, but which was ruled by a Mongolian regime recently placed there by the Red Army. Russia's unwillingness to permit China to control this buffer area was the stumbling block which prevented three Russian missions from effecting formal inter-governmental relations with Peking. In September 1923 the deputy commissar for foreign affairs, Lev M. Karakhan, arrived in Peking as envoy plenipotentiary to try once more to open negotiations.

China fitted into Russia's world revolutionary strategy as a region which should be liberated from capitalist exploitation. In 1919 Lenin organized the Third, or Communist, International to be the general staff of world revolution with its headquarters in Moscow. At its Second Congress in 1920 he articulated a strategy for undermining the great capitalist states by driving a wedge between them and their colonies. The Comintern, as well as the communist parties in the dominant countries and in their colonies, should concentrate on this liberation struggle as a preliminary stage of the world revolution. Lenin foresaw that the rising bourgeoisie in the colonies must inevitably lead these liberation movements, and he argued that it was the duty of each nascent communist party in a colony to assist the bourgeoisie in the national liberation struggle. This was a united front strategy. However, the communist party must maintain its separate identity, grow in strength by organizing and training the proletariat and poor peasantry, and prepare for the second revolutionary stage – the struggle to overthrow the bourgeoisie and establish a socialist state. The Communist International elaborated this basic strategy and propagated it in such colonial regions as its emissaries could penetrate. China, though not a colony, was fitted into this scheme and the Comintern sent its agents there.

Soviet emissaries had a double task in China: to help create a communist movement, and to find that national revolutionary organization which Soviet Russia and the Comintern would assist in the liberation struggle. Ignorant about China, the Russian revolutionary leaders needed several years of exploration by scouts before they settled upon the Nationalist Party. (The origin and circumstances of the Chinese Communist Party are discussed in chapter 10.) Once it had been organized, Hendricus Sneevliet – a Dutch Comintern agent who used the pseudonym Maring – went beyond the united front strategy by inducing the Communist Party's members, much against their will, to enter the Kuomintang, since Sun Yat-sen would not agree to an alliance between the parties. The Comintern's Executive Committee (ECCI) approved this tactic as a way for the infant party to gain access to the proletariat in South China, but, more importantly, in the hope that communists could radicalize the Kuomintang and steer it into alliance with Russia. The Russian leaders planned to be at the helm of the revolution.

There was a five-year courtship between Sun Yat-sen and Soviet Russia. At various times in his revolutionary career Dr Sun solicited aid from all the leading powers. Shortly after the Bolshevik Revolution he sent out feelers for an alliance between his party and Lenin's. Later he conceived the hope that the new revolutionary state would help him militarily into the presidency at Peking. Lenin and Gregorii Chicherin, the commissar for foreign affairs, cultivated Sun through occasional correspondence. Three Comintern agents – Voitinsky, Sneevliet and Dalin – tried to persuade him of the need to reform his party. After his defeat by Ch'en Chiung-ming in June 1922 Dr Sun was more than ever eager for foreign assistance, and he began to pin great hopes on Soviet Russia. In the latter part of 1922 he corresponded with Adolf Joffe, Russia's diplomatic delegate in Peking. Joffe failed in his efforts to negotiate a treaty with the Chinese government and went to Shanghai where he had extensive discussions with Dr Sun in January 1923, just after troops in Sun's pay had recovered Canton. The inner details of their deliberations have never been disclosed, but soon thereafter the Soviet leadership made a definite decision to assist Dr Sun and the Kuomintang financially, and to send advisers to help the party's revitalization.[3] Borodin was the person selected to direct this work.

Borodin had very good credentials from the Comintern's point of view. Born on 9 July 1884 he had been a revolutionary since his youth in Latvia. Expelled from Russia in 1906 he spent 11 years in the United States. He then returned to his homeland in the summer of 1918 and plunged into revolutionary work once more. He became well known to Lenin and translated one of his major works. After the founding of the Communist International he became one of its emissaries, visiting Spain, Mexico and the United States for organizational work, and then being arrested and imprisoned in England where he had gone to help reorganize the British Communist Party. Soon after his return to Moscow in the spring of 1923 he was chosen for the China assignment. When he arrived in Canton he was 39 years old, and by all accounts a man of intelligence and magnetic personality.

Borodin's instructions have not been published, but probably he had familiarized himself with past Comintern resolutions regarding China. The ECCI had sent a directive to the Chinese Communist Party in May 1923 that spelled out its role in the national revolution and the terms under which it should cooperate with the Kuomintang. The main thrust of the directive was the necessity to broaden the revolution by aggressively preparing for agrarian revolt and the need to reform the Kuomintang to make it the leader of a democratic anti-imperialist and anti-feudal front.

3 Details of the moves of Dr Sun and Soviet leaders towards an alliance may be found in C. Martin Wilbur, *Sun Yat-sen: frustrated patriot*.

The 'basic demand' of the Kuomintang must be its unconditional support of the workers' movement in China. The Kuomintang should draw the broadest possible masses into the struggle against the northern militarists and foreign imperialism. The Communist Party must continuously influence the Kuomintang in favour of agrarian revolution, insisting on confiscation of land in favour of the poorest peasantry; and it must do whatever possible to prevent alliances between Sun Yat-sen and the militarists. It must demand the earliest possible convocation of a Kuomintang convention to focus upon creation of a broad national democratic front, and it must insist on the abrogation of treaties and agreements imposed upon China by the imperialist powers.[4] Borodin's objectives probably were similar; this is clearly evident in his early activities in Canton.

Rejuvenating the Kuomintang

Borodin met frequently with Sun Yat-sen to discuss Kuomintang problems and offer advice on the coming revolution. He also met with local communists to reassure them of his intention in the long run to work for the strengthening of the Communist Party.[5] On 25 October Dr Sun appointed a Provisional Executive Committee to draft a new party programme and constitution and to prepare for a national congress. He appointed Borodin its adviser. Borodin drafted a new constitution for the Kuomintang, modelling its structure on that of the Russian Communist Party/Bolshevik. His draft, which is similar to the one later adopted, described five levels of organization – national, provincial, county, district and sub-district. An annual National Congress of Representatives was to elect a Central Executive Committee (CEC) and a Central Supervisory Committee (CSC). Between congresses the CEC would run the party, appoint its chief officers, manage finances, and direct its organs and all lower executive committees. Kuomintang members were all to be under strict party discipline. Those having membership in other organizations such as labour unions, merchants associations, provincial assemblies or

4 Xenia Joukoff Eudin and Robert C. North, *Soviet Russia and the East, 1920–1927: a documentary survey*, 344–6. Jane Degras, *The Communist International, 1919–1943: documents selected and edited by Jane Degras*, 2. 25–6, extracts.

5 Borodin's reports on his early meetings are found in N. Mitarevsky, *World-wide Soviet plots, as disclosed by hitherto unpublished documents seized in the USSR embassy in Peking*, 130–8. This is a hostile source, but the documents prove genuine when tested by other historical evidence. The best scholarly account of Borodin's life and his work in China until Dr Sun's death is Lydia Holubnychy, *Michael Borodin and the Chinese revolution, 1923–1925*. A biography of Borodin covering his entire life is Dan N. Jacobs, *Borodin: Stalin's man in China*.

the national parliament were to organize themselves into 'party fractions' (*tang-t'uan*) and must always present a united position in the other body in order to steer it.

The Provisional Executive Committee met 28 times, drafted a ringing proclamation and a new party programme. It supervised the re-registration of party members; established a journal to publicize the intended reorganization and explain the party's revolutionary ideology; and set up a school to train members of district and sub-district executive committees. It set the agenda for the National Congress and supervised the selection of delegates from the provinces and major cities of China and from branches abroad.[6]

Sun Yat-sen's hold on Canton became precarious in November 1923, as forces under Ch'en Chiung-ming menaced the city. It was feared the generalissimo might be forced to flee. During this crisis Borodin urged a radical programme to mobilize mass support. He urged Sun and a group of Kuomintang leaders to have the party issue decrees promising land to the peasants through confiscation and distribution of landlord holdings, and promising labour an eight-hour day, a minimum wage and other rights. He argued that these promises would rally support for the troops fighting Ch'en Chiung-ming. However, Dr Sun declined to issue the land decree because of strong opposition among some important followers. After considerable bargaining, he agreed – according to Borodin's reminiscent account – to a decree reducing land rent by 25 per cent and to another providing for establishment of peasant unions.[7] Fortunately for the Nationalists, the troops supporting Sun drove the enemy off. The military crisis passed. Sun did not issue the decree reducing land rents.

Another problem, which would haunt both the Nationalists and the Communists, arose shortly after Borodin and Liao Chung-k'ai, one of the staunchest advocates of Dr Sun's Soviet orientation, left for Shanghai at the end of November to explain to leading comrades the need for party

6 Details of the work of the Provisional Executive Committee were published in eight issues of *Kuo-min-tang chou-k'an* (Kuomintang weekly), Canton, 23 Nov. 1923–13 Jan. 1924. See also *Ko-ming wen-hsien* (Documents of the revolution; hereafter *KMWH*), 8. 1077–9; 1079–80 for proclamation; 1080–4 for draft of the party programme (trans. in Shieh, *The Kuomintang*, 73–85). Borodin's draft constitution is in *Kuo-min-tang chou-k'an*, 25 Nov. 1923; reprinted in *Hsiang-tao chou-pao* (Guide weekly; hereafter *HTCP*) no. 50, 29 Dec. 1923 (this was a communist journal).

7 Louis Fischer, *The soviets in world affairs: A history of the relations between the Soviet Union and the rest of the world*, 637–8. Also A. I. Cherepanov, *Zapiski voennogo sovetnika v Kitae; iz istorii pervoi grazdanskoi revolutionnoi coiny, 1924–1927* (Notes of a military adviser in China: from the history of the first revolutionary civil war in China, 1924–1927), 37–43. Draft trans. of vol. 1 by Alexandra O. Smith, 45–9. The military crisis is well covered in the chronological biography of Sun Yat-sen, *Kuo-fu nien-p'u* (hereafter *KFNP*), 2. 1020–33, but Borodin's recommendation and Sun's rejection are not mentioned.

reorganization. Eleven prestigious members of the Kuomintang's Kwangtung headquarters, party veterans all, sent a petition to Dr Sun, warning
him of communist influence in the new system of party organization and
in the draft documents. They accused Ch'en Tu-hsiu, head of the Communist Party, of being the man behind the scenes, and charged that the
policy of cooperation between the two parties was an element in the
Communist International's scheme to stir up class struggle in the capitalist countries to hasten social revolution and, in nascent capitalist
countries, to unite labour, peasants and petty bourgeoisie to produce
national revolution. Ch'en Tu-hsiu had brought his adherents into the
Kuomintang to take it over, they asserted; and they warned Dr Sun that
within five years Ch'en might be elected leader of the Kuomintang. This
petition was an early evidence of continuing opposition among conservative party veterans towards the Soviet orientation and the admission
of communists into the senior party.

Sun Yat-sen rejected the criticism. In a written reply, he explained
that Borodin was author of the new constitution and that Ch'en Tu-hsiu
had nothing to do with it. It was Russia's idea to befriend the Kuomintang
and it was Russia which had advised the Chinese communists to work
within the Kuomintang. He asserted that Russia must cooperate with the
Kuomintang and not with Ch'en Tu-hsiu. 'If Ch'en Tu-hsiu disobeys
our party he will be ousted.' Sun cautioned against suspicion of Russia
because of suspicion of Ch'en Tu-hsiu.[8] Despite this show of confidence,
the new draft constitution was revised to eliminate the election of the
party leader; instead, it named Sun Yat-sen as leader, made him chairman
of the National Congress of Representatives and the Central Executive
Committee, and gave him veto power over the decisions of both.

The Canton customs crisis, which peaked in mid December, sharpened
Sun Yat-sen's anti-imperialism, though Borodin's earlier advice – he was
not in Canton during the crisis – must have had its effects as well. The
generalissimo and his government demanded a share of the revenues collected at Canton by the foreign-controlled Maritime Customs Service,
for which there was a precedent. When the diplomatic corps in Peking
declined to instruct the inspector-general to allocate revenues as Sun's
foreign minister requested, Generalissimo Sun announced that he would

8 'Petition to impeach the Communist Party, presented by the Kwangtung Branch of the
  Chung-kuo Kuomintang and Tsung-li's criticisms and explanations' (in Chinese) in Central
  Supervisory Committee of the Kuomintang, *T'an-ho Kung-ch'an-tang liang ta yao-an* (Two
  important cases of impeachment of the Communist Party), 1-11. Reprinted in *KMWH*,
  9. 1271-3, but lacking Sun's comment. The comments are translated in Conrad Brandt,
  Benjamin Schwartz and John K. Fairbank, *A documentary history of Chinese communism*,
  72-3.

seize the Canton customs house and appoint his own officials. This threatened the unity of the customs service, an agency of the Peking government, which all the powers recognized; and the action might have started a trend that would undermine the security of two major indemnities and many foreign loans. The interested powers met Sun's challenge by sending gunboats to Canton to prevent the seizure. The Nationalists were much too weak to fight; instead, they turned to mass demonstrations and propaganda in foreign capitals. The crisis passed, but Sun had made great political capital in China by his challenge to foreign domination. The Nationalist Party became more overtly nationalistic: anti-imperialism became its central theme, exactly as the Comintern advocated.[9]

The National Congress of Kuomintang Delegates convened in Canton on 20 January 1924 with 196 delegates appointed or elected and with 165 present on the opening day. Most were party veterans and about 40 represented overseas branches. Some 20 of the delegates were members of the Chinese Communist Party as well as of the Kuomintang. The 10-day congress heard seven speeches by Sun Yat-sen, reports on party activity in various regions of China and abroad; it debated and adopted a proclamation, party programme and constitution; and it elected two central committees. A report on party membership stated that, after intensive recruitment, there were more than 23,360 registered members in China and about 4,600 members abroad. The congress adjourned for three days to mourn the death of Lenin.[10]

In his opening address Sun Yat-sen called for unity and sacrifice among all party members. The proclamation emphasized anti-imperialism, anti-militarism and the function of the masses, especially poor peasants and workers, in the national revolution. Yet Borodin, who played an important role back-stage, was unsuccessful in persuading Sun Yat-sen to include a clear statement of the movement's united front with Soviet Russia. Nor could he get a statement included in the proclamation on expropriation of lands of large and absentee landlords and distribution of such lands to tenants.[11] The party platform was a reformist programme designed to appeal to many sectors of Chinese society; it promised to solve China's problems through legal instruments.

9 The customs crisis and evidence of Sun's growing hostility towards the imperialist powers are presented in Wilbur, *Sun Yat-sen, 183–90.*

10 *Chung-kuo Kuo-min-tang ch'üan-kuo tai-piao ta-hui hui-i-lu* (Minutes of the National Congress of the Kuomintang of China). *KMWH,* 8. 1100–60 for systematic details on the congress, and *KFNP,* 2. 1052–70 for an overview.

11 Cherepanov, *Zapiski,* 1. 67–71; draft trans., 85–92. Cherepanov states that his account is based upon Borodin's notes.

The issue of communists within the Kuomintang arose once more when a group of delegates tried to include an amendment in the constitution forbidding any Kuomintang member to belong to another party. Li Ta-chao presented a defence of communist intentions in joining the Kuomintang: they did so to contribute to the revolutionary work of the senior party, not to use its name to promote communism. Theirs was an open and upright action and not a secret plot, he assured the delegates, and he begged them not to harbour suspicions. After debate the amendment was rejected. Dr Sun clearly indicated his acceptance of communists within his party by naming 10 as regular or alternate members of the Central Executive Committee, about a quarter of the total.[12]

The newly elected Central Executive Committee met after the Congress closed and organized the party's central headquarters, which were now to be in Canton. They decided upon a Secretariat, an Organizational Bureau to manage party affairs, and eight functional bureaus: propaganda, labour, farmers, youth, women, investigation (later dropped), Overseas Chinese and military affairs. Party veterans were appointed to head the bureaus, two of which were placed under communists who had prior affiliations with the Kuomintang, T'an P'ing-shan for organization and Lin Tsu-han for farmers. A three-man Standing Committee was to manage daily business; it consisted of Liao Chung-k'ai, Tai Chi-t'ao and T'an P'ing-shan, a leftist group. Other members of the CEC residing in Canton were to meet at least once a week thereafter, but a majority of the members and alternates returned to cities in the north where they set up regional executive headquarters in Peking, Szechwan, Shanghai, Hankow, and Harbin, to promote the party. Gradually the central bureaus were given small staffs and the regional headquarters began to function. The leadership devoted much effort to creating propaganda on a nationwide scale; enrolling new members throughout China; organizing labourers, poor farmers and students in Kwangtung; and creating a military force loyal to the party. The work was carried on with a small budget, to which it appears that Borodin initially contributed some Ch.$30,000 a month.[13] Thus the Kuomintang started on its way to becoming a mass organiza-

---

12 Accounts of the debate, based on minutes, are in Chiang Yung-ching, *Hu Han-min hsien-sheng nien-p'u* (Chronological biography of Mr Hu Han-min), 301–3; and Li Yun-han, *Ts'ung jung-Kung tao ch'ing-tang* (From admitting the communists to the purification of the Kuomintang; hereafter *TJK*), 176–82. The earliest version of Li Ta-chao's statement is probably in *Chung-kuo Kuo-min-tang chou-k'an*, 10 (2 March 1924) 5. The text in Li's handwriting is in *KMWH*, 9. 1243–54.

13 *KMWH*, 8. 1160–7. Borodin's early financial contributions are inferred from Tsou Lu, *Chung-kuo Kuo-min-tang shih kao* (A draft history of the Kuomintang of China), 2nd edn, 390 and 399, f.ns. 21 and 22. Although Tsou says that the party leaders decided to replace Borodin's subsidy with other funds, there is considerable evidence that it continued.

tion with a strong leadership structure, a revolutionary ideology, and a plan for the ultimate seizure of political power in China.

Creating a revolutionary military force

Soviet military advisers who arrived with Borodin or joined him in Canton were appalled at the condition of the military forces supporting Sun Yat-sen in the winter of 1923–4. Most of the troops were poorly trained, badly equipped and led by incompetent officers, in the Russians' opinion. Only Sun's bodyguard of 150–200 men were completely loyal to him; the rest were the private armies of their commanders and their fighting value was nil, it seemed to the Russians. This situation had to be remedied if the Nationalists were to launch a campaign to unify the country with any hope of achieving military success. Necessary reforms would be the centralization of revenue collection, arms procurement, and pay of military units; standardized military training, and the indoctrination of officers and men in a common revolutionary ideology; and the creation of a unified and effective command structure. These were difficult measures to carry out, given the government's slender resources and the fact that unification of finances and command ran against the particularistic interests of the senior officers upon whom the government depended for its territorial base. The local arsenal, when it operated, could producd only enough rifles and machine guns in a year to equip one, or at most two, full-strength divisions, but the arsenal was run like a commercial enterprise: it sold its arms to any general who could pay for them. Importation of arms was difficult, though not impossible, because of an international arms embargo which the Maritime Customs Service attempted to enforce.

Dr Sun tried to strengthen his authority and bring his commanders together by appointing them to important positions within the Kuomintang. He chose Generals T'an Yen-k'ai and Yang Hsi-min, the titular commanders of the Hunan and Yunnan forces in Kwangtung, to be members of the Central Executive Committee. As reserve members of the Central Supervisory Committee he nominated General Hsu Ch'ung-chih, in titular command of Kwangtung Army units which supported Sun, and Gernerals Liu Chen-huan and Fan Chung-hsiu, who commanded small Kwangsi and Honan forces. In March the CEC delegated them, together with Generals Chu P'ei-te, who led a separate Yunnan force, and Lu Shih-t'i, a Szechwanese commanding a mixed corps, to organize party cells in their units. Periodically the generalissimo tried to persuade the various commanders to allow his appointees to collect the taxes and pay their troops, but he had little success. In fact, he seemed compelled to appoint or confirm certain commanders to control such lucrative revenue sources as bureaus for licensing gambling or 'suppressing opium'.

The most important step worked out by Borodin and Sun Yat-sen was the establishment of a military academy to train junior officers who would also be thoroughly indoctrinated with loyalty to the Kuomintang and imbued with its increasingly nationalistic ideology. Planning began just after the Party Congress and by May 1924 the Army Officers Academy (Lu-chün chün-kuan hsüeh-hsiao) at Whampoa, on an island south of Canton, was ready to open its gates to the first entering class of some 500 patriotic students drawn from middle schools and colleges all over China. Dr Sun appointed Chiang Kai-shek as commandant, and the principal military instructors were graduates of Japanese military schools or the Paoting and Yunnan military academies. They were aided by a few Russian officers, graduates of the Frunze Military Academy and the Russian civil war. General Chiang, Liao Chung-k'ai, the Kuomintang representative in the management of the Academy, and such veteran revolutionaries as Hu Han-min, Wang Ching-wei, and Tai Chi-t'ao, gave political instruction. The school was supported from the start by Russian funds supplemented by local taxes.

In June Russia sent a skilled commander, General P. A. Pavlov, to be Dr. Sun's military adviser. He recommended the creation of a military council, and this was organized on 11 July, made up of the principal commanders supporting the military government and a few party veterans. The council was a step towards creating a unified command and a political apparatus in the allied armies. Their military schools were to be improved and elite units be formed in each army for retraining. Unfortunately, General Pavlov drowned while on a reconnaissance on the East River front a month after his arrival in Canton. General Vasilii K. Blyukher, his replacement who used the pseudonym 'Galen' in China, did not arrive until October 1924. By that time the Whampoa Academy had its second class of cadets and a training regiment was being formed which later became the First Division of the National Revolutionary Army, the 'Party Army'. The first substantial batch of Russian arms reached Canton also in October 1924 on the *Vorovsky*, a yacht which had sailed from Odessa bringing a third group of Russian military advisers. Later shipments came from Vladivostok.[14]

14 'The National Revolutionary Army: a short history of its origin, development and organization'. This document was found in the Soviet military attaché's office on 6 April 1927. A translation was forwarded by Colonel S. R. V. Steward, the British military attaché in Peking, to the Foreign Office. It may be seen in the Public Record Office, London, FO 371: 12440/9156. A study of militarism as institutionalized in China is Ch'i Hsi-sheng,

Efforts to create a mass movement

Comintern representatives had repeatedly urged Sun Yat-sen to bring the masses into the national revolution, and this was also on the agenda of the Chinese Communist Party, which intended to organize the proletariat and link it to the poor peasantry, also under its direction. In the mass movement the two parties became rivals. The CEC of the Kuomintang set up its bureaus for labour, farmers, youth and women early in 1924, but the first two bureaus soon fell under the influence of vigorous young communists. The Socialist Youth Corps, the Communist Party's adjunct, was gaining a wide influence among educated youth.

Liao Chung-k'ai, as head of the Labour Bureau, tried to bring all unions in Canton into a single federation under his office, but was unsuccessful since many well-established unions were suspicious that communists on his staff would penetrate the unions and control the workers. The Communist Party hoped to bring railway workers, seamen, telegraph and telephone operators, postal employees and electricity workers into a single federation under its control. These were industries vital to a successful revolution. Despite such rivalries, Canton labour did rally in support of Chinese employees in the British and French concessions on the island of Shameen, who struck to protest at a system of passes the foreign authorities tried to impose after a Vietnamese revolutionary attempted on 19 June to assassinate the governor-general of Indo-China, who was visiting the island. Liu Erh-sung, a communist labour leader, is credited with being the main organizer of a complete strike and blockade of Shameen that lasted over a month, with strongly anti-imperialist overtones. Experience gained in the strike was well used a year later in the great Canton-Hong Kong strike and boycott.

The Communist International gave much attention during its Fourth Congress in November-December 1922 to the problem of organizing the peasantry in oriental countries. Its 'General theses on the oriental question' stated that in order to draw the peasant masses into the national liberation struggle the revolutionary parties must force the bourgeois-nationalist parties to adopt a revolutionary agrarian programme of land expropriation and redistribution to the landless. In May 1923 the ECCI instructed the Chinese Communist Party to draw in the peasant masses and press forward in preparation for agrarian revolution.[15] Actually, the Chinese Socialist Youth Corps could claim some credit already for the

Warlord politics in China, 1916–1928. The efforts of Soviet military advisers are treated systematically in Dieter Heinzig, *Sowjetische militärberater bei der Kuomintang 1923–1927.*
15 Eudin and North, *Soviet Russia and the East,* 151 and 233; and 344–6.

work of one of its leaders, P'eng P'ai, who organized tenant farmers in his native Hai-feng hsien east of Canton during 1922 and 1923, with the help of other Youth Corps members. A large-scale rent strike ended in arrests of many members, but P'eng escaped and came to Canton in the spring of 1924 and was soon the leading figure in the Kuomintang's Farmers Bureau.[16]

Planning for work of the Farmers Bureau began slowly, but by June 1924 the Kuomintang announced a simple scheme for farmers' associations (*nung-min hsieh-hui*), which were to be autonomous bodies permitted to organize guards recruited only from their own members. Local units were to be made up of farmers owning less than 100 *mou* (16 acres) of land and must exclude certain undesirable types. The CEC authorized the appointment of 20 special deputies to go into the field to investigate rural conditions, spread propaganda, and organize farmers' associations. In July the Bureau set up a Farmers' Movement Training Institute to prepare such workers, and P'eng P'ai directed the first class; the students received theoretical and practical instruction, including military training. (Other communists directed each of the successive classes up to the sixth, of which Mao Tse-tung was director from May to October 1926.) By October 1924 some 175 students had graduated from the Institute's short courses, and most of them were organizing farmers' associations in their native counties. The plan was to unite such associations on a county-wide, province-wide, and finally into a national organization that would not be under the control of the Kuomintang nor of its government. Why such autonomy was necessary became the topic of much theoretical argument.[17]

The Chinese Communist Party intended to control the peasant movement. A communist writer, probably Lo Ch'i-yuan, who was director of the Institute's second class and influential in the farmers' movement, revealed in a 1926 report that the CCP organized a peasant committee in 1924 'to direct the Kuomintang Farmers Bureau'. He asserted that the committee directed the Provincial Farmers Association when it was

16 See his biography in Donald W. Klein and Ann B. Clark, *Biographic dictionary of Chinese communism, 1921-1965*, 2. 720-4; Howard L. Boorman and Richard C. Howard, *Biographical dictionary of Republican China*, 3. 71-3. On his organizing work, see Shinkichi Etō, 'Hai-lu-feng – the first Chinese soviet government', pt I, *The China Quarterly (hereafter CQ)*, 8 (Oct./Dec. 1961) 160-83; and for P'eng's own account, Donald Holoch, trans. *Seeds of peasant revolution: report on the Haifeng peasant movement by P'eng P'ai*. P'eng is treated extensively in Roy Hofheinz, *The broken wave: the Chinese communist peasant movement, 1922-1928*.
17 'First proclamation of the revolutionary government on the farmers' movement', in *Chung-kuo Kuo-min-tang chung-yao hsuan-yen hui-pien* (Collection of Important Proclamations of the Kuomintang of China), 247-51. Lo Ch'i-yuan, 'Short report on the work of this [Farmers] Bureau during the past year,' *Chung-kuo nung-min*, 2 (1 Feb. 1926) 147-207; 158-9 for CEC decision. There is considerable detail on the Training Institute.

organized in May 1925, as well as local farmers' committees and the special deputies. The report also boasts that 99 per cent of the special deputies were 'comrades'.[18] During a confidential discussion among the Russian military advisers on reasons for Kuomintang hostility towards Chinese Communists, 'Nilov' (Sakanovsky) cited the communists' attempt to monopolize the labour and peasant movements, with the result that in setting up a preparatory committee for the National Peasant Conference, which was to meet in May 1926, the communists tried to place a few Kuomintang members on the committee 'for the sake of appearances'. They failed, he said, 'because there are no KMT members working among the peasantry'. In a resolution on the peasant movement dated July 1926 the Communist Party's Central Committee stated that peasant associations must be kept organizationally independent of the Kuomintang and not become its appendages. However, 'our party must devote the utmost effort to gaining the position of leadership in all peasant movements'.[19] The 'soul and spirit of the movement' in Kwangtung were Lo Ch'i-yuan, P'eng P'ai, and Juan Hsiao-hsien;[20] all had been early recruits to the Socialist Youth Corps in Kwangtung, and then became members of both the Communist Party and the Kuomintang.

The organizing of farmers' associations began in the Canton suburbs and nearby counties; by April 1925 there were some 160 associations with a reported membership of 20,390 – a tiny fraction of the rural population in areas under the revolutionary Canton government.[21] Communist organizers had greater success in Kwang-ning county, bordering Kwangsi, where graduates of the Training Institute led by P'eng P'ai organized tenant farmers and succeeded, with military help from Canton, in defeating landlords in a protracted rent reduction struggle. Thereafter they were able to organize many more associations in the county, reportedly 294 with nearly 55,000 members by April 1925.[22] P'eng P'ai was able to return to Hai-feng county on the heels of the Eastern Expedition at the

18 *Kwang-tung nung-min yun-tung pao-kao* (A report on the farmers' movement in Kwangtung), 124 and 53.

19 C. Martin Wilbur and Julie Lien-ying How, eds. *Documents on communism, nationalism, and Soviet advisers in China, 1918–1927*, 258 and 301.

20 T. C. Chang [Chang Tzu-ch'iang], *The farmers' movement in Kwangtung*, 23.

21 Figures from a map discovered after the Canton Commune of December 1927. See J.F. Brenan, 'A report on results of translations of Russian documents seized in the Russian Consulate, December 14, 1927'. Great Britain: Foreign Office, 405/256. Confidential. *Further correspondence respecting China*, 13583 (Jan.–March 1928) 117. We deduce the date.

22 *Idem*. Ts'ai Ho-sen, 'The Kwangtung farmers' movement on May First this year', *HTCP*, 112 (Special Issue for 1 May 1925) 1030–6. *Kwang-tung nung-min yun-tung pao-kao*, 64–83 and 98–100. 'Experiences in the rent reduction movement of Kwang-ning farmers', in *Ti-i-tz'u kuo-nei ko-ming chan-cheng shih-ch'i ti nung-min yun-tung* (The Farmers' movement during the First Revolutionary Civil War period), 139–47. Reprinted from *Kwang-tung nung-min yun-tung ching-kuo kai-k'uang*, Jan. 1927.

end of February 1925 and to revive his shattered movement there. Membership grew rapidly to a reported 70,000, with 12,000 in neighbouring Lu-feng county, but Ch'en Chiung-ming's troops recovered these counties in the summer and again the movement was driven underground.[23]

Rural revolt brought on suppression. Farmers' associations tried to protect their members from oppression, mobilize them against heavy taxation, and pit tenants against landlords in rent reduction movements. Men of property frequently sent hired toughs, bandits, or militia (*min t'uan*) to enforce customary payments. Organizers were murdered and some villages burned. Farmers fought back, sometimes supported by Nationalist troops, as in the two most successful areas.[24] Rural revolution could not be easily constrained; it threatened the alliance between an essentially reformist Kuomintang and the militant Communist Party.

Conflict within the revolutionary camp and in the Kwangtung base

By June 1924, what Kuomintang leaders in Shanghai and Canton had learned about the Communist Party's infiltration tactics and efforts to steer their party generated strong anti-communist sentiments in both cities.[25] Members of the Central Supervisory Committee petitioned Sun Yat-sen about the dangers and confronted Borodin with documentary evidence found in resolutions of the Socialist Youth Corps and the Communist Party's Central Committee that showed how communists intended to use the senior party for their revolutionary purposes. They objected particularly to the system of communist fractions within all levels of the Kuomintang, which contradicted Li Ta-chao's assurances at the Kuomintang Congress that the Communist Party was not 'a party within the Party'. The petitioners feared for the Kuomintang's future. In his debate with Chang Chi and Hsieh Ch'ih, two Kuomintang stalwarts, Borodin made clear that Russian assistance depended upon continued communist participation in the Kuomintang.[26]

23 A letter from P'eng P'ai reporting his triumphal reception and organizing work is quoted in Ts'ai, 'The Kwangtung Farmers' Movement . . .', 1031. For other details, see Shinkichi Etō, 'Hai-lu-feng', 149-81; See 151-2.

24 *Ibid.* 159 for a list of 195 peasant leaders killed up to May 1926, based upon Juan Hsiao-hsien, 'An outline report on the farmers' struggles in Kwangtung province during the past year', in *Chung-kuo nung-min*, 6/7 (July 1926) 611-29. This journal reports many specific cases.

25 Su-ch'ing (pseud.), *Kung-ch'an-tang chih yin-mou ta pao-lu* (The plots of the Communist Party exposed). This gives an extensive account of the discoveries and the mounting controversy.

26 Central Supervisory Committee of the Kuomintang, *T'an-ho Kung-ch'an-tang liang ta yao-an* (Two important cases of impeachment of the Communist Party), reprinted in *KMWH*,

In July the Kuomintang Central Executive Committee discussed the problem and issued a proclamation urging members not to be suspicious of each other. Dr Sun, on the advice of Borodin, created a special organ, the Political Council, to deal with major policy issues: it was made up of a few trusted Kuomintang leaders, and he appointed Borodin its adviser. Borodin was uneasy about the growing tide of opposition in the Kuomintang: he feared that left and right were coming together against the communists, though they dared not take decisive action for fear of their party's total isolation – that is, from external (that is, Russian) support.[27]

Chinese communist leaders were also restive. Ch'en Tu-hsiu, Ts'ai Ho-sen, and Mao Tse-tung of the Central Committee advocated a break with the Kuomintang. The committee even sent a secret circular letter to all district committees of the party and to all cells, directing them to prepare for a break.[28] But Borodin and Voitinsky, now the Comintern's official representative, insisted that the advantageous arrangement continue.

The issue was temporarily set at rest by decisions of the Political Council endorsed by the Second Plenum of the Kuomintang Central Executive Committee in August. The Plenum issued an 'Instruction on questions relating to admission of communists', which credited the Communist Party with special responsibility for the proletariat, recognized its need for secrecy, and exhorted the comrades to cooperate with each other to complete the national revolution.[29] This was a victory for Comintern policy and for those in the Kuomintang who formed the emerging left wing.

Another conflict arose from the heavy taxation imposed by Sun's military government and by the voracious 'guest armies', as well as from the increasing evidences of radicalism and social conflict. To protect themselves, merchant leaders created a militia as a counter force. When the generalissimo discovered in August 1924 that the merchants had imported a large shipment of arms from Europe, he ordered the arms confiscated, which was accomplished by Chiang Kai-shek's Whampoa cadets with

9. 1278–86. The impeachment is also given in Tsou Lu, *Chung-kuo Kuo-min-tang shih kao* (A draft history of the Kuomintang of China) Taipei edn, 413–21. 'Records of the questions of Central Supervisory members, Hsieh Ch'ih and Chang Chi, and the answers of Borodin' in *T'an-ho kung-ch'an-tang*, 25–30, and *KMWH*, 9. 1286–91.

27 V. I. Glunin, 'Comintern and the formation of the communist movement in China (1920–1927)', (in Russian), in *Komintern i Vostok; bor'ba za Leninskuiu strategiiu i taktiku v natsional'no-osvoboditel'nom dvizhenii* (Comintern and the Orient; the struggle for the Leninist strategy and tactics in the national liberational movement), 242–99; see p. 271. The article, based upon Russian archives, was abstracted for me by the late Lydia Holubnychy.

28 *Ibid.* 271–3.

29 The instruction is reprinted in *KMWH*, 16. 2773–6. See *TJK*, 324–31, and *KFNP*, 2. 1117–19 for discussions of the debates at the plenum.

the help of a Cantonese naval vessel. After two months of indecisvie bargaining and one bloody clash Dr Sun ordered all the forces he could command to suppress the Merchants' Corps. They did so on 15 October, destroying much of Canton's commercial quarter by fire and looting. This action seriously tarnished Dr Sun's reputation in Cantonese commercial communities in China and abroad.[30] However, on 13 November, the ageing leader left for Peking, his hopes for the presidency revived by Feng Yü-hsiang's *coup d'état* against his superior, Wu P'ei-fu, on 23 October 1924.

While Dr Sun was in Peking dying of cancer, units of the Kwangtung Army under General Hsu Ch'ung-chih, together with the two training regiments of the Party Army, commanded by Chiang Kai-shek and staffed by officers and cadets of the Whampoa academy, launched a campaign against Ch'en Chiung-ming and his supporters. This is now known as the First Eastern Expedition. During February, March and April 1925 the combined revolutionary forces, with only diversionary help from the Yunnan and Kwangsi 'guest armies', succeeded in driving clear to the eastern borders of Kwangtung, taking major cities and capturing much equipment, but failing to destroy Ch'en's army. In June the Eastern Expedition turned back, abandoning most of the captured territory, in order to deal with the Yunnan and Kwangsi armies, which had taken firm control of Canton.

Several features of the Eastern Expedition presaged the later Northern Expedition. One was the good discipline and high morale of the lower officers and troops of the Party Army, who were thoroughly indoctrinated and who fought under a harsh 'law of collective responsibility' (*lien-tso fa*), decreed by General Chiang. Another was the propaganda squads that preceded or accompanied the revolutionary army, distributing leaflets and haranguing the populace to obtain support. As a result, farmers brought supplies and acted as spies, message carriers, guides and porters. As in the later Northern Expedition, Russian officers served as military advisers, planning strategy, aiding on transport and commissary, and directing artillery fire. The 19 Russian officers learned a great deal about the realities of Chinese warfare as practised in the south and thereafter worked energetically to prepare the revolutionary forces for more effective combat. Finally, there was the rivalry and disunity on the enemy side, and the friction between the commanders in the revolutionary camp. Even in the lower officer ranks there were the seeds of conflict between communists organized in the League of Military Youth, and other Kuo-

---

30 An extended account of the 'Merchants' Corps incident' is found in C. Martin Wilbur, *Forging the weapons: Sun Yat-sen and the Kuomintang in Canton, 1924*, 89-93, 100-5.

mintang officers who created a rival organization, the Society for the Study of Sun Yat-sen's Doctrines.[31]

The intensified revolutionary atmosphere in 1925

Dr Sun Yat-sen died on 12 March 1925, leaving behind a testament for his followers that was drafted by Wang Ching-wei and signed by the dying leader on 11 March. During the following month there were memorial meetings in all the major cities of China with much emphasis upon Dr Sun's revolutionary goals.[32] Shanghai University, conducted jointly by the Kuomintang and Chinese Communist Party, actively engaged in revolutionary propaganda and encouraged students to become involved in organizing labour. Communist leaders were reviving their labour movement with strongly anti-imperialist overtones and directed primarily towards Japanese-owned textile mills in Shanghai. During the first week of May a conference of some 280 delegates of unions throughout the country met in Canton and organized a National General Labour Union under communist leadership. It was designed to bring all unions into the national revolution under a single militant organization, though many anti-communist unions stayed aloof. The 26 man executive committee was dominated by communists, while all its principal officers were members of the party.[33] Then in Shanghai a strike in a Japanese factory lit the fuse that led to the May Thirtieth Incident.

On 15 May Japanese guards fired on a group of Chinese workers who invaded the temporarily closed mill, demanding work and smashing machinery. One of the leaders, a communist, died from his wounds. Other labour leaders and students of Shanghai University immediately

31 Sources on the First Eastern Expedition are Ch'en Hsun-cheng, *Kuo-min Ko-ming-chün chan-shih ch'u-kao* (A preliminary draft of the National Revolutionary Army's battle history), in *KMWH*, 10 and 11. 1523–677; Mao Ssu-ch'eng, comp. *Min-kuo shih-wu nien i-ch'ien chih Chiang Chieh-shih hsien-sheng* (Mr Chiang Kai-shek up to 1926; hereafter Mao, *CKSHS*) Taipei reprint, 403–63. National Government of the Republic of China, Ministry of Defence, *Pei-fa chan-shih* (A battle history of the northern punitive expedition; hereafter *PFCS*), 1. 137–276; National Government of the Republic of China, Ministry of Defence. *pei-fa chien-shih* (A Brief History of the northern punitive expedition), 13–25; and Cherepanov, *Zapiski*, 138–202, draft trans. 183–263.

32 The death-bed wills and a farewell letter to the leaders of Soviet Russia, and memorial services are discussed in Wilbur, *Sun Yat-sen*, 277–82.

33 Accounts of the congress are [Lo] I-nung, 'Chung-kuo ti-er-tz'u ch'uan-kuo lao-tung ta-hui chih shih-mo', *HTCP*, 115 (17 May 1925) 1063–4; Teng Chung-hsia, *Chung-kuo chih-kung yun-tung chien-shih* (A brief history of the Chinese labour movement). Many eds. I used Central China, New China Bookstore, 1949, 116–38; Ch'en Ta, *Chung-kuo lao-kung wen-t'i* (Chinese labour problems), 122–8 and 593; Chung-kuo lao-kung yun-tung shih pien-tsuan wei-yuan-hui, comp. *Chung-kuo lao-kung yun-tung shih* (A history of the Chinese labour movement), 2. 356–61; Chang Kuo-t'ao, *The rise of the Chinese Communist Party, 1921–1927*, 414–22; Jean Chesneaux, *The Chinese labor movement, 1919–1927*, 258–61.

began wide-scale agitation directed against imperialist capitalists, making a martyr of the slain communist worker, and then demanding the release of students arrested in the International Settlement for demonstrating. The communist leaders of a recently organized labour union that operated in the safety of the native city strove in every way to persuade workers of the Japanese factory to stay on strike. Demonstrators took up another issue, four new regulations for the International Settlement that were to be voted upon by the foreign rate-payers on 2 June: they objected to foreigners determining rules for Chinese within the Settlement. Chinese wanted to roll back the 'unequal treaties', not to permit extensions.[34]

Probably no one planned a riot nor anticipated a shooting when, on Saturday, 30 May, students from eight colleges in the Shanghai area gathered in the International Settlement to preach against the unequal treaties and the military rulers of China, and to demand that their six arrested colleagues be freed. Police of the Settlement under orders from their commissioner attempted to stop the street demonstrations, arrested students who refused to desist, and soon were in head-bloodying conflict with students and sympathetic Chinese bystanders. When a large and angry crowd pressed on the Lousa Police Station where the arrested students were held and where arms were stored, the officer in charge, Inspector Everson, feared the crowd would rush the station, according to his testimony at the later inquest and trial hearings. To stop it he ordered his Chinese and Sikh constables to fire into the infuriated throng.

34 Important sources on the May 30th Incident and its aftermath include *Kuo-wen chou-pao*, 2. 21 (7 June 1925) and 22 (14 June) and subsequent issues into Sept.; *Tung-fang tsa-chih* (hereafter *TFTC*), special issue in July 1925; *HTCP*, 117 (6 June 1925) to 134 (30 October); U.S. Department of State, *Records relating to internal affairs of China, 1910–1929*, Microcopy no. 329, Roll no. 137, for USDS 893.5045/112, dispatch from Edwin S. Cunningham, American consul-general in Shanghai, 10 June 1925, enclosure 1: 'Extracts from police reports for period May 16 to June 5; enclosure 2: Inquest; enclosure 5: 'Extract from Mixed Court register for Tuesday, 2 June, 1925' (preliminary trial hearing); USDS 893.5045/147: 'Extract from Mixed Court register for Tuesday, 9 June, 1925' (175 pp. of testimony and cross-examination followed by nine exhibits). The trial record is available in *Report of the trial of the Chinese arrested during the riots of May 30, 1925* (I have not seen this); USDS 893.5045/158, dispatch by Ferdinand Mayer, chargé d'affaires, Peking, 3 July 1925: report of the investigation by a delegation sent to Shanghai by the diplomatic corps, with 23 annexes; USDS 893.5045/274: separate findings of a commission of three judges – American, British and Japanese – who conducted an inquiry from 12 Oct. onwards. The covering letter from Justice E. Finley Johnson, chairman of the International Commission of Judges, to Secretary of State Frank B. Kellogg, is dated Shanghai, 14 Nov. 1925. The proceedings of the inquiry were published as: International Commission of Judges, 1925, *A report of the proceedings of the International Commission of Judges* (I have not seen this work). The gist of a vast number of letters, press clippings, translations of Chinese publications, photos of propaganda posters, etc., included in reports of U.S. diplomatic and consular personnel in the above mentioned Microcopy no. 329, Rolls 43–45 and 136–38, may be found in U.S. Department of State, *Papers relating to the foreign relations of the United States*, 1925 (hereafter *FRUS*), 1. 647–721. A good recent account is in Nicholas R. Clifford, *Shanghai, 1925: urban nationalism and the defense of foreign privilege*.

That volley at 3.37 p.m. left four Chinese dead and many wounded on the pavement. Eight later died of their wounds. Five or possibly six of the slain were students. Relations between Chinese and foreigners were never to be the same again.

The May Thirtieth Incident gave a tremendous spur to the national revolution. Local leaders and political activists in Shanghai immediately organized a city-wide protest which developed into a general strike on Monday morning, 1 June. Further rioting, countered by police repression, lasted several days and 10 more Chinese lost their lives. The International Settlement became an armed camp as the Shanghai Volunteer Corps and some 1,300 marines from five powers patrolled the streets. The Chinese press spread detailed accounts and student groups issued innumerable pamphlets and cartoons and dispatched telegrams and letters to other cities calling for support to the strikers and opposition to the imperialists. Demonstrations occurred in at least 28 cities. Anti-foreign riots broke out in the British concession in Chinkiang, in Hankow where more Chinese were killed and wounded, and in Kiukiang where the Japanese and British consulates were destroyed. Funds poured into Shanghai from all over the country, from Chinese overseas, and from Soviet Russia to support the strikers. The Canton tragedy of 23 June, in which scores of parading Chinese were machine-gunned from the Shameen concessions, intensified the hatred of foreign privilege. As a result of the protracted strikes and boycotts, the policies of Great Britain and the other powers changed significantly. Thus the 'May Thirtieth movement' was a nation-wide protest; it also aroused public opinion throughout the world against the archaic treaty system.

The Kuomintang and the Communist Party both grew rapidly. Students flocked to Canton to enter the Military Academy. The Communist Party's vigorous leadership of strikes and boycotts attracted thousands of new members. The party suddenly found the key to rapid unionization of Shanghai's labour force through relief payments to the strikers, and became dominant in the labour movement there. During the Hong Kong-Canton strike and boycott, Canton labour became much more militant. At the same time an anti-communist tide grew within the Kuomintang in Shanghai, and Chinese entrepreneurs in many cities became wary of communist leadership of their workers. In short, while nationalism flamed and social revolution grew more intense, the seeds of counter-revolution were also nourished.

Consolidating the southern revolutionary base

Canton's reaction to the May Thirtieth Incident was delayed due to the precarious situation of the remaining radical leadership there. The city was controlled by the Yunnan and Kwangsi armies under Generals Yang Hsi-min and Liu Chen-huan, because most of the other Nationalist forces were in eastern Kwangtung regrouping after the successful Eastern Expedition. They planned to return to Canton and subdue the forces of Yang and Liu, but until this battle was fought it was scarcely possible to mount anti-foreign demonstrations in Canton against the opposition of the two generals, who were courting foreign support.

The battle for Canton lasted from 6 to 12 June inclusive. The Eastern Expeditionary troops marched back and, on 8 June, captured Shih-lung on the south-eastern approaches to Canton along the railway from Kowloon. Other Nationalist units closed the ring west and north of the city. At dawn on 12 June the main Nationalist force attacked enemy emplacements north of Canton while a mixed force led by Whampoa cadets wearing red scarves crossed the river from Ch'ang-chou Island and landed east of Canton at Tung-shan to plunge into the fray. The battle raged from Tung-shan to White Cloud Mountain, north-west of the city, when at noon Cantonese troops crossed from Honam Island to deal with enemy forces in the city. By 3 p.m. the Nationalists were victorious. General Liu abandoned his troops, fled to the British concession in Shameen, and took steamer for Hong Kong; two days later General Yang followed him there.[35] Russian military advisers led by General Blyukher played important roles both in developing the strategy and overseeing its execution.[36] Chiang Kai-shek, who played a leading part in this campaign, became garrison commander and soon brought disorders in the city under control. It was now possible to create a new government with some grip on the city's finances, and also to join in the nationalistic agitation that was sweeping the country.

As soon as Canton had been secured, the Nationalist leaders set out to

35 Ch'en Hsun-cheng wrote a general account of the campaign, reprinted in *KMWH*, 11. 1704–6. This is the basis for a similar account in *PFCS*, 1. 280–7, with two maps. Also Mao, *CKSHS*, (1–14 June 1925) 484–6; USDS 893.00/6396 and /6458, dispatches of Consul-General Douglas Jenkins, Canton, 12 and 17 June 1925; and *New York Times*, 7–13 June.
36 Cherepanov gives a detailed account of the campaign, in which he participated with the Whampoa cadets, though the account is based in part on the Soviet mission archives, apparently. He portrays General Blyukher as author of the plan of attack and in charge of all operations, and depicts the Russian advisers with the scattered Nationalist units as forming a communications net and enforcing Blyukher's orders exactly. Cherepanov, *Zapiski*, 1. 201–38, draft trans., 291–314. This account is marked by a hostile bias towards Chiang Kai-shek. There were only some 20 Russian advisers with the Nationalist armies at this time.

establish a 'national government' in Canton, replacing the generalissimo's headquarters, which had been Dr Sun's central organ. The Kuomintang Political Council resumed meetings in Canton on 14 June with Borodin advising, and decided on a structure of government with nine ministries united by a Government Council, a reorganization of the armies into the National Revolutionary Army, and reform of military and financial administration to bring the sword and the purse under Kuomintang control. All organs were to be under the party's direction. The Government Council and a parallel Military Council were to take policy direction from the Kuomintang Central Executive Committee, but effectively this meant direction from the extra-statutory Political Council, consisting of Wang Ching-wei, Hu Han-min, Liao Chung-k'ai, Wu Ch'ao-shu (C.C. Wu), and Hsu Ch'ung-chih after early July. Wang, Hu and Liao seemed to be a triumvirate in the Political Council, Government Council, and Military Council, but Wang became chairman of each of these bodies. Generals T'an Yen-k'ai and Hsu Ch'ung-chih were also prominent along with Wu Ch'ao-shu, the mayor of Canton. Chiang Kai-shek had not yet risen to political importance, though he was a member of the Military Council, commandant of the Military Academy, and commander of the Party Army. Wang's rise was apparently at the expense of Hu Han-min, whose position declined from deputy generalissimo after Sun Yat-sen's departure, to minister of foreign affairs in the new government, which had no formal foreign relations.[37] The national government was proclaimed on 1 July 1925.

One week earlier the tragic 'Shakee massacre' of 23 June set off the massive Canton-Hong Kong strike and boycott that lasted for 16 months.[38] With the Yunnan and Kwangsi troops defeated, patriots in Canton began to organize an appropriate protest against the May Thirtieth Incident in Shanghai and subsequent repressions of demonstrations in other foreign concession areas. Labour leaders travelled to Hong Kong to persuade union leaders there to join in a strike and boycott planned to begin on 21 June, with Canton to provide sanctuary for Hong Kong workers who went on strike. While four communist-dominated unions in Hong Kong went out earlier, a general strike began simultaneously on the appointed day in the British concession on Shameen and in Hong Kong. Striking

---

37 Basic documents in *KMWH*, 20. 3801–20. *TJK*, 373 quotes the resolution from the minutes of the 14th Session of the Central Political Council of 14 June 1925, preserved in the Kuomintang Archives. Mao, *CKSHS*, 494 gives resolutions adopted by the Central Executive Committee the next day. Other details in Chiang Yung-ching, *Hu Han-min hsien-sheng nien-p'u*, 331–2.

38 The paragraphs on the beginnings of the Hong Kong-Canton strike and boycott are condensed from a manuscript based upon research by the author in Chinese, Russian, British and American sources.

workers poured into Canton, where organizers planned a massive demonstration on 23 June. Apprehensive British and French authorities brought up gunboats and marines and prepared the defences of their concession, fearing it would be attacked.

On 23 June after a huge noon-time rally directed against the unequal treaties, an orderly parade of Chinese passed through the crowded Canton streets and approached the bund facing Shameen Island. It was composed of more than a hundred contingents of workers, farmers, merchants, school children, boy scouts, college students, Whampoa cadets, and units from the Party Army and the Hunan and Kwangtung armies. As the parade was passing the heavily-guarded British bridge across the narrow strip of water which separated the two sides, someone started firing. Which side fired first immediately became a matter of dispute.[39] In the subsequent fusillades from both sides, one foreigner was killed and eight or nine wounded on Shameen, but fire from the British and French side killed at least 52 Chinese and wounded 117, including students, civilians of various occupations, cadets and troops.

Cantonese fury at this slaughter is scarcely describable. Many clamoured for war, but the political and military authorities strove to calm the populace to prevent an attack on the concessions. The Canton authorities adopted a policy of economic warfare against their foreign enemies coupled with diplomacy. They supported the strike of Chinese workers in Hong Kong, which was only partially successful in crippling the colony, and stoppage of all trade with Hong Kong and a boycott of British goods. On the diplomatic front they attempted to divide the powers and concentrated vengeance on Great Britain. These measures lasted for many months, and only came to an end in October 1926, after the Northern Expedition was under way and after many efforts to negotiate a settlement.[40] Canton became the driving force of the Chinese nationalist

---

39 The most extensive source giving the Chinese side of this dispute is Ch'ien I-chang, ed. 'Sha-chi t'ung shih' (The tragic history of Shakee), original in Kuomintang Archives 230/1780; partially reprinted in KMWH, 18. 3330–58 and intermittently to p. 3419. Also June Twenty-third: the report of the Commission for the Investigation of the Shakee Massacre June 23, 1925, Canton China, distributed 'With compliments of the Commission'. For testimony presented by Shameen observers that the firing began from the Chinese side, see Great Britain, Foreign Office, Cmd. 2636, China no. 1 (1926), Papers respecting the first firing in the Shameen affair of June 23, 1925. Also US Department of State, 893.00/6464, dispatch, Douglas Jenkins, Canton, 26 June 1925; 893.00/6314, telegram, Shameen, 24 June; and two telegrams from commander-in-chief, Asiatic Fleet to Operation Department of the U.S. Navy, delivered to the State Department in paraphrase, 893.00/6352 and /6359. I find it impossible to determine the fact of the first firing on the basis of evidence available to me.

40 A full account of periodic attempts to negotiate, primarily based on Foreign Office archives but also using Chinese sources, is found in David Clive Wilson, 'Britain and the Kuomintang, 1924–28: a study of the interaction of official policies and perceptions in Britain and China', University of London, School of Oriental and African Studies, Ph.D. dissertation, 1973.

movement. Citizens rallied behind its government. Patriotic students flocked to the city and many enrolled in the Whampoa Military Academy. Canton was filled with unemployed strikers whose support became a drain upon the city's financial resources, though contributions poured in from other parts of China, from overseas Chinese, and from Soviet Russia. The Chinese merchant community suffered serious losses due to the enforced stoppage of their normally extensive trade with Hong Kong. The well-organized strikers, with armed pickets and led by the Chinese Communist Party, became an imperium within the revolutionary movement. Thus, while the strike and boycott helped at first to consolidate the revolutionary base, it also divided the leadership. These results were part of the skein of conflict that led to the crushing of the organized left in Canton in April 1927.

COMPETITION AND DISSENSION WITHIN

Aborted counter-revolution

Counter-revolution showed its hand on 20 August 1925 in the assassination of Liao Chung-k'ai, an ardent supporter of Sun's alliance with Soviet Russia and his efforts to mobilize the masses. Immediately after the tragedy, Borodin proposed the formation of a special committee of three with full powers to deal with the crisis. Hsu Ch'ung-chih, Wang Ching-wei and Chiang Kai-shek made up the triumvirate, with Borodin as adviser. Investigations revealed a plot among a group of conservative Kuomintang leaders and some commanders in the Kwangtung Army to overthrow the radicals in the Canton power establishment. Within a week many suspects were arrested, some executed, while others of the plotters had fled. Chiang and Borodin decided to send Hu Han-min to Russia, and within a month Chiang Kai-shek expelled his rival, Hsu Ch'ung-chih, titular commander of the Kwangtung Army. Two party veterans who obstructed the expansion of Russian influence, Lin Sen and Tsou Lu, were sent north on a 'diplomatic mission'. These men later became leaders of a prestigious faction within the Kuomintang opposing the remaining leadership in Canton.[41]

There were other important consequences of the crisis. Wang Ching-wei and Chiang Kai-shek became key figures in the revolutionary movement and for six months held greatest influence in the Canton regime.

---

41 Sources on this complex series of events: *TJK*, 375–92; Wang Ching-wei, 'Political report' made to the Second Kuomintang Congress, in *KMWH*, 20. 3851–70; Chiang Kai-shek, 'Military Report' in *KMWH*, 11. 1756–63; Chiang's 'Diary' for the period 15 Aug.–23 Sept.; and reports of British and American consuls in Canton.

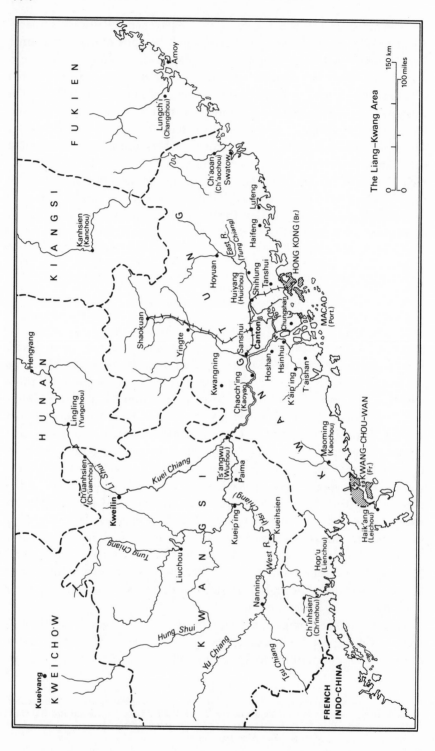

MAP 13. Kwangtung and Kwangsi in the early 1920s

The military forces upholding the regime were reorganized into five corps of the National Revolutionary Army: First Corps from the Party Army, commanded by Chiang Kai-shek; Second Corps of Hunanese, commanded by T'an Yen-k'ai; Third Corps of Yunnanese, Commanded by Chu P'ei-te; Fourth Corps drawn from the Kwangtung Army, placed under the command of Li Chi-shen; and Fifth Corps made up of Li Fu-lin's private army. To consolidate the Kwangtung Army, with its scattered units lodged in local bases, was not easy, but the newly designated Fourth Corps was gradually converted into a unified and effective fighting force. Another effort to unify financial administration was also ultimately successful.[42]

From October 1925 through January 1926 the reorganized National Revolutionary Army fought three campaigns which solidified its hold on Kwangtung. By early October Canton was menaced once more by the revived forces under Ch'en Chiung-ming on the east, a Szechwanese corps under Hsiung K'o-wu in the north-west, and Kwangtung troops under Teng Pen-yin and Wei Pang-p'ing in the south-west. The Second Eastern Expedition, made up principally of divisions of the First and Fourth Corps and a mixed force under Ch'eng Ch'ien, which later became the Sixth Corps, decisively defeated Ch'en Chiung-ming's coalition. The Fourth Regiment of the First Corps captured Ch'en's seemingly impregnable bastion of Hui-chow (Waichow) on 14 October with great courage and much loss of life, according to Cherepanov, who witnessed the battle and describes the courage of communist officers and political commissars.[43] Thereafter in a series of battles, the expeditionary force under Chiang Kai-shek's overall command captured towns *en route* to Swatow, while Ch'eng Ch'ien cut off the enemy's escape into Kiangsi and Fukien.[44] As in the previous eastern expedition political workers mobilized popular support and Russians advised each of the main units.

Also during October units of the Second and Third Corps drove the Szechwanese north across the Kwangtung border. Before the Eastern Expedition was finished parts of the First and Fourth Corps had to be

42 Wilbur and How, *Documents*, 186–99, contains a valuable report by 'Kisan'ka' (N.V. Kuibyshev), probably dated early in 1926, detailing important elements in the military reorganization and centralization. I have dealt with military unification in Kwangtung in 'Military separatism and the process of reunification under the Nationalist regime, 1922–1937', in Ping-ti Ho and Tang Tsou, eds. *China in crisis*, 1. 203–63, especially, 227–33.

43 Cherepanov, *Zapiski*, draft trans., 334–54. See *supra*, f.n. 31 for other accounts of the three campaigns.

44 N.I. Konchits, 'In the ranks of the National Revolutionary Army of China', (in Russian), *Sovetskiie dobrovoltsy v pervoi grazhdanskoi revolutsionnoi voine v Kitae; vospominaniia*, (Soviet volunteers in the First Revolutionary Civil War in China; reminiscences), 24–95. Pages 37–62 follow Ch'eng Ch'ien's campaign in a diary account.

sent to the southern front where, with help of units from the Second and Third Corps, they defeated the enemy by late December and went on to take Hainan Island. Thus were most of the elements of the National Revolutionary Army battle-tested and hardened before the Northern Expedition.

After Kwangtung had been brought under Nationalist control, three generals in neighbouring Kwangsi brought their province into alliance with Canton. Huang Shao-hsiung, Li Tsung-jen and Pai Ch'ung-hsi joined the Kuomintang and permitted the party to operate in regions they controlled. Their forces were designated the Seventh Corps, with General Li in command. General T'ang Sheng-chih, who commanded a division in southern Hunan, also negotiated in the spring of 1926 for incorporation of his troops, which were designated the Eighth Corps. These eight corps were the major units of the National Revolutionary Army when the Northern Expedition began. The total force numbered some 150,000, though only about 100,000 could be used outside the two-province base.[45] The NRA was still a rather heterogeneous force, but had been improved in training, equipment, indoctrination and battle experience during two-and-a-half years of reorganization with Russian help.

Polarization of the Kuomintang

In the summer of 1925 Tai Chi-t'ao issued two books, both of which presented a conservative interpretation of Sun Yat-sen's philosophy and arguments against communist participation in the Kuomintang.[46] Tai argued that the Three Principles of the People were the sole doctrine of the Kuomintang, which, he asserted, was the only party working for the national revolution. Communists and any others who did not accept these principles unreservedly should be excluded from the Kuomintang. In effect, Tai called for an end to the system by which communists were permitted to work within the senior party; he accused them of being parasitic, stirring up conflict between leaders, seeking to oust non-communists from Kuomintang posts, and absorbing its members into their party and youth corps. Tai's friend, Shen Ting-i, who had joined the Communist Party, turned against it. On 5 July he called a meeting of the Kuomintang's Chekiang Provincial Committee, which issued a manifesto echoing Tai's ideas and denouncing the concept of class struggle.

---

45 *KMWH*, 12. 1802-5 and *Pei-fa chien-shih*, chart following p. 46.
46 Boorman, *Biographical dictionary*, 3. 202. The late Miss Julie How analysed the main points in *Kuo-min ko-ming yü Chungkuo Kuomintang* in Wilbur and How, *Documents*, 206-7.

The Shanghai Executive Headquarters printed this document and sent it to all Kuomintang offices under its jurisdiction; it also issued an instruction forbidding Kuomintang members to advocate class struggle.[47]

The Communist Party responded to this challenge. Ch'en Tu-hsiu, the party's leader, published an open letter to Tai, dated 30 August, in which he defended communist motives in joining the Kuomintang and warned that Tai's writings were being used by reactionaries as propaganda.[48] The Central Committee held an enlarged plenum in Peking in October which passed a resolution on relations between the Communist Party and the Kuomintang. The resolution attacked Tai and others like him as the principal enemies and re-emphasized the policy of alliance with the left wing of the Kuomintang against the right. The resolution attempted to set standards for classifying members of the two factions but expressed doubts as to the real strength of the left.[49]

A group of Kuomintang veterans met in the Western Hills near Peking in November 1925 in what they called a plenum of the Central Executive Committee of the Kuomintang. Actually the party was so riven by controversy over the radical course being followed in Canton that neither the Peking group nor the leaders in Canton could muster a quorum of the CEC. Nevertheless, the 'Fourth CEC Plenum' decided to expel communists from the Kuomintang and declared that national revolution and class revolution could not go forward together. The group declared Borodin's relationship with the party terminated, dissolved the Political Council, which had no constitutional basis, and suspended Wang Ching-wei from party membership for six months. These measures had no binding effect. In retaliation the leaders in Canton used the CEC name to issue a manifesto denouncing Tsou Lu and Hsieh Ch'ih for their leadership of the Western Hills group, and in an open letter, Chiang Kai-shek defended Wang, Borodin and the Chinese communists. The Western Hills faction set up headquarters in Shanghai, seized the local membership records, took over the *Min-kuo jih-pao* as its mouthpiece, and planned to call the Second National Congress of the Kuomintang.[50]

The leaders in Canton succeeded, however, in assembling their Second National Congress first. It met in Canton from 4 to 19 January 1926, with 253 voting delegates, and heard a variety of reports on party work, includ-

47 *TJK*, 411–12, based on the documents preserved in Kuomintang Archives.
48 Ch'en Tu-hsiu, 'Letter to Tai Chi-t'ao', *HTCP*, 130 (18 September 1925) 1196–7.
49 Wilbur and How, *Documents*, 234–7.
50 'Important documents of the Western Hills Conference expelling communists from the Kuomintang, November 1925', *Kuo-wen chou-pao*, 4. 14 (17 April 1927) 14–16; Tsou Lu, *Hui-ku-lu* (Reminiscences), 1. 180–9; Tai Chi-t'ao, *Tai Chi-t'ao hsien-sheng wen-ts'un* (Collected writings of Mr Tai Chi-t'ao), edited by Ch'en T'ien-hsi, 3. 975–8 and 985; *TJK*, 413–34 (based on Kuomintang Archives); Wilbur and How, *Documents*, 209–12.

ing T'an P'ing-shan's discussion of party membership. This was still under 200,000, though later T'an spoke of half a million in China and overseas – an exaggeration. He gave round-number figures for membership in each of 11 formally organized provinces, five in the process of organization, and three special municipalities, which totalled 183,700; but he had to omit figures for Shanghai and Hankow, which had failed to report, and he left out figures for enrolments in army corps, naval vessels and the Canton police, all of which had special branches.[51]

Some 90 of the Kuomintang delegates, more than one third, were members of the Communist Party as well.[52] They operated as a caucus. The Congress debated the culpability of the dissident conservatives and how they should be punished. Opinion was sharply divided, but in the end Wang Ching-wei's plea for leniency – for not splitting the party further – was passed by a show-of-hands majority. Hsieh Ch'ih and Tsou Lu were to be expelled, 12 others who had attended the Western Hills conference should receive letters of warning, and Tai Chi-t'ao would be exhorted to repent.[53] As a direct response to the Western Hills group's expulsion of Borodin, the Second Congress unanimously passed a resolution to send him a letter of thanks together with a silver vessel inscribed with the words 'united struggle'.[54]

Since one of the principal demands of the Western Hills group was the expulsion of communists from the Kuomintang, that issue could not be avoided. Indeed, the debates showed an undercurrent of criticism of communist secret activities and implied doubts about their ultimate loyalty to the senior party. Several communist spokesmen heatedly defended their party. Then the issue was again set aside with a decision that the Central Executive Committees of the two parties should meet together to work out a solution.[55] No such joint meeting was ever held.

Another triumph for the left was the election of the new central committees of the Kuomintang. None of the dissident Peking group was re-elected. Communists won seven, and possibly eight, of the 36 seats on the CEC, and six among the 24 alternate positions, a slightly higher proportion than they held in the first CEC. Only two won positions on the Central Supervisory Committee, but there had been no communist in the previous CSC. Leftists, whose identification is less certain, won nine

51 *Chung-kuo Kuo-min-tang ti-erh-tz'u ch'üan-kuo tai-piao ta-hui hui-i chi-lu* (Minutes of the Second National Congress of Kuomintang Delegates; hereafter *Minutes*). CEC of the Kuomintang, April 1926, pp. 29 and 31.
52 *TJK*, 463.
53 *Minutes*, 134, and Li Yun-han, *TJK*, 466-9.
54 *Minutes*, 18-19.
55 *Ibid.* 165-9.

seats in the regular CEC and three among the alternates; they won two in the CSC. Chiang Kai-shek became a new member of the CEC, sharing the highest number of votes with Wang Ching-wei, T'an Yen-k'ai and Hu Han-min. Hu clearly was a potential right-wing leader and was still in exile in Russia for his alleged role in the Liao Chung-k'ai assassination plot. His virtually unanimous election must have been carried through by prearrangement.[56]

The clearest evidence of the drift leftward was the election by the new Central Executive Committee of its nine-man standing committee, the actual operating body. This contained three leftists – Wang Ching-wei, Ch'en Kung-po and Kan Nai-kuang; three communists – T'an P'ing-shan, Lin Tsu-han and Yang P'ao-an; and Chiang Kai-shek, T'an Yen-k'ai and Hu Han-min.[57] The leftist and communist leaders in Canton enjoyed their triumph for only two months.

Politicization and communist penetration of the National Revolutionary Army

The National Revolutionary Army of the Kuomintang was deliberately politicized to make it an effective revolutionary instrument. The armed forces were to be under the Kuomintang's civilian control and officers and troops to be indoctrinated with the party's ideology. The main instruments of control were the National Government Military Council, subordinate to the Political Council of the Kuomintang Central Executive Committee, the Political Training Department, which was directly under the Military Council, and party representatives in all major units of the armed forces. The Political Training Department was modelled on the Soviet Central Political Administration (PUR), and party representa-tives were equivalent to the political commissars in the Red Army. The system of control and indoctrination was worked out gradually, begin-ning with the establishment of the Whampoa Military Academy in the spring of 1924; by mid March 1926, shortly before the start of the Nor-thern Expedition, a political structure had been created within most larger units of the armed forces. Politicization was a partial substitute for

56 Election scores in *Minutes*, 145–6. The top four each won 248 of the 249 valid votes cast. Naturally, the three highest scorers at the meeting could not vote for themselves on signed ballots. According to Chang Kuo-t'ao, who attended the congress, the absent Hu actually received 249 votes but at Wang Ching-wei's instigation, the secretary-general of the congress, Wu Yü-chang, reduced Hu's vote by one and placed his name third in the rank order, behind those of Wang and Chiang (actually behind Wang and T'an, but ahead of Chiang, according to the published Minutes). Chang, *The rise of the Chinese Communist Party*, 1. 282 and 708, f.n. 14.

57 *TJK*, pp. 473 and 519, f.n. 33, based upon minutes in the Kuomintang Archives, with the scores in the voting.

technical modernization; it also was conceived of as a means to control military officers whose loyalty to the Kuomintang might be questionable.[58]

The Political Training Department was an instrument both for control and indoctrination. It was established in about June 1925 and by October had begun to function. The Military Council appointed the head of the department, with confirmation by the Kuomintang Political Council. Ch'en Kung-po held the position in March 1926, but was to be replaced. A table of organization of that date showed some 29 officers, who operated in three sections: general affairs, propaganda and party affairs. Actual work within the armed forces was carried out through party representatives and political sections, and the department, at least in theory, controlled all party representatives in army corps, independent divisions, the bureaus of the navy and the air force, in the Central Political and Military Academy, and in the General Staff and Administration of Supplies. All party, political and cultural work in the armed forces was supposed to be done under the Political Training Department's instructions, but instructions issued to higher level party representatives had to bear the signature of the chairman of the Military Council as well as that of the head of the department. However, there were elements of friction and conflict between the department and high level party representatives, who were mostly party veterans. Chou En-lai, a communist, was deputy and often acting head of the department.

As of mid March 1926, the Political Training Department had planned a three-month programme of political instruction for officers and for troops; had set up a commission to prepare a textbook in reading and writing for illiterate soldiers; and it issued a daily newspaper, *Political work*, which was distributed in 18,000 copies, mostly to officers and political workers in the armed forces. The editor of *Political work* was a communist and the local committee of the Chinese Communist Party wrote its feature articles as a means of instructing political personnel and,

58 The following discussion is based primarily on a series of unpublished documents seized in the raid on the Soviet military attaché's offices in the Russian embassy in Peking on 6 April 1927. The original documents were in Russian, and the British military attaché in Peking, Colonel J.R.V. Steward, sent an English translation to the British minister, Sir Miles Lampson, who forwarded them to the Foreign Office. They are now in the Public Record Office in London, filed under F.O. 371–12502 (F8322/3241/10). The documents in the series consist of 'Political work in the National Revolutionary Army' and 15 annexes, of which three are missing. They date from around mid March 1926, and the first annex, 'Regulations governing the political directorate of the National Revolutionary Army', dated 15 March 1926, and the undated sixth annex, 'Regulations governing political commissaries [*sic*] in the National Revolutionary Army', are confirmed by almost identical regulations issued by the National Government Military Council on 19 March 1926, and reprinted in *KMWH*, 12. 1814–21. It is planned to publish these Soviet documents in a revised and enlarged edition of Wilbur and How, *Documents*.

through them, the officers and troops. To coordinate publishing efforts of political sections in various army corps and divisions, a committee of representatives from these units planned to issue 16 pamphlets with such titles as 'What and how to teach soldiers', 'What are the "Unequal treaties"?' and 'The history of the Kuomintang'. Five were already in press, and in addition other pamphlets, leaflets, books, journals, wall newspapers and cartoon posters were being published in large numbers by various organs.

Party representatives were the political watch-dogs and official propagandists of the Kuomintang within units of the National Revolutionary Army. By March 1926 the system operated in all army corps and ships of the navy as well as in central military administrative organs. The first article of the 'Regulations for party representatives in the National Revolutionary Army' announced their purpose – 'to inculcate the revolutionary spirit, to increase fighting power, to tighten discipline, and to develop San Min Chu-i (Three Principles of the People) education'.[59] The party representative was responsible for the political and moral condition of his unit, overseeing the execution of Kuomintang instructions, guiding the party nucleus, and carrying out all political and cultural work. He had to be well acquainted with the officers and men of his unit, study their states of mind, and try to remedy all defects. He was an officer with the right to command, and his orders were be obeyed just as those of the unit commander. In battle he was to be an exemplar of bravery, protecting the civilian population from the army during campaigns, and was expected to establish connections with farmers' associations and labour unions in localities where the troops were quartered.

Party representatives were part of a separate chain of command, parallel but not subordinate to the military chain. They were observers of the loyalty of military officers. Higher level party representatives were appointed by the Military Council to headquarters of corps and divisions, to the Navy Bureau, the General Staff, and other high organs, and were to act jointly with their opposite numbers of the military command. Orders issued by the military commander without their signature were invalid. In case of disagreement, the party representative should sign but report the case to his superior; but if the commander committed some illegal act, the party representative should frustrate it and report immediately to his superior and to the chairman of the Military Council. The party representative, or 'commissar', and the military commander 'being one and an indivisible whole, should always and everywhere work toge-

---

59 *KMWH*, 12. 1818, with a different translation in annex 6, cited above.

ther trying to attain one common aim: the unification of China under the banner of the Kuomintang'.

According to the information available to the Russian author of our basic source as of about mid March 1926, there were 876 political workers in the National Revolutionary Army. About 75 per cent of them were communists or members of the Kuomintang left, about 20 per cent were careerists without principles, and the remaining 5 per cent were right wing members of the Kuomintang, who were extremely hostile to both the communists and leftists. One of the annexes numerates 241 communists doing political work in the National Revolutionary Army or more than a quarter of the known political workers. There were 887 communists known to be in the army, more than half of them in the First Corps and the Central Political-Military Academy – still a minute fraction of the 65,000 combat troops at that time. A Russian adviser, V. A. Sakanovsky ('Nilov'), in discussing the reasons for the 20 March coup, stated that communist political workers manned the most important posts in the army, appointed members of their own cliques to various positions, and secretly pursued tasks unknown to the respective commanding officers, which aroused the jealousy and indignation of the military officers of all ranks as well as of non-communist workers. He reported that the chief of the Political Department of the First Corps, four out of five commissars of its divisions, and five of the 16 regimental commissars were communists.[60]

All communists received directives to penetrate Kuomintang organizations and gain influence therein, according to the Russian author of 'Political work in the National Revolutionary Army'. The current slogan was 'A good communist is a good member of the Kuomintang nucleus'. This penetration, and particularly in the key area of political indoctrination of troops, intensely concerned some Kuomintang leaders. Furthermore, the Kwangtung Provincial Committee of the Chinese Communist Party had established a special Military Section at Canton to direct the work of communists in the army. It was a small, secret body whose membership was unknown to the mass of party comrades, and it directed the secret work of communist nuclei in the army. It was also supposed to organize armed detachments of workers and peasants, establish nuclei in secret societies, landowners' detachments and other armed groups, and organize nuclei on trunk railways and waterways to disrupt the enemy's

---

60 Wilbur and How, *Documents*, 259, deductively dated as between 10 and 16 April 1926. A disappointingly vague account of communist penetration of the Political Department is in *Kuo-chün cheng-kung shih-kao* (Draft history of political work in the National Army) 1. 212–221, esp. p. 221, where such penetration is blamed upon Ch'en Kung-po.

rear and put down counter-revolutionary uprisings. Communists who, in the guise of Kuomintang members, penetrated clubs and societies in the army, such as the League of Military Youth and the Society for the Study of Sun Wen-ism, were to follow the directives of the Military Section. They were also to watch the behaviour of officers and report any harmful activity to higher organizations of the Communist Party. In short, it was the communist intention to influence insofar as possible the politicization of the National Revolutionary Army even though they could not entirely direct it.

How well this secret system was kept from knowledge of the Kuomintang leadership is unknown. Nevertheless, communist organizational and propaganda work within the military could not be entirely concealed.

Communist leadership of mass movements before the Northern Expedition

The Chinese Communist Party committed itself to organizing the Chinese masses – labourers, peasants, soldiers and students – and to radicalizing these groups in preparation for that future day when the revolution would move to its second stage, the socialist revolution. The leadership intended both to control mass organizations and to infuse the party's own ranks with proletarians in order to make it a mass party. An enlarged plenum of the Party's Central Committee held in Peking in October 1925 adopted a series of 'Resolutions on the question of organization' which show these intentions. The second resolution exhorted:

... We must on the one hand assemble and organize the proletariat; on the other hand, we must provide it with political training and education. Through study we have come to understand the means of unifying the peasantry and allying it with other democratic elements. Before we can perform this historically significant duty, however, we must first of all expand our party by absorbing into the party the proletariat and the most revolutionary elements of the advanced intelligentsia. . . . It is absolutely true that the future destiny of the Chinese revolutionary movement depends entirely upon whether or not the Chinese Communist Party will be able to organize and lead the masses.[61]

The following year was marked by considerable success in enlarging the Communist Party and its Youth Corps and changing the social composition of their memberships. For example, the Communist Youth Corps, as it was renamed in February 1925, grew from less than 2,500 in early 1925 to some 12,500 in November 1926. Prior to 30 May 1925, 90 per cent of its members were students but by September they made up only

61 Wilbur and How, *Documents*, 100–1. Other parts of the resolutions instruct party members how to absorb proletarian elements and they criticize past mistakes in mass organization.

49 per cent. In November 1926 students constituted 35 per cent; workers, 40 per cent; and peasants, 5 per cent.[62] The Communist Party also grew rapidly as a result of the revolutionary upsurge in mid 1925. Near the end of 1926 the Party, which had been made up almost entirely of intellectuals, had changed its composition with a reported 66 per cent classified as proletarians, 22 per cent as intellectuals, 5 per cent as peasants, and 2 per cent as soldiers.[63] These proportions may, however, include both the Party and the Youth Corps.

Communists worked diligently to try to expand the National General Labour Union (Ch'üan-kuo tsung-kung hui) which they organized at a conference in Canton in May 1925, and which they controlled.[64] By the time of the next congress in May 1926 the membership in constituent unions was said to have grown from 540,000 to 1,241,000.[65] Because of repression, however, many of the unions had been driven underground. For example, in Shanghai the General Labour Union announced on 28 July 1925 that it had 218,000 members in 117 unions. This rapid growth was a result of the great patriotic June strikes and the fact that many workers received strike pay only through their unions. There was also coercion and intimidation by the unions' pickets. A year later the Shanghai General Labour Union claimed only 43,000 members (another account gives 81,000 for May 1926)[66] after the union's headquarters had been forcibly closed and such militant leaders as Li Li-san and Liu Shao-ch'i

62 See 'Report of the communistic movement of youth of China', *China illustrated review*, Peking, 28 Jan. 1928, 14–16. This is a document seized in the Peking raid; it was brought to my attention by Mrs Carol Andrews. Also, 'Report of the Young Communist International at the Sixth World Congress of the Communist International', *Lieh-ning ch'ing-nien*, 1. 10 (15 Feb. 1929) 69–94, 84. Files are in the Library of Congress.

63 Robert C. North, *Moscow and Chinese communists*, 131, citing *Report on the activity of the Communist International, March-November, 1926*, 118. Another account of membership composition at the time of the Fifth CCP Congress in May 1927 gives the following: Workers, 53.8 per cent; intellectuals, 19.1; peasants, 18.7; military men, 3.1; middle and small merchants, 0.5 per cent. Pavel Mif, *Chin-chi shih-ch'i chung ti Chung-kuo Kung-ch'an-tang* (The Chinese Communist Party in critical days) (trans. from the Russian), 37.

64 See *Supra*, f.n. 33.

65 'Lo-sheng' (pseud.), 'Ti-san-tz'u ch'üan-kuo lao-tung ta-hui chih ching-kuo chi ch'i chieh-kuo' (Experiences and results of the Third National Labour Congress), *HTCP*, 155 (5 May 1926) reprinted in *Ti-i-tz'u kuo-nei ko-ming chan-cheng shih-ch'i ti kung-jen yun-tung* (The workers' movement during the First Revolutionary Civil War period), 219. An important item which I have not seen used is Liu Shao-ch'i's report on the Chinese labour movement in the past year, i.e., up to May 1926, in *Cheng-chih chou-pao*, 14 (Canton, 5 June 1926) which is available in U.S. National Archives Microfilm 329, Reel 56, 893.00/ 7980.

66 Numbers in Chesneaux, *The Chinese labor movement*, 269 (based upon police daily report for 7 August 1925. I believe the exact figure was 217,804); and Chesneaux, 339. A British labour expert visited Shanghai in 1926 and was told that the Shanghai Federation of Labour Unions – i.e., the General Labour Union – claimed only 81,000 members in 15 unions with 47 branches in May 1926. Col. C. L'Estrange Malone, *New China, report of an investigation. Pt. II. Labour conditions and labour organizations 1926*.

had been driven from Shanghai the previous September. Despite such reverses and the rivalry and opposition of non-communist unions and federations, there were now many experienced labour organizers in the Communist Party after five years of work, and not a few among them were actual proletarians.[67] Moreover, Canton communists dominated the strike committee, which managed the Hong Kong-Canton strike, controlled the armed picket corps, and assumed some aspects of judicial and police authority.

The farmers' movement was greatly expanded in the year between May 1925 and May 1926, when the First and Second Congresses of the Kwangtung Farmers' Associations met in Canton. A fairly reliable figure for April 1925 showed 172,185 members in 557 villages or *hsiang*, in only 22 of Kwangtung's 94 counties.[68] A detailed report for May 1926 showed 626,457 members in 4,216 *hsiang* associations in 66 counties.[69] Still, this was a small proportion of the millions of farm families in the province. The nearly five-fold increase resulted from active organizing by graduates of the Farmers' Movement Training Institute, always headed by a communist member of the Kuomintang, which turned out 478 specialists, many of them farmers, from the five classes held between July 1924 and December 1925.[70] When the associations are plotted by counties on a map of Kwangtung, the greatest concentrations appear in the south-east (Hai-feng, Lu-feng and Wu-hua counties, where P'eng P'ai was the leader), in a few delta counties near Canton (especially Shun-te, Tung-wan and Hsiang-shan), and in Kwang-ning county in the north-west, where the movement had its first great success. In regions not controlled by the National Revolutionary Army, such as the north-east, or only recently conquered, such as the south-west, there were very few farmers' associations and memberships were small. The reason seems clear. Farmers' associations were agents of social revolution as well as instruments for the national revolution. It was difficult to organize and sustain them in areas where nationalist military power did not reach.

Local associations repeatedly engaged in struggles to eliminate socio-economic grievances, which pitted them against local power-holders such as wealthy landowners and taxing authorities, who often controlled local

67 This theme is developed by Chesneaux, *The Chinese labour movement*, 400–2.
68 See *Supra*, f.n. 21. The official figures for May 1925 were 210,000, but I consider them unreliable.
69 Lo Ch'i-yuan, 'Hui-wu tsung pao-kao' (General report of the association's work), *Chung-kuo nung-min*, 6/7 (July 1926) 639–87, 654. This gives exact figures for each county. There are detailed figures for later in 1926, showing 823,338 members in 6,442 associations, in 71 counties. See Chang, *The farmers' movement in Kwangtung*, 15–16.
70 Etō, 'Hai-lu-feng', 1. 182, based upon detailed reports in *Chung-kuo nung-min*. Hofheinz, *The broken wave*, 78–92 discusses the Institute.

militia. Better organized farmers' associations had their trained and armed guards. A good deal of bloodshed and intimidation by both sides marked these struggles. A list of 164 incidents of conflict during the first three-and-a-half months of 1926 categorizes the majority as struggles against oppression by *min t'uan*, 'local bullies and evil gentry'; looting and killing by bandits; and harassment by army units and oppression by officials. Others arose from more strictly economic causes.[71] Statements by the communist leadership emphasized the support given by farmers' associations to the National Revolutionary Army's campaigns in Kwangtung and to the Hong Kong strike and boycott. In short, they supported the revolution as well as engaged in class struggle.

The Russian role by early 1926

Soviet Russia and the Comintern advised and financed the Chinese revolutionary movement, and attempted to steer it to success in the defeat of imperialism and Chinese militarism. (A detailed account is beyond the scope of this chapter, but a summary as of early 1926 may help to explain developments.)

The extent of Russian financing of Chinese revolutionary activities is still secret; here it is possible only to give scattered examples based upon seemingly reliable evidence. In March 1923 the Russian leadership decided to assist Sun Yat-sen and voted to render financial aid in the amount of Ch.\$2 million.[72] Borodin provided part of the initial financing of Whampoa Military Academy, and he later told Louis Fischer that the Soviet government had made a grant of 3 million roubles (about Ch.\$2.7 million) for the organization and initial running expenses of the school.[73] Entries in Blyukher's diary show that the monthly subsidy was Ch.\$ 100,000 in November 1924.[74] The shipment of arms which came to Canton on the *Vorovsky* in October 1924 was a gift, but later the Canton government was expected to pay for arms and munitions shipped from Vladivostok, as shown by documents seized in the Soviet military attaché's office in Peking in April 1927. Egorov, the attaché, drafted a tele-

71 Lo Ch'i-yuan, 'Hui-wu tsung pao-kao', 667–8; summarized with examples in Chang, *The farmers' movement*, 24–30.

72 R. A. Mirovitskaia, 'Mikhail Borodin (1884–1951)' in *Vidnye Sovetskie kommunisty – uchastniki Kitaiskoi revolutsii* (Outstanding Soviet communists – the participants in the Chinese revolution), 22–40, esp. p. 24, based on Soviet archives.

73 Fischer, *The soviets in world affairs*, 640. 'The National Revolutionary Army', written by members of the Soviet military mission in Canton, ending about 19 April, states that 'This school was organized by us in 1924 and at first was maintained at our expense.'

74 A. I. Kartunova, 'Vasilii Blyukher (1889–1938)', in *Vidne Sovetskie kommunisty – uchastniki Kitaiskoi revolutsii* (The outstanding Soviet communists – participants in the Chinese revolution), 41–65, pp. 62–3.

gram to 'Galen' (Blyukher) on 4 July 1926 informing him that military supplies already provided to Canton as of 1 December [1925] had cost 2.5 million roubles, and must be paid for immediately; in future Canton's orders were to be executed as far as possible only for cash payments.[75] In August 1924, when Dr Sun established a central bank in Canton, Russia promised to underwrite the bank to the extent of Canton $10 million, though apparently only $30,000 was transmitted at that time.[76] Russia also subsidized the Kuomintang, through Borodin, at the rate of about Ch.$35,000 a month in 1924, according to Ma Soo, a confidant of Dr Sun, who visited Canton in October; and Blyukher's diary entry for 1 December indicates that Borodin had been making payments for salaries of Kuomintang officials and providing subsidies for party newspapers and journals.[77]

When Chinese workmen went on strike at the Japanese textile mills in Shanghai in February 1925, *Izvestia* stated on 3 March that Profintern, 'The Red International of Trade Unions,' was sending 30,000 roubles to support the workers; it also published a translation of the strike committee's acknowledgment of assistance.[78] After the explosive May Thirtieth Incident, Russian trade unions quickly sent 148,000 roubles to support the striking Chinese workers in Shanghai, according to the Moscow press.[79] Probably one would need to see Borodin's account books to know how much was provided to support Hong Kong workers who settled in Canton during the protracted strike and boycott of 1925–26, for a document found in the Peking raid, which provides a history of the strike as of March 1926, mentions only that funds were 'partly subscribed throughout China and abroad among the Chinese and the proletariat.'[80] In the north, Soviet advisers trained and equipped the army of General Feng Yü-hsiang. Between April 1925 and March 1926 Russia supplied Feng

75 Reprinted in *The China yearbook 1928*, 802. Alexandr Il'ich Egorov, a hero of the Russian civil war, came to Peking late in 1925 to take over the position of military attaché.

76 C. Martin Wilbur, *Sun Yat-sen: frustrated patriot*, 212 and 352, f.n. 99.

77 USDS 893.00/6393, dispatch, Mayer, Peking, 9 June 1925, enclosing Jenkins' dispatch from Canton, 29 May, reporting an interview with Ma Soo published in the *Hong Kong Telegraph* on 27 May. Kartunova, 'Vasilii Blyukher', 62–3. Both accounts identify Liao Chung-k'ai as the Kuomintang official negotiating with Borodin and, later, with Blyukher for allocation of Russian funds.

78 USDS 893.5045/53, dispatch, Coleman, Riga, 9 March 1925, trans. from Moscow *Izvestia*, No. 51, 3 March.

79 USDS 893.00B/156, telegram, Coleman, Riga, 17 June 1925. In addition Rub. 5,000 contributed in other countries was transmitted through Moscow.

80 GBFO F6462/3241/10 (now filed in FO 371/12501) and printed in FO 405/254. Confidential. *Further correspondence respecting China*, 13315, July–Sept. 1927, no. 27. Teng Chung-hsia, who was a leader of the strike, gives a total of Ch.$5,170,000 as the income of the strike committee to June 1926, with sources specified in round numbers; among these is 'other sources – 200,000'. Teng Chung-hsia, *Chung-kuo chih-kung yün-tung chien-shih*, 184.

with more than 6 million roubles' worth of arms and ammunition, according to his signed receipts.[81] I have seen no verifiable estimate of the extent of the Comintern's financial assistance to the Chinese Communist Party.

Money bought influence, but not absolute authority. The Russians in China suffered frustrations and disappointments. Despite the great growth of membership in the Chinese Communist Party and the Socialist Youth Corps in the latter half of 1925, and the apparent success of the party in organizing striking workers from Hong Kong and Kwangtung farmers, leaders of the Chinese party were restive at the constraints of working within the Kuomintang. Comintern advisers had to curb efforts to withdraw the Communist Party from the internal alliance.[82] On 13 March 1926, the Executive Committee of the Comintern passed a resolution on China which insisted on the 'fighting alliance of the Kuomintang with the communists'; scolded the party for slowness in organizational development because of its 'narrow sectarian views' on admission of workers; and warned against two deviations: 'right-wing deviationism' – a formless merging with the general democratic national movement – and 'left moods' – trying to skip over the revolutionary-democratic stage straight to the proletarian dictatorship and Soviet power, forgetting the peasantry. Once more the ECCI insisted, as it had since 1923, that 'the fundamental problem of the Chinese national liberation movement is the peasant problem'. It called upon the Chinese comrades 'to unite all existing peasant organizations into common revolutionary centres . . . which would be capable of rousing the whole peasantry to an armed struggle against the militarists and the administrators, middlemen and gentry who bolster up the semi-feudal order in the villages'.[83] This was an assignment easy to make in Moscow but not so easy to execute in China where, as late as July 1926, a plenum of the Executive Committee of the Communist Party admitted that there were barely 120 persons responsible for party work, when at least 355 directing personnel were needed.[84]

Russia had made a large investment in North China, attempting to strengthen and win over the Kuominchün, The National People's Army, organized by Feng Yü-hsiang and other generals after the coup against Wu P'ei-fu in October 1924. Beginning in late April 1925 a team of Soviet

---

81 Wilbur and How, *Documents*, 333 and 521, f.n. 93. The total may have been nearly Rub. 11 million.

82 *Ibid.* 92.

83 'Resolution on the Chinese question of the Sixth ECCI plenum' in *International press correspondence*, 6. 40 (6 May 1926) as quoted in Helmut Gruber, *Soviet Russia masters the Comintern*, 457-61.

84 Wilbur and How, *Documents*, 115.

military advisers began working with General Feng's First Kuominchün and by November there were 42 Russians working in his base at Kalgan. They did not succeed in getting close to Feng – let alone control him in Russia's interest – but they laboured hard to improve the junior officer corps by establishing a variety of technical schools. They had no such success politically as their colleagues seemed to be having in Canton. In June 1925, a team of 43 Russians arrived in Kaifeng, Honan, to work with the Second Kuominchün, commanded by Yueh Wei-chün. They were frustrated on every hand, and only a few of them remained to see the collapse of Yueh's army in early March 1926 under attack from rural 'Red Spears'. Russian advisers tried, but failed, to link up with the Third Kuominchün; it, too, disintegrated in February 1926.

By the end of 1925 Kuo Sung-ling's effort to overthrow Chang Tso-lin, Russia's enemy, had failed. This was partly due to ineffective support from the Kuominchün – though 18 members of the Russian Kalgan mission assisted Feng's offensive – and partly because the Japanese army in Manchuria intervened to protect Chang Tso-lin. General Feng then went into retirement and the commanders of his First Kuominchün were preparing to withdraw beyond the Great Wall to avoid war with the combined forces of Chang Tso-lin and a revived Wu P'ei-fu, who was no more friendly to Russia than was General Chang.[85] During Kuo Sungling's rebellion, Chang Tso-lin had sent for reinforcements from Heilungkiang, but the Russian manager of the Chinese Eastern Railway, A. N. Ivanov, refused to allow the troops to be moved on the railway without prepayment of the expense. The troops proceeded south by another route, but after suppression of the rebellion the returning troops commandeered several trains for the return to Harbin. Ivanov retaliated by shutting down the Changchun-Harbin section of the railway, and was in turn arrested by the Chinese troops on 22 January 1926. Karakhan issued an ultimatum, and the problem was settled through negotiations at Mukden. Chang Tso-lin was now fully aware of Russian power in the north of his domain and of Russian assistance to his domestic enemies.[86]

In February, shortly after and during these events, a commission from Moscow, headed by A. S. Bubnov, was in Peking studying the work of

85 Based upon a chapter written by the late Mrs Julie How Hwa for the forthcoming expanded version of Wilbur and How, *Documents*. Her basic sources were documents seized in the Peking raid as clarified by other contemporary evidence. A young Russian woman worked as an intepreter with the advisers in Kalgan and was in Peking during the first month of 1926. Her vivid account of these events is in Vera Vladimirovna Vishnyakova-Akimova, *Dva goda v vosstavshem Kitae, 1925–1927: vospominania,* trans. by Steven I. Levine, *Two years in revolutionary China, 1925–1927,* see 80–122.

86 Sow-theng Leong, *Sino-Soviet diplomatic relations, 1917–1926,* 282–3; and O. Edmund Clubb, *China and Russia: the 'great game',* 217–19.

the Russian advisers in North and South China and looking into general questions of Soviet aid to the Chinese revolution. The commission met with Ambassador Karakhan, the military attaché, Egòrov, and some advisers who had worked with Feng Yü-hsiang and in Canton. In spite of apprehensions about General Feng's true dedication to revolution, Bubnov and Karakhan decided he should continue to be courted.[87]

On 18 March a grave incident occurred in Peking which strained relations of the First Kuominchün with the Kuomintang and Communist Party, and may have further discouraged the Russian embassy. The incident was an outgrowth of an ultimatum which eight Boxer Protocol powers handed to Tuan Ch'i-jui's government on 16 March, demanding removal of all obstacles to their communications between Peking and the sea, in conformity with the Boxer Protocol of 1901. Next day representatives of Chinese civic and political organizations in Peking petitioned the government to reject the ultimatum, but were driven off and many petitioners were injured. On the morning of 18 March a mass meeting adopted resolutions demanding abrogation of the Boxer Protocol and all 'unequal treaties'. Leaders of the Kuomintang and the Communist Party jointly organized the protest, which iterated a basic objective of both parties. About two thousand demonstrators, many of them students, marched towards the cabinet offices but were attacked by government guards and 47 demonstrators were killed, almost as many Chinese as had been slain in the Shakee massacre. The government issued a warrant for the arrest of five prominent Kuomintang figures in Peking, one of whom, Li Ta-chao, was a founder of the Communist Party. All went into hiding, Li taking sanctuary in the Russian embassy. Tuan Ch'i-jui's government had survived through Feng Yü-hsiang's support. A Kuominchün general was garrison commander and chief of police in Peking, but seemingly did nothing to prevent the massacre. Hence, the Kuomintang's Peking municipal headquarters laid the blame for the incident upon Kuominchün leaders and stated in a resolution that the Kuomintang would break off friendly relations with the Kuominchün unless Tuan and other high officials were arrested and executed. This did not occur.[88]

In South China, the Russian aid mission probably numbered fifty or more adult workers early in March 1926. Six Russian ships plied regularly between Vladivostok and Canton bringing oil, weapons and disassembled aircraft.[89] The head of the military mission was N. V. Kuybyshev

87 See *supra*, f.n. 85.
88 *Idem.*
89 This is an estimate, for the numbers changed as new advisers arrived, some coming from

('Kisan'ka'), who had replaced General Blyukher, but his relations with Chiang Kai-shek, head of the Party Army and commandant of the Military Academy, were strained.

These problems and uncertainties help to explain a remarkably interesting resolution on China and Japan passed by a special commission of the Politburo of the Russian Communist Party on 25 March 1926, and formally approved by the Politburo a week later.[90] The Politburo commission, headed by Leon Trotsky, expressed considerable apprehension concerning the correlation of Chinese internal forces and the danger of consolidation of imperialist forces after the signing of the Locarno treaties of December 1925. The commission feared that Great Britain and Japan might join against the Chinese revolution and Soviet Russia. The Soviet Union needed an extended respite and the Chinese revolutionary movement needed to gain time. To meet these dangers and to protect Russian interests in Manchuria, the commission decided it was necessary to reach an understanding with Japan and Chang Tso-lin that would assure both the Japanese and the Russian positions in Manchuria. It was necessary to be 'reconciled to the fact that southern Manchuria will remain in Japanese hands during the period ahead'. The accommodation policy had to be submitted for approval to the Chinese Communist Party and the Kuomintang, recognizing how difficult it would be for them to accept the line in view of Chinese hatred for Japan. The orientation towards coming to 'a certain understanding with Japan' was to be carefully prepared so that Chinese revolutionary forces would not interpret it incorrectly as 'a sacrifice of Chinese interest, for the purpose of a settlement of Soviet-Japanese political relations'. To orient public opinion properly it would be necessary to strengthen revolutionary and anti-imperialist influences on the Chinese press.

If Manchuria were to become autonomous, which the commission said Japan desired, Russia should get Chang Tso-lin to give up 'meddling in the internal affairs of the rest of China'. The Chinese Eastern Railway should be brought completely under Russian control, though masked by

---

reduced or abandoned military missions in the north. C.C. Wu told the German consul, probably late in October 1925, that there were 38 Russians in the Canton government's service, GBFO 405/248 No. 251 (F 5914/194/10). Vishnyakova-Akimova, who arrived in Canton 28 February 1926, mentions six newcomers on her ship, and describes many she met in Canton, but does not give a total figure. She names the six Russian vessels. *Dva goda v vosstavshem Kitae*, Levine trans., 141, 149, 176–88.

90 The document is in the Trotsky Archives at Harvard University. 'Problems of our policy with respect to China and Japan' in Leon Trotsky, *Leon Trotsky on China: introduction by Peng Shu-tse*, 102–10. Abstract in Gruber, *Soviet Russia masters the Comintern*, 462–7, under a different title and translation; and commented upon in Leong, *Sino-Soviet diplomatic relations*, 286–9. Other members of the special commission were Chicherin, Dzerzhinsky and Voroshilov.

measures of a cultural nature called Sinification. In negotiations with Chang Tso-lin, Russia should encourage Chang to maintain good and stable relations with Japan. Russia would not encroach on such relations, but should make clear that it was to the Manchurian government's advantage to maintain good relations with Russia also, to guarantee itself a certain independence in relation to Japan. It could be pointed out to Chang Tso-lin that certain Japanese circles were ready to have him replaced by another buffer general, 'but that we see no reason for him to be replaced . . . while normal relations exist.' One of the points of agreement with Chang, and later with Japan, should be to protect revolutionary Mongolia from Chang's encroachment.

Before entering negotiations with Japan, Russia should concentrate on actually improving relations and influencing Japanese public opinion. The commission contemplated a possible tripartite agreement (Soviet Union, Japan, China), but 'the ground should be prepared politically and diplomatically in such a way that it will be impossible for the Chinese to interpret any concessions China may find itself temporarily forced to make to Japan as a division of spheres of influence with our participation'. Left-wing circles should be made aware that Russia was prepared to tolerate only those Chinese concessions to Japanese imperialism that were necessary to defend the revolutionary movement from a united imperialist offensive. The possible joint negotiations should have as their objective, at the cost of some concessions, to drive a wedge between Japan and Britain.

Russia was openly to declare its full sympathy with the struggle of the Chinese masses for a single independent government; however, it would reject the idea of any military intervention by Russia: the Chinese problem must be solved by the Chinese people themselves. Until realization of a unified China, the Soviet government 'attempts to establish and maintain loyal relations with all governments existing in China, central as well as provincial.' Hence, looking southwards, the commission considered that if the people's armies [that is, Kuominchün] had to surrender ground to Wu P'ei-fu for a long period it might be expedient to reach an agreement with Wu in order to weaken his dependence on Britain, 'the main and implacable foe of Chinese independence'. The Canton government was to be encouraged to perceive its area not only as a temporary revolutionary beach-head but also a country needing a stable administration, and to concentrate all its efforts on internal reform and defence. Stalin added to the approved text that in the present period the Canton government should 'emphatically reject any idea of an aggressive military campaign and, in general, any activity that would push the imperialists onto the path of military intervention' – a caution against Chiang Kai-shek's plan for a Northern Expedition. A note directed that the Soviet ambassador in Paris should explore the possibility that the Canton government might work out a *modus vivendi* with France and send a representative there to sound out this possibility.[91]

In short, as one specialist on Sino-Soviet relations during this period summarized the thrust of the document, the Russian tactic 'was to divide the imperialist camp by isolating Britain as the chief target of antiforeignism and buying off Japan at China's expense.'[92] Events transpiring in Canton at this very time make it evident, however, that Russia could not control the direction of the national revolution. Apparently the implications of Chiang Kai-shek's 20th March coup were not yet appreciated by the top leadership in Moscow by the end of March, or at least did not affect their basic strategy, which was concerned with the north.

Readjustment of power relations in Kwangtung

The reasons for the '*Chung-shan* gunboat incident' of 20 March 1926 and Chiang's power-play thereafter are too complex and confused to detail here.[93] Apparently Chiang developed a hostility towards three of the top Russian military advisers in Canton because of their domineering attitudes and control over allocation of Russian arms and funds, their lack of support for a Northern Expedition, and his suspicions that N. V. Kuybyshev was conniving with Wang Ching-wei and others to have him sent off to Russia. He also became hostile to Wang, his main political rival, whom he suspected of working hand-in-glove with the Russians against him.[94]

Suspicious comings and goings of the gunboat *Chung-shan* on 18 and 19 March, which was anchored off Chiang's headquarters at Whampoa with full steam up, may have led Chiang to believe that a plan to abduct him and send him to Russia was underway. On the morning of 20 March he had the vessel seized, arrested Li Chih-lung, the acting chief of the Naval Bureau and a communist, declared martial law in Canton, and had

---

91 The Gruber translation says, to send 'the president of the Canton government', rather than 'a representative' of the government. This is interesting in view of the fact that one outcome of Chiang's 20 March *coup d'état*, was that Wang Ching-wei left for France in May.
92 Leong, *Sino-Soviet diplomatic relations*, 287.
93 Two valuable recent studies are Wu Tien-wei, 'Chiang Kai-shek's March twentieth coup d'etat of 1926', *JAS*, 27 (May 1968) 585–602, and *TJK*, 489–94. A brief account is in Wilbur and How, *Documents*, 218–24.
94 Evidences of Chiang's growing suspicions are found in his 'Diary' (Mao, CKSHS) for the period from 19 Jan. to 15 March 1926. He made a series of charges against Wang early in April in Chiang Kai-shek, 'A letter of reply to Wang Ching-wei', later published in Wen-hua yen-chiu she, comp. *Chung-kuo wu ta wei-jen shou-cha* (Letters of China's five great leaders), 246–53.

his troops disarm the guards protecting the residences of the Russian advisers and the headquarters of the communist-controlled Hong Kong-Canton strike committee.[95] This sudden action, executed without consultation with Wang Ching-wei or forewarning to the Russian advisers, created a political storm which only ended with the Russians' agreement to deport the three advisers to whom Chiang most objected, the withdrawal of communist political workers from the First Corps, and the departure of Wang Ching-wei for France on 9 May.

On 29 April Borodin returned to Canton, together with Hu Han-min, Eugene Chen, and several leftist leaders. Thereafter there was intense bargaining between Chiang and Borodin, in which it seems that Borodin made most of the concessions. Chiang agreed to expel a group of more conservative Kuomintang officials and to continue cooperation with Soviet Russia and the Chinese Communist Party, while Borodin agreed to continue Russian aid and to support the Northern Expedition, which had been opposed by the Russian advisers and the Chinese Communist Party. Communists would restrict very considerably their activities in the Kuomintang.

Chiang called for a plenary meeting of the Kuomintang Central Executive Committee, which was held from 15 to 25 May, and which worked out severe restrictions on Communist Party influences within the Kuomintang. Chiang formulated most of the proposals that were adopted, with verbal modifications. Once more a joint council of high-level Kuomintang and communist representatives was planned to settle obstacles to inter-party cooperation with the help of a representative of the Third International. Members of 'another party' in the Kuomintang were forbidden to criticize the leader and his Three Principles of the People. The other party must turn over to the chairman of the Kuomintang CEC a list of its members who had joined the senior party, and such members might not occupy more than one third of the positions in executive committees of the Kuomintang in central, provincial or metropolitan headquarters, nor serve as heads of bureaus of the central organ. All orders of another party to its members in the Kuomintang must first be submitted to and passed by the joint council, and members of the Kuomintang might not join another party without permission. Violators of these conditions were to be expelled immediately. A new office was created with large powers, that of chairman of the standing committee of the Kuomintang's Central Executive Committee. Chiang Kai-shek's patron, Chang Jen-chieh (Ching-chiang), was elected to the position,

95 Mao, *CKSHS*, entries for 22 and 23 March, and 20 April, reprinted in *KMWH*, 9. 1291–300, give Chiang's account of the incident.

though he was not even a member of the committee. All Kuomintang members were to be re-registered; they were to pledge their allegiance to specified major writings of Sun Yat-sen and to the manifestos and resolutions of the First and Second Congresses; and those who had joined other political bodies not authorized by 'our party' must withdraw from them.[96] As an earlier part of the settlement, the Communist Party withdrew its members who were Kuomintang party representatives in the Army's First Corps on 10 April.[97] But many others retained their positions.

Such were some results of the negotiations between Chiang and Borodin. Communists within the Kuomintang must restrain their criticisms and curtail their active roles in high levels of the parent party; a mechanism was devised to adjudicate inter-party conflict; and the Kuomintang was somewhat further centralized. Communists relinquished important posts in the Kuomintang's Organization Bureau and the bureaus of propaganda and farmers, and in the Secretariat. Chiang, himself, became head of the Organization Bureau with his close associate, Ch'en Kuo-fu, as his deputy. Rightists also were curbed with the departure of Hu Han-min for Shanghai on 9 May, the imprisonment of Wu T'ieh-ch'eng on the 30th, and the expulsion of C.C. Wu, the foreign minister, who was replaced by the leftist, Eugene Chen. Planning for the Northern Expedition now resumed with full purpose.

THE DRIVE TO UNIFY CHINA – FIRST PHASE

Planning for the Northern Expedition

Planning had long been underway for a military campaign from Kwangtung province northwards to the Yangtze. General Blyukher presented a partial plan in March and June 1925, and drew up a more complete one in September while in Kalgan recuperating from Canton's sultry climate, both thermal and political.[98] The September plan estimated the enemy's potential resistance against an expedition made up of regrouped and better trained Nationalist forces, and predicted no difficulty in the ex-

---

96 Abstracted from the minutes of the plenum, quoted in *TJK*, 504–9, and Mao, *CKSHS*, 15–25 May.
97 Wilbur and How, *Documents*, 222.
98 A. I. Kartunova, 'Blucher's "grand plan" of 1926', trans. by Jan J. Solecki with notes by C. Martin Wilbur, *CQ*, 35 (July–Sept. 1968) 18–39. In Oct. 1925 the Russian embassy in Peking sent A. Khmelev to Canton to investigate conditions, and he reported on the constant friction between 'Galen' and Borodin, as a consequence of which Blyukher had been compelled to leave Canton. 'Extract (pp. 27–30) from the "Report *Journey to Canton* in October, 1925" by A. Khmeloff', a document from the Peking Raid of 6 April 1927. Trans. now in Hoover Institution on War, Revolution and Peace, Stanford, California, Jay Calvin Huston Collection.

pedition taking the Wuhan cities on the middle Yangtze and then capturing Shanghai. It was a remarkably prescient prediction.

On 16 April 1926 a joint meeting of the Kuomintang Political Council and the Military Council appointed Chiang Kai-shek, Chu P'ei-te and Li Chi-shen as a committee to plan for the Northern Expedition.[99] After Borodin's return and promise of support for the northern campaign, Chinese and Russian staff members did further planning, and when Blyukher returned to Canton late in May he refined the plans and presented them to the Military Council on 23 June.[100] Blyukher emphasized a single thrust through Hunan towards Hankow, with forces deployed to protect Kwangtung from Fukien on the east and other forces to protect the expedition's right flank from attack by Sun Ch'uan-fang in Kiangsi. The expedition was to begin only when all troops were in position, because of the difficulty of coordination, given the primitive facilities for communication between units.

In preparation for the campaign Chiang Kai-shek organized a General Headquarters of the National Revolutionary Army, which eventually replaced the Military Council, a collegial group of leading political and military figures, as the principal command organ. General Li Chi-shen was appointed chief-of-staff, with General Pai Ch'ung-hsi as his deputy. Li was commander of the Fourth Corps and was to remain in Canton with two divisions as garrison commander. General Pai was a graduate of the Paoting Military Academy and was one of the triumvirate of young Kwangsi officers (the others being Li Tsung-jen and Huang Shao-hsiung) who had unified Kwangsi and brought it into alliance with the Nationalist government in Kwangtung. Pai was a noted strategist. As part of the reorganization, the Political Training Department of the Military Council was placed under General Headquarters, and renamed the General Political Department. Teng Yen-ta was appointed its chief, replacing Ch'en Kung-po, and Kuo Mo-jo became deputy chief and head of the Propaganda Department. Teng, an ardent revolutionist, had been a student at Paoting Military Academy, a regimental commander in the Kwangtung First Division that brought Sun Yat-sen back to Canton in 1923, one of the organizers of Whampoa Military Academy and assistant director of its training department. In 1925 Teng went to Germany where he became acquainted with a number of Chinese communists, and returned to China through Soviet Russia. Chiang Kai-shek then appointed him dean of the

99 Minutes of the Kuomintang Political Council, no. 131. Strangely this meeting is not mentioned in Chiang's diary, although he did attend.

100 A. I. Kartunova, 'Vasilii Blyukher (1889–1938)', 62–3. For that date Chiang's 'Diary' does not mention any such meeting, though he chaired a meeting of the Political Department of the commander-in-chief's headquarters on work to be done when battle began.

academy, but he was arrested along with a number of communists during the 20 March coup, and soon sent to Ch'ao-chow to head the branch of the academy there. Teng's appointment as head of the General Political Department put a leftist in charge. Kuo Mo-jo was a noted literary figure, who had been active in the May Thirtieth movement and had helped to transform the Creation Society, a literary group, into an agency promoting the national revolution. A devotee of Marxism-Leninism, Kuo later joined the Chinese Communist Party. Under the General Political Department there were political departments attached to the headquarters of the various corps and divisions making up the National Revolutionary Army.[101]

Three military coalitions stood in the way of the Nationalists' hopes of reunifying China through a military-political campaign in the late spring of 1926. Wu P'ei-fu had been trying since mid 1925 to form a coalition in Hupei, Honan and northern Hunan that could overthrow both the Kuominchün in the north and the Kuomintang in the south. Divisions under his direct command were reputed to be well-disciplined and excellent fighters, but he was also dependent upon many unreliable generals. Nationalist historians portray Wu's coalition as numbering more than 200,000 troops, probably a greatly exaggerated figure. Sun Ch'uanfang headed an 'Alliance of Five Provinces' in east China – Fukien, Chekiang, Kiangsu, Anhwei and Kiangsi. Based on the wealthy lower Yangtze region, this coalition had great financial resources, but the alliance was one of convenience. It too, was reputed to number more than 200,000 men. Chang Tso-lin headed the most formidable coalition, whose members dominated Manchuria, Shantung and much of Chihli. This relatively well-armed force was believed to number about 350,000 men. Chang Tso-lin and Wu P'ei-fu, though enemies of long standing, jointly supported a government in Peking and were attempting to drive Feng Yü-hsiang's forces out of their base around Nan-k'ou and Kalgan. Russia supported Feng's army, the First Kuominchün, with arms and advisers. In May 1926 Feng went to Moscow to seek more aid, and he sent delegates to Canton to work out an alliance with the Nationalists. Other military groups in West China had to be considered in strategic planning, though they were not strong enough to be menacing. Two naval concentrations on the east coast might play an important strategic role, one at Foochow and the other at Shanghai. The Shanghai ships were particularly dangerous because of the possibility that they might be

---

101 Biographies in Boorman, *Biographical dictionary*. The organizational system of the General Political Department and its subsidiaries is given in *Kuo-chün cheng-kung shih-kao*, 1. 264–72. Pictures of Teng and Kuo, p. 281.

used to disrupt military crossings or transport of troops on the lower Yangtze.[102]

The National Revolutionary Army had been enlarged by the recent addition of Kwangsi forces under the triumvir of Li Tsung-jen, Huang Shao-hsiung and Pai Ch'ung-hsi, designated as the Seventh Corps, and by a South Hunan division under T'ang Sheng-chih which was to become the Eighth Corps. The total force may have reached 150,000 men, but since many would have to guard the base area, the forces available for the campaign probably were less than 65,000 at the beginning.

Provincial origin, past history and recent politics determined the orientation of the corps and divisions making up the National Revolutionary Army. The First Corps was initially built up from training regiments at the Whampoa Military Academy. Many of the troops in these regiments had been recruited in Chekiang, Kiangsu and Anhwei. There were also regiments and divisions formed out of units in the Second Kwangtung Army. Ho Ying-ch'in, the commander, was a native of Kweichow and a graduate of a Japanese military school. He had participated in the Revolution of 1911–12 on the staff of Ch'en Ch'i-mei, a patron of Chiang Kai-shek. Before joining the staff at Whampoa he had been an officer in the Kweichow Army and then dean of studies at the famed Yunnan Military Academy. At Whampoa he was responsible for training the regiments which became the First Division. Most of the officers of the First Corps had been instructors or cadets at the Whampoa Military Academy commanded by Chiang Kai-shek, and the corps was considered his base of power. Members of the conservative Society for the Study of Sun Wen-ism dominated the political apparatus of the First Corps. The corps had five divisions and a total strength of 19 regiments, much more than any other in the National Revolutionary Army.

The Second Corps was made up largely of Hunanese. Its commander was the scholar-politician, T'an Yen-k'ai, who had several times been governor of Hunan after the 1911 Revolution, and also been associated with Sun Yat-sen's separatist governments in the south. He was a leading member of the coalition which ruled Kwangtung after Dr Sun's death. The actual field commander of the corps was Lu Ti-p'ing, a Hunanese general. A French-trained communist, Li Fu-ch'un, headed the political department, and many of the political workers at regimental level were communists. The Second Corps had four divisions and a strength of 12 regiments.

The Third Corps was mainly a Yunnanese force, commanded by Chu P'ei-te. General Chu was a long-time revolutionary who had commanded

102 *KMWH*, 12. 1780–9 *PFCS* 1. 62–8; *Pei-fa chien-shih*, charts, 46ff.

units of the Yunnan Army campaigning in neighbouring provinces, had assisted Sun Yat-sen's return to Canton in 1923, and Dr Sun selected him to head his personal guard. The Third corps had three divisions, made up of eight regiments and two battalions, one being artillery.

The Fourth Corps was a battle-hardened force built up from the old First Division of the Kwangtung Army, loyal to Sun Yat-sen. Li Chi-shen commanded the corps, and most of the officers were men of long revolutionary association. Besides its four divisions there was an independent regiment commanded by Yeh T'ing, a communist who had studied in the Red Army Academy and the University of the Toilers of the East, and he had recruited a number of communist cadets from Whampoa Academy as platoon commanders. The Fourth Corps had a total strength of 13 regiments and two artillery battalions and it rivalled the First Corps.

Li Fu-lin's Fifth Corps was essentially a garrison force south of Canton. Some of its units participated only briefly in southern Kiangsi.

The Sixth Corps was the last to be formed in the revolutionary base. Ch'eng Ch'ien was its commander. General Ch'eng was a Hunan military officer with a long career as a revolutionary and supporter of Sun Yat-sen. The Kuomintang party representative in the Sixth Corps was Lin Po-ch'ü (Lin Tsu-han), a Hunanese revolutionary associate of Ch'eng Ch'ien. Lin was a leader of both the Kuomintang and the Chinese Communist Party. Communist political workers who left the First Corps after the March 20th incident were assigned to the Sixth Corps. This rather mixed force had three divisions with nine regiments and two artillery battalions.

The Kwangsi force, named the Seventh Corps, was organized in brigades rather than divisions, and consisted of 18 regiments and two artillery battalions. Li Tsung-jen commanded the units which participated in the Northern Expedition, about half the force. The head of its political department was Huang Jih-k'uei, a communist who had been active in the student movement and was appointed secretary of the Kuomintang Youth Bureau after the Second Kuomintang Congress. However, Li Tsung-jen left Huang at rear headquarters and appointed Mai Huan-chang, a non-communist trained in France, to be in charge of political work among troops at the front.

The Eighth Corps of T'ang Sheng-chih was only being formed. It soon grew into six divisions in 17 regiments. The Kuomintang party representative was Liu Wen-tao, a man of considerable revolutionary experience, educated in China, Japan and France. He joined the Kuomintang in 1925.

There were also two infantry regiments made up of cadets at the Central

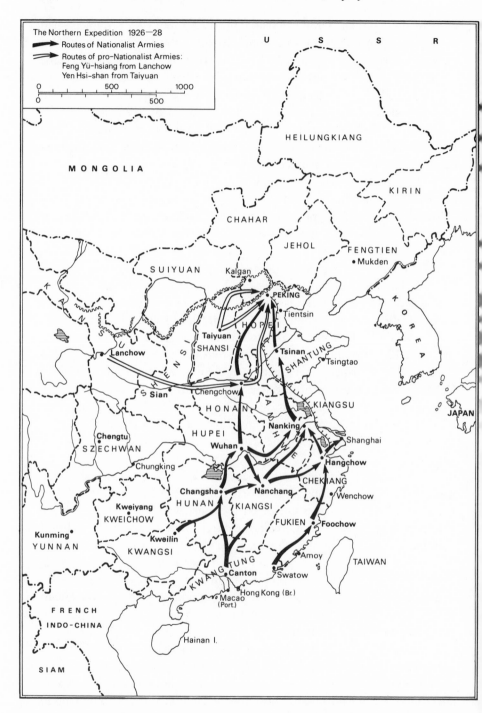

MAP 14. The Northern Expedition 1926–28

Military Political Academy, as the Whampoa Academy had been renamed, and two regiments of students of the fifth class; also a police regiment, and Lai Shih-huang's independent regiment, which was soon to become the Fourteenth Corps.[103]

Two routes from the provinces in the south led into Hunan, the first target of the Northern Expedition. A railway led northwards from Canton about 140 miles to Shao-kuan, from which point there was a toilsome ascent to a pass and a 30-mile portage to a tributary of the Hsiang River, which flows northwards through Hunan towards the Yangtze. The other route led from Kweilin in northern Kwangsi province through an easy connection to the headwaters of the Hsiang River in south-western Hunan. Hengyang, an important town in southern Hunan, was the place where the two routes joined. It was also T'ang Sheng-chih's main base, but in May 1926 General T'ang's hold on it was threatened from the north by another Hunanese general, Yeh K'ai-hsin. The first military movements in what became the Northern Expedition were the dispatches into Hunan of a brigade from Kwangsi and Yeh T'ing's independent regiment from Kwangtung to stiffen T'ang's resistance. On 2 June General T'ang accepted the post of commander of the Eighth Corps of the National Revolutionary Army, and on 5 June the Nationalist Government appointed Chiang Kai-shek as commander-in-chief of the army.

The Northern Expedition begins

By early July two divisions of the Fourth Corps, the 10th under Ch'en Ming-shu and the 12th under Chang Fa-k'uei, had joined Yeh T'ing's independent regiment in south-eastern Hunan, and more brigades of the Seventh Corps had entered South-west Hunan. Two rivers join the Hsiang about 50 kilometres south of Changsha, the Lien from the west and the Lu on the east. Advance Commander T'ang Sheng-chih ordered an offensive by the units of the three corps now in place on the west and east of the Hsiang River. Units of the Eighth Corps crossed the Lien, while on 10 July the Fourth Corps captured Li-ling on the P'ing-hsiang – Chu-chow railway line in the east. This breach of the Lien – Lo line left Changsha exposed; General Yeh K'ai-hsin retreated through the provincial capital into northern Hunan, and General T'ang entered Changsha

---

103 The careers of commanders and chief political workers are outlined in Boorman, *Biographical dictionary*. Tables of organization showing commanders of corps, divisions, regiments and battalions are given in *KMWH*, 12. 1802–3 (which I have followed), and in *PFCS* 2. 322ff., and *Pei-fa chien-shih*, 46ff.

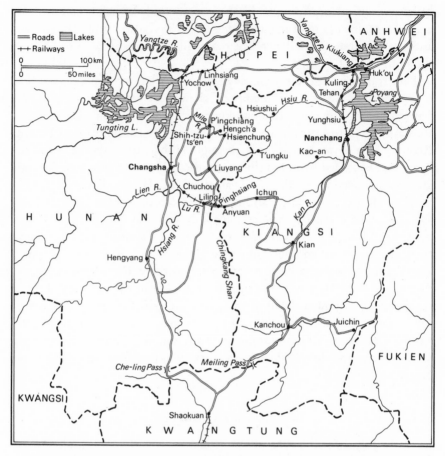

MAP 15.   Hunan and Kiangsi during the Northern Expedition

on 11 July. While this campaign was underway Chiang Kai-shek formally accepted the post of commander-in-chief of the National Revolutionary Army during a ceremony which officially launched the Northern Expedition on 9 July. Thus, with little fighting the revolutionary forces had captured most of the Hsiang River valley.

Major battles lay ahead as Wu P'ei-fu began to send divisions southwards and as the Second Division of the First Corps and the Sixth Corps were brought into Hunan as general reserves, and the Second and Third Corps were brought up to guard the right flank against an attack by Sun Ch'uan-fang from Kiangsi in the east. However, the Nationalists in Canton had been negotiating with Sun Ch'uan-fang to try to keep him neutral as long as possible. They also were negotiating with Yuan Tsu-ming, the military governor of Kweichow on the west, and on 11 July Chiang Kai-shek telegraphed T'ang Sheng-chih to say that Yuan and a subordinate general had joined the revolutionary side. On 20 July the Military Council of the national government appointed his two subordinates, P'eng Han-chang as commander of the Ninth Corps and Wang T'ien-p'ei as commander of the Tenth Corps. (This system of co-opting potential enemies or enrolling turncoat forces went on during most of the Northern Expedition, resulting in a tremendously bloated National Revolutionary Army, greatly diluted in quality.)[104]

Chiang Kai-shek left Canton for the front on 27 July accompanied by members of his staff and General Blyukher and a group of Russian advisers. Arriving at Changsha on 11 August he called a military conference to decide on next moves. The conference was attended by Pai Ch'ung-hsi, Teng Yen-ta, Ch'en Kung-po as head of the War Area Political Affairs Committee, Ch'en K'o-yü, deputy commander of the Fourth Corps, Li Tsung-jen, T'ang Sheng-chih, and various division commanders, Blyukher, and other advisers. The group finally decided to drive straight for Wuchang, the capital of Hupei province, and postpone the attack on Nanchang, the capital of Kiangsi, which apparently was Chiang Kai-shek's first objective. The Fourth Corps was to lead an attack on P'ing-chiang, a strongly held fortress on the Milo River and then race for Ting-ssu bridge on the railway leading to Wuchang. The Seventh Corps was to proceed north-east towards Wuchang, and the Eighth Corps to proceed on the west along the railway itself.

The Fourth Corps, with much dash and bravery, took P'ing-chiang on 19 August, with Huang Ch'i-hsiang's 36th Regiment of the 12th Division the first to enter the city. The victory at Ting-ssu bridge, defended by a strong force brought down by Wu P'ei-fu, and considered impossible to take from the south, was accomplished on the night of August 26/27, when local farmers guided the 36th Regiment through shallow waters for an attack on the bridge from behind. This was one of the crucial battles of the first phase of the campaign. General Wu P'ei-fu personally supervised the defences of Ho-sheng bridge, the next objective. Again the 12th Division led the fight, supported by the 10th Division and elements of the Seventh Corps. Despite Wu's desperate efforts to prevent his troops from retreating, they were defeated at many points on 30 August and fled.

---

104 An interesting report on Canton's negotiations is found in a document dated 3 June, 1926 and based upon reports from Borodin. Wilbur and How, *Documents*, p. 269. Donald A. Jordan, *The Northern Expedition: China's national revolution of 1926–1928*, 276–86, treats defections systematically. See also C. Martin Wilbur, 'Military separatism and the process of reunification', 244–5. A valuable account of the Northern Expedition as remembered by one of its top commanders is in Te-kong Tong and Li Tsung-jen, *The memoirs of Li Tsung-jen.*

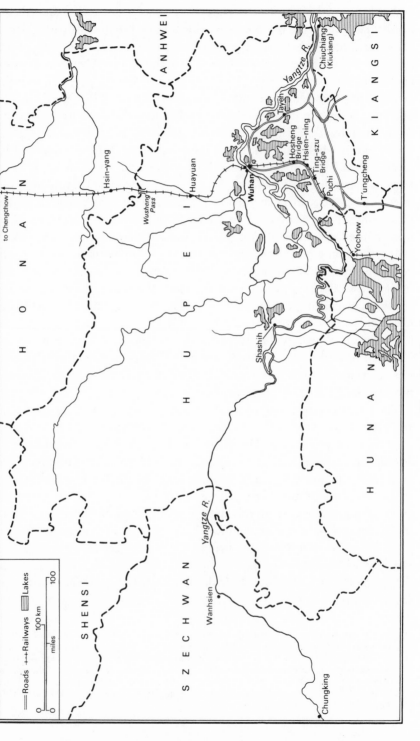

MAP 16. Hupei

General Wu narrowly escaped by train to Wuchang and crossed the Yangtze to Hankow. The Fourth Corps suffered heavy casualties in these battles and, together with the Seventh and Eighth Corps, captured thousands of enemy troops and mountains of equipment.[105] The road to Wuchang was now open.

Pursuing revolutionary forces arrived in the suburbs of Wuchang on 31 August, too late to prevent the enemy from withdrawing behind the city's massive walls. After three costly night-time attempts by 'dare-to-die' troops to scale the walls, in which Yeh T'ing's independent regiment lost heavily, the Fourth and Seventh Corps and the Second Division of the First Corps settled down to what became a seige of forty days. On 6 and 7 September the Eighth Corps, which had crossed the Yangtze, took Hanyang and Hankow after General Liu Tso-lung, the garrison commander, defected; later, Liu was given the title of commander of the Fifteenth Corps. Wu P'ei-fu retreated north along the Peking-Hankow Railway with his remaining troops to Wu-sheng Pass on the northern border of Hupei, but the pursuing Eighth Corps took the pass on 15 September, and Wu retreated into Honan. Finally, on 10 October, the Wuchang garrison surrendered and Hupei had been brought under the authority of the national government.

The assault on Kiangsi proved much more difficult. The most important topographical feature of that province is the Kan River, which starts near the northern border of Kwangtung and flows northeastwards into the great Po-yang Lake, which joins the Yangtze. Nanchang, the capital, lies in the northern part of the province on the east bank of the Kan in a rich plain which extends to the lake. The city was connected with Kiukiang on the Yangtze by a 79-mile railway. While Chiang Kai-shek and Sun Ch'uan-fang negotiated through representatives, both sides sent troops into the province. The general plan of the National Revolutionary Army was to send forces, which had so far done little fighting, eastwards from Hunan to capture Nanchang, while other units from Hupei would capture the railway and take Kiukiang. The southern part of Kiangsi was left to the Fourteenth Corps of Lai Shih-huang, who had defected to the Nationalist side. These movements took place during the first two weeks of September.

Then on 19 September Ch'eng Ch'ien's Sixth Corps by rapid march

---

105 These battles are described in *KMWH*, 12. 1904–31, and *PFCS*, 2. 355–431, both with lists of casualties, enemy prisoners, and booty; *Pei-fa chien-shih*, 55–9; Jordan, *The Northern Expedition*, 75–9; and in A. I. Cherepanov, *Severnyi pokhod Natsional'-no-Revoliutsionnoi Armii Kitaia (zapiski voennogo sovetnika 1926–1927)* (The Northern Expedition of the National Revolutionary Army of China – Notes of a military adviser 1926–1927), 158–64, from a Russian viewpoint.

succeeded in capturing Nanchang with help from the local garrison and students and workers within the city, and with support from the First Division of the First Corps. But an enemy counter-attack drove these forces from the city and the railway with very heavy losses, while the Third Corps allegedly stood by without giving support. Chiang Kai-shek personally directed a second attempt to take Nanchang with the Second Division of First Corps and two divisions of the Second. By 13 October this attack had failed, as well as efforts by elements from the Third, Sixth and Seventh Corps to capture towns on the railway, which they proved unable to hold. The double failure brought on a general retreat and reorganization while General Blyukher and his Russian staff directed careful preparations for a coordinated general attack with all units in proper communication and working on a single timetable. Four regiments of the Fourth Corps were called in from Wuchang as well as the Second Independent Division of Ho Yao-tsu, a Hunanese commander who had recently joined the Nationalists. Chiang Kai-shek was still negotiating with a representative of Sun Ch'uan-fang as late as 28 October, but by then negotiations were obviously a screen. More importantly several enemy regiments and brigades were negotiating to turn over.

The general offensive began at the end of October with the Seventh Corps, the Second Independent Division, and the 12th Division of the Fourth Corps attacking the centre and northern sector of the railway to take Kiukiang; the Third and Sixth Corps attacking stations near Nanchang; and the Second and Fourteenth Corps moving on Nanchang from the south. This well-planned and hard-fought campaign lasting a week succeeded in clearing the railway, capturing Kiukiang on 5 November and Nanchang on the 8th. Aside from some 7,000 of the enemy who defected, the Nationalists disarmed more than 40,000 of Sun Ch'uan-fang's troops. The National Revolutionary Army lost nearly 15,000 killed and wounded in the two months' campaign in Kiangsi.[106]

---

106 An account dated 5 Dec. 1926 and based upon information in Blyukher's headquarters was written by A. Khmelev, who was in Nanchang 24–30 Nov. Preserved in Russian archives, his report quotes a 15 Nov. telegram from 'Galen' which gives these casualty figures, and adds another 10,000 for the previous campaigns. Apparently Blyukher was counting losses only of the corps which had been organized in Kwangtung, the original NRA. He deprecated the actual fighting of the Seventh Corps and Ho Yao-tsu's Independent Second Division in the Kiangsi campaign, though these forces captured most of the enemy's arms. Blyukher's mid Nov. figures for forces campaigning outside Kwangtung are as follows:

Corps from Kwangtung	Outside Corps
First: more than 3,000	Seventh: about 7,000
In Fukien 8,000	Eighth: 25–30,000 (15,000 as
Second: 6,000 of inferior battle-fitness	battle-fit)
Third: around 3,000	Ninth and Tenth: unclear

While the campaign in Kiangsi was being fought, General Ho Ying-ch'in was directing another campaign in the coastal province of Fukien. Two divisions of the First Corps, the Third and 14th, guarded the eastern border of Kwangtung against a possible attack from the Fukien military governor, Chou Yin-jen, an ally of Sun Ch'uan-fang. General Ho nego-tiated with an enemy corps commander, Li Feng-hsiang, and his division commanders, Ts'ao Wan-hsun and Tu Ch'i-yun, to defect to the Nation-alist side, and with leaders of the navy stationed at Foochow. Kuomintang members in Fukien negotiated with various 'people's armies' to assist in ousting Chou Yin-jen, a northerner. Chiang Kai-shek instructed General Ho to negotiate for peace on condition that Chou not send troops into Kwangtung or Kwangsi. These preliminaries occurred in August and September.[107]

The enemy in Fukien reportedly outnumbered the Nationalist forces in men and equipment by the order of five to one. Chou Yin-jen on 27 September sent forces to invade Kwangtung with the purpose of captur-ing the major East River cities, but General Ho received inside informa-tion on these plans and ordered an offensive against Chou's base at Yung-ting across the border. On 10 October the First Corps' Third Division captured the city and then returned to Kwangtung to deal with the in-vaders at Sung-k'o. In these initial battles the Nationalists captured thou-sands of prisoners with their rifles, machine guns and cannon. On 14 October the enemy's Third Fukien Division defected, as planned, and was reorganized as the Seventeenth Corps of the National Revolutionary Army. These initial battles were so successful that on 16 October Chiang Kai-shek appointed General Ho as commander of the Eastern Route Army made up of the First, Seventeenth and Forteenth Corps (Lai Shih-huang's force, which was to enter Fukien from Kiangsi), and ordered him to proceed to conquer the province.

Fourth:	3,500 original and 2,500 newcomers	Fourteenth:	about 500
		Fifteenth:	5–6,000 inferior
Sixth:	more than 3,000	Seventeenth:	8,000

'Iz istorii severnogo pokhoda Natsional'no-Revolutsionnoi Armii' (From the history of the Northern Expedition of the National Revolutionary Army), in *Istoricheskii arkhiv* (The historical archives), 4 (1959) 113–26, Doc. 3, 116. Other accounts of the Kiangsi campaign are *KMWH*, 13. 2047–179 (with many telegrams); *PFCS*, 2. 499–564; *Pei-fa chien-shih*, 69–90; Cherepanov, *Severnyi*, 189–201 (with a hostile bias towards Chiang Kai-shek); Jordan, *The Northern Expedition*, 83–92.

107 I have used Ch'en Hsun-cheng's account of the Fukien campaign as the basic source. *KMWH*, 14. 2187–212, and 2212–20 for documents. A. I. Cherepanov was Ho Ying-ch'in's military adviser, but his account of the campaign is brief and not always accurate because he lacked documents. *Severnyi*, 172–8. Other accounts in *PFCS*, 2. 575–96; *Pei-fa chien-shih*, 91–8; Jordan, *The Northern Expedition*, 93–6. The Kuomintang Archives con-tain *Kuo-min ko-ming-chün tung-lu-chün chan-shih chi-lueh* (A brief record of the battle history of the Eastern Route Army of the National Revolutionary Army), 465/30, which gives voluminous details.

Pacification of Fukien proceeded methodically, with the main forces following the coastal route and taking major centres such as Chang-chou (8 November) and Ch'üan-chou (21 November). As the forces approached the Min River, the navy switched sides, trapping retreating troops who were disarmed by the thousands. On 3 December the navy occupied Foochow, the provincial capital, and on 18 December Ho Ying-ch'in occupied the city with two divisions of the First Corps. In the more mountainous central part of the province 'people's armies' assisted the Seventeeth Corps' advance. Chou Yin-jen retreated with his remnants to the Chekiang border, hoping to link up with Sun Ch'uan-fang, but was blocked by General Ch'en I, who was negotiating to join the Nationalist side.

Thus, by the end of December 1926 the Nationalists had taken the capitals and major cities of Hunan, Hupei, Kiangsi and Fukien, adding them to the original base of Kwangtung and the adjacent province of Kwangsi, which had joined through negotiations. The military governor of Kweichow had also brought his province nominally under the Nationalist government. These seven provinces had a population of approximately 170 million, and the four conquered provinces of 110 million.[108]

Many factors account for this success in only six months. Of prime importance was two years of training and equipping the original National Revolutionary Army with Russian help, and the battle-hardening of campaigns in Kwangtung during 1925. Another was the political indoctrination of troops and officers, giving them the cause for which to fight – essentially an ardent spirit of nationalism. Important, too, was the fiscal reform carried out in Kwangtung, which brought most of the province's tax revenues into the Nationalists' treasury, created trust in the currency and made it possible to borrow by selling treasury notes. Negotiations with enemy forces and the use of silver bullets to induce defections were also useful. The decisive factor, however, was the valour of the National Revolutionary Army in the long-awaited Northern Expedition, particularly the sacrificial spirit of the First and Fourth Corps, though some other units also fought well when committed to battle.

Russian advisers played an important role in the campaigns. General Blyukher developed the general strategy and he and his staff executed detailed, professional plans for particular campaigns. Each of the engaged corps had its Russian advisers, as did some of the divisions. These men tried to assure that plans were executed exactly by their units, and they provided Blyukher an intelligence network during the battles and valuable

108 George Babcock Cressey, *China's geographic foundations: a survey of the land and its people*, 55, based upon the Chinese Post Office estimate of 1926.

summations thereafter. Some actually led attacks. They also provided political assessments of the Chinese generals whom they advised. A few daring Russian aviators scouted enemy dispositions, dropped leaflets into beseiged cities, terrorized enemy troops, and lofted bombs onto strategic targets. Several Russians became seriously ill, one with cholera, others with dysentery. After the Kiangsi campaign, 'a considerable per cent of our workers' were admitted to the Nanchang American hospital.[109]

Mobilizing the masses

Another important reason for the quick military success was political work. Special political officers accompanying the armies, as well as Kuomintang and Communist Party members behind enemy lines, supported the campaign by winning over local populations and attempting to suborn enemy units. Troops of the National Revolutionary Army, coached to treat the populace well, were forbidden to loot or to press-gang labourers. There are many reports of their enthusiastic welcome, of farmers selling food to the troops, acting as spies, guides and porters, and serving as litter bearers for the wounded. In some cases crudely armed units of farmers attacked the enemy rear. Railway workers sabotaged enemy communications. Some 400 miners from An-yuan joined Yeh T'ing's independent regiment. Within beseiged Wuchang, revolutionaries secretly posted placards and distributed subversive leaflets to undermine enemy morale. Students and police in Nanchang helped with the first brief capture of that city and many paid with their lives when it was lost.[110]

As soon as major cities were taken by the National Revolutionary Army, labour organizers began to form or to revive labour unions. Most of the organizers were communists, some with much experience in the labour movement through work in Shanghai after the May Thirtieth Incident and in Canton directing the great strike and boycott against Hong Kong.

109 Khmelev's report in 'Iz istorii', 125. Cherepanov, *Severnyi*, 124–69, and Vishnyakova-Akimova, *Two Years*, 242–3 and 247. Three reports from the front by Russian advisers are translated and published in Wilbur and How, *Documents*, nos. 43, 44 and 49. Other reports are briefed in the forthcoming revision of that work. Ch'en Hsun-cheng's accounts of the capture of Wuchang and Nanchang praise the work of 'our airforce', without mentioning that the aviators were Russians. *KMWH*, 13. 1991–2, 2163–4.
110 Two early accounts of specific forms of assistance to the advancing army are reprinted in *Ti-itz'u . . . nung-min*, 293–7 (14 Sept. 1926) and 298–301 (4 Nov 1926). An early account by an Australian observer is H. Owen Chapman, *The Chinese revolution 1926–27: a record of the period under communist control as seen from the Nationalist capital, Hankow*, 21–7. Jordan, *The Northern Expedition*, 75–9, 241–6, for examples and an appraisal. Angus McDonald, 'The Hunan peasant movement: its urban origins', *Modern China*, 1.2 (April 1975) 188–9, and in his book, *The urban origins of rural revolution*, 264–70, deprecates the role of farmers in assisting the troops, crediting urban workers as more important.

In Hunan the labour movement was quickly revived under the direction of Kuo Liang, a Hunanese communist, who had been active in organizing railway workers in 1922, only to see the union crushed in the repression of 1923. He joined the Kuomintang and was a member of the party's underground nucleus in Changsha in 1924. At the Third Congress of the All China General Labour Union held in Canton in May 1926, he was elected to the Central Committee, and then returned to Changsha. Soon after the city was taken by the Eighth Corps, scores of unions had been formed and there followed a wave of agitation and strikes for higher wages and better working conditions. Political officers supported the unionization movement, and armed picket corps enforced the strikes. In September a provincial federation of Hunan unions was established and a December congress passed a series of resolutions which sought to regularize union structure and governance, to impose discipline in the labour movement, and prevent unauthorized strikes. Twenty-seven-year-old Kuo Liang became chairman of the Hunan General Labour Union. By spring of 1927 the provincial federation claimed over 400,000 members, of whom 90,000 were industrial workers.[111]

Revolutionary fervour mounted steadily in Hankow and Hanyang after their capture early in September. The cities were soon plastered with posters denouncing imperialism and warlords, and calling for support of the national revolution. The political department organized daily meetings and parades, and the Kuomintang began recruiting among students, lower level officials, women, labourers and others groups. By the end of December it had taken in some 31,000 new members. The Central Committee of the Communist Party sent Chang Kuo-t'ao from Shanghai to direct work in Wuhan; he arrived on 11 September and was followed by several comrades with rich experience in labour organizing, Li Li-san, Liu Shao-ch'i, Hsiang Ying, and Hsu Pai-hao. The labour movement had been repressed but not destroyed in the years after the brutal suppression of the Peking-Hankow Railway strike in February 1923. Now it quickly revived. On 14 September a preliminary meeting of union delegates planned the formation of a Hupei General Labour Union, which was officially inaugurated on 10 October. A list of unions published towards the end of November named 73 in the Wuhan cities with a reported membership of 82,000, and six unions in the iron mining centre of Ta-yeh with 11,000 members. Sometime in November the communist-dominated All China General Labour Union set up a management office in Hankow to direct the unionization process.[112]

---

111 *Ti-i-tz'u . . . kung-jen*, 316-74 for documents on unionization in Hunan. Chesneaux, *The Chinese labor movement*, 322.

112 *Ibid.* 321-2; Chang, *The rise of the Chinese Communist Party*, 1. 532-50; *Chung-kuo lao-kung yun-tung shih*, 2. 597-601.

In November a wave of strikes hit the Wuhan cities, directed against both native business and foreign concerns. Printers, postal workers, clerks in silk shops, coolie labourers, servants and employees in Japanese homes and businesses walked out, and the British cigarette company was closed down. Unions used armed picket corps to enforce strikes, which they did with brutality in some cases. Most strikes were quickly settled by wage increases, but unions tried to impose their authority on management, which stiffened resistance. The strikes had a depressing effect on business. Eleven Chinese banks failed on settlement day, 19 November, including two of the largest. Chinese business leaders began to organize to protect themselves and even threatened a commercial stoppage if the government did not respond to two demands: that pay increases be negotiated directly between employers and employees without interference of unions, and that coercion by picket corps be forbidden. The government responded by establishing a mediation commission with two representatives each from the Nationalist government, the Kuomintang, the Chamber of Commerce and the General Labour Union. The commission was to investigate the rising cost of living and the ability of business to pay increased wages. A number of government leaders arrived on 11 December from Canton, via Nanchang, and quickly sought to establish more orderly government. However, disruptive economic forces had already been set in train that ultimately contributed to the demise of the Wuhan government.[113]

The most dramatic and portentous involvement of the masses in the revolution was the rapid expansion of the farmers' movement in the newly liberated provinces. Before the Northern Expedition began, the Canton headquarters of the movement knew of only 161 local associations in Hunan, Hupei, and Kiangsi, with a total of 43,423 members. Six months later, at the end of 1926, communist leaders of the movement were claiming more than one-and-a-half-million farmers organized in associations spread through 91 counties of Hunan and Hupei alone. Such figures cannot be accurate, but they point to a frenzy of organizing by the few hundred cadres able to devote themselves to this phase of the revolution.[114]

Local communists who had worked surreptitiously before the Nationalist troops arrived, could now organize farmers openly with the help

113 *Ibid.* 612–22 on strikes, business reaction and the mediation commission. USDS 893.504/
40 Consul-general Lockhart, Hankow, to secretary of state, 28 Dec. 1926, p. 15 on strikes
and bank failures. *China year book 1928*, p. 984 on picket brutality. Wang Chien-min, *Chung-kuo Kung-ch'an-tang shih kao* (A draft history of the Chinese Communist Party), 1. 400–4,
for a general treatment of communist labour organizing in Hupei.

114 Enrolment figures from *Ti-i-tz'u . . . nung-min*, 17–18 for 3 June 1926; 257–62 for Hunan
in November; 395 for Hupei at end December. Li Jui asserts that more than 40,000 farmers had been organized in Hunan before the expedition began, but does not substan-
tiate it. *Ibid.* 267.

and protection of political officers. Among the organizers of the rural mass movement were graduates of the Farmers Movement Training Institute in Canton, 65 of whom were natives of Hunan, Hupei and Kiangsi. Another 85 graduated early in October from the class which Mao Tse-tung directed. Local organizers knew the poor farmers' grievances, and they had a repertoire of propaganda slogans and organizing techniques. In Hunan, they first concentrated on enlisting farmers to help the revolutionary troops, then turned to drawing them into associations and defence corps. At first they played down rural class struggle and emphasized benefits to the poorer farmers by opening granaries and calling for reduction of rent and interest rates, renegotiation of land contracts, and reducing food prices by prohibiting export of grain from one district to another. Such policies could only arouse fierce opposition from the powerful, and rural Hunan was soon embroiled in conflict. 'Local bullies and evil gentry' became the targets for attack and humiliation, along with large landlords and 'corrupt officials'. Their property should be confiscated, and when possible it was. However, it was not only communists and Kuomintang leftists who were organizing farmers' associations. More conservative provincial Kuomintang members as well as local notables organized associations or gave an official name to existing agricultural societies. A Left Society based in Changsha attempted to steer the farmers' movement into reformist channels. Thus there was inter-organizational conflict as well as class conflict within the agrarian movement.[115]

As violence spread there were reports of local tyrants being executed and, on the other side, of villages attacked and burned, and of farmer leaders slain. In some regions poor farmers, or their spokesmen, were demanding 'solution of the land problem' – that is, expropriation and division of landlords' land, or other forms of 'land equalization'. The farmers' movement spread geographically but was strongest in the Hsiang River valley and along the borders of Hupei, areas conquered by the National Revolutionary Army. By November there were reported to be 6,867 local farmers' associations in Hunan with a total membership of more than 1,267,000. Local groups were linked in a structure of 462 district associations and 29 formally organized county associations, with more being formed. An analysis of the class composition of the associations showed that over 60 per cent were hired agricultural workers or tenants, with 'semi-independent peasants' making up 18 per cent. 'Independent

---

115 Etō, 'Hai-lu-feng', 1. 182 for graduates of the FMTI. On early developments see accounts in *Ti-i-tz'u . . . nung-min*, 270-5, 281-4, 293-301, 322-5; Hofheinz, *The broken wave*, 130-4. McDonald 'The Hunan peasant movement', 190-5 argues the variety of associations in rivalry.

peasants' and handicraftsmen made up most of the remaining 20 per cent. The movement as organized by the leftist leadership seems clearly to have attracted the rural poor.[116]

The Hunan provincial farmers' association was organized at a congress at Changsha which lasted most of December. One-hundred-and-seventy delegates reportedly represented the more than 1.3 million organized farmers. The opening meetings were held jointly with a congress of labour delegates who were said to represent more than 326,000 unionized workers in Hunan. Many days were spent in discussing and then adopting resolutions that had been prepared by the organizers in advance. A proclamation adopted on 2 October by a conference of the Hunan provincial Communist Party branch had set forth the minimal political and economic demands of the farmers, and this provided the outlines for the resolutions adopted by the congress in December. The resolutions called for local self-government in which farmers' associations must participate, self-defence organizations controlled by farmers themselves, the smashing of domination by 'local bullies and evil gentry', support for the revolutionary policies of the Kuomintang and Chinese Communist Party, reduction of rent and of interest on loans, abolition of exorbitant taxes and likin, storage of grain against famine and other relief measures, and confiscation of property of reactionaries – that is, warlords and their subordinates, corrupt officials, 'local bullies and evil gentry'. One of the architects of the provincial association, who became its secretary-general, was Liu Chih-hsun, a Hunanese communist, aged 19, a graduate of Ya-li (Yale-in-China at Changsha), and friend of Mao Tse-tung. Mao, who had recently become head of the Communist Party's peasant committee, attended the latter part of the congress and delivered two speeches in which he insisted that the peasant problem was the central issue of the national revolution; unless it were solved, imperialism and warlordism could not be overthrown nor industrial progress be achieved. He excoriated those who would restrain the peasantry and called for unremitting struggle.[117] After the congress Mao travelled in five counties near

---

116 On executions, see reports in GBFO 405/252. Confidential. *Further correspondence respecting China*, 13313, Jan.–March 1927, nos. 44, 74, and 91; *North China Herald* (hereafter *NCH*), 15 Jan. 1927, p. 62; Mitarevsky, *World-wide Soviet plots*, 139–40, trans. of a report by a Kuomintang official. Communist writers emphasized how few executions of tyrants there were. See *Ti-i-tz'u . . . nung-min*, 281, 312, 381; and 282–3, 329 on killing of rural leaders. Hofheinz, *The broken wave*, 49–50, leans towards this interpretation. Apparently killings increased after the turn of the year. On November membership and class composition, *Ti-i-tz'u . . . nung-min*, 257–62, and Suguru Yokoyama, 'The Peasant movement in Hunan', *Modern China*, 1. 2. 204–38, chart on p. 217, but possibly based upon a different source.

117 *Ti-i-tz'u . . . nung-min*, 275–8 for Li Jui's account of the congress and Mao's speeches; 322–5 for the Communist Party proclamation (trans. in Yokoyama, cited, 220–2); and 326–80 for the proclamation and resolutions adopted by the congress.

Changsha to investigate the agrarian revolution; he then wrote a stirring – and later famous – report.

In Hupei the agrarian movement followed a similar course. From a small base of 38 associations with a membership of a little more than four thousand as reported on 3 June, the membership rose by December to a reported 287,000 in 34 counties. In Kiangsi, which was conquered only with great difficulty, development was not so rapid. In June there were only 36 associations with about 1,100 members; in October a reported 6,276 members (probably mostly in the south); and in November, after the capture of Nanchang, when a preparatory conference for a provincial association was held, the figure of 50,000 was being used. However, Kiangsi was Chiang Kai-shek's special sphere: the agrarian movement apparently was held in check.[118]

The anti-imperialist movement

At the heart of the Nationalist movement was opposition to the political and economic privileges of foreigners in China, privileges which derived from 'unequal treaties' imposed by the powers during the previous 80 years. The Nationalist leaders systematically sought to arouse the populace with barrages of propaganda in support of their pledge to win back China's lost rights. Although nationals of many countries enjoyed special treaty rights, the Nationalists' strategy (and behind it, Russian advice) was to focus hostility upon Great Britain in order to avoid a simultaneous confrontation with Japan, the United States and France. Great Britain held the predominant position in China and hence was a natural target. Anti-imperialism was, of course, a fundamental tenet of the world communist movement, and Bolshevik Russia, which supported and advised the Nationalists, regarded Great Britain as its major foe. Russia was particularly fearful of being drawn into conflict with Japan. The strategy of focusing Chinese hostility upon Great Britain became clear after the May Thirtieth and June Twenty-third Incidents of 1925, for Japan was an initial target in the first incident and France had been as guilty as Great Britan in the second, but in efforts at retaliation their roles were played down. The anti-imperialist movement brought great benefits in popular support for the Nationalists and the Communists – both parties grew rapidly from mid 1925 on – but it involved risks also. It seemed likely that Great Britain, if pushed too far, might retaliate militarily against

---

118 *Ti-i-tz'u . . . nung-min*, 17–18 for June figures; 395 for Hupei; 420 for Kiangsi. As late as May 1927 Kiangsi reported only 82,617 members. Hofheinz, *The broken wave*, 104, presents figures claimed by organizers from 1924 to 1927 for four provinces, but not Kiangsi.

Canton, or that the powers might adopt a policy of outright support for the Nationalists' enemies, the northern 'warlords'.

The strike against Hong Kong and the boycott against trade with Great Britain had gone on for a full year in Kwangtung when the Northern Expedition began. There had been several circuitous attempts to negotiate a settlement, for both sides wanted the conflict ended. The strike no longer inconvenienced Hong Kong but the boycott seriously harmed British trade and shipping in South China. Support for the strikers was a heavy drain on the resources of the Canton government, and the independent power in Canton which the strike committee had developed was an embarrassment. Armed and unruly pickets created many problems for the Canton leadership. The strike committee itself was the prime obstacle to a termination of the boycott because it insisted upon a large financial settlement to pay off the strikers for their year of unemployment, but the Canton government could not find the money and the Hong Kong government refused absolutely to pay what it regarded as blackmail. There was also the serious problem for the Canton authorities of employment for thousands of former Hong Kong workers when their financial relief ended. Eager to end the conflict, the Nationalist government consented to negotiate directly with the Hong Kong government, instead of continuing the pretence that it played only a mediating role. Formal negotiations from 15 to 23 July foundered again on the issue of payment. Then, on 4 September a brief action by ships of the British navy in Canton harbour and the unrelated Wan-hsien incident on the upper Yangtze the next day, apparently convinced the Canton authorities that Great Britain intended to try to force an end to the boycott by military action, though this was not the case. A telegram to Chiang Kai-shek at the front warned of this imagined danger and he ordered the strike and boycott ended. On 18 September Eugene Chen, acting foreign minister, told the acting British consul-general in Canton that the boycott would end on or before 10 October, and that his government would levy extra taxes in order to pay off the strikers. Thus, on 10 October the strike and boycott ended by unilateral decision on the Chinese side, and the Canton government imposed surtaxes on imports and exports that accorded with the 2.5 per cent surtaxes promised at the Washington Conference, though never officially brought into effect. To this imposition of new tariffs the British government turned a blind eye. The Foreign Office was happy to see the troublesome boycott ended and was trying to formulate a new policy more friendly towards the Nationalists.[119]

119 Wilson, 'Britain and the Kuomintang', 335–401, gives a judicious account of the settlement based upon British Foreign Office Archives and Chinese published sources. The minutes

Foreign missionary activity had long been a target of hostility for ardent Chinese nationalists, many of whom scorned religion and objected particularly to a foreign religion which, they argued, enslaved the minds of its converts. Missionary schools were a particular target because of foreign control over the education of Chinese youth. The nationwide propaganda campaign against missionary education that began in 1922 was not particularly associated with the Kuomintang, but soon that party and the Communist Party supported a vituperative anti-Christian movement. During 1925 Kwangtung saw many evidences: explicitly anti-Christian parades, street lectures and inflammatory handbills, and invasion and destruction of some mission properties, on two occasions by Nationalist troops. Disruptive activities occurred in a number of mission colleges and middle schools in central China where communist and Kuomintang influences were strong among students. For example, in both 1924 and 1925 provocateurs stirred up 'student storms' in Ya-li (Yale-in-China) in Changsha. The Second National Congress of the Kuomintang held in Canton in January 1926 endorsed a strong resolution supporting the anti-Christian movement, and charging schools, journals and churches run by missionaries as being 'the tongues and claws of imperialism'. In Kwangsi, after it had been brought into alliance with the Nationalist government, there were several anti-Christian riots with some looting of mission properties during the first half of 1926. The anti-Christian movement was, in short, a part of the broader anti-imperialist movement, but foreign missionaries and their institutions were immediate and very vulnerable targets.[120]

There was, however, an ambivalence. Some leaders of the Kuomintang were Christians, as Sun Yat-sen had been, and some were themselves graduates of missionary institutions. Violent attacks on Christian institutions damaged the reputation of the Kuomintang abroad as well as among Chinese Christians. The Nationalist military campaign seemed, at the beginning, to face dangerous odds; there was good reason to try to avoid arousing foreign opposition. In a resolution adopted by a plenary

of the Kuomintang Political Council for the first half of 1926, contain many cases of action by the strike committee or the pickets, which the Political Council found unruly and attempted to curb. Teng Chung-hsia and Su Chao-cheng of the strike committee often attended these meetings when such issues were on the agenda. Teng Chung-hsia, *Chung-kuo chih-kung yun-tung chien-shih*, 188–94; *Chung-kuo lao-kung yun-tung shih*, 2. 544–6, 551–6, 583–90 for varying Chinese accounts of ending the strike and boycott.

120 Much information on anti-Christian activities is in Leon Wieger, *Chine moderne*, 5, 6 and 7, covering the years 1924 through 1927; and in volumes of *Foreign relations of the United States* dealing with China for those years. Also Jessie G. Lutz, 'Chinese nationalism and the anti-Christian campaigns of the 1920s', *Modern Asian Studies*, 10. 3 (1976), 394–416; and Ka-che Yip, 'The anti-Christian movement in China, 1922–1927', Columbia University, Ph.D. dissertation, 1970, published as *Religion, nationalism and Chinese students*, 1980.

session of the Chinese Communist Party's Central Committee, which met in Shanghai from 12 to 18 July 1926 just as the Northern Expedition was getting under way, the following attitude towards the Christian church was laid down:

In our verbal propaganda, we should do our utmost to depict the [Christian] Church as the vanguard of imperialism. . . . The Church wishes to deceive all oppressed peoples and lead them to forget their own actual sufferings in order to ensure a strong and lasting foundation for imperialist oppression.

We must not at this time create any opportunity of actual conflict with the Church. This condition is imposed by our present situation (the Church is allied with militarists everywhere under the pretext of treaty protection) . . .

On 20 August after he reached Changsha, the commander-in-chief, Chiang Kai-shek, issued a proclamation to the world in which he explained the patriotic purposes of the Northern Expedition to liberate China from the warlords and win its rightful place of equality among the nations, with friendship for all. He promised protection of life and property for all foreigners in China who did not obstruct the operation of the revolutionary forces or assist the warlords. Two days later, Hsiang-ya, the Yale-in-China hospital and medical college in Changsha, received an order to send doctors to attend General Chiang. The American missionary surgeon who extracted an impacted tooth was favourably impressed by Chiang Kai-shek's apparent friendliness. The Hsiang-ya faculty had feared their hospital would be expropriated, but instead Chiang's headquarters set up a well equipped military hospital across the street, and for a time the two hospitals cooperated. General Chiang permitted no attacks on foreigners by troops under his control.[121]

After fighting had moved beyond Hunan, conditions changed markedly. An anti-British boycott was started in the province. Demonstrations in Changsha and other towns took on a fiercely anti-foreign character. In October many mission stations were under harassment, their buildings plastered with hostile posters and their Chinese employees or the students in their schools organized into unions that made demands that clearly had a common orchestration. Missionaries were driven from their stations in Li-ling and Nan-hsien. In Changsha all mission schools were under attack. As concern mounted, an American journalist submitted

121 Communist resolution, Wilbur and How, *Documents*, 299–300. Chiang's proclamation in Mao, *CKSHS* for 20 Aug. 1926; trans. in Wieger, *Chine moderne*, 7. 113–15 (dated 19 Aug.). The next item in *Chine moderne* is an anti-Christian statement issued by the Political Department of the Fourth Corps, dated 25 August. On the tooth episode, Ruth Altman Greene, *Hsiang-Ya journal*, 45–7. Reuben Holden, *Yale in China: the mainland, 1901–1951*, 157, states that at this time Chiang 'maintained excellent discipline among his troops and permitted no offenses against foreigners.'

questions to Chiang Kai-shek in Nanchang. He replied on 19 November 'I have no quarrel with Christianity and missionaries will always be welcome as heretofore. The elimination of missions from China is not part of our programme, and they may function in this country without interference as always.' Yet in Hunan threats of violence and other forms of pressure grew so intense that by the year's end most mission schools were closed and missionaries of several nationalities had fled to the Hankow sanctuary or were preparing to do so. No one had been killed, but many churches and mission properties had been seized by unions or military units. American businesses in Changsha had not been molested, and Japanese and Germans were generally left undisturbed.[122]

The British Foreign Office began work during November on a policy statement that might open the way to fuller accommodation to Chinese nationalism and improved relations with the Nationalist regime. Austen Chamberlain, the foreign secretary, personally directed the attempt to formulate a fresh and forward-looking policy, and his memorandum was approved by the cabinet on 1 December 1926. The text was cabled to the new British minister to China, Miles Lampson, who was then in Shanghai on his way to Peking. The statement (later known as the Christmas Memorandum because of its publication on 26 December) was actually directed to the other powers. It urged each to declare its willingness to negotiate on treaty revision and all other outstanding questions as soon as an authoritative Chinese government should emerge; but that pending such time, they should deal with local authorities and consider sympathetically any reasonable proposals, even if contrary to strict interpretation of treaty rights, in return for fair treatment of foreign interests by them. Protests should be reserved for attempted wholesale repudiation of treaty obligations or attacks upon the legitimate and vital interests of foreigners in China; and such protests should be made effective by united action of the powers. The memorandum stated the British government's view that some of the Commission on Extra-territoriality's recommendations for revision should be carried out at once, and that the powers should immediately and unconditionally authorize the Washington surtaxes without specifying how the proceeds were to be handled or used.[123] The memorandum, while showing a desire to accommodate to the aspirations of Chinese

---

122 Chiang Kai-shek's statement in *NCH*, 12 Feb. 1927, p. 230; but a very different summary in Wieger, *Chine moderne*, 7. 51. Catherine M. McGuire, 'The union movement in Hunan in 1926–1927 and its effect on the American community', Columbia University, M.A. essay in history, 1977, citing U.S. Consular archives from Changsha and correspondence from Hunan mission stations.

123 Wilson, 'Britain and the Kuomintang', 434–41; Dorothy Borg, *American policy and the Chinese revolution, 1925–1928*, 228–30.

patriots, was much too restrictive to satisfy the demands of the Nationalist movement.

Recognizing that the Nationalists seemed well established on the Yangtze, the British Foreign Office was considering the possibility of diplomatic recognition as soon as the Kuomintang government was sufficiently established to assume full responsibilities for all treaties and other obligations of the government it would succeed. Until that time Great Britain would endeavour to deal in a friendly spirit with any Kuomintang administration exercising *de facto* authority in any part of China. The Foreign Office authorized Lampson to visit Hankow even before taking up his post in Peking. Thus it was that the British minister to China held his first diplomatic discussions with Eugene Chen, the Nationalist foreign minister, from 9 to 17 December. The central issue in their exploratory discussion was the conditions for possible British recognition, and the main difficulty was Lampson's insistence that the Nationalists accept the existing treaties as binding until new treaties had been negotiated. The talks allowed each side to appraise the limits to which the other side would go in accommodation. Eugene Chen tried imaginatively to find a formula to bridge conflicting positions, for he seemed eager to win the advantage that recognition would bring his government. He insisted that Minister Lampson's departure be arranged to appear as only a temporary suspension of talks, and Lampson obliged him in this.[124]

Seizure of the British concession in Hankow

There were, however, others among the Wuhan leaders who opposed an attempt to come to an agreement with Great Britain. Anti-British agitation, which had mounted in November, causing alarm in the Hankow British concession, was held in check during Lampson's visit. After his departure on 18 December the public was again systematically subjected to propaganda against British imperialism. Evidently Borodin was eager to keep the anti-British fever burning, as evidenced by his advice in meetings of the Provisional Joint Council of Party and Government leaders (the top policy making body in Wuhan) and corresponding resolutions adopted by a Committee of Wuhan Citizens to Oppose British Imperialism which held a giant rally on 26 December. Li Li-san, a veteran communist labour leader who had won his spurs directing the anti-

---

124 Wilson, 'Britain and the Kuomintang', 464–7, based upon Lampson's cables, which the writer also has read in the Public Record Office. Eugene Chen's account as presented to the Kuomintang Third CEC Plenum on 13 March 1927 is in Chiang Yung-ching, *Bo-lo-t'ing yü Wu-han cheng-ch'üan* (Borodin and the Wuhan regime; hereafter, *Borodin*), 89–90. Professor Chiang bases his study on original documents in the Kuomintang Archives.

British strike in Shanghai during the summer of 1925, presided and gave a speech, as did other communist leaders. The Christmas Memorandum was published in China on the same date, and Borodin proposed the propaganda line to use in denouncing British policy, and this was adopted by the Kuomintang Central Propaganda Department. An issue which troubled relations was the arrest of 17 Kuomintang members in the British and French concessions in Tientsin on 23 November. After trial they were handed over to Chinese authorities and the Kuomintang office was sealed. The Nationalist government, still in Canton, had protested and announced that it held Great Britain responsible for what might happen to the Kuomintang members in enemy hands. Towards the end of December the Nationalist leadership, now in Hankow, revived the issue when seven of their Tientsin fellows were executed. This incident became part of the propaganda argument for the recovery of foreign concessionary areas. Yet direct conflict with Great Britain, the main enemy, had to be avoided.[125]

With the revival of anti-British demonstrations, the authorities of the Hankow British concession placed barricades at the entrances and manned them with police, small detachments of marines, and members of the Hankow Volunteers. Individual Chinese were permitted to pass through but not crowds or armed soldiers. The first two days of January saw celebrations and parades in the Wuhan cities to welcome – that is, to hasten – the Nationalist government's establishment there. The third saw a giant anti-British rally. That afternoon a large crowd of Chinese gathered outside one of the barricades listening to the anti-imperialist harangues of members of a propaganda squad. The crowd was being aroused to a passion of hatred for British imperialism when suddenly someone began flinging stones at the men on the barricades. This led to a clash between marines, using their bayonets, and the angry crowd. Five Chinese and three marines were injured, though no shots were fired. First reports said one or many Chinese had been killed. The Provisional Joint Council was just in meeting when this dangerous situation was reported. It decided immediately to try to forestall a worse conflict by persuading the crowd to disperse and by demanding that the British authorities withdraw the marines and leave the Chinese police, backed by troops,

125 Chiang Yung-ching, *Borodin*, 93–8. Borodin summarized his thoughts on the Christmas memorandum thus, 'Our present policy is to bring Britain and Japan, and Japan and Fengtien into increasing conflict.' In a speech on 20 December before several thousand delegates – possibly of the Committee to Oppose British Imperialism – Borodin stated that Lampson 'has been here with sweet words but his heart is sour. The British are working behind our backs to destroy us. The only way to combat this is first a boycott of everything British.' *NCH*, 24 Dec. 1926, as quoted in Wilson, 'Britain and the Kuomintang,' 468. An account of the 26 December anti-British rally is in *Ti-i-tz'u . . . kung-jen*, 383–4.

to maintain order. The crowd did disperse upon the urging of Hsu Ch'ien and Chiang Tso-pin, who promised that the government would solve the problem in 24 hours. The British consul-general, Herbert Goffe, in consultation with Rear-Admiral Cameron, prudently accepted Eugene Chen's proposal – delivered virtually as an ultimatum – in order to avoid a repetition of the May Thirtieth and June Twenty-third Incidents. The Volunteers withdrew and the marines went back to their ships. Chinese police replaced them on the 4th.

But in fact, the barricades were now open. Urged on by agitators, crowds rushed into the concession and the consul-general had to ask for Chinese troops to maintain order. Next day the Chinese and Sikh members of the concession police quit and the situation became tense when a mob began to stone the police station. The municipal council decided to hand the station over to the Nationalist authorities, making them responsible. British and American women and children were put on board ships and sent to Shanghai, while the men were concentrated in a building near the shore from which they could be evacuated quickly in case of necessity. The Nationalists set up a commission to administer the concession. Thus was the British concession wrested from British control, not by design but in response to a dangerously escalating development. On 6 January the small British enclave in Kiukiang was also taken over by crowd action, without British resistance, but with considerable looting and destruction. These victories for Chinese nationalism added enormously to the Kuomintang's prestige. They also had unforeseen consequences.[126]

One consequence was an increasing number of missionary refugees from interior stations ordered by their consuls to leave for places of safety. Another was concern for the security of the International Settlement in Shanghai, which had the greatest concentration of foreign residents and was a hub of British economic interests in China. Shanghai was clearly the next objective of the Nationalist military campaign. On the basis of predictions and estimates of the British naval commander-in-chief for the Far East and H.M. consul-general in Shanghai, the Cabinet in London debated sending a greatly augmented military force to protect the Settlement from enforced take-over. On 21 January the Cabinet

---

126 Accounts from the Chinese side are in Chiang Yung-ching, *Borodin*, 99–104, based upon minutes of the Provisional Joint Council; *Kuo-wen chou-pao*, 4.2 and 3, 9 Jan. (with pictures of Hsu Ch'ien and Chiang Tso-pin) and 16 Jan. 1927; *Ti-i-tz'u . . . kung-jen*, 384–93, reprinting Canton *Min-kuo jih-pao* accounts; and Chang, *The rise of the Chinese Communist Party*, 1. 562–6, for a reminiscent account. Wilson, 'Britain and the Kuomintang', 484–97, using British archives and Kuomintang documents, concludes convincingly that the seizure of the concession was not planned by the Nationalist leadership. A British eye-witness account is by E.S. Wilkinson in *NCH*, 15 Jan. 1927, pp. 46–7; also the *Hankow Herald* for January.

made the final decision to send a cruiser squadron and an entire British division instead of the single Indian battalion then on stand-by basis in Hong Kong. News of this decision, which reached China very quickly, created for the Nationalists the spectre that Great Britain might attempt to retake the concessions in Hankow and Kiukiang, or that the British force would assist Sun Ch'uan-fang against the planned capture of the Shanghai area. In fact, the British government had quickly set aside the idea of retaking either concession by force, and Miles Lampson, now in Peking, sent two members of his legation staff to Hankow to negotiate for their retrocession.

Owen O'Malley, the counsellor, and Eric Teichman, the Chinese secretary of the British legation, arrived in Hankow on 11 January and negotiations between Eugene Chen and O'Malley over the Hankow concession lasted until 12 February. For the Nationalist side the negotiations conveyed the appearance of British recognition, and a successful conclusion would add to the Nationalist government's prestige. For the British, the negotiations were seen as a test of the utility of conducting relations with the Nationalists: what the British government wanted was a restoration of face in China and assurance that the Nationalists would make no new attempt to abrogate treaty terms by force. In order to set a favourable stage, the Nationalist foreign ministry proclaimed on 10 January that during the negotiations the anti-British and anti-Christian campaigns were to cease. To reciprocate for the lull which did occur O'Malley persuaded the Hankow British community to resume business on 24 January. The shut-down had begun on 5 January because of the perceived danger, but it had continued as a form of economic pressure on a city already struggling with a depression of trade and unemployment. Some 30 out of 140 Chinese banks failed at Chinese New Year (26 January). Eugene Chen also issued a statement to the effect that the Nationalist government preferred to have all questions outstanding between itself and the foreign powers settled by negotiations and agreement. On the retrocession issue the two sides worked out a face-saving formula by which the Chinese commission would continue to administer the concession while the British Municipal Council wound up financial affairs; then a ratepayers' meeting would formally approve the passing of authority to a joint Chinese-British committee having a Chinese chairman and a Chinese majority – an arrangement based on the precedent of the retrocession of the German concession in Hankow some years earlier. The agreement was to be signed on 30 January, but a new issue arose with the arrival in Shanghai of the Indian battalion on 27 January and knowledge that many more British contingents were on the way. Eugene Chen now demanded assurances that the British force in Shanghai was intended only for defensive purposes; and he threatened not to sign the agreement unless the forces *en route* were stopped short of Shanghai. The compromise was a formal statement by Minister Chen that it was not the policy of his government to use force to effect changes in the status of concessions and international settlements, and British foreign secretary Chamberlain's statement in Parliament that if the Hankow agreement were signed, and no further emergency arose, the remaining British forces would be held in Hong Kong. After these gestures, the Chen-O'Malley agreement was signed on 19 February and a similar agreement on Kiukiang on 2 March. The Chinese side emerged from the negotiations with enhanced prestige while Great Britain had tested its new policy of accommodation towards the Nationalists. Furthermore, the Wuhan leftists had scored a triumph that strengthened their position relative to their rivals in Nanchang.[127]

CONFLICT OVER REVOLUTIONARY GOALS

Dissension within the revolutionary camp

Disunion was inherent in the composition of the Kuomintang leadership, a group riven by factionalism, and also in the situation of the Communist Party, with its distinct philosophy and separate goals, participating with the Kuomintang in guiding the national revolution. There was no consensus as to what forms of activity 'national revolution' embraced. By early in 1927 the Nationalist leadership was divided over a number of issues. What should be the next move in the military campaign – towards Shanghai or towards Peking? Where should the organs of authority be located – in Wuhan or in Nanchang? Behind this issue was a more important one – which leaders within the Kuomintang should make the major decisions? And behind the issue of authority lay a more divisive problem – how much social revolution should be encouraged and how rapidly should it be allowed to proceed? A similar problem, with strategic implications, was whether to stimulate or to restrain the anti-imperialist movement. Conflict over such issues during the first three months of the year resulted in disruption among the Kuomintang leaders, a realign-

---

127 This account is based primarily on Wilson, 'Britain and the Kuomintang', 498–530, which examines evolving British and Chinese response to the Hankow Incident on the basis of documents and accounts from both sides. Nationalist documents on the case are in *KMWH*, 14. 2343–78. See also, Iriye, *After imperialism*, 101–3; Chiang Yung-ching, *Borodin*, 104–09. Mr Chiang believes Borodin engineered the delay in signing of the agreement.

ment in April, and a purge of communists within much of the revolutionary domain.

When the remaining leadership in Canton proceeded northwards to set up the Nationalist government in Wuhan, they went in two separate parties, going overland to Nanchang, where Chiang Kai-shek had established the headquarters of the National Revolutionary Army. After a week of conferences, the first contingent went to Hankow, arriving 10 December. On Borodin's advice this group on 13 December formed the Provisional Joint Council, composed of a few members of the Kuomintang Central Executive Committee and of the National Government Council. They elected Hsu Ch'ien their chairman and Borodin their adviser. This small, extra-constitutional body soon became the chief policy-making group in Wuhan, in effect usurping the authority of the Kuomintang Political Council. Leftists predominated and the Joint Council became an important instrument of Borodin's influence.[128] The authority it began to assert was soon contested by another prestigious group in Nanchang that included not only Chiang Kai-shek, but Chang Ching-chiang (Chang Jen-chieh), acting chairman of the CEC Standing Committee, and T'an Yen-k'ai, acting chairman of the Nationalist Government Council, who arrived in the second travelling party from Canton on 31 December, together with central party headquarters and some government ministers.

In the first days of January, Chiang Kai-shek held a military conference at his headquarters in Nanchang to discuss the financing and reorganization of the swollen armies and to plan the next phase of the campaign. Chiang's intention was a drive on Shanghai by two routes, one down the Yangtze and the other northeastwards through Chekiang. General Blyukher opposed this strategy, as did T'ang Sheng-chih and Teng Yen-ta, the powerful head of the Political Department. The reasons on both sides were strategic and political. For Chiang and his followers, success would mean dominance of the wealthy and relatively industrialized lower Yangtze region and a potential capital at Nanking. For the Hankow group, a campaign northwards could mean a juncture with the Russian-assisted army of Feng Yü-hsiang and then the possibility of the big

128 Initial members were Soong Ch'ing-ling (Mme Sun Yat-sen), Hsu Ch'ien, Teng Yen-ta, Wu Yü-chang, Wang Fa-ch'in, T'ang Sheng-chih, Chan Ta-pei, Tung Yung-wei (Tung Pi-wu), Yü Shu-te, Chiang Tso-pin, Sun Fo, Eugene Chen, and T.V. Soong. All were either regular or reserve members of the Second CEC except T'ang Sheng-chih, commander of the strongest military force in the area and emerging as a rival to Chiang Kai-shek, and Chiang Tso-pin, an important Hupei leader in revolutionary activities and long-time associate of Sun Yat-sen. Wu Yü-chang, Tung Pi-wu and Yü Shu-te were also leading members of the Communist Party. The list is from Chiang Yung-ching, *Borodin*, 33, based on minutes of the Joint Council.

political prize, Peking. The strategy adopted by the conference conformed to Chiang Kai-shek's wishes, though it did include the concentration of T'ang Sheng-chih's troops on the southern section of the Peking-Hankow Railway in a defensive position.[129]

The Nanchang groups set up a Provisional Central Political Council, and most of the Central Committee members there advocated that party headquarters and the Nationalist government should be temporarily located at Nanchang, where the military headquarters were. Hsu Ch'ien and his associates demanded, on the contrary, an immediate move to Wuhan. Both factions, one claiming authority of the Joint Council and the other using the name of the Political Council, resolved to call a plenary session of the Central Executive Committee – each at its own locale! – to readjust party affairs. Chiang Kai-shek travelled to Wuhan on 11 January to try to win over his comrades there, but he left a week later, unsuccessful and apparently embittered. He had been publicly denounced by Borodin and had excoriated him in return the next day. From henceforth the two factions operated more and more independently and antagonistically, though emissaries went back and forth trying to patch up differences. However, the breach between Chiang Kai-shek and Borodin on the personal as well as policy level grew steadily worse. In fact, there is reason to believe that Borodin personally instigated a campaign against Chiang in hopes of weakening his position.[130]

The Chinese Communist leadership supported the Wuhan leftists in these controversies. In a political report dated 8 January 1927, the communist party Central Committee stressed that the next military campaign should drive northwards along the Peking–Hankow Railway and that all military forces should be concentrated there. It favoured a movement then emerging for an autonomous Shanghai that would create a buffer zone between Nationalist forces and the Mukden-Shantung troops. (If effective, this might at least delay Chiang Kai-shek's seizure of the Shanghai prize.) The report also approved the Joint Council, though it deplored the emerging conflict among the Nationalist leadership and urged a reconciliation between Chiang and Wang Ching-wei, who had already been invited by the Kuomintang to return and resume his leadership roles. However, in February, communists in Wuhan began a propaganda

129 *PFCS* 2. 606–14. This lists all corps and some divisions that would participate.
130 Chiang Yung-ching, *Borodin*, 33–43; *TJK*, 530–41; Chang, *The Rise of the Chinese Communist Party*, 556–62, 567–8. (All these writers discuss the rift and see Borodin as the instigator.) On Borodin's insulting speech, see also 'The letter from Shanghai', in Leon Trotsky, *Problems of the Chinese revolution*, 407. Chiang Kai-shek's account of the confrontation is translated in Wieger, *Chine moderne*, 7. 140–2. On the broadening rift, see also Wilbur and How, *Documents*, 381–8; and from a Soviet Russian point of view, Cherepanov, *Severnyi*, 205–10.

campaign against 'military dictators' and 'new warlords', and began specifically to denounce Chiang Kai-shek's strong supporter, Chang Ching-chiang. Chiang Kai-shek retaliated with a speech on 21 February, denouncing the Wuhan Joint Council as the usurper of party authority and Hsu Ch'ien as the autocrat, defending his own position and his determination to support the loyal old associates of Sun Yat-sen, and threatening to curb the aggressive Communist Party. On 25 February the Nanchang group received word from Ch'en Kung-po of what the Wuhan group planned to achieve through the Third CEC Plenum – essentially a reversion to the organizational system before Chiang Kai-shek acquired the concentration of powers in his own person through decisions of the Second Plenum the previous May, and by his appointment as commander-in-chief. They detected Borodin's machinations and on the next day the Nanchang Political Council resolved to telegraph the Comintern asking it to recall Borodin. When there was no reply, the Council is said to have telegraphed Borodin directly, urging him to leave, but he simply disregarded it. The breach was now very wide.[131]

The revolutionary leadership divided over other issues. Should the anti-imperialist movement be restrained for fear the powers would come to the support of Sun Ch'uan-fang and Chang Tso-lin? More difficult to grapple with was the question whether to rein in the mass movement for fear a powerful counter-revolutionary tide would so strengthen the enemy as to prevent victory in the campaign to unify the country under Nationalist control. Already the violence of the agrarian movement and the ebullience of the labour movement were creating a tide of opposition within Nationalist territory. Some leaders in Wuhan believed labour must be restrained because successive strikes were disrupting commerce, reducing government revenues, and creating a problem of relief for the unemployed. In the countryside, aroused farmers were executing local enemies, and larger landlords and merchants were fleeing to the cities where they spread word of a rural terror. Their flight disrupted rural commerce, particularly in rice, tea and other farm products, which led to depression in trade in Changsha, Wuhan and other cities in the Nationalist domain. The Communist Central Committee in its political report of 8 January expressed concern:

131 Wilbur and How, *Documents*, no. 47, 427-30; and 388-93 on the communist offensive. *KMWH*, 16. 2782-9 for Chiang's speech, and abstract in *NCH*, 12 March, p. 402 and 19 March, p. 439. Chiang Yung-ching, *Borodin*, 42, gives Ch'en's telegraphic report and Nanchang's reaction. *TJK*, 540, mentions the telegram to Borodin but without a substantiating source. 'The letter from Shanghai', dated 17 March 1927 states that Voitinsky, the Comintern representative, visited Chiang Kai-shek and then requested Moscow to recall Borodin because 'otherwise Chiang Kai-shek would not make any serious concessions.' Trotsky, *Problems*, 406.

In the provinces of Hunan, Hupei, and Kiangsi now occupied by the Northern Expeditionary Forces, the mass movement has entered the revolutionary path and revolutionary work has penetrated deeply into the villages. . . . Assassinations of local bullies and bad gentry continue to occur without end. . . . A violent reaction would ensue should there be a military setback.[132]

Just at this time Mao Tse-tung was making a field study of farmers' revolt in the counties around Changsha. In his report, which later became a classic revolutionary declaration, Mao gloried in the violence and the peasants' seizure of local power. He urged his comrades to support this absolutely necessary period of violence if the poor were to overthrow their centuries-old oppressors. As Mao presented it, peasant violence was entirely spontaneous.[133]

But the communist leaders became extremely apprehensive. A Central Committee Political report of 26 January surveyed emerging attitudes among the powers and the trend of political opinion in China towards the communists' role in the developing revolution. The following are key passages:

The right wing of the Kuomintang is daily becoming more powerful. . . . There is currently an extremely strong tendency within the Kuomintang to oppose Soviet Russia, the Communist Party, and the labour and peasant movements.

The tendency towards the right is due first to the belief of Chiang Kai-shek and Chang Ching-chiang that only one party should exist in the country, that all classes should cooperate, that class struggle should be prohibited, and that there is no need of a Communist Party. . . .

The second reason is their idea that the national revolution will soon succeed, that there will soon be a movement for class revolution, and that the greatest enemy at present is not imperialism or militarism but the Communist Party. . . . For these reasons, a great anti-Communist tide has developed within the Kuomintang. . .

The most important problem which requires our urgent consideration at the moment is the alliance of foreign imperialism and the Kuomintang right wing with the so-called moderate elements of the Kuomintang, resulting in internal and external opposition to Soviet Russia, communism, and the labour and peasant movements. This would be an extremely dangerous thing and is, furthermore, entirely within the realm of possibility . . .

How did the communist leadership propose to combat this danger? First, the party should quiet the Kuomintang's fears, based on the belief that the Communist Party, close to the masses, opposed the national

132 Wilbur and How, *Documents*, 428.
133 *Selected works of Mao Tse-tung*, 1. 21–59 ('corrected' in spots). Partial translations in Brandt, Schwartz and Fairbank, *A documentary history*, 80–9, and Stuart R. Schram, *The political thought of Mao Tse-tung*, rev. edn, 250–9. Hofheinz, *The broken wave*, 310–11, for a bibliographic note on various versions of Mao's report. It has been commented on by all Mao's biographers.

government, and that there would soon be a communist revolution. To do so, the party should urge the masses to give financial and military support to the government, and, through propaganda, explain that victory for the national revolution was still distant, discredit the bourgeoisie and its ideology, and warn the Kuomintang not to join the bourgeoisie against 'the real revolutionaries', the workers and peasants. In foreign policy, the party should concentrate on the anti-British movement and delay extending the anti-imperialist movement to Japan, France and the United States, in order to isolate Great Britain. 'These policies', the report concluded with a show of confidence, would, if properly executed, 'lead to complete success. They will prevent united attack on us by the foreign powers and eliminate the Kuomintang's fear of the Chinese Communist Party.'[134]

Still, the tide of events – events such as myriads of actions and reactions in the Chinese countryside and cities (strikes, business failures, land seizures, murders), propaganda, developing sentiments among Chinese of local and regional influence, and decisions in major power centres in China, and in Moscow, London, Tokyo, Paris and Washington – this tide was leading inexorably to head-on conflicts within the revolutionary movement.

The growing split among the revolutionaries

In February and early March the rift between the Wuhan group and Chiang Kai-shek and his supporters became clearly evident. They took separate roads, the radical left establishing itself more firmly in Wuhan and attempting to curb Chiang's power, and the commander-in-chief suppressing communists in his domain, sending forces off to conquer the lower Yangtze, and searching for new support, Chinese and foreign.

Leaders of the Kuomintang left, Hupei communist leaders, and some Russian advisers had worked for several months to create a military alliance around T'ang Sheng-chih against Chiang Kai-shek. On 5 March a secret Russian report, apparently written in Hankow, reported a line-up of armies opposed to Chiang, naming the Third Corps (Chu P'ei-te), the Fourth (Chang Fa-k'uei, now deputy commander), the Seventh (Li Tsung-jen), the Eighth (T'ang Sheng-chih), the Eleventh (reformed from the 10th Division of the Fourth Corps, Ch'en Ming-shu), and other less effective units. The document warned, however, that the internal struggle to destroy Chiang had not been entirely successful.[135] The Russian author misjudged the sentiments of Ch'en Ming-shu, the garrison commander at Wuchang, who had been sent to Nanchang to persuade CEC members to come to Wuhan to attend the controversial plenum there. He returned from Nanchang on 6 March and that very evening was forced to give up his command of the Eleventh Corps and depart.[136] The corps was turned over to Chang Fa-k'uei, a leftist.

In Nanchang, meanwhile, General Blyukher and members of his Russian staff at Chiang's headquarters worked on plans for a campaign to take the lower Yangtze area, although they opposed an immediate breakthrough to the east. Blyukher favoured an advance on Honan against the Mukdenese, a juncture with Feng Yü-hsiang's army, and then a move east along the Lunghai Railway. Borodin favoured a move directly against Chiang Kai-shek, according to Cherepanov, whose work is based in part on Russian archives. As planned by Blyukher, the lower Yangtze campaign should be preceded by a thrust north along the Peking–Hankow railway towards Chengchow and Loyang for the juncture with Feng, whose forces were now concentrated on the Shensi-Honan border.[137] Both sides were negotiating with Feng Yü-hsiang's representatives. In fact, both sides negotiated in the first months of 1927 with various commanders to ease the path of victory – among them Generals Chin Yun-ao and Wei I-san in Honan, Ch'en T'iao-yuan and Wang P'u in Anhwei, Meng Chao-yueh in Kiangsu, and Admiral Yang Shu-chuang and General Pi Shu-ch'eng in Shanghai.

Chiang Kai-shek negotiated indirectly with Chang Tso-lin, the most powerful of the 'warlords'. He did so on the basis of a decision reached at a conference with Borodin and a group of Kuomintang leaders on 7 December to eliminate Sun Ch'uan-fang and ally with Chang Tso-lin.[138] If Sun were to be eliminated it was important to persuade Chang Tso-lin

135 Wilbur and How, *Documents*, 435–6 and discussion of the anti-Chiang alliance, 393–96. Cherepanov, *Severnyi*, 299–300, quotes Blyukher's opinion in January 1927 that the Second, Fourth, Sixth and Eighth Corps would support the leftists and communists against a conspiracy of the rightists, but that the Third and Seventh Corps would constitute a serious obstacle.

136 *TJK*, 541–2 and Chiang Yung-ching, *Borodin*, 43–4; Wilbur and How, *Documents*, 531. Basing themselves on Kuomintang Archives, Professors Li and Chiang attribute Ch'en's enforced departure to T'ang Sheng-chih, Teng Yen-ta and Borodin.

137 Cherepanov, *Severnyi*, 300, and 225 for planning. R. A. Mirovitskaia, 'Pervoe destiatiletie' (The first decade), in *Leninskaia politika SSSR v otnoshenii Kitaia* (The Leninist policy of the USSR with regard to China). Moscow, 'Nauka', 1968, 20–67, p. 44 for quotation from a 'Memorandum on the liquidation of the enemy in the area of the Lower Yangtze', dated 6 Jan 1927 and now in the archives of the Ministry of Defence of the USSR. Marc Kasanin, *China in the twenties*, trans. from the Russian by Hilda Kasanina, 194–201, provides a colourful account of his work on Blyukher's staff in Nanchang.

138 Mao, *CKSHS*, for 7 Dec.

not to support him. Sun, however, had already effected an alliance with Chang and his subordinate, Chang Tsung-ch'ang; the latter then sent his Shantung army southwards to support – or displace – Sun. Chiang Kai-shek's negotiations went on through intermediaries well into March, and were intended to postpone war with the powerful Fengtien Army; but possibly Chiang was looking for additional strength against his rivals in Wuhan. Chang Tso-lin's terms for neutrality and divided spheres apparently included the condition that Chiang break with the Chinese Communist Party and suppress it.

In February and March communist writers protested against Chiang Kai-shek's 'crimes' in negotiating with Chang Tso-lin and with Japan.[139] There is ample evidence that Chiang was seeking an understanding with Japan, both to aid his negotiations with Chang Tso-lin and in anticipation of the drive on Shanghai. Through various means he tried to assure Japan, as well as the other powers, that they need not fear the consequences of the capture of Shanghai by his forces.[140] The Japanese government, well briefed on the developing rift in the Nationalist camp, moved towards the opinion that accommodation might be reached with Chiang.[141]

As always, Chiang needed money for the campaign to take Shanghai; one of his complaints against the Wuhan government was that it did not provide the funds. Being a native of the Ningpo area and having long been a resident of Shanghai with its large Ningpo community, powerful both in business and the underworld, Chiang had useful connections in the metropolis. Late in 1926 the chairman of the Shanghai Chinese Chamber of Commerce, Yü Hsia-ch'ing (better known as Yu Ya-ching) visited Chiang at Nanchang and allegedly offered handsome support

139 Letter from the CC of the CCP to the Northern Regional Committee dated 13 Feb. 1927, in Mitarevsky, *World wide Soviet plots*, 119–20; 'A warning', signed in the name of the Chinese Communist Party and a number of communist-dominated organizations and dated Canton, 27 Feb., in Robert C. North and Xenia J. Eudin, *M. N. Roy's mission to China: the Communist-Kuomintang Split of 1927*, 150–5. Ch'en Tu-hsiu in *HTCP*, 190 and 191 (6 and 12 March) 2045–6, 2056–7.

140 In an interview with a Japanese visiting Nanchang and published in *Jiji press* on 9 Feb., Chiang is reported to have said he did not think of taking the Shanghai concessions by force, and that if any country were to assist the Nationalists out of sympathy 'we would not refuse such assistance; rather we would shake hands with that country. . . . We would be glad to shake hands with Japan.' Dispatch, Sir John Tilley, Tokyo, to Sir Austen Chamberlain, 14 Feb. 1927, in GBFO 405/252. Confidential. *Further correspondence respecting China,* no. 13313 (Jan.–March 1927), no. 172 enclosure. Chiang sent Tai Chi-t'ao to Japan as an emissary. In a press interview in Tokyo on 27 February Tai explained that his mission was to secure Japan's proper understanding of the Nationalist position and future policy, and stated the conviction that the foreign concessions would be recovered by peaceful means. *NCH*, 5 March p. 352. Huang Fu was another important intermediary, according both to contemporary press reports and the autobiography of his widow, Shen I-yün, *I-yun hui-i* (Reminiscences of Shen I-yun), 247–90.

141 Much presumptive evidence of both sets of negotiations is presented in Wilbur and How, *Documents*, 389–91. See also, Iriye, *After imperialism*, 110, 119–21.

from the Chinese business leadership to help him take the city. Huang Chin-jung, leading underworld figure and also chief of Chinese detectives in the French concession, is said to have been another caller. Huang Fu, Chiang's sworn brother, served as an intermediary in Shanghai fund raising. He carried Chiang's confidential message to Chang Chia-ao, deputy governor of the Bank of China, requesting additional financial aid from the bank, and Chang complied with several hundred thousand Chinese dollars in January 1927. Chiang also sent his quartermaster-general, Yü Fei-p'eng, to Shanghai to arrange loans; Yü succeeded in extracting a million more from the Bank of China and presumably, by using similar tactics, a good deal more elsewhere. George Sokolsky may have helped in persuading the British–American Tobacco Company to advance two million dollars against future tax stamps, the money being deposited in the Bank of China to finance Ho Ying-ch'in's First Corps.[142]

Actions and counter-actions

Chiang Kai-shek's plans to capture Shanghai moved a step forward when Hsueh Yueh's First Division of the First Corps captured Hangchow on 18 February 1927. His drive on the capital of Chekiang from eastern Kiangsi was aided by the Second Division and by the Twenty-sixth Corps under General Chou Feng-ch'i, who had defected to the Nationalists in December. General Ho Ying-ch'in was in overall command of the Eastern Route Army but General Pai Ch'ung-hsi commanded the troops at the front.[143] After the capture of Hangchow, 130 miles by rail from Shanghai, the Nationalist forces pushed cautiously forward to Kashing, a vital point about 47 miles away, and both sides prepared for the inevitable battle for Shanghai. Marshal Sun Ch'uan-fang conferred with his new ally, Marshal Chang Tsung-ch'ang in Nanking and ceded the defence of Shanghai to the Shantungese. During a transitional period Sun's subordinate, General Li Pao-chang, retained his position as Shanghai-Woosung defence commander. During this transition the city's communist leaders, with as much cooperation as they could get from

142 Yen-p'ing Hao, *The Comprador in nineteenth century China: bridge between East and West*, 290, f.n. 83, cites a late source to the effect that Yü Hsia-ch'ing promised Chiang a loan of $60 million from the Chekiang financial clique. Harold Isaacs, *The tragedy of the Chinese revolution*, rev. edn, 143, tells of Huang's visit to Chiang, 'on behalf of the Shanghai bankers and merchants'. Chang Chia-ao in an unpublished autobiography on file in Columbia University reports Chiang's efforts to have the Bank of China support his campaign. Mr Sokolsky recounted his role in an interview with the writer in 1962, now on deposit in Special Collections Library of Columbia University.

143 Jordan, *The Northern Expedition*, 102–5; *PFCS*, 2. 619–29; *Pei-fa chien-shih*, 104–8. Cherepanov, *Severnyi*, 227–36. Cherepanov was adviser to Ho Ying-ch'in.

other groups, brought about the second 'Shanghai uprising' against Marshal Sun, which lasted from 19 to 24 February, effectively disrupting the city.[144]

The uprising apparently had two purposes: to disrupt Sun Ch'uan-fang's rear and thus to assist the Nationalist's advance; and to seize as much control of the Chinese cities as possible for instruments of the Communist Party and the left Kuomintang before the National Revolutionary Army arrived. The uprising was enforced by intimidation squads of the General Labour Union and by several assassinations of Chinese labour foremen and others opposing the strike.[145] Li Pao-chang suppressed the uprising ruthlessly, sending broadswordsmen into the streets of the Chinese city to behead agitators, many of them students. Nevertheless, the uprising brought some hundreds of thousands of workers (reported numbers differ widely) out on a political strike, and demonstrated the power of the Shanghai communists. It also hardened the resolve of leaders in the Chinese business community and rightists within the Kuomintang to oppose them. It strengthened the British government's determination to prevent another 'Hankow incident', and France, Japan and the United States advanced their preparations to protect their nationals. Thus the uprising probably assisted Chiang Kai-shek in his search for allies and sharpened the danger foreseen in the 26 January political report of the Communist Central Committee – 'an alliance of foreign imperialism and the Kuomintang right wing with the so-called moderate elements of the Kuomintang' against Soviet Russia, communism, and the labour and peasant movements.

On 10 March the long-awaited and much debated Third Plenum of the

144 There are many sources on this brief uprising. Primary ones are Chao Shih-yen ('Shih-ying'), 'Records of the Shanghai general strike' in *HTCP*, no. 189, 28 Feb. 1927, with documents: reprinted in *Ti-i-tz'u . . . kung-jen*, 450–72; 'Three Shanghai uprisings', *Problemi Kitaii*, 2. 10–11. 'Letter from Shanghai', 409–12; *NCH*, 26 Feb. 1927, pp. 317–21, and 19 March p. 472, for Municipal Gazette Police Reports for February; *China Yearbook 1928*, 820–3, reprinting 'Minutes of the military section', a communist document found in the 6 April raid on the Soviet embassy in Peking. USDS 893.00/8822, Dispatch, Gauss, Shanghai, 9 April 1927, 'Labour, student and agitator movements in Shanghai during February, 1927'. 34 pp. containing much factual detail.
   Secondary accounts are *Chung-kuo lao-kung yun-tung shih*, 2. 637–40; Wang, *Chung-kuo Kung-ch'an-tang*, 1. 276–9; Jordan, *The Northern Expedition*, 209–11 (all with a hostile bias). Harold Isaacs, *The tragedy of the Chinese Revolution*, 132–6; Chesneaux, *The Chinese labor movement*, 354–5 (both favourable).
145 Evidence for this statement comes from *NCH*, 19 March p. 472, Municipal Gazette News: police reports for February; and 'Minutes of the military section', 823 in a report by comrade Chow (probably Chou En-lai), dating before 10 March, which states 'The campaign of red terror has been successfully carried out at Shanghai. More than 10 strike-breakers, provokers and people opposed to the workers at the factories have been killed. This campaign had a sobering effect on the above mentioned people. . .'. (The figure may have included some executions after 24 Feb.)

Kuomintang Central Executive Committee opened in Hankow with 33 delegates, but without Chiang Kai-shek, who remained in Nanchang preparing for the campaign down the Yangtze. All but three of the participants were identifiable as Kuomintang leftists (at that time) or as communist members of the party.[146] Meeting for a week, the plenum passed a series of resolutions designed 'to restore power to the party'. These restructured all top party and government committees and councils, elevating Chiang's rival, Wang Ching-wei, who was still en route from Moscow, to the first position in all of them. They placed Chiang as one among equals in several committees, but left him out of the praesidium of the Political Council, the party's main policy-making body. The plenum re-established the Military Council, which had been abolished in favour of the commander-in-chief's headquarters when the Northern Expedition was about to begin. Chiang was chosen to be a member of its seven-man praesidium but Wang Ching-wei's name headed the list and three of the other members were Chiang's opponents, T'ang Sheng-chih, Teng Yen-ta and Hsu Ch'ien. Wang Ching-wei was elected head of the Party's important Organization Department, replacing Chiang, and Wu Yü-chang, a communist member of the Kuomintang, was to head the office until Wang arrived.

Another affront to Chiang Kai-shek and his faction was a resolution to invalidate the elections to the Kwangtung and Kiangsi Provincial Party Headquarters and the Canton Party Headquarters, which had been reorganized under the direction of Chang Ching-chiang and Ch'en Kuo-fu. A resolution on unifying foreign relations forbade any party members or government officials – including specifically military officers – not in responsible foreign office positions to have any 'direct or indirect dealings with imperialism', unless directed to do so, on pain of expulsion from the Kuomintang. This pointed to Chiang Kai-shek, whose forces would inevitably soon come in contact with foreign powers in Shanghai.[147] Other resolutions called for greater cooperation between the Kuomintang and the Communist Party; determined to cease criticism of the other party in Kuomintang journals; revived the idea of a joint commission with participation of representatives of the Comintern to settle inter-party conflicts; called on the Communist Party to appoint members to

---

146 *TJK*, 545. Li gives a detailed account of the plenum based upon documents in the Kuomintang Archives, some of which are published in *KMWH*, 16. 2689–95. See also Chiang Yung-ching, *Borodin*, 46–51; Wilbur and How, *Documents*, 397–400, based largely on translations of resolutions published in *Min-kuo jih-pao*, official organ of the Kuomintang, 8–18 March 1927, in USDS 893.00/8910, a dispatch from American Consul-General F. P. Lockhart, Hankow, 6 April 1927.
147 Li, *TJK*, 547.

join the Nationalist government and provincial governments; urged joint direction of mass movements, particularly of farmers and labourers; and decided to send a three man delegation to the Comintern to negotiate on problems of the Chinese revolution and its relation to world revolution.[148]

While these decisions were being taken in Hankow to reduce Chiang's power, his faction took action against communists and leftists in Kiangsi. On 11 March one of Chiang Kai-shek's subordinates executed Ch'en Tsan-hsien, the communist leader of the General Labour Union in Kanchow, a major town in the southern part of the province, and broke up the union. On 16 March, as he was about to launch the campaign down the Yangtze, Chiang Kai-shek ordered the dissolution of the Nanchang Municipal Headquarters of the Kuomintang, which supported the Wuhan faction, and ordered his subordinates to reorganize it. A few days later, after he reached Kiukiang, his subordinates violently suppressed the communist-led General Labour Union and the Kuomintang Municipal Headquarters there. On 19 March Chiang arrived in Anking, the capital of Anhwei, which had come over to the Nationalist side through the defection of Generals Ch'en T'iao-yuan and Wang P'u. On the 23rd a struggle between five hastily organized anti-communist provincial associations (one of them taking the name of General Labour Union) and communist partisans culminated in the dispersal of the latter.[149] These were portents.

The capture of Shanghai and Nanking

Chiang Kai-shek organized the drive to capture the important lower Yangtze cities along two routes. One was to drive down both banks of the great river, with the right bank army under Ch'eng Ch'ien aimed at Nanking and the left or north bank army under Li Tsung-jen directed towards cutting the Tientsin–Pukow Railway, the enemy's north–south lifeline. The other route was directed against Shanghai, which stands at the east end of a triangle with Hangchow at the south-west and Nanking at the north-west corners, and with the Grand Canal and Lake Tai forming a baseline on the west. By mid March, the forces that had taken Hangchow

148 *Ibid.* 548; Chiang Yung-ching, *Borodin*, 50.
149 *TJK*, 565–8, 594–8, and 660–2; Chang, *The rise of the Chinese Communist Party*, 578; Liu Li-k'ai and Wang Chen, *I-chiu i-chiu chih i-chiu er-ch'i nien ti Chung-kuo kung-jen yun-tung*, 55. Chesneaux, *The Chinese labor movement*, 352, summarizes these actions. Tom Mann, British labour leader and member of the International Workers' Delegation to China in 1927, passed through Kanchow on 19 March where he learned details of the execution of Ch'en Tsan-hsien. When he arrived in Nanchang on 25 March 'revolutionaries were in the ascendency but other forces had been dominant.' Tom Mann, *What I saw in China*.

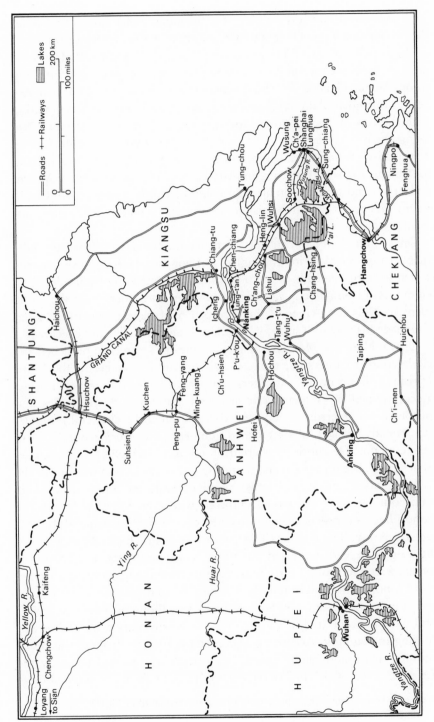

MAP 17. The Lower Yangtze region

were positioned only a few miles from Shanghai under front commander
Pai Ch'ung-hsi, while Ho Ying-ch'in's army was ready to press northward
on both sides of Lake Tai to cut the Shanghai–Nanking Railway, the
main escape route for Sun Ch'uan-fang's remnants and the fresh Shantung
troops under General Pi Shu-ch'eng. The commander of the Chinese
fleet at Shanghai, Admiral Yang Shu-chuang, had long been negotiating
with the Kuomintang through its chief representative in Shanghai, Niu
Yung-chien. On 14 March Admiral Yang declared his flotilla for the
Nationalists; he had already sent three vessels up the Yangtze to Kiukiang
for Chiang Kai-shek's use. Preliminary battles in the third week of March,
and strikes and sabotage on his railway lines, made it imperative for Chang
Tsung-ch'ang to withdraw his troops towards Nanking or face entrapment.

On 18 March a Nationalist attack broke the Sungkiang front and northern troops retreated into Shanghai, but not into the foreign settlements
which were protected by a multi-national army manning barricades at all
entrances. Pi Shu-ch'eng negotiated his own surrender, gave the battle
plans to Niu Yung-chien,[150] then escaped by Japanese ship to Tsingtao
and made his way to Tsinan, where he was apprehended and executed.

On 21 March, a Monday, as Pai Ch'ung-hsi's forces approached the
city's southern outskirts, the General Labour Union began the 'third
uprising'. By now the Workers' Inspections Corps numbered some
3,000, trained by Whampoa cadets, and some armed with rifles and
pistols. Some guerrilla groups had also infiltrated the city, and intimidation squads – called 'black gowned gunmen' in Western reports – were
active again. The uprising started at noon with pickets and gunmen
attacking police on the streets, capturing police stations in sections of the
Chinese cities, and seizing arms. Simultaneously thousands of workers
came out on a general strike, enforced where necessary, although the
atmosphere was one of celebration and welcome for the National Revolutionary Army. The city was filled with Nationalist flags. After a day of
fighting in a very confused situation, it appeared that a communist-
organized underground force with support from the masses had liberated
the Chinese cities, although the amount of joint planning with Kuomintang agents is unclear. Some four to five thousand northern troops
still were concentrated in Chapei near the North Station on the railway
leading to Nanking. According to contemporary reports there was much
looting, arson and killing, some by northern troops and some by the
irregular forces which had seized parts of the city. Probably some of these

150 Ch'en Hsun-cheng, 'The capture of Chekiang and Shanghai' in *KMWH*, 14. 2231–309,
    p. 2288 on Pi's defection.

irregulars were not affiliated with either the Nationalist or the Communist parties. The uprising, nevertheless, had the appearance of an effort by some of the Communist Party leadership to seize control of the Chinese sections of Shanghai in preparation for a provisional government that they already had formed. Chou En-lai, Chao Shih-yen, Lo I-nung, and Wang Shou-hua were among the guiding hands.

General Pai Ch'ung-hsi arrived on 22 March with 20,000 troops and set up his headquarters at the Arsenal on the southern edge of the city. His subordinate, General Hsueh Yueh, commanding the powerful First Division, subdued the remaining northern troops, most of whom were thereupon interned behind the foreign defence lines. General Pai proclaimed his authority for maintaining order, demanded that all irregulars be incorporated into his army or surrender their arms, and promised the foreign authorities that he would not permit an effort to take over the foreign settlements by force. He ordered an end to the general strike, and his order was carried out on 24 March. Between the 23rd and the 26th General Pai's troops in a variety of attacks against guerrilla centres rounded up 20 self-styled generals, including a communist leader, and many 'black gunmen'; most of the leaders reportedly were executed. Several large units of the Labour Inspection Corps, well armed, remained in three centres, and the Corps extended its control into Pootung, across the Whangpoo River.[151]

Northern troops retreated from Nanking on 23 March, followed during the night by entering troops of the Nationalists' Right Bank Army, commanded by General Ch'eng Ch'ien. On the morning of the 24th groups of Nationalist soldiers systematically looted the British, American and Japanese consulates, wounded the British consul, attacked and robbed foreign nationals throughout the city, killed two Englishmen, an American, a French and an Italian priest, and a Japanese marine. At 3 : 30 pm. two American destroyers and a British cruiser laid a curtain of shells around the residences of the Standard Oil Company to assist the escape of some fifty foreigners, mostly American and British. The bombardment of this sparsely populated area killed, according to separate Chinese inves-

151 Some contemporary accounts of Shanghai's capture are in *Kuo-wen chou-pao*, 27 March 1927. An article by Chao Shih-yen, using the pseudonym 'Shih-ying', and several GLU proclamations in *HTCP*, no. 193, 6 April 1927, and reprinted in *Ti-yi-tz'u . . . kung-jen*, 473–90. *NCH*, 26 March, pp. 481–8, and 515; 2 April p. 16. USDS 893.00/8406, 8410, 8414, 8415, 8421, 8422, telegrams from Consul-General Gauss, Shanghai, 19–24 March, some published in *FRUS*, 1927, 2. 89–91; and 893.000/8906, Gauss' long dispatch dated 21 April 1927, 'Political conditions in the Shanghai Consular District', covering the period 21 March to 20 April. 'Report on the situation in Shanghai', by British Vice-Consul Blackburn, dated 15 April, in GBFO 405/253. Confidential. *Further correspondence respecting China*, 13304, April–June 1927, no. 156, enclosure 2. Secondary accounts, as in the note on the 'Second Uprising'.

tigations, four, six or 15 Chinese civilians and 24 troops.[152] Early published Chinese and Russian reports asserted that thousands of Chinese had been killed. The bombardment quickly discouraged further attacks on foreigners. General Ch'eng, who entered the city in the afternoon, restored order among his troops and, on the 25th all foreigners who wished to leave were evacuated without harm, although foreign properties were looted and burned for several more days.[153]

Who the persons directly responsible for the Nanking Incident were, aside from the soldiers in Nationalist uniform actually engaged, seems not to have been judicially established. On March 25 Ch'eng Ch'ien issued a public statement asserting that 'reactionary elements in Nanking … incited enemy forces and local ruffians to loot foreign property, burn houses and there were even incidents of wounding and slaying.' On the same day Yang Chieh, commander of the 17th Division, Sixth Corps, told the Japanese consul, Morioka Shōhei, that the soldiers had been instigated by communists in Nanking. The consul reported to his government that the acts of violence had been planned by party commissars and communist officers of lower grade within the Second, Sixth and Fortieth Armies, and by members of the Communist Party's Nanking branch. Reports to Wuhan by Nationalist officers continued to attribute the attacks to northern troops and rascals dressed in Nationalist uniforms, but Western diplomats in China, and their home offices, very soon accepted the Japanese consul's version – communist instigation.[154] This explanation was also later adopted by the Chiang Kai-shek faction of the Kuomintang.

The Nanking Incident was a unique event during the Northern Expedition: previously there had been no such extensive attacks on resident foreigners resulting in killings and wide-scale property losses. The event

152 *NCH*, 16 April 1927, p. 108, for the 'diligent inquiry' of a Chinese man, who reported four Chinese killed; *KMWH*, 14. 2381–2 for telegraphic report of General Chang Hui-tsan of the Nationalist Fourth Division, dated 5 April, who reported five or six killed; and telegraphic report of Li Shih-chang, head of the Political Bureau of the commander-in-chief of the Right Bank Army, dated 5 April, reporting an officer and 23 soldiers killed and 15 civilians.

153 Foreign eye-witness accounts in *FRUS*, 1927, 2. 146–63; GBFO, China no. 4 (1927), *Papers relating to the Nanking Incident of March 24 and 25, 1927.* vol. 36, comd. 2953; *China yearbook*, 1928, pp. 723–36 'The Nanking outrages'; Alice Tisdale Hobart, *Within the walls of Nanking*, 157–243. Chinese documents and studies, *KMWH*, 14. 2378–92; Chiang Yung-ching, *Borodin*, 117–24; *TJK*, 584–8. Other accounts in Borg, *American policy and the Chinese revolution, 1925–1928*, 290–317. Iriye, *After imperialism*, 126–33.

154 *KMWH*, 14. 2379 for Ch'eng Ch'ien's report as published in *TFTC*, 24. 7 (10 April) 128–9; and 2378–83 for other reports. Iriye, *After imperialism*, 128–9, for Morioka's report. Iriye suggests that Yang Chieh's statement may have been a fabrication. The American consul, John K. Davis, came to believe that troops of the Fourth Division (Second Corps), commanded by Chang Hui-tsan, were responsible for the attacks. *FRUS*, 1927, 2. 158.

created an atmosphere of crisis in the foreign settlements in Shanghai. In Peking the British, American, Japanese, French and Italian ministers consulted among themselves and with their governments concerning reprisals. They reached agreement on a set of demands for retribution but their governments could not agree on sanctions if apologies from the Nationalist government and punishments of those guilty were not forthcoming. The Japanese government under the influence of Foreign Minister Shidehara Kijūrō, attempted to restrain Great Britain and the other powers from too bellicose a posture, while at the same time hoping to persuade Chiang Kai-shek and the other moderate leaders of the Kuomintang 'to solve the present issue and eventually stabilize conditions throughout the south.' In short, Chiang was to be encouraged to act against the radicals in his party. The Japanese consul-general in Shanghai, Yada Shichitarō, passed this advice to Chiang Kai-shek through his close associate, Huang Fu. The British government's policy towards the Nationalists hardened. Great Britain now had the power in place to execute a variety of punishments, but the American government would not consent to participate in sanctions. In the end, after protracted international debate, the powers did not take direct sanctions: developments in the power struggle within the Kuomintang superseded such ideas.[155]

The Wuhan government was at first poorly informed on the Nanking Incident. The foreign minister, Eugene Chen, learned the details of what had happened to the foreign community in Nanking from Eric Teichman, the British representative in Hankow, with confirmation from the American and Japanese consuls. Not until 1 April did the Political Council, now fully informed about the Incident and with some inkling as to reaction in foreign capitals, consider seriously how to deal with the situation. Great Britain and America, it appeared, were preparing to intervene, while Japan's policy was still unclear. Borodin put the matter bluntly – 'if the imperialists should actually help the counter-revolutionaries, it could bring about the destruction of the Revolutionary Army.' His proposals were rather familiar: divide Great Britain and Japan. This could be done by allaying Japanese fears of the revolution and by ensuring that Japanese in China were protected, particularly in Hankow where, according to Eugene Chen, Japanese residents were fearful their concession would be seized. Propaganda laying the blame for the Nanking Incident upon imperialism, and with moral appeals, should be addressed

155 Iriye, *After imperialism*, 130–3, describes Shidehara's policy and instructions to his officials in China, based on Japanese Foreign Office documents. Wilson, 'Great Britain and the Kuomintang', 575–91 describes the British reaction based on British Foreign Office and Cabinet documents. American policy is covered in *FRUS*, 1927, 2. 164–236; and in Borg, *American policy and the Chinese revolution*, 296–317.

daily to foreign countries, and particularly to the Japanese and British people to arouse them against intervention. At the same time the policy of the Political Council that foreigners in China should be protected must be clearly explained to all Chinese mass organizations and 'especially to our armed comrades.' To this prescription, the Political Council assented.[156]

Events soon overran the Political Council's determination to reassure Japan about the safety of its concession in Hankow. On 3 April, after a fight between a Japanese sailor and a rickshaw coolie in which the coolie was killed, an angry crowd killed two Japanese (or, according to a Chinese account, seized 10). In this inflamed situation Japanese marines were landed and opened fire with machine guns, killing nine Chinese and wounding eight. Japanese authorities evacuated most of the Japanese women and children, closed and manned the concession boundaries, and brought up more warships. In keeping with its policy, the Wuhan government tried both to minimize the gravity of the incident and to cool Chinese passions. It gave strict orders against retaliation.[157] Its order was one of many efforts by the Wuhan leadership to gain control over fast-moving revolutionary developments.

The struggle for control of Shanghai

Chiang Kai-shek arrived in Shanghai on the afternoon of Saturday, 26 March, and there immediately began an alignment of forces in a complicated struggle for control of the Chinese city, although this was but one aspect of the larger contest for authority over the national revolution. Communists and Kuomintang leftists had on their side the General Labour Union with its armed picket corps; several 'mass organizations' of students, women, journalists and street merchants; and the local Communist Party members. To this side Soviet Russia lent advice and some material support. On the other side were ranged the commanders of the Nationalist armies in and around the city, except perhaps for Hsueh Yueh; members of the Kuomintang 'old right wing', who had long made Shanghai their stronghold and who had good connections

---

156 From the minutes of the Political Council, 1 April 1927, in the Kuomintang Archives. Chiang Yung-ching, *Borodin*, 124-26, quotes Borodin's recommendations to the Council in full. The Wuhan reaction to the Nanking Incident is well analysed in Wilson, 'Great Britain and the Kuomintang', 562-75.

157 H. Owen Chapman, *The Chinese revolution 1926-27*, 72. Chapman was an Australian missionary doctor, in Hankow at the time. Chiang Yung-ching, *Borodin*, 138-9. USDS 893.00/ 8555, /8608, /8609 Telegrams, Lockhart, Hankow, 3, 4 and 6 April and 8952 dispatch, 14 April 1927; *NCH*, 9 April, pp. 53 and 55; and 16 April, p. 112, based on a letter from Hankow.

with Chinese financial, commercial and industrial leaders, persons who had their own reasons to oppose the militant labour movement; and, ultimately, leaders of Shanghai's underworld gangs, whose control of the city's workers the General Labour Union challenged. Benevolently inclined towards this side – the side of law and order and the continuation of privilege – were the foreign administrations and the police of the International Settlement and the French Concession; behind these most of the foreign consuls; and behind them the power of some 40 warships and 16,000 foreign troops. It seemed an unequal contest, but it took more than three weeks to work itself through.

The leftists tried to arouse the support of the Shanghai masses. On Sunday the General Labour Union opened new offices in the Huchow Guild in Chapei and Wang Shou-hua presided over a meeting at which representatives of many organizations passed resolutions demanding retrocession of the concessions, pledging support for the National government and the Shanghai citizens' government, and urging General Hsueh Yueh to remain in Shanghai, it being rumoured that his division was to be sent away. In Pootung a number of Chinese workers charged with being counter-revolutionaries were reportedly executed by order of the General Labour Union. In the afternoon a huge rally at the West Gate near the French Concession heard fiery speeches demanding the immediate occupation of the concessions on pain of a general strike. Nationalist troops prevented the parade which followed from bursting into the French Concession. The American consul-general reported the situation extremely tense and he doubted that Chiang Kai-shek had either the will or the power to control it.[158]

General Chiang tried to quiet the tense situation and possibly to lull his opponents. That same evening, 27 March, he met with several American reporters and expressed friendliness for their country. He deprecated the foreign preparations to defend the concessions as signs of 'panic'. He denied any split in the Kuomintang and said he recognized the communists as participants in the revolutionary movement regardless of their political creed. He also blamed the Nanking Incident on northern troops in southern uniform. In another interview on 31 March he protested at the foreign bombardment of Nanking, which had aroused enormous anti-foreign feeling, and pleaded that the Incident itself not be exaggerated. He requested the foreign authorities at Shanghai to take measures to lessen the tension between the Chinese populace and the foreign community, and stated that he had already issued instructions

158 *NCH*, 2 April, pp. 6, 16, 19, 37 and 3; USDS 893.00/8506, telegram, Gauss, Shanghai, 27 March, 6 p.m.

against mob violence or any acts harmful to foreign lives and property. He asked the foreign authorities to end martial law, withdraw their troops and warships, and leave protection of the foreign settlements to the Nationalists. The General Labour Union, too, had issued a proclamation the previous day denouncing rumours of a breach between the Nationalist Army and the labouring class; and it declared it false that the foreign settlements would be stormed by pickets under its guidance.[159]

Chiang Kai-shek was urged from several directions to suppress the militant labour movement in Shanghai and to curb the communists, but preparations took time. Leaders of the Chinese business community headed by Yü Hsia-ch'ing, Wang I-t'ing, compradore of a large Japanese shipping firm, and C.C. Wu, formed a federation of commercial and industrial bodies and sent a delegation to see Chiang on 29 March. They emphasized the importance of restoring peace and order in the city immediately, and offered financial support.[160] The Japanese consul-general, Yada, saw Chiang's sworn brother, Huang Fu, several times shortly after Chiang's arrival to urge the general to suppress disorderly elements as well as make amends for the Nanking Incident. An editorial of *North China Daily News*, Shanghai's leading British paper, commented that if General Chiang were 'to save his fellow countrymen from the Reds he must act swiftly and ruthlessly'.[161]

A prestigious group of Kuomintang veterans led by Wu Chih-hui pressed Chiang to purge their party of its communist members. The group was part of the Central Supervisory Committee, elected in January 1926 at the 'leftist' Second National Congress in Canton. On 28 March five of the 12 regular members met informally and passed a resolution proposed by Wu Chih-hui to expel communists from the Kuomintang. The effort would be called 'The movement to protect the party and rescue the country.' Others at the meeting were Ts'ai Yuan-p'ei, 'dean' of Chinese intellectuals, Chang Ching-chiang, the wealthy patron of both Sun Yat-sen and Chiang Kai-shek, Ku Ying-fen, veteran of the 1911 Revolution and Sun Yat-sen's financial commissioner, and Li Shih-tseng, a leader among the French returned students. On 2 April the group met again, with Ch'en Kuo-fu, Chiang's protégé and deputy head of the party's

159 *NCH*, 2 April, pp. 2, 9 and 18.
160 *NCH*, 2 April, pp. 7 and 20; *CWR*, 9 April. The amounts actually advanced to Chiang are uncertain, but three, seven and 15 million dollars are mentioned in Western reports, according to Isaacs, *The tragedy of the Chinese Revolution*, 151-2 and 350, f.n. 27. On 8 April Consul-General Gauss learned that local bankers had advanced Chiang three million dollars, but were insisting they would not support him further unless the communists were ejected from the Kuomintang. USDS 893,00B/276.
161 Iriye, *After imperialism*, 130-1 and footnotes. *NCH*, 2 April, p. 13, editorial dated 28 March.

Organization Department, and two alternate members of the Central Supervisory Committee, Generals Li Tsung-jen and Huang Shao-hsiung, attending. Li and Huang were leaders of the Kwangsi group, and Huang had come to Shanghai in response to a telegraphic request from Chiang Kai-shek. This meeting produced a list of 197 communists or near-communists holding important positions in the Kuomintang and resolved to send the list to the Central Executive Committee with the request that the persons thereon be placed under surveillance.[162]

Chiang Kai-shek conferred with the principal generals of the National Revolutionary Army who would accept his request to come to Shanghai. They included Ch'eng Ch'ien, Ho Yao-tsu, and Ho Ying-ch'in from Nanking; Li Tsung-jen from the Left Bank Army, Huang Shao-hsiung from Kwangsi and Li Chi-shen from Kwangtung; and Pai Ch'ung-hsi, already at Shanghai. Others were Ch'en Ming-shu, who had been driven from Wuhan; Po Wen-wei and Wang P'u of Anhwei, and Chou Feng-ch'i of Chekiang. All of them were anti-communist.

Wang Ching-wei arrived in Shanghai on 1 April, having returned from his 'vacation' in Paris, via Moscow, where he received a handsome welcome. Probably he was the only leader with enough prestige to bridge the widening split in his party. During the next few days he was in a swirl of discussions with T.V. Soong, who had been sent from Wuhan; with Wu Chih-hui, Ts'ai Yuan-p'ei and Li Shih-tseng of the Supervisory Committee faction; with his old colleague, Hu Han-min; with his rival, Chiang Kai-shek; and with Ch'en Tu-hsiu, the general-secretary of the Chinese Communist Party. On 3 April Chiang issued a telegram to all commanders of the National Revolutionary Army announcing Wang's return in most flattering terms and stating that now the administration of all military, civil, financial and foreign matters should be centralized under Chairman Wang's direction; Chiang only had general direction of the several armies and would obey the chairman, as should all other commanders. Thus would authority in the party truly be centralized in order to complete the national revolution and hasten fulfilment of the Three Principles of the People. Privately, Chiang urged on Wang the necessity of expelling Borodin and purifying the party of its communist members. He warned Wang against going to Wuhan where he could not escape becoming a communist pawn. Others begged Wang to join the party purge, but he advocated a plenary meeting of the Central Executive Committee to decide so serious a matter, and urged his comrades not to act independently.[163]

162 KMWH, 17. 3086–93 (list on 3091–92); TJK, 611–14; Chiang Yung-ching, Borodin, 158–60.
163 TJK, 615–17. Chiang's telegram in KMWH, 16. 2797–8; it was abstracted in NCH, 9 April, p. 52.

The outcome of discussions between Wang and Ch'en Tu-hsiu was their joint statement published in the Shanghai papers on the morning of 5 April. The statement first emphasized the continuing need for unity within the revolutionary camp and denied that the Communist Party, 'no matter what its faults', had ever advocated overthrowing its friendly party, the Kuomintang. China was unlikely to have a proletarian dictatorship even in the future; what was needed now was a democratic dictatorship of all oppressed classes to deal with counter-revolution. The statement called for a spirit of cooperation between members of the two parties and reminded Kuomintang members of Leader Sun's policy of allying with the communists. It tried to set at rest two 'rumours' current in Shanghai – that the Communist Party intended to organize a workers' government, invade the foreign concessions, subvert the northern expeditionary army, and overthrow the Kuomintang; and that the Kuomintang leaders planned to expel the Communist Party and suppress the labour unions and their inspection corps. Neither party had any such intentions. The statement ended by exhorting all comrades to rid themselves of suspicions, end rumours, and consult with mutual respect and good will 'for the good of the revolution and the good of the two parties.'[164]

That same morning Wang attended a stormy meeting with an enlarged group of party veterans and Nationalist generals determined to expel the communists, and then in the evening he secretly boarded a steamer for Hankow. In letters to Chang Jen-chieh (Chang Ching-chiang) and Chiang Kai-shek, he explained that he was going to Wuhan to arrange for a plenary meeting of the Central Executive Committee to be held in Nanking on 15 April to settle the disputes within the Kuomintang.[165] The Wuhan centre was reasonably well informed of the Shanghai meetings, both through the Chinese press, and from Ch'eng Ch'ien's personal report about April 6. General Ch'eng had left his army at Nanking to come

164 KMWH, 16. 2798–800; trans in Warren Kuo, Analytical history of the Chinese Communist Party, 1. 424–6; abstract in NCH, 9 April, p. 74. According to Wang Ching-wei's later account, Ch'en Tu-hsiu wrote the statement to refute the charges against the Communist Party that Wu, Ts'ai and Li had made to Wang. See his speech of 5 November 1927 in Wang Ching-wei hsien-sheng tsui-chin yen-shuo chi (Mr Wang Ching-wei's most recent speeches collected), 126. Ch'en, himself, later called it a 'shameful' statement, and blamed its position on Comintern policy of that time. Ch'en Tu-hsui, 'A letter to all comrades of the party', 10 Dec. 1929, trans. in Chinese Studies in History, 3. 3 (Spring 1970) 231.
165 TJK, 617–19, with a list of those attending. New names included Generals Li Chi-shen and Pai Ch'ung-hsi; and Po Wen-wei, T.V. Soong and Kan Nai-kuang of the Central Executive Committee. Kan was a member of the Standing Committee and had been considered a leftist. Wang's reminiscent account is in his speech of 5 Nov., cited above, 123–5. Wu Chih-hui wrote a very critical account of Wang's position, 'Shu Wang Ching-wei hsien-sheng hsien tien hou' (Written after Mr Wang Ching-wei's telegram of the 16th [i.e. of April]), Chih-hui wen-ts'un, first collection, 1–14.

to Wuhan after conferring with Chiang Kai-shek in Shanghai, and also meeting with Wu Chih-hui and Li Shih-tseng.[166] There was nothing effective the Wuhan centre could do to restrain Chiang Kai-shek and his fellow plotters, and besides, Wuhan was absorbed with its own problems.

Mounting violence among the revolutionaries

Radical and counter-radical actions broke out in widely scattered cities during the two weeks prior to 12 April, manifestations of the now intense conflict within the revolutionary camp itself. These actions were not merely struggles for power; behind the conflicts were issues of great revolutionary import. Was the goal of the national revolution, at least in its current phase, simply the reunification of China by eliminating the warlords and ending imperialist privileges, or was it also to be a class revolution to emancipate the impoverished masses from their bondage? In the countryside, were mobilized tenant farmers to seize the land or be content with rent reduction? In the cities, was the proletariat to force upon the capitalists not only better wages and working conditions but also, through the unions, some control over their enterprises? Was mass violence, including murders, an acceptable way to achieve lower class emancipation from the bonds of feudalism and capitalism? In short, what degree of social revolution should accompany the national revolution? Nationalism unites; social revolution divides.

Leaders at all levels held passionate beliefs about these issues, but they differed across a broad spectrum from radical to conservative. Struggles for control over local Kuomintang headquarters and governing councils, and competition in the indoctrination of junior officers and troops, arose from these differences in commitment. Among the revolutionaries – for all considered themselves as such – there were rival organizations of youth, labour, farmers, merchants and shopkeepers. Some were strongly influenced or dominated by the Communist Party; others were anti-communist. In the labour movement, rivalry between non-communist labour union organizers and the communist activists who had been determined to dominate the union movement as the preserve of the Communist Party dated from the previous six years.

There was a pattern to the conflicts that erupted in the cities. The radicals tried to win support by propaganda and street lecturing, and by

---

166 *TJK*, 623, citing minutes of an emergency meeting of the Wuhan Political Council, 7 April. Ch'eng's written report dated 5 May tells of his meetings in Shanghai, and of a military conference which he refused to attend. The conferees were anti-communist. Report is in the Kuomintang Archives, no. 1–5/804.

mobilizing the masses in patriotic rallies and parades, with handbills and slogans, some among which denounced conservative Kuomintang leaders. Armed workmen of the General Labour Union – the so-called 'inspection corps' – which were characteristically controlled by communists, protected the radicals' establishments and enforced strikes. Counter-radical action also followed a pattern which points to central direction: for example, the same slogans – 'Uphold Commander-in-Chief Chiang', 'Expel Borodin' – were used in widely scattered places. As conflict intensified in some locality, military commanders might order the arrest of suspected communists and closure of the organizations they dominated. In several cases Whampoa cadets loyal to Chiang were involved. Assisted by troops, a rival labour organization would attack the local offices of the General Labour Union and disarm its inspection corps. The crushing of the Shanghai Inspection Corps on 12 April could not have been a surprise.

In Hangchow, the capital of Chekiang, conflict developed after its capture on 18 February between leftist Kuomintang party headquarters, the General Labour Union, and the Students' Association on the one side, and an anti-communist Labour Federation, the Whampoa Cadets Association, and the rear-guard of the Eastern Route Army on the other. Hsüan Chung-hua, a communist very influential in the provincial Kuomintang headquarters, attempted to have the leaders of the Labour Federation arrested and the Federation broken up, but he was opposed by the head of the Public Security Bureau and the commander of the rear guard. After a bloody conflict on 30 March between parading clerks and workers of the Federation and the armed inspection corps of the General Labour Union, the rear-guard commander forbade the Union to hold a rally and parade the next day on pain of suppression by arms. When students and workers led by the inspection corps paraded anyway, troops fired on the marchers, surrounded and fired on the leftist Kuomintang headquarters, and disarmed the inspection corps. Rioters wrecked the headquarters of the General Labour Union.[167]

On the same day, 31 March, but far in the west, Chungking in Szechwan witnessed the crushing of the General Labour Union and other leftist organs, and the execution of many suspected communists. Conflict in

167 *TJK*, 645–60. Li reports Hsüan Chung-hua and another influential communist, An T'i-ch'eng, executed early in May. *Chung-kuo lao-kung yun-tung shih*, 2. 669–70. According to this source, the Chekiang Political Council called together representatives of the GLU and the army and worked out a settlement, which permitted the GLU to continue, but restricted the inspection corps to the union's headquarters. Later, under a reregistration procedure both the federation and the union were dissolved. *NCH*, 9 April, p. 67, report dated 5 April.

Chungking between left and right factions of the Kuomintang went back to 1925. One of the chief rightist leaders was Shih Ch'ing-yang, a party veteran and a member of the anti-communist Western Hills Conference of late 1925. During most of 1926 there were two provincial party headquarters, two general labour unions, and other competing organizations. Rival propaganda squads brawled in the streets. Two communists among the leftist leaders were the veteran revolutionary, Wu Yü-chang, and the later famous Liu Po-ch'eng. In November 1926 Liu Hsiang, the Szechwanese general controlling Chungking, suddenly turned towards the left and ordered the dispersal of right-wing organizations.[168] This was during the flush of the first phase of the Northern Expedition when the leftists in the Kuomintang seemed ascendant. Probably early in 1927 Chiang Kai-shek and the Nanchang Political Council ordered two anti-communists, Hsiang Fu-i and Lü Ch'ao, back to Szechwan to urge Liu Hsiang and Wang Ling-chi, the Chungking garrison commander, to take action against the communists. In February Lü brought a contingent of Whampoa cadets to work in Liu Hsiang's army. Other anti-communist groups were also organizing, and apparently most of the military commanders developed hostile sentiments towards the radicals. To strengthen their side, the Kuomintang leftists planned a great rally for 31 March, ostensibly to oppose British and American imperialism in response to the bombardment of Nanking a week before, but also to arouse sentiment against Chiang Kai-shek. Garrison Commander Wang, with General Liu Hsiang's concurrence, sent soldiers to surround the meeting place and arrest suspected communists; he also sent troops to search two schools that had been managed by Wu Yü-chang, and to seal up the provincial, county and municipal headquarters of the Kuomintang, the offices of the provincial farmers' association, the city General Labour Union, and the *Szechwan daily*, all controlled by communists, according to our source.[169] When the workers inspection corps resisted the troops in their arresting, much blood was shed. Six important local communists were beaten to death, and according to a report by another communist to the Wuhan centre, over 400 persons were killed and the inspection corps was completely smashed. Thereafter the purge spread throughout Szechwan.[170]

Leftists had their turn to overthrow their rivals on 2 April in Nanchang. Kiangsi was an arena of competition between the two Kuomintang fac-

168 *Chung-kuo lao-kung yun-tung shih*, 2. 566–9.
169 Li, *TJK*, 666.
170 *Ibid*. 666–8. *Chung-kuo lao-kung yun-tung shih*, 2. 649, estimates the killed at more than 70 and the wounded at more than 100. *NCH*, 9 April, carried a brief Reuters dispatch from Peking dated 1 April (presumably deriving from the British consulate in Chungking) on the clash.

tions. After the province was taken by the Northern Expeditionary troops, many communists were active there, though their influence was checked during the period when Chiang Kai-shek made Nanchang his headquarters. The Kuomintang provincial executive committee and the government council were made up predominently of 'pure' Kuomintang members. A prestigious old revolutionary, Li Lieh-chün, served as provincial governor. The Kuomintang's Nanchang city headquarters, however, was controlled by leftists. When Chiang Kai-shek left Nanchang in mid March 1927 he ordered the dissolution of the municipal party headquarters; but with his departure, the Wuhan centre increased its influence in Kiangsi. On 26 March the Central Executive Committee in Wuhan appointed a committee of eight to reorganize the provincial executive committee and the provincial government; six of the eight were dual party members. On 30 March the CEC appointed Chu P'ei-te, commander of the Third Corps, as governor, in a bid for his support. In order to carry out Wuhan's decisions, leftists mobilized their supporters among students and labourers, and staged a riotous coup on 2 April. In this case, Nanchang's garrison commander, Wang Chün, a subordinate of Chu P'ei-te, apparently cooperated or remained neutral. The later famous communist general, Chu Te, who then was in command of an officers training regiment and a military academy in Nanchang, supported the coup. A number of Kuomintang members holding positions in the provincial government were arrested and some twenty people were killed. Li Lieh-chün departed and Chu P'ei-te assumed the coveted governorship and restored order. After receiving a stern telegram from Chiang Kai-shek, he protected the Kuomintang officials who had been arrested, though some had been tried by a people's court and condemned to execution.[171]

In Foochow the balance of forces seems to have been more even, and developments took a somewhat different course. Two communist members of the Kuomintang, Ma Shih-ts'ai and Li P'ei-t'ung, came to dominate the provincial party headquarters, sent deputies to organize Kuomintang branches in various counties, and established a political training institute in which a number of the teachers were communists. Through party headquarters they set up the usual organizations of youth,

---

171 *TJK*, 594-8, Chiang Yung-ching, *Borodin*, 128, naming persons executed. Kao, *Chronology*, 252, mentions more than 20 persons killed by the General Labour Union and some 800 arrested. Mr Ch'eng T'ien-fang, who, as provincial educational commissioner, was one of those arrested, described his harrowing experiences in an interview with the writer in Taipei in 1962. His book, *A history of Sino-Soviet relations*, 138-9, gives a brief account. Chu Te's American biographer, Agnes Smedley, describes his work at Nanchang but passes over the incident of 2 April. Smedley, *The great road: the life and times of Chu Teh*.

women, farmers and workers. On the other side, 'pure' Kuomintang activists created anti-communist organizations of youth, women workers, and even a general labour union and a provincial farmers' association. Furthermore, General Ho Ying-ch'in while still in Foochow did not permit the communist-controlled labour union to form an inspection corps nor allow creation of farmers' guards. During March both sides tried to rally their forces in demonstrations of power and there were street conflicts between them, which the garrison commander suppressed. On 19 March a Foochow branch of the Whampoa Cadets Association was established, adding to the strength of the anti-communist side. On 4 April the conservative forces rallied in a meeting 'To uphold Commander-in-Chief Chiang and to protect the party.' They passed resolutions to support the commander-in-chief as leader of the revolutionary army, to expel Borodin, and to punish Hsu Ch'ien, Teng Yen-ta and T'an P'ing-shan. The inspiration for such resolutions could only have come from Shanghai. The meeting also resolved to punish those local communists and leftists who had 'destroyed party work'. including Ma and Li. The American consul in Foochow reported 'what virtually amounts to anti-communist *coup d'état* involving complete change in provincial administration . . . said to have been directly under orders of Chiang Kai-shek.' On 7 April, a group of more conservative party leaders formally established a new provincial headquarters. On the same day, Ma Shih-ts'ai and a few others fled from Foochow, but some ten of the defeated faction 'sooner or later fell into the net and were executed.'[172]

On 6 April the foreign diplomatic corps gave permission for the Peking metropolitan police to conduct a raid on certain buildings in the Soviet embassy compound. The grounds for the search warrant was the suspicion that Chinese communists were using the offices of the Chinese Eastern Railway and the Dalbank in planning an insurrection in Peking. During the raid the police arrested 22 Russians and 36 Kuomintang members in hiding there, including Li Ta-chao, one of the founders and principal theoreticians of the Chinese Communist Party. Six of the nine members of the Executive Committee of the Kuomintang Municipal Headquarters were taken. The police discovered documents of the Chinese Communist Party, as well as Kuomintang and communist banners and seals, and some arms and ammunition. Furthermore, when they saw that Russians in the Soviet military attaché's office were burning their papers,

---

172 *TJK*, 650–5, based upon archival materials including a report from Ma Shih-i. What happened to Li P'ei-t'ung is not stated. USDS 893.00/8615, telegram, MacMurray, Peking, 7 April.

they put out the fire and removed seven truckloads of documents.[173] The immediate effects of the raid were to disrupt Kuomintang and communist operations in the north and, probably, to disrupt the communications of the Russian military advisers with the military attaché's office in Peking. On the next day the authorities of the French Concession in Tientsin searched Soviet establishments there, and in Shanghai the Municipal Council ordered police to surround the Soviet consulate and prevent access. Thus did the Western powers attempt to cripple Soviet assistance to the revolutionaries. After trial by a Chinese court in Peking, Li Ta-chao and 19 other Chinese seized in the raid were executed on 25 April. Ten others received prison sentences. Among those executed were several Kuomintang members regarded with suspicion by the Peking communist organization.

In Shanghai many actions presaged the final break of Chiang Kai-shek and his supporters with the Wuhan centre and the Chinese Communist Party. Two of Chiang's intimates, Yang Hu and Ch'en Ch'ün, reportedly were his intermediaries with Tu Yueh-sheng, one of the top leaders of the Ch'ing-pang, the most powerful underworld society in the lower Yangtze region. They persuaded Tu to lead an anti-communist action. Tu created a 'Society for Common Progress' to carry this through. By 3 April the International Settlement police department had learned that leaders of the Ch'ing-pang had recruited several hundred armed gangsters for the society and that they were lodged in the French Concession where, incidentally, Tu had his lavishly appointed home. Allegedly, Chiang had paid the leaders Ch.$600,000. By 7 April the International Settlement police learned that the gangsters' purpose was to attack the headquarters of the General Labour Union.[174] Tu and Wang Shou-hua, the communist head of the Shanghai General Labour Union, were acquainted. More exactly, they were rivals for control over some sectors of the Shanghai labour force.

During the first three days in April, General Liu Chih, commander of

173 An account of the raid and of the authenticity of the documents discovered is given in Wilbur and How, *Documents*, 8–37. In the months following the raid many of the documents were published, revealing details of Russian espionage and aid to the Kuomintang and Feng Yü-hsiang, as well as much historical information about the revolutionary movement as it involved both parties.

174 Yang and Ch'en had been part of Ch'en Ch'i-mei's organization during the 1911 Revolution and after, as had Chiang. Rather shadowy figures, they were appointed by Chiang to important posts in the Shanghai garrison command. Tu Yueh-sheng was one of the most obscure but influential Chinese in Shanghai. See Y.C. Wang, 'Tu Yueh-sheng (1888–1951): a tentative political biography', *JAS*, 26. 3 (May 1967) 433–55. On the 'Society for Common Progress', see Chesneaux, *The Chinese labor movement*, 393–4, citing Police Daily Reports of 3 and 7 April. *Ti-i-tz'u . . . kung-jen*, 492–3, from a report of the GLU dated 15 April, which says that several days before 12 April the union received repeated reports that the gangsters would attack the union and the inspection corps.

the Second Division of the First Corps, on orders from Chiang Kai-shek and Pai Ch'ung-hsi, sent troops to attack concentrations of armed guerrillas, including one detachment of the inspection corps, killing some dozens and arresting others, who were sent to Lung-hua for trial. His adjutant told a reporter for the *North China Daily News* on 4 April that 'approximately a division' of irregulars had been disarmed but that, since the labour corps under the General Labour Union did not interfere with military affairs, 'the members would not be disarmed yet.' If, however, the corps caused any breaches of the peace, 'they would also be suppressed and disarmed.' On 5 April Chiang Kai-shek instituted martial law and ordered the disarming of all bearers of arms not properly enrolled in the Nationalist Army. Next day, Pai Ch'ung-hsi sealed the office of the Central Political Bureau established by order of the Wuhan centre, and ordered censorship of all telegrams and letters from Hankow. On the 8th he conducted a raid on a union headquarters in Nanshih, the formerly walled city adjacent to the French Concession. Nineteen suspected communists were arrested.[175] About the same time, General Chiang transferred the First and Second Divisions to Nanking,[176] where he had business to perform.

Chiang's purpose in going to Nanking was to gain control of the site of the government he and his allies intended to establish. To do this it was necessary to defend the city from the northern forces and to eliminate potentially subversive elements within. Chiang ordered the Second and Sixth Corps to cross the Yangtze to face the enemy and sent two divisions of the First Corps to the city as reinforcement. Most of the officers of the two divisions were former Whampoa instructors or graduates, and Chiang could count on them to obey his orders.[177]

Within Nanking a complex struggle was under way. The political departments of the Second and Sixth Corps were headed by dual party members, Li Fu-ch'un, a young returned student from France on the radical wing, and Lin Tsu-han, a veteran of the 1911 Revolution and an

175 *NCH*, 9 April, pp. 50, 51, 55, 77; Chesneaux, *The Chinese labor movement*, 346, from police daily report of 8 April.
176 Kao, *Chronology*, 9 April, implying the divisions had arrived. Leon Trotsky in *Problems of the Chinese revolution*, 276, quotes from a report by Chitarov, who had returned from China, that Hsueh Yueh offered to the Central Committee of the Chinese Communist Party that he not submit to Chiang's order to move his division, but instead stay in Shanghai and fight together with the workers. The responsible communist leaders turned him down because they did not want a 'premature conflict' with Chiang Kai-shek.
177 *TJK*, 623, states that Chiang ordered the crossing to be completed by 6 April. General Ch'eng, who was then in Wuhan, telegraphed his commanders not to go, but the telegram was discovered by Chiang's headquarters so 'Ch'eng's plot was foiled'. On 5 May Ch'eng Ch'ien wrote a bitter letter to the CEC in Wuhan describing these events and the destruction of his army. Kuomintang Archives 1–5/804.

important Kuomintang leader and member of its Central Executive Committee. After Nanking was occupied on 24 March the usual pattern of setting up a general labour union and other mass associations began under the leadership of the two political departments. Lin Tsu-han had not been with the Sixth Corps when it captured Nanking, but travelled there at the end of March and stayed a few days to develop support for the Wuhan side. On 1 April the Kiangsu Provincial Party Headquarters moved from Shanghai to Nanking; it was a leftist group in which two alleged communists, Chang Shu-shih and Hou Shao-ch'iu, were prominent. Chang had represented the Kiangsu Provincial Party Headquarters at the Third CEC Plenum, and came down from Hankow to Nanking on 3 April. His later report to Wuhan central is a first-hand if biased source of information on the developing conflict in Nanking. He learned that two 'counter-revolutionary gangsters' had organized a rival Kuomintang municipal headquarters, but the political department of the Sixth Corps shut this down and arrested some of its partisans. He also learned the ominous news that Chiang Kai-shek had appointed 'the wrecker of the Anhwei Provincial Party Headquarters, the gangster Yang Hu' to be in charge of the Nanking special area, and another 'counter-revolutionary gangster' to carry out the wrecking. These men organized a Labour Association 'especially to hire gangsters'. The political department was unable to shut this down because it was protected by the chief of the Public Security Bureau. The leftists planned a rally to close down the Labour Association by mass action, but the Public Security Bureau forbade this meeting on pain of forcible suppression. Provincial Party Headquarters then decided to hold an assembly to celebrate the union of soldiers and the people on 8 April, and on the next day to hold a rally to celebrate Wang Ching-wei's return. The first meeting was a disappointment because the Second and Sixth Corps had already crossed the Yangtze, and only the political department of the Sixth Corps and a few armed comrades attended. None came from the First Corps.[178] This signalled the shift in military power. Meanwhile in Hankow, Borodin called an emergency meeting of the Political Council on 7 April after hearing reports from Ch'eng Ch'ien and Li Fu-ch'un on Chiang's plans. The meeting

178 Chang Shu-shih, 'Kiangsu sheng tang-pu tai-piao pao-kao' (Report of the representative of the Kiangsu provincial party headquarters), Kuomintang Archives, Kiangsu collection, 2/99; date about 27 April. Quoted in Chiang Yung-ching, Borodin, 133-5. According to Pai Ch'ung-hsi, lower and middle ranking communist officers in Hsueh's division and the 21st Division of Yen Chung had either been dismissed or arrested. Pai Ch'ung-hsi, Shih-liu nien ch'ing-tang yun-tung ti hui-i (Recollections of the party purification movement of 1927), Propaganda Department of the Kuomintang Kwangsi Party Reconstruction Committee, 1932, p. 10.

resolved that central party headquarters and the National government should move to Nanking.[179] But it was already too late.

Chiang Kai-shek and Ho Ying-ch'in arrived in Nanking on the morning of 9 April, leaving Pai Ch'ung-hsi and Chou Feng-ch'i to hold Shanghai. Nanking was put under strict martial law. Those who had planned the great rally to welcome Wang Ching-wei found it advisable to add some posters and banners welcoming Chiang! But apparently that rally was never held. A gang of armed ruffians – hired for four Chinese dollars a day – attacked and smashed the Kuomintang provincial and city head-quarters, bound up staff members, including the heads of the provincial farmers department and merchants department, the secretaries of the propaganda department and women's department, and officials of the secretariat, and dragged them off to the public security office. Several were alleged communists. Chang Shu-shih hid during this raid, but later was captured and held overnight. It was thus he learned that Commander-in-chief Chiang was behind these acts. To counter this attack, the leftists sent labourers to the commander-in-chief's headquarters to petition him to protect the provincial and city headquarters of the Kuomintang and the General Labour Union, but to no avail. Next day the leftists succeeded in holding a rally, after which 'the masses' went again to the commander-in-chief to beg for protection. This time they came into conflict with troops and police, and many persons were wounded. There were two days of terror on 10 and 11 April: armed gangsters attacked the General Labour Union, and military police searched hotels and other places where Chang Shu-shih's comrades lived, arresting a number. Hou Shao-ch'iu was among those killed. Chang, himself, escaped through the water gate in a small boat and finally made his way to Hankow.[180] Nanking no longer was safe for Wuhan supporters.

Similar conflicts in Amoy and Ningpo on 9 and 10 April resulted in victories for the conservative side. In Canton the American consul reported on 9 April that the situation was becoming very tense and a clash between moderates and communists was expected at any time. The Chinese press had published telegrams from Li Chi-shen stating that, since the Hankow administration was controlled by communists, its mandates need not be obeyed.[181] This was only a hint of the terrible purge that was to begin on 15 April.

In spite of all these acts and portents, there was little the communist

179 Li, *TJK*, 623.
180 This paragraph is a synthesis of Chang's first-hand account and that of Li Yun-han, based on archival material. It is unclear how many of those arrested were executed. *Chung-kuo lao-kung yun-tung shih*, 2. 646–7 stresses the other side of the story.
181 *Ibid.* 670–1; *NCH*, 16 April, p. 100. USDS 893.00/8642, MacMurray, Peking, 11 April.

leadership in Shanghai could do to ward off an attack. Since no inner party documents are available for the first two weeks of April, it is difficult to learn what preparations the Central Committee and the leaders of the General Labour Union made. Ch'en Tu-hsiu later revealed that the Comintern instructed the Communist Party to hide or bury all the workers' weapons to avoid a military conflict with Chiang Kai-shek. The telegram was sent on 31 March, according to A. Mandalian. Apparently the order to hide the arms was not carried out.[182] Rather, the leadership tried to assert strict discipline over the unions and the inspection corps, to win public support, and prepare for a general strike in case the enemy tried to disarm the workers. After a secret meeting aboard a strike-bound ship in the river, the Shanghai General Labour Union held a more open meeting on 4 April under the chairmanship of its dynamic leader, Wang Shou-hua, where it was resolved – that is, announced – that the pickets must obey explicitly the General Labour Union regulations on the use of their fire-arms, and workers must not declare strikes without orders from the union. The public should be informed why it was necessary to maintain armed pickets. The joint statement by Wang Ching-wei and Ch'en Tu-hsiu the next day aimed at easing tension and gaining public support. But the Executive Committee of the General Labour Union resolved to order a general strike if anyone tried to disarm the workers. In Chapei the workers inspection corps held a parade, arms in hand, in a show of power: and on the 7th an assembly of labour union delegates resolved that, should anyone harm the picket corps or take armed action against it, all Shanghai workers must rise in support and use the power of the masses to stop it. Resolutions passed at a leftist meeting the same day indicate the radicals' concerns: the right wing of the Kuomintang in Rue Vallon should be suppressed and its members arrested and punished; the Kuomintang in Shanghai should come under the control and direction of the CEC in Hankow; General Liu Chih should be dismissed and punished, and General Hsueh Yueh be urged to stay in Shanghai and control military affairs; all counter-revolutionaries should be suppressed and all workers be armed.[183]

The spreading anti-communist purge

Pai Ch'ung-hsi, Yang Hu, Tu Yueh-sheng and their associates planned carefully for the disarming of the powerful workers inspection corps in

---

182 Ch'en Tu-hsiu, 'A letter to all comrades of the party', 231; North and Eudin, *M.N. Roy's mission to China*, 54, quoting an article in *Pravda*, 159 (16 July 1927) 2–3; and Chang, *The rise of the Chinese Communist Party*, 1. 587.
183 *NCH*, 9 April, p. 80; *TJK*, 570–1; *NCH*, 9 April, p. 50, resolutions 8–12 and 18.

Shanghai. Tu's gangster recruits were armed with pistols, formed into squads with specific targets of attack, and dressed in workmen's outfits with armbands carrying the word 'worker.' Several hundred troops from Pai's force were similarly disguised. On the night of 11 April Wang Shou-hua came by invitation to dinner at Tu Yueh-sheng's house. As he was leaving he was abducted, killed and the corpse dumped at Lung-hua. Chou Feng-ch'i's troops were positioned during the night near concentration points of the inspection corps and the headquarters of the General Labour Union. Authorities of the International Settlement and the French Concession were informed in advance. After midnight they were told of the impending attack; they ordered the barricades around the two settlements closed, preventing escape into the foreign sanctuaries. Yet Tu's 'workers' were permitted to move out from the French Concession and Pai's disguised troops to pass through the International Settlement just before dawn on 12 April.[184]

Between 4 and 5 a.m. the attacking parties, numbering about 1,000 in all, began firing upon concentrations of the inspection corps in Chapei, adjacent to the International Settlement, in the old south city next to the French Concession, in Pootung across the river, and in Woosung where the Whangpoo enters the Yangtze. In some places the defenders resisted fiercely but in others they were tricked into submission. In some places uniformed troops of Chou Feng-ch'i's Twenty-Sixth Corps joined the attack, in others they pretended to restore order between feuding labour organizations. According to early reports, some 25 to 30 of the resisters died in the fighting. Captured leaders on the leftist side were sent to General Pai's headquarters where, according to a news report, 145 were executed. Chou En-lai and Ku Shun-chang, a communist leader of the inspection corps, were among those arrested, though both escaped. General Chou Feng-ch'i made a great haul of workers' arms, some 3,000 rifles, 20 machine guns, 600 pistols, much ammunition, and quantities of axes and pikes. After disarming the inspection corps, troops and gangster-workers searched and sealed up the offices of various leftist organizations.[185]

184 On Wang's death, *Chuan-chi wen-hsueh*, 11. 1 (July 1967) 97; Taipei *Hua pao*, 4 and 5 Oct. 1961, an article on Tu Yueh-sheng by a former secretary, Hu Shu-wu. Both say Tu's subordinates did the killing, and imply Yang Hu and Ch'en Ch'ün were involved. A written reply to questions asked of Pai Ch'ung-hsi in 1962, stated, 'I arrested Wang Shou-hua . . . and the chief communist representative Hou Shao-ch'iu and others . . . the leaders were punished according to law . . .'. USDS 893.00/8906, dispatch, Gauss, Shanghai, 21 April 1927, 'Political conditions in the Shanghai consular district', states that Wang was arrested 11 April and executed at Pai Ch'ung-hsi's headquarters. For Pai Ch'ung-hsi's reminiscent account of the preparations, see Pai Ch'ung-hsi, *Shih-liu nien*, 11.
185 *Ti-i-tz'u . . . kung-jen*, 494–500, for an early account from the communist side; and *NCH*, 16 April, pp. 102–4, and USDS 893.00/8906, just cited, for outsiders' reports. Secondary accounts in Isaacs, *The tragedy of the Chinese revolution*, 175–7; Chesneaux, *The Chinese labor*

The defeated tried to rally their supporters. The leaders of the General Labour Union called a general strike and, despite General Pai's order forbidding it, more than 100,000 workers, many under picket intimidation, stayed away next day. But the strike could not be sustained for long. After a rally in Chapei on the 13th, demonstrators marched on Chou Feng-ch'i's headquarters to petition for the release of those arrested and the return of the workers' arms. Among the marchers were both armed men, and women and children. When guards at the headquarters fired on the procession, scores of innocents were slain. Among the 90 or so captured, more than 40 were former soldiers of the Shantung Army, hired as corps members. That evening a newly organized Committee on the Unification of Trade Unions took over the headquarters of the General Labour Union; it was to be Chiang's instrument to bring the labour movement under conservative control. The fearful repression of 12-14 April shattered the left-directed mass movement in Shanghai. Hundreds had been killed and thousands fled in terror. The leaders of the General Labour Union could do nothing but call off the strike on 15 April, and send to the Wuhan government a report bitterly denouncing Chiang Kai-shek and begging for help.[186]

Canton, the nursery of the revolution, underwent an equally brutal suppression of communist-led organizations, and many noted radicals were slain. General Li Chi-shen, who had been 'dismissed' by the Wuhan centre, returned to Canton on 14 April, fresh from the conservative conferences in Shanghai. He called a secret emergency meeting that night. The conferees set up a special committee, headed by General Li, to plan and execute 'party purification'. General Ch'ien Ta-chün, Canton garrison commander, proclaimed martial law beginning 15 April, and the head of the Canton Police Bureau issued a similar proclamation saying he had received orders from the commander-in-chief of the National Revolutionary Army to arrest without delay all Communist Party elements in Canton and to disarm the pickets of various labour unions. In the pre-dawn hours of 15 April the purge began.

Battalions of troops and 2,000 armed police surrounded the headquar-

movement, 369-70; and Tien-wei Wu, 'Chiang Kai-shek's April 12 coup of 1927', in F. Gilbert Chan and Thomas H. Etzold, eds. China in the 1920's: nationalism and revolution, 146-59, 155-7. General Pai Ch'ung-hsi told the writer there is no truth whatsoever in André Malraux's account, in Man's fate, of arrested radicals being executed by pitching them into the flames of a locomotive fire-box.

186 TJK, 628-9. Ti-i-tz'u . . . kung-jen, 516-18; GLU report on pp. 530-3. The original handwritten report dated 15 April, with a covering letter on the stationery of the GLU and with its seal, are in the Kuomintang Archives, Shanghai file, 1.8/423. They were to be brought to Wuhan by Wang Ssu-tseng, and were transmitted to the CEC on 27 April. The version in Ti-i-tz'u . . . kung-jen is the same. The original is quoted in part in Chiang Yung-ching, Borodin, 161-2.

ters of the Hong Kong strike committee, the Canton Congress of Workers' Delegates, and scores of radical unions, where they disarmed the guards and arrested the leaders. At Wongsha station, the terminus of the railway leading towards Hankow, a pitched battle broke out between the railwaymen's union and their old rivals, the conservative mechanics union. Supported by troops, the mechanics prevailed. There were raids also on Chung-shan University and two middle schools where radical influences were strong, and upon the offices of two Nationalist newspapers, which were then reorganized under conservative direction. Posters appeared on the streets on 16 April in support of Chiang Kai-shek and removal of the government to Nanking, which he was about to effect. Because communist influence was thought to be strong among cadets at Whampoa, they were all disarmed, but the majority supported the commander-in-chief. On 18 April some 200 cadets suspected of being communists were arrested while some others fled. A few unions were able to mount a protest strike which lasted from 23 to 25 April, but as a result some twenty or thirty more labour leaders were arrested. Seven persons caught distributing anti-government propaganda were executed, including two girl students. Forty-three unions were forced to reorganize. Raids continued until 27 April. By then some 2,000 suspected communists had been captured. Among the scores executed were Liu Erh-sung, Li Sen (Li Ch'i-han) and Hsiao Ch'u-nü, all well-known leftist militants, who had joined the Communist Party.[187]

Li Chi-shen and the special committee also reorganized the provincial government. Ku Ying-fen, an old associate of Sun Yat-sen and a conservative nationalist, became the leading civil official in Canton, while General Li remained, in effect, the military governor. The new government declared its independence from the Wuhan centre, and this had two serious consequences for the leadership there. The Central Bank at Canton, with eight million Chinese dollars in silver reserves, no longer supported Wuhan, thus weakening its already suspect currency. Further, the three provinces adhering to Wuhan were now cut off from the sea on the south; they were already only tenuously connected on the east via the Yangtze.

187 GBFO 405/253. Confidential. *Further correspondence respecting China,* 13304, April-June 1927, no. 127, a dispatch from British Consul-General J.F. Brenan, Canton, 21 April 1927, which includes translations of proclamations of the 15th and of other documents concerning the purge. Also GBFO 228, F3609/8135. USDS 893.00B/286, 290, 292 and 296, telegrams from American consul-general. Canton, 15, 16, 22 and 25 April. *Ti-i-tz'u ... kung-jen,* 534–9, an article published in 1931. *TJK,* 655–9, and Chiang Yung-ching, *Borodin,* 164–5, both based partly on a report by Han Lin-fu to the Wuhan leaders on 15 May. (Han, a communist, escaped from Canton and made his way to Hankow.) *Chung-kuo lao-kung yun-tung shih,* 2. 673–7. Liu Li-k'ai and Wang Chen, *I-chiu i-chiu,* 57.

Similar repressions took place in several cities in Kwangsi province on orders from General Huang Shao-hsiung, one of the Shanghai conferees, and also in the port cities of Swatow, Amoy and Ningpo. Yang Hu supervised the reorganization in Ningpo. Kuomintang branches and labour unions in several lesser cities in Kwangtung, Chekiang and Kiangsu were also purged of leftist leaders. These actions in the southern and eastern coastal provinces did not spell the end of the labour union movement, which had grown rapidly since 1920, but communist influences were sharply reduced. Party members had either to go underground or flee to the sanctuary of Wuhan – a temporary sanctuary only, as it proved to be.

The radical labour leaders in Wuhan may have felt a sense of revenge for the killing of their comrades in Shanghai with the execution on 14 April of eight veteran union organizers who had opposed the Communist Party's domination of the unions in Hupei. They were arrested by Teng Yen-ta's political department and denounced as 'labour thieves'. On 10 April communist labour leaders in Wuhan called a meeting of delegates of the Hupei General Labour Union and the meeting resolved that the eight be turned over to 'the masses' for execution. A few days later, Kuo P'in-po, Lu Shih-ying, Yuan Tzu-ying, and five others were condemned by a court and executed by firing squad on the streets of Hankow.[188] In Changsha, a focus of radicalism, an estimated 30 to 40 Chinese who had foreign business connections were reported to have been executed.[189] Among them was the noted scholar and conservative, Yeh Te-hui.

Establishing a government at Nanking

The conservative Kuomintang leaders in Shanghai widened their breach with Wuhan by setting up a rival central apparatus and a separate Nationalist government in Nanking. They had gathered there ostensibly to await the Wuhan members of the Central Executive Committee for the plenum that Wang Ching-wei was supposed to arrange. When Wang and the others did not come, nine members of a self-styled Central Political Council coopted nine others, and this group resolved on 17 April to establish the central government in Nanking the next day. Of those who made this decision, only five were members of the Central Executive Committee, which numbered 36 with 24 alternates. Eight were members of the Central Supervisory Committee, which had 12 members and eight

---

188 *TJK*, 568-9; Chiang Yung-ching, *Borodin*, 129; *Chung-kuo lao-kung yun-tung shih*, 601-2; Chesneaux, *The Chinese labor movement*, 326.
189 USDS 893.00/8802, telegram, Lockhart, 17 April, 'wantonly killed by the Communists', was the way Lockhart reported the information.

alternates. The remaining five were generals.[190] The Wuhan group had more legitimacy if measured by the number of Central Committee members active there, yet the Nanking group had several very prestigious persons, notably Hu Han-min, Wu Chih-hui, Ts'ai Yuan-p'ei, Li Shih-tseng, Chang Ching-chiang and Teng Tse-ju. After the formal inauguration of the government, which Hu Han-min now chaired, there was a manifesto both revolutionary and anti-communist in tone, for it was important to legitimize the 'party purification movement' already underway. After the Political Council had discussed the 2 April resolution of the Central Supervisory Committee, which urged expulsion of communists from the Kuomintang, the new government issued an appropriate order to the commander-in-chief and other officers and officials, naming Borodin, Ch'en Tu-hsiu, Hsu Ch'ien, Teng Yen-ta, Wu Yü-chang and Lin Tsu-han as particularly evil, but warning against communist leaders everywhere and appending a list of 197 persons to be arrested. Not all were members of the Communist Party so far as is known; probably the Central Supervisory Committee in drawing up the list had mainly to rely on its suspicions.[191] The next few weeks were occupied in setting up a central and various local purge committees to supervise the cleansing of the Kuomintang in those places where the influence of the Shanghai-Nanking group could reach. The government, itself, had little substance and its locale was quite insecure.

On 17 April the Central Executive Committee in Wuhan expelled Chiang Kai-shek from the Kuomintang and relieved him from all his posts. The Nationalist government at Wuhan issued a mandate elaborating his 12 great crimes, and the Chinese Communist Party issued a declaration on 20 April in support. This explained the class basis of the new reactionary tide and stated that the proletariat now no longer need be restrained from direct struggle against feudal-bourgeois elements.[192] Such verbal onslaughts scarcely touched the real power structure.

MOUNTING PROBLEMS FOR THE WUHAN REGIME

Wuhan's struggle to survive

The leadership in Wuhan now faced enormous difficulties. To the north were the powerful military forces of Chang Tso-lin; elements of the National Revolutionary Army on the east and south seemingly supported

---

190 *TJK*, 632; minutes of the meetings on the 17th in *KMWH*, 22. 4211–16.
191 An imperfect list in *KMWH*, 16. 2826–7; corrected lists in *KMWH*, 17. 3091–2 and *TJK*, 635–7.
192 *Chinese correspondence: weekly organ of the Central Executive Committee of the Kuomintang*, 2. 6 (1 May 1927); and *China yearbook, 1928*, 1367–70.

Chiang Kai-shek; and on the west were Szechwanese commanders apparently in league with him. The only bright patch on the military horizon as seen from Wuhan was in the north-west where Feng Yü-hsiang's revived army stood poised to descend down the Lung-Hai Railway into Honan; it was being re-equipped with Russian arms and had a cadre of experienced southern political officers working among the troops. Imperialism appeared menacing. The Arcos raid in London and raids on Soviet establishments in China, which had required international sanction, raised fears of concerted action against Russian support for revolutionary movements. The Nanking Incident, with the threat of foreign retaliation, had still to be settled, and foreign forces in Shanghai now had the power to retaliate. The river that divided the Wuhan cities was filled with foreign gunboats. Relations with Japan were strained because of the April Third Incident in the Japanese concession in Hankow.

However menacing the external scene may have seemed, it was internal economic problems that threatened the regime's survival. The confluence of rivers and two railway lines made the Wuhan cities the gathering place for agricultural and mineral products from a vast hinterland and the distribution point for manufactured goods from down river and abroad. Yet by April this trade was stagnating as a result of class warfare in Hunan and Hupei, and strikes and business failures in the main cities. There was even fear of a rice shortage in the revolutionary capital because revolutionaries in Hunan were holding back rice on the theory that if it were not shipped out from a community, prices there would remain low and the poor could afford to eat. In Wuhan there was massive unemployment: more than 100,000 workers idle, a potential danger and costly charge on the government. Foreign business activity was much curtailed, partly due to the exodus of foreigners from Hankow (on 12 April the foreign population was down from a normal 4,500 to 1,300), and partly due to strikes and lockouts. Mills and wharves in the Japanese concession were deserted. A strike of the Chinese staffs of foreign banks, which had begun on 21 March, contributed to the stagnation since the banks could not perform the financial functions essential to trade. Shipping on the middle Yangtze was much reduced, partly because China Merchants' Steam Navigation Company ships had been withdrawn to avoid commandeering, and partly because pilfering of cargoes and labour disorders on Hankow wharves discouraged foreign shipping. Business stagnation reduced the government's tax revenues while its currency was under inflationary pressures. To protect dwindling reserves of specie, the government on 18 April forbade Chinese banks to redeem their own notes in silver and imposed an embargo on its export. As the British legation's Chinese secretary, Eric Teichman, noted after three months in Hankow, 'The revolution has dislocated the whole economic life of Central China.' He wondered whether 'the puny figures of the Nationalist government, riding like froth' on the revolutionary wave, could control 'the storm and turmoil they have created'.[193]

At this very time the Wuhan centre planned to resume the Northern Expedition to link up with Feng Yü-hsiang. In view of the critical situation, Borodin recommended a 'tactical retreat.' On 20 April he proposed to the Central Political Council five ameliorative measures which amounted to a sharp change of course. (1) The government and the unions should set up a commission to enforce 'revolutionary discipline' on the workers, and the unions should form a tribunal to try and punish recalcitrant workers. (2) The government should reach agreement with foreign banks and other enterprises so they could conduct business freely in the areas under Wuhan's jurisdiction; and the government and unions should form a committee to enforce the agreement, using, if necessary, the inspection corps and armed forces. (3) Workers in foreign banks and other enterprises should not be allowed to strike without permission of this committee. (4) The government should do all in its power to fix maximum prices of commodities in terms of copper currency. (5) The government should set up a relief bureau and mess halls to take care of the unemployed, and the Finance Ministry should allocate $30,000 in copper coins to the General Labour Union to be used to exchange the workers' notes for cash. These measures, Borodin assured the councillors, would eliminate the excuse for foreign intervention, while restoration of foreign economic activity would benefit the workers themselves. After only brief discussion to clarify the powers of the proposed new organizations, the Council resolved to adopt Borodin's proposals and to appoint the head of the Kuomintang's Labour Bureau, the head of the Government's Labour Department, the foreign minister and the finance minister to implement the new course.[194]

The Wuhan leaders then acted decisively. Eugene Chen met with foreign business men on 23 April and promised them an improved climate

---

193 GBFO 405/253. Confidential. *Further correspondence respecting China,* 13304, April–June 1927, no. 112, enclosure, a dispatch by Eric Teichman from Hankow on 7 April. The economic situation in Wuhan was well reported by the American consul-general, Frank P. Lockhart, in telegrams and dispatches, including his monthly 'Review of commerce and industries'. Figures on exodus of foreigners, by nationality, in *China Yearbook, 1928*, 755.

194 Chiang Yung-ching, *Borodin,* 175–9, and *TJK,* 680–2, both based on minutes of the Political Council for 20 April in the Kuomintang Archives. The four persons appointed were Ch'en Kung-po, Su Chao-cheng, Eugene Chen, and Chang Chao-yuan, to replace the absent T.V. Soong. Ch'en was chairman.

for their enterprises; thereafter he attempted to solve their particular problems. The new policy was announced in the *People's Tribune* the same day, along with the new restraints imposed upon workers. Wang Ching-wei called a discussion meeting of leaders of the Nationalist and Communist Parties, and on 25 April a joint session of the Central Committee of the Communist Party and communist leaders of the Hupei General Labour Union issued a declaration which repeated the substance and much of the wording of the resolution passed by the Kuomintang's Political Council five days earlier, though altering the sequence to emphasize the relief measures for unemployed workers. Point five stated, 'Not a single strike can take place in foreign enterprises or firms without consent of the commission' that was to implement an agreement with foreign enterprises and banks. The resolution concluded, 'The basic requirement of the present moment is revolutionary discipline, self-sacrifice and the unity of the revolutionary forces.'[195] On 30 April at a meeting of all major political and military figures, army political bureau workers, and delegates of various local mass organizations, presided over by Sun Fo, Borodin made a long report on foreign policy, differentiating as always between Great Britain, America and Japan, but emphasizing the present need for conciliation. The finance minister sought to reassure the gathering that the government's financial situation was sound, and that even though economic conditions were serious, the city would be supplied with grain from Hunan through the cooperation of the people there; coal would begin to arrive soon; river boats could now freely sell salt; the government had bought a large supply of copper and intended soon to mint copper coins; remittances for trade with Shanghai would be facilitated by a deposit of more than a million dollars sent to banks in that city; and the government's paper currency was to be made stable by limiting the amount that might be printed and backing it with silver. So, 'all may rest easy'.[196]

The Wuhan leaders also forbade provincial leaders from deciding foreign policy questions, such as the Hunan decision to confiscate the American Standard Oil Company stocks and to form a committee to sell them. They sent Lin Tsu-han to Changsha and Ch'en Ch'i-yuan to Nanchang to explain the new foreign policy, and both emissaries on their return reported unanimous endorsement by the leadership meetings

---

195 Quoted in North and Eudin, *M.N. Roy's mission to China*, 186-7; Lockhart's telegrams in *FRUS*, 1927, 2. 112-13 and 115-16; *People's tribune* for 23 and 24 April. Isaacs writes disapprovingly of the measures followed by the Wuhan regime to curb labour and restore amicable foreign relations. *The tragedy of the Chinese revolution*, 204-6.

196 Minutes of the meeting of 30 April 1927 in the Kuomintang Archives.

they assembled. Tax revenues had declined alarmingly in the provinces due to the business recession. Yet it was not possible to cool down the revolutionary fever quickly. Both passion and power were involved. In some parts of Hupei mission properties, churches and schools were returned to their Chinese custodians, while near Wuhan several foreign-owned properties that had been occupied by Chinese troops were restored to their owners. Settling strikes on terms acceptable both to the unions and the owners proved difficult and protracted (some negotiations extended into June), and foreign managers in Hankow complained to Eugene Chen in May that union inspection corps still interfered with resumption of business. Yet discipline was quickly restored on the wharves and shipping took a turn for the better. Larger Chinese enterprises and their workers had similar difficulties in getting operations resumed. Relief for the unemployed was only beginning to be implemented by mid May. The result of a variety of remedial measures in Wuhan was a slight revival of commerce and industry there in May and June, but economic disruptions had been so widespread and severe that a real revival would take much longer to accomplish.[197]

Trying to manage rural revolution

The Wuhan government held only tenuous authority over three provinces – Hunan, Hupei and Kiangsi – with a combined population of some 80 millions and a territory larger than France. In parts of this huge area a rural revolution (arising from poverty, inequity and land hunger) spurred on by radicals among the farmers' movement activists, was gathering momentum, with executions of local despots and land seizures by tenants, all without sanction of the central authorities. These local actions disrupted the rural economy and brought on fierce retaliation just when a tide of reaction was endangering the regime at Wuhan. The leadership of both the Nationalist and the Communist Parties became deeply concerned. What could be done to restore order in the affected areas?

Participants at the Third Plenum of the Kuomintang's Central Executive Committee had passed resolutions and issued a 'Manifesto to the Farmers' on 16 March, which stressed the party's determination to help them. All local armed groups must be controlled by new self-governing village bodies. Self-defence units were authorized to press the struggle

197 Chiang Yung-ching, *Borodin*, 186–94 and 228–9; Chapman, *The Chinese revolution*, 134–6. On settlement of strikes and relief measures, the Kuomintang Archives has minutes of the Committee on Relations between Labour and Foreign Capital for May and June. Consul-General Lockhart, Hankow, to secretary of state, 6 June 1927, 'Review of commerce and industries for the month of May' in US National Archives, Record Group 59.

against 'local bullies and evil gentry', and lawless landlords. The CEC affirmed the Kuomintang's support for farmers in their struggle to possess the land, and suggested confiscation of the lands of counter-revolution-aries which, together with public and temple lands, should be turned over to local land commissions under the jurisdiction of district and village self-governing organs for distribution among the people. Most of these proposals had appeared as resolutions of the December congress of the Hunan Farmers' Association, and were Comintern policy. The plenum also authorized establishment of a Central Land Commission to work out details of the new, more militant, social policy.[198]

On the basis of this lead, local organizers, particularly in Hunan, began a campaign in March to extend self-government under the direction of farmers' associations to all villages. In mid April the Hunan Provincial Farmers' Association, on the authority of the Third Plenum resolutions, sent a directive to all county associations to set up farmers' self-defence forces; and the provincial Kuomintang Propaganda Office issued a pro-paganda outline that emphasized the need for struggle against feudalism: the time had come, it said, to support the peasants' demand for land. At the end of the month the Provincial Farmers' Association held a pro-paganda week, presenting what became the radicals' standard argument for the need to 'solve' the land problem now: the peasantry must be mobilized behind the Nationalist government to save it, but the govern-ment, to mobilize them, must solve their need for land. Solution of the land problem, it was argued, would also solve the government's financial problem, for the new owner-farmers could pay more taxes since they would no longer pay rent to landlords. Solving the land problem would provide the basis for a flourishing economy in the future; but nothing could be accomplished unless the existing feudal system in the villages was eradicated: landlords must be overthrown and the tillers be given land and political power.[199] By April leaders of the Provincial Farmers' Association were estimating between five and six million members in

---

198 The CEC Plenum's resolution of 10 March is quoted in full in Tien-wei Wu, 'A review of the Wuhan debacle: the Kuomintang-Communist split of 1927,' *JAS*, 29 (November 1969) 129-30. Also, Carol Corder Andrews, 'The policy of the Chinese Communist Party towards the peasant movement, 1921-1927: the impact of national on social revolution', Columbia University, Ph.D. dissertation, 1978, ch. VII, 61-2, based upon a collection of documents issued by the Kuomintang Central Farmers Bureau on 30 June 1927. Kuo-mintang Archives, 436/138. Chiang Yung-ching, *Borodin*, 268-71, quoting some passages from the resolutions. The Manifesto is also in *Chung-kuo Kuo-min-tang chung-yao hsuan-yen hui-pien*, 359-65. December resolutions in *Ti-i-tz'u . . . nung-min*, 332-40; 373-4. 'Thesis on the situation in China', of the Seventh Plenum of the ECCI, 22 Nov-16 Dec. 1926, in North and Eudin, *M.N. Roy's mission to China*, 139.

199 Andrews, *The policy of the Chinese Communist Party*, ch. 7, based upon contemporary documents in the Kuomintang Archives.

Hunan, though six months earlier they had been under 1.4 million.[200] Whatever the actual figures may have been, a rapid expansion of farmers' associations probably gave the organizers a sense of new power to force the pace of rural revolution.

There were many scores to be settled. During the latter part of 1926 land-owning gentry in many parts of the province had tried to quell the rising farmers movement that threatened their prestige, power and property. They had banded together in property protection societies, used local corps to suppress incipient farmers' associations and searched out activists for arrest and execution.[201] Most of the repression probably came from the landlord side at first, but the tide apparently began to turn in some areas of Hunan, Hupei and Kiangsi late in 1926, to judge from Mao Tse-tung's report of his investigation in counties around Changsha in January, and the alarm expressed by a resolution of the Communist Party's Central Committee on 8 January, which said 'Assassinations of local bullies and the bad gentry continue to occur without end. . . . A violent reaction would ensue should there be a military setback.'[202]

In the countryside theories were being translated into action. Struggle against local despots meant arrests and killings; struggle for the land led to flight of landlords and dividing their property. A report by the finance commissioner of Hunan about executions by farmers' associations in his province – he was concerned about losses of tax revenues as a result of the terror – brought on a debate in the Wuhan Joint Council at the end of January. How should such actions be managed? Tung Pi-wu reported executions in several hsien in Hupei; he thought the government should adopt a tolerant attitude towards the demands of the masses. Borodin advised that the people should not be permitted to act on their own but should submit requests for executions to local party and government offices, which should have authority to decide such cases. The Joint

200 Chiang Yung-ching, *Borodin*, 269, report of Ling Ping on 19 April: over five million organized farmers in Hunan representing some 20 million. Mann, *What I saw in China*, 27, was told in Changsha about 20 April that no less than 5,130,000 peasants were organized in unions in Hunan, in 53 of the 75 counties. Lin Tsu-han, 'Report on an investigation of the Hunan land question, financial question, and party conditions', 2 May (1927), Kuomintang Archives, Hunan 5/53: Now (ca. 30 April) there are farmers' associations in 65 hsien with more than six million members. Lin named six 'most advanced' hsien with a combined membership of 1.6 million, but all his figures were given in the hundred thousand. November 1926 figure in *Ti-i-tz'u . . . nung-min*, 258–62.

201 Li Jui, *The early revolutionary activities of Comrade Mao Tse-tung*, 302–6, for quotations from contemporary leftist Changsha journals concerning actions against the farmers' movement and brutal killings. Li insists that far more peasants were killed than local bullies and evil gentry.

202 'Report of an investigation into the peasant movement in Hunan', in *Selected works of Mao Tse-tung*, 1. 21–59, particularly the final section, 'Fourteen great deeds'. Wilbur and How, *Documents*, 428.

Council then resolved that the revolutionary government forbid executions carried out by the people or their organizations; they must make their accusations to local party and government offices, which would decide on appropriate punishments. The resolution also provided for a revolutionary court at the provincial level with final authority to grant executions. Apparently the central authorities wished to bring rural retributive violence under some system of control. In March Hsia Hsi, a prominent young communist member of the Hunan provincial Kuomintang headquarters, reported approvingly that by then party headquarters in eight hsien, which he named, were able to represent the masses in beating down 'local bullies and evil gentry' through executions and imprisonments. Debate continued at the Third CEC Plenum, with Mao Tse-tung favouring direct action by the masses, and Tung Pi-wu introducing regulations proposed by the Hupei provincial Kuomintang headquarters for punishing local despots, including execution or a lifetime prison sentence, in accordance with the gravity of their offences. The county courts issuing sentences were to be revolutionary commissions of persons elected by specified mass organizations, meeting under the chairmanship of the county magistrate, with majority vote prevailing. A similarly elected provincial court of appeals would hold final authority. The special provincial court in Changsha was established on 5 April and, according to a hostile source, it granted numerous group executions, as did the special courts at the county level. Changsha was filled with people who fled there from their rural homes. Ling Ping, another Hunan communist leader, reported on 19 April to the Central Land Commission that the provincial Kuomintang headquarters had executed several tens of 'local bullies and evil gentry', but this was not enough. What really was needed to suppress the counter-revolutionaries, he argued, was the power of the farmers' own guards.[203]

In the heat of revolution there were many anomalies and irregularities, of which the following are merely examples. The father of the prominent communist labour leader, Li Li-san, was executed by the farmers' association of his home village in Li-ling county, in spite of a letter from the son guaranteeing that his father would not oppose the association. The magistrate of Hsin-hua county, also in Hunan, reported to Central (Kuomintang Central Headquarters) the case of a group that dominated

203 Chiang Yung-ching, *Borodin*, 257-64, 269. Hofheinz, *The broken wave*, 49-51, infers that executions of despots were not numerous, but without substantiating evidence. Li Jui, *The early revolutionary activities*, 306, says that no more than several dozen persons were directly executed by the peasants. Angus W. McDonald, Jr. tabulated the reported executions of bad gentry and local bullies in Hunan up to early May and found 'perhaps 119 province-wide'. McDonald, *The urban origins of rural revolution*, 312. (However, some cases probably never were reported in media still available.)

the local revolutionary organs, using their authority to wreak private vengeance on opponents and to execute local despots without trial so as to divide the property among themselves under the guise of official confiscation. During 'red week', according to the accusation, they executed more than 10 people, and no one dared to interfere. They even shot the head of the likin bureau without trial; he was under arrest and should have been sent to the magistrate for trial. The well-known authoress, Hsieh Ping-ying, in an autobiographical account, described a mass trial of three persons over whom, as a girl soldier, she had stood night guard. The judge who passed the sentence was a mere lieutenant of the company passing through. The three were summarily shot.[204]

There was great disagreement among the leaders of the Comintern in Moscow and of the Chinese Communist Party at Wuhan, as well as between Borodin and a newly arrived Comintern figure, the Indian, M.N. Roy, whether the agrarian revolution should be pressed forward or restrained at this time, that is April 1927.[205] Verbally, all could agree that an agrarian revolution was essential, but if this meant large-scale confiscation and redistribution of farm lands, such action would imperil, and probably destroy, the united revolutionary front between the communists and the Kuomintang, which was sacrosanct Comintern policy. A renewed northern campaign was just then being mobilized. Borodin believed the agrarian revolution should be restrained while that operation to 'widen' the revolutionary base was underway. Roy opposed the campaign northward and argued for 'deepening' the revolution in the present base, that is, to encourage rural revolt in Hunan and Hupei. By April, however, farmers in some regions were already seizing and dividing the lands of the wealthy and of those they saw as enemies. Reports of these actions implied they were spontaneous with the poor farmers themselves.[206]

204 Chang, *The rise of the Chinese Communist Party*, 1. 606. Mr Chang uses the case of Li's father to illustrate how seriously the peasant movement had got out of hand. Telegram of Magistrate Li Hsien-p'ei and others, dated 6 June, 1927 in Kuomintang Archives, Hankow Archive: Hunan dispute, 1–5/704. Most of the members of the ring were killed in a conflict with the magistrate's force but the leaders escaped. The telegram urges their capture 'to rid the people of this scourge for good'. Hsieh Ping-ying, *Autobiography of a Chinese girl*, 120–5. The event apparently occurred in Hupei during the resumed northern expedition in the spring of 1927, but the book in translation is not without errors.

205 North and Eudin, *M.N. Roy's mission to China*, 32–83, trace the controversy from Dec. 1926 to May 1927, with quotations from various parties to the dispute.

206 Mann, *What I saw in China*, 27, recalling what he was told in Changsha, about 20–25 April and Lin Tsu-han, 'Report on a investigation of the Hunan land question', on what he learned at the end of April. The 'Resolution on the agrarian question' adopted at the Fifth Congress of the CCP on 9 May states 'Furthermore, in Hupei and Hunan the peasants are starting to resolve the land problem by confiscating and distributing lands belonging to the gentry and the bandits.' In a speech on 13 May Stalin said the peasants of Hunan, Hupei, and other provinces were already 'seizing the land from below'. North and Eudin, *M.N. Roy's mission to China*, 86 and 260.

During this time of rising turbulence and mounting hostility towards the militant farmers' movement, the Central Land Commission met in Hankow between 2 April and 9 May to draw up a land policy for adoption by the Kuomintang leadership. Teng Yen-ta was the commission's chairman; he had recently been made head of the Kuomintang Farmers Bureau, but his main position was chief of the National Revolutionary Army Political Department. Other members were the eminent jurist, Hsu Ch'ien, and Ku Meng-yü, a former professor of economics at Peking University, both of whom were at the pinnacle of the left-wing Kuomintang leadership alignment. Two communist members were T'an P'ing-shan, fresh back from the Seventh ECCI Plenum in Moscow, and Mao Tse-tung, head of the Communist Party Peasant Department. The commissioners met five times but found the problem so complex that they decided to gather more information and opinion by holding enlarged conferences. Five of these were held between 19 April and 6 May, participated in by provincial level Kuomintang leaders, functionaries involved with the farmers' movement in various provinces, military commanders and political officers, and some persons familiar with conditions in northern provinces which the Wuhan leaders hoped to bring under their control through the renewed military campaign. Some Russian advisers attended to recount experiences in 'solving the land question' in the Soviet Union, and to provide what information they had gathered about agrarian conditions in China. Borodin appeared once and cautioned against too hasty and too drastic a programme in actuality.[207]

The result of many hours of discussion and clash of opinion was a report signed by the commissioners on 9 May, and drafts of seven resolutions. All conferees were agreed, the commission reported, that the land problem required urgent solution, but there was much discussion whether all land should be confiscated and nationalized, or whether there should be only partial confiscation now. They had agreed that, in view of the objective situation, it was only possible at present to carry out partial, that is, political confiscation. The land of small landlords and of Nationalist military men should be protected, for it was believed that most officers came from landlord families, and there seemed to be a growing animosity among the troops towards the farmers' movement. The central authority should only establish general principles, leaving details of implementation to provincial authorities in the light of local conditions.

207 Chiang Yung-ching, *Borodin*, 276–308, provides texts of the resulting draft resolutions and an account of the debates. A lively and rather different account of positions taken by various protagonists, is in Hofheinz, *The broken wave*, 36–45, based partly on notes taken by the present writer from minutes of the meetings now in the Kuomintang Archives. The following account is based on these notes.

The draft 'Resolution on solving the land question' indicated that land of large landlords and officials, public land and wasteland should be distributed to farmers with no land or insufficient land to sustain themselves. To assure that the land problem was indeed solved, it was necessary for the farmers to have political power; hence, the Nationalist government should assist them in their struggle against big landlords and other feudal elements. A draft for a 'Law on disposition of rebel property' defined 'rebels' as all who were enemies of the national revolution, instruments of imperialism, those who fleece and oppress the people, currency manipulators, militarists, bureaucrats, corrupt officials, 'local bullies', gentry, and other counter-revolutionaries. All their property should be confiscated. Yet the draft also carefully specified which governmental organs should do the confiscating on the basis of what kinds of evidence, all in accordance with law. Furthermore, the proceeds of enemy property distributed during the war were to be used for expenses of the army and the government. In the case of confiscated village land, 30 per cent was to be used for village improvement (such as farmers' banks), and the remainder held for distribution to revolutionary soldiers returning from the war. Distributed property might not be sold or transferred by the recipient and was subject to governmental redistribution after his death. The more detailed draft 'Decision on the land question' showed that the writers considered the land given out was to be on tenure, for the recipients were to pay rent, the proceeds to go to the government.

The commission clearly intended to regularize confiscation instead of having lands and other property seized spontaneously by the masses. Yet no one could answer the 'prior question' asked by Professor Ku Meng-yü: could the comrades 'in the peasant movement in Hunan and Hupei' say whether or not the villagers would obey the regulations drawn up so carefully in the commission's chambers?

The commission also wrestled with the complex problems of farm tenancy. Its draft resolution on this subject stipulated that no tenant should have to pay more than 40 per cent of the crop and should not pay anything else. It even went into details about rental contracts, perpetual lease, times of payment, reduction of rent in times of hardship, and other complexities of Chinese tenancy systems. Clearly, the commission hoped the Kuomintang would actually start on its unfulfilled promise to protect and benefit tenant farmers.

Leaders of the Chinese Communist Party were also struggling to develop a policy towards the agrarian revolution, with some of the top leadership urging restraint while some who worked at the provincial level wanted to press the pace. On the same day that the Kuomintang

Land Commission submitted its report, 9 May, the Fifth Congress of the CCP adopted a somewhat more radical 'Resolution on the agrarian question'.[208] All communal, ancestral, temple and school lands, and lands belonging to the Christian church, and company-owned property, should be confiscated and transferred to the tenants who tilled them. Land committees should decide whether such lands would be cultivated communally or be divided among the peasants. Landlord estates should be transferred through land committees to those who had tilled them, but land belonging to small owners and to officers of the revolutionary army should not be confiscated. Soldiers who had no land were to be granted some after the revolutionary war was over. Confiscated land should be exempt from all duties except the progressive land tax payable to the state, and rent rates should be lowered to a level corresponding to that tax. Tenants cultivating unconfiscated land should enjoy permanent tenure, pay a fixed rent, and be exempt from all other dues. Landlords and gentry were to be deprived of all political rights, and their military forces disarmed and replaced by peasant militia. Accumulated debts were to be annulled and interest rates lowered and limited by law. This slightly more radical disposition of the agrarian question, and the underlying analysis in the preamble of the resolution, put the Communist Party on record in support of social revolution – 'revolution from below' – during the national revolution, but social revolution must still be guided by regulations.

When the Land Commission's recommendation for solving the land question came to the Kuomintang Political Council for decision on 12 May, several leaders expressed fears that if it were passed and publicized it would adversely effect the national revolution's chances for victory. In the end, the three who voted to adopt the resolution, even though it would be kept secret – Lin Tsu-han, Wu Yü-chang (both dual party members) and Teng Yen-ta – were outvoted by their eight colleagues. The proposed law was set aside 'temporarily'. Some of the other resolutions were adopted, though not all were to be publicized. In the end it made very little difference because events on the battlefield, and those soon to occur within the revolutionary base, would nullify these efforts of the leaders in Wuhan to legislate revolution.

Soldiers decide

During May both wings of the Nationalist Party resumed their north-ward campaigns along the railways, the Wuhan wing into Honan and the

---

208 North and Eudin, *M.N. Roy's mission to China*, doc. 16, pp. 254–63.

Nanking group into northern Anhwei and northern Kiangsu. Feng Yü-hsiang drove eastwards out of Shensi along the Lunghai Railway in coordination with Wuhan's campaign. Each wing also stationed defensive forces to guard against attack by the other. The Wuhan drive under the overall command of T'ang Sheng-chih, was opposed first by the remnants of Wu P'ei-fu's armies and then by the powerful Fengtien Army. Nanking faced the remnants of Sun Ch'uan-fang's forces and the stronger Shantung Army of Chang Tsung-ch'ang. By 1 June Feng Yü-hsiang's Kuominchün and T'ang Sheng-chih's armies met at Chengchow, where the Peking–Hankow Railway crosses the Lunghai, and the Fengtien Army had retreated north of the Yellow River. Two days later, the Nanking forces took Hsuchow, where the Lunghai crosses the Tientsin–Pukou Railway, and Sun and Chang retreated into Shantung to regroup their forces.[209] Somewhat concerned by the campaign towards Shantung, where there were many Japanese residents, the Japanese government dispatched troops to Tsingtao, and later to Tsinan, the provincial capital, arousing a storm of protest among nationalistic Chinese.

The Wuhan drive began first with the Fourth Front Army under Chang Fa-k'uei and the Thirty-Fifth and Thirty-Sixth Corps under T'ang Sheng-chih, some sixty to seventy thousand strong, moving up the railway towards the border of Honan, the remaining preserve of Wu P'ei-fu and his generals. Wu's subordinates were divided into two factions, one wishing to join Chang Tso-lin in opposition to Wuhan and the communists, and the other opting for Feng Yü-hsiang. Several of the second group were receiving subsidies from the Wuhan Military Council and they opened the way into Honan. Wu P'ei-fu attempted a stand at Chu-ma-tien, and was decisively beaten on 14 May. This ended his long and illustrious military career. Wu fled to eastern Szechwan under the protection of Yang Sen.[210] His defeat opened the way for major battles against heavily-armed Fengtien forces under the command of Chang Hsueh-liang, the son of Chang Tso-lin. Chang Fa-k'uei's 'Ironsides' defeated the Fengtien forces in northern Honan in bloody battles on 17 and 28 May, while Feng Yü-hsiang rushed eastwards against little

209 Accounts of these campaigns are in *PFCS*, 3. 677–755, with maps; *KMWH*, 15. 2412–92, with documents; Jordan, *The Northern Expedition*, 129–32; James E. Sheridan, *Chinese warlord: The career of Feng Yü-hsiang*, 220–4, with maps.

210 Odoric Y. K. Wou, *Militarism in modern China: the career of Wu P'ei-fu, 1916–1939*, 143, for the factionalism among Wu's subordinates and his defeat. Kuomintang Archives, 441/22, a military budget and accounting for April 1927, shows Chin Yün-ao receiving $320,000, Wei I-san receiving $100,000, and Fan Chung-hsiu, $44,000 that month. Feng Yü-hsiang, who the Wuhan group hoped to hold as an ally, was given $730,000, and his representative at Wuhan, Liu Chi, was paid $37,360. Feng's stipend was more than any other commander received except Chang Fa-k'uei, who got a little over $900,000 for his two corps.

opposition to seize the lion's share of the spoils. The Wuhan armies suffered some 14,000 casualties, while Feng lost a mere 400. Hospitals in Hankow were soon filled with wounded.[211] Nanking's effort, spearheaded by Ho Ying-ch'in, Li Tsung-jen and Pai Ch'ung-hsi, was much less costly.

In sending its best troops northwards and leaving only light garrison forces to protect the rail lines and major cities in Hunan and Hupei, the Wuhan regime created a golden opportunity for its enemies. General Yang Sen, one of those who came over to the Nationalist side during the early phase of the Northern Expedition and was rewarded by being appointed commander of the Twentieth Corps – his own Szechwanese troops – seized the opportunity to move eastwards from his base at Wan-hien to attack Ichang in western Hupei. Hsia Tou-yin, commander of the 14th Independent Division, who guarded Ichang and was subsidized by the Wuhan Military Council, withdrew in order to launch an attack on the Wuhan cities. Hsia claimed to be opposing communism, and sought support from generals garrisoning the revolutionary base. Both moves seem to have been inspired by Chiang Kai-shek.[212]

Wuhan's crisis came in mid May, when a regiment of Hsia's division, estimated by aerial reconnaissance to number five or six hundred, came within striking distance of Wuchang from the south, with the rest of the division only 50 miles away. Apparently most of the garrison forces in the tri-city areas were secretly in sympathy, if not in league, with Hsia.[213]

The Wuchang garrison commander, General Yeh T'ing, and his recently organized and only partially equipped 24th Division of the Eleventh Corps, stiffened by a few hundred cadets of the Wuhan Military Academy led by Yün Tai-ying, determined to drive Hsia away. Both men were members of the Communist Party, and another communist, Chang Kuo-t'ao, directed emergency security in Wuchang city. He was particularly concerned that collaborators might try to topple the leftist regime from within. M.N. Roy prepared a declaration for the Communist Party in which the party of the proletariat sought to reassure its partners, the 'petty bourgeoisie', that it had no intention of overthrowing them, and

211 Sheridan, *Chinese warlord*, 346, f.n. 45, citing a report by Wang Ching-wei in the Kuomintang Archives, and a dispatch from Consul-General Lockhart of 30 June 1927.

212 USDS 893.00/8929, telegram, Lockhart, Hankow, 18 May, reporting Hsia only 40 miles from Hankow and 'Believed to have allied self with Chiang Kai-shek'. On 1 June M. N. Roy implied the same in an article prepared for *International press correspondence*, calling Yang, Hsia and Hsu K'e-hsiang, who by then also had revolted, 'marionettes who are brought into motion by strings which are pulled from Shanghai by way of Nanking.' Sun Fo also made the charge against Chiang in a report dated 20 June, now in the Kuomintang Archives, 484/283. Chiang Yung-ching, *Borodin*, 311, 313; and *TJK*, 693–4, for the same assertion and a document of 20 May showing Chiang's close knowledge of the developments.

213 *TJK*, 696, citing a report to Nanking of an anti-communist organization in Wuhan.

also disclaiming responsibility for the 'excesses' of the peasant movement. He also prepared a propaganda appeal to the troops of Hsia Tou-yin, begging them not to be deceived by their commander's profession of anti-communism; he was really against their 'brother-peasants in Hunan' because they were taking the land from landlords and gentry. On the morning of 19 May Yeh T'ing's force routed the invading troops.[214]

The fighting south of Wuchang cut all communications with Changsha, the most revolutionary city in China at that time, where mass organizations led by communists were growing ever more militant and where there had been many executions of their opponents in April. A bitter anti-communist sentiment was gaining adherents, and there were plots to suppress the radicals. The city was full of rumours: that Wuhan had fallen, Wang Ching-wei had fled and Borodin been executed. Because the Wuhan regime had sent its most effective forces northwards, Changsha was sparsely garrisoned. General Ho Chien, commander of the Thirty-fifth Corps of T'ang Sheng-chih's Hunan Army, left one regiment under Hsu K'o-hsiang as his rearguard in Changsha, and there were other Hunanese units in the city and scattered throughout the province. In some of these outlying places troops clashed with farmers' associations, killing some of the leaders, while in Changsha there was mounting friction between garrison forces and armed pickets of the General Labour Union. Apparently both sides were preparing for a showdown.[215] There were rumours that farmers' guards and labour union pickets planned to disarm the troops. Merchants closed their shops. To lessen the tension some communists organized a joint meeting of mass organizations and troop units on 18 May, with pledges of revolutionary discipline and support for the Nationalist government.[216] But the situation was fast growing beyond anyone's control. The next day, according to a later report from the acting provin-

---

214 Chiang Yung-ching, *Borodin*, 311–25, and *TJK*, 693–9, give hostile accounts of communist activity in respect of Hsia's threat, but also quote a valuable account of the battle by Kao Yü-han. For the communist side, Chang, *The rise of the Chinese Communist Party*, 1. 627–32 and North and Eudin, *M. N. Roy's mission to China*, doc. 21 and 22, pp. 286–92. Sun Fo, in his report of 20 June, cited, did not mention Yeh T'ing's role, saying, 'But fortunately the Sixth and Second Corps returned and drove off Hsia Tou-yin, then defeated Yang Sen.' (In 1930, Hsia became garrison commander of the Wuhan cities, and in 1932, chairman of the Hupei Provincial government.)

215 Ho Chien in *KMWH*, 25. 5284–5, names four persons who planned a coup. Self-justifying telegrams, signed by Acting Provincial Chairman Chang I-p'eng, and by many officers, accused the radicals of planning an attack upon the garrison forces. Kuomintang Archives, Hankow Archive, Hunan dispute, 1–5/692, 695, and 700, dated 1, 4 and 7 June 1927. A reminiscent communist account says that communist leaders knew an attack was coming, and tried to prepare. *Ti-i-tz'u . . . nung-min*, 383.

216 Chiang Yung-ching, *Borodin*, 328–30, quoting from reports to the Wuhan government by various persons in Changsha in early June. Professor Chiang interprets the joint meeting as a communist defensive strategy.

cial governor, banners carried in a parade were inscribed, 'Overthrow the Thirty-fifth Corps; confiscate their arms'. On the same day, some troops in the city clashed with the General Labour Union, and the union's inspection corps reportedly invaded Ho Chien's residence and arrested and beat up his father.[217]

Two days later, on the night of 21 May, Hsu K'o-hsiang, with the support of many other commanders, took violent repressive measures against the headquarters of the provincial labour union and farmers' association, killing those who resisted and arresting a large number of suspected communists, closing down many radical organs and, in effect, dissolving the provincial government. A grain purchasing mission which had been sent from Hankow to persuade the Provincial Farmers' Association to release grain for the capital, got caught in the conflict and some of its members were killed.[218] For several days thereafter, the provincial capital witnessed a bloodbath, and the counter-revolution spread to many other counties.[219] In Hupei, Hsia Tou-yin's defeated troops went on a rampage of smashing farmers' associations and the terror spread to other districts in South and West Hupei.[220] Those slain in the two provinces probably numbered in the thousands.

The Changsha coup threw the Communist Party into confusion and presented the Kuomintang leaders with terrible dilemmas. While part of their army was in combat, troops in the rear had apparently taken counter-revolutionary action with no authorization from the centre. Whether Hsu K'o-hsiang and the other Hunanese commanders could be disciplined would depend upon the attitude of Generals T'ang Sheng-chih and Ho Chien, who were at the Honan front. Unsure of what had

---

217 Kao, *Chronology*, 258, and Boorman and Howard, *Biographical dictionary of Republican China*, 2. 61. Li Jui, *The early revolutionary activities*, 314, states that, 'Ho Chien had his father-in-law beaten only once'. He lists a series of murderous actions against peasants' associations in places other than Changsha from mid May to 21 May. I have not seen contemporary documentary evidence of the invasion of Ho Chien's home.

218 Kuomintang Archives, Hankow Archive, Hunan dispute, 1-5/709, 14 June 1927, gives an accounting of the purchase money given to the commission, most of which was lost, and an eye-witness account of the attack on the Provincial Farmers' Association head-quarters.

219 Many accounts of the 'Horse Day incident' (21 May) are listed in Wu, 'A review of the Wuhan debacle', 133, f.n. 30. Isaacs, *The Tragedy of the Chinese revolution*, 235-6 gives a vivid but essentially unsourced description of the executions. *TJK*, 699 and 702, says 3,000 per-sone were arrested and 70 organs closed. In his *TJK* Li Yun-han names three communist leaders executed and several others who fled in disguise.

220 A report submitted by the Hupei Farmers' Association dated 15 June 1927, in the Kuo-mintang Archives, cited in detail 19 specific places and estimated that four to five thousand persons were killed and many villages devastated. The association begged the Nationalist government to suppress these attacks and punish the perpetrators. Also *TJK*, 699. Isaacs, *The Tragedy of the Chinese revolution*, 227, quotes a pitiful report on the massacre of farmers in Hupei.

actually happened in Changsha, the Political Council, on the advice of Borodin, decided to send a special commission to investigate and, if possible, to restore order. It appointed T'an P'ing-shan, a communist who had just been made head of the government's Famers Department, Ch'en Kung-po, P'eng Tse-hsiang and two others nominated by General T'ang, together with Borodin. The commission started on 25 May but got no further than the Hunan border, where it was stopped and threatened with death in a telegram from Hsu K'o-hsiang. The commission returned hastily to the revolutionary capital. In Changsha, Hsu and other anti-communists set up a party purification commission to reregister all Kuomintang members and reorganize party affairs in the province.[221] A group of communist leaders in Hunan planned a counter-attack for 31 May, and started to mobilize farmers' guards in counties near Changsha.

Both in Wuhan and in Moscow, men trying to steer the revolution debated how to meet the crisis. On 24 May M.N. Roy, possibly still unaware of the gravity of the situation, drafted a resolution for the communist Politburo on relations with the Kuomintang, which proposed a declaration that 'At the present stage of the revolution, collaboration of the Communist Party with the Kuomintang is still necessary'. He then attempted to define the conditions for such collaboration: development of the democratic forces; persevering with the struggle against reactionary elements in the Kuomintang with the aim of isolating and then forcing them out of the party; seizure of leadership by the left wing closely linked with the masses; and defence of the interests of the proletariat and the peasantry.[222] This resolution, with its many details for moderation within the framework of collaboration, was shelved. The communist Politburo, caught in the vice of the Comintern's dominant policy of continuing membership in the other party and cooperation with its left wing, resolved on 26 May that the land problem first had to pass through a propaganda stage; for the time being soldiers were to be exposed to propaganda, and self-governing bodies were to be organized in the villages and counties.[223] This temporizing resolution merely reaffirmed the party's stand. More concretely, on the same day a telegram was sent in the name of the All-China General Labour Union and the National Peasants' Association (which had not yet been formally established) to the Hunan Provincial Farmers' Association and labour unions informing them that the government had appointed a commission, which was on

221 Chiang Yung-ching, *Borodin*, 332–3 and 337.
222 North and Eudin, *M. N. Roy's mission to China*, doc. 23, 302.
223 Brandt, Schwartz and Fairbank, *A documentary history*, 112, quoting the 7 Aug. 1927 'Circular letter of the CC to all party members'.

its way to settle the Changsha incident; it instructed them 'to be patient . . . in order to avoid further friction'.[224]

In far-off Moscow, the Executive Committee of the Communist International was holding its Eighth Plenum (18–30 May) during which Trotsky and the opposition bitterly attacked Stalin and Bukharin for their policy on the Chinese revolution, in particular for continuing to support the Wuhan faction of the Kuomintang, restraining the Chinese peasantry, and for rejecting the immediate creation of soviets.[225] The Chinese Commission was debating whether the time for land revolution in China had come or not. On 27 May Stalin joined the discussion, producing telegrams from Borodin showing that the Kuomintang was resolved to fight against the agrarian revolution even at the price of a break with the Comintern. Should the Communist Party fight or manoeuvre? Stalin asked, according to the later report of Albert Treint, who opposed him in the meeting. Stalin insisted that to fight meant certain defeat; to manoeuvre meant to win time, to become stronger, and to fight later in conditions where victory would be possible. He proposed to send instructions to Borodin directing him to oppose the confiscation and dividing of land belonging to members of the Kuomintang or to officers of the national army.[226] The final ECCI resolution called for the creation of a truly revolutionary army, 'but the Communist Party of China must exert all its efforts directly in alliance with the left Kuomintang.'[227]

The Hunan Provincial Committee of the Chinese Communist Party had mobilized a strong force of farmers' guards in counties near Changsha for a general attack on the city and nearby towns. Just before the appointed day, 31 May, Li Wei-han ordered a halt, probably in response to instructions from Hankow.[228] The order failed to reach the contingent at Liu-yang, which had already begun its march on Changsha. Their

224 North and Eudin, *M. N. Roy's mission to China*, 103, quoting *The people's tribune* of 28 May.
225 *Leon Trotsky on China*, 220–48, for Trotsky's speeches and writings during the session.
226 'Documents on the Comintern and the Chinese revolution', with an introduction by Harold Isaacs, *CQ*, 45 (January–March 1971) 100–15, with English and French versions of Albert Treint's retrospective account, written in 1935, but based on a version published in Nov. 1927. The English translation is reprinted in Gruber, *Soviet Russia masters the Comintern*, 490–4. (Stalin's proposed instruction to Borodin would merely reinforce the established policy of the Chinese Communist Party at that time.)
227 North and Eudin, *M. N. Roy's mission to China*, 92–3. They give an extended discussion of the debates on China raging in Moscow in May.
228 Both Ts'ai Ho-sen and P'eng Shu-chih charge Li with the order to halt. North and Eudin, *M. N. Roy's mission to China*, 106, and Brandt, Schwartz and Fairbank, *A documentary history*, 487, f.n. 8. Schram asserts that Mao Tse-tung gave the order on the instruction of Stalin. Li Jui, *The early revolutionary activities*, 315, note. Klein and Clark, *Biographic dictionary*, accept Li's responsibility for the order.

attack was crushed on the afternoon of 31 May, and another force attempting to seize Hsiang-t'an was destroyed to a man.[229]

The day after this disaster Stalin's famous telegram instructing his subordinates arrived in the revolutionary capital.[230] Stalin called for seizure of land by the masses 'from below', and also for combating 'excesses', not with the help of troops but through peasant unions. Vacillating and compromising leaders of the Kuomintang Central Committee were to be replaced by peasant and working-class leaders. Dependence upon unreliable generals had to cease, and several new army corps were to be created by mobilizing 20,000 communists and about 50,000 revolutionary workers and peasants from Hunan and Hupei. A revolutionary tribunal headed by a prominent non-communist Kuomintang leader had to be organized to punish officers who maintained contact with Chiang Kai-shek or who set soldiers on the people. 'Persuasion is not enough', Stalin exhorted. 'It is time to act. The scoundrels must be punished.'

Under the circumstances in China at that moment, with the mass movement suffering cruel oppression and the Communist Party in disarray, such orders were 'like taking a bath in a toilet', as Ch'en Tu-hsiu later characterized them. All Central Committee members realized the orders could not be executed. Everyone present knew not 'whether to laugh or cry', as Chang Kuo-t'ao recalled. Therefore, the party's Politburo telegraphed accepting the instructions in principle, but made it clear they could not be realized immediately.[231] (Roy's indiscretion in showing Stalin's telegram to Wang Ching-wei is discussed below.)

229 *Ti-i-tz'u . . . nung-min*, 338, from the reminiscences of Liu Chih-hsün, published a year later. This has been translated in part in Li Jui, *The early revolutionary activities*, 315–16. On 1 June the Kuomintang CEC sent a letter to the Hunan Special Committee, containing copies of telegrams received from Hsiang-t'an party headquarters and from the farmers' association describing attacks by units of the Eighth, 35th and 36th Corps on labour and farmer groups, making one believe the aggression came from the military before 31 May. Kuomintang Archives, Hankow Archive, Hunan dispute, 1–5/693. The acting governor, Chang I-p'eng, telegraphed Hankow on 30 May describing mass rallies in a number of counties and attacks on various places; then an attack on Changsha 'today at 10 a.m.' by 'hundreds of men with guns and thousands of men with wooden staves'. After a two-hour battle 'the peasants were totally routed'. He quotes prisoner interrogations to the effect that the provincial farmers' union had given the order on the 20th to break into the city and plunder. 'Therefore we came to slaughter.' Kuomintang Archives, Hankow Archive, Hunan dispute, 1–5/692. (The dates are puzzling.)

230 The text is given in North and Eudin, *M. N. Roy's Mission to China*, 106–7, translated from two articles by Stalin, dated 1935. Also in Eudin and North, *Soviet Russia and the East*, 303–4. In 1929 Ch'en Tu-hsiu gave the gist of the Stalin's instructions, which he said came from the Comintern, in 'A letter to all comrades of the party', 333–4, and this was used by Isaacs in *The Tragedy of the Chinese Revolution*, 245–6. It is unclear whether the telegram was addressed to Borodin, Roy or the Central Committee of the CCP.

231 Ch'en Tu-hsiu, 'A letter to all comrades of the party,' 234–5; Chang, *The rise of the Chinese Communist Party*, 1. 637. Roy provided the text of a telegram to the Comintern, dated 15 June, which he said was sent by Ch'en Tu-hsiu at the instruction of the Politburo. North and Eudin, *M. N. Roy's mission to China*, Doc. 29, pp. 338–40. The telegram describes the

Apparently the best that the communist leaders could do was to organize mass demonstrations in Wuhan on 4 and 5 June, with petitions addressed to the national government begging it to halt the slaughter in the provinces and to punish Hsu K'o-hsiang and his allies. The petitioners admitted that the agrarian movement had been marred by puerile actions, but contended that these were inevitable in the early stages of a revolution. They were nothing compared with the atrocities committed by Hsu and his fellow conspirators in league with Chiang Kai-shek; their actions disrupted the rear of the northern campaign and threatened the entire revolutionary movement.[232] The ever loquacious Roy prepared an open letter to the Central Committee of the Kuomintang from the Central Committee of the Communist Party, which called for a punitive expedition to suppress the Changsha counter-revolutionaries, the dissolution of its various committees, and a decree by the national government guaranteeing complete freedom to worker and peasant organizations and the Communist Party in Hunan. It requested an order to return the arms confiscated from workers' and peasants' detachments, and the arming of the peasants as a guarantee against future counter-revolutionary flare-ups. Roy also wrote an 'Appeal to the peasants' in which the Chinese Communist Party called on the Hunan peasants to continue the struggle against large landlords, the gentry, and counter-revolutionary militarists by seizing their land. But the lands of small landlords and of officers fighting at the front should be inviolate. The peasants should not regard soldiers as enemies but should establish close ties with them, drawing the mass of soldiers into peasant unions. Roy's words exhorted the Hunan peasants to demand the surrender of the counter-revolutionary gang in Changsha and to organize an armed uprising to overthrow it. 'Help the national government to restore [its] power in Hunan! Support the Kuomintang against the counter-revolutionary militarists!'[233]

The issue was not to be settled by words but by soldiers. Hsu K'o-hsiang was in telegraphic communication with Generals Ho Chien and T'ang Sheng-chih from the beginning, and he may have been their agent. After the commission of investigation was turned back, T'ang Sheng-chih appointed General Chou Lan, deputy commander of the Thirty-sixth Corps, as his commissioner to go to Changsha, and the Kuomintang

critical situation and the Communist Party's inability at present to carry out the Comintern's instructions.

232 Kuomintang Archives, Hankow Archive, Hunan dispute, 1-5/696 and 697, dated 4 and 5 June, one from the Provisional Assembly of Representatives of Various Circles in Wuhan, the other from the Wuhan Assembly to Celebrate the Capture of Chengchow and Kaifeng. (There are clear evidences of common drafting.)

233 North and Eudin, *M. N. Roy's mission to China*, docs. 26 and 27, pp. 314-20, dated 3 and 4 June.

Central Committee made him its special deputy. General Chou was instructed to take command of all troops in Hunan and enforce discipline. Both sides should cease their conflict. The provincial party apparatus, the provincial government, and farmers' and workers' organizations were to be reconstituted under Central's orders. After Chou Lan arrived in Changsha, Central received a telegram dated 7 June and signed in the names of Chang I-p'eng, four educational officials, and 41 commanders and political officers, including Hsu K'o-hsiang, expressing gratitude for the instructions transmitted by Deputy Commander Chou, justifying their own actions on 21 May, and pledging to carry out absolutely all orders of the central government.[234]

Though the tone was submissive the formidable list of officers who purportedly signed could only have been meant to convey their solidarity. Chou Lan was warmly welcomed by a citizens' gathering on 9 June, where he was urged to join the party purification movement. In fact, he found such a strong anti-communist sentiment in Changsha that he felt unable to carry out his even-handed instructions. He telegraphed Central reporting that farmers' associations opposed the government and asked for troops to exterminate them.[235]

The agrarian movement in Hunan was too widespread, and its communist leaders too few and divided for the disorders to be brought under control quickly. Several more reports came to Central describing conflicts that were blamed on the farmers' movement, including the seizure of the P'ing-hsiang–Chu-chou Railway and the surrounding of the P'ing-hsiang collieries, preventing coal from being shipped or food going to the miners.[236] In a discussion of the Hunan problem in the Political Council on 13 June Wang Ching-wei reported that in an immediately prior meeting of the Military Council Mao Tse-tung had admitted that farmers' associations had damaged the homes of soldiers, but he threw the blame on members of the Ko-lao hui, a powerful secret society in Hunan who he said, had infiltrated the associations. 'They knew neither the Kuomintang nor the Communist Party, but only the business of killing and setting fires', Wang quoted Mao as saying. With respect to the May Twenty-first Incident in Changsha, Mao maintained that it was the troops who had attacked the association, which had only tried to defend itself and was not trying to seize soldiers' rifles. With the concurrence of Mao and Wu Yü-chang, the Political Council then decided to send T'ang Sheng-chih,

234 Kuomintang Archives, Hankow Archive, Hunan dispute, 1–5/700.
235 Chiang Yung-ching, *Borodin*, 338, citing discussion in the Kuomintang Political Council, 13 June.
236 *Ibid.* 343–4, citing documents. The railway seizure was reported in the Political Council on 15 June.

recently back from the Honan battles, to restore order in Hunan, but he should do so without using military force.[237]

After arriving at his base and having been appraised of the situation, T'ang telegraphed on 26 June, recommending that two persons who had been leaders in Hsu K'o-hsiang's party purification movement should be expelled from the Kuomintang, and that Hsu, himself, should be given a demerit. Hsu, however, was not to be humbled by T'ang. He led his troops to South Hunan, where he received a commission from Chiang Kai-shek to join in the party purification struggle.[238]

Another soldier took action against the Communist Party in Kiangsi. Chu P'ei-te and his Third Corps guarded the province against a possible attack from the Nanking faction. Influenced by anti-communist sentiments in his army and by the May Twenty-first Incident in Changsha, he decided to dismiss the political officers in his army, many of whom were communists. On 29 May he sent 142 of them off to Wuhan where they arrived on 1 June. He also freed Ch'eng T'ien-feng and other Kuomintang leaders who had been imprisoned since 2 April and feared execution. On 5 June he ordered 22 leading communists to leave the province, though he treated them with great courtesy and provided them with travel money. Furthermore. he ordered the provincial General Labour Union and Farmers' Association to supend activities, and his gendarmes confiscated 800 rifles and other equipment from the Nanchang farmers' guards. Apparently, General Chu, who was also governor of Kiangsi, was trying to prevent the sort of conflicts that had erupted in neighbouring Hunan. He announced that sending away the political workers had no other purpose than to calm the environment. The Kuomintang organizations were to continue and mass organizations to maintain their structures, though suspending activities until orders came from Wuhan Central. He proclaimed his support for the National government in Wuhan and his opposition to the Nanking government. Still, he sent his resignation as head of the Kuomintang's special commission to manage party affairs, and asked for a new group of commissioners. Presumably he was testing Wuhan's reaction. Out in the province, Chu P'ei-te's order for suspension of activity by the farmers' and workers' movements was interpreted as an opportunity to suppress them. A report sent to Wuhan

---

237 *Ibid.* 348, and *TJK*, p. 707, both quoting the minutes of the Political Council. Also quoted in Kuo, *Analytical history*, 1. 243. According to Ts'ai Ho-sen, Borodin, too, used the explanation that misdeeds of the Hunan Farmers' Association had been 'led by local villains and the Ko Lao Hui, not by us.' Chiang Yung-ching, *Borodin*, 336, though not exactly dated.

238 A translation of General T'ang's telegram of 26 June is reprinted from *The people's tribune* of 29 June in North and Eudin, *M. N. Roy's Mission to China*, 120-1. The Chinese version in *TJK*, 708; also Chiang Yung-ching, *Borodin*, 350-1.

by the Provincial Farmers' Association stated that some 200 leaders of the movement were slain and that 'local bullies and evil gentry' in a number of named counties had gone on a rampage of smashing local associations and were cruelly killing farmers.

How could this development be dealt with? In Wuhan the communist leadership was in great disagreement. Some, including Roy, demanded that Chu be punished, and planned a general strike to back up their proposal. Borodin was furious at this idea. Others feared that an unsuccessful attempt to topple General Chu would have terrible consequences. When Wang Ching-wei returned from his conference with Feng Yü-hsiang at Chengchow, Hsiang Chung-fa demanded that he order Chu to restore the leaders of the mass movements to their positions. Then, when the Kuomintang Political Council considered Chu P'ei-te's resignation, Wang Ching-wei stated the problem plainly: if Chu were not excused for his actions he might immediately turn over to Nanking, greatly strengthening that overriding source of evil. Therefore the Political Council resolved not even to consider Chu's resignation. Searching for a compromise, the Council decided to send Ch'en Kung-po and Ch'en Ch'i-yuan, together with a few communist cadres, to Kiangsi to confer with Chu P'ei-te, while T'an P'ing-shan, in compliance with a request from Chu, offered to send 40 recent graduates of the Farmers' Movement Training Institute for low-level work in Kiangsi. On 20 June the two Ch'ens and the communist cadres arrived in Kiukiang where they conferred with General Chu. All agreed to a rather vague formula: concentration of power in the Kuomintang; all who did not maintain discipline would immediately be restrained. Thus was the issue compromised, though communist influence in the province, never as strong as in Hunan, had markedly declined.[239]

Separating communists from the left-wing Kuomintang

M.N. Roy revealed the contents of Stalin's telegram to Wang Ching-wei on 5 June, the day before Wuhan notables were to depart for a conference with General Feng Yü-hsiang. At Wang's request, Roy later gave him a translation of the text. Wang was appalled, but it took him and his closest associates some weeks to decide how to meet this menacing turn in Russian policy towards their party.[240]

239 This brief account is synthesized from Li, *TJK*, 709–15, and Chiang Yung-ching, *Borodin*, 354–68, both based on contemporary documents.
240 Wang reported the date and circumstances on 15 July to an enlarged meeting of the CEC Standing Committee, as quoted from the minutes in *TJK*, 736 and Chiang Yung-ching, *Borodin*, 403–4. The first public revelation of the major points in the telegram came in

On 6 June the praesidium of the Kuomintang Political Council travelled to Chengchow to confer with Feng Yü-hsiang.[241] Feng held the whip-hand, for Wuhan's armies had suffered heavy casualties and their rear was in great disorder. The conferees agreed to give Feng control of Honan province and confirmed his appointees in Shensi and Kansu, who were now to be officials of the Nationalist government. Feng's army and a variety of Honan units were to be reorganized into seven front armies under his command. Wuhan's forces were to return to defend their bases. Feng would not agree to join in a campaign against the Nanking faction, although he spoke privately to Wang about Chiang Kai-shek's perfidy. Some of the conferees also discussed Stalin's telegram and laid plans to curb the activities of the Communist Party.[242] The Wuhan contingent then hurriedly left for Hankow on 12 June, leaving Hsu Ch'ien with General Feng – they were old associates – and bringing Yü Yu-jen with them. Ku Meng-yü also stayed behind. Borodin quickly realized that from his point of view the conference had been a failure.[243]

The Wuhan regime faced a precarious strategic situation. At great sacrifice of manpower in Chang Fa-k'uei's Fourth and Eleventh Corps, Honan had been somewhat cleared of opposing armies, but Feng Yü-hsiang, an uncertain ally, now dominated the province. Kwangtung, the original revolutionary base, was controlled by Li Chi-shen, who opposed

August 1927 as a report of the Presidium of the Kuomintang Political Council dated 19 July, and published by the Kuomintang Central Propaganda Office. This is in the Kuomintang Archives. See *TJK*, 745, f.n. 94. On 5 Nov. 1927 Wang recounted the circumstances in a speech in Canton but gave 1 June as the date of Roy's revelation. Wang's speech was published in *Min-kuo jih-pao*, 9 Nov., and is reprinted in *KMWH*, 16. 2851-65, the pertinent section being 2861-2.

241 Wang's report at the 28th meeting of the Political Council on 13 June names T'an Yen-k'ai, Ku Meng-yü, Sun Fo, Hsü Ch'ien and himself as members of the presidium. Other participants mentioned by Wang were Yü Shu-te (the only communist), Wang Fa-ch'in, Teng Yen-ta, and T'ang Sheng-chih from the Wuhan group, and Feng Yü-hsiang, Lu Chung-lin, and Yü Yu-jen. Kuomintang Archives, 005/3. Chiang Yung-ching, *Borodin*, 380, adds Chang Fa-k'uei. Anna Louise Strong and Rayna Prohme accompanied the party, and Miss Strong in a colourful account, says that General Galen (Blyukher) also went, but Borodin could not go as he was sick with fever and had a broken arm. Anna Louise Strong, *China's millions*, 46-8.

242 Chang Fa-k'uei, in an interview with Julie Lien-ying How, remembered that Wang reported the contents of the Comintern resolution – i.e., Stalin's telegram? – and that T'ang Sheng-chih reported on peasant disturbances in Hunan. The decision was made to 'separate the communists', General Chang recalled. Sheridan, *Chinese warlord: the career of Feng Yü-hsiang*, 225-7, for an account of the Chengchow conference based on a variety of sources. See p. 346, f.n. 50, for later reports that the communist problem was discussed. Presumably Yü Shu-te and Blyukher were not included in those talks.

243 USDS 893.00/9106, telegram, Hankow, Lockhart to secretary of state, 15 June 1927, reporting Borodin's depression and his belief that had he been able to attend, the outcome of the conference would have been more favourable. Lockhart added, 'There appears to be a growing [belief] that there will be a gradual elimination of the Russians and the Chinese radicals from Kuomintang councils here.'

the radicalism of the workers and peasants, and was a quasi-ally of Chiang Kai-shek. He blocked Wuhan's access to the sea. To the east, the armies affiliated with the Nanking faction might launch an attack on Wuhan, now that they had driven the forces of Sun Ch'uan-fang and Chang Tsung-ch'ang into Shantung, and there were suspicions that Chiang Kai-shek was still negotiating for a truce with Chang Tso-lin. Within the three-province base – Hunan, Hupei and Kiangsi – the loyalty of T'ang Sheng-chih and his subordinates was uncertain due to their opposition to the militant peasant movement. Chu P'ei-te had just expelled leading communists from Kiangsi and ordered a halt to the activities of the peasant and worker movements, and he seemed to be attempting to play a mediating role between the two Nationalist factions. Complicating these difficulties was the problem of Stalin's order to Borodin and the Chinese Communist Party to encourage land seizures, create an independent military force, punish unreliable generals, and reform the left Kuomintang from below.

Should the left Kuomintang break with the communists in order to placate the generals whose support was essential, but thereby lose Soviet Russia's support? If the break were to be made, when and how should it be carried out? Was there a military solution: a continued drive on Peking, a campaign against Nanking, or a drive southwards to retake Kwangtung? These were the problems that gripped the Nationalist leaders when they returned from Chengchow. A successful drive on Peking would depend on the active participation of Yen Hsi-shan in Shansi, whose army might drive eastward to cut the P'ing-Han railway at Shih-chia-chuang. An attempt was underway to persuade Yen to join with Feng in a northward campaign but his agreement was unlikely. (In fact, he soon declared himself in favour of Nanking.) An eastward campaign against Nanking might succeed if the Kwangsi clique headed by Li Tsung-jen, Pai Ch'ung-hsi, and Huang Shao-hsiung could be induced to turn against Chiang Kai-shek, but for such a campaign Chu P'ei-te's support was essential. A southern campaign was urged by Roy and a few communist leaders and might be attractive to Chang Fa-k'uei, the most loyal military supporter of the left, but his armies had still to recover from casualties in Honan. The Hanyang Arsenal was working night and day, but there were shortages in essential supplies: could it provide arms enough for a second campaign?

By 15 June the Kuomintang Political Council had decided to prepare for an Eastern campaign. According to Ts'ai Ho-sen, this was Borodin's recommendation, and Wang Ching-wei and T'ang Sheng-chih accepted it in the expectation of Russian funds to finance it. In preparation for the campaign, the Military Council proposed new army designations. T'ang Sheng-chih should command the Fourth Group Army made up of two front armies: the First, under T'ang's direct command, made up of the Eighth, Thirty-fifth, and Thirty-sixth Corps; and the Second, commanded by Chang Fa-k'uei, made up of the Fourth, Eleventh, and the newly enrolled Twentieth Corps, commanded by Ho Lung. Before the campaign began, however, they must suppress Yang Sen and Hsia Tou-yin, who were still rampaging in Hupei, send T'ang Sheng-chih to settle matters in Hunan, and send Ch'en Kung-po to negotiate with Chu P'ei-te in Kiangsi (related above).[244]

The communist leaders faced a dilemma. They knew it was impossible to carry out Stalin's orders. Should Communist Party members try to stay within the Kuomintang and continue working for the national revolution under its banner? That policy had brought great benefits in a large membership and influence among students, urban workers and poorer farmers. But many signs pointed to growing hostility among important Kuomintang leaders, and a tide of reaction among the generals against the mass movements and the Communist Party itself. Only by curbing social revolution could the policy of working within the Kuomintang be continued, but many communists saw social revolution as the essence of national revolution. The mass organizations were the Communist Party's real base of support. After heated debate, the communist leadership, on Borodin's advice, seems to have decided about the middle of June to temporize: party members should stay within the Kuomintang and attempt to restrain social revolution. The party would support a campaign against Chiang Kai-shek in the hope, after victory, of rebuilding the shattered ranks and the mass organizations.[245] Their calculations, however, failed to give due weight to Feng Yü-hsiang.

After the Chengchow conference, General Feng sent his representative,

244 Chiang Yung-ching, Borodin, 393-4. Kuo, Analytical history, 1. 255, for excerpts from Ts'ai Ho-sen, 'History of opportunism'.
245 The fervour of the debate may be sensed from Roy's documents of 9 and 15 June, in North and Eudin, M.N. Roy's mission to China, nos. 28, 31 and 32, and the critique of the Central Committee's policy in the 7 Aug. 1927 'Circular letter of the CC to all party members', abstracted in Brandt, Schwartz and Fairbank, A documentary history, 102-18. Also Ts'ai Ho-sen's account of debates in the weeks following, in the 'History of opportunism', written a few months later, excerpted in Kuo, Analytical history, 1. 255-61, and Chiang Yung-ching, Borodin, 393-4. Chang Kuo-t'ao gives a retrospective account in The rise of the Chinese Communist Party, 1. 647-9. The Comintern's Executive Committee resolution on the Chinese Question adopted by the Eighth Plenum towards the end of May had forecast a campaign against Chiang Kai-shek in the instruction, 'and conduct intensive demoralization work in the rear and within the armies of Chiang Kai-shek with the aim of liquidating them, which does not exclude, of course, conducting military operations against them at the appropriate moment.' Eudin and North, Soviet Russia and the East, 275. Presumably such instructions had been sent by radio to Borodin.

Mao I-heng, to Hsuchow where he met with Pai Ch'ung-hsi and Li Tsung-jen, and it was agreed that Feng and Chiang Kai-shek should meet. An imposing group of Nanking and Shanghai notables then hastened to Hsuchow, where they conferred with General Feng on 20 and 21 June.[246] One important result of the conference was the apparent recruitment of Feng to the Nanking side in consideration of a promised subsidy, reportedly Ch.$2,000,000 a month,[247] which was far more than Wuhan had been paying him. Feng also agreed to use his influence to compel Wuhan to send Borodin back to Russia – something that Chiang had been trying to effect since February – to expel communists, and to persuade loyal Kuomintang members there to come to Nanking to reunite the party and form a single government.[248] On 21 June General Feng sent an ultimatum-like telegram to Wang Ching-wei and T'an Yen-k'ai. After recalling that at Chengchow they had talked about the radicals who had wormed their way into the party and oppressed merchants, factory owners, gentry, landowners, and soldiers, and who refused to obey orders, Feng laid down his terms: Michael Borodin should return to his country immediately; those members of the Central Executive Committee who wished to go abroad for a rest should be allowed to do so; and the rest might join the Nationalist government at Nanking if they so desired. 'It is my desire that you accept the above solution and reach a conclusion immediately.' The next day he told reporters of his 'sincere desire to cooperate with the Nationalists and to extirpate militarism and communism.' He gave them a copy of the telegram.[249]

Within the communist leadership debate raged over strategy. In hopes of overcoming 'the present, dangerous crisis of the revolution', the secretariat of the Chinese Communist Party proposed a desperate scheme on 23 June: the underground Shanghai committee must create within one

---

246 Mao I-heng, O Meng hui-i-lu (Recollections of Russia and Mongolia), 244–5. The participants from Nanking and Shanghai, besides Chiang, were Hu Han-min, Ts'ai Yuan-p'ei, Chang Jen-chieh (Ching-chiang), Li Shih-tseng, Huang Fu, Niu Yung-chien, Li Lieh-chün, Li Tsung-jen, Huang Shao-hsiung, Pai Ch'ung-hsi, and Wu Chih-hui, who presided. On Feng's side were Li Ming-chung and Ho Chi-kung. TJK, 718, based on Wu Chih-hui's report reprinted in KMWH, 15. 2566. Isaacs, The Tragedy of the Chinese revolution, 256, says that Hsu Ch'ien and Ku Meng-yü accompanied Feng to Hsuchow.

247 Mao I-heng, O Meng hui-i-lu, 245. The British consul-general in Shanghai, Sir Sidney Barton, reported on 30 June that there had been a great drive in the last two weeks in June to collect funds in Shanghai, which he speculated were needed to carry out Chiang's agreement at Hsuchow to finance Feng in return for Feng's support against Hankow and Peking. GBFO 405/254. Confidential. Further correspondence respecting China, no. 13315, July–Sept. 1927, no. 43, enclosure.

248 Chiang Kai-shek's report of 6 July, quoted by Li Yun-han in TJK, 718–19.

249 Isaacs, The Tragedy of the Chinese Revolution, 256, who quotes part of the telegram as published in CWR, 2 July 1927. The Chinese text was published in Kuo-wen chou-pao on 3 July, and is given in TJK, 719–20 and Chiang Yung-ching, Borodin, 382–3.

month a militant anti-imperialist movement more powerful than the May Thirtieth movement of two years before, with students, merchants and workers declaring a general strike and demonstrating within the foreign settlements – even, if necessary, demanding confiscation of imperialist property and taking back of the foreign concessions. If a powerful anti-foreign sentiment were fostered among all sectors of the population – particularly against Japan, which had sent troops into Shantung – and if this were especially virulent among the ranks of Chiang Kai-shek's armies, it would force the imperialists to occupy Nanking and Shanghai – so the secretariat reasoned. This would lead to a nationwide protest which would destroy the roots of Chiang's power and smash the danger from the right in the Wuhan government. 'This movement must burst like an explosion just at the moment when either Chiang Kai-shek attacks Wuhan, or Wuhan attacks Chiang Kai-shek.' The Communist Party could then carry on the social revolution under the banner of a new anti-imperialist war.[250] The Politburo[251] countermanded this scheme with its suicidal potentialities for the remnants of the shattered mass movement in the east. An increasingly hostile situation in the Wuhan cities forced new decisions upon the party leaders.

The Fourth Congress of the National General Labour Union had begun its meetings in Hankow on 19 June with more than 400 delegates, some from the shattered unions of Shanghai and Canton.[252] Also attending were a fraternal delegation from the Profintern (the Red Trade Union International), headed by its president, Aleksandr Lazovskii, representatives from the Kuomintang, the Chinese Communist Party and the Communist Youth League. Both the National General Labour Union and the Congress were controlled by the Communist Party, yet Feng Yü-hsiang now clearly demanded that the Wuhan regime separate itself from that party, and there were rumours that some of Wuhan's generals planned to arrest communists and suppress the labour movement. Who was safe? While the congress proceeded under the chairmanship of Su Chao-cheng, even being favoured by an address by Wang Ching-wei, the communist

---

250 North and Eudin, M. N. *Roy's mission to China*, Doc. 35, pp. 361–5. According to Roy, the secretariat sent the letter bearing these instructions to Shanghai, but the Politburo after lengthy debate replaced it by a resolution on the anti-imperialist struggle. Roy does not cite this but quotes his own speech, presumably to the Politburo, opposing this fool-hardy order to the Shanghai comrades. *Ibid.* 366–9.

251 After the Fifth CCP Congress, the Politburo consisted of Ch'en Tu-hsiu, Chang Kuo-t'ao, Chou En-lai, Ch'ü Ch'iu-pai, Li Li-san, Li Wei-han (pseudonym Lo Mai), T'an P'ing-shan, and Ts'ai Ho-sen, according to Bernadette Yu-ning Li, 'A biography of Ch'ü Ch'iu-pai: from youth to party leadership (1899–1928)', Columbia University, Ph.D. dissertation, 1967, 197.

252 An account of the meetings and some resolutions are reprinted in *Ti-i-tz'u . . . kung-jen*, 545–2; a description is in Strong, *China's millions*, 74–88.

Politburo debated what to do about the armed and uniformed pickets – the 'inspection corps' – of the General Labour Union and of the Hupei Provincial Union headed by Li Li-san. The pickets were a source of great animosity in the business community – both Chinese and foreign – which the Wuhan regime was encouraging in every way in order to revive the depressed economy, and provide work for scores of thousands of unemployed. Should the pickets give up their arms as a concession to the Kuomintang? Should they cross the river to Wuchang and enrol in Chang Fa-k'uei's forces? Apparently on 28 June, which was the last day of the congress, the Politburo met in Borodin's home and decided on a further retreat: the pickets would be disarmed voluntarily. That night – either by coincidence or after an understanding – police and troops of the Hankow garrison seized the headquarters of the National Labour Union and the Hupei Provincial Union, and pickets turned in their rifles and removed their insignia and uniforms. Yet the next day the offices were returned to the unions with face-saving apologies, and pickets reappeared, in smaller numbers and without arms. That evening the delegates to the congress were hosts at a festival for soldiers. Wang Ching-wei ordered that no harm should befall the unions.[253]

Pressures for a break between the two parties continued to mount. T'ang Sheng-chih's telegram of 26 June from Changsha, placing the blame for disorders in Hunan upon those who led the peasant movement, was published on 29 June. On the same day General Ho Chien, commander of the Thirty-fifth Corps, issued a proclamation demanding that the Kuomintang expel its communist members. He threatened to arrest any communists his troops could capture. In the face of this threat, the communist leadership decided to move the party's headquarters across the river to Wuchang, and there to hold an enlarged plenum of the Central Committee to fix a policy line. A meeting was first held on 30 June in Borodin's home, attended by Politburo members and two newly arrived Comintern delegates. After acrimonious debate, the participants accepted a series of resolutions that were then adopted on 1 July by the Central Committee. They marked the ultimate retreat of the Communist Party in order to retain working relations with the left Kuomintang. The party of the proletariat resolved that the worker and peasant movements should

253 *TJK*, 731 for Ts'ai Ho-sen's later account of the emergency Politburo meeting; also, Chang, *The rise of the Chinese Communist Party*, 649. Chiang, Yung-ching, *Borodin* 397, for Wang Ching-wei's description of the raids, and USDS 893.00/9159, telegram, Hankow, Lockhart to secretary of state, 29 June, describing the seizures. Miss Strong observed the return of the National Union's headquarters to Su Chao-cheng and describes the festival sardonically. Her account was written in Moscow. See *China's millions*, 87–8. General Li P'in-hsien, garrison commander in Hankow, apparently ordered the raids.

take their orders from, and be supervised by, Kuomintang offices, though the Kuomintang and the government must protect their organizations; armed units of workers and peasants should submit to the government's supervision and training, while those inspection corps in Wuhan that were still armed should be reduced in number or be enrolled in the army; workers and their inspection corps should not exercise judicial authority such as arresting and trying, nor patrol streets and markets without permission from Kuomintang headquarters or the government. Very soon the communist leadership severely reproached itself for these accommodations to the demand for law and order. Another resolution dealt with communists working in the national or local government organs. They should do so as Kuomintang members, not as communists, and to avoid conflict they might ask for leave of absence.[254]

The last days of June saw the beginning of an exodus of Russian military advisers and members of Borodin's staff, persons who had employed much talent and spent great energy in assisting the Nationalist Revolution, for now the end of Russian aid was approaching. Correspondents who called on Borodin early in July found him sick and weary, but determined to stay on as long as hope remained. His wife was in a Peking prison, having been seized on 28 February when the Soviet vessel *Pamiat Lenina*, on which she was travelling to Hankow, was captured by Shantung troops. Mme Borodin's release had to be arranged before he could leave, and apparently Japan was willing to be the intermediary. In the early morning of 12 July a Chinese judge dismissed the charges against her and other Russians who had been seized on the *Pamiat Lenina*. The judge then disappeared, only to show up later in Japan, and the Russian erstwhile prisoners were spirited out of Peking, except for Mme Borodin who was secreted in the city. Her presence was concealed by a series of false news accounts of her arrival in Vladivostok, an interview on the Trans-Siberian, and her arrival statement in Moscow. Towards the end of August she successfully left Peking disguised as a nun.[255]

254 Ho Chien's proclamation is in *Kuo-wen chou-pao*, 4. 29 (21 July 1927), which reprints eight important Wuhan documents concerning the inter-party split. The documents continue in succeeding issues. Chiang Yung-ching, *Borodin*, 399, quotes four of the 11 resolutions as given in the 'Letter to the comrades' from the 7 Aug. [1927] Central Committee Conference, so called. Kuo, *Analytical history*, 259-60, gives seven from the same source.
255 USDS 893.00/9128 telegram, Peking, MacMurray to secretary of state, 23 June, transmitting Hankow telegram of June 22, reporting early departure of Russian aviators. Vishnyakova-Akimova, *Two years in revolutionary China*, 326, tells of her departure soon after 20 June, on Borodin's orders, together with several military advisers. Others followed in contingents during July, and General Blyukher left on 11 Aug, according to Kasanin, *China in the twenties*, 291-2. Interviews with Borodin in Henry Francis Misselwitz, *The dragon stirs: an intimate sketchbook of China's Kuomintang revolution, 1927-1929*, 125; and Vincent Sheean, *Personal history*, 240-1. Sheean details Mme Borodin's escape, in which he nearly played a part (pp. 255-8), and his account is supplemented by Kasanin, cited, 295-6.

The breaking point between the two parties came in the middle of July. Feng Yü-hsiang and Chiang Kai-shek exerted pressure by repeated telegrams from Hsu Ch'ien urging his Wuhan colleagues to dismiss Borodin, and by Chiang bringing his crack First Corps back to Nanking and ordering the Seventh and two other corps to proceed towards Kiangsi. T. V. Soong, Wuhan's finance minister, who had stayed in Shanghai during the previous several months, suddenly returned to Hankow on 12 July, doubtless bearing messages from the Nanking faction. Private meetings in Wang Ching-wei's home were dominated by the more conservative Wuhan leaders, who hoped to find a peaceful settlement with their Nanking rivals. This would require separating from the communists and asking Borodin to leave. (Borodin had already made preparations for departure by an overland route through Mongolia.)[256]

On 14 July the praesidium of the Political Council accepted two proposals by Wang Ching-wei: to send a high-level representative to Moscow to explain Sun Yat-sen's policy of allying with Russia and the Communist Party under the Three Principles of the People, so as to clarify future relationships; and to find a method to manage communists within the Kuomintang so as to avoid intra-party ideological and policy conflicts, and expecially to end the system of two separate and conflicting policy organs. Next day an expanded meeting of the Kuomintang CEC Standing Committee heard Wang's account of Stalin's 1 June telegram, which had so exercised the Political Bureau, and learned that M. N. Roy had left and that Borodin wished to depart. The meeting resolved to call a plenum of the Central Executive Committee within one month to consider the recommendations of the Political Council praesidium – clearly implying separation of communists from the Kuomintang – and before that date entrusting Party headquarters to deal with recalcitrant members. The conferees also agreed that the Political Council should select the delegate to go to Moscow, and it passed resolutions ordering the protection of workers and farmers, as well as the personal freedom of Communist Party members. The decisions were to be kept secret from the rank and file.[257] Thus it appears that at this point the party's civilian leaders planned to postpone the separation and then to take the step peacefully. One element at stake was the hoped for continuation of Russian aid. But on that very day, General Ho Chien's troops were searching the streets for communists,

---

256 USDS 893.00/9165/9194/9213, telegrams from Peking to secretary of state transmitting information from Hankow and Nanking of 5, 11 and 13 July; and George Sokolsky on the Kuomintang, in *The China Yearbook, 1928*, 1371, for an account of the private meetings, for which T.V. Soong probably was the source.
257 Chiang Yung-ching, *Borodin*, 401–2, and *TJK*, 736–40, citing minutes.

including two Kuomintang Central Committee members, Wu Yü-chang and T'an P'ing-shan, both of whom had disappeared.

They may have gone into hiding along with many other prominent Chinese communists in the Wuhan cities as a result of decisions taken at a meeting on 13 July in response to urgent instructions from the Comintern. Besides blaming the Chinese Communist Party for its opportunistic mistakes, and ordering Borodin back to Russia, the Comintern demanded a proclamation demonstratively announcing the withdrawal of communists from the government. It forbade them, however, to withdraw from the Kuomintang. Even if they were expelled, they should secretly work with the Kuomintang's lower level masses to create resistance to decisions of the leadership and demands for changes in that party's leading organs. On this foundation, communists should then prepare to call a Kuomintang congress.[258] This duplicity was too much for Ch'en Tu-hsiu, the founder of the Chinese Communist Party and its secretary-general, who had often advocated withdrawal from the Kuomintang but always had been overruled. Now he resigned his position. The Communist Party's declaration of 13 July denounced the Nationalist government for failing to protect the workers and peasants but actually encouraging reaction, and it announced that T'an P'ing-shan and Su Chao-cheng had resigned their positions. Yet it also stated that communists were neither withdrawing from the Kuomintang nor abandoning the policy of cooperation with it. Borodin then left for a recuperative rest at a mountain resort near Kiukiang. It was just after his wife had been freed from the Peking prison. Accompanying him was the Russian speaking Ch'ü Ch'iu-pai, who was soon to become the party's new secretary-general, at the age of 28.[259]

Separation of the two parties now became a reality. On 16 July, the day the Kuomintang Central Committee published its resolutions restricting communists but ordering their personal protection and no harm to the workers' and farmers' movements, the Communist Party statement of 13 July appeared on posters and in the press. This stimulated the praesidium of the Political Council to publish its account of Stalin's menacing

258 Quoted by TJK, 735-6, from Hua Kang's History of the Chinese Communist Party during the great revolution of 1925-1927. Isaacs, The tragedy of the Chinese revolution, 266-7, quotes 'Resolution of the E.C.C.I. on the present situation of the Chinese revolution,' from Imprecor, 28 July, which carries the instructions, but he gives 14 July as its date.

259 The proclamation was reprinted in Kuo-wen chou-pao, 4. no. 29 (21 July 1927), and is partially translated in T.C. Woo, The Kuomintang and the future of the Chinese revolution, 182. Ch'en Tu-hsiu's position is stated in his 'A letter to all comrades of the Party', 323-33. Vishnyakova-Akimova gives a guarded account of the meeting, presumably based on Russian archives. Two Years, 331. Li, A Biography of Ch'ü Ch'iu-pai, 221-2. The 13 July 'Manifesto of the Central Committee of the CCP' is translated in Hyobom Pak, Documents of the Chinese Communist Party, 1927-1930, 21-9.

telegram, together with a denunciation of communists for withdrawing from the government while planning to stay within the Kuomintang. This amounted to destroying the Kuomintang's policy of admitting communists, the praesidium charged. It ordered all dual party members to resign from one party or the other. Each side issued more excoriating documents. But some leftist Kuomintang leaders deplored the split. Teng Yen-ta issued a condemnation and resigned his positions as head of the National Revolutionary Army's Political Department and of the Kuomintang Farmers Bureau. He had already disappeared and soon was on his way to Russia. Mme Sun Yat-sen issued a statement condemning the anti-revolutionary course on which her colleagues had embarked, and left for Kuling, and later for Shanghai and Russia. Both statements emphasized what was now the underlying and central issue – social revolution. They charged that Wuhan's compromising leaders had turned against it.[260] Eugene Chen also was preparing to leave.

Counter-revolution now moved into the leftist capital. The Wuhan cities went under martial law, troops seized labour union headquarters again, as well as other suspected communist strongholds, and executed many hapless militants. For the communist leaders there seemed to be only two options: flight or revolt. The well-known communists in the Wuhan area went underground or fled to northern Kiangsi, to which province Chang Fa-k'uei's armies were being transferred. There were many communist officers among his forces. By the last week in July, with the inter-party collaboration policy wrecked upon the rocks of class struggle, the Communist Party's core leadership was already planning revolts, now with Comintern encouragement.

Michael Borodin's departure from Hankow symbolized the end of Russia's effort to foster revolution in China through the Nationalist Party – as the first stage. On the afternoon of 27 July, still suffering from fever, Borodin left for Chengchow with a small party of Russian advisers and bodyguards, the two sons of Eugene Chen and an American journalist, Anna Louise Strong, on a train loaded with trucks and heavy-duty touring cars, a great quantity of petrol, and baggage, for a long and uncertain journey homeward. The most important remaining officials in Wuhan saw him off with great courtesy, and Wang Ching-wei presented

260 A variety of the documents are in *Kuo-wen chou-pao*, as cited above, and a few are in *KMWH*, 16. 2828-40. Teng Yen-ta's statement is briefed in USDS 893.00/9216, transmitting Lockhart's telegram of 15 July. Chiang Yung-ching, *Borodin*, 409, gives evidence that Teng was in Chengchow by 18 July. Mme Sun's statement is reprinted in T. C. Woo, *The Kuomintang*, 270-3. General accounts of the split, based on KMT documents, are in Chiang, *Borodin*, 401-12, and *TJK*, 741-3. Isaacs, *The tragedy of the Chinese revolution*, devotes a chapter to 'Wuhan: the debacle'.

him with a testamentary letter addressed to the 'Comrades of the Central Politburo of the Communist Party of Soviet Russia.' This expressed the undying gratitude of the Chinese comrades for Borodin's brilliant achievements as adviser to the Kuomintang. The letter also announced that the Kuomintang hoped in the nearest future to send important comrades to Russia to discuss ways of uniting the two countries. Methods of cooperation between the Kuomintang and the Chinese Communist Party still awaited instruction, but Wang professed confidence that Borodin could give a thorough account of the complexities of this matter. The letter closed 'With Revolutionary Greetings', and was subscribed as from the praesidium of the Kuomintang Political Council.[261]

In Chengchow, Borodin received courteous attention from Feng Yü-hsiang, who ordered that he be protected *en route*, and then he travelled westward by rail, taking with him some of General Feng's Russian advisers who knew the route. At the end of the Lunghai Railway, the party loaded its five trucks and five touring cars for the precarious trip west and north through Shensi and Kansu to Ninghsia city, and thence across the Gobi desert to Ulan-Bator, where they arrived in mid September. After a long rest Borodin flew to Verkhne-Udinsk, where he boarded the express train for Moscow. He arrived there on 6 October, at the age of 43.[262]

The two nationalistic parties with their conflicting social philosophies now followed separate ways – the Communists into revolt and the Nationalists into uneasy reconciliation among the various factions. It was not easy for politicians, labour leaders, propagandists and military commanders, who had called each other 'comrade' and worked together for years to rescue China from imperialism and militarism, to disengage. Some simply withdrew, but most of the activists went in one direction or the other. The breach set the main course of Chinese political life for decades thereafter.

261 Wang's draft, dated 25 July 1927, is in the Kuomintang Archives, 445/35.
262 An account of the trip is in Strong, *China's millions*. Arrival date from *Pravda*, 7 Oct. 1927. Borodin was born 9 July 1884. In Moscow he held such posts as deputy people's commissar for labour, deputy to the head of Tass, manager of the paper industry and, beginning in 1932, editor of the English language *Moscow news*. Louis Fischer interviewed him 10 times between 26 Feb. and 29 June 1929, according to his *Men and politics: an autobiography*, 138. Fischer recounts, indirectly, what Borodin told him about the Chinese revolution in one chapter of *The Soviets in world affairs*, 2. 632-79. Borodin was arrested in 1949, along with many other Jewish intellectuals, and sent to a prison camp, where he died in 1951 at about the age of 67. *New York Times*, 3 Sept. 1953 and 1 July 1964. More recently, Borodin's reputation has been rehabilitated in the USSR and there are scholarly publications concerning his contributions to the Chinese revolution.

THE COMMUNISTS TURN TO REBELLION

Beginnings of communist revolt

During the latter half of July the Chinese Communist leadership debated plans for a general uprising in four provinces, with encouragement from a newly arrived Comintern delegate, Besso Lominadze, and advice from General Bluykher and some of his staff. An important element of the plan was to seize control of elements in Chang Fa-k'uei's Second Front Army that had moved into northern Kiangsi and in which there were a number of communist commanders and many communist political workers. Details for the revolt were worked out by a group of communists in Nanchang and Kiukiang, and discussed on 26 July in Hankow at a meeting of available members of the party's Central Standing Committee – Ch'ü Ch'iu-pai, who had returned with the plan, Li Wei-han, Chang T'ai-lei and Chang Kuo-t'ao. Lominadze and Bluykher attended together with several other Russians. The plotters hoped that Chang Fa-k'uei could be persuaded to join and lead his troops back to Kwangtung, but if not, then communists would stage a revolt and take over his troops anyway. Moscow had been informed, but at this meeting the Comintern representative reported telegraphic instructions that no Russians were to participate in the uprising, and he also said that no funds were available. Bluykher, who had held a discussion with General Chang only the day before, predicted that should he join the insurrection, there might be 30,000 troops, which would be plenty to fight through to eastern Kwangtung, at which time the communists could cut Chang out; but if the communists split his forces at Nanchang, the uprising would only gain from 5,000 to 8,000 troops. A Moscow telegram cautioned against the uprising unless victory was assured. Therefore Lominadze sent Chang Kuo-t'ao that very night to Nanchang to inform the plotters of Comintern's ambiguous instructions.[263]

263 This description of the Nanchang Uprising is based primarily on accounts by planners and participants in the revolt, Chang T'ai-lei, Li Li-san, Chou I-ch'ün, and Chang Kuo-t'ao, written between early Oct. and early Nov. 1927, shortly after the defeat, and published in the Chinese Communist Party's new journal, *Chung-yang t'ung-hsun* (Central newsletter), 30 Oct. and 30 Nov. They are translated in C. Martin Wilbur, 'The ashes of defeat', *CQ*, 18 (April–June 1964) 3–54. The same documents and some Kuomintang sources are the basis for Wang Chien-min's excellent account in *Chung-kuo kung-ch'an-tang shih-kao*, 1. 534–52. He gives useful order of battle tables. Another valuable reconstruction based on these primary sources and on the memoirs of Chang Kuo-t'ao and Kung Ch'u, is Hsiao Tso-liang, 'From Nanchang to Swatow' in his *Chinese communism in 1927: city vs. countryside*, 81–104. Chang Kuo-t'ao gives an emotional reminiscent account in *The rise of the Chinese Communist Party*, 1. 672–7, and 2. 3–55, based in part on his own contemporary reports. See also, Harrison, *The long march to power*, 120–3, and Jacques Guillermaz, *A history of the Chinese Communist Party, 1921–1949*, 150–6.

The main architects of the Nanchang uprising were T'an P'ing-shan, Teng Chung-hsia, Yun Tai-ying, Li Li-san, P'eng P'ai, Yeh T'ing, and later Chou En-lai, who was sent by the Centre to supervise. The Chinese Communist Party celebrates 1 August, when the uprising broke out, as the founding date of the Red Army. Several of the commanders who participated went on to illustrious careers in that army – Yeh T'ing, Ho Lung, Liu Po-ch'eng, Chu Te, Nieh Jung-chen, Lo Jui-ch'ing, Ch'en Yi, Hsiao K'o and Lin Piao.[264] Planning had gone so far when Chang Kuo-t'ao arrived and tried to stop the action that 'the arrow was on the bowstring and had to be shot'. General Yeh T'ing, commanding the 24th Division, was prepared to take over the Eleventh Corps, while General Ho Lung, commander of the Twentieth Corps and not yet a member of the Communist Party, was eager to take action in the expectation of re-placing Chang Fa-k'uei, who was just then in conference with Wang Ching-wei, T'ang Sheng-chih, Chu P'ei-te, Sun Fo, and other generals and notables in the mountain resort of Lu-shan.[265]

The uprising was a quick success militarily. Troops under Generals Yeh and Ho disarmed opposing units in the city before daybreak, and Chu Te brought in the remnants of his training regiment to form the cadre of a new division. The conspirators got quantities of arms and ammunition, and a great deal of cash and banknotes from the city's banks and the provincial treasury. Political preparations had not been well worked out, however. Still pretending to be acting under the Kuomintang banner, the leadership announced a 31 member Central Revolutionary Committee of the Kuomintang, naming such absent leaders as Teng Yen-ta, Mme Sun Yat-sen and Mme Liao Chung-k'ai (Ho Hsiang-ning), Eugene Chen, Chang Fa-k'uei and two of his displaced corps commanders, and 17 communists. The only present members of the 'praesidium' were T'an P'ing-shan, Ho Lung, Kuo Mo-jo, and Yun Tai-ying, and all the various named committees were headed by communists, except for Ho Lung and Kuo Mo-jo, who reportedly joined the party *en route*.[266] In setting up a Kuomintang Revolutionary Committee, the leaders claimed legitimacy, but, by their own later admission, they had no firm policies

264 Klein and Clark, *Biographic dictionary*, 1066, lists 40 known participants in the planning or action. Chu Te gave a reminiscent account to Agnes Smedley, published in *The great road*, 200-9.

265 An interesting account of how the news of the Uprising was reported to this conference, of Chang Fa-k'uei's unsuccessful effort to get to Nanchang, and of Wang Ching-wei's outrage at the event, is given in Wang's report on 5 August to the Wuhan Kuomintang Central Standing Committee meeting, reprinted from the minutes held in the Kuomin-tang Archives, in *Kung-fei huo-kuo shih-liao hui-pien* (A compilation of documents on the communist bandits' destruction of the nation) 1. 485-8.

266 Wilbur, 'The ashes of defeat', 31.

on such issues as land revolution, attitudes towards local power-holders, and methods of financing, and they even disputed whether to head for Canton or the East River district of Kwangtung, and about the route of march.

The armies started marching south on the fourth in blistering heat, but lost much equipment along the way. Troop strength dwindled through desertion, dysentery and battle casualties. General Ts'ai T'ing-k'ai escaped with his 10th Division to Chekiang, leaving only the 24th and 25th Divisions of the Eleventh Corps. After suffering serious casualties in battles near Jui-chin and Hui-ch'ang, the marchers were able to leave their seriously wounded in the care of a British missionary hospital at Ting-chou in western Fukien.[267] The army found no support along the way, for the farmers' movement scarcely existed in mountainous eastern Kiangsi and Fukien. Arriving along the Fukien-Kwangtung border after more than a month of marching, the expedition briefly held Chao-chou and Swatow (24–30 September), but found no mass support where only a year before the Hong Kong strike and boycott movement had been very active. By the end of September the scattered units had been completely defeated. Some of the remnants of the 24th Division and of the Twentieth Corps made their way to Lu-feng, on the coast, where the peasant movement organized by P'eng P'ai still had strength; but there Ho Lung's divisional commanders turned over to the enemy side. Many of the communist leaders then escaped in small boats to Hong Kong, and some took ship for Shanghai. The remnants of the 25th Division, commanded by Chou Shih-ti, and the troops under Chu Te, which had served as a rearguard, fled to the mountains. Later Chou and Chu led their force across southern Kiangsi and then split up, Chu Te leading his 600 or so poorly armed men to a junction with Mao Tse-tung in southern Hunan in the spring of 1928.[268]

An immediate result of the Nanchang uprising was the wide-scale arrest of suspected communists in Kiukiang and the Wuhan area and many executions. However, most of the leading communists who were not campaigning southwards were already in hiding and escaped this purge. They were secretly planning to stage a series of rural revolts during the autumn harvest season – normally a time of great tension in the villages when rents had to be paid.

267 Smedley, *The great road*, 205. In recalling this in 1937, Chu Te seemed still impressed that 'Dr Nelson Fu and the British doctors in that foreign hospital took charge of our wounded men!'
268 Klein and Clark, *Biographic dictionary*, 247.

Autumn harvest revolts

On orders from the Comintern, Besso Lominadze called a conference of available members of the party's Central Committee on 7 August to reorganize the leadership structure, repudiate past errors – they were to be blamed upon Chinese rather than Comintern strategists – and to ratify a new policy line. Some 22 Chinese communists met for one day in Wuhan under the 'guidance' of Lominadze; 15 of these were members or alternates of the Central Committee, less than half the total number. They elected a new provisional politburo, headed by Ch'ü Ch'iu-pai, to manage party affairs until a new congress convened. The party was now to be rigidly centralized and secret.[269] The August 7th conferees also issued four documents. One, which reportedly was dictated by Lominadze, censured the past Chinese leadership for opportunism, naming particularly, T'an P'ing-shan, but also the party patriarch, Ch'en Tu-hsiu. The other documents laid down an insurrectionist line: the Communist Party would seek to overthrow both the Wuhan and the Nanking regimes, and would organize revolts in the provinces wherever objective situations permitted, looking towards the future establishment of soviets. The revolts were to be conducted under the banner of the 'revolutionary left Kuomintang'.[270]

While the original plan called for rural revolts in Hupei, Hunan, Kiangsi and Kwangtung during the autumn harvest season, the exodus of most of the Kiangsi leaders on the march south after the Nanchang Uprising made another revolt in that province impossible. The new Politburo dispatched Chang T'ai-lei to be in command in Kwangtung as

269 These interpretations are based on the careful study by Bernadette Li, 'A biography of Ch'ü Ch'iu-pai', 232–48. Dr Li identified 14 participants and named the following as the new Politburo: Ch'ü, Hsiang Chung-fa, Li Wei-han, Lo I-nung, P'eng P'ai (in absentia), Su Chao-cheng, and Ts'ai Ho-sen; with four alternates, Chang Kuo-t'ao (in absentia), Chang T'ai-lei, Mao Tse-tung, and P'eng Kung-ta. Hsiao Tso-liang gives a different list based on the memoirs of Chang Kuo-t'ao, who did not attend, and locates the meeting in Kiukiang. Hsiao, *Chinese communism in 1927*, 39–46. Wang Chien-min, *Chung-kuo Kung-ch'an-tang*, 1. 503, and Harrison, *The long march to power*, 123, conclude that Hankow was the meeting site.

270 Documents from the August 7th Conference were published in *Chung-yang t'ung-hsun*, no. 2, 23 Aug. 1927. Some have been reprinted or abstracted in Wang, *Chung-kuo Kung-ch'an-tang*, 1. 504–28 and in *Kung-fei huo-kuo shih-liao hui-pien*, 1. 445–84 (both sanitized to remove references to Chiang Kai-shek). The 'Resolution on the political tasks and tactics of the Chinese Communist Party' is translated in Pak, *Documents*, 45–57, while the 'Circular letter from the conference to all party members' and the resolutions are abstracted in Brandt, Schwartz, and Fairbank, *A documentary history*, 102–23.

Ch'ü Ch'iu-pai, who became head of the Politburo as a result of this conference, made a long report in Moscow about a year later concerning the problems of the Chinese Communist Party in the period leading up to the conference and during his time of leadership. The second half of his report is translated by Man Kwok–chuen and published in *Chinese studies in history*, 5. 1 (Fall 1971) 4–72.

secretary of the Communist Party Southern Bureau and the Provincial Committee. They divided Hupei into seven districts and Hunan into three, hoping to mount extensive peasant revolts in those provinces, but because of a shortage of guiding personnel the theatre was narrowed to the part of Hupei south of Wuhan and the Hunan region east of Changsha. The plotters put Mao Tse-tung in charge of the Hunan operation, to work together with the provincial secretary, P'eng Kung-ta. The provincial secretary for Hupei, Lo I-nung, was involved in the planning, but not the execution of the South Hupei operation, which was directed by a hastily organized special committee. The date set for the two-province insurrection to burst out was 10 September.[271]

Peasant uprisings were to carry through a land revolution, overthrow the Wuhan government and T'ang Sheng-chih's regime, and lead to a people's government. The insurrection must be carefully prepared in its organizational, technical and political aspects, and once launched must never flinch or retreat. Peasants must constitute the main force, though existing troop units and bandit gangs, if converted to the revolutionary cause, could be used as auxiliaries. 'Land to the tillers!', 'Resistance to taxes and rent!', 'Confiscate the land of large and middle landlords!', and 'Exterminate local bullies, evil gentry, and all counter-revolutionaries!' – such were the slogans that should arouse the rural masses. Slaughter of class enemies and local officials would commit the peasantry to a broad rural revolt and to the capture of county seats. Then would follow insurrection in Wuhan and Changsha. So theorized the fugitive Politburo members. Implementation was more difficult.

In southern Hupei the revolt started prematurely with a train robbery on the night of 8 September in which the special committee captured a shipment of money and a few arms. But when it came to attacking two walled and well-defended county seats, as called for in the plan, the local communist leaders backed off, for they lacked the military capability to do

---

271 Basic information on the uprisings is in *Chung-yang t'ung-hsun*, nos. 4–7 and 11, dated 30 Aug. 12, 20 and 30 Sept., 30 Oct., and probably late Nov. 1927. Selected documents from this source are translated in Pak, *Documents*, no. 9 (pp. 59–66) 'Resolution on the plan for insurrection in Hunan and Hupei'; nos. 12–18 (pp. 87–113) on Hunan; nos. 30–32 (pp. 201–15) on Hupei; and no. 23 (pp. 133–45), a post-mortem. Abstracts of the 'Resolution on the plan' and some other items are in Wang Chien-min *Chung-kuo Kung-ch'an-tang*, 1. 533–60; and that resolution and the 'Resolution on political discipline', of 14 Nov. 1927, in which blame for failure was passed out, are translated in Kuo, *Analytical history*, 1. 462–7. The extensive 'Report on the Autumn Harvest Revolt in Hupei', in *Chung-yang t'ung-hsun*, no. 11, was found in corrupt form in Japan, and is translated into Japanese by Taicho Mikami, Tadao Ishikawa and Minoru Shabata, and published by Kansai University Institute of Oriental and Occidental Studies, Osaka, 1961.

Scholarly reconstructions are Roy Hofheinz, Jr. 'The Autumn Harvest Uprising', *CQ*, 32 (Oct.–Dec. 1967) 37–87 with maps; Hsiao, *Chinese communism in 1927*, 39–80, with maps; and Li, 'A biography of Ch'ü Ch'iu-pai', 249–60.

so with their poorly armed and untrained peasant force. Central had forbidden the special committee to contact military units still having some communist officers. This was to be a peasant movement. Thus, the committee was reduced to setting up a revolutionary government in a small town in the mountains on 12 September. Only shortly afterwards they began a move to a market town, Hsin-tien, expecting to get support from a local self-defence force, a group of ex-bandits with 38 rifles, for a joint attack on another county seat. If this proved impossible, then a move towards Yo-chow, across the provincial border, might link them with the uprising in eastern Hunan. Unfortunately for the committee, the leader of the self-defence force, with whom they had been negotiating and who had participated in the train robbery, betrayed them. He disarmed their small force, though allowing the committee members to escape. Thus collapsed the insurrection in south Hupei, after less than 10 days of scattered rioting and killings.[272]

The revolt in Hunan, which Mao Tse-tung was charged with directing, was initially more successful, but also ended in failure. During the organizing stage Mao was in conflict with the Politburo members in Wuhan over several issues. He sensed that without organized military units a revolt could not be sustained, whether or not the troops were called auxiliaries. He also insisted that the available leadership should not be spread too thinly and, in defiance of Central, he restricted his efforts to the Hsiang River counties near Changsha. He also wished the uprising to be fought under the communist banner, not that of the Kuomintang, and he favoured complete land confiscation and the immediate establishment of soviets. Central criticized Mao severely and sent a Russian adviser to Changsha to assist in the directing; it is from reports of this Comrade Ma K'e-fu that some useful information on the uprising and on Mao's 'mistakes' is available.[273]

By the first week in September there were four military units that Mao could throw into the battle. The first was an under-strength regiment made up of fugitives from Chang Fa-k'uei's guards, which had missed the Nanchang Uprising and become depleted through desertions. Its commander and assistant commander were communists, and it was lodged at Hsiu-shui in Kiangsi near the Hunan border. The second was a 'rag-tag' unit made up of deserters from Hsia Tou-yin's force. It was headed by a

272 Hofheinz, 'The Autumn Harvest Uprising', 51-7; Hsiao, Chinese communism in 1927, 62-7.
273 An authoritative discussion of Mao's conflict with the Politburo is in Stuart R. Schram, 'On the nature of Mao Tse-tung's "deviation" in 1927', CQ, 18 (April-June 1964) 55-66, based on contemporary Russian and Chinese communist documents. The disagreements are also discussed in Hofheinz, 'The Autumn Harvest Uprising', 61-6, and Hsiao, Chinese communism in 1927, 46-53.

former bandit and had been in conflict with the so-called first regiment, which had driven it out of Hsiu-shui. The third unit, called the P'ing-chiang–Liu-yang Self-Defence Force, was made up partly of peasants, who had attempted to storm Changsha at the end of May, and partly of local corps and bandits. A graduate of the Wuhan branch of the Nationalist Military Academy commanded this unit, which was based in the mountains east of Changsha. The backbone of the fourth regiment, the P'ing-hsiang–Li-ling Self-Defence Force, consisted of unemployed miners from An-yuan, a very militant group under communist leadership. The Hunan Provincial Committee designated these four 'regiments' – scattered in three localities across 150 kilometres, and two of them hostile to each other – as the First Division of the First Army of the Chinese Workers' and Peasants' Revolutionary Army, and gave them communist flags.[274]

The final battle plan called for the first two regiments to attack P'ing-chiang, to the north-east of Changsha, and for the other two to attack Liu-yang, directly east of the provincial capital. Preliminary riots on or before 11 September in the countryside around Changsha were to distract attention from these attacks on walled towns, and guerrilla forces were supposed to harass troops going out to oppose the attackers. The railways leading to Changsha should be cut north and south. After P'ing-chiang and Liu-yang had been captured, all forces would descend on Changsha on the 15th, and the city would respond with a mass uprising from within. However, the Communist Party members who would carry through this plan had been much reduced from the days before the May Twenty-First Incident – from about 20,000 to 5,000 for the province, with only about 1,000 of these in Changsha. Furthermore, the attacking units had relatively few arms.

The An-yuan fourth regiment began its march on schedule on 10 September. Unable to capture P'ing-hsiang, it went on to take Li-ling, a county seat on the railway leading to Changsha, on the 12th. It held the city for a little more than a day, setting up a revolutionary committee and announcing a land confiscation programme. A communist-led peasant unit with only 60 rifles was able to capture Chu-chow, only 50 kilometres from Changsha, throwing the provincial capital into panic on the 13th. According to Comrade Ma, in this area thousands of peasants armed with hand weapons entered the fray and many rifles were captured. Farther

274 This account is based upon Hofheinz and Hsiao, cited, and an interesting reconstruction of Mao's role in Stuart R. Schram, *Political leaders of the twentieth century: Mao Tse-tung*, 120–5. All are based primarily on the *Chung-yang t'ung-hsun* documents, but differ considerably in detail.

north, however, the two regiments that were supposed to take P'ing-chiang actually fought each other, and the remnants of the first regiment retreated to the mountains of Kiangsi on the 15th. In the face of this disaster, the Hunan Provincial Committee called off the uprising scheduled for Changsha that day. The third regiment having lost its right flank through the betrayal to its north, gave up its attack on Liu-yang just before the fourth regiment managed to capture the city on the night of the 16th. The next day this best of the communists' regiments was surrounded and almost totally destroyed, and the largely peasant force, the third regiment, met the same fate. 'Comrade Ma' denounced the leadership for cowardice and demanded the attacks be renewed, but to no avail.

Mao Tse-tung had a narrow escape while moving between units in Liu-yang county. He was captured by *min t'uan* and probably would have been shot had he not successfully fled and hid. The exact day on which this happened, and how long Mao was a captive, are not clear, but after his escape he made his way on foot to a mountain town where remnants of the third regiment had gathered and where he ordered the rest of the first regiment to assemble. Overcoming opposition, Mao persuaded the battered force of soldiers, miners, peasants and bandits to retreat to a mountain fastness on the Hunan-Kiangsi border, the famous bandit bastion, Ching-kang-shan.[275] There he took the first step on his long march to power. He did not learn until much later of his dismissal from the Politburo and the punishment meted out to other local communist leaders, whom the Politburo blamed for the Hunan failure.

In Kwangtung, the third area where autumn harvest revolts were ordered, there existed ill-equipped peasant forces in the south-eastern coastal counties of Hai-feng and Lu-feng, where P'eng P'ai had once been able to create a strong movement. In reaction to Li Chi-shen's anti-communist coup of mid April, a communist-led band had succeeded in capturing Hai-feng city on 1 May, executing most of the officials and other counter-revolutionaries who had not escaped. This force was driven out after 10 days, but insurgent units in the hinterland conducted sporadic raids and peasants defied their landlords where possible. On 22 August, heartened by the news that the forces of Yeh T'ing and Ho Lung were approaching, the Communist Party's Kwangtung Committee planned an insurrection timed for their arrival. Communist-led peasant corps were able to capture Lu-feng city on 8 September and Hai-feng on the 17th. Again they evacuated the cities after a period of looting and killing, and regrouped in a prepared mountain base. As the Yeh-Ho

275 In 1936, Mao gave Edgar Snow a vivid account of his escape, immortalized in *Red star over China*.

armies approached Swatow, peasants briefly captured two other county seats, Ch'ao-yang and Chieh-yang, but there was very little coordination between the local forces and the oncoming troops. With the help of a battalion of Yeh T'ing's troops, peasants fought a battle for P'u-ning city, but the battalion commander, a communist, would not permit the peasant force into the city for fear of excessive slaying. With the defeat at Swatow at the end of September, communist hopes of establishing a worker and peasant government in eastern Kwangtung faded temporarily.[276]

In the face of all these defeats, and under increasing danger of being discovered in Wuhan, Ch'ü Ch'iu-pai and some other members of the Politburo made their way in disguise to Shanghai where they re-established the secret headquarters of the Chinese Communist Party about the first of October 1927.

Attempts to unify the Kuomintang leadership

Conciliatory negotiations between the three main factions of the Kuomintang began as soon as the communist leaders had been expelled from Wuhan. The Shanghai faction was made up of a group of prestigious revolutionary veterans united in their opposition to the results of Sun Yat-sen's Russian orientation and admission of communists into the Kuomintang. Some, but not all of this group, had met in the Western Hills outside Peking in November 1925, where they strongly denounced the Communist Party's penetration of the Kuomintang, demanded the dismissal of Borodin, and censured Wang Ching-wei. This dissident group maintained the old Kuomintang headquarters in Shanghai as the party's true centre, and had even held a separate Second Kuomintang Congress in March 1926. A number of the Shanghai leaders cooperated with Chiang Kai-shek and his followers from Nanchang in the anti-communist action in the spring of 1927 and helped in the formation of the Nanking government in April but the group still retained their central party headquarters in Shanghai. A number of them nursed the grievance of having been 'expelled' from the Kuomintang by the Canton leadership, some of whom were now heading the Nanking faction. By late July the Wuhan group had made its break with the Chinese Communist Party and also had lost its most outspokenly radical – and idealistic – members. Reconciliation was not to be easy, because the Wuhan group at its Third

276 Hofheinz, *The broken wave*, 239–48; Eto, 'Hai-lu-feng – the first Chinese soviet government,' II, *CQ*, 9 (Jan.–March 1962) 165–70; and Wilbur, 'The ashes of defeat', 21, 36 and 43.

CEC Plenum in March 1927 had attempted to reduce Chiang Kai-shek's stature and authority, while after Wang Ching-wei's return to China, the Wuhan and Nanking factions had indulged in mutual public denunciations. Each claimed to be the true centre of party authority.

By August, military reverses suffered by the Nanking group and communist-led insurrections in territories claimed by the Wuhan group spurred on the negotiations. Nanking had weakened its northern front to send troops against Wuhan and this led to a recovery by the northern military coalition. Chang Tsung-ch'ang recaptured Hsu-chow on 25 July, and Sun Ch'uan-fang launched a drive towards his old base in the Yangtze delta. In mid to late July Feng Yü-hsiang telegraphed both Nanking and Wuhan urging reconciliation but neither side trusted him, and they were exchanging telegrams and emissaries of their own in early August.[277]

Within the Nanking group there was conflict between the Kwangsi clique, headed by Li Tsung-jen and Pai Ch'ung-hsi, and Chiang's Whampoa adherents. Even Ho Ying-ch'in's support for Chiang was uncertain. It seems the commander-in-chief had many political enemies because of his domineering ways, and that he was an obstacle to reconciliation. Now Chiang's reverses on the northern front, and the Nanking government's financial difficulties in spite of extortionate fund-raising in Shanghai, weakened his prestige. At a meeting of the Military Council at Nanking on 12 August, Chiang stated his intention to resign as commander-in-chief and to leave the defence of the capital to the other generals. When they raised no objection, an intolerable insult, he departed for Shanghai, and was soon followed by Chang Ching-chiang, Hu Han-min, Ts'ai Yuan-p'ei, Wu Chih-hui, and Li Shih-tseng, to try to dissuade him. Chiang's retirement statement published on 13 August, emphasized his sole desire to serve the party; if his retirement would promote unity, he was happy to retire. He reviewed the party's history, Sun Yat-sen's decision to ally with Russia and admit the communists, and justified his own role in expelling the communists for their intrigues within the Kuomintang. He urged his comrades to come together at Nanking and then to complete the Northern Expedition.[278]

After Chiang's departure, emissaries from the two sides met at Lu-

277 The complicated process of unification is explored by Professor Li Yun-han on the basis of Kuomintang archival material in his *TJK*, 756-812. *KMWH*, 17. 3104-09, for telegrams exchanged by Nanking and Hankow from 8 Aug. to 20 Sept.
278 There are differing interpretations of Chiang's retirement at this critical moment. His retirement statement is in *KMWH*, 15. 2567-73, and *The China Yearbook 1928*, 1380-5. On extortionate fund-raising by Chiang's agents, see the well-documented study by Parks M. Coble, Jr., 'The Kuomintang regime and the Shanghai capitalists, 1927-29', *CQ*, 77 (March 1979) 1-24, esp. pp. 7-12. See also Dr Coble's book on the same subject.

shan to discuss terms of reconciliation and decided that on 15 September the Central Executive and Central Supervisory Committees should meet in Nanking to settle differences. But before this could happen, Nanking itself was in danger of being captured by the revived forces of Sun Ch'uan-fang, which succeeded in crossing the Yangtze just 15 miles east of the city and had cut the railway leading to Shanghai. This was on 26 August, at a time when elements of Li Tsung-jen's old Seventh Corps and of Ho Ying-ch'in's old First Corps were holding the city, though the two commanders were at odds. Furthermore, T'ang Sheng-chih had sent two corps under Ho Chien and Liu Hsing towards Nanking in coordination with Sun's drive. In this critical situation, Generals Li and Ho set aside their differences and sent their forces into battle, assisted by Pai Ch'ung-hsi and all other available troops. The Nationalists finally defeated the northern invaders in a six-day, seesaw battle which ended on 31 August. Some 30,000 of Sun's troops, their retreat cut off by the Nationalist navy, were taken prisoner, along with a mountain of arms. The Lung-t'an battle was one of the key engagements of the entire campaign. It saved Nanking and the rich delta region, and made possible the reconstitution of the Nationalist government.[279] The First Army then drove Sun's shattered remnants back up the Tientsin–Pukow Railway towards Hsu-chow.

T'an Yen-k'ai and Sun Fo, representing the Wuhan faction, had gone to Nanking for preliminary discussions of party unification, and in early September, with Nanking saved, Wang Ching-wei and most of the other Wuhan leaders followed them to negotiate with their recent rivals. T'ang Sheng-chih, though already in Anking supervising Wuhan's 'Eastern Expedition', declined to come. During talks in Nanking and Shanghai between 5 and 12 September the three factions worked out an ingenious compromise which gave 'face' to all. They would create a Special Central Committee to manage party affairs, to reconstruct the national government and the Military Council, and to prepare for and call the Third Party Congress in January 1928. The congress would then start the party on a new course. Even the method for holding election of delegates to the congress was specified. Thus the Special Central Committee would replace the Central Executive Committees that had been elected at the two rival Second Congresses. In constituting the committee, each faction nominated six representatives and three alternates, and this group was then to elect 14 most prestigious political and military persons – Wang Ching-wei, Hu Han-min, Chang Chi, Wu Chih-hui, Tai Chi-t'ao, Chang

<hr>

279 *PFCS*, 3. 851–916; *Kuo-min Ko-ming Chün Tung-lu-chün chan-shih chi-lueh*, 94–105; Jordan, *The Northern Expedition*, 138–41. In interviews, Generals Li and Pai remembered the Lung-t'an battle as crucial to the success of the Northern Expedition.

Ching-chiang, Chiang Kai-shek, T'ang Sheng-chih, Feng Yü-hsiang, Yen Hsi-shan, Yang Shu-chuang, Li Chi-shen, Ho Ying-ch'in and Pai Ch'ung-hsi. Thus the Special Central Committee would have 32 members and nine alternates and would include, at least nominally, the most important military leaders. No communists were listed, of course, but the names of Soong Ch'ing-ling, Eugene Chen and even T. V. Soong, were omitted as well.[280]

On 13 September, however, Wang Ching-wei resigned and departed for Kiukiang with some of his close followers. He was dissatisfied that his proposal to call a Fourth Plenum of the Central Executive Committee had been rejected by those who refused to accept the validity of the Third Plenum that had met in Hankow the previous March. Wang professed to consider the Special Central Committee illegal. He followed Chinese practice by issuing a formalistic resignation statement of repentence for his past errors.[281] The other leaders went right ahead to set up the Special Central Committee in Nanking on 15 September by the agreed-upon process. They also issued a telegram rejecting Wang's resignation and requesting Hu Han-min, Wu Chih-hui and Chiang Kai-shek to resume their duties. The Special Central Committee then elected a new Government Council, with Wang Ching-wei, Hu Han-min, Li Lieh-chün, Ts'ai Yuan-p'ei, and T'an Yen-k'ai as its Standing Committee, and appointed four ministers to carry out governmental operations.[282] Neither Wang nor Hu would serve.

The compromise settlement faced obstacles from the beginning. The new committee was vulnerable to the objection of being extra-constitutional, several former Nanking and Shanghai leaders had not been mollified, Chiang Kai-shek still absented himself, and Wang Ching-wei openly opposed it. Early in October the new Nanking group sent a delegation to try to persuade Wang and by the 10th it appeared that a new compromise had been reached. Next day, T'an Yen-k'ai, Li Tsung-jen, Ho Ying-ch'in, and Ch'eng Ch'ien in Nanking issued a circular telegram proposing that the Fourth Plenum of the Central Executive Committee convene in Nanking on 1 November. Even this concession apparently was not enough for Wang and his military prop, T'ang Sheng-chih, who demanded to be appointed commander-in-chief in place of Chiang Kai-shek. On the 21st the Wuhan Political Council, a mere shadow of its former self, issued a manifesto claiming exclusive authority over party, military and political affairs in its territory pending restoration of the

280 Names and details are in *TJK*, 766–69. Also, Kao Yin-tsu, *Chronology*, 268–9.
281 Wang's resignation telegrams are in *KMWH*, 17. 3105–6, and *China Yearbook*, *1928*, 1391.
282 *The China Yearbook, 1928*, 1390–7 for lists of names.

Central Executive Committee, and T'ang Sheng-chih denounced Nanking in a circular telegram and announced plans to overthrow the usurpers there. Wang Ching-wei secretly departed for Canton via Shanghai, arriving in the old revolutionary base on 29 October.[283]

T'ang Sheng-chih's challenge probably was a response to the Nanking Government's order of 20 October for a punitive campaign against him. His alleged intrigues with Sun Ch'uan-fang and Chang Tso-lin reportedly had been discovered after the Lung-t'an battle. The campaign against him was to be commanded by Ch'eng Ch'ien, an old Hunanese rival, but the force he led included the armies of Li Tsung-jen and Chu P'ei-te, a naval flotilla, and some aircraft. T'ang, it appears, had many enemies, for Feng Yü-hsiang threatened him from the north, Li Chi-shen from the south, while T'an Yen-k'ai's field commander, Lu Ti-p'ing, sent his forces down the Yangtze from the west. Li Tsung-jen's army methodically pushed Ho Chien's forces on the north side of the Yangtze back towards Hupei, while Ch'eng Ch'ien's army on the south bank drove Liu Hsing's troops towards Kiangsi, where they faced the army of Chu P'ei-te. By early November Nanking's naval units had captured the gateway to the Wuhan cities and Lu Ti-p'ing was pressing on Yo-chow, endangering T'ang Sheng-chih's escape route to Hunan. T'ang's subordinate generals, Ho Chien, Liu Hsing, Yeh Ch'i, Chou Lan, and Li P'in-hsien, decided to retreat to their old bases in Hunan where each would fend for himself. On 12 November, T'ang announced his retirement and secretly fled on a Japanese vessel for safety in Japan.[284] The Northern Expedition military coalition was beginning to fall apart.

Wang Ching-wei returned to Canton to set up a party headquarters in opposition to the Special Central Committee in Nanking. A few leftist Central Committee members such as Ch'en Kung-po, Ku Meng-yü, Kan Nai-kuang, and Ho Hsiang-ning (Mme Liao Chung-k'ai) joined him, while his principal military supporter continued to be Chang Fa-k'uei. After the Nanchang Uprising, General Chang sent his remaining troops – three infantry divisions, an artillery regiment, and a training regiment – on a march to Shao-kuan, near the northern border of Kwangtung at the end of the rail line to Canton, while Chang returned to Canton by sea on the invitation of Li Chi-shen, arriving about 27 September. When his troops reached Shao-kuan he ordered them to Canton, where they probably were a more powerful force than Li Chi-shen commanded, for

283 *TJK*, 775–7 and *FRUS*, 1927, 2. 31–2. Kao Yin-tsu, *Chronology*, 273.
284 *TJK*, 780–2, based in part on Ch'en Hsün-cheng's account of the anti-T'ang campaign and documents in *KMWH*, 17. 2996–3064. Jordan, *The Northern Expedition*, 145. *FRUS*, 1927, 2. 36–7.

Li's troops were spread through the delta towns and he had sent a number of regiments to the Swatow area to suppress the Ho Lung–Yeh T'ing incursion. After that successful operation, General Li began bringing back his troops so that when Wang Ching-wei arrived on 29 October, the military balance between the two generals seemed approximately equal. Li Chi-shen's support for Wang was only nominal, for he had close connections with Huang Shao-hsiung of the Kwangsi clique that supported the Nanking Special Committee and its government. However, the campaign against T'ang Sheng-chih had weakened the Kwangsi clique's hold on Nanking, and the Special Committee itself was in trouble.[285]

Upon arrival, Wang Ching-wei issued a call for the Fourth Plenum of the Central Executive Committee to meet in Canton, inviting the members in Nanking and Shanghai to attend. Li Chi-shen declined to join in this call. More telegraphic negotiations with the Nanking leaders ensued, since they had previously agreed to begin the plenum on 1 November, but in Nanking. It did not meet, but on that day Wang opened central Kuomintang headquarters in Canton. The city's leftist labour movement, which had been severely repressed under Li Chi-shen's anti-communist regime, showed signs of life after Chang Fa-k'uei and Wang Ching-wei returned. Several thousand workers carrying red flags marched on Wang's home, begging him to free labour leaders who had been imprisoned, but the police dispersed them. An effort to revive the anti-British boycott may have indicated a communist initiative, for communists had dominated the old strike committee. Wang's branch political council and the provincial government arranged to disband the remaining strikers from Hong Kong with a monetary gift for each.[286] Apparently Wang's faction was not eager for labour disturbances. As it turned out, Wang's stay in Canton was only fleeting, for early in November Chiang Kai-shek re-entered the political arena with a proposal for a Chiang-Wang alliance against Nanking.

General Chiang had departed for Japan on 28 September where, among other activities, he won agreement from Mme Soong that he might marry her youngest daughter, Mei-ling. This would relate him by marriage with Sun Yat-sen's widow, with T. V. Soong, and with the wife of H. H. Kung.[287] He also met privately with the Japanese prime minister, Tanaka Giichi, on 5 November. Baron Tanaka commended Chiang on his timely retirement but told him that only he could save the Chinese revolution.

285 Kao Yin-tsu, *Chronology*, 269–73. *TJK*, 777, has Wang arrive in Canton on 28 Oct.
286 Kao Yin-tsu, *Chronology*, 14 Oct., 1 and 8 Nov. Also S. Bernard Thomas, '*Proletarian hegemony' in the Chinese revolution and the Canton Commune of 1927*, 21.
287 Hollington K. Tong, *Chiang Kai-shek*, 100–1. The marriage was on 1 December, in both civil and Christian ceremonies. Later Chiang Kai-shek adopted Christianity.

He advised Chiang to consolidate the Nationalist position south of the Yangtze and not to become entangled in warlord politics of the north. Japan, the prime minister said, would assist Chiang in his anti-communist efforts so long as international considerations permitted and Japan's own interests were not sacrificed. Chiang responded that a northward drive was imperative and appealed for Japanese assistance so as to wipe out the impression that Japan was aiding Chang Tso-lin. Only thus, he said, could Japan ensure the safety of its nationals in China.[288] Each man had issued an appeal and a warning.

Chiang Kai-shek arranged for T. V. Soong to go to Canton to effect a reconciliation with Wang Ching-wei. Soong arrived on 2 November and Chiang returned to Shanghai on the 10th, when he telegraphed inviting Wang to join him for discussions, agreeing with Wang's fundamental point that the Central Executive Committee should convene to settle all problems in the party. There should be preparatory discussions in Shanghai. T'an Yen-k'ai on behalf of the Nanking Special Committee also telegraphed Wang proposing Shanghai as the site for discussions preparatory to calling the Fourth CEC Plenum.[289]

As Wang Ching-wei and Li Chi-shen prepared to depart for the meeting in Shanghai, General Li asked his associate, Huang Shao-hsiung, to come to Canton to take over control of Li's troops and Wang seconded the invitation. Chang Fa-k'uei agreed to take a trip abroad if Li would support Wang; the trip was financed by a grant of Hong Kong $50,000 from the provincial treasury – that is, by courtesy of General Li, who was happy to see Chang Fa-k'uei gone. General Chang placed his troops under command of his trusted associate, General Huang Ch'i-hsiang, and left for Hong Kong on the 14th, whence he was to sail for Shanghai with Wang and Li.

It was all a ruse, a classic double-cross. Chang Fa-k'uei 'missed' the boat when Wang and Li departed Hong Kong on the 16th. In the pre-dawn hours of the 17th Huang Ch'i-hsiang staged a coup in Canton, supported by Generals Hsueh Yueh and Li Fu-lin. Their troops surrounded the various headquarters and barracks of the Li-Huang forces in Canton and disarmed them. They meant to arrest Huang Shao-hsiung, who, being forewarned, narrowly escaped. Chang Fa-k'uei returned to Canton on the 17th when the coup was over and, together with Ch'en Kung-po and others of Wang Ching-wei's supporters, set up a new

288 Iriye, *After imperialism*, 157–8, based upon Japanese Foreign Office records.
289 Kao Yin-tsu, *Chronology*, 274. GBFO 405/255. Confidential. *Further correspondence respecting China*, no. 13448, Oct.–Dec. 1927, no. 116, enclosure, Consul-General J. F. Brenan, Canton, to Miles Lampson in Peking, 22 Nov. 1927, describing Canton politics of the past few weeks, including T.V. Soong's visit.

provincial government. The coup went by the name of 'Protecting the party'. On board ship between Hong Kong and Shanghai, Li Chi-shen could do nothing, and Wang Ching-wei could profess ignorance of the whole affair.[290]

Very few in Shanghai believed Wang. His political position there was weakened by the coup, though it had strengthened his supporters' hold on wealthy Kwangtung. Party veterans in Shanghai – Hu Han-min, Wu Chih-hui, Ts'ai Yuan-p'ei, Li Shih-tseng and Chang Ching-chiang – scorned Wang for his treachery and some of them refused to see him. Li Chi-shen denounced the coup as a communist plot, recounting a number of incidents before the coup and reports he received shortly after, to back his charge, which Wang, of course, denied. According to Wang the coup was directed entirely against the illegal Special Central Committee. Nevertheless, the charge – not necessarily the facts – proved very damaging to Wang within a few weeks. Li Tsung-jen and Pai Ch'ung-hsi of the Kwangsi clique, who had just won Wuhan from T'ang Sheng-chih, were furious. They even discussed a military campaign to restore Li Chi-shen in Canton. Thus the preliminary discussions in Shanghai towards convening the Central Executive Committee Plenum started off in discord. The discord was particularly intense between those who upheld the Special Central Committee and those, like Wang, who opposed it. An old feud between Hu Han-min and Wang Ching-wei continued unabated. Chiang Kai-shek, having had nothing publicly to do with Kuomintang politics during the past three months, was in a favoured position to mediate. Preliminary 'chats' began in his house in Shanghai's French Concession on 24 November.[291]

A more formal 'preparatory conference' to plan the CEC Plenum met in Chiang's place between 3 and 10 December, with some 35 of the 80 members and alternates of the Central Executive and Central Supervisory Committees attending, but controversy between various factions was as intense as ever. Conflict was fanned by the Nanking government's order on 2 December – the day before the conference was to open – for a military expedition to punish Chang Fa-k'uei and Huang Ch'i-hsiang for their coup 'in league with the Communist Party', since the Nanking government was the creation of the questionable Special Central Com-

290 Li Yun-han provides a vivid account, quoting from Huang Shao-hsiung, and from Li Chi-shen's bitter accusation against Chang Fa-k'uei: *TJK*, 790–4. Kao Yin-tsu, *Chronology*, 275; *FRUS*, 1927, 2. 35–6. Consul-General Brenan, in the account cited above, speculated that Li Chi-shen was not tricked but, knowing his position in Canton was undermined, went to Shanghai leaving Huang Shao-hsiung to 'hold the baby'. On the evidence available, this seems unlikely.

291 *TJK*, 792–4; Kao Yin-tsu, *Chronology*, 275–6. *KMWH*, 17. 3113–22 for related documents.

mittee. Charges and threats of impeachment flew back and forth, and only four meetings could be held as one group or another absented itself to caucus. Finally, on 10 December, after Chiang Kai-shek had issued a plea for compromise and unity, Wang Ching-wei offered a resolution requesting Chiang to resume his duties as commander-in-chief. He also intimated his own intention to retire in the interest of party unity. Wang's motion passed unanimously. Indeed, there had been a campaign of circular telegrams from Feng Yü-hsiang, Yen Hsi-shan, Ho Ying-ch'in and other generals demanding that Chiang resume command – a campaign quite probably engineered by Chiang himself. Though General Chiang did not immediately indicate his decision, the preparatory conference also voted to request him to take charge of calling the Fourth CEC Plenum, which should be held between 1 and 15 January. All contentious problems should be settled by that plenum. In short, the Kuomintang leadership was so torn by dissension that the preparatory conference could resolve only routine matters. Chiang's position in the party had been considerably enhanced, and now he might influence strongly, if not determine, which CEC members and alternates might attend the forthcoming plenum that was supposed to reunite the party.[292]

No sooner had the preparatory committee adjourned than Shanghai learned the devastating news of a communist-led uprising in Canton, which began before dawn on 11 December. At first apparently successful in gaining control of parts of the city, the uprising was marked by looting, burning and many executions. Most of Chang Fa-k'uei's troops were off on a campaign against Huang Shao-hsiung, or in the East River district, but he ordered them back. Enough had returned by the third day that General Chang with the help of Li Fu-lin, could suppress the revolt – ferociously. The devastation of Canton had been severe. Wang Ching-wei's political position was irreparably compromised. He first went into a hospital for safety and then sailed for France on a second exile on 17 December. Other leading members of his faction were simply excluded from further participation in high-level Kuomintang work for several years.[293]

292 Kao Yin-tsu, *Chronology*, 276–8; *The China Yearbook, 1928*, 1400; GBFO 405/256. Confidential. *Further correspondence respecting China*, 13583, Jan.–March 1928, No. 154, enclosure, Consul-General Sidney Barton, Shanghai, to Miles Lampson, Peking, 11 Dec. 1927, a well-informed report on the Preparatory Conference. Sir Sidney listed 35 who attended, Hu Han-min was the most conspicuous for his absence. Sir Sidney listed the following as the 'Nanking die-hards', who opposed Wang Ching-wei's faction: T'an Yen-k'ai, Ts'ai Yuan-p'ei, Li Shih-tseng, Li Tsung-jen, Ho Ying-ch'in, Sun Fo, Chang Ching-chiang, Li Chi-sen, Wu Ch'ao-shu, and Wu T'ieh-ch'eng, a very interesting combination. *KMWH*, 16. 2875–9 for Chiang's appeal to the conferees. *Ibid*. 17. 3122–4, for orders for a punitive campaign against Chang and Huang.
293 Wang's apologia and retirement statement is in *KMWH*, 17. 3134–5.

The Canton commune

The disastrous Canton uprising, engineered by a small group of daring Chinese communist leaders to carry out general instructions of the new Provisional Politburo in Shanghai, marked a low point in the Communist Party's long struggle for power. The last large-scale communist-led urban insurrection in China for two decades, it was a convincing failure of the insurrectionist policy mandated by the Comintern in July 1927. The international communist movement put on a brave face about the disaster, emphasizing the heroism of the participants and pronouncing the uprising a symbolic victory, but it was, nevertheless, a major miscalculation in itself, and another failure in the Comintern's effort to direct revolution in another country. The defeat and brutal suppression which followed struck a fearful blow to the radical labour movement in Canton, and had adverse effects in major cities elsewhere. Reports of the slaughter, burning and looting in Canton during the first two days, and assumed Russian involvement, turned Chinese public opinion against the Communist Party and Soviet Russia. The Nationalist government severed relations with Russia, and the Kuomintang terminated its tattered 'alliance' with the Comintern. Since there are many reportorial and analytic accounts of the uprising and its suppression, we present here only a factual sketch.[294]

294 Nearly all histories of the Chinese Communist Party describe the Canton uprising, which was well reported in the world press.

The following are reports by observers: J. Calvin Huston, 'Peasants, workers, and soldiers revolt of December 11-13, 1927 at Canton, China.' Dispatch no. 699 to J.V.A. MacMurray, U.S. minister to Peking, 30 Dec. 1927, in Hoover Institution, Stanford, California, J. Calvin Huston Collection, package II, pt II, folder 5, item 20. (Item 12 is an original handbill in Chinese dated 11 Dec. 1927, announcing the Soviet and giving a list of officials.) The gist of Consul-General Huston's telegraphic reports may be read in *FRUS*, 1927, 2. 39-40; they are available in US National Archives microfilm. GBFO 405/ 256. Confidential. *Further correspondence respecting China*, 13583, no. 71, enclosure 1, James Brenan, Canton, to Miles Lampson, Peking, 15 Dec. 1927, a description; enclosure 3, a handbill distributed in Canton on Dec. 11 (trans.); and *ibid.* no. 80, enclosure 4, Cecil Clementi, governor of Hong Kong to Mr Amery, colonial secretary, London, 15 Dec., a description; and enclosure 5, translation from *Red flag* of 11 Dec., announcing the Canton Soviet and list of officials. GBFO 371/13199, contains many dispatches from Governor Clementi giving intelligence on conditions in Canton and Kwangtung from December to February 1928. A vivid eye-witness account by Earl Swisher, who went into Canton while the insurrection was underway and after it was crushed, is in Kenneth W. Rea, ed. *Canton in revolution: the collected papers of Earl Swisher, 1925-1928*, 89-125, including translations of documents and grim photographs. *Kung-fei huo-kuo shih-liao hui-pien*, 1. 510-65, reprints Chinese newspaper reports of 13-15 December, and a valuable document, a Resolution of the CCP Politburo of 3 January 1928 on 'The meaning and lessons of the Canton insurrection'.

Scholarly and well-annotated analyses that use the extensive retrospective literature are S. Bernard Thomas, *'Proletarian hegemony' in the Chinese revolution*; Hsiao, *Chinese communism in 1927*, 134-56; and *TJK*, 794-9.

The Communist Party's Provisional Politburo held an enlarged meeting in Shanghai on 10 and 11 November to assess the recent defeats and develop plans to rebuild the party. To 'start on the path of true revolutionary bolshevik struggle', it laid down a general strategy for revolution,[295] after which plans for an insurrection in Kwangtung were worked out with Chang T'ai-lei, secretary of the Kwangtung Provincial Committee. News of Huang Ch'i-hsiang's coup against Huang Shao-hsiung in Canton on 17 November, made it seem likely there would soon be conflict between the armies of Chang Fa-k'uei and Li Chi-shen. To take advantage of this opportunity, the Politburo issued an 11-point programme on 18 November, which instructed the Kwangtung communists to unleash peasant insurrections in the countryside, worker uprisings in county centres, a general political strike in Canton, and military mutinies.[296] On 26 November the Kwangtung Provincial Committee resolved to stage an insurrection and appointed a five-man Revolutionary Military Council, with Chang T'ai-lei as chairman and Yeh T'ing as commander-in-chief. The council developed a political programme, began military preparations, selected officers for a soviet, mobilized workers in the remaining red unions, secretly recruited among the troops, and tried to establish contacts with nearby peasant movements. On 7 December the Kwangtung Provincial Committee secretly convened a meeting in Canton that was called a 'worker-peasant-soldier congress', and this adopted a soviet of 15 deputies, of whom nine were listed as workers and three each as peasants and soldiers, though the Provincial Committee later admitted that all were intellectuals. This meeting picked 13 December as the date for the Canton uprising.[297]

By then the Revolutionary Military Council had considerable resources. The cadet Training Regiment, which Chang Fa-k'uei had brought from Wuhan where its men had been under the influence of Yun Tai-ying, had some communist officers and Yeh Chien-ying was its deputy commander. The council had organized a Red Guard made up of about 500 former strike pickets from the Hong Kong–Canton strike organization and some 1,500 workers from unions still under communist leadership. There were also some communists among the cadets at the Whampoa Academy. The main difficulty was a shortage of arms. Canton was lightly protected in early December, since Chang Fa-k'uei had sent most of his troops out of the city to ward off the forces of Huang Shao-hsiung and

---

295 The plan appeared as 'Central announcement number 16', dated 18 Nov, in *Chung-yang t'ung-hsun*, 13, (30 Nov. 1927), 1–6.
296 Thomas, '*Proletarian hegemony*' in the Chinese revolution, 21–2.
297 *Ibid.* 23.

Li Chi-shen, leaving only small units to guard various headquarters and the arsenals. Li Fu-lin still controlled Honam Island, but with only a small guard since most of his troops were at Kongmoon. Canton had an efficient and well-armed police force. An intangible factor was the leftist sentiments of General Huang Ch'i-hsiang, commander of the Fourth Corps, who had been much influenced by Teng Yen-ta. Liao Shang-kuo, who was close to the communists, headed the political department of the Fourth Corps, and General Huang knew that communist leaders were slipping into Canton from Hong Kong; he even kept Yun Tai-ying in his home in Tung-shan.

News of communist activity in Canton and radical articles appearing in the journal published by the political department of the Fourth Corps apparently alarmed Wang Ching-wei in Shanghai, for on 9 and 10 December he telegraphed Ch'en Kung-po and Chang Fa-k'uei, directing them to take action against the communists. They should send troops to surround and search the Soviet consulate which, Wang charged, was the headquarters of a planned insurrection, and they should expel the Soviet consul. Huang Ch'i-hsiang should retire temporarily while the clean-up of communists was carried out.[298]

On 9 December the police discovered a cache of bombs. This, and news that Chang Fa-k'uei planned to disarm the Training Regiment, led the Revolutionary Military Council to advance the date of the uprising. They hastily called General Yeh T'ing to Canton from Hong Kong. Inauspiciously, he arrived to take command only a few hours before the revolt began. Also, advancing the date by two days may have made it impossible for some peasant units that had been recruited to reach the city. Reportedly only 500 came in from nearby suburbs to join the insurrection.

The insurrectionists had the advantage of surprise. At 3.30 a.m. Sunday, 11 December, workers' Red Guards attacked the Bureau of Public Safety – police headquarters – and were soon reinforced by most of the cadet Training Regiment, which had revolted and shot 15 of its officers. It was now commanded by Yeh Chien-ying. After subduing the Bureau of Public Safety, the attackers released some 700 prisoners who had been taken in raids during the past two days. These men, mostly from communist dominated labour unions, also joined the fight. By noon most police stations in Canton city had been taken, and several, though not all, the Canton headquarters of various military units in the field had been captured. The rebels controlled the railway stations, telegraph and post

298 *KMWH*, 17. 3124-5.

offices, and had taken over governmental offices and Kuomintang provincial headquarters. They captured the Central Bank but were unable to open the vault where silver and banknotes were stored. A fire soon gutted the building. They also looted other banks and money shops. The Bureau of Public Safety became the centre of the new soviet government. By nightfall there had been considerable private looting, burning of property, and shooting of suspected enemies, including about 300 of the police. However, Honam island escaped because it was protected by gunboats and Li Fu-lin's guards, and it was to Honam that Ch'en Kung-po, Chang Fa-k'uei, Huang Ch'i-hsiang and other Kuomintang loyalists fled early Sunday morning. Shameen remained a foreign sanctuary, and the British consul general assisted the loyalists by sending their telegrams to recall troops from the West River region.[299]

On the morning of the attack the soviet government proclaimed itself. The Kwangtung Provincial Committee of the Communist Party had printed several thousand leaflets announcing the formation of the Canton Soviet and its political programme, and appealing for mass support. *Red Flag* came out with a similar flier listing the officials of the new regime, which was to be headed by the popular leader of the Seamen's Union, Su Chao-cheng, who was at the moment away. His position was filled temporarily by Chang T'ai-lei. Nine other persons held the other 11 positions in the worker-peasant-soldier soviet, most of them, and possibly all, being communists. Four, in addition to Su Chao-sheng, were labour leaders.[300] Although some 3,000 workers, by police estimate, joined in the fighting or looting, they were a very small proportion of Canton's unionized work force, estimated at 290,000. Others had been so intimidated by the previous eight months of repression, or were already so hostile to the communist labour leadership, that they either remained passive or opposed the uprising. Very little popular support for the soviet emerged. Shopkeepers followed the classic tactic during a coup, shuttering their shops for fear of looting. Their apprentices and clerks remained passive. Few of the disarmed soldiers joined the revolt, and the populace simply stayed away from the two meetings that were called to show mass support.[301] Would a general strike called in advance of the

299 Stated in Consul-general Brenan's report of 15 Dec., in GBFO 405/256. Confidential . . . 13583, no. 71, enclosure 1, cited above f.n. 294.
300 Translations in *Ibid.* enclosure 3, and no. 80, enclosure 5. Photos and Swisher's translations in Rea, ed. *Canton in revolution*, 99–102. Biographies of Su, Chang, Ch'en Yü, P'eng P'ai (listed in absentia), Yang Yin, Yeh T'ing and Yün Tai-ying are in Klein and Clark, *Biographic dictionary*. The others listed were Chou Wen-yung, Huang P'ing, Ho Lai and Hsu Kuang-ying.
301 Yeh T'ing later described eloquently the hostility or apathy of the Cantonese towards the uprising; quoted in Hsiao, *Chinese communism in 1927*, 141–2.

uprising have made any difference? The Revolutionary Military Committee had decided against trying to call out a strike because the communist position with labour was too weak; but later the Politburo reproved them for this mistake.

On the second day, Chang T'ai-lei was killed in action at the age of 29. Chang had been one of the founders of the Socialist Youth Corps and an early member of the Chinese Communist Party. He was a central figure in both organizations, and particularly in relations with the Comintern. He was one of the organizers of the Hong Kong – Canton strike and boycott movement in 1925, had served as chief secretary in Borodin's Canton office, and later was Borodin's Chinese secretary in Wuhan. His death left General Yeh T'ing in command, but he had not been in Canton for 18 months, and was unfamilar with local conditions, party personnel, and sources of support. His hastily assembled military force soon faced overwhelming odds.

Generals Chang Fa-k'uei and Li Fu-lin recalled their troops from the West River region and they began arriving in Honam and on the outskirts of Canton on the night of December 12/13, as did a regiment of Hsueh Yueh's division and the independent regiment led by Mo Hsiung. On the morning of the 13th gunboats machine-gunned the bund to clear it for the landing of troops crossing from Honam. Other units closed in from west, north and east. Fighting squads from the Mechanics Union, eager to settle old scores, joined in the attack. The battle to recover the Public Security Office, the headquarters of the soviet, lasted four hours. By dusk all fighting had ceased. Many of the revolting workers and troops died at their posts, others went into hiding, and some escaped towards the north-west. Virtually all the planners and leaders of the revolt succeeded in escaping one way or another. Heinz Neumann, the resident Comintern agent, who helped in the planning and financing, also slipped away.

Two Russians were killed in the battle against Hsueh Yueh's troops and two others participating in the defence of the workers, peasants and soldiers soviet headquarters were captured. When Vice-consul M. Hassis, armed with grenades, attempted to reach the headquarters in a consulate car, he was seized. Searchers arrested two other Russians hiding near their consulate. All five men were marched through the streets and then shot. In a raid on the Russian consulate, Boris Pokvalisky, the consul-general, was arrested together with his wife and several Russian women and children, but the consular body intervened and persuaded the outraged authorities to spare their lives. A new regime in Canton deported them at the end of the year.[302] Documents found in the consulate allegedly implicated it in the conspiracy. The Russian Foreign Office denied any relationship between the consulate and the uprising.

Three days of fighting, incendiarism and looting devastated Canton. When the fighting ceased, the streets were littered with dead, and nearly 900 buildings on 46 streets were burned out, according to later police reports. The Communist Party's Kwangtung Provincial Committee estimated a few weeks after the event that more than 200 communist comrades and more than 2,000 Red Guards and Red Army men were killed, but that no more than 100 deaths were reported on the enemy side. Those killed during the uprising probably were fewer than those slaughtered after it had been put down. Execution squads rounded up several thousand suspects and dispatched them in an orgy of revenge. The American consulate estimated than between three and four thousand men and women, many of them innocent of any connection with the uprising, were executed, and the authorities admitted the killing of 2,000. Later communist sources reported even larger losses.[303]

The Nationalist government in Nanking ordered all Russian consulates and other facilities in nationalist areas to be closed and the personnel deported in consequence of the assumed responsibility of the Soviet consulate for the Canton uprising. In Hankow, Garrison Commander Hu Tsung-to ordered a raid on the Soviet consulate and all other institutions thought to harbour communists. On 16 December troops, police and plain-clothesmen raided and searched the consulate and other establishments, rounding up more than 200 suspected foreigners and Chinese in the French Concession and the three former concessions. Troops surrounded Sun Yat-sen University in Wuchang and other schools, and arrested hundreds of students. Then followed executions of labour leaders and students, many of them women. Two noted leftists were seized in the Japanese concession on 17 December and executed forthwith: Li Han-chün, one of the founders of the Chinese Communist Party, but no longer a member; and Chan Ta-pei, a noted anti-Manchu revolutionary,

302 Huston, 'Peasants, workers, and soldiers revolt', 36–8. Pictures of the slain men are in Hoover Institution, J. Calvin Huston Collection, package II, pt II. folder 3, no. 11. The collection also contains the personal papers of Vice-consul Hassis.

303 Hsiao, *Chinese communism in 1927*, 142, citing 'Resolution on the Canton Uprising', adopted by the Kwangtung Provincial Committee, 1–5 Jan. 1928; Huston, 'Peasant, workers and soldiers revolt', 28; and Thomas, '*Proletarian hegemony' in the Chinese revolution*, 27, citing *Bolshevik*, no. 12, Jan. 1928, in L. P. Deliusin, ed. *Kantonskaia Kommuna* (The Canton Commune), 207.

associate of Sun Yat-sen, and a member of the Kuomintang Central Executive Committee.[304]

In Canton, most of the members of the government set up by Wang Ching-wei, left in disgrace, some taking with them funds from the provincial treasury. Chang Fa-k'uei and Huang Ch'i-hsiang accepted pro-forma responsibility for the Canton uprising and resigned their commands. They sent their troops to the East River region, where they were defeated by forces under Ch'en Ming-shu. Li Chi-shen's troops retook Canton on 29 December and he returned in early January.

Thus by the end of the year, the Wang Ching-wei faction had lost its base of power, Wang was on his way to France and most of his important adherents were in eclipse. The Chinese Communist Party had been devastated by eight months of suppressions and abortive uprisings. A score of its best leaders and many thousands of its members and followers were slain. It would take many years of desperate struggle to rebuild the shattered party.

THE FINAL DRIVE – PEKING CAPTURED AND NANKING THE NEW CAPITAL

Preparations for a renewed drive on Peking

In order to complete the military unification of China, Chiang Kai-shek, now the most influential member of the Nationalist Party, had to secure adequate finances, regroup the widely scattered military forces, and attempt to reunite the party leadership. He persuaded T. V. Soong to resume the post of finance minister, in which he had been extraordinarily effective in the Canton days, and Soong planned in various ways to increase revenues, which were coming to the government only from Kiangsu and Chekiang. On taking his post on 7 January Soong announced that monthly income was less than three million yuan but expenses were 11 million. He hoped by March to increase income to 10 million a month.[305]

To rebuild a victorious military coalition could not be easy, for the

---

304 GBFO 405/256. Confidential . . . 13583, no. 144, enclosures 1–6, Acting Consul-General Harold Porter, Hankow, 21 Dec. 1927 to Miles Lampson in Peking, with extracts from the *Hankow Herald*, 17 to 21 Dec. 1927, describing the raids, reporting more than 700 Chinese suspects and 17 Russians arrested, and giving names of 20 persons executed, including five women students ranging in age from 20 to 26. Biographies of Li in Klein and Clark, *Biographic dictionary* and Chan in Boorman and Howard, *Biographical dictionary*.

Strangely, the raids apparently failed to apprehend any of the 39 communist leaders who attended a Hupei Provincial Party Congress in Hankow on 14 and 15 December, described in Hsiao Tso-liang, 'The dispute over a Wuhan insurrection in 1927', *CQ* 33 (Jan.–March 1968) 108–122, p. 133.

305 Kao, *Chronology*, 281.

original valiant Fourth Corps was now much reduced and its top commanders were in retirement; most of the old Eighth Corps had been driven back to Hunan and its commander was in Japan; and the Seventh Corps, now building its power base in Hupei, was led by Chiang's rivals, Li Tsung-jen and Pai Ch'ung-hsi, who, in turn, were linked to Huang Shao-hsiung and Li Chi-shen in the south. Chang Tso-lin's Manchurian Army and Chang Tsung-ch'ang's Shantungese were still formidable opponents for the conglomeration of forces Chiang could command; but there was hope that Feng Yü-hsiang and Yen Hsi-shan, the boss of Shansi, who had hoisted the Nationalist flag the previous June but maintained cautious relations with Chang Tso-lin until conflict between them erupted in October, might now cooperate in a drive on Peking. Chiang Kai-shek returned to Nanking on 4 January and announced resumption of his duties as commander-in-chief on the 9th. He also issued a preparatory call for the Fourth CEC Plenum.

It soon became evident that Chiang and his close supporters intended to reform and cleanse the Kuomintang as well as attempt to reunite a leadership body. The CEC Standing Committee of the moment issued instructions that provincial party headquarters in five provinces should cease activities pending reorganization, and that the Chekiang and Kiangsu party branches were being reorganized. It took from 13 January to 1 February for Chiang to get everything in place for the long-postponed Fourth Plenum of the Second Central Executive Committee. Besides getting agreement on the agenda and persuading certain factions not to bring up sensitive issues, an important question that Chiang had to get settled was: Who might be permitted to attend? Certainly none of the 13 communists elected two years earlier by the Second National Congress as members or alternates of the Central Executive Committee would be admitted to this plenum. But what of the Wang Ching-wei faction that many considered culpable, at least by negligence, for the communist devastation of Canton in December? Five members of the Central Supervisory Committee recommended that Wang and eight associates be excluded. In the end, however, only Wang, Ch'en Kung-po, Ku Meng-yü and Kan Nai-kuang were not permitted to attend. The others came. Hu Han-min, Sun Fo, and C. C. Wu, three opponents of Chiang Kai-shek, were conveniently persuaded to leave on a well-financed tour of inspection abroad, and there were some others who probably would not wish to attend.[306]

Twenty-nine members and alternates of the Central Executive and

306 *TJK*, 804–06, and Kao, *Chronology*, 281–84.

Central Supervisory Committees attended the opening ceremony of this joint plenum on 2 February. There were 77 living members and alternates of whom about 50 might have been available. Thereafter the numbers attending sessions fluctuated around 30.[307] The plenum had three main tasks: setting a new direction to party policy, putting old disputes to rest, and electing new governing bodies.

The participants listened to Chiang Kai-shek's policy proposals: to replace the communist-inspired ideology of class struggle, the Kuomintang should promote a spirit of mutual help and cooperation within the nation. All propaganda should be based upon the late leader's 'Plan for national reconstruction' – that is, on Dr Sun's ideas prior to direct Bolshevik influence – and all slogans used during the period of communist influence should be eliminated. The party's publications should be strictly supervised; no anti-party or anti-government propaganda should be permitted; and all publicity regarding foreign affairs must be in conformity with the government's policy. The Kuomintang should be cleansed by the dissolution of all provincial party bodies pending reregistration of members, and by the abolition of the departments for farmers, workers, merchants, women and youth at central headquarters and in party branches. There should be only three departments for the present: organization, propaganda and party-training. All mass movements must be brought under Kuomintang control, communist influence in them be eliminated, and armed corps of farmers' associations and workers' unions should be dealt with strictly. Education should emphasize science, and students should direct their attention to national reconstruction.[308] This conservative proposal won quick approval from the plenum, now shorn of all its radicals and all but a few of its leftist members. It foretold the direction in which the Nationalist Party would develop.

To paper over the earlier conflicts between the Wuhan and Nanking rivals, the plenum accepted a compromise formula: all previous resolutions related to the policies of allying with Russia and admitting communists should be annulled, while, on the other hand, all removals of persons from Kuomintang membership as part of Nanking's anti-communist drive would be set aside. However, there was to be a complete

---

307 Counting alternates, the total of the two committees was 80, but 3 were deceased, 15 were communists, 8 had been excluded or sent abroad, and 3 were in Russia. Names for the opening ceremony in *TJK*, 806. Eleven attenders were regular CEC members (total 36), 10 were alternates (total 24); 5 were CSC members (total 12), and 3 alternates (total 8).
308 *KMWH*, 17. 3138-52 presents in detail the proposals for reforming the Kuomintang as worked up by Ting Wei-fen, Ch'en Kuo-fu, and Chiang Kai-shek, and preserved in the Kuomintang Archives. For a brief account, GBFO 405/257. Confidential. *Further correspondence respecting China*, 13612, April–June 1928, no. 36, enclosure 3. Sidney Barton, Shanghai, to Miles Lampson, Peking, 16 Feb. 1928.

reregistration of party members; and this plenum specifically expelled all the communists from membership on the two central committees. It also expelled P'eng Tse-min and Teng Yen-ta on the grounds of being accessories to rebellion, and it suspended the rights of Hsu Ch'ien as a CEC member, and of two alternates of the CSC. To fill the empty slots, alternates were moved up systematically.[309]

The plenum considered and passed a number of bills. The Nationalist government should now be organized in a more elaborate way, with an Executive Yuan having seven ministries, a Supreme Court, an Examination Yuan and a Control Yuan, an Academy, an Auditing Yuan, a Legislative Drafting Office, and four Commissions, for Reconstruction, Military Affairs, Mongolian and Tibetan Affairs, and Overseas Chinese Affairs. It was not quite the five yuan system envisaged by Sun Yat-sen but tended in that direction, and most of it was still only a plan. The Kuomintang was to be reconstructed under the direct supervision of the new Central. A standard system of military organization, and reform of political work in the armed forces – an enterprise that had been deeply infiltrated by communists – were approved. (Chiang Kai-shek had chosen the anti-communist ideologist, Tai Chi-t'ao, who was also his close friend, to head the Political Training Department.) The plenum also held elections, but it is not clear what the process was in preparing the slates for voting. Elected to the Standing Committee of the Central Executive Committee were Chiang Kai-shek, Yü Yu-jen, Tai Chi-t'ao, Ting Wei-fen, and T'an Yen-k'ai, with four posts held open for leaders abroad. Forty-nine persons were named to the Government Council, with a Standing Committee consisting of T'an Yen-k'ai, chairman, Ts'ai Yuan-p'ei, Chang Ching-chiang, Li Lieh-chün, and Yü Yu-jen. The new Military Council named 73 persons, with a Standing Committee of 11, chaired by Chiang Kai-shek. Thus the new councils had room for all prominent Kuomintang figures and military leaders then in good repute, but the standing committees were stacked with conservative party veterans or military commanders with real power. Chiang was in charge of military matters and T'an Yen-k'ai seemed charged with supervising governmental affairs.[310]

With these political arrangements completed, Chiang Kai-shek began

309 *TJK*, 807; expulsions shown in *Chung-kuo Kuo-min-tang cheng-li tang-wu chih t'ung-chi pao-kao* (Statistical report on the work of party adjustment of the Chinese Nationalist Party), Organization Department of the CEC, March 1929.

310 Kao, *Chronology*, 285–86; GBFO 405/257. Confidential. *Further correspondence respecting China*, 13612, no. 36, cited, enclosures 1 and 2 (the latter lists the members of the Government Council). *KMWH*, 16. 2887–96 for the plenum's proclamation issued 8 February; and *KMWH*, 17. front plates and pp. 3153–5, for other documents.

preparations for a final military drive on Peking. Two months before, Feng Yü-hsiang had sent an army eastwards along the Lunghai Railway and Ho Ying-ch'in had sent part of the First Route Army north along the Tientsin-Pukow Railway. The two forces had met on 16 December at the strategic city of Hsuchow where the railways cross. On 9 February General Chiang left Nanking with his staff to review the troops at Hsuchow, and then went to Kaifeng for a conference with General Feng on 16 February to discuss a renewed offensive. Feng's Kuominchün was partly financed and provided with some military supplies by Nanking. Feng also had several associates in the Nanking government, Huang Fu as foreign minister, H.H. Kung as minister of industry, and Hsüeh Tu-pi as minister of interior. Hankow also provided Feng with some money and arms, perhaps as tribute, for the Kwangsi generals were busy campaigning in Hunan. They showed no interest in a northward campaign, nor did Li Chi-shen in Canton. On 28 February the newly established Central Military Council announced that Chiang Kai-shek would command the First Group Army, Feng Yü-hsiang the Second, and Yen Hsi-shan the Third. Ho Ying-ch'in, former commander of the First Route Army, had been appointed chief-of-staff of the combined Northern Expeditionary forces.[311]

It took about a month more to assemble troops, munitions, rations and the finances necessary for a resumed Northern Expedition. On paper General Chiang commanded a vast force in the First Group Army with more than 60 divisions grouped in 18 corps, and these into four principal armies commanded by Liu Chih, Ch'en T'iao-yuan, Ho Yao-tsu and Fang Chen-wu. The first of these armies had grown out of the original First Corps, officered by instructors and cadets from the Whampoa Academy, but it also had some other divisions and corps contributed by Chang Fa-k'uei and Chu P'ei-te. As usual, the First Army was the best equipped of the participating armies.[312] General Ch'en, a northerner and formerly military governor of Anhwei, had turned over to the Nationalist side in March 1927, opening the way for the drive on Nanking; but he

311 Kao, *Chronology*, 278-9, 286-7; *FRUS*, 1928, 2. 123-5.
312 According to the *History of the First Group Army*, a commission made a careful inspection of this army between 22 and 26 March 1928. Charts on pp. 10-14 show that the Headquarters and 1st, 2nd and 22nd Divisions of the First Corps had 2,681 officers and 30,269 troops equipped with 16,236 rifles, 502 machine guns and 93 cannon. The Ninth Corps, also made up of headquarters and three divisions, had 2,810 officers and 24,310 troops equipped with 12,436 rifles, 221 machine guns, and 77 cannon. However, the Tenth Corps from Kweichow with only two divisions had 1,437 officers and 8,263 troops with 2,953 rifles, 19 machine guns, and 29 cannon. Total combatants, 70,770, but only 31,625 rifles, plus 1,457 pistols for the officers. In addition there were 5,117 porters and 673 pack horses in the First and Ninth Corps. The average age of 22 commanding officers in the three corps was 33 years (the range was 24 to 43), or about a year less, if *sui* was meant.

was an old-time militarist still. General Ho had brought his Hunanese division into the National Revolutionary Army during the first phase of the Northern Expedition and had participated in the capture of Kiukiang and Nanking. His division had expanded into a corps, the Fortieth, and garrisoned the Nanking area. Fang Chen-wu's revolutionary credentials went back to the 1911 Revolution, and he had been associated with various opposition governments in Canton. More recently he had been a commander in Feng Yü-hsiang's Kuominchün, and participated in Feng's move out of Shensi into Honan in May 1927. He then enrolled his small force in the National Revolutionary Army. These four armies, some other miscellaneous units, and part of Feng Yü-hsiang's Second Group Army were responsible for the drive through Shantung. This motley force was a far cry from the highly indoctrinated and moderately well-trained five corps that had started north from Kwangtung nearly two years before.[313] Peking was about 500 miles distant.

Shortly before campaigning began, Foreign Minister Huang Fu and the American minister to China, J. V. A. MacMurray, negotiated a settlement of the Nanking Incident. This came after considerable effort on both sides, and after the Nanking government had issued two mandates on 16 March, one of which announced that a group of soldiers and others implicated in the Incident had been executed, while the other ordered that full protection must be given to foreigners and foreign property. The two representatives exchanged agreed upon notes, which offered regrets and explanations, and these were signed on 30 March, a little more than a year after the violence and shelling in Nanking. So far as the United States was concerned this ended the diplomatic difficulties with Nanking, although recognition came much later. To some Chinese officials, however, the settlement was far from satisfactory, for the American side only expressed regrets that 'circumstances beyond its control should have necessitated the adoption of such measures [that is, the naval bombardment] for the protection of its citizens at Nanking.' To many Chinese, the Nanking Incident *was* the American and British shelling of the city. The British minister, Miles Lampson, had also visited Nanking and held discussions with Huang Fu, but they had failed to find an acceptable formula.[314]

313 *PFCS*, 4. map facing p. 1170 shows the main thrusts of the campaign against Peking in four stages; order of battle following p. 1180. All this volume and the following items deal with the final campaign: *KMWH*, 18. 3169–271; 19. 3479–503; 20. 3671–773; 21. 3925–70. There are brief accounts in Jordan, *The Northern Expedition*, 151–68; Sheridan, *Chinese warlord: Feng Yü-hsiang*, 236–9; and Donald G. Gillin, *Warlord: Yen Hsi-shan in Shansi province, 1911–1949*, 108–9.

314 *FRUS*, 1928, 2. 323–69, for details of the long negotiations and the notes. Summarized in Borg, *American policy and the Chinese revolution*, 380–4. Lampson's difficulties are ex-

The final military campaign

Marshal Chang Tso-lin had overall command of the An-kuo Chün, a shaky alliance of his own Manchurian troops (the Fengtien Army), the remaining troops of Sun Ch'uan-fang, and the Chihli and Shantung provincial forces, under Ch'u Yü-p'u and Chang Tsung-ch'ang. The Manchurians were responsible for the defence of Peking and the railways leading south and west; Sun Ch'uan-fang and the Shantungese for defending the Tientsin-Pukow Railway on the east. But much of Chihli and western Shantung are open plains, making defence difficult, particularly against cavalry. Yen Hsi-shan on the western flank complicated the defence of the Peking-Hankow line.

Feng Yü-hsiang's Second Group Army commenced the Nationalists' spring campaign with a drive into south-western Shantung and a holding operation in the west against the Fengtien Army. The Nationalists' First Group Army joined the battle in Shantung about 9 April, advancing along the railway and sending another column northward near the coast to intercept the rail line leading from Tsinan, the provincial capital, to the port of Tsingtao. Chang Tsung-ch'ang's troops showed little fight, but Sun Ch'uan-fang attempted a counter attack. He was badly defeated, leaving the way open for the capture of Tsinan, which cavalry units of the Kuominchün under General Sun Liang-ch'eng entered on 30 April. On the western front, however, the Manchurians strongly resisted the Second Group Army, which had advanced only as far as Chang-te (An-yang), at the northern tip of Honan, still some 400 miles from Peking. During April the Manchurians had also engaged in preemptive attacks against Shansi along the Peking–Suiyuan Railway and the line leading from Shihchiachuang to Taiyuan, the provincial capital. At this point in the battle, during the first week in May, a bitter and bloody conflict broke out between advancing Nationalist troops and Japanese regular army units that had been sent to Tsinan to protect resident Japanese nationals.

The Tsinan Incident, 3-11 May 1928

The Tanaka government, while favourably impressed by the Nationalist movement under Chiang Kai-shek's leadership, remembered the Nanking

plained in Wilson, 'Britain and the Kuomintang', 644-9. Private letters of appreciation to Foreign Minister Huang Fu from Miles Lampson and J. V. A. MacMurray, both in very cordial terms, are reproduced in the reminiscences of Huang's widow, Shen I-yün, *I-yün hui-i*, 356-9.

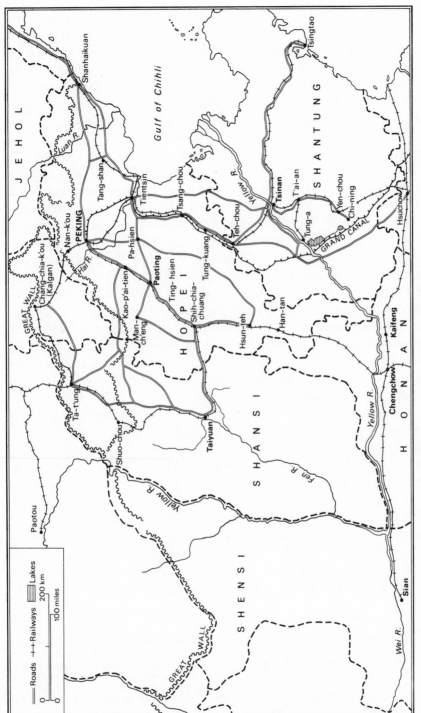

MAP 18. North China about 1928

Incident and other anti-foreign disorders during earlier stages of the Northern Expedition. In preparation for the time when the National Revolutionary Army would resume its drive, the Japanese Cabinet, the War Ministry and the General Staff debated how best to protect Japanese nationals in north China: some favoured and some opposed sending an expeditionary force.[315] Chiang Kai-shek and Foreign Minister Huang Fu tried to reassure Japan that the Nationalist government and its army would protect Japanese lives and property in areas that came under its control. However, when it became evident in early April that the military campaign would probably drive through Tsinan despite Baron Tanaka's earlier request to Chiang and Feng Yü-hsiang that they bypass the city where 2,000 Japanese civilians resided, the Japanese government decided to act. By 18 April Prime Minister Tanaka was persuaded by the War Ministry, and the Japanese Cabinet agreed, to send an expeditionary force of 5,000 from the Sixth Division to Shantung. The public announcement sought to reassure China that Japan did not intend to interfere in the civil war and that the troops would be withdrawn when no longer needed to protect Japanese nationals. Both the Peking and the Nanking governments protested this intrusion on China's sovereignty, and public sentiment against Japan rapidly heated up. Yet the Nationalists wished to avoid a conflict. The Kuomintang and the commander-in-chief issued strong orders against anti-Japanese agitation and hostile acts in places where Japanese resided.

General Fukuda Hikosuke, commanding the Sixth Division, which arrived in Tsingtao between 25 and 27 April, ordered troops to Tsinan on his own initiative, and some 500 had arrived there by 30 April, when the northern forces withdrew from the city. The small Japanese force immediately staked out the area within Tsinan where most Japanese lived – it was called the Japanese Settlement – set up barricades, and forbade any Chinese troops to enter. Next day troops of General Sun Liang-ch'eng followed by others of the First Group Army poured into Tsinan. When Chiang Kai-shek arrived on 2 May he requested General Fukuda to withdraw his troops, pledging to maintain peace in the city. General Fukuda consented, and that night Japanese troops demolished their barricades

---

315 The following is based primarily on the scholarly account in Iriye, *After imperialism*, 193–205, which made use of the extensive documentation from both sides. Reports and other documents on the Chinese side are in *KMWH*, 19. 3504–657; 22. 4443–537; 23. 4783–815. *China Yearbook, 1929–30*, 878–93 for some documents from each side. Initial American reports in *FRUS*, 1928, 2. 136–9. Eye-witness reports from J. B. Affleck, British Acting Consul-General in Tsinan, in GBFO 405/257. Confidential. *Further correspondence respecting China*, 13612, April–June 1928, nos. 238 and 239, enclosures.

and seemed to be preparing to leave. A peaceful transition to Nationalist rule looked possible.

Unhappily, fighting broke out between small units on each side on the morning of 3 May. The origin of and responsibility for the fighting were in absolute dispute between the two sides. The local incident rapidly developed into fighting throughout the city between intensely nationalistic Japanese and Chinese troops, despite the efforts of Generals Chiang and Fukuda to stop it. Both sides committed atrocities which inflamed the conflict.[316] Finally a truce was worked out, with the Chinese side agreeing to withdraw all troops from the city except for a few thousand that would remain to keep order. Chiang Kai-shek obviously wished to avoid entrapment in a dangerous conflict that could only obstruct his drive on Peking.

General Fukuda, however, was determined to uphold the prestige of the Japanese Army by punishing the Chinese. He asked for reinforcements and Prime Minister Tanaka and the Cabinet decided on 4 May, to send additional troops from Korea and Manchuria. On 7 May, with Japanese reinforcements in Tsinan, the Japanese generals prepared for drastic action.[317] That afternoon, General Fukuda sent an ultimatum to the acting Chinese commissioner for foreign affairs with a 12-hour time limit. It demanded punishment of responsible high Chinese officers; the disarming of responsible Chinese troops before the Japanese army; evacuation of two military barracks near Tsinan; prohibition of all anti-Japanese propaganda; and withdrawal of all Chinese troops beyond 20 *li* (about seven miles) on both sides of the Tsinan-Tsingtao Railway. Such humiliating demands were more than any Chinese commander could accede to. That night, Chiang Kai-shek and his aides, who had left Tsinan, conferred on this new problem, and next morning General Chiang sent back a conciliatory reply that met only some of the demands. General Fukuda insisted that, since his ultimatum had not been accepted within twelve hours, he was forced to take action to uphold the prestige of the Japanese army.

316 The British Acting Consul-General, Mr Affleck reported that on 5 May he was taken to the Japanese hospital and shown the bodies of 12 Japanese, most of the males having been castrated. GBFO 405/257, cited, no. 238, 'Account of the Tsinan Incident', dated 7 May 1928. In a report dated 21 May Mr Affleck stated his belief that blame for beginning the incident on 3 May lay with Chinese troops, who were looting Japanese shops. GBFO 504/258. Confidential. *Further correspondence respecting China*, 13613, July–Sept., no. 37, enclosure. The American Vice-Consul, Ernest Price, blamed the poor discipline of the Chinese troops for the outbreak of the incident.

A Japanese atrocity was the blinding and then killing the Chinese Commissioner for Foreign Affairs, Ts'ai Kung-shih, and the murder of 16 of his staff. This happened on 4 May, according to Kao Yin-tsu, *Chronology*, 291.

317 Professor Iriye places the blame for renewed fighting squarely upon the Japanese. See *After imperialism*, 201.

On the afternoon of 8 May the Japanese attacked within the city and the surrounding area. By the 11th, after fierce fighting, the remaining Chinese troops had been overcome. There was great damage to the city and thousands of Chinese soldiers and civilians had been killed. Nothing could have done more to inflame Chinese hatred against Japan.[318]

The Tsinan Incident brought to an end the Chinese Nationalists' attempt at a *rapprochement* with Japan, but the government did what it could to prevent further trouble with its powerful neighbour. The Nationalist government requested the League of Nations to investigate and appealed to the American government for support, but these requests were of little effect – as was repeatedly to be the case thereafter. The arbitrary action by Japanese commanders in the field was the first of a series that led three years later to the Japanese Kwantung Army's seizure of Manchuria, then to an ever-spreading Sino-Japanese conflict, and ultimately to Japan's utter defeat in 1945.

Who shall have Peking?

In the spring of 1928 the major concern of the Japanese government with respect to China was to protect and enhance its special position in Manchuria. This might be done through cooperation with Chang Tso-lin or with the Nationalists. While attempting to present an appearance of impartiality between the contestants, Japan was determined to prevent the conflict from being carried into Manchuria. As early as January Prime Minister Tanaka had warned Chang Ch'ün, Chiang Kai-shek's special envoy in Tokyo, that Japan would not permit Nationalist troops to pursue the Fengtien Army beyond the Great Wall, but in return, Japan would assure the swift withdrawal of Chang Tso-lin to Mukden if he were defeated. By April the Japanese government had decided to maintain the peace in Manchuria by arranging a truce between the contestants if possible, and by the use of force if necessary.

To avoid embroilment with Japan, Chiang Kai-shek had pulled back most of the troops that had invaded Tsinan and sent them west for a crossing of the Yellow River and regroupment on the north bank. During the second week in May, even as the Japanese army was crushing Chinese forces in and around Tsinan, the Nationalists' three Group Armies began a general offensive, while the An-kuo Chün pulled back towards Peking and Tientsin. Yen Hsi-shan's troops pushed down on Shihchiachuang where, on 10 May, they met with a body of Feng Yü-hsiang's soldiers

318 Iriye, *After imperialism*, 207-8, based upon Japanese records.

following the retreating Manchurians on the Peking-Hankow Railway. Other units of Yen's army were recovering northern Shansi and moving along the Peking-Suiyuan Railway towards Peking's back door. The An-kuo Chün tried to establish a shorter line between Paoting on the west and Techow, at the northern tip of Shantung, on the east, reinforcing the Shantungese with Chihli provincial troops under Ch'u Yü-p'u, stiffened with some Manchurians. But the eastern end could not hold against Feng Yü-hsiang's attack; Techow fell on 12 May and its defenders fell back towards Tientsin. On 18 May Generals Chiang and Feng met at Chengchow to plan the advance on Tientsin, which, if taken and held, would cut the rail line that the Manchurian army would need should it retreat to its home base.

By this time it was becoming evident that the Manchurians were preparing to withdraw from North China. Officers were sending their families and valuables back home. Units of the Fengtien army on the Peking-Suiyuan Railway began to pull back on Kalgan and then beyond. At this late date the Kwangsi faction entered the campaign. General Pai Ch'ung-hsi, as field commander, led a force into Honan, which the Military Council designated the Fourth Group Army, with Li Tsung-jen its commander. General Pai met Commander-in-Chief Chiang at Chengchow on 20 May to receive his instructions. The troops were former elements of T'ang Sheng-chih's Hunanese Army.[319]

Japan and the Western powers were concerned for the safety of their nationals in Tientsin, with its five separate foreign concessions, and for the foreign community in Peking, should the cities be captured in battle. The experiences of Nanking and the more recent troubles in Tsinan made them wary of disorderly Chinese troops whether in defeat or in victory. The powers had kept contingents of troops in Tientsin for many years in accordance with the Boxer Protocol of 1901, and these garrisons had recently been reinforced so that there were thousands of foreign troops on hand. On 11 May the general commanding the Japanese force in Tientsin proposed excluding Chinese troops from a zone of 20 *li* around the city in accordance with the 1902 treaty between China and various powers. The United States had not been party to that treaty, nor did it have a concession in Tientsin. The American marine commander, Smedley Butler, devised his own plan for the protection of Americans, while the others drew up joint defence plans.

319 General Pai told the writer in 1962 that he had been urged by Commander-in-Chief Chiang to bring a force to the aid of the hard-pressed Feng and Yen. His three sub-commanders were Li P'in-hsien, Liao Lei and Yeh Ch'i. 'When the Fengtien Army saw the advance of such a large reinforcement, it hastily retreated outside the Great Wall', General Pai reminisced.

In Tokyo the Foreign Ministry was preparing the text of a warning that would be presented to both Chinese contestants, stating Japan's determination to prevent extension of the civil war into Manchuria. On 17 May Prime Minister Tanaka met with British, American, French and Italian representatives to explain the purpose of the memorandum that would be delivered next day to the Peking and Nanking governments. He said, in part:

> Our policy was devised to prevent fighting at Peking, in order to keep disturbances from spreading into Manchuria. If Chang Tso-lin withdraws from Peking quietly, maintaining discipline among his soldiers, and if he is not pursued by the Southerners, we will permit him to enter Manchuria; but if he fights at Peking, and retreats towards Shanhaikuan, or to some other point which we may fix, fighting the Southerners as he goes, we will prevent him and the Southern army from passing into Manchuria. I believe this plan will have the effect of encouraging Chang Tso-lin to leave Peking quietly and without fighting. I think also that, if Chang Tso-lin retreats from Peking at the present moment, the Southerners will not molest him. I therefore look forward to Peking being evacuated and passing quietly into the hands of the Southerners.[320]

Baron Tanaka instructed his minister to Peking, Yoshizawa Kenkichi, to urge Chang Tso-lin to lose no time in withdrawing to Manchuria; and Consul-General Yada in Shanghai was instructed to let the Nationalists understand that once Chang Tso-lin had returned to his base, Japan would not permit him to interfere in affairs south of the Wall. Thus did Baron Tanaka and his government plan to divide China, and to protect Japan's special sphere in Manchuria. The War Ministry sent telegraphic instructions and explanations of Japan's policy to commanders in Manchuria, Korea and Formosa. Chang Tso-lin would not be advised to retire from public life and Fengtien soldiers need not be disarmed if they returned to Manchuria in good order, but the Japanese army would not permit the southern forces beyond the Wall. The Kwantung Army was to prepare itself to carry through this programme.

Minister Yoshizawa called on Marshal Chang on the night of 17/18 May and handed him the Japanese Memorandum. He told him that the northern army was on the verge of defeat, but that the Japanese government could save him and his army if he accepted the advice to return speedily to Manchuria. But Chang Tso-lin resisted. In Yoshizawa's opinion, he had expected assistance from Japan without having to give up Peking.[321]

---

320 GBFO 504/258. Confidential. *Further correspondence respecting China*, 13613, cited above f.n. 316, no. 2, enclosure. This is a memorandum on the meeting by Eugene Dooman of the U.S. Embassy. See also *FRUS*, 1928, 2. 224–5 and 229.
321 Iriye, *After imperialism*, 210–11, based upon Japanese records.

Next night, Marshal Chang sent an aide to tell the British minister, Miles Lampson, of Yoshizawa's midnight discussion and to seek Lampson's advice. Was it time to leave Peking and the foreigners to the forces of anarchy? he asked. Mr Lampson, who doubtless knew of Prime Minister Tanaka's explanation to the foreign diplomats the previous day, advised that Chang Tso-lin and his staff consider the matter carefully. He gave his opinion that Japan did not have aggressive designs, but that they would protect their interests in Manchuria. Chang should avoid at all costs a clash with Japan.[322]

Japanese representatives conveyed similar warnings against disturbing the peace of Manchuria to Feng Yü-hsiang, Yen Hsi-shan and Chiang Kai-shek, and probably encouraged all sides to negotiate a termination of the civil war. The American government would have no part in the Japanese *démarche*. Secretary of State Frank B. Kellogg telegraphed Minister MacMurray on 18 May and instructed: 'There will be no participation by the United States in joint action with the Japanese government or any other power to prevent the extension of Chinese hostilities to Manchuria or to interfere with the controlled military operation of Chinese armies, but solely for the protection of American citizens.'[323]

Events now moved very fast. The Fengtien Army had difficulty in holding its position at Paoting, and the line eastward of that strong point was very shaky. The Nationalists had agents in Peking attempting to negotiate defections. Chang Tso-lin and his generals had to consider the risks of holding on too long to north-eastern Chihli, which shielded Peking and Tientsin, for fear of being trapped therein. But if Chang Tso-lin and his army were to depart, who should be allowed to take over Peking? Feng Yü-hsiang was an old enemy of Chang Tso-lin. As early as mid April, the American minister had noted that the Peking regime hoped to defeat and drive off Feng's army, but to reach some compromise with Shansi and Nanking. Now, in May, Feng's army could certainly have captured the city, but a deal was worked out for the Fengtien Army to withdraw in such a way that Yen Hsi-shan's army would be first in the Peking-Tientsin area and Feng Yü-hsiang would be excluded from that rich prize.[324] By the end of May the Fengtien Army had given up Paoting

322 GBFO 504/258. Confidential. *Further correspondence respecting China*, 13613, no. 6, enclosure. Miles Lampson to Austen Chamberlain, Peking, 23 May 1928. 'Record of a conversation with Mr Ou Tching.' [Wu Chin].
323 *FRUS*, 1928, 2. 226, and Iriye, *After imperialism*, 321.
324 Sheridan, *Chinese warlord*, 238. GBFO 504/258. Confidential, *Further correspondence respecting China*, 13613, no. 40, Miles Lampson to Austen Chamberlain, Peking, 8 June 1928, a dispatch.

and was drawing back on Peking. Chang Tso-lin was preparing to depart from the capital.

On 1 June General Chiang, Feng and Yen met at Shihchiachuang to plan for the take-over of Peking and Tientsin and to settle on arrangements thereafter. Perhaps it was then – though it may have been earlier – that Feng Yü-hsiang learned he was not to get Peking; nor would Chiang, who returned to Nanking on the 3rd. Next day the Nationalist government appointed – that is, confirmed – Yen Hsi-shan as Peking's garrison commander.

Chang Tso-lin called in the diplomatic corps on 1 June for what turned out to be a valedictory address. He had already made arrangements to turn over governance of the city to a Peace Preservation Commission made up of Chinese elder statesmen, headed by Wang Shih-chen, once a close associate of Yuan Shih-k'ai and once a premier. Internal security was in the hands of Peking's efficient police and a brigade of Manchurian troops under General Pao Yü-lin, who would stay behind until the city passed to Yen Hsi-shan and then be permitted to return unmolested to Fengtien. Next day Marshal Chang issued a farewell telegram to the Chinese people, expressing regret that he had not successfully concluded the anti-Red campaign, and announcing his return to Manchuria in order to spare further bloodshed. He left Peking with pomp, accompanied by most of his cabinet and high ranking officers, on a special train on the night of 2/3 June, but the train was wrecked by bomb explosions early in the morning of 4 June as it neared Mukden. The Marshal died of his wounds within two hours. He had been assassinated by a group of officers of Japan's Kwantung Army, who plotted the deed on their own in opposition to Tanaka's policy.[325]

Chang Hsueh-liang, the Marshal's eldest son, and Yang Yü-t'ing his chief-of-staff, left together with Sun Ch'uan-fang on 4 June for Tientsin, which had to be held until the large Manchurian army had been evacuated toward Shanhaikuan. The Peace Preservation Commission then sent emissaries to Paoting to welcome Yen Hsi-shan to Peking. On 8 June a commander of the Third Army Group, General Shang Chen, led his Shansi troops into the capital, and on 11 June Yen Hsi-shan himself, accompanied by General Pai Ch'ung-hsi, entered the city. Another of his generals, Fu Tso-i, took over Tientsin by prearrangement on the 12th. The transition had been effected peacefully, except for one incident. General Han Fu-ch'ü, a subordinate of Feng Yü-hsiang, who had led the drive on Peking and whose troops were now barracked on the city's

325 Iriye, *After imperialism*, 213–14 and 324, f.ns. 52 and 53.

outskirts, surrounded and disarmed the departing Manchurian brigade that had been promised safe conduct. Peking's diplomatic corps had underwritten the safe passage, and protested to Nanking strenuously. Ultimately, the Manchurian troops were released and some of their arms returned.[326]

Launching on national reconstruction

The commanders of the Four Army Groups met in Peking on 6 July at a solemn ceremony before the coffin of their late Leader, Sun Yat-sen, in a temple in the Western Hills outside Peking. They reported that the long-cherished northern campaign had been accomplished with the capture of Peking and the elimination of its government. A few days later, the commanders and their staffs met in informal military conference to discuss the problem of troop disbandment. Ho Ying-ch'in had reported that the National Revolutionary Army now had about 300 divisions grouped in 84 corps, with troops numbering 2.2 million. (Apparently this counted all organized units as part of the NRA.) If properly paid, the normal cost of this vast army would be at least 60 million dollars a month. The commander-in-chief's office hoped to reduce the total to 80 divisions and 1.2 million men, which would consume only 60 per cent of the nation's revenues. Chiang Kai-shek presented his military colleagues with a memorandum prepared for the forthcoming meeting of the Central Executive Committee, which proposed a Military Rehabilitation Conference for the special purpose of formulating a disbandment scheme, fixing the number of troops and military expenses, and dividing the country into a definite number of military districts. He suggested 12, each having 40 to 50 thousand troops.[327] A disbandment conference was to be held in January 1929, but it achieved very little because, by then, the regional military factions had virtually divided the country. An indication of what was to come appeared in Peking at that July meeting of the commanders. Feng Yü-hsiang nursed a grievance at being cut out of the Peking and Tientsin spoils. When a Branch Political Council for Peking was established, with Yen Hsi-shan as chairman, General Feng would

326 FRUS, 1928, 2. 235–42; GBFO 504/258 confidential, *Further correspondence respecting China*, 13613, nos. 50 and 89, reports by Miles Lampson.
327 Kao Yin-tsu, *Chronology*, 300, 2 July 1928. (The figure for the victorious NRA in July 1928 was about 1.6 million.) *KMWH*, 21. 4067–71 for Chiang's preliminary disbandment plan. *Ibid.* 4076–85 for a list of divisions and corps counted as making up the NRA as of July 1928 (including many units that had no part in the Northern Expedition), and their commanders. GBFO 405/259. Confidential. *Further correspondence respecting China*, 13616, Oct.–Dec. 1928, no. 46, enclosure 7, 'Summary of military memorandum by Chiang Kai-shek' issued by Kuomin News Agency, Peiping, 15 July 1928.

not accept a position on it; ominously, he left Peking on 14 July to tend the graves of his ancestors, and thence to his military headquarters in Honan.[328]

The Fifth Plenum of the Kuomintang's Second Central Executive Committee met in Nanking from 8 to 14 August, to plan the nation's future. Generals Feng Yü-hsiang and Yen Hsi-shan, and Admiral Yang Shu-chuang were invited to attend as special guests.[329] The plenum faced important matters of national policy. The most contentious issue was how rapidly and rigorously to move towards centralization of political, financial and military power. Should the branch political councils, which, in effect, divided Nationalist China into satrapies, be abolished? After much wrangling between proponents of centralization and those who wished to retain local power – it almost ended the meeting – the plenum passed a resolution which affirmed that the Central Political Council should be appointed by the Central Executive Committee and pass its decisions through it to the national government to execute; branch political councils should be terminated by the end of the year, and in the meantime should not issue orders nor appoint and remove officials in their own names. Thus, the Political Council, originally created by Sun Yat-sen on Borodin's advice as his inner council, was not to be independent of and above the elected Central Executive Committee; and the recently created branch councils should be no more. However, when the list of Central Political Council members was announced, there were 46 persons, including nearly all regular members of the Central Executive and the Central Supervisory Committees, most major military figures, and some conservative veterans of the party who now were back in the fold.[330] It was very likely to be a figure-head organ, with decisions made by a small, inner group, as before. Another gesture toward centralization was passage of a resolution which stated, as a guiding principle, that all members of the party's Central Committees should reside at the capital and must not disperse to various places.

---

328 Kao Yin-tsu, *Chronology*, 300, 6 July 1928; GBFO 405/259. Confidential. *Further correspondence respecting China*, 13616, no. 9, Miles Lampson to Austen Chamberlain, Peking, 1 Aug. 1928.

329 *KMWH*, 21. 4092-100, for some documents on the Fifth Plenum. Kao Yin-tsu, *Chronology*, 305-7, for resolutions passed. Kao states that 24 regular members and one alternate, eight CSC members and one alternate, and Feng and Yang attended.

330 Beside Hu Han-min and Wang Ching-wei, who had missed the Plenum, two of Wang's followers who had been excluded from the Fourth and Fifth Plenums, Ch'en Kung-po and Ku Meng-yü, were included, as were Mme Sun Yat-sen and Eugene Chen. Important military men not members of either committee but included in the Central Political Council were Yen Hsi-shan, Feng Yü-hsiang, Yang Shu-chuang, Pai Ch'ung-hsi, and Ch'en Ming-shu. A list is in GBFO 405/259. Confidential. *Further correspondence respecting China*, 13616, no. 46, enclosure 3, from the Kuomin News Agency.

How might governmental finances be unified? T. V. Soong, the minister of finance, had convened two conferences, one on financial and one on economic reconstruction, drawing together leading private bankers, merchants and industrialists, provincial finance officers, representatives of the various armies, and financial experts. He described the nation's financial chaos and presented the plenum with detailed proposals coming from these conferences. They dealt with demarcation between national and provincial sources of revenue, abolition of internal transit taxes, recovery of tariff autonomy, liquidation of national indebtedness, unification of currency, promotion of commerce, stabilization of the money market, founding of a government central bank and regulating the private banking system, and issuance of public bonds to provide the cost of troop disbandment and reconstruction. Dr Soong insisted that unification of finance and adoption of a national budget were essential; it would be idle to talk of financial rehabilitation unless these two things were done. His plea was backed by a delegation of nearly 100 Shanghai bankers and merchants led by Yu Ya-ching (Yü Hsia-ch'ing), which threatened that no more loans could be exacted from them unless these reforms were carried out. They had had enough of extortion and blackmail by Chiang's agents. To Dr Soong, financial unification meant unified employment of financial personnel and centralized administration of the collection and expenditure of revenue. During the Northern Expedition, he complained, there was no budgeting at all; the minister of finance could only assemble funds and turn them over on command to the highest military authority for disposition. Now, he insisted, all revenues should be placed in the national treasury, while a powerful budget committee should decide on appropriations for all branches of government, and no deviations should be allowed without the committee's approval. 'Rehabilitation of finance and establishment of clean and efficient government cannot be realized unless a sound system of national budget is enforced', he concluded. The plenum considered his proposals 'proper and suitable' and turned them over to the Government Council for careful consideration and execution; and it agreed that establishment of a budget committee was imperative, and instructed the same council to organize the committee. A little later the Central Executive Committee's Standing Committee appointed a 13-man budget committee with a preponderance of the more powerful regional military men, but stipulated that the budget as drawn must be approved by the Government Council.[331]

331 On continued extortion of funds from Shanghai merchants and Soong's efforts to create a more orderly fiscal system, see Coble, 'The Kuomintang and the Shanghai capitalists,

The crucial problem in respect to centralization of power lay in the military sphere. So long as commanders had their independent bases and sources of revenue, there could be no real centralization. They might be persuaded to join the centre in reality, or they might be subdued by the centre. There seemed to be no other way. Chiang Kai-shek made an eloquent opening plea that those having military power should make a public vow that, despite differences in political views, they would never resort to arms and fight each other. The National Army hereafter should be used only for national defence and the suppression of bandits; it should never fight internal wars. 'If this principle is strictly adhered to, political differences among those in power will not develop into serious conflicts involving the entire country', he asserted.[332]

The plenum debated the problem of military reorganization and passed a resolution on fundamental principles: (a) military administration and military orders must be absolutely unified; (b) the army must quickly be reduced considerably in size, and annual military expenditures must not exceed half the national revenue; (c) military education must be unified and centralized and all military academies be established by the central government, no armies or local authorities being allowed to establish military academies or similar institutions; (d) all disbanded troops should be used as labourers for colonization and reconstruction purposes; and (e) in order to prepare for national defence, practical measures must be adopted to develop the navy and an airforce, and to strengthen forts and naval bases.

The last of these principles expressed the dream of 60 years; others sought to address problems that had grown out of China's protracted effort to protect itself from foreign aggression and internal disorder. Those problems could not be quickly solved. The plenum referred two other resolutions, one concerning party control of government and the army, and the other prohibiting military organs from interfering with mass movements, to the CEC Standing Committee and the highest military organ of the government, 'with instructions to formulate detailed measures based upon the principle of party supremacy in the state', and to carry them out.[333]

1927-29', 14-19. GBFO 405/259. Confidential. *Further correspondence respecting China*, 13616, no. 46, enclosure 6 for Soong's proposals, and no. 70, enclosure 1, Acting Consul-General Garstin, Shanghai, to Miles Lampson, 4 Sept. 1928. *KMWH*, 22. 4336-9 for the budget committee regulations and those appointed. They were Chiang Kai-shek, Yen Hsi-shan, Yang Shu-chuang, Wang Po-ch'ün, T'an Yen-k'ai, Ho Ying-ch'in, Feng Yü-hsiang. Li Tsung-jen, T.V. Soong, Yü Yu-jen, Li Chi-shen, Ts'ai Yuan-p'ei, and Chiang Tso-pin. Members unable to attend could send deputies.

332 GBFO, just cited, no. 46, enclosure 4, summary of a memorandum submitted by Chiang Kai-shek, from Kuomin News Agency, 9 Aug. 1928.

333 *Ibid.* enclosure 3.

Since the military campaigns were now thought to be over and the period of political tutelage was about to begin, the plenum resolved that a provisional constitution should be drawn up, adopted and enforced, and that the five-yuan system of government should come into effect. It also tried to legislate on a problem of conflicts between party and government, which, apparently, were more serious at lower levels than at the top, where the leaderships were fused. Should any party organ consider the action of a government organ at its same level as being improper, it should report the case upward to its superior party organ, which would then bring the matter to the attention of the governmental organ at its own level; that government organ would then discipline the offending lower organ according to law. The procedure was to be the same when a lower government organ had a complaint against a party organ at its level; it should report upward and after lateral consultation, the offending party organ would be disciplined by its superior.[334] But this regulation could not solve the problem inherent in two authorities – three, if the military be added – each with its own hierarchy and with separate lines of command.

The national revolution had been mounted to rid China of foreign domination. The 'unequal treaties', which gave extraordinary privileges to foreign nationals in China, outraged many patriotic Chinese. The Peking government had struggled to the last to revise such treaties as it could. On 7 July the Nationalist foreign minister, Wang Cheng-t'ing, had announced that all treaties that had expired, or were soon to do so, would be replaced by new ones, and that all other treaties would be abrogated and renegotiated. During a transition period, all foreign nationals in China, and their property, would be protected according to Chinese law, but foreigners must be subject to the laws of China and the jurisdiction of Chinese courts, and they must pay Chinese taxes and conventional tariffs. The ministry followed this order, which it lacked the power to enforce, with formal requests to a number of foreign governments to appoint negotiating delegates. The American minister, J. V. A. MacMurray, on instructions from Secretary of State Frank B. Kellogg, did negotiate a new tariff treaty with T. V. Soong, which they signed on 25 July. This accepted the principle of complete national autonomy for China and equal treatment of nationals of both countries in tariff matters. The new treaty would go into effect on 1 January of the next year, but this was contingent upon the 'most favoured nation' clause, which meant that it would not become operative until all other governments had acknowledged China's autonomous rights in respect of its tariffs. The

334 *Idem.*

negotiations and signing, with the approval of the secretary of state, seemed a form of *de facto* recognition of the Nanking government.[335] Furthermore, on 8 August Great Britain settled the Nanking Incident with the Nationalist government on terms similar to those of the United States.

It was in this nationalistic climate and mood of some elation that the Fifth Plenum had before it a memorandum on foreign policy prepared by T'an Yen-k'ai and Ts'ai Yuan-p'ei, which called for complete and unconditional abrogation of all the unequal treaties, set 1 January 1929 as the date for ending the treaties which imposed fixed tariffs upon China, demanded unconditional abolition of consular jurisdiction and the immediate retrocession of foreign concessions and settlements, and forbade the stationing of foreign troops and warships in China. No more than a year should be allowed for the process of negotiating new and reciprocal treaties.[336] This ambitious programme actually took 15 years to accomplish.[337]

The plenum ended on 15 August, leaving many proposals to the CEC Standing Committee to deal with. Then official Nanking busied itself preparing to establish a new government, both in form and in personnel. Hu Han-min returned from abroad on 3 September and, after some hesitation, agreed to participate together with Tai Chi-t'ao and Wang Ch'ung-hui in the drafting of an Organic Law of the National Government. Their work was completed on 3 October and the Kuomintang's Central Executive Committee promulgated the law on 8 October. It first promulgated 'The general principles governing the period of political tutelage', which made it quite clear that the Kuomintang, through its National Congresses and its Central Executive Committee, exercised sovereign power during the period in which the Chinese people were being prepared for democratic life. The Kuomintang's Political Council would guide and superintend the national government in the execution of important national affairs, and the Council might amend and interpret the Organic Law.[338]

On 10 October 1928, the seventeenth anniversary of the outbreak of the revolution which ended the Manchu dynasty, a refurbished Nationalist government was inaugurated at Nanking with pomp and fanfare. Its

335 Kao Yin-tsu, *Chronology*, 300-4; Borg, *American policy*, 400-2.
336 GBFO 405/259. Confidential. *Further correspondence respecting China*, 13616, no. 46, enclosure 5.
337 William L. Tung, *China and the foreign powers: the impact of and reaction to unequal treaties*, 249-57 for a systematic account of treaty revision before the 'Mukden Incident' of Sept. 1931.
338 *KMWH*, 22. 4356-63 for the Guiding Principles and the Organic Law; the former is translated in Shieh, *The Kuomintang*, 137-8.

structure was of Sun Yat-sen's conception: Five separate boards or yuan – executive, legislative, judicial, examination and control. The Standing Committee of the Kuomintang Central Executive Committee chose the five heads of these yuan, all prestigious veterans: T'an Yen-k'ai, Hu Han-min, Wang Ch'ung-hui, Tai Chi-t'ao, and Ts'ai Yuan-p'ei – although Ts'ai declined to accept the appointment, which was later given to Yü Yu-jen. Above these boards was a State Council made up of these men and 12 others, some powerful, some prestigious, and several far from Nanking: Feng Yü-hsiang, Sun Fo, Ch'en Kuo-fu, Yen Hsi-shan, Li Tsung-jen, Li Chi-shen, Ho Ying-ch'in, Chang Hsueh-liang, Lin Sen, Yang Shu-chuang and Chang Chi, with Chiang Kai-shek as its chairman, and hence the highest official of the government, its president. A few days later the Political Council appointed the ministers in the Executive Yuan.

The era of the Nanking government – ruled by the Kuomintang Political Council – had begun.

China's prospects in 1928

Seen from the perspective of late 1928, China's future seemed bright. It was a time of optimism that verged on jubilation. The Nationalists had destroyed the corrupt and bankrupt Peking government and a new government was in place, staffed by well educated and patriotic men who had long been concerned for the condition of the country, and who intended that the new government should solve the nation's many political, economic and social problems. The leaders of the Nationalist Party planned to control the government and to set its policies; they conceived their role as a stewardship during a period of tutelage. Theirs was a popular party in 1928. Few Chinese questioned its right to manage public affairs. It had a respected revolutionary history, and had just proved itself an effective organization for mobilizing and channelling power to achieve popular goals.

Four years of close Russian involvement with the Kuomintang had left upon it a Leninist stamp. It was very different from the loosely linked congeries of revolutionaries that had coalesced around Sun Yat-sen from time to time. Now it practised 'democratic centralism', with the inevitable emphasis on centralism and dictation by a very few. The party was better prepared to exercise tutelage than it had been before its reorganization in 1924. It had improved its propaganda techniques, though keeping nationalism as the central theme, and it had learned the utility of mobilizing 'the masses', as well as some of the risks involved. The Kuomintang had created a military force under its own leadership, which, through a system of political training, had proved an effective instrument of revolution. Now the Kuomintang had a new leader, the 41-year-old Chiang Kai-shek, respected and admired, who had shown determination and ability at careful planning, intrigue and conciliation. He understood well the ultimate power of the purse and the sword. The party's leadership was now much more conservative in outlook than it had been during the first two years after Sun Yat-sen's death, when Borodin's influence was strongest. Most of the party's liberal-minded leaders were away, and communists had been driven out. The group which now intended to lead the party was, as we have seen, riven by factionalism – entirely familiar in the Chinese setting, yet an incubus.

The Chinese Communist Party, instead of being a temporary partner of the Kuomintang and growing rapidly in numbers and influence, was now in revolt against it, driven to that position long before it was ready for the 'second stage' of revolution, the socialist stage. Reduced, probably, to fewer than ten thousand members, if that many, the party's fortunes were at a low ebb. Some 20 of its youthful leaders, idealistic activists from the May Fourth student generation, had been executed, including the two sons of Ch'en Tu-hsiu, and one of its most prestigious leaders, Li Ta-chao. Hundreds of their members had died in battle or been killed in ill-conceived uprisings; and thousands had simply withdrawn from the dangerous party. The rest of its members lived furtively in cities, or in a few remote rural areas trying to hold on to essential bases. Some of the remaining leaders had journeyed secretly to Russia for the Sixth Congress of the Chinese Communist Party, held during June and July 1928 in a village outside Moscow. The Congress elected a 40-year-old proletarian, Hsiang Chung-fa, as secretary-general, and vowed to drive imperialism out of China, really unify the country, and abolish the landowning system of the landlord class. It called upon the Chinese people to overthrow the Kuomintang, establish soviets of workers', peasants', and soldiers' deputies, confiscate foreign enterprises, and carry out a variety of social reforms, for this was still the epoch of bourgeois-democratic revolution. Those leaders faced an enormously difficult task of rebuilding their party in a hostile environment, and of emancipating themselves from Comintern direction.

Yet seven years since the party's founding had provided the leadership with valuable experience on which to draw, and many lessons. It had learned in a practical way how to organize a political movement directed towards a nationalistic revolution, and how to recruit patriotic youth through the party's subsidiary organization, the Communist Youth League. Mostly people of education, the leaders had perfected the art of propaganda through a variety of journals directed towards different groups in society; and they knew how to organize patriotic demonstrations in which they discovered activists, and how to manipulate such movements towards the party's other goals. They had gained experience in 'united front work', joining with a variety of other organizations in common patriotic efforts, usually anti-imperialist. Some of them had learned how to come 'close' to the real proletariat; how to organize workers into unions and federations that were controlled by the party, and in this process, how to mount and finance strikes, the importance of coercion, and the need to generate public support. Other leaders had been able to organize a vast number of poor farmers in South China, had learned what grievances and hopes would bring them into group action; but also, how fragile and weak such rapidly created organizations were in the face of established local power. Not a few of the remaining leaders had been involved in military work, either as cadets in Whampoa Academy and its branch at Wuhan, or as political instructors and combat officers. Starting from the school room, the workshop, or the farm, almost all the leaders had, by 1928, undergone their baptisms of violence. A screening process had removed the faint-hearted. In short, the Chinese Communist Party still had a vigorous young leadership with many talents, wide contacts, and much useful experience in revolutionary work, but the odds against them must have seemed enormous.

Enormous problems faced any group, party, or regime that hoped to remake China according to some more humane blueprint. In the field of foreign relations there was a 70-year legacy of treaties, many signed under duress, which restricted China's sovereignty and gave foreigners extraordinary privileges, which their governments enforced with gunboats and marines. Although Great Britain and the United States were moving towards negotiating the return of China's 'lost rights' step by step, a more determined imperialist power, Japan, was acting forcefully to protect and enhance its economic dominance of Manchuria.

Internally, warlordism had scarcely been ended, though a few militarists such as Wu P'ei-fu, Sun Ch'uan-fang, Chang Tsung-ch'ang, and Chang Tso-lin had been overthrown. They had been replaced by others out of the Northern Expedition. Now the country had five main agglomerations of regional military power – the group proclaiming itself the Nationalist government, based in the lower Yangtze valley; the Kwangsi faction holding much of Hupei, Hunan and Kwangsi; Feng Yü-hsiang's Kuominchün with its base in Shensi and populous Honan, and now stretching into Shantung and Hopei; Yen Hsi-shan of Shansi, with subordinates ensconced in the Peking-Tientsin area as well; and Chang Hsueh-liang and other Manchurian generals controlling domestic affairs in the North-east. Most of West and South-west China had scarcely been touched by the Northern Expedition; local commanders in Szechwan, Kweichow and Yunnan defended and exploited their territories as before. Even Kwangtung, the home of the nationalist revolution, was only loosely attached to the Nanking centre. This deeply rooted phenomenon of nearly autonomous regional power – a product of geography and history – must be a major obstacle to all efforts at centralization and nationwide rehabilitation.

Many other inheritances from the past created intractable problems – a chaotic monetary system; a taxation system characterized by exploitation of the poor and riddled with corruption; an inadequate transportation system for a modernizing nation; very little factory industry, and that concentrated in a few cities where the workers lived in slums and were overworked and underpaid. Most serious of all was the condition of rural life, with a dense population struggling with enormous industry to sustain itself on too little arable land and without benefit of scientific agricultural techniques. Education and public health needed great expansion because the vast populace was largely illiterate and was plagued by preventable diseases. Parts of the country were periodically ravaged by famine.

Thus, though the politically aware looked forward with hope in 1928, progress towards creating a modern nation-state was sure to be slow even under the most favourable conditions. And such were not to be.

CHAPTER 12

THE CHINESE BOURGEOISIE, 1911–37

The Revolution of 1911 marked – if not the advent of the bourgeoisie – at least its establishment as a major force in the economic and social life of China. The appearance of a bourgeoisie in the large coastal cities was made possible by the development of the merchant class under the Ming and Ch'ing. During the eighteenth century urbanization was accelerated by a demographic upsurge and an expansion in inter-regional exchanges: the urban population is estimated to have reached 24 million.[1] Merchants intensified and diversified their activities. Local guilds (*hui-kuan*) multiplied throughout the whole country, and new forms of credit made their appearance in Ningpo and Shanghai well before the Treaty of Nanking opened these ports to foreign trade.[2]

In the second half of the nineteenth century the intervention of the West gave a new impetus to the growth of the coastal cities and brought about tremendous economic change. From this the dominant urban classes quickly sought to profit. Mandarins and merchants each had certain advantages: the former had access to the administration and the public purse, a sense of responsibility, a capacity for initiative; the latter enjoyed personal wealth, group solidarity and a willingness to adopt innovations. From the uneasy collaboration and the partial fusion of these classes there sprang an elite of ill-defined configuration, that of the 'gentry and merchants' (*shen-shang*). At the beginning of the twentieth century, the decline of the central government weakened the position of the mandarins within this elite. But while the Revolution of 1911 reflected and accelerated this development, it was not until the First World War that the new bourgeoisie really sprang into action. The withdrawal of foreign competition opened new markets to it, both inside and outside the country. The expansion and diversification of these new fields of activity favoured a new breed of businessmen: bankers and industrialists began to take the

---

1 Gilbert Rozman, *Urban networks in Ch'ing China and Tokugawa Japan*, 6. Mark Elvin, *The pattern of the Chinese past*, 268.
2 Ho Ping-ti, *Studies on the population of China*, 197–204. Susan Jones, 'Finance in Ningpo: the "ch'ien-chuang" ', in W. E. Willmott, ed. *Economic organization in Chinese society*, 47–51.

lead from merchants. These wartime and post-war years formed the golden age of the Chinese bourgeoisie. But the restoration of a bureaucratic and military administration in 1927 ushered in an era of reaction. The most dynamic, the most enterprising element of the bourgeois class lost ground, to be supplanted by a state capitalism which more often than not was merely the capitalism of the higher officials.

The story of the Chinese bourgeoisie in the twentieth century is thus the story of a set-back, for which we shall try to pick out the causes as we proceed. To draw lessons from it is more difficult. We can of course hark back to certain familiar themes: is not the Third Force merely a mirage, the projection of a narcissistic West on a Third World which is incapable of resembling it, and little desirous of so doing? From another point of view we may query the necessity of the bourgeois revolution: is it possible to by-pass this stage? or can the responsibility of the bourgeois revolution be entrusted to other social classes than the bourgeoisie?

Every trend that has been defeated by history runs a grave risk of being regarded as merely a deviation of no significance. However, the return in force of the Chinese bureaucracy, first under the Kuomintang, then under the communist regime, could not obliterate the bourgeoisie's contribution to the modern, democratic and internationalist tradition that emanated from the May Fourth movement, any more than it could prevent the eventual resurrection of this tradition. Paradoxically, it is only over the long term that the balance-sheet can be drawn up for a bourgeois experiment that was marginal and transitory at the time.

THE BIRTH OF A CHINESE BOURGEOISIE

The economic upheavals in the late nineteenth and early twentieth centuries

The centuries that preceded the opening of China to foreigners were centuries of prosperity and growth. An intensive agriculture with refined techniques had ensured yields greater than those of pre-industrial Europe. The Chinese population, which had doubled during the eighteenth century, was estimated to be more than 400 million around 1850. A well-organized and inexpensive system of river transport carried the growing flow of inter-regional traffic. The pace of urbanization accelerated, and a network of markets hemmed in ever more closely a countryside in which craftsmanship had become a secondary vocation. Traditional techniques had been brought to such a level of perfection that further improvements seemed neither possible nor profitable without an industrial revolution – a revolution deterred by demographic pressure, low per capita income, and insufficient consumer demand, as well as by the abundance of labour and the relative scarcity of raw materials. The Chinese economy seemed caught in the 'high-level equilibrium trap' so well described by Mark Elvin.[3]

The intervention of the West had a deeply upsetting effect on the functioning of this system, which had become introverted because the Ming and Ch'ing governments had discouraged trade and seafaring. 'It was the historic contribution of the modern West to ease and then break the high-level equilibrium trap in China.'[4] During the mid century crises of war and rebellion, the elements of a new dynamism were mustering. Foreign trade grew rapidly from 1860 onwards; China set up its first modern business enterprises: armament factories, steamship companies, iron- and steel-works, and textile mills. The foci of this new development were the urban coastal centres, among which Shanghai soon established its pre-eminence. These new port-cities differed considerably from the previous generation of Chinese towns. Cities of medium importance, markets or administrative centres, places of residence for a bureaucratic and landed elite with which the merchant community was eager to be assimilated, the towns of the sixteenth to eighteenth centuries seemed perfectly integrated into a political and social order of which their leading elements were, at one and the same time, the most active agents and the principal beneficiaries. The originality of the coastal ports at the close of the Ch'ing dynasty lay not only in the remoteness of their location on the fringes of the rural and continental empire, nor even in the concentration of their population – which was to make Shanghai one of the largest cities in Asia in the twentieth century: had not Marco Polo already numbered the inhabitants of the Chinese towns of the middle ages in the millions? The great coastal centres that sprang up in the second half of the nineteenth century escaped the Chinese urban tradition by becoming foci of technological innovation and political subversion. This double evolution of the city was fostered by the presence of the foreigners from whom the Chinese borrowed the new techniques of production and organization, and from the shelter of whose concessions they denounced the abuses and the impotence of the imperial government. Despite all its efforts the dynasty could not control these new urban centres as completely as it had the cities of the interior in former days. To be sure, the Shanghai–Canton–Hong-Kong axis formed only a narrow corridor on the flank of the continental empire. But through this breach surged the ideas, the techniques, and the men who were to topple

3 Elvin, *Pattern of the Chinese past*, 298.   4 *Ibid.* 314.

(or perhaps merely to rock on its foundations?) a civilization that had lasted a thousand years.

The Chinese bourgeoisie was born in these new cities. Its growth was linked to that of this peripheral China, opened to Western influences and stigmatized by some as foreign to the 'true' China of Confucius and the countryside.[5] This same accusation was also levelled against the bourgeoisie, which was repudiated as consisting of compradors – but when necessary, was forgiven, as being Chinese. However, just as the concept of the treaty ports was in the tradition of China as a sea-going nation – a tradition as authentic as the dominant one of the continental empire – so also was the modern bourgeoisie welded onto the traditional society.

A complex social base

When a modern economic sector began to take shape in the second half of the nineteenth century, the dominant urban classes – mandarins and merchants – tried to seize control of it and reserve its benefits for themselves.

The civil servants were doubly privileged by their easy access to the authorities and by their command of public funds. As indeed in all 'underdeveloped' countries, the public authorities played an essential role in the process of modernization. Acting in the name of the state, the higher officials gathered information, and granted authorizations, monopolies, exemptions and loans. In China the tradition of state control over the merchant community could only reinforce the administration's stranglehold on modernization. The bureaucrats were supported by their natural allies, the gentry. Since the eighteenth century numerous landed proprietors had made their way back to the towns. Leaving to others the task of overseeing the running of their estates, these new notables devoted themselves both to their private affairs such as money-lending or commerce and to the public affairs of the community. From this era dates the rise of the charity associations (*shan-t'ang*) and of the various offices (*chü*) in which, in collaboration with the lower ranks of the administration, the elite in actual fact assumed responsibility for the conduct of municipal affairs.[6] Their sense of initiative, their aptitude for management, and the

5 Cf. for example, the theses presented by Rhoads Murphey, *The outsiders: The Western experience in India and China.*
6 On the transfer of power from the landed gentry to the urban, commercial, or bureaucratic elites, cf. Elvin, *Pattern of the Chinese past*, 235, 248–60. The decline of serfdom, which Elvin uses to explain this transfer, remains a controversial problem; but it seems certain that the regime of property, and social structures in general, underwent profound upheavals during the eighteenth century. Cf. Thomas A. Metzger, 'On the historical roots of modernization in China: the increasing differentiation of the economy from the polity during late Ming

favours of the administration notwithstanding, the paucity of public funds and the complexity of the new techniques of production and organization obliged the officials more often than not to seek the assistance of the merchants.

With a tradition that went back to the origins of the empire, the merchant class had blossomed forth during the economic revolution of the middle ages: from the eighteenth century onwards it had enjoyed a renewal of prosperity and prestige, evidenced by the increase in its regional and professional guilds. From their long history the Chinese merchants had inherited a high degree of competence in both the commercial and the financial spheres. The complexity of the institutions, the multiplicity of middlemen, and the specialization of functions allowed the merchants to commercialize – without, however, controlling – the production of the small artisans and farmers, and thus to integrate it into a local, an inter-regional, or, more rarely, a national market.

The Chinese merchants' exceptional capacity for seizing and exploiting every opportunity for enrichment encouraged their collaboration with the foreigners. In the open ports investors in Western factories and transport companies were numerous: and around 1900 the number of compradors who had placed or were placing their talents in the service of foreign businessmen was estimated at 20,000.[7] Through these professional contacts, the merchants acquired the modern techniques of management and production. They constituted a pioneer group, open to the outside world, and perhaps closer to the foreign communities than to traditional Chinese society. However, far from collapsing under these foreign contacts – as might have been suggested by the number of religious conversions, or the fetish of wearing Western apparel – the national and social identity of the Chinese merchants asserted itself with renewed force in the bosom of the regional guilds, the professional associations, and – from 1904 – the chambers of commerce.

However, various obstacles slowed down the transformation of the merchant class into a modern bourgeoisie of businessmen and industrialists. These obstacles had their origin partly in the merchant tradition itself: for example, in the strict separation between the two networks of marketing and production. Before the second half of the nineteenth century, the Chinese made hardly any use of the system of 'putting-out', the general adoption of which marked the dawn of industrial capitalism in

and early Ch'ing times', in The Institute of Economics, ed. *Conference on modern Chinese economic history*, Academia Sinica (Taipei, 1977), 33–44. On the role of the notables in urban administration, cf. Mark Elvin, 'The administration of Shanghai 1905–1914', in M. Elvin and G. William Skinner, eds. *The Chinese city between two worlds*, 241.

7 Yen-p'ing Hao, *The comprador in nineteenth century China, bridge between East and West*, 102.

Manchester or Lyons. In the same way their penchant for speculation led these merchants to run considerable risks in return for quick and large profits, which were rarely to be obtained from industrial investments. But above all it was the inferiority of their social status which, in the final days of the empire, handicapped the merchant class in their economic and political transformation. Care most certainly has to be taken not to interpret too literally Confucianism's condemnation of commerce. Over the centuries practice had continually counteracted rigidity of principle.[8] In actual fact the very real enfeoffment of the merchants to the public authorities manifested itself not in the repression of commercial activities, but in the various forms of control and collaboration, the most classic example of which was the salt trade in the seventeenth and eighteenth centuries. However, this enfeoffment allowed a wide margin of initiative and enrichment: the prosperity and power of the merchants of Yang-chou bore witness to that.[9] Either co-opted by the bureaucracy, or seeking to force their way into it by success in the examinations or by the purchase of titles, members of the merchant class abandoned their class origins and climbed up the social ladder. But this upward mobility was partly compensated for by a counter-movement on the part of some members of the gentry who devoted themselves to the clandestine or roundabout practice of business.

The business bourgeoisie thus came into being at the end of the nineteenth century as the result of intensified collaboration between mandarins and gentry on the one hand, and merchants on the other; and of a partial fusion of these two groups. On the initiative of the public authorities mixed enterprises (*kuan-tu shang-pan* or *kuan-shang ho-pan*) were developed in the modern sector, financed by both private and public funds, and managed by merchants under the responsible supervision of higher officials. As the years went by this bureaucratic capitalism became less institutionalized. When it reached its most advanced state of evolution, in the first decade of the twentieth century, it was in fact based solely on the double adherence, as individuals, of the leaders of an enterprise to the mandarin and merchant classes – as, for example, Chang Chien or Yen Hsin-hou.[10] The appearance of this new group of urban gentry-merchants (*shen-shang*) was acknowledged in and encouraged by the massive sale of mandarin titles dating from the middle of the nineteenth

8 Wellington K. K. Chan, *Merchants, mandarins and modern enterprise in late Ch'ing China*, 15–25.
9 Ho Ping-ti, 'The salt merchants of Yang-chou: a study of commercial capitalism in eighteenth century China' in *Harvard Journal of Asiatic Studies*, 17 (1954) 130–68.
10 Chan, *Merchants, mandarins and modern enterprise*, ch. 6, 'State control and the official entrepreneur'.

century, by the upgrading of the status of merchants at the beginning of the following century (by an edict of 1903), and by the ever-growing interest in business openly displayed by numerous mandarins or ex-mandarins.

The balance was shifting between the constituent elements of this new hybrid class. At the dawn of the twentieth century the mandarins seemed to be presiding over its destiny. Mandarins were to be found at the head of the charity associations (ai-yü shan-t'ang) of Shanghai and Canton, the embryonic municipal councils such as the Tsung-kung chü (Head Office of Public Works) of the Chinese city of Shanghai, and even as presidents of the new chambers of commerce (which numbered about 800 at the end of the Ch'ing).[11] But in the years that followed, the abolition of the official examinations (1905), the decline of the central government, and the militarization of the regional authorities weakened the mandarinate. The merchants came to assume more importance within the urban elite. Their intervention in the anti-American boycott of 1905 revealed their new significance in both the economic and the political spheres. The officials or sons of officials who had joined the ranks of the bourgeoisie of business behaved more and more like heads of corporations and private capitalists – such as the grandson of Tseng Kuo-fan, who around 1920 under the name of Nieh Yun-t'ai (C. C. Nieh) was to become one of the principal leaders and the spokesman of the great body of Chinese industrial employers.

The role of the treaty ports

The formation of the Chinese bourgeoisie sprang also from extraneous circumstances: foreign intervention and the growth of concessions in the treaty ports.

First seen during the Ming, the buds of capitalism had withered without blossoming either into a technological revolution, or into a modern bourgeoisie. The reasons for this set-back are not yet clearly defined by historians, who have variously blamed bureaucratic oppression (E. Balazs), institutional unwieldiness (A. Feuerwerker), scarcity of supplies and raw materials and the lack of coordination between the small producers bound by routine and the better informed merchants (M. Elvin), or even the insufficiency of energy resources.[12] At the most we may note,

11 Chow Tse-tung, The May Fourth movement: intellectual revolution in modern China, 380.
12 Étienne Balazs, Chinese civilization and bureaucracy: variations on a theme, 44. Albert Feuerwerker, China's early industrialization, Sheng Hsuan-huai 1844–1916 and mandarin enterprise, 242. Elvin, Pattern of the Chinese Past, 284–301. S. A. M. Adshead, 'An energy crisis in early modern China', Ch'ing-shih wen-t'i, 3. 2 (Dec. 1974).

following E. Balazs, that the blossoming of merchant communities coincided, over the centuries, with the diminution of the powers of the state and of bureaucratic restraints. However, whenever the buds of capitalism opened out thanks to a weakening of the dominant political and ideological order, they were stifled more or less quickly by the troubles that followed on this weakening. Thus, the only alternative to a paralysing imperial and Confucian power seemed to be a destructive anarchy.

The upsurge of the bourgeois class at the end of the nineteenth century and the beginning of the twentieth originated in the coincidence between the decline of bureaucratic restraints (which released the energies of the merchants), and the existence of islands of relative security and order – 'the refuge of the concessions' – (which preserved these energies).[13] Although they were treated as second-class citizens – liable to taxation, but long denied all municipal responsibilities – the Chinese residents of the concessions benefited from the presence of the foreigners. The concession police, reinforced if necessary by the volunteer corps recruited from among the foreign residents, sheltered the treaty ports from the disturbances and small rebellions which were continually springing up in the provinces from the end of the nineteenth century onwards. Not that the strength of these armed forces was very impressive: but the threat that lay behind the foreign gunboats, anchored in the principal ports or cruising up and down the Yangtze, was enough to preserve the peace of these 'states within the state'. In the shelter of this peace, the public services (customs, post) introduced new administrative virtues of honesty and regularity. The 'model concessions' offered utilities (the supply of low-cost domestic and industrial electricity, running water, networks of tramways and urban telephones) which equalled those of the great Western cities. But what the Chinese elite seemed above all to be looking for in the concessions was the safety of their goods and persons. They entrusted their fortunes to foreign banks whose vaults the Peking government would never be able to break open; and against the high-handedness of the imperial officials they appealed to the jurisdiction of the mixed courts.[14] The foreigners' desire to ensure for local commercial interests the development that they considered normal – by shielding them from all interference by the public authorities – in fact led the Shanghai Municipal Council in 1902 to suggest in principle that no Chinese resident should be handed over to the imperial authorities until he had

13 For a more detailed analysis, cf. M. Claire Bergère, ' "The other China": Shanghai from 1919 to 1949' in C. Howe, ed. *Shanghai: revolution and development in an Asian metropolis.*
14 A. Feuerwerker, 'The foreign presence in China', ch. 3 above.

first been judged and found guilty by the Mixed Court. In 1903 this principle was signally illustrated in the *Su-pao* (Kiangsu daily) case, when the British majority on the municipal council put pressure on the Mixed Court to ensure that the radical anti-Manchu journalists whose immediate extradition was being demanded by the governor-general at Nanking should be judged according to Western rules of law and should be sentenced only to a short term in jail.[15]

Equally favoured by the existence of these international enclaves into which the concessions had developed, opposition to the imperial regime and the formation of a bourgeois class marched forward side by side, each reinforcing the other.

1911: THE INVISIBLE BOURGEOIS REVOLUTION

Was there a bourgeois revolution in 1911?

Let us reject a more or less widely accepted hypothesis right away: the Revolution of 1911 was not a bourgeois revolution. On the morrow of their victory in 1949 the Chinese Communists, reinterpreting their national history in Marxist terms, have described the 'old democratic revolution' (*chiu min-chu chu-i ko-ming*) of 1911 as a more or less indispensable bourgeois stage between feudalism and socialism, with the bourgeoisie supposedly directing the revolution and becoming its principal beneficiary. Such was not the case – unless one defines the bourgeoisie very broadly to include, besides the business circles and the urban intelligentsia, also higher officials, landlords, officers, and heads of secret societies and armed bands. The specific and original character of these diverse groups argues against such an interpretation, which would equate the bourgeoisie with the ruling classes of a society that by and large remained agrarian and traditional in nature.[16] By the more restrictive definition – that of an urban bourgeoisie tied to modern business – it seems clear that this bourgeoisie played only a secondary part in the events of 1911. Armed insurrections, uprisings led by the local elite – this first revolution outstripped the bourgeoisie and escaped its control.[17]

When the bourgeoisie tried, after the success of the revolution, to exploit the situation to its own advantage, it was only half successful.

15 John Lust, 'The Su-pao case: an episode in the early Chinese nationalist movement' in *Bulletin of the School of Oriental and African Studies*, 27. 2 (1964) 408–29.
16 M. Claire Bergère, 'La Révolution de 1911 jugée par les historiens de la République Populaire de Chine', *Revue historique*, 230 (Oct.–Dec. 1963) 403–36.
17 M. Claire Bergère, 'The role of the bourgeoisie', in Mary C. Wright, ed. *China in revolution: the first phase 1900–1913*, 229–95.

It succeeded in getting its essential interests respected, but not in seizing power other than at the local level.

Although one cannot call the Revolution of 1911 a bourgeois revolution, the fact remains that it played an important part in the destiny of the bourgeoisie. It marked the bourgeoisie's first political involvement, its official entry onto the scene of Chinese history – a début of which it was said: 'The present revolution has brought out very clearly the influence and stability of the powerful merchant community, acting through the intermediary of the chambers of commerce.'[18] However, at this particular time the bourgeoisie had only a fragile economic base, the modern sector being as yet little developed and largely controlled by foreign interests. Its social definition was still imprecise: its *rapprochement* with the mandarinate had increased its strength, but weakened its identity. Whence then sprang the importance of its political role?

In 1912 the Ministry of Agriculture and Commerce listed 794 main and subsidiary chambers of commerce mustering 196,636 members.[19] As the membership of chambers of commerce included not only individuals but also numerous societies, guilds or corporations represented by their directors, the number of merchants enrolled in the chambers of commerce – either as individuals or through their appointed representatives – was clearly much greater than suggested by the official statistics. If one takes families into account the richest and most respected section of the merchant class must have been about 1.5 to 2 million strong, and represented almost 0.5 per cent of the total population. This seems a very small percentage. However, in comparison with other groups of the ruling class, the number of merchants is much greater than that of military officers (17,000),[20] students (30,000), graduates returned from abroad (35,000),[21] officials (50,000), and even than that of members of the upper gentry (200,000).[22] The existence of 794 chambers of commerce shows that merchant communities were widespread throughout the land. For the reasons outlined above (new possibilities of enrichment, security of property and person) it was in the large treaty ports, and in particular Shanghai, that the most numerous, the most dynamic, and the richest communities were concentrated – those which participated most directly in the modern world. Although it constituted but a small fraction of the total population, the merchant class was numerically one of the largest

18 *NCH*, 1 Nov. 1913, p. 352.
19 Cf. f.n. 11.
20 Chang Chung-li, *The Chinese gentry: Studies on their role in nineteenth century Chinese society,* 117–20.
21 Wang Y. C., *Chinese intellectuals and the West 1872–1949,* 367, 64, 73.
22 Cf. f.n. 20.

ruling groups. Allied to the gentry, this class represented the dominant elite of the new modernized China of the treaty ports.

The importance of the role the Chinese bourgeoisie set out to play at that time can also be explained as a phenomenon of ideological super-determination. The emergence of this new class coincided in fact with the diffusion throughout China of ideas of democracy and nationalism imported from the West, where during the eighteenth and nineteenth centuries their formulation had generally been associated with the coming to power of national bourgeoisies. As the inheritors of a body of ideas transmitted (not without some distortion and omissions) by the intellectual youth and certain officers of the New Army, the Chinese bourgeoisie tried to link this imported ideology to the national reality. The democracy, constitutionalism and nationalism preached by the leaders of the anti-Ch'ing opposition coincided with the aspirations of a bourgeoisie whose sudden awakening was correspondingly accelerated.

The bourgeoisie actively supported the opposition parties. Reformers and revolutionaries profited equally from its aid. At a time when ideologies were feeling their way, when the influence of personality was compensating for the imprecision of programme, the indecisiveness demonstrated by the bourgeoisie was in no way surprising. Far from following any strict line of division between lower and upper bourgeoisie, between compradors and businessmen of national stature, the differentiation between reformist bourgeoisie and revolutionary bourgeoisie seemed unpredictable: here, as in so many other spheres, personal relations played a part – thus the importance of the contacts which the leaders of the opposition established with the merchant communities during their frequent travels. However, on the eve of the revolution reformism seemed to be favoured by the continental bourgeoisie, while the emigrant communities overseas appeared more radical. The business establishment in the treaty ports, always closely allied with the gentry class, shared with it a very real social conservatism, and doubtless a more realistic view of the Chinese situation as a whole. Through the chambers of commerce the merchants played an active part in the constitutionalist movement: in 1909, they were elected to provincial assemblies, and in 1910 they participated in the campaign for the convening of a national assembly.[23]

The Chinese merchants living overseas dreamed of restoring international prestige to their native land by endowing her with the most modern forms of political and economic organization. The communities of Hong Kong, Yokohama and Singapore therefore were among the first to

23 M. Claire Bergère, *La bourgeoisie chinoise et la révolution de 1911*, 53.

finance the activities of Sun Yat-sen. When the acceptance of Sun spread, after 1905, to intellectual and military circles, his bonds with the merchants remained as firm as before. Of course, this assimilation of the overseas bourgeoisie into the radical wing of the opposition could not be pushed too far. The reform leaders K'ang Yu-wei and Liang Ch'i-ch'ao were also able to win the understanding of their émigré compatriots, and received substantial financial assistance from them. In addition, during the final years of the Ch'ing government its reform-minded ministers found valuable collaborators overseas such as the rich merchant Chang Pi-shih who returned from Singapore to help Sheng Hsuan-huai develop the national railway system and set up the Ministry of Commerce (Shang-pu).[24] Within China, the participation of the treaty-port merchants in the constitutional movement and in policies of reform did not prevent them, when the time came, from switching over into the revolutionary camp, supporting the insurrection, and managing affairs locally while awaiting the establishment of the new regime.

The merchants and the revolutionary uprising

The insurrection at Wuchang on 10 October 1911 was carried out by the military. The merchants played no immediate role, even though they were no strangers to the troubles leading up to the revolutionary explosion. The campaign against the nationalization of the railways, which disturbed the province of Szechwan during the spring and the summer of 1911, had received the active support of the chambers of commerce and the guilds of Chungking and Chengtu. In October the merchants of Wuchang hastened to lend their support to the military insurgents. On 12 October, these insurgents gave the merchants guarantees, proclaiming:

'Those who mistreat merchants will be beheaded; Those who interfere with trade will be beheaded; Those who attempt to close the shops will be beheaded; Those who encourage the success of business will be rewarded.'[25]

In exchange for this protection merchants took part in the maintenance of order and organized militia to hunt down looters and arsonists. The president of the chamber of commerce was even promoted to the position of chief of police. The chamber of commerce granted the insurgents an immediate loan of 200,000 taels.

24 Chan, *Merchants, mandarins and modern enterprise*, 131, 164, 168, 183.
25 Bergère, *La bourgeoisie chinoise*, 59–60.

In Shanghai the cooperation of the bourgeoisie with the revolutionaries did not follow the uprising: it preceded it and paved the way for it.[26]

In April 1911 contact was established with the leaders of the T'ung-meng hui (Revolutionary Alliance): Ch'en Ch'i-mei, Chu Shao-p'ing and the banker Shen Man-yun. The last-named was the official representative of the Association of Chinese Citizens (Chung-kuo kuo-min hui), a newly created patriotic organization: he was also one of the directors of the General Chamber of Commerce (Shang-wu tsung-hui) and a member of the Municipal Council of the Chinese city (Tzu-chih kung-so). At the same time the merchant militia created in 1906 was reorganized and placed under a unified command. Their effective strength, which had been estimated as between 350 and 700, rose to 2,000 at the beginning of November 1911. Command of this national corps of volunteers from Shanghai to which was linked – politically at least – the Chinese Company of Volunteers from the International Settlement, was entrusted to the president of the Municipal Council of the Chinese city, Li Chung-chueh (P'ing-shu). Li belonged to the mandarin wing of the local elite of *shen-shang*. But in Shanghai the elite presented a united front.[27] Whether their background was that of business or of letters, whether they lived in the concessions or in the Chinese quarter, they seemed to have the same sympathy for the revolutionary undertaking. Were disaffection with the central authorities and patriotic uneasiness enough to explain this unanimity? Should one not also recognize the workings of an elitist organization which kept the initiative within a small circle of responsible persons – a few dozen in all – who were to be found in charge of the Chamber of Commerce as well as of the militia and the Municipal Council of the Chinese city? After the revolt at Wuchang a regular collaboration came into being between Ch'en Ch'i-mei and Li Chung-chueh as a consequence of the daily meetings that took place on the premises of the revolutionary daily *Min-li pao* (The interest of the people), which was financed by Shen Man-yun. The merchant militia controlled the town; the Municipal Council of the Chinese city neutralized the local police; the Chamber of Commerce promised subsidies to the revolutionaries.[28]

26 Mark Elvin, 'The gentry democracy in Shanghai 1905–1914' (Harvard University, Ph.D. dissertation, 1967), 230–46.

27 The appearance at the end of 1911 of an ephemeral rival to the Shanghai Chamber of Commerce perhaps reflects, as J. Sanford suggests, political divergences in the bosom of the merchant community. If indeed a conflict existed, it was rapidly resolved, since the two chambers amalgamated at the beginning of 1912. James Sanford, 'Chinese commercial organization and behavior in Shanghai of the late nineteenth and early twentieth century' (Harvard University, Ph.D. dissertation, 1976), 259.

28 Bergère, *La bourgeoisie chinoise*, 62.

When Ch'en Ch'i-mei overcame the Manchu garrison on 3 November and seized the Kiangnan Arsenal, Shanghai became republican.

In the great outburst of sentiment for Chinese unity which marked the Revolution of 1911 each province and each town had a different story to tell. The role of the entire bourgeoisie cannot properly be judged by the admittedly exceptional experience of Shanghai. At Canton the news of the revolt of 10 October had at first no other effect than to induce the governor-general, Chang Ming-ch'i, to preserve his powers by declaring his neutrality in the civil war and strengthening provincial autonomy. His plan, approved by the gentry, was thwarted by the merchants who gathered at the Ai-yü Charity Association on 29 October when they opted for the republic and proclaimed the independence of Kwangtung.[29] But the merchants were unable to translate their decision into action; and it was not until 9 November that Chang Ming-ch'i, yielding to the growing pressure of the revolutionary forces, left town and abandoned power to the representative of the T'ung-meng hui, Hu Han-min. Thus, in spite of Canton's commercial importance, the merchants of the city played only a limited role in the events of the revolution. Their divisiveness was the cause of their weakness. Here, the chamber of commerce was unable to assert itself over the 72 guilds and nine charity associations, and act as spokesman for the business community. Then again, the slower rhythm of economic modernization hampered the integration of the urban elite. Facing a gentry that clung to its prerogatives and its traditional interests, the merchants formed an isolated group of relatively minor importance.

Thus the role of the bourgeoisie varied from one city to another. They were unobtrusive in the recently-colonized areas of the north-east, where the merchants contented themselves with maintaining order and adopting a 'wait and see' attitude, or in the provinces of the interior such as Hunan where the competition lay between the army, the gentry and secret societies. They were more active in the coastal regions like Shantung, Chekiang and Kiangsu, or in the big treaty ports of the middle Yangtze – Hankow, for example.

Generally speaking, the bourgeoisie did not take the initiative in the uprisings. It contented itself with reacting, in accordance with its own strength, to the local political situations brought about by other groups. Even in Shanghai it played only a contributory role. Nevertheless it welcomed the revolution sympathetically and confidently. The events of the revolution did not bring about any grave economic crisis. The inter-

29 Edward J. M. Rhoads, *China's republican revolution: the case of Kwangtung, 1895–1913*, 222–3.

ruption of transport and the shortage of liquid assets caused a momentary slowing-down of commercial and industrial activity. But panic was avoided; and in Shanghai recovery began to take place in mid December.

Some historians of the People's Republic of China emphasize the internal contradictions inherent among the bourgeoisie, evidenced by their plunging into the revolution on the side of the intellectuals and the young officers, and then – scared by the extent of the upheavals – beating a hasty retreat in order to preserve their class interests and taking their place alongside the gentry.[30] The reversal of feeling which set in among the Cantonese merchants in December 1911, or among those of Chengtu at the beginning of 1912, gives some colour to this proposition; but more generally speaking, it would seem that the Chinese merchants were no more aware than their contemporaries of the gap between the conservative character of the uprising and the revolutionary ideas in the name of which it had taken place. Should we then talk here of 'ideological disorder' and 'political immaturity'?[31] If we acknowledge, as does J. W. Esherick, that in the Chinese political tradition liberalism is not to be defined in terms of the individual, but rather as opposition to the authoritarianism of the central government,[32] there is nothing inconsistent in the suggestion that the local elites saw in the establishment of their own power the triumph of liberty and democracy.

The merchants and the common front of the elite

On the morrow of the revolution, the lack of a central power and the decay of public authority frequently led the urban elites to undertake the running of their cities. 'After the fall of the Manchu regime, the government of most of the Chinese cities was in actual fact carried out over a period of months by the chambers of commerce and the guilds working in cooperation.'[33]

This intervention by the merchant communities in local political and administrative life, reflected the importance that the urban elites had acquired throughout the country (including inland China) since the nineteenth century. It was not, however, a new political experience. It continued – and amplified – the tradition of the guild federation, whose role

---

30 Cf. the celebration of the 50th anniversary of the revolution of 1911 by Tung Pi-wu, *Current Background*, 667 (6 Nov. 1961).

31 M. C. Bergère, *La bourgeoisie chinoise*, 41–2, 125–6.

32 Joseph W. Esherick, *Reform and revolution in China: the 1911 Revolution in Hunan and Hubei*, 237–50.

33 *NCH*, 1 Nov. 1913, p. 352.

had been established during the crisis of the Taiping Rebellion.[34] Going
beyond the corporatist framework, these federations had at that time
devoted themselves to the service of the urban collectivity. Moved by a
Confucian sense of civic responsibility, they had tried to remedy the
inefficiency of the public authorities and protect the immediate interests
of their cities.

The objective of the chambers of commerce, which in 1912 imposed
their authority on many towns, both large and small, was no different.
It was a question of maintaining the social order, and contending with
the pirates, brigands, undisciplined soldiers and secret societies. The
merchants made common cause with the gentry: and in this common
front of notables, there was nothing to single them out, save perhaps
the vigour of their action. It was the chambers of commerce and the
guilds that paid the soldiers, bribed the bandits to depart, started disband-
ing the troops, and stepped in between the rival generals. 'Of all the
constituent elements of Chinese society', a contemporary observed, 'the
merchant group is both the most solid and the most conservative.'[35]

However general it may have been, the involvement of the merchants
acquired only a limited political importance. In effect, they were insinuat-
ing themselves into the framework of an established system, and simply
attempting to correct its faulty functioning. The merchants did not
seek power for themselves. More often than not, they were content to
negotiate with the existing authorities: mandarins who had remained at
their posts, generals or militant revolutionaries who had been swept into
power. This method of indirect control involved many risks: local power-
holders frequently turned against the merchants, taxing them, threatening
them, having them kidnapped. And despite the means of financial pressure at their disposal (in that they either advanced funds or guaranteed
the issues of bills), the merchants then became the first victims of the
authorities whose establishment they had facilitated. However, for the
most part, the merchants were not ready to assume directly the political
responsibilities from which tradition had always excluded them. Their
involvement was merely short term.

In the general crisis that spread throughout the political system, this
expedient proved ineffective. Insecurity persisted, and grew worse.
Kwangtung became nothing but a 'Pirate Republic'.[36] Transit duties
(likin), which the merchants had tried to abolish, reappeared under other

34 Tou Chi-liang, T'ung-hsiang tsu-chih yen-chiu (Studies of regional associations), ch. 2 (quoted
here from Elvin, Pattern of the Chinese past, 337, f.n. 18).
35 NCH, 1 Nov. 1913, p. 352. On the role of the merchants in the administration of provincial cities, cf. Bergère, La bourgeoisie chinoise, 69–80.
36 Jean Rodes, Scènes de la vie révolutionnaire en Chine: 1911–1914, 301, 117.

names – *shang-chüan* (imposts on trade) or *t'ung-chüan* (general taxes). In the absence of any regular fiscal revenues, the merchants could not for long cover the costs of public administration by themselves. Lack of coordination between the local authorities and lack of interest in the countryside doomed to failure the efforts at pacification as well as the project for the unification of the market. In the Chinese provinces the power of the merchants could not take the place of the bureaucratic power of the central and provincial governments. All it could do was attempt to limit the destructive anarchy which remained, as in the past, the only alternative to the imperial system.

The Shanghai bourgeoisie and the government at Nanking

In Shanghai, however, a more powerful and better organized merchant elite, while freeing themselves from the restraints of the past, continued to enjoy relative security and order within the concessions. They seized the opportunity offered by the revolution to assert their political ambitions, both locally and nationally.

After the defeat of the imperial garrison, in 1911, the principal business-men of the International Settlement and of the Chinese city did not hesitate to take part in the military government organized by General Ch'en Ch'i-mei. Ch'en recruited his advisers from among the directors of the General Chamber of Commerce (Yü Hsia-ch'ing and Chou Sun-ch'ing). He entrusted the conduct of financial affairs to bankers such as Chu Pao-san and Shen Man-yun, assisted by a comprador, Yü P'ing-han. Business management was placed in the hands of the shipowner and industrialist Wang I-t'ing. Municipal administration went to a public works contractor in service utilities, Li Chung-chueh, and to a grain merchant, Ku Hsing-i, who acted as his assistant.[37]

In the environment which best suited it – that of the Chinese coast, cosmopolitan and modernized – the bourgeoisie asserted itself to become a dominant political force. If the treaty ports had really been the enclaves, lacking all communication with the interior, that some authors have made them out to be, perhaps the merchants of Shanghai would not have dreamed of extending their activities to the whole of China. But the economy of the coastal fringe was turned as much towards the hin-terland as towards the ocean. Its prosperity depended on its relations

---

37 Kojima Yoshio, 'Shingai kakumei ni okeru Shanhai dokuritsu to shōshinsō' (The gentry and the merchant classes and Shanghai's independence during the Revolution of 1911), *Tōyō shigaku ronshū*, 6 (Aug. 1960) 113–34, special issue: *Chūgoku kindaika no shakai kōzō: Shingai kakumei no shiteki ichi* (The social structure of Chinese modernization: the historical position of the Revolution of 1911) edited by Tōkyō Kyōiku Daigaku, Ajiashi Kenkyūkai.

with the provinces just as much as on its contacts with foreign countries. Its economic solidarity strengthened the need and the desire for national unity. The bourgeoisie of Shanghai adopted Sun Yat-sen's republican programme and joined him in his striving for modernization. Like Sun Yat-sen, and with him, they wanted to fashion a new China, calling for this purpose on the aid of the Chinese overseas: they wanted to take control of a vast hinterland and transform it in the image of the coastal fringe, so that there the buds of capitalism and democracy might blossom forth at last.

By their loans, estimated at seven million taels,[38] the merchants of Shanghai facilitated the establishment of the Chinese Republic, proclaimed by Sun Yat-sen at Nanking on 1 January 1912, and given legitimacy by the vote of the provincial delegates. The programme of the new government, which straight away established itself as the national government, repeated that of the T'ung-meng hui. In his manifesto of 5 January 1912 Sun levelled an indictment against the obscurantist empire of the Manchus: they 'governed the country to the lasting injury ... of the people, creating privileges and monopolies ... they have levied irregular and unwholesome taxes upon us, have restricted foreign trade to treaty ports, placed likin embargoes upon merchandise in transit and obstructed internal commerce', and Sun promised: 'We will revise ... our commercial and mining codes ... abolish restrictions to trade and commerce. . . .'[39]

At the prompting of Chang Chien, who had been appointed minister of industry, industrial bureaus were set up to relay the directives of the central government to the provinces and to coordinate their efforts.[40] The banker Shen Man-yun obtained five million dollars from overseas Chinese for the creation of a Chinese Industrial Bank (Chung-hua shih-yeh yin-hang), under the joint patronage of Sun Yat-sen and the president of the Shanghai General Chamber of Commerce, Chou Chin-chen.[41] However, the Nanking government only remained in power for three months, which meant it was unable to go very much further. Would it have been capable of doing so, in any case? A few weeks after Sun Yat-sen assumed the presidency, 'the bankers, the rich merchants and com-

38 NCH, 13 July 1912, p. 109; 1 March 1913, p. 650; Bergère, La bourgeoisie chinoise, 82–85.
39 Translation of the manifesto in F. McCormick, The flowery republic, 457.
40 Chin-tai-shih tzu-liao (Materials on modern history) Special issue, 'Hsin-hai ko-ming tzu-liao' (Materials on the 1911 Revolution), 1 (1961) 58, 201.
41 'Hsin-hai ko-ming tzu-liao', 96. Cf. also Shen Yun-sun, 'Chung-hua shih-yeh yin-hang shih-mo' (History of the Chinese Industrial Bank) in Chin-tai-shih tzu-liao (Materials on modern history) 6 (1957) 120–39.

pradors . . . began to find the regime very hard to bear'.[42] Relations deteriorated between the business community and Ch'en Ch'i-mei, the military governor of Shanghai, who sometimes resorted to harsh measures in order to obtain the necessary funds.[43] When the government decided, at the beginning of February, to mortgage the China Merchants' Steam Navigation Company to guarantee a loan from abroad, it ran into violent protests from the shareholders, among whom was Chou Chin-chen.[44]

The conflict that arose in Shanghai in 1912 does not seem analogous to the resistance put up during the 1920s by the Cantonese bourgeoisie, adherents of provincial particularism, to a Kuomintang government anxious to extend its activities on a national basis, even at the price of the difficult Northern Expedition. The Shanghai bourgeoisie shared with Sun a very keen sense of national unity. However, they no doubt hoped that the Nanking government, which had been established thanks to their help, would be able rapidly to widen its foundations and find other sources of support within the country. They soon discovered the extent of their illusion. Deprived of an adequate social base, the Nanking government could not count on the effectiveness of a party machine. At the beginning of 1912 new parties started competing with the T'ung-meng hui, which had always been very loosely structured; and before long it consisted of little more than Sun's immediate entourage. Faced with the Peking–Wuchang axis, which embraced the vast majority of the regular armed forces and enjoyed the support of the mandarinate and the traditionalist gentry, Sun was forced to take a back seat, and surrendered the presidency of the republic to Yuan Shih-k'ai in February 1912.

Thus the first political experiment of the bourgeoisie in the spring of 1912 ended in a double failure. True, the bourgeoisie was able to make its weight felt at that time. In the provinces, it had helped to ensure the continuation of business as usual and the maintenance of a certain degree of public order. Their support of the Nanking government had prevented an unwanted return of the Manchu dynasty, and had contributed to the formation of the republican regime. However, it had not succeeded in setting up the political structures that were indispensable to its development. In the provinces its social base was too poorly defined for its actions to be truly distinguishable from those of the gentry. Nor could the businessmen of Shanghai keep a national government in their hands

42 Report of the consul-general of France, Shanghai, 13 Jan. 1912. Quai d'Orsay Archives: China-Interior politics, Chinese Revolution.
43 Report of the consul-general of France, Shanghai, 13, 17 and 18 Jan. 1912, *ibid.*
44 *NCH*, 10 Feb. 1912, p. 356; 10 Aug. 1912, p. 405; 17 Aug. 1912, p. 458. Report of the consul-general of France, Shanghai, 2 March 1912.

alone. They were unable to graft onto the rural and bureaucratic society of the Chinese interior the new order founded on trade and technology, on free competition and the relatively harmonious attitudes of democracy, which the foreign presence had made possible in the treaty ports.

Despite the bourgeoisie of coastal China, the destiny of the nation continued to be embodied in continental China and in the military and bureaucratic apparatus which alone was capable of governing it.

The recession

The accession of Yuan Shih-k'ai to the presidency of the Chinese Republic ushered in a period of political recession for the Chinese bourgeoisie. After several months of disorder business circles were anxious for a return to calm and security. Their somewhat hesitant rallying to Yuan Shih-k'ai marked the beginning of this political reorientation. The bonds with the revolutionary republicans grew looser. In Shanghai, the 'dare-to-die' troops accused the General Chamber of Commerce of treason when their commander Liu Fu-piao[45] was arrested in April 1912 in the International Settlement. The bourgeoisie's adherents became attracted to new and more moderate political parties, which in May 1912 were reorganized into the Republican Party (Kung-ho tang). In the national elections of December 1912–January 1913 moderates supported this party in Shanghai. In addition, Yuan Shih-k'ai took pains to give compensation and assurances to the merchants: he recognized the contractual obligations of the Nanking government to the business circles of Shanghai,[46] and promised indemnification to the merchants of Hankow whose shops had been destroyed in October 1911.[47] In a lengthy appearance before the provisional senate in Peking, on 29 April 1912, he announced a series of reforms designed to win him the support of the bourgeoisie: suppression of the transit tax (likin), reductions in export taxes, unification of the currency, a policy of industrial development.

After the stagnation of the first few months of 1912 the resumption of businese diverted the bourgeoisie from political action. Helped by an abundant crop and by the rise in value of silver on the world market, foreign trade figures showed only a very small falling-off in comparison with 1911: 843 million haikwan (maritime customs) taels as against 848 million.[48] This prosperity spread to industry. In Shanghai, in 1912, it

45 *NCH*, 27 April 1912, p. 217.
46 *NCH*, 1 March 1913, p. 650.
47 *NCH*, 9 Nov. 1912, p. 40.
48 Hsiao Liang-lin, *China's foreign trade statistics 1864–1949*, table 1, pp. 2–3.

became necessary to quadruple the supply of industrial electric current to meet the demands of new plants – especially those of the rice mills which were being built on both sides of Soochow Creek, and of the textile mills which were developing their capacity.[49] During this same period the milling trade experienced a rapid upsurge (out of 53 Chinese firms recorded in 1913, 14 had been formed after 1911, in Shanghai, in Manchuria, and in cities on the Yangtze).[50] Machine shops increased in number: nine were set up in 1912–13, most of them in Shanghai.[51] The blast furnaces at Hanyang, which had been abandoned during the uprising of October 1911, were brought back into operation by teams which henceforth were exclusively Chinese.[52] In the mining industry, prospecting and mine work were expanding, sometimes with the aid of capital from overseas.[53] Construction of the tramway system of the Chinese city of Shanghai (Nantao) was planned and completed within a few months, without any help from abroad.[54] This overall effort was sustained and coordinated by a dozen or so provincial or national societies for the encouragement of industry, formed during 1912.[55]

In these conditions what business circles feared most was a recrudescence of political and military disorder. The assassination of Sung Chiao-jen on 22 March 1913 at the instigation of President Yuan caused profound uneasiness among the big merchants of Shanghai.[56] However, they were less disturbed by Yuan Shih-k'ai's treason than they were by Sun Yat-sen's hostile reactions. At a time when the newly established public institutions and freedoms were in danger, the only concern of the bourgeoisie was the immediate inconvenience that would come from a new crisis. Disappointment with the revolutionary experiment, the attractions of an orderly regime and the hopes aroused by the economic expansion, all combined to push them towards a collusive neutrality.[57] The crisis of the summer of 1913 was to force them to make up their minds.

When the conflict between Yuan Shih-k'ai and Sun Yat-sen broke out in July 1913 the military leaders of the southern provinces declared their independence. Shanghai was drawn into the movement: Ch'en Ch'i-mei took command of the rebel troops. The merchants hesitated between open

---

49 Wang Ching-yü, comp. *Chung-kuo chin-tai kung-yeh-shih tzu-liao, ti-erh chi, 1895–1914 nien* (Source materials on the history of modern industry in China, second collection, 1895–1914; hereafter *Kung-yeh-shih tzu liao*), 2. 848.
50 *Ibid.* 2. 908.
51 *Ibid.* 2. 920.
52 *NCH*, 16 Nov. 1912, p. 479.
53 *NCH*, 7 Dec. 1912, p. 665.
54 *NCH*, 13 Aug. 1913, p. 558.
55 Wang Ching-yü, *Kung-yeh shih tzu-liao*, 2. 860–7.
56 *NCH*, 26 April 1913, pp. 226, 252; 10 May 1913, p. 427; 24 May 1913, p. 531.
57 Cf. the telegram from the Guild of (old style) Chinese Banks, *NCH*, 17 May 1913, p. 495.

hostility to the rebel movement and the opportunism necessary for the preservation of their interests. The General Chamber of Commerce refused to approve the declaration of independence or to supply Ch'en Ch'i-mei with the funds he demanded. The merchants hoped above all to avoid a confrontation between the rebel troops and the garrison, now re-established in the Kiangnan Arsenal: 'Since Shanghai is a trading port and not a battlefield . . . the party, whichever it may be, that first opens hostilities will be regarded as the enemy of the people.'[58] In highly simplistic fashion, the interests of the group were thus identified with those of the people.

At Canton the governor Ch'en Chiung-ming, who had announced the city's independence on 21 July, himself encountered the hostility or passivity of the local merchants.[59] The few Kuomintang supporters came from among the overseas communities or from Hong Kong and Macao. But it was not long before the most active among them, Chan Chik-yue (Ch'en Hsi-ju), was excluded from residence in Hong Kong by the British authorities. In the principal ports of the Yangtze, in Chungking, Changsha, Wuhu, and Nanking, the merchants showed the same cautiousness, the same veiled hostility towards the rebellion.[60] With varying degrees of success, the local chambers of commerce devoted their energies to preserving their city, bribing the rebel soldiers to leave, and preparing the way for the peaceful return of the northerners. These efforts failed at Nanking, where the merchants had had to supply a good deal of money to the southerners; now they saw themselves ruined by the entry of the northern troops and the pillaging that followed (1–3 September 1913).[61]

The bourgeoisie's hostility to the 'second revolution' of 1913 was manifested only in the most circumspect fashion, especially in those provinces that had declared their independence. Chambers of commerce showed no overt opposition, they merely refused their financial cooperation – as long as the pressure was not too great. In any case, the outcome of the struggle depended above all on the military leaders, and on the number and quality of their troops. In this sphere Yuan Shih-k'ai's superiority was overwhelming. The opposition, or rather the abstention, of the bourgeoisie did not carry any decisive weight in 1913, any more than its

58 *NCH*, 26 July 1913, p. 283.
59 *South China morning post* (hereafter *SCMP*), 27 July, 29 July, 30 July, 1 Aug. 1913.
60 *Foreign Office, Embassy and Consular Archives, China*, Correspondence. F.O. 228: 2499, vol. 277, Revolution, North and South, 24–31 July 1919. F.O. 228: 2500, vol. 278, Revolution, North and South, 1–15 Aug. 1913. F.O. 228: 2501, vol. 279, Revolution, North and South, 16–31 Aug. 1913. Cf. more particularly the communications from Chinkiang, Nanking, Chungking, Wuhu.
61 Communication from Nanking, 29 Aug. 1913, F.O. 228: 2502, vol. 280, Revolution, North and South, Sept. 1913.

adherence had really influenced the course of events in 1911. Whether for or against the revolution, the bourgeoisie remained but a secondary force.

The failure of the 1913 uprising, which brought in its train heavy taxes and pillaged shops, forced the bourgeoisie to defend its short-term interests. Yuan Shih-k'ai encouraged the merchants' return to their traditional social isolation and political abstention. Once victorious, Yuan did not in fact content himself with eliminating the revolutionary opposition by forcing its leaders into exile and ordering the dissolution first of the Kuomintang (November 1913) and then of the parliament (December 1913). He also directed his attacks against all the representative systems that had been set up for the benefit of the local elites before and after the revolution. On 4 February 1914 he suppressed the provincial and local assemblies which had just been resuscitated during the winter of 1912–13 on the basis of a much enlarged electorate (25 per cent of the adult male population).[62] Since the revolution, these local assemblies had taken over many of the administrative, fiscal and military functions normally reserved for the state bureaucracy.[63] In addition, they served as forums and staging-posts for the new associations of industrialists, educators, artisans and women, which were growing ever more numerous at that time. Through these associations a whole stratum of society – the gentry, but also men of letters and small merchants – found itself integrated into the political life of the nation. These assemblies represented something which within the Chinese political tradition came very close to liberalism: the defence of local interests and social groups shut out or neglected by the mandarinate. In the eyes of Yuan they thus represented a threat both to his personal power and to the maintenance of national unity, which he equated with a rigorous administrative centralization.

For the merchants of Shanghai this was the end of an exceptional experience. In the municipality of the Chinese city, which had been re-baptized after the revolution (*shih-cheng t'ing*), the urban gentry of the *shen-shang* had been able to give proof of its capacity for management, its aptitude for modernization, its comprehension of democratic procedures, and its interest in major national problems.[64] The Shanghai business circles would never again recover this local administrative and political autonomy. The bureaus of public works, police, and taxes (*kung-hsün-*

---

62 Cf. Ernest P. Young, 'Politics in the aftermath of revolution: the era of Yuan Shih-k'ai 1919–16', ch. 4 above.
63 On the reduction of the powers of the bureaucracy for the benefit of the local elites, and on the alliance of these elites with private businessmen between 1911 and 1913, cf. Esherick, *Reform and revolution in China*, 246–255.
64 M. Elvin, 'The gentry democracy in Shanghai 1905–1914', 73; 'Shang-hai shih-chih chin-hua shih-lueh' (Brief history of progress of the Shanghai municipal system) in Shang-hai t'ung she, ed. *Shang-hai yen-chiu tzu-liao* (Research materials on Shanghai), 75–8.

chüan chü) which Yuan had substituted for the former municipality remained strictly subordinated to the local officials. The law of 1914, which strengthened government control over the chambers of commerce, succeeded in depriving the merchants of their means of political expression.

Thus deprived of initiative, the merchants seemed to lose interest in the great ideals which had inspired them for a dozen years. Unable to achieve a countrywide acceptance of the modernity which they themselves had pioneered in China, they became absorbed in the defence of their short-term interests. Faced with a military and bureaucratic regime, which they had not sought but had found no great difficulty in accepting, they strove to strengthen the autonomy of their geographic and social base, in the shadow of the foreign presence. Thus we see them requesting the British consul at Nanking to extend the concession to the harbour and commercial quarter of Hsia-kuan, which would thus be better protected. At Shanghai some of the notables of Chapei, in the Chinese city, asked for the intervention of the International Settlement police and sought, to quote the ironic words of a foreign resident, 'the protection of our municipal Tyranny'.

However, Yuan Shih-k'ai's accession to power did not represent a simple restoration of the former regime. His presidency was characterized by a new determination to further economic development by completing commercial legislation, stabilizing the fiscal and monetary system, and encouraging private enterprise.[65] Chang Chien, who was minister of agriculture and trade from October 1913 to December 1915, had laws passed on the registration of commercial enterprises and corporations, and on corporation establishment; he set up model stations for growing cotton and sugar-cane; and he planned to standardize the system of weights and measures. Then again in February 1914, at the instigation of Liang Shih-i, the Yuan Shih-k'ai dollar was established, as the first step towards monetary unification. This willingness to encourage business contrasted oddly with the refusal to grant the smallest scrap of power to the bourgeoisie. Here Yuan returned to the tradition of a modernizing bureaucracy, of which he had been one of the principal representatives during the last years of the Ch'ing. As dictator whose power rested upon the army and the mandarinate Yuan Shih-k'ai had no need to woo the merchants. It would be wrong, therefore, to see in his economic policy any pledge to support the bourgeoisie. It would also be wrong to attribute to it the prosperity enjoyed by the great treaty ports during the years of Yuan's

---

65 On the economic policy of Yuan Shih-k'ai cf. Kikuchi Takaharu, *Chūgoku minzoku undō no kihon kōzō – taigai boikotto no kenkyū* (Basic structure of the Chinese national movement: a study of anti-foreign boycotts), 154–78.

regime. The decisive impulse which was to propel the Chinese bourgeoisie into its golden age came from elsewhere: from the transformation of the international situation brought about by the First World War.

THE GOLDEN AGE OF CHINESE CAPITALISM, 1917–23

The limited participation of the bourgeoisie in the revolutionary movement and its conservative reactions when faced with social disorder are not, however, sufficient to dismiss the concept of bourgeois revolution. Further study of the consequences of the Revolution of 1911 is called for. Though of little use for the clarification of the events of 1911–13, perhaps the concept of bourgeois revolution can usefully be reintroduced in a longer-term socio-economic analysis. The idea of a transition (between 'feudal methods of production' and 'capitalist methods of production', between a bureaucratic society and a class society) would then replace the idea of a revolutionary rupture. Such mutations spring from a long-term secular process. In China this process began in the sixteenth to eighteenth centuries with the appearance of the so-called buds of capitalism within the traditional economy. This evolution then became very plain in the nineteenth century, as already noted. After 1911 it continued as part of the economic modernization and social change of the twentieth century. Hence it is impossible to encapsulate a development such as the rise of the bourgeoisie within a single revolutionary occurrence.

But can one not ask whether in the middle term of 10 to 15 years the Revolution of 1911 did not precipitate industrialization, alter the balance of power in the bosom of society, and promote the rise of a true bourgeoisie? Certain historians of the French Revolution, when referring to 'this savage capitalism' the forces of which the revolution was considered to have unleashed, have stressed how slowly it got under way.[66] In China, by contrast, 10 years after the revolution, at the beginning of the 1920s, national capitalism was in full swing and a new generation of businessmen had appeared, who were directly linked to industrial production and the exploitation of a salaried work-force. But this upswing in the urban economy and society resulted less from a revolution which had long since been taken over by the militarists than from an economic miracle caused by the First World War. In semi-colonial China, the logic of the bourgeois revolution was governed, from outside, by the evolution of international relations.

66 François Furet, *Penser la révolution française.*

The boom during the war and after, 1914–23

The war restored to the Chinese market part of the protection of which the 'unequal treaties' of the nineteenth century had deprived it. Absorbed in their strife, the belligerent powers turned away from China. This European decline, which favoured the development of national industries in replacement, also encouraged the expansion of Japanese and American interests – thus sowing the seeds of fresh difficulties and future conflicts.

At the same time the war caused a marked increase in the world demand for alimentary products and raw materials (non-ferrous metals, vegetable oils). As a major supplier of primary products China was well placed to meet this demand. Then again, the increase in purchases made by the Western powers in countries with a silver-based currency, such as China and India, stimulated the rise in the international price of silver, which had been under way since the closing of the mines in Mexico in 1913. The tael thus became a strong currency. Its purchasing power on Western markets tripled within a few years. Although external debt charges were reduced thereby, imports, and in particular the import of industrial equipment, were nevertheless not facilitated; for if the war offered the Chinese economy opportunities for development, these opportunities could be grasped and exploited only within the restrictive framework of an 'underdeveloped' economy, dependent on the dynamism of a semi-colonial system suffering deeply from certain handicaps which themselves had arisen from the world-wide conflict.

The requisitioning of merchant fleets by the belligerent states, the reduction in world commercial tonnage, and the consequent rise in freight rates hampered international trade. Exchange controls, and the embargoes on silk and tea imposed by France and Great Britain in 1917, denied certain traditional outlets to Chinese products. In the end the priority given to war industries by the European powers adversely affected the supply of equipment to China. At the moment when the lessening of foreign competition was stimulating the upsurge of national industries, it became very difficult for these same industries to acquire the machinery they needed.[67] At the time of the First World War China had not yet attained the level of development which would allow it to reap the full benefit of the relative withdrawal of the foreign presence. The difficulties caused by the war involved, it is true, a lack of profit rather than actual losses. For the modern sector of the Chinese economy

67 TR (1915, 1917, 1919), reports from Shanghai and Canton.

the years of warfare were a time of prosperity. However, it was not until the return of peace that the 'golden age' dawned for the national business concerns.

It was not until 1919 that the modern sector began to reap the benefits offered by the world war and the regained peace. Far from flagging, the demand for primary products intensified. The needs of war had been replaced by those of reconstruction. In Shanghai, in 1919, the value of exports was 30 per cent higher than the preceding year. The upsurge in exports was all the more remarkable in that the price of silver continued to rise, and with it the exchange rate of the tael. However, the urgency of their needs was such that European buyers were willing to pay high prices. The greater availability of sea freight and the reconversion of war industries allowed the Chinese industrialists to return to Western markets for their supplies. Their purchases of textile material rose from 1.8 million taels in 1918 to 3.9 million in 1919.[68] By an extraordinary concatenation of circumstances Chinese business now benefited from the demand created previously on the national market by Western imports, from the relative protection resulting from the decline of foreign competition, from the facilities for the procurement of supplies on the European and American markets, and finally from a favourable rate of exchange.

After a moderate expansion up to 1917 the value of foreign trade rose from 1,040 million taels in 1918 to 1,670 millions in 1923. Progress was measured by the growth and diversification of exports.[69] Imports increased less rapidly, but underwent considerable restructuring: consumer products, and in particular cotton goods, the manufacture of which was developing in China, declined in favour of hard goods, which in 1920 represented 28.5 per cent of the total value of Chinese purchases abroad.[70] This inequality of growth in imports and exports contributed to restoring the balance of trade. In 1919 the deficit was no more than 16 million taels.[71] The composition of Chinese foreign trade remained that of an 'underdeveloped' economy; but this trade was no longer exactly that of a dependent economy: it corresponded, rather, to the first phase of growth of a modern national economy.

Stimulated by the demands of the market, both domestic and foreign, production increased. Traditional sector and modern sector combined to satisfy the new needs. The scarcity of ocean freight and of equipment, which had hampered the upsurge of modern industries until 1919, had

68 H. G. W. Woodhead, ed. *The China yearbook 1921–22*, 1004–6.
69 Hsiao Liang-lin, *China's foreign trade statistics, 1864–1969*, 73–124.
70 Yen Chung-p'ing, comp. *Chung-kuo chin-tai ching-chi shih t'ung-chi tzu-liao hsuan-chi* (Selected statistical materials on modern Chinese economic history), 72–3.
71 Hsiao Liang-lin, *Trade statistics*, 23.

not affected the handicraft sector. From 1915–16 weaving-looms had been increasing in number in the northern and central provinces. Production was directed towards the domestic market. Urban workshops were developed, and commercial capitalism spread throughout the countryside near the major urban centres. The progress made in weaving, ready-to-wear clothing, hosiery, glassware, matches, oil production, did not consist merely of a resurrection of the former methods of production. Often using improved techniques and raw materials of industrial origin (yarn, chemical products), this handicraft activity represented, on the contrary, an attempt to adapt, a particularly good example of what we referred to above as transitory modernization. Thus we cannot subscribe to the opinion of H. H. Fox, shared by many of his contemporaries, that 'industrial progress was limited to the most important of the treaty ports'.[72]

The upsurge of modern business in the coastal cities represents only one aspect of a more general expansion; but it is, without a doubt, the most striking aspect. From 1912 to 1920, the growth-rate of modern industries reached 13.8 per cent.[73] (Such a rapid tempo of development would not be encountered again until the days of the First Five-Year Plan, from 1953 to 1957.) The leading example was cotton yarn. The number of spindles in the national capacity rose from 658,748 in 1919 to 1,506,634 in 1922: at that time Chinese spinners owned 63 per cent of all the spindles installed in China.[74] Out of 120 spinning mills listed in 1928, 47 had been established between 1920 and 1922. The upsurge in the food industries is evidenced by the opening of 26 flour mills between 1917 and 1922,[75] and by the re-purchase of foreign-owned oil mills. Considerable progress was also made in the tobacco and cigarette industry. But the enthusiasm of the golden age scarcely spread to the heavy industries. The ephemeral prosperity of the exploitation of non-ferrous metals (in particular antimony and tin) in the southern provinces was strictly determined by international speculations, and disappeared with them. Modern coal and iron mines remained 75 to 100 per cent controlled by foreign interests. The most notable progress was made in the machine-building industry.[76] Shanghai and its surroundings were the main beneficiaries of this expan-

72 Department of Overseas Trade, *Trade and economic conditions in China* ... Report by H. H. Fox.

73 John K. Chang, *Industrial development in pre-communist China: a quantitative analysis.*

74 Yen Chung-p'ing, *T'ung-chi tzu-liao*, 134.

75 Chou Hsiu-luan, *Ti-i-tz'u shih-chieh ta-chan shih-ch'i Chung-kuo min-tsu kung-yeh ti fa-chan* (The development of national industries during the First World War; hereafter *Kung-yeh ti fa-chan*), ch. 2.

76 *Ta-lung chi-ch'i-ch'ang ti fa-sheng fa-chan yü kai-tsao* (Origin, development, and transformation of the Ta-lung Machine Works), comp. by the Academy of Sciences, Shanghai Institute for Economic Research, *et al.* Thomas G. Rawski, 'The growth of producer industries' in Dwight H. Perkins, ed. *China's modern economy in historical perspective*, 231.

sion, which also affected Tientsin and, to a lesser degree, Canton and Wuhan.

During the whole of the boom period the growth of trade and of production was sustained by the development of credit and stimulated by the rise in prices and profits. The decline of foreign banks, which hampered the operations of foreign trade, did not affect the domestic market, the financing of which had never passed from Chinese control. On the contrary, this domestic market made important resources available to national businesses, such as the capital funds of notables or compradors, who for reasons of security or interest had until then chiefly funded foreign activities. The rise of the modern Chinese banks dated from the First World War. In the years 1918 and 1919 alone, 96 new banks were founded.[77] However, most of these banks maintained close ties with the public authorities. This was the case with the official Bank of China (Chung-kuo yin-hang) and Bank of Communications (Chiao-t'ung yin-hang), some dozen provincial banks, and numerous 'political' banks founders of which belonged to government circles or maintained close relations with higher officials. The activity of all these establishments was limited to the handling of state funds and loans. A dozen modern banks, situated mostly in Shanghai, were run on a purely commercial basis; but their involvement in the financing of national business remained hampered by the archaic structures of the market. Before the war no Chinese exchange for securities or commodities had existed. The Shanghai Stock Exchange in the International Settlement only handled foreign stocks. The creation and success of the Shanghai Stock and Produce Exchange (Shang-hai cheng-ch'üan wu-p'in chiao-i so) inspired many imitations. At the end of 1921 Shanghai had 140 establishments, most of which traded only in their own shares until a general collapse, the stock exchanges crash (hsin-chiao feng-ch'ao), put an end some months later to this mushroom growth.[78]

In order to finance businesses, the modern banks were thus obliged, just like the old-style banks (ch'ien-chuang), to resort to direct loans. However, the modern banks demanded guarantees from their clients in the form of property mortgages or deposits of goods. This put them at a disadvantage vis-à-vis the ch'ien-chuang which, operating under customary rules and on a basis of personal relations, granted loans 'on trust'. Consequently, despite the spectacular but essentially speculative rise of the modern banking sector, the real business banks remained the ch'ien-

77 D. K. Lieu, China's industries and finance, 48.
78 Sha Yao-shu, 'Lun chiao-i-so chih shih-pao yuan-yin' (The causes of failure of the Chinese exchanges), TSHYP, 2. 8 (Aug. 1922) 8–13.

chuang. In Shanghai there were 71 of them in 1920 (as against 31 in 1913), and the capital they controlled – 7.7 million Chinese dollars – was five times greater than that on the eve of the world war.

In the absence of a stock exchange market and of a national discount system, a useful barometer of economic progress was the interest rate on inter-bank loans on the Shanghai market (*yin-che*). The monthly average rose from 0.06 (one candareen per day per 1,000 taels) in 1919 to 0.17 in 1922. Although this rise in the cost of money can be explained as being due to purely financial reasons (repatriation into the metropolis of the bullion reserves of the foreign banks, speculative purchases of gold on the world market), there is no doubt that the needs of an expanding economy played their part: for example, the marketing of crops earmarked for export involved larger and larger capital levies on the financial markets of the big cities.

Constructed according to various methods and based upon heterogeneous surveys, the available price-indices did not permit of very precise analyses.[79] They did, however, show a rise in wholesale prices during the First World War from 20 to 44 per cent. This development, which was quite moderate in comparison with that in Western countries during the same period, was due to the stability of agricultural prices in contrast with the soaring of industrial costs. In a traditional rural economy this stability of agricultural prices (from which, however, the prices of certain export products were excluded) was evidence less of the stagnation of the market than of the favourable character of the climatic conditions – that is, the relative equilibrium of the rural world. The stability of agricultural prices and the rise in industrial prices were to be seen as complementary signs of prosperity.

It was above all the business world that profited from this prosperity. From 1914 to 1919 the average profit for cotton-spinning mills per ball of yarn rose by 70 per cent, and that of the *ch'ien-chuang* by 74 per cent.[80] The most important companies increased their profits twenty-fold, some even fifty-fold. Dividends reached 30 to 40 per cent, and sometimes even 90 per cent.[81] The gains of the businessmen were all the more significant in that they hardly shared them at all with their employees: indeed, the

79 Nan-k'ai ta-hsueh ching-chi yen-chiu so (Nankai Institute for Economic Research) comp. *1913 nien-1952 nien Nan-k'ai chih-shu tzu-liao hui-pien*) (Nankai price indexes 1913–1952), 2–7; 'Methods of price investigation', *The Chinese economic bulletin,* 21 June 1924.
80 Yen Chung-p'ing, *T'ung-chi tzu-liao,* table 61, p. 165; *Shang-hai ch'ien-chuang shih-liao* (Material for the history of the *ch'ien chuang* banks of Shanghai), comp. Chung-kuo jen-min yin-hang Shang-hai-shih fen-hang (The Shanghai branch of the Chinese People's Bank), 202.
81 Cf. the case of the Ta-sheng spinning-mills cited by Samuel Chu, *Reformer in modern China, Chang Chien 1853–1926,* 31.

TABLE 38

Increase in population of some Chinese cities over the war years[83]

City	Year	Inhabitants
Peking	1912	725,235
	1921	863,209
Tientsin	1900	320,000
	1921	837,000
Tsingtao	1911	54,459
	1921	83,272
Shanghai		
Foreign settlements		
Foreign population	1910	13,536
	1920	23,307
Chinese population	1910	488,005
	1920	759,839
Chinese Town	1910	568,372
	1920	1,699,077

salaries of the artisans and labourers rose only by 6.9 per cent in Canton, and by 10 to 20 per cent in Shanghai.[82]

It was on the basis of this material prosperity that an urban society developed in the great coastal cities which was increasingly open to occidental influences.

The rise of urban society and transformation of the bourgeoisie

The economic boom was accompanied by an accelerated urbanization. The annual growth rate of the urban population seemed to be considerably greater than that of the population as a whole. The phenomenon was particularly evident in Shanghai, where the population of the Chinese quarter tripled in 10 years (see table 38); but the other treaty ports of Tientsin and Tsingtao also attracted many newcomers.

The cities of the interior also experienced a rapid, though less marked, expansion: in Tsinan (Shantung) the growth-rate was 3 per cent per annum between 1914 and 1919, while the rate for the population of the province as a whole was only 1 per cent.[84]

This urban thrust did not coincide with either any great famine or with

82 Jean Chesneaux, *Le mouvement ouvrier chinois de 1919 à 1927*, 197; *TSHYP* 4.4 (April 1924) 35–6.
83 After H. O. Kung 'The growth of population in six Chinese cities', *The Chinese economic journal and bulletin*, 20. 3 (March 1937) 301–14. Cf. also Dwight Perkins, *Agricultural development in China, 1368–1968*, app. E, 290–1.
84 David D. Buck, *Urban change in China: politics and development in Tsinan, Shantung, 1890–1949*, app. B.

any particular worsening of civil unrest in the interior. Essentially it reflected the attraction exercised on the rural society by the new centres of development. The poor peasants, misfits of rural society, came to seek employment in the workshops and the new mills. They signed on as dockers in the ports; hired themselves out as coolies or rickshaw-men. Many rural notables were also drawn to the provincial capitals and the regional metropolises, partly by the prospect of a career in local administration or the self-government organizations, and partly anxious to ensure a modern education for their children – a privilege exclusive to the cities.

The urban zones spread out; suburbs were built, communicating with difficulty with the heart of the city through the monumental gates of the old city walls. In many cities, however – for example, Changsha, Wuchow and Canton – the city walls were demolished to allow new quarters to be developed. Although most of the new construction was residential, commercial buildings were the most imposing. The New World shops at Hankow rivalled those of the Sincere (Hsien-shih) Company and the Wing-on (Yung-an) Company department stores which opened in Shanghai in 1919. In Canton the nine stores of the Ta-hsin shops had dominated the Bund since 1918. The Shanghai Municipal Council, which had granted 41 construction permits in 1915 (for buildings in foreign style), granted 109 of them in 1920. Taking into account houses in Chinese style, workshops, warehouses, and various other buildings, the value of the construction authorized by the Municipal Council rose during this same period from 5 to 11 million taels.[85]

In these rapidly-expanding cities, in which the population never stopped increasing, social groupings became both more complex and better differentiated. A working proletariat appeared; a modern intelligentsia and a modern bourgeoisie emerged from the urban elite (*shen shang*). These social transformations did not fail to catch the attention of foreign historians aware of how these new elites echoed the Western experience, and also the attention of Marxist historians, who sometimes tried to isolate these phenomena from their context (which was still largely traditional), the better to illustrate their thesis.[86]

In fact, these transformations remained marginal: not only as regards Chinese society as a whole, but also as regards its urban and relatively modernized fringe. It is impossible to understand the role of the new

85 Richard Feetham, *Report of the Hon. Richard Feetham to the Shanghai Municipal Council*, 2 vols. 1. 347.
86 Jean Chesneaux, *The Chinese labour movement, 1919–1927*. Since the publication of this work in 1962, the author seems to have reverted to a more realistic conception of the world of Chinese labour.

businessmen (any more than that of the new intellectuals) without first studying the persistence and the evolution of the group of notables who, on the eve of the revolution, formed that 'urban reformist elite' described by J. W. Esherick, which was so similar to the Old Regime bourgeoisie celebrated in French historiography.[87]

Although these notables found themselves engaged in economic, social and political activities very different from those of the rural gentry, they remained linked to the structures of the Old Regime both through their interest in landed property and by their close relations with the public authorities. The Revolution of 1911 had in general increased their importance. Their leaders were always in the forefront; for example, Chang Chien (1853–1926), a metropolitan degree holder (*chin-shih*), minister of industry under Yuan Shih-k'ai. His Ta-sheng cotton mills at Nan-t'ung (Kiangsu) doubled their number of spindles between 1914 and 1921.[88] Or Yü Hsia-ch'ing (1868–?), director of the Shanghai General Chamber of Commerce and of the Ningpo guild, who had invested two million taels in steamship companies during the war – San-pei (1917), Ning-shao (1917), Hung-an (1918).[89] Or again Chu Pao-san (1847–?), who was still president of the General Chamber of Commerce in 1919, at the age of 72. The war also consolidated the fortune of the Jung brothers – Jung Tsung-ching (1873–1938) and Jung Te-sheng (1875–1952).[90] Coming from a family of merchants and minor civil servants of Wusih, the Jung brothers had built the Mao-hsin flour mills in 1901, and the Fu-hsin mills in 1913. Between 1914 and 1920 these two companies opened eight new factories, some of which had capital of 1.5 million taels. At the same time the Jung brothers extended their activities into the textile world by setting up the Shen-hsin spinning mills. The economic success of all these pioneers was due to exceptional personal qualities which, through an incomplete initiation gained from their contact with foreigners in the treaty ports, had enabled them to grasp the importance of modern technology and management.

However, the majority of the urban elite were distinguished more by their political orientation and their social role than by their participation in modern business. After the Revolution of 1911, bureaucratic institutions were taken over by the new network of authorities created by the

87 Esherick, *Reform and revolution*; F. Furet, *Penser la révolution francaise*, 159.
88 Chu, *Reformer in modern China.*
89 Fang T'eng, 'Yü Hsia-ch'ing lun' (On the subject of Yü Hsia-ch'ing), *Tsa-chih yueh-k'an* (Monthly miscellany) 12. 2 (Nov. 1943) 46–51; 12. 3 (Dec. 1943) 62–7; 12. 4 (Jan. 1944) 59–64.
90 *Mao-hsin Fu-hsin Shen-hsin tsung-kung-ssu sa-chou-nien chi-nien ts'e* (Book commemorating the 30th anniversary of the Mow Sing mills and the Foh Sing and Sung Sing cotton works).

organizations representing local interests – provincial assemblies, chambers of commerce, educational and agricultural societies. This, however, clashed on the national plane with Yuan Shih-k'ai's unitary centralizing efforts, and on the regional plane with the rival ambitions of the militarists. Yet the power of the urban elite increased. Although they did not succeed in retaining for their local organizations the administrative prerogatives (and in particular the right of taxation) which they had seized in 1912–14, they exerted a much stronger influence on the bureaucracy than before the revolution. Without doubt this was basically because for the most part this bureaucracy was being recruited locally. The proportion of officials of local origin, which had been very high on the morrow of the revolution (five out of seven in the upper ranks of the Chekiang provincial administration in 1912), had fallen off later (four out of eight in Chekiang in 1920).[91] But the law of 'avoidance' – which, under the empire, had precluded the choosing of magistrates from among the local scholars – had not been re-established. Whether it was expressed directly through the intermediary of local representative organizations, or indirectly through pressures on the bureaucracy, the urban elite tended to preserve their interests against interference by the public authorities, against encroachment by foreigners, and against claims by the populace.

This Old Regime bourgeoisie thus appeared as a stable force in the bosom of Chinese society. In one of the district capitals in Chekiang, 40 per cent of the personalities who were running the local organizations in 1925 had already been active in 1911. However, within this group the balance of the component parts tended to change. The degree-holding literati (*chin-shih, chü-jen, kung-sheng*) played a less important role. In 1918–21 they no longer represented more than 6 per cent of the strength of the new provincial assembly of Chekiang (as against 46 per cent on the eve of the revolution).[92] Death thinned their ranks, which were not renewed after the abolition of the examination system in 1905. In their traditional roles as financiers and managers of philanthropic institutions, they were more and more often replaced by the public authorities and by specialists in hygiene or public works. This was the case in Tsinan, for example, where in 1917 the Benevolent Association (Kuang-jen shan-chü) was replaced by a public Bureau of Philanthropy.[93]

This development accentuated the split between the urban elites and the gentry, who had originally been the dominant component. At the same

91 Robert Keith Schoppa, 'Politics and society in Chekiang, 1907–1927: elite power, social control and the making of a province' (University of Michigan, Ph.D. dissertation, 1975), 218.
92 Schoppa, 'Society in Chekiang', 254, 307.
93 Buck, *Urban change*, 147–8.

time it widened the gap between town and country, making the latter provide funds for urban services. In Tsinan, for example, the upkeep of a police force responsible for the omnicompetent tasks of hygiene, public highways, law and order, and fire-fighting was met from provincial receipts just as much as from municipal revenues.

Henceforth, the urban notables were recruited from among the merchants, the landowners and the graduates of the modern schools. This elite, with its somewhat ill-defined limits, achieved cohesion in the provincial assemblies, in which it provided the greater part of their working strength – 88 per cent in Chekiang, in 1921–6.[94] The new notables continued to defend the interests of the landowners (regrouped into agricultural societies), but now they applied themselves to protecting the interests of the merchants. These latter often dominated the provincial assemblies. It was by no means rare for the president of the chamber of commerce also to be president of the district assembly. Moreover, in some cases the chamber of commerce completely took the place of the district assembly; for example, Shao-hsing, in Chekiang, in 1922. Chambers of commerce proliferated during the 1920s: the district of Chia-hsing, in Chekiang, which had been authorized to set up two, had no less than 13 in 1924. Progressively these chambers took the lead over the other local representative organizations.[95]

From this world of urban notables there emerged, at the time of the First World War, a narrow social fringe devoted to the ideology of industrial growth, free enterprise and economic rationality: a true modern bourgeoisie. This mutation took place quite naturally under the influence of the economic miracle, but in a semi-colonial environment dominated by the West. The businessmen of the new generation in whom this modern bourgeoisie was embodied had carried out their studies abroad. They were at once better informed as to the realities of the contemporary world and enjoyed greater freedom from the traditional restraints. The best-known among them was without doubt Mu Hsiang-yueh (Mu Ou-ch'u, H. Y. Moh, 1876–1942). Born in Shanghai, of a cotton-merchant father, he learned English and in 1900 passed the entrance examination for the Maritime Customs Service. Called upon to resign on account of the active part he had played in the anti-American boycott of 1905, Mu went to the United States, at the age of 33, to complete his technical education. He studied agronomy at the University of Illinois, and then

---

94 Schoppa, 'Society in Chekiang', 254.
95 Buck, *Urban change*, 149. Schoppa, 'Society in Chekiang'. For other examples, in the province of Hopei, cf. Linda Grove, 'Rural society: the Gaoyang district 1910–1947' (University of California, Ph.D. dissertation, Dec. 1975), 49–52.

went on to learn the techniques of the textile industry at Texas Agricultural and Mechanical College. On his return to China in 1914 he sought to modernize his own textile plants by improving equipment and introducing long-fibred cottons imported from America. In 1915 he built the Hou-sheng spinning mill in Shanghai; in 1916, the Te-ta mill; and in 1920, the Yü-feng mill in Chengchow (Honan). The same year, he played a part in the organization of the Cotton Exchange (one of the few establishments to survive the storm of speculations in 1921), of which he remained president until 1926. Anxious to assist Chinese industry to educate the leaders it needed, he gave his best apprentices scholarships to study in the United States. Among them, in 1921, was Fang Hsien-t'ing (H. D. Fong), the future professor of economics at the Nankai Institute in Tientsin.[96]

The career of Ch'en Kuang-fu (K. P. Chen) (1880?–1974), the banker, was very similar to that of Mu Ou-ch'u. Born into a family of merchants, and apprenticed at the age of 11, Ch'en left in 1904 for six years to study business in the United States. On his return, he sought the cooperation of some old fellow-pupils and some employees of the customs and postal services versed in modern accountancy methods, to form the Shanghai Commercial and Saving Bank in 1915; this was one of the most prosperous of the private banks, managed by Ch'en himself until 1940.

Certain engineers, who came from families that enjoyed comparatively easy circumstances and who had also been trained abroad, pursued two careers simultaneously – civil servant and businessman; examples were Chiang Shun-te (S. T. Kong, 1880–?), one of the pioneers of the modern paint and dye industry; and the geologist Ting Wen-chiang (V. K. Ting, 1887–1936), who founded and directed from 1921 to 1925 the Pei-p'iao coal company in Jehol.

Finally, the new generation figured largely among the businessmen from overseas, who shared with the foreign-trained students a direct practical experience of the modern world. Before the First World War the Chien brothers – Chien Chao-nan (1875–1923) and Chien Yü-chieh (1877–1957) – had formed the Nanyang Brothers Tobacco Company in Hong-Kong (Nan-yang hsiung-ti yen-ts'ao kung-ssu), the products of which were sold to the émigré Chinese communities in Thailand and Singapore. The war opened the Chinese market to the Nanyang company. Between 1912 and 1917 its production rose 610 per cent.[97] It set up branches in Ningpo, Hankow and Shanghai, the last mentioned becoming

96 Mu Ou-ch'u (Hsiang-yueh) Ou-ch'u wu-shih tzu-shu (Autobiography of Mu Ou-ch'u at 50 years of age); H. D. Fong, Reminiscences of a Chinese economist at 70.
97 Nan-yang hsiung-ti yen-ts'ao kung-ssu shih-liao (Material for the history of the Nanyang Brothers Tobacco Company) comp. Shanghai Institute of Economic Research and Institute of Economic Research, Shanghai Academy of Social Sciences, 19.

the main office in 1919. Chien Chao-nan, as one of the most influential businessmen in the Shanghai community, then joined the board of the General Chamber of Commerce. His brother, Yü-chieh, succeeded him after his death and continued his career as a national capitalist under the communist regime after 1949.

The achievements of Ma Yü-shan (M. Y. San, 1878–1929) were more ephemeral. He began his career as a biscuit-manufacturer in the Philippines. The Revolution of 1911 brought him back to Canton and Hong Kong, where he built some new factories. Thereafter, he ran his network of subsidiary companies from Shanghai. In 1921 M. Y. San tried to give China a modern sugar industry. The National Refineries Company of China (Chung-hua kuo-min chih-t'ang kung-ssu) was set up at Woosung. The Shanghai capitalists subscribed capital of 10 million taels. The following year M. Y. San travelled in the West to gather information on the techniques of sugar-making. He even tried to introduce sugar beet growing into Manchuria. However, it was not long before the experiment faltered, and M. Y. San went back to South-East Asia.[98]

Nieh Yun-t'ai (C. C. Nieh), who enjoyed a special authority and prestige among the Shanghai business community, formed the link between the generation of the urban notables and that of the businessmen. Grandson of Viceroy Tseng Kuo-fan he was a member of the upper gentry. Though living in China, he acquired a perfect mastery of English. He was 24 years of age when his father, then governor of Chekiang, put him in charge of a small spinning-mill which he himself had just taken over, thanks to public funds. Under the name of Heng-feng, the mill thrived during the war; in 1919, its capital was one million dollars, and the workshops employed 1,300 workers. In 1921 C. C. Nieh built the Ta Chung-hua mills. He also invested in the I-chung machine-shops. Nieh was an organizer as well as a businessman. In 1918 he took part in the foundation of the China Cotton Millowners' Association (Hua-shang sha-ch'ang lien-ho-hui) and of a committee for the improvement of raw cotton; he succeeded in getting Tung-nan University and various American experts to participate in this latter project. At the time of the crisis in 1919–20, when the conservative and the radical factions of the Shanghai General Chamber of Commerce were at each other's throats, C. C. Nieh stepped forward as mediator: and his accession to the presidency opened the road to a settlement.[99]

Let us end our review here. We could cite other names, some less

98 Ch'en Chen *et al.* comps. *Chung-kuo chin-tai kung-yeh shih tzu-liao* (Source materials on the history of modern industry in China; hereafter *Kung-yeh shih tzu-liao*) 4 vols. 1. 502–9.

99 Ch'en Chen, *Kung-yeh shih-liao*, 1. 397–401; Yen Chung-p'ing, *Chung kuo mien-fang-chih shih-kao* (Draft history of the cotton industry in China; 3rd edn.), 328. Nieh Ch'i-chieh, ed. *Ch'ung-te lao-jen tzu-ting nien-p'u* (Chronological autobiography of Nieh Ch'ung-te).

prestigious. However, they would not be very numerous in total –
perhaps a few hundred. Is this really enough to constitute a bourgeoisie?

First of all, we must point out that a modern intelligentsia was taking
shape simultaneously with the emergence of this group of businessmen.
The new intellectuals were men like Ts'ai Yuan-p'ei, Hu Shih, Chiang
Meng-lin (Mon-lin) and Kuo Ping-wen. They too were mostly educated
abroad. They too returned to China at the outbreak of the war, with new
skills and new ideas. They too had moved away from the old society, and
cut the bonds by which the state had made officials out of the men of
letters and had united politics (*cheng*) with orthodoxy (*chiao*). At the same
time they had preached a new form of education (*hsin chiao-yü*) based on
respect for individuality (*ko-hsing chu-i*).[100] The presence of this intelligentsia was a comfort to the new bourgeoisie. The solidarity of these two
groups strengthened the effectiveness of both. However, their influence
lay essentially in the relations they continued to maintain with the body
of urban notables, with that reformist elite of the Old Regime from which
they themselves had sprung.

The young intellectuals and the young businessmen found their elders
afforded them considerable support, which both facilitated their action
and assured their influence and success. What would have become of
Chiang Meng-lin's movement for the New Education, if it had not been
supported by organizations as representative and as powerful as the
Kiangsu Educational Association (Chiang-su sheng chiao-yü-hui)? How
could Mu Ou-ch'u have put together the capital necessary for the establishment of his first spinning-mill if certain traditional merchants had
not entrusted him with the enormous profits they had made by their
speculations in dyes after imports from Germany had been stopped at
the beginning of the war? No sooner had he arrived from Hong Kong
than Chien Chao-nan was co-opted by the board of governors of the
Shanghai General Chamber of Commerce. The solidarity between the
urban notables on the one hand, and the intelligentsia and the modern
bourgeoisie on the other, was based on a common ground of social
conservatism, nationalism and mistrust of the power of the state.

The economic and political strategy of the new bourgeoisie was formulated in the bosom of the business associations created at the end of
the First World War. They differed from the professional or craft guilds
and from the regional same-place societies (*t'ung-hsiang hui*) which gave
the merchants only a somewhat departmentalized representation; also
from the chambers of commerce which had been foisted on local com-

100 Barry Keenan, *The Dewey experiment in China: educational reform and political power in the
early republic*, 56–63.

munities by the imperial administration. The business associations were the result of action that was both unified and spontaneous. In fact, the initiative came from the interested parties themselves. Formed in 1918, the Chinese Cotton Millowners' Association (Hua-shang sha-ch'ang lien-ho-hui) gave official status to a defensive group which had been organized the year before to press for the retention of an export tax on raw cotton that Japanese buyers were seeking to have abolished. In Peking the Association of Modern Bankers came into being in 1920 as a result of friendly dinner-meetings which had been held twice a week for some time by the principal bankers of the city. The Chinese Cotton Millowners' Association quickly grew to national stature; only three years lay between the appearance of the first local banking associations and the creation of a National Bankers' Association (Ch'üan-kuo yin-hang tsung-hui) in December 1920.

The new business associations showed their modernity by their perception of their role. They avoided religious and philanthropic works, to which the traditional associations had devoted a large part of their resources. They adopted the viewpoint of an international capitalism dominated by the themes of growth, progress and competition. They began disseminating economic information and publishing specialized reviews on which the best economists of the day had collaborated. Thus, over the next few years, the following publications were launched: the *Shanghai Bankers' Weekly* (*Yin-hang chou-pao*) in 1917; the *China Cotton Journal* (*Hua-shang sha-ch'ang lien-ho-hui ch'i-k'an*) in 1919; the Peking *Bankers' Monthly* (*Yin-hang yueh-k'an*) in 1921; the *Hankow Bankers' Magazine* (*Yin-hang tsa-chih*) in 1923. These reviews provided an exceptionally rich and precise testimony as to the activities of the modern sector during that period, and as to the obstacles that lay in the path of its development, while the importance attached to the study of foreign markets bore witness to the efforts expended on locating this Chinese development in the stream of world economic forces.

Here, class interests took on a modern aspect. Solidarity was no longer – as it was in the guilds – the solidarity of interests acquired, but rather that of interests to be acquired. The ideology of growth had taken the place of the tradition of monopoly.

This young body of employers obviously represented only a very narrow fringe of the business bourgeoisie. However, the influence of this *avant-garde* made itself felt in the official institutions of merchant power – the chambers of commerce, which were forced to modernize and to some extent democratize themselves.

The Shanghai General Chamber of Commerce still appeared, on the morrow of the war, as a federation of guilds dominated by the powerful *pang* (group) of Ningpo. Very high annual subscriptions (several hundred taels) limited the number of its members to 300. Apart from the guilds, only the most important businesses were represented in the chamber. The power of decision was monopolized by a board of 35 directors selected mainly from among the merchants and compradors of the old generation presided over by the venerable Chu Pao-san. From 1919–20 onwards, influenced by the external and internal pressures working upon it, the Chamber of Commerce elected a new board of directors. Although its scope of selection seemed scarcely any wider, the institution did in fact become thereafter a little more representative. Since its creation the Shanghai General Chamber of Commerce had always accepted representatives from the modern sector. But this modern sector had generally been represented by merchants who remained equally tied to traditional business: Wang I-t'ing, Yü Hsia-ch'ing. After the First World War, the Chamber's board was widened to include bankers (Sung Han-chang, Fu Hsiao-an, Chao Hsi-en, known in Western circles as S. U. Zau); cotton millowners (Mu Ou-ch'u, Nieh Yun-t'ai); industrialists (Chien Chao-nan, Jung Tsung-ching), whose interests and activities were completely oriented towards the modern sector. Within the Chamber of Commerce, they continued the course of action already commenced within the framework of the business associations: dissemination of economic information, encouragement of new technologies, development of professional education, negotiations with public authorities.

However, collaboration between the Old Regime bourgeoisie and the new-style businessmen did not develop entirely smoothly. In the Shanghai General Chamber of Commerce, a crisis erupted during the May Fourth movement of 1919.[101] The opposition did not emanate from the new business associations, but from the old regional same-place societies which (as opposed to the professional guilds) remained open to small businessmen and even to ordinary workers. The Ningpo Regional Association (Ning-po lü-Hu t'ung-hsiang-hui), created in 1909 by Ch'en Hung-lai, had a much less aristocratic membership than the Ningpo Guild to which it was affiliated, and to some extent subordinate. However, the most radical of the societies was the Canton Guild, the president of which was T'ang Fu-fu (T'ang Chieh-chih, or F. C. Tong). Nevertheless, in the very bosom of the Chamber, an opposition group of about 60 members forced

---

101 *Wu-ssu yun-tung tsai Shang-hai shih-liao hsuan-chi* (Selected materials for the history of the May Fourth movement at Shanghai; hereafter *Wu-ssu yun-tung*), comp. Institute of Historical Research of the Shanghai Social Sciences Academy, 221–247, 376–94. Chow Tse-tung, *The May Fourth movement*, ch. 6. Sanford, 'Chinese commercial organization and behavior', ch. 5.

the resignation of Chu Pao-san in July 1919 and presented a programme of reform offering liberal conditions of membership, the lowering of annual subscription rates, expansion of the board of directors, and the creation of economic information services. The August 1920 elections for the renewal of the board of directors gave 20 seats (out of 35) to the reformers. Who were they? Some of them – for example T'ang Fu-fu or Feng Hsiao-shan – were distinguished by their Cantonese origin and their political activism. Many of them simply belonged to the new generation of businessmen.

The reformers did not succeed in democratizing the membership of the Chamber. However, their influence made itself felt in the chronicles of the *Monthly Journal of the Shanghai General Chamber of Commerce (Shanghai tsung-shang-hui yueh-pao)*, which was started in 1921, and presented a new viewpoint on the problems of economic development and political involvement. Among its most distinguished analysts, the *Journal* numbered Fang Chiao-po (Chi-fan), born in 1884, heir of one of the great families of Ningpo, a banker and industrialist, and vice-president of the General Chamber of Commerce in 1922; and especially Feng Hsiao-shan, also born in 1884, a Cantonese, and a shareholder in the Nanyang Brothers' Tobacco Company.

The role of political *avant-garde*, which the General Chamber of Commerce refused to play, was taken over by new organizations that came into being with the great nationalist mobilization of the spring of 1919 and lived on thereafter. From its creation in March 1919 the Shanghai Commercial Federation (Shang-hai shang-yeh kung-t'uan lien-ho-hui) appeared as the spokesman of the regional societies. The Cantonese activists – T'ang Fu-fu, Feng Hsiao-shan – played an important role in this. Although the radicalism of the Federation often clashed with the conservatism of the Chamber of Commerce, the same men (and in particular Yü Hsia-ch'ing) were often prominent in both organizations. Their social structures scarcely differed: they represented two faces of the same bourgeoisie.

A few months later street associations (*ma-lu lien-ho-hui*) were formed representing the interests of the Chinese merchants of Shanghai's principal commercial arteries. They mobilized their members – shopkeepers with premises of their own – against the taxation policy of the Shanghai Municipal Council. Since Shanghai was the citadel of foreign imperialism, this local strife assumed particular importance in the struggle for national emancipation.

Thus, the voices which the Shanghai General Chamber of Commerce sometimes sought to suppress were raised in other assemblies. 'The Chamber of Commerce is no longer as representative of the Chinese community as it was in former days; other institutions have overthrown its supremacy' – so said the chairman of the Shanghai Municipal Council in 1920.[102] Guided by these new men who created their own organizations or acted within the framework of traditional institutions, the bourgeoisie was about to make its reappearance on the political scene.

Since the decline of the gentry this bourgeoisie constituted the dominant element of the urban elite. It integrated the bulk of Old Regime notables and the fringe of the new businessmen into a lively coalition that borrowed from the former their social stability and from the latter their spirit of innovation and initiative. Far from being atypical, it seemed on the contrary very representative of the urban society of the day. However, the cities themselves were more and more isolated from the Chinese body politic. Their very progress and their Westernization – which was inevitably associated with their modernization – helped to widen the gap which separated them from the rural word. As a vast empire of peasants how could China be governed from these few great coastal cities?

THE POLITICAL FAILURE OF THE BOURGEOISIE

Accepted with reluctance, cooperation with Yuan Shih-k'ai's regime did not last long. The dictatorial style of the government and the arbitrary imposition of new taxes had caused considerable discontent among the merchants, which was echoed in the Shanghai Chamber of Commerce. The merchants might be forcibly gagged; but it was useless to resort to force in an effort to prevent their sympathies from cooling.[103] The provincial rebellions against the attempt to restore the monarchy in 1915, the financial failure of the government in 1916, and the imposition of a moratorium on the official banks all combined to disrupt the market, and ended up by estranging the bourgeoisie from the regime.

Unable to change the direction of government policy, part of the bourgeoisie retired within itself and dreamt of creating islands of security and prosperity in the bosom of society. Encouraged by the philanthropic tradition it imagined exemplary communities – sometimes even going so far as to try to achieve them. Chang Chien made a model city of Nantung; and Chu Pao-san bought 1,000 *mu* on the outskirts of Shanghai with the intention of establishing a model city there.[104]

102 On the Federation, see *Wu-ssu yun-tung*, 648–64. On the chairman of the SMC, Feetham, *Report of the Hon Richard Feetham*, 1. 126–7.
103 *NCH*, 19 Feb. 1916, 467.
104 *The Chinese economic bulletin*, 23 Dec. 1922, 2.

Towards political involvement

The rapid development of Chinese businesses nevertheless called for some institutional reforms – monetary unification, fiscal reforms, a return to customs autonomy. These once again challenged the nature and the actions of the central government as well as the semi-colonial status of China resulting from the international treaties. The economic ambitions of the modern bourgeoisie inevitably led it towards wider battlefields: and more and more businessmen began to realize that their lot was bound up with the general evolution of society and state. 'Men cannot quit society and live alone; we cannot separate ourselves from the Chinese society of today, which is disordered and disorganized, and form a group apart.'[105]

At the annual conference of the Federation of Chambers of Commerce in 1921, T'ang Fu-fu launched an impassioned appeal for political involvement. It was no longer a question, as it had been in the past, of supporting this party or that, of adhering to this strong man or that: 'We can have confidence in nobody . . . there is no saviour. . .'. The Chambers of Commerce had to assume some direct responsibilities:

It was time for merchants faced with the present situation to renounce their outmoded traditions of non-intervention in politics. They had refused to become involved in what had long been called 'filthy politics', but if politics are filthy, it was the merchants who had allowed them to become so. The Chambers of Commerce had always made a point of abstaining from politics but today this abstention had become shameful.[106]

In more sober vein, H. Y. Moh repeated the same message:

The old idea that we held that businessmen should only care for businesses, is no more useful to-day. It is the duty of our businessmen to get together and devise every way and means to force our government to improve our internal affairs. . . . We believe that only by so doing can we find hope in the recovery of the business of our country and that our failure to take such steps will result in the complete failure of all business, the impossibility for our people to make livings and finally the destruction of our nation.[107]

The sudden political awareness of the bourgeoisie, linked as it was to the institutional obstacles encountered in economic development, had been encouraged by the intellectual effervescence of the May Fourth

---

105 Ai Lu, 'Chin-yung-chieh chin-hou chih chueh-wu ju-ho?' (How will financial circles gain awareness from now on?), *YHYK*, 2. 5 (May 1922).
106 *NCH*, 15 Oct. 1921, 151.
107 H. Y. Moh, 'Causes for the high price of cotton and the low price of yarn', *CWR*, 23 Dec. 1922, 140–1.

movement. The future of the country, its economic development, and the role of Chinese capitalists in industrial construction were the central topics of every discussion. Everything started from one fixed fact: China's poverty and backwardness. There was one single prescription: industrial development – one single recommendation: that China profit by the experience of Europe and the United States, and that she refuse to allow a conflict to develop between capital and labour. These themes dominated *The international development of China* written by Sun Yat-Sen after the 1918 armistice, a work touched by an industrial lyricism in the style of Saint-Simon. Similar ideas were elaborated by John Dewey during his many lectures at Chinese universities between 1919 and 1921, and defended, under his influence, by the liberal intelligentsia (Chang Tung-sun, Hu Shih) and in transitory fashion by the future founder of the Communist Party, Ch'en Tu-hsiu.[108]

The ideologists of May Fourth had in mind a development partially controlled by the state and based on the rise of a class of producers which would include the bourgeoisie as well as the working class. During the years 1919–20 the emphasis was not on the class struggle but on the deeply-felt solidarity of the Chinese people faced with the task of development. 'The primary force of human evolution is co-operation and not struggle.'[109] Anticipating the arguments between liberals and radicals which broke out in 1921–2, the necessity for economic development seemed to call for a certain merging of options: nationalism, industrial growth and social harmony. In highly classical fashion, contemporary Chinese political thought commenced its apprenticeship by striving for Utopia.

These discussions which centred directly or indirectly on the role of the bourgeoisie were closely followed by business circles. John Dewey and Bertrand Russell were received by the Shanghai General Chamber of Commerce. Chang Tung-sun, in his paper *China Times* (*Shih-shih hsin-pao*), seemed very close to the young Shanghai businessmen whose actions he supported in the Chamber of Commerce. Sun Yat-sen commanded such prestige among business circles that in 1921 a group of merchants wanted to build at Shanghai the Chinese outer harbour described in *The international development of China*.[110]

However, in more general fashion the ideas of the bourgeoisie sprang more from the practice of business than from theoretical speculations.

---

108 Robert W. Clopton and Tsuin-chen Ou, trans. and ed. *John Dewey, lectures in China, 1919–1920.*
109 Sun Yat-sen, *The international development of China*, 2nd edn. p. 158.
110 *CWR*, 26 March 1921, 176

In this regard, the decisive experience of the war and the period immediately following it was that of economic prosperity in the midst of political chaos. It seemed that the bourgeoisie was more aware of the advantages of the former than of the inconveniences of the latter. It had had almost no experience of modern economic cycles. The euphoria of the moment outweighed uncertainties over the future. The optimism of the bourgeoisie befitted the Utopias of the theoreticians. Illusions born of incomplete experience were joined with those of still-hesitant political thinking.

Great expectations

The ideas of the bourgeoisie as expressed in the positions taken in the chambers of commerce, in the articles in the specialized press, and in the declarations of the merchants and industrialists were centred around certain great themes that in themselves were paradoxical: both nationalism and international cooperation, both industrial revolution and social peace.

The Chinese bourgeoisie added its voice to all those who were demanding the righting of wrongs, the abolition of the Twenty-one Demands, the suppression of extraterritoriality, and the return to customs autonomy.[111] None of these themes was specifically of the bourgeoisie. Its nationalism seemed mainly tributary to the trend which at that time was setting urban society against foreign encroachments. Like all elites in big cities the businessmen were suffering from what one of them – the banker Chao Hsi-en (S. U. Zau) – called 'social inequality'. 'Foreign merchants in Shanghai seem to have formed an exclusive set. Individual Chinese merchants or firms have not the privilege of associating with them. . . . Such an aristocratic manner of living without due regard for their hosts and customers hurts the feelings of our merchants.'[112]

However, the foreign expansion, even though it worked to the detriment of the general interests of the dominated nation, involved in more immediate fashion areas of commerce, industry and finance which were the special field of action of the business bourgeoisie. The Chinese merchants thus found themselves doubly affected: both as citizens anxious to save the country (*chiu-kuo*), and as businessmen subjected to competition. The secretary of the Tientsin Chamber of Commerce in addressing

111 Cf. for example the demands presented by the Federation of Chambers of Commerce and the Federation of Educational Associations at their joint congress in Shanghai, in October 1921. *TSHYP*, 1. 4 (Oct. 1921).
112 *CWR*, 16 Dec. 1922, 86.

the National Conference of Banking Associations in 1921 underlined their special responsibilities: 'I really hope that you will consider the development of industry and the administration of finances as tasks which, in the interests of the Chinese people, should fall only on your shoulders.'[113]

However, the bourgeoisie realized that this economic development, the control and benefits of which it was claiming for itself, remained dependent on foreign cooperation: 'If we now wish to give fresh impetus to our industries, we must first adopt the principle of free trade, make use of foreign capital, introduce machine power into our country. . . . Should the country try to develop its industries through its own resources, the objective could never be achieved.'[114]

Chinese businessmen thus counted on foreign support. 'We expect you to make use of every chance to render assistance to our commercial and industrial enterprises.'[115] But they laid down precise conditions for this assistance. 'Cooperation must not in any way interfere with our national finances, nor hinder our development.'[116] It was not so much a question of control as of 'an intelligent action of mutual benefit'.[117] To establish what Henri Madier, president of the French Chamber of Commerce in China, so aptly called 'the economic *entente cordiale*', the Chinese bourgeoisie counted on the intelligence and good will of the foreigners, hoping that 'the healthier elements of the allied and friendly nations will be able to influence their governments to abolish or revise treaties detrimental to the spirit of cooperation'.[118] Above all, it was to the United States that Chinese business circles turned, captivated by the Wilsonian mirage. In 1918 they gave an enthusiastic welcome to the president's envoy, the millionaire Charles Crane, who had come from Chicago to express his sympathy for China, and his desire to help her.

This lack of means, this inevitable recourse to the good will of others, involved the risk that what was an effort of original forethought should be regarded simply as utopian. From 1919–20, the Chinese bourgeoisie in fact faced a problem which has continued to remain of prime importance ever since: the problem of foreign aid to 'under-developed' countries. The nature of the problem is very clear: how to get economic cooperation while maintaining respect for national independence, and

113 'Ch'üan-kuo yin-hang kung-hui lien-ho-hui-i chi' (Notes on the National Conference of Banking Associations), *YHYK*, 1. 6 (June 1921).
114 Report of the High Commissioner for Industry, Yeh Kung-ch'o, to the Peking Chamber of Commerce, *La politique de Pekin*, special no. Jan. 1920, 21–2; 29 Jan. 1920, 147.
115 Mu Ou-ch'u (H. Y. Moh) quoted by *NCH*, 13 Jan. 1923, 95.
116 Third resolution of the National Conference of Chinese Banking Associations, *Bulletin commercial d'Extreme Orient*, Oct. 1921, 17–18.
117 Mu Ou-ch'u, *NCH*, 13 Jan. 1923, p. 95.
118 *La politique de Pekin*, special no., Jan. 1920).

for the mutual benefit of the associated powers. This idea, which has become commonplace, even though seldom put into practice, was at that time revolutionary. It ran counter to the concepts of an international diplomacy devoted since the nineteenth century to the search for privileges and zones of influence; and in addition it broke with the Confucian tradition that held China to be the centre of the world and knew nothing of reciprocal relationships between nations.

The theme of international cooperation was matched on the domestic political level by that of social harmony in the service of the industrial revolution.

The interest in the working class shown by the bourgeoisie at that time possibly reflects the preoccupations of certain Christian employers: C. C. Nieh, Ou Pen (co-founder of the Nanyang Brothers Tobacco Company), and the banker Hsu En-yuan. At all events it coincided with the campaign conducted from 1920 onwards by the Y.M.C.A. and personalities such as C. F. Remer and Sherwood Eddy. From the meeting of these influences and the communal tradition of the guilds sprang a paternalist ideology which sought to reconcile the well-being of the workers and the interests of the employers. Founded in 1920 the *Kung shang chih yu* (*The friend of workers and merchants*) advocated reduced hours of work, increased wages and profit-sharing for the workers.[119] The necessity for social progress was acknowledged under the guise of efficiency. The energy of the workers represented in the words of H. Y. Moh spoken at the inauguration of one of his new spinning mills in 1920, 'the invisible capital of industry . . . this capital must not be squandered'. Faced with the immense task of development, the bourgeoisie felt itself interdependent with the working class. 'The new industrial system will practice mutual aid between employers and workers',[120] and this idea found a ready response in certain working class circles.[121] The awareness of a common danger, which national industries found themselves facing from foreign competition, strengthened this spirit of solidarity. The progress of the working class was thus not the result of struggles detrimental to all; it was not brought about *despite* the bourgeoisie, but, rather, *with* it, and on its initiative. Hu Shih felt that 'until a sufficiently intelligent and powerful public opinion had taken shape, and effective

119 *Wu-ssu shih-ch'i ch'i-k'an chieh-shao* (Introduction to the periodicals of May Fourth period; hereafter *Ch'i-k'an chieh-shao*) comp. by the Research Department of the Bureau of Translation of the Works of Marx, Engels, Lenin and Stalin, Central Committee of the Chinese Communist Party, 3. 292–4.
120 *Ning-po kung-ch'ang chou-k'an* (Weekly paper of the Ningpo workshops), *Ch'i-k'an chieh-shao*, 3. 289.
121 'Kung-chieh' (The world of labour), *Ch'i-k'an chieh-shao*, 3. 301.

legislation had been passed, a solution to the labour problems in China could come only from a policy voluntarily applied by enlightened employers such as Messrs Nieh and Moh, to improve the situation of the workers.'[122]

The Chinese press in Shanghai repeated this theme of a bourgeoisie that was 'intelligent' (*ts'ung-ming*), and 'farsighted' (*yuan-chien*). It underlined the necessity for 'a sudden awareness on the part of Chinese capitalists' (*chung-kuo tzu-pen-chia ti chueh-wu*) and worked to that end. The great liberal organ, the *Shen-pao* (Shanghai Times), pleaded for a rise in wages, and explained that this would not be detrimental to shareholders' interests.

The propaganda put out by industrial circles on behalf of popular education carried on the theme of social solidarity. The immediate objective was obviously to provide industry with the staff and qualified manpower that it lacked. However, the publication *Chiao-yü yü chih-yeh* (Education and vocation), founded in 1917, maintained that improvement in the living conditions of the masses came about as the result of coordinated development of industry and education: 'Employers and schools cooperate, labour and education progress together'.[123]

The philosophy of the Chinese bourgeoisie in 1919 was one of expansion. The resemblances it bore to certain aspects of French socialism (Saint-Simonism in particular) or of Anglo-American liberalism do not belong solely to intellectual history. All things considered, they resulted from an analogous experience – that of growth. Thus the bourgeois Utopia of the golden age occupied a special place in the evolution of modern Chinese economic thinking. It reflected the fugitive reality of its times: an economic miracle born of the First World War but with no future.

The nationalist mobilization

The bourgeoisie did not form a homogeneous class, and its various constituent groups did not react in the same manner to the presence and encroachments of foreigners. In this respect, the distinction drawn by Marxist analysis between national bourgeoisie and comprador bourgeoisie does not seem to be valid. On the one hand, most of the national businesses in the modern sector depended on foreigners – even if only in the area of finance. Foreign banks were making direct loans to Chinese industries. Examples were the Asia Banking Corporation, which acquired an interest in the Yü-feng spinning mills at Chengchow, or the Japanese

122 Hu Shih, *CWR*, 10 July 1920, p. 324.   123 *Ch'i-k'an chieh-shao*, 3. 303.

holding companies Tōyō Takushoku Kaisha (Oriental Colonization Society), Tōa Kōgyō Kaisha (Oriental Prosperity Company), or Chū-Nichi Jitsugyō Kaisha (Sino-Japanese Industrial Company).[124] Meanwhile lack of funds in the treasury (inherent in their system of management) forced Chinese businessmen to take out regular short-term loans from the old-style banks (*ch'ien-chuang*), who were themselves partially financed by foreign banks. On the other hand, even if any purely national capital had existed, it could hardly have been considered an essential condition of nationalist involvement. In certain cases, the benefits they enjoyed from their economic collaboration with the foreigners naturally predisposed Chinese businessmen to compromise. Thus the pro-Japanese position of the Shanghai General Chamber of Commerce at the start of the May Fourth movement can be partly explained by the business relationship maintained with Japanese finance and trade circles by the president of the Chamber, Chu Pao-san, and by some of the principal directors: the Cantonese merchant Ku Hsing-i, the comprador Wang I-t'ing, and Hsieh Heng-ch'uang, a coal merchant from Ningpo.[125] However, economic dependence did not always involve political submission. At the same time the Tientsin guild of compradors was the principal support of the vice-president of the local chamber of commerce, Pien Yin-ch'ang, an ardent partisan of resistance to Japan.[126] A bourgeois nationalism thus did not depend on the development of purely Chinese-owned enterprises.

The statements made and the positions taken by the various commercial and professional organizations showed that this nationalism was split into radical and moderate wings. We have already remarked on the hesitation of the Shanghai General Chamber of Commerce to involve itself in the May Fourth movement. When it later decided to do so, on 13 May, its involvement was tempered with prudence: on 3 June it refused to approve the call for a commercial strike launched by the students. Faced with a *fait accompli* its chief preoccupation was the maintenance of order; and its interim president Yü Hsia-ch'ing assisted the efforts of the civil and military authorities to get the shops open again. On 9 June the Chamber declared itself officially against the strike: but its lead was not followed. During the whole of this period the initiative lay elsewhere. It was the Shanghai Commercial Federation which addressed a telegram to the president of the republic on 6 May protesting against the decision of the Versailles Conference: 'The students are expressing the sentiments

124 Chou Hsiu-luan, *Kung-yeh ti fa-chan*, 80.
125 *Wu-ssu yun-tung*, 243–4.
126 *Peking Times*, 21 Nov. 1919.

of the whole nation . . . we beg the government not to punish them, otherwise the troubles will spread throughout the country'.[127] In a further telegram on 10 May the Federation reproached the General Chamber of Commerce for its pro-Japanese stand. On 4 June the strike plan was discussed in the District Chamber of Commerce. These were the merchants who on 5 June decided on their own initiative to close their shops and placard them with notices: 'The failure of diplomacy has robbed us of any taste for business.'[128] On 9 June the regional guilds of Ningpo, Canton and Shantung, and the Ningpo Regional Association sent a stinging refusal to the General Chamber of Commerce's appeal for a return to work.[129]

The contrast between the active participation of these various associations and the moderation of the General Chamber of Commerce reflects in part the difference in their social composition: bankers, compradors, industrialists and businessmen on the one hand, merchants and shopkeepers on the other. But how far can these associations, only a few members of which can be identified, be regarded as representative of a particular stratum of the bourgeoisie? Complex bonds united the various groups of this class, which was as yet but poorly structured. The same persons found themselves at the head of the two types of organization – the activist and the conservative: Chu Pao-san, president of the General Chamber of Commerce, and Yü Hsia-ch'ing, one of its principal directors, were also numbered among the influential directors of the Shanghai Commercial Federation. Ku Hsing-i, who presided over the District Chamber of Commerce, belonged also to the old guard of the General Chamber. Their attitudes were changeable, and apparently contradictory. In the General Chamber of Commerce at the end of May, Yü Hsia-ch'ing, who supported the reformist party, associated himself with the campaign demanding the return of Chu Pao-san, whose pro-Japanese attitude had just caused his removal from the presidency; while one of the founders of the Shanghai Commercial Federation, the Cantonese comprador and industrialist Ch'en Ping-ch'ien, was the leader of the conservative faction.[130]

This confusion of loyalties reflects a social organization in which the class structures were but poorly separated from the complex network of family and geographical ties. In addition, out of respect for Confucian principles and need for social prestige, the radical bourgeoisie continued

127 *Wu-ssu yun-tung*, 172–3.
128 *Ibid.* 386.
129 *Ibid.* 389.
130 Sanford, 'Commercial organization and behavior', 342, 361.

to look towards their elders: and for its part, the haute bourgeoisie, in order not to dissociate itself from the business community, often had to ratify decisions which it had not managed to prevent. During the struggle of 1919–20 between the Chinese residents of the International Settlement and the Shanghai Municipal Council, the Chamber of Commerce – not without reluctance – supported the fiscal strike declared by the shop-keepers of the street unions (*ma-lu lien-ho-hui*) for, as Chu Pao-san said, 'if you merchants oppose these payments, I suppose we shall have to take the same attitude since we also are merchants, and we must work together'.[131]

This merchant solidarity, and this Confucian-style democracy, which lessened the differences of interests, were helped by the economic pro-sperity and the rise of modern businessmen: sometimes they were as conservative as their elders. H. Y. Moh (Mu Ou-ch'u) for example, was resolutely hostile to the business strike of June 1919. They were, how-ever, more prepared to make the necessary concessions. On them lay the responsibility for settling the conflicts between radicals and moderates. In 1920 the election of C. C. Nieh to the presidency of the chamber of commerce prepared the ground for reconciliation. In the same way, after having protested against the Shanghai General Chamber of Com-erce which 'professes to represent the taxpaying Chinese without having been approved by them', the Chinese merchants and residents of the International Settlement elected to the Advisory Committee, charged with representing them at the Shanghai Municipal Council, Mu Ou-ch'u, Sung Han-cheng and the banker K. P. Chen ... all three of them direc-tors of that very Chamber.[132]

This cooperation between radical elements and moderate elements seemed to repeat itself in Tientsin, where the chamber of commerce was somewhat unwillingly inveigled into anti-Japanese resistance by its vice-president, Pien Yin-ch'ang, supported by the compradors, the cotton-spinners, and various activist elements gathered together into a commercial federation and a Group of Ten.[133]

Thanks to its internal cohesion the bourgeoisie benefited from the alliance formed between its most radical wing and the students, the em-ployees, and, to a certain degree, the workers. By associating itself with the demands of the urban masses, it contributed to their success. It was at the insistence of the Shanghai General Chamber of Commerce and of the various banking associations that the Peking government agreed on

131 *NCH*, 24 April 1920, p. 185.
132 *NCH*, 12 June 1920, p. 660; 11 Dec. 1920, p. 745.
133 *Peking Times*, 21 Nov. 1919.

10 June 1919 to dismiss its three pro-Japanese cabinet ministers. But the enthusiasm of the mass movement also allowed the bourgeoisie to strengthen its own position vis-à-vis foreign interests, in the name of the national interest.

The economic boycott represented the bourgeois method *par excellence* for nationalist mobilization. During the anti-American movement of 1905 and the anti-Japanese ones of 1908 and 1915, the merchants had protested in their own way against the denials of justice and the foreign encroachments: their reactions, as short-lived as they were violent, were often tainted with xenophobia and with mediocre effectiveness on both the political and economic planes. After 1919, and in the nationalist excitement created by the May Fourth movement, the boycott became semi-permanent. The movement of 1919–21 was followed by that of 1923, which carried over into 1924, became general in 1925–26, and thereafter was incorporated into the strategy of the revolutionary struggle. Between times the bourgeoisie tried to use the boycott to win the national market and promote a new industrial society.

From 1919 to 1923 the boycott movements were directed exclusively against Japan. Profiting from the withdrawal of the Western powers during the First World War, Japan flooded the Chinese market with low-price goods of poor quality (*lieh-huo*), which competed directly with the products of Chinese enterprise. Declared by the students and put into practice by the merchants, the boycott of 1919–20 thus sought to make up for the absence of customs protection. The slowing-down in the establishment of Japanese industries and the decline in imports from Japan are perhaps partly due to this movement. However, it is hard to distinguish the consequences of the boycott from those of the reconversion crisis which gripped Japan at that time. The boycott of Japanese 'shoddy goods' was accompanied by an extensive campaign to promote national products and patriotic products (*ai-kuo-huo*), which transformed the very nature of the movement. From a manifestation of hostility to this particular measure or that particular policy, the boycott became 'a far-reaching plan' and 'the principle of a permanent organization', stimulating China to create her own industries. 'When everywhere resound the cries of: "Long live the joint-stock industrial societies created by the Chinese people" . . . only then will the objectives of the boycott have been attained.'[134] In place of xenophobia and ephemeral passion, the

---

134 *Gaimushō* (Ministry of Foreign Affairs), Diplomatic archives *Shina ni oite Nihon shōhin dōmei haiseki ikken. zakken* (The boycotting of Japanese goods in China; various matters) series M.T. 3. 3 8. 5–I (1919). Enc. to consular despatch from Chefoo, 29 Aug. 1919 (nos. 740856–740873).

bourgeoisie wished to substitute an ideology of national salvation (*chiu-kuo*) through industry. Reactions of sentiment had to give way to 'state policy'.[135] The boycott had to make allowances above all for 'the interests of the national economy'.[136] 'It is an end and not a means.'[137] Taken to its extreme limits by C. C. Nieh, this analysis became transformed into a Gandhi-like defence of non-cooperation.[138]

In this context responsibility for the boycott returned to the merchants who would henceforth enact its rules and 'themselves ensure its super-vision'. 'The students must not get mixed up in it.'[139] It was in fact a matter of stopping incidents and disorders, of avoiding useless financial losses, and of placing the mass movement at the service of economic develop-ment organized by the bourgeoisie.

The economic reports for the years 1919-20 are full of references to the boycott's stimulating effect on the founding of Chinese industries.[140] But how can one isolate these specific effects from the extremely favour-able general economic setting of which they formed a part?

When the bourgeoisie joined battle on clearly-defined ground it was easier to appreciate the result of its efforts. In October 1920 the great powers signed an agreement for an international consortium which would be responsible for the financing of all public loans sought by the Chinese authorities. By way of guarantee the lenders proposed to take control of certain public revenues: railway receipts and even – according to rumour, constantly denied – the land tax. The articles of the New Consortium stated, baldly, that 'the cooperation of Chinese capital will be welcome'.[141] When the Chinese banking associations held their first national conference in December 1920 in Shanghai, they decided not to ask to be admitted into the Consortium, but to take up the foreign challenge by creating their own consortium: 'The International Consortium has repeatedly declared its intention to help China . . . and for it we feel very grateful.

135 'T'i-ch'ang kuo-huo chih wo chien' (My views on the promotion of national merchandiz-ing), *TSHYP*, 4. 5 (May 1924), heading *Yen-lun*.
136 Wen Han, 'Yu kung-yeh chien-ti shang lun wei-ch'ih kuo-huo yü ti-chih Jih-huo' (The promotion of national merchandizing and the anti-Japanese boycott considered from the industry's point of view), *Shih-yeh tsa-chih* (Industrial review), 71 (Sept. 1923).
137 'Ti-ch'ang kuo-huo', *TSHYP*, 4. 5 (May 1924).
138 Nieh Yun-t'ai (C. C. Nieh), 'Wei Jih-ping ch'iang-sha shih-min shih ching-kao kuo-min' (Warning to the nation concerning the incident when Japanese soldiers shot and killed citizens), *TSHYP*, 3. 6 (June 1923), heading *Yen-lun*. French translation in: M. Claire Bergère and Fou-jouei Tchang, *Sauvons la Patrie: Le nationalisme chinois et la mouvement du 4 mai 1919*, 103-14.
139 Chih Ping, 'Kuo-ch'üan hui-fu yü ching-chi chueh-chiao' (The return of sovereign rights and the rupture of economic relations), *TSHYP*, 3. 4 (April 1923), heading *Yen-lun*.
140 M. Claire Bergère, 'Le mouvement du 4 mai 1919 en Chine: la conjoncture économique et le rôle de la bourgeoisie nationale', *Revue historique*, 241 (April–June 1969) 309-26.
141 H. G. W. Woodhead, ed. *The China yearbook 1923*, 674.

But the fundamental reform of administrative affairs of this country lies with the Chinese.'[142]

In forceful editorials the *Journal of the Shanghai General Chamber of Commerce* denounced the hidden ambitions of the great powers, and exposed 'the mechanism of economic dismemberment' (*ching-chi kua-fen*) to which China was in danger of finding itself subjected. 'They wish to make us take stags as horses. . . . Whilst beforehand special privileges were accorded only to certain powers, henceforth all the powers will enjoy these privileges in common.'[143]

The persistent hostility of Chinese official and financial circles finally prevented the International Consortium from investing as it had planned. This was a political victory for the bourgeoisie. During the preceding years it had tried – not without success – to supplant foreigners in the task of economic modernization; now it sought to supplant them in their role as providers of government funds and controllers of public revenue. By underestimating the strength and determination of the Chinese bankers, the great powers had committed an error which the Washington Conference of November 1921–February 1922 gave them an opportunity to correct. American diplomacy and, following its lead, British diplomacy gambled on the Chinese bourgeoisie; and following a policy which foreshadowed the neo-colonialism of the second half of the twentieth century, they tried to ensure that power in China should pass to the local elite, and more particularly to the business community.

In China, with the announcement of the Washington Conference, public opinion was mobilized in a vast campaign for 'a popular diplomacy' (*kuo-min wai-chiao*) in which the chambers of commerce and the banking associations took the lead. This popular diplomacy seemed like the last resort of a nation which no longer had a unified government, and which was represented by negotiators (*cheng-fu tai-piao*) whose mandate was in dispute. Thus, at the meeting which took place in Shanghai from 12 to 17 October 1921, the representatives of the educational societies and of the chambers of commerce, Chiang Monlin (Chiang Meng-lin) and David T. Z. Yui (Yü Jih-chang) were instructed to go to Washington to make known 'the will of the people' (*min-i*).[144] Those who (to distinguish them from the official delegation) were known as the 'popular' delegates (*kuo-min tai-piao*) were mainly teachers. But neither of

142 Interview of Chang Chia-ngau, *CWR*, 29 January 1921, p. 470.
143 Ju Hsuan, 'Hsin yin-hang-t'uan yü ching-chi kua-fen' (The New Consortium and the economic dismemberment of China), *TSHYP*, 1. 6 (Dec. 1921), heading *Yen-lun*.
144 'Ch'üan-kuo shang-chiao lien-hsi hui-i shih-mo chi' (Notes on the progress of the joint Conference of the National Federations of Chambers of Commerce and the Educational Societies), *TSHYP*, 1. 4 (Oct. 1921), heading *Chi-shih*.

the two popular delegates were strangers to the world of business. Chiang was the grandson of a banker, and his family had held shares in Shanghai *ch'ien-chuang*. He had first become interested in economic affairs in 1918 when he collaborated in the publication of Sun Yat-sen's work *The international development of China*. In his capacity as secretary-general of the Y.M.C.A., David T. Z. Yui, for his part, maintained numerous contacts with heads of businesses; and as a member of the Chinese Consultative Committee (which represented the interests of the Chinese residents on the Shanghai Municipal Council), he was in touch with the bankers Sung Han-chang and K. P. Chen as well as the spinning-mill owner Mu Ou-ch'u, all of whom were close colleagues of his.[145]

In Washington the popular delegates played an indirect but active role, and spent their time defending China's rights to Shantung and the return to a status of complete international equality, which was demanded in particular by the banking associations and the chambers of commerce. The Washington Conference partly realized the hopes set on it by the Chinese nationalists. Doubtless the strategic hazards of world diplomacy contributed to this success more than the mobilization of Chinese popular diplomacy. 'If a blind cat catches a mouse, it's purely a matter of luck!' remarked a British journalist.[146] But it is still necessary for the cat to have its claws out . . . the Chinese bourgeoisie, through its organizations, had asserted its presence and its ambitions. This was what led Anglo-American diplomacy to gamble on it.

In fact, after the Washington Conference the foreign diplomats and businessmen living in China increased their appeals. 'It is the duty of those who represent the economic life of China to take part directly in its political reorganization' – so said the new British minister in Peking, Sir Ronald Macleay, as he assumed his duties.[147] A. O. Lang, president of the Hong Kong and Shanghai Bank, stated for his part: 'It is the great body of the Chinese commercial opinion and vested interests . . . which will prove to be the force of the immediate future'.[148] E. F. Mackay, president of the Butterfield and Swire Company as well as of the China Association made up of British residents, developed the same themes.[149] These appeals were based on the declared identity of interest of *all* the merchants of the treaty ports: Chinese and foreigners would gain equally from the cessation of the unrest that was paralysing economic development. It was the responsibility of the Chinese merchants to secure the

145 W. S. A. Pott, 'The people's delegates to the Pacific Conference', *CWR*, 22 Oct. 1921.
146 *NCH*, 18 Feb. 1922, p. 420.
147 'Sir Ronald Macleay and China's merchants', *NCH*, 17 Feb. 1923, pp. 446–7.
148 *NCH*, 10 March 1923, pp. 664–5.
149 *NCH*, 19 May 1923, pp. 471–2; 23 June 1923, p. 818.

political reform for which the foreigners were praying whole-heartedly. This reform, for which the initiative had to come from within, could be assisted from without. Thus, the urgings of the foreigners directed at the Chinese merchants were larded with various proposals for assistance. The editorial writer of the *North China Daily News* suggested that 'a well-qualified counsellor, enjoying the support of the commercial class, could rapidly reorganize public finances on behalf of an honest government'.[150] And E. F. Mackay forecast that after having dismissed corrupt officials, 'the merchant class will take power with the aid of foreign counsellors, if necessary'.[151]

The foreigners sought discreetly to set up a political movement, the latent powers of which they were impatient to use. The initiative seemed to come from Hankow where in November 1922 an association of foreigners (*wan-kuo kung-min ta-hui*) was formed and contact was made with the delegates of the Chinese Chambers of Commerce, who were gathered together at the time for their national federation's annual conference.[152] Agreement was reached on a programme providing for the disbandment of troops and the establishment of a constitutional regime. The bourgeoisie warmly welcomed this political cooperation, but vigorously denied any wish to set up 'a feudal bourgeois regime subordinated to the foreigners' – an accusation made by the editorial writer of the communist publication *The Guide Weekly* (*Hsiang-tao chou-pao*).[153] 'To invite a friendly power to help you is a matter of spontaneous initiative, not one of imposed constraint.'[154] Sun Yat-sen himself, in his declaration on the peaceful unification of China on 26 January 1923 seemed to back 'a policy of disbandment of the troops which would involve the raising of a demobilization loan . . . the use of which would be supervised by a foreign expert'.[155]

The proposed collaboration with the Chinese bourgeoisie, as envisaged by Anglo-American diplomacy, was intended to push the Chinese bourgeoisie into playing a progressively more important role in the political life of the country. However, the attempt seemed strangely premature,

150 'Plain words to the merchants', *NCH*, 14 April 1923, p. 77.
151 *NCH*, 23 June 1923, p. 818.
152 *NCH*, 16 Dec. 1922, pp. 711–2; Shirley Garrett, *Social reformers in urban China: the Chinese Y.M.C.A., 1895–1926*, 171.
153 (Ts'ai) Ho-sen, 'Wai-kuo ti-kuo-chu-i-che tui-Hua ti hsin chiu fang-fa' (New and old methods of the foreign imperialists with regard to China), *Hsiang-tao chou-pao* (The guide weekly; hereafter *HTCP*), 22 (25 April 1923) 158–60.
154 (Ts'ai) Ho-sen, 'Fan tui "tun-ch'ing i yu-pang" kan-she Chung-kuo nei-cheng' (Against 'the cordial invitation to a friendly power' to intervene in the internal government of China), *HTCP*, 19 (7 Feb. 1923) 150.
155 'Ho-p'ing t'ung-i hsuan-yen' (Manifesto on peaceful unification), *Kuo-fu ch'üan-shu* (Complete works of the national father [Sun Yat-sen]), ed. by Chang Ch'i-yun, 755.

for the bourgeoisie was incapable of assuming the political destiny which, for the moment, its foreign mentors dreamed of placing in its hands.

Liberalism in action

It is impossible to understand the political game which the bourgeoisie played and lost in the 1920s without taking into consideration the precise framework within which the game developed. In classes excluded from power the formation of a political conscience is of necessity conditioned by the nature of the established regime. Having acquired a certain social and economic maturity the Chinese bourgeoisie was called upon to accept responsibilities in a world which the decline of the traditional ideology and elites had deprived of its proven forms of organization without introducing it to new liberties in compensation. Despotism was no longer bound up with the imperial system or with the military dictatorship of a Yuan Shih-k'ai: but it lived on nonetheless, embodied henceforth in the local warlords whose very numbers removed all meaning from the partial victories their opponents might gain at their expense. If the involvement of the bourgeoisie often seemed ambiguous, disordered and ineffective, this was due in part to the very nature of the political environment within which it was slowly being formulated.

The era of the warlords was a period of generalized insecurity and exploitation. Every social group was affected. In the foreign concessions the bourgeoisie of the treaty ports escaped the pillaging and the exactions suffered by the merchants of the interior. But inasmuch as its economic activities were developing within an inter-regional framework, this bourgeoisie was directly and adversely affected by the decline in reliable social relationships, and by the disorganization of the transport and the monetary systems. The impact of militarism on a society of semi-autonomous agricultural producers had a rather punctilious character. If one village was ravaged by the passage of an army, the next one, a little off to the side, might be spared. But the proliferation of these civil disturbances succeeded in spreading the disaster over vast regions without altering the essentially local and fragmentary nature of the phenomenon: it was an accumulation of separate disasters. The merchants suffered from these dangerous hazards no less than others: their shops were sacked, their depots were burnt down. But they suffered equally from the disorders that were taking place *elsewhere*, and sometimes even when very far away from them. The wars in Szechwan posed no threat to the peasants of Kiangsu; but they deprived the mill-owners of Shanghai of one of their principal markets. At the beginning of the 1920s the business bourgeoisie was the only class the development and prosperity of which were *immediately* identified with the internal peace of China and with its national unity. In this respect it could be considered as the principal victim of a militarism which was the negation both of peace and of unity.

The political remedies which the bourgeoisie recommended sprang both from the motions adopted by the chambers of commerce and the banking associations, and from the editorials in the business reviews. It closely followed on many points the thinking expressed by Hu Shih and the liberal theoreticians of his entourage in their new weekly, *Endeavour (Nu-li chou-pao)*. Both groups made the same appeal for the involvement of the elite (*hao-jen*), the same search for professional competence to solve specific problems (*wen-t'i*), the same prescription for good government (*hao cheng-fu*), (that is, a public government (*kung-k'ai ti cheng-fu*) submitting financial accounts to the nation), and for a planning process (*chi-hua*) capable of laying down the stages of development while still preserving individual initiative.[156]

This community of views can be partly explained by the ties – personal, familial and institutional – which bound the urban elites together. For example, in October 1922 the delegates from the Federation of Educational Societies and those from the Federation of Chambers of Commerce (Ch'üan-kuo shang-chiao lien-hsi-hui-i) met together in Shanghai to work out political proposals.[157] Now the businessmen could in no way be regarded as disciples of Hu Shih. Most of them had acquired their political awareness solely through their perception of the obstacles standing in the way of their own economic development: militarism, financial disorder, bureaucratic arbitrariness. There was no question of Hu Shih's becoming the spokesman of the Chinese bourgeoisie: the predominant part played by foreign influences in his political thinking precluded such an interpretation. However, the two currents – intellectual and bourgeois – remained closely bound together, and the involvement of the bourgeoisie gave Chinese liberalism, often considered a somewhat aberrant episode in China's intellectual history, its political and social significance.

Though the positions taken by the philosophers of *Endeavour* and the practical men of the chambers of commerce were often identical, liberalism in action did however run into inevitable distortions, or, rather, necessary adaptations. The most striking feature of this Sinification of liberalism

---

156 Hu Shih, 'Wo-men ti cheng-chih chu-chang' (Our political proposals), *Nu-li chou-pao* (Endeavour; hereafter *NLCP*), 2, 14 May 1922. Trans. by Jerome B. Grieder, *Hu Shih and the Chinese renaissance*, 191.
157 'Ch'üan-kuo shang-chiao lien-hsi hui-i shih-mo chi'.

was the substitution of the defence of local liberties for that of individual liberties. Influenced by Western example, Hu Shih and his friends defended the rights of the individual. Based on their associative and interdependent practices, the businessmen took care above all to protect their communities against excessive interference on the part of the civil power (or powers). Having learnt, however, from the failure of the Revolution of 1911, the bourgeoisie sought to reconcile its autonomous aspirations with a more generalized system of organization, which alone would be likely in the long run to ensure a liberal fulfilment. Thus, there was a shift from the traditional theme of autonomy (*tzu-chih*) to that of a federation of provinces (*lien-sheng tzu-chih*). The decline of the central government gave the bourgeoisie the opportunity to redefine its relations with the state. It sought to break the vicious circle which for centuries past had associated freedom of enterprise with civil disturbances on the one hand, and political order with economic exploitation (or repression) on the other, whenever new state structures were envisaged; autonomy and federalism became, for a time, the instruments of the bourgeoisie's liberal policy and class ambitions.

From 1920 onwards, the autonomy movement seemed to bring together supporters who were fundamentally at odds; conservative notables, and enlightened or ambitious militarists; the revolutionary intelligentsia and the chambers of commerce. The bourgeoisie made use of this movement to try to realize its contradictory aspirations for liberty and for order. By encouraging the drawing-up of provincial constitutions and the revival of the organs of local government, the merchants hoped to consolidate their power in the face of interference from the civil or military bureaucracy. Among the non-official local elites who would be the first to benefit from the movement, the merchant class, as we have seen, played an increasing role.

In addition, the provincial or local framework appeared particularly appropriate for bringing into play the professionalism (*chih-yeh chu-i*) then being preached by liberal intellectuals from Ting Wen-chiang to Wu Yü-kan.[158] Partly derived from the guild socialism preached by John Dewey, professionalism advocated the transfer of public responsibilities to the experts. 'Long live the government of the artisans, the agriculturists, the professors and the intellectuals! Long live the government of those who work. . . . Down with the government of those who have

---

158 Ting Wen-chiang, 'Shao-shu jen ti tse-jen' (The responsibilities of a minority), *NLCP*, 67, 26 August 1923. Wu Yü-kan, 'Lien-sheng tzu-chih yü chih-yeh chu-i' (Provincial federalism and professionalism), *T'ai-p'ing yang* (The Pacific), 3. 7 (Sept. 1922).
159 *NCH*, 28 Oct. 1920, p. 223.

nothing else to do!'[159] Repeated in frankly polemic fashion by the monthly journal of the Shanghai General Chamber of Commerce, the theme became that of government by professionals (*chih-yeh cheng-chih*): all non-professionals (*wu chih-yeh che*) were to be deprived of civil rights – that is, 'the aristocrats, the militarists, the bureaucrats and the politicians'.[160]

Without going as far as that, most of the proposals for provincial constitutions reserved special representation for professional interests, and handed over very broad economic powers to local authorities: for example, management of the railways, telephones and telegraphs, founding of note-issuing banks.[161]

Through autonomy the bourgeoisie was not only seeking to ensure its emancipation from the bureaucracy: it was also attempting to establish, in its own interests, an effective system of social control. Recent studies have emphasized the concomitance between the development of the organs of self-government and that of systems of fiscal levy of the *li-chia* type, or security organizations of the *pao-chia* type.[162] The growth of merchant militia at the beginning of the 1920s bears witness to this same solicitude on the part of business circles to take charge of the maintenance of order. In 1916 the organization of these militia had been strictly regulated. This came about as a result of Yuan Shih-k'ai's dissolution of the district assemblies in 1914, which represented an offensive return of bureaucracy. With the development of the movement for autonomy, the merchants demanded that this control be relaxed. 'We ask the government to allow every chamber of commerce to train its own militia to ensure its self-defence.'[163] Quoting the precedent of the Hanseatic League, the Hankow Chamber of Commerce even demanded the creation of a genuine League of Cities. 'If throughout the whole of the country the cities succeed in establishing a real union, our power will be immense.'[164]

160 (Teng) Chih-ping 'Shih-chü tsa-kan' (Various impressions of the current situation), *TSHYP*, 3. 2 (Feb. 1923), heading *Yen-lun*.
161 Sie Ying-chow, *Le fédéralisme en Chine. Études sur quelques constitutions provinciales,* 83, 204.
162 Philip A. Kuhn, 'Local self-government under the republic: problems of control, autonomy and mobilization', in Frederic Wakeman, Jr. and Carolyn Grant, eds. *Conflict and control in late imperial China,* 257–98.
163 ' "Ch'ing ho-ch'eng cheng-fu t'e-hsu ch'üan-kuo shang-hui tzu-lien shang-t'uan an": Ssu-ch'uan Ch'eng-tu tsung-shang-hui tai-piao t'i-i,' ('That a common approach be made to the government requesting that Chambers of Commerce be specially authorized to train merchant militia'. Motion put forward by the General Chamber of Commerce of Chengtu, Szechwan), *TSHYP*, 3. 4 (April 1923).
164 'Pao-hu shang-pu an-ch'üan i-an, Han-k'ou tsung-shang-hui t'i-i' (Proposal concerning the protection of commercial centres. Motion put forward by the General Chamber of Commerce of Hankow), *TSHYP*, 3. 5 (May 1923).

However, although the decline of Peking's authority encouraged autonomist tendencies, there were also negative effects experienced by the merchants: no arrangement could preserve the social order, or guide an economic modernization the accelerated tempo of which called for the introduction of unitarian structures, either monetary or customs. This nostalgia for a strong state appeared in the numerous motions put forward by the chambers of commerce asking the 'centre' (*chung-yang*) for directives, prohibitions, righting of wrongs, and so forth. Thus, the merchants refused to renounce the benefits of centralization even as they were demanding autonomy. They felt that the adoption of a federal regime would enable this contradiction to be overcome, and a satisfactory adjustment could be made between the central power and local organization.

In intellectual circles there was much rivalry in constitutional erudition, and much comparison of the German, Austrian or American systems. But the Shanghai General Chamber of Commerce insisted, for its part, that the organization of municipalities, and the police functions, should be left to local bodies: and that industrial undertakings should not fall under the authority of the central government 'not only because industrial development would find itself paralysed thereby, but also because the central government would be in a position to mortgage or to sell the rights accruing to these industrial undertakings'.[165] The bourgeoisie thus continued to dread the arbitrary action of a state the deficiencies of which, on the other hand, they found themselves deploring.

After a decade of usurpations and strong-arm tactics, the bourgeoisie felt it would be difficult to revive the legal entity of the republic set up by the provisional constitution of 1912. In October 1921, the Federation of Chambers of Commerce backed the idea of a constituent national convention (*kuo-min hui-i*) bringing together delegates from the provincial assemblies and the business and educational associations, which would be charged with deciding on the political regime, and ensuring reunification, disbandment of troops, and financial reorganization.[166]

When this convention met, from March to September 1922, it confined itself to presenting certain constitutional projects. Meanwhile, it is true, the hopes of the liberals and of the bourgeoisie had turned to General Wu P'ei-fu who, by recalling to Peking the members of the old parliament (dissolved in 1917), seemed ready to play the card of reunification in the name of the republic as a legal entity. However, the political spring which Peking enjoyed in 1922 was too short to produce the constitutional

165 NCH, 6 Jan. 1923, p. 8.
166 Ju Hsuan, 'Kuan yü kuo-shih hui-i chih p'ien-yen' (A few notes on the subject of the Convention on National Affairs), TSHYP, 1. 5 (Nov. 1921), heading *Yen-lun*.

renewal sought by business circles. The attempt to restructure the state with respect to local liberties and republican principles ended in complete failure.

At the provincial level the autonomy movement, made use of by generals who were clever enough to take advantage of it, became a simple variant of warlordism; while at the national level the constitution promulgated on 10 October 1923 was a triumph of centralist and unitarian tendencies.

The text of this still-born constitution mattered less, however, than the conditions in which it was promulgated. The coup of Ts'ao K'un, who removed Li Yuan-hung from the presidency on 14 June 1923, did in fact initiate the final crisis which ended in the foundering of the very republican legal entity which the constitution was meant to restore. To resolve this national crisis, the Shanghai General Chamber of Commerce tried to establish 'a merchant power' – the early collapse of which illustrated in half-comic, half-tragic fashion the limits to the role of the bourgeoisie in China.

On 23 June the General Chamber of Commerce held an extraordinary meeting during which it 'declared its independence'.[167] Secession, which in Chinese history represents a classic display of opposition, is generally an act of regional powers: and on the geographic plane it displays itself in those sudden displacements of the political centre of gravity which are so characteristic of troubled times. It is surprising to see this strategy applied here by a constituted body – the General Chamber of Commerce – in the absence of any territorial base and any military forces. Breaking with a republican legal entity which had fallen into total discredit, Shanghai business circles reverted to the idea that the solution to China's political problem should be referred back 'into the hands of the people' – that is, to a national convention. However, unwilling to extend this convention to include all the various urban elites, the business circles sought to ensure a return to 'democracy' by themselves setting up a Popular Government Committee (Min-chih wei-yuan-hui) of 70 members, which included *ex officio* the 35 members of the board of directors of the General Chamber of Commerce. Abandoning the shelter of provincialism as well as constitutional alibis, the merchant power demanded, in actual fact, the government of the country.

The audacity of this step provoked ironic comments from Hsu Ch'ien and Yang Ch'üan, both of them members of the Kuomintang. 'It is

---

167 *TSHYP*, 3. 7 (July 1923), heading *Hui-wu chi-tsai*; United States National Archives (hereafter *USNA*), dispatch from Consul-General Edward S. Cunningham, Shanghai, 26 June 1923, 893 00/5095.

really laughable ... the Shanghai Chamber of Commerce wants to organize a government of merchants (*shang-jen cheng-fu*), as if no one existed other than the merchants of Shanghai. . .'. 'Up till now, our merchants have lacked political culture ... they grope their way forward, they act foolishly, and are radically wrong: the Shanghai merchants' government is merely the venture of a very small group. This type of government handles the interior problems arising from the Chamber of Commerce itself.'[168] Curiously, the only encouragement came from Mao Tse-tung, by that time converted to the policy of the united front: 'The merchants of Shanghai ... have adopted revolutionary methods; they have overwhelming courage to take charge of national affairs. . .'.[169] The American and English diplomats who had encouraged the merchants to get involved were not congratulating themselves on the course of events; and the *North China Daily News*, poked fun at the Chamber of Commerce's approach to the militarists, who were asked to abstain from any political intervention, and compared the merchants to Aesop's mice, asking: 'Who will bell the cat?'[170]

The mirage of merchant power did in fact vanish very quickly, and from the month of August the Shanghai General Chamber of Commerce was once again negotiating the maintenance of local peace with the warlords: the popular government committee had given way to an association opposing the war between Chekiang and Kiangsu.

Thus the merchants, unable to set up a new political regime, were compelled to negotiate – as they had always done – with the existing authorities. However, during the years of the Golden Age, the traditional pragmatism had assumed a new significance. Beyond the obvious defence of certain group interests, it was now a matter of ensuring progress by the successive solution of specific problems (*wen-t'i*). Advocated by Hu Shih, this approach was the one adopted by the Chinese bankers in their relations with an enfeebled central government on which they hoped to impose their views. 'In a situation in which progress is impossible, *some* steps must be taken.'[171]

After the First World War the financial straits of the central government and the lack of availability of foreign loans (imposed since 1920 under the agreements of the New Consortium) put the Chinese bankers in a strong

168 ' "Shang-jen cheng-fu" ti p'i-p'ing' (Critique of the 'government of the merchants'), *Tung-fang tsa-chih* (The eastern miscellany; hereafter *TFTC*), 20. 11 (20 June 1923).
169 (Mao) Tse-tung, 'Pei-ching cheng-pien yü shang-jen' (The Peking coup d'etat and the merchants), *HTCP*, 11 July 1923, 31–2.
170 *North China Daily News*, 26 June 1923.
171 Ai Lu, 'Chin-yung-chieh chin-hou chih chueh-wu ju-ho?' ('How will financial circles gain awareness from now on?'), *Yin-hang yueh-k'an* (Banker's monthly; hereafter *YHYK*) 2: 5 (May 1922) heading *P'ing-t'an*.

position. Isolated by foreign establishments from the financing of external trade, and by the old-style banks from the circuits of internal trade, the modern banks took advantage of the possibilities offered by the increase in internal borrowing. These investments were often more profitable than would have seemed possible, given the parlous state of public finances. Interest on loans was in fact calculated in relation to the nominal value of the securities, which were generally acquired at enormous discounts. The profits were proportional to the risks: both were very high – for the placement and negotiation of loans were made extremely hazardous by the risks inherent in a chaotic political situation.

Most of the banks engaged in this business had either an official status or some links with government circles. Nearly always set up in Peking or Tientsin, they numbered among their directors and their loan-sources many past or future cabinet ministers: for example, Liang Shih-i, Chou Tzu-ch'i, Wang K'o-min, Ts'ao Ju-lin and Yeh Kung-ch'o.

The osmosis between the banking and political circles of Peking was aptly illustrated by the activity of the Bank of Communications clique. It leads one at first glance to consider the confrontations which since 1920 had separated bankers and ministers, as only an expression of factional rivalries in the bosom of the ruling politico-military bureaucracy.[172] Such an analysis, though pertinent, would present only a partial picture. It would fail to take into account the solidarity that developed among the bankers, faced by the incompetencies and errors of the government's performance.

The Peking Bankers' Association embodied the unity and power of the local banking community. Its influence in the National Federation of Banking Associations balanced that of the Shanghai banks. At its first Congress in Shanghai on 6 December 1920 the National Federation warned the government that if it wished to obtain funds, it must reduce its military expenditure, readjust its internal debt, and reform the monetary system.[173] The intransigence of the bankers was merely, in the words of Chang Kia-ngau, 'the expression of their patriotism'. 'They are ready to offer very strong backing to any public loan which is truly designed to help the country.'[174] The formation of a Chinese Consortium in January 1921 corresponded to this willingness to assist the government to the extent that it agreed to work for the common good. The Rolling Stock

172 See above ch. 5, pp. 272–4; and Andrew J. Nathan, *Peking politics 1918–1923: factionalism and the failure of constitutionalism*, 74–90.
173 'Ch'üan-kuo yin-hang kung-hui chih chien-i-an' (Motion put forward by the National Federation of Banking Associations), *TFTC*, 18. 3 (10 Feb. 1921); trans. in *CWR*, 22 Jan. 1921, pp. 412–14.
174 *CWR*, 29 Jan. 1921, p. 470.

Loan (Ch'e-liang chieh-k'uan), the Shanghai Mint Loan (Hu tsao-pi-ch'ang chieh-k'uan) and the Peking October Loan, which were granted shortly afterwards by the Consortium, were larded with rigorous control clauses and mandatory recommendations on monetary reform and the reorganization of the internal debt. The government complied: it appointed a Commission for Monetary Reform, and published a plan for the redemption of its long-term loans.

As vigilant censors of the Peking government, the banking circles appeared at that time to be spokesmen for the higher interests of the country. 'It is the assertion of a part of the populace – which perforce must begin with a part – towards its ruler which spells democracy ... from the standpoints of both financial prosperity and democracy the recent development of the Chinese bankers must be praised as wholly good.'[175] However, between controls established in the interests of all and controls established for private interests – between democracy and plutocracy – the margin is dangerously narrow. By granting a loan to Liang Shih-i's cabinet in January 1922, the Consortium abandoned its own principles and consigned itself to oblivion. The bankers had been granted exceptionally high interest rates under the loan contract, and they renounced their control over the government, preferring to place themselves once more at its service and to gamble on its fortunes. The only alternative to an inconclusive liberalism was an ineffective pragmatism.

Now the bourgeoisie's political capability was brought into question. Should the Chinese merchants and bankers be accused of passivity – as they were by those disappointed Pygmalions, their foreign critics? Were they really 'incapable of any effective and constructive collective effort',[176] 'always ready to pay rather than to assume their responsibilities'?[177]

No doubt the failure was due in part to the lack of political maturity in a versatile bourgeoisie, which was sometimes quick to leap into action, but incapable of carrying that action, once undertaken, tenaciously through to a conclusion. 'In our chambers of commerce, we do not lack elite elements ... but one thing worries me: after the conference adjourns, all the birds fly away ... and who will look after the unfinished business?'[178]

175 Upton Close (pseud. of J. W. Hall), 'The Chinese Bankers assert themselves', *CWR*, 19 (Feb. 1921).
176 *Peking and Tientsin Times*, 19 April 1923.
177 *CWR*, 8 Oct. 1921, editorial.
178 ' "Ch'ing wei-ch'ih ch'üan-kuo-shang-hui lien-ho-hui t'ung-kuo i-an li-cheng shih-hsing an". Hu-pei I-tu shang-hui t'i-i' ('That the motions passed by the Conference of the National Federation of Chambers of Commerce be supported, and that every effort be made to have them put into practice.' Motion put forward by the Chamber of Commerce of I-tu, Hupei), *TSHYP*, 3. 4 (April 1923).

The failure can be explained much more completely by the methods used, the objectives chosen, and the permanent data of Chinese political life. The methods were those of compromise and negotiation. The merchants put their trust in public declarations and circular telegrams to induce the militarists to lay down their arms. 'Who would have believed that the warlords would turn a deaf ear and continue to muster troops as in the past?'[179] There were some who recognized the unreality of such an approach very clearly. 'Negotiating with the militarists and the politicians over the disbandment of the troops . . . is like negotiating with a tiger to get him to give you his skin.'[180] But was not this tactic itself indissolubly linked to the objective towards which it was headed? Was it not an integral part of the **very** liberalism the triumph of which it sought to ensure? Was it not already an expression of this liberalism?

What then were the chances of liberalism in the China of 1920? By a historical tautology – which was not acknowledged by the exporters of the model nor by the Westernized elite anxious to draw inspiration from it, the American Minister Jacob Gould Schurman as well as the philosopher Hu Shih – a liberal regime, under its elaborate forms of self-government and parliamentary procedure, seems unable to function except in a liberal society, that is, a stable society in the bosom of which a minimum consensus allows different interests to confront each other without their differences degenerating into violence, without a permanent rupture being involved. It is not enough to say that liberalism was powerless to cure the ills of a China in the grip of civil war and threatened in its national sovereignty: the very excess of these ills made it impossible for liberalism to take root.

However, the liberal endeavour of the years 1920–23 represented more than an avatar of intellectual history. It coincided with the rise of a marginal and urban society, based on big business and modern industry, and concentrated in the treaty ports. Relatively autonomous in comparison with the vast rural hinterland, this society could not however survive economically or politically without it. But it showed itself incapable of ensuring the integration of that hinterland, far less control over it. In fact, the unification and development of the Chinese continent, with its innumerable multitudes of small market-towns, villages and peasants, called for the bringing into play of ideological, bureaucratic and military

---

179 'Ch'ing fen-ch'eng ko hsun-yueh-shih ko tu-chün hsi-cheng pao-min li-mou t'ung-i an̄
   ('That the marshals and the *tu-chün* be instructed to stop fighting among themselves, and
   to protect the people and work their hardest for unification'), *TSHYP*, 3. 6 (June 1923).
180 (Teng) Chih-ping, 'Shih-chü tsa-k'an' (Various impressions), *TSHYP*, 3. 2 (Feb. 1923).

forces other than those of liberalism – even a Sinified liberalism. In the Golden Age of its short life, the Chinese bourgeoisie, despite its growing economic prosperity, remained incapable of overcoming this contradiction.

FROM ECONOMIC CRISIS TO POLITICAL ABDICATION, 1923–27

From 1923 onwards the end of the economic miracle and the rise of the revolutionary movement condemned the bourgeoisie to a growing isolation. Cooperation with the foreigners, already difficult when it came to sharing the profits, gave way to a desperate rivalry when the economic crisis struck. However, the retreat of the bourgeoisie to an anti-imperialist stand was not enough to weld its alliance with the radical intelligentsia or the proletariat, whose revolutionary nationalism carried with it social demands that were just as dangerous for the employer class as was foreign competition. Refusing to compromise itself in a collaboration which its foreign partners no longer even took the trouble to disguise as cooperation, the bourgeoisie nevertheless would not follow the path of a revolution that threatened its immediate interests. It preferred to encourage the restoration of a state power of the traditional type – that is, bureaucratic and military – which it hoped would be able both to ensure national emancipation and to preserve the social order.

The economic crisis and the aggressive return of imperialism

After the political failure of the bourgeoisie, the economic crisis succeeded in dispelling the mirage of Sino-foreign cooperation. The spirit of the Washington Conference disappeared, and in 1923 the Western powers were induced to reaffirm their solidarity with Japan while deprecating her policy of expansion in China. This aggressive return of imperialism shattered the hopes the Chinese bourgeoisie had built upon the 'intelligence' and 'good will' of foreigners.

The crisis in the national industries

China had stood up relatively well to the crisis of reconversion which, from 1920 onwards, had affected the Western and Japanese economies. The closure of their foreign outlets had hit the tea and silk exporters, and the overall volume of exports had fallen from 630 million Haikwan taels in 1919 to 540 million in 1920. But the immensity and vitality of the domestic market had stopped the crisis from spreading and prices from collapsing: 'Goods intended for abroad, which the foreigners were unable

to buy, were consumed within the country itself.'[181] The difficulties experienced during the same period by importers who were unable to take
delivery of the goods they had ordered (the disastrous fall of silver had
caused a parallel devaluation of the tael), resembled many other speculative shocks which since the nineteenth century had shaken the markets
of the treaty ports without causing them to crash. However, the essential
fact remained – the Chinese industries were now undergoing vigorous
development and continually making significant profits. It was not until
1923 that the crisis hit this sector, at the very time that the first signs of
recovery were becoming apparent on the Western and Japanese markets.

The difficulties began in the autumn of 1922 when the prices of cotton
moved in different directions – that of raw cotton going up, that of yarn
going down. The Chinese spinning mills, in full production, had increased
their consumption of raw cotton from 2.7 million piculs in 1918 to 6.3
million in 1922 – at the very moment when the cotton-crop, hit by the
bad weather of 1920–21, was beginning to decline.[182] Obliged to import
an increasing quantity of raw material (about 1.1 million piculs in 1922,
or almost a third of their consumption), the Chinese spinning mills thus
felt the effects of the world-wide increase in prices. The famine of 1920–22
in the northern provinces, and civil disturbances in Chihli, Szechwan
and Fukien in 1922 also reduced sales of yarn. In 1921 the mills were
still making an average profit of 25 taels per bale of yarn: in 1923, there
was a loss of about 15 taels per bale. Many mills reduced production.
While the installation of new spindles, ordered one or two years earlier,
increased production capacity, the number of machines standing idle also
increased. Yet at the same time the Japanese mills were continuing to
work day and night, and paying their shareholders dividends of 30 per
cent. Most of the British spinning mills also escaped the crisis.

Competition and domination

Chinese industrialists made various analyses of this crisis. They blamed
'the unfavourable market', and 'insufficient capital', 'the excessive proportion of fixed capital',[183] 'the permanent indebtedness',[184] 'lack of fore-

---

181 *Bulletin commercial d'Extreme-Orient*, Jan. 1922.
182 Marie-Claire Bergère, *Capitalisme national et impérialism: la crise des filatures chinoises en 1923*.
183 Chih I, 'Hua-shang sha-ch'ang tzu-chin wen-t'i yü mien-yeh ch'ien-t'u chih kuan-hsi'
    (The problem of capital for the Chinese spinning-mills, and its effect on the future of the
    cotton industry), *The China Cotton Journal* (*Hua-shang sha-ch'ang lien-ho-hui chi-k'an*) (Quar-
    terly review of the Chinese spinning-mills; hereafter *HSSC*), 4. 2 (Oct. 1923) 2–8.
184 Ch'ien Yüan, 'Fang-chi-yeh ken-pen cheng-li chih ssu-chien' (My opinion on the radical
    reorganization of the cotton textile industry), *HSSC*, 3. 4 (20 Oct. 1922) 2–6; Chu Hsien-
    fang, 'Cheng-li mien-yeh hsin-i' (New debate on the reform of the textile industry),
    TSHYP, 3. 5 (May 1923) 1–12.

sight on the part of management',[185] 'over-inflated dividends'.[186] But for all that they did not join in the opinion of the British commercial attaché, according to whom: 'The Japanese and British mills weathered the storm better thanks to better management and healthier financing'.[187] For, said the Chinese businessmen, 'even if our techniques and our management had been as good as those of the foreigners, we could not have escaped their competition'.[188]

In their eyes the obvious weakness of Chinese businesses stemmed from a more general context – that of a dominated economy; and the economic superiority of foreign businesses was due to their strong connections round the world. From this point of view, the principal responsibility for the crisis in the national industries lay with Japan, whose economic strategy was considered the instrument of a veritable policy of colonization.

'Our textile industry has one enemy, and only one: Japan.'[189] This accusation did not merely reflect the hostility roused among the Chinese bourgeoisie by the attempt at territorial expansion and seizure of political control by the Japanese in China. Japanese businessmen's exceptional drive in the Chinese market was also a matter for anxiety. Between 1918 and 1924 the number of Japanese spindles installed in China increased by 388 per cent.[190] 'They (the Japanese) swoop down on China with the violence of a crashing mountain, of the turning tide.'[191] Those industrial investments were accompanied by numerous instances of financial involvement in Chinese spinning-mills. Out of a total of 19 foreign loans negotiated by these mills between 1917 and 1922, 14 were granted by Japanese companies. And when the Chinese industrialists could no longer pay their creditors in 1922 the participation of the Japanese turned into control, as happened with the Hua-feng mills in 1923, and the Pao-ch'eng mills in 1925.[192]

What alarmed the Chinese industrialists was not merely the force of

185 Chen Te, 'Min-kuo shih-i nien-tu ko sha-ch'ang ying-yeh pao-kao' (Operational report for various spinning-mills for the year 1922), TSHYP, 3. 5 (May 1923).
186 B. Y. Lee, 'The present situation of cotton mills in China', CWR, 6 Oct. 1923.
187 Department of Overseas Trade, Report on the industrial and economic situation of China in June 1923, by H. G. Brett, Shanghai.
188 Ch'ien Yuan, 'Ch'ing-tao fang-chi-yeh chih chuang-k'uang yü hsi-wang' (The situation and prospects of the textile industries of Tsingtao), HSSC, 4. 1 (Jan. 1923) 29–32.
189 Li Shou-t'ung, 'Kuan-shui chia-tseng yü wo kuo fang-chih-yeh chih ch'ien-t'u' (The increases in customs duty and the future of our spinning-mills), HSSC, 3. 2 (20 March 1922) 9–14.
190 H. D. Fong, Cotton industry and trade in China, 2 vols. 1. 6–7; NCH, 25 Feb. 1922, p. 518.
191 Li Shou-t'ung, 'Kuan-shui chia-tseng'.
192 Yen Chung-p'ing, Chung-kuo mien-fang-chih shih-kao (Draft history of the cotton industry in China; 3rd edn. 1963), 180–5.

this economic offensive: it was the concerted and systematic way in which it was pursued. They saw in it the expression of a veritable 'textile policy' (*fang-chih cheng-ts'e*),[193] the bringing into play of a 'conspiracy' aimed at 'extinguishing the flame that had just been lit in China'.[194] They denounced Japan's desire to dominate and monopolize.

The establishment of an embargo on raw cotton in the spring of 1923 witnessed a trial of strength between Chinese and Japanese industrialists. The rise in price of raw cotton, which inconvenienced the Chinese mill-owners, led them in fact to demand that all export be forbidden.[195] At that time Japanese mill-owners were buying almost all the Chinese cotton being exported (803,000 piculs out of 974,000 in 1923).[196] These exports represented only 10 to 13 per cent of the Chinese production: but they were taken from that portion of the crop set aside for trade (about half), and thus deprived the Chinese spinning mills of a quarter of the supply normally left to them after the traditional spinning and quilting of clothing.

Although the Chinese analysts were not unaware of the role played in the crisis by the insufficiency of agricultural production, the acceleration of industrialization and the evolution of world prices,[197] they considered the embargo as the key to the problem posed by the rise in price of raw cotton. There is no doubt that they were right. Even though this embargo could not resolve the fundamental problem of preserving the right balance between agricultural development and industrialization; even though it could not prevent the Japanese spinning mills set up in China from obtaining supplies on the local market; it would nonetheless, in the short term, have alleviated the difficulties of the mill-owners. 'A temporary remedy', the Chinese themselves called it; but one easy to apply and quick to produce results.

Presented at the end of 1922 by the Association of Chinese Spinning-mill Owners, the request for an embargo was approved by the Peking

193 Ch'ien Yüan, 'Fang-chi-yeh ken-pen cheng-li'.
194 Tzu Ming, 'Shih-chieh mien-hua chih hsu-kei yü Chung Jih mien-yeh chih kuan-hsi' (Supply and demand of cotton on the world market, and the textile industries in China and Japan), *Yin-hang chou-pao* (Bankers' weekly; hereafter *YHCP*), 7. 10 (20 March 1923), and 7. 11 (27 March 1923).
195 Ts'ang Shui, 'Chin mien ch'u-k'ou yü chin-hou Chung Jih sha-shih chih kan-hsiang' (Impressions on the ban of exportation of raw cotton and on the future of the market for Chinese and Japanese yarns), *YHCP*, 7. 6 (6 Feb. 1923) 14–15; Fang Tsung-ao, 'Chin-chih mien-hua ch'u-k'ou chih wo-chien' (My viewpoint on the ban of exportation of raw cotton), *Shang-hsüeh chi-k'an* (Quarterly review of commercial studies; hereafter *SHCK*), 1. 1 (Feb. 1923) 1–3 (sep. pag.).
196 Fong, *Cotton industry and trade*, vol. II app. 5.
197 Mu Ou-ch'u, 'Hua-kuei sha-chien chih yuan-yin' (Causes of the dearness of raw cotton and the cheapness of yarn), *TSHYP*, 3. 2 (Feb. 1923).

cabinet, and an official decree was promulgated.[198] Japan protested, supported by the Diplomatic Corps, who invoked the treaties. Faced with the unanimous opposition of the 'interested nations', the Chinese government was obliged to abrogate its interdictory decree in May 1923.[199]

Thus the attempt at an embargo on cotton, to meet an urgent need of the Chinese industries, led to a reappearance of the common front of the great powers. When the warning was sounded, the solidarity of the imperialist nations prevailed over their differences. The United States then added its voice to that of Japan to defend 'treaty rights'.

Heightened by the crisis, economic rivalries made political cooperation more and more improbable. In 1923 many foreign observers and residents felt that the deterioration of their relations with the Chinese bourgeoisie – which they considered to be both too weak and too rigid – called for a complete revision of the diplomatic line adopted at the Washington Conference. One incident, among many others, was to be the occasion for this change of policy.

Cooperation at an impasse: the Lin-cheng Incident, May 1923

On 6 May 1923 an express train was stopped at Lin-cheng (Shantung) by bandits who captured numerous travellers – among whom were 24 foreigners. The incident aroused public opinion and exasperated foreign residents, who called for the return to a policy of armed intervention. For the old China hands, who had never stopped denouncing what they called 'Washington's illusions', this was the opportunity for a shattering revenge: they felt they must take advantage of this incident. The foreign governments must present as stringent demands as possible.[200]

An official note from the Diplomatic Corps dated 10 August 1923 and signed by all the powers (including those who were not directly affected by the incident) demanded, in addition to indemnities and penalties, the creation of a special railway police force under foreign officers.[201]

Thus, a return had been made to the most classic practices of imperialism. The Lin-cheng Incident was added to the list of many others – murders of missionaries, kidnappings of merchants – which, in the second half of the nineteenth century, had generally been the starting-point for military and diplomatic reprisals by the powers.

The foreigners were quite certain that this return to tradition would be understood and supported by the Chinese bourgeoisie. Whether they

198 *Bulletin commercial d'Extreme Orient,* March 1923, 41–2; *NCH,* 17 Feb. 1923, p. 426.
199 'Shih-t'uan yü chin-mien ch'u-k'ou-ling chih ch'ü-hsiao' (The diplomatic corps and the abrogation of the decree banning the exportation of cotton), *YHYK,* 3. 7 (July 1923).
200 *NCH,* 19 May 1923, pp. 471–2.
201 H. G. W. Woodhead, ed. *The China yearbook 1924,* 819.

were Chinese or foreign, did not the merchant communities have the same need for security? They must unite and work together for the re-establishment of order. The Americans and Englishmen of Shanghai were so confident of the implicit agreement of the local bourgeoisie that the statement of the common programme of their chamber of commerce and their residents' associations for the strengthening of foreign control over China mentioned, in conclusion, 'the approval of the principal Chinese commercial and banking circles which deplore the chaos but dare not take action themselves'.[202]

Did the Chinese merchants really not dare to take action? The *North China Herald* reproached them with 'masterly inactivity';[203] but did this not, rather, indicate a refusal to associate themselves with a step they judged incompatible with their interests, their dignity, and their very existence? Indeed, the Chinese merchants regarded the Lin-cheng Incident as a national disgrace, and they had tried to the best of their ability to help put the matter to rights; delegates from the major chambers of commerce had even gone to the site to take part in the negotiations with the bandits. Deplorable as it was, this incident could not, however, justify the establishment of international control over China.

'It is certainly not because of some local disorder that they suddenly wish to attack our sovereignty.'[204] With that, the guilds and chambers of commerce passed to the offensive and placed the responsibility for the incident on 'the foreign bankers and traders who, by their loans and their deliveries of arms, keep civil war and disorder alive in China'.[205]

This action by the chambers of commerce and the merchant communities was hailed by the communists as a recognition of 'the imperialist curse'. 'We call upon the comrades of the commercial world to rejoin the path of revolutionary nationalism.' Were the foreigners, by hardening their position and rejecting the collaboration of the Chinese bourgeoisie, about to drive it towards revolution? How could the bourgeoisie resign itself to this deadly alternative? But how could it escape it?

---

202 *CWR*, 7 July 1923, p. 172.
203 *NCH*, 30 June 1923, p. 859.
204 'Wei wai-jen kan-yü hu-lu shih chih Fu ling-hsiu kung-shih han' (Letter addressed to Mr Fu (Batalha de Freitas), doyen of the Diplomatic Corps, on the subject of foreign interference in the protection of the railways), *TSHYP*, 3. 9 (Sept. 1923), heading *Hui-wu chi-tsai*.
205 (Ts'ai) Ho-sen, 'Shang-jen kan-chüeh tao wai-kuo ti-kuo-chu-i chu-chang Chung-kuo nei-luan ti ti-i-sheng' (The merchants begin to realize that foreign imperialism promotes internal troubles in China), *HTCP*, 44 (27 Oct. 1923) 333.

The rise of the revolutionary movement
and the growing isolation of the bourgeoisie

From 1923 the *rapprochment* of Sun Yat-sen with the communists and the elaboration of a 'united front' policy gave new impetus to the revolutionary movement: events that stood out as landmarks in its progress were the establishment of the Canton base, the rise of trade-unionism, the great anti-imperialist movement of 30 May 1925, and the Northern Expedition recounted in the preceding chapter. In the cities workers and intellectuals rallied to this revolution in great numbers, while the bourgeoisie – both that of the Old Regime and that of the new businessmen – drew further and further away from it. The nationalist slogans around which unanimity had been built at the time of the May Fourth movement could no longer restrain the social and political antagonisms of the present. So clash followed upon clash – between the chambers of commerce and Sun Yat-sen, between the merchant volunteers and the cadets of the nationalist army, between the trade unions and the business associations.

In the autumn of 1923 the affair of the surplus customs revenue at Canton led to a direct confrontation between Sun and the powers. Despite the atmosphere of tension created several months before by the Lin-cheng Incident, the bourgeoisie refused to support Sun's initiatives, for the ground on which he had chosen to give battle was the very one the bourgeoisie considered as its private preserve. The Cantonese government's offensive in fact ran the risk of compromising the system of repayment of internal loans.

Towards the end of the war the increase in customs receipts had produced a sizeable annual surplus which the foreign banks placed at the disposal of the central government. In 1919 the Canton military government had asked for, and received, a portion (13.7 per cent) of this surplus for its own use. Thrown out in March 1920 the Canton government had then ceased to assert its claim. On his return to power in March 1923 Sun Yat-sen demanded the resumption of the payments, as well as the payment of arrears. Meanwhile, however, a presidential decree of 29 July 1922 had assigned the total customs surpluses to the funds for the repayment of the consolidated internal loans. In September 1923 the diplomatic corps warned Sun Yat-sen, in the name of the treaties: if he tried to seize the revenues of the local customs by force, the powers would resort to military intervention. By way of warning they moved 23 gunboats into Canton waters in December.

During this time the bourgeoisie was constantly thinking of the cost of their existing obligations; the various commercial and banking associations of Shanghai and Tientsin begged San Yat-sen not to jeopardize their interests: 'You founded the Republic. . . . You have the life of the merchants at heart. We earnestly hope that you will maintain the integrity of the customs revenues, so that the repayment funds may be kept up and the merchants saved from ruin.'[206]

In spite of Sun's stressing that the internal loans had been arranged by the Peking government, the authority of which Canton did not recognize, the bankers had no wish to get involved in political quarrels: 'Whether the government of the south has recognized these loans or not; whether the government of the north wishes to use them in this way or that . . . these are questions which the people do not have to ask themselves. And since the customs surpluses form an important part of the repayment funds, if they are touched in the slightest degree, the people are injured.'

Sun's communist allies came to his assistance. They defended his policies by trying to raise the level of debate to enlighten the bourgeoisie as to its real interests, and to contrast the prospects of future development with that of immediate profit: 'Sun's one policy is the restoration of customs sovereignty. . . . Not merely does this policy in no way seek to harm the commercial and banking world, but it is aimed particularly at serving the sovereignty of the state and the interests of the middle classes. Poor Chinese merchants! Poor bankers! They are really lacking in elementary knowledge, and are unfamiliar with politics.'[207]

However, the Chinese merchants preferred to appeal to Sir Francis Aglen, the inspector-general of Customs, to 'save the public credit'.[208]

If the Lin-cheng Incident had marked the limits of Sino-foreign collaboration, the affair of the customs surplus showed the limitations of bourgeois nationalism. In this affair, Sun Yat-sen came up against the opposition of the great modernized bourgeoisie – bankers and merchants of the treaty ports – the principal holders of the bonds covering government loans. However, the hostility of the traditional urban elites was no less bitter: it came to a head a few months later in the clash with the Canton Merchant Volunteers.

Driven out of Canton in 1922 Sun returned at the beginning of the following year, thanks to the aid of mercenaries from Yunnan and Kwangsi. The military government he then set up was feeble and incapable of

206 'Yin-hang-chieh ch'ing Sun Wen wei-ch'ih nei-chai chi-chin (Banking circles ask Sun Yat-sen to support the sinking fund for internal debts), YHYK, 3. 12 (Dec. 1923), heading Yin-hang-chieh hsiao-hsin hui-wen.
207 (Ts'ai) Ho-sen, 'Wei shou-hui hai-kuan chu-ch'üan shih kao ch'üan-kuo kuo-min' (Notice to the Chinese people of the restitution of rights over the Maritime Customs), HTCP, 48 (12 Dec. 1923) 365.
208 NCH, 5 Jan. 1924, p. 1. See also above, pages 536–7.

controlling the generals who were protecting him while at the same time ceaselessly demanding fresh funds. To meet these financial needs, Sun tried to negotiate a loan of a million dollars from the Canton Chamber of Commerce. He imposed numerous surtaxes; permitted the reopening of gambling-houses, the exploitation of which he handed over to his mercenaries; and pillaged the communal temples, several 'public' pro-perties supporting religious or local collectives, and private enterprises which he 'nationalized'. Municipal revenue tripled in one year and reached nine million dollars in 1923. However, such a degree of exploitation had the effect of turning against Sun, and against his government and his mercenaries, every creditor in the city, and all the rich Cantonese mer-chants overseas whose backing had been so valuable to him at the time of the Revolution of 1911. They felt that since Sun returned to Kwang-tung, bandits and vagabonds had been swarming like ants. How could there still be any hope that anyone would invest his money in the indus-trial development of the mother country? 'He would do better to throw it into the Pacific.'[209]

Tension between Sun and the local bourgeoisie continued to mount. In 1924 merchants and traders refused to accept the promissory notes issued by the authorities, went on strike with increasing frequency, and called on the Volunteer Corps for support.

This merchant militia, the creation or reactivation of which had been recommended by the chambers of commerce, developed rapidly in Canton. By the end of 1923 the Volunteer Corps was 13,000 strong. The cost of their equipment was borne by businesses, some of which maintained more than 30 militiamen.[210] The network of these militia corps spread over some hundred cities in Kwangtung. In June 1924 all these Volunteers banded together into a provincial corps, command of which was assumed by Ch'en Lien-po (Chan Lin-pak), a comprador of the Hong Kong and Shanghai Banking Corporation and the brother of the president of the Canton Chamber of Commerce. Ch'en Lien-po him-self aligned the movement with the defence of local interests: 'We are tired of the frequent interruption of inland traffic, the drop of our trade, the inability of our raw materials to reach their proper market, the loss of our investments. . . . The new Merchants Volunteer Corps of Kwang-tung has no other outside object than to be a non-partisan military unit for local self-defence. . . . Experience has taught us that people must rely on themselves. . . . A united effort for common defence and home

209 *SCMP*, 24 July 1923.
210 C. Martin Wilbur, *Sun Yat-sen, frustrated patriot*, 249–64. *CWR*, 24 Nov. 1923, pp. 534–535; 22 Dec. 1923, 130. On the Merchants Volunteers see also above, pp. 545–6.

rule will be but a beginning for other equally helpful policies to be later considered and put into practice.'[211]

The demands of the Cantonese merchants in 1924 repeated the familiar themes of local autonomy: return of the urban police and of monetary control to the guilds, and abolition of surtaxes. The ideology and political tendencies embodied in these merchant militia thus did not seem to have changed very much. However, the very swift radicalization of Sun's government in 1923 and 1924 highlighted their conservative character.

The merchants' revolt against the greed and the arbitrariness of the Canton authorities became partially identified with the resistance movement which all over the country was setting local communities and chambers of commerce against the militarists. Although he often used their methods, Sun was not like the warlords. Since the Kuomintang's reorganization congress in January 1924, his government had been trying to win the support of the masses. On May Day 1924 Sun continued to celebrate the unity of the Chinese workers and capitalists in their struggle against foreign imperialism. However, at the same time, the Canton Workers' Delegates Conference (Kung-jen tai-piao ta-hui), convened by Liao Chung-k'ai, requested the government to prohibit business employees from serving in the Volunteer Corps of the merchants, and asked and obtained for the workers the right to organize themselves also into self-defence militia.

The conflict which broke out in the summer of 1924 between the merchant organizations on the one hand, and the revolutionary government and the workers' unions on the other, clarified the options implicit in the autonomy slogans. Once assimilated into the concept of democracy the defence of local interests appeared to be no more than the protection of the elite. The 'people' to whom these slogans constantly referred formed only a minority of creditors. Just as the bourgeoisie of Shanghai had refused in 1912 to finance the establishment of a national government on its own, so in 1924 the Canton bourgeoisie declined to bear the cost of a Northern Expedition designed to reunify the country. But the Cantonese merchants' resistance to Sun Yat-sen's plans was increased twofold by their profound aversion to his pro-communist and pro-Soviet tendencies. While the failure of the Nanking Republic in 1912 reflected merely the narrowness of its social base, which accorded ill with Sun Yat-Sen's national ambitions, the armed confrontation with which the struggle between the Canton government and the merchants ended in 1924, had all the violence of a class war.

211 *CWR*, 21 June 1924, 82.

Deprived of the popular support which until then they had used in the defence of their interests, the urban elite were obliged to seek the assistance of foreigners. It is impossible not to be impressed by the widespread network and cunning schemes which the Cantonese merchants set going within the British consulate, the Hong Kong and Shanghai Banking Corporation, and the customs administration, to order, pay for and import the arms intended to equip their Volunteer Corps. This flow of arms not unnaturally provoked the final confrontation during which, on 15 October 1924, the merchant militia were crushed by the government troops, and the commercial quarter of Hsi-kuan, west of Canton, was set on fire and pillaged.

In a China in which the defence of liberties was often identified with that of local privileges, it was not surprising to see a class struggle break out in connection with provincial autonomy. Branded as fascists by communist historiography, the merchant militia bore witness to the bourgeoisie's attachment to those vital interests which were, for it, its local interests. However significant it may have been, the crushing of the Canton merchant militia in 1924 figures as an isolated incident. But the problem of the relations between the bourgeoisie and the revolution was raised on a national scale one year later, when the May Thirtieth movement of 1925 broke out in all the major Chinese cities.

Like that of May Fourth 1919, the May Thirtieth movement of 1925 developed under the standard of nationalism and anti-imperialism. It sprang from a local incident: the death of a striker in a Japanese spinning mill in Shanghai, and the bloody repression of a demonstration organized in his memory. It spread quickly to other areas of China, where equally serious incidents broke out in Hankow on 12 June, and in Canton on 23 June. It resulted from the foreign presence in China, the regime imposed by the treaties, and the administration of the concessions.

The Thirteen Demands presented by the General Chamber of Commerce in June 1925 and retained as the platform for negotiation between the Peking government commissioners and the representatives of the diplomatic corps provided, in addition to the punishment of those responsible and the compensation of the victims, for the return to Chinese jurisdiction of the Mixed Court (Article 6), representation of Chinese residents on the Municipal Council of the International Settlement (Article 9), the surrender to the Chinese authorities of the external roads constructed outside the Settlement (Article 10), the cancellation of plans for decrees dealing with the increase of port rights and with censorship (Article 11). However, the demonstrators and the Chinese press (in particular the underground press which was at that time enjoying a remarkable success in the factories, schools and army)[212] went much further: they demanded the complete abolition of the 'unequal treaties' and the declaration of war on Great Britain and Japan.

The methods of action had hardly changed. The general strike called in Shanghai on 31 May continued until 25 June. It spread to other cities: in Canton, it lasted six months. It was accompanied by a boycott aimed first against Japan, then against Great Britain. The institution of this boycott caused the usual collisions between students and merchants.

As was ultimately the case in 1919, splits became apparent within the bourgeoisie. On the one hand there were moderate elements, for example, the leaders of the Shanghai General Chamber of Commerce, who only passed on to the authorities 13 of the 17 demands presented by most of the organizations: en route they cut out the requests dealing with trade union rights, the suppression of extraterritorial consular jurisdiction, and the evacuation of foreign gunboats. On the other side were more radical elements grouped in Shanghai into the street unions and the Commercial Federation, and militants in the Association of Workers, Merchants and Students (Kung-shang-hsueh hui), formed on 7 June to unify the movement.

The new feature in 1925 was the presence, in the large Chinese cities and in particular in Shanghai, of a powerful workers' movement, officered by a Leninist-type revolutionary party. Formed in Shanghai in 1925, and controlled by the communists, the General Labour Union grouped together 117 workers' organizations with a membership totalling 218,000. It was a well-organized force. This massive intervention of the working class changed, on the one hand, the conditions of the dialogue (or the confrontation) between Chinese and foreigners, and on the other hand, the proportional strengths in the very heart of the nationalist movement.

In 1925 the foreigners resident in China became afraid. Not since the Boxer crisis had they experienced such serious alarm. However, the strikes and the boycott which were paralysing the port of Hong Kong and the factories of Shanghai could not be handled by an international military expedition; what they called for was negotiations, and compromise. The foreign chambers of commerce, the residents' associations, the official press of the Shanghai International Association (and in particular the *North China Daily News* which had recently still been disapproving of 'the absurd generosity' of the Washington Conference), henceforth asserted their sympathy for the Chinese demands,[213] and kept in contact

212 Nicole Dulioust, 'Quelques aspects de la press chinoise pendant le mouvement du 30 mai 1925', *Cahiers du Centre d'Études Chinoises de l'INALCO*, no. 1 (1980).
213 *NCH*, 18 July 1925, p. 20.

much more frequently. In Shanghai their privileged correspondents were naturally the leaders of the General Chamber of Commerce. To obtain an alliance with them the foreigners were ready to grant them the return of the Mixed Court, effective representation of Chinese residents on the Shanghai Municipal Council, and the progressive re-establishment of customs autonomy. Thanks to the intervention of the working class, the nationalist movement thus acquired a new effectiveness, and the bourgeoisie were finally granted the requests they had been making without stopping since 1905.

If the foreign residents were counting on these concessions to win the support of the Shanghai bourgeoisie, their manoeuvre was only half successful. Their first attempt, on 16 July, met with a favourable reception from the president and the vice-president of the General Chamber of Commerce, Yü Hsia-ch'ing and Fang Chiao-po respectively. However, these two were disavowed by their colleagues, who were swayed by the banker Sung Han-chang.[214] And although after the conclusion of the agreement Yü Hsia-ch'ing expressed his gratitude and enthusiasm in the warmest of terms, the *Journal* of the Chamber of Commerce viewed the matter differently: 'The British did not take this step until they had disgraced us, abused us and done us every possible harm. We therefore cannot thank or praise them.'[215]

During the summer of 1925 the Shanghai bourgeoisie thus appeared split along the lines that existed before the crisis: the old guard of compradors, the new generation of bankers and businessmen, and the radical shopkeepers of the Cantonese guild or the street associations. The complexity of the crisis stemmed from the divergent and contradictory attitudes of these various groups much more than it did from a sharp volte-face by a bourgeoisie that had suddenly become scared. At the beginning the crisis offered the commercial organizations an opportunity to play a mediating role, which they grasped for the sake of their own interests. It was doubtless to oust the bourgeoisie from this position as arbitrators, and force them to join in a common front with the employers – and hence to abandon the cause of anti-imperialism – that the authorities of the International Settlement cut off the electric power supply on 6 July, thus forcing the Chinese factories – hitherto spared from strikes – to close down.

Was this really enough to cause a rift between the bourgeoisie and the revolutionary movement? To put it another way: had there ever been a real alliance between them?

214 *NCH*, 25 July 1925, p. 54.   215 *NCH*, 12 Sept. 1925, p. 348.

In 1925 numerous journals took up the familiar theme of national unity again, and continued to present the development of Chinese capitalism as the path of safety for the proletariat.[216] At the same time, the dialectic of the united front supplied the theoretical bases for cooperation between two parties deemed to represent, one, the working class, and the other, the bourgeoisie. However, the ties between the bourgeoisie and the Kuomintang had already become very loose when Sun Yat-sen died in March 1925. With him disappeared the old revolutionary leader in whom the merchant communities had so often trusted, and who – despite recent disappointments – continued to inspire in them a feeling of gratitude and admiration for the work he had accomplished in 1911. In a political setting in which personalities often take precedence over programmes, Sun's death certainly helped to widen the rift between the bourgeoisie and the revolutionary party.

Nevertheless, in the immense patriotic *élan* of 30 May 1925, the Shanghai bourgeoisie supported the strikers through the agency of its organizations. The General Chamber of Commerce collected and distributed 2.2 million Chinese dollars.[217] With the aid of the trade unions, of students and educational societies, it organized a Provisional Relief Association and a strike fund financed by a special tax levied on goods originating from British or Japanese warehouses.[218] However, it would be incorrect to interpret these acts of mutual aid as manifestations of a true political alliance. In the patriotic enthusiasm of the summer of 1925, in fact, there was a general movement in support of the strikers. Warlords and the Peking government themselves provided funds.[219]

Furthermore, the leaders of the Shanghai General Chamber of Commerce had a tendency to negotiate with the strikers just as they would have negotiated with any other trouble-makers. Like all notables of provincial cities, they considered themselves responsible for the maintenance of local order, and were prepared for considerable financial sacrifices to ensure 'the public peace'. Yü Hsia-ch'ing, whose extraordinary activity dominated these months of crisis, and who was the leading figure in all the negotiations, did not act only in his capacity as president of the Shanghai Chamber of Commerce and spokesman for the merchants. His nomination as administrator (*hui-pan*) of a future autonomous municipality, the establishment of which he had actively negotiated during February and March, made him the official representative of local in-

216 *Hsueh hen* (Bloody scars), no. 2, 19 June 1925; no. 3, 12 July 1925. *Chiu wang* (Salvation), no. 2, 16 June 1925.
217 *NCH*, 14 Nov. 1925, p. 294.
218 *NCH*, 1 Aug. 1925, p. 78.
219 *NCH*, 29 Aug. 1925, p. 251; Chesneaux, *The Chinese labor movement*, 266.

terests.[220] Anxious to maintain his popularity, he was very attentive to public opinion: 'We will heed the smallest criticism from a tiny Chinese organization'.[221] With more justification, he was ready to give in when the strikers resorted to violence – as was the case with the 5,000 dockers who on 13 August sacked two boats of the San-peh Company, owned by Yü, in order to obtain strike pay from the Chamber of Commerce.[222]

In addition to the employers' sympathy for the cause of the workers, the aid given to the strikers by the Shanghai General Chamber of Commerce in the summer of 1925 reflected their fear in the face of mass movements, and their habit of compromise practised in the name of a Confucian ideal of social consensus (and freely stigmatized by foreign observers and historians as running with the hare and hunting with the hounds). The progressive abandonment of the movement by the bourgeoisie during the summer reflected the new equilibrium of forces, rather than actually creating it. The initiative came at that time from the foreigners who alternated between concessions and blackmail, and from the labour unions who extended the strikes into the Chinese factories and administrations. As always, the bourgeoisie reacted to the event, but did not take the initiative in it. It granted increases of wages, attempted to split the workers' organizations, and intervened between the strikers and the foreign owners to negotiate a return to work in the Japanese companies (in August) and the British (in October). Atavistic prudence? Paralysis due to its own inner contradictions? The bourgeoisie coped with specific situations but the course of history escaped it once again.

The turn to Chiang Kai-shek, April 1927

The rally to Chiang Kai-shek, which was to involve the rapid elimination of the bourgeoisie as a political force, was not merely a last resort imposed by the revolutionary explosion of 1927. It was a choice arrived at by a process of political thought which had been going on since the years 1923–4.

The movement stemmed from the liberal intellectual circles close to the new bourgeoisie. In 1924 Chiang Meng-lin drew attention to the established fact of the failure of liberalism[223] and of the New Education, both of which stressed the advancement of the individual. Under the direction of its new editor, Ch'en Ch'i-t'ien, the journal *Chinese Educational*

220 *NCH*, 21 March 1925, p. 478; 25 April 1925, p. 140; 13 June 1925, p. 440.
221 *CWR*, 24 July 1926, 188–90.
222 *NCH*, 15 Aug. 1925, p. 167.
223 Keenan, *The Dewey experiment*, 119.

Changes preached a nationalist education designed above all to produce a citizen useful to the country. Associated with the Young China Party and its journal, the *Awakened Lion* (*Hsing-shih chou-pao*), the statist current played a more important role than has been generally thought in the May Thirtieth movement. The Young China leaders Tseng Ch'i (1892–1951) and Li Huang (1895–), who had perhaps come under the influence of Charles Maurras during their time in France at the beginning of the 1920s, preached the 'eternal structure' of the country, which transcends social changes, and called for a national revolution (*ch'üan-min ko-ming*); that is to say, a redressing of the economic, political and cultural balance but excluding any restructuring of the social order.

Similar on certain points to the ideology of self-strengthening, the statist movement constituted a reaction against Marxism and proletarian internationalism. Although it indeed contained strains of totalitarianism and fascism, it did not exclude, at the outset, all democratic practices; its elitism was tempered by a certain populism.

Within the Kuomintang, Tai Chi-t'ao (1894–1949) followed a rather parallel line at the same time. From his former allegiance to communism he retained the importance of Leninist methods of organization which he dreamt of putting into action in a nationalist revolution (*kuo-min ko-ming*) in order to achieve 'a corporate state directed by a unitary political leadership'.[224]

After the establishment of the Nanking government in 1927–8, the bulk of the themes of nationalism, corporatism and *étatism* were officially adopted by the Kuomintang. It is therefore difficult to evaluate their specific influence prior to 1927. Their success meanwhile seems to have been greatest amongst the urban elites, both traditional and modern. Preserving certain fundamental values – anti-imperialism, economic modernization – while excluding class struggle, this ideology responded both to the aspirations and the interests of the bourgeoisie. On the essential points, such as social harmony, national independence and material advance, the programmes of 1925 recalled those of 1919. But the spirit was not the same. The realization of these objectives that the bourgeoisie and intelligentsia had previously assessed as conditional upon access to the West, seemed now to depend on a renaissance of traditional culture and nationalism. Nothing was more significant in this respect than the reinterpretation of the thought of Sun Yat-sen in Confucian terms by Tai Chi-t'ao. This return to China's origins was not to frighten off the bourgeoisie. The preachings of, say, Nieh Yun-t'ai, who advocated

224 Herman Mast, III and William G. Saywell, 'Revolution out of tradition: the political ideology of Tai Chi-t'ao', *JAS*, 34. 1 (Nov. 1974) 73–98.

frugality to the gilded youth of the cities, or of Mu Ou-ch'u, who drew lots in a Buddhist temple to resolve problems of administration, were following ancient practices.

It is more surprising to see the bourgeoisie rallying to the idea of an all powerful state as the guardian of unity and national prosperity. This recourse to the state was contrary not only to recently imported and incompletely assimilated liberalism, but above all was contrary to the traditional autarchy of the merchant class. If the bourgeoisie had come to view the establishment of a nationalist-unitary state as the final solution, this was because (as most writers emphasized) it saw such a state as the most effective protection against workers' demands and revolutionary troubles. But it was also, and perhaps above all, because the bourgeoisie saw that only a strong state was capable of regaining and preserving national independence.

The Chinese bourgeoisie was not resigned to the arrival in power of Chiang Kai-shek – as once it had been to that of Yuan Shih-k'ai – merely out of lassitude and fear. It hoped also he would rid them of their inherent contradictions, thereby reconciling capitalism and nationalism. The reconciliation of Chiang Kai-shek and the bourgeoisie was made easier by the existence of old personal ties and the weakening of the merchant community of Shanghai.

The personal ties seem to have been established in Shanghai at the time of the Revolution of 1911, among the entourage of the military governor Ch'en Ch'i-mei. After Ch'en's death, his old allies in the General Chamber of Commerce and the Chekiang set, Yü Hsia-ch'ing and Chang Jen-chieh (Ching-chiang), aided the career of his protégé Chiang Kai-shek. When in 1920, responding to Sun Yat-sen's demands for funds, Yü Hsia-ch'ing created the Shanghai Stock and Commodity Exchange, he brought Chiang into the enterprise. There were gathered together all the people who later played an important role in the rise of Chiang – Ch'en Kuo-fu, Ch'en Ch'i-mei's nephew, Tai Chi-t'ao, one of the most brilliant Kuomintang theoreticians, Wen Lan-t'ing, friend of Yü Hsia-ch'ing and director of the General Chamber of Commerce.

The importance of these personal ties also appeared in 1925 when the death of Sun Yat-sen forced a realignment of forces at the centre of the Kuomintang and the formation of a faction on the right. This Western Hills group, which was against the presence of communists at the heart of the Kuomintang, referred to the writings of Tai Chi-t'ao. From the evidence one tends to think that Yü Hsia-ch'ing and Chang Jen-chieh were not exactly strangers to the solid infiltration of the group into Shanghai. In Canton the link between the Sun Yat-senism Study Society and the business elements is more difficult to establish. Up to their final defeat in November 1925 the moderate merchants seemed to prefer to turn to Sun's rival, Ch'en Chiung-ming. Moreover the radical orientation of the Kuomintang government up to Chiang's coup of 20 March 1926 hindered the regrouping of the right-wing forces. But the arrival in Canton and the periodic participation in the government of Chang Jen-chieh or Chien Chao-nan, head of the Nanyang Brothers Tobacco Company, hint that contact had never ceased between the Kuomintang right wing, Chiang Kai-shek and the business elements.

The connections between the Chinese bourgeoisie and the Kuomintang extended beyond this alliance. In Canton, in particular, they reflected all the political ambiguities of the years 1925–6. Up against a business community it had severely tested by the repression of the autumn of 1924, the Kuomintang government tried in succession both seduction – the obligatory doctrine of a united front – and caution. The objective was to prevent the resurrection of an autonomous bourgeois political force. The reconstitution of Merchant Volunteer Corps was forbidden and all social aid and philanthropic activities were put under rigorous control.[225] At the same time the government sought to reach an understanding with the merchants who were prepared to collaborate with it. It encouraged the formation of new organizations to compete with the established bodies. While waiting for the chambers of commerce to come around, it opposed to them a Canton Merchants' Association.[226] It sought to substitute for the Merchant Volunteers a Citizens' Corps whose expenses would be paid by the firms but whose political and military structure would be controlled by government authorities.[227] Any recalcitrants were listed as 'merchants of comprador type' and would be placed under the direct authority of the Kuomintang Department of Commerce.[228] The Nanyang Company which refused a loan to the government was accused of repressing the unions and put under a boycott.[229]

These actions were not just political manipulation. T. V. Soong, educated in the West, an advocate of economic modernization and the expansion of democracy, became commercial commissar in the government and director of the Central Bank established in 1925. He seems to have been a sincere and conciliatory intermediary with the merchants. The Kuomintang – even during its radical period – aimed at neither the ruination nor destruction of the merchant community but rather sought

225 *NCH*, 17 Jan. 1925, p. 91; 31 Oct. 1925, p. 194.
226 *CWR*, 7 March 1925, p. 21; 21 Nov. 1925, p. 288.
227 *CWR*, 17 April 1926, p. 179.
228 *CWR*, 13 Feb. 1926, p. 316.
229 *NCH*, 24 June. 1925, p. 146.

to place it under the tutelage of the party and in its service (*tang-hua*). After the coup of 20 March 1926, by which Chiang Kai-shek confirmed his power, the principles of this policy were not changed. But the bourgeoisie benefited from the repression of the workers' movement, which was initiated as early as June and intensified after the departure of the Northern Expedition in July. The Canton base served as a testing ground for what was to become the strategy of the Nanking government. The success of this policy in Canton had been helped by the defeat and elimination of the city's merchant militia in October 1924; by the desertion of the richest traders fleeing the 'Reds' and also by the relatively archaic character of a bourgeoisie that was more tied to the landed classes than to entrepreneurs.

The Canton bourgeoisie was thus subdued. That of Shanghai was being won over. The classic interpretations of Harold Isaacs and André Malraux see this as the counter-revolutionary choice of a bourgeoisie threatened by the insurrectionist strikes of November 1926, and of January 1927. The move towards Chiang Kai-shek, in fact, constituted the triumph of the progressive elements at the core of the merchant community. Since the summer of 1926, after the victorious march of the Northern Expedition and the uprisings which preceded and accompanied it, the mass movement had put the Shanghai bourgeois community on the defensive. There was no real alternative: support the mass movement or resist it. The choice devolved exclusively on the means of resistance. Some recommended an alliance with the local military embodied in Chekiang by General Sun Ch'uan-fang. Others more subtle or better informed as to Chiang Kai-shek's true objectives, sought to ally themselves with the non-communists of the Kuomintang.

The elections of June 1926 for the General Chamber of Commerce clearly illuminated the political divisions in the merchant class. Supported by Sun Ch'uan-fang, the old pro-Japanese group who had been brushed aside in 1919–20, reappeared in force. As a sign of protest against these gerrymandered elections, the out-going president Yü Hsia-ch'ing left for a voyage to Japan and 150 members of the Chamber refused to take part in the election. Their abstention helped the accession to power of a directory that was homogeneous but not very representative. The banker Fu Hsiao-an (Tsung-yao) had trouble taking up his functions and his role remained disputed as was his suitability.[230] The overthrow of the majority at the core of the chamber of commerce, thus achieved, forced it into a radical political reorientation. During his presidency (1924–6),

230 'Power and politics of the Chinese Chamber of Commerce', *CWR*, 24 July 1926, p. 190; *CWR*, 17 July 1926, p. 176.

which had coincided with the start of the civil wars and the large military concentrations in Chekiang and Kiangsu, Yü Hsia-ch'ing had employed many methods to establish the neutrality of Shanghai and its surroundings, to ensure the evacuation of defeated soldiers who became refugees in the city and the closure of the Kiangnan Arsenal. He had pressed equally strongly for the establishment of a special zone, Shanghai-Woosung, endowed with municipal autonomy, free from the authority of the provincial administration.[231] Faithful to the ideology and practice of local elites, Yü Hsia-ch'ing's actions had been received as favourably by the Shanghai community as by the Peking government.

Anxious to reassert his control over Shanghai and its financial resources, Sun Ch'uan-fang presented in 1926 his own particular plan for a Greater Shanghai municipality. He gave its organization to a friend of Hu Shih, the geologist Ting Wen-chiang, but at the outset he limited its jurisdiction to keep it subordinate to the provincial administration.[232] Hostile to this policy, a large faction among the merchant community grouped around Yü Hsia-ch'ing, and started to agitate in favour of autonomy. This campaign was particularly strong in the autumn of 1926.[233] But henceforth Sun Ch'uan-fang was able to count on the support of the chamber of commerce. It made no attempt to oppose the re-opening of the Kiangnan Arsenal and the president, Fu Hsiao-an, helped General Sun transport his troops by putting at his disposal the ships of the China Merchants Line, of which he was director.[234] However, at the time of the insurrectionist strike on 17 February 1927 the brutally effective repression imposed in Shanghai by the police and troops of Sun Ch'uan-fang was not sufficient to rally the bourgeoisie to a military whose defeat on the battlefield was already accomplished.

The alliance which helped Chiang Kai-shek to establish his power in Shanghai at the end of March and beginning of April 1927 was made, then, not with the right wing of the bourgeoisie but with those elements that were the most nationalist, modern and, to a certain extent, democratic.

As in Canton in 1924 the development of a revolutionary situation in Shanghai in the spring of 1927 provoked a general realignment in the structure of society. The old radical bourgeoisie of the beginning of the 1920s continued to fight for Chinese representation on the Municipal

231 NCH, 21 March 1925, p. 478; 25 April 1925, p. 140; 13 June 1925, p. 409. Chiang Shen-wu, 'Shang-hai shih-cheng-chi-kuan pien-ch'ien shih-lueh' (Short history of the structural changes in the municipal government of Shanghai), in Shang-hai yen-chiu tzu-liao (Research material on Shanghai; 1st edn. 1926), 78–82.
232 NCH, 8 May 1926, p. 252.
233 HTCP, 177 (1926), p. 1832.
234 NCH, 20 Nov. 1926.

Council, for the rendition of the Mixed Court and against the encroachments of the military. But its place on the political chess board had completely changed. Behind the cliché of a nationalist bourgeoisie betraying the revolution under the influence of a group of compradors, lies another reality: that of a bourgeoisie whose radicalism was transmuted to conservatism by the simple fact of a general evolution of socio-political tensions which changed the relations of the bourgeoisie with other political groups and personalities. This brand of conservatism appears to be much like that defined by Karl Mannheim: a dynamic movement existing essentially as a conscious repudiation of progressivism.[235]

This analysis finds confirmation in the study of the reorganization and the groupings occurring in the institutions of the merchant community in the spring of 1927. The General Chamber of Commerce, as constituted after the elections of 1926, lost its leading role to the Federation of Commerce and Industry (Shang-yeh lien-ho-hui), the brain-child of Yü Hsia-ch'ing. It was this federation which made contact with Chiang Kai-shek on his arrival in Shanghai on 26 March and immediately agreed to advance a loan of three million dollars to him, his charge for re-establishing order: in other words, for him to smash the power of the communist unions. The federation was the political mouthpiece of the main commercial organizations in the city, which, from a firm base of corporate solidarity, at the same time rejoined the Shanghai Merchant Collaborative Association (Hu-shang hsieh-hui). As with all the Merchant Collaborative Associations – either official or clandestine – set up during 1926, the Shanghai Association was a Kuomintang organization under the control of the Department of Merchants (Shang-min pu) created at the Second Party Congress in January 1926. Little is known of the Shanghai Association before it ceased being clandestine on 20 March 1927. But it seems to have been closely linked with the Federation of Street Associations whose branches were taken over in order to speed up the growth of the Merchants' Collaborative Association during the events of April 1927.[236] In this way one can see the amalgamation and intermingling of the Federation of Commerce and Industry, set up to help the rise of Chiang Kai-shek, and the Federation of Street Associations which many historians consider, from its appearance during the May Fourth movement, as the voice of the progressive petit bourgeoisie.

Approved by the majority of the merchant community, the collabora-

235 Karl Mannheim, *Essays on sociology and social psychology*, ch. 2.
236 Joseph Fewsmith, 'Merchant associations and the establishment of Nationalist rule in Shanghai' (paper prepared for the annual meeting of the Association for Asian Studies Chicago, 31 March–2 April 1978).

tion of the bourgeoisie was vital to Chiang Kai-shek. By refusing to sit on the Provisional Municipal Government, created on 29 March under the auspices of the communist trade unions, the merchants effectively paralysed the political initiative of the workers' organizations.[237] The money lent to Chiang Kai-shek allowed him to recruit and pay body-guards, for the most part members of the Green Gang (Ch'ing-pang), who at dawn of 12 April attacked and disarmed the workers' militia.

Almost immediately the relationship that was originally based on cooperation gave way to one based on subordination and exploitation. Once the coup of 12 April was over, Chiang Kai-shek exacted a new payment of seven million dollars, imposed a loan of 30 million dollars, blackmailed, and extorted money at every opportunity; he caused terror to reign among the merchants.[238] The Shanghai bourgeoisie were as powerless as the notables of any provincial Chamber of Commerce held to ransom by a passing *condottiere*. In this case, its congenital weakness, that of shopkeepers and financiers faced by men of arms, was exacerbated by dissension arising out of internal divisions. The Chamber of Com-merce had lost the political authority it had possessed in earlier years. Chiang Kai-shek negotiated one by one with the organizations, which were unable to set up any resistance against their assimilation into the Kuomintang apparatus. On the other hand, the repression directed against the bourgeoisie by Chiang Kai-shek from the second half of April 1927, appeared as a continuation of the internecine faction-fighting amongst the bourgeoisie. The arrest warrant against Fu Hsiao-an; the confiscation of a large part of his goods; the annulment of his election to the presidency of the General Chamber of Commerce and the latter being put under tutelage; all this gave a great deal of satisfaction to Yü Hsia-ch'ing and his friends. Ousted from the direction of the Chamber of Commerce in 1926, they regained control at the end of April 1927, when three of this group (Yü Hsia-ch'ing, Wang Chen (I-t'ing) and Feng Hsiao-shan (P'ei-hsi)) were called to sit on the government committee charged with the supervision of the Chamber's activities.

The bourgeoisie did not rebel against abuses of power that at other times and in other places they had vigorously condemned and fought against: in this case they served the direct interests of the largest faction. The betrayal of 1927 was not only that of the proletariat by the bour-geoisie; it was also the bourgeoisie betraying itself. By abdicating all

---

237 Harold Isaacs, *The tragedy of the Chinese revolution*, rev. edn. 2nd printing, 166.
238 Parks Coble, Jr. 'The Kuomintang régime and the Shanghai capitalists, 1927–29', *CQ*, 77 (March 1979) 1–24.

political autonomy the bourgeoisie subjected itself to the blows of the very state power that it had helped to restore.

THE RETURN OF BUREAUCRACY AND DECLINE OF THE BOURGEOISIE, 1927–37

For a long time the Nanking decade (1927–37) seemed to coincide with the apogee of the Chinese bourgeoisie. Accepted by observers and journalists of the 1930s, this thesis has been taken up by most historians who have studied the period. As late as 1975 Jean Chesneaux wrote: 'its power [of the Kuomintang] was founded on the coalition of the conservative managerial classes and the pro-Western business classes.'[239] According to this interpretation, the merchant bourgeoisie and, more particularly, the Shanghai capitalists, along with the landowners, were the principal supporters and beneficiaries of the regime.

Chinese communist historians generally adopt a similar interpretation.[240] With rhetorical caution they are content to denounce the compradors and capitalist-bureaucrats, but it is in fact quite clear that the whole of the bourgeoisie is implicated in an assumed support of the Chiang Kai-shek regime. Indeed it is this support of the regime which, in the eyes of communist historians, confers on this or that entrepreneur his character as either comprador or bureaucrat. Meanwhile no one knows what happened to the old nationalist bourgeoisie, who are strangely absent from the political and economic scene.

Recent studies[241] have begun to look again at the difficult question of relations between the Kuomintang and the bourgeoisie. In its most extreme form, this revised thesis contends that the 'urban economic interest did not control or significantly influence the Nanking regime' and that Chiang Kai-shek's government was only concerned 'to emasculate politically the urban elite and to milk the modern sector of the economy.'[242]

If, as we believe, this revised theory is well-founded, why has the idea of a bourgeois Kuomintang regime prevailed for so long? The difficulty of interpretation bears striking witness to the very real ambiguities in a regime that is difficult to analyse and describe. In a moment of discourage-

239 Jean Chesneaux and Francoise LeBarbier, *China from the 1911 revolution to liberation*, 188.
240 Ch'en Po-ta, *Chung-kuo ssu-ta-chia-tsu* (China's four great families). Hsu Ti-hsin, *Kuan-liao tzu-pen lun* (On the subject of bureaucratic capitalism).
241 Lloyd E. Eastman, *The abortive revolution: China under Nationalist rule 1927–1937*. Parks M. Coble, Jr. 'The Shanghai capitalists and the Nationalist government 1927–1937' (University of Illinois, Ph.D. dissertation, 1975). M. C. Bergère, '"The other China": Shanghai from 1919 to 1949' in C. Howe, ed. *Shanghai: revolution and development in an Asian metropolis*.
242 Coble, 'The Kuomintang regime', 1–2.

ment a historian may well ask himself if he is indeed dealing with a regime without a class basis.[243] But the misapprehension seems to have been knowingly fostered by the Chinese themselves. Chinese theoreticians who are anxious to present the development of China as conforming with Marxist inevitability, have sought to establish the existence of a bourgeois stage, be it comprador, bureaucratic or semi-feudal. On the other hand the Chiang Kai-shek government skilfully created the image most advantageous to its own interests, an image likely to attract the sympathies and financial aid of the West. Just as the China of Mao Tse-tung sought to dazzle the eyes of leftists or radicals of the West, exuding frugality and fraternity, so the China of Chiang Kai-shek was keen to convince and win over the democracies of Europe and America by unduly highlighting its urban, modernized and liberal character – in a word, its bourgeois character. In both cases, the success of these projected images marked the measure of our ignorance about China. Because foreigners have only limited access to China, they are usually forced to use an intermediary or interpreter on whom they remain dependent. For Kuomintang China T. V. Soong was best known for this role. He was educated at Harvard and had a perfect command of English. He held press conferences, received businessmen and foreign advisers. 'It was easy for me to deal with T. V. Soong whose culture was European', said Jean Monnet.[244] It was doubtless far more difficult for him, as indeed for others like him, to see that the solicitude of T. V. Soong for the Chinese capitalists was not shared by the Nanking government. Behind the myth created by T. V. Soong for the consumption of his foreign contacts, one begins today to see a totally different picture: that of a bourgeoisie subordinated and integrated into the apparatus of the state; a bureaucracy in a state of change, as unsure of its objectives as of its methods; and of a modern economic sector always dominated by the risks of the international scene.

The alienation of the bourgeoisie

Reconstituted in its prerogatives and authority after 1927 the government captured from the bourgeoisie the political initiative which it had enjoyed since the Revolution of 1911 and even more after the May Fourth movement of 1919. A bureaucracy which was far more ambitious in its objectives than was its counterpart under the old dynasty succeeded in taking away a part of the social autonomy that had benefited the merchant class

243 L. Eastman, *Chinese Republican Studies Newsletter*, I. 1 (Oct. 1975), 14.
244 Jean Monnet, *Memoires*, 134.

in the preceding century. Against these encroachments by the public authorities, the foreign concessions offered only an increasingly fragile and illusory refuge. The bourgeoisie had no choice but to allow itself to be sucked into the state apparatus for better or worse.

Subordination of bourgeois organizations to the Kuomintang regime

The Nanking government's offensive to subordinate the merchant organizations developed from 1927 to 1932 by means of diverse and complementary strategies: establishment of parallel bodies, reorganization or eradication of old institutions, progressive reduction of the bourgeoisie's political and social activity. Shanghai, the stronghold of capitalism and headquarters of the Kuomintang, provides the best example of the unfolding of this offensive and its success.

In the first stage, the Shanghai Merchants' Alliance (Shang-min hsieh-hui), established in March 1927, multiplied its subsidiary organizations (*fen-hui*): this occasioned a certain unification among traditional corporate bodies. The guilds encompassing the same type of professional activity – silk manufacture and raising cocoons, for example, or the trade in beans and rice – were called on to regroup. The adoption of unitary organizational structures generally coincided with a profound change in the governing bodies. Discredited by charges of elitism and compradorism, the old office-holders were forced to give way to successors who were deemed suitable above all for their subservience to the Kuomintang.

Once they had established their control over the organizations at the bottom, the authorities attacked the chambers of commerce, whose suppression was claimed, without success, at the Third National Congress of the Kuomintang (March 1929). In Shanghai the General Chamber of Commerce was reorganized from May 1929 until June 1930 by a committee presided over by Yü Hsia-ch'ing. Under the pretext of unifying the representation of commercial interests, the General Chamber was merged with the branch chambers of Nantao and Chapei and one third of the seats were reserved for delegates of the Merchants' Alliance. Most of the leading figures in the International Settlement were removed: they were the men who had made the Chamber a prestigious and influential institution earlier in the 1920s. In future the Chamber was controlled by the small entrepreneurs from the Chinese districts and by the Merchants' Alliance, who were not capable or willing to challenge the regime in power. The new Chamber of Commerce of the Municipality of Greater Shanghai was no more than a simple cog of local government.[245]

245 Shirley Garrett, 'Chambers of Commerce' in Elvin and Skinner (eds.), *The Chinese City between two worlds*. 227–8. Coble, 'The Kuomintang regime', 23.

By the laws of July 1927 and May 1930, the municipality of Shanghai was granted very large, important powers and jurisdiction which were to be used under tight control by the central government. Its Bureau for Social Affairs was to supervise all the commercial organizations. The development, which since the nineteenth century had enabled these organizations to assume control of the management of the urban communities, was savagely reversed. Henceforth it was the municipal authorities who, encroaching on areas that hitherto had been the preserve of the chambers of commerce and the guilds, were called to settle professional disputes, collect economic statistics and carry on philanthropic works.

Deprived of autonomous representative institutions, ousted from local management, and from their most traditional activities, the bourgeoisie equally lost control of a certain type of anti-foreign movement which for two decades it had developed while often using it for profit.

The Chinese Ratepayers' Association which continued to protest against the taxes imposed by the Municipal Council of the International Settlement, was no longer to ask for directives from the dignitaries of the Chamber of Commerce but from the Kuomintang Merchants' Department in Shanghai.[246] The government finally sought to institutionalize the boycott, which had been the means of merchant protest, an autonomous social resistance against foreign ascendancy. The government at last had a two-edged weapon, directed against imperialism and the bourgeoisie at the same time. The initiative in the movement of June 1927, triggered by Japanese troop landings at Tsingtao, escaped the students as well as the merchants. It was at the Shanghai headquarters of the Kuomintang that the mass organizations gathered, where regulations were published and where sanctions against offenders were decreed. Even if the cages intended to hold fraudulent merchants seem often not to have been used, the boycott still gave the authorities the opportunity to reassert their control over the business community. This institutionalization of the boycott became more precise during the course of later movements. Organized in reply to a new Japanese troop landing in Shantung, the 1928 boycott was controlled and directed by the government from the outset. 'Universal wrath against the sending of Japanese troops. Concentrate power under party leadership' was the *Central Daily News* (*Chungyang jih-pao*) headline at the beginning of May.[247] At the end of July a national anti-Japanese conference determined the correct procedures for

---

246 Feetham, *Report*, 1. 243.
247 *Shen Pao*, 24 June 1927, p. 13; 30 June 1927, p. 13; 2 July 1927, p. 13.

all boycott organizations in China and this time the cages did not stay empty, at least in Hankow.[248]

The boycott of 1931-2 marked the climax of this development. The national protest campaign against Japanese aggression in Manchuria was entirely in the hands of the Kuomintang authorities. The Japanese claims before the League of Nations that the Chinese authorities had organized the movement themselves were not without proof. The Japanese cited a document – a memorandum dated 25 September 1931 addressed by the Executive Yuan to provincial and municipal authorities, entitled 'Plan of action against Japan'. It was explicit: 'All the party committees will organize a "Fight Japan and Save the Nation Society" by means of popular groups.'[249] C. F. Remer who sought to defend before the world the Chinese thesis that it was a spontaneous, autonomous action, beyond the domain of the public authorities, acknowledged that this boycott was far better coordinated than all the previous outbursts. The strategy of controlled 'spontaneous' mass movements does not date from the Cultural Revolution.

Deprived of any initiative, the bourgeoisie saw turned against it a type of struggle that it had long practised 'to save the country'. At the end of 1932, in fact, the punishments which penalized non-observation of the boycott, real or imagined, took on a new character. It was no longer a matter as before of being put on the index, fined or suffering destruction of stocks. Now there were distinctly terrorist expeditions directed against offending merchants by clandestine groups with highly evocative names: 'Shanghai Bloody Group for the Extermination of the Traitors', 'Iron Blood Groups', and so forth. In the hands of state officials, Kuomintang militants and the gangsters whom they protected, the boycott had become an instrument of intimidation and terror, another means of subduing the bourgeoisie to the power of the state.

The threatened sanctuary of the concessions

The development of the Chinese bourgeoisie during the nineteenth century had been encouraged by the existence of the concessions, the foreign enclaves where merchants set up shop to avoid the high-handed and often extortionate Chinese authorities. At the end of 1927 the system of the concessions – in law and in practice – was increasingly threatened by a nationalist resurgence which the bourgeoisie had encouraged, only to become one of its first victims.

Following the example of Great Britain, which had given up its conces-

248 C. F. Remer, *A study of Chinese boycotts*, 1st edn. (1933) 138-40.
249 Remer, *Chinese boycotts*, 269.

sions at Hankow and Kiukiang when they were occupied by nationalist and communist forces in the spring of 1927, the great powers opted for a policy of compromise: 20 concessions out of 33 were handed back to the Nanking government. Of course the most important concessions continued, those of Shanghai in particular. But the foreigners had had to accept the return to China of the Shanghai Mixed Court, which was replaced in 1930 by a district court (the Shanghai special area district court) and a provincial court of appeals (the Second Branch of the Kiangsu high court). Here all foreign interference was excluded. The Chinese residents of the International Settlement had finally won the fight to have three representatives in the municipal council; in May 1930 it was raised to five. At the same time the municipality of Greater Shanghai led a veritable war of attrition against the foreigners, bringing up case after case of incidents and problems, presenting an ever more restrictive interpretation of the treaties and sometimes ignoring them completely. The foreigners prudently refused to resort to arms. But compromise after compromise wore down their privileges and the Chinese authorities won the right to oversee the administration of the Settlement.[250]

In particular they succeeded in developing their control over public opinion or, at least, its formation and dissemination in schools and in the press. They demanded and obtained the registration of all teaching establishments, then all newspaper offices. When they had regained their judicial power over Chinese residents, they made the full weight of their administrative power felt by the foreign community.

In April 1927 the Kuomintang concluded an alliance with the underworld of Shanghai which further allowed them to enforce their control over the concessions. Gangsters and hooligans would no longer be stopped by administrative frontiers, as were the police and the inspectors. Under the direction of Tu Yueh-sheng, Huang Chin-jung and Chang Hsiao-lin the members of the Green Gang (Ch'ing-pang) – 20,000 or even 100,000 strong – became agents of the Kuomintang as well: not only ready to hunt down trade union and communist leaders but also to kidnap or kill rich merchants who refused to pay money to the government. From May to August 1927 a wave of terror engulfed the merchant community, who were obliged to finance the nationalist troops' expedition against the northern provinces.[251]

The concessions were by now increasingly susceptible to the influence, legal or illegal, of the Kuomintang, and could offer no more than an illusory refuge to the Chinese. Like Chinese merchants of the preceding

250 Bergère, '"The other China": Shanghai from 1919 to 1949'.
251 Coble, 'The Kuomintang regime', 1–2.

century, they found themselves defenceless in the face of increasing pressure from the bureaucratic apparatus.

The bourgeoisie: victim or accomplice?

The capitalists protested against the exploitation and indignities to which they were subjected. In the summer of 1928, after the completion of the Northern Expedition, they enjoyed a degree of political détente and protection which T. V. Soong, then minister of finance, granted: they could present their complaints and claims before the national Conferences on the Economy (June 1928) and on Finances (July 1928). The national Federation of Chambers of Commerce, reformed in October 1928, claimed five seats in the Legislative Yuan for its representatives. The merchants even threatened to stop their loans to the government, if they were not given satisfaction.[252]

The Third Kuomintang Congress (March 1929), closely followed by the reorganization of the Shanghai General Chamber of Commerce, put a halt to these manifestations of independence and the bourgeoisie seemed to give up all attempts at resistance. Were the numerous pressures exerted on the bourgeoisie by the Kuomintang sufficient to explain this passivity? Without reviving the thesis of the bourgeois base of the regime, is one able to believe, as J. Fewsmith does, for example, that the Kuomintang gave sufficient reparations to the capitalists – at least to a certain few amongst them – to obtain their support?[253]

The entrepreneurs for whom the regime did the most for their personal careers and their financial interests, were the bankers. Under the early republic, the bankers of Peking, closely linked with political and adminis-trative cliques, had built their fortunes on public loans. At the end of 1927 the Shanghai bankers, until then jealous of their independence, be-came in their turn the principal lenders through public loans, thereby linking their cause to that of Chiang Kai-shek. From 1927 to 1931, they covered the majority (50 to 75 per cent) of the domestic loans which reached one billion Chinese dollars. Sold by the government at a price well below their nominal value, the bonds brought into the banks a real interest of about 20 per cent, which easily outweighed the official interest rate of 8.6 per cent. The first years of the regime were a prosperous period for the banking sector. But during the crisis of 1931-2 market saturation, the invasion of Manchuria and political uncertainty caused the price of public bonds to plummet. This was followed, in 1936, by the government imposing an authoritarian reduction in repayments. In the meantime

252 Coble, 'The Shanghai capitalists', ch. 4.   253 Fewsmith, 'Merchant associations'.

reform of the monetary system and the banking coup of 1935 had given it control of the principal credit agencies, which were henceforth run by Kuomintang officials.

With their prerogatives already diminished and in any case bereft of any other course of action, certain bankers chose then to join the upper echelons of the administration. This was the case with Wu Ting-ch'ang (1884–1950). He began his career in the Bank of China in 1912, introduced a reform which helped private shareholders and reorganized the private banks on the American model, centralizing their resources in a Joint Treasury and Savings Society. But in 1935 Wu broke all links with private enterprise and became minister of industry before taking over the office of governor of Kweichow province in 1937.[254]

Chang Kia-ngau (Chang Chia-ao) (1888–) was similarly one who in the Bank of China had always, both in Peking and Shanghai, defended a liberal conception of banking activities. He played an active role in the establishment of the Shanghai Bankers' Association, and in launching the review Yin-hang chou-pao (Shanghai bankers weekly); at the head of the Chinese Consortium he had tried to force on the Peking government rigorous financial controls and the adoption of budgetary reforms. Forced out of the Bank of China by the crash of 1935, Chang became head of the Ministry of Railways before leaving, in 1942, on an official mission to the United States to study the problems of economic reconstruction.[255]

Ch'ien Yung-ming (1885–1950) opted for a career in politics and the administration as early as 1927. It was Ch'ien who had defended the Communications Bank so energetically against the interference of the government and who had been president of the Shanghai Bankers' Association at a time in 1920–22, when it was asserting itself as a potent and powerful political force. He swiftly joined Chiang Kai-shek and received the post of vice-minister of finance before becoming financial commissioner for Chekiang the next year.[256]

Other bankers joined Chiang Kai-shek in order to keep, as Kuomintang officials, responsibilities in businesses they had formerly managed as entrepreneurs. This was the case with the former director-general of the Bank of China, Sung Han-chang, who after the 1935 reforms assumed, under the control of T. V. Soong, the chairmanship of the executive committee of the board of directors of the bank. Sung Han-chang, who

254 Howard L. Boorman and Richard C. Howard, eds. *Biographical dictionary of Republican China*, 3. 452. Y. C. Wang, *Chinese intellectuals and the West, 1872–1949*, 418.
255 Boorman and Howard, *Biographical dictionary*, 1. 26.
256 *Ibid.* 1. 379.

had done everything in 1915–16 to disassociate the Bank of China from the political manoeuvres of Yuan Shih-kai, placed himself from then on in the service of the Nanking government.

Even if they did not join the administration, others were induced to carry on under the more or less direct control of the government authorities and to shift their careers by accepting official missions. Ch'en Kuang-fu (K. P. Chen), for example, continued until 1937 to manage his private bank, the Shanghai Commercial and Saving Bank, which he had founded in 1915. An old friendship which linked him to H. H. Kung – his fellow-student in the United States and, some say, his blood brother – perhaps made more acceptable to him the control which the latter, as the minister of finance, wielded over his banking activities. It certainly facilitated Ch'en's public career. He was sent to the United States to negotiate the conversion of the Chinese silver stocks within the framework of the monetary reform. After 1937 Ch'en devoted himself entirely to official duties: he managed the Chinese borrowing in the United States and became, from 1938–41, president of the Foreign Trade Commission at the Finance Ministry.[257]

Without undergoing so clear a change in direction, the career of Li Ming (1887–1966), promoter of the Chekiang Industrial Bank, also took on a more official character. Appointed president of the National Bonds Sinking Fund Committee in 1927, Li ensured good administration of the internal debt, as well as strengthening the government's credit. After 1935 the government appointed him to reform the organization of the banking sector.[258]

The financial advantages that the borrowing policy of the new regime brought them from 1927 to 1931 and the prospects of official or semi-official careers which were open to them in the economic administration, both encouraged the bankers' support for the regime and hastened their transformation from entrepreneurs to civil servants or semi-civil servants. The banking coup of 1935 by which the government established its control over 66 per cent to 70 per cent of the banking sector left them very little choice, moreover. The industrialists and the tradesmen, in comparison, had been constrained rather than seduced. The capital levies were operated through an ever more burdensome fiscal system: the consolidated excise tax in 1928, customs duties revised in 1928, 1929 and 1939. When in 1935 the great spinning factory and mill-owner, Jung Tsung-ching, was adjudged bankrupt, he pointed out to the government, from whom he wanted help, that in the three preceding years his total in

257 *Ibid.* 1. 192.   258 *Ibid.* 2. 316–17.

taxes and duties had come to 10 million dollars.[259] Leaving aside a few
exceptional cases, such as Mu Ou-ch'u (H. Y. Moh) who, during the crisis
of 1923 had lost control of his spinning factories and accepted in 1929
the post of financial vice-minister,[260] there is no sign amongst industrialists
and tradesmen of the massive conversion to bureaucratic careers that
was so striking in the banking sector. Industrialists and tradesmen were
evidently unable to finance the government's deficit as did the bankers.
They also did not benefit from the same favourable treatment. Until 1935
they preserved a certain autonomy in their business. By then the government controlled no more than 11 to 14 per cent of the factories owned by
Chinese capital.[261] When in the following years, the government, supported by the powerful network of official banks, undertook to extend
its control over an industrial and commercial sector that was weakened
by the world economic crisis, the entrepreneurs were not summoned to
put their skills into the service of the state: they were usually thrown out,
to the profit of Kuomintang officials already installed.

The integration of the bourgeoisie into the state apparatus was thereby
achieved through constraints combined with granting of privileges.
The constraints hit the entrepreneurs above all and the privileges profited
the bankers more.

The regime's conception of its immediate interests explains the difference in the treatment it gave the principal groups of the bourgeoisie.
Certainly the operations of modern banks, almost exclusively funded by
the financing of public expenditures, prepared entrepreneurs for restructuring by the bureaucracy much better than could be done by the autonomist and corporatist tradition of Chinese merchants and artisans.
Alienated, the bourgeoisie ceased to be its own master. Henceforth its
destiny depended on the government that had put it in tutelage: the bourgeoisie depended on the action of this government, more profoundly,
on its real nature and on the idea it had of its proper role. The study of
the Chinese bourgeoisie now moves on to an analysis of the Nanking
regime.

Symbiosis of bureaucracy and bourgeoisie

The subordination of the bourgeoisie to the state suggests that as in one
of those cyclical movements so well described by E. Balazs, the triumphant
bureaucratic apparatus would again extinguish the spirit of enterprise.

259 Coble, 'The Shanghai capitalists', 173.
260 Wang, Chinese intellectuals, 477.
261 Coble, 'The Shanghai capitalists', 362.

The symbiosis, which was established during the course of the 1930s between the civil servants of the Kuomintang and a bourgeoisie that was docile to governmental initiatives, bears a resemblance to the bureaucratic capitalism of the imperial regime during its decline. Under the Kuomintang, as under the Ch'ing, the government tried to use enterprises of modernization to consolidate its basic authority, and the high officials diverted to their own profit the material and human resources mobilized in the name of economic development. But does the role which the theme of modernization played in its ideology, the key place which the resources of the treaty ports occupied in its financial system, allow a comparison between the Nanking government and the Confucian agrarian empire?

In the light of the institutional reforms undertaken by the Kuomintang regime, could the symbiosis between bureaucracy and bourgeoisie have been a temporary relief offered to a class of entrepreneurs, still very weak, by which the state endeavoured to encourage its development through a policy of national independence and internal peace? The capitalist societies of Germany and Japan had no different origin. Or should we consider that state intervention, far from representing an initial impulse given to private capitalism, rather announced a very real take-over of development by the public authority? The partial absorption of the bourgeoisie by the bureaucracy coincided with the formation of a class of technocrats and managers. In contrast with the old official capitalism of the Ch'ing, characterized by the bureaucratization of enterprises, this was a new state capitalism based on the professionalization of the bureaucracy.

Within the Kuomintang, the ideological currents appear sufficiently contradictory to sustain alternative theses. To support the thesis of a modernizing bureaucracy, open to dialogue with the entrepreneurs, anxious to help them and for them to participate in the government, one can examine the career of T. V. Soong, minister of finance from 1928 to 1933. His first attempts at cooperation with the bourgeoisie go back to the national conference on the economy which he called in June 1928 to promote meetings between businessmen and high office-holders. In 1932, because he wanted to obtain the support of the business world against Chiang Kai-shek's policy of military expenditure, T. V. Soong organized at the General Chamber of Commerce in Shanghai a conference against the civil war which constituted the last great political manifestation of the bourgeoisie. The following year T. V. Soong tried to associate the Shanghai capitalists with the leadership of the National Economic Council, a government agency set up to develop and manage the financial and technological aid from the Western countries to China.

His departure from government in October 1933 interrupted this collaboration and deprived the business world of its principal spokesman.

In fact the regime was still dominated by an anti-capitalist ideology, borrowed from the doctrines of Sun Yat-sen and strengthened by experience of the world crisis. At the time of its Third Congress, in March 1929, the Kuomintang reaffirmed its condemnation of private capitalism. This condemnation became yet more severe after 1930 when under the influence of Chiang Kai-shek, from now on the dominating force, the official doctrine was developed by the addition of Confucian precepts and fascist axioms. Despite the fact it found its justification in a revolutionary past, this anti-capitalist current was often dependent on a traditional sensibility, hostile to mercantilism: as voiced, for example, by Han Fu-ch'ü, governor of Shantung from 1930 to 1936, who was anxious to improve the administration of the countryside and distrustful of too rapid industrialization and urbanization.[262]

The modernizers for their part sought a model in the German and Italian dictators and advocated, in the name of efficiency, economic development planned and coordinated by the state. This was the position adopted by, among others, Liu Chien-ch'ün, the theoretician of Chinese fascism and the inspirer of the Blue Shirts secret organization. Their disciplinary code classed 'traitorous merchants' among the 'rotten elements' to eliminate from society, and they aimed to restore direct state management over heavy industries, mines, transport and foreign trade.[263] Economic development was to be pursued as an element of grandeur and national might; in itself, it was not a high-priority objective.

Behind the ideologies, there were plenty of other forces at work: greed for lucre, nepotism and cliquism. Numerous high officials considered that building up the economy was simply a chance for self-enrichment, even more so were wives in the top echelon: particularly Madame Chiang Kai-shek and Madame H. H. Kung.

The uncertainty over objectives gave birth to divergent policies. Both the re-establishment of peace and internal security (particularly in the middle and lower Yangtze basin) and the suppression of workers' strikes and the trade union movement encouraged the activity of entrepreneurs. More specifically the government put into operation a series of institutional reforms, which had been demanded for a long time by the chambers of commerce and by the bankers' and employers' associations. Likin was abolished in 1931. China recovered her customs autonomy: import duty moved from 4 per cent in 1929, to 10 per cent in 1930 to reach

262 Buck, *Urban change in China*, 167.   263 Eastman, *The abortive revolution*, 47.

25 per cent in 1934. The opening of a new mint in Shanghai in 1932 cleared the way for the abolition of the tael, which was decreed in March 1933. The disappearance of this very old unit of accounting simplified the monetary system, which was henceforth based on the silver dollar. Monetary unification was achieved at a time when the world silver price was rising: China was obliged in November 1935 to adopt a legal currency (*fa-pi*) whose issue was the exclusive privilege of the four large government banks under the control of a Currency Reserve Board.[264]

In 1928 the new Central Bank of China regrouped under its authority the old semi-official Bank of Communications and the Bank of China, and also the more recently established Farmers' Bank. This enabled the modern banking sector to be restructured. The Central Bank of China removed from foreign banks the custody of custom's receipts; their increasing quantity augmented the bank's funds. In 1933 the Shanghai Clearing House took over from the Hong Kong and Shanghai Banking Corporation the clearing of inter-banking accounts.

Since 1911 the burden of likin, the lack of customs autonomy, the chaos in the monetary and banking system had been denounced, justifiably, as so many obstacles blocking the rise of the modern sector and the blossoming of the bourgeoisie. The reforms of the Nanking government removed these obstacles but it immediately gave birth to others, just as big. In the areas controlled by the government the likin was abolished only to be replaced by multiple taxes on production: on cigarettes and flour (1928), cotton thread, matches and alcohol (1931), ore (1933), and so forth. The newly recovered customs autonomy served less to protect home industries than to fill the state's coffers: import duties were imposed equally on primary materials, machinery and finished goods.

The rationalization and centralization of the banking system led to the 'coup' of November 1935 which was equivalent to nationalization. While the establishment of a paper money system allowed the government in future to finance its own deficit with multiple issues, it also opened the way to chronic inflation.

Indeed all the reforms sought by the bourgeoisie appeared to rebound on them. While noting certain apparent similarities, one cannot compare the policy of Nanking with that of the Japanese leaders of the Meiji era. Even if the reforms had sometimes favoured the activities of the bourgeoisie, the essential objective of the Kuomintang government was not to create an institutional framework favourable to private enterprise. It gave plenty of proof of this lack of interest: the most striking without

264 Paul T. K. Shih, ed. *The strenuous decade: China's nation-building efforts 1927–1937*; Arthur N. Young, *China's nation-building effort, 1927–1937: the financial and economic record*.

doubt was the absence of all aid during the first years of the commercial and industrial depression of 1932–5.

Is it therefore possible to trace in the policies of Nanking the beginning of a state capitalism? The quasi-nationalization of the banks in November 1935 does not, in itself, amount to a control of the principal economic activities since the rise of the modern banking sector was due in China to the financing of public expenditures far more than to productive investments. This nationalization however greatly increased the government's opportunities to intervene in the industrial and commercial sectors. Brought to heel by the crisis, the business community itself solicited these interventions which at first took the form of credits: 20 million yuan were distributed by a Committee for Commercial and Industrial Relief Loans, set up rather late, in June 1935 and put under the control of Tu Yueh-sheng.[265] Thereupon, under the impetus of its new director, T. V. Soong, the Bank of China took control of some 15 spinning mills (totalling about 13 per cent of Chinese spindles) and spread its interventions into various areas of light industry: tobacco, flour, the processing and trade in rice.

The Central Bank of China under H. H. Kung was relatively less active. But in both these cases, the tangle of public and private interests was very complex. For example, H. H. Kung and T. V. Soong were the principal stockholders in a private enterprise, the China Development Finance Corporation (founded in 1934 to attract foreign capital into Chinese business), its principal role after 1935 being that of acting as an intermediary between the government banks and public agencies – like the Finance Ministry and National Economic Council – which initiated the principal development projects. It transpires that these two high-ranking officials and their families invested privately as well. Started by H. H. Kung, in association with Tu Yueh-sheng, the Ch'i-hsin company speculated in bonds, gold, cotton and flour. Finally, there were numerous companies that were mixed. Some arose out of the redemption of private companies in difficulties, such as the Nanyang Brothers Tobacco Company, in which T. V. Soong became majority shareholder at the end of 1937. Many of them – China Vegetable Oil Refinery Company, China Tea Corporation, Shanghai Central Fish Market – were directly organized by Wu Ting-ch'ang, industry minister from 1936 to 1937, with the collaboration of provincial governments and financial backing from private capitalists, who generally belonged to government factions. These companies which received subsidies, monopolies and privileges, were usually not afraid to crush any private opposition.[266]

265 Coble, 'The Shanghai capitalists', 267–71.   266 *Ibid.* 286–301.

Only the National Resources Commission, under the direct authority of Chiang Kai-shek and the Military Affairs Commission, followed a policy of confiscation which resulted in putting under government control most heavy industry and mine workings.

The public sector of the economy, in a strict sense, remained limited. But it is not possible to view industrial and commercial enterprises which did not belong to the public sector as purely part of the private sector. The role played by the regime's senior officials with a diversity of holdings gave these businesses an ambiguous status, characteristic of bureaucratic capitalism. Though generally denounced by historians, the corruption and confusion between the interests of the state and those of its servants are not, however, enough to define the system. And the similarities with the official-supervision and merchant-management enterprises (*kuan-tu shang-pan*) of the nineteenth century are only partially useful. The bureaucrats of 1930 did not, in fact, resemble at all the mandarins of 1880. Despite the view that seeks similarities between Wu Ting-ch'ang and the mandarin provincial governors, the initiative behind development came essentially from the centre and it was limited (if not to four 'great families' – Soong, K'ung, Chiang, Ch'en – as is still contended in communist historiography) at least to a small number of very high ranking officials. The most active of them had studied abroad and their initiation into the modern world, and to its industrial and financial methods, was incomparably superior to those of their predecessors in the Ch'ing era. By taking in banking and economic experts this bureaucracy (which included at least the upper echelons of the central administration) had accelerated its proper development. The dwindling of the entrepreneurial bourgeoisie accompanied this modernization of the bureaucracy. For reasons of political strategy communist historians have set up a close correlation between these two phenomena, making the first the direct consequence of the second and calling on the bourgeoisie to line up against the Kuomintang regime.

It is not certain, for all that, that this double evolution did not obey far more general imperatives: those imposed by the economic and technological take-off of an immense rural country. In its Golden Age the bourgeoisie had provided proof that this take-off was impossible in the absence of a state apparatus capable of maintaining (or restoring) unity and national independence. Insofar as the Chinese historical tradition excludes the coexistence of a strong (or relatively strong) state and autonomous groups in the bosom of a pluralist society, symbiosis with the bureaucracy could have appeared as the bourgeoisie's only possible form of survival.

Being much closer in these respects to the 'new class' of today's socialist regimes than to the Western liberal bourgeoisie, this bourgeoisie – bureaucracy amalgam must then be judged neither on its relations with private enterprise nor on the corruption of its morals (which is common in various ways to all the 'new classes') but rather on its capacity to secure the economic development of the country.

Was it responsible for the stagnation denounced by Douglas S. Paauw or Lloyd E. Eastman?[267] Or on the contrary should it be credited with the expansion described by Ramon Myers[268] or Thomas G. Rawski?[269] The uncertainty surrounding the economic balance sheet of the Nanking decade does not make the diagnosis any easier. This uncertainty, nevertheless, applies mainly to the evolution of the rural world and these authors agree in recognizing the progress of the small modern sector. The index of industrial production, drawn up by J. K. Chang, indicates that with the rate rising annually at 8–9 per cent the Nanking decade saw a rhythm of development comparable to that which prevailed during most of the republican era (1912–37). T. Rawski insists on the other hand on the qualitative progress made in that period by the developmental industries.

Nevertheless, beneath this general tendency to expand, a cycle emerges parallel enough to that of the 1920s. After the post-war economic miracle, interrupted by the crisis of 1923–4 which was prolonged by three years of revolution and civil war, the modern sector, at the end of 1928, experienced a new period of prosperity until the following crisis in 1932. In 1935 a quarter of Chinese factories had ceased working. Work had barely resumed when, in 1937, the Sino-Japanese war broke out.

In the 1930s, just as in the preceding decade, these economic fluctuations were essentially determined by outside events. Coinciding with the world crisis, the substantial depreciation of silver, which between 1928 and 1931 lost more than half its value on the international market, in effect meant devaluation for China. The resultant stimulating effect on exports compensated the effects of the Western crisis and by acting as a brake on certain imports acted as a substitute for customs tariffs that were incapable of protecting the national industries.

When the devaluation of the pound sterling, in 1931, and of the American dollar, in 1934, caused a strong revaluation of silver, the fall in prices had immediate repercussions for Chinese producers, but in the

267 Douglas S. Paauw, 'The Kuomintang and economic stagnation 1928–1937', *JAS*, 16. 2 (Feb. 1957) 213–20; Eastman, *The abortive revolution*, ch. 5.
268 Ramon H. Myers, *The Chinese peasant economy: agricultural development in Hopei and Shantung 1890–1949*.
269 Thomas G. Rawski, *China's republican economy: an introduction*. (Joint Centre on Modern East Asia, University of Toronto-York University, Discussion paper no. 1. 1978).

treaty ports the importers sought to maintain the prices of the preceding period. The buying power of silver did not increase as quickly in China as on the foreign markets and this disparity provoked a massive outflow of metal and a violent inflation. These surges of inflation and deflation, combined with the effects of the Japanese aggression in Manchuria and Shanghai, contributed more than all other factors to shake the economy of the treaty ports during the 1930s.

Compared with this permanent phenomenon of dependence vis-à-vis the world market, the return in force of the bureaucracy and the decline of the entrepreneurial bourgeoisie assumed only secondary importance. It was not bureaucratization that hampered the take-off of the modern sector and eventually that of the entrepreneurial bourgeoisie: it was the weakness of China, as a nation. In the absence of any political and social revolution, the symbiosis between the bourgeoisie and the bureaucracy, which gave the Kuomintang regime its urban flavour, would not have been able to open up the way to a real modernization of the economy.

The failure of the Chinese bourgeoisie (whether as a bourgeoisie of the classic type, 'liberal and Western', in the 1920s or as the bureaucratized bourgeoisie of the following decade) inhered in a much more general cause of failure: that of economic take-off.

If we abandon the illusions of the liberals who wished to see it as the source of a third force, and abandon too the exaggerated dogma of the Marxists who have identified it as a necessary stage of the revolution, is it necessary then to consider this experience of the Chinese bourgeoisie as merely a sneeze in history – an episode without posterity? In later phases of the revolution the bourgeoisie was to be eliminated as a class. Yet a heritage survived: urban, modernist, democratic and cosmopolitan. This tradition – of a national development opening onto the rest of the world – inspired the modernizing bureaucracy of later times. The Chinese bourgeoisie was the first – as a class – to take on the challenge of modernization; that is why the tradition which it founded continued to inspire those who dreamt of succeeding where it had failed.

BIBLIOGRAPHICAL ESSAYS

I. INTRODUCTION: THE REPUBLICAN PERIOD IN GENERAL

Historical research and writing on China 1912–49 have flourished in four major parts of the world – China, Japan, the Atlantic community and the Soviet Union – but communication among them has been less than perfect. No doubt this is due to the fact that most historians have but one lifetime at their disposal. They should try to take account of work on China published in Chinese, Japanese, English, French, German, Russian, Korean and other languages, just as they should also be interested in concepts derived from economics, political science, sociology, psychology, anthropology and other disciplines. It is an imperfect world.

The Chinese recording of events after the end of the dynasty in 1912 was aided by the rise of the press and publishing industry. Historical compilation and publication were pursued after 1949 on Taiwan under the Nationalist government of the Kuomintang, and in the People's Republic both before and after the Cultural Revolution. The 1980s are witnessing an enormous outpouring of Chinese documentation, research and discussion on republican history.

Meanwhile Japan's expansion on the continent and then the victory and revolution of the CCP stimulated a growing flood of China studies in Japanese while the Soviet involvement in China's revolution squeezed forth a more meagre flow of work in Russian. War and revolution also led British, French, German, Dutch and American Sinology to cohabit with the social sciences under the tent of 'area study'. A considerable outflow of historical scholarship has resulted.

But few Chinese scholars feel at home in the Japanese language and are able to work in Japanese collections of Chinese materials. Westerners who use Chinese easily are not always as facile in Japanese or in Russian, and so on around the circle. In dealing with Republican China we are far from the state of multi-archival scholarly competence achieved by historians working on modern and contemporary Europe – for example, on the origins of the First World War.

For the English-speaking historian it can be argued that mastery of the historical facts concerning the Chinese Republic requires the use of Japanese almost equally with Chinese. This is because the Japanese panoply of reference works and research aids is still fully equal, if not in some respects superior, to the Chinese. Indications may be found in two survey volumes on *Japanese studies of modern China* – the first dated 'to 1953' by J. K. Fairbank, Masataka Banno and Sumiko Yamamoto and the second covering 1953 to 1969 by Noriko Kamachi and others. The more than 2,000 Japanese books and articles described in these two volumes cite the whole universe of Chinese documentation.

British and American studies of China are aided by wide access to their governments' consular and diplomatic correspondence as well as by a large body of memoirs left by missionary and other residents of China. The lesser volume of available Soviet documents and memoirs leaves a smaller base for work on Republican China in the Soviet Union. But the vicissitudes of Soviet involvement in China, both in the 1920s and in the 1950s, and the problems of ideology, national interests and diplomatic relations, have all combined to create a constantly increasing body of Soviet studies of China. The greatest failure of China scholarship in the Atlantic community has been its inability to take adequate account of this body of work, even though foreign contact with Soviet historians of China has, needless to say, been inhibited by the Soviet authorities.

Since bibliographical essays in *CHOC* 10 and 11 have provided a considerable coverage already, we have tried to limit the present survey essays to works important for the topic covered plus additional items of value. The most eye-opening view of China's traditional scholarship is provided in Ssu-yü Teng and Knight Biggerstaff, comps. *An annotated bibliography of selected Chinese reference works*, 3rd edn 1971. It shows the background from which republican scholarship emerged. The most illuminating and well informed view of the Ch'ing and other archives inherited by the republic is in Frederic Wakeman, Jr. ed. *Ming and Qing historical studies in the People's Republic of China.*

The very extensive project on republican history of the Chinese Academy of Social Sciences in Peking (Beijing) is planned to produce a multi-volumed narrative *History of Republican China* ca. 1905–49 and several multi-volumed sets of source materials including chronologies, biographies and primary materials arranged under some 600 topics! See the report by Barry Keenan in *Chinese Republican Studies Newsletter* 6.1 (Oct. 1980) 18–19.

Andrew Nathan, *Modern China, 1840–1972: An introduction to sources and research aids*, is a useful bibliographic guide to Chinese and Western materials. For secondary literature see T. L. Yuan (Yuan T'ung-li), *China in Western literature*, and G. W. Skinner, *et al.*, eds. *Modern Chinese society: an analytic bibliography*, 3 vols., which has a heavy emphasis on the twentieth century. For an annotated guide as of 1950 to 1000 Chinese works on the period of the present volume, see John King Fairbank and Kwang-Ching Liu, *Modern China: A bibliographical guide to Chinese works, 1898–1937*, corrected reprint, 1961. Recent listings may be found in the annual *Bibliography of Asian Studies* sponsored by the Association for Asian Studies. The most useful survey of events in English is by O. Edmund Clubb, *20th century China.*

Two atlases of the republican period were based both on foreign maps and on actual surveys conducted by the Chinese Geological Survey under Ting Wen-chiang and Weng Wen-hao: *Chung-kuo fen-sheng hsin-ti-t'u* (New atlas of China by provinces; 1933) and *Chung-hua min-kuo hsin-ti-t'u* (New atlas of the Republic of China; 1934). For coastal provinces, more accurate maps may be found in county gazetteers compiled during the 1920s, often with the cartographic discipline acquired from Japan.

In the field of chronology, the most recent Chinese work is that of the founding director of the Modern History Institute of Academia Sinica, Taipei: Kuo T'ing-i, *Chung-hua min-kuo shih-shih jih-chih* (A chronology of the Republic of China: 1912–25), published posthumously in 1979.

Certain early works may well be noted here, even though they were later outdated. In the wake of the Nationalist Revolution of 1924–7, for instance, a group of Chinese scholars with modern disciplines launched a major project for a series of historical surveys of the epochal changes in the preceding three decades. Under the aegis of the Pacific (T'ai-p'ing-yang) Bookshop in Shanghai, the series' most prestigious work was Li Chien-nung, *Tsui-chin san-shih-nien Chung-kuo cheng-chih shih* (A political history of China in the past thirty years), published in 1931, enlarged and re-issued in 1947 as *Chung-kuo chin-pai-nien cheng-chih shih* (A political history of China during the last century); an abridged English version came out in 1956: S. Y. Teng and J. Ingalls, *The political history of China, 1840–1928*. Another product of this '30 Years History' project was Wen Kung-chih (Wen Ti), *Tsui-chin san-shih-nien Chung-kuo chün-shih shih* (History of Chinese military affairs in the past thirty years), 2 vols.; it is more comprehensive but less meticulous than Ting Wen-chiang's earlier *Min-kuo chün-shih chin-chi* (Recent accounts of the military affairs of the Republic). F. F. Liu, *A military history of modern China, 1924–1949*, supplements the above.

Kinship relations and other kinds of personal 'connections' (*kuan-hsi*) are cited in the present volume as playing a role in China's factional politics, in warlord cliques, and in power relations within the KMT and CCP. Official biographies of course made up the great bulk of the old dynastic histories. Modern biographical studies now make possible a fuller exploration of this important personal-relations level of Chinese life.

Chao Erh-hsun, *et al.*, eds. *Ch'ing-shih kao* (A draft history of the Ch'ing dynasty), 536 *chüan*, included useful information on the early republic among the multitude of biographies. More biographical data are added in the revised edition edited by Chang Ch'i-yun, Hsiao I-shan and others entitled *Ch'ing-shih* (A history of the Ch'ing dynasty), which also adds an index. A first product from the Chinese Academy of Social Sciences' mammoth compilation project on republican history is by Li Hsin, *et al.*, eds. *Min-kuo jen-wu chuan* (Who's who of the Republic of China), vol. 1, Peking, 1978. It includes biographical entries on political, military, cultural and business leaders.

A series of comprehensive biographical dictionaries has been compiled in English. A. W. Hummel, ed. *Eminent Chinese of the Ch'ing period,* 2 vols., comes down to the early republic. Howard L. Boorman and Richard C. Howard, eds. *Biographical dictionary of Republican China*, 5 vols., centres on the period. Donald W. Klein and Ann B. Clark, eds. *Biographic dictionary of Chinese communism, 1921–65*, 2 vols., continues the sequence. More inclusive is Hashikawa Tokio, *Chūgoku bunkakai jimbutsu sōkan* (Biographical dictionary of Chinese cultural personalities).

In the field of full-length modern-style biography, Hu Shih, 'Ting Wen-chiang ti chuan-chi' (A biography of Ting Wen-chiang), which took 20 years to complete, was written deliberately as a model for clarity, accuracy and comprehensiveness. Another landmark on a financier-industrialist was *Chou Chih-an hsien-sheng pieh-chuan* (An unorthodox biography of Mr Chou Hsueh-hsi), by his daughter, Chou Shu-chen, written as a Yenching University master's thesis. Shen Yun-lung, a specialist in the maze of personal and factional relations during the late Ch'ing and early republican periods, has written on two early republican presidents, *Li Yuan-hung p'ing-chuan* (A critical biography of Li Yuan-hung) and *Hsu Shih-ch'ang p'ing-chuan* (A critical biography of Hsu Shih-ch'ang).

Nien p'u, annals or chronological records of an individual's career, the traditional form of biographical compilation, have been used to trace the confusing and complex personal relationships of leaders in the early republic. For political history, note *San-shui Liang Yen-sun hsien-sheng nien-p'u* (Annals of Mr Liang Shih-i of San-shui). For intellectual history as well as early republican politics, researchers have benefited by the publication in 1958 of the monumental *Liang Jen-kung hsien-sheng nien-p'u ch'ang-pien ch'u-kao* (Extended annals of Mr Liang Ch'i-ch'ao, first draft), 3 vols., compiled by Ting Wen-chiang, *et al.* Other *nien-p'u* compilations have covered a broad range: Tuan Ch'i-jui; T'an Yen-k'ai; Ma Liang; Wang Kuo-wei. The most elaborate of all *nien-p'u* have been the annals of Sun Yat-sen. Based on several earlier works, the Kuomintang Archives in Taipei have thrice revised and expanded *Kuo-fu nien-p'u* (A chronological biography of the Father of the Country; 1958, 1965, 1969). In Canton, a major project was launched in 1979 to compile even more comprehensive annals of Sun Yat-sen's career. For Chiang Kai-shek, the authorized *Min-kuo shih-wu nien i-ch'ien chih Chiang Chieh-shih hsien-sheng* (Mr Chiang Kai-shek up to 1926), in 20 *ts'e*, comp. by Mao Ssu-ch'eng in the early 1930s, has been reprinted in Hong Kong. For his canonization, a most elaborate *nien-p'u* has been completed in 1980, for publication in Taipei, 'Tsung-t'ung Chiang-kung ta-shih ch'ang-pien' (Extended annals of the important events in President Chiang [Kai-shek's career]).

Collective biographies include *Ko-ming jen-wu chih* (Biographies of revolutionary figures), a multi-volumed reprint collection, and Wu Hsiang-hsiang, ed. *Min-kuo pai-jen chuan* (100 biographies of the republican period) in 4 volumes. The traditional-style biographical sketches in Min Erh-ch'ang, comp. *Pei-chuan chi-pu* (Supplement to the collection of biographies from stone inscriptions), in 24 *ts'e*, are often cited in historical studies of the 1912–27 period. For personalities in business, see Hsu Ying, ed. *Tang-tai Chung-kuo shih-yeh jen-wu chih* (Biographies of modern Chinese economic leaders). For regional histories, a recent example is Chou K'ai-ch'ing, comp. *Min-kuo Ssu-ch'uan jen-wu chuan-chi* (Biographies of republican personalities in Szechwan). Note also two journals, *Kuo-shih-kuan kuan-k'an* (Bulletin of the State History Office or National Historical Commission); and *Chuan-chi wen-hsueh* (Biographical literature) in Taipei.

On China's modern publishing industry see the important series of volumes compiled and annotated by Chang Ching-lu, *Chung-kuo chin-tai ch'u-pan shih-liao* (Historical materials on modern Chinese publications), *Ch'u-pien* (pt I), 1953; *Erh-pien* (pt II), 1954; *Chung-kuo hsien-tai ch'u-pan shih-liao* (Historical materials on contemporary Chinese publications), *Chia-pien* (pt I), 1954; *I-pien* (pt II), 1955; *Ping-pien* (pt III), 1956; *Ting-pien* (pt IV), 1959, 2 vols.; *Chung-kuo ch'u-pan shih-liao* (Historical materials on Chinese publications), *Pu-pien* (Supplement), 1957. This supplement to the first and second series came out before the two volumes of the fourth part of the second series. Publisher: Chung-hua (Peking). Chow Tse-tsung, *Research guide to the May Fourth movement: intellectual revolution in modern China, 1915–1924* (1963) describes some 600 periodicals of the 1915–23 period. Also important is CCP, Central Party Committee, Office for editing and translation of the works of Marx, Engels, Lenin and Stalin, ed. *Wu-ssu shih-ch'i ch'i-k'an chieh-shao* (Introduction to the periodicals of the May Fourth period), in 3 vols.

Among the most important Chinese documentary compilations, which cover more topics than the individual bibliographical essays to follow, are *Chin-tai-shih tzu-liao* (Materials on modern history), sponsored by the Institute of Modern History, Peking, since the 1950s; *Ko-ming wen-hsien* (Documents on the revolution), sponsored by the National Historical Commission since the 1950s (vols. 1–3, 5–23, 42–00 concern the 1912–27 period); *Chung-kuo wai-chiao-shih tzu-liao* (Compendia of materials on Chinese diplomatic history), a series sponsored by the Institute of Modern History, Academia Sinica, Taipei, based on the archives of the Ministry of Foreign Affairs, open up to 1925.

Among documentary collections in English translation see W. T. deBary et al., eds. *Sources of Chinese tradition*; Ssu-yü Teng and John King Fairbank, eds. *China's response to the West*; and Milton J. T. Shieh, *The Kuomintang: selected historical documents, 1894–1949*.

For reprints of government gazettes and learned journals, see the *Newsletter* of the Center for Chinese Research Materials, Washington, DC; for non-communist magazines reprinted in Taiwan, see the catalogues of the Chinese Materials Center in San Francisco.

Scholarly journals in English include the *Journal of Asian Studies, The China Quarterly, Modern China, Modern Asian Studies* and *Pacific Affairs*, among others; in Chinese, the *Bulletin (Chi-k'an)* of the Institute of Modern History, Academia Sinica, Taipei, and the new *Chin-tai-shih yen-chiu* of the Institute of Modern History, Chinese Academy of Social Sciences, Peking; in Japanese, *Kindai Chūgoku kenkyū* of Toyo Bunko, among many others. There are, of course, many solid research articles in the academic journals (*hsueh-pao*) emanating from universities in Japan, Taiwan and Hong Kong as well as from the Chinese mainland. Occasionally special issues are devoted to symposia on special topics, e.g. *Kuo Mo-jo yen-chiu chuan k'an* (Special issue on studies of Kuo Mo-jo) in *Ssu-ch'uan ta-hsueh hsueh-pao: che-hsueh she-hui k'o-hsueh pan* (Journal of Szechwan University: philosophy and social sciences), no. 2, 1979. Many centres for Chinese studies in the Atlantic community issue established series of books or booklets, usually through their university presses, in numbers too extensive to pursue here.

2. ECONOMIC TRENDS, 1912–49

National economic statistics that are either comprehensive or reliable are a regrettable lacuna even for twentieth-century China. The Ministry of Agriculture and Commerce of the Peking government did publish a series of annual statistical tables (Ministry of Agriculture and Commerce, *Nung-shang t'ung-chi piao* [Tables of agricultural and commercial statistics; Shanghai, 1914–19; Peking, 1920–24]). The volumes for 1914 and 1918 are relatively better than the others; as a whole the data are estimates rather than the products of controlled surveys. Statistical reports were issued, for example, by the national railways (Ministry of Communications [from 1925 issue, Ministry of Railways, Bureau of Railway Statistics], *Statistics of government railways, 1915–36* [from 1922 issue, *Statistics of railways*] [Peking, 1916–28; Nanking, 1931–36]). And of course the generally excellent foreign trade statistics of the foreign-administered Chinese Maritime Customs appeared annually. The customs statistics are usefully collated, with full references to the original sources, in Hsiao Liang-lin, *China's foreign trade statistics, 1864–1949*. For the most part, however, before 1928 the central government was so weak and ineffectual that no systematic national effort was made to collect economic data.

With the establishment of the Kuomintang Nationalist government, the statistical situation improved somewhat. The *Annual reports* of the Ministry of Finance for the years 1928–34 are the only genuine reports on Chinese national finance ever issued (Ministry of Finance, *Annual reports for the 17th, 18th, 19th, 21st, 22nd, and 23rd fiscal years* [Nanking, 1930–6]). For the 1930s agricultural statistics, including acreage and crop production, were compiled by the National Agricultural Research Bureau of the Ministry of Industries and made available in its monthly publication *Nung-ch'ing pao-kao* (Crop reports, 1933–9). These estimates, together with the privately-sponsored work of J. L. Buck covering the late 1920s and early 1930s at the College of Agriculture, University of Nanking, are about the best data available on Chinese agriculture (John Lossing Buck, *Land utilization in China: a study of 16,786 farms in 168 localities, and 38,256 farm families in twenty-two provinces in China, 1929–33*. Vol. 2 presents Buck's statistics in 475 folio pages). The only year for which we have detailed industrial statistics is 1933. These are the product of a large-scale survey made by D. K. Lieu for the National Resources Commission of the National Military Council (Liu Ta-chün [D. K. Lieu], *Chung-kuo kung-yeh tiao-ch'a pao-kao* [Report on a survey of China's industry; 3 vols.]). Lieu's data exclude both Manchuria and foreign-owned factories in China outside of Manchuria. Japanese studies of Manchurian industry are, however, available (see John Young, *The research activities of the South Manchurian Railway Company, 1907–45: a history and bibliography*). There are also a number of estimates of foreign-owned industry in China, but none of them is comparable to Lieu's survey. In addition to government-sponsored collections of statistics, good but fragmentary private collections of data were carried out by the Nankai Institute of Economics in Tientsin (mainly price data: see *1913 nien-1952 nien Nan-k'ai chih-shu tzu-liao hui-pien* [Nankai price indexes, 1913–52]), and in Shanghai by the China Institute of Economic and Statistical Research (published in its bilingual monthly journal, *Ching-chi t'ung-chi yueh-chih* [The Chinese economic and statistical review, 1934–41]). Shanghai price indices are collected in Academy of Sciences, Shanghai Institute of Economic Research, *Shang-hai chieh-fang ch'ien-hou wu-chia tzu-liao hui-pien (1921 nien-1957 nien)* (Collected materials on Shanghai prices before and after Liberation, 1921–57).

Although in quantity and quality they were much superior to pre-1928 data, the economic statistics of the Kuomintang period still leave much to be desired, in part because China was still far from being politically unified; in part because a large proportion of economic activity continued to be carried on outside of any market transactions and thus could not easily be measured; and finally because of the continued technical backwardness of the statistical services. But even the relatively deficient data of 1928–37 are a godsend when compared to what is available thereafter. War and civil war did not spare statistical collection any more than other parts of the administrative organization. For 1937–49, macrodata of any kind, apart from fiscal and monetary statistics, are scarce and unreliable. Chang Kia-ngau, *The inflationary spiral: the experience of China, 1939–50* includes data available only to the author, who was governor of the Central Bank of China.

The statistical publications that I have noted are, of course, only examples. There was more – the publications of the Ministry of Industry and the Bureau of Foreign Trade of the Nanking government, for instance, or the rural surveys prepared for the Executive Yuan's Rural Recovery Commission and the comprehensive mineral output data for China proper and Manchuria published by the Geological Survey of China. In addition to these official reports, Chinese and Japanese researchers (the latter mainly on behalf of the South Manchurian Railway Company) produced hundreds of fragmentary local studies. But none of these individually – nor all of them collectively – supply or easily permit the derivation of the comprehensive data on population, employment, capital stock, national product and expenditure, prices, taxation, monetary flows and the like, which the economic historian might use for a definitive analysis of China's economy in the first half of the twentieth century. The introductory matter to each of the 36 sections of National government, Directorate of Statistics, *Chung-hua min-kuo t'ung-chi t'i-yao, 1935* (Statistical abstract of the Republic of China, 1935) includes useful descriptions of most of the statistical publications of republican China. Yen Chung-p'ing, comp. *Chung-kuo chin-tai ching-chi t'ung-chi tzu-liao hsuan-chi* (Statistical materials on modern Chinese economic history) draws on a wide range of sources which are carefully noted and – in spite of its tendentious arrangement and commentaries, not to speak of the compiler's apparent innocence about 'the index number problem' – is of substantial value. Other collections of source materials and monographic works are cited in the footnotes to chapter 2.

It is under these handicaps that the Chinese economy in the period of the republic must be surveyed. That so much of the macroeconomic description included in this chapter hangs on what are, after all, only intelligent guesses for 1933 makes it admittedly a hostage to fortune. Chinese domestic materials, inadequate as they are, have not yet been fully exploited, and careful use of studies of the twentieth-century Chinese economy by such Japanese agencies as the South Manchurian Railway will probably show them to contribute more than we have seemed to credit them with. *Caveat lector.*

3. THE FOREIGN PRESENCE IN CHINA

Westel W. Willoughby, *Foreign rights and interests in China* (2nd edn 1927; 2 vols.) is a useful, although excessively legalistic, introduction to this whole subject. It was well translated by Wang Shao-fang as *Wai-jen tsai Hua t'e-ch'üan ho li-i*, Peking: San-lien, 1957.

The many faces of the foreigner in China in the early twentieth century are reflected in substantial detail in the published and unpublished diplomatic correspondence and consular records of each of the principal treaty powers. Microfilm copies of the British, Japanese and American diplomatic archives for these years are available in major research libraries. The Chinese side of the diplomatic story may be pursued in that part of the archives of the Wai-chiao pu (Ministry of Foreign Affairs) which is in the possession of the Institute of Modern History, Academia Sinica, Taipei.

Eighty or ninety foreign-owned newspapers and periodicals circulated in China in the second decade of the century. Some of these were missionary newsletters and journals, in Chinese or a foreign language. The principal secular publications as of approximately 1920 at the major ports and Peking, but excluding Manchuria, are listed below. This foreign press provides an important supplement to the diplomatic record.

The immense literature on Christian missions in China was naturally produced mainly by the missionaries themselves. It reflects their viewpoint. Clayton H. Chu, *American missionaries in China: books, articles, and pamphlets extracted from the subject catalogue of the Missionary Research Library* lists 7,000 items arranged by a detailed subject classification and, its title notwithstanding, is not limited to

TABLE 39

Principal Secular Foreign Periodicals in China

Place of Publication	Title	Nationality	Frequency
Peking	North China Standard	Japanese	Daily
	Journal de Pékin	French	Daily
Tientsin	Peking & Tientsin Times	British	Daily
	China Illustrated Review	British	Weekly edn of the above
	North China Daily Mail	British	Daily
	China Advertiser	Japanese	Daily
	Tenshin Nichi-nichi Shimbun	Japanese	Daily
	L'Echo de Tientsin	French	Daily
	North China Star	American	Daily
Hankow	Central China Post	British	Daily
Shanghai	North-China Daily News	British	Daily
	North-China Herald	British	Weekly edn of the above
	Shanghai Mercury	British	Daily
	Shanghai Times	British	Daily
	Shanghai Sunday Times	British	Weekly
	Finance and Commerce	British	Weekly
	New China Review	British	Monthly
	Shanhai Nippō	Japanese	Daily
	L'Echo de Chine	French	Daily
	China Press	American	Daily
	Evening Star	American	Daily
	China Weekly Review	American	Weekly
	Far Eastern Review	American	Monthly
Hong Kong	Hongkong Daily Press	British	Daily
	South China Morning Post	British	Daily
	Hongkong Telegraph	British	Daily
	China Mail	British	Daily

American missions. Although first published in 1929, Kenneth Scott Latourette, *A history of Christian missions in China* remains a good starting place. The principal Protestant journal published in China was *The Chinese Recorder* (Shanghai, 1867–1941). *The China Missions Year Book*, 1910–25, continued as *The China Christian Year Book* (1926–40), provides annual assessments of all aspects of Church endeavour. Recent studies of twentieth-century missionary activities include Paul A. Varg, *Missionaries, Chinese, and diplomats: the American Protestant missionary movement in China, 1890–1952*; John K. Fairbank, ed. *The missionary enterprise in China and America*; Jessie Gregory Lutz, *China and the Christian colleges, 1850–1950*; Shirley Garrett, *Social reformers in urban China: the Chinese Y.M.C.A., 1895–1926*; James C. Thomson, Jr. *While China faced West: American reformers in Nationalist China, 1928–37*; and Philip West, *Yenching University and Sino-Western relations, 1916–52*. For the development of independent and indigenous church movements among Chinese Protestant Christians, see Yamamoto Sumiko, *Chūgoku Kiristokyōshi kenkyū* (Studies on the history of Christianity in China).

On the foreign role in the Maritime Customs, see Stanley F. Wright, *China's customs revenue since the Revolution of 1911*, and Stanley F. Wright, *China's struggle for tariff autonomy: 1843–1938*. Sir Robert Hart, who epitomized – and ran – the Customs for four decades is revealed in Stanley F. Wright, *Hart and the Chinese customs*, and John King Fairbank, Katherine Bruner, *et al.*, eds. *The I.G. in Peking: letters of Robert Hart, Chinese Maritime Customs, 1868–1907*. S. A. M. Adshead, *The modernization of the Chinese Salt Administration, 1900–20*, analyses the role of Sir Richard Dane in the salt gabelle. The series *Ti-kuo chu-i yü Chung-kuo hai-kuan* (Imperialism and the Chinese Maritime Customs), of which I have seen 10 volumes published in Peking by K'o-hsueh ch'u-pan-she between 1957 and 1962, reprints important documents translated from the Customs archives, but has not included twentieth-century materials except in Vol. 10 on the handling of the Boxer indemnity payments during the republic.

Non-ideological treatment of the foreign economic role in twentieth-century China is scarce. For basic data, see Carl F. Remer, *Foreign trade of China*; Carl F. Remer, *Foreign investments in China*; Yu-Kwei Cheng, *Foreign trade and industrial development of China*; and Chi-ming Hou, *Foreign investment and economic development in China, 1840–1937*. Robert F. Dernberger, 'The role of the foreigner in China's economic development, 1840–1949', in Dwight H. Perkins, ed. *China's modern economy in historical perspective*, 19–47, concludes that the foreign sector 'clearly made a positive *direct* contribution to the Chinese domestic economy'.

4. THE ERA OF YUAN SHIH-K'AI

The first four or five years of the Republic of China, which comprehended Yuan Shih-k'ai's presidency and separated the 1911 Revolution from the onset of warlordism, have only rarely been taken by researchers and compilers as a unit. The great bulk of relevant collection and comment has come as a by-product of interest in the 1911 Revolution. Scholarly attention rapidly tapers off with the Ch'ing abdication and usually ceases entirely with the defeat of Sun Yat-sen's group in the summer of 1913. This limitation applies to the great documentary collections that have so stimulated studies of the republican revolution: Peking's eight volumes of *Hsin-hai ko-ming* (The 1911 Revolution); and the relevant volumes in the series *Chung-hua min-kuo k'ai-kuo wu-shih-nien wen-hsien* (A documentary collection in celebration of the 50th anniversary of the founding of the Republic of China), especially pt II, vols. 3–5, under the sub-title of *Ko-sheng kuang-fu* (Restoration [to Chinese rule] in the provinces), sponsored by the Kuomintang Archives in Taipei and others. Some memoirs in *Hsin-hai ko-ming hui-i-lu* (Memoirs of the 1911 Revolution) carry on into the early republic, but usually not far. The period has been better, though still sparsely, served by the documentary series that serve the whole modern period, or at least the first half of the twentieth century: from Taipei, *Ko-ming wen-hsien* (Documents of the revolution), and from Peking, *Chin-tai-shih tzu-liao* (Materials on modern history). This tendency to concentrate on the 1911 Revolution while neglecting the aftermath has had the effect of insuring the continuing value of some older collections, notably Pai Chiao, *Yuan Shih-k'ai yü Chung-hua min-kuo* (Yuan Shih-k'ai and the Republic of China), issued in 1936, as well as the more recent Shen Yun-lung, comp. *Yuan Shih-k'ai shih-liao hui-pien* (Compendium of sources on Yuan Shih-k'ai). The prospect of an expansion of published materials impends, as the Chinese Academy of Social Sciences in Peking proceeds with ambitious plans to document and narrate the history of the Republic of China.

General views of the period were for a long time dominated by writings based on contemporary newspapers and anecdotes. The central theme has been the obloquy of Yuan Shih-k'ai and his warlord progeny. The ablest representative of this tradition has perhaps been T'ao Ch'ü-yin, especially his *Pei-yang chün-fa t'ung-chih shih-ch'i shih-hua* (Historical tales about the period of rule by the Peiyang warlords), in six volumes (1957). This situation – an orthodoxy only thinly buttressed by research – presented obvious temptations to any historian out to reverse judgments. The challenge has been recognized in recent years, but no one has seen fit to attempt a full reversal of interpretation. In the last section of a biography, Jerome Ch'en, *Yuan Shih-k'ai, 1859–1916* (rev. edn 1972), offers a textured account of Yuan as a creature of his times. Edward Friedman follows some of Yuan's revolutionary opponents through these years in *Backward toward revolution: the Chinese Revolutionary Party* (1974). He complicates our picture of Sun Yat-sen's revolutionary impulses without diminishing the justness of Sun's opposition. In *The presidency of Yuan Shih-k'ai: liberalism and dictatorship in early Republican China* (1977), Ernest P. Young attempts to analyse the presidency's policies apart from private motives and in terms of new constellations of issues and political groups but finds the policies deficient and, often enough, pernicious. The president of the first years of the republic still lacks his champion.

Close attention to secondary figures has led to a more refined understanding of the period. Liang Ch'i-ch'ao presents the most conspicuous opportunity in this respect, since he was strategically placed and left a voluminous record, including an unparalleled set of letters collected by Ting Wen-chiang as noted above. Chang P'eng-yüan has been developing these possibilities: *Liang Ch'i-ch'ao yü min-kuo cheng-chih* (Liang Ch'i-ch'ao and republican politics). Biographies of Huang Hsing by Hsueh Chün-tu and of Sung Chiao-jen by K. S. Liew are helpful. Foreign advisers played some part in the dramatic events of Yuan's presidency. The abundant papers of one, George Ernest Morrison, have been selectively published for these years: *The correspondence of G. E. Morrison, vol. 2, 1912–20*, edited by Lo Hui-min.

The social and economic history of the early republic has to be patched together in the first instance from various local or provincial studies centred on the preceding revolution: see the publications of Mark Elvin, Joseph W. Esherick, Mary Backus Rankin and Edward Rhoads. A discussion of the economic policies of Yuan's regime occurs in Kikuchi Takaharu, *Chūgoku minzoku undō no kihon kōzō – taigai boikotto no kenkyū* (Basic structure of the Chinese national movement – a study of anti-foreign boycotts). Articles on early republican economic programmes, local peasant struggles, and the emerging women's movement appear in major Japanese scholarly compendia: *Chūgoku kindaika no shakai kōzō: Shingai kakumei no shiteki ichi* (The social framework of China's modernization: the historical position of the 1911 Revolution); *Kindai Chūgoku nōson shakaishi kenkyū* (Studies on modern Chinese rural social history); and Onogawa Hidemi and Shimada Kenji, eds. *Shingai kakumei no kenkyū* (Studies on the 1911 Revolution). Philip Richard Billingsley's 1974 Ph.D. dissertation at the University of Leeds, 'Banditry in China, 1911 to 1928, with particular reference to Henan province', treats White Wolf's bandit group of the early republic.

Foreign relations have been more systematically served by scholars, although arguments about the domestic ramifications are hardly settled. The diplomacy of the Reorganization Loan has been given detailed examination by P'u Yu-shu, in an unpublished Ph.D. dissertation at the University of Michigan of 1951, 'The Consortium reorganization loan to China, 1911–14; an episode in pre-war diplomacy and international finance'. British relations and the intrigue over Tibet are analysed in: Alastair Lamb, *The McMahon line: a study in the relations between India, China and Tibet, 1904 to 1914*; and Parshotam Mehra, *The McMahon line and after: a study of the triangular contest on India's northeastern frontier between Britain, China and Tibet, 1904–47*. The other critical relationship in these years was with Japan. The literature is large. Among the book–length studies, these are noteworthy: Li Yü-shu, *Chung-Jih erh-shih-i-t'iao chiao-she, I* (Sino-Japanese negotiations over the Twenty-one Demands, vol. I); Madeleine Chi, *China diplomacy, 1914–18*; and Usui Katsumi, *Nihon to Chūgoku – Taishō jidai* (Japan and China: the Taishō period). The focus is naturally on the Twenty-one Demands, from which Sino-Japanese relations did not fully recover before the relationship radically worsened.

About the effort to prevent Yuan's enthronement and then to seek his ouster, there has been an enduring interest but no comprehensive treatment, perhaps because the movement was so diverse. The Yunnan component has received the lion's share of attention, and legitimately so. Chinese scholarship has amended the consignment of full credit to Ts'ai O and has brought out the importance of pre-existing planning among junior officers in Yunnan well before Ts'ai's arrival from Peking: Chin Ch'ung-chi, 'Yun-nan hu-kuo yun-tung ti chen-cheng fa-tung che shih shui?' (Who was the true initiator of the Yunnan National Protection movement?), *Fu-tan hsueh-pao*, 2 (1956). Terahiro Teruo has seconded this judgment: *Chūgoku kakumei no shiteki tenkai* (The historical unfolding of the Chinese revolution). New meanings are added to the episode by the work of Donald S. Sutton, *Provincial militarism and the Chinese Republic: the Yunnan Army, 1905–25*, which places the affair in the context of the Yunnan Army's evolution and its contribution to the emergence of warlordism. As one might expect, then, if the subsequent warlord period was conceived in the early republic, the paternity was multiple.

5. THE PEKING GOVERNMENT, 1916–28

Although the primary sources are rich and the contemporary phenomena of warlordism and intellectual revolution have received considerable attention, the Peking government has been little studied. For an overview of the 1916–28 period in historical context, see J. E. Sheridan, *China in disintegration: the republican era*. For institutional studies of the central government, see Ch'ien Tuan-sheng, *The government and politics of China, 1912–49*, reprinted paperbound, and Franklin W. Houn, *Central government of China, 1912–28: an institutional study*. More recent is Andrew J. Nathan, *Peking politics, 1918–23: factionalism and the failure of constitutionalism*.

These works rely in part on contemporary Chinese newspapers, such as the *Shun-t'ien shih-pao* (Peking), *Shen pao* (Shanghai), and *Shih pao* (Shanghai), as well as on the foreign press in China. The newspapers are available for further research, as is an invaluable clipping service, Hatano Ken'ichi, *Gendai Shina no kiroku* (Records of contemporary China), which from 1924 to 1932 reprinted some 400 pages per month of key articles from Chinese newspapers. For a deeper understanding of political events, it is useful to supplement newspapers with contemporary Chinese, Western and Japanese memoirs and observations; for initial guidance, see George William Skinner, *et al.*, eds. *Modern Chinese society: an analytical bibliography*. Many essential facts and verbatim documents are also recorded in roughly contemporary Chinese works like Liu Ch'u-hsiang, *Kuei-hai cheng-pien chi-lueh* (A brief record of the 1923 coup); Sun Yao, *Chung-hua min-kuo shih-liao* (Historical materials of the Chinese Republic); and Ts'en Hsueh-lü's *nien-p'u* of Liang Shih-i.

Much more can be learned from less used types of materials. Chinese government organs documented their work in voluminous gazettes which throw light on what government officials at and below the cabinet level believed in, hoped to achieve, and did achieve. Among those surviving are *Cheng-fu kung-pao* (Government gazette), the gazettes of many of the ministries, those of the 1916–17 House and Senate, and those of such miscellaneous organizations as the 1925 Reconstruction Conference. In addition, the government published the quarterly *Chih-yuan lu* (Register of officials), through which researchers can trace continuity and change in higher bureaucratic appointments.

Diplomatic archives represent another under-used source. Whether one interprets the diplomacy of the early republic in conventional terms as a disaster for China, or more positively as in this chapter, the story of how the Chinese and the powers conducted themselves needs to be looked at more closely. The only modern work on the subject is Sow-theng Leong, *Sino-Soviet diplomatic relations, 1917–26*. Leong's bibliography lists the published and archival Chinese Foreign Ministry documents he consulted. For the Ministry's collection on Sino-Japanese relations, see Kuo T'ing-yee, comp. and J. W. Morley, ed. *Sino-Japanese relations, 1862–1927: a checklist of the Chinese Foreign Ministry Archives*, with a useful glossary of Chinese, Japanese and Korean names. American, British and Japanese diplomatic materials, in both published and archival form, were similarly important; for a brief description of each see Andrew J. Nathan, *Modern China, 1840–1972: an introduction to sources and research aids*. Diplomatic reports are of course important for their information on internal Chinese politics.

An understanding of Peking politics requires work on related topics in intellectual, economic and social history. So far, we know little about the specific content of the debates over constitutional provisions that went on from the late Ch'ing into the Nanking decade and beyond. This topic can be studied further in government gazettes, newspapers and intellectual journals such as *Tung-fang tsa-chih*. Meanwhile, thanks to the work of Chang P'eng-yuan (in particular his *Li-hsien p'ai yü Hsin-hai ko-ming, Liang Ch'i-ch'ao yü Ch'ing-chi ko-ming*, and *Liang Ch'i-ch'ao yü min-kuo cheng-chih*) and others like Chang Yü-fa, we know a good deal about the basic rationale for constitutionalism and the social and political nature of the forces promoting it.

Banking and government finance is another important topic that needs study. Chia Shih-i's compendious *Min-kuo ts'ai-cheng shih* provides materials whose import has yet to be fully analysed; Frank Tamagna, *Banking and finance in China*, was an early effort that needs a successor. Numerous more or less contemporary Japanese analyses are important for this subject. These include *Shina kin'yū jijō* and Kagawa Shun'ichirō, *Sensō shihon ron*; others are listed in Skinner, *Modern Chinese society*; John King Fairbank *et al. Japanese studies of modern China*; and Noriko Kamachi *et al. Japanese studies of modern China since 1953*. The Chinese banking magazines, *Yin-hang chou-pao* and *Yin-hang yüeh-k'an*, are also revealing.

To both foreign scholars and Chinese participants, factionalism is an important theme in modern Chinese history. Nathan, *Peking politics*, provides one analysis of what factionalism was and how it worked; slightly different interpretations have been offered for the 1910s and 1920s by, among others, Ch'i Hsi-sheng, *Warlord politics in China 1916–18*, and Odoric Y. K. Wou, *Militarism in modern China: the career of Wu P'ei-fu, 1916–1939*. See also Jerome Ch'en, 'Defining Chinese warlords and their factions'. To explain why this problem was so severe in modern China we need more studies of biography. In addition to Howard L. Boorman and Richard C. Howard, eds. *Biographical dictionary of Republican China*, note the series of Gaimushō dictionaries under various titles.

6. THE WARLORD ERA

The sources for the study of warlordism are, like the warlord period itself, disordered and confusing. Most work to date has been in the form of political biographies of individual warlords. A beginning has also been made in regional studies. The challenge now is to find biographical materials for those who have not yet been investigated, and local and regional historical materials for thematic studies of the warlord era. Convenient approaches to general categories of sources are through Stephen Fitzgerald's essay 'Sources on Kuomintang and Republican China', in *Essays on the sources for Chinese history*, edited by Donald O. Leslie, as well as A. J. Nathan, *Modern China, 1840–1972*.

The best overall study of warlordism is Ch'i Hsi-sheng, *Warlord politics in China 1916–1928*; Ch'i's analysis of warlord relations in balance-of-power terms may be controversial, but he offers a great deal of well-documented information. Lucian W. Pye, *Warlord politics: Conflict and coalition in the modernization of Republican China,* delivers less than its title promises, but nonetheless raises many useful questions. C. Martin Wilbur offers a thoughtful discussion in 'Military separatism and the process of reunification under the Nationalist regime, 1922–1937'. James E. Sheridan devoted one chapter to a summary description of warlordism in *China in disintegration: The republican era in Chinese history*.

Li Chien-nung, *Chung-kuo chin-pai-nien cheng-chih shih* (A political history of China in the last century) is the standard survey of modern political history in Chinese – a clear, reliable, and well-written outline of major political events. The English translation of this work by Teng Ssu-yü and Jeremy Ingalls, *The political history of China 1840–1928*, is abbreviated and so does not do justice to the original. More specifically focused on the warlords is T'ao Chü-yin, *Pei-yang chün-fa t'ung-chih shih-ch'i shih-hua* (Historical tales about the period of rule by the Peiyang warlords); not rigorously documented, but widely used. The same author's *Tu-chün-t'uan chuan* (Chronicle of the association of warlords) on the early warlord period has much on the intrigues preceding the 1917 restoration. An important Japanese work is Hatano Yoshihiro, *Chūgoku kindai gumbatsu no kenkyū* (Studies of the warlords of modern China).

There is no satisfactory military history in English for the warlord period. Ralph L. Powell, *The rise of Chinese military power, 1895–1912*, stops when the republic begins, and F. F. Liu, *A military history of modern China: 1924–1949*, is largely devoted to the late republic. The basic Chinese work is still Wen Kung-chih, *Tsui-chin san-shih-nien Chung-kuo chün-shih shih* (History of Chinese military affairs in the past thirty years), written in 1930, with a great deal of very specific information about military organizations. *Pei-fa chan-shih* (History of the northern expeditionary war) gives the Kuomintang view of the struggle with the warlords. *Ko-ming wen-hsien* (Documents of the revolution) from the Kuomintang Archives includes documents relating to military affairs.

Howard L. Boorman and Richard C. Howard, eds. *Biographical dictionary of Republican China*, has useful details but treats only a small number of personages. It may be supplemented with the biographical sections of *The China year book*, edited by H. G. W. Woodhead, and the 1925 edition of *Who's who in China: biographies of Chinese leaders*, published by *The China Weekly Review*, Shanghai. Sonoda Kazuki's biographical dictionary in Japanese has been translated into Chinese by Huang Hui-ch'üan and Tiao Ying-hua: *Fen-sheng hsin Chung-kuo jen-wu-chih* (A record of personages of new China by provinces). See also Chia I-chün, ed. *Chung-hua min-kuo ming-jen chuan* (Biographies of famous men of the republic). The many small biographical dictionaries in Chinese, some devoted to specific regions, produced in the mid republican years, must be used carefully; their entries are often sketchy and sometimes in error.

A substantial number of figures active in the early republic have published their recollections. Examples are Huang Shao-hsiung (Huang Shao-hung), *Wu-shih hui-i* (Recollections at fifty); Ch'in Te-ch'un, *Ch'in Te-ch'un hui-i lu* (Recollections of Ch'in Te-ch'un); Liu Ju-ming, *Liu Ju-ming hui-i lu* (Recollections of Liu Ju-ming); Liu Chih, *Wo-ti hui-i* (My recollections); Ts'ao Ju-lin, *I-sheng chih hui-i* (A lifetime's recollections). Hsu Shu-cheng's son has published his father's biography in Hsu Tao-lin, *Hsu Shu-cheng hsien-sheng wen-chi nien-p'u ho-k'an* (Selected writings and chronological biography of Mr Hsu Shu-cheng). Shorter recollections, and other biographical and autobiographical materials appear regularly in the periodical *Chuan-chi wen-hsueh* (Biographical literature).

Of great interest to warlord studies are the autobiographical materials in the Chinese Oral History Project of the East Asian Institute, Columbia University. Te-kong Tong, ed. *The memoirs of Li Tsung-jen*, has been published. 'The Reminiscences of General Chang Fa-k'uei as told to Julie Lien-ying How' (the portions relating to the warlord period are open under certain conditions) is a candid and fascinating account.

Among political biographies in English, Donald Gillin has written about the 'Model Governor' in *Warlord: Yen Hsi-shan in Shansi province 1911–1949*. The 'Christian General' has been studied by James E. Sheridan, *Chinese warlord: the career of Feng Yü-hsiang*. Odoric Wou, cited above, examines the one-time head of the Chihli Clique, Wu P'ei-fu. Winston Hsieh discusses the intellectual life of a southern militarist in 'The ideas and ideals of a warlord: Ch'en Chiung-ming (1878–1933)'. Each of these men left a substantial body of writings. For books and articles about them in Chinese and Japanese, see the bibliographies of the above studies.

Diana Lary, *Region and nation: The Kwangsi Clique in Chinese politics 1925–1937*, studies one of the main warlord groupings and offers acute insights into the nature of regionalism and militarism in modern China. Also focused on region rather than individuals is Robert A. Kapp, *Szechwan and the Chinese Republic: provincial militarism and central power, 1911–1938*. David D. Buck, *Urban change in China: politics and development in Tsinan, Shantung, 1890–1949*, is a study in urban history, but throws a good deal of light on economic and social problems. Gavan McCormack, *Chang Tso-lin in Northeast China 1911–1928: China, Japan and the Manchurian Idea*, studies not only the most powerful of the northern warlords, but also Japanese activities in Republican China.

Reports from foreign diplomats, journalists, missionaries and travellers are extremely useful, even when coloured by the prejudices or preconceptions of foreigners. The large British consular network in China made the Foreign Office archives very valuable. The Foreign Office file FO 228 contains consular correspondence from 1834 to 1930. FO 371 contains political correspondence from 1906 to 1932. Many files in the Public Record Office in London have been microfilmed for major research repositories such as the Center for Research Libraries in Chicago. Slightly less full, but still very useful are the United States State Department's 227 microfilmed rolls of correspondence relating to internal Chinese affairs from 1910 to 1929. Japanese diplomatic archives constitute an extraordinarily rich source that most warlord studies have utilized only slightly, if at all. Two helpful guides are Cecil H. Uyehara, comp. *Checklist of archives in the Japanese Ministry of Foreign Affairs, Tokyo, Japan, 1868–1945*, and John Young, comp. *Checklist of microfilm reproductions of selected archives of the Japanese Army, Navy, and other government agencies, 1868–1945*. C. Martin Wilbur and Julie Lien-ying How, eds. *Documents on communism, nationalism and Soviet advisers in China, 1918–1927* contains documents relating to warlords, especially Feng Yü-hsiang.

Few have attempted what might properly be called a social history of warlordism. One interesting work – an attempt at 'social history through popular literature' – is Jeffrey C. Kinkley, 'Shen Ts'ung-wen's vision of Republican China', Harvard University Ph.D. dissertation, 1977. Materials compiled by Chang Yu-i, *Chung-kuo chin-tai nung-yeh shih tzu-liao* (Source materials on China's modern agricultural history) vol. 2, deal with the period from 1912 to 1927, with excerpts from books, reports, periodical articles and other sources, reflecting social conditions of the time.

The confusion of the warlord years makes a clear and reliable chronology essential. That of Kuo T'ing-i has been noted above. Kao Yin-tsu, *Chung-hua min-kuo ta-shih chi* (Chronology of Republican China) is not complete but nonetheless useful. *Tung-fang tsa-chih* (Eastern miscellany) included a chronology in each issue, much of the material from which has formed the core of a six-volume *A chronology of twentieth century China, 1904–1949*, prepared by the Center for Chinese Research Materials.

Ting Wen-chiang, Weng Wen-hao and Tseng Shih-ying, comps. *Chung-hua min-kuo hsin-ti-t'u* (New atlas of the Republic of China) is useful for warlord studies because of its contemporary place names.

7. INTELLECTUAL CHANGE, 1895–1920

The basic sources on the intellectual history of the reform generation are the collected writings of the leading intellectuals together with the periodical literature on reform which so many of them edited. Howard L. Boorman and Richard C. Howard, eds. *Biographical dictionary of Republican China* (5 vols) is the best starting point for brief English-language accounts of individual figures, together with bibliographies of their published writings. However, T'an Ssu-t'ung died early and is therefore covered in A. W. Hummel, ed. *Eminent Chinese of the Ch'ing period.* The most interesting and intimately informed survey is in Jonathan Spence, *The Gate of Heavenly Peace: the Chinese and their revolution 1895–1980.*

In the 1950s and 1960s widespread scholarly interest in early modern Chinese reform and radical thought led to the publication of photolithographed reprint editions of many of the best known reform journals. *Shih-wu pao* (Current affairs), *Ch'ing-i pao* (Upright discussion), *Hsin-min ts'ung-pao* (New people's journal) and *Yung-yen* (Justice) all edited by Liang Ch'i-ch'ao, are available in reprints from Taiwan. The T'ung-meng hui organ, *Min-pao* (People's journal) was reprinted in Peking in 1957. Japanese publishers have supplied editions of Wu Chih-hui's *Hsin shih-chi* (New century), and Liu Shih-p'ei's *T'ien-i* (Natural morality), while a Hong Kong edition of Liu Shih-fu's *Min-sheng* (People's voice) is available. More conservative journals have generally not benefited from re-publication, but remain essential sources. These include *Kuo-ts'ui hsueh-pao* (National essence journal), Liang Ch'i-ch'ao's *Ta Chung-hua* (Great China), *Chia-yin* (Tiger magazine) edited by Chang Shih-chao, and K'ang Yu-wei's *Pu-jen* (Compassion magazine).

A variety of divergent Chinese interpretations of the reform era can be surveyed in the relevant chapters of the richly documented histories of Chinese thought by several leading scholars. The best Marxist analysis is Hou Wai-lu, *Chin-tai Chung-kuo ssu-hsiang hsueh-shuo shih* (Interpretive history of modern Chinese thought). See also Hou Wai-lu *et al. Chung-kuo chin-tai che-hsueh shih* (History of modern Chinese philosophy). Hsiao Kung-ch'üan, *Chung-kuo cheng-chih ssu-hsiang shih* (A history of Chinese political thought) offers the perspective of an eminent Chinese liberal, of which the elegant translation by Frederick Mote has come out in vol. 1 (1979). A neo-traditional view may be found in Ch'ien Mu, *Chung-kuo chin san-pai-nien hsueh-shu shih* (An intellectual history of China during the past three hundred years). Two earlier studies by republican intellectuals offer interesting, if contrasting, insights: Kuo Chan-po, *Chin wu-shih-nien Chung-kuo ssu-hsiang shih* (An intellectual history of China in the last fifty years) published in 1936, and Ho Lin, *Tang-tai Chung-kuo che-hsueh* (Contemporary Chinese philosophy), published in 1947. A recent major work in this field is by Wang Erh-min, *Chung-kuo chin-tai ssu-hsiang shih lun* (On the history of modern Chinese thought). For an example of careful Japanese work in this field, see Nishi Junsō and Shimada Kenji, eds. *Shimmatsu minkoku sho seiji hyōron shū* (Collected political essays of the late Ch'ing and early republic), who translate and annotate 63 key essays and articles of the nineteenth and twentieth centuries.

English language scholarship on China's intellectual transition beginning in the 1890s was pioneered by the late Joseph R. Levenson, first in his biography of Liang Ch'i-ch'ao, *Liang Ch'i-ch'ao and the mind of modern China* (1953), and then in his wide-ranging *Confucian China and its modern fate* (3 vols, 1958–65). These works remain models of interpretive method and elegant style even as their analysis of the erosion of the traditional high culture under the impact of alien ideas has come to be modified. More recent revisionist works stressing continuities between modern thought and aspects of the indigenous intellectual heritage include the fascinating survey by Jonathan Spence cited above, which traces the intellectual career of K'ang Yu-wei, among others; the essays in Charlotte Furth, ed. *The limits of change: essays on conservative alternatives in Republican China*; and the book by Thomas A. Metzger, *Escape from predicament: Neo-Confucianism and China's evolving political culture*. Wolfgang Bauer, translated from the German as *China and the search for happiness: recurring themes in four thousand years of cultural history*, weaves modern utopianism into a rich historical tapestry.

Monographs in the field have been dominated by intellectual biography. Here Benjamin Schwartz has offered a model analysis of Chinese interpretations of Western ideas, in *In search of wealth and power: Yen Fu and the West*. In general, the leaders of the 1898 reform movement have received the most attention. In addition to Levenson's study there are two other full length biographies of Liang Ch'i-ch'ao: *Liang Ch'i-ch'ao and intellectual transition in China* by Chang Hao, and *Liang Ch'i-ch'ao and modern Chinese liberalism* by Philip C. Huang. Hsiao Kung-ch'üan has provided a major biography of K'ang Yu-wei, *A modern China and a new world: K'ang Yu-wei, reformer and utopian 1858–1927*; this is supplemented by the collection of Lo Jung-pang, ed. *K'ang Yu-wei, a biography and a symposium*. Supporters of Sun Yat-sen's republican revolution are considered as a group in *Chinese intellectuals and the Revolution of 1911* by Michael Gasster, while useful article-length studies of a number of minor figures appear in Chün-tu Hsueh, ed. *Revolutionary leaders of modern China*. The gap in the biographical literature on neo-traditionalists has begun to be closed with Guy Alitto's *The last Confucian: Liang Shu-ming and the Chinese dilemma of modernity*.

Most of the thematic treatments of intellectual developments in this period have focused upon the sources of revolutionary ideology. These include two studies of the origins of Chinese socialism, Don C. Price, *Russia and the roots of the Chinese revolution 1896–1911*, and Martin Bernal, *Chinese socialism to 1907*. The anarchists are given a brief introduction in Robert A. Scalapino and George Yu, *The Chinese anarchist movement*.

Intellectual historians of China have as yet scarcely begun to develop research linking the history of thought in this period with that of popular consciousness, or with the evolution of institutions. To do so will require substantial diversification both in the use of primary sources and in methodological innovation.

8. THE MAY FOURTH ERA

The indispensable starting point on the May Fourth movement is Chow Tse-tsung's pioneering *The May Fourth movement: intellectual revolution in modern China* (1960) and its bibliographic companion, *Research guide to the May Fourth movement* (1963). The research guide provides an annotated list of important periodicals and newspapers. Chun-jo Liu, *Controversies in modern Chinese intellectual history*, provides a good rudimentary introduction to the periodical literature of the era. A more extensive guide is *Wu-ssu shih-ch'i ch'i-k'an chieh-shao* (Introduction to periodicals of the May Fourth period).

An original study of the May Fourth phenomenon is Lin Yü-sheng's challenging work *The crisis of Chinese consciousness: radical anti-traditionalism in the May Fourth era*. Interpretative surveys can be found in Benjamin I. Schwartz, ed. *Reflections on the May Fourth movement*. Charlotte Furth, ed. *The limits of change: essays on conservative alternatives in Republican China* offers the conservative perspective. O. Brière's *Fifty years of Chinese philosophy 1898–1950* is a handy summary of major philosophical controversies and movements.

Surveys in Chinese from a Marxist viewpoint, focused on the period around 1919, include Hua Kang, *Wu-ssu yun-tung shih* (History of the May Fourth movement) for which there is a well-edited Japanese version by Amano Motonosuke, *et al.* under the same title, but with glossary sections on historical terms and personal names; and Ch'en Tuan-chih, *Wu-ssu yun-tung chih shih ti p'ing-chia* (Historical evaluation of the May Fourth movement). The most important documentary collections are *Wu-ssu ai-kuo yun-tung tzu-liao* (Materials on the May Fourth patriotic movement) and *Wu-ssu yun-tung tsai Shang-hai shih-liao hsuan-chi* (Selected materials for the history of the May Fourth movement at Shanghai). A valuable recent collection of 22 essays is P'eng Min, ed. *Wu-ssu yun-tung lun-wen chi* (Collected essays on the May Fourth movement).

The best work on the intellectual history of the May Fourth generation has been in the form of biography. Perhaps the single most noted May Fourth intellectual is Hu Shih, on whom Jerome B. Grieder has written *Hu Shih and the Chinese renaissance: liberalism in the Chinese revolution, 1917–1937*. Hu's own writings, published in several collections from 1920 through the 1960s, are accessible through a handy index compiled by T'ung Shih-kang, *Hu Shih wen-ts'un so-yin* (Index to the collected works of Hu Shih). Hu Shih's American mentor, John Dewey, was in China from 1919 to 1921. Barry Keenan, *The Dewey experiment in China: educational reform and political power in the early republic*, tells of Dewey's Chinese sojourn and of Chinese efforts to implement his ideas. Dewey lectured extensively while in China, but apparently lost his notes later. Robert W. Clopton and Tsuin-chen Ou have translated 32 of the published

Chinese translations back into English in *John Dewey, lectures in China, 1919–1920*.

On Ts'ai Yuan-p'ei, see William J. Duiker, *Ts'ai Yüan-p'ei: educator of modern China*. There are available in Chinese an abundance of writings, for example, a richly compiled *nien-p'u* in traditional style by T'ao Ying-hui (vol. 1, 1976), in the monograph series of the Institute of Modern History, Academia Sinica, Taipei; an intellectual biography, *Ts'ai Yuan-p'ei hsueh-shu ssu-hsiang chuan-chi* (An academic and intellectual biography of Ts'ai Yuan-p'ei) by Ts'ai Shang-ssu; a major compilation of his writings, *Ts'ai Yuan-p'ei hsien-sheng i-wen lei-ch'ao* (Posthumous collection of Ts'ai Yuan-p'ei's writings arranged by types) comp. by Sun Te-chung; and several autobiographical sketches by himself.

On the conservative Confucian thinker Liang Shu-ming, Hu's philosophical and ideological rival, see Guy S. Alitto's *The last Confucian: Liang Shu-ming and the Chinese dilemma of modernity*, which suggests that Maoism had far more in common with Confucianism than with Hu's liberalism and that Mao himself may have been influenced by Liang.

Maurice Meisner, *Li Ta-chao and the origins of Chinese Marxism*, is the best intellectual biography of the first prominent Chinese intellectual to respond to the stimulus of the Russian revolution and pledge allegiance to Bolshevism. Meisner sees two themes throughout Li's thought: a voluntaristic interpretation of Marxism (an uneasiness with determinism) and a militant Chinese nationalism. The translations of ten of Li's essays in Huang Sung-k'ang, *Li Ta-chao and the impact of Marxism on modern Chinese thinking*, have some documentary value. *Li Ta-chao hsuan-chi* (Selected writings of Li Ta-chao), handily brings together all his important writings. Ch'en Tu-hsiu still needs a satisfactory intellectual biography.

Charlotte Furth, *Ting Wen-chiang: science and China's new culture*, gives a lucid portrait of another important personality and sheds light on the nature of 'science' and 'scientific attitude' in twentieth-century Chinese intellectual history. Ting and Science also feature prominently in D. W. Y. Kwok, *Scientism in Chinese thought 1900–1950*, which describes the triumph of extreme scientism and also touches upon the thinkers mentioned above, plus Wu Chih-hui, Jen Hung-chün and Chang Chün-mai. Chang was a central figure in the Science versus Philosophy of Life debate of 1923. His life to the time of the debate is exhaustively covered in Roger B. Jeans' Ph.D. dissertation, 'Syncretism in defense of Confucianism: an intellectual and political biography of the early years of Chang Chün-mai, 1887–1923' (George Washington University, 1974). The next important public debate on an intellectual issue was the Chinese social history controversy of the late 1920s and 1930s. In his *Revolution and history: origins of Marxist historiography in China 1919–1937* Arif Dirlik gives an excellent summary of it.

9. LITERARY TRENDS: 1895–1928

The history of modern Chinese literature has been extensively researched by Chinese and Japanese scholars. Compilations, compendiums, anthologies of works by individual authors, as well as studies and surveys are numerous and readily available (see the bibliography for standard titles under the names of Chao Chia-pi, Chang Ching-lu, Wang Yao, Wang Che-fu, Li Ho-lin and Liu Shou-sung). However, much research and, in particular, rethinking remains to be done, since most of the available secondary literature, especially by Chinese scholars, lacks in-depth and original analysis. The standard approach to the subject has been leftist and naively Marxist, in the sense that it follows superficial ideology without much rigour of dialectical analysis. The Maoist canon, as formulated in the famous Yenan talks in 1942, dominated literary scholarship in China from 1949 to 1979. It was subtly challenged in the subsequent ideological 'thaw'.

Western scholarship on modern Chinese literature lags behind Chinese and Japanese in its control and publication, not to mention translation, of primary sources. The most useful and up-to-date guide, especially for the uninitiated reader, is Donald Gibbs and Yun-chen Li, eds. *A bibliography of studies and translations of modern Chinese literature, 1918–1942*. Perusal of the *Modern Chinese Literature Newsletter* suggests that this field is a rapidly developing discipline.

Until about a decade ago Western scholarship was led by European scholars, particularly those centered around Prague under the late Professor Jaroslav Průšek. (See his *The lyrical and the epic: studies of modern Chinese literature*, ed. by Leo Ou-fan Lee, 1980.) In the United States, the first major scholarly effort was C. T. Hsia, *A history of modern Chinese fiction*, first published in 1961, now in its third revision. A Chinese translation edited by Liu Shao-ming, with a new preface by Hsia, was published in Taipei and Hong Kong in 1979 under the title *Chung-kuo hsien-tai hsiao-shuo shih*. In spite of its political biases, the book remains unchallenged.

Most studies in the West, unlike Hsia's comprehensive treatment, have been confined to individual writers. Among well known May Fourth authors there are studies of Kuo Mo-jo (by David Roy), Hsu Chih-mo (by Cyril Birch), Yü Ta-fu (by Anna Doleželová), Mao Tun (by Marian Galik), Ting Ling (by Yi-tsi Feuerwerker), Chou Tso-jen (by David Pollard and Ernest Wolf), Pa Chin (by Olga Lang), Lao She (by Ranbir Vohra) and, of course, Lu Hsun (by Huang Sung-k'ang, Berta Krebsova, William Lyell and Harriet Mills). Several important dissertations await publication. These include Gaylord Leung on Hsu Chih-mo (School of Oriental and African Studies, London), Michael Egan on Yü Ta-fu (Toronto), and Frank Kelly on Yeh Sheng-t'ao (Chicago). These and many other sources on Lu Hsun, Ch'ü Ch'iu-pai, Hsu Chih-mo and Ting Ling are used in Jonathan Spence's survey, *The Gate of Heavenly Peace: the Chinese and their revolution 1895–1980*. Perhaps the best available sampling of

the work by both established and younger scholars in the West can be found in
Merle Goldman, ed. *Modern Chinese literature in the May Fourth era*, which contains
biographical and literary studies resulting from a Harvard conference and workshop in the summer of 1974. For a critical appraisal of Western scholarship
on modern Chinese literature, see the article by Michael Gotz in *Modern China*
2.3 (July 1976).

The beginning of modern Chinese literature has been traditionally attributed
to the literary revolution of 1917 – a myth fostered by some leaders, Hu Shih
in particular. Recent scholarship traces its origins to the late Ch'ing. There was,
to be sure, much that was truly 'new' in May Fourth literature, but the significance of late Ch'ing beginnings cannot be over-emphasized.

The most erudite and indefatigable scholar of the late Ch'ing period remains
the late A Ying (Ch'ien Hsing-ts'un) whose many compilations (especially
Wan-Ch'ing wen-hsueh ts'ung-ch'ao) and surveys (*Wan-Ch'ing hsiao-shuo shih, Wan-
Ch'ing wen-i pao-k'an shu-lueh*) are essential for all students of the subject. Aside
from A Ying, Chinese and Western scholars have generally ignored this important period until recently. A conference volume edited by Professor Milena
Doleželová, *Chinese novels at the turn of the century*, contains detailed analyses of a
number of late Ch'ing works of fiction. These papers are generally literary in
their approach, but the period offers fertile ground for historians interested in
researching modern China's popular culture. The rise of journalism and public
opinion, the beginnings of para-translations of Western history and literature,
the growth of urban readership, the development of urban popular values and
forms of communication – these are but some of the obvious avenues for
exploration.

The late Ch'ing period also witnessed initial formulations of the nature and
function of 'new literature', which paved the way for the ideology of the literary
revolution. C. T. Hsia has analysed the views of two leading figures, Yen Fu
and Liang Ch'i-ch'ao (in Adele Rickett, ed. *Chinese approaches to literature from
Confucius to Liang Ch'i-ch'ao*). Their original formulations were subsequently
expanded and adulterated by a host of popular 'theoreticians'. The process of
popularization, in both theory and practice, is an intriguing topic awaiting
analysis.

The period from 1911 to 1917 has been perceived by most historians of
modern Chinese literature as a 'dark' interval before the 'dawn' of the May
Fourth movement. This may not have been the case. Much of the late Ch'ing
popular trends continued; some interesting novels, especially of a sentimental
variety (such as *Yü-li hun* by Hsu Chen-ya) were published. The journalistic and
publishing enterprises in Shanghai continued to thrive, as exemplified by its
leading representative, The Commercial Press (see Chang Ching-lu, *Chung-kuo
chin-tai ch'u-pan shih-liao*). Perry Link's research on the 'Mandarin Duck and
Butterfly' school of popular fiction, which prospered in the 1910s and persisted
in the 1920s, demonstrates again the importance of late Ch'ing precedents and
the vitality of the popular strains of literature.

An elitist alternative to Butterfly fiction can be found in the poetry of the

Southern Society (Nan she), composed of eminent politicians and littérateurs of the period. It has been briefly treated in Liu Wu-chi's book on *Su Man-shu* (Professor Liu's father, Liu Ya-tzu, was a leader of the society), but awaits further study.

May Fourth literature has of course been approached by historians in the context of the intellectual ferment associated with the May Fourth movement. The standard work in any language, by Chow Tse-tung, remains useful for general information concerning the literary revolution. A more in-depth study of three major thinkers of the May Fourth period – Ch'en Tu-hsiu, Hu Shih, and Lu Hsun – can be found in Yü-sheng Lin. The romantic temper of the early May Fourth period has been treated in Leo Ou-fan Lee, *The romantic generation of modern Chinese writers*, although it does not deal extensively with the feminist movement. This obvious gap has been filled by Yi-tsi Feuerwerker, particularly in her studies of the foremost woman writer, Ting Ling.

Of all the May Fourth writers the most renowned figure – and the most challenging subject for study – is undoubtedly Lu Hsun. Ever since his death in 1936, there has been a veritable tradition of Lu Hsun studies in China. His subsequent deification in the People's Republic has further triggered countless ideologically-oriented articles and books. Lu Hsun research in China is comparable to that of 'Hung-hsueh' (scholarship on *The dream of the red chamber*): both survived the 'gang of four' and then flourished as never before with newly organized societies, study groups, and publications too numerous to catalogue. Japanese works on Lu Hsun are equally massive. The leading Japanese scholar, the late Takeuchi Yoshimi, whose biography of Lu Hsun has undergone several editions, is being challenged by a spate of brilliant new studies – notably those by Itō Toramaru and Maruyama Noboru.

Western scholarship on Lu Hsun is represented by two early dissertations (Harriet Mills, Columbia; and William Schultz, University of Washington), a number of monographs by European scholars (Huang Sung-k'ang, Berta Krebsova), articles by Doleželová, Fokkema, Lee, and Mills in the Goldman volume on *Modern Chinese literature in the May Fourth era*, and a recently published book by William Lyell, *Lu Hsun's vision of reality*. Few of these works can rival the two ground-breaking papers by the late Tsi-an Hsia ('Lu Hsun and the dissolution of the League of Leftwing Writers' and 'Aspects of the power of darkness in Lu Hsun', included in his *The gate of darkness: studies on the leftist literary movement in China*) which offered, for the first time, the darker and tormented side of this 'revolutionary writer'. The most penetrating analysis of Lu Hsun's short stories is Patrick Hanan's long article, 'The technique of Lu Hsun's fiction'. Vladimir Semanov's *Lu Hsun and his predecessors*, translated into English by Charles Alber, is an example of Soviet scholarship.

Despite all these secondary works, perhaps the best introduction to Lu Hsun for an uninitiated reader is his own work as translated into English by Gladys and Hsien-yi Yang in *Selected works of Lu Hsun* (4 vols.). William Lyell is currently at work on a complete translation of *all* of Lu Hsun's stories.

The general scholarly inclination, in both China and the West, toward studies of individual authors – Lu Hsun in particular – has both its strength and its limitations. To be sure, writers of the May Fourth era attained an unprecedented status of glamour and renown. Yet neither biographical nor literary concentration on a single author is adequate for a general understanding of modern Chinese literature. As a new anthology on *Modern Chinese stories and novellas, 1919–1949*, edited by C. T. Hsia, Joseph Lau and Leo Lee, indicates, the corpus of creative writing in these three decades is rich and varied in spite of its generally realistic mode.

10. THE CCP TO 1927

The principal bibliographic work on the CCP before 1949 has been done by Japanese scholars, who have listed especially documents held in archives in Taiwan and articles published in major serials. See Tokuda Noriyuki, 'Chūkyōtō shi kankei shiryō mokuroku' (Bibliography of materials on the history of the CCP). This is item 5.6.63 in Noriko Kamachi *et al.*, eds. *Japanese studies of modern China since 1953*. (See also items 5.6.64–70.) For a list in English, though now 20 years old, see Chün-tu Hsueh, comp. *The Chinese Communist movement 1921–1937*.

To celebrate the 16th anniversary of the founding of the CCP, selected documents on the party were issued as *Hung-se wen-hsien* (Red documents), and brought out by the Chieh-fang (Liberation) Publishing House, Yenan, 1938. There are, however, only 21 items in this compilation, which may be compared with over 850 in the recent 12 volumes of *Chūgoku Kyōsantōshi shiryōshu* (Collected materials on the history of the CCP) down to 1945, compiled by Nippon Kokusaimondai Kenkyūjo, Tokyo 1970–. After 1949 major collections published by the PRC included 16 volumes of pre-1927 reminiscences, *Hung-ch'i p'iao-p'iao* (Red flags flying), and two volumes of documents entitled *Ti-i-tz'u kuo-nei ko-ming chan-cheng shih-ch'i ti nung-min yun-tung* (The farmers' movement during the first revolutionary civil war period), 1953 (cited as *Nung-min*) and . . . *kung-jen yun-tung* (The labour movement . . .), 1963 (cited as *Kung-jen*).

Translations of selected documents may be found in Jane Degras, comp. and trans. *Soviet documents on foreign policy*, 2 vols., and Jane Degras, ed. and trans. *The Communist International 1919–1943: documents*, 3 vols.

Among the periodicals, the more easily available are *Hsin ch'ing-nien* (New youth), which is invaluable for the study of conversion to Marxism and contemporary social problems and *Hsiang-tao chou-pao* (The Guide weekly), indispensable for the study of CCP attitudes and policies towards current problems. The less easily available periodicals of the May Fourth period, for example, the *Mei-chou p'ing-lun* (Weekly review), *Ch'en-pao* (Morning post, Peking), the *Hsiang-chiang p'ing-lun* (Hsiang River review), are to be found in digest form in *Wu-ssu shih-ch'i ch'i-k'an chieh-shao* (Introduction to the periodicals of the May Fourth period). Views from Moscow are in the *International Press Correspondence* (Imprecor), 1925–35 and other Soviet publications including

Materialy po Kitaiskomu voprosu (Materials on the Chinese question) from Sun Yat-sen University in Moscow, 1925–27.

The *dramatis personae* of this period left behind a wealth of material. Among the founding members who were at the CCP first congress, three who abandoned the movement have given their stories. Ch'en Kung-po, *The communist movement in China*, edited and with an introduction by C. Martin Wilbur in 1960, has factual reliability inasmuch as it was written in 1924, originally as a Columbia University degree thesis. Chang Kuo-t'ao's lengthy memoirs, 'Wo-ti hui-i' (My recollections), first serialized in *Ming pao yueh-k'an* (Hong Kong), has been translated in two volumes under the title of *The rise of the Chinese Communist Party*. Volume one concerns 1921–27. Chou Fo-hai's memoirs, *Wang-i chi* (What has passed), is yet to be translated. Chu Hsin-fan, the author of *Chung-kuo ko-ming yü Chung-kuo she-hui ko chieh-chi* (The Chinese revolution and the social classes in China; 1930) produced a political story of the CCP movement under the pseudonym of Li Ang, *Hung-se wu-t'ai* (The red stage), published in wartime Chungking as the first major piece of defector literature. It must be used with great caution. From the military side, there is also Kung Ch'u's *Wo yü Hung-chün* (I and the Red Army).

The Trotskyist view of early CCP history is systematically presented by P'eng Shu-chih (known in French as Peng Shu-tse), a founding member of the Socialist Youth League in 1920, who served on the CCP Politburo and as editor of *The Guide Weekly* and *New Youth* during 1925–27. P'eng was a leader of the Chinese Trotskyist movement after he was expelled, along with Ch'en Tu-hsiu, from the CCP in 1929. His reassessment is in his 67-page 'Introduction' to *Leon Trotsky on China* (1976). This anthology, edited by L. Evans and R. Block, supersedes the 1932 collection of Trotsky papers, *Problems of the Chinese revolution*.

Ch'en Tu-hsiu published a great deal, among which his *Wen-ts'un* (Collected essays) and *Pien-shu-chuang* (My defence; 20 Feb. 1933, n.p.) are the most relevant. Li Ta-chao, *Shou-ch'ang wen-chi* (Collected essays, 1933) and *Hsuan-chi* (Selected essays, 1959) record the intellectual transition of an early Chinese Marxist. Because of his rising importance in the communist movement, Mao Tse-tung's writings have received the closest editorial attention. S. R. Schram's *The political thought of Mao Tse-tung* is both useful and reliable. But for comprehensiveness of coverage and skill in textual collation, *Mao Tse-tung chi* (Collected writings) edited by Takeuchi Minoru (Tokyo, 1970–2) remain the best 10 volumes of Mao's writings up to 1949. It is a pity that the publisher, Hokubōsha, went bankrupt and consequently the 11th volume, a chronological bibliography, remains unpublished.

Significant secondary works on the CCP are numerous; only a few can be mentioned here. Neither Hu Ch'iao-mu, *Chung-kuo Kung-ch'an-tang ti san-shih-nien* (Thirty years of the CCP) nor Ho Kan-chih *Chung-kuo hsien-tai ko-ming shih* (A history of the modern Chinese revolution, Chinese edn 1957 and English edn 1959 with considerable differences) can be considered an official history.

However, an author's seniority in the party may give him access to important documents. Ho Kan-chih's treatment of the Tsunyi Conference is a case in point. The multi-volumed *Hsin-min-chu chu-i ko-ming shih* (A history of the new democratic revolution), edited by Li Hsin and others and published before the Cultural Revolution, is scheduled for reprinting. Based upon it, a major project on party history has been launched at the Institute of Modern History in the Chinese Academy of Social Sciences. Wang Chien-min, *Chung-kuo Kung-ch'an-tang shih kao* (A draft history of the CCP), 3 vols., is a rather reliable collection of facts based on Taipei collections. Kuo Hua-lun, *Chung-kung shih-lun* (Analytical history of the CCP), also 3 vols., is more judicious and readable. An excerpted English version was published earlier as Warren Kuo, *An analytical history of the Chinese Communist Party*. As a general history by a participant in the revolution, P. Mif, *Heroic China: fifteen years of the Communist Party of China*, represents the Stalinist view. To date, James Pinckney Harrison, *The long march to power: a history of the Chinese Communist Party, 1921–72* remains the most detailed and balanced account.

In English, O. E. Clubb's pioneer consular report, *Communism in China, as reported from Hankow in 1932* (published 1968) was followed by Edgar Snow's celebrated *Red star over China* and Harold R. Isaacs, *The tragedy of the Chinese revolution*. With these books paving the way, American research in the CCP matured in 1951 with the publication of B. Schwartz's *Chinese communism and the rise of Mao*. Thereafter M. Meisner, *Li Ta-chao and the origins of Chinese Marxism*, Robert C. North and Xenia J. Eudin, *M. N. Roy's mission to China: the Communist-Kuomintang split of 1927*, A. Whiting, *Soviet policies in China, 1917–1924*, Conrad Brandt, *Stalin's failure in China, 1924–1927*, Roy Hofheinz, *The broken wave: the Chinese communist peasant movement, 1922–1928*, and Angus W. McDonald, *The urban origins of rural revolution*, among others, have each contributed to the understanding of the early CCP.

In France, Jacques Guillermaz, *Histoire du parti communiste chinois, 1921–49*, has appeared also in an English edition. In Japan, Hatano Ken'ichi, *Chūgoku Kyōsantōshi* (A history of the Chinese Communist Party), in seven volumes, has been a major reference since its publication in 1961.

Mao Tse-tung's early revolutionary activities are related and analysed by Li Jui, *Mao Tse-tung t'ung-chih ti ch'u-ch'i ko-ming huo-tung* (Peking, 1957; English translation under the title, *The early revolutionary activities of Comrade Mao Tse-tung*, trans. by Anthony W. Sariti and edited by James C. Hsiung, 1977). Biographies of Mao include S. Schram, *Political leaders in the twentieth century: Mao Tse-tung*, Jerome Ch'en, *Mao and the Chinese revolution*, and Ross Terrill, *Mao, a biography*. Studies of Mao and his collected works will be discussed in vol. 13.

II. THE NATIONALIST REVOLUTION: CANTON TO NANKING

For the activities of the Nationalist and Communist parties in cooperation and competition during the years 1923 to 1928, the Kuomintang Archives in Taiwan are fundamentally important. They contain minutes of party congresses and of weekly meetings and plenums of the Central Executive Committee; records of the Political Council and Military Council, and of the so-called Joint Council in Wuhan; a great variety of documents of the Kuomintang's central bureaux (such as those for Organization, Farmers, Workers, Youth, Women) as well as now rare publications, collections of news clippings arranged by subject, correspondence of important party personnel, field reports and the like. Thousands of documents from these archives are available in *Ko-ming wen-hsien* (Documents of the revolution), a multi-volume series published under the Kuomintang Central Executive Committee (vols. 8 through 22 especially pertain to the Nationalist Revolution). Two books based primarily on the Kuomintang Archives and written by staff members are Li Yun-han, *Ts'ung jung-Kung tao ch'ing-tang* (From admitting the communists to the purification of the Kuomintang), and Chiang Yung-ching, *Bo-lo-t'ing yü Wu-han cheng-ch'üan* (Borodin and the Wuhan regime). The National Historical Commission has published important collections such as the two volume chronological biography of Sun Yat-sen, entitled *Kuo-fu nien-p'u*, and a multi-volume collection of Dr Sun's writings, speeches, and correspondence, *Kuo-fu ch'üan-chi*. (There are at least 22 different collections of Dr Sun's works.)

Also in Taiwan are archives on the career of Chiang Kai-shek, not readily available to scholars at the time this was written. Mao Ssu-ch'eng compiled a chronological account of Chiang's life up to the end of 1926, which included excerpts of many documents, *Min-kuo shih-wu-nien i-ch'ien chih Chiang Chieh-shih hsien-sheng* (Mr Chiang Kai-shek up to 1926). The library of the National Government Ministry of Justice contains much archival material on the Chinese communist movement from about 1927, including the valuable intra-party journal, *Chung-yang t'ung-hsin* (Central newsletter). Many documents from this journal are translated in Hyobom Pak, *Documents of the Chinese Communist Party, 1927–1930*. Other important archival collections in Taiwan come from the various ministries of the Peking Government (including notably, the Foreign Office or Ministry of Foreign Affairs, held by the Institute of Modern History, Academia Sinica) and ministries of the Nationalist government.

The vast archives in the People's Republic of China are being energetically developed. Archives of the Communist International are preserved in Moscow and have been used by Soviet scholars. Books and articles cited in this volume have also used the records of the Russian aid missions in China and other valuable historical collections. Chinese police in Peking raided the Soviet military attaché's office on 6 April 1927 and carted off a great volume of documents generated by Soviet Russian activities in China in assisting the Nationalist Revolution, and some documents of the Chinese Communist Party. Many of these documents were translated and published; see the list of publications in C. Martin Wilbur and Julie Lien-ying How, eds. *Documents on communism, nationalism, and Soviet advisers in China, 1918–1927: papers seized in the 1927 Peking raid*, 565–68.

British archives in the Public Record Office in London have the correspondence with the Foreign Office and Colonial Office from China and Hong Kong.
Particularly informative is the series of 'confidential print', FO 405, which contains important documents from and about China, printed for high-level circulation in the government and missions abroad, then cumulated and bound semi-
annually or quarterly. (See Nathan, 69, for two guides to this series.)

American government archives concerning China, preserved in the National
Archives in Washington, are also well arranged and open. Dispatches from the
American legation in Peking and from consular officials in Canton, Changsha,
Hankow, Nanking and Shanghai are useful for the period treated. The State
Department's publication, *Papers relating to the foreign relations of the United States*,
in annual volumes, gives excerpts, arranged by topic, from important corre-
spondence between diplomatic and consular officials in China and the State
Department. Most of the dispatches and telegrams are available on microfilms.
(See Nathan, *Modern China, 1840–1972*, for series listing). The National Archives
also contain information provided by military and naval intelligence, and from
commercial attachés in China.

Two useful guides to Japanese collections that have been microfilmed are
by Cecil H. Uyehara, and John Young, cited above.

Periodicals contemporary to the events are numerous and constitute important sources of historical information. Invaluable guides to Chinese periodicals are Contemporary China Institute, *A bibliography of Chinese newspapers
and periodicals in European libraries*, and Library of Congress, *Chinese periodicals
in the Library of Congress*. For the Nationalist Revolution the following are most
important: *Tung-fang tsa-chih* (The eastern miscellany) and *Kuo-wen chou-pao*
(The Kuowen weekly, illustrated) as non-party journals of news and opinion,
which also published documents; *Hsiang-tao chou-pao* (The guide weekly) as
an organ of the Chinese Communist Party; and *People's Tribune*, March to August
1927, as an organ of the Nationalist government in Hankow. Useful sources of
foreign reporting are *North China Herald* (weekly edn of the British *North
China Daily News*) and the American *China Weekly Review*, both published in
Shanghai; *South China Morning Post*, Hong Kong; *The New York Times* and
The Times, London. A valuable series of translations from the Chinese press is
Léon Wieger, S.J., *Chine modérne*, particularly Tomes V-VII, covering the years
1924–27. Important collections which reprint materials from Chinese journals
and other sources of the day are: *Kung-fei huo-kuo shih-liao hui-pien* (A compilation of documents on the communist bandits' destruction of the nation), vols
1 and 4, published in Taipei; *Ti-i-tz'u kuo-nei ko-ming chan-cheng shih-ch'i ti kung-
jen yun-tung* (The labour movement during the first revolutionary civil war
period); and *Ti-i-tz'u . . . nung-min yun-tung* (The farmers' movement during
the first revolutionary civil war period), both published in the People's Republic
of China.

Other compilations reprint documents, such as *Chung-kuo Kuo-min-tang chung-
yao hsuan-yen hui-pien* (Collection of important proclamations of the Kuomintang

of China), and *Chung-kuo wu ta wei-jen shou-cha* (Letters of China's five great leaders, i.e., Sun Yat-sen, Chiang Kai-shek, Wang Ching-wei, Hu Han-min and Liao Chung-k'ai). Collected writings and speeches are numerous, for example, for Chang Chi, Chiang Kai-shek, Hu Han-min, Tai Chi-t'ao, Teng Yen-ta, Wang Ching-wei and Wu Chih-hui, among others, on the Nationalist side, and for Ch'en Tu-hsiu, Ch'ü Ch'iu-pai, Li Ta-chao and Mao Tse-tung among those on the Communist side. Several documentary collections are available in English, for example, Milton J. T. Shieh, *The Kuomintang: selected historical documents, 1894–1969*, and Conrad Brandt, Benjamin Schwartz and John K. Fairbank, *A documentary history of Chinese communism*, though each has only a few documents from this period. For Soviet Russian and Comintern policies, *Soviet Russia and the East, 1920–1927: a documentary survey* by Xenia Joukoff Eudin and Robert C. North is most useful. The Wilbur and How collection has been noted; see also *M. N. Roy's mission to China: the Kuomintang-Communist split of 1927*, by Robert C. North and Xenia J. Eudin.

Many participants have left memoirs. Of particular interest is *The memoirs of Li Tsung-jen*, with Dr Te-kong Tong as interviewer, research scholar, writer and editor. General Li, who commanded the original Seventh Corps from Kwangsi, gave an extended account of the battles and politics of the Northern Expedition. For military organization and campaigns, the major compilations, which remain invaluable sources for research, are: *Kuo-min ko-ming-chün chan-shih* (A military history of the National Revolutionary Army); *Ti-ssu-chün chi-shih* (Factual account of the Fourth Army), on the 'Ironsides' of Chang Fa-k'uei; *Pei-fa chan-shih* (A battle history of the northern punitive expedition), 5 vols., comp. by the Ministry of National Defence, Historical Bureau, Taipei; *Kuo-chün cheng-kung shih-kao* (Draft history of political work in the National Army), 2 vols., comp. by the Ministry of National Defence, Historical Bureau, Taipei.

Several Russians who assisted the Nationalist Revolution and who survived the Stalin purges wrote their memoirs with the help of younger scholars, who were given access to archives. The most extensive is a two volume account by General A. I. Cherepanov. It is marred, however, by anachronistic biases. A rough translation of volume one is *Notes of a military adviser in China*. Two other interesting and rather charming reminiscences have been translated into English: Vera Vladimirovna Vishnyakova-Akimova, *Two years in revolutionary China, 1925–1927*, translated by Steven I. Levine; and Marc Kasanin, *China in the twenties*, translated by his widow, Hilda Kasanina. An important source for information on the Russian military aid mission, as well as for recent Russian scholarship concerning it, is Dieter Heinzig, *Sowjetische militärberater bei der Kuomintang 1923–1927*. The posthumously published study by Lydia Holu-bnychy, *Michael Borodin and the Chinese revolution, 1923–1925* used and lists many recent works by Soviet scholars having access to Russian archives. The Russian sources have been used most recently by Dan Jacobs, *Borodin: Stalin's man in China*. The beginnings of cooperation between the two parties is detailed in Benjamin I. Schwartz, *Chinese communism and the rise of Mao*, a classic for its time

of publication, and C. Martin Wilbur, *Sun Yat-sen: frustrated patriot*. Harold
Isaacs, *The tragedy of the Chinese revolution*, first published in 1938, revised and
reissued in 1951, has been very influential in its presentation of the 'under dog'
communist and proletarian cause and for its anti-Stalin and anti-Chiang Kai-
shek views. In similar vein is the path-breaking study by Jean Chesneaux, *The
Chinese labor movement, 1919–1927*, translated from the French by H. M. Wright.
In the field of foreign relations, two excellent works are Dorothy Borg, *American
policy and the Chinese revolution, 1925–1928*, and Akira Iriye, *After imperialism:
the search for a new order in the Far East, 1921–1931*.

12. THE CHINESE BOURGEOISIE

No work comprehensively studies the history of the Chinese business class or
bourgeoisie during the whole of the republican period. However, numerous
documents and several studies exist that describe its economic and political
activities. On the formation of the bourgeoisie from the urban gentry and the
merchant class see Mark Elvin, 'The gentry democracy in Chinese Shanghai,
1905–14', On the progress made by the urban elites at the expense of the
bureaucracy see Joseph Esherick, *Reform and revolution in China: the 1911 Revolution in Hunan and Hubei*.

The involvement of the Chinese bourgeoisie in the revolution of 1911 marked
its emergence on the political scene. On this see M. Claire Bergère, *La bourgeoisie
chinoise et la Révolution de 1911*, Kojima Yoshio's excellent article 'Shingai
Kakumei ni okeru Shanhai dokuritsu to shōshinsō', and Edward J. M. Rhoads'
more general study, *China's republican revolution: the case of Kwangtung 1895–1913*.
The Revolution of 1911 was, however, far from a bourgeois revolution in the
English or the French sense. Chinese historiography on this point complies
first and foremost with the desire to integrate China in the plans for universal
evolution elaborated by Marx – as M. Claire Bergère is at pains to show in
'La Révolution de 1911 jugée par les historiens de la République Populaire de
Chine'. The revolution none the less consolidated the role of the bourgeoisie
in local administration. Although this evolution has not been the subject of a
systematic study, it has been tackled by several authors: see E. Young, chapter
4 in this volume; Robert Keith Schoppa, 'Politics and society in Chekiang,
1907–1927: elite power, social control and the making of a province'; and
Elvin and Esherick already cited.

The part played by the bourgeoisie in the very rapid rise of the modern
sector is underlined in Chou Hsiu-luan's *Ti-i-tz'u shih-chieh ta-chan shih-ch'i
Chung-kuo min-tsu kung-yeh ti fa-chan*. Substantial information may be found in
the major compilations of documents from leading Chinese business firms'
archives, ranging from cotton mills to cement companies, the publication of
which is proceeding apace, especially under the auspices of the Shanghai
Academy of Social Sciences in the series *Chung-kuo tzu-pen-chu-i kung shang yeh
shih-liao ts'ung-k'an* (Collection of historical materials on capitalist industry and
commerce). Among these are Shang-hai she-hui k'o-hsueh-yuan ching-chi

yen-chiu so, comp. *Jung-chia ch'i-yeh shih-liao* (Historical materials on the enterprises of the Jung family). On such compilations are based recent monographic studies like Sherman Cochran's on the tobacco industry and Chao Kang's English and Chinese books on the cotton textile industry, which supplement earlier studies by H. D. Fong and Yen Chung-p'ing in English and Chinese, respectively. These sources and studies give one a better grasp of the importance of the social and cultural factors (family spirit, geographical solidarities, etc.) in the organization of production. Note, for example, *Nan-yang hsiung-ti yen-ts'ao kung-ssu shih-liao* (Historical materials on the Nanyang Brothers Tobacco Company) and the study of the Heng-feng cotton mill.

While traditional gilds and other organizations have been the subject of numerous studies, the chambers of commerce and the business associations, despite the essential roles they played between 1911 and 1927, remain but poorly known. James Sanford's research on 'Chinese commercial organization and behavior in Shanghai of the late nineteenth and early twentieth century' (Harvard University, 1976 Ph.D. dissertation) is not primarily on the republican period. Most of these organizations published their own journals: *Shang-hai tsung-shang-hui yueh-pao, Yin-hang chou-pao, Yin-hang yueh-k'an, Hua-shang sha-ch'ang lien-ho-hui chi-k'an.* These reviews offer additions and amendments to the information given in the foreign newspapers and periodicals published in the treaty ports, such as the *North China Daily News, China Weekly Review, Bulletin Commercial d'Extreme Orient.* The rivalries and solidarities among the Chinese and foreign business communities form a subject easy to approach but as yet little explored.

Widely-dispersed but plentiful, the periodicals of the 1920s enable one to study the political and economic role of the bourgeoisie of the treaty ports. It is much harder to catch the men of the period. Rather few biographies exist, but note Samuel C. Chu, *Reformer in modern China: Chang Chien 1853–1926.* For a notable such as Yü Hsia-ch'ing (Yü Ya-ch'ing in Shanghai dialect), who dominated the life of the Chinese business community of Shanghai for nearly half a century, all we have is one single article, by Fang T'eng – 'Yü Hsia-ch'ing lun'! Only a few merchants or industrialists followed Mu Ou-ch'u's example and published their own memoirs. See Chang Chien, *Nan-t'ung Chang Chi-chih hsien-sheng chuan-chi* (A biography of Mr Chang Chien from Nan-t'ung), by his son, Chang Hsiao-jo, and his major collection, *Chang Chi-tzu chiu-lu* (Nine collections of Chang Chien's writings); Mu Hsiang-yueh, also known as Mu Ou-ch'u, *Ou-ch'u wu-shih tzu-shu* (Autobiography of Mu Ou-ch'u at 50 years of age); and Jung Te-sheng, *Lo-nung tzu-ting hsing-nien chi-shih* (An autobiographical chronology by Jung Te-sheng). Ts'ao Ju-lin's published memoirs include information on government and private banks. For collective biographies see Hsu Ying, *Tang-tai Chung-kuo shih-yeh jen-wu chih* (Biographies of modern Chinese economic leaders); and Li Hsin and Sun Ssu-pai, eds. *Min-kuo jen-wu chuan* (Who's who of the Republic of China), of which vol. 1, published in 1978, includes 12 entries on 14 business leaders.

Noteworthy among recent and important contributions to the historiography of the Chinese bourgeoisie, is Parks Coble, *The Shanghai capitalists and the National government 1927–1937*. Coble's interpretation, which stresses the decline of the Chinese bourgeoisie after 1927, should take the place of the classic – but erroneous – thesis of the triumph of the bourgeoisie under the Kuomintang. However, this revisionist interpretation raises, without really resolving, the problem of the relations between the bourgeoisie and bureaucratic capitalism in the 1930s. For a recent survey see M. Claire Bergère, ' "The other China": Shanghai from 1919 to 1949'.

The rarity of studies on the bourgeoisie, which contrasts with the relative abundance of source-material, betrays the relative lack of interest of contemporary historians. In the context of a revolution that was dubbed rural by its principal leader, the business bourgeoisie of the 1920s and 1930s has appeared as a marginal class – or simply a group – of ephemeral importance. The changes of orientation that have occurred in Chinese policy since the death of Mao Tsetung should lead – if not to a reversal of the verdict – at least to a renewal of interest and to further publication.

BIBLIOGRAPHY

CHINESE AND JAPANESE PUBLISHERS

Cheng-chung 正中 (Taipei)
Chuan-chi wen-hsueh 傳記文學 (Taipei)
Chung-hua 中華 (major cities)
Commercial Press 商務印書館 (major cities)
Daian 大安 (Tokyo)
Jen-min 人民 (Shanghai and other cities)
K'o-hsueh 科學 (Peking)
San-lien 生活讀書新知三聯書店 (Peking, Shanghai)
Wen-hai 文海 (Taipei)
Wen-hsing 文星 (Taipei)

WORKS CITED

A Ying 阿英 (Ch'ien Hsing-ts'un 錢杏邨), ed. *Wan-Ch'ing wen-hsueh ts'ung-ch'ao* 晚清文學叢鈔 (Anthology of late Ch'ing literature) series. Peking: Chung-hua, 1960–

A Ying. *Wan-Ch'ing hsiao-shuo shih* 晚清小説史 (A history of late Ch'ing fiction). Peking: Tso-chia ch'u-pan-she 作家出版社, 1955. Hong Kong reprint: T'ai-p'ing shu-chü 太平書局, 1966

A Ying. *Wan-Ch'ing wen-i pao-k'an shu-lueh* 晚清文藝報刊述略 (A brief account of late Ch'ing literary journals and newspapers). Shanghai: Ku-tien wen-hsueh ch'u-pan she 古典文學出版社, 1958

Abrams, M. H. *A glossary of literary terms*. New York: Holt, Rinehart & Winston, 3rd edn, 1971

Academia Sinica. See Chung-yang yen-chiu-yuan

Academy of Sciences. See Chung-kuo k'o-hsueh-yuan

Adshead, S. A. M. *The modernization of the Chinese Salt Administration, 1900–1920*. Cambridge, Mass.: Harvard University Press, 1970

Adshead, S. A. M. 'An energy crisis in early modern China'. *Ch'ing-shih wen-t'i*, 3.2 (Dec. 1974) 20–28

Ai Lu 藹廬. 'Chin-yung-chieh chin-hou chih chueh-wu ju-ho?' 金融界今後之覺悟如何 (How will financial circles gain awareness from now on?). *YHYK*, 2.5 (May 1922)

Akademiia Nauk SSSR. Institut Narodov Azii (Academy of Sciences of the USSR. Institute of the Peoples of Asia). *Sovetskiie dobrovoltsy v pervoi grazhdanskoi revolutsionnoi voine v Kitae; vospominaniia* (Soviet volunteers in the first revolutionary civil war in China; reminiscences). Moscow: Oriental Literature Publishing House, 1961

Alitto, Guy S. *The last Confucian: Liang Shu-ming and the Chinese dilemma of modernity.* Berkeley: University of California Press, 1978

Allen, G. C. and Donnithorne, Audrey G. *Western enterprise in Far Eastern economic development: China and Japan.* London: George Allen & Unwin, 1954

Altman, Albert A. and Schiffrin, Harold Z. 'Sun Yat-sen and the Japanese: 1914–16'. *Modern Asian Studies*, 6.4 (Oct. 1972) 385–400

Amano Motonosuke 天野元之助. *Shina nōgyō keizai ron* 支那農業經濟論 (On the Chinese agricultural economy). 2 vols. Tokyo: Kaizōsha 改造社, 1940–2

Amano Motonosuke *et al.*, trans. and eds. *Goshi undōshi* 五四運動史 (History of the May Fourth movement) by Hua Kang 華岡. Osaka: Sōgensha 創元社, 1952

Amano Motonosuke. *Chūgoku nōgyō no shomondai* 中國農業の諸問題 (Problems of Chinese agriculture). 2 vols. Tokyo: Gihōdō 技報堂, 1952–3

Amano Motonosuke. *Chūgoku nōgyō shi kenkyū* 中國農業史研究 (A study of the history of Chinese agriculture). Tokyo: Ochanomizu 御茶の水, 1962

American Bankers Association, Commission on Commerce and Marine. *China, an economic survey, 1923.* New York, 1928

Andersen, Meyer and Company Limited of China. Shanghai: Kelley and Walsh, 1931

Andrews, Carol Corder, 'The policy of the Chinese Communist Party towards the peasant movement, 1921–1927: the impact of national on social revolution'. Columbia University, Ph.D. dissertation, 1978

Ash, Robert. *Land tenure in pre-revolutionary China: Kiangsu province in the 1920s and 1930s.* London: Contemporary China Institute, School of Oriental and African Studies, University of London, 1976

Balazs, Étienne. *Chinese civilization and bureaucracy: variations on a theme,* trans. by H. M. Wright. New Haven and London: Yale University Press, 1964

Barnett, A. Doak. *China on the eve of Communist takeover.* New York: Praeger, 1963

Bastid, Marianne. *Aspects de la réforme de l'enseignement en Chine au début de XXᵉ siècle, d'après des écrits de Zhang Jian.* Paris and the Hague: Mouton, 1971

Bauer, Wolfgang. *China and the search for happiness: recurring themes in four thousand years of Chinese cultural history.* Trans. from the German by Michael Shaw. New York: Seabury Press, 1976

Bergère, M. Claire. 'La Révolution de 1911 jugée par les historiens de la République Populaire de Chine'. *Revue Historique,* 230 (Oct.-Dec. 1963) 403–36

Bergère, M. Claire. *La bourgeoisie chinoise et la Révolution de 1911.* Paris and the Hague: Mouton, 1968

Bergère, M. Claire, 'The role of the bourgeoisie', in Mary C. Wright, ed. *China in revolution: the first phase 1900–1913*, 229–95. New Haven and London: Yale University Press, 1968

Bergère, M. Claire, 'Le mouvement du 4 mai 1919 en Chine: la conjuncture économique et le rôle de la bourgeoisie nationale'. *Revue Historique,* 241 (April–June 1969) 309–26

Bergère, M. Claire and Tchang, Fou-jouei. *Sauvons la Patrie! Le nationalisme chinois et le mouvement du 4 mai 1919.* Paris: Publications Orientalistes de France, 1978

Bergère, M. Claire, '"The other China": Shanghai from 1919 to 1949', in C. Howe, ed. *Shanghai: revolution and development in an Asian metropolis.* Cambridge: Cambridge University Press, 1981

Bergère, Marie-Claire. *Capitalisme national et impérialisme: la crise des filatures chinoises en 1923.* Cahiers du Centre Chine 2, Centre de Recherches et de Documentation sur la Chine Contemporaine. Paris: École des Hautes Études en Sciences Sociales, 1980

Bernal, Martin. 'The triumph of anarchism over Marxism 1906–1907', in Mary Wright, ed. *China in revolution: the first phase 1900–1913*, 97–142. New Haven: Yale University Press, 1968

Bernal, Martin. 'Chinese socialism before 1913', in Jack Gray, ed. *Modern China's search for a political form,* 66–95. London: Oxford University Press, 1969

Bernal, Martin. *Chinese socialism to 1907.* Ithaca: Cornell University Press, 1976

Bernal, Martin. 'Liu Shih-p'ei and national essence', in Charlotte Furth, ed. *The limits of change: essays on conservative alternatives in Republican China,* 90–112. Cambridge, Mass.: Harvard University Press, 1976

Berninghausen, John and Huters, Ted, eds. *Revolutionary literature in China: an anthology.* White Plains, N.Y.: M. E. Sharpe, 1977. First published in *Bulletin of Concerned Asian Scholars,* 8.1–2 (1976)

Bibliography of Asian Studies. Annual. Ann Arbor: Association for Asian Studies. Inc. Annual from 1969 (pub. 1971).

Bien, Gloria, 'Baudelaire and the Han Garden', paper presented at the Chinese Language Teachers Association panel, Modern Languages Association annual meeting, New York, Dec. 1976

Bien, Gloria. 'Shao Hsun-mei and the flowers of evil', paper presented at the Association for Asian Studies annual meeting, Chicago, April 1978

Billingsley, Philip Richard. 'Banditry in China, 1911 to 1928, with particular reference to Henan province'. University of Leeds, Ph.D. dissertation, 1974

Birch, Cyril. 'Lao She: the humourist in his humour'. *CQ*, 8 (Oct.–Dec. 1961) 45–62

Birch, Cyril. 'English and Chinese meters in Hsu Chih-mo'. *Asia Major*, NS 8.2 (1961) 258–93.

Birch, Cyril. 'Change and continuity in modern Chinese fiction', in Merle Goldman, ed. *Modern Chinese literature in the May Fourth era,* 385–406. Cambridge, Mass.: Harvard University Press, 1977

Blackburn, V. 'Report on the situation in Shanghai', dispatch dated 15 April

1927 in Great Britain: Foreign Office 405/253. Confidential. *Further correspondence respecting China*, 13304 (April–June 1927) no. 156, enclosure 2

Boorman, Howard L. and Richard C. Howard, eds. *Biographical dictionary of Republican China*. New York: Columbia University Press, 4 vols. 1967–71 and index volume (vol. 5) 1979

Borg, Dorothy. *American policy and the Chinese revolution, 1925–1928*. New York: Macmillan, 1947

Brandt, Conrad, Schwartz, Benjamin and Fairbank, John K. *A documentary history of Chinese communism*. Cambridge, Mass.: Harvard University Press, 1952

Brandt, Conrad. *Stalin's failure in China, 1924–1927*. Cambridge, Mass.: Harvard University Press, 1958

Braudel, Fernand. *The Mediterranean and the Mediterranean world in the age of Philip II*. Paris: Colin, 1949, 2nd rev. ed 1966. New York: Harper & Row, trans. by Sian Reynolds, vol. 1, 1972, vol. 2, 1973

Brenan, J. F. 'A report on results of translation of Russian documents seized in the Russian Consulate, December 14, 1927' in Great Britain: Foreign Office, 405/256. Confidential. *Further correspondence respecting China*, 13583, Jan.– March 1928

Brière, O., S. J. *Fifty years of Chinese philosophy 1898–1950*. Trans. from the French by Laurence G. Thompson. London: George Allen and Unwin, 1956; reprinted with a new introduction by J. Doolin, New York: Praeger, 1965. Originally in *Bull. de l'Université l'Aurore*, Shanghai, ser. 3 vol. 10.40 (Oct. 1949) 561–650

Brown, Edward J. *Russian literature since the revolution*. New York: Collier, 1963; rev. edn, 1969

BSOAS: *Bulletin of the School of Oriental and African Studies*

Buck, David D. *Urban change in China: politics and development in Tsinan, Shantung, 1890–1949*. Madison: University of Wisconsin Press, 1978

Buck, John Lossing. *Land utilization in China: a study of 16,786 farms in 168 localities, and 38,256 farm families in twenty-two provinces in China, 1929–1933*. 3 vols. Nanking: University of Nanking, 1937

Bulletin Commercial d'Extrême-Orient. Monthly. Shanghai: Chambre de commerce française en Chine, 1916–

Bulletin of the Institute of Modern History, Academia Sinica. See *Chung-yang yen-chiu-yuan chin-tai-shih yen-chiu-so chi-k'an*

Calinescu, Matei. *Faces of modernity: avant-garde, decadence, kitsch*. Bloomington: Indiana University Press, 1977

Catalogues of the Chinese Materials Center, 809 Taraval Street, San Francisco, Cal. 94116

CCP: Chinese Communist Party

CEC: Central Executive Committee (of the KMT or the CCP)

Center for Chinese Research Materials. *Chung-kuo ta-shih chi* 中國大事記 (A chronology of twentieth-century China, 1904–1949). 6 vols. Washington, DC: Association of Research Libraries, 1973

Central Committee of the Chinese Communist Party. Research Department of the Bureau of Translation of the Works of Marx, Engels, Lenin and Stalin. See *Wu-ssu shih-ch'i ch'i-k'an chieh-shao*

Central Ministry of Agriculture, Planning Office 中央農業部計劃司. *Liang-nien-lai ti Chung-kuo nung-ts'un ching-chi tiao-ch'a hui-pien* 兩年來的中國農村經濟調查彙編 (Collection of surveys of the rural economy of China during the past two years). Shanghai: Chung-hua, 1952

Chan, Adrian. 'Development and nature of Chinese communism to 1925'. Australian National University, Ph.D. dissertation, 1974

Chan, Agnes. 'The Chinese anarchists'. University of California, Ph.D. dissertation. Berkeley, 1977

Chan, Gilbert F. and Etzold, Thomas H., eds. *China in the 1920's: nationalism and revolution*. New York and London: New Viewpoints, 1976

Chan, Wellington K. K. *Merchants, mandarins and modern enterprise in late Ch'ing China*. Cambridge, Mass.: Harvard University Press, 1977

Chan, Wing-tsit 陳榮捷. *Religious trends in modern China*. New York: Columbia University Press, 1953

Chang, Carsun. See Chang Chün-mai

Chang Chi 張繼. *Chang P'u-ch'üan hsien-sheng ch'üan-chi* 張溥泉先生全集 (A complete collection of works of Chang Chi), ed. by Chung-yang kai-tsao wei-yuan-hui tang-shih pien-tsuan wei-yuan-hui 中央改造委員會黨史編纂委員會 (Committee on party history, Central Committee of Reconstruction). Taipei: Chung-yang wen-wu kung-ying-she 中央文物供應社, 1951 ... *pu-pien* 補編 (supplement), 1952

Chang Ch'i-yun 張其昀 *et al.*, eds. *Ch'ing-shih* 清史 (A history of the Ch'ing dynasty). 8 vols. Taipei: Kuo-fang yen-chiu-yuan 國防研究院, 1961. A revision of Chao Erh-hsun, *et al. Ch'ing-shih kao*

Chang Ch'i-yun, ed. *Kuo-fu ch'üan-shu* 國父全書 (Complete works of the national father [Sun Yat-sen]). Taipei: Kuo-fang yen-chiu-yuan, 1960

Chang Chia-ao. See Chang Kia-ngau

Chang Chien 張謇. *Chang Chi-tzu chiu lu* 張季子九錄 (Nine collections of Chang Chien's writings). Shanghai: Chung-hua, 1931

Chang, C. M. 'Local government expenditure in China'. *Monthly Bulletin of Economic China* (formerly *Nankai Weekly Statistical Service*), 7.6 (June 1934) 233–47.

Chang Ching-lu 張靜廬, ed. *Chung-kuo chin-tai ch'u-pan shih-liao* 中國近代出版史料 (Historical materials on modern Chinese publications). *Ch'u-pien* 初編 (Part I), 1953; *Erh-pien* 二編 (Part II), 1954. Peking: Chung-hua

Chang Ching-lu, ed. *Chung-kuo hsien-tai ch'u-pan shih-liao* 中國現代出版史料 (Historical materials on contemporary Chinese publications). *Chia-pien* 甲編 (Part I), 1954; *I-pien* 乙編 (Part II), 1955; *Ping-pien* 丙編 (Part III), 1956; *Ting-pien* 丁編 (Part IV), 1959, 2 vols. Peking: Chung-hua

Chang Ching-lu, ed. *Chung-kuo ch'u-pan shih-liao* 中國出版史料 (Historical materials on Chinese publications). *Pu-pien* 補編 (Supplement), 1957. Peking: Chung-hua

Chang Chün-mai 張君勱. 'Jen-sheng kuan' 人生觀 (Philosophy of life), in *K'o-hsueh yü jen-sheng kuan* 科學與人生觀, prefaces by Hu Shih 胡適 and Ch'en Tu-hsiu 陳獨秀. Shanghai: Ya-tung shu-chü 亞東書局, 1923

Chang Chung-li 張仲禮. *The Chinese gentry: studies on their role in nineteenth century Chinese society*. Seattle: University of Washington Press, 1st edn, 1955; 2nd edn paperback, 1970

Chang Fa-k'uei 張發奎. 'The reminiscences of General Chang Fa-k'uei as told to Julie Lien-ying How'. MS. The Chinese Oral History Project of the East Asian Institute, Columbia University

Chang, Hao 張灝. *Liang Ch'i-ch'ao and intellectual transition in China, 1890–1907*. Cambridge, Mass.: Harvard University Press, 1971

Chang Hsiao-jo 張孝若. *Nan-t'ung Chang Chi-chih hsien-sheng chuan-chi* 南通張季直先生傳記 (A biography of Mr Chang Chien from Nan-t'ung). Shanghai: Chung-hua, 1930; Taipei reprint: Wen-hai, 1965

Chang I-lin 張一麐. *Hsin-t'ai-p'ing-shih chi* 心太平室集 (Collection of Chang I-lin's works), 1930. Taipei reprint: Wen-hai, 1966

Chang Jen-chia 張人价. *Konan no kokumai* 湖南の穀米 (Rice in Hunan). Trans. of 1936 report by Hunan provincial economic research institute. Tokyo: Seikatsusha 生活社, 1940

Chang Jo-ku 張若谷, ed. *Ma Hsiang-po hsien-sheng nien-p'u* 馬相伯先生年譜 [馬良] (Chronological biography of Mr Ma Hsiang-po [Ma Liang]). Changsha: Commercial Press, 1939

Chang Jo-ying 張若英, ed. *Hsin wen-hsueh yun-tung shih tzu-liao* 新文學運動史資料 (Materials concerning the new literary movement). Shanghai: Kuang-ming shu-chü 光明書局, 1934

Chang, John K. *Industrial development in pre-communist China: a quantitative analysis*. Chicago: Aldine, 1969

Chang Kia-ngau 張嘉璈. *China's struggle for railway development*. New York: John Day, 1943

Chang Kia-ngau. *The inflationary spiral: the experience of China, 1939–1950*. New York: M. I. T. Press and Wiley, 1958

Chang Kuo-t'ao 張國燾. 'Wo-ti hui-i' 我的回憶 (My recollections), in *Ming-pao yueh-k'an* 明報月刊 (Ming Pao monthly), 1.3–6.2 (March 1966–Feb. 1971); reprinted in 3 vols. Hong Kong: Ming-pao yueh-k'an, 1971–4

Chang Kuo-t'ao. *The rise of the Chinese Communist Party, 1921–1927; ... 1928–1938*. 2 vols. Lawrence, Kansas: University Press of Kansas, 1971–2

Chang, Kwang-chih 張光直. *The archaeology of ancient China*. 3rd rev. and enlarged edn, New Haven and London: Yale University Press, 1977

Chang Man-i 張曼儀 *et al. Hsien-tai Chung-kuo shih-hsuan, 1917–1949* 現代中國詩選, 1917–1949 (Modern Chinese poetry: an anthology 1917–49). 2 vols. Hong Kong: Hong Kong University Press and the Chinese University of Hong Kong Publications Office, 1974

Chang P'eng-yuan 張朋園. 'Ch'ing-chi tzu-i-chü i-yuan ti hsuan-chü chi ch'i ch'u-shen chih fen-hsi' 清季諮議局議員的選舉及其出身之分析 (China's first election of provincial assemblies in 1909 and an analysis of the background of the members). *Ssu yü yen* 思與言, 5.6 (March 1968) 1435-45

Chang P'eng-yuan. *Liang Ch'i-ch'ao yü Ch'ing-chi ko-ming* 梁啓超與清季革命 (Liang Ch'i-ch'ao and the late Ch'ing revolution). Taipei: Chung-yang yen-chiu-yuan chin-tai-shih yen-chiu-so, 1964

Chang P'eng-yuan. *Li-hsien p'ai yü Hsin-hai ko-ming* 立憲派與辛亥革命 (The Constitutionalists and the 1911 Revolution). Taipei: Chung-kuo hsueh-shu chu-tso chiang-chu wei-yuan hui, 1969

Chang P'eng-yuan. 'Wei-hu kung-ho – Liang Ch'i-ch'ao chih lien-Yuan yü t'ao-Yuan' 維護共和 – 梁啓超之聯袁與討袁 (Guarding the republic – Liang Ch'i-ch'ao's allying with Yuan and opposing him). *Chung-yang yen-chiu-yuan chin-tai-shih yen-chiu-so chi-k'an*, 3.2 (Dec. 1972) 377-96

Chang P'eng-yuan. *Liang Ch'i-ch'ao yü min-kuo cheng-chih* 梁啓超與民國政治 (Liang Ch'i-ch'ao and republican politics). Taipei: Shih-huo ch'u-pan she 食貨出版社, 1978

Chang Ping-lin 章炳麟. 'Chü-fen chin-hua lun' 俱分進化論 (Progress as differentiation). *Min-pao* 民報, 7 (5 Sept. 1906) 1-13

Chang Ping-lin. *Ch'iu shu* 訄書 (Book of raillery). Shanghai, 1904; Taipei, photolithographed reprint: Chung-kuo Kuo-min-tang tang-shih shih-liao pien-tsuan wei-yuan-hui 中國國民黨黨史料編纂委員會, 1967

Chang Ping-lin. 'She-hui t'ung-ch'üan shang-tui' 社會通詮商兌 (Discussion of the 'History of politics'). *Min-pao*, 12 (6 March 1907) 1-24

Chang Ping-lin. 'Wu-wu lun' 五無論 (The five negatives). *Min-pao*, 16 (25 Sept. 1907) 1-22

Chang Ping-lin. 'Po shen-wo hsien-cheng shuo' 駁神我憲政說 (Against 'soul' as a foundation for constitutional government). *Min-pao*, 21 (10 June 1908) 1-11

Chang Ping-lin. 'Ssu-huo lun' 四惑論 (On four delusions). *Min-pao*, 22 (10 July 1908) 1-22

Chang Ping-lin. *Kuo-ku lun-heng* 國故論衡 (Critical essays on antiquity). Shanghai, n.d.; photolithographed reprint, Taipei: Kuang-wen shu-chü 廣文書局, 1971

Chang Shou-yung 張壽鏞, *et al.* comps. *Huang-ch'ao chang-ku hui-pien* 皇朝掌故彙編 (Collected historical records of the imperial dynasty). 100 *chüan*. 1902; Taipei reprint: Wen-hai, 1964, 3 vols.

Chang, T. C. *The farmers' movement in Kwangtung,* trans. by the Committee on Christianizing Economic Relations. Shanghai: National Christian Council of China, 1928

Chang Tung-sun 張東蓀. 'Yü chih K'ung-chiao kuan' 余之孔教觀 (My view of Confucianism). *Yung yen* 庸言, 1.15 (July 1913) 1-12

Chang Yu-i. See Li Wen-chih

Chang Yü-fa 張玉法. 'Min-ch'u kuo-hui chung ti pao-shou p'ai cheng-tang' 民初國會中的保守派政黨 (Conservative parties in the early republican parliament), in *Chung-yang yen-chiu-yuan chin-tai-shih yen-chiu-so chi-k'an*, 8 (Oct. 1979) 21-63

Chao Chia-pi 趙家璧, ed. *Chung-kuo hsin-wen-hsueh ta-hsi* 中國新文學大系 (Comprehensive compendium of China's new literature). 10 vols. Shanghai: Liang-yu t'u-shu yin-shua kung-ssu 良友圖書印刷公司, 1935–6; Hong Kong reprint, 1963

Chao Erh-hsun 趙爾巽 *et al.*, eds. *Ch'ing-shih kao* 清史稿 (Draft history of the Ch'ing dynasty). 536 *chüan*, in 12 cases. Peking: Ch'ing-shih kuan 清史館, 1928; Mukden, 1928, rev. edn 1937; Shanghai reproduction, etc.

Chao Kang. 'Policies and performance in industry', in Alexander Eckstein, Walter Galenson, and Ta-chung Liu, eds. *Economic trends in communist China*, 549–95. Chicago: Aldine, 1968

Chao Kang. 'The growth of a modern cotton textile industry and the competition with handicrafts', in Dwight H. Perkins, ed. *China's modern economy in historical perspective*, 167–201. Stanford: Stanford University Press, 1975

Chao Kang. *The development of cotton textile production in China*. Cambridge, Mass.: East Asian Research Center, Harvard University. Distributed by Harvard University Press, 1977

Chao Kang and Ch'en Chung-i 趙岡, 陳鍾毅. *Chung-kuo mien-yeh shih* 中國棉業史 (History of Chinese cotton textile industry). Taipei: Lien-ching ch'u-pan shih-yeh kung-ssu 聯經出版事業公司, 1977

Chao Shih-yen 趙世炎 ('Shih-ying' 施英 pseud.), 'Record of the Shanghai general strike', *HTCP* 嚮導週報, 189 (28 Feb. 1927); reprinted in *Kung-jen*, 450–72, with documents

Chao Shih-yen ('Shih-ying', pseud.). 'A record of Shanghai workers' March insurrection'. *HTCP*, 193 (6 April 1927); reprinted with documents in *Kung-jen*, 473–90

Chapman, H. Owen. *The Chinese revolution 1926–27: a record of the period under communist control as seen from the Nationalist capital, Hankow*. London: Constable & Co., Ltd., 1928

Chen, C. S. 'Profits of British bankers from Chinese loans, 1895–1914'. *Tsing Hua Journal of Chinese Studies*, NS 5.1 (July 1965) 107–20

Chen, P. T. 'Public finance'. *The Chinese year book, 1935–1936*, 1163–428. Shanghai: Commercial Press, 1935

Chen Pan-tsu (Ch'en T'an-ch'iu). 'Reminiscences of the First Congress of the Communist Party of China'. *Communist International*. American edn, 14.10 (Oct. 1936) 1361–6; British edn, 13.9 (Sept.–Oct. 1936) 593–6

Chen Te 振德. 'Min-kuo shih-i nien-tu ko sha-ch'ang ying-yeh pao-kao' 民國十一年度各紗廠營業報告 (Operational report for various spinning-mills for the year 1922). *TSHYP*, 3.5 (May 1923)

Ch'en Chen 陳真 *et al.*, comps. *Chung-kuo chin-tai kung-yeh shih tzu-liao* 中國近代工業史資料 (Source materials on the history of modern industry in China). 6 vols. Peking: San-lien, 1957–61

Ch'en Cheng-mo 陳正謨. *Chung-kuo ko-sheng ti ti-tsu* 中國各省的地租 (Land rents in China by province). Shanghai: Commercial Press, 1936

Ch'en Hsun-cheng 陳訓正 (Ch'en Pu-lei 陳布雷?), *Kuo-min ko-ming-chün chan shih ch'u-kao* 國民革命軍戰史初稿 (A military history of the National Revolutionary Army). 4 vols. Taipei: Wen-hai, 1972

Ch'en, Jerome (Ch'en Chih-jang 陳志讓). *Mao and the Chinese revolution*. London: Oxford University Press, 1965

Ch'en, Jerome. *Yuan Shih-k'ai, 1859–1916*. Stanford: Stanford University Press, 1961; 2nd edn, 1972

Ch'en, Jerome. 'The left-wing Kuomintang – a definition'. *BSOAS*, 25.3 (1962) 557–76

Ch'en, Jerome. 'Defining Chinese warlords and their factions'. *BSOAS*, 31 (1968) 563–600

Ch'en, Jerome. *The military-gentry coalition: China under the warlords*. Toronto: University of Toronto-York University, Joint Centre on Modern East Asia, 1979

Ch'en Kung-po 陳公博. *Han-feng chi* 寒風集 (Cold wind). Shanghai: Shanghai ti-fang hsing-cheng she 上海地方行政社, 1944

Ch'en Kung-po. *The communist movement in China: an essay written in 1924*. Ed. with an introduction by C. Martin Wilbur. New York: Octagon Books, 1966

Ch'en-pao 晨報. (Morning post) Peking: 15 Aug. 1916–

Ch'en Po-ta 陳伯達. *Chung-kuo ssu-ta-chia-tsu* 中國四大家族 (China's four great families). Hong Kong: Nan-yang shu-tien, 1947

Ch'en Po-ta. *Ch'ieh-kuo ta-tao Yuan Shih-k'ai* 竊國大盜袁世凱 (Yuan Shih-k'ai, the great thief who stole the country). 1945; Peking reprint: Jen-min, 1962

Ch'en Ta 陳達. 'Labour unrest in China'. *Monthly Labour Review*, 6 (Dec. 1920) 23

Ch'en Ta. *Chung-kuo lao-kung wen-t'i* 中國勞工問題 (Chinese labour problems). Shanghai: Commercial Press, 1929

Ch'en Tu-hsiu 陳獨秀. 'Ching-kao ch'ing-nien' 敬告青年 (A call to youth). *Hsin ch'ing-nien* 新青年, 1.1 (Sept. 1915) 1–6 (Sep. pag.)

Ch'en Tu-hsiu. 'K'ung-tzu chih tao yü hsien-tai sheng-huo' 孔子之道與現代生活 (Confucianism and modern life). *Hsin ch'ing-nien*, 2.4 (1 Dec. 1916) 1–7 (sep. pag.)

Ch'en Tu-hsiu. 'Tui-yü Liang Chü-ch'uan [Liang Chi] hsien-sheng tzu-sha chih kan-hsiang' 對於梁巨川先生自殺之感想 (Impressions of the suicide of Mr Liang Chü-ch'uan). *Hsin ch'ing-nien*, 6.1 (15 Jan. 1918) 19–20

Ch'en Tu-hsiu. 'Letter to Tai Chi-t'ao'. *HTCP* 129–30 (11 and 18 Sept. 1925) 1186–90, 1196–7

Ch'en Tu-hsiu. *Tu-hsiu wen-ts'un* 獨秀文存 (Collected essays of Ch'en Tu-hsiu). 4 vols. Shanghai: Ya-tung t'u-shu-kuan 亞東圖書館, 1922

Ch'en Tu-hsiu. *Pien-shu-chuang* 辯述狀 (My defence). 20 Feb. 1933, n.p.

Ch'en Tu-hsiu. *Kao ch'üan-tang t'ung-chih shu* 告全黨同志書 (A letter to all comrades of the Party). Reprinted in *Kung-fei huo-kuo shih-liao hui-pien*, 427–44; trans. in *Chinese Studies in History*, 2.3 (Spring 1970) 224–50

Ch'en Tuan-chih 陳端志. *Wu-ssu yun-tung chih shih ti p'ing-chia* 五四運動之史的評價 (Historical evaluation of the May Fourth movement). Shanghai: Sheng-huo shu-tien 生活書店, 1936

Cheng Chen-to 鄭振鐸, *et al. Chung-kuo hsin wen-hsueh ta-hsi tao-lun hsuan-chi* 中國新文學大系導論選集 (Selected introductory essays to *Comprehensive compendium of China's new literature*). Hong Kong: Ch'ün-i ch'u-pan she 群益出版社, 1966

Cheng, Ch'ing-mao 鄭清茂. 'The impact of Japanese literary trends on modern Chinese writers', in Merle Goldman, ed. *Modern Chinese literature in the May Fourth era*, 63–88

Cheng-fu kung-pao 政府公報 (Government gazette). Peking, 1912–28

Cheng Tien-fang. *A history of Sino-Russian relations.* Washington: Public Affairs Press, 1957

Cheng, Ying-wan. *Postal communication in China and its modernization, 1860–1896.* Cambridge, Mass.: Harvard University Press, 1970

Cheng, Yu-Kwei. *Foreign trade and industrial development of China.* Washington, D. C.: University Press of Washington, 1956

Ch'eng Chi-hua 程季華 *et al. Chung-kuo tien-ying fa-chan shih* 中國電影發展史 (History of the development of modern Chinese cinema). 2 vols. Peking: Chung-kuo tien-ying 中國電影, 1963

Cheong, W. E. *Mandarins and merchants: Jardine Matheson & Co., a China agency of the early nineteenth century.* Scandinavian Institute of Asian Studies Monograph Series, no. 26. London and Malmö: Curzon Press, 1979

Cherepanov, A. I. *Severnyi pokhod Natsional'-no-Revoliutsionnoi Armii Kitaia (zapiski voennogo sovetnika 1926–1927)* (The Northern Expedition of the National Revolutionary Army of China – notes of a military adviser 1926–7). Moscow: Izdatel'stvo 'Nauka', 1968

Cherepanov, A. I. *Zapiski voennogo sovetnika v kitae: iz istorii pervoi grazdanskoi revolutsionnoi coiny, 1924–1927* (Notes of a military adviser in China; from the history of the first revolutionary civil war in China, 1924–1927). Moscow: Academy of Sciences of the USSR, Institut Narodov Azii, 'Nauka'. 2 vols., 1964, 1968. Draft trans. of vol. 1 by Alexandra O. Smith, edited by Harry H. Collier and Thomas M. Williamson, Taipei: (U. S. Army) Office of Military History, 1970

Chesneaux, Jean. *Le mouvement ouvrier chinois de 1919 à 1927.* Paris, La Hague: Mouton, 1962

Chesneaux, Jean. *The Chinese labor movement, 1919–1927.* Trans. from the French by H. M. Wright. Stanford: Stanford University Press, 1968

Chesneaux, Jean. 'The federalist movement in China, 1920–3', in Jack Gray, ed. *Modern China's search for a political form*, 96–137. London, New York and Toronto: Oxford University Press, 1969

Chesneaux, Jean and LeBarbier, Francoise. *La Chine: la marche de la révolution 1921–1949.* Paris: Hatier, 1975

Chi, Madeleine. *China diplomacy, 1914–1918.* Cambridge, Mass.: Harvard University Press, 1970

Ch'i Hsi-sheng. *Warlord politics in China 1916–1928*. Stanford: Stanford University Press, 1976

Ch'i-wu lao-jen 栖梧老人. 'Chung-kuo Kung-ch'an-tang ch'eng-li ch'ien-hou ti chien-wen' 中國共產黨成立前后的見聞 (My impressions before and after the founding of the Chinese Communist Party). *Hsin kuan-ch'a* 新觀察 (New observer), Peking, 13 (1 July 1957) 16–18

Chia I-chün 賈逸君, ed. *Chung-hua min-kuo ming-jen chuan* 中華民國名人傳 (Biographies of famous men of the republic). 2 vols. Peiping: Wen-hua hsueh-she 文化學社, 1932–3

Chia Shih-i 賈士毅. *Min-kuo ts'ai-cheng shih* 民國財政史 (Fiscal history of the republic). 2 vols. Shanghai: Commercial Press, 1917

Chia Shih-i. *Min-kuo hsü ts'ai-cheng shih* 民國續財政史 (A history of public finance under the republic, supplement). 7 vols. Shanghai: Commercial Press, 1932–4

Chia Shih-i. *Min-kuo ts'ai-cheng shih san-pien* 民國財政史三編 (A history of public finance under the republic, second supplement). 2 vols. Taipei: Commercial Press, 1962

Chia Shih-i. *Min-kuo ch'u-nien ti chi-jen ts'ai-cheng tsung-chang* 民國初年的幾任財政總長 (Several finance ministers of the early republic). Taipei: Chuan-chi wen-hsueh ch'u-pan she, 1967

Chia Te-huai 賈德懷. *Min-kuo ts'ai-cheng chien-shih* 民國財政簡史 (A short fiscal history of the republic). Shanghai: Commercial Press, 1946

Chia-yin 甲寅. Tokyo and Shanghai, May 1914–

Chia-yin (The Tiger). Peking and Tientsin, 1925–

Chia-yin jih-k'an 甲寅日刊 (1914 daily)

Chiang Kai-shek 蔣介石. 'A letter of reply to Wang Ching-wei', in Wen-hua yen-chiu she, comps. *Chung-kuo wu ta wei-jen shou cha* (q.v.), 246–53

Chiang Kai-shek. *Soviet Russia in China*. Authorized trans. by Wang Chung-hui, with an introduction by Lin Yutang. New York: Farrar, Straus and Cudahy, 1957

Chiang Kai-shek. 'Military report' to the Second Kuomintang Congress (in Chinese), in *KMWH*, 11 (Dec. 1955) 1756–63

Chiang Kai-shek. *Chiang wei-yuan-chang ch'üan-chi* 蔣委員長全集 (Complete works of Generalissimo Chiang), ed. Shen Feng-kang 沈鳳崗. Taipei: Min-tsu ch'u-pan she 民族出版社, 1956

Chiang K'ang-hu 江亢虎. *Hung-shui chi: Chiang K'ang-hu san-shih sui i-ch'ien tso* 洪水集：江亢虎三十歲以前作 (Flood tide: collection of writings by Chiang K'ang-hu before the age of thirty). n.p. Title page dated Sept. 1913

Chiang Shen-wu 蔣慎吾. 'Shang-hai shih-cheng-chi-kuan pien-ch'ien shih-lueh' 上海市政機關變遷史略 (Short history of the structural changes in the municipal government of Shanghai), in Shang-hai t'ung-she 上海通社, ed. *Shang-hai yen-chiu tzu-liao* 上海研究資料 (Research materials on Shanghai). 1st edn Shanghai, 1936; Taipei: China Press, 1973

Chiang Yung-ching 蔣永敬. *Bo-lo-t'ing yü Wu-han cheng-ch'üan* 鮑羅廷與武漢政權 (Borodin and the Wuhan regime). Taipei: China Committee for Publication Aid and Prize Awards, 1964

Chiang Yung-ching. *Hu Han-min hsien-sheng nien-p'u* 胡漢民先生年譜 (Chronological biography of Mr Hu Han-min). Taipei: Chung-kuo Kuomintang
Central Executive Committee, Party History Committee, 1978

Chien Po-tsan 翦伯贊 *et al.*, comps. *Wu-hsu pien-fa* 戊戌變法 (1898 reforms).
4 vols. Chung-kuo chin-tai shih tzu-liao ts'ung-k'an 中國近代史資料叢刊.
Chung-kuo shih-hsueh hui 中國史學會 ed. Shanghai: Jen-min, 1961

Chien-she 建設 (Construction). Shanghai, Aug. 1919–

Ch'ien Chia-chü 千家駒. *Chiu Chung-kuo kung-chai shih tzu-liao, 1894–1949* 舊中國
公債史資料, 1894–1949 (Source materials on government bond issues in old
China, 1894–1949). Peking: Ts'ai-cheng ching-chi 財政經濟, 1955

Ch'ien Chih-hsiu 錢智修. 'Shuo t'i-ho' 說體合 (On adaptation). *TFTC* 東方雜誌,
10.7 (1 Jan. 1914) 1–4 (sep. pag.)

Ch'ien Chung-shu. *Fortress Besieged*, trans. by Jeanne Kelly and Nathan K.
Mao. Bloomington and London: Indiana University Press, 1979

Ch'ien-feng 前鋒 (Vanguard). Canton, July 1923–

Ch'ien Hsing-ts'un. See A Ying

Ch'ien I-chang 錢義璋, ed. 'Sha-chi t'ung shih' 沙基痛史 (The tragic history of
Shakee). Canton?, n.p., 1925?; reprinted in *KMWH*, 18 (Sept. 1957), 3330–
3419

Ch'ien Mu 錢穆. *Chung-kuo chin san-pai-nien hsueh-shu shih* 中國近三百年學術史
(An intellectual history of China during the past three hundred years). Taipei:
Commercial Press, 1966

Ch'ien Tuan-sheng 錢端升. *The government and politics of China, 1912–1949*. Cambridge, Mass.: Harvard University Press, 1950

Ch'ien Yuan 潛園. 'Fang-chi-yeh ken-pen cheng-li chih ssu-chien' 紡績業根本整
理之私見 (My opinion on the radical reorganization of the cotton textile
industry). *HSSC*, 3.4 (20 Oct. 1922) 6–14

Ch'ien Yuan. 'Ch'ing-tao fang-chi-yeh chih chuang-k'uang yü hsi-wang' 青島紡
績業之狀況與希望 (The situation and prospects of the textile industries of
Tsingtao). *HSSC*, 4.1 (Jan. 1923) 29–32

Chih I 之一. 'Hua-shang sha-ch'ang tzu-chin wen-t'i yü mien-yeh ch'ien-t'u
chih kuan-hsi' 華商紗廠資金問題與棉業前途之關係 (The problem of capital for
the Chinese spinning mills, and its effect on the future of the cotton industry).
HSSC, 4.4 (Oct. 1923) 2–8

Chih Ta 志達. 'Nan-tao nü-ch'ang chih Shang-hai' 男盜女娼之上海 (Shanghai,
where men are robbers and women are whores). *T'ien-i* 天義, 5 (10 Aug.
1907) 95–7

Chih-yuan lu 職員錄 (Register of officials). Quarterly. Peking, 1918–23

Chin Ch'ung-chi 金冲及. 'Yun-nan hu-kuo yun-tung ti chen-cheng fa-tung-che
shih shui?' 雲南護國運動的真正發動者是誰? (Who was the true initiator of the
Yunnan National Protection movement?). Chou K'ang-hsieh 周康燮 *et al.* eds.
*Chin-erh-shih-nien Chung-kuo shih-hsueh lun-wen hui-pien, ch'u-pien: Hsin-hai ko-
ming yen-chiu lun-chi ti-i-chi* (1895–1929) 近廿年中國史學論文彙編初編：辛亥革
命研究論集第一集 (1895–1929) (First collection of Chinese historical articles

of the last 20 years: first volume of studies on the 1911 Revolution (1895–1929), Hong Kong: Ch'ung-wen shu-tien 崇文書店, 1971

Chin-tai-shih tzu-liao 近代史資料 (Materials on modern history) series. Peking: The group for compiling materials on modern history in the Institute of Modern History of the Chinese Academy of Sciences, 1954–

Ch'in Te-ch'un 秦德純. *Ch'in Te-ch'un hui-i-lu* 秦德純回憶錄 (Recollections of Ch'in Te-ch'un). Taipei: Chuan-chi wen-hsueh ch'u-pan she, 1967

China Continuation Committee. *The Christian occupation of China: a general survey of the numerical strength and geographical distribution of the Christian forces in China made by the Special Committee on Survey and Occupation, China Continuation Committee, 1918–1921*. Shanghai, 1922

China. Inspectorate General of Customs. *Decennial reports . . ., 1902–1911*. 2 vols. Shanghai, 1913

China. Inspectorate General of Customs. *Decennial reports . . ., 1912–1921*. 2 vols. Shanghai, 1924

China. Inspectorate General of Customs. *Documents illustrative of the origin, development, and activities of the Chinese Customs Service*. 7 vols. Shanghai: Inspectorate General of Customs, 1937–40

China. The Maritime Customs. *Handbook of customs procedure at Shanghai*. Shanghai: Kelly & Walsh, 1921

The China Mission Year Book. Shanghai, 1910–25; continued as *The China Christian Year Book*. Shanghai, 1926–40

China Quarterly. London, 1960–

China Weekly Review. Shanghai, 1917–

The China year book. H. G. W. Woodhead, ed. London: George Routledge & Sons, Ltd., 1912–21; Tientsin: The Tientsin Press, 1921–30; Shanghai: The North China Daily News & Herald, Ltd., 1931–9

Chinese Academy of Sciences. See Chung-kuo k'o-hsueh-yuan

Chinese Correspondence: weekly organ of the Central Executive Committee of the Kuomintang. Wuhan 2.6 (1 May 1927)

Chinese Ministry of Information. *China handbook, 1937–1945*. New York: Macmillan, 1947

The Chinese Recorder. Shanghai, 1867–1941

Chinese Republican Studies Newsletter. Semi-annual (Oct. and Feb.), 1975–

Chinese Social and Political Science Review. Quarterly. Peking, 1916–

Chinese Studies in History: A Journal of Translation. White Plains, N.Y.: International Arts and Sciences Press, Inc., Fall 1967–

Ching-chi t'ung-chi yueh-chih 經濟統計月誌 (The Chinese economic and statistical review). Monthly. Shanghai: 1934–41

' "Ch'ing ho-ch'eng cheng-fu t'e-hsu ch'üan-kuo shang-hui tzu-lien shang-t'uan an": Ssu-ch'uan Ch'eng-tu tsung-shang-hui tai-piao t'i-i' 請合呈政府特許全國商會自練商團案：四川成都總商會代表提議 ('That a common approach be made to the government requesting that Chambers of Commerce be specially authorized to train merchant militia'. Motion put forward by the

General Chamber of Commerce of Chengtu, Szechwan). *TSHYP*, 3.4 (April 1923)

Ch'ing-i pao 清議報 (Upright discussion), 1–100 (Dec. 1898–Nov. 1901); reprinted by Ch'eng-wen ch'u-pan she 成文出版社. 12 vols. Taipei, 1967

' "Ch'ing wei-ch'ih ch'üan-kuo-shang-hui lien-ho-hui t'ung-kuo i-an li-cheng shih-hsing an": Hu-pei I-tu shang-hui t'i-i' 請維持全國商會聯合會通過議案力爭實行案：湖北宜都商會提議 ('That the motions passed by the conference of the National Federation of Chambers of Commerce be supported, and that every effort be made to have them put into practice'. Motion put forward by the Chamber of Commerce of I-tu, Hupei). *TSHYP*, 3.4 (April 1923)

Chiu wang 救亡 (Salvation). Weekly. Peking: Kuo hun she 國魂社 (Society for the national soul), 2 (16 June 1925), 3 (23 June 1925)

CHOC: Cambridge History of China

Chou Fo-hai 周佛海. *Wang-i chi* 往矣集 (What has passed). Hong Kong, 1955

Chou Hsiu-luan 周秀鸞. *Ti-i-tz'u shih-chieh ta-chan shih-ch'i Chung-kuo min-tsu kung-yeh ti fa-chan* 第一次世界大戰時期中國民族工業的發展 (The development of national industries during the First World War). Shanghai: Jen-min, 1958

Chou K'ai-ch'ing, 周開慶, comp. *Min-kuo Ssu-ch'uan jen-wu chuan-chi* 民國四川人物傳記 (Biographies of republican personalities in Szechwan). Taipei: Commercial Press, 1966

Chou Shu-chen 周叔娗. *Chou Chih-an hsien-sheng pieh-chuan* 周止菴先生別傳 (An unorthodox biography of Chou Hsueh-hsi). 1947. Taipei: Wen-hai, 1966

Chou, Shun-hsin. *The Chinese inflation, 1937–1949*. New York: Columbia University Press, 1963

Chou Tso-jen 周作人. 'Jen ti wen-hsueh' 人的文學 (A humane literature), *Hsin ch'ing-nien*, 5.6 (Dec. 1918) 575–84

Chou Yü-t'ung 周予同. *Ching ku-chin wen-hsueh* 經古今文學 (Old and new text classical learning). Shanghai: Commercial Press, 1926

Chow Tse-tsung 周策縱. *The May Fourth movement: intellectual revolution in modern China*. Cambridge, Mass.: Harvard University Press, 1960

Chow Tse-tsung. *Research guide to the May Fourth movement: intellectual revolution in modern China, 1915–1924*. Cambridge, Mass.: Harvard University Press, 1963

Chu, Clayton H. *American missionaries in China: books, articles, and pamphlets extracted from the subject catalogue of the Missionary Research Library*. 3 vols. Cambridge, Mass.: Harvard University Department of History, 1960 (dittographed)

Chu Hsieh 朱偰. *Chung-kuo ts'ai-cheng wen-t'i* 中國財政問題 (Problems of China's public finance). Shanghai: Commercial Press, 1934

Chu Hsien-fang 朱仙舫. 'Cheng-li mien-yeh hsin-i' 整理棉業新議 (New debate on the reform of the textile industry). *TSHYP*, 3.5 (May 1923)

Chu Hsin-fan. See Li Ang

Chu P'ei-wo 朱佩我. *Chung-kuo ko-ming yü Chung-kuo she-hui ko chieh-chi* 中國革命與中國社會各階級 (The Chinese revolution and the social classes in China). 2 vols. Shanghai: Lien-ho shu-tien 聯合書店, 1930

Chu P'ei-wo. See Chu Hsin-fan, Li Ang

Chu, Samuel. *Reformer in modern China, Chang Chien 1853–1926.* New York, London: Columbia University Press, 1965

Ch'u Min-i [Min] 褚民誼 [民]. 'Wu-cheng-fu shuo' 無政府説 (On anarchism). *Hsin shih-chi* 新世紀, 31–47 (25 Jan.–16 May 1908)

Ch'ü Ch'iu-pai 瞿秋白. *Ch'ü Ch'iu-pai hsuan-chi* 瞿秋白選集 (Selected writings of Ch'ü Ch'iu-pai). Peking: Jen-min, 1959

Ch'ü, T'ung-tsu 瞿同祖. *Han social structure*, ed. by Jack L. Dull. Seattle: University of Washington Press, 1972

Chuan-chi wen-hsueh 傳記文學 (Biographical literature). Monthly. Taipei, 1962–

'Ch'üan-kuo shang-chiao lien-hsi hui-i shih-mo chi' 全國商教聯席會議始末記 (Notes on the progress of the joint conference of the National Federation of Chambers of Commerce and the Educational Societies). *TSHYP*, 1.4 (Oct. 1921) heading *Chi-shih*

'Ch'üan-kuo yin-hang kung-hui chih chien-i-an' 全國銀行公會之建議案 (Motion put forward by the National Federation of Banking Associations). *TFTC*, 18.3 (10 Feb. 1921) 127–9

'Ch'üan-kuo yin-hang kung-hui lien-ho-hui-i chi' 全國銀行公會聯合會議記 (Notes on the National Conference of Banking Associations). *YHYK*, 1.6 (June 1921)

Chueh-wu 覺悟 (Enlightenment). Tientsin, 20 Jan. 1920–

Chūgoku kindaika no shakai kōzō: Shingai kakumei no shiteki ichi 中国近代化の社会構造：辛亥革命の史的位置 (The social framework of China's modernization: the historical position of the 1911 Revolution), comp. by Aziashi Kenkyūkai アジア史研究会, *Tōyō shigaku ronshū* 東洋史學論集 (Studies in Oriental History), no. 6. Tokyo: Daian, 1960

Chūgoku Kyōsantōshi shiryōshū. See Hatano Ken'ichi, *Shina Kyōsantōshi*

Chūgoku Kyōsantōshi shiryōshū 中国共産党史資料集 (Collected materials on the history of the Chinese Communist party), ed. by Nippon Kokusaimondai Kenkyūkai Chūgoku Bukai 日本国際問題研究会中国部会. Tokyo: Keisō shobō 勁草書房, 1970–5

Ch'un-ch'iu tsa-chih 春秋雜誌 (Spring and autumn magazine). Taipei: 1964–

Chung-kuo chin-tai-shih tzu-liao hui-pien 中國近代史資料彙編 (Collections of historical materials on modern Chinese history), a series pub. by Institute of Modern History, Academia Sinica, Taipei, concerning maritime defence (*Hai-fang tang* 海防檔, 9 vols., 1957), mining affairs (*K'uang-wu tang* 礦務檔, 8 vols., 1960), and diplomatic negotiations

Chung-kuo ch'ing-nien 中國青年 (The Chinese youth). Wuchang, June 1937–; Chungking, July 1938–

Chung-kuo hsien-tai wen-hsueh shih ts'an-k'ao tzu-liao 中國現代文學史參考資料 (Research materials on the history of modern Chinese literature), ed. by Pei-ching shih-fan ta-hsueh Chung-wen hsi hsien-tai wen-hsueh chiao-hsueh kai-ke hsiao-tsu 北京師範大學中文系現代文學教學改革小組 (Peking Normal University, Chinese Literature Department, Contemporary literature teaching reform group). 3 vols. Peking: Kao-teng chiao-yü 高等教育, 1959

Chung-kuo hsien-tai wen-i tzu-liao ts'ung-k'an ti-i chi 中國現代文藝資料叢刊第一輯 (Sources of modern Chinese literature, first series), ed. by Shang-hai wen-i ch'u-pan-she pien-chi pu 上海文藝出版社編輯部 (Editorial department of *Shanghai Literature*). Shanghai: Shang-hai wen-i, 1962

Chung-kuo hsin wen-hsueh ta-hsi 中國新文學大系 (A comprehensive compendium of China's new literature), general ed. Chao Chia-pi 趙家璧. 10 vols. Shanghai: Liang-yu t'u-shu kung-ssu 良友圖書公司, 1935–6; Hong Kong reprint, 1963

Chung-kuo k'o-hsueh yuan chin-tai shih yen-chiu-so 中國科學院近代史研究所, *Chin-tai shih yen-chiu* 近代史研究 (Researches on modern history) Peking, Oct. 1979–

Chung-kuo k'o-hsueh-yuan li-shih yen-chiu-so 中國科學院歷史研究所, ed. *Chin-tai-shih tzu-liao* 近代史資料 (Materials on modern history), 1 (1961): (special issue) *Hsin-hai ko-ming tzu-liao* 辛亥革命資料 (Materials on the 1911 Revolution)

Chung-kuo k'o-hsueh-yuan Shang-hai ching-chi yen-chiu-so 中國科學院上海經濟研究所 (Academy of Sciences, Shanghai Institute of Economic Research). *Shang-hai chieh-fang ch'ien-hou wu-chia tzu-liao hui-pien (1921 nien–1957 nien)* 上海解放前後物價資料匯編 (1921年–1957年) (Collected materials on Shanghai prices before and after Liberation, 1921–57). Shanghai: Jen-min, 1958

Chung-kuo k'o-hsueh yuan Shang-hai ching-chi yen-chiu-so 中國科學院上海經濟研究所 and Shang-hai she-hui k'o-hsueh yuan ching-chi yen-chiu-so 上海社會科學院經濟研究所, comps. *Nan-yang hsiung-ti yen-ts'ao kung-ssu shih-liao* 南洋兄弟烟草公司史料 (Materials for the history of the Nanyang Brothers Tobacco Company). Shanghai: Jen-min, 1958

Chung-kuo Kuo-min-tang cheng-li tang-wu chih t'ung-chi pao-kao 中國國民黨整理黨務之統計報告 (Statistical report on the work of party adjustment of the Kuomintang of China). Nanking: KMT CEC Organization Department, March 1929

Chung-kuo Kuo-min-tang chou-k'an 中國國民黨週刊 (Kuomintang of China weekly). Canton, 1924

Chung-kuo Kuo-min-tang ch'üan-kuo tai-piao ta-hui hui-i-lu 中國國民黨全國代表大會會議錄 (Minutes of the national congress of the Kuomintang of China). Reprinted, Washington, D.C.: Center for Chinese Research Materials, 1971

Chung-kuo Kuo-min-tang chung-yao hsuan-yen hui-pien 中國國民黨重要宣言彙編 (Collection of important proclamations of the Kuomintang of China). n.p.: Tang-i yen-chiu hui 黨義研究會, May 1929

Chung-kuo Kuo-min-tang ti-erh-tz'u ch'üan-kuo tai-piao ta-hui hui-i chi-lu 中國國民黨第二次全國代表大會會議記錄 (Minutes of the Second National Congress of Kuomintang delegates). n.p.: Central Executive Committee of the Kuomintang of China, April 1926

Chung-kuo lao-kung yun-tung shih pien-tsuan wei-yuan-hui 中國勞工運動史編纂委員會, comp. *Chung-kuo lao-kung yun-tung shih* 中國勞工運動史 (A history of the Chinese labour movement). 5 vols. Taipei: Chinese Labour Welfare Publisher, 1959

Chung-kuo nung-min 中國農民 (The Chinese farmer). Canton: Farmers' Bureau of the Central Executive Committee of the Kuomintang of China, 1926. Photolithographic reprint edn, Tokyo: Daian, 1964

Chung-kuo wu ta wei-jen shou-cha. See Wen-hua yen-chiu she.

Chung-yang t'ung-hsin 中央通信 (Central newsletter). Organ of the Central Committee of the Chinese Communist Party, Aug. 1927–

Chung-yang yen-chiu-yuan chin-tai-shih yen-chiu-so chi-k'an 中央研究院近代史研究所集刊 (Bulletin of the Institute of Modern History, Academia Sinica). Taipei, Aug. 1969–

CI: Communist International, Comintern

Clifford, Nicholas R. *Shanghai, 1925: urban nationalism and the defense of foreign privilege.* Ann Arbor: Center for Chinese Studies, University of Michigan, 1979

Clopton, Robert W. and Ou Tsuin-chen, trans. and ed. *John Dewey, lectures in China, 1919–1920.* Honolulu: East-West Center, 1973

Close, Upton (pseud. of Hall, Joseph W.). 'The Chinese bankers assert themselves'. *CWR* (19 Feb. 1921)

Clubb, O. Edmund. *Communism in China as reported from Hankow in 1932.* New York: Columbia University Press, 1968

Clubb, O. Edmund. *China and Russia: the 'great game'.* New York: Columbia University Press, 1971

Clubb, O. Edmund. *20th century China.* New York: Columbia University Press, 1964; 3rd edn, 1978

Coble, Parks, Jr. 'The Shanghai capitalists and the Nationalist government 1927–1937', University of Illinois, Ph.D. dissertation, 1975. Published as a book by Harvard University Press, 1980

Coble, Parks M., Jr. 'The Kuomintang regime and the Shanghai capitalists, 1927–29'. *CQ*, 77 (March 1979) 1–24

Cochran, Sherman G. 'Big business in China: Sino-American rivalry in the tobacco industry, 1890–1930'. Yale University, Ph.D. dissertation, 1975

Cohen, Paul A. *Between tradition and modernity: Wang T'ao and reform in late Ch'ing China.* Cambridge, Mass.: Harvard University Press, 1974

Commission for the Investigation of the Shakee Massacre. *June Twenty-Third: the report of the Commission for the Investigation of the Shakee Massacre June 23, 1925, Canton, China.* Canton: Wah On Printing Co., n.d. (1925), distributed 'with compliments of the Commission'.

Conference on the limitation of armament, Washington, November 12, 1921–February 6, 1922. 2 vols. Washington, D.C.: U.S. Government Printing Office, 1922

Contemporary China Institute. *A bibliography of Chinese newspapers and periodicals in European libraries.* Cambridge: Cambridge University Press, 1975

CP: Commercial Press

CQ: See *China Quarterly, The*

Cressey, George Babcock. *China's geographic foundations: a survey of the land and its people.* New York and London: McGraw Hill Book Co., 1934

CSC: Central Supervisory Committee of the Kuomintang

CWR: China Weekly Review. Shanghai, 1917– (formerly *Millard's Review*)

CYB: The China Yearbook

Darwent, C. E. *Shanghai, a handbook for travellers and residents*. Shanghai: Kelly & Walsh, n.d.

deBary, W. T. *et al.*, eds. *Sources of Chinese tradition*. New York: Columbia University Press, 1960

Degras, Jane, comp. and trans. *Soviet documents on foreign policy*. 2 vols. London: Oxford University Press, 1951–3

Degras, Jane. *The Communist International, 1919–1943: documents selected and edited by Jane Degras*. 3 vols. London: Oxford University Press, 1956–65

Deliusin, L. P., ed. *Kantonskaia Kommuna* (The Canton Commune). Moscow: Akad. Nauk SSSR, Institut Dal'nego Vostoka, 'Nauka', 1967

Denby, Charles. *China and her people*. 2 vols. Boston: L. C. Page, 1906

d'Encausse, H. and Schram, S. R., eds. *Marxism and Asia: an introduction with readings*. London: Allen Lane, Penguin Press, 1969

Department of Overseas Trade, ed. *Report on the commercial, industrial and economic situation in China*. Annual. London: H. M. Stationery Office, 1922–

Dernberger, Robert F. 'The role of the foreigner in China's economic development, 1840–1949', in Dwight H. Perkins, ed. *China's modern economy in historical perspective*, 19–47. Stanford: Stanford University Press, 1975

Dirlik, Arif. *Revolution and history: origins of Marxist historiography in China 1919–1937*. Berkeley: University of California Press, 1978

Doležalová, Anna. *Yü Ta-fu: specific traits of literary creation*. New York: Paragon, 1971

Doleželová-Velingerová, Milena. 'The origins of modern Chinese literature', in Merle Goldman, ed. *Modern Chinese literature in the May Fourth era*, 17–36. Cambridge, Mass.: Harvard University Press, 1977

Doleželová-Velingerová, Milena, ed. *Chinese novels at the turn of the century* (forthcoming)

Dreyer, Edward L. 'The Poyang campaign, 1363: inland naval warfare in the founding of the Ming dynasty', in Frank A. Kierman, Jr. and John K. Fairbank, eds. *Chinese ways in warfare*, 202–40. Cambridge, Mass.: Harvard University Press, 1974

Dulioust, Nicole. 'Quelques aspects de la presse chinoise pendant le mouvement du 30 mai 1925'. *Cahiers du Centre d'Etudes Chinoises de l'INALCO*, 1 (forthcoming)

Eastman, Lloyd E. *The abortive revolution: China under Nationalist rule 1927–1937*. Cambridge, Mass.: Harvard University Press, 1974

Eastman, Lloyd E. 'Some themes on wartime China'. *Chinese Republican Studies Newsletter*, 1.1 (Oct. 1975) 8–12

ECCI: Executive Committee of the Communist International

Eckstein, Alexander, Galenson, Walter and Liu Ta-chung, eds. *Economic trends in communist China*. Chicago: Aldine, 1968

Eckstein, Alexander, Chao Kang and Chang, John. 'The economic development of Manchuria: the rise of a frontier economy'. *The Journal of Economic History*, 34.1 (March 1974) 239–64

Egan, Michael. 'Yü Dafu and the transition to modern Chinese literature', in Merle Goldman, ed. *Modern Chinese literature in the May Fourth era*, 309–24

Egan, Michael. 'The short stories of Yü Ta-fu: life through art'. University of Toronto, Ph.D. dissertation, 1979

Elvin, Mark. 'The gentry democracy in Chinese Shanghai, 1905–14', in Jack Gray, ed. *Modern China's search for a political form*, 41–65. London: Oxford University Press, 1969

Elvin, Mark. *The pattern of the Chinese past*. Stanford: Stanford University Press, 1973

Elvin, Mark and Skinner, G. William, eds. *The Chinese city between two worlds*. Stanford: Stanford University Press, 1974

Elvin, Mark. 'The administration of Shanghai, 1905–1914', in Mark Elvin and G. William Skinner, eds. *The Chinese city between two worlds*, 239–69. Stanford: Stanford University Press, 1974

Elvin, Mark. 'Mandarins and millennarians: reflections on the Boxer uprising of 1899–1900'. *Journal of the Anthropological Society of Oxford*, 10.3 (1979) 115–38

Esherick, Joseph W. *Reform and revolution in China: the 1911 Revolution in Hunan and Hubei*. Berkeley: University of California Press, 1976

Etō, Shinkichi 衛藤瀋吉. 'Hai-lu-feng – the first Chinese soviet government'. Pt I. *CQ*, 8 (Oct./Dec. 1961) 160–83; pt II (Jan./March 1962) 149–81

Eudin, Xenia Joukoff and North, Robert C. *Soviet Russia and the East, 1920–1927: a documentay survey*. Stanford: Stanford University Press, 1957

Evans, Lee and Block, Russell, eds. *Leon Trotsky on China: introduction by Peng Shu-tse*. New York: Monad Press, 1976

Fairbank, John King and Liu, Kwang-Ching 劉廣京. *Modern China: a bibliographical guide to Chinese works, 1898–1937*. Cambridge, Mass.: Harvard University Press, 1950; corrected reprint, 1961

Fairbank, John King, Banno Masataka 坂野正高 and Yamamoto Sumiko 山本澄子, eds. *Japanese studies of modern China: a bibliographical guide to historical and social-science research on the 19th and 20th centuries*. Harvard-Yenching Institute Studies, XXVI. Tuttle, 1955; reissued Cambridge, Mass.: Harvard University Press, 1971

Fairbank, John K., Reischauer, Edwin O., and Craig, Albert M. *East Asia: the modern transformation*. Boston: Houghton Mifflin, 1965

Fairbank, John King, ed. *The Chinese world order: traditional China's foreign relations*. Cambridge, Mass.: Harvard University Press, 1968

Fairbank, John King, Bruner, Katherine Frost and Matheson, Elizabeth MacLeod, eds. *The I.G. in Peking: letters of Robert Hart, Chinese Maritime Customs, 1868–1907*. 2 vols. Cambridge, Mass.: Harvard University Press, 1975

Fairbank, John K., ed. *The missionary enterprise in China and America*. Cambridge, Mass.: Harvard University Press, 1974

Fang, Achilles. 'From imagism to Whitmanism in recent Chinese poetry: a search for poetics that failed', in Horst Frenz and G. A. Anderson, eds. *Indiana University conference on Oriental-Western literary relations*, 177–89. Chapel Hill: University of North Carolina Press, 1955.

Fang T'eng 方騰. 'Yü Hsia-ch'ing lun' 虞洽卿論 (On the subject of Yü Hsia-ch'ing). *Tsa-chih yueh-k'an* 雜誌月刊 (Monthly miscellany), 12.2 (Nov. 1943) 46–51; 12.3 (Dec. 1943) 62–7; 12.4 (Jan. 1944) 59–64

Fang Tsung-ao 方宗鰲. 'Chin-chih mien-hua ch'u-k'ou chih wo-chien' 禁止棉花出口之我見 (My viewpoint on the ban of exportation of raw cotton). *SHCK*, 1.1 (Feb. 1923) 1–3 (sep. pag.)

Feetham, Richard. *Report of the Hon. Richard Feetham to the Shanghai Municipal Council*. 2 vols. Shanghai: North-China Daily News and Herald, 1931

Feng Hsueh-feng 馮雪峯. *Hui-i Lu Hsun* 回憶魯迅 (Reminiscence of Lu Hsun). Peking: Jen-min wen-hsueh 人民文學, 1952

Feng Yü-hsiang 馮玉祥. *Wo ti sheng-huo* 我的生活 (My life). 3 vols. Canton: Yü-chou-feng she 宇宙風社, 1939; many later editions

FEQ: Far Eastern Quarterly

Feuerwerker, Albert. *China's early industrialization, Sheng Hsuan-huai 1844–1916 and mandarin enterprise*. Cambridge, Mass.: Harvard University Press, 1958

Feuerwerker, Albert, Rhoads Murphey and Mary C. Wright, eds. *Approaches to modern Chinese history*. Berkeley: University of California Press, 1967

Feuerwerker, A. 'Handicraft and manufactured cotton textiles in China, 1871–1910'. *Journal of Economic History*, 30.2 (June 1970) 338–78

Feuerwerker, A. 'Economic trends in the late Ch'ing empire, 1870–1911', in J. K. Fairbank and Kwang-Ching Liu, eds. *Cambridge history of China*, vol. 11, *Late Ch'ing, 1800–1911*, Part 2. Cambridge: Cambridge University Press, 1980

Feuerwerker, A. *The foreign establishment in China in the early twentieth century*. Ann Arbor: Center for Chinese Studies, University of Michigan, 1976

Feuerwerker, Yi-tsi 梅儀慈. 'Women as writers in the 1920s and 1930s', in Margery Wolf and Roxane Witke, eds. *Women in Chinese society*, 143–68. Stanford: Stanford University Press, 1975

Feuerwerker, Yi-tsi. 'The changing relationship between literature and life: aspects of the writer's role in Ding Ling', in Merle Goldman, ed. *Modern Chinese literature in the May Fourth era*, 281–308. Cambridge, Mass.: Harvard University Press, 1977

Fewsmith, Joseph. 'Merchant associations and the establishment of Nationalist rule in Shanghai', paper prepared for the annual meeting of the Association for Asian Studies, Chicago, 31 March–2 April 1968

'First proclamation of the revolutionary government on the farmers' movement', in *Chung-kuo Kuo-min-tang chung-yao hsuan-yen hui-pien* (q.v.) 247–51

Fischer, Louis. *The soviets in world affairs: a history of the relations between the Soviet Union and the rest of the world*. 2 vols. London and New York: Jonathan Cape, 1930

Fischer, Louis. *Men and politics: an autobiography*. New York: Duell, Sloan and Pearce, 1941

Fitzgerald, Stephen. 'Sources on Kuomintang and Republican China', in Donald D. Leslie, Colin Mackerras and Wang Gungwu, eds. *Essays on the sources for Chinese history*, 229–40. Columbia, South Carolina: University of South Carolina Press, 1973

Fokkema, Douwe W. 'Lu Xun: the impact of Russian literature', in Merle Goldman, ed. *Modern Chinese literature in the May Fourth era*, 89–102. Cambridge, Mass.: Harvard University Press, 1977

Fong, H. D. (Fang Hsien-t'ing) 方顯廷. *Cotton industry and trade in China*. 2 vols. Tientsin: Chihli Press, 1932

Fong, H. D. *Reminiscences of a Chinese economist at 70*. Singapore: South Seas Press, 1975

Forsythe, Sidney A. *An American missionary community in China, 1895–1905*. Cambridge, Mass.: Harvard University Press, 1971

Freedman, Maurice. *Lineage organization in southeastern China*. Monographs on Social Anthropology, no. 18, London School of Economics; reprinted with corrections, University of London, 1965

Freedman, Maurice. *The study of Chinese society: essays by Maurice Freedman*, selected and introduced by G. William Skinner. Stanford: Stanford University Press, 1979

Friedman, Edward. *Backward toward revolution: the Chinese Revolutionary Party*. Berkeley: University of California Press, 1974

Fung Yu-lan 馮友蘭. *Hsin shih lun* 新事論 (New culture and society). Changsha, 1941; 3rd printing Shanghai: Commercial Press, 1948

Furet, François. *Penser la Révolution française*. Paris: Gallimard, 1978

Furth, Charlotte. *Ting Wen-chiang: science and China's new culture*. Cambridge, Mass.: Harvard University Press, 1970

Furth, Charlotte, ed. *The limits of change: essays on conservative alternatives in Republican China*. Cambridge, Mass.: Harvard University Press, 1976

Gaimushō. See Japan, Ministry of Foreign Affairs

Gale, Esson M. *Salt for the dragon: a personal history of China, 1908–45*. East Lansing: Michigan State College Press, 1953

Galik, Marian. *Mao Tun and modern Chinese literary criticism*. Wiesbaden: Franz Steiner, 1969

Garrett, Shirley. *Social reformers in urban China: the Chinese Y.M.C.A., 1895–1926*. Cambridge, Mass.: Harvard University Press, 1970

Gasster, Michael. *Chinese intellectuals and the Revolution of 1911: the birth of modern Chinese radicalism*. Seattle: University of Washington Press, 1969

Gauss, C. E. 'Labor, student and agitator movements in Shanghai during February, 1927'. Dispatch dated 9 April 1927, in U.S. Department of State. Records relating to the internal affairs of China, 1910–29. USNA 893.00/8822

Gauss, C. E. 'Political conditions in the Shanghai consular district'. Dispatch covering period 21 March to 20 April 1927, in U.S. Department of State. Records relating to the internal affairs of China, 1910–29. USNA 893.00/8906

Gibbs, Donald and Li, Yun-chen, eds. *A bibliography of studies and translations of modern Chinese literature, 1918–1942*. Cambridge, Mass.: East Asian Research

Center, Harvard University. Distributed by Harvard University Press, 1975

Gillin, Donald G. *Warlord: Yen Hsi-shan in Shansi province 1911–1949*. Princeton: Princeton University Press, 1967

GLU: General Labour Union

Glunin, V. I. 'Komintern i stanovlenie kommunisticheskogo dvizheniia v Kitae (1920–1927)'. (The Comintern and the formation of the communist movement in China (1920–1927)). *Komintern i Vostok; bor'ba za Leninskuiu strategiiu i taktiku v natsional'no-osvoboditel'nom dvizhenii* (Comintern and the Orient; the struggle for the Leninist strategy and tactics in the national liberational movement). Moscow: Glav. Red. Vost. Lit., 1969, 242–99

Goldblatt, Howard. *Hsiao Hung*. New York: Twayne, 1976

Goldman. See Goldman, Merle, ed. *Modern Chinese literature in the May Fourth era*. Cambridge, Mass.: Harvard University Press, 1977

Goldman, Merle. *Literary dissent in Communist China*. Cambridge, Mass.: Harvard University Press, 1967

Gotz, Michael. 'The development of modern Chinese literature studies in the West: a critical review'. *Modern China*, 2.3 (July 1976) 397–416

Great Britain. Foreign Office. Archives, Public Record Office, London; cited as FO

Great Britain. Foreign Office. comd. 2636, China No. 1 (1926). *Papers respecting the first firing in the Shameen affair of June 23, 1925*. London: H. M. Stationery Office, 1926

Great Britain. Foreign Office. Comd. 2953. China No. 4 (1927). *Papers relating to the Nanking Incident of March 24 and 25, 1927*. London: H. M. Stationery Office, 1927

Great Britain. Foreign Office. 405/240–259. Confidential. *Further correspondence respecting China*. Jan.-June 1923–Oct.-Dec. 1928

Greene, Ruth Altman. *Hsiang-Ya journal*. Hamden, Conn.: Shoe String Press, 1977

Grieder, Jerome B. *Hu Shih and the Chinese renaissance: liberalism in the Chinese revolution, 1917–1937*. Cambridge, Mass.: Harvard University Press, 1970

Grove, Linda. 'Rural society: the Gaoyang district 1910–1947'. University of California, Ph.D. dissertation. Berkeley, 1975

Gruber, Helmut. *Soviet Russia masters the Comintern*. Garden City, N.Y.: Anchor Press/Doubleday, 1974

Guillermaz, Jacques. *A history of the Chinese Communist Party, 1921–1949*. New York: Random House, 1972. Trans. of *Histoire du parti communiste chinois 1921–49*. Paris: Payot, 1968

Gunn, Edward Mansfield, Jr. 'Chinese writers under Japanese occupation (1937–45)'. Report on research in progress, Columbia University, Sept. 1976

Gunn, Edward Mansfield, Jr. 'Chinese literature in Shanghai and Peking (1937–45)'. Columbia University, Ph.D. dissertation, 1978

Hanan, Patrick. 'The technique of Lu Hsun's fiction'. *Harvard Journal of Asiatic Studies*, 34 (1975)53–96

Hao, Yen-p'ing 郝延平. *The comprador in nineteenth century China: bridge between East and West.* Cambridge, Mass.: Harvard University Press, 1970

Harrison, James Pinckney. *The long march to power: a history of the Chinese Communist Party, 1921–72.* New York & Washington, D.C.: Praeger, 1972

Hashikawa Tokio 橋川時雄. *Chūgoku bunkakai jimbutsu sōkan* 中國文化界人物總鑑 (Biographical dictionary of Chinese cultural personalities). Peking: Chunghua fa-ling pien-yin-kuan 中華法令編印館, 1940

Hatano Ken'ichi 波多野乾一, comp. *Gendai Shina no kiroku* 現代支那之記錄 (Records of contemporary China). Monthly. Peking: Enjinsha 燕塵社, 1924–32

Hatano Ken'ichi. *Shina Kyōsantōshi* 支那共産党史 (A history of the Chinese Communist Party), 7 vols., 1st vol. published in 1931, the last, 1937, by Gaimushō, Jōhōbu 情報部; reprinted as *Chūgoku Kyōsantōshi* 中国共産党史. Tokyo: Jiji tsushinsha 時事通信社, 1961

Hatano Yoshihiro 波多野善大. *Chūgoku kindai gumbatsu no kenkyū* 中国近代軍閥の研究 (Studies on the warlords of modern China). Tokyo: Kawade Shobo Shinsha 河出書房新社, 1973

Heinzig, Dieter. *Sowjetische militärberater bei der Kuomintang 1923–1927.* Baden-Baden: Momos Verlagsgesellschaft, 1978

Heng-feng sha-ch'ang ti fa-sheng fa-chan yü kai-tsao: Chung-kuo tsui-tsao ti i-chia mien-fang-chih-ch'ang 恒豐紗廠的發生發展與改造：中國最早的一家棉紡織廠 (The birth, growth and reform of the Heng-feng cotton mill: China's earliest cotton spinning and weaving factory), ed. by Chung-kuo k'o-hsueh yuan, Shang-hai ching-chi yen-chiu-so 中國科學院上海經濟研究所 and Shang-hai she-hui k'o-hsueh-yuan, Ching-chi yen-chiu-so 上海社會科學院經濟研究所. Shanghai: Shang-hai Jen-min, 1958

Hewlitt, Sir Meyrick. *Forty years in China.* London: Macmillan, 1943

Hidy, Ralph W. and Hidy, Muriel E. *Pioneering in big business, 1882–1911.* New York: Harper, 1955

Higham, John. 'The matrix of specialization', in Alexandra Oleson and John Voss, eds. *The organization of knowledge in modern America, 1860–1920*, 3–18. Baltimore and London: The Johns Hopkins University Press, 1979

History of the First Army Group. See *Kuo-min Ko-ming Chün Ti-i Chi-t'uan Chün* . . .

Ho Ch'ang-kung 何長工. *Ch'in-kung chien-hsueh sheng-huo hui-i* 勤工儉學生活回憶 (Memoirs of the work-study programme). Peking: Kung-jen ch'u-pan-she 工人出版社, 1958

Ho Chen 何震. 'Nü-tzu fu-ch'ou lun' 女子復仇論 (On women's revenge). *T'ien-i*, 3 (10 July 1907) 7–23

Ho Chen. 'Lun nü-tzu tang chih kung-ch'an chu-i' 論女子當知共產主義 (On why women should know about communism). *T'ien-i*, 8–10 (30 Oct. 1907) 229–32

Ho Kan-chih 何幹之, ed. *Chung-kuo hsien-tai ko-ming shih* 中國現代革命史 (A history of the modern Chinese revolution). Peking: Kao-teng chiao-yü ch'u-pan-she 高等教育出版社, 1957; Hong Kong: San-lien, 1958; English edn, 1959

Ho Lin 賀麟. *Tang-tai Chung-kuo che-hsueh* 當代中國哲學 (Contemporary Chinese philosophy). Nanking: Sheng-li ch'u-pan kung-ssu 勝利出版公司, 1947

Ho Ping-ti 何炳棣. 'The salt merchants of Yang-chou: a study of commercial capitalism in eighteenth century China'. *Harvard Journal of Asiatic Studies*, 17 (1954) 130–68

Ho Ping-ti. *Studies on the population of China 1368–1953*. Cambridge, Mass.: Harvard University Press, 1959

Ho Ping-ti. *The ladder of success in imperial China: aspects of social mobility, 1368–1911*. New York: Columbia University Press, 1962

Ho Ping-ti and Tsou Tang 鄒讜, eds. *China in crisis*. 3 vols. Chicago: University of Chicago Press, 1968

Hobart, Alice Tisdale. *Within the walls of Nanking*. London: Jonathan Cape, 1928

Hofheinz, Roy, Jr. 'The Autumn Harvest uprising'. *CQ*, 32 (Oct.–Dec. 1967) 37–87

Hofheinz, Roy, Jr. *The broken wave: the Chinese communist peasant movement, 1922–1928*. Cambridge, Mass.: Harvard University Press, 1977

Holden, Reuben. *Yale in China: the mainland, 1901–1951*. New Haven: The Yale in China Association, 1964

Holoch, Donald, trans. *Seeds of peasant revolution: report on the Haifeng peasant movement by P'eng P'ai*. Ithaca: Cornell University China-Japan Program, 1973

Holubnychy, Lydia. *Michael Borodin and the Chinese revolution, 1923–1925*. Ann Arbor: University Microfilms International, 1979. Published for the East Asian Institute, Columbia University

Hou, Chi-ming 侯繼明. *Foreign investment and economic development in China, 1840–1937*. Cambridge, Mass.: Harvard University Press, 1965

Hou Chien 侯健. *Ts'ung wen-hsueh ko-ming tao ko-ming wen-hsueh* 從文學革命到革命文學 (From literary revolution to revolutionary literature). Taipei: Chung-wai wen-hsueh yueh-k'an she 中外文學月刊社, 1974

Hou Wai-lu 侯外廬. *Chin-tai Chung-kuo ssu-hsiang hsueh-shuo shih* 近代中國思想學說史 (Interpretive history of modern Chinese thought). Shanghai: Sheng-huo, 1947

Hou Wai-lu *et al. Chung-kuo chin-tai che-hsueh shih* 中國近代哲學史 (History of modern Chinese philosophy). Peking: Hsin-hua shu-tien 新華書店, 1978

Houn, Franklin W. *Central government of China, 1912–1928: an institutional study*. Madison: University of Wisconsin Press, 1957

Howard, Richard C. 'The concept of parliamentary government in 19th century China: a preliminary survey'. Paper delivered to University Seminar on Modern East Asia – China and Japan, Columbia University, New York, 9 Jan. 1963.

Howe, Christopher. *Wage patterns and wage policy in modern China, 1919–1972*. Cambridge: Cambridge University Press, 1972

Howe, Christopher, ed. *Shanghai: revolution and development in an Asian metropolis*. Cambridge: Cambridge University Press, 1981

Howe, Irving, ed. *The idea of the modern in literature and the arts.* New York: Horizon Press, 1967

Hsia, C. T. 'The travels of Lao Ts'an: an exploration of its art and meaning'. *Tsing Hua Journal of Chinese Studies,* NS 7.2 (Aug. 1966) 40–66

Hsia, C. T. *A history of modern Chinese fiction.* New Haven: Yale University Press, 2nd edn, 1971

Hsia Chih-ch'ing 夏志清. *Chung-kuo hsien-tai hsiao-shuo shih* 中國現代小説史 (A history of modern Chinese fiction), trans. from English by Liu Shao-ming 劉紹明 (Joseph S. M. Lau) *et al.* Hong Kong: Yu-lien shu-tien 友聯書店, 1979

Hsia, C. T. 'Obsession with China: the moral burden of modern Chinese literature', in his *A history of modern Chinese fiction,* 533–54

Hsia, C. T., ed. *Twentieth-century Chinese stories.* New York: Columbia University Press, 1971

Hsia, C. T. 'The fiction of Tuan-mu Hung-liang', paper delivered at the Dedham conference on modern Chinese literature (Aug. 1974)

Hsia, C. T. 'Yen Fu and Liang Ch'i-ch'ao as advocates of new fiction', in Adele A. Rickett, ed. *Chinese approaches to literature from Confucius to Liang Ch'i-ch'ao,* 251–57. Princeton: Princeton University Press, 1978

Hsia, C. T., Lau, Joseph and Lee, Leo, eds. *Modern Chinese stories and novellas, 1919–1949.* New York: Columbia University Press, 1980

Hsia Tseng-yu 夏曽佑. *Chung-kuo li-shih chiao-k'o-shu* 中國歷史教科書 (Textbook on Chinese history).

Hsia, Tsi-an. *The gate of darkness: studies on the leftist literary movement in China.* Seattle: University of Washington Press, 1968

Hsiang-chiang p'ing-lun 湘江評論 (Hsiang River review). Changsha, 14 July 1919–

Hsiang-tao chou-pao 嚮導週報 (The guide weekly). Shanghai and Canton: Chung-kuo Kung-ch'an-tang, Sept. 1923–July 1927

Hsiao Chün. See T'ien Chun

Hsiao Hung 蕭紅. *Two novels of northeastern China: the field of life and death and tales of Hulan River,* trans. by Howard Goldblatt. Bloomington: Indiana University Press, 1979

Hsiao Kung-ch'üan 蕭公權. *Chung-kuo cheng-chih ssu-hsiang shih* 中國政治思想史 (A history of Chinese political thought). Vol. 1, Chungking, April 1945, Shanghai, Dec. 1945; vol. 2, Shanghai, 1946, Taipei: Chung-hua ta-tien pien-yin-hui 中華大典編印會, 1964

Hsiao, Kung-chuan. *A modern China and a new world: K'ang Yu-wei, reformer and utopian 1858–1927.* Seattle: University of Washington Press, 1975

Hsiao Kung-chuan. *A history of Chinese political thought. Volume one: from the beginnings to the sixth century A.D.,* trans. by F. W. Mote. Princeton: Princeton University Press, 1979

Hsiao Liang-lin. *China's foreign trade statistics, 1864–1949.* Cambridge, Mass.: Harvard University Press, 1974

Hsiao Tso-liang, 'The dispute over a Wuhan insurrection in 1927'. *CQ,* 33 (Jan.–March 1968) 108–22

Hsiao Tso-liang. *Chinese communism in 1927: city vs. countryside*. Hong Kong: The Chinese University of Hong Kong, 1970

Hsieh Pen-shu 謝本書. 'Lun Ts'ai O' 論蔡鍔 (On Ts'ai O). *Li-shih yen-chiu* 歷史研究 (Historical studies) (Nov. 1979) 47–61.

Hsieh Ping-ying. *Autobiography of a Chinese girl*, trans. by Tsui Chi. London: Allen & Unwin, 1943

Hsieh, Winston 謝文蓀. 'The ideas and ideals of a warlord: Ch'en Chiung-ming (1878–1933)'. *Papers on China*, 16 (Dec. 1962) 198–252

Hsieh, Winston W. 'The economics of warlordism'. *Chinese Republican Studies Newsletter*, 1.1 (Oct. 1975) 15–21

Hsien K'o 獻可. *Chin pai-nien-lai ti-kuo chu-i tsai-Hua yin-hang fa-hsing chih-pi kai-k'uang* 近百年來帝國主義在華銀行發行紙幣概況 (The issue of bank notes in China by imperialist banks in the past 100 years). Shanghai: Jen-min, 1958

Hsin ch'ing-nien 新青年 (New youth). Sept. 1915-July 1926. Reprinted Tokyo: Daian, 1962

Hsin-hai ko-ming 辛亥革命 (The 1911 Revolution), comp. by Chung-kuo shih-hsueh-hui 中國史學會 (Chinese Historical Association). 8 vols. Shanghai: Jen-min, 1957

Hsin-hai ko-ming hui-i-lu 辛亥革命回憶錄 (Memoirs of the 1911 Revolution), comp. by Chung-kuo jen-min cheng-chih hsieh-shang hui-i ch'üan-kuo wei-yuan-hui wen-shih tzu-liao yen-chiu wei-yuan-hui 中國人民政治協商會議全國委員會文史資料研究委員會. 5 vols. Peking: Chung-hua, 1961–3

Hsin-hai shou-i hui-i-lu 辛亥首義回憶錄 (Memoirs of the initial uprising of 1911), ed. by Chung-kuo jen-min cheng-chih hsieh-shang hui-i Hu-pei-sheng wei-yuan-hui 中國人民政治協商會議湖北省委員會 (Hupei committee of the Chinese People's Political Consultative Conference). 3 vols. Wuhan: Hu-pei jen-min ch'u-pan-she, 1957–8

Hsin kuan-ch'a 新觀察 (New observer). Peking, 1 July 1950–

Hsin-min-hsueh-hui hui-yuan t'ung-hsin-chi 新民學會會員通信集 (Correspondence of members of the New Citizens' Society), in *Wu-ssu shih-ch'i ch'i-k'an chieh-shao* 五四時期期刊介紹, 1.154–5

Hsin-min ts'ung-pao 新民叢報 (New people's journal), 1–96 (8 Feb. 1902–20 Nov. 1907); reprinted in 17 volumes by I-wen yin-shu-kuan 藝文印書館, Taipei, 1966

Hsin she-hui 新社會 (New society). Peking, Nov. 1913–

Hsin shih-chi 新世紀 (New century), 22 June 1908–11 Dec. 1908; reprinted in *Chung-kuo tzu-liao ts'ung-shu* 中國資料叢書 (A collection of materials on China), series 6, no. 1 in *Chung-kuo ch'u-ch'i she-hui chu-i wen-hsien chi* 中國初期社會主義文獻集 (A collection of documents on early Chinese socialism). Tokyo: Daian, 1966

Hsin Shu-pao 新蜀報 (New Szechwan daily). Chungking, 1 Feb. 1921–

HSSC: Hua-shang sha-ch'ang lien-ho-hui chi-k'an

Hsu Chen-ya 徐枕亞. *Yü-li hun* 玉黎魂 (Jade pear spirit). Shanghai: Ta-chung shu-chü 大衆書局, 1939

Hsu I-sheng 徐義生. *Chung-kuo chin-tai wai-chai shih t'ung-chi tzu-liao, 1853-1927* 中國近代外債史統計資料, 1853-1927 (Statistical materials on foreign loans in modern China, 1853-1927). Peking:Chung-hua, 1962

Hsu, Kai-yu, trans. and ed. *Twentieth-century Chinese poetry: an anthology.* New York: Anchor, 1964

Hsu Tao-lin 徐道鄰. *Hsu Shu-cheng hsien-sheng wen-chi nien-p'u ho-k'an* 徐樹錚先生文集年譜合刊 (Selected writings and chronological biography of Mr Hsu Shu-cheng). Taipei: Commercial Press, 1962

Hsu Ti-hsin 許滌新. *Kuan-liao tzu-pen lun* 官僚資本論 (On the subject of bureaucratic capitalism). Hong Kong: Nan-yang shu-tien 南洋書店, 1947

Hsu Ying, 徐盈, ed. *Tang-tai Chung-kuo shih-yeh jen-wu chih* 當代中國實業人物志 (Biographies of modern Chinese economic leaders). Shanghai: Chung-hua, 1948

Hsueh Chün-tu 薛君度, comp. *Chinese communist movement, 1921-1937.* Stanford: Hoover Institution on War, Revolution and Peace, Stanford University, 1960

Hsueh, Chün-tu. *Huang Hsing and the Chinese revolution.* Stanford: Stanford University Press, 1961

Hsueh, Chün-tu, ed. *Revolutionary leaders of modern China.* New York: Oxford University Press, 1971

Hsueh Fu-ch'eng 薛福成. *Ch'ou-yang ch'u-i* 籌洋芻議 (Preliminary proposals on foreign affairs, 1886); partially reprinted in Yang Chia-lo, vol. 1, 151-61

Hsueh-hen 血痕 (Bloody scars). No. 2 (19 June 1925); no. 3 (12 July 1925). Shanghai: Association des étudiants de l'école technique des Beaux Arts.

HTCP: Hsiang-tao chou-pao

Hu Ch'iao-mu 胡喬木. *Chung-kuo Kung-ch'an-tang ti san-shih-nien* 中國共產黨的三十年 (Thirty years of the Chinese Communist Party). Peking: Jen-min, 1951

Hu Feng 胡風. *Min-tsu chan-cheng yü wen-i hsing-ko* 民族戰爭與文藝性格 (The national war and the character of literature). Chungking: Hsi-wang she 希望社, 1946

Hu Han-min 胡漢民. *Hu Han-min hsien-sheng yen-chiang chi* 胡漢民先生演講集 (Collection of Mr Hu Han-min's speeches). 4 vols. in 1. Shanghai: Min-chih shu-chü 民智書局, 1927

Hu Han-min. *Hu Han-min hsuan-chi* 胡漢民選集 (Selected writings of Hu Han-min). Taipei: P'a-mi-erh shu-tien 帕米爾書店, 1959

Hu Hua 胡華, ed. *Chung-kuo hsin-min-chu-chu-i ko-ming-shih ts'an-k'ao tzu-liao* 中國新民主主義革命史參考資料 (Historical materials on the Chinese new democratic revolution). Shanghai: CP, 1951

Hu, John Y. H. *Ts'ao Yü.* New York: Twayne, 1972

Hu-nan li-shih tzu-liao 湖南歷史資料 (Historical materials of Hunan). Quarterly. Changsha: Hu-nan jen-min ch'u-pan she, 1958–

Hu-nan shih-yeh tsa-chih 湖南實業雜誌 (The industrial magazine). Bimonthly. Changsha, 1918-35

Hu Shih 胡適. 'Wo-men ti cheng-chih chu-chang' 我們的政治主張 (Our political proposals). *NLCP*, 2 (14 May 1922)

Hu Shih. 'Ting Wen-chiang ti chuan-chi' 丁文江的傳記 (A biography of Ting Wen-chiang), in Chung-yang yen-chiu-yuan yuan-k'an 中央研究院院刊, no. 3, 1956. Also separately printed, n.p., n.d.

Hu Shih. 'Pi-shang Liang-shan' 逼上梁山 (Forced to the Liang mountain), in his *Ssu-shih tzu-shu* 四十自述 (Autobiography at forty), 91–122. Shanghai, 1933; Taipei reprint: Yuan-tung t'u-shu kung-ssu 遠東圖書公司, 1967

Hu Shih. *The Chinese renaissance.* Chicago: University of Chicago Press, 1934

Hu Shih. *Hu Shih wen-ts'un* 胡適文存 (Collected works of Hu Shih). 4 vols. Taipei: Yuan-tung t'u-shu kung-ssu 遠東圖書公司, 1953

Hu Shih. 'Wu-shih-nien-lai Chung-kuo chih wen-hsueh' 五十年來中國之文學 (Chinese literature of the past fifty years), in *Hu Shih wen-ts'un* 胡適文存 (Collected works of Hu Shih), 2.180–260. Taipei: Yuan-tung t'u-shu kung-ssu 遠東圖書公司, 1953

Hua-ch'iao jih-pao (Wah Kiu Yat Po) 華僑日報 (Overseas Chinese daily news). Hong Kong, 1926–

Hua Kang 華崗. *Chung-kuo min-tsu chieh-fang yun-tung shih* 中國民族解放運動史 (A history of the Chinese national liberation movement). 2 vols. Shanghai: Chi-ming 雞鳴 and Tu Shu 讀書, 1940. (Many later edns.)

Hua Kang. *Wu-ssu yun-tung shih* 五四運動史 (History of the May Fourth movement). Shanghai: Hai-yen shu-tien 海燕書店, 1951; rev. edn, 1952

Hua Kang. See Amano Motonosuke

Hua-shang sha-ch'ang lien-ho-hui chi-k'an 華商紗廠聯合會季刊 (The China cotton journal). Shanghai: Chinese Cotton Millowners Association, Sept. 1919–Oct. 1930

Hua-tzu jih-pao 華字日報 (The Chinese mail). Hong Kong, 1864–

Huang Chieh 黃節. 'Huang shih' 黃史 (Yellow history). *Kuo-ts'ui hsueh-pao* 國粹學報 (National essence journal), nos. 1–9 (1905)

Huang, Philip 黃宗智. *Liang Ch'i-ch'ao and modern Chinese liberalism.* Seattle: University of Washington Press, 1972

Huang Shao-hsiung (Huang Shao-hung) 黃紹竑. *Wu-shih hui-i* 五十回憶 (Recollections at fifty). Hangchow: Yun-feng ch'u-pan she 雲風出版社, 1945; Hong Kong reprint, 1969

Huang Shih-hui 黃世暉. 'Ts'ai Chieh-min chuan-lueh' 蔡孑民傳略 (Biographic sketch of Ts'ai Yuan-p'ei), in *Ts'ai Chieh-min hsien-sheng yen-hsing-lu* 蔡孑民先生言行錄 (Mr Ts'ai Yuan-p'ei's words and deeds), 1–36. Peking: Hsin-ch'ao-she 新潮社, 1920; Taipei reprint: Wen-hai, 1973

Huang Sung-k'ang. *Lu Hsun and the new culture movement of modern China.* Amsterdam: Djambatan, 1967

Huang Sung-k'ang. *Li Ta-chao and the impact of Marxism on modern Chinese thinking.* The Hague: Mouton, 1965

Huang Yuan-yung 黃遠庸. *Yuan-sheng i-chu* 遠生遺著 (Posthumous collection of writings of Huang Yuan-yung). 1920; Taipei reprint: Wen-hsing, 2 vols., 1962

Hummel, A. W., ed. *Eminent Chinese of the Ch'ing period, 1644–1912.* 2 vols. Washington: United States Government Printing Office, 1943–4

Hung-ch'i p'iao-p'iao 紅旗飄飄 (Red flags flying). 16 vols. Peking: Chung-kuo ch'ing-nien ch'u-pan-she 中國青年出版社, 1957–61

Hung-se wen-hsien 紅色文獻 (Red documents). n.p., 1938

Huston, J. Calvin. 'Peasants, workers, and soldiers revolt of December 11–13, 1927 at Canton, China'. Dispatch no. 669 to J. V. A. MacMurray, U. S. Minister to Peking, 30 Dec. 1927. In Hoover Institution on War, Revolution, and Peace, Stanford, California, J. Calvin Huston Collection, Package II, Part II, Folder 5, Item 20.

Hutchison, James L. *China hand.* Boston: Lothrop, Lee, and Shepard, 1936

Imperial Japanese Government Railways. *An official guide to Eastern Asia,* vol. 4, *China.* Tokyo, 1915

'Important documents of the Western Hills Conference expelling communists from the Kuomintang, November 1925'. *Kuo-wen chou-pao,* 4.14 (17 April 1927) 14–16

Imprecor. See *International Press Correspondence*

Institute of Modern History, Academia Sinica, Taipei. See Chung-yang yen-chiu-yuan chin-tai-shih yen-chiu-so

International Commission of Judges, 1925. *A report of the proceedings of the International Commission of Judges.* Shanghai: reprinted from *Shanghai Mercury,* 1925

International Press Correspondence. Organ of the Executive Committee of the Communist International. English edn

Iriye, Akira, ed. *The Chinese and the Japanese: Essays on Political and Cultural Interactions.* Princeton, N.J.: Princeton University Press, 1980

Iriye, Akira. *After imperialism: the search for a new order in the Far East, 1921–1931.* Cambridge, Mass.: Harvard University Press, 1965

Isaacs, Harold R. *The tragedy of the Chinese revolution.* 1st edn, London: Secker and Warburg, 1938; rev. edn, Stanford; Stanford University Press, 1951

Isaacs, Harold R. 'Documents on the Comintern and the Chinese revolution'. *CQ,* 54 (Jan.-March 1971) 100–15

Itō Toramaru 伊藤虎丸 *Ro Jin to shūmatsuron* 魯迅と終末論 (Final assessment of Lu Hsun). Tokyo: Ryūkei shosha 竜溪書舎, 1975

'Iz istorii severnogo pokhoda Natsional'no-Revolutskionnoi Armii' (From the history of the Northern Expedition of the National Revolutionary Army), *Istoricheskii Arkhiv,* 4 (1959) 113–26

Jacobs, Dan. *Borodin: Stalin's man in China.* Cambridge, Mass.: Harvard University Press, 1981

Jamieson, George. 'Tenure of land in China and the condition of the rural population'. *Journal of the North China Branch of the Royal Asiatic Society,* 23 (1889) 59–117

Japan. Ministry of Foreign Affairs. Archives at the Gaikō Shiryōkan 外交史料館, Tokyo, and microfilm at the Library of Congress, Washington, D.C.

Japan. Ministry of Foreign Affairs (Gaimushō) 外務省. *Nihon gaikō nempyō narabi ni shuyō bunsho* 日本外交年表並主要文書 (Important documents and chronological tables of Japanese diplomacy). 2 vols., 1955

Japan. Ministry of Foreign Affairs (Gaimushō). *Shina ni oite Nihon shōhin dōmei haiseki ikken. zakken* 支那ニ於テ日本商品同盟排斥一件, 雜件 (The boycotting of Japanese goods in China; various matters). Series M.T.3.3.8.5–1 (1919)

Japan. Ministry of Foreign Affairs (Gaimushō). Asia Bureau (Ajiyakyoku) 亞細亞局. *Shina yōhei gaikokujin jimmeiroku* 支那傭聘外國人人名錄 (List of foreign employees of China). Tokyo, 1925

Japan. Ministry of Foreign Affairs (Gaimushō). Asia Bureau (Ajiyakyoku). Biographical dictionaries of Chinese with various titles were published in 1937, 1953 and 1972

Japan. Ministry of Foreign Affairs. Office of Trade, second section. *Shina kin'yū jijō* 支那金融事情 (The financial situation in China). Tokyo: Gaimushō tsūshōkyoku dainika, March 1925

JAS: Journal of Asian Studies

Jaynes, Julian. *The origin of consciousness in the breakdown of the bicameral mind.* Boston: Houghton Mifflin, 1976

Jeans, Roger B. 'Syncretism in defense of Confucianism: an intellectual and political biography of the early years of Chang Chün-mai, 1887–1923'. George Washington University, Ph.D. dissertation, 1974

Johnson, Chalmers. *Peasant nationalism and communist power: the emergence of revolutionary China, 1937–1945.* Stanford: Stanford University Press, 1962

Johnson, David G. *The medieval Chinese oligarchy.* Boulder, Colorado: Westview Press, 1977

Johnston, Reginald F. *Twilight in the Forbidden City.* London: Victor Gollancz, 1934

Jones, Susan. 'Finance in Ningpo: the "ch'ien-chuang", 1780–1880', in W. E. Willmott, ed. *Economic organization in Chinese society*; 47–77. Stanford: Stanford University Press, 1972

Jordan, Donald A. *The Northern Expedition: China's national revolution of 1926–1928.* Honolulu: University Press of Hawaii, 1976

Journal of Asian Studies, 1956– (formerly *Far Eastern Quarterly*, 1941–56)

Ju Hsuan 茹玄. 'Hsin yin-hang-t'uan yü ching-chi kua-fen' 新銀行團與經濟瓜分 (The New Consortium and the economic dismemberment of China). *TSHYP*, 1.6 (Dec. 1921) heading *Yen-lun*

Ju Hsuan. 'Kuan yü kuo-shih hui-i chih p'ien-yen' 關於國是會議之片言 (A few notes on the subject of the Convention on National Affairs). *TSHYP*, 1.5 (Nov. 1921) heading *Yen-lun*

June Twenty-third: the report of the Commission for the Investigation of the Shakee Massacre June 23, 1925, Canton China. Canton: Wah On Printing Co., n.d.

Jung Te-sheng 榮德生. *Lo-nung tzu-ting hsing-nien chi-shih* 樂農自訂行年紀事 (An autobiographical chronology by Jung Te-sheng)

Kagan, Richard C. 'Ch'en Tu-hsiu's unfinished autobiography'. *CQ*, 50 (April–June 1972) 295–314

Kagawa Shun'ichirō 香川峻一郎. *Sensō shihon ron* 錢莊資本論 (On [Chinese] money shop capital). Tokyo: Jitsugyō no Nihonsha 実業之日本社, 1948

Kamachi, Noriko 蒲地典子, Fairbank, John K. and Ichiko Chūzō 市古宙三, eds. *Japanese studies of modern China since 1953: a bibliographical guide to historical and social-science research on the 19th and 20th centuries.* Cambridge, Mass.: East Asian Research Center, Harvard University, 1975

K'ang Yu-wei 康有為. *Ta-t'ung shu* 大同書 (Book of the Great Commonwealth). Shanghai: Chung-hua, 1935

K'ang Yu-wei. Trans. by Laurence G. Thompson. *Ta Tung Shu: Book of the Great Commonwealth.* London: Allen & Unwin, 1958

K'ang Yu-wei. 'Chung-hua chiu-kuo lun' 中華救國論 (On China's salvation). *Pu-jen tsa-chih* 不忍雜誌, 1 (March 1913) 21-2

K'ang Yu-wei. 'Ta-chieh-chai po-i' 大借債駁議 (A critique of the large loan). *Min-kuo ching-shih wen-pien* 民國經世文編 (Republican essays on public affairs), 1913. Taipei: Wen-hsing reprint, 4 vols., 1962, 3.893-5

Kao Yin-tsu 高蔭祖. *Chung-hua min-kuo ta-shih chi* 中華民國大事記 (Chronology of Republican China). Taipei: Shih-chieh she 世界社, 1957

Kapp, Robert A. *Szechwan and the Chinese Republic: provincial militarism and central power 1911–1938.* New Haven and London: Yale University Press, 1973

Kartunova, A. I. 'Blucher's "grand plan" of 1926', trans. by Jan J. Solecki with notes by C. Martin Wilbur. *CQ*, 35 (July–Sept. 1968) 18–39

Kartunova, A. I. 'Vasilii Blyukher (1889–1938)', in *Vidnye Sovietskie kommunisty – uchastniki Kitaiskoi revolutsii* (The outstanding Soviet communists – participants in the Chinese revolution), 41–65. Moscow: Akad. Nauk SSSR, Institut Dal'nego Vostoka, 'Nauka' 1970

Kasanin, Marc. *China in the twenties.* Trans. from the Russian by Hilda Kasanina. Moscow: Central Department of Oriental Literature, 1973

Kashiwai Kisao. 柏井象雄. *Kindai Shina zaisei shi* 近代支那財政史 (History of modern Chinese finance). Kyoto: Kyōiku Tosho 教育圖書, 1942

Keenan, Barry. *The Dewey experiment in China: educational reform and political power in the early republic.* Cambridge, Mass.: Harvard University Press, 1977

Kelly, Frank. 'The writings of Yeh Sheng-t'ao'. University of Chicago, Ph.D. dissertation, 1979

KFNP: Kuo-fu nien-p'u

Khmeloff, A. 'Journey to Canton in October, 1925'. (A document from the Peking raid of 6 April 1927). Trans. in Jay Calvin Huston Collection, Hoover Institution on War, Revolution and Peace, Stanford, California

Kierman, Frank A., Jr. and Fairbank, John K., eds. *Chinese ways in warfare.* Cambridge, Mass.: Harvard University Press, 1974

Kikuchi Saburō 菊池三郎. *Chūgoku gendai bungaku shi* 中國現代文學史 (History of contemporary Chinese literature). 2 vols. Tokyo: Aoki 青木, 1953

Kikuchi Takaharu 菊池貴晴. *Chūgoku minzoku undō no kihon kōzō – taigai boikotto no kenkyū* 中国民族運動の基本構造―対外ボイコットの研究 (Basic structure of the Chinese national movement – a study of anti-foreign boycotts). Tokyo: Daian, 1966

Kindai Chūgoku kenkyū 近代中國研究 (Studies on modern China), ed. by Kindai

Chūgoku Kenkyū Iinkai 近代中國研究委員會 (The Seminar on Modern China) series. Tokyo: Tōyō Bunko 東洋文庫, 1958–

Kindai Chūgoku nōson shakaishi kenkyū 近代中国農村社会史研究 (Studies on modern Chinese rural social history), in *Tōyōshigaku ronshū* 東洋史学論集 (Studies in oriental history), no. 8. Tokyo: Daian, 1967

King, F. H. *Farmers of forty centuries.* Madison, Wis., 1911; 2nd edn, London: J. Cape, 1927

Kinkley, Jeffrey C. 'Shen Ts'ung-wen's vision of Republican China'. Harvard University, Ph.D. dissertation, 1977

Klein, Donald W. and Clark, Ann B. *Biographic dictionary of Chinese communism, 1921–1965.* 2 vols. Cambridge, Mass.: Harvard University Press, 1965

KMT: Kuomintang

KMT Archives. Chung-kuo Kuo-min-tang chung-yang wei-yuan-hui tang-shih shih-liao pien-tsuan wei-yuan-hui

KMT Department of Organization. *Ti-i-tz'u ch'üan-kuo ta-hui hsuan-yen* 第一次全國大會宣言 (Manifesto of the First National Congress). n.p., Aug. 1927

KMWH: Ko-ming wen-hsien

Ko-ming jen-wu chih 革命人物誌 (Biographies of revolutionary figures), ed. by Chung-kuo Kuo-min-tang chung-yang wei-yuan-hui tang-shih shih-liao pien-tsuan wei-yuan-hui 中國國民黨中央委員會黨史料編纂委員會 (Committee on the composition of party history and documents, Central Committee, KMT) series. Taipei, 1969–

Ko-ming wen-hsien 革命文獻 (Documents of the revolution), comp. by Lo Chia-lun 羅家倫 and others. Taipei: Central Executive Committee of the Chung-kuo Kuomintang, many volumes, 1953–; cited as *KMWH; KMWH* printed in vols. 10–21 excerpts from Ch'en Hsün-cheng, *Kuo-min ko-ming-chün chan-shih ch'u-kao* (q.v.)

Ko-sheng kuang-fu 各省光復 (Restoration in the provinces), comp. by Chung-hua min-kuo k'ai-kuo wu-shih-nien wen-hsien pien-tsuan wei-yuan-hui 中華民國開國五十年文獻編纂委員會. 3 vols. Taipei: Committee on the compilation of documents on the fiftieth anniversary of the founding of the Republic of China, 1962

K'o-hsueh yü jen-sheng kuan 科學與人生觀 (Science and the philosophy of life). Prefaces by Hu Shih 胡適 and Ch'en Tu-hsiu 陳獨秀. Shanghai: Ya-tung 亞東, 1927

Kojima Yoshio 小島淑男. 'Shingai Kakumei ni okeru Shanhai dokuritsu to shōshinsō 辛亥革命における上海独立と商紳層 (The gentry and the merchant classes and Shanghai's independence during the Revolution of 1911). *Tōyō shigaku ronshū*, 6 (Aug. 1960) 113–34. (Special issue: *Chūgoku kindaika no shakai kōzō: Shingai Kakumei no shiteki ichi* 中国近代化の社会構造：辛亥革命の史的位置 [The social structure of Chinese modernization: the historical position of the Revolution of 1911])

Komintern i Vostok: bor'ba za leninskuiu strategiiu i taktiku v natsional'no-osvo-

boditel'nom dvizhenii (Comintern and the Orient: the struggle of the Leninist strategy and tactics in national liberation movements). Moscow: Glav. Red. Vost. Lit., 1969

Konchits, N. I. 'In the ranks of the National Revolutionary Army of China', (in Russian), in *Sovetskiie dobrovoltsy v pervoi grazhdanskoi revolutsionnoi voine v Kitae; vospominaniia* (Soviet volunteers in the First Revolutionary Civil War in China; reminiscences), 24–95. Moscow: Akademiia Nauk SSSR, Institut Narodov Azii, 1961

Kracke, E. A., Jr. *Civil service in early Sung China, 960–1067.* Cambridge, Mass.: Harvard University Press, 1953

Kracke, E. A., Jr. 'Sung society: change within tradition'. *FEQ*, 14.4 (Aug. 1955) 479–88

Krebs, Edward. 'Liu Ssu-fu and Chinese anarchism 1905–15'. University of Washington, Ph.D. dissertation, Seattle, 1977

Krebsova, Berta. *Lu Sün, sa vie et son oeuvre.* Prague, Editions de l'Académie tchécoslovaque des sciences, 1953

Ku Ch'un-fan (Koh Tso-fan). 谷春帆 *Chung-kuo kung-yeh-hua t'ung-lun* 中國工業化通論 (A general discussion of China's industrialization). Shanghai: Commercial Press, 1947

Ku Lang 顧琅. *Chung-kuo shih ta k'uang-ch'ang tiao-ch'a chi* 中國十大礦廠調查記 (Report of an investigation of the 10 largest mines in China). Shanghai, 1916

Kuhn, Philip A. 'Local self-government under the republic: problems of control, autonomy and mobilization', in Frederic Wakeman, Jr. and Carolyn Grant, eds. *Conflict and control in late imperial China*, 257–98. Berkeley: University of California Press, 1975

Kung-ch'an-tang 共產黨 (The Communist party). Shanghai, Nov. 1920–

'Kung-chieh' 工界 (The world of labour), in *Wu-ssu shih-ch'i ch'i-k'an chieh-shao*, 3.300–2

Kung Ch'u 龔楚. *Wo yü Hung-chün* 我與紅軍 (I and the Red Army). Hong Kong: Nan-feng ch'u-pan-she 南風出版社, 1954

Kung-fei huo-kuo shih-liao hui-pien 共匪禍國史料彙編 (A compilation of documents on the communist bandits' destruction of the nation). 4 vols. Taipei: Committee for Compilation of Documents on the Fiftieth anniversary of the Founding of the Republic, 1964

Kung, H. O. 'The growth of population in six large Chinese cities'. *Chinese Economic Journal*, 20.3 (March 1937) 301–14

Kung-jen. See *Ti-i-tz'u kuo-nei ko-ming chan-cheng shih-ch'i ti kung-jen yun-tung.*

Kuo Chan-po 郭湛波. *Chin wu-shih-nien Chung-kuo ssu-hsiang shih* 近五十年中國思想史 (An intellectual history of China in the last fifty years). Peiping: Jen-min, 1936

Kuo-chün cheng-kung shih-kao. See Ministry of Defence

Kuo-fu ch'üan-chi. See Sun Yat-sen

Kuo-fu nien-p'u 國父年譜 (A chronological biography of the Father of the Country). 3rd edn, comp. by Lo Chia-lun 羅家倫 and Huang Chi-lu 黃季陸. 2 vols. Taipei: Central Executive Committee of the Chung-kuo Kuomintang, 1969; abbreviated as *KFNP*

Kuo Hua-lun (Warren) 郭華倫. *Chung-kung shih-lun* 中共史論 (An analytical history of the Chinese Communist Party). Taipei: Kuo-chi-kuan-hsi yen-chiu-so 國際關係研究所, 1969

Kuo-min-tang chou-k'an 國民黨週刊 (Kuomintang weekly). Canton, 23 Nov. 1923–13 Jan. 1924

Kuo-min Ko-ming-chün Ti-i Chi-t'uan-chün Ti-i Chün-t'uan li-shih 國民革命軍第一集團軍第一軍團歷史 (A history of the First Army Group of the First Group Army of the National Revolutionary Army), comp. by Chief of Staff, Office of the First Army Group. N.p., Sept. 1929

Kuo-min Ko-ming-chün Tung-lu-chün chan-shih chi-lueh 國民革命軍東路軍戰史紀略 (A brief record of the battle history of the Eastern Route Army of the National Revolutionary Army). Hankow, n.p., July 1930. Seen in the Kuomintang Archives

Kuo Mo-jo yen-chiu chuan-k'an 郭沫若研究專刊 (Special issue on studies of Kuo Mo-jo), in *Ssu-ch'uan ta-hsueh hsueh-pao: che-hsueh she-hui k'o-hsueh pan* 四川大學學報：哲學社會科學版 (Journal of Szechwan University: Philosophy and Social Sciences), no. 2. Chengtu: Ssu-ch'uan ta-hsueh, 1979

Kuo-shih-kuan kuan-k'an 國史館館刊 (Bulletin of the State History Office or National Historical Commission). Nanking: Dec. 1947– (vol. 1, nos. 1–4 [1947–48]; vol. 2, no. 1 [1949])

Kuo, Thomas C. *Ch'en Tu-hsiu (1879–1942) and the Chinese communist movement*. South Orange, N. J.: Seton Hall University Press, 1975

Kuo T'ing-yee, comp., and Morley, J. W., ed. *Sino-Japanese relations, 1862–1927; a checklist of the Chinese Foreign Ministry Archives*. New York: East Asian Institute, Columbia University, 1965

Kuo T'ing-i 郭廷以. *Chung-hua min-kuo shih-shih jih-chih* 中華民國史事日誌 (A chronology of the Republic of China: 1912–25). Vol. 1, Taipei: Institute of Modern History, Academia Sinica, 1979

Kuo-ts'ui hsueh-pao 國粹學報 (National essence journal), 1–82 (Jan. 1905–June 1911). Reprinted in 13 vols, Taipei: Wen-hai, 1970

Kuo, Warren (Kuo Hua-lun). *Analytical history of the Chinese Communist Party*. Book One, Taipei: Institute of International Relations, 1966

Kuo-wen chou-pao 國聞週報 (Kuowen weekly, illustrated). Tientsin Kuowen Weekly Association, 1924–37

Kwang-tung nung-min yun-tung pao-kao 廣東農民運動報告 (A report on the farmers' movement in Kwangtung). Canton, 1926. (On microfilm, the Hoover Library, Stanford University)

Kwok, D. W. Y. 郭穎頤 *Scientism in Chinese thought 1900–1950*. New Haven and London: Yale University Press, 1965

Kwok, Sin-tong E. 'The two faces of Confucianism: a comparative study of anti-restorationism of the 1910s and 1970s', paper presented to the Regional

Seminar on Confucian Studies, University of California, Berkeley, 4 June 1976

Lamb, Alastair. *The McMahon line: a study in the relations between India, China and Tibet, 1904 to 1914*. 2 vols. London: Routledge and Kegan Paul, 1966

Lan Hai 藍海. *Chung-kuo k'ang-chan wen-i shih* 中國抗戰文藝史 (A history of Chinese literature during the war of resistance). Shanghai: Hsien-tai 現代, 1947

Lang, Olga. *Pa Chin and his writings: Chinese youth between the two revolutions*. Cambridge, Mass.: Harvard University Press, 1967

Lao Ts'an. See Liu Ê, C. T. Hsia, and Harold Shadick

Lao-tung chou-pao 勞動週報 (Labour weekly). Hankow, Dec. (?) 1922–

Lary, Diana. *Region and nation: the Kwangsi Clique in Chinese politics, 1925–1937*. Cambridge: Cambridge University Press, 1974

Latourette, Kenneth Scott. *A history of Christian missions in China*. New York: Macmillan, 1929

Lau, Joseph S. M. 劉紹銘. *Ts'ao Yü: the reluctant disciple of Chekhov and O'Neil, a study in literary influence*. Hong Kong: Hong Kong University Press, 1970

Lee, B. Y. 'The present situation of cotton mills in China'. *CWR* (6 Oct. 1923)

Lee, Leo Ou-fan 李歐梵. *The romantic generation of modern Chinese writers*. Cambridge, Mass.: Harvard University Press, 1973

Lee, Leo Ou-fan. 'Two emancipated Noras: an intimate portrait', paper submitted to the Conference on 'Women in Chinese Society', San Francisco, June 1973

Lee, Leo Ou-fan. 'Literature on the eve of revolution: reflections on Lu Xun's leftist years, 1927–1936'. *Modern China*, 2.3 (July 1976) 277–91

Lee, Leo Ou-fan. 'Genesis of a writer: notes on Lu Xun's educational experience, 1881–1909', in Merle Goldman, ed. *Modern Chinese literature in the May Fourth era*, 161–88. Cambridge, Mass.: Harvard University Press, 1977

Leong, Sow-theng. *Sino-Soviet diplomatic relations, 1917–1926*. Honolulu: University of Hawaii Press, 1976

Leslie, Donald, Mackerras, Colin and Wang Gungwu, eds. *Essays on the sources for Chinese history*. Canberra: Australian National University Press, 1973

'The letter from Shanghai'. See Nassanov

Leung, Gaylord Kai-loh. 'Hsu Chih-mo: a literary biography'. University of London, Ph.D. dissertation, 1973

Levenson, Joseph R. *Liang Ch'i-ch'ao and the mind of modern China*. Cambridge, Mass.: Harvard University Press, 1953

Levenson, Joseph R. *Confucian China and its modern fate*. 3 vols. Berkeley: University of California Press, 1958–65

Levenson, Joseph R., ed. *European expansion and the counter-example of Asia, 1300–1600*. Englewood Cliffs, N. J.: Prentice-Hall, Inc., 1967

Levine, Steven I. See Vishnyakova-Akimova

Leyda, Jay. *Dianying: an account of films and the film audience in China*. Cambridge, Mass.: M.I.T. Press, 1972

Li Ang (Chu P'ei-wo, Chu Hsin-fan) 李昂 (朱佩我, 朱新繁). *Hung-se wu-t'ai* 紅色舞台 (The red stage). Peking: Sheng-li ch'u-pan-she 勝利出版社, 1946

Li Chien-nung 李劍農. *Tsui-chin san-shih-nien Chung-kuo cheng-chih shih* 最近三十年中國政治史 (A political history of China in the past thirty years). Shanghai: T'ai-p'ing-yang shu-tien 太平洋書店, 1931

Li Chien-nung. *Chung-kuo chin-pai-nien cheng-chih shih* 中國近百年政治史 (A political history of China during the last century). Shanghai: Commercial Press, 1947

Li, Chien-nung. *The political history of China, 1840–1928*, trans. by Teng Ssu-yü and Jeremy Ingalls. Princeton, N. J.: Van Nostrand, 1956

Li Ch'uan 李川. *Chün-fa i-wen* 軍閥軼聞 (Warlord anecdotes). Taipei: Hai-yen ch'u-pan-she 海燕出版社, 1966

Li Ho-lin 李何林. *Chin-erh-shih-nien Chung-kuo wen-i ssu-ch'ao lun* 近二十年中國文藝思潮論 (Chinese literary trends in the recent twenty years). Shanghai: Sheng-huo, 1947

Li Ho-lin *et al. Chung-kuo hsin wen-hsueh shih yen-chiu* 中國新文學史研究 (Studies on the history of China's new literature). Peking: Hsin chien-she tsa-chih she 新建設雜誌社, 1951

Li Ho-lin, ed. *Chung-kuo wen-i lun-chan* 中國文藝論戰 (Chinese literary polemics). Hong Kong: Hua-hsia 華夏, 1957

Li Hsin 李新 *et al.*, eds. *Min-kuo jen-wu chuan* 民國人物傳 (Who's who of the Republic of China), vol. 1. Institute of Modern History, Chinese Academy of Social Sciences. Peking: Chung-hua, 1978

Li Jui 李銳. *Mao Tse-tung t'ung-chih ti ch'u-ch'i ko-ming huo-tung* 毛澤東同志的初期革命活動 (Comrade Mao Tse-tung's early revolutionary activities). Peking: Chung-kuo ch'ing-nien ch'u-pan-she 中國青年出版社, 1957

Li Jui. *The early revolutionary activities of Comrade Mao Tse-tung*, trans. by Anthony W. Sariti, ed. by James C. Hsiung. White Plains, N.Y.: M. E. Sharpe, Inc., 1977

Li, Lillian Ming-tse. 'Kiangnan and the silk export trade, 1842–1937'. Harvard University, Ph.D. dissertation, 1975

Li Mu 李牧. *San-shih nien-tai wen-i lun* 三十年代文藝論 (On the literature of the 1930s). Taipei: Li-ming 黎明, 1973

Li, Peter 李培德. *Tseng P'u*. New York: Twayne Publishers, 1978

Li Po-yuan 李伯元. *Wen-ming hsiao-shih* 文明小史 (A little history of modern times). Shanghai, 1903. Reprinted, Peking: T'ung-su wen-i ch'u-pan-she 通俗文藝出版社, 1955

Li San-pao, 'K'ang Yu-wei's iconoclasm: interpretation and translation of his earliest writings 1884–87'. University of California, Ph.D. dissertation, Davis, 1978

Li Shih-tseng [Chen] 李石曾 [真]. 'San-kang ko-ming' 三綱革命 (Revolution against the three bonds). *Hsin shih-chi*, 11 (31 Aug. 1907) 1–2

Li Shou-k'ung 李守孔. *Min-ch'u chih kuo-hui* 民初之國會 (National assemblies in the early republic). Taipei: Commercial Press, 1964

Li Shou-t'ung 李壽涃. 'Kuan-shui chia-tseng yü wo kuo fang-chih-yeh chih ch'ien-t'u' 關稅加增與我國紡織業之前途 (The increase in customs duty and the future of our spinning-mills). *HSSC*, 3.2 (20 March 1922) 9–14

Li Ta-chao 李大釗. 'Yen-shih hsin yü tzu-chueh hsin' 厭世心與自覺心 (On misanthropy and self awareness). *Chia-yin* (The tiger), 1.8 (10 Aug. 1915)

Li Ta-chao. 'Ch'ing-ch'un' 青春 (Spring). *Hsin ch'ing-nien*, 2.1 (1 Sept. 1916) 1–12 [sep. pag.]

Li Ta-chao. 'Chin' 今 (Now). *Hsin ch'ing-nien*, 4.4 (15 April 1918) 307–10

Li Ta-chao. 'Hsin chi-yuan' 新紀元 (A new era). *Mei-chou p'ing-lun* (15 Jan. 1919)

Li Ta-chao. *Shou-ch'ang wen-chi* 守常文集 (Collected essays of Li Ta-chao). Shanghai: Jen-min, 1952

Li Ta-chao. *Li Ta-chao hsuan-chi* 李大釗選集 (Selected writings of Li Ta-chao). Peking: Jen-min, 1959

Li Tsung-jen. See Tong, Te-kong

Li Wen-chih 李文治 and Chang Yu-i 章有義, comps. *Chung-kuo chin-tai nung-yeh shih tzu-liao* 中國近代農業史資料 (Source materials on China's modern agricultural history). 3 vols. Peking: San-lien, 1957

Li Yu-ning, Bernadette 李又寧. 'A biography of Ch'ü Ch'iu-pai: from youth to party leadership (1899–1928)'. Columbia University, Ph.D. dissertation, 1967

Li Yü-shu 李毓澍. *Chung-Jih erh-shih-i-t'iao chiao-she, I* 中日二十一條交涉(上) (Sino-Japanese negotiations over the Twenty-one Demands, volume one). Taipei: Institute of Modern History, Academia Sinica, 1966

Li Yun-han 李雲漢. *Ts'ung jung-Kung tao ch'ing-tang* 從容共到清黨 (From admitting the communists to the purification of the Kuomintang). Taipei: China Committee on Publication Aid and Prize Awards, 1966; cited as *TJK*

Li Yun-han. *Huang K'o-ch'iang hsien-sheng nien-p'u* 黃克強先生年譜 (Chronological biography of Huang Hsing). Taipei: Chung-yang wen-wu kung-ying-she 中央文物供應社, 1973

Liang Ch'i-ch'ao 梁啓超. *Yin-ping-shih ho-chi* 飲冰室合集 (Combined writings from the Ice-drinker's Studio) in 40 vols. (*wen-chi*, 16 vols.; *chuan-chi*, 24 vols.). Shanghai: Chung-hua, 1936; Taiwan reprint: Chung-hua, 1960

Liang Ch'i-ch'ao. *Yin-ping-shih wen-chi* 飲冰室文集 (Collected essays from the Ice-drinker's Studio). Shanghai: Chung-hua, 1936; Taipei: Chung-hua, 16 vols., 1960. Note that this is also published as part of the preceding item

Liang Ch'i-ch'ao. 'Shuo-ch'ün hsu' 説群序 (Preface to Groups 1896). *YPSWC*, ts'e 2.3–4

Liang Ch'i-ch'ao. 'Shuo tung' 説動 (On dynamism, 1898). *YPSWC*, ts'e 2.37–40

Liang Ch'i-ch'ao [Jen-kung] [任公]. 'Lun ch'iang-ch'üan' 論強權 (On power). *Ch'ing-i pao*, 31 (1899) 4–7

Liang Ch'i-ch'ao. 'Chung-kuo shih hsu-lun' 中國史敍論 (Introduction to Chinese history, 1901). *YPSWC*, ts'e 3.1–12

Liang Ch'i-ch'ao. 'Kuo-chia ssu-hsiang pien-ch'ien i-t'ung lun' 國家思想變遷異同論 (On similarity and difference in alterations in national thought, 1901). *YPSWC*, ts'e 3.12–22

Liang Ch'i-ch'ao. 'Kuo-tu shih-tai' 過渡時代 (A transitional age, 1901). *YPSWC, ts'e* 3.27–32

Liang Ch'i-ch'ao. 'Pao-chiao fei so-i tsun-K'ung lun' 保教非所以尊孔論 (To 'save the faith' is not the way to honour Confucius). *Hsin-min ts'ung-pao*, 2 (22 Feb. 1902) 59–72

Liang Ch'i-ch'ao. 'Hsin shih-hsueh' 新史學 (The new history, 1902). *YPSWC, ts'e* 4.1–32

Liang Ch'i-ch'ao. 'K'ai-ming chuan-chih lun' 開明專制論 (On enlightened despotism). *Hsin-min ts'ung-pao*, 73–75 (25 Jan.-23 Feb. 1906); reprinted in *YPSWC, ts'e* 6.13–83

Liang Ch'i-ch'ao. 'Chung-kuo tao-te chih ta-yuan' 中國道德之大原 (Fundamentals of Chinese morality). *Yung-yen*, 1.2 (Dec. 1912) 1–8; 1.4 (Feb. 1913) 1–8 (sep. pag.)

Liang Ch'i-ch'ao. 'Kuo-hsing p'ien' 國性篇 (Essays on the national character). *Yung-yen*, 1.1 (Jan. 1913) 1–6 (sep. pag.)

Liang Ch'i-ch'ao. 'Fu-ku ssu-ch'ao p'ing-i' 復古思潮評議 (Critique of the restorationist thought tide). *Ta Chung-hua*, 1.7 (20 July 1916) 1–10 (sep. pag.)

Liang Ch'i-ch'ao. 'Wu-nien-lai chih chiao-hsun' 五年來之教訓 (Lessons of the past five years). *Ta Chung-hua*, 2.10 (20 Oct. 1915) 1–5 (sep. pag.)

Liang Ch'i-ch'ao. 'Ts'ung-chün jih-chi' 從軍日記 (Diary of my military enlistment, 1916). *Shun-pi-chi* 盾鼻集. Taipei reprint: Wen-hai, 1966

Liang Ch'i-ch'ao. 'Ou yu hsin-ying lu chieh-lu' 歐遊心影錄節錄 (Reflections on a trip to Europe) in *Yin-ping-shih ho-chi, chuan-chi, ts'e* 5, 1–162. Shanghai: Chung-hua, 1936

Liang Ch'i-ch'ao. See *Ch'ing-i pao, Hsin-min ts'ung-pao, Shih-wu pao*

Liang Shu-ming 梁漱溟. *Tung Hsi wen-hua chi ch'i che-hsueh* 東西文化及其哲學 (Eastern and Western civilizations and their philosophies). 1922; reprinted, Taipei: Hung-ch'iao shu-tien 虹橋書店, 1968

Library of Congress. *Chinese periodicals in the Library of Congress*, comp. by Han Chu Huang. Washington: Library of Congress, 1977

Lieh-ning Ssu-ta-lin lun Chung-kuo 列寧斯大林論中國 (Lenin and Stalin on China). Peking: Jen-min, 1963

Lieu, D. K. *China's industries and finance*. Peking: Chinese Government Bureau of Economic Information, 1927

Lieu, D. K. See Liu Ta-chün

Liew, K. S. *Struggle for democracy: Sung Chiao-jen and the 1911 Chinese Revolution*. Berkeley: University of California Press, 1971

Lin Ch'in-nan hsien-sheng hsueh-hsing p'u-chi ssu-chung 林琴南先生學行譜記四種 (The life and works of Mr Lin Shu, four records), ed. by Chu Hsi-chou 朱羲冑; includes 'Ch'un-chueh chai chu-shu chi' 春覺齋著述記 (Works from the Ch'un-chueh study). 3 *chüan*. Taipei: Shih-chieh shu-chü 世界書局, 1961

Lin, Julia C. *Modern Chinese poetry: an introduction*. Seattle: University of Washington Press, 1972

Lin Tsu-han 林祖涵. 'Report on an investigation of the Hunan land question, financial question, and Party condition'. 2 May 1927 (in Chinese). KMT Archives, Hunan 5/53

Lin Tsung 林淙. *Hsien chieh-tuan ti wen-hsueh lun-chan* 現階段的文學論戰 (Current literary debates). Shanghai: Kuang-ming 光明, 1936

Lin, Yü-sheng 林毓生. 'The dialectic of Lu Hsun's iconoclastic consciousness', paper presented at the Association for Asian Studies annual meeting, New York, April 1973

Lin, Yü-sheng. *The crisis of Chinese consciousness: radical anti-traditionalism in the May Fourth era.* Madison: University of Wisconsin Press, 1978

Link, E. Perry. 'The rise of modern popular fiction in Shanghai'. Harvard University, Ph.D. dissertation, 1976

Link, Perry. 'Traditional-style popular urban fiction in the teens and twenties', in Merle Goldman, ed. *Modern Chinese literature in the May Fourth era*, 327–50

Link, E. Perry. *Mandarin ducks and butterflies: popular urban fiction in early twentieth-century China.* Berkeley and Los Angeles: University of California Press, 1980

Lippit, Victor D. *Land reform and economic development in China.* White Plains, N.Y.: International Arts and Sciences Press, 1974

Liu Chih 劉峙. *Wo-ti hui-i* 我的回憶 (My recollections). Taipei: Kuang-lung wen-chü yin-shua kung-ssu 廣隆文具印刷公司, 1966

Liu Ch'u-hsiang 劉楚湘. *Kuei-hai cheng-pien chi-lueh* 癸亥政變紀略 (Brief record of the 1923 coup). 1924; Taipei reprint: Wen-hai, 1967

Liu Chun-jo. *Controversies in modern Chinese intellectual history: an analytic bibliography of periodical articles, mainly of the May Fourth and post-May Fourth era.* Cambridge, Mass.: East Asian Research Center; distributed by Harvard University Press, 1964

Liu Ê 劉鶚. *The travels of Lao Ts'an*, trans. by Harold Shadick. Ithaca: Cornell University Press, 1966

Liu, F. F. *A military history of modern China: 1924–1949.* Princeton: Princeton University Press, 1956

Liu Hsin-huang 劉心皇. *Hsien-tai Chung-kuo wen-hsueh shih-hua* 現代中國文學史話 (Discourse on the history of modern Chinese literature). Taipei: Cheng-chung shu-chü 正中書局, 1971

Liu Ju-ming 劉汝明. *Liu Ju-ming hui-i lu* 劉汝明回憶錄 (The recollections of Liu Ju-ming). Taipei: Chuan-chi wen-hsueh, 1966

Liu Li-k'ai 劉立凱 and Wang Chen 王真. *I-chiu i-chiu chih i-chiu erh-ch'i nien ti Chung-kuo kung-jen yun-tung* 一九一九至一九二七年的中國工人運動 (The Chinese labour movement from 1919 to 1927). Peking: Workers Publishing House, 1953

Liu Shao-ch'i 劉少奇. 'Report on the Chinese labour movement in the past year'. *Cheng-chih chou-pao* 政治週報 (Political weekly), 14 (5 June 1926). Canton. Available on U.S. National Archives microfilm 329, reel 56, 893.00/7980

[Liu] Shih-fu [劉] 師復. [Shang-hai wu-cheng-fu kung-ch'an chu-i t'ung-chih she kung-pu] 上海無政府共產主義同志社公佈 [Manifesto of the Shanghai anarchist-communist fellowship]. 'Wu-cheng-fu kung-ch'an-tang chih mu-ti yü shou-tuan' 無政府共產黨之目的與手段 (Goals and methods of the anarchist-communist party). *Min-sheng* 民聲 (Voice of the people), 19 (18 July 1914)

Liu Shih-p'ei 劉師培. 'Jen-lei chün-li lun' 人類均力論 (On the equalization of human powers). *T'ien-i*, 3 (10 July 1907)

Liu Shih-p'ei and Ho Chen 何震. 'Lun chung-tsu ko-ming yü wu-cheng-fu ko-ming chih te-shih' 論種族革命與無政府革命之得失 (On the strengths and weaknesses of racial revolution as opposed to anarchist revolution). *T'ien-i* 6 (1 Sept. 1907)

Liu Shih-p'ei. 'Lun hsin-cheng wei ping-min chih-ken' 論新政為病民之根 (On why the new politics injures the people). *T'ien-i*, 8–10 (30 Oct. 1907)

Liu Shih-p'ei. *Liu Shen-shu hsien-sheng i-shu*, 劉申叔先生遺書 (Posthumous collection of the works of Liu Shih-p'ei). 4 vols. Taipei reprint: Ta-hsin shu-chü 大新書局, 1965

Liu Shih-p'ei. *Jang shu* 攘書 (Book of the expulsion). 1903. Reprinted in *Liu Shen-shu hsien-sheng i-shu*, 2.751–65

Liu Shou-lin 劉壽林. *Hsin-hai i-hou shih-ch'i nien chih-kuan nien-piao* 辛亥以後十七年職官年表 (Tables of officials by year, 1911–28). Peking: Chung-hua, 1966

Liu Shou-sung 劉綬松. *Chung-kuo hsin wen-hsueh shih ch'u-kao* 中國新文學史初稿 (A preliminary draft history of China's new literature). 2 vols. Peking: Tso-chia ch'u-pan-she 作家出版社, 1956

Liu Ta-chün (D. K. Lieu) 劉大鈞. *Chung-kuo kung-yeh tiao-ch'a pao-kao* 中國工業調查報告 (Report on a survey of China's industry). 3 vols. Nanking, 1937

Liu Ta-chung 劉大中 and Yeh Kung-chia 葉孔嘉. *The economy of the Chinese mainland: national income and economic development, 1933–1949*. Princeton: Princeton University Press, 1965

Liu Wu-chi 柳無忌. 'The modern period', in Herbert A. Giles. *A history of Chinese literature*, 445–500. Reprinted, New York: Frederick Ungar, 1967. 1st edn, 1901

Liu Wu-chi. *Su Man-shu*. New York: Twayne Publishers, 1972

Liu Ya-tzu 柳亞子. *Nan-she chi lueh* 南社紀略 (A brief account of the Southern Society). Shanghai, 1940

Lo Ch'i-yuan 羅綺園. 'Short report on the work of this [Farmers] Bureau during the past year'. *Chung-kuo nung-min*, 2 (1 Feb. 1926) 147–207

Lo Ch'i-yuan. 'Hui-wu tsung pao-kao' 會務總報告 (General report of the [Farmers'] Association work). *Chung-kuo nung-min*, 6/7 (July 1926) 639–87

Lo Chia-lun 羅家倫, ed. *Chung-hua min-kuo shih-liao ts'ung-pien chieh-shao* 中華民國史料叢編介紹 (An introduction to historical materials on the Republic of China), vol. 1. Taipei: Chung-kuo Kuo-min-tang chung-yang wei-yuan-hui tang-shih shih-liao pien-tsuan wei-yuan-hui, 1968

Lo Chia-lun. See *Ko-ming wen-hsien*

Lo-fu (Chang Wen-t'ien) 洛甫 (張聞天). *Ch'ing-nien hsueh-hsi wen-t'i* 青年學習問題 (Problems of young people's study). Shanghai: Hua-hsia shu-tien 華夏書店 1949

Lo, Hui-min, ed. *The correspondence of G. E. Morrison, Vol. II, 1912–1920.* London, New York and Melbourne: Cambridge University Press, 1978

Lo I-nung 羅亦農. 'Chung-kuo ti-erh-tz'u ch'üan-kuo lao-tung ta-hui chih shih-mo' 中國第二次全國勞動大會之始末 (A complete account of the Second National Labour Congress). *HTCP,* 115 (17 May 1925) 1063–4

Lo, J. P. (Lo Jung-pang). 'The emergence of China as a sea power during the late Sung and early Yuan periods'. *FEQ,* 14.4 (1955) 489–504

Lo, J. P. (Lo Jung-pang). 'The decline of the early Ming navy'. *Oriens extremus,* 5.2 (Dec. 1958) 149–68

Lo, Jung-pang, ed. and introduction. *Kang Yu-wei: A biography and a symposium.* Tucson: University of Arizona Press, 1967

Lo, J. P. (Lo Jung-pang). 'Maritime commerce and its relation to the Sung navy'. *Journal of the Economic and Social History of the Orient,* 12.1 (1969) 57–101

Lo-sheng 樂生 (pseud.). 'Ti-san-tz'u ch'üan-kuo lao-tung ta-hui chih ching-kuo chi ch'i chieh-kuo' 第三次全國勞動大會之經過及其結果 (Experiences and results of the Third National Labour Congress). *HTCP,* 155 (5 May 1926). Reprinted in *Ti-i-tz'u kuo-nei ko-ming chan-cheng shih-ch'i ti kung-jen yun-tung,* 219–24. 3rd edn, Peking: Jen-min ch'u-pan she, April 1963

Loewe, Michael. *Military operations in the Han period.* London: The China Society, 1961

Loewe, Michael. 'The campaigns of Han Wu-ti', in Frank A. Kierman, Jr. and John King Fairbank, eds. *Chinese ways in warfare,* 67–122. Cambridge, Mass.: Harvard University Press, 1974

Lu Hsun 魯迅. 'Mo-lo shih li shuo' 摩羅詩力説 (On the power of Mara poetry, 1907), in *Fen* 墳 (Graves) 53–100

Lu Hsun 魯迅. 'Wen-hua p'ien-chih lun' 文化偏至論 (On the pendulum movement of culture), 1907), in *Fen* 墳 (Graves) 36–52

Lu Hsun. *Fen* 墳 (Graves). Shanghai: Ch'ing-kuang shu-chü 青光書局, 1933.

Lu Hsun. 'No-la ch'u-tsou hou tsen-yang' 娜拉出走後怎樣 (What happens after Nora goes away), in *Fen* (Graves). Reprint from *Lu Hsun ch'üan-chi* 魯迅全集, 1938 edn, 141–50. Hong Kong: Hsin-i 新藝, 1967

Lu Hsun. *Selected stories from Lu Hsun,* trans. by Yang Hsien-yi and Gladys Yang. Peking: Foreign Languages Press, 1960

Lu Hsun. *Selected works of Lu Hsun,* trans. by Yang Hsien-yi and Gladys Yang. 4 vols. Peking: Foreign Languages Press, 1960

Lu Hsun. *Na-han* 吶喊 (A call to arms). Reprint from *Lu Hsun ch'üan-chi,* 1938 edn. Hong Kong: Hsin-i 新藝, 1967

Lu Hsun. *P'ang-huang* 彷徨 (Wandering). Reprint from *Lu Hsun ch'üan-chi,* 1938 edn. Hong Kong: Hsin-i 新藝, 1967

Lu Hsun. *Yeh-ts'ao* 野草 (Wild grass). Reprint from *Lu Hsun ch'üan-chi,* 1938 edn. Hong Kong: Hsin-i 新藝, 1967

Lu Hsun. *Lu Hsun ch'üan-chi* 魯迅全集 (Complete works of Lu Hsun). 20 vols. Peking: Jen-min, 1973

Lu Hsun. See Gladys Yang, Harriet Mills.

Lunt, Carroll, ed. *The China who's who (foreign).* Shanghai, 1922, 1925

Lust, John. 'The Su-pao case: an episode in the early Chinese nationalist movement'. *BSOAS*, 27.2 (1964) 408–29

Lutz, Jessie G. 'Chinese nationalism and the anti-Christian campaigns of the 1920s'. *Modern Asian Studies*, 10.3 (July 1976) 395–416

Lutz, Jessie Gregory. *China and the Christian colleges, 1850–1950.* Ithaca: Cornell University Press, 1971

Lyell, William. *Lu Hsun's vision of reality.* Berkeley: University of California Press, 1976

Ma Huan. See Mills, J. V. G.

MacKinnon, Stephen R. *Power and politics in late imperial China: Yuan Shi-kai in Beijing and Tianjin, 1901–1908.* Berkeley: University of California Press, 1980

MacMurray, John V. A. *Treaties and agreements with and concerning China, 1894–1919.* 2 vols. New York: Oxford University Press, 1921

Mah Feng-hwa. *The foreign trade of mainland China.* Chicago: Aldine, 1971

Malone, Col. C. L'Estrange. *New China: report of an investigation. Part II. Labour conditions and labour organizations 1926.* London: Independent Labour Party Publication Department, 1927

Malraux, André. *Man's fate.* Trans. by Haakon M. Chevalier from the French *La condition humaine.* New York: Smith and Haas, 1934

Mann, Tom. *What I saw in China.* London: National Minority Movement, 1927?

Mannheim, Karl. *Essays on sociology and social psychology.* London and New York: Oxford University Press, 1953

Mao-hsin Fu-hsin Shen-hsin tsung-kung-ssu sa-chou-nien chi-nien ts'e 茂新福新申新總公司卅週年紀念冊 (Book commemorating the 30th anniversary of the Mow Sing mills and the Foh Sing and Sung Sing cotton works). Shanghai: Shih-chieh shu-chü 世界書局, 1929

Mao I-heng 毛以亨. *O Meng hui-i-lu* 俄蒙回憶錄 (Recollections of Russia and Mongolia). Hong Kong: Asia Book Co., 1954

Mao, *CKSHS*. See next item Mao Ssu-ch'eng.

Mao Ssu-ch'eng 毛思誠. *Min-kuo shih-wu-nien i-ch'ien chih Chiang Chieh-shih hsien-sheng* 民國十五年以前之蔣介石先生 (Mr Chiang Kai-shek up to 1926). N.p. (1936); Taipei edn (1948?) Often referred to as 'Chiang's Diary'.

Mao Tse-tung 毛澤東, 'Min-chung ti ta-lien-ho' 民眾的大聯合 (Great union of the popular masses), in *Hsiang-chiang p'ing-lun* 湘江評論 (Hsiang River review), 21 July–4 Aug. 1919; reprinted in Takeuchi edn, *Mao Tse-tung chi* 毛澤東集, 1.57–69

Mao Tse-tung. *Selected works of Mao Tse-tung.* Vol. 1. London: Lawrence & Wishart, 1954. Abbrev. *SW*

Mao Tse-tung. *Mao Tse-tung on art and literature.* Peking: Foreign Languages Press, 1967

(Mao) Tse-tung (毛) 澤東. 'Pei-ching cheng-pien yü shang-jen' 北京政變與商人 (The Peking coup d'etat and the merchants). *HTCP*, 31–32 (11 July 1923)

Mao Tse-tung. *Mao Tse-tung chi* 毛澤東集 (Collected writings of Mao Tse-tung), ed. by Takeuchi Minoru 竹內実 10 vols. Tokyo: Hokubōsha 北望社, 1970–2. Cited as Takeuchi edn

Mao Tse-tung. 'Ch'üan-kuo nung-hsieh tsui-chin hsun-ling' 全國農協最近訓令 (A recent decree of the National Peasant Association), in Takeuchi edn, 2.9

Maruyama Noboru 丸山昇. *Ro Jin sono bungaku to kakumei* 魯迅その文学と革命 (Lu Hsun, his literature and revolution). Tokyo: Heibonsha 平凡社, 1965

Masson, Michel. 'The idea of Chinese tradition: Fung Yu-lan, 1939–1949'. Harvard University, Ph.D. dissertation, 1978

Mast, Herman, III, and Saywell, William G. 'Revolution out of tradition: the political ideology of Tai Chi-t'ao'. *JAS*, 34.1 (Nov. 1974) 73–98

Materialy po Kitaiskomu voprosu (Materials on the China question). Moscow: Sun Yat-sen University, 1925–7

McCormack, Gavan. *Chang Tso-lin in Northeast China, 1911–1928: China, Japan and the Manchurian idea.* Stanford: Stanford University Press, 1977

McCormick, F. *The flowery republic.* New York: Appleton, 1913

McDonald, Angus W., Jr. *The urban origins of rural revolution: elites and masses in Hunan province, China, 1911–1927.* Berkeley, Los Angeles and London: University of California Press, 1978

McDonald, Angus W., Jr. 'The Hunan peasant movement: its urban origins'. *Modern China*, 1.2 (April 1975) 180–203

McDougall, Bonnie S. *The introduction of Western literary theories into modern China, 1919–1925.* Tokyo: Centre for East Asian Cultural Studies, 1971

McDougall, Bonnie S., trans. and ed. *Paths in dreams: selected prose and poetry of Ho Ch'i-fang.* Queensland, Australia: University of Queensland Press, 1976

McElderry, Andrea Lee. *Shanghai old-style banks (ch'ien-chuang), 1800–1935.* Ann Arbor: University of Michigan, Center for Chinese Studies, 1976

McGuire, Catherine M. 'The union movement in Hunan in 1926–1927 and its effect on the American community'. Columbia University, M.A. essay in History, 1977

Mehra, Parshotam. *The McMahon Line and after: a study of the triangular contest on India's northeastern frontier between Britain, China and Tibet, 1904–47.* Delhi: Macmillan, 1974

Mei-chou p'ing-lun 每週評論 (Weekly review). Peking: Dec. 1918–

Meisner, Maurice. *Li Ta-chao and the origins of Chinese Marxism.* Cambridge, Mass.: Harvard University Press, 1967

Meserve, Walter and Meserve, Ruth, eds. *Modern drama from Communist China.* New York: New York University Press, 1970

Metzger, Thomas A. *Escape from predicament: Neo-Confucianism and China's evolving political culture.* New York: Columbia University Press, 1977

Metzger, Thomas A. 'On the historical roots of modernization in China: the increasing differentiation of the economy from the polity during late Ming and early Ch'ing times', paper presented at the Conference on Modern Chinese Economic History, Taipei, 1977

Mif, Pavel. *Chin-chi shih-ch'i chung ti Chung-kuo Kung-ch'an-tang* 緊急時期中的中國共產黨 (The Chinese Communist Party in critical days). Moscow: Sun Yat-sen University, 1928. (Translated from the Russian.)

Mif, Pavel. *Heroic China: fifteen years of the Communist Party of China*. New York: Workers Library Publisher, 1937

Mikami Taichō 三上諦聽, Ishikawa Tadao 石川忠雄 and Shibata Minoru 芝田稔. *Kohoku shūshū bōdō keika no hōkoku* 湖北秋収暴動経過の報告 (A report on the Autumn Harvest uprising in Hupei). *Kansai daigaku tōzai gakujutsu kenkyūjo shiryō shūkan* 関西大学東西学術研究所資料集刊 (Sources of the Kansai University Institute of Oriental and Occidental Studies), no. 1. Osaka: Kansai Daigaku Tōzai Gakujutsu Kenkyūjo, 1961. This is a translation of the whole text of the *Chung-yang t'ung-hsun* 中央通訊 (Central Committee circular), no. 11: *Hu-pei ch'iu-shou pao-tung chuan-hao* 湖北秋收暴動專號 (Special issue on the Autumn Harvest uprising in Hupei), which was probably published on 24 or 25 November, 1927

Miller, Stuart Creighton. 'Ends and means: missionary justification of force in nineteenth century China', in John K. Fairbank, ed. *The missionary enterprise in China and America*, 249–82

Mills, Harriet C. 'Lu Hsun: 1927–1936, the years on the left'. Columbia University, Ph.D. dissertation, 1963

Mills, Harriet C. 'The essays: some observations on form and substance', paper presented at the annual meeting of the Association for Asian Studies, New York, March 1972

Mills, Harriet. 'Lu Xun: literature and revolution – from Mara to Marx', in Merle Goldman, ed. *Modern Chinese literature in the May Fourth era*, 189–220. Cambridge, Mass.: Harvard University Press, 1977

Mills, J. V. G., trans. and ed. *Ma Huan, Ying-yai sheng-lan, the overall survey of the ocean's shores (1433)*. Cambridge: Cambridge University Press, 1970

Min Erh-ch'ang, 閔爾昌, comp. *Pei-chuan chi-pu* 碑傳集補 (Supplement to the collection of biographies from stone inscriptions). 24 ts'e. Peking: Yen-ching ta-hsueh 燕京大學, 1932

Min-kuo jih-pao 民國日報 (National daily). Shanghai and Canton, *ca.* 1914–

Min-li pao 民立報 (Independent people's newspaper). Shanghai, 1910–13

Min-pao 民報 (People's journal). 1–26 (Sept. 1905–Sept. 1908). Reprinted by K'o-hsueh, Peking, 1957. 4 vols.

Min-sheng 民聲 (People's voice). 1–29 (Aug. 1913–June 1921). Reprinted by Lung-men shu-tien 龍門書店, Hong Kong, 1967

Min to 民鐸 (People's tocsin). Shanghai: 1916–

Ming-pao yueh-k'an 明報月刊 (Ming-pao monthly). Hong Kong, 1966–

Ministry of Agriculture and Commerce. *Nung-shang t'ung-chi piao* 農商統計表 (Tables of agricultural and commercial statistics). Shanghai, 1914–19; Peking, 1920–4

Ministry of Communications (Ministry of Railways, Bureau of Railway Statistics, from 1925 issue). *Statistics of government railways, 1915–1936*. Peking, 1916–28; Nanking, 1931–6

Ministry of Defence. Kuo-fang-pu shih-cheng-chü 國防部史政局. *Pei-fa chan-shih* 北伐戰史 (A battle history of the northern punitive expedition). 4 vols. Taipei, 1959; another set bound in 10 *ts'e*; another edn published at Yang-ming-shan: Chung-hua ta-tien pien-yin hui, 5 vols., 1967; our citations are to the 4 vols. 1959 edn.

Ministry of Defence. General Political Department. *Kuo-chün cheng-kung shih-kao* 國軍政工史稿 (Draft history of political work in the National Army). 2 vols. Taipei: General Political Department of the Ministry of Defence, 1960

Ministry of Defence. *Pei-fa chien-shih* 北伐簡史 (A brief history of the northern punitive expedition). Taipei: Ministry of Defence, 1961

Ministry of Finance. *Annual reports for the 17th, 18th, 19th, 21st, 22nd, and 23rd fiscal years.* Nanking, 1930–6

Ministry of Industries, National Agricultural Research Bureau, *Nung-ch'ing pao-kao* 農情報告 (Crop reports). Nanking, 1933–9

Ministry of the Interior. *Nei-cheng nien-chien* 內政年鑑 (Yearbook of the Interior Ministry). 4 vols. Shanghai: Commercial Press, 1936

'Minutes of the Military Section on . . . 1927', in *Soviet plot in China,* 143–8; also in *Chinese Social and Political Science Review,* 7 (1927) 232–9. (A document seized in the Peking raid of 6 April 1927.)

Mirovitskaia, R. A. 'Pervoe destiatiletie' (The first decade), in *Leninskaia politika SSSR v otnoshenii Kitaia* (The Leninist policy of the USSR with regard to China). Moscow: 'Nauka', 1968

Mirovitskaia, R. A. 'Mikhail Borodin (1884–1951)', in *Vidnye sovietskie kommunisty – uchastniki kitaiskoi revolutsii,* 22–40

Misselwitz, Henry Francis. *The dragon stirs: an intimate sketchbook of China's Kuomintang revolution, 1927–1929.* New York: Harbinger House, 1941

Mitarevsky, N. *World-wide soviet plots, as disclosed by hitherto unpublished documents seized in the USSR embassy in Peking.* Tientsin: Tientsin Press, Ltd., 1927

Miyashita Tadao 宮下忠雄. *Shina ginkō seido ron* 支那銀行制度論 (A treatise on the Chinese banking system). Tokyo: Ganshōdō 巖松堂, 1941

Miyazaki, Ichisada 宮崎市定, trans. by Schirokauer, Conrad. *China's examination hell: the civil service examinations of imperial China.* New York and Tokyo: Weatherhill, 1976. Originally *Kakyo: Chūgoku no shiken jigoku* 科挙：中国の試験地獄. Tokyo: Chūō Kōronsha 中央公論社, 1963

Modern China: an international quarterly. Beverly Hills, Cal.: Sage Publications, 1975–

Modern Chinese Literature Newsletter, ed. by Michael Gotz, 1975–

Moh, H. Y. 'Causes for the high price of cotton and the low price of yarn'. *CWR,* (23 Dec. 1922) 140–1

Moh, H. Y. See Mu Ou-ch'u

Monnet, Jean. *Mémoires.* Paris: Fayard, 1976

Moore, John A., Jr. 'The Chinese consortiums and America-China policy, 1909–1917'. Claremont Graduate School, Ph.D. dissertation, 1972

Morrison, George Ernest. Private papers, Mitchell Library, Sydney, New South Wales

Morrison, G. E. See Lo Hui-min

Morrison, Esther. 'The modernization of the Confucian bureaucracy: an historical study of public administration'. Radcliffe College, Ph.D. dissertation, 3 vols. 1959.

Morse, H. B. *The international relations of the Chinese empire.* 3 vols. London: Longmans, 1910–18

Mote, Frederick W. 'The T'u-mu incident of 1449', in Frank A. Kierman, Jr., and John K. Fairbank, eds. *Chinese ways in warfare*, 243–72. Cambridge, Mass.: Harvard University Press, 1974

Mote, F. W. See Hsiao Kung-chuan

Mu Ou-ch'u 穆藕初. 'Hua-kuei sha-chien chih yuan-yin' 花貴紗賤之原因 (Causes of the dearness of raw cotton and the cheapness of yarn). *TSHYP*, 3.2 (Feb. 1923)

Mu Ou-ch'u (Hsiang-yueh) (湘玥). *Ou-ch'u wu-shih tzu-shu* 藕初五十自述 (Autobiography of Mu Ou-ch'u at 50 years of age). Shanghai: Commercial Press, 1926

Muramatsu Yūji. 'A documentary study of Chinese landlordism in late Ch'ing and early republican Kiangnan'. *Bulletin of the School of Oriental and African Studies*, 29.3 (1966) 566–99

Muramatsu Yūji 村松祐次. *Kindai Kōnan no sosan – Chūgoku jinushi seido no kenkyū* 近代江南の租棧—中国地主制度の研究 (Bursaries in modern Kiangnan – a study of the Chinese landlord system). Tokyo: Tokyo University Press, 1970

Murphey, Rhoads. *The outsiders: the Western experience in India and China.* Ann Arbor: The University of Michigan Press, 1977

Myers, Ramon H. *The Chinese peasant economy: agricultural development in Hopei and Shantung, 1890–1949.* Cambridge, Mass.: Harvard University Press, 1970

Myers, Ramon H. 'Agrarian policy and agricultural transformation: mainland China and Taiwan, 1895–1954'. *Hsiang-kang Chung-wen ta-hsueh Chung-kuo wen-hua yen-chiu-so hsueh-pao* 香港中文大學中國文化研究所學報 (Journal of the Institute of Chinese Studies of the Chinese University of Hong Kong), 3.2 (1970) 521–44

Nan-hai yin-tzu 南海胤子 (pseud.). *An-fu huo-kuo chi* 安福禍國記 (How the Anfu Clique brought disaster on the country). 3 vols. n.p., 1920

Nankai Institute of Economics. See Nan-k'ai ta-hsueh ching-chi yen-chiu so

Nankai Institute of Economics. *Nankai Weekly Statistical Service.* Tientsin, 1928–

Nan-k'ai ta-hsueh ching-chi yen-chiu so 南開大學經濟研究所 (Nankai Institute of Economics), comp. *1913 nien–1952 nien Nan-k'ai chih-shu tzu-liao hui-pien* 1913年–1952年 南開指數資料彙編 (Nankai price indexes 1913–52). Peking: T'ung-chi ch'u-pan-she 統計出版社, 1958

Nan-yang hsiung-ti yen-ts'ao kung-ssu shih-liao. See Chung-kuo k'o-hsueh yuan

Nassanov, N., Fokine, N. and Albrecht, A. 'The letter from Shanghai', 17 March 1927. Trans. from the French in Leon Trotsky. *Problems of the Chinese revolution*, 397–432

Nathan, Andrew James. *A history of the China International Famine Relief Commis-*

sion. Cambridge, Mass.: Harvard University East Asian Research Center, 1965

Nathan, Andrew J. *Modern China, 1840–1972: an introduction to sources and research aids*. Ann Arbor: University of Michigan, 1971

Nathan, Andrew J. *Peking politics 1918–1923: factionalism and the failure of constitutionalism*. Berkeley: University of California Press, 1976

National Agricultural Research Bureau. *Crop reporting in China, 1934*. Nanking, 1936

National Economic Council. Bureau of Public Roads. *Highways in China*. Nanking, 1935

National Government. Directorate of Statistics. *Chung-hua min-kuo t'ung-chi t'i-yao, 1935* 中華民國統計提要 (Statistical abstract of the Republic of China, 1935). Nanking, 1936

National Government. Directorate of Statistics. *Chung-kuo tsu-tien chih-tu chih t'ung-chi fen-hsi* 中國租佃制度之統計分析 (Statistical analysis of China's land rent system). Shanghai: Cheng-chung 正中, 1946

National Land Commission. *Ch'üan-kuo t'u-ti tiao-ch'a pao-kao kang-yao* 全國土地調查報告綱要 (Preliminary report of the national land survey). Nanking, 1937

'The National Revolutionary Army. A short history of its origin, development and organization', Trans. from a document seized in the Soviet Military Attache's office in Peking, 6 April 1927. In British Foreign Office Archives, FO 371: 12440/9156

NCH. North China Herald

Needham, Joseph. *Science and civilisation in China*. Vol. 4: *Physics and Physical Technology, Part 3: Civil Engineering and Nautics*. Cambridge: Cambridge University Press, 1971

Newsletter of the Center for Chinese Research Materials, 1527 New Hampshire Ave., N.W., Washington, D.C., 20036

Nieh Ch'i-chieh 聶其傑 (杰) ed. *Ch'ung-te lao-jen tzu-ting nien-p'u* 崇德老人自訂年譜 (Chronological autobiography of Nieh Ch'ung-te). Taipei: Wen-hai, 1966

Nieh Yun-t'ai 聶雲台 (Ch'i-chieh, C. C. Nieh 聶其傑). 'Wei Jih-ping ch'iang-sha shih-min shih ching-kao kuo-min' 為日兵鎗殺市民事警告國民 (Warning to the nation concerning the incident when Japanese soldiers shot and killed citizens). *TSHYP*, 3.6 (June 1923) heading *Yen-lun*

Nihon gaikō bunsho 日本外交文書 (Documents on Japan's diplomacy), comp. by Gaimushō (Ministry of foreign affairs). Tokyo, 1936–

Ning-po kung-ch'ang chou-k'an 寧波工廠週刊 (Weekly paper of the Ningpo workshops) in *Wu-ssu shih-ch'i ch'i-k'an chieh-shao*, 3.288–91

Nishi Junsō 西順藏 and Shimada Kenji 島田虔次, eds. *Shimmatsu minkoku sho seiji hyōron shū* 清末民国初政治評論集 (Collected political essays of the late Ch'ing and early republic), in *Chūgoku koten bungaku taikei* 中国古典文学大系 (Comprehensive compendium of Chinese classical literature), no. 58. Tokyo: Heibonsha 平凡社, 1971

Nivison, David S. and Wright, Arthur F., eds. *Confucianism in action*. Stanford: Stanford University Press, 1959

NLCP. See *Nu-li chou-pao*

North China Daily News. Shanghai, 1864–

The North China Herald and Supreme Court and Consular Gazette. Weekly. Shanghai, 1850–

North, Robert C. *Moscow and Chinese communists*. Stanford: Stanford University Press, 1952

North, Robert C. and Eudin, Xenia J. *M. N. Roy's mission to China: the Communist-Kuomintang split of 1927*. Berkeley and Los Angeles: University of California Press, 1963

Nu-li chou-pao 努力週報 (Endeavour). Weekly. Peking, 1922–3

Nung-min. See *Ti-i-tz'u kuo-nei ko-ming chan-cheng shih-ch'i ti nung-min yun-tung*

Oleson, Alexandra and Voss, John, eds. *The organization of knowledge in modern America, 1860–1920*. Baltimore: Johns Hopkins University Press, 1979

Onogawa Hidemi 小野川秀美 and Shimada Kenji 島田虔次, eds. *Shingai kakumei no kenkyū* 辛亥革命の研究 (Studies on the 1911 Revolution). Tokyo: Chikuma shobō 筑摩書房, 1978

Ortega y Gasset, José. 'The dehumanization of art', in Irving Howe, ed. *The idea of the modern in literature and the arts*, 83–96

Osaka Tokushi 尾坂德司. *Chūgoku shin bungaku undō shi* 中国新文学運動史 (History of the new literature movement of China). 2 vols. Tokyo: Hosei daigaku 法政大学, 1965

Ou Pao-san. See Wu Pao-san

Pa Chin 巴金. *The family*. Trans. by Sidney Shapiro with introduction by Olga Lang. New York: Anchor, 1972

Paauw, Douglas S. 'Chinese national expenditure during the Nanking period'. *FEQ*, 12.1 (Nov. 1952) 3–26

Paauw, Douglas S. 'Chinese public finance during the Nanking government period'. Harvard University, Ph.D. dissertation, 1950

Paauw, Douglas S. 'The Kuomintang and economic stagnation 1928–1937'. *JAS*, 16.2 (Feb. 1957) 213–220

Pacific Affairs. Vancouver, etc. 1926–

Pai Chiao 白蕉. *Yuan Shih-k'ai yü Chung-hua min-kuo* 袁世凱與中華民國 (Yuan Shih-k'ai and the Republic of China). Shanghai: Jen-wen yueh-k'an she 人文月刊社, 1936; Taipei, 1961

Pai Ch'ung-hsi 白崇禧. *Shih-liu nien ch'ing-tang yun-tung ti hui-i* 十六年清黨運動的回憶 (Recollections of the party purification movement of 1927). Kuomintang Kwangsi Party Reconstruction Committee, Propaganda Department, 1932

Pak, Hyobom. *Documents of the Chinese Communist Party, 1927–1930*. Hong Kong: Union Research Institute, 1971

Pan Wei-tung. *The Chinese Constitution: a study of forty years of constitution-making in China*. Washington, D.C.: Sponsored by the Institute of Chinese Culture, 1946

'Pao-hu shang-pu an-ch'üan i-an, Han-k'ou tsung-shang-hui t'i-i' 「保護商埠安全議案」. 漢口總商會提議 (Proposal concerning the protection of commercial centres. Motions put forward by the General Chamber of Commerce of Hankow). *TSHYP*, 3.5 (May 1923)

Pearl, Cyril. *Morrison of China*. Sydney: Angus & Robertson Ltd., 1967

'Pei-ching ta-hsueh-t'ang chih kuo-hsueh wen-t'i' 北京大學堂之國學問題 (The problem of national learning at Peking University). *Hsin-min ts'ung-pao*, 34 (July 1903) 61–2

Pei-fa chan-shih. See Ministry of Defence

Pei-fa chien-shih. See Ministry of Defence

P'eng Min 彭民. *Wu-ssu yun-tung lun-wen chi* 五四運動論文集 (Collected essays on the May Fourth movement). Canton: Jen-min, 1978

P'eng Tse-i 彭澤益, comp. *Chung-kuo chin-tai shou-kung-yeh shih tzu-liao, 1840–1949* 中國近代手工業史資料, 1840–1949 (Source materials on the history of handicraft industry in modern China, 1840–1949). 4 vols. Peking: San-lien, 1957

People's Tribune. Organ of the National Government in Hankow. March–Aug. 1927

Perkins, Dwight H. *Agricultural development in China, 1368–1968*. Chicago: Aldine, 1969

Perkins, Dwight H., ed. *China's modern economy in historical perspective*. Stanford: Stanford University Press, 1975

Perkins, Dwight H. 'Growth and changing structure of China's twentieth-century economy', in Dwight H. Perkins, ed. *China's modern economy in historical perspective*, 115–65. Stanford: Stanford University Press, 1975

PFCS: *Pei-fa chan-shih*. See Ministry of Defence

Pickowicz, Paul. 'Ch'ü Ch'iu-pai and the Chinese Marxist conception of revolutionary popular literature'. *CQ*, 70 (June 1977) 296–314

Pollard, David E. *A Chinese look at literature: the literary values of Chou Tso-jen in relation to the tradition*. Berkeley: University of California Press, 1973

Pott, W. S. A. 'The people's delegates to the Pacific Conference'. *CWR* (22 Oct. 1921)

Powell, Ralph L. *The rise of Chinese military power, 1895–1912*. Princeton: Princeton University Press, 1955

'Power and politics of the Chinese Chamber of Commerce'. *CWR* (17 July 1926) 176; (24 July 1926) 190

Price, Don C. *Russia and the roots of the Chinese Revolution, 1896–1911*. Cambridge, Mass.: Harvard University Press, 1974

'Problems of our policy with respect to China and Japan'. (A resolution of the Politburo of the Russian Communist Party, 25 March 1926). Translated in Leon Trotsky. *Leon Trotsky on China*, 102–10; abstract in Gruber, *Soviet Russia masters the Comintern*, 462–7; and in Leong, *Sino-Soviet diplomatic relations*, 286–9

Průšek, Jaroslav. 'Subjectivism and individualism in modern Chinese literature.' *Archiv Orientalni*, 25.2 (1957) 261–83

Průšek, Jaroslav. 'A confrontation of traditional oriental literature with modern European literature in the context of the Chinese literary revolution.' *Archiv Orientalni*, 32 (1964) 365–75

Průšek, Jaroslav. 'Lu Hsun's "Huai-chiu": a precursor of modern Chinese literature.' *Harvard Journal of Asiatic Studies*, 29 (1969) 169–76

Průšek, Jaroslav. *The lyrical and the epic: studies of modern Chinese literature.* Ed. with a preface by Leo Ou-fan Lee. Bloomington: Indiana University Press, 1980

Pu-erh-sai-wei-k'e 布爾塞維克 (Bolshevik). Shanghai, Oct. 1927–

Pu-jen tsa-chih 不忍. (Compassion magazine). Shanghai, Feb. 1913–

P'u, Yu-shu. 'The Consortium reorganization loan to China, 1911–1914; an episode in pre-war diplomacy and international finance'. University of Michigan, Ph.D. dissertation, 1951

Pye, Lucian W. *Warlord politics: conflict and coalition in the modernization of Republican China.* New York: Praeger, 1971

Rankin, Mary Backus. *Early Chinese revolutionaries: radical intellectuals in Shanghai and Chekiang, 1902–1911.* Cambridge, Mass.: Harvard University Press, 1971

Rankin, Mary Backus. 'The emergence of women at the end of the Ch'ing: the case of Ch'iu Chin', in Margery Wolf and Roxane Witke, eds. *Women in Chinese society*, 39–66. Stanford: Stanford University Press, 1975

Rawski, Thomas G. 'The growth of producer industries, 1900–1971', in Dwight H. Perkins, ed. *China's modern economy in historical perspective*, 203–234. Stanford: Stanford University Press, 1975

Rawski, Thomas G. *China's republican economy: an introduction.* Discussion paper no. 1. Toronto: Joint Centre on Modern East Asia, University of Toronto-York University, 1978

Rea, Kenneth W. See Swisher, Earl.

Reinsch, Paul S. *An American diplomat in China.* Garden City, N.Y.: Doubleday, Page & Co., 1922

Remer, Carl F. *Foreign trade of China.* Shanghai: Commercial Press, 1926

Remer, C. F. *Foreign investments in China.* New York: Macmillan, 1933

Remer, C. F. *A study of Chinese boycotts.* Baltimore: The Johns Hopkins Press, 1933; Taipei: Ch'eng-wen Publishing Co., 1966

Renditions: A Chinese-English Translation Magazine. Chinese University of Hong Kong, Hong Kong, 1973–

'Report of the communistic movement of youth of China'. *China Illustrated Review*, Peking (28 Jan. 1928) 14–16

Report of the trial of the Chinese arrested during the riots of May 30, 1925. Shanghai: North China Daily News and Herald, Ltd., 1925

'Report of the Young Communist International at the Sixth World Congress of the Communist International'. *Lieh-ning ch'ing-nien* 列寧青年 (Leninist youth), 1.10 (15 Feb. 1929) 69–94

'Resolution on the Chinese question of the Sixth ECCI Plenum', in *International press correspondence*, 6.40 (6 May 1926) as quoted in Gruber, *Soviet Russia masters the Comintern*, 475–61

'Review symposium' on Thomas A. Metzger's *Escape from predicament: Neo-Confucianism and China's evolving political culture*. *JAS*, 39.2 (Feb. 1980) 237–90

Reynolds, David. 'Iconoclasm, activism and scholarship: the tension between "spontaneity" and "obligation" in the thought of Fu Ssu-nien', paper presented at the Regional Seminar on Confucian Studies, Berkeley, 4 June 1976

Reynolds, Bruce Lloyd. 'The impact of trade and foreign investment on industrialization: Chinese textiles, 1875–1931', Ph.D. dissertation, University of Michigan, 1974

Rhoads, Edward J. M. *China's republican revolution: the case of Kwangtung, 1895–1913*. Cambridge, Mass.: Harvard University Press, 1975

Rickett, Adele, ed. *Chinese approaches to literature from Confucius to Liang Ch'i-ch'ao*. Princeton, New Jersey: Princeton University Press, 1978

Riskin, Carl. 'Surplus and stagnation in modern China', in Dwight H. Perkins, ed. *China's modern economy in historical perspective*, 49–84. Stanford: Stanford University Press, 1975

Rodes, Jean. *Scenes de la vie révolutionnaire en Chine: 1911–1914*. Paris: Plon Nourrit, 1917

Romanov, B. A. *Russia in Manchuria (1892–1906)*, trans. by Susan W. Jones. Ann Arbor, 1952. Trans. of Rossiya v Manchzhurii, publication 26 of the A. S. Enukidze Oriental Institute, Leningrad, USSR, 1928

Roy, David. *Kuo Mo-jo: the early years*. Cambridge, Mass.: Harvard University Press, 1971

Rozman, Gilbert. *Urban networks in Ch'ing China and Tokugawa Japan*. Princeton: Princeton University Press, 1973

Sanford, James. 'Chinese commercial organization and behavior in Shanghai of the late nineteenth and early twentieth century'. Harvard University, Ph.D. dissertation, 1976

Sanetō Keishū 實藤惠秀. *Chūgokujin Nihon ryūgaku shi* 中国人日本留學史 (A history of Chinese students in Japan). Tokyo: Kuroshio Shuppan くろしお出版, 1960

Sansom, G. B. *The Western world and Japan: a study in the interaction of European and Asiatic cultures*. New York: Knopf, 1950

Scalapino, Robert A. and Yu, George. *The Chinese anarchist movement*. Berkeley: University of California Press, 1962

Schafer, Edward H. *The golden peaches of Samarkand: a study of T'ang exotica*. Berkeley: University of California Press, 1963

Schiffrin, Harold Z. 'Military and politics in China: is the warlord model pertinent?' *Asia Quarterly: A Journal from Europe*, 3 (1975) 193–206

Schneider, Laurence A. *Ku Chieh-kang and China's new history*. Berkeley: University of California Press, 1971

Schneider, Laurence A. 'National essence and the new intelligentsia', in C. Furth, ed. *The limits of change: essays on conservative alternatives in Republican China*, 57–89. Cambridge, Mass.: Harvard University Press, 1976

Schoppa, Robert Keith. 'Politics and society in Chekiang, 1907–1927: elite power, social control and the making of a province'. University of Michigan, Ph.D. dissertation, 1975

Schram, Stuart R. 'On the nature of Mao Tse-tung's "deviation" in 1927'. *CQ*, 18 (April–June 1964) 55–66

Schram, Stuart R. *Political leaders in the twentieth century: Mao Tse-tung.* Harmondsworth, England: Penguin Books, Ltd., 1966

Schram, Stuart R. *The political thought of Mao Tse-tung.* Rev. edn, New York: Praeger, 1969

Schram, Stuart, 'The great union of the popular masses'. *CQ*, 49 (Jan.–March 1972) 88–105

Schràn, Peter. *Guerrilla economy: the development of the Shensi-Kansu-Ninghsia border region, 1937–1945.* Albany: University of New York Press, 1976

Schrecker, John E. *Imperialism and Chinese nationalism: Germany in Shantung.* Cambridge, Mass.: Harvard University Press, 1971

Schultz, William. 'Lu Hsun: the creative years'. University of Washington, Ph.D. dissertation, 1955

Schurmann, F. and Schell, O., comp. *The China reader.* Vol. 2. *Republican China: nationalism, war, and the rise of communism 1911–1949.* New York: Random House, 1967

Schwartz, Benjamin, 'Ch'en Tu-hsiu and the acceptance of the modern West'. *Journal of the History of Ideas,* 12 (1951) 61–72

Schwartz, Benjamin I. *Chinese communism and the rise of Mao.* Cambridge, Mass. Harvard University Press, 1951; paperback edn with new introduction, 1980

Schwartz, Benjamin. 'Some polarities in Confucian thought', in David S. Nivison and Arthur F. Wright, eds. *Confucianism in action,* 50–62. Stanford: Stanford University Press, 1959

Schwartz, Benjamin. *In search of wealth and power: Yen Fu and the West.* Cambridge, Mass.: Harvard University Press, 1964

Schwartz, Benjamin. 'Some stereotypes in the periodization of Chinese history'. *Philosophic Forum,* 1.2 (Winter 1968) 219–230

Schwartz, Benjamin, ed. *Reflections on the May Fourth movement: a symposium.* Cambridge, Mass.: Harvard East Asian Monographs, 1972

SCMP. South China Morning Post

Semanov, Vladimir. *Lu Hsun and his predecessors,* trans. by Charles Alber. New York: M. E. Sharpe, 1980

Shadick, Harold, trans. *The travels of Lao Ts'an.* Ithaca: Cornell University Press, 1966

Shang-hai ch'ien-chuang shih-liao 上海錢莊史料 (Material for the history of the *ch'ien-chuang* banks of Shanghai), comp. by Chung-kuo jen-min yin-hang Shang-hai-shih fen-hang 中國人民銀行上海市分行 (The Shanghai branch of the Chinese People's Bank). Shanghai: Jen-min, 1960

'Shang-hai shih-chih chin-hua shih-lueh' 上海市制進化史略 (Brief history of progress of the Shanghai municipal system), in Shang-hai t'ung she 上海通社, ed. *Shang-hai yen-chiu tzu-liao* 上海研究資料 (Research materials on Shanghai), Shanghai: Chung-hua shu-chü, 1936; Taipei: Chung-kuo ch'u-pan-she, 中國出版社, 1973, 75–8.

Shang-hai tsung-shang-hui yueh-pao 上海總商會月報 (Journal of the General Chamber of Commerce). Monthly. Shanghai, 1921–

Shang-hai t'ung-she 上海通社, ed. *Shang-hai yen-chiu tzu-liao* 上海研究資料 (Research materials on Shanghai). Shanghai, 1936; Taipei: China Press, 1973

Shang-hsueh chi-k'an 商學季刊 (Quarterly review of commercial studies). Peking: Chung-kuo ta-hsueh, 1919–25(?)

' "Shang-jen cheng-fu" ti p'i-p'ing' 「商人政府」的批評 (Critique of the 'government of merchants'). *TFTC*, 20.11 (20 June 1923) 124–5

SHCK. See *Shang-hsueh chi-k'an*

She Yao-shu 佘耀樞. 'Lun chiao-i-so chih shih-pai chih yuan-yin' 論交易所之失敗之原因 (The causes of failure of the Chinese exchanges). *TSHYP*, 2.8 (Aug. 1922) 8–13

She-hui hsin-wen 社會新聞 (The social mercury). Shanghai, Oct. 1932–

Sheean, Vincent. *Personal history*. Garden City, N.Y.: Doubleday, Doran & Co., 1935

Shen I-yun 沈亦雲. *I-yun hui-i* 亦雲回憶 (Reminiscences of Shen I-yun). Taipei: Chuan-chi wen-hsueh, 1968

Shen pao ('Shun Pao') 申報. Daily, Shanghai, 1872–1949

Shen Yun-lung 沈雲龍. *Li Yuan-hung p'ing-chuan* 黎元洪評傳 (A critical biography of Li Yuan-hung). Taipei: Institute of Modern History, Academia Sinica, 1963

Shen Yun-lung, comp. *Yuan Shih-k'ai shih-liao hui-k'an* 袁世凱史料彙刊 (Collected historical materials on Yuan Shih-k'ai), a multi-volume collection, various titles. Also *Hsu-pien* 續編 (Supplement) and further volumes. Taipei reprint: Wen-hai, 1966

Shen Yun-lung. *Hsu Shih-ch'ang p'ing-chuan* 徐世昌評傳 (A critical biography of Hsu Shih-ch'ang). Taipei: Chuan-chi wen-hsueh, 1979

Shen Yun-lung, ed. *Chin-tai Chung-kuo shih-liao ts'ung-k'an* 近代中國史料叢刊 (Library of historical materials on modern China). 1st series Taipei: Wen-hai, 1966

Shen Yun-sun 沈雲蓀. 'Chung-hua shih-yeh yin-hang shih-mo' 中華實業銀行始末 (History of the Chinese Industrial Bank). *Chin-tai-shih tzu-liao* 近代史資料 (Materials on modern history), 6 (1957) 120–39

Sheridan, James E. *Chinese warlord: the career of Feng Yü-hsiang*. Stanford: Stanford University Press, 1966

Sheridan, James E. *China in disintegration: the republican era in Chinese history*. New York: Free Press, 1975

Shieh, Milton J. T. *The Kuomintang: selected historical documents, 1894–1969*. Jamaica, N.Y.: St. John's University Press, 1970

Shih Chün, 石峻, ed. *Chung-kuo chin-tai ssu-hsiang-shih tzu-liao – wu-ssu shih-ch'i chu-yao lun-wen-hsuan* 中國近代思想史資料—五四時期主要論文選 (Materials on modern Chinese intellectual history – selected important essays of the May 4 period). Tokyo: Daian, 1968

Shih-fu. See Liu Shih-fu

Shih-pao 時報. Shanghai, 1904–

Shih, Paul T. K. *The strenuous decade: China's nation-building efforts 1927–1937*. Jamaica, N.Y.: St. John's University Press, 1970

'Shih-t'uan yü chin-mien ch'u-k'ou-ling chih ch'ü-hsiao' 使團與禁棉出口令之取銷 (The Diplomatic Corps and the abrogation of the decree banning the exportation of cotton). *YHYK*, 3.7 (July 1923) heading *Kuo-nei ts'ai-cheng ching-chi*

Shih-wu pao 時務報 (Current affairs, 'The China progress'). Shanghai, Aug. 1896–July 1898

Shin, Linda. 'China in transition: the role of Wu T'ing-fang (1842–1922)'. University of California, Los Angeles, Ph.D. dissertation, 1970

Shina kin'yū jijō. See Japan, Gaimushō

Shun Pao. See *Shen-pao*

Shun-t'ien shih-pao 順天時報. Peking, 1901–30

Sie, Ying-chow. *Le fédéralisme en Chine. Étude sur quelques constitutions provinciales*. University of Paris, thèse de la Faculté de Droit, 1924

Sigel, Louis T. 'T'ang Shao-yi (1860–1938): the diplomacy of Chinese nationalism'. Harvard University, Ph.D. dissertation, 1972

Skachkov, P. E., ed. *Bibliografiia Kitaia* (Bibliography of China). Moscow: Izdvo vostochnoi literatury, 1960

Skinner, G. William. *Chinese society in Thailand: an analytical history*. Ithaca: Cornell University Press, 1957

Skinner, G. William. 'Marketing and social structure in rural China'. Part I, *JAS*, 26.1 (Nov. 1964) 3–44. (Part II and III in subsequent issues)

Skinner, George William, *et al.*, eds. *Modern Chinese society: an analytical bibliography*. 3 vols. Stanford: Stanford University Press, 1973

Skinner, G. William, ed. *The city in late imperial China*. Stanford: Stanford University Press, 1977

Slupski, Zbigniew. *The evolution of a modern Chinese writer: an analysis of Lao She's fiction with biographical and bibliographical appendices*. Prague: Oriental Institute, 1966

SMR: Mantetsu Chōsabu 滿鐵調查部 (South Manchurian Railway Research Department). *Chū-shi no minsengyō* 中支の民船業 (The junk trade of central China). Tokyo: Hakubunkan 博文館, 1943

Smedley, Agnes. *The great road: the life and times of Chu Teh*. New York: Monthly Review Press, 1956

Snow, Edgar. *Red star over China*. New York: Random House, 1938; 1st rev. and enlarged edn, Grove Press, 1968

So, Kwan-wai. *Japanese piracy in Ming China during the 16th century*. East Lansing: Michigan State University Press, 1975

Solomon, Richard H. *Mao's revolution and the Chinese political culture*. Berkeley: University of California Press, 1971

Sonoda Kazuki 園田一龜, comp. *Fen-sheng hsin-Chung-kuo jen-wu-chih* 分省新中國人物誌 (A record of personages of new China by provinces). Trans. from the

Japanese by Huang Hui-ch'üan 黃惠泉 and Tiao Ying-hua 刁英華. Shanghai: Liang-yu 良友, 1930

South China Morning Post. Hong Kong, 1903–

South Manchurian Railway, various offices. See SMR

Soviet plot in China. Peking: The Metropolitan Police Headquarters, 1928

Spence, Jonathan D. *The death of Woman Wang.* New York: The Viking Press, 1978

Spence, Jonathan D. *The Gate of Heavenly Peace: the Chinese and their revolution 1895–1980.* New York: Viking Press, 1981

Spence, Jonathan D. and Wills, John E., Jr., eds. *From Ming to Ch'ing: conquest, region, and continuity in seventeenth-century China.* New Haven: Yale University Press, 1979

State Statistical Bureau. Industrial Statistics Department. *Wo-kuo kang-t'ieh, tien-li, mei-t'an, chi-hsieh, fang-chih, tsao-chih kung-yeh ti chin-hsi* 我國鋼鐵, 電力, 煤炭, 機械, 紡織, 造紙工業的今昔 (Past and present of China's iron and steel, electric power, coal, machinery, textile and paper industries). Peking: T'ung-chi ch'u-pan-she 統計出版社, 1958

Strand, David. 'Peking in the 1920s: political order and popular protest'. Columbia University, Ph.D. dissertation, 1979

Strong, Anna Louise. *China's millions.* New York: Coward McCann, 1928

Su-ch'ing 蕭清 (pseud.). *Kung-ch'an-tang chih yin-mou ta pao-lu* 共產黨之陰謀大暴露 (The plots of the Communist Party exposed). Canton: San Min Chü-lo-pu, 1924

Su Wen 蘇汶, ed. *Wen-i tzu-yu lun-pien chi* 文藝自由論辯集 (Debate on the freedom of literature and art). Shanghai: Hsien-tai 現代, 1933

Suleski, Ronald S. 'Manchuria under Chang Tso-lin'. University of Michigan, Ph.D. dissertation, 1974

Sun K'o-fu 孫克復 and Fan Shu-sheng 樊樹生. *Yuan Shih-k'ai tsun-K'ung fu-p'i ch'ou-chü* 袁世凱尊孔復辟醜劇 (The ugly drama of Yuan Shih-k'ai's veneration of Confucius and imperial restoration). Peking: Chung-hua, 1975

Sun Te-chung 孫德中, comp. *Ts'ai Yuan-p'ei hsien-sheng i-wen lei-ch'ao* 蔡元培先生遺文類鈔 (Posthumous collection of Ts'ai Yuan-p'ei's writings arranged by types). Taipei: Fu-hsing shu-chü 復興書局, 1961

Sun Yao 孫曜. *Chung-hua min-kuo shih-liao* 中華民國史料 (Historical materials of the Chinese Republic) 1930. Taipei: Wen-hai, 1967

Sun Yat-sen. *The international development of China.* Preface 1921. 2nd edn, London Office of the Chinese Ministry of Information. London: Hutchinson, 1928

Sun Yat-sen 孫逸仙. 'Ho-p'ing t'ung-i hsuan-yen' 和平統一宣言 (Manifesto on peaceful unification), in Chang Ch'i-yun, 張其昀, ed. *Kuo-fu ch'üan-shu* 國父全書 (Complete works of the national father Sun Yat-sen). 754–5 Taipei: Chung-kuo hsin-wen, 1960

Sun Yat-sen. *Kuo-fu ch'üan-chi* 國父全集 (The collected works of the national father Sun Yat-sen). 6 vols. Rev. edn, Taipei: Chung-kuo Kuomintang Central Executive Committee, 1961

Sutton, Donald S. *Provincial militarism and the Chinese Republic: the Yunnan Army, 1905–25*. Ann Arbor: University of Michigan Press, 1980

Swisher, Earl. *Canton in revolution: the collected papers of Earl Swisher, 1925–1928*, ed. by Kenneth W. Rea. Boulder, Colorado: Westview Press, 1977

Ta Chung-hua 大中華 (Great China). Shanghai, Jan. 1915– Dec. 1916

Ta-lung chi-ch'i-ch'ang ti fa-sheng fa-chan yü kai-tsao 大隆機器廠的發生發展與改造 (Origin, development and transformation of the Ta-lung Machine Works). Comp. by Chung-kuo k'o-hsueh-yuan Shang-hai ching-chi yen-chiu-so 中國科學院上海經濟研究所. Shanghai: Jen-min, 1958

Tagore, Amitendranath. *Literary debates in modern China, 1918–1937*. Tokyo: Centre for East Asian Cultural Studies, 1967

Tai Chi-t'ao 戴季陶. *Kuo-min ko-ming yü Chung-kuo Kuo-min-tang* 國民革命與中國國民黨 (The national revolution and the Kuomintang of China). Shanghai: 'Chi-t'ao's Office', July 1925

Tai Chi-t'ao. *Tai Chi-t'ao hsien-sheng wen-ts'un* 戴季陶先生文存 (Collected writings of Mr Tai Chi-t'ao), ed by Ch'en T'ien-hsi 陳天錫. 4 vols. Central Executive Committee of the Kuomintang, 1959

Tai Chi-t'ao. *Tai T'ien-ch'ou wen-chi* 戴天仇文集 (Collected essays of Tai Chi-t'ao). Original title: *Sung Yü-fu Tai T'ien-ch'ou wen-chi ho-k'o* 宋漁父戴天仇文集合刻 (Collected essays of Sung Chiao-jen and Tai Chi-t'ao, 1912). Taipei reprint: Wen-hsing, 1962

Tai, Yih-jian. 'The contemporary Chinese theater and Soviet influence'. Southern Illinois University, Ph.D. dissertation, 1974

T'ai-p'ing yang 太平洋 ('The Pacific Ocean'). Monthly, then bimonthly. Shanghai: Commercial Press, 1917–

Takeuchi Katsumi 竹內克己 and Kashiwada Tenzan 柏田天山. *Shina seitō kessha shi* 支那政黨結社史 (A history of political parties and societies in China). 2 vols. Hankow: Ch'ung-wen ko 崇文閣, 1918

Takeuchi edn. See Mao Tse-tung

Takeuchi Yoshimi 竹內好. *Ro Jin* 魯迅 (Lu Hsun). Tokyo: Miraisha 未來社, 1961; 10th printing, 1973

Tamagna, Frank M. *Banking and finance in China*. New York: Institute of Pacific Relations, 1942

T'an, Chester. *Chinese political thought in the twentieth century*. New York: Doubleday, 1971

T'an-ho Kung-ch'an-tang liang ta yao-an 彈劾共產黨兩大要案 (Two important cases of impeachment of the Communist Party). n.p.: Kuomintang Central Supervisory Committee, Sept. 1927; reprinted in *KMWH*, 9 (June 1955) 1271–3

T'an Ssu-t'ung 譚嗣同. 'Jen hsueh' 仁學 (On humanity). *Ch'ing-i pao* 清議報. 2–14 (2 Jan. 1899–10 May 1899)

T'an Ssu-t'ung. 'Chih shih p'ien' 治事篇 (Essay on public affairs), in Yang Chia-lo 楊家駱, *Wu-hsu pien-fa wen-hsien hui-pien* 3.83–92

T'an Ssu-t'ung. *T'an Ssu-t'ung ch'üan chi* 譚嗣同全集 (Complete works of T'an Ssu-t'ung). Tokyo, 1966

Tang, Peter S. H. *Russian and Soviet policy in Manchuria and Outer Mongolia, 1911–
1931*. Durham, N.C.: Duke University Press, 1959

T'ao Chü-yin 陶菊隱. *Wu P'ei-fu chiang-chün chuan* 吳佩孚將軍傳 (Biography of
General Wu P'ei-fu). Shanghai: Chung-hua, 1941; reprinted as *Wu P'ei-fu
chuan* 吳佩孚傳, Taipei: Chung-hua, 1957

T'ao Chü-yin. *Tu-chün-t'uan chuan* 督軍團傳 (Chronicle of the association of
warlords). Shanghai; Taipei reprint: Wen-hai, 1971

T'ao Chü-yin. *Chiang Po-li hsien-sheng chuan* 蔣百里先生傳 (A biography of Mr
Chiang Po-li). Shanghai: Chung-hua, 1948; Taiwan reprint: Wen-hai, 1972

T'ao Chü-yin. *Pei-yang chün-fa t'ung-chih shih-ch'i shih-hua* 北洋軍閥統治時期史話
(Historical tales about the period of rule by the Peiyang warlords). 7 vols.
Peking: San-lien, 1957–61

T'ao Meng-ho 陶孟和 [T'ao Lü-kung] 陶履恭. 'Lun tzu-sha' 論自殺 (On suicide).
Hsin ch'ing-nien, 6.1 (15 Jan. 1918) 12–18

T'ao Ying-hui 陶英惠, comp. *Ts'ai Yuan-p'ei nien-p'u* 蔡元培年譜 (A chronological biography of Ts'ai Yuan-p'ei). Vol 1. Taipei: Institute of Modern History, Academia Sinica, 1976

(Teng) Chih-ping (鄧) 峙冰. 'Shih-chü tsa-kan' 時局雜感 (Various impressions
of the current situation). *TSHYP*, 3.2 (Feb. 1923) heading *Yen-lun*

(Teng) Chih-ping. 'Kuo-ch'üan hui-fu yü ching-chi chueh-chiao' 國權回復與經
濟絕交 (The return of sovereign rights and the rupture of economic relations).
TSHYP, 3.4 (April 1923) heading *Yen-lun*

Teng Chung-hsia 鄧中夏. *Chung-kuo chih-kung yun-tung chien-shih* 中國職工運動簡史
(A brief history of the Chinese labour movement). Original edn, Moscow,
1930; Central China: New China Bookstore, 1949

Teng, Ssu-yü and Fairbank, John K., comps. *China's response to the West: a documentary survey, 1839–1923*. Cambridge, Mass.: Harvard University Press,
1954; with a new preface, 1979

Teng, Ssu-yü and Biggerstaff, Knight, comps. *An annotated bibliography of
selected Chinese reference works*. 3rd edn. Cambridge, Mass.: Harvard University
Press, 1971

Teng Yen-ta 鄧演達. *Teng Yen-ta hsien-sheng i-chu* 鄧演達先生遺著 (A posthumous
collection of Mr Teng Yen-ta's writings). Preface (1949) by Yang I-t'ang 楊逸
棠. Hong Kong: n.p., n.d.

Terahiro Teruo 寺廣映雄. 'Unnan gokokugun ni tsuite – kigi no shutai to undō
no seishitsu' 雲南護國軍について―起義の主體と運動の性質 (The main constituents of the uprising of Yunnan's National Protection Army and the
nature of the movement). *Tōyōshi kenkyū* 東洋史研究, 17.3 (Dec. 1958) 27–53

Terahiro Teruo. *Chūgoku kakumei no shiteki tenkai* 中国革命の史的展開 (The
historical unfolding of the Chinese revolution). Tokyo: Kyūko shoin 汲古書
院, 1979

Terrill, Ross. *Mao: a biography*. New York: Harper & Row, 1980

TFTC. See *Tung-fang tsa-chih*

Thomas, S. Bernard. '*Proletarian hegemony' in the Chinese revolution and the Canton*

Commune of 1927. Ann Arbor: University of Michigan Center for Chinese Studies, 1975

Thomson, James C., Jr. *While China faced West: American reformers in Nationalist China, 1928–1937.* Cambridge: Harvard University Press, 1969

'Three Shanghai uprisings'. *Problemi Kitaii,* Moscow, 2 (1930); mimeographed

Ti-i-tz'u kuo-nei ko-ming chan-cheng shih-ch'i ti kung-jen yun-tung 第一次國內革命戰爭時期的工人運動 (The labour movement during the first revolutionary civil war period). 3rd edn, Peking: Jen-min, 1963; cited as *Kung-jen*

Ti-i-tz'u kuo-nei ko-ming chan-cheng shih-ch'i ti nung-min yun-tung 第一次國內革命戰爭時期的農民運動 (The farmers' movement during the first revolutionary civil war period). Peking: Jen-min, 1953; cited as *Nung-min*

Ti-kuo chu-i yü Chung-kuo hai-kuan 帝國主義與中國海關 (Imperialism and the Chinese Maritime Customs). 10 vols. Peking: K'o-hsueh, 1957–62

Ti-ssu-chün chi-shih 第四軍紀實 (Factual account of the Fourth Army), comp. by Compilation Committee on the Factual Account of the Fourth Army. Canton: Huai-yuan wen-hua shih-yeh fu-wu-she 懷遠文化事業服務社, 1949

'T'i-ch'ang kuo-huo chih wo-chien' 提倡國貨之我見 (My views on the promotion of national merchandizing). *TSHYP,* 4.5 (May 1924) heading *Yen-lun.*

T'ien Chun (Hsiao Chün). *Village in August,* trans. by Evan King, with an introduction by Edgar Snow. New York: Smith & Durrell, 1942

T'ien Han 田漢, Ou-yang Yü-ch'ien 歐陽予倩, *et al. Chung-kuo hua-chü yun-tung wu-shih-nien shih-liao chi, 1907–1957* 中國話劇運動五十年史料集, 1907–1957 (Historical materials on the modern Chinese drama movement of the last fifty years, 1907–1957). Peking: Chung-kuo hsi-chü 中國戲劇, 1957

T'ien-i 天義 (Natural morality), 3–19 (10 July 1907–15 March 1908); reprinted in *Chung-kuo tzu-liao ts'ung-shu* 中國資料叢書, series 6 *Chung-kuo ch'u-ch'i she-hui chu-i wen-hsien chi* 中國初期社會主義文獻集, no. 2 Tokyo: Daian, 1966

Ting, Leonard G. 'Chinese modern banks and the finance of government and industry'. *Nankai Social and Economic Quarterly,* 8.3 (Oct. 1935) 578–616

Ting Ling 丁玲 *et al. Chieh-fang ch'ü tuan-p'ien ch'uang-tso hsuan* 解放區短篇創作選 (Selected short works from the liberated areas). 2 vols. N.p., 1947

Ting Wen-chiang 丁文江 and Weng Wen-hao 翁文灝. *Chung-kuo fen-sheng hsin-t'u* 中國分省新圖 (New atlas of China by provinces). Shanghai: Shen-pao kuan, 申報館, 1933

Ting Wen-chiang, Weng Wen-hao and Tseng Shih-ying 曾世英. *Chung-hua min-kuo hsin-ti-t'u* 中華民國新地圖 (New atlas of the Chinese Republic). Shanghai: Shen-pao kuan 申報館, 1934

Ting Wen-chiang. 'Shao-shu jen ti tse-jen' 少數人的責任 (The responsibilities of a minority). *NLCP,* 67 (26 Aug. 1923)

Ting Wen-chiang. *Min-kuo chün-shih chin-chi* 民國軍事近紀 (Recent accounts of the military affairs of the republic). Peking: Commercial Press, 1926

Ting Wen-chiang, *et al.,* eds. *Liang Jen-kung hsien-sheng nien-p'u ch'ang-pien ch'u-kao* 梁任公先生年譜長編初稿 (Extended annals of Mr Liang Ch'i-ch'ao, first draft). 3 vols. Taipei: Shih-chieh shu-chü 世界書局, 1958

TJK: See Li Yun-han, *Ts'ung jung-Kung tao ch'ing-tang*

Tokuda Noriyuki 德田教之. 'Chūkyōtō shi kankei shiryō mokuroku' 中共党史関係資料目錄 (Bibliography of materials on the history of the CCP.) *Kindai Chūgoku kenkyū sentā ihō* 近代中国研究センター彙報 9 (July 1967) 8–20; 10 (Oct. 1967) 8–24

Tokunaga Kiyoyuki 德永清行. *Shina chūō ginkō ron* 支那中央銀行論 (A treatise on central banking in China). Tokyo: Yūhikaku 有斐閣, 1942

Tong, Hollington K. (Tung Hsien-kuang 董顯光). *Chiang Kai-shek*. Rev. edn, Taipei: China Publishing Co., 1953

Tong Te-kong and Li Tsung-jen. *The memoirs of Li Tsung-jen*. Boulder & Folkestone: Westview Press and Wm. Dawson and Sons, Studies of the East Asian Institute, Columbia University, 1979

Tou Chi-liang 竇季良. *T'ung-hsiang tsu-chih chih yen-chiu* 同鄉組織之研究 (Studies of regional associations). Chungking: Cheng-chung, 1943

Trotsky, Leon. *Problems of the Chinese revolution*. 2nd edn, reprint, New York: Paragon Book Gallery, 1962

Trotsky, Leon. *Leon Trotsky on China: introduction by Peng Shu-tse,* eds. Les Evans and Russell Block. New York: Monad Press, 1976

Tsa-chih yueh-k'an 雜誌月刊 (Monthly miscellany). Shanghai, May 1938–

(Ts'ai) Ho-sen 蔡和森. 'Fan-tui "tun-ch'ing i yu-pang" kan-she Chung-kuo nei-cheng' 反對「敦請一友邦」干涉中國內政 (Against 'the cordial invitation to a friendly power' to intervene in the internal government of China). *HTCP*, 19 (7 Feb. 1923) 150

(Ts'ai) Ho-sen. 'Wai-kuo ti-kuo-chu-i-che tui-Hua ti hsin chiu fang-fa' 外國帝國主義者對華的新舊方法 (New and old methods of the foreign imperialists with regard to China). *HTCP* 22 (25 April 1923) 158–60

(Ts'ai) Ho-sen. 'Wei shou-hui hai-kuan chu-ch'üan shih kao ch'üan-kuo kuo-min' 為收回海關主權事告全國國民 (Notice to the Chinese people of the restitution of rights over the Maritime Customs). *HTCP*, 48 (12 Dec. 1923) 365–6

(Ts'ai) Ho-sen. 'Shang-jen kan-chueh tao wai-kuo ti-kuo-chu-i chu-chang Chung-kuo nei-luan ti ti-i-sheng' 商人感覺到外國帝國主義助長中國內亂的第一聲 (The merchants begin to realize that foreign imperialism promotes internal troubles in China). *HTCP*, 44 (27 Oct. 1923) 333

Ts'ai Ho-sen. 'The Kwangtung farmers' movement on May First this year'. *HTCP*, 112 (1 May 1925) 1030–6

Ts'ai Shang-ssu 蔡尙思. *Ts'ai Yuan-p'ei hsueh-shu ssu-hsiang chuan-chi* 蔡元培學術思想傳記 (An academic and intellectual biography of Ts'ai Yuan-p'ei). Shanghai: T'ang-ti ch'u-pan-she 棠棣出版社, 1950

Ts'ai Yuan-p'ei 蔡元培. 'Wu-shih-nien lai Chung-kuo chih che-hsueh' 五十年來中國之哲學 (Chinese philosophy in the past 50 years). *Shen pao* 申報 anniversary issue, *Tsui-chin wu-shih nien* 最近五十年 (The last 50 years), 1–10 (sep. pag.). Shanghai: Shen pao, 1922

Ts'ai Yuan-p'ei. 'Wo so-shou chiu-chiao-yü chih hui-i' 我所受舊教育之回憶 (Reminiscences on the traditional education I have received), *Jen-chien-shih* 人間世, 1 (5 April 1934) 8–9

Ts'ai Yuan-p'ei. 'Wo ch'ing-nien-shih-tai ti tu-shu sheng-huo' 我青年時代的讀書生活 (My experiences as a student), *Tu-shu sheng-huo* 讀書生活, 2.6 (July 1936)

Ts'ai Yuan-p'ei. See Huang Shih-hui

Ts'ang Shui 滄水. 'Chin mien ch'u-k'ou yü chin-hou Chung Jih sha-shih chih kan-hsiang' 禁棉出口與今後中日紗市之感想 (Impressions on the ban of exportation of raw cotton and on the future for Chinese and Japanese yarns). *YHCP*, 7.6 (6 Feb. 1923) 14–15

Ts'ao Chü-jen 曹聚仁. *Wen-t'an san i* 文壇三憶 (Three reminiscences of the literary scene). Hong Kong: Hsin wen-hua ch'u-pan-she 新文化出版社, 1954

Ts'ao Chü-jen. *Wen-t'an wu-shih nien hsu-chi* 文壇五十年續集 (Sequel to fifty years on the literary scene). Hong Kong: Hsin wen-hua, 1969

Ts'ao Ju-lin 曹汝霖. *I-sheng chih hui-i* 一生之回憶 (A lifetime's recollections). Hong Kong: Ch'un-ch'iu tsa-chih she 春秋雜誌社, 1966

Ts'ao Yü 曹禺. *Jih-ch'u* 日出 (Sunrise). Shanghai: Wen-hua sheng-huo 文化生活, 1936

Ts'en Hsueh-lü 岑學呂 [Feng-kang chi-men ti-tzu 鳳岡及門弟子], comp. *San-shui Liang Yen-sun hsien-sheng nien-p'u* 三水梁燕孫先生年譜 (A chronological biography of the life of Mr Liang Yen-sun [Shih-i] of San-shui hsien). 2 vols. 1930. Taipei: Wen-hsing, 1962

TSHYP. See *Shang-hai tsung-shang-hui yueh-pao*

Tso-lien shih-ch'i wu-ch'an chieh-chi ko-ming wen-hsueh 左聯時期無產階級革命文學 (Proletarian revolutionary literature in the period of the Leftwing League), ed. by Nan-ching ta-hsueh Chung-wen hsi 南京大學中文系 (Department of Chinese, Nanking University). Nanking: Chiang-su wen-i 江蘇文藝, 1960

Tsou Lu 鄒魯. *Chung-kuo Kuo-min-tang shih kao* 中國國民黨史稿 (A draft history of the Kuomintang of China). 2nd edn. Chungking: Commercial Press, 1944; Taipei: Commercial Press, 1970

Tsou Lu. *Hui-ku-lu* 回顧錄 (Reminiscences). 2 vols. Nanking: Tu-li 獨立, 1946; reprint 1947

Tung, William L. *China and the foreign powers: the impact of and reaction to unequal treaties.* Dobbs Ferry, N.Y.: Oceania Publications, Inc., 1970

Tung-fang tsa-chih 東方雜誌 (The eastern miscellany). Shanghai, 1904–48; cited as *TFTC*

Tung Hsien-kuang 董顯光 (Hollington Tong). *Chiang Tsung-t'ung chuan* 蔣總統傳 (A biography of President Chiang). Taipei: Chung-hua wen-hua ch'u-pan shih-yeh wei-yuan-hui 中華文化出版事業委員會, 1954

T'ung Shih-kang 童世綱. *Hu Shih wen-ts'un so-yin* 胡適文存索引 (Index to the collected works of Hu Shih). Taipei: Hsueh-sheng shu-chü 學生書局, 1969

Tzu Ming 子明. 'Shih-chieh mien-hua chih hsu-kei yü Chung Jih mien-yeh chih kuan-hsi' 世界棉花之需給與中日棉業之關係 (Supply and demand of cotton on the world market, and the textile industries in China and Japan). *YHCP*, 7.10 (20 March 1923), 7.11 (27 March 1923)

U. S. Bureau of the Census. *Historical statistics of the United States, 1789–1945.* Washington, D.C., 1949

U.S. Department of State. *Papers relating to the foreign relations of the United States.* Washington, D.C.: U.S. Government Printing Office, annual volumes.

U.S. Department of State. 'Records relating to the internal affairs of China, 1910–1929'. Washington, D.C.: U.S. National Archives, Microcopy 329

USFR. See U.S. Department of State, *Papers relating to. . . .*

USNA. United States National Archives

Usui Katsumi 臼井勝美. *Nihōn to Chūgoku – Taishō jidai* 日本と中国―大正時代 (Japan and China – the Taishō period). Tokyo: Hara shobō 原書房, 1972

Uyehara, Cecil H., comp. *Checklist of archives in the Japanese Ministry of Foreign Affairs, Tokyo, Japan, 1868–1945, microfilmed for the Library of Congress, 1949–1951.* Washington, D.C.: Library of Congress, 1954

Varè, Daniele. *Laughing diplomat.* New York: Doubleday, Doran & Co., 1938

Varg, Paul A. *Missionaries, Chinese, and diplomats: the American Protestant missionary movement in China, 1890–1952.* Princeton: Princeton University Press, 1958

Vidnye sovietskie kommunisty – uchastniki kitaiskoi revolutsii (Outstanding Soviet communists – participants in the Chinese revolution). Moscow: Akad. Nauk SSSR, Institut Dal'nego Vostoka, 'Nauka', 1970

Vincent, John Carter. *The extraterritorial system in China: final phase.* Cambridge, Mass.: Harvard University Press, 1970

Viraphol, Sarasin. *Tribute and profit: Sino-Siamese trade, 1652–1853.* Cambridge, Mass.: Harvard University Press, 1977

Vishnyakova-Akimova, Vera Vladimirovna. *Dva goda v vosstavshem Kitae, 1925–1927: vospominania.* Moscow: Akad. Nauk SSSR, Institute of the Peoples of Asia, Izd-vo 'Nauka', 1965. Trans. by Steven I. Levine, *Two years in revolutionary China, 1925–1927.* Cambridge, Mass.: Harvard University Press, 1971

Vohra, Ranbir. *Lao She and the Chinese revolution.* Cambridge, Mass.: Harvard East Asian Monographs, 1974

Wakeman, Frederic, Jr. *History and will: philosophical perspectives of Mao Tse-tung's thought.* Berkeley: University of California Press, 1973

Wakeman, Frederic, Jr., ed. *Ming and Qing historical studies in the People's Republic of China.* Berkeley: Center for Chinese studies, China research monograph no. 17, 1980

Wales, Nym (Helen Foster Snow). *Red dust: autobiographies of Chinese Communists as told to Nym Wales.* Stanford: Stanford University Press, 1952

Walker, Kenneth R. *Planning in Chinese agriculture: socialisation and the private sector, 1956–1962.* Chicago: Aldine, 1965

Wallerstein, Immanuel. *The modern world-system: capitalist agriculture and the origins of the European world-economy in the sixteenth century.* London: Academic Press, 1976

Wang Che-fu 王哲甫. *Chung-kuo hsin wen-hsueh yun-tung shih* 中國新文學運動史

(A history of the new literary movement in China). Hong Kong: Yuan-tung t'u-shu kung-ssu 遠東圖書公司, 1965

Wang Chi-chen, ed. *Stories of China at war*. New York: Columbia University Press, 1947

Wang Chi-shen 王季深. *Chan-shih Shang-hai ching-chi* 戰時上海經濟 (The economy of wartime Shanghai). Shanghai: Shang-hai ching-chi yen-chiu-so 上海經濟研究所, 1945

Wang Chien-min 王健民. *Chung-kuo Kung-ch'an-tang shih kao* 中國共產黨史稿 (A draft history of the Chinese Communist Party). 3 vols. Taipei: published by the author, 1965

Wang, C. H. 王靖獻. 'Chou Tso-jen's Hellenism'. *Renditions*, 7 (Spring 1977) 5–28

Wang Ching-wei 汪精衛. 'Political report' to the Second Kuomintang Congress, in *KMWH*, 20 (March 1958) 3851–70

Wang Ching-wei. *Wang Ching-wei hsien-sheng tsui-chin yen-shuo chi* 汪精衛先生最近演說集 (Mr Wang Ching-wei's most recent speeches collected). N.p., n.d. (1928?)

Wang Ching-yü 汪敬虞, comp. *Chung-kuo chin-tai kung-yeh-shih tzu-liao, ti-erh chi, 1895–1914 nien* 中國近代工業史資料第二輯, 1895–1914年 (Source materials on the history of modern industry in China, second collection, 1895–1914). 2 vols. Peking: K'o-hsueh, 1957

Wang Erh-min 王爾敏. *Chung-kuo chin-tai ssu-hsiang shih lun* 中國近代思想史論 (On the history of modern Chinese thought). Taipei: Hua-shih ch'u-pan-she 華世出版社, 1977

Wang Fu-sun 汪馥蓀. 'Chan-ch'ien Chung-kuo kung-yeh sheng-ch'an-chung wai-ch'ang sheng-ch'an ti pi-chung wen-t'i' 戰前中國工業生產中外廠生產的比重問題 (The proportion of industrial production by foreign-owned factories in total industrial production in pre-war China). *Chung-yang yin-hang yueh-pao* 中央銀行月報, 2.3 (March 1947) 1–19

Wang Fu-sun. 'Chan-shih Hua-pei kung-yeh tzu-pen chiu-yeh yü sheng-ch'an' 戰時華北工業資本就業與生產 (Wartime industrial capital, employment and production in North China). *She-hui k'o-hsueh tsa-chih* 社會科學雜誌, 9.2 (Dec. 1947) 48

Wang, Gungwu. 'The Nanhai trade'. *Journal of the Malayan Branch of the Royal Asiatic Society*, 31 (1958) pt 2.1–135

Wang, Gungwu. *Power, rights and duties in Chinese history*, the 40th George Ernest Morrison Lecture in Ethnology, 1979. Canberra: The Australian National University, 1979

Wang P'ing-ling 王平陵. *San-shih-nien wen-t'an ts'ang-sang lu* 三十年文壇滄桑錄 (Changes on the literary scene in thirty years). Taipei: Chung-kuo wen-i-she 中國文藝社, 1965

Wang Shao-fang 王紹坊, trans. *Wai-jen tsai-Hua t'e-ch'üan ho li-i* 外人在華特權和利益 (Foreigners' rights and interests in China), a translation of Westel W. Willoughby, *Foreign rights and interests in China*. Peking: San-lien, 1957

Wang T'ao 王韜. 'Pien-fa' 變法 (Reform), reprinted in Yang Chia-lo 楊家駱, comp, *Wu-hsu-pien-fa wen-hsien hui-pien* 戊戌變法文獻彙編 (Documentary collection of literature of the 1898 reform movement), 1.131-5

Wang Te-i 王德毅. *Wang Kuo-wei nien-p'u* 王國維年譜 (Chronological biography of Wang Kuo-wei). Taipei: Chung-kuo hsueh-shu chu-tso chiang-chu wei-yuan-hui 中國學術著作獎助委員會, 1967

Wang Yao 王瑤. *Chung-kuo hsin-wen-hsueh shih-kao* 中國新文學史稿 (A draft history of China's new literature). 2 vols. Shanghai: Hsin-wen-i ch'u-pan she, 1953

Wang, Y. C. 汪一駒. *Chinese intellectuals and the West, 1872-1949*. Chapel Hill: University of North Carolina Press, 1966

Wang, Y. C. 'Tu Yueh-sheng (1888-1951): a tentative political biography'. *JAS*, 26.3 (May 1967) 433-55

Watanabe Atsushi 渡辺惇. 'En Seigai seiken no keizaiteki kiban – hokuyō-ha no kigyō katsudō' 袁世凱政権の経済的基盤—北洋派の企業活動 (The economic basis of the Yuan Shih-k'ai regime: the industrial activity of the Peiyang Clique), in *Chūgoku kindaika no shakai kōzō: Shingai kakumei no shiteki ichi* 中国近代化の社会構造：辛亥革命の史的位置 (The social framework of China's modernization: the historical position of the 1911 Revolution), 135-71. Tokyo: Daian, 1960

'Wei wai-jen kan-yü hu-lu shih chih Fu ling-hsiu kung-shih han' 為外人干預護路事致符領袖公使函 (Letter addressed to Mr Fu [Batalha de Freitas], doyen of the Diplomatic Corps, on the subject of foreign interference in the protection of the railways). *TSHYK*, 3.9 (Sept. 1923) heading *Hui-wu chi-tsai*.

Wellek, René. *Concepts of criticism*. New Haven, 1963

Wen Han 文漢. 'Yu kung-yeh chien-ti shang lun wei-ch'ih kuo-huo yü ti-chih Jih-huo' 由工業見地上論維持國貨與抵制日貨 (The promotion of national merchandizing and the anti-Japanese boycott considered from the industry's point of view). *Shih-yeh tsa-chih*, 71 (Sept. 1923)

Wen-hua yen-chiu she 文化研究社, comps. *Chung-kuo wu ta wei-jen shou-cha* 中國五大偉人手札 (Letters of China's five great leaders). Shanghai: Ta-fang 大方, 1939

Wen Kung-chih 文公直 (Wen Ti 文砥). *Tsui-chin san-shih-nien Chung-kuo chün-shih shih* 最近三十年中國軍事史 (History of Chinese military affairs in the past thirty years). 2 vols. Shanghai: T'ai-p'ing yang shu-tien 太平洋書店, 1930, reprinted Taipei, 1962

West, Philip. *Yenching University and Sino-Western relations, 1916-1952*. Cambridge, Mass.: Harvard University Press, 1976

Whiting, Allen S. *Soviet policies in China, 1917-1924*. New York: Columbia University Press, 1954

Who's who in China. 3rd edn, Shanghai: The China Weekly Review, 1925

Wieger, Léon, S.J. *Chine moderne*. Hien-hien (Hsien hsien, Shantung). 7 vols. 1921-7

Wilbur, C. Martin and How, Julie Lien-ying 夏連蔭, eds. *Documents on com-*

munism, nationalism, and Soviet advisers in China, 1918–1927: papers seized in the 1927 Peking raid. New York: Columbia University Press, 1956

Wilbur, C. Martin. *Forging the weapons: Sun Yat-sen and the Kuomintang in Canton, 1924.* New York: East Asian Institute of Columbia University, 1966 (mimeograph)

Wilbur, C. Martin. 'The ashes of defeat'. *CQ*, 18 (April–June 1964) 3–54

Wilbur, C. Martin. 'Military separatism and the process of reunification under the Nationalist regime, 1922–1937', in Ho Ping-ti and Tsou Tang, eds. *China in crisis*, 1.203–63. Chicago: University of Chicago Press, 1968

Wilbur, C. Martin. 'Problems of starting a revolutionary base: Sun Yat-sen in Canton, 1923'. *Bulletin of the Institute of Modern History*, Academia Sinica (Taipei), 4.2 (1974) 665–727

Wilbur, C. Martin. *Sun Yat-sen: frustrated patriot.* New York: Columbia University Press, 1976

Wilbur, C. Martin. See Ch'en Kung-po

Wile, David. 'T'an Ssu-t'ung: his life and major work, the Jen Hsueh'. University of Wisconsin, Ph.D. dissertation, 1972

Willoughby, W. W. *Constitutional government in China: present conditions and prospects.* Washington, D.C.: Carnegie Endowment for International Peace, 1922

Willoughby, Westel W. *Foreign rights and interests in China.* 2 vols. Baltimore: Johns Hopkins University Press, rev. and enlarged edn, 1927. See Wang Shao-fang

Wills, John E., Jr. *Pepper, guns and parleys: the Dutch East India Company and China, 1662–1681.* Cambridge, Mass.: Harvard University Press, 1974

Wills, John E., Jr. 'Maritime China from Wang Chih to Shih Lang: themes in peripheral history', in Jonathan D. Spence and John E. Wills, Jr., eds. *From Ming to Ch'ing: conquest, region and continuity in seventeenth-century China*, 201–38

Wilson, David Clive. 'Britain and the Kuomintang, 1924–28: a study of the interaction of official policies and perceptions in Britain and China'. University of London, School of Oriental and African Studies, Ph.D. dissertation, 1973

Wolf, Margery and Witke, Roxane, eds. *Women in Chinese society.* Stanford: Stanford University Press, 1975

Wolff, Ernest. *Chou Tso-jen.* New York: Twayne Publishers, 1971

Woo, T. C. *The Kuomintang and the future of the Chinese revolution.* London: George Allen & Unwin Ltd., 1928

Woodhead, H. G. W., ed. *The China yearbook 1921–22.* Tientsin: Tientsin Press, 1921

Wou, Odoric Y. K. 'A Chinese "Warlord" faction: the Chihli Clique, 1918–1924', in Andrew Cordier, ed. *Columbia essays in International affairs vol. III, the Dean's papers, 1967*, 249–74. New York: Columbia University Press, 1968

Wou, Odoric Y. K. 'The district magistrate profession in the early republican period: occupational recruitment, training and mobility'. *Modern Asian Studies*, 8.2 (April 1974) 217–45

Wou, Odoric Y. K. *Militarism in modern China: the career of Wu P'ei-fu, 1916–1939*. Studies of the East Asian Institute, Columbia University. Folkestone, Kent: Wm. Dawson and Sons; Canberra: Australian National University, 1978

Wright, Arthur F., ed. *Studies in Chinese thought*. Chicago: University of Chicago Press, 1953

Wright, Arthur F. 'The study of Chinese civilization'. *Journal of the History of Ideas*, 21.2 (April–June 1960) 233–55

Wright, Mary Clabaugh, ed. *China in revolution: the first phase, 1900–1913*. 'Introduction', 1–63. New Haven: Yale University Press, 1968

Wright, Stanley F. *China's customs revenue since the Revolution of 1911*. Shanghai: Inspectorate General of Customs, 3rd edn, 1935

Wright, Stanley F. *China's struggle for tariff autonomy: 1843–1938*. Shanghai: Kelly & Walsh, 1938

Wright, Stanley F. *Hart and the Chinese customs*. Belfast: Wm. Mullan & Son, 1950

[Wu Chih-hui 吳稚暉]. 'T'ui-kuang jen-shu i i shih-chieh kuan' 推廣仁術以醫世界觀 (On curing the world through the extension of medical care). *Hsin shih-chi* 新世紀, 37 (7 March 1908) 3–4

[Wu Chih-hui]. 'T'an wu-cheng-fu chih hsien-t'ien' 談無政府之闚天 (Casual talk on anarchism). *Hsin shih-chi*, 49 (30 May 1980) 3–4

Wu Chih-hui. *Chih-hui wen-ts'un* 稚暉文存 (Wu Chih-hui's writings). 1st collection. Shanghai: Hsin-hsin Book Store, 1927

Wu Chih-hui. 'Shu Wang Ching-wei hsien-sheng hsien tien hou' 書汪精衛先生銑電後 (Written after Mr Wang Ching-wei's telegram of the 16th [April 1927]). *Chih-hui wen-ts'un*, 1–14

Wu Chih-hui. *Wu Chih-hui hsien-sheng ch'üan chi* 吳稚暉先生全集 (Complete works of Mr Wu Chih-hui). 18 vols. Comp. by Chung-kuo Kuo-min-tang chung-yang wei-yuan-hui tang-shih shih-liao pien-tsuan wei-yuan-hui, Taipei, 1969

Wu Hsiang-hsiang 吳相湘, ed. *Chung-kuo hsien-tai shih-liao ts'ung-shu* 中國現代史料叢書 (Collected historical materials on contemporary China), 6 collections. 30 vols. Taipei: Wen-hsing, 1962

Wu Hsiang-hsiang. *Sung Chiao-jen: Chung-kuo min-chu hsien-cheng ti hsien-ch'ü* 宋敎仁：中國民主憲政的先驅 (Sung Chiao-jen: precursor of Chinese democracy and constitutional government). Taipei: Wen-hsing, 1964

Wu Hsiang-hsiang, ed. *Min-kuo pai-jen chuan* 民國百人傳 (100 biographies of the republican period). 4 vols. Taipei: Chuan-chi wen-hsueh, 1971

Wu Pao-san (Ou Pao-san) 巫寶三. *Chung-kuo liang-shih tui-wai mao-i ch'i ti-wei ch'ü-shih chi pien-ch'ien chih yuan-yin, 1912–1931* 中國糧食對外貿易其地位趨勢及變遷之原因, 1912–1931 (Causes of trends and fluctuations in China's foreign trade in food grains, 1912–1931). Nanking, 1934

Wu Pao-san (Ou Pao-san). *Chung-kuo kuo-min so-te, i-chiu-san-san-nien* 中國國民所得, 1933年 (China's national income, 1933). 2 vols. Shanghai: Chung-hua, 1947

Wu Pao-san (Ou Pao-san). 'Chung-kuo kuo-min so-te i-chiu-san-san hsiu-cheng' 中國國民所得，一九三三修正 (Correction to China's national income, 1933). *She-hui k'o-hsueh tsa-chih*, 9.2 (Dec. 1947) 92–153

Wu Pao-san (Ou Pao-san). 'Chung-kuo kuo-min so-te, 1933, 1936, chi 1946' 中國國民所得，1933, 1936, 及 1946 (China's national income, 1933, 1936, and 1946). *She-hui k'o-hsueh tsa-chih*, 9.2 (Dec. 1947) 12–30

Wu-ssu ai-kuo yun-tung tzu-liao 五四愛國運動資料 (Materials on the May Fourth patriotic movement). comp. by Institute of History, Academy of Sciences, Peking: K'o-hsueh, 1959

Wu-ssu shih-ch'i ch'i-k'an chieh-shao 五四時期期刊介紹 (Introduction to the periodicals of the May Fourth period), comp. by Research Department of the Bureau of Translation of the Works of Marx, Engels, Lenin and Stalin, Central Committee of the Chinese Communist Party. 3 vols. Peking: Jen-min, 1958–59

Wu-ssu yun-tung tsai Shang-hai shih-liao hsuan-chi 五四運動在上海史料選輯 (Selected materials for the history of the May Fourth movement at Shanghai), comp. by Shang-hai she-hui k'o-hsueh-yüan li-shih yen-chiu-so 上海社會科學院歷史研究所 (Historical research section of the Shanghai Academy of Social Science). Shanghai: Jen-min, 1966

Wu Tien-wei. 'Chiang Kai-shek's March twentieth coup d'état of 1926'. *JAS*, 27 (May 1968) 585–602

Wu Tien-wei. 'A review of the Wuhan debacle: the Kuomintang-Communist split of 1927'. *JAS*, 29 (Nov. 1969) 125–43

Wu Tien-wei. 'Chiang Kai-shek's April 12 coup of 1927', in Gilbert F. Chan and Thomas H. Etzold, eds. *China in the 1920s*, 146–59

Wu T'ing-hsieh 吳廷燮, ed. 'Ho-fei chih-cheng nien-p'u' 合肥執政年譜 (Chronological biography of Tuan Ch'i-jui), in Wu Hsiang-hsiang, ed. *Chung-kuo hsien-tai shih-liao ts'ung-shu*, vol. 4, 1962

Wu Wo-yao 吳沃堯. *Vignettes from the late Ch'ing: bizarre happenings eyewitnessed over two decades*, trans. by Shih Shun Liu. Hong Kong: Chinese University of Hong Kong, 1975. A translation of *Erh-shih-nien mu-tu chih kuai-hsien-chuang* 二十年目睹之怪現狀

Wu Yü-kan 武堉幹. 'Lien-sheng tzu-chih yü chih-yeh chu-i' 聯省自治與職業主義 (Provincial federalism and professionalism). *T'ai-p'ing yang* 太平洋 (The Pacific), 3.7 (Sept. 1922), 1–8 (sep. pag.)

Wu Yueh 吳樾. 'Wu Yueh i-shu' 吳樾遺書 (Wu Yueh's testament). *T'ien t'ao: Min-pao lin-shih tseng-k'an* 天討：民報臨時增刊 (Demand of heaven: Min-pao special issue), 25 April 1907

Ya Hsien 瘂弦, ed. *Tai Wang-shu chüan* 戴望舒卷 (Collected works of Tai Wang-shu). Taipei: Hung-fan 洪範, 1970

Yamamoto Sumiko 山本澄子. *Chūgoku Kiristokyōshi kenkyū* 中国キリスト教史研究 (Studies on the history of Christianity in China). Tokyo: Tōkyō Daigaku Shuppankai 東京大学出版会, 1972

Yang Chia-lo 楊家駱, ed. *Wu-hsu pien-fa wen-hsien hui-pien* 戊戌變法文獻彙編

(Documentary collection of the literature of the 1898 reform movement). 5 vols. Taipei: Ting-wen shu-chü 鼎文書局, 1973

Yang Ch'üan 楊銓. 'Chung-kuo chin san-shih nien lai chih she-hui kai-tsao ssu-hsiang' 中國近三十年來之社會改造思想 (Social reform thought in China in the last thirty years). *TFTC*, 21.17 (10 Sept. 1924) 50–6

Yang, Gladys, ed. and trans. *Silent China: selected writings of Lu Xun*. Oxford: Oxford University Press, 1973

Yang, Lien-sheng. 'Historical notes on the Chinese world order', in John King Fairbank, ed. *The Chinese world order: traditional China's foreign relations*, 20–33. Cambridge, Mass.: Harvard University Press, 1968

Yang Tuan-liu 楊端六 *et al*. *Liu-shih-wu-nien-lai Chung-kuo kuo-chi mao-i t'ung-chi* 六十五年來中國國際貿易統計 (Statistics of China's foreign trade during the last sixty-five years). National Research Institute of Social Sciences, Academia Sinica, 1931

Yeh Kung-ch'o 葉恭綽. 'Rapport devant la Chambre de Commerce de Pekin'. *La Politique de Pekin*, special no. (Jan. 1920)

Yen Chi-ch'eng 嚴既澄. '*Shao-nien Chung-kuo tsung-chiao wen-t'i hao p'i-p'ing*' 少年中國宗教問題號批評 (Critique of the special issue on religious questions in the *Young China* magazine). *Min-to*, 3.2 (1 Feb. 1922) 1–12

Yen Chung-p'ing 嚴中平 comp. *Chung-kuo chin-tai ching-chi-shih t'ung-chi tzu-liao hsuan-chi* 中國近代經濟史統計資料選輯 (Selected statistical materials on modern Chinese economic history). Peking: K'o-hsueh, 1955

Yen Chung-p'ing. *Chung-kuo mien-fang-chih shih-kao* 中國棉紡織史稿 (Draft history of the cotton industry in China). 1st edn, 1955; 3rd edn, Peking: K'o-hsueh, 1963

Yen Fu 嚴復. *Yen Chi-tao hsien-sheng i-chu* 嚴幾道先生遺著 (Posthumous works of Mr Yen Fu). Singapore: Nan-yang hsueh-hui 南洋學會, 1959

Yen Fu. 'Lun shih-pien chih chi' 論世變之亟 (On the speed of world change, 1895), reprinted in *Yen Chi-tao shih wen ch'ao* 嚴幾道詩文鈔 (Essays and poems of Yen Fu, preface 1916), 1.1–5

Yen Fu. 'Yuan ch'iang' 原強 (On strength, 1896), reprinted in *Yen Chi-tao hsien-sheng i-chu*, 1.6–26

Yen Fu *et al*. 'K'ung-chiao-hui chang-ch'eng' 孔教會章程 (The programme of the Society for Confucianism). *Yung-yen*, 1.14 (June 1913) 1–8

Yen Fu. *Yen Chi-tao shih wen ch'ao* 嚴幾道詩文鈔, (Essays and poems of Yen Fu), preface 1916. Taipei: Wen-hai, 1969

Yen, W. W. *East-West kaleidoscope 1877–1944: an autobiography*. New York: St. John's University Press, 1974

YHCP. See *Yin-hang chou-pao*

YHYK. See *Yin-hang yueh-k'an*

'Yin-hang-chieh ch'ing Sun Wen wei-ch'ih nei-chai chi-chin' 銀行界請孫文維持內債基金 (Banking circles ask Sun Yat-sen to support the sinking fund for internal debts). *YHYK*, 3.12 (Dec. 1923) heading *Yin-hang-chieh hsiao-hsin hui-wen*

Yin-hang chou-pao 銀行週報 (Bankers' weekly). Shanghai, 1917–50

Yin-hang yueh-k'an 銀行月刊 (Bankers' monthly). Peking, 1921–8

Yip, Ka-che. 'The anti-Christian movement in China, 1922–1927'. Columbia University, Ph.D. dissertation, 1970

Yokoyama, Suguru. 'The peasant movement in Hunan'. *Modern China*, 1.2 (April 1975) 204–38

Young, Arthur N. *China and the helping hand, 1937–1945.* Cambridge, Mass.: Harvard University Press, 1963

Young, Arthur N. *China's wartime finance and inflation, 1937–1945.* Cambridge, Mass.: Harvard University Press, 1965

Young, Arthur N. *China's nation-building effort, 1927–1937: the financial and economic record.* Stanford: Hoover Institution Press, 1971

Young, Ernest P. *The presidency of Yuan Shih-k'ai: liberalism and dictatorship in early Republican China.* Ann Arbor: University of Michigan Press, 1977

Young, Ernest P. 'Chinese leaders and Japanese aid in the early Republic', in Akira Iriye, ed. *The Chinese and the Japanese,* 124–39

Young, John, comp. *Checklist of microfilm reproductions of selected archives of the Japanese Army, Navy, and other government agencies, 1868–1945.* Washington, D.C.: Georgetown University Press, 1959

Young, John. *The research activities of the South Manchurian Railway Company, 1907–1945: a history and bibliography.* New York: East Asian Institute, Columbia University, 1966

Young, L. K. *British policy in China, 1895–1902.* Oxford: Oxford University Press, 1970

YPSWC. See Liang Ch'i-ch'ao, *Yin-ping-shih wen-chi*

Yuan, T. L. (Yuan T'ung-li 袁同禮). *China in Western literature.* New Haven: Far Eastern Publications, Yale University, 1958

Yung-yen 庸言 (Justice), 1.1–2.6 (Jan. 1913–June 1914); Taipei reprint: Wen-hai, 1971, 10 vols.

GLOSSARY-INDEX

There is a considerable number of trees in this forest. It is difficult to view it overall or even in the sections created by chapters. Indexing has been pursued with this problem in mind, to give the reader access to all the content on a given topic. This list also contains characters for the names of some Chinese or Japanese authors whose works in English are listed in the Bibliography.

927

174

unions, *see* labour unions; trade
    unions
united front 800, 804; proposed
    519; goals of CCP 519–20;
    Russian advice on 525; break in
    526
United Nations 108
United States: trade in Far East
    21–2; agricultural population of
    35; grain production in 73;
    loans from 95, 108, 231; trade
    with 125, 126; residents in China
    149; armed forces, 152–3; in
    Diplomatic Body 155; diplomatic
    pressure by 163; consular service
    of 164; missionaries of 169;
    Christian colleges of 175; postal
    service of 187; and the warlords
    307; in the anti-foreign campaign
    598; and Shanghai campaign 612;
    attacks on citizens of 617–18;
    settlement of Nanking Incident
    701; and Japanese memorandum
    709; new tariff treaty with 715;
    as model and partner 766
U.S. Court for China 150
U.S.S.R., *see* Russia
Unity Party (T'ung-i tang 統一黨)
    220
Universal Postal Union 187
University of the Toilers of the
    East 579
urban elite, *see* elite
urban population 28; growth of 32;
    in 18th century 721
urban sector: pre-1949 29;
    handicrafts in 52–3; government
    financed by 99; missionaries in
    168–9, 177; served by foreign
    industry 202; popular fiction of
    436, 462
urbanization: during 19th century
    723; post-First World War

751–62

utilities: and national income 36–7,
    51; investment in 119
utopia: K'ang Yu-wei's vision of
    330, 414; Liang Ch'i-ch'ao on
    338, 348; in antiquity 345;
    social, and May Fourth movement
    373, 764; defined by radicals 380;
    of Paris group 380; of Tokyo
    group 381; and family system
    384–5; without barriers 388; and
    individual emancipation 389;
    in Chinese novels 459; of
    bourgeoisie 765–8

Valéry, Paul 495
Vanguard (*Ch'ien-feng* 前鋒) 520
Varé, Signor 155
Verlaine, Paul 495, 496
vernacular: as vehicle for literature
    424, 466–8; Hu Shih on
    development of 435, 469–70; *see
    also* Chinese language
Versailles Conference, *see* Paris
    Peace Conference
Versailles, Treaty of 267, 402, 407,
    430, 506, 769
Vietnam 14
Vijñanavada school of Buddhism
    418
villages 29–31, 62, 88;
    self-government for 644; *see also*
    farms; peasants
Vladivostok 540, 566, 570, 668
Voitinsky, G. 514, 533; in China
    515, 545

wages: 61, agricultural 70–1;
    during First World War 751;
    see also labour
wai 外 (outside; foreign) 4, 8
wai-fan 外藩 (outer feudatories) 4
wai-kuo 外國 (foreign states) 4
Waichow 555